THE MILITARY ENGINEER IN INDIA.

1997

THE MILITARY ENGINEER IN INDIA

BY

LIEUT.-COLONEL E. W. C. SANDES,
D.S.O., M.C., R.E. (*Ret.*),

LATE PRINCIPAL, THOMASON CIVIL ENGINEERING COLLEGE, ROORKEE, INDIA,
AND AUTHOR OF
"IN KUT AND CAPTIVITY" AND "TALES OF TURKEY"

The
Naval & Military
Press

FIELD-MARSHAL LORD NAPIER OF MAGDALA, G.C.B., G.C.S.I.

To My Comrades

of

The Corps

of

Royal Engineers.

FOREWORD.

WHEN I happen to think of it, I always congratulate myself on my good fortune in that my service of thirty-two happy years in India included nearly all the " 'seventies " of the nineteenth century, when I was privileged to see a great deal of the British Government of India at the zenith of its success.

India, then and since, as never before in its history, enjoyed good and honest government with the best administration of justice that has ever been arrived at in this imperfect world. There was order and contentment everywhere from Cape Comorin to the farthest land frontiers in the north ; and throughout this vast territory, peace and prosperity reigned. So we who were proudly taking part in maintaining the British Raj at that time saw every reason to regard it as a glorious and splendid success, likely to survive for many generations.

Now in the establishment of this glorious and splendid state of things, the men who directed and carried out the engineering works, defensive and other, in the early days of the East India Company, and their successors who gradually created and carried on the great Public Works Department of India in later times, had no small share. And these were the same Military Engineers and Corps of Military Engineers afterwards, whose names, titles and achievements are recorded by my friend and comrade, Lieut.-Colonel Sandes, in this book ; inasmuch as in their time they were the only Engineers in British India, and did all the Engineering work there.

The Corps of Military Engineers that I have referred to were the famous Bengal, Madras, and Bombay Engineers, which were established in the middle of the eighteenth century and carried on all the engineering work in British India for more than a hundred years, creating in that time the great Public Works Department of India, completing a vast number of engineering works in all departments, and so contributing most importantly to the success of our rule in India, which began after we occupied Delhi in 1803.

These three distinguished Corps were amalgamated with the Royal Engineers in April, 1862, which Corps had begun to send officers to India in 1860. At that time also, owing to the great expansion of Civil Engineering work in India, and to the rise of the Civil Engineering profession, the Public Works Department began to be largely recruited with Civil Engineers ; while in 1881 the Military Works Department was transferred from it to the Military Department. So at present the Royal Engineers furnish Officers for the Military Engineer Services in India, Officers and Warrant and N.C. Officers for the three Corps of Sappers and Miners, and a few Officers and other ranks for other branches of the Indian public service.

Colonel Sandes gives in this book most complete details of all these matters, and also of the war services of the Military Engineers in India and on expeditions out of India, together with very judicious remarks on various Indian military subjects. He also gives very interesting information about the three Sapper Corps from their origins, about the beginning of the nineteenth century, until the present day, when they enjoy long-established reputations for efficiency in every respect.

I venture to think that the great majority of people who read this book, which Colonel Sandes has written after most extensive and laborious research and investigation, will learn a vast deal that they did not know before about the British connection with and position in India ; and accordingly I commend it to the notice of all who desire to increase their knowledge of the truth about that most interesting sub-continent.

BINDON BLOOD.

2nd November, 1932.

PREFACE.

WHEN Major-General Whitworth Porter, late R.E., wrote the Preface of his Volume I of the *History of the Corps of Royal Engineers* in 1889, he remarked that he had intended, when he first began his task, to have included the Indian branch of the Corps, but he found that its records were so numerous and full of picturesque interest that it demanded separate treatment. " The history of the Indian Engineers," said he, " remains to be written, and a valuable and interesting record it will prove. It is to be hoped that before long some member of that service will supply the void. The names of two men, pre-eminently qualified for the task, naturally suggest themselves—Lieutenant-General George Chesney and Colonel Henry Yule. In the hands of either of these, full justice would be done to a most attractive subject." Again, the author of Volume III, Colonel Sir Charles M. Watson, K.C.M.G., C.B., M.A., late R.E., wrote in July, 1914 : " The work done by the Royal Engineers in India and the countries connected with it during the period 1886–1912 has been so important that it is hoped that a separate volume dealing with it may some day be published by the Royal Engineers' Institute ; but it will have to be written by an officer who has served in India and is personally acquainted with the civil and military duties of the Corps in that part of the British Empire."

General Sir George Chesney, K.C.B., C.S.I., C.I.E., died in 1895, Colonel Sir Henry Yule, K.C.S.I., C.B., in 1899, and Colonel Sir Charles Watson, K.C.M.G., C.B., in March, 1915, within eight months of completing Volume III of the Corps History, and for many years the project remained in abeyance during the Great War and the difficult times which followed it. It was revived, however, in 1929, when I was greatly honoured by an invitation from the Institution of Royal Engineers to undertake the task, the magnitude of which I could not then foresee. While still in India, where I had served in military and civil employment for 28 years, I began to collect all possible information ; and in June, 1930, in England, I wrote the first words of this volume, the completion of which has taken more than two and a half years.

The activities of military engineers in India having been equally conspicuous in military and civil engineering, it seemed advisable to deal with military and civil work in separate volumes. My plan was to devote Volume I to a history of the achievements of British Military Engineers and Indian Sappers and Miners in fortification and war, and to describe in Volume II the work of the former in the various civil departments of the Government of India, such as Irrigation, Roads and Buildings, Railways, Telegraphs, Mints, Education and Survey. Volume I, accordingly, is purely military in nature. The field of three centuries which it covers is so enormous that it has been necessary to omit a number of entertaining episodes and adventures in the lives of the military engineers of the earliest times. The demands of compression are inexorable, but many personal touches are still to be found in the narrative.

The spelling of the names of places and persons in India has always been a matter of controversy. The " Hunterian System," under which Lucknow becomes Lakhnau, and Cawnpore appears as Khanpur, has such obvious drawbacks that I have adopted as far as possible the spelling given in the *Imperial Gazetteer of India* which is reasonable and modern. No separate bibliography is included, as the titles of the hundreds of historical works, despatches and records which I have consulted or studied are given in footnotes. A complete set of general maps will be found at the end of the volume.

In the course of my work I have received valuable and prompt assistance from a great number of Royal Engineer and other officers, for which I am deeply grateful. But my particular acknowledgments are due to General Sir Bindon Blood, G.C.B., G.C.V.O., the Representative Colonel Commandant of the Corps, who has written a Foreword to this volume and has shown unfailing interest in its progress ; to Brigadier-General Sir James Edmonds, C.B., C.M.G. (late R.E.), to Sir William Foster, C.I.E., and to Lieut.-Colonel P. H. Kealy (R.E., retired), the Secretary of the Institution of Royal Engineers, who have read the typescript, chapter by chapter, and have offered most valuable suggestions. I desire also to thank the officials of the Military Secretary's Branch, the Records Department, and the Library of the India Office, and in particular, the Assistant Librarian, Dr. H. N. Randle, who has given me every facility in making use of the fine collection of historical works in his charge, without which this volume could never have been written.

Further acknowledgments are due to Lieut.-General Sir Fenton Aylmer, V.C., K.C.B., Major-General S. H. Sheppard, C.B., C.M.G., D.S.O., Brigadier-General P. T. Buston, C.B., C.M.G., D.S.O., Brigadier E. F. J. Hill, D.S.O., M.C., and Lieut.-Colonels E. P. Le Breton, D.L., *J.P.*, and F. G. Drew, O.B.E., all retired or serving officers of the Corps, for copious notes of their personal experiences ; and to Lieut.-General Sir George MacMunn, K.C.B., K.C.S.I., D.S.O., Major-General G. H. Addison, C.M.G., D.S.O. (Engineer-in-Chief, India), the Commandants of the three Corps of Sappers and Miners, Brigadier-General F. J. Moberly, C.B., C.S.I., D.S.O., Sir Evan Cotton, C.I.E., Colonel C. B. Thackeray, D.S.O. (late R.A.) and Major V. C. P. Hodson (I.A., retired) for useful information and advice. I have received energetic help also from Mr. J. G. Scott, the Librarian of the Corps Library in Whitehall.

My aim has been to write a readable story rather than a precise and exhaustive (and perhaps exhausting) military record—a tale which may encourage and guide others in a more detailed research into the engineering history of the campaigns which I have outlined. The growth of British power in India has been due to those campaigns, supplemented by wise administration; and a goodly part of the foundation on which our Eastern Empire has been built is the work of the military engineers of India.

E. W. C. SANDES.

13th February, 1933.

CONTENTS.

CHAPTER I.
THE FIRST BRITISH ENGINEERS.

Formation of the East India Company—First settlements in India—The "Gunner and his Crew" as the only Engineers—Fort St. George founded in 1640—The Fort in 1653—Gunners Jeremy Roote and Hugh Dixon—Parsimony of the Directors—Gunner William Dixon—First issue of uniforms ... ...   PAGE 1

CHAPTER II.
BOMBAY AND MADRAS IN THE SEVENTEENTH CENTURY.

Bombay ceded to the British in 1661—Humphrey Cooke takes possession—Bombay Castle—Bombay transferred to East India Company—Presidents Oxenden and Aungier—"Wilful and conceited Engineers"—Captain Samuel Smith and Colonel Herman Bake, Engineers—The defences in 1671—Bombay City taken by Mughals—Restored to British in 1690—Edward Fowle, Engineer in Madras in 1684—Danger from Mughals and Marathas—War against France—Von Werlinhoffe, Engineer in Madras in 1696—Dismissed in 1702—Paymasters and doctors as Engineers—Fort St. George in 1724 13

CHAPTER III.
THE BUILDING OF OLD FORT WILLIAM.

Early Bengal factories—Job Charnock abandons Hugli in 1686—He leaves Bengal, but returns in 1690—President Charles Eyre founds Old Fort William in 1700—Description of the Old Fort—Designers unknown—Winder's proposed ditch—Improvements to Old Fort William—Gunners and sailors as Engineers—The Fort completed in 1716—Badly planned and with inadequate defences... 30

CHAPTER IV.
THE END OF OLD FORT WILLIAM.

Environs of Old Fort William—Maratha invasion in 1742—The Maratha Ditch—Major Knipe and Mr. Forresti, Engineers—Career of Bartholomew Plaisted, Sailor and Engineer—Captain Alexander Delavaux, Chief Engineer in 1748, deserts—Benjamin Robins, Engineer-General, dies in 1751—Committee of Works—King's and Company's Engineers—Colonel Caroline Scott succeeds Robins—Various plans for a new Fort William—Scott dies in Madras, 1754—Siraj-ud-Daula advances on Old Fort William in 1756—Charles O'Hara, Engineer, deserts—Governor Holwell defends the Fort, but finally surrenders—The Black Hole—Colonel Clive and Admiral Watson recapture Calcutta in 1757 42

CHAPTER V.
MADRAS FROM 1707 TO 1773.

The "Gunroom Crew" as Engineers—Marathas invade Carnatic in 1740—Dupleix at Pondicherry—Major Knipe advises on defences of Fort St. George in 1743—He dies—Joseph Smith tries to strengthen the defences—La Bourdonnais captures the Fort in 1746—Madras returned to the British in 1749—Benjamin Robins, Engineer-General, arrives in 1750—Dies in following year—Colonel Caroline Scott, new Engineer-General, advises on defences in 1753—Captain John Brohier strengthens the defences—Brohier goes to Calcutta in 1757, and Captain John Call succeeds him in Madras—The French fail to capture Madras—First companies of Pioneers formed—Colonel Eyre Coote defeats the French—Paul Benfield, Contractor—Captain Patrick Ross relieves Call in 1770—Engineers become combatant officers in 1775—Description of Madras 61

CHAPTER VI.

BOMBAY IN THE EIGHTEENTH CENTURY.

Description of old Bombay—Naval operations against pirates in 1721— President Boone encourages engineering—Defences strengthened when Marathas occupy Salsette in 1738—Joseph Smith, Engineer, digs a Town Ditch in 1742—Captain de Funck, Engineer in 1753—He recommends fortification of Dongri Hill—Superseded by Major Mace in 1758—Mace recommends demolition of Dongri Hill—He dies in 1761—Captain Thomas Keating, Engineer in 1764—He fortifies the city—Colonel Archibald Campbell arrives to advise Keating—Dongri Hill fortified in 1769—Captain Lawrence Nilson acts as Chief Engineer in 1774—Bombay in 1775 84

CHAPTER VII.

THE BUILDING OF NEW FORT WILLIAM.

Initiated by Robert Clive—Captain Robert Barker, Engineer, improves Old Fort William in 1757—Clive defeats Siraj-ud-Daula and crushes the French—Barker proposes a new Fort William—He resigns and Captain John Brohier becomes Engineer—Major Mace ordered to Bengal, but does not come—Battle of Plassey—Brohier proposes a new citadel—Clive favours a site at Govindpur—Brohier submits designs for a new Fort William at Govindpur in October, 1757—Work begins—Directors complain of expense—Clive destroys Chandarnagar (French) and defeats the Dutch—He leaves India in 1860—Bribery and corruption—Malpractices in building Fort William—Brohier arrested and absconds—Calcutta society 100

CHAPTER VIII.

FORT WILLIAM COMPLETED.

Political situation in Bengal—History of labour difficulties in building New Fort William—Difficulties in obtaining materials—Fraudulent contractors—Dishonest officials—Thomas Amphlett succeeds Brohier as Engineer in 1760—Captain Anthony Polier follows Amphlett in 1762—Captain Fleming Martin becomes Engineer in 1764—He criticizes the deplorable state of the fortifications—Directors restrict extent of the work—Martin a rigid economist—Calcutta Council distrusts his ability—Martin resigns in 1768—Mrs. Kindersley describes Calcutta—Lieut.-Colonel Archibald Campbell becomes Chief Engineer in 1769—He reports on state of the works—He plans a dockyard—He stops defence work of the French at Chandarnagar—Major Lillyman follows Campbell in 1772—He completes the main fortifications—Colonel Henry Watson succeeds Lillyman in 1776 and finishes the works in 1781 119

CHAPTER IX.

THE COMPLETION OF FORT ST. GEORGE.

Early definition of a Military Engineer—Innes Munro on an officer's kit—Lieut.-Colonel Patrick Ross succeeds Call as Chief Engineer in 1770—He plans alterations to Fort St. George—Benfield begins them—Political situation—Maratha soldiers—Haidar Ali and Tipu Sultan—The Mysore Army—British capture Tanjore in 1773—Growth of Madras Army—Ross greatly strengthens Fort St. George—War against France—General Hector Munro takes Pondicherry in 1778—Major George Maule, Engineer in Madras—Fort St. George completed in 1783—Innes Munro on the Fort, its garrison, and Madras society 138

CHAPTER X.

THE MYSORE WARS, 1780-1799.

Second Mysore War—Haidar Ali invades the Carnatic in 1780—Madras in danger—Disaster at Pollilur—Lieutenant Moorhouse raises two companies of Madras Pioneers—Defects of Engineer organization—Eyre Coote defeats Mysoreans—War against Dutch—Tipu of Mysore annihilates Braithwaite's detachment—Peace with Mysore in 1784—General Archibald Campbell, the famous Engineer, becomes Governor of Madras in 1786—Third Mysore War begins in 1790—An officer's equipment and retinue—Lord Cornwallis takes

Bangalore, with Major Maule as Chief Engineer—He fails to reach Seringapatam —Capture of hill fortresses—Cornwallis advances again on Seringapatam in 1792 with Colonel Patrick Ross as Chief Engineer—He captures the Mysore capital— War against the French—Pondicherry taken in 1793—Maule killed—War against the Dutch—Colombo taken in 1795—Expedition to Malay Peninsula— Madras Pioneers increased to ten companies—Fourth Mysore War—General Harris marches on Seringapatam in 1799 with Colonel William Gent as Chief Engineer—Tipu fights and retires into his capital—Gent submits plans of attack—Harris accepts advice of Major Beatson—Colonel Arthur Wellesley present—Seringapatam stormed and Tipu slain 154

CHAPTER XI.

THE FIRST MARATHA WAR, 1774–1782.

First Rohilla War—Bengal Engineers—British occupy Salsette near Bombay in 1774—First Maratha War—Lieut.-Colonel Keating, an Engineer, commands a mixed force—He supports Raghuba against Sindhia and Holkar—Battle of Adas, 1775—Keating court-martialled but acquitted—Cadre of Bombay Engineers formed—It becomes a Corps under Major Nilson in 1777—Conditions of Service—Pay—Uniform—Scheme for German artificers—Unit of "Pioneer Lascars" raised in Bombay in 1777—Disastrous operations against Marathas —Treaty of Wargaum, 1779—General Goddard marches across India—He takes Bassein and advances on Poona—Repulsed by the Marathas—First Maratha War ends in 1782—Treaty of Salbai, 1783—Operations in Malabar during Second Mysore War—General Matthews capitulates at Bednore— Captain Sartorius, Engineer—Operations in 1800 against Dhundia Nag— Expedition to Egypt in 1801—Madras Pioneers increased to 16 companies— Three companies of Bengal Pioneers raised in 1803 under Lieutenant John Swinton 179

CHAPTER XII.

THE SECOND MARATHA WAR, 1803–1806.

Native warfare—Treaty of Bassein, 1802—War declared in 1803 against Sindhia of Gwalior and the Raja of Berar—Pontoon train formed—Colonel Arthur Wellesley takes Ahmadnagar with Captain Johnson as Engineer— Unwieldy transport—Wellesley defeats Sindhia at Assaye on September 23rd, 1803—Asirgarh taken—Wellesley crushes Sindhia and Berar at Argaon—He besieges and captures Gawilgarh—Sindhia and Berar make peace—General Lake with the Grand Army meanwhile captures Aligarh—Bravery of Lieutenant John Swinton, Bengal Pioneers—Lake defeats Marathas before Delhi in September, 1803—French officers surrender—Lake annihilates Marathas at Laswari in November—British converge on Holkar of Indore—Colonel Monson's disastrous retreat—Lake captures Dig in December, 1804—He besieges Bhurtpore and fails—Treaty signed in April, 1805, at Bhurtpore—Inexperienced engineers—Lake pursues Holkar to the Punjab 202

CHAPTER XIII.

THE NEPAL AND THIRD MARATHA WARS, 1814–1819.

Widespread unrest—Cadres of Engineers expanded—Bengal "Pioneers and Sappers" increased to eight companies in 1808—Their uniform—Four companies of Bombay Pioneers—Their status in 1812—Two battalions of Madras Pioneers—Bengal Sappers and Miners formed as a Corps in 1819 under Major Anbury—Their uniform—A company of Bombay Sappers and Miners raised in 1820—Bombay Pioneers expanded to eight companies in 1822—Major de Havilland's reorganization proposals—Gradual absorption of all Pioneers into Sappers and Miners—Capture of Mauritius in 1810—Expedition to Java in 1811—Nepal War begins in October, 1814—Repulse at Kalanga—Elephants in hill warfare—General Ochterlony captures all Gurkha positions near site of Simla—Amar Singh surrenders in May, 1815—Second phase opens in February, 1816—Ochterlony advances on Katmandu—Gurkhas conclude Treaty of Sagauli in March, 1816—Siege of Hathras—Third Maratha War commences —Operations against Pindaris begin in November, 1817—Lack of engineer equipment—Battles of Kirkee, Sitabaldi, Nagpur, Mehidpur and Ashti— Marathas subdued—Hill forts taken—War ends with capture of Asirgarh in April, 1819—Minor operations in Arabia 223

CHAPTER XIV.

THE FIRST BURMA WAR AND THE CAPTURE OF BHURTPORE, 1824–1826.

Truculence of Burmese—General Archibald Campbell (late of 38th Foot) leads an expedition to Burma in May, 1824—Engineer casualties—Rangoon occupied easily—Failure at Kemmendine—Burmese stockades—Kemmendine taken—Gallantry of Madras Pioneers at Pagoda Point—Minor local expeditions —Maha Bandula encircles Rangoon in December, 1824—He attacks skilfully but is repulsed and retires to Donabyu—Unfortunate British expeditions in Cachar and Arakan—Campbell advances northwards in February, 1825—He captures Donabyu and Prome in April—He resumes his advance up the Irrawaddy in December—Burmese overwhelmed—Treaty of Yandabu signed in February, 1826—Trouble meanwhile in India—Lord Combermere lays siege to Bhurtpore in December, 1825—Lieut.-Colonel Anbury, Chief Engineer— Well-planned attack by powerful force—Mining and counter-mining—Bhurtpore taken by assault on January 18th, 1826—Engineers praised—Minor operations up to 1838 in Assam, Central India, Coorg, Malay Peninsula and at Jhansi 251

PAGE

CHAPTER XV.

THE FIRST AFGHAN WAR, AND CAMPAIGNS IN CHINA, SIND AND GWALIOR, 1839–1843.

The First Afghan War—Political control—Army of the Indus marches for Afghanistan in December, 1838—Captain Thomson, B.E., bridges the Indus —Advance to Quetta—General Keane occupies Kandahar in April, 1839—He assaults Ghazni on July 23rd—Engineers and Sappers blow in the Kabul Gate— Keane enters Kabul in August—General Cotton takes command in Kabul with General Nott at Kandahar—Broadfoot's Sappers—General Elphinstone succeeds Cotton in April, 1841—Afghans attack Kabul in November— Disastrous British retreat through snow-bound passes—One survivor of an army—General Sale defends Jalalabad with Captain George Broadfoot as Engineer—General Pollock relieves Jalalabad in April, 1842—He enters Kabul in September, punishes the Afghans, and returns to India—Expedition to China in 1840 under General Sir H. Gough—Chinese defeated—Treaty of Nanking concluded in August, 1842—Bengal Sappers and Miners increased to ten companies in 1844—Known as " Bengal Sappers and Pioneers " from 1847 to 1851—Changes in Madras Corps—Armament—Campaign in Sind under General Sir Charles Napier—He defeats the enemy at Miani and Hyderabad in February and March, 1843—Annexation of Sind—Gwalior Campaign under General Sir H. Gough—Marathas routed on December 29th, 1843, by General Gough at Maharajpur and by General Grey at Panniar 267

CHAPTER XVI.

THE SIKH, SECOND BURMA AND SECOND CHINA WARS, 1845–1860.

Sikhs cross River Sutlej in December, 1845—General Sir Hugh Gough concentrates the Army of the Sutlej to oppose them—War declared on December 13th—Gough defeats enemy at Mudki on 18th and Ferozeshah on 22nd— Baptism of fire of Major Robert Napier, B.E., at Mudki—Captain George Broadfoot, B.E., killed at Ferozeshah—General Sir Harry Smith defeats Sikhs at Aliwal on January 28th, 1846—Gough routs them at Sobraon on February 11th and enters Lahore—Treaty of Lahore—Expansion of Engineer cadres— Military engineers normally found in civil employment—Explanation of this anomaly—Insurrection at Multan—General Whish besieges Multan in September, 1848, with Napier as Chief Engineer—Gallantry of Lieutenant A. Taylor, B.E.—Operations interrupted—Siege resumed in December with Colonel Cheape as Chief Engineer—Multan captured on January 2nd, 1849—Sikhs rise meanwhile in the Punjab—General Gough assembles the Army of the Punjab —Battle of Ramnagar on November 21st, 1848—Action at Sadulapur—Gough wins desperate battle at Chilianwala on January 13th, 1849—He routs the Sikhs at Gujarat on February 21st—General Gilbert pursues them to Rawalpindi—Annexation of the Punjab—Second Burma War—General Godwin occupies Rangoon in April, 1852—Major Fraser, B.E., Chief Engineer—Godwin takes Prome in October—Burmese army disperses—General Cheape (Engineer) operates against dacoits—War ends in June, 1853—Fighting in Persia in 1856-57—Second China War in 1860—General Sir Hope Grant, with General R. Napier as a Divisional Commander, leads expedition to China—He captures Taku Forts in August—Occupies Tientsin—Battle of Chang-kia-wan—Peking surrenders on October 7th, 1860 291

CHAPTER XVII.

THE INDIAN MUTINY: ROORKEE, MEERUT AND DELHI.

Causes and phases of the Mutiny—Outbreak at Meerut on May 10th, 1857—Events in Delhi—Captain Fraser, B.E., leaves Roorkee for Meerut on May 12th with six companies of Bengal Sappers and Miners—Four of these companies mutiny at Meerut and join the rebels—Fraser murdered—Major Baird Smith, B.E., safeguards Europeans in Roorkee—General Anson marches from Ambala towards Delhi on May 25th—He dies, and General Barnard assumes chief command—General Archdale Wilson marches from Meerut and defeats rebels on May 30th—Barnard routs rebels at Badli-ki-Serai on June 8th and occupies Delhi Ridge—Delhi in 1857—British position—Lack of Sappers and Miners—Rebels attack the Ridge repeatedly—Early assault on Delhi planned but abandoned—Engineers gradually make British position secure—Major Laughton, B.E., Chief Engineer, removed on June 29th—Captain Alexander Taylor, B.E., arrives from Punjab—Major Baird Smith, B.E., becomes Chief Engineer on July 3rd—List of Engineers at Delhi—Death of Barnard on 5th—General Reed succeeds him—Reinforcements of Pioneers—Archdale Wilson takes command on July 17th—Casualties among Engineers—General Nicholson arrives on August 7th—The "Baird Smith–Taylor controversy"—Baird Smith urges Wilson to assault—Siege train arrives on September 4th—Taylor's reconnaissances—British attack begins on 7th—Breaching batteries constructed and open fire—Assault launched in four columns on September 14th—Blowing in of the Kashmir Gate by party led by Lieutenants Home and Salkeld, B.E.—List of party—Various accounts of exploit—V.C. awards—Fighting in the city—Nicholson mortally wounded—Lieutenant Thackeray, B.E., gains V.C.—Delhi City cleared gradually—Fort occupied on 21st—Columns sweep the surrounding country... 316

CHAPTER XVIII.

THE INDIAN MUTINY: CAWNPORE, LUCKNOW AND CENTRAL INDIA.

Mutiny at Cawnpore on June 4th, 1857—General Wheeler makes a gallant defence—He capitulates to Nana Sahib on 27th—Cawnpore massacres—General Havelock marches from Allahabad to Cawnpore—Captain Crommelin, B.E., bridges the Ganges—Havelock and Outram advance on Lucknow in September—Events in Lucknow—British defeated at Chinhut on June 30th—They concentrate in Residency—Sir Henry Lawrence mortally wounded—Rebels invest Residency and resort to mining—Their assaults fail—British countermining under Captain Fulton, B.E.—Sorties—Fulton killed—Havelock and Outram reach Residency and reinforce garrison on September 25th—Outram assumes command—Colonel R. Napier acts as Chief Engineer—Underground warfare—No serious assaults by rebels—British position extended—First R.E. unit in India (23rd Company) lands in Calcutta on August 11th, 1857—General Sir Colin Campbell advances early in November from Cawnpore—Heavy fighting in Lucknow—Campbell rescues Residency garrison and non-combatants on November 17th and retires to Cawnpore—Outram holds the Alambagh—British columns scour the country—Campbell advances again in March, 1858, to attack Lucknow—Brigadier R. Napier as Chief Engineer—List of Engineers—Attack begins—Capture of Lucknow completed on March 21st, 1858—Minor operations in Malwa—Campaign in Central India—General Sir Hugh Rose moves northwards from Mhow in January, 1858—He defeats Tantia Topi on the Betwa in April, 1858, and captures Jhansi—He defeats Tantia Topi again on the Jumna in May—He takes Gwalior in June—Napier succeeds Rose in chief command—He pursues rebels in Central India and ends the rebellion in April, 1859 348

CHAPTER XIX.

THE SECOND AFGHAN WAR, 1878-1880.

End of the East India Company—Reorganization of the Indian Army— PAGE
Amalgamation of Company's and Royal Engineers on April 1st, 1862—Strength of Engineer cadres—Civil employment—Causes of Second Afghan War—Declaration of War on November 2nd, 1878—Invasion by Generals Sir S. Browne, F. Roberts and D. M. Stewart through the Khaibar Pass, Kurram Valley and by Kandahar respectively—Browne takes Ali Masjid—He reaches Dacca on November 23rd—Operations in Bazar and Bara Valleys—Roberts captures the Paiwar Kotal on December 2nd and advances to Ali Khel—Stewart occupies Kandahar easily—Survey operations—Nondescript dress of Engineers—Pause in hostilities—Treaty of Gandamak signed on May 26th, 1879—Khaibar and Kurram Columns withdraw—Murder of British envoy at Kabul on September 3rd, 1879—Second invasion of Afghanistan—Main thrust by Roberts through Kurram Valley—He defeats Afghans near Charasiab and camps outside Kabul on October 9th—He is surrounded in Sherpur Cantonment and repulses heavy attack on December 23rd—Reinforcements arrive—Sherpur made impregnable—Railway opened between Sukkur and Sibi—Stewart marches from Kandahar towards Kabul on March 29th, 1880—He routs enemy at Ahmad Khel on April 19th and reaches Kabul—Disaster at Maiwand on July 27th, 1880—Gallantry of Lieutenant Henn, R.E., and Bombay Sappers—Terrible retreat to Kandahar—Ayub Khan besieges Kandahar—Roberts sets out from Kabul on August 8th to relieve Kandahar—No Sappers and Miners with the force—Roberts relieves Kandahar on August 31st and routs Ayab Khan—Gradual evacuation of British troops—Reorganization of Sappers and Miners in 1885—Presidency armies merged into Army in India in 1895 368

CHAPTER XX.

OVERSEAS EXPEDITIONS AND THE THIRD BURMA WAR.

Expedition to Abyssinia in 1867 under Lieut.-General Sir Robert Napier (late B.E.)—Troops land at Zula—Engineers prepare track towards interior—Napier arrives on January 7th, 1868—He leads the army southwards—Magdala carried by assault on April 13th, 1868—King Theodore commits suicide—Troops return to Zula—Napier raised to peerage—Expedition to Malay Peninsula in 1875—Occupation of Cyprus in 1878—Expedition to Egypt in 1882—Operations in the Sudan in 1885—Madras Sappers in the Tofrek *zariba* on March 2nd—Third Burma War, 1885—Insolence of King Thibaw—General Sir H. Prendergast (late M.E.) leads expedition up Irrawaddy—He advances on Mandalay in November—Burmese driven back—Thibaw sues for peace—Mandalay occupied on November 28th and Thibaw deported—British occupy Bhamo—Annexation of Upper Burma—Gradual pacification of country—Design of military posts—Burma Company of Sappers formed in 1887—Operations in Somaliland in 1890—Madras Sappers at Suakin in 1896—Bombay Sappers in Mekran in 1898 and 1900—Third China War, 1900—General Sir A. Gaselee commands British contingent—Peking legations relieved on August 14th—Extensive engineering follows—Operations in Aden Hinterland, 1901-1904—Campaign in Somaliland, 1903-1904—Early operations—General Sir C. Egerton advances from Berbera—He routs the Mad Mulla at Jidballi on January 10th, 1904—Lord Kitchener's reforms in India—Changes in Sapper Corps—Brief History of the Military Works Department or Services (now M.E.S.) 396

CHAPTER XXI.

THE NORTH-WEST FRONTIER.

Frontier tribes—Expeditions between 1849 and 1888—Singular dearth of Sappers—Ambela Campaign in 1863—Desperate fighting—Black Mountain, 1888—Tribesmen become better armed—Zhob Valley, 1890—Black Mountain, 1891—Miranzais, 1891—Demolition of towers—Hunza-Nagar, 1891—" A war on the roof of the world "—Captain Aylmer, R.E., wins V.C. at Nilt—Waziristan, 1894—Chitral, 1895—General Bindon Blood as Chief of Staff—Aylmer bridges the

CONTENTS. xix.

Panjkora—Colonel Kelly's wonderful march from Gilgit—Lieutenant Oldham, PAGE
R.E., at Nisa Gol—Chitral relieved—General rising in 1897—Frontier medals—
Swatis attack Malakand in July—General Sir Bindon Blood defeats them at
Landakai on August 17th—He advances into Bajaur—Lieutenants Watson
and Colvin, R.E., win V.C. at Bilot—Sir B. Blood repulses attacks—Mamunds
submit—Sir B. Blood crushes Bunerwals in January, 1898—Operations under
General Elles against Mohmands—General Sir W. Lockhart invades the Tirah
in October, 1897—He punishes Afridis—Difficult retreat down Bara Valley—
Lord Curzon's frontier policy—General Sir J. Willcocks defeats Zakka Khels
in February, 1908—He overruns Mohmand country in May—Frontier remains
quiet until 1914 421

CHAPTER XXII.

THE NORTH-EAST FRONTIER.

Territory and tribes—Expeditions between 1772 and 1861—" Sibandi Sappers"
—Expeditions after 1861—Bhutan Expedition in December, 1864—Invasion
by four columns—Early success—Country annexed—Bhutias rise again—
British reverse near Diwangiri in January, 1865—General Tombs, V.C., attacks
Diwangiri in April—Captain Trevor and Lieutenant Dundas, R.E., win V.C.—
Bhutias submit—Chin-Lushai Expedition in 1889—Columns from Chittagong
and Burma meet in enemy's territory—They build and garrison posts, and
then withdraw—Road construction through forests—Expedition to Tibet—
Negotiations fail—Occupation of Chumbi Valley in December, 1903—Colonel
Younghusband heads Tibet " Mission "—General J. R. L. Macdonald (late
R.E.) commands troops—Arctic conditions—Younghusband moves from
Chumbi on March 24th, 1904—Tibetans defeated at Guru—Gyantse reached
on April 14th—Engineer work on communications—Captain Sheppard, R.E.,
in attack on Palla Village opposite Gyantse on June 26th—Lieutenant Garstin,
R.E., killed—Macdonald captures Gyantse Jong on July 6th, 1904—Mission
sets out for Lhasa on 14th—Action at Karo-la at over 18,000 feet—Crossing of
the Tsan-po—Entry into Lhasa on August 3rd—Treaty signed on September
7th, 1904—Mission returns to India—Abor Expedition under General Bower
in 1911—Jungle warfare—Mishmi Mission in 1911 to the borders of China ... 456

CHAPTER XXIII.

THE GREAT WAR, 1914-1918.

R.E. officers sent to Home Army—Expansion of Sappers and Miners—
Indian Corps embarks for France in August and September, 1914, under
General Sir J. Willcocks—20th and 21st Companies, Bombay Sappers and
Miners, in attack on Neuve Chapelle on October 28th—Bengal Sappers and
Miners at Neuve Chapelle and Festubert in November—Manufacture of trench
appliances and grenades—Indian Corps goes into reserve after Battle of
Givenchy in December, 1914—Sappers return to front line in March, 1915, for
attack on Neuve Chapelle—Battle of Ypres—Battle of Loos in September,
1915—Indian Corps leaves France in December, 1915—Campaign in Mesopotamia—6th Indian Division occupies Basra on November 22nd, 1914—
General Townshend leads advance up Tigris in June, 1915—He captures Kut,
fights at Ctesiphon, and retreats to Kut in November, 1915—6th Division
defends Kut, but surrenders on April 29th, 1916—Exploits of Bridging Train
under Captain Sandes, R.E.—Operations of Kut Relief Force under General
Sir F. Aylmer, V.C., and General Sir G. Gorringe (Engineers)—Relief fails—
General Sir F. Maude advances with large army in January, 1917—Crossing
of Tigris at Shumran Bend on February 23rd—Maude captures Baghdad on
March 11th and Samarra on April 23rd—Sapper work in Persia—Operations
outside Aden during the war—Operations in Egypt and Palestine—Defence of
Suez Canal in 1915-16—General Sir E. Allenby captures Gaza and Jerusalem in
1917—Engineering preparations for final attack—Allenby breaks Turkish
front on September 19th, 1918, and sweeps northwards—Campaign in East
Africa—Disaster at Tanga in November, 1914—General Sheppard (late R.E.)
commands a brigade—Von Lettow Vorbeck's prolonged resistance—He surrenders in November, 1918—Engineer work mostly on railways—Minor
operations on North-West Frontier of India during the Great War 475

CONTENTS.

CHAPTER XXIV.

CAMPAIGNS AFTER THE GREAT WAR, 1919–1932.

Third Afghan War begins on May 6th, 1919—General Sir A. Barrett commands N.W. Frontier Force; General Climo, Waziristan Force; and General Wapshare, Baluchistan Force—Afghans advance on Landi Kotal in Khaibar Pass—They are defeated at Bagh on May 11th and retreat to Dacca—Fighting near Dacca—Armistice concluded on June 3rd—Meanwhile Afghans under Nadir Khan invade the Tochi—Thal relieved by General Dyer on May 31st—British evacuate Upper Tochi posts—Wapshare takes Spin Baldak Fort on May 26th—Construction of Khaibar Railway—Operations in Waziristan, 1919–20—General Skeen subdues Tochi Wazirs in November, 1919—He moves to Southern Waziristan and advances up the Tank Zam against Mahsuds in December—Desperate assaults by enemy—Heavy losses on both sides—Skeen destroys Makin on February 20th, 1920—He occupies Kaniguram on March 6th—Construction of Razmak Circular Road—Arab Rising in Mesopotamia in 1920—General Sir J. A. Haldane commands British troops—General E. H. de V. Atkinson as Chief Engineer—Relief of many besieged garrisons—Building of blockhouses—Atkinson becomes Divisional Commander and relieves Samawa in October—Arabs submit—Moplah Rebellion in Malabar in 1921—Kajuri Plain operations, 1930–31—Afridis attack Peshawar in June, 1930—British advance to Kajuri Plain in October—Sappers bridge the Bara River—Permanent occupation of Kajuri Plain—Operations in Burma in 1931—Abolition of Pioneers in 1932 and their partial absorption into Sappers and Miners 505

APPENDIX I—THE MILITARY ENGINEER SERVICES 531

APPENDIX II—Q.V.O. MADRAS SAPPERS AND MINERS... 536

APPENDIX III—K.G.O. BENGAL SAPPERS AND MINERS 541

APPENDIX IV—ROYAL BOMBAY SAPPERS AND MINERS 546

APPENDIX V—THE ABOLITION OF PIONEER CORPS AND THE REORGANIZATION OF THE SAPPERS AND MINERS IN 1932 551

APPENDIX VI—SUBMARINE MINING IN INDIA... 554

INDEX 557

ILLUSTRATIONS.

	FACING PAGE
FIELD-MARSHAL LORD NAPIER OF MAGDALA, G.C.B., G.C.S.I.	*Frontispiece*
THE RIVER FACE, OLD FORT WILLIAM	38
SIR ARCHIBALD CAMPBELL, K.B., OF INVERNEIL	134
COLONEL COLIN MACKENZIE, C.B., F.R.S.	164
OFFICER, MADRAS PIONEERS, 1780	196
LIEUT.-GENERAL ROBERT NICHOLSON	208
GAWILGARH	210
STORMING A STOCKADE AT PAGODA POINT, RANGOON	254
STORMING OF THE KABUL GATE AT GHAZNI	272
LIEUT.-COLONEL RICHARD BAIRD SMITH, BENGAL ENGINEERS	322
GENERAL SIR ALEXANDER TAYLOR, G.C.B.	336
THE BLOWING IN OF THE KASHMIR GATE, DELHI, 14TH SEPTEMBER, 1857	342
"LYING IN WAIT." CAPTAIN G. W. W. FULTON, B.E.	352
THE RESIDENCY, LUCKNOW, AT THE END OF THE SIEGE	354
ALI MASJID FORT IN THE KHAIBAR PASS	378
"BOUND FOR KANDAHAR." COLONEL "JACKY" HILLS, R.E.	380
THE DEVIL'S STAIRCASE, SURU, ABYSSINIA	400
FIELD-MARSHAL EARL KITCHENER OF KHARTOUM, G.C.B., G.C.M.G., G.C.S.I., G.C.I.E., COLONEL COMMANDANT R.E.	418
GENERAL SIR BINDON BLOOD, G.C.B., G.C.V.O., COLONEL COMMANDANT R.E., AS A COLONEL	440
THE MALAKAND PASS	446
THE POTALA AT LHASA, TIBET	470
YAMBUNG FERRY, DIHANG RIVER	472
CROSSING OF THE SHUMRAN BEND, RIVER TIGRIS	488
LANDI KHANA AND THE AFGHAN FRONTIER	508
THE BARA BRIDGE ACROSS THE BARA RIVER, KAJURI PLAIN	526

THE MILITARY ENGINEER IN INDIA

CHAPTER I.

THE FIRST BRITISH ENGINEERS.

AMONG the earliest British settlers in India, military engineering seems to have been a hobby of the more ingenious—a duty to be done when the serious business of trading was finished, and then only if danger threatened. For more than a century after the arrival of the servants of the East India Company, there was not a trained engineer between Cape Comorin and the Himalayas. Any man might be called upon to dig and build if his companions admired his practical ability and he seemed to have an average share of common sense. The doubtful blessings of trades unions were unknown. Every man was a pioneer in the truest sense of the word. Soldiers, sailors, traders, parsons and doctors, all became, at one time or another, the engineers of the Company.

The original East India Company, under the name of " The Governor and Company of Merchants of London trading into the East Indies," was incorporated at the end of 1600 and granted the monopoly of trade with India for 15 years. The first Governor, Thomas Smythe, and his 24 committee-men, knew little of the country; but they were guided to some extent by the experience of the Dutch companies which were already in existence, and by that of the Portuguese who had settled in India in the sixteenth century. The infant British company received small encouragement. Parliament stood aloof, and investors were suspicious. The company of merchants, however, was not deterred, and expeditions were despatched to the East under such brave sea-captains as Lancaster, Middleton and Hawkins, the last of whom landed at Surat, north of Bombay, in 1608, and actually reached Agra. Four years later, after the defeat of a Portuguese fleet by the Company's ships, the Mughal Emperor, Jahangir, permitted the Company to establish a factory at Surat, 150 miles north of where Bombay now stands, and so the English traders made their first permanent settlement. Thomas Aldworth hired a building as a factory, and to him belongs the credit for the entry of British trade into India. Becoming popular with the natives, he pressed his advantage, and established agencies inland against the bitter opposition of the Portuguese. The work so ably begun by Aldworth was carried on by Sir Thomas Roe, " of a pregnant understanding, well-spoken, learned, industrious, and of a comelie personage,"[1] who arrived in 1615 and lived at the Mughal court for three years.

The Company's factories were naturally established on the sea coasts, at first chiefly on the west coast as being nearer to England, and later more on the east coast. It is curious that England gained the lead in the race for India by defeat in the farther East. Both the Dutch and British adventurers coveted the Spice Islands in the Malay Archipelago, and the Dutch eventually securing them, the British consoled themselves with India. And so England, out of defeat, won a prize of untold value. The early factories, surrounded by warlike nations which could annihilate them in a day, existed on sufferance. Only by following rigidly a policy of conciliation could the adventurous souls in each factory hope to survive, and they felt safer on the coast where at least they were in occasional touch with the Company's ships. On the coast, also, their merchandise could be stored in safety, and trade could be extended gradually into the interior as far as local native rulers would permit. These British settlers desired to be known only as peaceful traders; they wasted no money on soldiery, and their motto was " Defence, not Defiance." Economy was the key-note of every letter from the East India Company to its employees in India, and an explanation was required for every penny spent otherwise than in trade.

A policy of peaceful penetration was forced upon the Company in the early seventeenth century by the refusal of the Mughals to allow any European nation to fortify its factories. Profits were swelled by the exercise of rigid economy on the military side; but a loss of prestige—the breath of life in the East—showed itself after a few years. Though investors were attracted to the Company by early profits, and British settlements spread along the Indian coasts, the structure of British trade had no sure foundation, for it lay at the mercy of European rivals and the fickle rulers of the country. Before the end of the century, Gerald Aungier, President at Surat, wrote: " The state of India is much altered of what it was; that justice and respect, wherewith strangers in general and especially those of our nation were wont to be treated with, is quite laid aside; the name of the honourable Company and the English nation, through our long and patient sufferings of wrong, is become slighted; our complaints, remonstrances, paper protests and threatenings are laughed at. In violent distempers violent cures are only successful. The times now require you to manage your general commerce with your sword in your hands."[2] The experience of 70 years was needed to teach the

---

[1] *The Embassy of Sir Thomas Roe*, ed. by W. Foster (Hakluyt Society), Vol. I, Introduction, p. 4.
[2] India Office Records, Original Correspondence Series, No. 4258.

lesson that trade follows the flag, or in other words that it must be backed by force and by force which is in evidence. Discipline soon became lax in the early settlements, controlled, as they were, by a body of directors separated from them by thousands of miles. The need to conciliate and bribe the avaricious rulers on all sides, arising from lack of military strength to enforce any demand, was bad for the self-respect of the Company's servants; and the men themselves, in the competition of private trade, became less scrupulous. Cases of insubordination, quarrelling and duelling multiplied; and after a few years it was apparent that the Company must maintain a military force of some sort if it was to succeed in the race for Indian trade or even to hold what it had got.

For defence against theft or assault, every factory was surrounded by a wall of brick or mud guarded by native *peons*. Even peaceful trade demanded so much security. For instance, the first little factory on the east coast, established at Masulipatam by Captain Hippon in 1611, had a guard, although little was manufactured there. The trade consisted only in the sale of goods imported from the Company's still earlier settlement at Bantam, in Java, or from England, and in the purchase of calicos, chintz and muslin which were the best products of the Coromandel coast. When, however, the coast factories increased in size and value, better systems of defence were needed, and these involved some degree of specialization. Higher walls were built, and being higher, demanded better materials and workmanship to withstand the torrential rains of the monsoon. The larger areas to be defended involved the traders in the details of elementary military engineering, and they began to recognize that this was a science which was essential to their welfare. The armies of the native potentates had primitive artillery; and so it came about that the Company's factories had to be armed with ordnance, taken as a rule from their ships, and mounted, and sometimes manned, by their sailors. So important were these guns that the walls were altered or rebuilt to suit them, and a " Gunner " was appointed from among the sailors, with a band of assistants known as his " Crew." It seems that the Gunner was acknowledged as the scientific expert of the little community; as such he advised them when they helped him to build his embrasures or to alter the defences to suit his needs. From advice to full control is but a step. The Gunner was soon recognized as the Military Engineer—the first British military engineer in India.

In these early days the most important English factory in India was at Surat, though the headquarters of the Company were at Bantam, in Java, where a settlement had been founded in 1603. Orders were issued through Bantam, and many ships cruised between the east coast settlements and that place. The importance of Surat increased, however, and that of Bantam waned, so that, in 1634, they became independent, Surat being recognized as the headquarters of the Company in the East and remaining so till supplanted by Bombay in 1687. The Masulipatam factory, established in 1611, failed after some years owing to Dutch opposition and intrigue and the exactions of the King of Golconda and his officers. The Dutch had a long start of the British. They had a rival factory at Masulipatam, another at Pulicat, 160 miles to the south, and others still farther south at Sadras and Negapatam; and the Danes had begun to trade at Tranquebar, close to Negapatam, though with little success. Undeterred, however, by the failure at Masulipatam, the East India Company went farther afield and established two settlements in Bengal in 1633, one at Hariharpur, near Cuttack, and another at Balasore, which was abandoned nine years later, and these paved the way for a settlement at Hugli in 1651, from which the British were driven by the Mughals in 1686, to return later and found Calcutta.

The failure of trade at Masulipatam, and the oppression of the Mughal rulers, led to the greatest achievement in British military engineering in India during the seventeenth century—the building of Fort St. George at Madras. Thomas Ivie, voyaging from Bantam to Masulipatam in 1639 as the newly-appointed Agent of the latter place, touched at a small settlement called Armagon where Francis Day was Agent, and at the earnest request of Day, allowed him to reconnoitre towards the south for a new British settlement where the interference of the Dutch might be less marked, though it was recognized that if the settlement were founded too far southwards, trouble might arise from the Portuguese, who occupied a place called St. Thomé, near the town of Mylapore. The Coromandel coast was rich in cheap and excellent muslins and printed calicos, so Day searched the coast most carefully until within three miles of St. Thomé, where at last, when 230 miles south of Masulipatam, he found a spot to his liking near a village called Madrasapatam. He prevailed upon the *Naik* of Chingleput, who had a keen eye for trade, to grant some land and certain privileges, including permission to build a fort and found a settlement, and he then returned to Masulipatam and reported his success to Andrew Cogan, a new agent who had superseded Ivie. Cogan and Day, losing no time, set sail with their followers in the galleys *Eagle* and *Unity*, on February 20th, 1640. With the two leaders were two other factors, a couple of writers, a surgeon, some European artificers, a native " powder-maker," a retinue of servants, 25 armed men to form a garrison under an officer and a serjeant, and lastly the valuable " Gunner." They reached their destination, disembarked through the surf on the tract of land granted by the *Naik*, and laid out a small fort, nearly square in plan, on a surf-bank of sand, south of the village of Madrasapatam and between the Elambore River (now known as the Coum) and the sea. The *Naik* of Chingleput had promised Day that he would build a fort

FOUNDATION OF FORT ST. GEORGE.

for him; but when it was found that the *Naik's* fort would be merely a stockade of toddy palms and earth, Cogan himself, with the Gunner and his crew and the other sailors, began to dig and build, living in palm huts on the beach till they could get a roof over their heads. These amateur engineers erected in time a three-storeyed building containing storerooms, offices and quarters, and around this factory they laid out four battlemented walls with bastions at the corners for batteries of guns and enfilade fire.

Some idea may be formed of the difficulties overcome by Cogan's men when it is stated that more than three years elapsed before the brick-in-mud bastions (afterwards cased in stone) were completed, while the curtain walls connecting them were not finished until 14 years after the work was begun. The south-east bastion, on the sea coast, was ready in a few months and cost £375;[1] the north-east bastion was completed a year later, and a third bastion was finished and stone-cased in 1643, when £4,150 in all had been spent on the buildings and fortifications.[2] Lack of funds may have been the cause of the great delay in completing the curtains, for the Company was parsimonious to a degree. Colonel H. D. Love, in his *Vestiges of Old Madras*, remarks: "Cogan has not hitherto received adequate credit for his share in the founding of Fort St. George. It is true that Day projected the new settlement, conducted the preliminary negotiations, chose the site and obtained the *Naik's* grant; but Cogan, his superior officer, was present from the beginning of the occupation and was mainly responsible for the erection of the Fort." Cogan handed over charge as Agent to Francis Day, on August 27th, 1643, and left India. He seems to have been the first British enthusiast in military engineering in India, and though he had other more important duties and responsibilities, he initiated, with the Gunner and his crew, the first British fortification in India which might be compared with some of those in Europe.

When Thomas Ivie relieved Francis Day as Agent at Fort St. George in 1644, the latter having held office for a short period only, he urged the Company to spend more money on the fort, and to increase the garrison which included only "37 souldiers and other professions" in addition to five factors and two writers. He estimated that 100 soldiers would soon be needed to defend the place. "The Moores,"[3] he wrote, "had advanced but 5 weekes past with their armies within three Myles of Pullicatt and sent unto the Duch Governour to Surrender up there Castle; and we did suddenly expect the same. But shortly after, the Jentues[4] came downe with a greate power, gave the Moores Battle, routed their Armie and put the Moores to flight beyond Armagon where they are now a gathering a head

---

[1] Original Correspondence Series, No. 1763, November 27th, 1640.
[2] *Ibid.*, No. 1751, January 13th, 1644-45.
[3] Indian Muhammadans. In this case the forces of Golconda.
[4] *Jentues* or *Gentues*. Hindus.

againe; soe the dainger that we live in is yet unknowne."[1] This letter, written during the building of Fort St. George—so named after the patron saint of England—shows the unsettled state of the country and the perilous existence of the little band of British traders.

Jeremy Roote, the first British military engineer whose name is recorded, now enters upon the scene. It is probable that he was the "Gunner" who sailed with Cogan and Day to Madrasapatam in 1640, for, in a Court Minute of December, 1647, he is recorded as having held that post for many years. In 1646, having survived a serious illness, he was sent by Henry Greenhill, the Agent at that time, to help Mir Jumla, the first Nawab of the Carnatic and Viceroy to the Muhammadan King of Golconda, who was blockading the Portuguese at St. Thomé, near Fort St. George; and six years later he was still showing great ability and tact in the native camp while his ordinary work in Fort St. George was carried out by one John Morris, Gunner's mate. In Mir Jumla's camp, however, Jeremy was training a youngster named Hugh Dixon who was to succeed later to the Gunner's post and to hold it for no less than 19 years. Jeremy Roote was followed in 1654 by Christopher Wilkins, and the latter by Hugh Dixon in 1658; but the credit for the building of the original Fort St. George must go to Jeremy Roote and his understudy, John Morris.

In 1653, according to Colonel H. D. Love,[2] Fort St. George had four battlemented curtain walls, disposed in a square whose sides were 60 yards in length. At the angles were four large bastions, also battlemented, the salient points of which were about 100 yards apart. The western curtain was pierced by the Fort Gate, and there was a smaller opening in the east curtain giving access to the factory or Fort House. This building, which was a flat-roofed structure fronting the sea, seems to have replaced an earlier domed edifice, which was built diagonally to the square of the fort so that its walls directly faced the gorges of the bastions, with the probable object of defending them. The centre of the fort was nearly 200 yards from the sea on the east, and about 100 yards from the river on the west. The whole establishment, civil and military, lived within the fort, the former in the factory house, the latter under the curtain walls. Outside were the houses of the European town and the Capuchin church of St. Andrew. In later years the town and church were enclosed by four walls forming an irregular quadrilateral with bastions at the angular points. The original or inner fort, which then became the citadel, survived until 1714, when it was rebuilt as the Fort Square.

As an example of the type of work designed by the Company's

---

[1] Original Correspondence Series, No. 1885, September 8th, 1644.
[2] *Vestiges of Old Madras*, by Colonel H. D. Love (late R.E.), Vol. I, p. 106. Colonel Love bases his description on a map prepared by Thomas Pitt in 1710.

servants, and supervised by the Gunner and his crew, this description is valuable; but these budding engineers had many difficulties to surmount, and suffered much through inexperience, for we come across this report :—[1]

"FORT ST. GEORGE TO THE HONBLE. COMPANY.

"Wee have yett one Curtaine of our Fort to seaward, the most part whereof is laid with Loose Bricks which a man may push downe with his hand; which although we are loathe to expend any of the Companys money in building, yet wee must bee forced to doe it Leest to save a penny wee Loose a pound; for untill that bee up we Cannot think ourselves safe in the place where we are, so long as we see such dayly broiles in our Towne."

The "Towne" alluded to was the native quarter, afterwards called *Black Town* to distinguish it from the *White Town* or European quarter which sprang up mostly north of the original fort and between it and Black Town. The White Town was enclosed at a later date within a quadrilateral of bastioned walls, thus concentrating the European community and their citadel in a defended area. The settlement at Fort St. George increased rapidly in size, for some of the retired servants of the Company remained there as private traders or contractors, and these pursuits attracted also a large number of Portuguese, Armenians and other aliens. The Company's officers would no longer tolerate a monastic life, and married accommodation was demanded in increasing amount. By 1654 several women had joined their husbands in Madrasapatam, or had been married there. Buildings sprang up like mushrooms, and the Gunner became a popular hero. It seems also that in time the Company itself began to encourage matrimony for, some years later, the Court of Directors sent out 20 single women to the new settlement at Bombay who were said to be of " sober and civil lives." They were each provided by the generous Directors with one " suit of wearing apparel," and were to " have victuals " at the expense of the said gentlemen for one year.[2] Alas, some of the sober maidens fell from grace! Within a few months they were reported to have grown " scandalous to our nation, religion and government," and the Bombay authorities were ordered " to give them all fair warning that they do apply themselves to a more sober and Christian conversation: otherwise the sentence is this, that they shall be confined totally of their liberty to go abroad, and fed with bread and water till they are embarked on board ship for England."[3] Perhaps this fierce threat produced the meek and godly maidens fitted to wed the factors; the

---

[1] Original Correspondence Series, No. 2311, February 5th, 1652-53.
[2] *Company to Surat*, in a letter dated August 24th, 1668.
[3] India Office Records. Court Book No. 26, p. 183, and Letter of Surat Council to Bombay, December 18th, 1657.

terrors of a rough sea voyage, after a starvation diet, may well have done so, but history does not relate how the ladies behaved thereafter. The Company, however, was not deterred from further experiments. Three maidens arrived at Fort St. George without warning—curiously enough by the ship *Society*—and greatly to the surprise of the honest factors :—

"FORT ST. GEORGE CONSULTATION.[1]

"The Honble. Company having been pleased to send out three single women who came upon *Ship Society*, vizt., Mary Gainsford, Anne Davys, Rebecca Randall, whose passage was paid for by the Honble. Company, as Capt. Thomson affirms ; and they having neither relations, nor recommendations to any person in this place but say they knew noe otherwayes but that they were sent out by the Honble. Company, and therefore have made their requests for subsistence upon their Accompt. They being in low condition, and not able to maintain themselves it was therefore resolv'd to allow them 40 *fanams*[2] per Mensem for their maintenance upon the Honble. Companys accompt soe long as they remaine unmarryed."[3]

For some years after 1653, the work of strengthening the position at Madrasapatam appears to have languished. A probable explanation is that after the bastions and curtains of the original fort had been built, the Company was determined not to spend another penny on military precautions. The garrison of the fort was much reduced, drawing bitter complaints from Henry Greenhill, the Agent in 1657, who wrote that he had only "ten Souldiers, a weake crew for such times," and that he had been forced to recruit "Portugals, Mestizoes[4] and Blackes" in consequence. But after the arrival of Edward Winter as Agent in 1662, engineering received a great impetus, and a number of buildings were erected under the guidance of Gunner Hugh Dixon, though the Company jibbed at the expense involved. The struggle to keep the garrison up to a strength sufficient to man the defences and assist in engineering schemes continued. Meagre reinforcements arrived, but Winter was not hopeful—indeed he was lugubrious. He wrote :—[5]

"Notwithstanding your Worships have taken care to furnish us with men for the Fort, yet wee may expect, according as t'is usuall, that most of them freshmen will Dy ; so that wee cannot well discharge any of the Portuguese soldiers. Twere good indeed if wee had all our owne Naĉon. But if it be your Worships pleasure to have

[1] *Public Consultations*, Vol. II, July 25th, 1678.
[2] Equivalent to ten shillings.
[3] Only Mary Gainsford remained unwed after six months, and she married within three years.
[4] Eurasians.
[5] Original Correspondence Series, No. 3406, January 12th, 1664-5.

all English in the Fort, then you would doe very well to send over people sufficient both of Men and Women to inhabit here. The Women may be such as have byn brought up to spinning and knitting, and then they may be imployed in makeing of Cotton stockings and gloves."

And again :—[1]

" You may be pleased also to take notice in what want wee are of Englishmen for Souldiers by the Mortillity that hath hapned amongst those last sent out, as per list of Dead men herewith sent, though we Cannot but Confess that their owne ill liveing and Debauchedness was the Chiefe outward cause that brought them to their ends."

William Langhorn, who followed Winter and Foxcroft, became Agent and Governor of Fort St. George in 1672. Foxcroft had been very careless in military matters; and thus when war was declared between England and Holland, it fell to Langhorn to improve the crumbling fortifications and to increase the garrison. A bastion known as the "Fishing Bulwarke" had fallen down, through encroachment by the sea, and the Council of Fort St. George consulted their engineering advisers :—[2]

"FORT ST. GEORGE CONSULTATION.

" Surveighed the Buildings and Fortifications, and findeing them goeing much to ruine for want of the needfull Repaires of the last yeares, by advice of the Bricklayer, Carpenter, Leiftenant Sutton and Gunner Dixon, resolved to proceede to repaire them without delay."

This extract shows that Hugh Dixon, who was an assistant of Jeremy Roote in 1652, and became Gunner of the Fort in 1658, still held the latter apointment 14 years later—an unusually long tenure of office, and of life itself, in the climate of Madrasapatam; indeed, he did not relinquish his office until 1677, when he was succeeded by William Dixon. In Fort St. George, in 1672, the gunner's crew was commanded by Hugh Dixon as Chief Gunner or Gunner of the Inner Fort. The outer fortifications, encircling the inner fort (or citadel) and the houses, barracks and church, were in the charge of the Assistant Gunner or "Matross." These outer works, from which developed the Fort St. George of the early nineteenth century, were erected between 1653 and 1666, and a wet ditch from the river was begun along the southern face.

The encroachment of the sea, the growing fortifications, and possibly the faulty material and workmanship of the defences, induced the Council of Fort St. George in 1676 to send an urgent though belated request for an expert engineer :—[3]

[1] Original Correspondence Series, No. 3038, January 21st, 1664–5.
[2] *Factory Records*, Fort St. George, February, 1671–2.
[3] Original Correspondence Series, No. 4215, August 22nd, 1676.

"FORT ST. GEORGE TO THE HONBLE. COMPANY.

"And here it is not improper to acquaint you how that the sea having come very near your fortifications in a great storm about three years since, and gone off again as far as ever it had been since Anno 1670, it has since the last yeare come nearer and nearer . . . Meanwhile it will be absolutely necessary that you send out some knowing and experienced person to make some peers[1] towards both monsoons, or what other fences most proper to keep off and drive back the sea whiles yet in time. We doubt not but there may be some ingenious persons now going home who, belonging to the sea, may give some satisfaction, the good choice of whom exceedingly imports, for there are crowds of undertakers, Dutchmen especially, but great difference between speaking and doing."

It is clear that the Council were afflicted with useless contractors and hoped fervently that a knowing and experienced engineer from England would save the crumbling walls from collapse. The thrifty Directors, however, threw cold water on the scheme; they replied, in December, 1677,[2] "Our business is trade not warr; and for the better making good your Fortifications both against an Enemy and the Sea, Wee have appointed ships to take in what quantity of stones they can at Johannah[3] where they may be had cheape, and question not but the Commanders of our ships, and others you have with you, will contrive the carrying on of that work to make it answer our ends without sending an Engineer from hence, those sort of men being alwaies found very expensive." The true Aberdonian spirit seems to have permeated the Court of Directors.

St. Thomé, the Portuguese settlement three miles south of Fort St. George, had been besieged and captured by the forces of Golconda in 1662, and it was held by them till they, in their turn, were ousted by the French ten years later. The proximity of the French was a threat to Fort St. George which could not be ignored. The area within the British fortifications now gave ample space for a larger garrison, and a strong contingent was needed to man the defences; and so it appears that, by 1673, the garrison had been increased to 241 British infantry in four companies, and 14 artillerymen, supplemented by 163 Portuguese militia and about 550 native soldiers—a total of nearly 1,000 fighting men. In this garrison, the engineer establishment was larger than before. The Chief Gunner, Hugh Dixon, and his Assistant Gunner, William Dixon, were helped by 12 other "Assistants."[4] But when the French were expelled from St. Thomé, in 1674, by the Muslims and the Dutch, the Company, to save expense, reduced the garrison, and the Gunner's crew dwindled

---

[1] Piers or groynes.
[2] *Public Despatches from England*, Vol. I, December 12th, 1677.
[3] An island in the Mozambique Channel.
[4] Original Correspondence Series, No. 3765, *cir.* January, 1673.

to 15 men. The reduction was temporary only, for the garrison had to be increased, three years later, on the approach of a Maratha army.

The statement by the Directors that "those sort of men were always found very expensive," when referring to the recruitment of engineers, must be considered in relation to the scale of pay of the Company's officers and soldiers. Compared with the wretched emoluments of these men, the cost of recruiting a "knowing and experienced person" from England might well have dismayed the Company's financial pundits. In 1665 the pay of a British "private sentinel" in the Company's army was exactly 13s. 4d. per mensem, and a serjeant received the munificent sum of £1 5s. for the same period. In the garrison of Bombay, as late as 1710, a private sentinel received only a guinea a month, a corporal £1 4s., and a serjeant £1 10s. but with an added bonus of one month's pay every year; and at that date an ensign was paid £3 a month, and a lieutenant £4. Civil officers, joining as apprentices in 1675, received the princely salary of £5 per annum during the first five years of their service. When promoted to writer a man might expect £10, and as a factor £20 per annum. The Governor himself received a yearly salary of only £300. The "Chirurgeon," a specialist, had to be content with £30 per annum. Both soldiers and civilians, however, received free board and lodging. One may marvel that the Company could obtain the services of any men on such pay, but the explanation lies in the fact that these salaries were purely nominal. Every officer aspired to be a contractor and a private trader, and thousands of pounds were earned, sometimes legitimately, by these subsidiary professions. The Company did not interfere provided that its own interests were safeguarded. But after a time the Directors recognized the bad effects of this system, increased the official salaries, and made every effort to stop private trade and other such exterior sources of income. The case of the private soldier in India in the seventeenth century differed from that of the officer, and it is difficult indeed to understand how a man from England could be induced to serve on the Coromandel Coast on fivepence a day.

In 1677, when the hard-hearted Directors had refused to send out to Fort St. George a knowing and experienced person as engineer, we find the first reference to an official military engineer in Madras,[1] though not the first in India, since Colonel Herman Bake had already been appointed in Bombay :—

"The outward wall of the House in the Fort being found to be very crazy and tottering through badness of the foundation, and many cracks more and more appearing therein, has upon surveigh by the Chief Gunner and *Ingenier* of the Fort, Wm. Dixon, Muttamarra the chief carpenter, and Nallana the chief Bricklayer, allready obliged

---
[1] *Factory Records*, Fort St. George, November 1st, 1677.

us to run up two Buttresses the last yeare to the North East, and one this yeare to the S.W. to support it."

William Dixon, the architect of St. Mary's Church in the Fort, had just taken over charge from Hugh Dixon, and the Council of Fort St. George recognized at last that an engineer should be shown as such on the military establishment of the settlement; so to William Dixon, in 1677, belongs the honour of being the first military engineer officially appointed in Madras, since there is no mention of his brother Hugh as *Ingenier* in addition to his duties as Gunner.

It appears that, up to 1672, the Company's officers and soldiers, including the Gunners and their crew, wore no distinctive uniform. The officers disported themselves on state occasions in good cloth coats of various colours, ornamented with silver lace, and for every-day wear used any other garments they possessed. Perukes were reserved for agents and other great men. The majority of officers copied the " Moors " in cutting their hair short. President Aungier of Bombay, a military enthusiast, seems to have been the first to see that uniforms would add to the prestige and improve the discipline of the Company's forces. In 1672 he obtained sanction for the supply of uniforms to the troops on the western coast " to be of one colour for the greater awe of the adversary."[1] But it was only natural that the small communities of white men, isolated in a strange country, should adopt to some extent the dress and customs of the teeming millions around them, and most of the Company's officers in these early days had Indian wives and fell largely into Indian ways —for instance, when they toured inland, they wore Indian dress and squatted or lay on carpets to take their meals.

The request of Aungier for uniforms for the Bombay troops induced the Directors to sanction provisionally the supply of uniforms to the Madras forces, but with an eye to profit rather than an increase in discipline or prestige. The astute gentlemen wished to advertise their cloth among the native princes. It seems probable that the Madras troops did not receive any uniform until 1674; but they certainly had it in 1679, when the cost was stopped out of their meagre pay. Discipline in the Company's forces must have improved greatly by that time, for there is no record of any protest against this deduction. The coats were red in colour, with green facings. There is no mention that trousers or pantaloons formed part of the outfit. In 1724, the three companies which then composed the garrison were distinguished by blue, yellow or green facings; but it is presumed that, in the latter part of the seventeenth century, the embryo military engineers of Madras were clothed in red tunics with green facings as were the other soldiers in Fort St. George. Only those who know the climate of Madras will realize what those men must have endured.

[1] Court of Directors to Surat Council, December 13th, 1672.

CHAPTER II.

BOMBAY AND MADRAS IN THE SEVENTEENTH CENTURY.

AFTER Vasco da Gama had anchored off Calicut on the western coast of India in 1498, his countrymen, the Portuguese, began to build forts along that coast in support of their trade ; and, in 1534, under the Treaty of Bassein, the Sultan of Gujarat bestowed the city of Bassein and several islands, including Bombay, on the King of Portugal. The Portuguese then divided their new territory into areas which they let out on leases, the second lessee of Bombay being Dr. Garcia da Orta, who occupied, and probably built part of, the " Quinta," or Manor House, which lay close to the site of the present Mint. The settlers prospered, and their ships swept the Indian seas until, with the opening of the seventeenth century, the combined supremacy of Portugal and Spain was challenged by England and Holland. On October 13th, 1626, a British and Dutch squadron, led by Captain David Davies in the *Discovery*, sailed into Bombay harbour, and afterwards landed a strong party who devastated the Portuguese settlement. Little did these Englishmen, the first to set foot in Bombay, imagine that the place was destined to become in time the most important sea port of the British Empire in the East.

The British settlement at Surat, near the mouth of the River Tapti, north of Bombay, was established in 1612 as a peaceful venture, and existed at the mercy of the Mughal Emperor of Delhi, who permitted its foundation. There were traders of other European nations in Surat who obstructed and rivalled the British, and thus the Company's merchants cast longing eyes on the Portuguese possessions in the Bombay Islands where a wonderful natural harbour existed which would serve as a base for their ships. Several times the Agent and Council of the Company at Surat represented to the Court of Directors in England the value of Bombay, and the Directors tried to induce Cromwell to buy it from the Portuguese, but with no success. With the Restoration, however, the position of the Company improved greatly. The Directors saw clearly that British trade interests could not prosper unless they secured " fortified stations yielding a revenue equal to the charges of them," and that such stations must be garrisoned so that they would be independent of the native intrigues and quarrels around them. As the might of Portugal waned in India, that of Holland increased, and the deposal of Shah Jahan in 1658[1] produced such disturbances near Surat that, by 1660, the need

[1] He was imprisoned in 1658 and died in 1666.

to establish a new colony, isolated from the Dutch and less subject to native interference, became imperative. The opportunity came in the signing of the marriage treaty between Charles II. of England and the Infanta Catherine of Braganza, on June 23rd, 1661, when the Portuguese princess brought with her, as part dowry, the Island of Bombay and " all rights, profits, territories and appurtenances thereunto belonging," and the Portuguese Viceroy of Goa, plunged into despair at the news, wrote : " India will be lost on the same day on which the English nation is settled in Bombay."

On September 18th, 1662, the Earl of Marlborough, with 400 King's troops and many officers, sailed into Bombay harbour to take over the island on behalf of the King of England. The Portuguese Governor refused to hand it over, affirming that the wording of the treaty was ambiguous. Reinforcements under Sir Abraham Shipman followed within a month, but not a man of the whole British expedition was allowed to land. The ships sailed to Swally, the seaport of Surat, where the force was rebuffed by Sir George Oxenden, the Company's President at Surat, who would not permit the men to disembark on the mainland lest the Mughals should take offence. The unfortunate expedition sailed to the south, and the men were landed at last on the desert island of Anjidevi, south of Goa, where they died by scores daily. It was not till January, 1665, that the survivors returned to Bombay under Humphrey Cooke and took possession of the island with the approval of the local Portuguese. According to Fryer's description of Bombay Castle in 1665,[1] it was " a pretty well Seated but ill Fortified House, four Brass Guns being the whole Defence of the island ; unless a few Chambers housed in small Towers, convenient Places to scower the Malabars who heretofore have been more insolent of late, adventuring not only to seize the Cattle but depopulate whole villages by their Outrages. . . . About the House is a delicate Garden, voiced to be the pleasantest in India, intended rather for wanton Dalliance, Love's Artillery, than to make resistance against an invading Foe." So after all, Garcia da Orta seems to have been more botanist than engineer, and his defences proof only against Cupid's darts.

Foster remarks[2] that Cooke's first care was to make his position safe against attack, but to do this he needed money. Oxenden, the Company's President at Surat, was unwilling to supply any money without permission from England and pointed out that, if King Charles had intended that Bombay should be fortified, he would have sent the requisite funds. However, at the end of 1665, Cooke was pleased with his fortifications, reporting that he had completed the work towards the sea where he had built a large platform " wherein cann play 18 peeces of large ordinance " and which would last " for

---

[1] *A New Account of East India and Persia*, by J. Fryer, p. 63.
[2] *The English Factories in India*, 1665–1667, by Sir William Foster, C.I.E., p. 41.

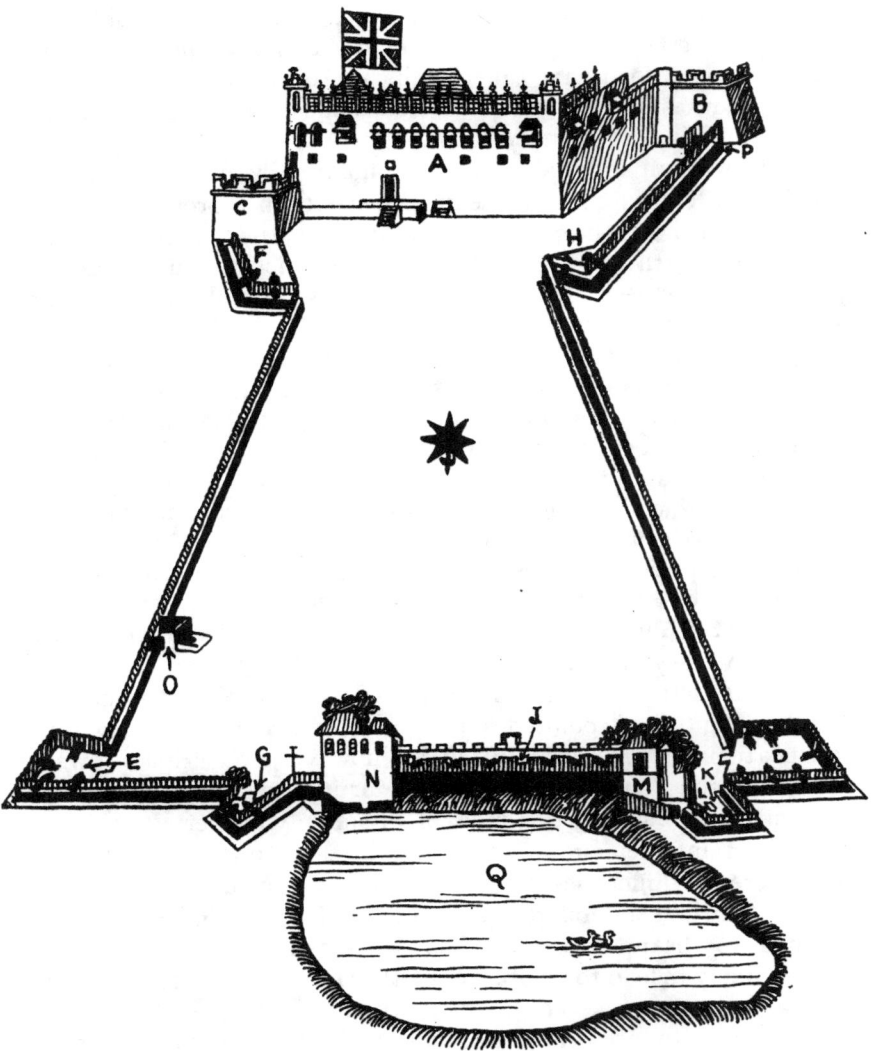

BOMBAY FORT, 1665.

A. The House to landward.
B. Fort Charles.
C. Fort James.
D. Fort Royall.
E. Fort St. George.
F. Fort St. Andrew.
G. Fort St. Patrick.
H. Fort St. David.
J. Plat Form Henerieta Maria.
K. Fort Rupert.
L. Well of water concealed.
M. Garden House.
N. Banqueting house.
O : P. Sally Ports.
Q. Pond fresh water.

many hundred yeares." To landward also he had been busy, and to show his progress he enclosed a "ruff draught" for the King to see. In describing it he remarked that: "It's all done with turffe and cocernutt trees, 14 foote hygh round. . . . This worke would have cost His Majesty 5,000 l. to have concluded it, but I hope it will not cost him 100 l., for I have taken such care to have all the islanders to work by turnes, some dayes 1,000 men, some dayes 800, without pay, only something to drinke." The "ruff draught" was probably identical with an undated plan of "Bombaim" which is preserved in the Public Record Office Museum and has been reproduced for this volume. It shows the original house or castle, the fortified enclosure, and at the north or lower end, a pond in which two ducks are disporting themselves. The sea-shore lay close outside the house and skirted the eastern line of defence.

Humphrey Cooke made a poor bargain: he received Bombay alone, with its dependencies Warli, Parel and Mazagon, and could enforce no demand with his weak contingent of 117 officers and men with 23 guns. The Portuguese, keeping hold of Mahim and Bandra in the north of the island, threw every difficulty in his way; and the mixed population, 10,000 strong, preferred the known rigour of the Portuguese rule to the unknown ways of their new masters. Tidings of the humiliating position reached England; and King Charles II., who was naturally furious at the turn of events, recalled Cooke and appointed Sir Gervase Lucas in his stead. Lucas died within a year, and Henry Gary became Governor under the Crown in 1667. Before Sir Gervase left England he had applied for 400 soldiers to garrison Bombay, and had pointed out that Cooke had condemned the fortifications of the island; little, however, was done towards increasing the garrison prior to 1668, for it seems that, in 1667, the total strength was only 285 men, of whom only 93 were British, and that the reinforcement of 400 was whittled down to 60 soldiers. Such were the difficulties faced by the pioneers of our Indian Empire.

King Charles soon found that his hopes of success in Bombay were doomed to disappointment. The settlement was costly, and it seemed likely to lead to trouble with other European nations and with the native powers. Accordingly the King was very willing to part with his unfortunate bridal gift, and on March 27th, 1668, he issued letters patent by which his Bombay possessions were handed over to the Company at an annual rental of £10 in gold. The Directors decided to appoint a Deputy Governor for Bombay, working under the jurisdiction of their President at Surat; and Sir George Oxenden, the President, sent Messrs. Goodwin, Coates, Streynsham Master (afterwards Governor at Madras) and Captain Young to take possession, which they did on September 23rd, 1668. The King's troops in Bombay were given the choice of becoming soldiers of the Company for a few years or returning to England. Most of them elected to serve the Company and formed its first European regiment, known afterwards as the Bombay Fusiliers, and later again as the 103rd Foot.

Oxenden visited Bombay in January, 1669, and appointed a committee under Captain Whitehorn, of the *Return*, to survey the island and its defences. The work was well done, for we read[1] that "Captain Whitehorn hath been a principall instrument and hath taken much paines in circulating the island." In the same letter, however, Oxenden records an event which should interest engineers—the appointment of the first Chief Engineer of Bombay. "Capt. Samuell Smith, late commander of your *Little Charles*," he writes, "is taken ashore and now appointed Chiefe Engineer of your island and Master Comptrouler of the Ordnance, hee being very aptly qualified in his ability and practicall experience, and likewise hathe the approbation of all that pretend to understand anything of fortifications or gunnery, being likewise well versed in all manner of fireworks and in playing the granadoes." So, with a reputation which to modern ears savours of musical pyrotechnics, Captain Samuel Smith, a jolly mariner, took charge of the Bombay fortifications and presented to the Council of War a scheme, or "modell in paper," for certain improvements.[2] These were approved, the scheme was sent to England, and work began at once. So well did Captain Smith and his men dig and build that Captain Young, the Deputy Governor, was able to report[3] in February that the foundations of the "bulwarkes," ten feet wide and six feet deep, had been completed, and the masonry was up to ground level. Though little progress was made after the break of the monsoon in May, the walls were 12 feet above ground in November and were faced with stone.[4] The "Quinta" was in a fair way to become a fort.

Under the direction of the famous President, Gerald Aungier, who succeeded Oxenden at Surat in July, 1669, Bombay grew and prospered. His instructions from England were explicit and dealt with many subjects. The Directors informed[5] the President, as already related, that they were sending out 20 maidens of "sober and civil lives," and they wound up with the remark that "the enterteining of a person of the quallitie above a soldier, whoe intended to proceed with his wife, hath alsoe encouraged some Gentlewomen, whoe though we did not invite thereto, yet being engaged therein, wee doe recommend them unto you, that they may bee there civilly treated, and have that respect from you as their virtues shall deserve." It will be seen that the Company took so keen an interest

[1] Oxenden, Streynsham Master, and Gary to Company. Letter dated January 15th, 1669.
[2] Proceedings of a Council of War, dated January 25th, 1669.
[3] Bombay to Surat. Letter dated February 22nd, 1669.
[4] Statement by Adams, Coates, Stirling and others, dated November 15th, 1669.
[5] India Office Records, Home Miscellaneous Series, No. 49, Vol. II, March 10th, 1668.

in its servants that there seems to have been no aspect of life, moral, social, spiritual, or temporal, which escaped the notice and copious remarks of the Directors.

Gerald Aungier was the soul of Bombay. A man of immense energy, he urged the Directors to make Bombay the headquarters of the Company on the western coast, to construct docks and a mole, to build a wall around the proposed town, to supply galleys or brigantines for the protection of commerce, and to clothe the troops in red uniforms. There can be no doubt that the rapid improvement and extension of the defences, hampered though they were by lack of funds, may be attributed primarily to the driving force of this President at Surat ; but even before the death of his predecessor (Sir Henry Oxenden), the Deputy Governor and Council of " Bombaim " were fully aware of the importance of the schemes for fortifications and harbour works. " Wee want much an Engineer," they wrote to Surat,[1] and added grimly, " Two or three would be convenient to bee provided for mortality sake." And they signed themselves " Your Honours' most faithfull and most affectionate Servants." But the Directors in London were adamant. " Wee desire you," they replied, " to enquire amongst our Factors and Soldiers, whither some of them are not skilful as Engineers, And, if they are, it wilbe far better to give them some encoragement, then to send one from hence on purpose, for that if able they wilbe very difficult to be procured and at a greate sallary and usually very willfull in their waies in putting persons upon extravagant and unnecessary charge, whereas a person not so much conceited of his owne abilities, but will be consulted with, will be much more suitable to our affaires. Your very loving friends, Wm. Thomson Govr., John Robinson, Andrew Riccard, etc."

The very loving old gentlemen in London seem to have held no exalted opinion of the professional engineer of the day, so wilful in his ways and so conceited ; but before this rebuff could reach the affectionate servants in Bombay, the latter had addressed headquarters at Surat, showing how well they were progressing with the work on Bombay Castle under the direction of one Captain Samuel Smith who was a capable engineer and surveyor.[2] The Directors were pleased to learn of the discovery of Captain Samuel Smith, and incidentally of another budding engineer called Toldervy ; it saved them the trouble and expense of sending an " extraordinary willfull " expert from home. So, in February, 1670, they addressed Aungier and his Surat Council in their usual careful manner, referring to Bombay :—[3]

" Wee wrote you at large the last yeare concerning the laying out of a Towne and Fortifications, and therefore shall forbeare to say

---

[1] India Office Records, Home Miscellaneous Series, No. 49, Vol. II, October 6th, 1668.
[2] *Ibid.*, March 17th, 1669.   [3] *Ibid.*, February 16th, 1670.

more as to those particulars now, and for the Enginier you write for, wee find Persons of great abilities difficult to be obteyned and extraordinary willfull in their way, and expensive, and therefore would have you make use of Captain Smith, Capt. Toldervy or any others that you are able upon the place, whom wee hope with your reasons will be sufficient to perform the worke in a regular manner, Fortifications being now more generally understood than formerly, and for their helpe therein have sent you bookes of Fortifications.

" Wee have perused the Paper mentioning places to bee fortified upon the Island of Bombay, but cannot approve thereof, for it mentions soe many that to be strongly fortified and mainteyned would cost more than the Island is like to be worth unto us. Wherefore, that which wee doe ayme at is, That as wee have directed, you lyne out a convenient place for the Towne and Castle and to fortifie them well and strongly, that there, (by God's blessing) may bee safety for our people and all Inhabitants."

At the end of 1669 the President and his Council were pressing on with the work, but found great difficulty in carrying out their schemes owing to lack of funds. Captain Samuel Smith, the leading engineer, having died earlier in the year, a Mr. Robert Barber was appointed to his post. " Thankes bee to God," wrote the Deputy Governor, Captain Young,[1] " our present Fortifications have gone on well hitherto, but wee shall find a great want of our deceased friend Capt. Smith who departed this life the night past of a flux,[2] Mr. Barber wee doubt not will give all assistance hee can, for the carrying them on, and wee hope you will remember him therein, for encouragement is the life of action. . . . As for the women that are come hither, wee thinke fitt to keepe them on the Company's charge, till disposed of, for we must not suffer them to wante, but wee expect your further order." Which effusion caused Aungier to send a letter to the Directors reporting progress and reassuring the old gentlemen about the proposed treatment of the virtuous gentlewomen till disposed of.[3]

We arrive now at the first instance of the appointment in India of a military engineer. It will be remembered that, on the Madras side, William Dixon held the post of " Chief Gunner and Ingenier " of Fort St. George in 1677. No mention is made, in any consultation or letter prior to that date, of an official engineer, though many of the Company's servants acted in that capacity. However, President Aungier of Surat realized, as early as 1671, that the engineering and surveying duties in his settlement at Bombay had become so responsible and diverse that an officer should be appointed under the proper

---

[1] India Office Records, Home Miscellaneous Series, No. 49, Vol. II, October 6th, 1669.
[2] Dysentery.
[3] India Office Records, Home Miscellaneous Series, No. 49, Vol. II, November 26th 1669.

title of Engineer and that a survey should be made of the Island :—[1]

"SURAT TO COMPANY.

"Your Island of Bombay enjoyes a great tranquility, and a considerable reputation, the Fortification is so farr raysed as to become notable defensive. . . . Colonel Herman Bake to whom you granted passage on shipp *Berkeley Castle* being defeated of his expectation in Persia offered his service to you to undertake some employment on your Island Bombay, whom Wee at first refused but having since discouvered his abillityes and being more sensible of the indispensible necessity you have of an able *Ingineer* for draining the coast overflowen Sands,[2] for lining out the new Towne, and for surveighing the Island, Wee have therefore entertained him in your Service allowing him together with his Assistant a chamber and diet at your Fort on Bombay and as to his sallary he himselfe desires to be referred wholly to your owne generosity. . . . Wee have found him a very ingenious, pious and well disposed person and receive him in the quality of Ingineer and Surveigher Generall of your Island Bombay during your pleasure."

Thus the name of Colonel Herman Bake, a German,[3] should head the long list of the professional engineers of India; and though his qualifications are summed up in the word "ingenious," and he was appointed in 1671 primarily for civil engineering work, there can be no doubt that this "pious and well disposed person" was also the military engineer of Bombay and was concerned in the further development of the defences. Bake was a wanderer who had no credentials except his practical ability; he was not recruited in England by the Company, whose hand indeed was forced by Aungier in appointing him before applying for permission to do so. Fortunately perhaps for Aungier, the Directors were in a complacent mood and replied as he desired :—[4]

"OUR PRESIDENT AND COUNSELL IN SURRATT.

"The good character you give of Captain Herman Bake makes us hope he may bee serviceable to us in that Imployment of Ingineer and Surveyor Generall of Bombay, which wee approve of, but as to his sallery wee must leave it to you to make him such allowance as shall be reasonable not exceeding £60 per annum with respect to the conveniency of his diet at the Companys Table. And wee desire especial care to be taken that wee be not put to any unnecessary charge in fortifying the Island but that all good husbandry and

---

[1] India Office Records, Home Miscellaneous Series, No. 49, Vol. II, April 7th, 1671.
[2] The "Drowned Lands," *i.e.*, unhealthy swamps partially covered at high tide.
[3] Court of Committees, January 11th, 1670 (Court Book, Vol. XXVI, p. 612).
[4] India Office Records, Home Miscellaneous Series, No. 49, Vol. II, March 15th, 1672.

frugality be used therein, for that menn under the Notion of Engineers are wont to be excessive in their charge. . . . Andrew Riccard, Govr., Robert Thomson, Dep., James Edwards, etc."

The following extracts, transcribed in modern spelling, from a letter written by President Aungier to the Court of Directors at the end of 1673, describe Bombay and its defences at that date :—[1]

" The Castle of Bombay lies upon a neck of land between two bays ; a quadrangular Fort whereof three points command the port and the two small bays, and the fourth with two of the others commands the town and the plain before the castle. It is of small circumference and irregularly built, owing to the ignorance of the engineers. The landward wall is 27 feet high and 25 feet broad, consisting of an outer and inner wall of stone and *terraphene*[2] of earth : the two seaward platforms are 20 feet high and 42 feet broad, to carry 36 ordnance besides those on the bastions. Three bastions are finished, mounted with 50 pieces of ordnance : the seaward bastion is incomplete. The powder rooms inside will contain 2,000 barrels of gunpowder. In the middle of the Fort is the Governor's house built formerly by the Portugals. A large spring or tank lies 100 paces outside the wall which the Engineers ought to have included. Instead they were obliged to build a new tank. There is no ditch or moat, but a *fausse-braye*[3] has been raised 20 feet from the wall outside the castle and two horn-works."[4]

The Directors continued to take a keen interest in the fortification of Bombay. They were resolved to make Bombay impregnable, and in this they succeeded so well that, when the Admiral of the Dutch fleet hoped to surprise the settlement in 1673, he found the defences so strong that he relinquished his plan for an assault. Work upon the Castle continued without a break, and in 1677 the Bombay Council informed headquarters at Surat that they were building their fourth, last and best bastion.

The rebellion of Captain Keigwin, the royalist commander of the garrison, who proclaimed himself Governor in the King's name and repudiated the authority of the Company, caused some dislocation of work in Bombay in 1683–84. The Directors soon afterwards adopted a new policy and resolved to declare war on the Mughals whose truculence had begun to exceed even the liberal bounds set by the Company ; they no longer addressed the native rulers in submissive terms, and they collected a fleet of 12 well-armed vessels of war. In 1687 they recognized the importance of Bombay by making it their

---

[1] *The Gazetteer of Bombay City and Island*, Vol. II, p. 67.
[2] *Terraphene, terraplane, terreplein.* The ground surface within a work.
[3] *Fausse-braye.* A low work built outside a higher parapet to provide a second tier of fire.
[4] *Horn.* A large outwork having a re-entering angle in front and two parallel flanks.

headquarters on the western coast in place of Surat, and their policy of aggression on that coast was directed from Bombay. It failed miserably. In 1689 the whole of Bombay, except the Castle, was captured by the Mughal fleet in retaliation for the supposed menace from the Company's armed ships, and the British in India were only saved by their sea power. Sir John Child, the able Governor of Bombay, acted with energy against the hostile fleet and trading vessels, and thus brought Aurangzeb, the Mughal Emperor, to reason; but Bombay was not restored to the British until, under the terms of a treaty signed in February, 1690, they had agreed to apologize to Aurangzeb, to pay a fine of £17,000, and to dismiss Child, who, however, died before he could undergo this last humiliation. After this disastrous war the garrison of Bombay was reduced to sore straits and consisted only of 70 English soldiers and a few Topasses and Gentues. The reputation of the British had received a shattering blow from which it did not recover for many years, and meanwhile the work of fortifying Bombay remained at a standstill. The original, or Old, East India Company was in the throes of a struggle against the New East India Company, which ended in the amalgamation of the two concerns. Until the union was completed in 1708, when the combined companies were incorporated under the title of "The United Company of Merchants of England trading to the East Indies," there was a lack of money, and of able direction, which prevented any large expansion of the settlement in Bombay.

On the eastern or Coromandel coast of India during the latter part of the seventeenth century, there was more engineering activity, and a greater expansion of trade, than on the Bombay side. The movements of the Maratha forces, under their renowned leader Sivaji, began to excite attention in Madras in 1676; and towards the end of the next year Governor Langhorn and his Council were in a state of considerable anxiety and much concerned with their defensive preparations. Sivaji, with a huge army, captured Gingee, but refrained from attacking the British settlement. This was perhaps fortunate considering the state of the defences. The threat, however, put new life into the engineers of the Fort, and they devoted themselves for a time to the improvement of the fortifications on the northern front of the White or Christian Town area.

Streynsham Master from the west coast, who succeeded Langhorn as Governor in 1678, was too independent in mind and nature to be a success, so he was superseded by William Gyfford three years later. But Master will ever be remembered for the building of St. Mary's Church, initiated by him and executed by Gunner William Dixon. He did not approve of Langhorn's alterations and additions to the Madras defences which he remarked upon adversely soon after he assumed charge. To use his own words:[1] "Those workes of the

[1] *Master Papers*, February 11th, 1678.

Fortifications built in his (Langhorn's) time have been most of them twice done, first with Turf, which was very chargeable and soone mouldered and washed downe, and then with Brick and Stone ; all done upon his owne fancy and humor without adviseing with anyone, at double the Expence need have been, and much washed into the Sea through folly." He was resolved not to act upon his own fancy and humour, so, in January, 1679, he summoned the captains of several of the Company's ships,[1] with some military officers, to report on the fortifications, and they advised him that certain bastions, curtains and gates should be rebuilt without delay and the warehouses and barracks enlarged. William Dixon, the Gunner and Engineer, served on the committee ; but four of the seven members were merely merchant captains passing through Madras, which shows in what small regard the scientific side of military engineering was held, or at least the straits to which the Governor was reduced to obtain advice in such matters owing to the parsimony of the Court of Directors. The rather ambitious recommendations of the committee were referred to the Directors, but the latter were not very sympathetic. They replied[2] that no new works should be started owing to financial stringency ; that the fort and town seemed to be strong enough to resist any sudden attack ; and that the Company's trade should not be supported by fortifications and guns but by " fayr complyance " with the King of Golconda and his chief minister. They added, naïvely, that if that monarch showed hostility at any time, £500 spent in *piscashes*[3] would probably be more useful than money expended in the upkeep of fortifications.

Reference has been made already to the approval accorded by the Company to the appointment of Colonel Herman Bake as Engineer and Surveyor-General of Bombay in 1672. This experiment must have proved a success, for nearly two years later, on the retirement[4] of William Dixon from the post of Chief Gunner and Engineer of Fort St. George in Madras, the Directors summoned up courage at last to face the expense of an engineer recruited from England. Mr. Edward Fowle was the first such military engineer to arrive in India. He sailed from London in October, 1683, and landed at Madras in the following year.[5] Fowle was appointed as " Engineer and Master Gunner," and not as " Chief Gunner and Engineer," as was his predecessor ; that is to say, he was recruited primarily for engineering work. He had no military rank. In those remote days, and for many years later, engineers were not considered as executive military officers, and indeed the Company's military officers in actual com-

---

[1] This seems to have been a common practice. It was adopted at Fort William, Calcutta, in 1706. See Chapter III.
[2] *Letter Book*, Vol. VI, January 3rd and December 3rd, 1679.
[3] Presents.
[4] He seems to have become a trader after retirement.
[5] *Public Despatches from England*, Vol. V, October 19th, 1683.

mand of troops were denied military rank. Several military officers in Madras petitioned for commissions in 1678 and their request was granted by the Governor; but the order was revoked by the Directors[1] with the biting comment that they looked upon the granting of commissions as a " vaine Ostentatious thing." Edward Fowle soon fell a victim to one of the diseases so fatal to the British settlers. He was succeeded in Madras by one Robert Ivory, who was said to have " behaved himself very soberly and diligently " during Fowle's absence, and Giles Scudimore was appointed as the Chief Gunner's mate.

The builders of the British fortifications in India during the seventeenth century were quite inexperienced and naturally they made many errors. They seem to have invited trouble particularly by neglecting to provide adequate foundations for their walls. The same fault is evident in many of the very old bungalows, and even in some large public buildings where the foundations are frequently quite insufficient according to modern practice. The engineers did not realize the effect of the seepage of water. There is no doubt that they were inclined to build their coast fortresses too near the high-water level, and time and again we read of the collapse of a bastion here, or a curtain there, from the effects of the encroachment of the sea which was probably accompanied by percolation through the sand below the shallow foundations. When criticizing the designs, however, due allowance should be made for the difficulties caused by lack of funds. There is nothing to show for money spent on foundations. Display and immediate protection were all-important in dealing with the turbulent and treacherous native rulers of the seventeenth century. The engineers of Fort St. George had many a bitter lesson before they learnt that it is dangerous for a man to build his house upon the sand.

The native inhabitants were required " with all gentleness " to pay for the erection of fortifications which they did not want—a custom which was copied from the Dutch and French. The ruler of each European settlement was an autocrat within its walls. His factory became the nucleus of a native town which added both trade and weakness. The inhabitants benefited greatly by the increasing trade which they could carry on without molestation under the protection of the Company's soldiers, and consequently the demand that they should pay handsomely for the defences of the settlement as a whole was reasonable as a form of insurance of life and property. This demand was made in every large British settlement. The money was well spent on fortifications, and this was recognized in the end by the native population which increased steadily in spite of taxes and so-called " voluntary subscriptions." In 1684 the Directors estimated that they had spent altogether

[1] *Public Despatches from England*, November 18th, 1681.

£300,000 on the fortifications and buildings of Fort St. George,[1] so they were justified in requiring financial assistance.

Madras was established definitely as a Presidency in 1684, and it entered then on a stormy period. Within a short time the new and aggressive policy adopted by the Company began to cause trouble in the south, just as it led to reverses in Bombay and complete disaster in Bengal. In 1685 the Mughal forces laid siege to the native stronghold of Golconda and frightened the Madras engineers into activity at Fort St. George, as it was but a step from Golconda to the British settlement. Materials and supplies were collected, reservoirs made, guns mounted and sallyports strengthened; and the captains of the ships in harbour and "other experienced men" were invited to inspect the defences with the Governor and Council and to make suggestions for improvements. Elihu Yale, who succeeded Gyfford as Governor in July, 1687, and after whom Yale University was named, was informed in October of that year that Golconda had been captured by the Mughals; and soon afterwards he learnt that they had appeared at Conjeveram, near Madras, and that a Mughal *subadar*[2] had been appointed to rule the adjacent country. In view of the hostile action by the Company against the Mughal Government in Bengal, it appeared to be certain now that Madras would be besieged; but the storm blew over, and the defences of Fort St. George were not put to the test.

The Company's expedition against Bengal failed. Job Charnock, the Agent in Bengal, having evacuated the northern factories, arrived at Madras in March, 1689, with a large retinue. The victorious Mughals seized the British factories at Vizagapatam, Masulipatam and Madapollam, and they beheaded the King of Golconda. Anxiety in Madras was relieved at last by the humiliating peace made with the Emperor Aurangzeb in March, 1690, after which Charnock sailed again for Bengal to found a settlement at Chuttanutee (Sutanuti) on the Hugli, below his former factory at Hugli village, and so to lay the foundations of Calcutta. In the same year a new English factory was established at Tegnapatam, south of Pondicherry and near Cuddalore. The place was called Fort St. David, and was bought from the Marathas whose fortifications were improved and strengthened by the British engineers. The position in Madras was precarious. In their weakness the British feared both the Muhammadan armies of the Mughals and their closer neighbours the Marathas, who were in the process of being defeated by the forces of Aurangzeb. The fortifications of Fort St. George, and the sea power of England, alone stood between them and complete disaster. To make matters worse, war had been declared by France against England and Holland; and a French squadron appeared off Fort St.

---

[1] *Public Despatches from England*, Vol. IV, July 2nd, 1684.
[2] Ruler of a *Suba* or province.

George on August 15th, 1690, and fought an action against the Company's ships and some Dutchmen. The lot of Governor Yale, worried by the threat of the Maratha forces, the hostility of the Mughals, and war against France, was unenviable.

During this period of alarms and excursions there were many changes in the cadre of engineers and gunners at Fort St. George, caused mostly by disease or accident. Robert Ivory, Engineer and Master Gunner for five years, died in 1690, and was succeeded, for two months only, by Captain Putsham (sometimes spelt Geesham). Putsham died suddenly, so Thomas Meddowes was appointed and held the post for five years till he was invalided. These men were Chief Gunners of the Fort. In May, 1689, a master mariner, one Captain John Spencer, was appointed " Chief Gunner of the out-Garrison " ; but he met a sudden end, one month later, by being blown up when charging grenades. Captain Barwick, who followed him, survived for only five months. Mr. Thomas Makreeth was then appointed as Provisional Surveyor " to direct and inspect what Bullwarks and Fortifications are ordered to be erected and repaired " because he was said to " have some skill in Fortification and Gunnery."[1] With such rapid changes in the technical staff there must have been great difficulty in carrying out the urgent engineering work necessitated by the dangerous political state of the country.

Following on the troubled period of the beginning of the war against the French, there seems to have been a lull in engineering activities in Madras as in Bombay. The Company was in low water. Both the British and the Portuguese were always under the threat of the Mughal domination. The Moslems, who had captured St. Thomé, leased it to the Portuguese in 1688 though it remained actually in their power. In 1696, when relations between Governor Higginson and the Mughal Nawab Zulfikar Khan became strained, the Portuguese tried to get leave to fortify St. Thomé ; but instead, in the following year, the Mughals began to demolish all the defences then existing, and the place soon became a waste of rubble. The hostile attitude of Zulfikar Khan towards the British was most marked in 1698 after the fall of Gingee which had been the seat of the Maratha Government for many years. All the British inhabitants of Madras were concentrated in White Town for safety, more guns were mounted, and the engineers raised some of the battlements. The problem of the defence of the large area covered by the adjoining Black Town, where many of the British had taken up their residence owing to lack of space in White Town, became acute. It was decided to rely on musketry alone for the defence of this area, to dismantle the bastions, and to strengthen the curtain walls, though it is probable that these measures were dictated more by lack of funds than a hope of improving the defences. The Company's factories acted every-

[1] *Factory Records*, Fort St. George, Vol. VI, November 14th, 1689.

where as magnets, attracting by the facilities for trade and the protection which they afforded, a heterogeneous and cosmopolitan population which became a source both of financial strength and military weakness. The fruit which grew on the tree weighed down its branches. The helpless and money-seeking population, clinging for life to the British battlements, was almost useless for their defence, and it fell to the engineers to ensure that the fortifications kept pace with the influx of private traders. It is greatly to their credit that they succeeded as well as they did.

So threatening were the clouds overhanging the settlement in 1696 that the Directors were forced at last to admit that a specialist in engineering, as distinct from gunnery, was essential on the Coromandel coast. They had approved of the appointment of Colonel Herman Bake as Engineer and Surveyor-General of Bombay in 1672, though he was not sent from England, and, as already related, they had recruited Mr. Edward Fowle in England in 1683 for engineering duty in Madras with gunnery work added. Now they sent to Fort St. George, Captain Frederick Mathew von Werlinhoffe (or Merlinhoffe) to relieve Mr. Fowle who was on contract for seven years only, and commissioned him, on April 24th, 1696, as Engineer and Miner General for an indefinite period, giving him military rank and high standing in the Madras settlement.[1]

Captain von Werlinhoffe did not remain long in the Company's service. After one year at Fort St. George he was transferred in 1698 to the new settlement at Fort St. David to construct the defences of that place and of Cuddalore. Four years later it seems that he was considered to be one of those "extraordinary willful persons so much conceited of their owne abillities, and apt to put persons upon extravagant and unnecessary charge," for his services were dispensed with on the ground that they entailed heavy expense to no purpose.[2] So, after all, the first experiment of the Directors in the direct recruitment from England of a commissioned military engineer was a failure, and in 1700 the well-tried gunners of the Fort, assisted by other officers, appear to have resumed their engineering duties. The failure of von Werlinhoffe threw the responsibilities of engineering on Mr. Robert Atkinson, who was Chief Gunner from 1695 till he died in 1711 in Madras.

Governor Pitt, once an "Interloper,"[3] held the reins of office in 1700. He was so much concerned with the weakness of Black Town that he undertook the permanent fortification of that area by a rampart, 1,500 yards in length and 17 feet thick, faced on both sides with brick and paved on the crest to carry guns. This huge wall, with flanking works at intervals, surrounded Black Town on all sides

---

[1] *Public Consultations*, Vol. XXV, February 25th, 1697.
[2] *Ibid.*, Vol. XXXI, December 3rd, 1702.
[3] A private trader, competing with the Company.

except the sea face, which was already protected, and part of the southern face which touched the northern rampart of White Town. It replaced the old earthen wall, and was completed in seven years. Pitt tried to clear a field of fire to the north-west, and with much difficulty raised money for the cost of the works by taxes or voluntary subscriptions from the native inhabitants. The new wall, and the flanking works, were finished in 1707.

When Captain von Werlinhoffe was sent to Fort St. David, the Council of Fort St. George had to look around for someone to help Gunner Robert Atkinson, and so we find a Paymaster acting as an engineer in 1700 :—[1]

"FORT ST. GEORGE CONSULTATION.

"The Governour and Councill having Surveigh'd and view'd Attapollam gate belonging to the black town, think it necessary to make a small work for clearing the curtains on both Sides, as also for the defence of the Gate; and therefore Order that the Paymaster forthwith gets all Materials together to do it as the Governour shall Direct; and likewise to carry on the wall on both sides of the aforesaid Gate."

In 1711 there was a still more curious instance of amateur engineering, or at least of the supply of engineering materials.[2] Surgeon Edward Bulkley, of Fort St. George, had left the ill-paid profession of medicine to become Paymaster, and the foundations at St. Thomas' Point having subsided, it was "order'd that the paymaster (Bulkley) make preparation of bricks and what else necessary to rebuild the said Point as soon as the rains are over, and that in the meantime the Gunner do take off the gunns to prevent the point falling on peoples heads as they pass by."

The history of military engineering in Madras during the seventeenth century may be concluded with a brief description of Fort St. George as it was at the end of that period. Thomas Salmon, who was once an Ensign in the Company's service, wrote as follows in his *Modern History or the Present State of All Nations*, which was published in 1724 :—

"The fort (Inner Fort) is a regular square, about a hundred yards on each side, with four bastions, built with what they call iron stone (laterite) being of the colour of unwrought iron and very rough on the outside like honeycomb. There is no ditch about the fort, and the walls are arched and hollow within, so that I question whether they are cannon proof. It has two gates, one to the east and the other to the west. The western gate which looks towards the land is pretty large; and here the main guard is kept, the soldiers of the

---

[1] *Public Consultations*, Vol. XXIX, December 4th, 1700.
[2] *Ibid.*, Vol. XLII, November 3rd, 1711.

guard lying on the right and left of it under the wall which, being hollow, serves them instead of a guard house. The east gate towards the sea is but small, and guarded only with a file of musqueteers. In the middle of the fort stands the Governor's house, in which also are apartments for the Company's servants; it is a handsome lofty square stone building; the first rooms are ascended by ten or twelve steps, and from thence another pair of stairs leads to the council chamber and the Governor's lodgings. The fort stands pretty near the middle of the White Town where the Europeans inhabit. This is an oblong square about a quarter of a mile in length, but not half so much in breadth. To the northward of the fort are three strait handsome streets, and as many to the south. The buildings are of brick, and several of the houses are two stories high. Their roofs are flat and covered with plaister made of sea shells, which no rain can penetrate; and being secured with battlements, they (the inhabitants) take the fresh air upon them morning and evening. The walls of these houses are very thick and the rooms lofty.

" To the northward, adjoining the White Town, stands a much larger town, called Black Town, where the Portuguese, Indians, Armenians and a great variety of other people inhabit. This is built in the form of a square, and is better than a mile and a half in circumference. The streets of Black Town are wide, and trees are planted in some of them, but except some few brick houses the rest are miserable cottages built with clay and thatched. In this Black Town stands an Armenian church and several little Pagodas or Indian temples; to the latter belong abundance of female choristers. . . . These seem also designed to serve the public in another capacity and make up the equipage of a great man when he goes abroad; for every man of figure in the country, I observed, had a number of these singing women run before him; even the Governor of Fort St. George was attended by fifty of them as well as by the country musick when he went out; but some of our late Governors, out of their excessive modesty, have thought fit to dispence with this piece of grandeur. The Governor has as much respect paid him at his going abroad as a sovereign Prince. The guards are drawn out, the drums beat as he passes by; and fifty or sixty armed blacks run before him, and some of the likeliest young fellows he can pick out of the European soldiers run by the side of the palanquin he is carried in, armed with blunderbusses. A numerous train of servants also, and the country musick, attend him, and with their harsh untuneable trumpets give notice of his march."

CHAPTER III.

THE BUILDING OF OLD FORT WILLIAM.

THE history of military engineering in Bengal centres naturally in Old Fort William : not in the elaborate fortress which now overlooks the Calcutta *maidan*, but in the small, ill-designed and badly-situated work, long since ruined and buried, where Holwell tried to retrieve the errors of his countrymen.

The pioneers of the European nations in Bengal, as in Western India, were the Portuguese, who entered the river Hugli about the year 1530, and at the end of the century built a fort and a church at the town of Hugli, some 26 miles upstream of the site of modern Calcutta. Villages began to multiply below Hugli ; and a group of three, named Chuttanutee (Sutanuti), Kalikata[1] (Calcutta) and Govindpur, sprang up on the eastern bank of the river on some high ground surrounded by jungles and swamps. Attracted by the Bengal trade, the British established a factory at Balasore[2] in 1637 ; and in 1650, through the good offices of Surgeon Gabriel Boughton at the Mughal Court at Agra, they were permitted by the Emperor Shah Jahan to build another at Hugli. By 1658 they were firmly installed in that place, with some Dutch traders at Chinsura as their nearest neighbours a few miles downstream. They built factories higher up the river at Cossimbazar and Patna, but were soon involved in serious difficulties, having no military power to cope with the depredations of pirates, the competition of the Dutch and Portuguese, and the impositions of the native Governors of Bengal and Hugli appointed by the Mughal Emperor. They were allowed to remain because of their trade. To use the metaphor of a certain babu of modern Bengal, the Mughals did not wish " to kill the fatted calf that laid the golden egg."

When the Court of Directors sent Streynsham Master to Bengal, in 1676, to reorganize the British factories, he could do little to remedy the administrative chaos which had developed ; and William Hedges, who became Agent at Hugli in 1682, could only advise the Court that the Company must resolve to quarrel with the Mughals and to build a fort at the mouth of the river.[3] But the Directors favoured instead a raid on Chittagong[4] as a counterblast to the Mughal threats. Such was the position when a remarkable man named Job Charnock

---

[1] From the goddess Kali.
[2] About 100 miles from the mouth of the Hugli River.
[3] Hedges' *Diary*, Vol. I, pp. 117, 121.
[4] A sea port east of the Hugli River.

JOB CHARNOCK FOUNDS CALCUTTA.

—the ultimate founder of Calcutta—became Agent in 1685. The project to capture and fortify Chittagong intrigued the Directors so much that they issued some instructions on field engineering which ended with the remark that " untill a City or an armie be intrenched, no man ought to think himself too good to give his helping hand to make all sure ; although after the danger is over, such work is only proper for Pioneers or such as you call Cooleys "—which is, perhaps, the first official reference to the humble Pioneer of the seventeenth century.

A crisis arrived in 1686 which forced Charnock to abandon Hugli and retire to the island of Hijili at the mouth of the river ; but on his voyage downstream he was so much impressed with the advantages of the Sutanuti locality for security and trade that, when he had patched up a truce with the Mughals, he returned to it in 1688 and spent some months there while his men died of dysentery and malaria. But the Directors disapproved of his movements, and sent a swaggering commander named Heath to remove all the British from Bengal ; so Charnock and most of his men quitted Sutanuti on November 8th, 1688, and sailed for Madras. The British venture into Bengal seemed to have come to a disastrous end.

However, the Mughal Emperor Aurangzeb[1] was sorry to lose the British traders, and accordingly invited Charnock and his men to return to Bengal from Madras after they had idled there for 15 months. So Charnock sailed for Bengal on July 30th, 1690, and arrived at Sutanuti for the third time, with his Council and only 30 soldiers, on August 24th. The monsoon rain was falling day and night, provisions were scarce, Charnock was old and feeble, his men were sick, and the only shelter was in three mud huts or in the ships and boats. Under these depressing conditions the little band of hardy Englishmen founded the " City of Palaces." They were completely isolated and defenceless in a malarial swamp.

The desperate situation of the English traders in Sutanuti was saved by the arrival of Sir John Goldsborough from Madras, in August, 1693, as " Commissary Generall, Admirall of the East India Fleet, and Chief Governour of the Right Honorable English East India Company's Affaires." Goldsborough found the settlement in a deplorable condition and proceeded at once to reform the administration. His first step was to appoint Charles Eyre, a son-in-law of Charnock, as Agent, and then to reduce the undisciplined garrison of so-called soldiers to an establishment of 25 men with some military value. In this measure of economy he followed the advice given by the Court in the previous year, that " a Penny saved is two Pence gott." From an historical point of view, however, his most notable act was that he ordered the construction of the first fortification in

---

[1] Shah Jahan fell ill in 1657, and in July, 1658, his third son, Aurangzeb, ascended the throne after a fratricidal war of succession.

Calcutta in the form of a mud wall to enclose part of the settlement; this wall was to be built as soon as the Mughals would accord permission. The site which he selected was not in Sutanuti itself but a short distance southwards in " Dhee Collecotta " (Dihi Calcutta). It was the highest spot in the Sutanuti area, and lay to the north of the burial ground, where he and Charnock now lie, and south of the Barabazar which supplied provisions to the settlement. It included the few small huts acquired by Charnock for his men. This was the site of Old Fort William. Sir John Goldsborough's mud wall was the first sign of the rise of British power in Bengal which continued thereafter with only one check, and it is probable that the wall was completed before his services were lost to his country by his untimely death in November, when he had been only three months in Bengal. His death was a serious blow to British interests in that province, but Charles Eyre carried on his traditions in a worthy manner.

There can be little doubt that the British would have liked to fortify each factory as it was established. They regarded with envious eyes the modest defences which the Dutch, through bribery and a display of some military power, were allowed to erect around their factory at Chinsura. The native government watched the British as a cat watches a mouse. The Directors in London, well aware of this fact, knew that if any of their servants in Bengal began to build works which might be considered defensible, the local native ruler would seize the excuse to attack and sack the offending settlement under the plea that his safety was threatened. Repeatedly we find instructions to Bengal that works which might be useful for defensive purposes must be very carefully disguised. A factory might safely be surrounded by a plain wall of mud or even brick, but there must be no provision for flanking fire from bastions; the wall must be designed to prevent theft and not to repel attack.

Each British factory, being a trading centre, became surrounded in a few years by a native town; consequently there was no field of fire whatever from the factory walls, for the traders did not dare to insist upon a clear space around their buildings. At Balasore, Patna, Malda, Hugli and Hijili, the factories were practically undefended and indefensible, and it seemed likely that Sutanuti would remain open to attack unless Fate intervened. The home authorities considered that the fortification of the factory would be worth the money spent on it; but no opportunity occurred for the British to claim the right to fortify their settlement until Charles Eyre wrung a grudging consent from the Nawab of Dacca, in 1696, and took full advantage of it. The factors then began to improve Goldsborough's simple wall, and applied to Madras on January 1st, 1697, for ten " proper Gunns for the points." In the following May, they discharged 50 " Gunmen " from their service, though they continued to fortify their position and built a strong point, or keep, within it by substituting a structure of brick and mud for the old thatched house which had contained the Company's provisions and stores. They disobeyed, without hindrance, a Mughal order which forbade permanent buildings. The fort was rising day by day, but there was little room for expansion. More ground was urgently needed, especially as trade had been concentrated in Sutanuti for safety and better supervision.

Eyre succeeded in extending the British settlement in 1698. The Court had informed him in the previous year[1] that he would do well to hire three or four miles of land around the factory, at a rent of 800 to 1,000 rupees a year, before its value rose; so, through a present of 16,000 rupees, he procured letters patent from Prince Azim-ush-shan, the Nawab of Bengal, allowing the Company to buy from the existing holders the right to rent the three villages of Calcutta, Sutanuti and Govindpur. The purchase, which Eyre and his Council considered to be " the best money that ever was spent," was concluded in the same year, and " Dihi Kalkatah, Sataluti and Gobindpur " came under the English rule for the trifling annual rent of 1,300 rupees. It is impossible to overestimate the importance of this acquisition. It brought great prestige to the Company at a time when its fortunes were at a low ebb. The Company's servants in Bengal became at once landed proprietors with the full recognition of the Mughal government. But the most valuable feature of the transaction, from a military point of view, was that the British could fortify their settlement without interference. The Court of Directors was not slow to remark on this point :—[2]

"COURT TO BENGAL.

" Your Present to the Prince was very considerable and made a large hole in our Cash, but since you were necessitated thereunto you did well to take that advantage for getting his Grant. You may go on now in making any necessary Additional Strength to our ffortification without fear of giving Umbrage to the Moors, because they can't pretend to make an inquisition in a Place where they having nothing to do withall."

Bengal was constituted as a separate Presidency in a general letter, dated December 20th, 1699, and Sir Charles Eyre became its first President in May, 1700. In that letter the Directors bestowed on Goldsborough's fort, then becoming of some military value, the historic name of Fort William, after King William III. of England. Old Fort William was an enclosure with a mud wall, possibly rebuilt with brick in parts, but having only one properly constructed bastion of brick masonry laid in mud mortar with some adjacent lengths of similar wall on each side of it. It lay on the highest ground on the river-bank, so that it commanded the Hugli, and, to some extent, the

---

[1] General letter, Court to Bengal, April 16th, 1697. Para. 6, *Letter Book*, No. 9.
[2] *Ibid.*, November 21st, 1699. *Letter Book*, No. 10.

native town outside its walls. The single bastion was approximately square in plan, and was at the south-east corner of the enclosure which contained a few houses and many huts. A second bastion, at the north-east corner, was added by President John Beard in 1701.[1] Beard was warned from England that, as Aurangzeb was reported to be dying, serious disturbances might be expected before his successor was settled on the throne, and that, during that period, " rich unfortifyed places would be a tempting bait to those perfidious people." The disturbances were heralded by a proclamation at the end of 1701, ordering the arrest of all Europeans in India. A Rohilla chieftain, named Daud Khan, blockaded Fort St. George in the next year, and the servants of the Old Company were seized at various places in Bengal. But John Beard had meanwhile made such additions to the meagre defences of Fort William on the landward side, where the fire from his ships was masked by intervening houses, that the place was strong enough to discourage any Nawab or Governor who was bent on loot. He took the precaution also to transfer some guns from his ships to the fort, with sailors to man them, and thus raised his garrison to 120 men. These preparations had their effect. Fort William escaped attack, the Mughals assured the English of their peaceable intentions, and, on October 6th, 1702, the Union Jack of those days was hoisted for the first time on the flagstaff within the walls, proclaiming to the eastern world that England had a sure footing in Bengal.

In 1883, Roskell Bayne, of the East Indian Railway, found by personal examination that the original masonry work of Fort William was of good material and very hard to demolish. H. E. A. Cotton, in his book *Calcutta Old and New*, remarks : " The small depth to which the foundation walls were carried astonished Mr. Bayne. Where the ground was faulty, *sal* timbers were freely used and built upon, but deep foundations appeared not to be thought of. The masonry, however, was of such strength that pickaxe and crowbar were of no avail, and blasting by gunpowder was resorted to." The curtain walls of the first or south-east bastion were more than six feet thick, and those of the north-east bastion still thicker. These walls were battered to a slope of one in ten, and their outer faces treated with a thin coat of lime plaster of a rich crimson tint and reticulated in imitation of stonework.[2] Stone being unobtainable in lower Bengal in those days, Beard thought, no doubt, that his walls of imitation ashlar masonry would impress the native government and make a brave show ; but he might have chosen a better colour than rich crimson in the heat and glare of Bengal. He was spared their contemplation for long, however, for he handed over charge to the " Rotation Government " on February 1st, 1704. In this absurd

[1] Beard succeeded Eyre in 1700.
[2] Bayne, in the *Journal of the Asiatic Society of Bengal*, Part I, 1883, p. 109.

system of diarchy, two members of the Council, with opposing views and representing the old and new companies respectively, presided over the United Company's affairs in alternate weeks; under such direction it is surprising that anything was done to strengthen Fort William during the next few years. The guiding hand of President Beard was gone. Trade, politics and self-aggrandisement were of greater importance than protection. The house was divided against itself; and a civil war, such as followed the death of Aurangzeb in March, 1707, was needed to revive military engineering in Bengal.

We come now to a most difficult question. Who were the engineers, if any, who designed and constructed the earlier defences of Old Fort William? It is a curious and regrettable fact that the historians of the eighteenth century, and the records of that period which still exist, omit the names of the men who executed these works. The names of the engineers in Madras are recorded, or their identities can be inferred. The names of several of the Bombay engineers are given. Why, then, are the names of the engineers of the more recent settlement in Bengal hidden in the mists of time? A theory has been advanced that there were no engineers in charge of the first structural operations in Calcutta—that, in fact, the walls grew at the whim, and according to the fancy, of a succession of the Company's servants advised from London. Yet the Directors had already found, both in Madras and Bombay, that it was worth their while to employ engineers, however "conceited and willful." Colonel Herman Bake had been appointed in 1671 as Engineer and Surveyor-General of Bombay; Edward Fowle had been sent from England to Madras as Engineer and Master Gunner twelve years later; and Captain von Werlinhoffe was made Engineer and Miner-General in the East Indies in 1696. Von Werlinhoffe probably reached Madras in 1697, when the English seized the opportunity to improve the walls of Fort William during a Hindu rebellion in Bengal. Did he, as Engineer-in-Chief, visit Calcutta to advise on the defences? It seems unlikely that he made the journey as he was transferred to Fort St. David in March, 1698, and dismissed in 1702. It is possible that, as the result of their experience of von Werlinhoffe, who appears to have been either a fool or a knave, the Directors may have been disinclined for a time to experiment further with military engineers.

In the absence of any mention of a British engineer, one is led to believe, from the meagre information which is available, that the early designers and constructors of Old Fort William were certain jolly mariners from the Company's ships in the Hugli, the "Buxey"[1] or Military Paymaster of the settlement, a French engineer employed by the British, and perhaps the Gunner and his crew. The following advice was penned in 1702 :—[2]

[1] *Bakhshi.*
[2] General letter, Court to Bengal, March 5th, 1702. *Letter Book*, No. 10.

"COURT TO BENGAL.

"We shall grudge at no reasonable Charge you may be at in Strengthening your ffortifications, and if you are not sufficiently instructed in forming them to a Pentagon or figure of 5 equall Sides and Angles, Scarce a Commander that Comes to you but will instruct you therein and give you his opinion what is necessary to be done to make your buildings more commodious, strong and tenable, ffortification being one part of the usuall Study of accomplisht Marriners.[1] If their stay is so short that you can't compleat what they advise in that time let them draw you out a plan or Scheme on paper, and do you perfect it at leisure."

Again, in 1706, the Court wrote[2] that " some of our Europe Commanders are doubtless able to give you their opinion wherein they think it may be strengthen'd by any additional building because Gunnery and ffortification is part of the study of an ingenious Mariner." So it is most probable that several ingenious and accomplished captains of ships hitched up their braces and went ashore to help in the design of the bastions and curtains of the old fort on the Hugli. The Paymaster, who was the Seventh Member of Council, was not allowed to escape the net of the fishers for engineers. In a Bengal Public Consultation of 1707,[3] it was agreed " that we make two regular Bastions to the Water Side to Answer those to the land, and the Buxey is Ordered to See it well perform'd out of hand, and to that end to take all materials in town that are necessary thereto." So it is reasonable to presume that the poor Buxey was caught and forced to serve as an engineer.

The French had a factory at Chandarnagar below Chinsura, and had availed themselves of the opportunity offered by a Hindu rebellion in 1697 to add to their works of defence. They had never been watched by the Mughals so carefully as the British, and consequently they had more scope for engineering. They could not equal the British in the volume of their trade, but they decided that they would be well advised to keep on good terms with their neighbours and rivals in Bengal though England and France were often at war. It seems that the French in Bengal had a capable engineer in 1707, whom they were prepared to hire out to the British, thus earning both money and goodwill ; for the Court of Directors, when discussing further measures for strengthening Calcutta in the following year, wrote as follows :—[4]

" Mr. Winder says that the ffrench have a very skillfull Engineer in their Service that has been employ'd by you in Severall businesses

---

[1] Exemplified by the case of Bartholomew Plaisted, a retired ship's captain, of whom more later.
[2] General letter, Court to Bengal, January 18th, 1706. *Letter Book*, No. 12.
[3] April 28th, 1707.
[4] General letter, Court to Bengal, April 7th, 1708. *Letter Book*, No. 13.

and that would be willing to earn money, for the ffrench have little business of their own to do. If so and you do find him or any other Person able to perform such a business[1] we give you leave to set instantly about it."

This French engineer, whose name is not mentioned, was probably concerned in the building of Old Fort William, that being the most important work which the British had undertaken. His services were not available for long, as he died in the beginning of 1709.[2]

The ideas of the home authorities on the nature and requirements of Fort William are well expressed in a general letter written in 1706:—[3]

"COURT TO BENGAL.

"It pleases us well to read the ffort is in so good a Condition and doubt not but it will be so preserved. Our aim is not to lay out the money to make it a compleat ffortification sufficient to resist the Attacks of an European Enemy, for we are not apprehensive of that danger, but to make it tenable against the Moors in Case they should assault you. We are told you are about new building Calcutta and making it more regular, if so we recommend you to order the Streets so as that the ffort Guns may be brought to bear on the Severall Streets to beat out an Enemy that should gett into them, and that the Houses may be at such a Distance from the ffort as not to prejudice any part of it in Case by accident or design they should be sett on fire."

This extract brings to light a rather curious point. Houses were not to be allowed close to the fort; but the primary reason for this prohibition was protection from fire and not the retention of a field of fire for the muskets of the garrison. It is obvious that the gentlemen in London were traders and not soldiers; and to crown their military blunders they permitted the construction of the Church of St. Anne by the Rotation Government in Calcutta. This building was completed in 1709,[4] and its roof and steeple dominated the east curtain and most of the interior of Fort William, for it lay only 50 yards from the walls. It had a tapering, octagonal spire until the time of the cyclone of 1737, and was a well-built structure, 80 feet long, with a high-pitched roof on massive pillars. St. Anne's Church was indeed by far the most prominent and lofty building in old Calcutta. And yet this point of vantage was not only near the walls of the fort, but it looked straight down on to them.

The third and fourth bastions of Old Fort William, on the river side,

---

[1] Digging a large ditch.
[2] General letter, Bengal to Court, February 18th, 1709. *Coast and Bay Abstracts of Letters received*, K.77.
[3] General letter, Court to Bengal, January 18th, 1706. *Letter Book*, No. 12.
[4] The merchants and sailors of Calcutta provided the funds.

were finished in 1707. They were designed to mount one gun each; but these guns were not mounted at once for fear of offending the suspicious native government. The two bastions were run up in great haste. Signs of this haste were disclosed in the remains of the north-west bastion when they were exposed by excavation in 1883: the courses of bricks were found to be irregular, the outlines confused, and the dimensions contracted. The Rotation Government tried to keep native huts away from the walls, but their efforts seem to have been half-hearted and were soon abandoned. The Calcutta engineers began to case the two inland bastions with good masonry in 1708, and the Court of Directors put forward proposals for what was, in those days, a large engineering work. The moving spirit was Mr. Jonathan Winder, a retired "Nabob" of Bengal, who had been chairman of the United Council when in Calcutta. The Directors were greatly impressed by Winder's advice, which, however well meant, must have made him very unpopular with the perspiring servants of the Company in steamy Calcutta.

Winder proposed that a large ditch should be dug round three sides of the settlement, and that the northern face should have a defensible wall. This wall was to run eastwards from the river between the northern, or Sutanuti, area, and the central, or Calcutta, area, thus excluding the Sutanuti native quarter from the fortified enclosure.[1] From the eastern end of the wall, a flooded ditch was to run southwards, and finally westwards, to form the eastern and southern defences of the Calcutta or European area, debouching into the river between that area and the southern, or Govindpur, area, which was native. Its proposed course was along the line of the present Chitpur Road, at that time about half a mile from the river bank; thence through the "Garden" or Calcutta Green[2] (now Dalhousie Square), past the Burying Place (now St. John's Churchyard) south of Fort William, and finally, gradually westwards till it entered the Hugli through a sluice to retain or admit the tide. The length of the ditch was to be 2,000 yards, and it was to be crossed by a defended drawbridge opposite Fort William. Winder suggested also that a wharf, or "Key," should be built on the river-bank alongside the fort. The Directors accepted his schemes provisionally, and ordered the Council in Calcutta to execute them at any reasonable cost if they agreed that the ditch would fulfil its various purposes which were to form a line of defence, to drain the Calcutta area, and to provide earth for filling up insanitary holes which had been dug by the inhabitants. Winder had evolved his scheme for a ditch before he left Bengal, for the Directors stated that, when Winder was in Calcutta, the native merchants and other inhabitants had been so much in favour of it that they had offered to pay one-half the cost of

[1] General letter, Court to Bengal, April 7th, 1708. *Letter Book*, No. 13.
[2] Also called the "Park."

THE RIVER FACE, OLD FORT WILLIAM.

the work. Fearing the suspicions of the Mughals, however, the Directors instructed the Council to pretend that the ditch, if made, was only for draining water-logged ground, though they stipulated that it must actually be a " proper ffortification to the Town." They were not satisfied with the design of the fort itself, complaining that its form was irregular and the curtains too long ;[1] they did not wish to dismantle and rebuild it, but suggested that the bastions might be enlarged or lengthened to provide better flanking fire, and that this proposal should be laid before " a good Engineer if you shall be so fortunate to get one into your Service." They wound up with the usual condition that not a penny should be spent beyond the requirements of bare necessity.

Old Fort William suffered greatly through having no professional engineer, and through the heavy mortality among the men who acted from time to time as engineers. Each enthusiast made proposals which, on examination, often proved to be impracticable or too expensive. And so it was with Winder's ditch. President Weltden, who assumed charge from the Rotation Government in 1710, wrote that he would go on with the ditch, but he seems to have wished to reduce its length as he proposed to keep it within range of the guns.[2] His successor, John Russell, a grandson of Oliver Cromwell, threw cold water on the scheme on the ground of expense. Other objections were raised, and finally, early in 1714, the Directors abandoned the whole project. The Calcutta Council recorded, at the end of the year,[3] that they did not want the ditch as a drain because the ground dried in a few hours after the heaviest rain : and that was the end of Winder's scheme which had been under discussion and correspondence for more than six years. It may have given birth to the idea of the Maratha ditch of later years, but it exemplifies the haphazard way in which engineering schemes were formulated, and time wasted, in the early days of the eighteenth century. There was no expert or unified control of engineering.

While the project for Winder's ditch was under discussion, the engineers of Old Fort William turned their hands to other work. For many years the only source of water supply had been from the Hugli, and this water was distinctly brackish during certain months ; so, in 1709, the Council decided[4] to enlarge and deepen the old tank or pond, called the Lal Dighi, situated east of the fort in the Calcutta Green, and thus to provide a supply of fresh water for their European servants. They hoped also that the enlarged tank would be an obstacle to any assault from the land side. The earth which was excavated was to form a bank or curtain on the western or river face

---

[1] General letter, Court to Bengal, April 7th, 1708.
[2] *Ibid.*, Bengal to Court, October 16th, 1710, *Coast and Bay Abstracts of Letters received*, K.77.
[3] *Ibid.*, December 11th, 1714, *Coast and Bay Abstracts of Letters received*, K.77.
[4] *Bengal Public Consultations*, March 8th, 1709, Range I, Vol. I.

between the two new river bastions, and was to be faced with rubble and ballast. The excavation was made, and the western curtain finished in 1712. Increasing trade demanded the provision of a proper landing stage for boats, so the Council, prompted from home, decided in 1710[1] to build a wharf alongside the fort with a breastwork for cannon; at the end of the year the wharf extended for three-quarters of the length of the fort, and the engineers were completing each end with a half-moon[2] to mount ten small guns, protected by wooden palisading. The Directors suggested also the construction of a dry dock for ships; but the Council said it would be a waste of money,[3] and the dock scheme was shelved. However, there was a considerable amount of engineering activity during these years.

Within the walls, buildings of solid masonry began to appear, for it was recognized at last that good materials were worth the money spent on them. The Company had, in fact, decided to abandon the " penny wise, pound foolish " policy, in regard to building, which had been hitherto a marked characteristic of its administration in Bengal. But the Directors could not face the great expenditure which they would incur in enlarging Fort William to accommodate the increasing number of their servants and the growing bulk of their merchandise. Gradually it was found that the area within the fort was becoming too restricted for this purpose; and thus it came about that warehouses and dwellings began to spring up near to, and even touching, Fort William, which led at last to its capture and humiliation at the hands of Siraj-ud-Daula.

The practice of employing the Gunner as an engineer seems to have been usual in Calcutta in 1711, following the example of Madras and Bombay. In a general letter of that year[4] the remark appears: " Wee should be glad to hear the works you were about were compleated, which now you have two Master Gunners may and wee hope will be more carefully and Speedily effected." In the same letter, the name of one of these gunners—Mr. Cooke—is given, the other being Captain William Adams; and in another letter, written more than a year later,[5] the Chief or Master Gunner is said to have been one Captain Harnett. These seem to be the first engineers of Bengal whose names are recorded. Harnett was also " Master of Attendance." He died at the end of 1718, when he was succeeded by Captain John Jones, a ship's captain, who, as a master mariner, was supposed to have a knowledge of fortification.

Towards the close of 1712 the British were well satisfied with the progress of their defences on the Hugli. The works at Fort William were said to be well forward though not completed, the wharf

---

[1] *Bengal Public Consultations*, February 9th, 1710, Range I, Vol. II.
[2] A bastion forming a quadrant.
[3] General Letter, Bengal to Court, December 30th, 1710.
[4] *Ibid.*, Court to Bengal, December 28th, 1711.
[5] *Ibid.*, Bengal to Court, February 7th, 1713.

finished and awaiting its breastwork, and a pier or "bridge," with a crane at its end, nearing completion. Little remained to be done except to make a broad walk round the walls, rebuild a block of quarters for the writers, and repair the river curtain. But the Directors were not so well satisfied as their councillors in Bengal :—[1]

"COURT TO BENGAL.

"We hear you make a very pompous Show to the Water side by high Turrets and Lofty Buildings which have the appearance but not the benefit of a Fortification.[2] This if so is contrary to our Aim and Orders. If you review all of them you will find our design was to obtain a Building that should be strong eno' to answer all the ends of a Fortification without the appearance and when you ever did any thing to make it stronger you shou'd colour it over with some specious pretence. We will keep our fort, yet We would have nothing appear to shew it is one and the less it is called by that name the better. . . . We don't propose it as a Fortress to withstand a Royal Army."

The building of Old Fort William may be said to have ended in the year 1716. Its defences, raised in piecemeal fashion by well-meaning but inexperienced men who were stinted of money, hardly justified its being called a fortress, nor did its sponsors desire it to be so known. Its cramped bastions could not ensure proper enfilade fire along its curtains, and its eastern and northern faces were commanded from the roof and spire of St. Anne's Church. Assaulting troops with ladders could scale its walls at any point. There was no ditch. There was no field of fire except from the western face across the river, from the south-east corner across the Green for perhaps 500 yards, and from the southern face for a lesser distance, where some attempt had been made to clear the ground and fill up holes. The only source of fresh water supply for the garrison was the Lal Dighi outside the walls. To the north and north-east, thatched houses lay within a few yards of the walls, and, if set on fire, might render the fort untenable. And lastly, the garrison was weak, ill-armed and undisciplined. The only redeeming features of the military situation in Calcutta were that Fort William was above flood level, and that it could be reinforced from the Company's ships which, in case of a reverse, could embark the garrison or cover their retreat along the river-bank if embarkation at Calcutta was too difficult. But the moral effect of the Union Jack, floating over the walls of Fort William, was worth a great deal to the Company ; and President Robert Hedges, who ruled the settlement at this period, was naturally proud of his domain.

---

[1] General letter, Court to Bengal, February 2nd, 1713.
[2] The Council denied this later, and pointed out that the French and Dutch factories looked as like forts as the British factory, and yet were unmolested by the natives.

CHAPTER IV.

THE END OF OLD FORT WILLIAM.

OLD Fort William changed little during the last years of its life. New warehouses and godowns sprang up within and without its walls, but its main features remained unaltered. It lay on the left bank of the Hugli[1] on the site now occupied by the General Post Office, the new Government Offices, the Custom House and the East India Railway House. Some warehouses, built along the south side of the fort, skirted Koila Ghat Street. The north side was in Fairlie Place, and the east front looked out on Clive Street and on Dalhousie Square which in those days was known as the Lal Bagh, or the Park. In shape it was an irregular tetragon.[2] At the four corners were small square bastions. The curtain walls were about four feet thick and 18 feet high, built of thin tile-bricks, strongly cemented together. Each bastion mounted ten guns, and the main east gate, which projected, carried five. The river face was defended by heavy cannon in embrasures along an outlying river-wall, but there were no military outworks or ditches on the three land faces. The interior was filled with barracks, quarters, magazines and stores; and near the east gate, against the outer wall, was a range of small rooms in one of which the tragedy of the Black Hole was enacted in 1756.

The ground around the fort was congested with houses and trees, relieved only by the green expanse of the Lal Bagh, or park, containing the tank.[3] Most of the European houses lay north of the fort in what is to-day Clive Street, but many were grouped on the other sides or around the Park. Outside the European buildings were four Indian villages of mud huts—Sutanuti, Calcutta, Govindpur, and the new hamlet of Chowringhee which was separated from Govindpur, in 1717, by a tiger-haunted jungle where the Calcutta *maidan* now extends. The Calcutta Esplanade was a wilderness of trees and shrubs with a few huts here and there. Towards the south stretched broken ground dotted with hovels, till Govindpur was reached where the second and existing Fort William was built in after years. In the words of Captain Alexander Hamilton : " The town, rising about this old Fort like one about a baronial castle in the mediæval times, was built without order, as the builders thought most convenient for their own affairs, every one taking what ground best pleased them for

---

[1] Two hundred years ago the Hugli flowed much farther east than it does now, and there was deep water where Strand Road now is.
[2] North side, 340 ft. ; south side, 485 ft. ; east and west sides, each 710 ft.
[3] A pond.

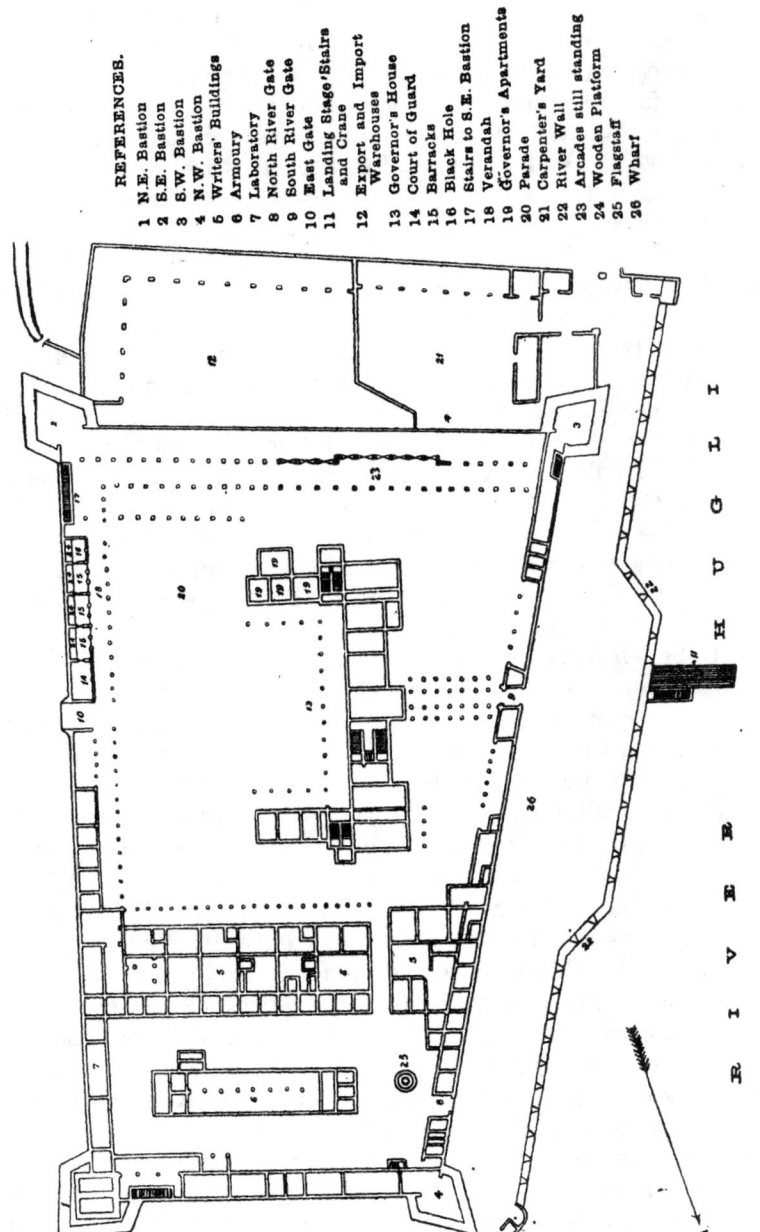

OLD FORT WILLIAM, 1756.

gardening, the English building near the riverside and the natives within land." The English houses were not luxurious : they had no flues nor *punkahs*. Cane lattice-work filled the window openings in place of glass. They were occupied mostly by the married servants of the Company who were allowed to have their own establishments. The bachelor factors and writers lived in the fort, where the Governor had his official residence. Overlooked as it was by St. Anne's Church, Fort William was as badly situated for defence as any work could be, and its garrison numbered less than 300 so-called soldiers.

By the year 1724, a new engineering appointment had appeared on the Company's books. The incumbent was called the " Master Builder,"[1] and was presumably in charge of the buildings, but whether his responsibilities extended to the military defences is not recorded. In that year, Captain Henry Cave was " Gunner and Master of Attendance " in Calcutta, and was concerned with a Captain Joseph Colson in extensive repairs to the river-bank at Govindpur,[2] south of the fort, where they drove lines of piles to check the erosion caused by floods. This area began to attract a good deal of attention as Calcutta seemed more likely to expand southwards, towards the good anchorage in Garden Reach, than towards the north. Cave died in 1728, more than one lakh of rupees in debt, and was followed by Captain Thomas Snow.[3] In this year the whole of the works—and incidentally the garrison—of Fort William were reported to be " in very bad repair," and Captain Snow was directed to survey and report on them with a certain John Aloffe,[4] carpenter, and later, Surveyor of Works. The name of John Aloffe appears constantly in the Calcutta records, in connection with engineering, between 1728 and the date of his death in 1745. He was the joint author, with an Italian engineer named Forresti, of two early plans of Calcutta, now in the British Museum. Aloffe must have been a man of some ability, and also of remarkable constitution to withstand the pestilential climate of Calcutta for so many years. The mortality from malaria was terrible in the early eighteenth century : for instance, Alexander Hamilton records that in one year, out of 1,200 British in Calcutta, no less than 460 died between August and the following January. Aloffe was associated with Gunner Thomas Gregory Warren from 1731 to 1739,[5] and also with Zachariah Gee,[6] Master of Attendance, chiefly in the construction of river wharfs, the repair of warehouses, and river protection works.

The period from 1716 to 1742 produced no military engineering work of much interest in Calcutta, except the construction of extensive palisades around the European settlement which was peopled

---

[1] *Bengal Public Consultations*, September 21st, 1724.
[2] *Ibid.*, November 16th and 23rd, 1724.
[3] General letter, Court to Bengal, February 21st, 1729.
[4] Aloffe, otherwise Alofze, Oliffe, or Olifres.
[5] *Bengal Public Consultations*, April 10th, 1732.
[6] *Ibid.*, September 8th, 1735.

by Armenians and Portuguese as well as British. At one time the settlement is said to have been completely encircled by wooden palisading. But the sudden irruption of the Maratha hordes into Bengal in 1742 changed mercantile Calcutta into the semblance of an armed camp where feverish activity in engineering overruled the dictates of peaceful trade. Ali Vardi Khan, a Tartar adventurer, was then leading a revolt which raised him to the position of Subadar of Bengal, Bihar and Orissa ; and the Marathas seized the opportunity to invade Bengal under Janoji, son of Raghuji Bhonsla, a Maratha general. They occupied Orissa, laid waste the country from Balasore to Rajmahal, and captured the town of Hugli. So close did they come to Fort William that they actually entered a Mughal fort at Thana, some miles below it. The native inhabitants on the right bank of the river implored the protection of the British who, to defend Calcutta, planted seven batteries of guns in different parts of the settlement as a second line of defence to the guns of their ships.

As an additional safeguard it was proposed that the entire British territory on the left bank should be encircled by a wet ditch ; and thus the incursion of the Maratha hordes into Bengal was the incentive for the largest engineering project undertaken since the building of Fort William. The work is known in history as the " Maratha Ditch." The proposal was to dig a moat, strengthened by a continuous rampart with bastions at intervals, for a distance of seven miles from Perrin's Point—the most northern point of Sutanuti, where a warship was moored—to the southern end of Govindpur which would be defended by another ship. The ditch was to follow roughly the line of the present Circular Road during its southerly course, enclosing an area about four miles long and one and a quarter miles wide, containing the British settlement and its surrounding villages on the left bank.[1] The scheme was launched in a panic, and ended, as such undertakings are prone to do, in labour thrown away. The ditch was never completed : it drained some ground, it marked a boundary, and there its utility ended. There is no record of the actual date on which the frightened inhabitants began to dig. By the end of 1743, however, they had made the ditch and rampart along the northern front from the inlet at Perrin's Point, and as far south as the road running due eastwards from the fort—a length of at least three miles in perhaps six months—so they must have worked harder than ever before in their lives. However, certain concessions in Orissa and money payments, made by Ali Vardi Khan to the Marathas in 1744, induced the latter to turn back ; and the merchants and other inhabitants, reassured by meeting no Marathas near their homes, discontinued their labours, and the ditch deteriorated gradually into stagnant drain.

[1] The line of the ditch is shown in a map inset in a corner of Upjohn's large map of 1793, in the British Museum.

A military engineer who was concerned in the improvement of the Calcutta defences, and probably in the digging of the Maratha ditch, was Major Charles Knipe.[1] As in the cases of other engineers of the period who were military officers, he held his military rank by virtue of his commission in an infantry regiment. Knipe reached Calcutta in the *Wilmington*, in 1742, with instructions from the Court to the Bengal Council that they would " do well to consult with the Major on the State of our Fortifications at your Place and transmit his Sentiments to us." He was on his way from England to Madras by way of Fort Marlborough (in Sumatra) and Bengal, having been posted to Fort St. George with the remark[2] that " This Gentleman, Major Knipe, offers also to serve Us in carrying on the Works that shall be judged necessary for the further Securing your Fortifications, in which we have reason to believe he may be very useful, as he has been employed in that way in Flanders ; and therefore You will do well to Advise with him." Knipe was accompanied by Ensign Moses Stephen Hollard, a young officer who was reputed to have " Applied himself very particularly to the Study of Fortifications," and had with him all the instruments for his work.[3] Hollard died soon after his arrival in Calcutta ; Knipe succumbed in Madras in 1743, after four months at that place ; and the surveying instruments never got beyond Calcutta ; but Knipe's wide experience as a soldier, and remarkable energy as an engineer, were of the greatest value in the Bengal settlement during his short stay there in the time of the Maratha scare.

Being in urgent need of engineers in 1742, the Calcutta Council let no opportunity slip to obtain them :—

" BENGAL PUBLIC CONSULTATIONS.[4]

" There being one Captain Robert Lennard come from Madras who we hear was very Serviceable raising the new Fortifications there on the Morattoes Approach, Agreed that he be Entertained for the present occasion and that he have a Suitable Reward for his trouble.[5] Resolved also that we write to the Gentlemen at Patna and desire they will prevail on Mr. Forresty to come hither from thence as we look upon him to be an able Engineer."

Forresti (or Forrestie) left Patna accordingly on July 11th, and, on arrival in Calcutta 18 days later, was asked for his advice and assistance in preparing a scheme of fortification and measures for defence. He responded with several schemes which were laid before

---

[1] His early history is uncertain, but he seems to have been commissioned on April 24th, 1706, and appointed a Captain in Colonel Long's Regiment of Foot on January 25th, 1741.
[2] *Public Despatches*, Court to Madras, March 26th, 1742, Vol. XLVI.
[3] He had a plane-table, a theodolite, a level and a telescope.
[4] April 24th and May 27th, 1742.
[5] Lennard was employed for seven months, and then discharged with a reward of Rs. 500.

Major Knipe, as Chief Engineer, in November. The latter disagreed with Forresti's recommendations, remarking[1] that they appeared to be impracticable. He proposed instead that the settlement should be encircled by a wall four feet thick with flanking towers at intervals, each mounting ten cannon; this, he said, would be sufficient to check any force which did not sit down to a regular siege. Forresti seems to have been an Italian, for Knipe, when addressing the Court of Directors from Madras in 1743,[2] wrote: " If my plan and directions are pursued, I will engage my life 'tis a Sufficient, Firm and lasting Fortification for the Place, and will be compleated at less than half the expence of the Scheem intended by the Italian Gentleman." The Directors sided with the confident Knipe, and Forresti declined in favour. We read his epitaph in a general letter of March, 1744, which runs: " Mr. Forrestie may be an Ingenious Skilful Engineer, but We don't see any Occasion that We have for him. Such Persons have generally Expensive Schemes in their Heads, therefore he must be Discharged from our Service." Exit poor Signor Forresti, having discharged but one salvo of the expensive schemes in his head.

When the post of Surveyor of Works became vacant in July, 1745, through the death of John Aloffe, Governor Braddyll and his Council invited Captain Bartholomew Plaisted, Master of the ship *Kent*, to accept it. Plaisted did so, and thereby embarked on a more stormy sea than he had ever sailed before. Early in 1747, when Commodore Griffin pointed out to Governor John Forster the weakness of Fort William, the Council decided[3] that Plaisted should draw up a plan to make the fort more defensible, and should receive for his work the same salary as Forresti had done. Plaisted responded with a criticism of the fort and a " scheem for the most Expeditious way of Fortifying Fort William with the Easyest Expence."[4] He said that the fort, as it stood, was irregular and weak, and could be taken easily ; that the bastions were so small as scarcely to deserve the name ; and further that, to demolish and rebuild them on a larger scale would cost 50,000 rupees and occupy his workmen for two years. He proposed therefore, at a cost of only 30,000 rupees, to surround the fort with a mud bastion, faced at first with turf and later with brick, of less height than the walls, this new rampart being 12 feet thick at the top and providing an ample *terreplein* for guns between it and the walls. His idea was to provide two tiers of fire by using the original elevated bastions as cavaliers[5] dominating the new ramparts, and to encircle the whole by a ditch. He proposed also to clear away some of the warehouses against the southern wall. Altogether, the scheme was practical and economical ; but, as it

[1] *Bengal Public Consultations*, November 15th, 1742.
[2] Letter from Major Knipe to Court, January 26th, 1743.
[3] *Bengal Public Consultations*, January 23rd, 1747, Range I, Vol. XIX.
[4] Plaisted to Council. Letter dated February 2nd, 1747.
[5] *Cavalier*. A work raised within another and several feet higher. Commonly a bastion within a bastion.

happened, too many cooks spoiled the broth. Plaisted's proposals were submitted to a committee of four officers,[1] who vetoed the ditch and made recommendations for palisading which drew from Plaisted the protest : " I therefore give it as my humble oppinion that the Scheem now on Foot will be both Expencive and Useless on which Account I transfer and make over to the Proposer thereof all the Honour that may accrue thereby, declaring the Maxim is new to me and passes my comprehension, indeed something of the kind is practiced on the Coast of Guiney to keep the Wild Negroes and Inhabitants of the Wood out."

Apparently this sarcasm about wild negroes, and the free offer of any honour accruing from palisading, killed the project to surround Fort William with this type of obstacle, for only the ends of the wharf were so protected.[2] The letter shows the pugnacious character of the man and explains his troubled career in Bengal. As a conscientious reformer, Plaisted fell foul of Messrs. Bellamy and Kempe, " Buxeys," in exposing certain malpractices during 1748 in the office of the military paymaster ; and, his allegations being disbelieved, he was suspended from his office as Surveyor of Works. Shortly afterwards, he threw up his appointment as Engineer and sailed for England ; but he was exonerated by the Court of Directors, and, against the wishes of the Council, reappointed in 1752 with the remark that he was an honest and capable man. With the blessing of the Court he returned to India, and resumed his former appointments in Calcutta in September.[3]

In spite of his unpopularity with some of the Council, Plaisted rose gradually in the estimation of his employers and was placed in charge of all the engineering works in Calcutta in 1755, becoming also Master Attendant in charge of the shipping.[4] Yet, by the end of that year, he had incurred the severe resentment of the Council once more by addressing two memorials direct to the Court, with the result that he was suspended from his office as Master Attendant. Again he resigned his other appointment as Engineer, and sailed for England. Like a bad penny, in the opinion of the Calcutta Council, he appeared for the third time in their settlement in November, 1758, appointed by the Court[5] as Surveyor of Works, with the remark that he was " a Person whom we deem in all respects most equal to this Trust." Success came to him at last. Three years later he had done such good work in surveying the Chittagong coast that the Council did not want to part with him, and in 1766 he earned a strong recommendation to the Directors for his long service ; but, worn out by his

[1] Letter, Bengal to Court, February 22nd, 1747. *Bengal Letters Received*, Vol. I (a).
[2] General letter, Bengal to Court, January 10th, 1748. *Bengal Letters Received*, Vol. I (a).
[3] *Bengal Public Consultations*, September 18th and 25th, 1752, Range I, Vol. XXV.
[4] *Ibid.*, November 2nd, 1755, Range I, Vol. XXVIII.
[4] General letter, Court to Bengal, March 3rd, 1758, Vol. I.

stormy career of 22 years, he died of fever in the following year.[1] The story of his life in Bengal shows the atmosphere of jealousy and intrigue in which the engineering operations of those days were conceived and executed. Bartholomew Plaisted will be remembered chiefly for his project to improve Old Fort William. If his ideas had been translated into brick and mortar in 1747, Holwell might have withstood the Mughal assault nine years later.

Measures for the defence of Calcutta received a fresh impetus in 1744 through the hostility of the French. The struggle between the British and French in southern India had its repercussion in Bengal, where the position was peculiar. The French garrison of Fort Orleans at Chandarnagar was not strong enough to risk an assault on Fort William, nor did the British in Calcutta wish to launch an attack against the French settlement. Reinforcements to either community might have changed armed neutrality into open warfare, but none came. The councillors in Calcutta, however, were aghast at the news of the surrender of Fort St. George in September, 1746, and, in 1747, directed Captain Commandant Robert Hamilton, a member of the committee which rejected Plaisted's scheme, to submit further proposals for defence. Hamilton recommended[2] that treble palisades, with ditches and breastworks, should be erected in all streets and alleys leading to Fort William, and that gabions and sandbags should be prepared. All small cannon should be mounted on field carriages. Banquettes should be raised behind garden walls bordering on avenues of approach, so that men could fire into the streets. Important localities should be held by British troops, and the rest by native levies. This advice he supplemented by the naïve statement that " if it is replied We cannot maintain so many Posts at Once, I answer neither can the Enemy attack so many Posts at once, and one man within is worth 4 without." Unfortunately, Siraj-ud-Daula proved, in after years, that he was fully able to attack many posts at once.

An inglorious figure appears now on the scene—one Captain Alexander Delavaux, Chief Engineer of all the settlements and Captain of the Train of Artillery. The Directors recognized that Madras and Calcutta were in need of a qualified military engineer, so they commissioned Delavaux as a Captain on January 20th, 1748. To what extent, if any, he was qualified for his responsible post, history does not relate; but it is certain that the Company made a bad bargain when it secured his services. He landed at Fort St. David in June, 1748, and deserted to the French in Pondicherry within 11 months, charged with fraud and manslaughter.[3] It was intended that he should proceed in time to Bengal, but he never did so. On

---

[1] General letter, Bengal to Court, December 10th, 1767.
[2] Hamilton to Governor John Forster, letter dated August 31st, 1747: *Bengal Public Consultations*, September 3rd, 1747, Range I, Vol. XX.
[3] *Public Despatches to England*, Madras to Court, November 2nd, 1749, Vol. XVII, and *Fort St. David Consultations*, May 24th, 1749, Vol. XVII.

July 12th, 1749, he was discharged from the Company's service, a dishonoured man. In Major Mosman, of the 55th Foot, however, the Council in Calcutta found an engineering adviser of some value in 1748, but he was then nearly 50 years of age and died of fever after a few months.

It was not till 1750 that a capable Chief Engineer was recruited in the person of Benjamin Robins, Quaker, mathematician and military engineer, who arrived at Fort St. David in the *Grantham*, on July 14th, 1750, and reached Calcutta in the following March.[1] His appointment as Engineer-General of all the English settlements was notified by the Court in a general letter,[2] in which he was referred to as a "Gentleman eminently Skilled in his Profession." Benjamin Robins was indeed in the first rank of his profession, and a Fellow of the Royal Society. He had studied civil engineering in England, and fortification and gunnery in Flanders. He was also an inventor and a writer. His instructions were to visit Fort St. David, Fort St. George, Fort William, Bombay and St. Helena, to prepare drawings of all their defences, and to report on the alterations or additions required. The chief command of the artillery was to devolve upon him, and he was to hold the exalted office of Third in Council. A staff of six assistants accompanied him to India—John Barker, ranking as a factor, and Nathaniel Carrington, Charles O'Hara, Sampson Morrice, Charles Knapton and Philip Glass ranking as writers. Carrington soon died, and was replaced by Achilles Preston;[3] and John Brohier, the first builder of the present Fort William, was attached to Robins' staff.[4] At last a small, but moderately efficient, cadre of engineers had been formed. Several of these men, and particularly Robins and Barker, did what they could to remedy an almost hopeless military position. Alas, they came too late to save the situation. Robins, though only 44 years of age, contracted malaria as soon as he arrived in India, and died at Fort St. David, as Robert Orme says, "with his pen in his hand," in July, 1751. When on the point of death he wrote a letter to the Court of Directors which, as an example of an heroic sense of duty, is hard to equal :—

"Fort St. David,
25th July, 1751.

"I am now upon my Death Bed, but cannot help giving You these few lines in relation to your Affairs. I have been labouring at the Account to be sent you of Bengall, in consequence of the Observations I made there. Many Accidents, and lastly my Sickness, prevented me from putting it together, so that it is of no Use, being only intelligible to myself. The Works here will be finished by Mr.

---

[1] *Bengal Public Consultations*, March 11th, 1751, Range I, Vol. XXIV.
[2] General Letter, Court to Bengal, January 12th, 1750. *Letter Book*, No. 27.
[3] *Public Despatches to England*, Madras to Court, October 24th, 1750, Vol. XVIII.
[4] *Public Despatches from England*, March 13th, 1751, Vol. LIV.

Brohier who has full instructions from me. . . . Pray Gentlemen, if possible, let Calcutta be well secured for it is a Place of infinite Consequence. I sincerely wish you the utmost Success in your Public Affairs, and to each of you in particular Health and Happyness. I must aver to you that I have served you with the most Disinterested Zeal.

"BENJAMIN ROBINS.

" *P.S.*—I request you to make John Call, a Youth who will be very usefull, One of my Young People before my Death."

Robins passed away four days after he penned these lines; but even in his dying moments his thoughts were only of his great responsibilities. He helped his masters to the last, for in John Call he provided another keen engineer who laboured to save Calcutta from the fate which overshadowed it, and to defend Fort St. George against the French.

In 1748 the Directors in London were much perturbed about the fortifications in Bengal and wrote copious instructions.[1] They feared that the French, elated by the capture of Madras, would take Calcutta by storm. Having no plan of Calcutta they were at a disadvantage in advising the Council, and had to rely on that body and Major Mosman to design suitable works; but they suggested that two small earthen redoubts might perhaps be dug on the bank of the Hugli at the northern and southern ends of the Company's territory, which, or part of which, could be surrounded by a broad ditch and rampart similar apparently to the Maratha ditch. Possibly they hoped that the Maratha ditch might be completed. The downstream redoubt was to be on the north side of a creek near Govindpur, and designed so that fire from its heavy guns would prevent French ships from approaching Fort William and would command the Thana (or Tannah) Reach[2] and the Mughal battery there. The site proposed must have been not far from that selected in after years for the new Fort William.

When Benjamin Robins died in 1751, the Council at Fort St. David decided[3] that, as John Brohier was the only person who was acquainted with Robins' schemes for defence, he should take entire charge of the works in Madras, pending further orders from England. Brohier had been given a passage to India at the end of 1749, to be employed " in a seafaring way," and was commissioned as a Lieutenant in the Artillery in the following year. He soon became invaluable to Robins, managing the work when the Engineer-General was present, and being left in entire charge when he was absent on tour. Robins thought highly of his ability, but perhaps not so highly of his integrity, for in his last letter he wrote regarding

[1] Court to the Governor of Fort William, June 17th, 1748. *Letter Book*, No. 27.
[2] Garden Reach.
[3] Fort St. David Consultations, July 29th, 1751. *Fort St. David Records*, No. 7.

Brohier: "He is certainly the properest person for the Work and I recommend him as Such. He has hitherto behav'd I believe with great Integrity. But if you employ him at Madras, His Trust will be Considerably great, pray therefore do not Stinct his Allowances too much." The doubt expressed in this phrase proved to be well founded. Brohier certainly justified his selection by his work in Calcutta; but he succumbed to temptation in the end.

The malpractices in the office of the military Paymaster in Calcutta, which were exposed by Plaisted in 1748, brought about the formation of a Committee of Works in 1751.[1] This body, advised by, and including, the Engineer-General, was ordered to examine the methods of paying for materials and labour and of employing skilled labour, to accumulate a stock of materials, to supervise the dealings of the Paymaster in engineering matters, and to issue materials for works. There were only three members—the Governor of Fort William, the Chief Factor of the out-factory at Cossimbazar, and the Engineer-General.[2] The Committee had extensive powers; for instance, we read their instructions that: "If you shall find any Money or Presents properly applyed may facilitate your Application to the Country Government, We do empower you to make such Presents and to such Persons as you shall find necessary provided the whole amount does not exceed One hundred thousand Current Rupees ... and provided you shall be fully satisfied of obtaining not only leave to Erect Fortifications but also of procuring Grants of any Place or Places out of our own Districts it may be thought to Fortify upon. This whole affair is to be transacted with great address, and the most inviolable Secrecy, and in particular it must not be known that We have empowered You to make any Presents." But the formation of a Committee of Works was a great step towards efficiency and proper administration. It helped to put down certain evil practices which had arisen in connection with building contracts and the supply of materials and labour. Control no longer rested in the hands of men who were perhaps interested financially in the undertakings. The Engineer-General had supreme technical control; but in financial matters, and in policy, the Committee of Works was paramount.

At the end of 1752, the Court of Directors having heard of the death of Benjamin Robins, decided to appoint another Engineer-General from England to succeed him. John Brohier, who was acting in the post, was too junior for it, and the choice fell upon Caroline Frederick Scott, a Lieutenant-Colonel in the 29th (Fuller's) Foot. Subject to Scott's control, Brohier was to take charge of the engineering works in Fort St. George and Fort St. David when relieved by the new Engineer-General. Scott was ordered to embark in the *Winchelsea*, bound for Fort St. George and Fort William, and, after a short stay

---

[1] General letter, Court to Bengal, August 21st, 1751. *Letter Book*, No. 28.
[2] *Ibid.*, January 24th, 1753. *Letter Book*, No. 28.

on the Coromandel coast, to proceed to Calcutta, the defence of which was to be his chief duty. He was instructed to examine the fortifications of Fort William and any other places which he visited, to prepare plans of the existing works, and to send in suggestions and estimates for improvements. He could visit any settlement at his discretion, and was entitled to be present when any Governor or Council discussed military plans. Inspectors were to be appointed by him to supervise disbursements by the paymasters. He was required to prepare large-scale plans of all proposed works, supplemented by models if necessary. This was a precautionary measure, and it could not have been reassuring to Scott, for the Directors gave as their reason " that the Works begun by You may not be interrupted by any Casualty that may happen to you."

The instructions gave permission to Scott to take with him, from Madras to Bengal, Brohier, O'Hara, Morrice, Knapton, Glass, Preston and Call, who were " the young people under Mr. Robins." Scott was directed to lay his plans before the President and Council at Fort William, and to require them to provide money, workmen and materials without delay ; and lastly he was enjoined to preserve the strictest secrecy to avoid interference by the Nawab. His instructions from the Court of Directors placed him in an exceedingly powerful and responsible position. In engineering matters he was almost a dictator. Governors and councils were to admit him to their most secret conclaves, and were ordered to supply him on demand with men, materials and money. Yet, with a salary of £650 a year, it is curious to find him as a contractor not only for the supply of clothing to his company of infantry, but for gunpowder to the whole settlement in Calcutta. The pernicious system under which engineer officers were allowed to add to their incomes by undertaking contracts remained in force for many years after Scott's death, but was finally suppressed.

Lieutenant-Colonel Caroline Scott, the new Engineer-General, accompanied by O'Hara, disembarked at Fort St. George on August 4th, 1753, and, having surveyed the Madras fortifications, sailed for Bengal nine days later. By September 7th, he had reached Fort William and was admitted to his seat on the Council.[1] He spent the cold weather in Bengal in working out elaborate, but much criticized, schemes for the defence of Calcutta, and was ready to sail for Madras in the following March. Embarking early in April, after handing over charge to Lieutenant William Wells,[2] he arrived in Madras once more about April 20th, but with his health so shattered by fever that he died on May 12th, 1754.[3] It can be said of Scott that he did well in the post of Engineer-General. During his six months in Calcutta

[1] *Bengal Public Consultations*, September 7th, 1753.
[2] Wells died on August 18th, 1755.
[3] *Madras Public Consultations*, May 12th, 1754, Vol. LXXXII.

he put new life into the work of the settlement at the cost of his own; and whether or not his schemes were sound, his administrative reforms were invaluable.

It would be interesting to know how Colonel Scott attained such eminence, and so high a reputation in engineering, that the Company was prepared to place him in the position of a dictator at Calcutta. There seems to be no record of the manner in which infantry officers of the first half of the eighteenth century received technical training in engineering, and it was from such officers that engineers were recruited. As no school of military engineering existed, it is presumed that the Company's officers learnt their engineering in the field under older officers who had specialized in it, and by the study of a few text-books on fortification. In England, a regular Corps of Engineers of the Royal Army was formed in May, 1716, consisting of a Chief Engineer, three Directors, six Engineers-in-Ordinary, six Engineers Extraordinary, six Sub-Engineers and six Practitioner Engineers, a total of 28 officers, which was raised to 34 in 1717 on the inclusion of the garrisons of Minorca and Gibraltar. But the formation of this cadre was not preceded by the foundation of a school to impart technical training; indeed, it was not until 1741 that the first step was taken to establish a military school in England for the officers of the Artillery and Engineers. This school developed into the Royal Military Academy, Woolwich, which was founded under a King's Warrant, dated July 30th, 1741. The engineer officers who were recruited and employed by the East India Company were on a different footing from King's engineer officers; they seem to have been trained only in the hard school of experience, which is perhaps the best school. In 1750, all cadets for the Company's army were appointed to the Infantry, and from that branch a few were selected for the less popular Artillery and Engineering services. Some officers for these " scientific " branches were even drafted from the Marine. Recognizing the value of proper training, the Company tried in 1765 to obtain officers for their Artillery and Engineers who had been educated at the Royal Military Academy, and a few were allowed to transfer from the King's to the Company's service, but most of them elected to join the Infantry. Engineering was in its infancy in the early days of Calcutta.

Colonel Scott, while in Calcutta, prepared two schemes—one for improving and enlarging Fort William to make it defensible against any enemy, whether European or Indian, and the other for securing the whole settlement against an attack by Indian forces alone. He submitted his first, and more ambitious, scheme to the Court of Directors in a letter dated January 6th, 1754, and laid his second scheme before the Calcutta Council on February 11th.[1] The Directors agreed with him that Fort William was better situated

---

[1] General letter, Court to Bengal, November 29th, 1754.

than any new fort which could be built downstream at Govindpur or upstream near Perrin's Point, and therefore they approved his proposal to enlarge the existing fort, though they stipulated that, before any work was undertaken, he must obtain the concurrence of the remainder of the Committee of Works who could review the political situation in Bengal before expressing their opinions. Scott was empowered to appoint as many assistant engineers as he desired, in addition to Captain Barker and Lieutenant Wells, who were mentioned by name. His scheme was to build a new fort, about three times the size of the existing one, on the site of that work and extending towards the south. The new fort was to be on an irregular pentagonal trace, with a very long riverside curtain, the four landward faces being protected by a wide ditch with a covered way and flanking redoubts beyond it. Many houses were to be demolished to provide space for the fort, ditch and glacis, and also for an extensive "Esplanade" outside the fortifications to allow a suitable field of fire. The project raised a storm of protest and criticism after Scott's death, and it was never executed, being first shelved by the Court on the ground of expense and finally dropped. It was severely criticized in particular by Mr. Colin Simson, Engineer and Surveyor in 1756, who proposed that a square fort should be built. There can be little doubt that Simson's criticisms killed Scott's more ambitious scheme.

The work proposed by Scott in his second scheme, for the defence of Calcutta against native forces alone, was put in hand[1] but never completed. This minor project was designed to provide protection to the settlement within a few months and at a small cost. Apparently Scott wished to make use of the remains of the Maratha ditch and its extensions southwards, with drawbridges and small redoubts at three or four places, and with two larger redoubts, one at Perrin's Point at the northern end of the ditch and the other south of Govindpur where the ditch would rejoin the river. Other small works, here and there, entered into the scheme. The redoubt at Perrin's Point, known as the Bagh Bazar Redoubt, was almost completed in February, 1756, at a cost of 29,000 rupees;[2] but as this amount proved to be greater than Scott had estimated, Simson was called upon to check Scott's estimate for the remaining works before they were taken in hand. Scott had proposed that the ditch around the settlement should be 36 feet wide and 12 feet deep; and Simson estimated that such a ditch, with all the redoubts and drawbridges, would cost more than 75,000 rupees. This proved too much for the Council, who stopped further work pending orders from home; and so the only result of Scott's second scheme was a redoubt at Perrin's Point. If that fortification had been made the pivot of well-con-

---

[1] General letter, Bengal to Court, February 28th, 1754. *Bengal Letters Received* Vol. II.
[2] *Ibid.*, February 21st, 1756. *Bengal Letters Received*, Vol. III.

ducted operations to the north of the British settlement when Siraj-ud-Daula advanced to attack it, instead of relying on the defence of Old Fort William and some scattered outposts in the labyrinth of streets and alleys around it, how different might have been the result of the struggle in 1756.

Most of the engineers of any standing in Bengal appear to have sent in schemes to improve Old Fort William, possibly at the invitation of the Council. Each scheme differed radically from its predecessors. There was Plaisted's scheme to add a second tier of fire by an encircling bastion at a lower level; Scott's scheme for an elongated pentagonal fort, and Simson's scheme for a large square one. Then, in August, 1755, Jaspar Leigh Jones, a Captain in the Artillery who urged his claim to succeed Scott as Engineer-General and was snubbed for his pains, produced a plan to add several fascine batteries along the river-bank " to terrify the enemy ";[1] and, within another two months, Captain Commandant George Minchin gave his " sentiments " of what works were necessary in case of war with France, recommending two extra river batteries, close below the fort, and a " Saluting Battery the same as in the Tower of London."[2] An officer, whose identity is unknown, submitted proposals to improve Fort William by enlarging its bastions, digging a broad ditch around it, deepening the tank outside the fort to make a basin for ships, and converting St. Anne's Church into a citadel with two tiers of guns.[3] This enthusiast pointed out that his scheme did not " depend on extraordinary Engineers or expensive works." Every engineer wished to have a finger in the pie, and some thrust in a whole hand; and so it was also with the new Fort William when it came to be built at Govindpur. The Directors in England, and the Council in Calcutta, deserve some credit for arriving at any decisions, however wrong, amid the welter of arguments, assertions and contradictions which engulfed them. Shielded, however, behind their traditional barrier of financial stringency, they could not be enticed into extravagance or haste.

The diversity of the engineering advice tendered to the Company originated not only in the lack of trained engineers, but also in the heavy mortality among such experts as could be recruited. The Calcutta Council, writing to Mr. Watts, Chief of the Cossimbazar factory, on August 22nd, 1755, remarked: " It has hitherto been very Unfortunate to this Settlement that every Gentleman who has had Capacity or has been appointed by Our Employers to Fortifye this Place have never Lived even to make a Beginning on the Plans proposed." In that sentence one may read the doom of Old Fort William. There could be no continuity of policy, no proper supervision of work, no unity of control. Madras was none too healthy; but in the pestilential climate of Calcutta hardly an engineer survived

---

[1] *Bengal Public Consultations*, August 4th, 1755, Range I, Vol. XXVIII.
[2] *Ibid.*, October 2nd, 1755, Range I, Vol. XXVII.
[3] *Correspondence Memoranda*, 1757.

for more than two years, and the experts sent from England died in a few months. Each builder of early Calcutta flits like a ghost across the stage and is lost in the gloom overhanging the settlement, his work uncompleted and himself soon forgotten.

We come now to the tragedy of 1756. Ali Vardi Khan, a shrewd and capable old man, had then ruled Bengal for 15 years. He had always seen the value of the British and French trade, and was prepared to turn a blind eye on the small improvements which both nations made in their settlements if these alterations or additions were supposed to be for protection against the Marathas or to drain the land. But Ali Vardi Khan grew feeble, and at the same time a renewal of the war between England and France seemed probable. The British and French in Bengal, foreseeing early hostilities on the Hugli and a weakening in the native government when the old Nawab died, began to fortify their settlements openly, thus contravening the orders of the Mughal government. Ali Vardi Khan died in 1756, and was succeeded by his grand-nephew Mirza Mohammed, generally known by his title Siraj-ud-Daula. This weak and vicious degenerate, only 20 years of age, decided to attack the British as the stronger of the two European powers in Bengal. Busteed writes[1] that Siraj-ud-Daula's action was brought about by the advice given to him by the old Nawab when dying. But whether this was the case, or whether it was caused by the enmity and jealousy which were developing between the Muhammadans and the wealthy Hindu merchants who were friendly to the British, the fact remains that the young Muslim ruler determined to drive the British from his province. Two months after his accession, while yet blind to the value of European trade, he gained possession of their factory at Cossimbazar on June 2nd, 1756, by capturing Mr. Watts, the chief factor, and holding him as a hostage. He then marched upon Calcutta with 50,000 men, and at the same time ordered the French at Chandarnagar, and the Dutch at Chinsura, to assist him. They refused to do so, and were punished with heavy fines. The British, in fear of annihilation, appealed to their European neighbours for help, and were met with a blank refusal from the Dutch and a sly invitation from the French to abandon Calcutta and migrate to Chandarnagar. Taken by surprise, their garrison insignificant, their supplies inadequate, and their fortifications despicable, the British were confronted by the disaster which they had courted so long. Their engineers planned a more contracted line of defence around Fort William which might perhaps be completed before the French or any other enemy could attack.[2] Every man was set to work, but the time for preparation was pitifully short. Siraj-ud-Daula advanced against Calcutta.

The fact that Cossimbazar had fallen on June 2nd was not known

[1] *Echoes from Old Calcutta*, by H. E. Busteed, p. 4.
[2] *Narrative of the Succession of Surajah Dowlah and the Siege of Calcutta*, by Governor Drake, July 19th, 1756. Orme Collection, India, IV.

in Calcutta till five days later. Nine days after the news arrived, Siraj-ud-Daula appeared outside the settlement. It is sad to relate that the hurried preparations for defence showed a lack of appreciation of the military situation and of the elements of strategy. The only fortification of strategical value—the Bagh Bazar Redoubt at Perrin's Point—was left " in the air " and weakly garrisoned. Fifty heavy guns lay rusting on the ground under the walls of Fort William. They had lain thus for three years because there were no carriages for them. Few of the guns which were actually mounted could fire with safety, for the shells did not fit properly and the platforms were weak. There was a deficiency of ammunition, and its quality was poor, though this was concealed for a time. The garrison was utterly inadequate to defend Calcutta, and hardly strong enough to hold Fort William alone. The British officers, with one or two exceptions, were inexperienced and inefficient, the worst being the Commandant himself, Captain George Minchin. About him, Holwell writes, " Touching the military capacity of our Commandant, I am a stranger. I can only say that we were unhappy in his keeping it to himself, if he had any." Cotton states[1] that there were only two engineers, of whom one, Charles O'Hara, deserted the garrison before the siege, and the other, Colin Simson, perished in the Black Hole after the siege, and that " they can have been little better than amateurs for they were constantly oscillating between a writership and their purely military duties." This, then, was the state of Calcutta when it met the assault of the invading thousands.

The story of the capture of Old Fort William by Siraj-ud-Daula has been told so often and so well that it would be superfluous to repeat it in any detail. Advancing from the north he attacked the Bagh Bazar Redoubt on June 16th, but was repulsed; then, gradually enveloping the town, he attacked on the following day from the east and entered the suburbs, while the British were burning the bazaars to the east and south of the fort in a belated attempt to secure a field of fire, and were collecting the European women and children within the walls. When the enemy burst into the town, the Portuguese and half-caste population flocked into Fort William to the number of 2,500, and there they obstructed the defenders, consumed the supplies, and were useless in the fight. On June 18th the enemy, advancing from house to house, fought hard to capture the east battery where Holwell was posted, and at last, by fire from the adjacent houses, rendered it untenable. It was abandoned after a stubborn contest, with the loss of two 18-pounder guns, which, being inadequately spiked, were repaired by the enemy and used against Fort William. When this key position had been lost, the defenders abandoned also the northern and southern battery positions and withdrew into the fort, though they took the precaution to occupy St. Anne's Church and a few other prominent buildings close outside the

[1] *Calcutta, Old and New*, by H. E. A. Cotton, p. 56, footnote.

walls. The signal for retirement was followed by the desertion, in a body, of 1,500 matchlock men and other native troops. After dark, a piquet in the "Company's House" outside the south-west bastion was driven in by overwhelming fire from neighbouring houses. During a Council of War that night, it was decided to embark the women and children on the ships anchored off the fort. Most of them went aboard at once, and the remainder, with few exceptions, on the following morning. At the same Council of War the artillery commander announced, for the first time, that he had ammunition for only three days, and that he was afraid that part even of that meagre supply was damp. During the hours of darkness, panic and disorder spread among the militia soldiery and refugees, and, early on June 19th, the defenders had to abandon the church and Mr. Cruttenden's house, the last remaining outposts, and to retire altogether within the walls of Fort William. The ships, with the women and children on board, began to drop downstream; and at half-past ten in the morning the garrison was basely deserted by Governor Drake, Captain Minchin and other officers, who rowed off to the last remaining ships which then weighed anchor.

Holwell took command of the little garrison. He made an heroic effort—a defence which did much to wipe out the infamy of Drake's desertion—but his situation was hopeless unless the ships returned, which they did not attempt to do. The enemy mounted guns on St. Anne's Church and other buildings, opened a devastating fire at point-blank range, and, after sustaining a minor repulse at the north curtain, collected troops for a general assault. Only 80 men in the garrison remained unwounded. In desperation, Holwell tried to make terms of surrender. The enemy then took advantage of a flag of truce to get close to the walls, so Holwell withdrew the flag and ordered fire to be reopened; but a gate had been opened treacherously by some of the garrison and the enemy were already swarming in. During the afternoon of June 20th, 30 hours after Drake had fled, Old Fort William surrendered. That evening was enacted the tragedy of the Black Hole, when all the European captives, 146 in number, were crowded into a small chamber, only 18 feet square, near the south-east bastion, and only 23 survived, among whom was Holwell. The survivors, and other refugees, sought refuge about 30 miles down the Hugli, near the village of Fulta, where they were joined in August, 1756, by some 230 men from Madras under Major Kilpatrick. There they led a wretched existence, decimated by fever, until the arrival of Colonel Clive and Admiral Watson in December, when these gallant commanders led a powerful force which recaptured Calcutta on January 2nd, 1757, and brought ruin and death to Siraj-ud-Daula. The sack of Calcutta by the Nawab did not result in the complete destruction of Old Fort William, though several buildings within the walls were demolished and the materials used to build a mosque; and thus, when the Union Jack floated once more over its walls, and the pretentious mosque had been destroyed, the old fort was restored in some degree to its former appearance, and, indeed, improved and strengthened. But its glory had vanished, it had betrayed the trust placed in it, and a new Fort William began to rise at Govindpur, an impregnable fortress on a grand scale, an emblem of the might of England.

The tale of Old Fort William may be closed with a few extracts from the speech delivered in 1902 by Lord Curzon, when he unveiled an obelisk in Dalhousie Square to the memory of the victims of the Black Hole.[1] "Gentlemen," said he, "how few of us ever pause to think about the past, and our duty to it, in the rush and scurry of our modern lives. How few of us who tread the streets of Calcutta from day to day ever turn a thought to the Calcutta of the past. Forgotten worthies in ancient costumes haunt the precincts of this historic square. Strange figures, in guise of peace or war, pass in and out of the vanished gateways of the vanished fort. A short drive of two miles will take us to the most pathetic sight in Calcutta, those dismal and decaying Park Street cemeteries where generations of bygone Englishmen and Englishwomen, who struggled and laboured on this stage of exile for a brief span, lie unnamed, unremembered and unknown. But if among these forerunners of our own, if among those ancient and unconscious builders of Empire, there are any who especially deserve commemoration, surely it is the martyr band whose fate I recall and whose names I resuscitate on this site; and if there be a spot which should be dear to an Englishman in India, it is that below our feet, which was stained with the blood and which closed over the remains of the victims of that night of destiny, the 20th of June, 1756."

[1] It took the place of an obelisk erected by Holwell and removed by order of the Marquess of Hastings in 1821.

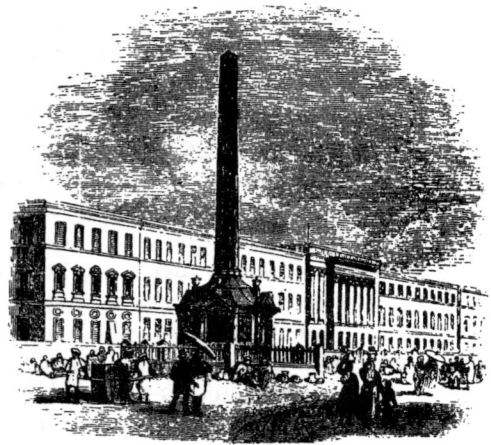

MONUMENT TO THOSE WHO PERISHED IN THE BLACK HOLE, CALCUTTA.

CHAPTER V.

MADRAS FROM 1707 TO 1773.

IN the early days of the eighteenth century, Fort St. George was the chief stronghold of the British traders in India. It had been affected less than the other settlements by the humiliating terms dictated by the Emperor Aurangzeb in 1690, when Bombay was crushed and Calcutta lost. The Coromandel coast lay so far from the centre of the Mughal web that the orders emanating from Delhi lost some of their force before they reached it; but this isolation naturally encouraged the subordinate officials of the Mughal government to break away from the crumbling monarchy, and the resulting diversity of petty rulers led to a peculiar and unstable situation in which the Council at Madras was obliged to act with the greatest wariness. New kingdoms were rising from the dwindling Mughal empire, while over all hung the gathering cloud of the Maratha confederacy. Under such conditions there could be little money for engineering undertakings. When the demands of trade had been satisfied, the balance went to sweeten the dispositions, and line the pockets, of the rulers and officials of Hyderabad and the Carnatic.

The unfortunate experience of the Directors in recruiting von Werlinhoffe as Engineer and Miner-General in 1696, made them suspicious of engineering experts from England. Such men being, as they affirmed, so unreliable and expensive, they were always on the look-out for others who might be useful as specialists in one department or another. They employed Dutchmen, Portuguese, Frenchmen and Swiss, and in 1751 they tried the experiment of enlisting two whole companies of Swiss soldiers for service in India. The Swiss companies reached Madras but were unsatisfactory; so they were absorbed after a few years into the English companies.[1] This experiment may have been tried because some Swiss soldiers had already shown a martial spirit and rendered valuable service in Madras. Lieutenant James Hugonin, of that nation, landed in Madras in 1696 with a few soldiers among whom was his younger brother Francis, then a Serjeant. Francis Hugonin became an Ensign in 1706, and was appointed Chief Gunner of Fort St. David,[2] and therefore an Engineer under the Company; and later, when at Fort St. George, he was employed with one Thomas Way, Surveyor of Buildings, in rebuilding the Inner Fort as planned by Governor

---

[1] *Public Despatches from England*, December 19th, 1755, and March 13th, 1761.
[2] *Public Consultations*, December 9th, 1706, Vol. XXXVI.

Harrison. He remained in Madras until 1724, when he was succeeded by David Murray.

At the end of 1712, the walls of the Inner Fort, surrounding the " Company's House," were in a state of collapse ;[1] but under Governor Harrison they were demolished and rebuilt after the Council had represented to the Directors the urgency of the work.[2] The new enclosure, called " the Fort Square," was finished in three years. Its angles coincided with the bastion points of the old Inner Fort. The work of dismantling the Inner Fort was attended with some difficulty because the debris could not be left in either White or Black Town and so was carried piecemeal across the river. Within the bounds of the new Fort Square, the playful writers and apprentices found themselves, much to their disgust, always under the official eye. The councillors had become tired of winking at the indiscretions of the junior officers ; indeed, the Directors themselves had remarked, in 1711,[3] that they were " sorry to hear that of late there had not been a Sufficient Decorum kept up among our People, and particularly among the Young Writers and Factors, and that there had been Files of Musqueteers Sent for to keep the peace at dinner time." Yet the new enclosure failed to effect a reformation, for it is recorded that, in 1719, Ensign Clarke was accused of " incorrigible sottishness " in being " so much disguised by liquor " that he was incapable of doing his duty.

In 1719 the Directors had so far recovered from their disappointment in von Werlinhoffe that they sent another Chief Engineer to Madras. They had planned an expedition to acquire the island of Divi, near Masulipatam, and considered that an expert engineer would be needed, so they engaged Captain James Johnson as Chief Engineer, Bombardier and Fireworker.[4] Johnson did not live up to his imposing array of titles—in fact he was as hopeless a failure as von Werlinhoffe and showed plainly the wilful character of the engineers of the eighteenth century. Soon after he reached Madras he was sent to Bombay because the Divi expedition had been abandoned, and during the voyage he received an order to transfer to another ship which was on its way to attack the pirate Angria. He refused to obey, was dismissed from the service, and died in Madras two years later.[5] Once again the Company was compelled to rely upon its trusty Gunners and Supervisors of Works to carry on the engineering operations in Fort St. George and Fort St. David.

In 1724, there were two Supervisors at Madras, Thomas Way and Henry Johnson, who were classed as " Particular Persons," an honour which they shared with the doctor's mates, the schoolmaster, the

---

[1] These were the original walls begun by Day and Cogan in 1640.
[2] *Public Letter to England,* January 11th, 1713, Vol. III.
[3] *Public Despatches from England,* January 3rd, 1711, Vol. XV.
[4] *Ibid.,* January 9th, 1719, Vol. XXII.
[5] *Public Consultations,* March 21st, 1721, Vol. LII.

bookbinder, some disabled men and a few poor widows.[1] The gun-room crew was feeling the strain of its combined artillery and engineering duties; and to add to its burden, a reduction in its strength was threatened. So the Paymaster wrote to Governor Elwick: " Formerly the Gun-room was lookt upon as a Lodging work-house to relieve poor seamen, and at the same time be of use to the Garrison. They were entertain'd and discharg'd at their pleasure, which encouragement was thought necessary, thereby to have always Sailors on any extraordinary occasion, so that their Number increas'd or decreas'd as Voyages offered. They now consist of Forty six Europeans, Fifty two Portuguese and thirty Lascars, most old Standars. And if a man will look about the Garrison and take notice how they are employ'd, I believe there will be found little reason for Alteration. However, I bow down to Your Honour, &cs, Better Judgement." But this appeal was rejected by Elwick, who was a rigid economist. During his tenure of office, little was done to improve the fortifications. He was followed in 1725 by James Macrae who, during his five years as Governor, did much to repair the ravages of time and climate, and built a Silver Mint and a new Powder House.[2]

It seems that while, in the absence of a Chief Engineer, the Chief Gunner was in charge of the fortifications, civil buildings in Madras were constructed and maintained at this time by the Supervisors, or Surveyors, of Works. In August, 1726, Stephen Newcome was appointed Surveyor of Works on the minute salary of five pagodas a month because he was said to have a tolerable knowledge of building. He earned his few shillings; and being an inventor of some capability, he erected a large water lift, driven by wind power, at Fort St. David, and a sawmill and power station at Fort St. George. Thomas Way had died in the previous year after retiring from the office of Surveyor to become a free merchant. Way was nominated one of the aldermen of Madras under the new charter of September, 1726, but did not live to assume office. The charter invested Madras with the dignity of a mayor and nine aldermen, and it was put into operation on August 17th, 1727, to the accompaniment of country music and the gyrations of native dancing girls, regarding which performances the Council remarked:[3] " The Country Musick is a privilidge bought of this government by the old Company at a very great charge, and is therefore kept up, it being look't upon here as one of the greatest Marks of Grandeur that can be; but if you please to have them discharged, it shall be done, they being far from Agreeable to your President or any of the Europeans."

There is little to record about military engineering in Madras during the next few years. Gunner David Murray died in 1732, and

---

[1] *Public Consultations*, September 3rd, 1724, Vol. LIV.
[2] *Ibid.*, Vols. LV to LVII.
[3] *Public Letter to England*, September 22nd, 1727, Vol. VI.

was followed by John Goulding, who held the post till he also died, in 1738. But, though engineering was at a standstill, political events crowded one on another in bewildering succession, and these must be described as briefly as possible to explain the circumstances which led to the siege and fall of Madras. Confusion and disorder reigned in the Carnatic after 1732. In March, 1741, Raghoji Bhonsla, the Maratha leader, advanced on Trichinopoly and captured and garrisoned it with 30,000 men under Morari Rao. Straggling bands of Marathas even entered the bounds of the British settlement at Fort St. David. The Marathas were everywhere. They assumed the right to collect one-fourth of the revenue over a large part of India. They upset the era of peaceful commerce, and substituted for it a situation fraught with peril for the Company. They disorganized the Company's affairs, and in this way hampered the British so that, in the general confusion, Fort St. George fell an easy prey to the French under Dupleix and La Bourdonnais.

When the first Maratha invasion took place in May, 1740, the garrison of Fort St. George was too small to man the defences. William Percival was Chief Gunner at the time, and, under his supervision, the re-excavation of the wet ditch on the north and west faces of Black Town was taken in hand, as it had been neglected and the ditch was choked up.[1] In addition, he repaired several large breaches in the walls and made some attempt to secure a better field of fire. Some 200 guns, from 24-pounders downwards, were in position on the walls, but the Gunner's detachment was utterly inadequate to man them or even to direct their operation by crews of volunteers. The Maratha advance on Trichinopoly at the end of the year spread alarm among the British. All civilians, including Portuguese and Armenians, were enrolled in a militia, and the Council decided to construct a rampart along the sea face of Black Town and to clear a field of fire, 200 yards wide, on the north and west faces of that quarter, being urged thereto by " great Clamours among the European Inhabitants that the Walls of the Black Town are so inclosed by houses and gardens that it would be impossible for the Guns to be of any service against any enemy."[2] The arrangements for the water-supply of Fort St. George were ludicrous : no pure water was obtainable nearer than two miles from the walls. The engineers accordingly busied themselves in making cisterns of masonry or timber to store an adequate supply, and were then confronted by the problem of filling them, and all available casks, without pipe-lines or water carts. The Council solved the difficulty. They ordered an official called the " Scavenger " to bring the water in his buffalo-drawn conservancy carts, designed and used for sanitary purposes. History does not relate what the doctors did or thought about this

[1] *Public Consultations,* May 12th to 30th, 1740, Vol. LXX.
[2] *Ibid.*; January 19th, 1741, Vol. LXXI.

scheme. Presumably their objections, if any, were over-ruled, and the Scavenger duly led his fleet of "Dreadnoughts" into action and filled each cistern with sparkling liquid.

The French under Dumas, secure in their fortified settlement at Pondicherry, opposed a bold front to the Marathas and rejected all their demands, softening their refusals with polite words and presents of liqueurs. Dumas was an energetic governor. On the first alarm, he strengthened the defences of the French settlement, formed a body of European infantry, and laid the first foundations of a sepoy[1] contingent by arming four or five thousand Muhammadans and training them like European soldiers. His preparations saved Pondicherry from the Marathas, and he became the hero and idol of the local Mughal rulers and of the Mughal Emperor. Thus, when Dupleix relieved him in January, 1742, and England and France were drifting towards open war, the French reputation in southern India stood at a very high level. Meanwhile Mahé de la Bourdonnais, the French governor of the Isles of France and Bourbon,[2] proceeded to fit out a privateering fleet to harry the English shipping. He sailed from France in 1741 and awaited, in Eastern seas, the declaration of war. In the following year, however, as war had not been declared, he was ordered to send his ships home and was thus defeated in his designs which were checked later by the arrival of an English fleet under Commodore Barnet, off Pondicherry, in 1745. In Admiral La Bourdonnais the French had a most enterprising commander, who, with the experienced and crafty Dupleix, was a menace to the British settlements on the Coromandel coast.

At the beginning of 1741 the defences of Fort St. George left much to be desired. It is true that by September of that year considerable progress had been made in improving the works, but the fort was in no condition to resist a French assault.[3] That part of it which was known as White Town was better defended on its sea face than on its western or land face, along the front of which ran the River Elambore. The width of the fort between the river and the sea was small in comparison with its length from north to south, and the long curtains of the western face were not properly flanked by their small bastions. The shallow river afforded no serious obstacle to a determined assault. In 1741, Governor Benyon revived the idea of extending the main fortifications to the island ; but the Directors refused to entertain it, and made alternative proposals,[4] though they sanctioned an increase in the strength of the garrison to bring the number of European soldiers to 600 men. At the same time they sent out Major Charles Knipe[5] and Mr. Moses Stephen Hollard as

[1] Fr. *Cipaye*.
[2] Mauritius and Réunion.
[3] *Public Letter to England*, September 26th, 1741, Vol. XIII.
[4] *Public Despatches from England*, January 20th, 1742, Vol. XLVI.
[5] See Chapter IV.

experts in engineering,[1] explaining that, next to the security of Madras, their chief reason for incurring such large expenses was to encourage people to flock thither for protection, and so to foster trade and obtain an increased revenue.

Knipe reached India by way of Sumatra, and after a few months in Calcutta, landed in Madras on January 11th, 1743. He proceeded at once to inspect the defences of White Town, and advised that the river should be diverted, the old bed filled in, and the western face rebuilt on the island :[2] in fact, he reiterated the assertions of the Governor to the Court. He strongly condemned the old western wall, remarking that it was " no more than a mere garden wall." His criticisms so impressed the Directors that they accepted his proposals in March, 1744,[3] when they informed the Madras Council that they were glad to learn that Black Town was well secured, though at a cost of nearly one lakh of rupees, and that as Knipe had said that the river could be diverted at a small cost, the Council could carry out his scheme in their own fashion. The projected works, however, were not far advanced when the French attacked Madras. In the same month in which the Directors signified their approval, war was declared in Europe between England and France, though news of this event did not filter through to Madras till September, 1744.

The defences were falling to ruin through lack of proper attention and expenditure. Fort St. George was little more than a walled town when Major Charles Knipe died in May, 1743. He commanded the garrison and was also its engineer, and after his death, Madras had no engineer for a time. William Percival relinquished gunnery and engineering in 1743 to become a factor, and John Waters then become Chief Gunner. As such he had to carry on the military engineering work of the settlement, but only for a few months, for he died in 1744. When Nicholas Morse became Governor in January, 1744, he saw the deadlock in engineering which had been caused by Knipe's death and applied at once to Bombay for a capable engineer, representing in strong terms the critical political situation on the Coromandel coast. Governor Wake of Bombay rose to the occasion, and sent Joseph Smith[4] to Madras in September, as " Bombardier and Engineer " on a salary of Rs. 140 a month, recommending him as " a person very capable and deserving who has also some knowledge of Engineering."[5]

Joseph Smith was asked to make bricks without straw and to produce them in an impossibly short time. He did his best ; but when he had worked only two years on the defences, he died, worn out by mental anguish and physical fatigue. We read that " Mr.

---

[1] *Public Despatches from England*, March 26th, 1742, Vol. XLVI.
[2] Knipe to Governor Benyon. Letter dated July 25th, 1743.
[3] *Public Despatches from England*, March 21st, 1744, Vol. XLVIII.
[4] He was the father of the General of the same name.
[5] Public letter, Madras to England, September 5th, 1744, Vol. XIV.

Smith, our Gunner, Having by that time discover'd that he was ill used by his Wife, and likewise that much would be laid to his Charge for having hardly anything that belonged to his province in that readiness which had all along been expected from him, dyed the day the Enemy landed." His chief task in 1744 was to examine Knipe's plan to extend Fort St. George on to the island, and in June, 1745, he submitted two schemes to the Council which they considered with the one prepared by Knipe.[1] They selected a design which provided for the construction of three new faces on the island, each 200 yards long, fronting north-west, west and south-west respectively, with large bastions at the points, the whole forming a line of fortification which was convex towards the west. The original bed of the Elambore River, which lay behind this extension, was to be filled up, and the stream diverted into a large wet ditch in front of the new works on the island. Some defences were to be added also to the sea face. The work was put in hand; but only the ditch, with its escarp and counterscarp walls, had been finished, with one important alteration, when the French attacked Fort St. George. It is unfortunate that Smith's plans have been lost or destroyed, but the general nature of his recommendations is known. His proposal to divert the river into the new ditch was fundamentally wrong, and luckily no attempt was made to carry out this part of his scheme. Instead, the river was diverted into a new channel across the island, well clear of the walls, and the ditch was flooded through a small cut leading to a backwater.

War was declared in Europe between England and France in 1744, and in 1746 a French fleet, under La Bourdonnais, engaged a British squadron which, after a drawn battle, retired towards the south, leaving Madras open to the French. La Bourdonnais hesitated for a time and then sailed unopposed to besiege Madras, where, by September 4th, he had landed a force of about 1,800 men, of whom 1,000 were Europeans. In his ships he had 1,700 sailors and marines. He attacked from the west, and subjected White Town to an artillery bombardment which lasted for several days though it caused very few casualties in the garrison. Yet the moral and material effect of the fire was such that the Governor of Madras, Nicholas Morse, surrendered Fort St. George on September 10th without any serious attempt at resistance. La Bourdonnais did not wish to keep Madras. He feared that he might be blockaded there by a British fleet and that his ships would be driven away or sunk by the monsoon storms, so he arranged to restore the place to the British on payment by them of £481,250, provided that he himself received a handsome bribe of £4,375. When Dupleix, at Pondicherry, heard of this proposal his fury knew no bounds; but the ransom in the form of bonds, and a bribe of £3,850, were paid, and La Bourdonnais

[1] *Public Consultations*, June 4th, 1745, Vol. LXXV.

sailed for Mauritius. Instantly Dupleix seized Madras, repudiated La Bourdonnais's convention in spite of the ransom already paid, and removed the British as prisoners to Pondicherry. He next attacked Fort St. David but was repelled by Stringer Lawrence, and then was himself besieged in Pondicherry by a powerful British fleet and a force on land. But Dupleix defended his settlement with such success that, in the end, the siege was raised and the British retired after losing 1,000 men. Finally, under the terms of the treaty signed between England and France at Aix-la-Chappelle in 1748, Madras was restored to England in return for concessions to France in North America.

As soon as La Bourdonnais left the Coromandel coast, the Nawab of the Carnatic advanced on Madras with a powerful force to claim it from the French, who had no intention of relinquishing it. Barthélemy, the French commander, defended the place with ability, and Dupleix sent a reinforcement of 400 men, under an officer named Paradis, to assist him. When Paradis arrived on the bank of the Adyar River, within a few miles of Fort St. George, he was confronted by a Mughal army of 10,000 men; but fearlessly adopting the offensive, he crossed the river, charged with the bayonet, routed the enemy and entered Madras. This small battle had a far-reaching effect. Fortescue writes:[1] "With this action it may be said that the dominance of a European nation in India was assured. Hitherto the native armies had been treated with respect. Their numbers had given the impression of overwhelming strength; and it had not occurred to Europeans that they could be encountered except with a force of man for man. Consequently all dealings of Europeans with native princes had been conducted in a spirit of humility and awe. . . . Now the spell was broken, and Dupleix from the courtier had become the master; so momentous was the change wrought by a single Swiss officer. . . . The memory of Paradis should be honoured in England since he taught us the secret of the conquest of India." It may be added that the man who thus taught Clive and his successors the value of the offensive in India, whatever the odds, was an engineer, though an enemy of the British. The prowess shown by the French had its effect on British fortification. From this time, the defences of the British settlements were planned to resist the attack of disciplined troops under European direction rather than the ill-directed assaults of Mughal or Maratha armies under their own leaders; they had to conform to European designs, and the uneducated Gunner could no longer be trusted to build them.

Soon after his arrival in captured Madras, Paradis became Governor, replacing an officer named d'Esprémenil, and he proceeded to make several alterations to the defences of Fort St. George. He destroyed the whole of the fortifications of Black Town, and

[1] *A History of the British Army*, by the Hon. J. W. Fortescue, Vol. II, p. 185.

demolished all the houses in that area within 120 yards of the northern wall of White Town, extending this clearance to a depth of 400 yards before the fort was given back to the British in 1749. About one-half of Black Town was thus razed to the ground. The French did not interfere much with the defences or buildings of White Town. It seems that their energies were directed mainly towards ridding White Town of the encumbrance of the thickly-populated Black Town which pressed against its northern wall.

While Fort St. George fell a victim, Fort St. David continued to weather the storm. The engineer in charge of its defences was Mr. George Jones, whose name alone was calculated to inspire confidence in British hearts. The Gunner who assisted him was Philip Baker, and Robert Clive was one of the garrison. The place was nearly captured by the French in March, 1747, but the opportune arrival of Commodore Griffin with a British squadron caused the besiegers to withdraw. Griffin advised the Governor to improve the fortifications without delay, so George Jones was directed to submit a scheme; but when he did so on April 25th, he prefaced his recommendations by the remark that Fort St. David was too weak and defective to make any effective resistance against the French, being merely a rectangular enclosure with four small bastions, a *fausse-braye* and a wide ditch, which was the standard design of the early fortifications. He proposed to add to these primitive works a horn-work on the north side to enfilade the approaches, lunettes for the east and west sides, a covered way, and a glacis; and in conclusion he stated that " a very able hand should be sent from England as it was highly necessary." These improvements were not completed until shortly before the French attacked Fort St. David in May, 1758, but the " very able hand " arrived on June 13th, 1748, in the person of Captain Alexander Delavaux, who has figured already in this narrative.[1]

The Gunner and his crew now make their farewell bow. The last Gunner of Fort St. George was Joseph Smith, Bombardier and Engineer, who died in 1746, when the French began their successful assault on Madras; and the last Gunner of Fort St. David was Philip Baker. In the days of simple defences and primitive artillery, the gunroom crew gave invaluable service as engineers; but those days were past. European troops, or disciplined native regiments, now attacked the British settlements under effective artillery fire. Fortifications had become highly complicated, and professional engineers were sent from England to design them. And so, under a reorganization of the military services of the Company initiated by Stringer Lawrence, regular companies of sepoys were recruited and trained at Madras, a squadron of European cavalry was formed, and the gunroom crew was replaced by two companies of Artillery, one

[1] See Chapter IV.

at Fort St. George and the other at Fort St. David, officered partly by men, such as Brohier, who were both engineers and gunners. The mixed gunroom crew failed to rise to the occasion in the French attack of 1746 when opposed to the expert Artillery of La Bourdonnais, and its replacement by a new organization became inevitable.

In February, 1748, Captain Alexander Delavaux was appointed as Chief Engineer of all the British settlements in India,[1] and on landing at Fort St. David, relieved Mr. George Jones in charge of the work. His brief and inglorious career ended in his desertion to the French at Pondicherry in May, 1749, and there is no record that he performed any useful service on the Coromandel coast. It was indeed fortunate that when Madras had been lost and Fort St. David and Cuddalore[2] were in jeopardy, a commander of ability and experience arrived in the person of Major Stringer Lawrence who had fought in Europe. Lawrence set foot in Fort St. David in January, 1748; and six months later, Admiral Edward Boscawen, with a powerful fleet and 1,400 troops, joined forces with Commodore Griffin's squadron at the same place. The tables were then turned on the French; and the British, under Boscawen as Commander-in-Chief on sea and land, sailed to lay siege to Pondicherry. This operation, however, was abandoned in October, shortly before the news arrived of the peace of Aix-la-Chappelle. The British and French in India could then no longer resort to open warfare, but they were bitterly hostile. Dupleix led the way in trying to turn the intrigues and wars of the native rulers to his advantage, and he forced the British to adopt a similar course; but the French intrigues were the more successful, and Dupleix himself attained the position of a dictator over the whole of Southern India. It is said that he received £200,000 in presents from his grateful *protégés*.

On August 21st, 1749, Madras was handed back to the British, very much the worse for wear, and history indicates that the only engineers available to repair the defences were men working under Admiral Boscawen in place of the renegade Delavaux. The names of Leonard Bickerstaff and John Apperley are mentioned. Bickerstaff had been a military engineer in Europe, and was selected in 1747 as a Chief Engineer with Boscawen's expedition to India. The mistakes of the siege of Pondicherry tarnished his reputation, and he left the Company's service in 1751. Apperley was a gunner's mate in India, who was promoted in 1747 to be an engineer and left the country three years later. Bickerstaff and Apperley made the plans, which are preserved in the War Office, showing Madras after its reoccupation by the British. The one by Apperley was prepared in August, 1749, and the other by Bickerstaff in the following month. Although

---

[1] *Public Despatches from England*, February 10th, 1748, Vol. LI.
[2] A small settlement two miles south of Fort St. David.

inaccuracies appear in both plans, they indicate the alterations made by the French during their occupation of Fort St. George, and to that extent are valuable.

When La Bourdonnais captured Fort St. George, the seat of the British government on the coast was transferred to Fort St. David as a temporary measure, pending the recovery of the larger fortress. Actually the Governor and Council remained in Fort St. David until 1752 ; but when Madras was reoccupied, the Directors determined to restore it without delay to its former strength and position, and to this end they sent out Benjamin Robins, with a staff of assistants, in 1750, appointing him as Engineer-General of all the settlements.[1] Robins landed at Fort St. David on July 14th, 1750,[2] and within two months prepared and sent to England plans of that place and also of Fort St. George. His proposals with regard to Madras included the fortification of two suburbs beyond the ruined part of Black Town, and the completion of Joseph Smith's design to extend White Town on to the island and divert the river. His scheme was sanctioned in 1751, and he was ordered to put it into execution without delay ;[3] but he was denied the satisfaction of doing so, as he died of fever in July of that year, after writing the pathetic letter which has been quoted earlier in this narrative.[4] On his death-bed, Robins wrote also to the Governor and Council of Fort St. David[5] requesting that John Brohier should be allowed to carry on and complete the works at that place, and that John Call should assist him. In his will he bequeathed to Brohier his choice of his swords and two-thirds of all his books on fortification, and to Call the remaining books. The Council recommended Brohier and Call to the Court, remarking that Brohier had often spoken of Call as a most promising youth with a genius for his profession, and that, as another engineer would no doubt be sent to replace Robins, they hoped the newcomer would be as capable and agreeable as the late Engineer-General. Brohier was then posted to Fort St. David as engineer, with Call and O'Hara to assist him.

In 1751, Clive began his triumphant rise to fame and power by seizing Arcot to induce Nawab Chanda Sahib[6] to raise the siege of Trichinopoly. He was then himself besieged in Arcot, where he resisted all the Nawab's efforts for 50 days and beat off his assailants. Stringer Lawrence, a redoubtable opponent of Dupleix and Bussy, the French General, returned from England as Commander-in-Chief on March 14th, 1752, and, with Clive, relieved Trichinopoly. These events impressed on the Directors the precarious situation of their

[1] See page 50.
[2] Letter from Fort St. David, July 15th, 1750, Vol. III.
[3] *Public Despatches from England*, August 23rd, 1751.
[4] See page 50.
[5] Letter from Benjamin Robins to the Hon. Thomas Saunders, Esq., dated Fort St. David, July 25th, 1751.
[6] Nawab of the Carnatic.

settlement in Madras. They had sent out a capable leader in Stringer Lawrence, and they were determined to find an equally efficient engineer. Their choice fell on Lieut.-Colonel Caroline Frederick Scott, whom they appointed and despatched to India at the end of the year as Engineer-General.[1] Although his chief duties were to be in Bengal, Scott was ordered to report on Forts St. George and St. David on his voyage to the Hugli, and John Brohier was appointed under his command as engineer in charge of both these forts. The new Engineer-General of all the settlements landed at Fort St. George on August 4th, 1753, attended a meeting of the Council on the following day, surveyed the defences with Brohier, and on August 13th delivered his report and sailed for Calcutta.[2] In the space of nine days Scott produced a complete scheme to remodel the defences of Fort St. George, a feat which is worthy of record. Orders arrived from England that he was to become Commander-in-Chief, in addition to his engineering appointment, if any accident happened to Stringer Lawrence; and he nearly became so, for when Lawrence, who was ill at the time, wrote in January, 1754, that he wished to resign his command at once to Scott, the Madras Council implored the latter to return forthwith from Bengal.[3] As soon as Scott could leave his engineering work in Calcutta, he sailed for Madras; but finding on his arrival on April 20th that Lawrence was no longer seriously ill, he declined to take the supreme command. He was then himself an invalid; and to the great regret of his officers, he died of fever on May 12th.[4]

Stringer Lawrence was superseded in September, 1754, as Commander-in-Chief by Lieutenant-Colonel Adlercron of the King's Army, who landed at Fort St. David with his regiment of King's troops,[5] from the ships of a squadron commanded by Admiral Charles Watson. This was the first unit of the Royal Army to set foot in India since Humphrey Cooke took possession of Bombay in the King's name in 1665. The Directors expected that trouble would ensue between the Royal and Company's soldiers, so they warned their servants in Madras " to carry it with great Respect to Colonel Adlercron " and to treat all His Majesty's officers " in a Gentleman like and Friendly manner." The fact that Royal troops were being sent to India showed the new interest taken by the British Government in the Company's affairs. It presaged the linking up of those affairs with the Imperial policy, and it strengthened the Company in its struggle against the French.

The scheme which Colonel Scott submitted for the improvement of the Madras fortifications was based mainly on extending the

[1] *Public Despatches from England*, December 15th, 1752, Vol. LVI. See Chapter IV.
[2] *Public Consultations*, August 5th and 13th, 1753, Vol. LXXXI.
[3] Letter to Colonel Scott from Fort St. George, January 24th, 1754, Vol. XXX.
[4] *Public Despatches from England*, May 12th, 1754, Vol. LXXXII.
[5] The 39th Foot, now the 1st Battalion Dorsetshire Regt.

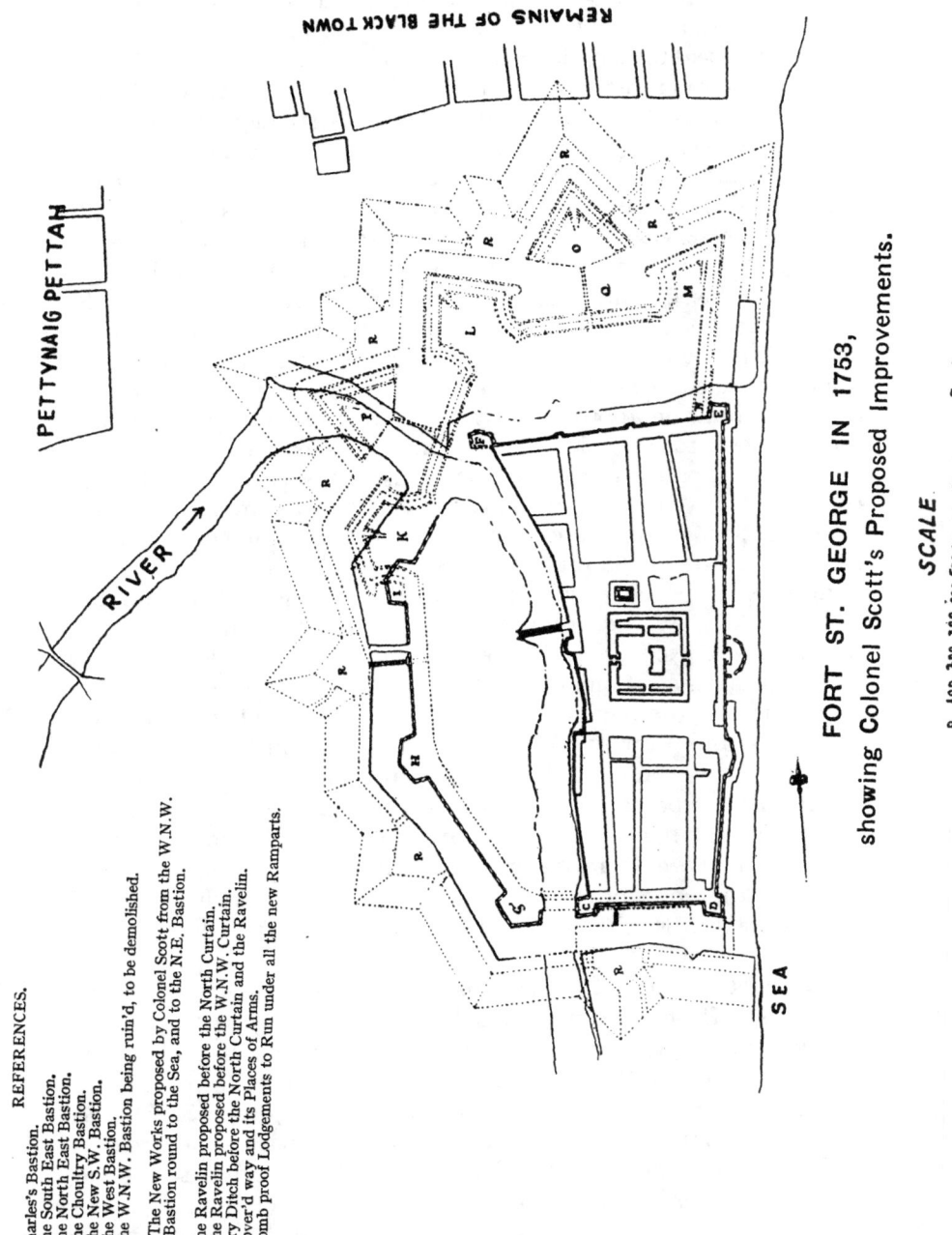

FORT ST. GEORGE IN 1753,
showing Colonel Scott's Proposed Improvements.

REFERENCES.

C. Charles's Bastion.
D. The South East Bastion.
E. The North East Bastion.
F. The Choultry Bastion.
G. The New S.W. Bastion.
H. The West Bastion.
I. The W.N.W. Bastion being ruin'd, to be demolished.
K. } The New Works proposed by Colonel Scott from the W.N.W.
L. } Bastion round to the Sea, and to the N.E. Bastion.
M. }
N. }
O. The Ravelin proposed before the North Curtain.
P. The Ravelin proposed before the W.N.W. Curtain.
Q. Dry Ditch before the North Curtain and the Ravelin.
R. Cover'd way and its Places of Arms.
S. Bomb proof Lodgements to Run under all the new Ramparts.

northern face of the enlarged Fort St. George bequeathed to him by Joseph Smith and Benjamin Robins, but it excluded the Black Town area.[1] He refused to agree with Robins that Black Town should be surrounded by a large wall, though he was willing to propose some more economical form of defence against native troops only. Scott's idea in proposing the extension of White Town northwards was merely to increase the area of that part of the settlement. His design included two very large bastions (K and L) and a demi-bastion (M), their adjacent curtains, a ditch, two ravelins (P and O), and a covered way and glacis around the fortress except on the sea face. He obtained the services of Lieutenant Robert Barker, who made the drawing of Scott's scheme, which is preserved in the King's Library of the British Museum and is reproduced here. Work was started on the western face, being carried out in part by negro women who were slaves of the Company, but the fort was not extended northwards. When Scott died, his scheme was modified, and although the northern face was rebuilt on approximately the plan approved by him, it was erected close to the old walls. This modification avoided any encroachment on the clearance, 400 yards wide, made by the French to the north of White Town, and thus a good field of fire was retained.

Scott was able to introduce some valuable reforms in Madras before his untimely death, notably in checking financial malpractices in engineering. He insisted that all materials should be bought publicly, and that wages should be paid in native coin at the exact current rate of exchange. His recommendations caused the Madras Council to form a " Committee of Works " to supervise engineering operations and the issue of materials, the first members being two councillors and Captain John Brohier as engineer.[2] A similar committee had been formed in Calcutta by Robins, three years after Plaisted had exposed the crooked dealings of the Paymaster and earned his undying hatred. No longer was it possible for a paymaster to make a lucrative business out of his profession at the expense of the works or the poor coolies employed on them. He had to be content with the rather meagre pay granted to him by the Company.

After Scott's death, Brohier took charge of the engineering work in Madras. He had been occupied for some time in damming the old river channel which ran through White Town, and improving the new channel across the island, and on March 1st, 1756, he sent in his own scheme for approval. It combined those of Joseph Smith and Scott. He adopted Scott's design for a large bastion and demi-bastion on the northern front, but rejected his proposal to rebuild that front 100 yards farther northwards, so Scott's north-west bastion vanished from the scheme. For the western front, Brohier proposed

---

[1] *Public Consultations*, August 13th, 1753, Vol. CXXXI.
[2] *Ibid.*, May 13th, 1754, Vol. LXXXII.

to build the three small bastions planned by Smith, and an extensive wall for Black Town with bastions at intervals. The new works on the northern front were begun in December, 1756, and such good progress was made that in February they were well above ground and the smaller works on the western front were almost finished.[1] The engineers worked with a will, for rumours of impending war with France had reached them in July, and the sad news of the loss of Calcutta arrived in August. Admiral Watson was then at Fort St. George, and on his advice the Council decided to despatch an expedition to Bengal to retrieve the situation. It sailed to the north on October 16th, 1756, under Clive and Watson—a band of picked men under two leaders of exceptional ability.

When Clive had driven Siraj-ud-Daula from the northern capital, the Calcutta Council wished to build a new Fort William without delay, but they lacked an experienced engineer for the work. While the defences of Madras were by no means perfect, Calcutta was in a far worse case for it had no fortifications of any value whatever. At the moment, John Brohier seemed to be the most capable military engineer available, and consequently he was transferred from Madras to Calcutta in June, 1757, to plan and build a new Fort William, his place at Fort St. George being taken by John Call, who had been till then at Fort St. David. In Call the Company found a worthy successor to Robins and Scott. He seems to have been honest, trustworthy, and at the same time an engineer of great merit. He proved his value during the siege of Madras by Lally, and rose to be Engineer-in-Chief after the " elopement " of Captain Brohier, thus justifying the high opinion which Robins and Scott had formed of his abilities.

Early in 1755, the British and French companies in India signed a provisional treaty ; but renewed hostilities broke out in 1756 and led in the end to the ruin of the French in India. Dupleix had returned in disgrace to France, and Clive was in Bengal, where he had recaptured Calcutta and destroyed the French fortifications at Chandarnagar. With the English leader they most dreaded so far from southern India, the moment seemed opportune to the French Government for an attack in the south, so Count Lally was sent from France to achieve this object, while Bussy made himself master of the coast from Masulipatam to Vizagapatam. Lally turned his attention first to the weaker settlements of his hereditary foes. Disembarking with a considerable force from the ships of a French fleet under Admiral d'Aché, he attacked Cuddalore on April 29th, 1758, and captured it in five days. He then proceeded to invest Fort St. David on June 2nd. He blew up its fortifications and reduced the place to a heap of ruins, wiping off the map for ever a settlement which was next in importance to Madras itself on the Coromandel coast. His way now

[1] *Military Letters to England*, February 28th, 1757.

lay open to Madras and he concentrated all his efforts on its capture which he hoped would drive the British out of southern India.

For some time before the loss of Fort St. David, the engineers of Fort St. George had made good progress on their defences under the able direction of John Call. It seems that he followed roughly the designs prepared by Brohier. His schemes are clearly shown in a plan headed " A Plan of Fort St. George with the Projects humbly proposed by John Call, 1758," which has been preserved in the King's Library of the British Museum. It is interesting to compare this plan of the fort as it was when besieged by the French, with the plan projected by Scott for enlarging it towards the north. Call's plan demonstrates the striking advance in the science of military engineering which was made in India during the first half of the eighteenth century.

Edward Cotsford, a practitioner (junior) engineer, writing in 1758,[1] says that it was fortunate for the British that Lally directed his attention first to Fort St. David and an expedition to Tanjore, for this respite enabled the engineers in Madras to press on with their work. They swept the surrounding country clear of coolies, labourers and tank-diggers, and so managed to keep 4,000 men at work daily on the defences, some of which were finished in earth as there was not time to build them in masonry. Call expected that the French would attack from the north through Black Town, which was defended only by a " Bound Hedge "[2] on its distant northern edge, so he arranged to inundate all low-lying ground around it and to barricade its streets with palm trees.[3] His preparations, however, were interrupted by the appearance of the French outside Madras on December 9th, 1758, with a force estimated as 3,000 Europeans, 500 native cavalry and 3,000 sepoys. To oppose this force the British had 1,758 Europeans and 2,200 sepoys. That Lally should have dared to attack the British in Fort St. George with so small a preponderance in numbers is remarkable. He paid dearly for his temerity.

Space does not admit of a full account of the siege of Madras, which lasted for 67 days and ended in victory for the British; but a brief report by the Madras Council shows how near the French came to success :—[4]

" FORT ST. GEORGE TO THE COMPANY.

" Fort St. George was invested on the 12th December by the whole force of the French commanded by Mr. Lally. We had received from Europe but a very small part of Colonel Draper's battalion. . . . We cannot too much commend the bravery of his Majesty's and your Officers and Men during the whole Siege. . . . The Enemy open'd

---

[1] Orme MSS., Vol. LXII.
[2] A fence of thorny shrubs and cactus.
[3] *Military Consultations*, November 20th, 1758, Vol. IX.
[4] *Military Letters to England*, February 21st, 1759, Vol. II.

their batteries on us the 6th January. Their greatest fire was from 26 pieces of Cannon and 9 Mortars. Their attack, being on the North from the vicinity of Black Town,[1] afforded them convenient Cover to advance immediately so near as 450 yards, which was the distance of their first and Royal Battery. Having fired a few days from this and their other batteries which enfiladed all the North side of the Town, they advanced by Sap to within 30 yards of the Crest of the Glacis, where they erected a battery against the right face of the north Ravelin. Their cannon were destroyed by the fire from the Ravelin as often as they opened their embrazures. They succeeded as ill in the next battery they opened, which was on the Crest of the Glacis where we had so superior a fire on them that they were unable to live there and were obliged to retire again to their Royal battery, but not untill they had sprung a Mine which opened the Counterscarp of our ditch before the Salient Angle of the demi Bastion."

Lally poured his troops into Black Town on December 14th. The British were not content with a passive resistance and tried to eject their assailants by a sortie in force under Colonel Draper, who was second-in-command to Stringer Lawrence, but unhappily they failed with heavy loss. There is no record that Lally ever attempted a general assault. He relied on a deliberate advance supported by artillery fire, and finally resorted to mining ; but neither his guns nor his mines were sufficient to open a way through Call's bastions and curtains.[2] He may have considered that his force was too weak to risk the heavy casualties of an assault unless the defences were reduced to ruin. Before that could happen, he was obliged to raise the siege on the approach of a British squadron under Admiral Pocock. On February 17th, 1759, the French abandoned their trenches and batteries, leaving behind them 52 guns ; the Union Jack still floated over Fort St. George and the French power in India was broken. From that date, Madras was never attacked until, on September 22nd, 1914, the German cruiser *Emden* bombarded the town and coast.

Two events during the siege may be of interest to engineers. In January, 1759, finding that infantry working parties were unable to cope with the damage done by the French artillery, Captain Call formed a pioneer company from European volunteers drawn from several corps and employed them in repairing the walls. Two pioneer companies of sepoys were formed on the same plan.[3] These units appear to be the first pioneer companies raised in India on a

---

[1] As Call had anticipated.
[2] Due credit for the fortifications should be given also to the Governor, George Pigot, who had insisted on expenditure being incurred on them against the wishes of his Council.
[3] *The Military History of the Madras Engineers*, by H. M. Vibart, Vol. I, p. 32.

proper military organization.[1] The other event which should be recorded was the grant of commissions on January 20th, 1759, to several of the Company's engineers in Fort St. George. John Call, "Sub-Director of Ingineers," was commissioned as a Captain; Alexander Leigh, "Engineer in Ordinary" became a Captain-Lieutenant; William Stevenson, a "Sub-Engineer," became a Lieutenant; and Edward Cotsford, "Practitioner Engineer," an Ensign. It is probable that this step was taken to give the Company's engineers some standing with the King's officers then serving in Madras. The concession was well merited, for engineers such as Robins and Scott had rendered excellent service, and Call was following their example. The siege led to important changes in the organization of troops other than engineers. The Select Committee[2] drew up a scheme, which was sanctioned in September, 1759, providing for a sepoy force of 7,000 men in seven battalions, each officered by "two subalterns, three Sergeant Majors and one Black Commandant." Thus, beyond the impetus given to military engineering, the siege of Madras brought about a valuable reorganization of the Company's army in southern India.

Lieutenant-Colonel Eyre Coote arrived from Calcutta in 1759 with the 84th Regiment, and embarked on a campaign which resulted in the battle of Wandiwash on January 22nd, 1760. In this decisive victory over Lally, he captured the French General, Bussy, and afterwards proceeded to reduce the French strongholds in southern India with such rapidity that soon only Pondicherry and a couple of hill forts remained to afford refuge to the shattered remnants of the French army. Towards the end of the year, when Coote was investing Pondicherry, John Call was sent from Madras to take charge of the siege operations and determine the front to be attacked. Lally, being in sore straits for food, turned 1,400 native inhabitants out of the town, and for eight days these wretched men, women and children wandered forlornly between the British and French lines, living on the roots of grass or dying of starvation, till the more humane British commander allowed them to pass through his entrenchments. This tragic episode has been recorded often in history, and has formed the basis of a stirring tale in modern fiction.[3] It shows to what lengths a ruthless commander will go in quest of victory. On December 9th

---

[1] Between 1761 and 1780, companies of pioneers and miners were formed when required and broken up when their services were no longer needed. They were employed at the siege of Vellore under Colonel John Caillaud in 1761. They accompanied the expedition against the Spanish settlements in the Philippine Islands, and were in action at the storming of Manila and the capture of the citadel on October 6th, 1762. They took part in the siege and surrender of Tanjore in 1771, when they earned the high praise of General Joseph Smith. They were engaged also at the second siege and storm of Tanjore two years later, at the siege and capture of Pondicherry by Sir Hector Munro in 1778, and at the capture of Mahé in 1779. (See *Historical Record of the 2nd Q.V.O. Sappers and Miners*, Vol. I, p. 5.)

[2] A Standing Committee formed in February, 1755, to deal with military and naval matters in consultation, if necessary, with a "Secret" Committee.

[3] *The Green Curve*, by Ole Luke Oie.

the English batteries opened a bombardment which lasted for six days and was renewed when more ammunition arrived on December 20th. A severe cyclone then interrupted the attack; but on January 15th, 1761, Lally was forced to propose terms of surrender. Pondicherry passed into British hands on the following day.

Eyre Coote was determined to leave nothing to chance. He directed that the French fortifications should be destroyed without delay, and entrusted the work to John Call. It is clear that the fortifications were dealt with effectively, for the Madras Council reported in October that they were entirely destroyed, including the outlying forts.[1] Lally was sent to England as a prisoner of war, whence he returned to France on parole to be tried, condemned and executed by his countrymen. The fall of Pondicherry completed the ruin of the French in India.

Having demolished the defences of Pondicherry, John Call and other engineers were employed afterwards in operations against Vellore. The engineers who remained in Madras repaired the breaches in the northern bastions and curtains and strengthened the sea face. At the end of 1762, however, Call found time to send in five alternative schemes for alterations to the southern defences of Fort St. George.[2] The selected design provided for an extension southwards by advancing the southern curtain and building a large bastion and some minor works. It was estimated that the work would occupy eight years and would cost more than 1,000,000 rupees; nevertheless it was begun, and continued steadily till it was finished. Call turned his attention also to Black Town—a never-failing source of argument—and proposed to surround it by an earthen bank topped with thorny shrubs. In Fort St. George itself he schemed to lay out a new system of streets, to rebuild a number of houses and erect new ones, and to put up a temporary riding school " by which convenience," the Council naïvely remarked, " the Cavalry may be render'd in some degree manageable."[3] In fact, John Call altered the face of Fort St. George during the years in which he was Engineer-in-Chief on the coast. He was more fortunate than Brohier and his other predecessors, for the Directors had loosened their purse-strings at last in the interests of military engineering.

There were many curious men on the Coromandel coast as elsewhere—clever men, dull men, ambitious men and dishonest men—but one of the cleverest was Paul Benfield. While Call was absent in 1764 as Chief Engineer with a force operating in Madura, Lieutenant Benfield remained in Fort St. George, with other assistant engineers, to carry on the works planned by his chief. He seems to have been a man of outstanding ability in his profession, but unhappily not too

---

[1] *Military Letters to England*, October 2nd, 1761, Vol. III.
[2] *Military Consultations*, December 28th, 1762, Vol. XVII.
[3] *Public Consultations*, October 24th, 1759, Vol. LXXXIX.

scrupulous in his dealings. When he arrived from England in 1764, as " Civil Architect and Assistant Engineer," he came with excellent credentials from the Directors who wrote :[1] " He is exceedingly well recommended to Us as having been regularly bred an Architect, Surveyor and draughtsman, and for his knowledge in Fortification and other Branches of Mathematicks." So much was Call himself impressed by young Benfield that when he resigned in 1768 he recommended him as his successor in the post of Engineer of Fort St. George. Benfield, however, had financial ambitions. He tendered for, and obtained, a contract for the fortification of Black Town, involving the construction of three and a half miles of rampart, and resigned his post as engineer after holding it for only a few months. As a contractor he was a brilliant success, for he carried out the work in a manner far superior to anything which had been seen in Madras. He introduced the use of the inverted arch into India, thereby economizing in masonry; and he employed foundation wells to support his heavy works, a method which he is said to have copied from the natives of Madras. But unfortunately his reputation was tarnished by his doubtful dealings in 1773 with Muhammad Ali, then Nawab of the Carnatic, in the scandal of the Nawab's debts. It is best to pass over this unsavoury business and to remember Benfield as a contractor without equal in the time of the rebuilding of Fort St. George.

While it is true that, in 1762, Call had advised against a scheme to rebuild a wall round Black Town, he seems to have altered his mind, for two years later he proposed that a defensive line of this nature should be provided to cover the north, west, and part of the south sides of the native quarter. The work was actually begun, but it was not till 1769 that it was undertaken in earnest after a raid by Haidar Ali in 1767 had frightened the inhabitants. Call then wrote[2] that he intended to build only a single line of bastions and curtains, varying in size and length according to the nature of the ground. His description erred on the side of modesty, for the defences, as constructed, included 17 bastions with curtains averaging 300 yards in length. They were almost completed in 1770 by Paul Benfield, and some of the northern bastions and curtains still remain as a testimony to his ability as a contractor. The cost was estimated at 150,000 pagodas,[3] but it did not fall on the Company as the Council taxed the patient inhabitants sufficiently to recover the amount in 12 years. This autocratic method provided an easy solution of a difficult financial problem. Such matters were settled more easily in the eighteenth century than they could be in the twentieth. Among the Councillors who sanctioned the tax was Warren Hastings, destined to become famous in the history of India.

[1] *Public Despatches from England,* December 30th, 1763, Vol. LXVII.
[2] *Military Consultations,* March 27th, 1769, Vol. XXXIII.
[3] Nearly 4 lakhs of rupees.

ENGINEERS BECOME COMBATANT OFFICERS.

As John Call's health was failing under the strain of campaigns against Haidar Ali and engineering in Madras, he was forced to resign in 1770 and proceed to England where he became a baronet in 1791, and died ten years later. The Directors were hard put to it to find a suitable successor to so eminent an engineer; but by applying to the Board of Ordnance they were fortunate enough to secure the services of Captain-Lieutenant Patrick Ross as Chief Engineer on the Coromandel coast, and he landed in Madras about September 15th, 1770. This appointment is remarkable as Ross held a commission in the Corps of Engineers of the Royal Army, having joined it as a Sub-Engineer and Lieutenant in 1751. He was an experienced military engineer who had seen much active service in many parts of the world. Soon after his arrival in Madras he took part in the siege of Tanjore, where he was wounded and lost almost all his engineer officers in various attacks. Thus early in the history of modern India did the engineers begin to pay heavily for the honour of leading the way in the assault. But their work in the field, and the casualties which they suffered, drew attention to their branch of the service; and in 1769, during a campaign against Haidar Ali, the ruler of Mysore, a sweeping change in the organization of the engineering branch came under discussion. Proposals were put forward to reorganize the Corps of Engineers in India by recruiting some officers from England, and to place it entirely on a military footing; and since this scheme was likely to affect the officers then serving in India, these were called upon to choose whether they would resign or remain. Some of them transferred into civil employment, but most elected to remain as engineers under the new régime.

The military duties which devolved at this period on engineers in the field and during sieges, seemed to justify them in demanding that they should be considered as combatant officers rather than mere technical experts. Colonel Patrick Ross accordingly addressed the Court of Directors in 1771,[1] asking that engineer officers might be allowed to take rank and command in the army. The petition was granted, and orders were issued that they were to command in the field or in garrison, according to their army rank, on the authority of the wording of their commissions. This ruling, however, led to an extended dispute. The officers of the other branches of the Company's army did not want the engineers to encroach on their preserves, and it was not till 1775 that the Directors decided[2] that, while officers of their Corps of Engineers were to hold rank in the army according to the dates of their commissions, as in His Majesty's army, they could rise in their ranks only in their own Corps. From that time, engineer officers in India were combatant soldiers. They well deserved this honour which they had fought so hard to obtain.

[1] *The Military History of the Madras Engineers*, by H. M. Vibart, Vol. I, p. 119.
[2] *Ibid.*, p. 126.

The town of Madras was now spreading in all directions, and Fort St. George was nearing completion. Not only were native suburbs springing up like mushrooms under the encouragement of the Company's protection and trade, but the civil and military officers were building country residences for themselves in the fertile tracts a few miles from the fort. This shocked the authorities who tried to discourage such extravagance by remarking[1] that "Buildings and Gardens of Pleasure tend to the Encouragement of Idleness, Expence and Dissipation." But their remonstrances fell on deaf ears. The British officials were bored with the monotonous seascapes visible from their quarters in Fort St. George, and wished to escape from official restraint. There is little doubt that they were incited to rebellion by the feminine element of the gay society in old Madras. The ladies won as usual, and the "Country House" habit, which started as a week-end relaxation, became a permanent arrangement. Good husbands flocked daily into the fort from their "buildings of pleasure" and returned in the evening to the bosoms of their families. Fort St. George ceased to be a town, and became instead a fortress containing the headquarters of the Madras Government and the barracks, quarters and storerooms of the military garrison.

Before we leave Madras to trace the development of engineering in Western India in the eighteenth century, it may be well to pause for a moment to view the settlement through the eyes of a visitor from Europe. Mrs. Kindersley, who was on her way in 1765 to join her husband in Bengal, writes :[2] " Madrass is, without exception, the prettiest place I ever saw. It is strongly fortified, and the walls and works as well as the barracks for the army, the storehouses, and every other public building are so calculated as to be both convenient and an addition to the beauty of the place. The town is laid out in streets and squares ; the houses neat and pretty, many of them large : in all the good houses the apartments are upstairs and all on one floor : the rooms are large and very lofty : most of the houses are built with a *verander*. But what gives the greatest elegance to the houses is a material peculiar to the place : it is a cement or plaster called *channam* made of the shells of a very large species of oysters found on the coast : these shells when burnt, pounded and mixed with water, form the strongest cement imaginable : if it is to be used as a plaster, they mix it with whites of eggs, milk, and some other ingredients : when dry it is as hard, and very nearly as beautiful, as marble : the rooms, staircases, etc., are covered with it. . . . The mode of living is so extraordinary that I can scarcely believe myself among English people. I shall only say that they are expensive in horses, carriages, palenqueens and number of servants ; are fond of

---

[1] *Public Consultations*, September 7th, 1769, Vol. CII.
[2] *Letters from the Island of Teneriffe*, etc., by Mrs. Jemima Kindersley, 1777; Letter XIX, June, 1765.

entertainments, dress and pleasure; sociable with each other; hospitable and civil to strangers."

And so farewell for a time to Madras, with its great fort, rolling surf, teeming Black Town, elegant country houses and indolent society. Once a small fishing village discovered by Cogan and Day, it had become, through 130 years of trade, war and engineering, a great commercial centre defying alike the attempts of European or native foes to snatch from it its hard-earned wealth.

FORT ST. GEORGE, MADRAS, 1754.
From a print by Van Ryne, Royal Library, British Museum.

CHAPTER VI.

BOMBAY IN THE EIGHTEENTH CENTURY.

BOMBAY recovered slowly from the effects of the humiliating treaty with Aurangzeb in 1690 and the disorganization caused by the struggle which preceded the formation of the United Company in 1708. Threatened by enemies without and pestilence within, the colony decreased in size; trade failed, money was scarce. The place was a veritable graveyard. In those days, Bombay was represented by a double chain of small tracts of hill or jungle—Mahim, Warli, Parel, Mazagon,[1] Bombay, and Old Woman's[2] Islands—which were islands only at high tide when the sea rushed through the channels between them and flooded the adjacent flat areas. When the tide ebbed it left behind it pestilential deposits; myriads of flies bred from the fish manure which the inhabitants used for their toddy palms, and malarial mosquitoes swarmed from the dense jungles obstructing most of the ground above water-level. But the Company was not disheartened by these scourges. Gradually the "drowned lands" were protected from the sea by causeways built across the breaches, and the territory thus gained was covered at first with salt-pans, similar to those in Portugal and France. Jungles were cut down, the use of fish manure was prohibited, and when Charles Boone arrived as President, in 1715, a brighter day dawned. For many years the energies of the engineers were devoted as much to their fight against the sea as to their fortifications, docks and buildings. Their success can be seen in the great modern city, and its far-reaching suburbs, which form the western gateway of India.

In the earlier part of the eighteenth century the town of Bombay, on the small original island of the same name, depended for its defence on its "Castle" and a few outlying forts or "watch-houses" on the other tracts of land which now form the large island. Considering these tracts as one island, we find, at the extreme north, a fort at Sion; on the west coast, forts at Mahim and Warli; and on the east, forts at Sewri and Dongri, the latter close to the ramparts of Bombay itself and a fruitful source of official argument. It is clear that the outlying defences of Bombay were very primitive. Each little fort, or loopholed house, was garrisoned only by a squad of *Topasses* and a few British soldiers, usually under a serjeant; though at the end of 1702, a fort of superior type, with a larger garrison, was nearing completion at Mahim, and the fort at Sion

[1] Mazgaon or Mazagaon. [2] Al Oman.

was of some value. In 1704 the Directors accorded the Bombay Council a "general liberty to fortifie the island,"[1] but the general liberty did not extend to the funds required for the work ; and, as a part of such money as was actually provided seems to have flowed into the pockets of the engineers,[2] it is not surprising that there was stagnation in engineering until steps were taken to reorganize the administration and to check abuses.

The growth of Bombay was hindered not only by internal troubles but by the activities of the pirates who infested the Indian seas. Captain Kidd, John Avery, and other adventurers under the Jolly Roger were succeeded by the famous Maratha corsair, Kanhoji Angria, who preyed on all the shipping along the western coast with his fast-sailing vessels and fifty-oared galleys called *gallivats* or *grabs*. At first he attacked only Mughal ships ; but later, when assisted by James Plantain, Taylor, England and other European buccaneers, he assailed even the largest of the Company's vessels. His methods were simple. Darting suddenly from a creek he would mass his craft astern of his victim while she lay becalmed, bring down her rigging with a few well-placed shots, and then board her with hordes of ruffians, sword in hand. Attacks were made in vain on Angria's lairs in 1717, 1718 and 1720, till at length, in desperation, the Directors induced the King to send an expedition against him at the end of 1721, and Commodore Matthews arrived in Bombay with some men-of-war.

The proceedings after the advent of the Royal Navy were worthy of a Gilbert and Sullivan opera. Commodore Matthews flew into a rage because the guns of President Boone failed to salute his squadron. The President, who considered himself senior to any commodore, refused to expend the necessary powder until the Commodore had fired first. Messages flashed to and fro. Neither would salute the other. At last the President gave in and fired his guns ; and the Commodore, stiff and haughty, consented to come ashore. A contemporary writer relates[3] that "the island of Bombay was now thronged with the Navy-officers, who looked as much superior to us as the greatness of their ambition could possibly lead them. There were daily duels fought by one or other of them, and challenges perpetually sent round the island by the gentlemen of the navy. Having such a great number of gallant heroes we were in great hopes of totally demolishing Angria." The Council then invited the Portuguese Viceroy of Goa, and his "General of the North" at Bassein, to take part in the attack on Angria at Alibag. "The Viceroy, with much pretended zeal, came in person, designing to head

---

[1] Company to Bombay, letter dated January 12th, 1704, alluded to in *Compilation of Orders*, 1704.

[2] Mr. John Cooper was the senior engineer in charge of the works at this time, Colonel Herman Bake having died in 1677.

[3] *A Compendious History of the Indian Wars*, 1737, by Downing.

such forces as he had raised. The General of the North also came down to Bombay and was most magnificently entertained by the President." It is sad to relate that, after so much gold lace had shone and wine had flowed, the Commodore and his eager allies failed to disturb Angria. On the very day fixed for the assault the Viceroy went aboard his ship saying he was seriously ill, and the Portuguese troops refused to advance. The final scene depicts the choleric Commodore " coming ashore in a violent rage, flying at the General of the North and thrusting his cane in his mouth, and treating the Viceroy not much better." The man who fared best was Angria himself, who was left at liberty for many years to continue his operations against the ships and defences of the smaller European settlements on the Bombay coast.

The first care of President Charles Boone was to render Bombay more secure from attack. With that object in view he carried out the plan originated by Aungier 40 years before, and built a fortified wall around the town, with gates to north, west and south, and a large bastion mounting 48-pounder guns at Mendham's Point.[1] Aungier had advised the Company to enclose the town from Dongri Hill to Mendham's Point in a polygonal line of fortification[2] to " secure trading people from the insults of their troublesome, beggarly neighbours in the continent " ; but his proposals were rejected and his scheme remained more or less in abeyance till Boone took it in hand and brought it to completion on Christmas Day, 1716. Until Boone arrived, Bombay was indeed, as Downing remarks, " in a declining posture " ; but the town wall set it on its feet. The wall, though a poor defence, had eight bastions and enclosed an area of about 153 acres of warehouses, residences, gardens and native bazaars. Before he retired in 1722, Boone extended the old dockyard begun by Nicholas Waite 15 years earlier, built some ships at Surat for an Indian Marine, and in 1718 opened the church which is now St. Thomas' Cathedral. He excelled in the advancement of engineering and gave a new lease of life to Bombay.

Up to the middle of the eighteenth century the policy of the Company in Bombay was dictated by prudence. Their servants were enjoined to placate the various native powers in western India, and during each respite so gained, to strengthen their political and commercial position. The Councillors in Bombay were often called upon to side with one or other of their natural enemies—Mughals, pirates, Marathas or Portuguese. To stand alone was to invite attack by any or all of these potential foes. Usually the British sided with one of the weaker parties, to prevent its extinction by a more potent neighbour, and thus maintained a balance of power which might avert hostilities. The Mughal dominance was vanishing

---

[1] The southern extremity of the original Bombay Island, near the site of the present Taj Mahal Hotel.
[2] *New Account*, by Hamilton, Vol. I, p. 88.

and the Portuguese were on the downward path. On land, the Marathas were becoming the most dangerous foe; on the sea, the piratical fleets of Angria harried the shipping. But of these two, by far the greater menace was from the Maratha confederacy; indeed it may be said that fear of the Marathas was responsible for more progress in the fortification of Bombay up to the middle of the eighteenth century than any other factor. So lowering was this cloud that the British and Portuguese, laying aside their old enmity, drew together against the common danger. It was an open question whether the defences of Bombay could keep pace with the Maratha advance.

Between 1717 and 1724 the annual expenditure on the Bombay defences increased to such an extent that, in the opinion of the Court, it became unbearable. The Directors looked on every side for money. To meet the cost of the town wall the Council imposed taxes designed to reimburse the charge in 14 years;[1] but the financial position in 1724 was so bad that the Directors sent instructions that no new buildings were to be begun without their permission, and gave warning that " to prevent anyone in future diverting our cash designed for trade by laying it out in buildings, we add that if hereafter any new buildings be set about without our previous leave from hence, we shall expect the President and Council to reimburse and repay into our cash whatever is expended thereon." No option was given. Even if the veto on building and fortification may have increased the amounts available for trade and for the naval and military forces, a more deadly encouragement to masterly inactivity in the face of danger could not have been devised. But the sea and land forces had certainly developed greatly by 1737 when a small Indian navy sailed the seas and the force on land amounted to more than 1,600 men, including 750 Europeans, making Bombay more powerful than either Madras or Calcutta. By that time matters had assumed a more cheerful aspect. The troops were paid regularly, their barracks had been enlarged, and a better hospital was available for the sick.

The ban imposed on building and fortification in Bombay could not last for long when the Marathas were extending their territory so effectively and ruthlessly. It seems to have been removed before 1734, for in that year the Bombay Government appointed Mr. Archibald Campbell,[2] First Lieutenant of the galley *Princess Carolina*, as Overseer of Works and Master of Arms, " hee being an ingenious person, having a good notion of architecture and other parts of mathematicks."[3] In 1737, when the Marathas had nearly ousted the Portuguese from Salsette, the gravest anxiety was felt in Bombay.

[1] Court to Bombay, letter dated February 21st, 1717.
[2] Not the Archibald Campbell, the famous military engineer, who became Governor of Madras.
[3] *Bombay and Western India*, by J. Douglas, Vol. I, p. 137.

The President, with all the military officers, inspected the fortifications in person, and the Council ordered that all coconut trees within 120 yards of the Bombay town wall should be cut down and the wall widened. Towards the close of the year, reports reached Bombay that the Marathas intended to launch an attack against it, so the President himself, accompanied by Mr. Cockell, the engineer, and various military officers, inspected the outlying forts. They decided that these defences were too weak to resist the invaders, and ordered the construction of small additional batteries between Warli and Mahim, and other minor works elsewhere along the coast. However, the invasion never came; and in 1738, when the Portuguese handed over Salsette to the Marathas, the Bombay Council were satisfied that they had made their territory secure from aggression.

Two large engineering projects next came under discussion. The first was for a ditch around the town wall, and the second concerned the treatment of Dongri Hill, a ridge which lay close outside the northern wall of the town. In spite of the assurance of the Council that Bombay was secure from invasion, the merchants remained so much in fear of the Marathas that they came forward at the end of June, 1739, with a suggestion that they should be taxed sufficiently to raise 30,000 rupees towards the cost of a ditch.[1] Although the work was estimated to cost three times that sum, the President, Stephen Law, decided to begin an excavation 50 feet wide and 14 feet deep. A ditch was dug, and it may have produced a good moral effect; but it became in time an open sewer and was the cause of much sickness in the town.

S. M. Edwardes gives a good description of the Bombay works and their garrisons at this period.[2] To protect the island, its population of 70,000, and its gardens, groves, ricelands, fisheries, graveyards and salt-pans, there were in existence the "Great Fort" with bastions and town wall; the Mazagon and Dongri forts; Sewri Fort, facing the village of Maula on Salsette and garrisoned by a *subadar* and 50 sepoys with eight to ten guns; a small tower and breastwork at Sion, facing Kurla, held by a captain and 60 soldiers with nine to ten guns; a "triple-bastioned fortress" at Mahim, in front of Bandra, manned by 100 soldiers with 30 guns; and lastly a fort at Warli, armed with eight guns and garrisoned by an ensign and 25 men. If these figures are correct, the Bombay Council were hardly justified in feeling, as they did in 1738, that they were safe from invasion.

Joseph Smith,[3] the father of General Joseph Smith,[4] was the

[1] Bombay Merchants' Representation to Government, June, 1739. *Public Diary*, No. 12, of 1738–39.
[2] *The Rise of Bombay*, by S. M. Edwardes, p. 169.
[3] *Bombay Consultations*, October 18th, 1742. *Public Diary*, No. 15, of 1741–42.
[4] General Joseph Smith served as a Colonel under Clive in the Carnatic, in 1752. He commanded the Trichinopoly garrison in 1757–58, and defeated Haidar Ali and the Nizam at Trinomalai on September 26th, 1767. As a Major-General he captured Tanjore in 1773. He died in 1790.

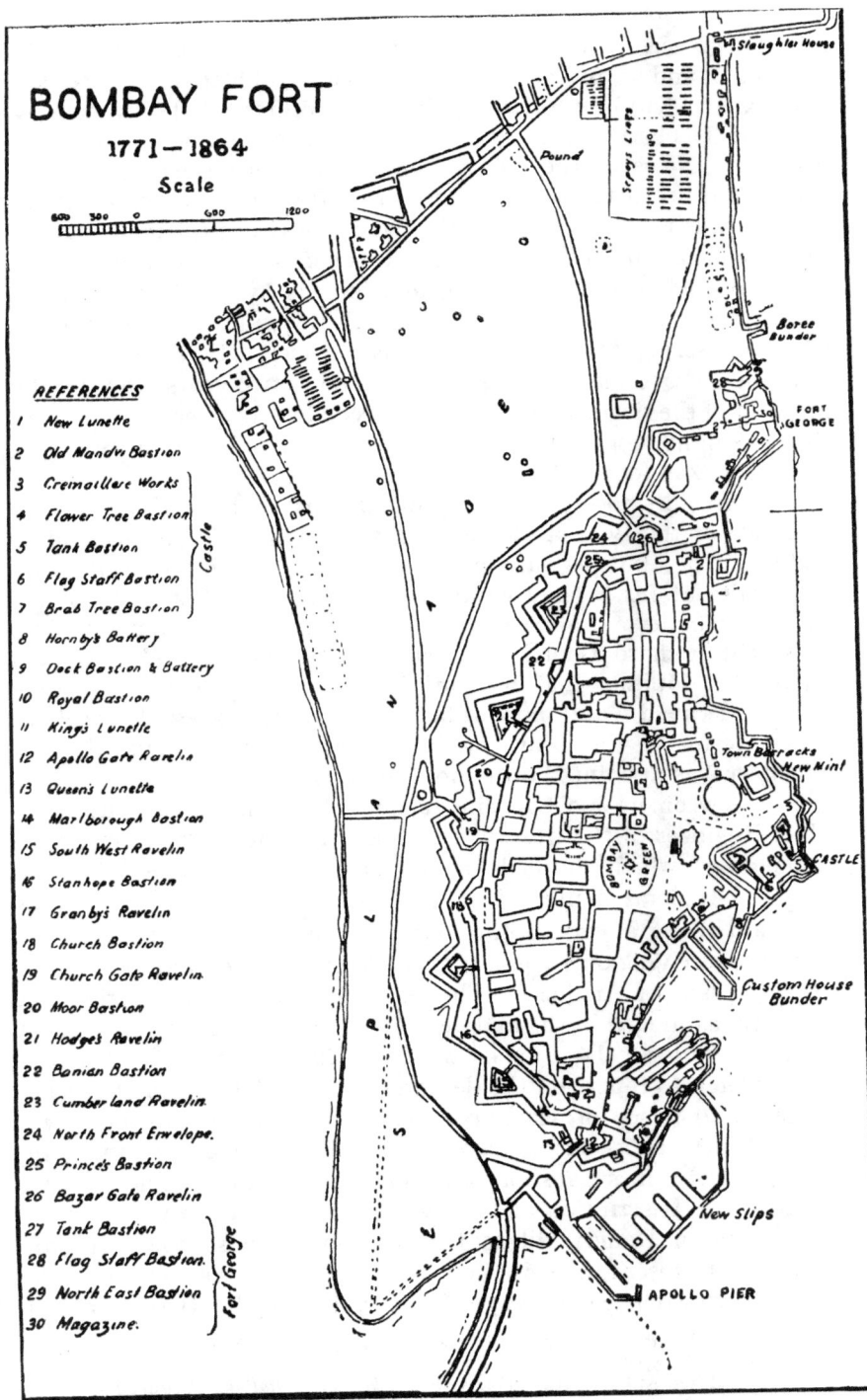

acting engineer of Bombay in 1742 when the town ditch was nearly completed, and he and his men seem to have had little to do after the last spadeful had been thrown. The scare of immediate invasion by the Marathas had died away. For a time, engineering languished in Bombay. News of the declaration of war between England and France did not reach the settlement till after the monsoon of 1744; Dupleix was busy in the Carnatic; and it was not till 1746 that La Bourdonnais launched his successful attack against Madras. Bombay appeared to be secure from interference by Dupleix or Bussy. Under these circumstances Joseph Smith was transferred to Madras where his services were more urgently needed. He left Bombay in 1744 for the Coromandel coast where he died, two years later, on the first day of the siege of Madras. For several years after his departure there was no engineering work of any importance in Bombay. Attention was focussed on the Southern Presidency.

The Directors hoped that Benjamin Robins would be able to advise them about the Bombay fortifications in 1750, as he did in Madras and Calcutta; but his untimely death in the following year upset all their calculations. They wrote in 1752[1] that the Bombay Council was not to undertake any expensive works without special permission. President Richard Bourchier, however, was not satisfied with such an order. Finding that his outlying defences were by that time " much decayed," and most of his gun-carriages useless, he wrote in strong terms to the Court[2] with the result that a qualified Chief Engineer was appointed once more to Bombay.

The newcomer was Captain Jacques de Funck, who was made Chief Engineer of the western settlement in March, 1753, under the same order which notified the appointment of Colonel Scott as Engineer-General of all the British settlements. Although de Funck was said to be a very skilful engineer, he was badly paid for his services, receiving only £40 a year as Chief Engineer and £200 a year as a Captain of Artillery. The relative value of engineering and gunnery, as judged in the middle of the eighteenth century, is shown by these figures. De Funck landed in Bombay in November, and was ordered to report on the defences without delay; but he was in no hurry to do so, for nearly two years elapsed before his report was handed in.[3] He seems to have been a man of ideas, but incurably lazy; fruitful in suggestion, but slow in execution. The report is headed " A Description of Bombay Town and Castle with the disadvantage of Dongri hill as the situation stands, how built and fortified at present, likewise how the same works are to be amended for its better defence, surveyed in the year 1755." It runs to more

---

[1] Court to Bombay, letter dated March 4th, 1752. *Public Department Court's Letters*, Vol. IV, of 1752–56.

[2] Report dated August 24th, 1752, with *Bombay Consultations*, August 25th, 1752. *Public Diary*, No. 25, of 1752.

[3] Report by Captain de Funck, dated September 23rd, 1755, appearing in *Public Diary*, No. 28, of 1755.

than 3,000 words, and is in great detail. De Funck criticized the lack of a field of fire around the town, the inadequacy of the ditch, and the weakness of Bombay Castle, and he drew particular attention to Dongri Hill which he described as the key of the island.

At the end of his long report on the defences, de Funck stated that Dongri Hill should be properly fortified and that certain works should be put in hand at once, such as the connection of the existing Dongri fortifications to the ramparts near the Bazar Gate, certain improvements to the Castle, a new battery on the sea coast, and three drawbridges for the town gates. These urgent works were carried out;[1] but still further expense was incurred in 1756, on his recommendation, because the situation between the British and French was then considered to be so critical that an attack by the French fleet seemed imminent. This touched the Directors on a sore spot, and they protested accordingly :[2] " We find you are carrying on several works upon the projects of Mr. de Funck. But as they seem to us to be calculated with little regard to expense we intended to have put an entire stop to your proceedings. Mr. Mace's going to Bombay gives us the opportunity of being more satisfactorily informed of what is necessary to be done. Without our directions you are to proceed no further on Mr. de Funck's general plan or any other unless Mr. Mace shall make it appear some works are evidently necessary for the immediate defence of the island."

The Court of Directors had lost confidence in de Funck, and they sent Major James Mace to supersede him. It was only to be expected that, when Mace arrived, the two engineers would disagree over the plans for defence. This occurred, and de Funck sent in his resignation on February 7th, 1758, refusing to carry out Mace's proposals.[3] When he was ordered to hand over to his rival the plans which he had prepared, or was believed to have prepared, showing the works which he proposed, he produced only some rough sketches without scales. As nothing more helpful could be got from him, and he was determined not to work under the direction of Mace, he was given a passage to England, a disappointed and discredited man. So the name of Captain Jacques de Funck passes from the pages of Indian history.

Meanwhile Admiral Watson and Colonel Clive had eliminated one of the most powerful foes of the European colonists on the western coast. The Angria pirates had renewed their excesses in 1748 and again in 1752, and the British, hard hit by their defeat in Madras, could not cope single-handed with these pests. Looking around for assistance they decided that their only course was to enlist the help

---

[1] *Bombay Government Consultations*, September 23rd, 1755. *Public Diary*, No. 28, of 1755.
[2] Court to Bombay, May 4th, 1757. *Public Department Court's Letters*, Vol. V of 1757-61.
[3] *Bombay Government Consultations*, February 7th, 1758. *Public Diary*, No. 31, of 1758.

of their quondam enemies the Marathas; and thus a coalition was formed in 1755 against Tulaji Angria, a descendant of Kanhoji, who had established himself in the stronghold of Gheria (Vijayadurg),[1] built on a rugged promontory which gave shelter to his ships and galleys. Admiral Watson, with a royal squadron and a large detachment of King's troops, happened to be on his way from England to attack the French in the Deccan, so the Bombay Government invited him to rid them of Angria before he sailed to the south. This he consented to do, and with Clive on board, appeared off Gheria on February 11th, 1756, finding a Maratha force already in position before it. Watson attacked and burned the pirate fleet, while Clive assaulted on land; and in two days the fortress was taken. Thereafter the Company's ships could sail the Indian seas in safety at least from organized piracy, and the engineers of Bombay were called upon to guard only against their uncertain friends the Marathas by land and the squadrons of the French by sea. Their position "between the devil and the deep sea" was not too enviable, and their large ideas on fortification were hampered by lack of funds and a scarcity of artisans. However, at the moment the Marathas seemed well disposed towards the British in acknowledgment of valuable presents and expressions of goodwill, and even went so far as to offer sanctuary at Thana to all European women and children when a French invasion was imminent.

In January and February, 1758, Major James Mace wrote several reports on the defences of Bombay, disagreeing with de Funck on almost every point. He said[2] that the gates were not sufficiently protected, the parapets were in a wretched condition, the landward curtains and bastions were not properly flanked, and at the north end, near the Bazar Gate, everything was in disorder. He drew particular attention to Dongri Fort which commanded the northern quarter of the town. Deprecating any attempt to spend money in improving the existing lines of defence and making a covered way, he remarked that "the works in Dongri are of little defence, and not being supported by any works on the town, an enemy might easily become master of the hill. Were an enemy to possess themselves of Dongri, they might from thence batter the Mandvi bastion, and, if they pleased, lay the town in ashes. These circumstances, I think, make it absolutely necessary either to enclose Dongri Hill with a good work and bring it within the town, or to destroy the tower and works entirely and endeavour to level the rock on which it stands. To remedy the inconveniences attending Dongri, and the bad situation of the town's fortifications, it will require many necessary additions and amendments to the old works or a work entirely new. The alternative which I should prefer is to construct a new line from sea

---

[1] 250 miles south of Bombay.
[2] Mr. Mace to Bombay Government. Reports dated January 30th and February 14th, 1758. *Public Diary*, No. 31, of 1758.

to sea, from Dongri to Back Bay. This will secure Dongri, enlarge the town, and not be liable to the insult of any eminence or hollow way. The expense of the line which I propose to be fortified cannot greatly, if at all, exceed that of putting the old works in any tolerable condition."

The proposal to isolate the southern portion of Bombay Island by a defensible wall from sea to sea had much to recommend it. The town could not then be partially enveloped by an army advancing from the mainland, and the forward line of defence would be secure on both flanks if these were protected by armed vessels ; but unfortunately the scheme involved heavy expenditure and much destruction of property. However, the President and Council accorded their approval, and ordered Mace to begin work " with all possible expedition."[1] This he proceeded to do, but when no more had been done than to clear the ground along the proposed line by felling coconut trees, the wrath of the Directors smote the Council. " Your wall and other outworks," they wrote,[2] " begun and carried on without our permission, we deem an absolute breach of orders. Even Mr. de Funck, so loudly complained of for expensiveness which you have already more than doubled, could never be brought into such measures. The town wall was always too large for your usual garrison to defend. Multiplying then of walls and detached distant batteries must surely be highly absurd ! "

Not only was Mace's scheme for a new line from sea to sea killed by this stern rebuke, but the unfortunate engineer himself survived the blow for only a few months, as he died in Bombay on August 11th, 1761. Again, the Directors wrote in 1762 :[3] " On the least opening given them the engineers will be ever forming new projects. Once for all we do positively tell you that we shall call upon you in another manner if our orders are thus disregarded." But in spite of this dire threat the engineers managed to complete some useful works before they could be stopped from London, such as clearing the Esplanade around the town walls and building a covered approach to the small defences on Dongri Hill.

No subject fills more pages of the correspondence on engineering in old Bombay than the treatment of Dongri Hill which lay so close to the northern wall of the town. The suggestions of the engineers, and the orders and counter-orders of the Directors, on this key to the gate of Bombay, might fill a volume in themselves. Each Chief Engineer had his own ideas, and usually the Council supported him. When the recommendations reached England, the Directors were often assailed by doubts ; they forbade or stopped the work on the

---

[1] *Bombay Government Consultations*, February 17th, 1758. *Public Diary*, No. 31, of 1758.
[2] Court to Bombay, letter dated April 25th, 1760. *Public Department Court's Letters*, Vol. V, of 1757–61.
[3] *Ibid.*, letter dated April 16th, 1672. *Public Department Court's Letters*, Vol. VI, of 1762–64.

score of expense, and appointed a new Chief Engineer to report on the situation ; and then we read once more the same cycle of recommendation, approval and veto. The discussion dealt, after all, with a simple question. Should Dongri Hill be fortified properly or should it be removed ? Some engineers said that it should be fortified ; others that it should be demolished. The Directors were in a fog, and the ink expended on Dongri Hill was sufficient almost to wash away its rocky slopes.

De Funck had said in 1755 that the hill should be fortified and held as a strong outwork to the existing defences. Mace, on the other hand, preferred to include it within his proposed line from sea to sea ; but if this line was not sanctioned, he considered that the hill should be removed although the work would occupy many years.[1] When he died, Captain Andrew Werner, the sub-engineer who succeeded him, gave his opinion[2] that all that was necessary was to mine the existing defences on the hill in case the enemy captured them, to repair them in places, and to mount a few small guns in them to oppose a landing beyond the hill. The Directors then became nervous and told the Council " you must be cautious in future and not suffer the work of one engineer to be undone by his successor." But it appears that, before this injunction reached Bombay in 1763, a great part of the old defences on the hill had been blown up ; and the Councillors, influenced, no doubt, by the opinion of the late Major Mace, wished to remove the entire hill by a very slow process—they ordered that all stones for building and all ballast for ships should be taken from it.[3] Werner, ignoring so futile a suggestion, then threw some figures at them. He told them that to demolish the hill would occupy 2,000 workmen for 15 years ! So the bewildered Councillors applied for orders from the Court—which meant a delay of a year or so—and before a reply could arrive, a new Chief Engineer was sent out who naturally had his own ideas.

Enter Captain Thomas Keating, appointed on April 3rd, 1764, as " Principal Engineer at the Presidency of Bombay " and " very well recommended for a gentleman of abilities in his profession." He was fortunate enough to receive £300 a year as Engineer, and a further £200 a year as Captain of Artillery—a great advance on the paltry £40 a year which de Funck received for his engineering duties. As soon as Keating had inspected the defences in November, 1764, he gave his " sentiments " in the usual way, winding up with the remark that " Fortifying Dongri is the most eligible and best method, as the removal will be attended with a very heavy and tedious

---

[1] Mr. J. Mace to Bombay Government, letter dated February 3rd, 1761. *Public Diary*, No. 36, of 1761.

[2] Sub-Engineer to Bombay Government, letter dated June 15th, 1762. *Public Diary*, No. 38, of 1762.

[3] *Bombay Government Consultations*, August 9th, 1763. *Public Diary*, No. 41, of 1763.

expense."[1] He might have added that it was actually attended with a very heavy and tedious correspondence. The tug-of-war was in full swing. On the one side, the ghost of Mace and the Council—for demolition; on the other, Werner and Keating—for fortification. Which would win?

While the engineers were thus engaged in a seemingly endless argument about Dongri Hill, Bombay had developed enormously. Indeed by the end of 1764, with a population of about 100,000 and greatly increased commerce, it was ready to enter the political arena and give proof of its power. It lacked only the military strength required to fight for the mastery of the whole of Western India. Against any native power, its defences were impregnable. Though the small island of Colaba was still separated from Bombay at high tide, the dam or causeway which had been completed at Warli by Captain Bates in 1727 to close the "Great Breach" on the west coast, had checked the inroads of the sea and reclaimed the central part of Bombay Island for cultivation and occupation. The original town known as "The Fort," with its Courts of Justice, Mint, church, schools, shops, bazaars and Green, was a great centre of business and life. Beyond its walls to the north, a new town was rising; and country residences, with fine gardens, were spreading along the breezy shore of Back Bay. Houses were dotted here and there along the ridge of Malabar Hill. Good roads were being made within the Fort and towards the north. The harbour and docks were filled with shipping. The Marathas were quiet, and the French had been defeated. Money flowed into the coffers of the Company, but the cost of expansion was heavy. It is a fact that at times the Bombay treasury was so depleted that all engineering was stopped; for instance, in February, 1765, the available balance being only 17,000 rupees, the Council decided to discharge all workmen employed on the fortifications, docks and other works, so that trade should not suffer.[2] But such crises were rare and of short duration. Bombay demanded, and ultimately secured, adequate protection against any foe, native or European.

Although the dispute over the fate of Dongri Hill raged for months and years, Keating found much other work to hand. Mace and Werner had devoted a good deal of attention to the main fortifications and Keating pushed on their schemes to such good purpose that in February, 1765, before all work was stopped by the Directors, masonry ravelins were nearing completion at the Church Gate to the west and the Apollo Gate to the south, and other redoubts, lunettes and the hundred-and-one elaborations of the Vauban system of defence were developing as they had done in Fort St. George and

---

[1] Captain Thomas Keating to Bombay Government, report dated November 20th, 1764. *Public Diary*, No. 43, of 1764.
[2] Bombay to Court, letter dated April 25th, 1765. *Public Department Letters to Court*, Vol. XII, of 1765.

were doing in Fort William. When money again became available, engineering was resumed; but it is impossible to follow in detail the growth of such a spider's web as was formed by the defences towards the end of the eighteenth century. Suffice it to say that the main fortifications of Bombay grew steadily, though retarded by a lack of skilled overseers till a few were sent from Europe.

But the case was otherwise with Dongri Hill. Here discussion reigned supreme. By the end of 1766, Keating was becoming so desperate over this matter that he wrote :[1] " I must once more beg leave to mention and recommend to the Board's most serious attention the absolute necessity for commencing the fortifying of Dongri Hill. To leave this post in its present defenceless state must in case of an attack infallibly cause the loss of Bombay. No wonder if the most alarming consequences are to be dreaded from the neglect of a post of so great importance. If strongly fortified and sufficiently garrisoned I will venture to affirm Dongri will most effectually secure the Honourable Company's settlements on this coast." Yet his protest and recommendations fell on deaf ears. Not till the summer of 1768 did a reply arrive from home; and even then, although it opened with definite orders that the hill was to be removed, it tailed off in doubt :—[2]

" COURT TO BOMBAY.

" Captain Keating's plan and profile of the works proposed to be erected on Dongri Hill, with his letter, have been considered. We have determined not to fortify the hill but to destroy it. . . . Building a fort will be attended with a great and almost constant expense. . . . From the ample testimonials we have received of the abilities of Lieutenant-Colonel Archibald Campbell, we have been induced to appoint him our Chief Engineer in Bengal. He takes passage first to your Presidency on the ship *Thames*. There he, in conjunction with Colonel Keating,[3] may take a survey of the works and fortifications thereat. Those gentlemen should also take a survey of Dongri Hill, and give their sentiments as to the propriety of its demolition or erecting a fort thereon. Their opinion must guide you in giving the necessary orders, notwithstanding it may be entirely opposite to our direction for demolishing the hill."

So the net result of this long-delayed reply was to convey nothing whatever. The futility of control attempted from more than 5,000 miles away was never more strikingly illustrated, for the ultimate

---

[1] Principal Engineer to Bombay Government, letter dated October 21st, 1766. *Public Diary*, No. 47, of 1766.
[2] Court to Bombay, letter dated March 18th, 1768. *Public Department Court's Letters*, Vol. VII, of 1765–68.
[3] Keating had been promoted to the rank of Lieut.-Colonel in the Artillery. He was assisted in his engineering work by Captains Lawrence Nilson and Lockhart Russell.

decision was left in reality to Colonel Campbell when Keating alone might have been trusted to make it two years earlier.

Archibald Campbell began a laborious inspection of Bombay soon after he landed, and with Keating at his elbow, produced for the digestion or indigestion of the Council and Directors, in 1768, a report nearly 4,000 words in length.[1] He ended it with a definite recommendation. " For those reasons alone," he wrote, " I declare it my fixed and determined opinion that not only the fortifying of Dongri is in every respect preferable to its being removed, but also that the work ought to be carried into immediate execution. I have only to add with extreme satisfaction that Lieutenant-Colonel Keating's sentiments are perfectly corresponding." It is satisfactory to note that Campbell's elaborate and exhaustive report induced the President and Council to order that the fortification of Dongri Hill and the strengthening of the northern front of the town, should be taken in hand forthwith.[2] So the greatest engineering work which Bombay had ever seen was begun. The solution to the riddle of Dongri had been found.

There remains little to record about the fortification of Bombay. The progress reports sent in by the Principal Engineer show that work proceeded steadily on both Dongri Hill and the town defences. To provide space for the new fort on the hill, masses of hard rock were removed by the engineers. This was started on October 23rd, 1768, and the old defences were blown up five months later. By November, 1769, Keating was able to report that nearly 400,000 cubic feet of solid rock had been removed in excavating the Dongri ditches and levelling the site, and that it was " one of the most obstinate works ever undertaken."[3] However, on January 1st, 1770, he had the satisfaction of laying the foundation stone of the new fort, which he named Fort George in honour of His Majesty King George III.[4] Dongri Hill ceased to be a danger to Bombay. As will be seen in the plan of Bombay Fort, which appears in this chapter, the hill was crowned in a few years with a work which formed an integral part of the general scheme of fortification, and which, by its high command, could bring a devastating fire to bear against the flank of any force which had the temerity to attack the town from the north. At the end of the year 1773, when Captain Lawrence Nilson was acting as Principal Engineer,[5] the construction of Fort George was far

[1] Lieut.-Colonel Archibald Campbell, Principal Engineer, Bengal, to Bombay Government. Letter dated October 18th, 1768. *Public Diary*, No. 52, of 1768.
[2] *Bombay Government Consultations*, October 18th, 1768. *Public Diary*, No. 52, of 1768.
[3] Principal Engineer to Bombay Government, letter dated November 15th, 1769. *Public Diary*, No. 54, of 1769.
[4] *Bombay Government Diary*, January 1st, 1770. *Public Diary*, No. 55, of 1770. The similarity of the name to that of Fort St. George at Madras is liable to cause confusion.
[5] Nilson seems to have acted for Keating for some time, and was finally confirmed as Principal Engineer. There were allegations against Keating for which he was tried by court martial.

E

advanced ; and although the final touches were not put to the work till seven or eight years later, the defences of the fort, and of the whole town, had by that time attained a strength which justified a claim that they were impregnable to any enemy who might attack them by land or sea. Bombay had become more powerful than Madras, and was rivalled only by Fort William in Calcutta.

Before leaving the western capital to follow the exploits of the engineers in Calcutta after its recapture by Clive and Watson, we may pause to read the excellent description of Bombay in 1775 which comes from the pen of Abraham Parsons, sailor and trader :—[1]

" The town of Bombay is near a mile in length from Apollo Gate to that of the bazaar, and about a quarter of a mile broad in the broadest part from the Bunda across the Green to Church Gate, which is nearly in the centre of the west side. There are likewise two marine gates, with a commodious wharf and cranes built out from each gate, besides a landing-place for passengers only. Between the two marine gates is the Castle, properly called Bombay Castle, a very large and strong fortification which commands the bay ; the works round the town are so many, and the bastions so very strong and judiciously situated, and the whole defended with a broad and deep ditch, so as to make a strong fortress.

" Here is a spacious green capable of containing many regiments exercising at a time ; the streets are well laid out and the buildings (viz. gentlemen's houses) so numerous and handsome as to make an elegant town. The soil is a sand mixed with small gravel, which makes it always so clean, even in the rainy season, that a man may walk all over the town, within half an hour after a heavy shower, without dirtying his shoes. The esplanade is very extensive, and as smooth and even as a bowling green. . . . Near the extreme point of Old Woman's Island next the sea is a very lofty light-house.[2] On this island are two large barracks for the military ; sometimes a camp is formed here. It has good grass, not many trees, and a few houses, but neither town nor village. It lies so very open to the sea all round as to be deemed a very healthy place whither people after recovering from illness frequently move for a change of air."[3]

And what of the life of the Englishman in Bombay in the good old days of George III. ? James Douglas describes it in picturesque fashion :—[4]

" To hunt the tiger from his lair in Salsette ; to course the hare on Malabar Hill ; to play cards and drink sack or arrack punch in a

---
[1] *Bombay and Western India*, by James Douglas, Vol. I, p. 393. Parsons reached Bombay from Bushire in the *Sea Horse*, on August 17th, 1775, and some historians state that Nelson was on board the ship as an invalid.
[2] The building of a lighthouse at Colaba was sanctioned in 1769.
[3] The hill station habit had not been formed in those days.
[4] *Bombay and Western India*, by James Douglas, Vol. I, p. 10.

bungalow on the Thana Creek until all was blue ; to send your sick daughter to Old Woman's Island and go yourself to the hot spring at Bankot ; to sit and moon over some speculation to Bantam or Amboyna, on which the comfort and happiness of your family depended, and then, sick of delay, deliver yourself body and soul into the hands of an astrologer ; to weary your life out for an hour under a hair-dresser so that you may appear the cynosure of neighbouring eyes in curl and bagwig at Parel or the Royal Bastion at the witching hour of sundown ; or peradventure on a Sunday at Church, with meek and placid countenance, as you sat with your feet on that old cowdung floor, gazing listlessly on, but not through, the oyster panes,[1] to hear from the pulpit the sentence which debars you from the communion ; to read Shakespeare by moonlight on the roof of the Custom House because you could not afford the wherewithal to purchase a candle ; to drive from the Breach to the ballroom in a bullock garry and return—royal—with lighted flambeaux ; and if you survived the ten or twenty years' conflict, to see *Hic Jacet* written over almost every friend you knew or cared about ; such were some of the environments of the Bombay merchant."

[1] Window panes made from the translucent lining of oyster shells. Glass was not available.

A GRAB.

CHAPTER VII.

THE BUILDING OF NEW FORT WILLIAM.

MANY instances may be found in history in which injustice is done to the efforts of those who executed a great work while honour is heaped upon the man who initiated it, but there can be little doubt that Calcutta owes its Fort William of to-day in no small degree to the indomitable energy and dynamic force of Robert Clive. It is true that John Brohier designed it, and that a long line of engineers laboured to complete the work which he began ; yet such was the confusion of the Company's affairs after the recapture of Calcutta in 1757, and so heavy were the drains on its exchequer, that without a man of such magnetic personality as Clive to father the scheme, it is difficult to believe that a project for a new Fort William could have got beyond the stage of correspondence. The idea was so grandiose, the expense so enormous, that a government might have hesitated before it. Clive induced a commercial body to embark upon it.

Before the fall of Old Fort William in 1756, the British in Bengal were successful in trade, but they stood on the edge of a precipice. Regarded by the native powers as of no military importance, and obsessed with a false idea of the might of the Nawab of Bengal, they had no thought of challenging that potentate to a trial of arms. If any dispute arose, the Nawab could, and often did, blockade their up-country settlements, and the interruption of trade which ensued soon brought them to reason. But the lesson of the disaster of 1756, caused through lack of skilled leaders, trained men and proper defences, was not lost on Clive ; and so, when he and Watson had retaken Calcutta by a series of well-planned operations, he turned his attention to two military schemes of prime importance. The first was the formation of an army to defend the British possessions in Bengal, and the second, as a natural corollary, the construction of a fortress large enough to hold that army, and also the whole European population of Calcutta, in case of need.

With Old Fort William in his hands on January 2nd, 1757, and Hugli recaptured by Major Kilpatrick 15 days later, Clive proceeded to consolidate his position. His small army was confronted on one side by the huge forces of Siraj-ud-Daula, who spurned all offers of negotiation and thirsted for revenge, and on the other by the French at Chandarnagar who were searching for an ally with whom they might attack him. He could expect no reinforcements of British troops for some time ; and so, even before the battle of Plassey had established his ascendancy in Bengal, he began to reorganize the Indian troops under his command by forming them into regular battalions, each with a small nucleus of British officers. He raised a battalion of Indian infantry from selected men, drilled and disciplined them as regular troops, and appointed a British captain and two subalterns, assisted by a serjeant-major and several British serjeants, to command and instruct them. This, the first Bengal native regiment, was known as the *Lal Pultan*,[1] and soon mustered 820 rank and file in ten companies, with 42 Indian officers, including an Indian commandant. The introduction of a few British non-commissioned officers as instructors of the native troops is a point which should interest officers of the Royal Engineers, for this system survives to the present day in the three Corps of Sappers and Miners in India. When Plassey had been fought, Clive raised a second battalion, and two more in 1758. Thus, with the European troops as a stiffening, the military forces in Calcutta soon took on the form of a small regular army—but an army without a proper base, without well-built barracks, without fortifications which it could hold against the overwhelming forces of the country. Old Fort William could not contain the troops and European inhabitants of the Calcutta of 1758: a much larger fortress was essential, well sited and well built.

The engineer in charge of Old Fort William, when it was attacked by Siraj-ud-Daula, was Charles O'Hara, who then deserted his post with Governor Drake, Captain Minchin and other gentlemen of greater discretion than valour. When Clive and Watson entered Calcutta in triumph in January, 1757, they brought with them from Madras Captain Robert Barker,[2] the engineer who drew Colonel Scott's design for the defences of Fort St. George. O'Hara slunk back to Calcutta and protested to the renegade Drake, who had actually reassumed office, that it was unfair that he should be superseded by Barker who was junior to him. He had the effrontery to request Drake to ask the Directors why he, O'Hara, should be considered " less capable and deserving of trust " than Barker; but his protests were ignored, even by Drake who was tarred with the same brush, and Robert Barker was confirmed as Engineer of Calcutta.[3]

Four days after the recapture of the settlement, the Bengal Select Committee ordered Clive and Barker to survey it and report what works should be thrown up for immediate defence, and what houses should be demolished, to prevent a second capture by Siraj-ud-Daula who was expected to advance again with his whole force,[4] and as a

---

[1] " The Red Regiment," on account of its uniform.
[2] Afterwards Brigadier-General Sir Robert Barker, Commander-in-Chief of the Bengal Army, from March, 1770, to December, 1773.
[3] O'Hara was afterwards transferred to Patna where he contracted a lingering illness of which he died in Calcutta on September 11th, 1759. (General Letter, Bengal to Court, January 16th, 1761.)
[4] *Bengal Select Committee Consultations*, January 6th, 1757. Orme Collection, O.V. 170.

result of this survey, Old Fort William was much improved before the end of January, 1757. By that time Barker had excavated a ditch, 30 feet wide and 12 feet deep, around the land faces, and had raised batteries to flank the northern and southern walls. He was completing the ravelin before the east gate, and had demolished the houses around the fort to a distance of nearly 150 yards. Indeed, such progress had been made that Clive was able to inform Madras that Old Fort William could not be retaken by the Nawab if the garrison remained staunch.[1]

At the outset, however, Clive had little confidence in Barker. He wanted an engineer from England, and the more so as his first sight of Old Fort William had decided him that it was useless to repair it, except as a temporary expedient, and that a new fortification was required ;[2] but he was occupied too closely at the time with military operations and political manœuvres to be able to select a site or suggest a plan. Before he could attend to defensive measures he had to deal with the French and the Nawab. Accordingly, after receiving some artillery reinforcements, he attacked Siraj-ud-Daula outside the Maratha Ditch at the beginning of February, and having defeated him after a precarious night march, forced him to conclude a treaty which allowed the British to fortify Calcutta as they wished ; but the treaty soon became a dead letter, for the rupture with the French which followed it caused an early resumption of hostilities against the Nawab. It is surprising that Clive consented to treat with the infamous scoundrel who permitted the Black Hole tragedy. The explanation may be that he wished to deal with his enemies in turn, and tempering valour with caution, he hoped by this treaty to gain time and prevent a combination of the Nawab and the French against him. In direct opposition to an order from the Nawab, and assisted by reinforcements from Bombay, he advanced on Chandarnagar. This was a combined naval and military affair. The passage of Admiral Watson's ships up the Hugli was a remarkable exploit ; but the defence made by Renault, the French Governor, for nine days, with a paltry garrison and without a military engineer, was even more praiseworthy. Nevertheless, the French were forced to strike their flag on March 23rd, 1757 ; and in the two following years, Captain John Brohier, as Engineer of Calcutta, razed the fortress and town of Chandarnagar to the ground. Thus the French power in Bengal was crushed utterly and finally. The Dutch at Chinsura were biding their time. Immediate danger threatened only from the vast but undisciplined hordes of Siraj-ud-Daula.

It will be remembered that, when Colonel Scott died in May, 1754, John Brohier became Chief Engineer on the Coromandel coast, where

---

[1] Colonel Clive to the Select Committee at Fort St. George, letter dated January 28th, 1757. *Madras Select Committee Consultations*, February 24th, 1757, Range C, Vol. LI.

[2] Letter dated January 8th, 1757. Orme Collection, India, X.

he remained for some time to re-design Fort St. George. In this work he showed enough ability to impress the Directors, and thus it came about that, against the wishes of the Select Committee of Fort St. George, he was sent to Bengal in the summer of 1757 :—[1]

"COURT TO BENGAL.

"The Death of Collonel Scott, and the want of able People for undertaking such an Important Work as the Fortifying Fort William, has almost totally disconcerted our Designs, but wee have some prospect of engaging in the Company's Service a Gentleman of tryed Abilitys and known Skill as an Engineer,[2] but this at present wee can only hint for your Information. In the meantime the War with France justly alarms us and wee cannot but be apprehensive that your Settlement may be liable to an Attack. . . . Wee are to inform you then that as Wee cannot at present think of any Person as fitt and capable in all respects to Fortifye Fort William in effectual manner as Captain John Brohier our present Engineer upon the Coast of Choromandel, wee hope in consequence of the orders sent by the Committee of Secrecy he has or will be able to proceed accordingly to Bengal. . . . He is to have all necessary Informations, Intelligence and Advice, from all of which he is to consider of and Form a Plann for a Fortification. If you approve thereof you are to carry the same forthwith into Execution in the Manner and Method laid down in our several Letters of late."

These instructions did not reach Calcutta till Brohier arrived early in July, 1757; but in the meantime, Robert Barker, more Gunner than Engineer, had submitted his "sentiments" on the best locality for a new Fort William.[3] His ideas were peculiar, if not quite original. He proposed to build a fort, 600 yards to the east of the old one, in the very centre of the settlement. His reasons for selecting this spot were that the ground was higher there than elsewhere, and that a fort at that place would be out of effective range of the guns of hostile ships; also it would be convenient for business, and as place of refuge for the inhabitants. He ended by impressing on the Council that the old fort must be repaired so that it could defend the new one while the latter was being built. The Council, however, refused to be hurried into precipitate action on so important a matter. They insisted that the scheme must await the approval of Brohier before any work was taken in hand. Brohier arrived, and disapproved. So Barker's scheme joined Plaisted's, Scott's, Simson's, Leigh Jones' and Minchin's in the dusty pigeonholes and tattered files of old Calcutta.

[1] Court to Bengal, General Letter dated March 25th, 1757. *Bengal Despatches*, Vol. I.
[2] Major James Mace, who never reached Calcutta. He died in Bombay.
[3] Captain Robert Barker to the Honourable President and Council of Fort William, letter dated May 2nd, 1757. *Bengal Public Consultations*, May 2nd, 1757, Range I, Vol. XXIX.

But unfortunately for his peace of mind, Barker detested inefficiency and unwisely tried to introduce regulations for the labourers in Old Fort William. He recovered from the rejection of his scheme, but the Indian cooly killed his love of engineering. "I was sorry," writes he,[1] "to see the Company imposed upon by a parcel of Cooleys who laugh'd at me as they sat in Groops Smoaking their Hookers. I was indeed obliged then to make use of a Rattan which I hear has since been represented in very strong colours. For want of regulations the Cooleys and People employ'd on the Works have been found Sculking in all Holes and Corners either Sleeping, Smoaking or counting of Cowries. Not above one Third of the People Employ'd really work, so that the Company are at a tribble Expence. When I had a kind of Authority to muster them, then I generally found two or three hundred more than appeared on the Works. . . . I now humbly beg leave as soon as the Works in Hand are finish'd to resign an Employ which has been so disagreable, difficult and detrimental to me in depriving me of the Honour of Conducting the Honourable Company's Artillery in the Field." It is evident that Barker had had little experience of the subtle habits of the cooly. He was better fitted to work his guns; and, as his name vanishes after this from engineering history, we presume that he returned forthwith to his regiment. In military employment he was most successful, and rose at last to be Commander-in-Chief in Bengal.

After a time the Directors divulged the secret about which they had hinted so coyly in March, and wrote[2] that they had selected Mr. James Mace to be Chief Engineer in Bengal on a salary of £300 a year, and had "furnished him with several mathematical instruments which were always to be looked upon as the property of the Company." Mace was ordered to break his journey at Bombay where the President was directed to "take advantage of Mr. Mace's Thoughts, Projects and Assistance during his Stay." If Brohier was in Calcutta when Mace arrived there, Brohier was to return to Madras. And then came the warning: "The object you are never to lose sight of must be That of Confining your Works to a Contracted Plan and avoiding those great Designs hitherto projected by making such Fortifications only as may be defended with a reasonable Number of Men against any enemy." This was the rock against which Clive had to beat. He could lead the Calcutta Council in most directions. But could he induce them to follow him so far that they would flout this order of the Directors and embark on a project for a new Fort William which could not, by the wildest stretch of imagination, be considered a contracted plan?

However, before Clive could take a hand in the project for a new

---

[1] Captain Robert Barker to the Honourable President and Council at Fort William, letters dated May 16th and June 13th, 1757. *Bengal Public Consultations* of those dates, Range I, Vol. XXIX.

[2] Court to Bengal, General Letter dated May 4th, 1757. *Bengal Despatches*, Vol. I.

fortress in Calcutta, he had to settle with Siraj-ud-Daula. By the exercise of great patience and some cunning he had contrived to prevent the Nawab of Bengal from interfering while he captured Chandarnagar. The hesitation shown by that ruler may have been due partly to the fact that Ahmad Shah Durani had sacked Delhi in January, and the Nawab thought that the British might prove useful allies if Bengal were invaded. A conspiracy was hatching in his court to dethrone him in favour of his chief officer, Mir Jafar, a brother-in-law of Ali Vardi Khan. Clive, ever ready to seize an advantage, supported the plot, and some questionable negotiations ended in an arrangement with Mir Jafar. The moment then seemed propitious for attack, so Clive wrote a peremptory letter to Siraj-ud-Daula demanding satisfaction for all injuries. Receiving no reply he marched northwards from Chandarnagar where he had managed to concentrate a small force of about 750 European and 2,100 Indian infantry, some sailors and gunners with a few field guns, and a sprinkling of *Topasses*. Siraj-ud-Daula advanced to meet him with 50,000 infantry, 18,000 horse and 53 heavy guns. The armies met on the historic field of Plassey, where, on June 23rd, 1757, the Nawab's troops were scattered in headlong flight and left everything they possessed in the hands of the British. Clive then advanced to Murshidabad where he installed Mir Jafar on the throne of Bengal, Bihar and Orissa, while the unhappy Siraj-ud-Daula was caught at Rajmahal, brought back a captive to his capital, and there assassinated by a son of the new ruler.

Under the terms of a treaty with Mir Jafar, the British were granted all the land within the Maratha ditch and for 600 yards outside it, and in addition, certain rights over a very large tract to the south of Calcutta, which included the district known as the "24 Parganas." It was agreed also that compensation to the amount of nearly $2\frac{3}{4}$ millions sterling should be paid to the Company for the losses sustained through the sack of Calcutta by Siraj-ud-Daula, and a further sum of 80 lakhs of rupees to the inhabitants. Seven hundred chests full of coined rupees actually reached Calcutta on July 6th, 1757, and more followed. The scandalous financial dealings which accompanied the payment of this indemnity, through which Clive himself is said to have received £234,000, do not concern us. The joint in Clive's armour was his fondness for money which led him into transactions which, perhaps, he did not himself consider to be dishonest, but which would appear in a different light to-day.

A few days after the victory of Plassey, Captain John Brohier arrived from Madras in the *Marlborough*[1] to take up his duties as Chief Engineer till replaced by Major James Mace from Bombay.

[1] Bengal to Court, General Letter dated August 20th, 1757. *Bengal Letters Received*, Vol. III.

E*

Actually, he was never superseded by Mace, for the latter was kept in Bombay till he died there in August, 1761. It fell to Brohier, therefore, to express his ideas on the subject of a new Fort William and ultimately to begin that great work, and he prepared his first scheme while Clive was immersed in the sea of political manœuvre which followed Plassey. At the end of July, when he had been only three weeks in Calcutta, Brohier submitted his rough ideas to the Select Committee;[1] and although the new Fort William was not built on the site which he proposed, it may be well to place his recommendations on record.

Brohier began his rather illiterate report by explaining that until Macdonald, one of his Assistant Engineers, had made a proper survey, he was unable to prepare any project for a new fort; but his general idea was to build an hexagonal citadel to the south of the "old Dock," which lay about 100 yards to the south of Old Fort William. The site was said to be a good one as the river-bank projected at that place. Three sides of the work were to flank the river and to mount 100 guns to prevent hostile ships from passing upstream, and the ramparts were to be of earth, though encased in brickwork to a height of four feet above high-water level. As an outer zone of resistance, Brohier wished to fortify along a line extending around part of the settlement from his citadel to a point above the Portuguese and Armenian churches which lay about 500 yards north of Old Fort William. This would entail the demolition of a great number of native houses on a belt 500 yards in width, and Brohier proposed that the owners should be given land in the "Park"[2] on which they could rebuild. Forrest states[3] that this report was twice read and considered in Council, and Brohier was then ordered to survey the ground and prepare a plan of the citadel.

A critical examination of these proposals shows that the old idea that a fort should meet the needs of a factory still existed in the minds of the Company's engineers. They could not rid themselves entirely of the notion that convenience of access for native traders and the Company's servants, and the provision of a place of refuge in the centre of the town, were the chief requirements. Brohier's new citadel was to be in almost the same situation as Old Fort William, which was built more for commerce than defence; but his selection of a site is readily explicable by the fact that he knew that the money for the work was to be voted by a purely commercial concern. Clive insisted, however, that if the requirements of defence and trade clashed in a country such as India in the eighteenth century, war must take precedence over commerce. There was land in plenty to the south of Calcutta which, if cleared of jungle and kept free of

[1] Captain Brohier to President Roger Drake, letter dated July 25th, 1757. *Bengal Public Consultations*, July 25th and August 2nd, 1757, Range I, Vol. XXIX.
[2] Dalhousie Square.
[3] *Life of Clive*, by G. W. Forrest, Vol. II, p. 39.

buildings, would give ample space for the greatest fortress which could be required. Certainly the fortress would be some distance from the native shops and bazaars; but it would be safe from capture by a sudden assault, and it could be built without wholesale destruction of private property. Also it would more effectually block the passage of hostile vessels up the Hugli, towards the centre of trade and finance in Calcutta, than any citadel in the town.

The Committee of Fortifications deliberated long and carefully on Brohier's first scheme for a new fort close to Old Fort William, and so far approved it that orders were actually given to pull down all the buildings in Calcutta lying to the south of the Dock and the Park.[1] Fortunately the news of this intended clearance must have reached Clive, for, soon after he had seen Mir Jafar seated on the *masnud*, he found time to put a stop to such an unsatisfactory project. It seems that the actual plan of the new fortress had not been decided by the end of August, 1757, or at least no details had been supplied to Clive at Murshidabad. After a visit to Calcutta, he wrote early in September,[2] in some anxiety, to the President and Council of Fort William. "It is with great concern that we understand no steps are yet taken towards fortifying Calcutta. We must beg to represent to you the absolute necessity of commencing the fortifications while every circumstance is so favourable for it. And though you may not immediately be able to fix on what plan to go, yet all materials should be collected, and necessary preparations made to execute, without loss of time, whatever plan may be determined on."

The present Fort William is roughly octagonal in shape, while the first design contemplated by Brohier at the end of July, 1757, was for an hexagonal work. It is clear, therefore, that when the site immediately south of Old Fort William was rejected, Brohier must have set to work on an entirely new design to suit the altered conditions, and we may conjecture that he began his great task in September after the receipt of Clive's urgent appeal. Clive came in person to Calcutta at the beginning of August, when no doubt he heard of Brohier's first scheme and the extensive demolitions which it involved, and he arrived in the nick of time to prevent the Committee of Fortifications from beginning a general clearance of all the buildings south of the Old Dock and the Park. He must have had some stormy meetings with the members, but he emerged victorious from the struggle and with an alternative plan rapidly taking shape in his fertile brain. He imagined a great stronghold to the south of the town where the village of Govindpur nestled amid jungles infested by tigers and boars, a village formed two centuries before by the Hindu Fathers of Calcutta, the Setts and Bysacks. Where those

[1] *Calcutta Old and New*, by H. E. A. Cotton, p. 843, and *The Building of the Present Fort William*, by C. R. Wilson, appearing in *The Calcutta Review*, Vol. CXIX, p. 375.
[2] Messrs. Clive, Watts and Mackett to the President and Council of Fort William, letter dated September 6th, 1757. Orme Collection, O.V. 170.

tigers roamed there was space for a grand structure: jungle could be cut down: houses removed and built elsewhere. Clive would take no denial, and it is believed that it was he who guided Brohier in the right direction and initiated the great undertaking. Hundreds of workmen demolished the huts of Govindpur, thousands hacked down the dense jungles around the village, and so, on a scene of complete desolation, Brohier and his men traced the lines of modern Fort William.

Brohier laid his plan for the new fort and some outlying works before the Council in a letter dated October 13th, 1757.[1] The Council entered this letter in their proceedings and ordered copies of the letter and plan to be sent at once to the Court of Directors, but they would express no opinion on either. However, at another meeting four days later, they issued definite orders[2] that the village of Govindpur was to be removed, the bazaar being reconstructed farther south near what is now Tolly's Nullah,[3] and the inhabitants migrating to a suburb called Similea[4] in the north of Calcutta, where they would be given building sites and monetary compensation. These measures were carried out, and Govindpur ceased to exist. Thus the great work was begun; but the engineers, who started with such light hearts and so much confidence in October, 1757, would have been appalled could they have foreseen the difficulties, delays and malpractices which they and their successors would have to overcome before the last brick was laid. It is probable that, if the fortification of Calcutta had rested in the feeble hands of Governor Roger Drake and his Council, the scheme for a new Fort William would have been discussed for years and then shelved in favour of some trumpery reconstruction of Old Fort William "at a minimum of expense." Brohier and his officers had much to learn of the control of labourers and contractors, the supply of materials and the keeping of accounts. They, and indeed any other British engineers in the country, had never before attempted engineering operations on such a scale; and, in spite of the disgrace of the many fraudulent dealings which are laid to their charge, it is clear that their technical knowledge was considerable and their efforts praiseworthy.

Fort William is built on a modification of the Vauban trace—an adaptation of the type of fortification introduced by de Vauban, the most famous French engineer of the seventeenth century,[5] with

---

[1] *Bengal Public Consultations*, October 13th, 1757, and letter from Captain Brohier of the same date, Range I, Vol. XXIX.

[2] *Ibid.*, October 17th, 1757, Range I, Vol. XXIX.

[3] Formerly known as "Govindpur Creek," and actually part of the old bed of the river. It was excavated by Major Tolly in 1775 at his own expense, and was known also as "Surman's Nullah or Creek."

[4] Simla (Calcutta). A native district north of the European quarter but within the Maratha Ditch. So called from the *Simul*, or cotton, trees which abounded there.

[5] Sebastian le Prestre de Vauban was born in 1633. He rose to be the recognized master of French military engineering under Louis XIV, and directed the siege operations in the wars on the Flemish frontier during the last half of the seventeenth century. He became a Marshal in 1703, and died in 1707.

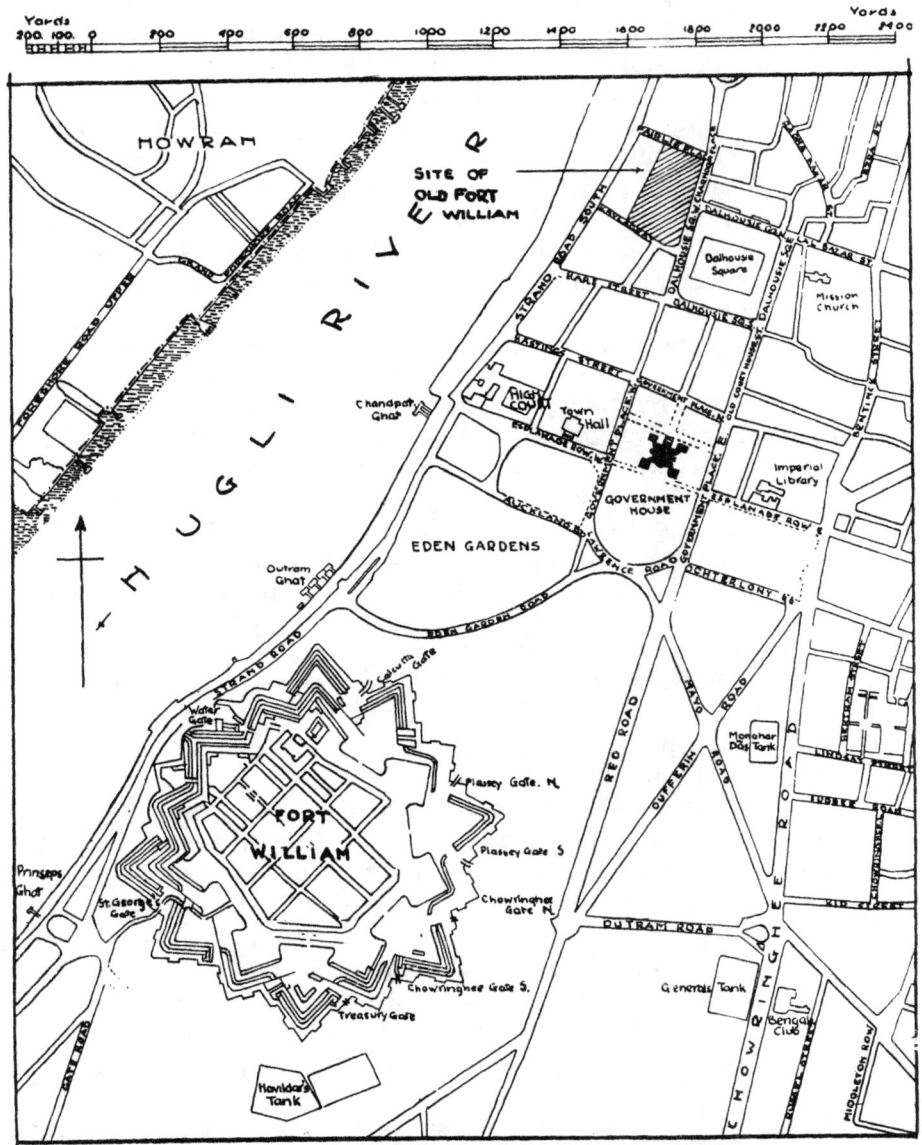

improvements copied, perhaps, from the designs of Cormontaigne, another celebrated French engineer who served his country in many sieges between 1734 and 1745. Is it possible that Captain John Brohier, a young engineer with only seven years' service in India, could have produced an original design for such a work as that which we can see to-day in Calcutta? A glance only is needed at the bewildering complications of the plan to foster the belief that Brohier must have copied or adapted the design of some fortress in Europe. He prepared his drawings in less than two months. His assistants were few and poorly trained, and he and they had other work to do in the steamy climate of Calcutta. That he should have been able even to modify or alter some existing design in so short a time is in itself astounding, and proves that, whatever his defects of character, he was, at least, a born engineer. During his brief career in Calcutta he laid the foundations of the first real fortress of the British in India: the others were mere developments of fortified settlements or factories.

Clive, having remained in Calcutta during August and part of September, 1757, was obliged to proceed to Patna in the middle of November to settle the country around that place, and as soon as his back was turned, engineering energy began to wane in the capital. Impatient at length of the incapacity of Governor Drake and the advisers of that peace-loving gentleman, he wrote to Calcutta in the beginning of 1758[1] that he wished to represent in the strongest terms the great stake the Company had in Bengal and the danger it ran through want of a proper fortification: that it pained him inexpressibly to hear from all sides that the work was going on very slowly because of the lack of "a few pice more," and that he did not think that such paltry saving of money should be considered for a moment or that it would be approved by the Court. Should Calcutta fall again into the hands of an enemy, it would be an eternal disgrace. To this protest he received an early reply[2] that the works were being carried on with great vigour, that many thousands of labourers were employed thereon, and that every nerve was being strained to finish them. The reply may have referred to Old Fort William; but if so, the reference to the "many thousands of workmen" is incomprehensible. Perhaps the Council hoped to satisfy Clive for the moment, and on his return to Calcutta, to transfer to his broad shoulders the responsibilities of the major engineering operations.

News that the construction of another Fort William was under discussion arrived in London during February, 1758; but it seems that Brohier's plan, which had been despatched from Calcutta in the

---

[1] Colonel Clive to Bengal Select Committee, letter dated January 22nd, 1758. *Bengal Select Committee Proceedings*, 1758.
[2] Select Committee to Robert Clive and William Watts, letter dated January 28th, 1758. *Bengal Select Committee Consultations*, Orme Collection, O. 170.

previous October, had not then reached the Directors, for, in the course of a last attempt to avoid the gigantic expense of a new fort, they make no mention of Brohier's plan in a letter written on March 3rd.[1] By the time the letter reached Calcutta, the preparations on the Govindpur site were too far advanced to permit a change of policy. The Company was committed irretrievably to a new fortress south of Calcutta which would demand a garrison, not of hundreds, but of thousands, for its defence against a civilized foe. But the Directors issued a warning on March 8th, restricting the size of a new Fort William to such as could be defended by 1,000 Europeans as a maximum.[2]

Some months, however, before these restrictive orders were received in Calcutta, Robert Clive had become President and Governor of Bengal in place of Drake. Having returned from Patna to Murshidabad in May, 1758, he was met by the news that the French were massing their forces on the Coromandel coast, and so he pushed on at once to Calcutta. It was soon after his arrival there that, at the urgent request of the Council, he became President. There was great anxiety in official circles. A French fleet might appear at any moment in the Hugli to attack the capital while Admiral Pocock and his ships were elsewhere, the old fort worthless, and the new fort hardly begun. In this crisis Brohier and his assistants[3] prepared to defend and block the river. They proposed[4] to erect fascine batteries, mounting heavy guns, at several places on the right bank downstream of the new fort; and upstream of it, to obstruct the channels with chains and to have fire-ships in readiness. The batteries were begun at once; but neither they nor the fire-ships were ever needed, for the French navy made no attempt on Calcutta.

Clive steadfastly refused to be stinted in money when it was really needed. In his political relations with native rulers, he did things in the grand manner, deliberately, it seems, and with the idea of the aggrandisement of his country rather than of himself. He dealt his cards with a lavish hand, whether in war, politics or engineering, and he required his masters to foot the bill. An example occurs in an account for 50,000 rupees, spent on entertaining the Nawab of Bengal during a short visit by that potentate to Calcutta in 1759, which Clive sent in for payment. Some of the items are interesting :—

Arcot Rupees.

" To 9 large Looking Glasses	517
To Nabob's diet	657
To 101 Gold Mohurs[5] gave to Nabob	1515

---

[1] General Letter, Court to Bengal, March 3rd, 1758. *Bengal Despatches*, Vol. I, 1758.
[2] *Ibid.*, March 8th, 1758. *Bengal Despatches*, Vol. I, 1758.
[3] Captain Wedderburn and Messrs. MacDonald, Smith and Scott.
[4] *Bengal Select Committee Consultations*, June 17th, 1758, Range A, Vol. II.
[5] Coins.

	Arcot Rupees.
Wax-work :—	
To 12 standing Venusses to pull off behind ...	840
To 6 kissing figures	72
To 8 ladies under glasses	160
To 2 ladies richly dressed in silver, playing two tunes	2080
To 18 pieces of flowered velvet, 837 yards	4708
Paid Louis Vaneet's Bill for sounding of Trumpets, Horns and Kettle Drums at the entertainment ...	54
To purchasing a coffre[1] boy	500
To presents to people who brought presents ...	310
To 15 chests of rose water	397
To 70 maunds[2] wax candles sent to Nabob ...	3430
To 61 Boat hire for Nabob going up river	1406 "

Well, perhaps the game was worth the candle, or even two tons of candles. Clive usually secured a return for his money.

But to revert to the sterner subject of fortification. At the end of 1758, President Clive was able to send to England a report on Fort William which was more reassuring than usual.[3] In it he estimated that the cost of finishing the main fortifications would not exceed 22 lakhs of rupees. "Notwithstanding this Expence may appear very large at first," he continued, "yet we are not without Hopes that the Company will in time be reimbursed a great part of it, as it is beyond all doubt that when the works are finished, and a proper Garrison kept up, it will be able to resist the largest Force that can be brought to the attack of it. This once known, the greatest part of the Riches of the country will, upon any Change of Affairs or sudden inroad of Foreign Enemys, be brought to this Fort as to a place of Entire Security, the proprietors whereof will be glad to pay a Duty to the Company for the Protection granted them and their Effects."

Oh, clever Clive, to coat the financial pill with so much sugar! But unhappily, before the sweetened pill could reach the Court, a querulous letter, written in March, 1759,[4] was already on its long journey from London to Calcutta :—

"COURT TO BENGAL.

"We esteem it a fortunate incident that we have given you our sentiments so fully by the last years ships on the subject of fortifying your subordinates[5] because we conceive you would not presume to go on with your extensive scheme of Fortifying Cossimbuzar. We cannot avoid remarking that you seem so thoroughly possessed with

---

[1] Slave.   [2] 5,600 lb.
[3] General Letter, Bengal to Court, December 31st, 1758.
[4] *Ibid.*, Court to Bengal, March 23rd, 1759.
[5] Outlying factories, the fortification of which had been forbidden but which Clive proposed, nevertheless, to fortify.

Military ideas as to forget your employers are Merchants and Trade their principal object, and were we to adopt your several plans for Fortifying, half our Capital would be buried in stone walls. Your reasons for erecting a Fort at Cossimbuzar by no means coincides with our opinion. We say in the first place it would be a most unpolitic step and would render you odious. . . . .

"By Mr. Brohier's letter and estimate addressed to our Secret Committee it appears that the erection of the Citadel of Calcutta only, exclusive of the town and enclosure, will cost us 1,911,569 Current Rupees, an enormous sum indeed. We wish you had mentioned what number of men would be required to Garrison it, for however willing we may be to bear an extraordinary expence for the security of this settlement and its acquisitions, yet a number of soldiers are seldom to be procured, and if His Majesty had not graciously condescended to give us one thousand men We should not have been able to have sent you any considerable assistance this season.

"From your representations and the judgment we form of this too extensive work, We send you double the number of men as was first settled for your garrison[1] and this we will endeavour to keep up. More must not be expected, we mean Europeans, for other troops must be left to your own prudence. The works ought not to be of greater extent than can be defended by a moderate garrison, even less than we have mentioned if possible. You must therefore have a particular regard to the directions in our letter of the 4th of May, 1757, and the instructions given at that time to Mr. Mace for confining your works to a contracted plan.

"Mr. Brohier in his letter to our Secret Committee expresses himself to be under great Difficulties for want of Assistant Engineers and mentions Mr. James MacDonald, whom he brought with him as such, to have declined that service. . . . Engineers shall be kept in their own line. We had rather bear an increased expence than have these important Branches filled with disqualified persons."

It was during the year 1759 that Brohier completed the devastation of the French settlement at Chandarnagar. This act of apparent vandalism was instigated by the conduct of Count Lally in the Madras Presidency, three years earlier, when he besieged Fort St. George. Clive resolved to pay the French back in their own coin. He feared that Chandarnagar might recover sufficiently to become once again a menace to Calcutta, and he was determined that it should not do so. But the last houses had not fallen in the French settlement when another challenge to British supremacy arose on the Hugli. This came from the Dutch. The good Hollanders at Chinsura had been jealous of the British for some time, and hoped, with

[1] 500 Europeans were originally deemed sufficient.

the assistance of the fickle Nawab, to defeat them if an opportunity offered. They increased the garrison of their settlement; and when, in October, 1759, a fleet of seven Dutch vessels full of troops entered the Hugli, the moment seemed favourable for an attack, the Dutch being then more powerful than the British on land and water. Early in November they opened hostilities by seizing some British ships and factories. But in Clive they soon found their master. Defeated in a naval action on November 24th, and driven back to Chinsura by a force on land under Colonel Forde, the Dutch were routed on the following day by the same commander in a short and bloody action at Badara, and forced to make peace and to pay an indemnity of ten lakhs of rupees. The British were then without European rivals in Bengal. Clive, whose health was breaking down, decided to return in triumph to England, and he sailed for home on February 25th, 1760, leaving Holwell, of Black Hole fame, to act as President. To use the words of one who saw his departure, " it seemed as if the soul were departing out of the body of Bengal."

After the departure of Clive, things went from bad to worse. When Holwell became acting Governor, a period began, which, to use the words of Alfred Lyall, was the only one in Anglo-Indian history to throw grave and unpardonable discredit on the English name. The political shams amid which the Company's servants existed in Calcutta could not fail to undermine their integrity. Raised suddenly, through the victories of Clive, from the position of needy traders to be actual rulers of a province, they could not resist the temptation to profit in illicit ways by their new-found power. The deadly contagion spread rapidly through the community and infected some of the men engaged on engineering work in Calcutta, among them Brohier himself, whose opportunities for personal gain were unique.

But before judgment is passed on a few dishonest engineers of Fort William it is well to remember that their failings, which look so black on the pages of history, were in some degree the outcome of the extraordinary circumstances in which they were placed. In every department of the civil administration they saw British officials amassing fortunes by corrupt practices and retiring in affluence to England as "returned Nabobs of the East." They watched their fellow engineers dying in the unhealthy climate of Lower Bengal, and knew that their own turn might come any day. Their pay was wretched; but the sums which they handled, and the contracts which they controlled, were enormous. Their contractors were unable to understand that the acceptance of " presents " was against the code of European morals, for bribery permeated every branch of every native administration. On all sides, Brohier and his men observed financial chaos. The Company's treasury was exhausted. Mir Jafar, the Nawab of Bengal, could not pay the subsidy demanded of him for the protection afforded by the British forces. Even the usual remittances from England were withheld by the Directors because they imagined that Calcutta was rolling in money. The engineers saw Mir Jafar deposed by the Bengal Council, on the advice of Holwell; and they noted that his son-in-law Mir Kasim, besides ceding Burdwan, Midnapore and Chittagong to the British, bestowed gratuities amounting to £200,000 on the Councillors and £50,000 on Vansittart, the Governor at that time, whose salary and allowances alone amounted to £18,000 a year and who supplemented this princely sum by private trade. Every signpost pointed the road to self-enrichment, and thus it came about that some of the engineers of Calcutta disgraced their honourable profession.

Soon after he became acting Governor, Holwell suspected, if he did not already know, that malpractices were developing rapidly in Calcutta and particularly in connection with the building of Fort William. The perpetrators of the frauds, hearing of this, sent him a bribe of 80,000 rupees to suppress any evidence which he might have collected; but he scorned the offer, paid the money into the Company's treasury, and continued his enquiries.[1] From these he got conclusive proof that wholesale frauds had been committed and that the man chiefly responsible for them was John Brohier. The latter, anticipating trouble, tried to escape from Calcutta; but, before he could do so, he was placed under arrest in June, 1760,[2] and made a prisoner in his own house, though he was released on parole after a few days. Brohier then demanded to be tried by a General Court Martial to vindicate his character. He offered to pay 76,000 rupees towards what he chose to describe as the defalcations of his assistants rather than his own fraudulent dealings. But he was never tried, nor did he make any restitution in cash, for he broke his parole and escaped from Calcutta with two other delinquents at the end of July. His companions were John Lowis (or Lowes), Assistant Engineer, and Louis Da Costa, a clerk.[3]

When the news reached the Directors they wrote:[4] " It seems very extraordinary that Capt. Brohier and Mr. Louis should, upon their absconding, evade all your searches to recover them as from Letters which some of the former's Friends here have received from him he was then no further off than Chinsura." However, the birds had flown, helped, no doubt, by the Company's money which they had stolen. It is said that Brohier wandered to Ceylon, where he took service with the Dutch. Lowis escaped to Batavia and died there shortly afterwards. Da Costa was apprehended at Madras and was held responsible for upwards of Rs. 30,000.[5] Brohier attributed his

[1] *The Building of the Present Fort William, Calcutta*, by C. R. Wilson, appearing in *The Calcutta Review*, Vol. CXIX, July, 1904.
[2] *Bengal Public Consultations*, June 12th, 1760.
[3] *Madras Public Consultations*, Vol. XC, September 24th, 1760.
[4] General Letter, Court to Bengal, September 30th, 1761.
[5] *Bengal Letters Received*, Vol. V, November 12th, 1761, and October 30th, 1762.

ruin to the "malevolence" of Governor Vansittart and Thomas Boddam, a Councillor; but, as five plans of the citadel and town of Calcutta were stolen from Brohier in Ceylon, in December, 1760, and he had no right to these papers, it seems that he was guilty.[1] A committee which investigated the frauds found evidence of overcharges to the amount of more than two lakhs of rupees between February, 1759, and February, 1760, and also of one and a quarter lakhs between April and November, 1760; but many of the more important papers were not forthcoming so the investigations were incomplete—an unsatisfactory ending to what was, from first to last, an unsavoury affair.

In December, 1760, when the frauds had been discovered and Brohier had fled, the Directors, in blissful ignorance of these happenings, wrote[2] that the construction of all the outworks provided for in the estimate for the new fort was to be stopped at once as they had been informed that the cost of these would nearly equal that of the main fortifications on which an excessive amount had been spent already; and then, in March, 1761, they elaborated these orders in a letter which was even more restrictive in tone and a very wail about expense. Wilson states[3] that it was Holwell himself who informed the Court that on Brohier's plan the fort would cost more than £600,000;[4] and further, that Holwell wrote that he had always thought that Brohier's powers were independent of the Governor and Council, though he had discovered that this was not so. Holwell is said to have expressed a hope that the main defences, the ravelins, and the glacis, would be completed before the monsoon of 1760, after which nothing more would be done to the outworks until further orders were received. The Court, pleased to find a man of frugal mind, replied as recorded, stopping all work on the ravelins, redoubts, counterguards and glacis—a most serious step to take when so much work was partly finished. From the point of view of the honest engineers in Calcutta, Holwell was a nuisance: from that of the dishonest ones, a devil. As head of the civil administration, he seems to have been a failure except as an exposer of fraud. He deserves some credit for his detective ability, but Calcutta had fallen on evil days to require it.

And while a new Fort William was rising foot by foot, and the Court was urging economy and more economy, the history of Old Fort William was one of departing glory. In July, 1758, the Council passed a resolution[5] that " as there are no Barracks for the Soldiers in the place and great inconveniences experienc'd from their being

---

[1] *On the Coromandel Coast*, by Mrs. F. E. Penny.
[2] General Letter, Court to Bengal, December 31st, 1760.
[3] *The Building of the Present Fort William, Calcutta*, by C. R. Wilson, appearing in *The Calcutta Review*, Vol. CXIX, July, 1904.
[4] It is stated to have cost about £2,000,000 before it was completed.
[5] *Bengal Public Consultations*, July 3rd, 1758, Range I, Vol. XXX.

dispers'd att different Houses, and the impossibility of preventing them committing great disorders and destroying themselves with spirituous Liquors when so dispers'd, It is Agreed for those reasons to remove the Honourable Companys goods from the old Factory that it may be converted into Barracks for the Military till proper Barracks are built within the new Works." This was done, and towards the end of the next year some apartments were built in the old fort to house the officers of Colonel Coote's battalion. In 1760, the space between the East Gate and the Black Hole prison was made into a place of worship, called St. John's Chapel, which remained in use until the construction of St. John's Church by Lieutenant James Agg was completed in 1787. The Select Committee proposed in 1766[1] to turn Old Fort William into a Custom House; and in the following year all the military were withdrawn and the place was altered for its new purpose by blocking or altering the gates and building sheds within the walls. Its last days are thus described by Cotton.[2] "The river," he writes, "gradually receded, and the tide of life left it to flow in other channels. The Old Custom House at the southern extremity of the Old Fort disappeared during the reforming administration of the Marquis of Hastings and with it the last vestige of the historic walls which had for so many years reminded Calcutta of an older and humbler order of things." Farewell, then, to Old Fort William, with all its tragic memories.

But to mention St. John's Chapel in the old fort is to recall a lively description of Calcutta society from the pen of Miss Sophia Goldborne,[3] a visitor to India shortly before the chapel was abandoned. She writes to a friend in England :—

"I have been at church, my dear girl, in my new palanquin (the mode of genteel conveyance) where *all* ladies are approached, by sanction of ancient custom, by *all* gentlemen indiscriminately, known or unknown, with offers of their hand to conduct them to their seat; accordingly, those gentlemen who wish to change their condition (which, between ourselves, are chiefly old fellows, for the young ones either chuse country-born ladies for wealth, or having left their hearts behind them, enrich themselves in order to be united to their favourite dulcineas in their native land) on hearing of a ship's arrival, make a point of repairing to this holy dome, and eagerly tender their services to the fair strangers; who, if this stolen view happens to captivate, often without undergoing the ceremony of a formal introduction, receive matrimonial overtures, and become brides in the utmost possible splendour, have their rank instantaneously established, and are visited and paid every honour to which the

---

[1] *Select Committee Proceedings,* April 4th, 1766.
[2] *Calcutta, Old and New,* by H. E. A. Cotton, p. 464.
[3] Extracts from the *Letters of Sophia Goldborne,* published in 1789 under the title of *Hartly House, Calcutta.*

consequence of their husbands entitles them. On my mentioning the church, you will perhaps fancy I ought to recount to you its magnificence and style of architecture, but the edifice dignified at present with that appellation does not deserve notice. It is situated at the Old Fort, and consists solely of a ground-floor, with an arrangement of plain pews; nor is the Governor himself much better accommodated than the rest, and of course the Padra, as the clergyman is called, has little to boast of. . . . You are liable to be plundered of your consent any evening of your life: and without time to collect yourself much less to retract, by the Padra's being one of the company you may be induced to give him a claim to twenty gold mohurs before he takes his leave: and so, being married in haste, left to repent at leisure."

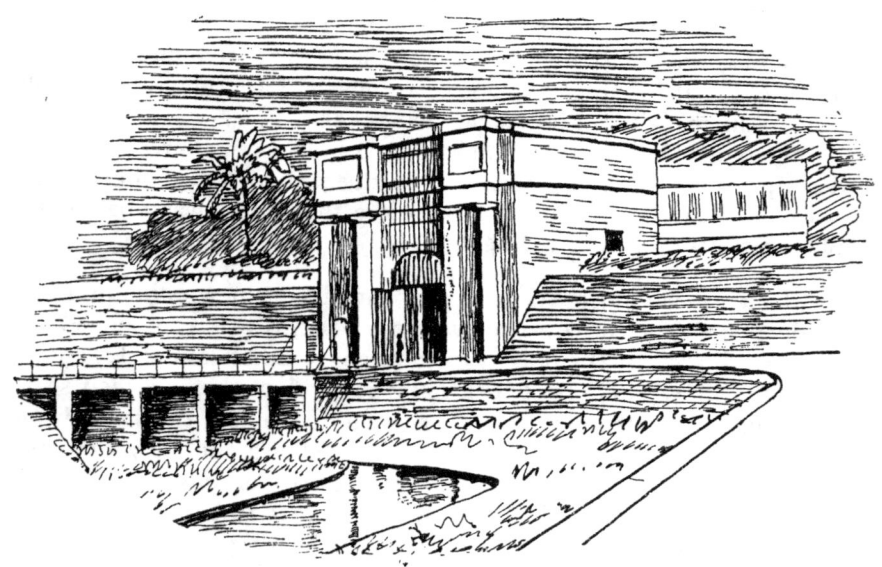

WATERGATE, FORT WILLIAM.

CHAPTER VIII.

FORT WILLIAM COMPLETED.

THE political situation in Bengal after Governor Henry Vansittart had deposed Mir Jafar in favour of Mir Kasim was certainly peculiar. Mir Kasim soon fell foul of his benefactors, seized a few of their servants, was defeated several times in battle, lost his capital, and then massacred 200 prisoners. The Mughal Emperor, Shah Alam, was the nominal overlord of Mir Kasim, and the latter the nominal ruler of Bengal in which the British posed as mere traders. Yet actually the British ruled the Nawab, and the Nawab dictated to the puppet emperor. In July, 1763, the British deposed Mir Kasim who fled to Oudh where, with Shuja-ud-Daula, the ruler of that province, and the Emperor Shah Alam, he suffered a crushing defeat from Major Munro[1] at the battle of Buxar in 1764. This was a desperate fight which, in the opinion of some historians, deserves far more than Plassey to be considered as the origin of British power in India. Old and ill as he was, Mir Jafar was placed once more on the throne of Bengal; but he died early in 1765, and his son consented to sell the sovereignty of Bengal, Bihar and Orissa to the Company. At last the British were the acknowledged rulers of Bengal.

Before this settlement was reached, the Directors were aghast at the military and political state of the province, and insisted in February, 1764, that Lord Clive should be sent to India to restore order and establish a proper government. On his arrival in Calcutta in May, 1765, he found the external position retrieved, the Mughal emperor and Shuja-ud-Daula humbled, and Oudh defenceless before the British armies. But Clive was wise enough to see the danger of acquiring too much territory. Ever a politician, he agreed to recognize and support Shah Alam, and then, turning to Shuja-ud-Daula, restored to him most of his lost province of Oudh after he had agreed to pay an indemnity of 50 lakhs of rupees and to allow his frontiers to be defended if necessary by British forces for whose maintenance he was to be charged. This was high strategy. It established a buffer state, north-west of the British territory, which was certainly a valuable shield to Bengal. But until it was formed, the province was in danger. During that period it was most important that the defences of Calcutta should be constructed with all possible speed, so that the army should have a strong base from which to operate, but Henry Vansittart was not the man to ensure that this was done.

[1] Afterwards General Sir Hector Munro.

The bastions and curtains of Fort William did not rise with that celerity which the political situation demanded and which the engineers would have liked to see. Money was stinted, orders were modified or countermanded, and months of delay were caused through the distance of India from England and the suspicions which had arisen in the minds of the Directors. Most of the engineers in Calcutta were mediocre in ability, and some were dishonest; and the Governors of Bengal, with the exception of Clive, were not helpful. More than 20 years elapsed before the fortress even approached completion. But the most formidable obstacles to progress were, firstly, a scarcity of artisans and labourers, and secondly, difficulties in the supply of materials. In these two matters the engineers waged a bitter and unceasing war in which the hand of every man seemed to be against them. It is necessary to depart for a time from a strictly chronological history of the progress of New Fort William in order to describe the difficulties which arose.

When Brohier began his task at the end of October, 1757, he proposed to import 12,000 men from Cossimbazar to dig trenches, and a further four or five thousand to clear and level the site of the new fort, to collect brushwood, and to help the bricklayers. His scheme was sound in conception, but he was too sanguine. He should have asked himself whether, in the first place, he could possibly secure so many men, and secondly, whether he could keep them if he got them. In his report he admitted that he could find employment for sixteen or seventeen thousand men, and that there were some at Cossimbazar who, with a little encouragement, might be brought to Calcutta. He trusted to the Nawab to get them for him. Mir Jafar, however, was a man of specious promises and tardy fulfilment unless he was interested personally. To supply labourers to help the invaders of his country could not give him much satisfaction, so he gave some orders and watched the result through the smoke of his hookah.

Calcutta was recovering in 1758 from the damage done by Siraj-ud-Daula. Trade was reviving, merchants were flocking to the shelter of Clive's army, and owing to the rapid extension of the town, labourers, and particularly skilled artisans, were in great demand. The services of men who had any experience in building were naturally secured by the highest bidders, and the Company was outbid on all sides by wealthy merchants. So obvious was this to Clive that, when he pointed out in January[1] that Calcutta was exposed because it had no proper fort, he added that the employment of labourers on private work should be stopped, and that it was poor economy to save a few pence and lose the available labour. This aspect of the problem had already struck the Council, for a resolution was passed by Governor Drake and his advisers on January 3rd,

---

[1] Letter from Colonel Clive to the President and Council of Fort William, dated January 22nd, 1758. *Bengal Public Consultations*, 1758.

1758,[1] which runs: " The Committee of Works send in a letter to the Board informing us of the difficulty they find in getting labourers and artificers for the fortifications, and desiring the Board will take some method to get them people to carry on the works. Ordered that they advertise (that) no artificers shall be employed by the private inhabitants after the first day of February. As to labourers, the Board imagine with proper encouragement a sufficient number may be procured after the harvest of paddy[2] is over."

This measure, however, failed to produce any radical improvement in the supply of labour to Fort William. For a time it had some effect, but, like all arbitrary regulations interfering with the freedom of the subject, it soon lost its force. Although Zamindars[3] agreed to supply labour for the Company's works, we read in the Select Committee Proceedings of March 10th, 1760, that " the works being much retarded for want of coolies, and the farmers not complying with their agreement, Ordered the Collector[4] to send peons into the pergunnahs[5] and to bring up by force 8,000, if to be procured." This harsh method of recruitment by the press-gang led to discontent and confusion on the works. And when at last an army of coolies had been collected and set to work, troubles arose about their payment. To simplify this laborious task, the engineers had arranged to pay the men in copper annas and pice instead of cowries, those minute shells which did duty for money among the poorer classes in Calcutta. The coolies, however, wanted cowries for their daily expenses, so they were obliged to exchange their annas for these shells in the bazaar. Instantly the cunning shopkeepers and *shroffs*[6] saw their opportunity, and by refusing to exchange at the authorized rate, added daily to their bulging money-bags and swelling paunches. The coolies, knowing that they were being cheated, then deserted in large numbers, and a severe check ensued in the progress of the fortifications until, in April, 1760,[7] the engineer in charge of the works induced the Council to force a fixed rate of exchange on the *shroffs*. A fortnight after this matter had been settled, regulations were announced governing the employment and payment of the coolies and artificers[8]. They were divided into gangs of 100 men, each commanded by a *banian*, whose duty it was to count his men every afternoon. A British overseer was appointed for every 1,000 coolies and artificers, as a check on the *banians* ; and, in supreme charge of the musters for payment, was a Sub-Engineer to watch every item of the proceedings. This organization led to some improvement.

Certain classes of labour were more difficult to obtain than others.

---

[1] *Bengal Public Consultations*, January 3rd, 1758, Range I, Vol. XXX.
[2] Rice.   [3] Landowners, farmers of revenue.
[4] An official appointed to collect revenue. Nowadays the Deputy-Commissioner of a district.
[5] Fiscal areas outside Calcutta.   [6] Moneylenders.
[7] *Bengal Public Consultations*, April 14th, 1760.
[8] *Ibid.*, April 28th, 1760.

There were "tank-diggers" in abundance because the population of Bengal, being mostly agricultural, was accustomed to dig. On the other hand, as their huts were of mud with thatched roofs, there were few bricklayers, and it was just these men who were most needed for the construction of Fort William. The native bricklayers also were unused to handling large bricks and were ignorant of European methods of bonding. Their own bricks were small and flat—easily burnt, but very extravagant in mortar. The bricklayers had to be taught their work, and men were required to teach them. Even when they had been taught European methods it was necessary to watch them constantly at work, for naturally, in their heart of hearts, they still imagined that the ways of their fathers and grandfathers were superior to the new-fangled ideas of their European employers.

Brohier's experience in Madras had taught him what to expect in Bengal, so he took the precaution to bring with him to Calcutta, in 1757, one John Dyer, a master bricklayer who had been sent from England, two years before, to help Colonel Scott.[1] Dyer proved so useful in Calcutta that Brohier then induced the Court to despatch another bricklayer, named John Raper, to India, in November, 1758,[2] and three more in the following January—Thomas Braiding, I. Daw and Charles Bonwick—the first two receiving £90 a year each, and the last £60 a year, as salary.[3] But the climate and the continual struggles with the local bricklayers were too much for John Raper who, in November, 1760, asked to be allowed to go home. Experts in trades other than bricklaying were sent from England occasionally to supervise the native craftsmen engaged in Fort William. For instance, three carpenters—Abraham Hathaway, Thomas Lyon and John Faux—sailed for Calcutta in March, 1763, with Mr. Fortnam, a "Civil Architect," on a contract to serve for five years on salaries of £90 a year each.[4] There is no doubt, however, that bricklaying presented a most difficult problem in the construction of Fort William; and the numerous complaints which were made in after years about the quality of the earlier defences were caused by defective work executed when British supervisors were scarce and the native bricklayers new to their job.

The indigenous bricklayer of Calcutta was as slippery as an eel —here to-day, and gone to-morrow.[5] In September, 1761, the senior engineer reported[6] that he was in great want of bricklayers and that the dilatory manner in which his work was being carried out would greatly enhance the expense. He renewed his complaint in March,

---

[1] Captain Brohier to the Hon'ble Roger Drake, President and Governor, and Council. Letter dated July 25th, 1757. *Bengal Public Consultations*, July 25th, 1757.
[2] General Letter, Court to Bengal, March 23rd, 1759, para. 67.
[3] *Ibid.*, January 23rd, 1759.   [4] *Ibid.*, March 9th, 1763.
[5] This is not surprising as the *monthly* wage of a bricklayer amounted to about six shillings.
[6] *Bengal Public Consultations*, September 7th, 1761, Range I, Vol. XXXIII.

1762, whereupon the Government empowered him to seize all the bricklayers in Calcutta.[1] Matters reached such a pass in May, 1766 that the senior engineer then reported[2] that, out of 900 to 1,000 bricklayers formerly in the Company's pay, all but 23 had been seduced into private employment by higher pay than the Company allowed. The Committee of Works accordingly resolved to checkmate the people who were outbidding them, and induced the Council to pass regulations that if any person paid more for labour than the rate fixed by the Company, he should forfeit the Company's protection; that all artificers residing in Calcutta should be obliged to register their names at once with the Company and receive a certificate; that nobody should be allowed to employ artificers without special permission, and that any artificer found at work without a certificate should be severely punished and obliged to work on the fortifications for five days on half-pay.

These stringent rules were introduced with a flourish; but, like most regulations of eighteenth-century Calcutta, they failed to impress the private employers of labour, or the labourers themselves, all of whom were well accustomed to gestures and threats. The new regulations were never fully enforced, and so the same trouble recurred two years later when the engineer twice complained of the difficulty of procuring workmen.[3] The Government then ordered that no private person should commence any building in or about Calcutta, and that all persons having buildings already in hand should register their buildings and workmen with the Company; and further that all unregistered workmen should be seized forthwith for the Company's works. But it was discovered that such restrictions were difficult, if not impossible, to enforce; so in January, 1770, the Government republished their regulations by beat of drum,[4] although, at that time, 4,000 men were employed in Fort William, of whom about 700 were artificers.

This is the history of the struggle of the military engineers of Fort William against the labour troubles in Calcutta. It was war to the knife against the private employer. In the end, victory lay with the engineers, though not till the middle of 1770, when the work was far advanced, could they get a satisfactory number of men. By that time, bricklayers were as common as pebbles on the beach.[5] But all danger of the invasion of Calcutta was then past. It was in the precarious times of Clive and Vansittart that skilled workmen were as rare as diamonds, and, to the Company, almost as valuable.

[1] *Bengal Public Consultations*, March 25th, 1762, Range I, Vol. XXXIV.
[2] *Ibid.*, May 19th, 1766, Range I, Vol. XXXIX.
[3] *Ibid.*, April 4th and August 22nd, 1768, Range I, Vol. XLIII.
[4] *Ibid.*, January 18th, 1770, Range I, Vol. XLVI.
[5] According to the Chief Engineer's weekly return the daily number of workmen for the week April 6th–14th, 1770, averaged 5,112; while for the week June 10th–16th, the average was 9,802. (*Bengal Public Consultations*, April 17th and July 13th, 1770, Range I, Vols. XLVI and XLVII.)

The second formidable obstacle to rapid progress in the building of Fort William was the defective and uncertain supply of the materials required for the work. The Committee of Works was greatly perplexed as to the best way of procuring the gigantic quantities of bricks and scantlings which were needed, and oscillated at first between the alternatives of making bricks and sawing wood by daily labour or procuring them from contractors. Brohier favoured supply by contract—for reasons which in his case are sufficiently obvious—and this system was adopted accordingly. But two inconveniences were soon apparent. The contractors began to defraud the Company, and they failed also to supply enough materials. In October, 1760, the engineer in charge of the works informed the Council[1] that when he was appointed to succeed Brohier, "all materials were received and delivered by Banyans who had it in their power (and I believe did not neglect the opportunity) to get at least 50 per cent. by false charges." To stop these malpractices he introduced some regulations, "but this affected the Banyans so much that they almost all deserted the works; the bricklayers likewise followed their example so much that out of 1,000 not 200 remained, and the coolies from 4,000 were reduced to 2 or 300 so that in the month of March and to the middle of April scarce anything was done."

The struggle for materials continued, month by month and year by year. In August, 1762, the engineer told the Council[2] that he was unable to place contracts for the supply of the number of bricks which he required: the merchants and brickmakers of Calcutta would not undertake to supply more than 2,500,000 bricks during that cold weather, while he wanted more than eight times that number. Realizing that, at this rate of supply, all work must soon cease in Fort William, the Government then appointed a "Superintendent of Brickmaking" and agreed to allow him a premium of several annas on every 1,000 bricks which he produced from his kilns. They authorized him also to collect all the brickmakers in Calcutta, and to prohibit any other person making bricks on pain of confiscation. This action broke the ring of contractors, but other difficulties were to follow. It is recorded that the post of Superintendent of Brickmaking proved to be so lucrative that it was very much in demand; indeed, the fortunate holder was said to enjoy an income which equalled at times that of the Chief Engineer himself! Naturally such affluence perturbed the minds of the Directors, who abolished the post at the end of 1765 and said that the Committee of Works must arrange to carry on the work.[3] The unfortunate Directors were

[1] Letter dated October 18th, 1760. *Bengal Public Consultations*, October 20th, 1760, Range I, Vol. XXXII.
[2] Letter dated August 3rd, 1762. *Bengal Public Consultations*, August 9th, 1762, Range I, Vol. XXXIV.
[3] General Letter, Court to Bengal, December 24th, 1765. *Bengal Despatches*, Vol. III.

forced to choose between dishonest and incapable contractors and officials whose primary object seemed to be their own gain.

By April, 1767, the Committee of Works had reached the conclusion that the contract system was both cheaper and quicker than Government manufacture, and took steps to introduce it for all the works. The Government at this time shared the hope of the Committee that the supply of almost all materials by contract would hasten the completion of Fort William, but they were soon confronted with new difficulties. From bricks the trouble passed to lime, and in February, 1768, the Committee informed the Council[1] that all work must soon cease for want of it; they proposed accordingly to manufacture lime, and execute earthwork, under their own direction. The root of the trouble, however, was the monthly wage paid to the Calcutta labourer. Living expenses were rising as they always do in thriving cities, and the labourer could no longer exist on the standard wage of Rs. 2/12/0 a month. If he could not eat, he would not work. So the authorized wage was increased to Rs. 3, and from this time all the materials and stores for the construction of Fort William were provided by contract. The middle of the year 1770 saw the problems of supply and labour solved to the satisfaction of all concerned, but Fort William had then been under construction for nearly 14 years.

It is necessary now to revert to the year 1760 when the departure of Brohier was a serious blow to the progress of the fortifications. He may have been dishonest, but he was certainly clever; and he alone had the experience necessary to cope with the difficulties which beset the path of the engineers. When he fled from Calcutta, the Council had to appoint someone in his place, and the mantle descended on Thomas Amphlett,[2] who had worked under Brohier for a time. This did not please the Directors, who wrote, in 1762,[3] that they had no great faith in Amphlett's capabilities and had accordingly told the Bombay Council to send James Mace at once to replace him. They added that no new projects were to be undertaken without the most serious consideration. James Mace, however, never reached Calcutta, so Amphlett acted as Chief Engineer from about June, 1760, to October, 1762, when he resigned his post on account of ill health.[4] He was a novice at engineering, but he did his best in most difficult circumstances. All departments of the work in Fort William were in a state of ferment when he was thrust suddenly into supreme charge. In April, 1760, Brohier being already under suspicion,

---

[1] *Bengal Public Consultations*, February 15th, 1768, Range I, Vol. XLIII.
[2] Thomas Amphlett was probably of the family of Amphlett of Hadsor and Clent. He was sent from Madras to assist Brohier. He was killed in October, 1763, at Patna, when Resident at the Nawab's Durbar, in the massacre ordered by Mir Kasim.
[3] General Letter, Court to Bengal, February 19th, 1762. *Bengal Despatches*, Vol. II.
[4] *Bengal Public Consultations*, October 11th, 1762, Range I, Vol. XXXIV; and General Letter, Bengal to Court, October 30th, 1762, *Bengal Letters Received*, Vol. V.

Amphlett tried to stem the tide of confusion and corruption by introducing stringent regulations, and it is said that as a sequel to his well-meant reforms, nearly all the labourers deserted. But if so, he was not to blame. "Strategic movements to the rear" were the delight of the Calcutta cooly. Amphlett departed with an unblemished character, if with little glory.

Next in the long line of Calcutta engineers comes Captain Anthony Polier, who followed Amphlett in October, 1762. A regular engineering establishment was formed after his arrival, consisting of Polier himself as Chief Engineer (on a salary of Rs. 4,000 a year as Engineer in addition to his pay as a Captain-Lieutenant), one Sub-Engineer, and a few Practitioner Engineers and volunteers. Polier held his appointment for nearly two years. It was at the end of 1763, during his tenure of office, that a letter came from England[1] saying how extremely disagreeable it was to the Directors to reflect on the immense sums Fort William had already cost them, amounting, up to December, 1761, to nearly £350,000, and how pleased they were that the President and Council had determined to curtail the outworks and "contract the plan." Ten months later, when Polier had just vacated his post, another letter arrived[2] expressing concern at the slow progress of the works as reported in a letter from Amphlett in October, 1762, and ending with the warning: "We have often taken notice of the heavy expence resulting from the extensive and extravagant projects of Mr. Brohier; we must therefore again recommend to your most serious consideration the contracting his plans as far as can be reasonably done." However, before either of these letters reached Calcutta, Polier had cleverly persuaded the Council, at a consultation held on June 20th, 1763, to sanction the completion of the works on the north side of the fort according to Brohier's design. He was inexperienced, as was Amphlett, and his energies were spent in trying to restore to order the confusion left by Brohier. The work on the fortifications went on, but very slowly and not too well.

When Amphlett was Chief Engineer he had been sorely handicapped by a lack of assistant engineers, and accordingly induced the Council to apply to England for help. Polier, who succeeded him, became the head of a small engineering establishment recruited in India and hoped, no doubt, that Amphlett's petition would lead to the reinforcement of his makeshift cadre by better material. He was disappointed. The reply from England[3] intimated that the Directors would gladly send out "young persons to be brought up as assistants in the Engineering branch," but as they found it very difficult to get them, Polier should employ any cadets or others in Calcutta who had a bent for engineering. Several of the writers then sailing for India,

---

[1] General Letter, Court to Bengal, March 9th, 1763.
[2] *Ibid.*, February 22nd, 1764.   [3] *Ibid.*, March 9th, 1763.

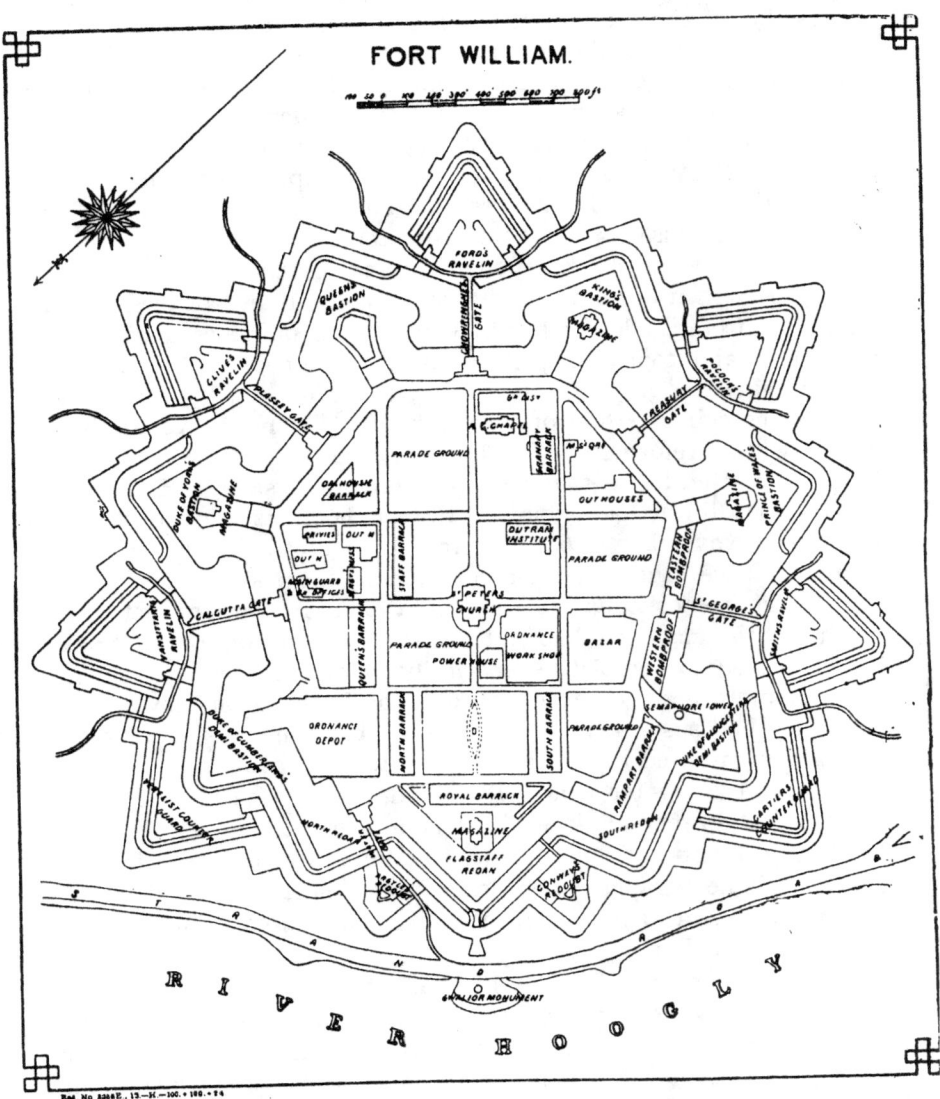

wrote the Directors, were said to be qualified in drawing, and they could be posted to the works on arrival. One can imagine the despair of the unfortunate Polier when he read this letter. A knowledge of drawing was considered a sufficient qualification for the supervision of engineering work costing thousands of pounds. Not many months after the letter reached Calcutta, Anthony Polier handed over charge to another engineer. No doubt he was glad to do so. The newcomer was Captain Fleming Martin, who, by order of the Court, superseded Polier in September, 1764.

Fleming Martin was lucky enough to be appointed when a reorganization of the engineering establishment was in progress, and he soon had under his orders two Sub-Directors, four Sub-Engineers and six Practitioner Engineers, though to what extent these men were qualified for their duties is not recorded. Few, if any, of them could have come from England; but they looked well on paper, and Martin was remarkably fond of paper and of ink. Immediately he became Chief Engineer he gave a foretaste of what was to come by remarking[1] that, in his opinion, the works were too far advanced " to admit of any essential reformation "; but that the ramparts demanded immediate attention as they were in a deplorable state. He refused to say much till he had examined the fortifications in detail, but at the end of November, 1764, he threw his bombshell.[2] He strongly condemned everything that had been done in the past. Fort William was by no means equal to its reputation: it was not yet half-finished: the engineers had not one-sixth of the number of bricklayers needed to complete even the body of the work apart from ravelins and other such excrescences: the fortifications now looked as if they had sustained a heavy siege. The ramparts, sloping the wrong way, allowed rain to wash away the parapets and choke the drains, so that water collected behind the revetment and burst through it. In several places, bricks might be taken out singly with finger and thumb. The magazines stood exposed several feet above the top of the parapet. The drains and sluices were so defective that it took eight days to drain the ditch, and three spring tides on the Hugli to refill it.

These were some of the criticisms offered by the new Chief Engineer. Having prepared his ground, he then proceeded to sow his seed, which was much to the liking of the Directors. Those worthy gentlemen, though on safety bent, always had a frugal mind. Martin was all for retrenchment and the reduction of the fortification to moderate dimensions. He may have been genuine, or, on the other hand, a sycophant. He presumed that the intention of Government was to provide a safe retreat for its servants and

---

[1] Captain Martin to Council, letter dated October 11th, 1764. *Bengal Public Consultations*, October 11th, 1764.
[2] *Ibid.*, letter dated November 26th, 1764. *Bengal Public Consultations*, November 26th, 1764.

property; if so, a work of far inferior strength would suffice. If the original scheme was carried out, the works would be much too extensive for any garrison which could be found in India. A force which was large enough to hold Fort William would be better employed in the field. To an unfinished fortress, extensive outworks were like fine clothes on a weak body. The *fausse-braye*[1] alone had already cost more than the probable expense of completing the body of the place with buttresses and proper revetments. It was too late now to propose any essential reformation, though something might be done to cut down the expense if Government would appoint a few properly qualified engineers. Such were the observations which Martin addressed to the Court of Directors, and which, unfortunately for themselves, the Governor and Council forwarded without remark. Martin then supplemented his report by an appeal to the Council,[2] in which he begged leave " to renew his apprehensions," and stated that " nothing less than an early Hand " could prevent the walls from collapsing in many places during the next rains.

As Martin's letter to the Court started on its voyage, a despatch left England for Calcutta[3] informing the Council that, although it might be necessary to finish the main body of Fort William, no more outworks were to be constructed unless they were absolutely necessary. The Directors, determined to leave nothing to chance or the whims of their engineers, called for plans of all finished works, and for drawings and estimates of all proposed works. Ten months later, Martin's bombshell exploded in the Court, producing great consternation. " Captain Martin's Account of the Fortifications in his letter of the 26th November, 1764," wrote the Directors to the Council,[4] " alarms us much, and we are surprised such a letter should have passed through your Hands without any Observations thereon. We must now depend upon your attention to remedy any apparent defects in the present Works and particularly to guard against the Encroachments of the River.[5] You are not to suffer Our Engineer to proceed on any thing material without your express Approbation." But river protection works had been started before the orders arrived. The waters of the Hugli at this time flowed close to Fort William and threatened to wash away the western defences, so the Chief Engineer was forced to take action to ward off this danger. He submitted a scheme for the protection of the river-bank by rows of teak and sal piling at a cost of more than six lakhs of Arcot rupees, and, the

---

[1] A platform and wall around a fort, forming a kind of outer *enceinte* at a lower level than the parapet, and providing a second tier of fire.
[2] Captain Martin to Council, letter dated February 4th, 1765. *Bengal Public Consultations*, February 4th, 1765.
[3] General Letter, Court to Bengal, February 15th, 1765. *Bengal Despatches*, Vol. II.
[4] *Ibid.*, December 24th, 1765. *Bengal Despatches*, Vol. III.
[5] Danger from this source was reported by the Engineer as early as 1760, *vide Bengal Public Consultations*, September 15th, 1760.

F

Council having sanctioned the estimate at the beginning of 1766,[1] the work was begun.

For three and a half years Captain Fleming Martin carried out his policy of retrenchment and rigid economy. His was a long tenure of office, as tenures went in Calcutta, and there can be little doubt that he held his post for that period because he voiced the wishes of the Directors. In modern slang parlance, he was, at least for a time, their " ditto-ditto man." However, he was obliged to agree with the remainder of the Committee of Works in July, 1767, that the piling operations must be continued and the counterscarp repaired.[2] The Council had at last become doubtful of his ability and distrustful of his extreme economy, so that, in November, they passed a resolution that the works should be inspected every week by one of their own number,[3] and this, in the end, led to a reversal of Martin's policy.

Colonel Smith, a member of the Council, visited Fort William in May, 1768, and afterwards wrote a report in which he strongly condemned the listless way in which Martin was carrying on the work.[4] He remarked that, although a strong fortress was urgently needed, no progress had been made since 1765. So rich a place as Calcutta, he argued, must be well protected. " Consider the great wealth and flourishing state of commerce in your opulent town of Calcutta. Remember that in the course of next year we may expect to have half a million sterling in our treasury, and that, at certain periods of every year, we have a very considerable investment deposited at the presidency until the despatch of our ships to Europe. These are additional and very strong arguments for our completing with all expedition such a fortification as may prove in time of danger a safe repository for the Company's treasures and effects as well as a sure asylum to the persons and properties of those who live under our protection."

This report roused Martin to restate his opinions that outworks were superfluous, and that a rampart, some bastions, a wet ditch and a covered way were sufficient. He refused to be convinced to the contrary by any arguments, and, on June 7th, 1768, addressed President Verelst and the Council in a long letter.[5] His sentiments, however, did not meet with approbation. Governor Verelst, an able and experienced man, considered the letter with his Council after they had taken the advice of a few military critics. They replied[6] that they had resolved to have a ravelin constructed in front of each curtain of Fort William, and to complete the covered way and glacis.

[1] *Bengal Public Consultations,* January 6th, 1766.
[2] Committee of Works to the Hon'ble Harry Verelst, Esq., President and Governor, etc., Council of Fort William. Letter dated July 3rd, 1767. *Bengal Public Consultations,* July 9th, 1767.
[3] *Bengal Public Consultations,* November 5th, 1767, Range I, Vol. XLI.
[4] *Ibid.,* May 4th, 1768, Range I, Vol. XLIII.
[5] Captain Martin to Council, letter dated June 7th, 1768. *Bengal Public Consultations,* June 7th, 1768.
[6] Council to Captain Martin, letter dated June 13th, 1768.

As soon as the counterscarp of the ditch was finished, the interior revetment was to be completed as quickly as possible. The ditches of the ravelins would help to supply the earth for the glacis, and thus reduce its cost. In fact, the Governor and Council refused absolutely to be parties to any scheme for a " contracted plan " with no outworks. They followed up these orders by calling the Chief Engineer before them and interrogating him on his objections to ravelins.[1] They concluded that he could not advance any argument in support of his point of view of sufficient weight to make them alter their decisions; and as Colonel Smith, Major Polier and Captain Watson agreed, they repeated their orders to Martin that he should build the ravelins. But he did not progress far with the work, for he resigned his appointment in November, 1768, and obtained leave to return to England.[2] On the whole, Fort William was better without him. Though a man of determination, he lacked imagination. He could not understand that the fort, as planned by Brohier, would be none too large for the troops and European population of Calcutta after a few more years had passed. An economist to the end, he failed to realize that rigid economy was a short-sighted policy in the construction of Fort William.

Meanwhile the development of Calcutta had been keeping pace with that of Fort William. When Clive returned from England in 1765, he found a different city from that of eight years before; and when he sailed homewards for the last time in 1767 it had altered still more. It lacked cohesion and beauty, but none the less it was a remarkable place. Few can describe it better than that enterprising traveller, Mrs. Kindersley:—[3]

" I think I have never given you any account of the town of Calcutta; indeed, after Madras, it does not appear much worthy describing; for although it is large, with a great many good houses in it, it is as awkward a place as can be conceived, and so irregular that it looks as if all the houses had been thrown up in the air and fallen down again by accident as they now stand. People keep continually building; and every one who can procure a piece of ground to build a house upon, consults his own taste and convenience without regard to the beauty or regularity of the town.[4] Besides, the appearance of the best houses is spoiled by the little straw huts which are built up by the servants for themselves to sleep in: so that all the English part of the town, which is the largest, is a confusion of very superb and very shoddy houses, dead walls, straw huts, warehouses and I know not what.

" The new fort, an immense place, is on the river side about a mile below the town. If all the buildings which are intended within its

[1] *Bengal Public Consultations*, July 18th, 1768, Range I, Vol. XLIII.
[2] *Ibid.*, November 7th, 1768, Range I, Vol. XLIII.
[3] Extracts from *Letters from the East Indies* (1777), by Mrs. Kindersley, p. 273 *et seq.*
[4] Mrs. Kindersley might almost have been writing of modern England.

walls are finished, it will be a town within itself; for besides houses for the engineers and other officers who reside at Calcutta, there are apartments for the Company's writers, barracks for soldiers, magazines for stores, etc.

"The Town of Calcutta is likewise daily increasing in size, notwithstanding which, the English inhabitants multiply so fast, that houses are extremely scarce. As I have given you a description of the houses at Madras, I need only say that these are much in the same style only they have not the beautiful channam;[1] for although they have had the same shells brought from the coast of Coromandel, and have mixed them with the same materials, and in the same manner, it has not the least of that fine gloss which is there so greatly admired. This is owing to all the water in Bengal partaking too much of the salt-petre with which the earth is in every part impregnated. Paper or wainscot are improper, both on account of the heat, the vermin, and the difficulty of getting it done; the rooms are therefore all whited walls, but plastered in pannels, which has a pretty effect, and are generally ornamented with prints, looking-glasses, or whatever else can be procured from Europe. The floors are likewise plaster, covered all over with fine matt, which is nailed down. The rooms are few, but mostly very large and lofty; many of the new-built houses have glass windows which are pleasant to the eye, but not so well calculated for the climate as the old ones, which are made of cane."[2]

Cotton, in his *Calcutta, Old and New*, remarks[3] that there could have been little to invite the pleasure of a drive, for the streets were unmetalled and there were other discomforts, not to say dangers. Carriages were not very common: the palanquin, gilded and covered with brocade, was the usual mode of conveyance. There was no Strand Road along the bank of the river, and the only drive was the "Course,"[4] where one swallowed ten mouthfuls of dust for one of fresh air; but it was the place to which everyone flocked before sun-down and was described as "the scene of various gradations of equestrian grace and charioteering excellence, the very Rotten Row of our Eastern emporium."

To quote from a poem entitled *Calcutta in 1811*:—

    "Sedate they quit the ruminating chair,
    And breathe abroad the evening dust and air,
    As dips the sun, of dazzling splendour shorn,
    When the wide Fort resounds the evening horn,
    Full many a soddened form, in jacket white,
    Wings on the thronging course his airy flight,
    Borne on the steed, or perched, with whip and reins,
    In a dear specimen of Steuart's[5] pains."

---

[1] Lime plaster. [2] Lattice-work of split bamboos.
[3] *Calcutta, Old and New*, by H. E. A. Cotton, p. 147.
[4] *The Corse.* From the *kos*, which is an Indian measure of distance.
[5] Steuart and Co., coachmakers of those and later times.

Lieutenant-Colonel Fleming Martin was succeeded on February 20th, 1769, by Lieutenant-Colonel Archibald Campbell,[1] under whom the works at Fort William were at last reduced to some order and system. The new Chief Engineer was fresh from his advisory duties in Bombay, where he had collaborated during the autumn with Lieutenant-Colonel Keating in settling the fate of the much disputed Dongri Hill. When he assumed charge in Fort William, he made his assistants keep books in which they were obliged to record every important engineering transaction. Also, he caused an exact survey to be made of all the engineering stores, and proper returns to be drawn up, and he prepared a careful plan and state of the works. Till his arrival, Calcutta had not been fortunate in her Chief Engineers. Brohier was clever and dishonest: Amphlett and Polier, well-meaning but inexperienced: Martin, upright, but obstinate and niggardly. In Archibald Campbell, however, she got at last the man she needed, energetic, methodical, of high integrity and good ability. He understood his work, and did it.

But Campbell was faced with a most difficult task. Much of the work already done was bad, and progress had been slow. His first report to Government,[2] which he submitted in 1769 after viewing the fortifications, described the obstacles which he had to overcome. Having dealt with the state of the fortifications, he proceeded to remark that the ditch had not been completely dug along part of the south front of Fort William, and that its sluices were so small that 16 tides would be necessary to fill it to a depth of $6\frac{1}{2}$ feet. He wished to devote his attention first to the completion of the counterscarp walls of the main defences, and the walls and ditches of the ravelins, all of which, he said, should be finished before the next monsoon began. After that, the retaining walls of the covered way and parapets should be taken in hand, and certain improvements carried

---

[1] *Bengal Public Consultations*, March 16th, 1769. Archibald Campbell had certainly the most distinguished career of any engineer in India during the eighteenth century, for he attained, as a Major-General, to the position of Governor and Commander-in-Chief of Madras. Commissioned in 1758 in the Corps of Engineers of the King's Army, he was selected in 1764, after service at Guadeloupe, to be Chief Engineer at Calcutta with the rank of Lieut.-Colonel in the Bengal Engineers, though he was then only a Captain-Lieutenant and 25 years of age. He did not reach India, however, till the autumn of 1768, when he advised on the Bombay defences before continuing his voyage to Calcutta. His resignation from the post of Chief Engineer at Calcutta was brought about by rules framed in 1771 under which he could not retain his position in both the King's and Company's armies. He saw more scope for his abilities in the Royal Army, so India lost his services for a time, though, on his voyage home, he inspected and advised on the defences of Madras. In 1775 he sailed for North America in command of the 71st Foot. Three years later he was in command of the troops in Georgia, and, in 1780, became Governor of Jamaica. In 1785, when a Major-General, he accepted the office of Governor and Commander-in-Chief of Madras and was created Knight of the Bath. Resigning in 1789 on account of ill health, he died in England in 1791 at the early age of 52 years, and was buried in Westminster Abbey. His portrait, as painted by Romney in 1790, appears in this chapter.

[2] Lieut.-Colonel Campbell to the Hon. H. Verelst, President and Governor, Council of Fort William. Letter dated March 1st, 1769. *Bengal Public Consultations*, March 16th, 1769.

out in the arrangements for flooding the ditch. These proposals met with the entire approval of the Council, and Campbell was ordered to put the works in hand at once. A general survey of his report shows that the upstream or north side of Fort William was elaborately fortified before March, 1769, both as regards the main body of the place and the outworks; but, on the inland or east side, the outworks were only partly finished, and on the south side they had scarcely been begun. This is interesting, as it seems to indicate that, during the earlier stages of construction, an attack on Fort William was expected from the direction of the town rather than from Dutch or French ships advancing up the Hugli in co-operation, possibly, with a force on land.

Campbell did not confine his attention solely to the fortifications. With Captain Henry Watson, one of his assistants, he planned to lay out a dockyard on the bank of the river. Considerable delay, and a long correspondence with Government, followed. In the end, however, Campbell's scheme led to the establishment, under Lieutenant-Colonel Henry Watson, of a Government Dockyard at Kidderpore, south of Fort William, where Watson launched the *Nonsuch*, a frigate of 36 guns, in 1781. Between that year and 1800, 35 vessels were launched; and before 1821 the total had reached 237, including the *Hastings*, a 74-gun ship. The credit for this maritime enterprise should rest with Campbell, though Watson carried it through, and it is a true indication of the energy and ability of the Chief Engineer of 1769. Presumably Campbell and Watson intended to act as contractors for building and repairing ships until Government would purchase their concern. If so, it was a legitimate business, as private trade was still allowed. Their adventure certainly led to great results.

Campbell had important work to do at the French settlement of Chandarnagar during the summer of 1769. While at Chinsura, he learnt that a large number of coolies were excavating a "drain" around Chandarnagar, so he took the opportunity to examine part of this work in April before announcing his arrival to the French Governor.[1] He found that the "drain" was about three miles long, some 50 feet wide and from 12 to 18 feet deep, the parts most nearly finished being those in the most secluded areas, and he reported to Calcutta that the drain could be converted into a powerful field defence in a very few days. The Council, being impressed by Campbell's further remarks that the ditch took a zigzag line and had a rampart, decided to send him to make an official survey of it, and wrote to M. Jean Chevalier, the French Governor, requesting that this inspection should be allowed. British troops were held in readiness to enforce the demand, and in spite of the protests of

---

[1] Lieut.-Colonel Campbell to Government, letter dated April 27th, 1769. *Bengal Public Consultations*, May 2nd, 1769.

SIR ARCHIBALD CAMPBELL, K.B., OF INVERNEIL.

Chevalier, Campbell inspected the ditch and reported that it was certainly designed for military defence. The Government in Calcutta then ordered that it should be demolished and filled in, which was accordingly done under Campbell's direction, and by September the secret defence of Chandarnagar had been stopped.[1]

In Major James Lillyman, who succeeded Colonel Campbell on December 17th, 1772,[2] the Company made a happy choice. He was not only a skilful engineer and an indefatigable worker, but had made a study of the works before he took charge of them. Lillyman was confident that he could soon complete what remained to be done, and judging by the outward appearance of the defences in the summer of 1773, it seemed that his hopes were justified. However, he was disappointed. Heavy rain in September, which brought down some lengths of the rampart, showed that the retaining walls were too weak everywhere, and that his predecessors, except Campbell, were not skilled in design. So, amid the crash of falling masonry, Lillyman wrote a full report to the Government.[3] Unfortunately his very sensible remarks did not receive much attention until October, 1774, when Warren Hastings became the first Governor-General, nominally of Fort William, but actually, in many respects, of British India. Hastings then instructed the Chief Engineer to lay before Government without delay an accurate statement of the fortifications, with estimates for repairing and completing them, and proposals for the immediate expenditure of six lakhs of rupees on very urgent repairs.[4] This Lillyman did in November,[5] and it became evident that, both in the outworks and in the body of Fort William, much still remained to be done. Of the outworks, the Ford ravelin was finished with the exception of the platforms; but the Clive, Pocock, Vansittart and Smith ravelins, the Verelst and Cartier counterguards, and the Argyll and Conway redoubts were all in an unfinished state.[6] Only one sluice had been altered. As for the body of the place, much was required—an interior retaining wall for the rampart, a powder magazine, dispense magazines for all the gates, two small flanking bastions for the Argyll and Conway redoubts, guardhouses, workshops, stores, barracks, kitchens, wells, a granary, a mint, public offices, and quarters for officers. There was no lack of work at the moment, nor was there likely to be for several years. In general it may be said that the main or interior line of fortification was almost completed by the year 1774, although the outworks had not reached that stage, and that a large part of the space within the fort had still to be filled with necessary buildings. By the irony of fate, the man

[1] General Letter, Bengal to Court, September 25th, 1769.
[2] *Bengal Public Consultations*, December 17th, 1772, Range II, Vol. I.
[3] *Ibid.*, September 9th, 1773, Range II, Vol. IV.
[4] *Ibid.*, October 28th, 1774, Range II, Vol. VII.
[5] *Ibid.*, November 7th, 1774, Range II, Vol. VII.
[6] These defensive works are shown in the plan of Fort William which is included in this chapter.

who was chiefly responsible for the construction of Fort William—Robert Clive—died in London on November 22nd, 1774, by his own hand, driven to this act by ill-health and persecution before he could see the creation of his mind translated fully into brick and mortar.

There is little more to record about the building of Fort William. During the last few years of the work, a Military Committee of higher standing and greater powers than the Committee of Works controlled all engineering affairs, and the latter body ceased to function about 1774.[1] As the Governor himself, four Councillors, the Military Storekeeper, the Naval Storekeeper, the Master Attendant, the Military Paymaster and the Paymaster of the Works all sat in the Military Committee[2] in addition to the Chief Engineer, the latter was of small account in such a galaxy, and his powers were necessarily more limited than in the Committee of Works. Lillyman received orders in 1774 to complete, as fast as he could, the Vansittart ravelin, the North and South and Flagstaff redans near the river, the drawbridges of several gates, the ditch sluices, and some barracks near the Plassey Gate, but he did not live to carry out his instructions, for he was buried in Calcutta on December 28th.[3] In default of a more experienced military engineer, Major Fortnam, the Civil Architect of Calcutta, who had built the Council Chamber ten years earlier,[4] was then appointed Chief Engineer with the rank of Lieutenant-Colonel, and carried on the work to the best of his ability till relieved, towards the end of 1776, by Lieutenant-Colonel Henry Watson, whose appointment had been approved by the Court of Directors in April of that year.[5]

Henry Watson, as the architect of Fort William in its final stages, is entitled to special recognition; but he is remembered also as the man who established wet and dry docks and a marine yard on the bank of the Hugli, who laid out the *maidan* around Fort William and made the Red Road which traverses that green expanse, and who seconded Philip Francis in his famous duel with Warren Hastings, the Governor-General, in 1780. Though Watson had the reputation of being difficult and quarrelsome, he was undoubtedly a fine engineer. Indeed, he did such brilliant work that his name is perpetuated in Watganj Street near the Kidderpore Docks.

By the end of 1781, Fort William was complete in all its more important details. After nearly a quarter of a century of labour, and the expenditure of some two millions sterling,[6] the military engineers

---

[1] C. R. Wilson states that the Committee of Works was abolished in March, 1771; but a letter from that Committee appears in the *Bengal Public Consultations* of August, 1774.
[2] *The Building of the Present Fort William, Calcutta*, by C. R. Wilson, appearing in *The Calcutta Review*, Vol. CXIX, July, 1904.
[3] *Bengal Burials*, Vol. II, p. 246.
[4] *Bengal Public Consultations*, October 25th, 1764, Range I, Vol. XXXVII.
[5] General Letter, Court to Bengal, April 5th, 1776.
[6] *The Building of the Present Fort William, Calcutta*, by C. R. Wilson, appearing in *The Calcutta Review*, Vol. CXIX, July, 1904.

of Bengal had given Calcutta a fortress of which she might well be proud. Nothing of importance remained to be done but to level the *maidan* and intersect it by roads, and these finishing touches were applied during the next few years. A general discharge of all the guns on December 24th, 1781, in honour of the surrender of Negapatam, announced also that Fort William was fully armed and prepared to defend herself against any foe.

So ends the story of the building of this great stronghold. It must be confessed that at times it makes doleful reading ; but to gloss over the frailty and incapacity of some of the builders, and to minimize their faults, would give a false idea of the tortuous path which led to ultimate success. Fort William has never been called upon to fulfil the purpose for which it was designed : it has stood no siege, and no gun has ever been fired from its ramparts against an enemy. It has remained a silent emblem of power. Guns are not mounted to-day upon its bastions. A battalion of British infantry and a section of armoured cars alone form its standing garrison. The old quarter of the Commander-in-Chief has become an officers' mess ; and of the seven original gates, only the Calcutta, Chowringhee, Plassey and Water Gates are now used for general traffic. The dry ditch still bounds the perimeter, and part of it can be filled with water from the river ; but the old " Dacoit Fencing " which once encircled the outer walls, has vanished. With the advance of science, Fort William has been modernized in every department other than fortification. Tube wells give an abundant supply of pure water to the garrison, and electric lights and fans make their lives more pleasant than in the days of old John Company.

Though obsolete as a fortification, Brohier's creation is replete with interest to the engineer whose footsteps may lead him through its labyrinth of walls and ditches. In imagination he will see again those hardy, rollicking and adventurous leaders of his own profession whose deeds and lives have been described in these pages : those pioneers who sweated and experimented in the steamy vapours of the Hugli, and after many and costly errors, finished their great work and gave their countrymen an impregnable stronghold in northern India.

CHAPTER IX.

THE COMPLETION OF FORT ST. GEORGE.

DURING the 40 years which followed the battle of Plassey, the extension of British territory and responsibility in India was rapid. Against the wishes of the Directors in Leadenhall Street, and in spite of their repeated instructions to curtail military expenditure, their agents in India were driven in self-defence to increase their military forces. The balance of military power became unstable from Cape Comorin to the Himalayas, but particularly in southern India where the ambitions of Haidar Ali, the intrigues of the French and the raids of the Marathas, kept the country in a state of constant turmoil. For the British, the era of defence behind walls then passed to one of active operations in the field or against fortified strongholds, and forces were used which included all arms and were larger than any which had yet been mobilized. Rivers had to be bridged, batteries raised, saps and parallels dug, and mountain roads prepared, and for such technical work trained men were needed—men who were disciplined soldiers and at the same time professional engineers rather than hired labourers or enthusiastic volunteers. Thus the launching of field operations on a large scale produced the engineering soldier of India who was known first as the " Pioneer " and later as the " Sapper and Miner." The deeds of these men are conspicuous in the history of the military conquest of India. Sappers and Miners prepared the way for every assault, often they led forlorn hopes against walls reputed to be impregnable. Their numbers were small, but their courage great. They died that others might reap the fruits of victory, and, by their heroism and skill, raised military engineering to the position which it holds in the Indian Army of to-day.

The appointment of military engineers to command trained soldiers in the field necessitated an increase in the establishment of engineer officers. Where formerly such officers were needed only to fortify the main settlements, they were now scattered over India and exposed to the constant dangers and casualties of minor campaigns. In the course of this history, it has been possible, hitherto, to deal with the exploits and careers of most of the military engineers of India ; but, with the development of engineering in the field, all that can be done is to mention those engineers who were pre-eminent in their profession or were concerned in some remarkable exploit. The names of scores of men who did excellent work must be omitted through lack of space. The value of that work is shown in the Empire which these less celebrated officers helped to build.

In 1763 the *Society of Gentlemen* thus defined a military engineer :[1]

"ENGINEER IN THE MILITARY ART.

"An able, expert man, who by a perfect knowledge in mathematics, delineates upon paper or marks upon the ground, all sorts of forts and other works proper for offence and defence. He should understand the art of fortification, so as to be able not only to discover the defects of a plan, but to find a remedy proper for them, as also how to make an attack upon, as well as to defend, the place. Engineers are extremely necessary for these purposes: wherefore it is requisite that, besides being ingenious, they should be brave in proportion. When at a siege the engineers have narrowly surveyed the place, they are to make their report to the general, by acquainting him which part they adjudge the weakest, and where approaches may be made with most success. Their business is also to delineate the lines of circumvallation and contravallation, taking all the advantages of the ground; to mark out the trenches, places of arms, batteries and lodgments, taking care that none of their works be flanked or discovered from the place. After making a faithful report to the general of what is a doing, the engineers are to demand a sufficient number of workmen and utensils, and whatever else is necessary."

The description is interesting for it shows that, until the time of the Company's serious entry into the campaigns in southern India, the military engineer was still considered primarily as an attacker or defender of fortresses. Field engineering, in the modern sense, formed no part of his normal duties, nor could it when he had no trained soldiers under him. It was not till 1772 that, at Gibraltar, an engineer officer found himself in command of a company of trained men called "Soldier Artificers," who replaced the civil labourers till then employed on the fortifications. The engineer officer of India, with the exception of the Chief Engineer, was badly paid, and although efforts were being made to discourage the system of undertaking contracts, certain perquisites survived which added a little to the meagre official salaries—for instance, gun platforms, which, after a siege, were considered as the personal property of the commanding engineer of the besieging force.[2]

When the fortress engineer made his *début* into the field, his kit appears to have expanded in proportion to his duties. The entertaining remarks of Captain Innes Munro, on the requirements of a

---

[1] *A New and Complete Dictionary of Arts and Sciences*, by a Society of Gentlemen, published in 1763. See *R.E. Journal*, Vol. II, July to December, 1905, p. 58.
[2] *Madras Artillery Records*, Vol. IX, 1839.

young officer on joining the Company's service at Madras, may be quoted,[1] for they apply as much to engineers as others :—

"When an European arrives at Madras he is obliged, in a short time afterwards, to get a fresh supply of cotton shirts, waistcoats, and breeches, not only because they are better adapted to the climate, but because the washermen seem to have come under an engagement to the cotton-vendors and tailors to destroy the European habiliments as soon as possible ; which indeed they do effectually and make no secret of their purpose ; for while they thump your linen upon the washing stones, at every blow they call out ' Europe ' ! and strike with ten times the force they would do the produce of their own country.[2]

"And this leads me to make you acquainted with the articles which seem most necessary for a gentleman to purchase in England before he embarks for the East-Indies. All that is necessary for a young adventurer to carry out with him to the East Indies is as much light cloth and other furnishings as will be sufficient for three or four coats ; a few fashionable waistcoats ; three hats, two black and one white ; four pairs of boots ; twelve or eighteen pair of neat shoes ; with only a few pairs of silk stockings, as those of the country are for the most part worn ; a neat saddle and bridle with a strong bit, and spare girths and straps. A fowling piece and a few books are to be added to the list.

"For the requisite conveniences on board ship, one should, in the first place, complete his stock to one dozen ruffled shirts for particular occasions, and three dozen coarse plain ones. He should likewise have a few black stocks or neckcloths, two pair of dark fustian trousers, and six neat white ones to button at the ancles, with his former stock of breeches and stockings ; a boat-cloak, a ship-cot with three pairs of sheets, six pillow cases and bedding ; two dozen hand towels, an huswife, a few quires of brown paper, some tea, sago and sugar ready pounded ; a cheese ; a few pounds of salt butter and some biscuits ; with a tin kettle and tea-equipage for six persons ; also two large and four small japanned mugs, a good stout case of spirituous liquors, particularly gin ; six dozen of Bristol water,[3] which ought to be sparingly dealt out in case of sickness ; some bottles of souring[4] and shrub,[5] and three dozen of wine ; and these I think will be quite sufficient for any private gentleman's stock for an East-Indian voyage."

[1] *A Narrative of the Military Operations on the Coromandel Coast against the combined forces of the French, Dutch and Hyder Ally Caun from the year 1780 to the peace in 1784; in a series of letters in which are included many Useful Cautions to Young Gentlemen destined for India*, by Innes Munro, Esq., Captain of the late 73rd Regiment of Highlanders (1789), p. 41.

[2] Yet this was before the days of Mr. Gandhi.

[3] *Bristol water.* Water of warm springs near Bristol, used medicinally. Probably used as table water during voyages.

[4] *Souring.* Vinegar.

[5] *Shrub.* A drink prepared from lemons, raspberries and currants, with spirits.

A remarkable man had succeeded John Call in September, 1770, as Chief Engineer on the Coromandel coast. This was Patrick Ross,[1] who was destined to carry out the final reconstruction of Fort St. George, and to finish it as Henry Watson did Fort William. Ross started his career as a Practitioner Engineer and Ensign in the Corps of Engineers of the Royal Army in 1758, and, following in the footsteps of Archibald Campbell, whose services had been placed at the disposal of the East India Company as Chief Engineer of Bengal, he was nominated to the like command in Madras, with the rank of Lieutenant-Colonel, when only 30 years of age. Resigning his royal commission, he served as Chief Engineer for the enormous period of more than 32 years, became a Major-General in 1796, retired in 1803, and died in England in the following year. Though he did not reach the heights attained by Campbell, who became Governor and Commander-in-Chief of Madras, his services were most notable in the technical line. This was the man who made Fort St. George an impregnable base for the military expeditions launched by the Company against the rulers of Mysore and other enemies. His ideas were bold and fearless, his execution masterly. The final stages in the construction of this fortress, whose history we have traced from 1649, must find a place in this chapter, for they were the culminating achievement of the life of an eminent military engineer of India.

In 1770, between the departure of Call and the arrival of Ross, Captain Henry Montresor officiated as Chief Engineer of Madras. The western or landward face of Fort St. George was then in a very bad state, and Montresor recommended that, as advised by Call before he left, the Pigot and Lawrence bastions should be reconstructed and the St. George's ravelin between them greatly enlarged —measures which would, in his opinion, make the western face sufficiently strong "at a minimum of expense." But Patrick Ross thought otherwise. He scorned half-measures and proposed a complete change of trace, converting the outline of Fort St. George from a half-decagon into a semi-octagon by the abolition of the two old bastions and the prolongation of the north-east and south-west curtains to meet in one large bastion on the site of the St. George's ravelin.[2] By this proposal the three faces on the west front would be reduced to two, and the works simplified. The scheme included also the enlargement of the Nabob's bastion at the southern end of the west front.

The project was bold and sound, and Ross was fortunate enough to secure the support and concurrence of his personal friend Archibald Campbell when the latter was on his way to England in 1773. At the invitation of the Madras Council, Campbell inspected Fort St. George, and his report[3] showed that he was in complete agreement with Ross.

[1] See Chapter V.
[2] See Plan of Fort St. George after completion, given in this chapter, and the plan of Fort St. George in 1753, given in Chapter V.
[3] *Public Consultations*, March 2nd, 1773, Vol. CIX.

Encouraged by this, Ross sent in proposals in November, 1774,[1] for the construction of the works which he considered necessary to complete Fort St. George, or, as he put it, " to render Fort St. George very formidable, and so uniformly strong that no particular part can be attacked with much Advantage." With it he sent an estimate amounting to 218,171 pagodas.[2] Now, Paul Benfield's tender of 130,279 pagodas[3] for the construction of the new west bastion had been accepted only in the previous year, and, though the Madras Council agreed with wry faces to Ross's further demand, it caused dismay in England :—[4]

" THE COMPANY TO FORT ST. GEORGE.

" When we review the Plan lately transmitted to us, we cannot but be greatly alarmed at the repeated multiplication of Outworks, which are not only too many for the Body of the Place, but must be productive of a vast increase in the amount of Our Garrison Charges. . . . As we have been under the necessity of limiting our Expence of Fortifications in Bengal, so we must confine those under your Presidency to 50,000 Pagodas[5] per Year, unless the most imminent danger should render an excess unavoidably necessary. We moreover direct that the Projects for the several Fronts be reconsidered with every degree of attention."

However, before these restrictive orders from England could reach Madras, the Council had approved Colonel Ross's estimate for the new works which he proposed and had accepted a tender from Benfield for their execution.[6] After that, a " reconsideration with every degree of attention " was useless. No doubt the Council considered that the situation was one of imminent danger, and in this they were fully justified. The course of political events may be summarized briefly. In 1773, before Warren Hastings conquered Rohilkhand in the north, the Madras Council had arbitrarily deposed the Raja of Tanjore[7] to oblige Muhammad Ali, Nawab of the Carnatic, and the latter had then proceeded to sow corruption throughout the British administration by his financial dealings with Benfield and others. In a period of seven years, two governors of Madras were dismissed, and another suspended ; and in 1776, a fourth, Lord Pigot, was deposed and imprisoned. These events led to a chaotic policy which drew Madras into the war which was raging on the western side of India against the Maratha confederacy, and a disastrous expedition from Bombay brought about the convention of Wargaum in 1779,

---

[1] *Public Consultations*, November 30th, 1774, Vol. CXII.
[2] About £127,000.
[3] About £52,000. Vibart, in his *Military History of the Madras Engineers*, Vol. I, p. 128, states that the total amount of the work contracted for by Benfield between 1775 and 1777 amounted to 603,857 pagodas, *i.e.*, more than £241,000.
[4] *Public Despatches from England*, April 5th, 1776, Vol. LXXIX.
[5] £20,000.   [6] *Madras Consultations*, April 17th, 1775, Vol. LI.
[7] A small state about 150 miles south of Madras.

by which the Bombay Government was shorn of all its territorial gains since 1773.

The disgraceful capitulation of General Egerton's army at Wargaum was one of the worst disasters which had befallen the British since they first arrived in India. It had its repercussions in all parts of the country. At the time, the Nizam of Hyderabad was nominally friendly, Haidar Ali of Mysore was biding his time, and the Raja of Berar stood aloof in his isolation from the remainder of his Maratha kinsmen. But now a spirit of dissatisfaction began to show itself in both the Nizam and Haidar Ali, and Berar grew cold and suspicious. The Nizam disliked the British alliance with Raghuba,[1] although he took no active part against the Madras Government until annoyed by their political manœuvres. Then he raised all the powerful native states against them. Mysore, Poona, and all the Maratha states except Baroda, conspired with him to destroy the British power in India. The leader in this confederacy was Haidar Ali of Mysore who had, for seven years, been concerting schemes with the French at Pondicherry for a campaign against the British. The moment had come. In July, 1780, the horsemen of Mysore streamed through the Changama Pass into the Carnatic, and laid waste the country almost up to the walls of Madras.

These, briefly, were the events which hastened the completion of Fort St. George by Patrick Ross and his men. The Madras Council did well to combat the financial objections of the Directors and to make the Company secure at least in one spot in southern India.

The most powerful and troublesome enemies of the British during these years, apart from the French, were the Marathas and the Mysoreans. The Marathas were curious folk, chiefly mounted freebooters, past masters in the art of guerilla warfare, elusive, treacherous, and so born to the saddle that they held the foot soldier in the greatest contempt. Their confederacy held undisputed sway over a wide band of territory stretching across Central India from the Bay of Bengal to the Indian Ocean. Leagued together, more by a common love of booty than the bonds of friendship, were the Bhonsla Raja of Berar, Holkar of Indore, Sindhia of Gwalior and the Gaikwar of Baroda, the first three of whom were hereditary generals of the Peshwa. Sindhia and Holkar had a family feud, Berar was too distant from the court at Poona to enter fully into its intrigues, and the Gaikwar was usually neutral or friendly towards the British; but when all except the Gaikwar combined against the Company, the situation was one of great peril.

The Marathas made up for their deficiencies in equipment by a natural bent for warfare. Major Dirom, a keen observer and a graphic writer, gives us a picture of them at war.[2] " The Maratha

[1] The British wished to establish Raghuba as "Peshwa," or ruling Maratha minister.
[2] *A Narrative of the Campaign in India which terminated the War with Tippoo Sultan in 1792*, by Major Dirom (1793), p. 10.

guns," says he, " are of all sorts and dimensions : and, having the names of their gods given to them, are painted in the most fantastic manner ; and many of them, held in esteem for the services they are said to have already performed for the state, cannot now be dispensed with, although in every respect unfit for use. . . . The Maratha infantry is composed of black Christians, and despicable poor wretches of the lowest cast, uniform in nothing but the bad state of their musquets. Few are provided with either ammunition or acoutrements. They are commanded by half-caste people of Portuguese and French extraction who draw off the attention of spectators from the bad clothing of their men by the profusion of antiquated lace bestowed on their own. . . . The Marathas do not appear to treat their infantry with more respect than they deserve, as they ride through them without ceremony on the march and on all occasions evidently consider them as foreigners. On a marching day, the guns and infantry move off soon after daylight, but rarely together : the bazaars and baggage move nearly about the same time. The guns and tumbrils,[1] sufficiently unweildy without further burden, are so heaped with stores and baggage that there does not seem to be any idea of its ever being necessary to unlimber and prepare for action on the march. There are sometimes a hundred and fifty bullocks, in a string of pairs, to one gun. The chiefs remain upon the ground without tents, smoking their hookers, till the artillery and baggage have gone on some miles ; they then follow, each persuing his own route, attended by his principal people, while the inferiors disperse to forage and plunder over the country."

Such were the undisciplined but martial hordes who threatened our armies and fortresses in many parts of India, but with whom, nevertheless, we were occasionally in alliance. If the Marathas included any engineers or pioneers among their troops in the field, we have no evidence of the fact : their engineers must have been humble folk who shared with the infantry the honour of being ridden through on the march by the swashbuckling cavalry. But the Maratha chiefs had some capable fortress engineers, men who built strongholds on rocky peaks which defied the assaults of native armies and even, on more than one occasion, resisted the storming troops of the Company. In the field the Marathas seem to have had no use or need for engineers ; as a swarm of locusts they spread over the country, collected, dispersed, ravaged and destroyed. They might invest a fortified town, smothering it with mounted men as with a blanket ; but they would no more dream of conducting regular siege operations than of re-clothing and re-arming their wretched and alien infantry.

Antagonists of a very different type were the soldiers of Mysore, led by the redoubtable Haidar Ali, who did more by his military ability to force the establishment of a proper engineering service on a

[1] Ammunition wagons.

reluctant British Government than any man before or since. He figures so prominently in the military events of the end of the eighteenth century in India, and his son Tipu[1] involved the British in such extensive siege operations before he was crushed at Seringapatam, that some space may be devoted to him and the troops which he organized and led with such marked success.

Haidar Ali of Mysore, the son of an obscure officer of infantry, was uneducated, amoral, irreligious, and cruel; but, being a man of rare energy and industry, swift in decision, ruthless in execution, and gifted with a keen judgment of character, he rose rapidly in the Mysore army which he joined in 1749. By his prowess in war he drove the Marathas back from the borders of his state, and by this exploit so ingratiated himself with the army and the population that, on the death of his sovereign, the old king of Mysore, he usurped the throne and kept the real heir a virtual prisoner in Seringapatam. He then became a terror to the neighbouring rulers for, combining as he did the shrewdness of a talented politician with the initiative of an able soldier, he proceeded to reorganize both the civil and military administrations of Mysore with such success that he was soon the most formidable prince in southern India. The innate savagery of his nature was tempered with caution, wisdom and common sense, qualities which were sadly lacking in his degenerate son, Tipu Sultan. This reprobate was a sad disappointment to his ambitious father. He outdid him in cruelty, wantonness and pride, without possessing his soldierly and statesmanlike attributes.

These were the successive rulers of Mysore who brought the East India Company nearer to ruin than ever before or since. Haidar Ali knew that he must defeat the British or admit their supremacy. His first care, after he had risen to power, was accordingly to establish an efficient army. His early conflicts against the Company's troops taught him that European discipline was essential to success, and so he tried by every possible means to attract to his standard military adventurers of all nations, but particularly artificers and sepoys from the British forces. He introduced English words of command, and clothed his regular soldiers in uniforms so like those of the British that his men were sometimes mistaken for the troops of the Company. He tried even to build a navy to challenge the power of England on the eastern seas, though in this he met with little success. In time, however, his land forces reached a state of discipline never before seen among the native armies of India; they were not uniform in training, equipment or military value, but they were formidable because they meant to fight, could fight, and did fight.

The Mysore troops are well described by Innes Munro.[2] Haidar Ali's regular cavalry, he writes, were chiefly clothed in quilted cotton

[1] Spelt also Tippoo.
[2] *A Narrative of the Military Operations on the Coromandel Coast*, by Captain Innes Munro, p. 130.

gowns, thick enough to be proof against a sword cut. They carried large, curved sabres and also pistols. Their brethren of the irregular or light cavalry, known as *Lootywallahs*, slung old rusty matchlocks and sometimes carried lances or spears six feet long ; if very irregular, they were content with bows and arrows alone. Regulars and irregulars, Mysore could put into the field, in 1780, 28,000 mounted men, and, a few years later, a much greater number. Haidar Ali's best infantry in 1780, a division of about 15,000 men, were clothed in red and green, with facings of different colours, and were armed with European muskets and bayonets. Thoroughly trained in European fashion, and sometimes led by Frenchmen, they could always give a good account of themselves. This division was supported by another 12,000 strong, not so highly trained, but well disciplined. Swarms of matchlock men, who skirmished around the regular troops in battle, and mobs of savage *poligars*, carrying 20-foot bamboo spears with which to repel cavalry or charge infantry, brought the total of the Mysore infantry to some 55,000 men when Haidar Ali invaded the Carnatic. His numerous French and Danish guns were drawn by teams of bullocks, and well served by gunners instructed by French officers. As a species of auxiliary artillery he employed several thousands of men for throwing rockets. The rocket, says Munro, had a " stalk " of thick bamboo, eight or ten feet long, ending in an iron tube, six to twelve pounds in weight, in which the fuse and charge were placed. Its range was a mile and a half, and, if pointed horizontally, it would ricochet on dry ground among cavalry and artillery and do great damage. It is said that Haidar Ali had at one time a corps of pioneers 5,000 strong, but it is doubtful if the men were much more than hired labourers. This was the army with which Mysore challenged British supremacy in southern India and against which our military engineers had to contend in the battles and sieges in which they took so prominent and honourable a part.

Though Colonel Patrick Ross was concerned chiefly with the alterations to Fort St. George, he acted also as Chief Engineer with some of the military expeditions which the Company was now obliged to despatch from Madras, and in this capacity he accompanied a column under General Joseph Smith which was sent to Trichinopoly in July, 1773, to besiege Tanjore. He directed the siege works with great skill, and, on September 17th, was able to report that a breach was practicable for assault. The attack was made by a force of four companies of British Grenadiers and six battalions of sepoys, and Tanjore was captured at a price of less than 200 casualties. Under Ross's orders were Captains William Campbell and George Maule, Lieutenants Mitchell and Dugood, and Assistant-Engineer Lieutenant Geils,[1] several of whom figure subsequently in

---

[1] *The Military History of the Madras Engineers and Pioneers*, by Major H. M. Vibart, Vol. I, p. 125.

this narrative. For so small an operation this was an ample cadre of engineers, and it shows how military engineering was rising in general estimation. Ross and most of his officers escaped lightly in the fighting at Tanjore, but Captain Campbell was killed. News was received of the death also of Captain Montresor, who had reverted to the infantry after acting as Chief Engineer of Madras between the departure of Call and the arrival of Ross.

The Madras army was growing rapidly at this time. While, in, 1776, there were only 12 battalions of Indian Infantry for the Carnatic[1] and six for the northern Circars,[2] in the following year the numbers were increased to 22 battalions for the Carnatic and Tanjore and eight for the Circars. As each battalion had 750 men, it will be seen that in 1777 the strength of the Madras Indian Infantry was nearly 22,000 men. In addition there were some battalions of British infantry, both King's troops and Company's men, several companies of artillery, and an establishment of Pioneers. It was indeed fortunate for the Company that it was able to place so many trained soldiers in the field before the struggle was renewed against Mysore.

Work on the defences of Fort St. George was much hindered by the confusion following a revolution in 1776 among the civil and military officers against the rule of Lord Pigot, the Governor, whom they actually arrested and imprisoned. Vibart states[3] that, at about this time, Fort St. George had taken its final form, but this is not quite correct, for several years were to elapse before the alterations planned by Ross were completed. The " body of the place " may have assumed its final shape, but not the outworks, which were numerous and intricate. During the revolution, Ross complained that he was short of materials and labour. His muster roll of labourers, which had swelled to 5,000 shortly before the outbreak, had sunk to 3,000, and work was confined to the west front where the main fortifications were complete, but two new ravelins and their four cunettes were still in hand. He reported, in September, 1776,[4] that nothing had been done for several years to fortify the Black Town area north of the fort, and it was there that an enemy would launch his attack. Its only existing defence, said he, was a wooden palisade. This report induced Colonel Stuart, the Garrison Commander, to enter a strong protest to Government, chiefly on the score of the limitation of expenditure on the fortifications to 50,000 pagodas annually. But Ross continued to impress on his superiors the importance of completing the whole scheme of fortification which he had planned, and

[1] The coastal region from the extreme south to near Masulipatam and including Madras, Pondicherry (Fr.), and the state of Tanjore.
[2] The coastal region north of the Carnatic up to near Cuttack and the River Mahanadi.
[3] *The Military History of the Madras Engineers*, by Major H. M. Vibart, Vol. I, p. 127.
[4] *Madras Consultations*, September 28th, 1776, Vol. LVI.

wrote a long letter about it in January, 1777.[1] As a result, he was allowed to strengthen the north-east and south-east angles of Fort St. George besides continuing his labours on the west front, which, by the end of the year was complete with outworks, gates and ditch. By that time he had built also 300 feet of sea wall at the south-east angle. In the spring of 1778, however, he was obliged to go on leave to England ; yet before he sailed he was able to guarantee[2] that the west front was strong enough to resist any European attack and that the other fronts were greatly improved.

When the directors heard of the revolution against Lord Pigot, they chose Mr. Thomas Rumbold to succeed Pigot as Governor of Madras and despatched him at once to India. Rumbold landed at Fort St. George in February, 1778, on the same day as the newly-appointed Commander-in-Chief, Major-General Sir Hector Munro, the victor of Buxar. Within a month of their arrival, war was declared between France and England, the French having united their forces in America with those of the revolted British colonies. England prepared to strike the first blow in India. An expeditionary force was mobilized at once under Munro to attack Pondicherry, and, at the end of August, siege operations were begun against the French settlement. With the investing force was Major W. Stevens as Chief Engineer, and so well did he advance his saps and dig his parallels that fire was opened against the French defences on September 18th. He did not live, however, to see the surrender of the place, for on October 4th, three days before M. Bellecombe, the French Governor, lowered his flag, Stevens was mortally wounded by a cannon ball. " In him," wrote Munro, " Society have lost an honest Man, and the Company a most valuable and gallant Soldier." It is curious that Captain George Maule, who succeeded Stevens as Acting Chief Engineer, should have been destined, like him, to be killed before Pondicherry. Yet so it was, though it happened some years afterwards. Among the engineers present at the siege was a young Ensign named William Gent, who figures prominently in the history of Madras engineering of a later date.

Writing of the fall of Pondicherry, Fortescue remarks[3] that in India, as in America, the command of the sea was essential to successful operations by land, and that war with France in the east opened with a naval action fought on August 10th between the French and British squadrons, which, though indecisive, ended in the withdrawal of the French ships, leaving Pondicherry at the mercy of Munro. The city, however, made a very fine defence at a cost to the besiegers of 800 killed and wounded. On the French side, the Chief Engineer was M. Dulac to whom credit should be given for the strong defence which caused such trouble to his enemies. On the advice of Sir

---

[1] *Madras Consultations*, January 28th, 1777, Vol. LVIII.
[2] *Ibid.*, March 6th, 1778, Vol. LXI.
[3] *A History of the British Army*, by the Hon. J. W. Fortescue, Vol. III, p. 438.

Eyre Coote, who arrived from England in December, 1778, orders were issued to demolish the fortifications of Pondicherry—orders which were carried out so effectually by Captain Thomas Geils,[1] that the Select Committee was able to report to the Secret Committee in October, 1779,[2] that, although the fortifications were four miles in circuit, they would all be demolished by the end of that month and the ditch filled up, when not a trace of the defences would remain.

Hastings[3] was not content with taking Pondicherry and Chandarnagar, but was resolved to leave the French no fortified bases in the whole of India; so all were attacked and fell easily with the exception of Mahé, a settlement a few miles south of Tellicherry, in Malabar, on the western coast. Haidar Ali of Mysore, who boasted that all European settlements in this region were under his protection, was notified that Mahé would be the next objective of the British and was extremely angry as he used the place to import munitions and supplies for his army and hoped that it would become a port of disembarkation of the French troops from Europe, whom he expected as allies. He replied accordingly that, if Mahé was attacked, he would help to defend it and would also invade the province of Arcot. He did, in fact, help the French at Mahé, and after the capture of the place by Braithwaite, complained bitterly to the victorious British that his trust in their good faith was shattered. The attitude of Haidar Ali was changed by the capture of Mahé from veiled to undisguised hostility. From that moment he made no secret of his designs. Mysore would enter on a struggle to the death with the British power in southern India. The capture of this French base was a very minor operation, typical of the desultory wars in southern India and hardly worth recording as a military undertaking; but its political effect was far-reaching, for it helped to precipitate the outbreak of the Second Mysore War.[4]

Before we embark on any account of the deeds and experiences of military engineers in the wars against Haidar Ali and his son Tipu Sultan, it may be convenient to trace the final stages in the remodelling of Fort St. George. Early in 1779, the Select Committee approved a plan for the reconstruction of the sea face on a line slightly in advance of the old wall. The new front was designed to give flanking fire and was to have two gates instead of the old Sea Gate. The Committee, which included the Governor, Thomas Rumbold, recorded[5] that "the ruinous State of the Fortifications on the Sea Line having been frequently represented, and the Committee having always had it in their Intention to put that part of the Fort in a proper State of defence as soon as the N.E. and S.E. Angles

[1] Geils had transferred from the Artillery to the Engineers ten years before.
[2] *Military Letters to England*, October 14th, 1779, Vol. XIV.
[3] Warren Hastings, who became Govenor-General in 1774.
[4] The First Mysore War (1767–69), had ended in a very ignominious treaty for the British, who nearly lost Fort St. George.
[5] *Madras Consultations*, April 5th, 1779, Vol. LXVI.

were secured, it is now Resolved that the Works planned for the defence of the Sea Line be constructed with all possible dispatch, agreably to the plan proposed by Major Maule."[1] Work began at once on that face, and, shortly afterwards, on the outworks still needed to complete the north front. So well did Maule push on the work that before the end of 1779, Rumbold was able to express " the pleasing Hope of seeing the Fortifications entirely compleated in the course of six or eight months." Maule had assured the Select Committee on October 11th that he had got through the heavy work of removing many of the original fortifications and excavating deep and wide foundations for the new ones, and that he could finish the alterations and additions in six months. On this the Government informed the Court of his opinion,[2] adding, in true Company style, that they trusted that the Directors would not for many years be put to any further expense on fortification. "What necessity," wrote they, " there might have been originally for executing such great and expensive Works as We have seen built since the year 1773 We will not pretend to say; but We may, upon the Authority of three successive Engineers,[3] pronounce that there will be no necessity for altering any of the present Fortifications when the Works now in hand are finished."

But Maule's hope that he could put the finishing touches to the defences of Fort St. George in six months was not fulfilled although he made substantial progress in that period. In November, 1780, he reported[4] to the Commander-in-Chief in India, Lieutenant-General Sir Eyre Coote, that the west front was in a perfect state, and the south and east fronts almost finished. He was concentrating his energies on the north front, but had been much hindered by a serious lack of materials, which was not surprising when we remember that a war was then raging against Haidar Ali, who had captured Arcot, and that the routine in the fort was upset by the return of Sir Hector Munro's army after a disastrous campaign in the south. Though Maule did well, it was fortunate perhaps that Patrick Ross returned in the middle of 1782, when he was able to report[5] that the works as a whole were in " a very respectable state," that the northern defences were much improved, and that the whole of the sea front had been finished some months before except the drawbridges required for the two gates. He was particularly pleased that Maule had levelled some rising ground known as Hoghill, which lay half a mile to the north-west of the fort in a native suburb. This was a large engineering work, involving the cutting away of about 214,000 cubic yards of soil and heavy compensation to house owners, but it was worth the expense as the hill commanded the defences. The field of fire

[1] Then Chief Engineer.
[2] *Military Letters to England*, October 14th, 1779, Vol. XIV.
[3] Presumably Ross, Montresor and Maule.
[4] *Madras Consultations*, November 13th, 1780, Vol. LXXII.
[5] *Ibid.*, July 9th, 1782, Vol. LXXXI.

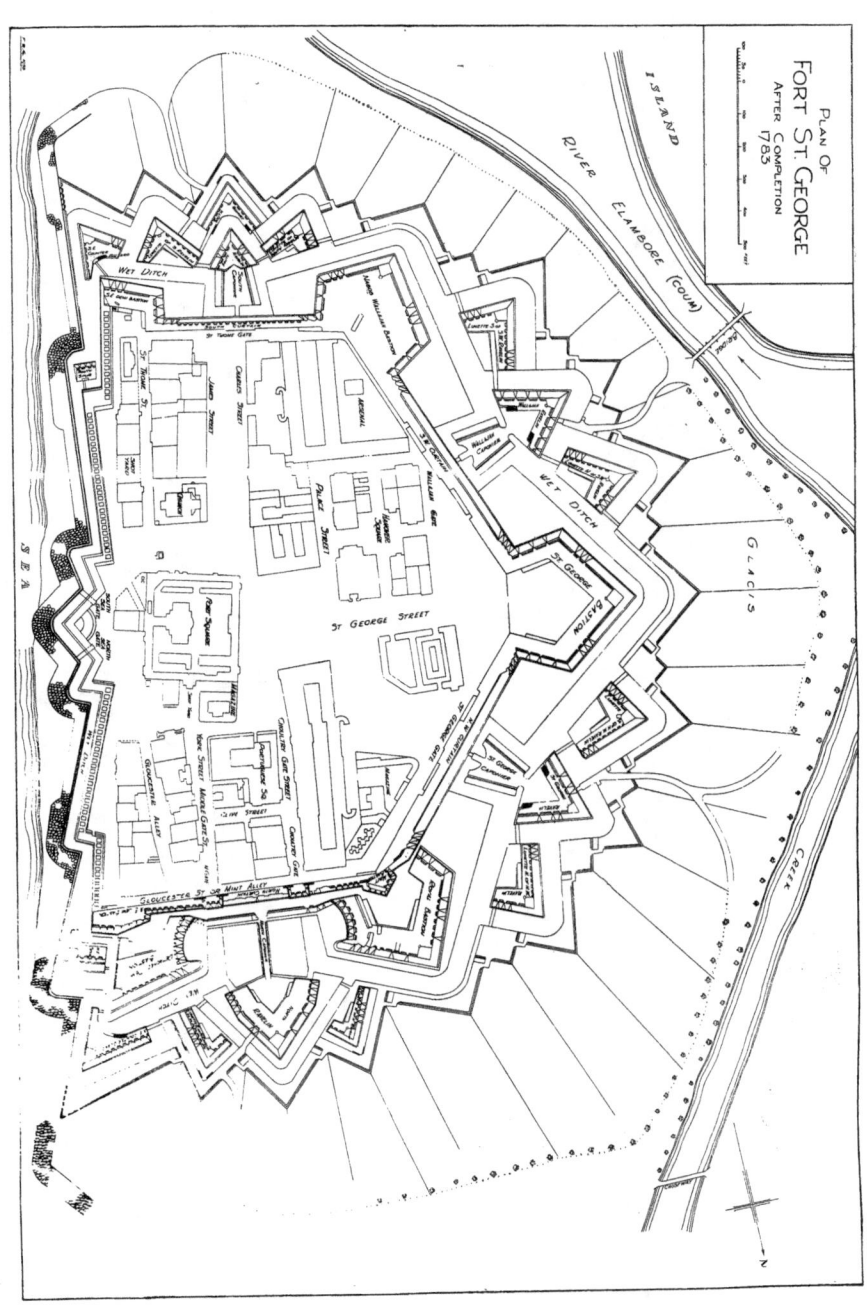

around Black Town had been improved, and this also earned the praise of Ross. In conclusion he urged that the defences of Black Town should be finished properly, and that arrangements should be made for storing more water in the fort itself in case of a siege, although 3,000 tons could be put into the new cisterns provided along the sea front and under the Treasury and Mint bastions.

The tale of Fort St. George is almost told. As time went on new buildings were added within it and improvements made to its outworks, but it may be said in general that the year 1783 undoubtedly saw the end of the reconstruction begun by John Brohier in 1756. For 27 years that scheme had been in hand—years of constant danger, uncertainty and difficulty. The results, however, were worthy of the few expert engineers who supervised the work in its latter stages. While the building of the new Fort William ended in 1781, and that of Bombay Fort in the same year, Fort St. George, whose walls first began to rise in 1640, was not completed till two years after her rivals in Calcutta and Bombay. For 143 years she struggled to reach her prime, and the amazing intricacies of her final shape are shown in the plan which is reproduced in this chapter. This plan agrees with one prepared by Major Maule in 1783, which is preserved in the King's Library of the British Museum, but it is more complete as it shows the buildings within the walls while Maule's plan shows only the fortifications.[1]

The history of Fort St. George since its completion is that of a seat of government rather than a fortress. Like Fort William in Bengal, its defences have never been tested in war, and those defences are not now what they were in 1783. After surviving for more than a century, the outworks on the south front were demolished to make room for a hospital, and, at about the same time, all the outworks on the other fronts, except the ravelins, were levelled to the ground. There is no obvious reason for these sweeping changes except a possible aversion by Government to "a multiplication of outworks." The demolitions secured a wider field of fire, and enabled the fort to be held by a smaller garrison. The place was perhaps unnecessarily strong and elaborate before it was shorn of its excrescences in the latter part of the nineteenth century. No enemies then roamed through the Carnatic as in the turbulent epochs of the French, Maratha and Mysore wars.

That vivid writer, Innes Munro, has much to say of the old fort and its defenders, and some of his remarks may form a fitting conclusion to its history.[2] With some friends he landed in a surf-boat

---

[1] The plan was drawn in 1931 in Madras from an old but undated plan of Fort St. George as completed, and from information taken from official records. It is probable that the undated plan was copied and elaborated from Maule's plan a year or so after the latter was drawn, say about 1785.

[2] *A Narrative of the Military Operations on the Coromandel Coast*, by Captain Innes Munro, p. 20 *et seq.*, Letter IV, March, 1780.

in 1780 on his first visit to India, and entered the fort through one of the new Sea Gates :—

"We were now ushered into the king's barracks, so magnificently described to us on shipboard, but which are nothing better than an old fabric of two stories in height, much resembling a Portuguese convent. The upper story is laid out into apartments for the officers, and in the under the soldiers are accomodated, both being of very mean appearance. The officers' rooms, the walls of which were black with dirt, had been for some time used as a granary, so that rats and mice were very numerous and familiar all over its quarters.[1]

"Fort St. George is the presidency of the Company's settlement on the Coromandel coast, and is said to be the handsomest fortification in the British dominions. It is situated in a flat sandy country, and is surrounded, both naturally and artificially, by water, excepting on the side next the Black Town, which has additional outworks to it on that account. Its form is an irregular hexagon, well built; having the faces towards the sea constructed in the shape of a contracted crownwork,[2] the curtains of which are built like the side of a ship of war, with a tier of large port-holes for heavy cannon. These are level with the water and covered by bomb-proofs. All the works, even the face next the sea, are encompassed by very handsome broad ditches which are kept continually full of clear salt water, and upon the scarps are occasionally found a supply of fine large oysters. This garrison is blessed with one of the finest fountains of fresh water in all India; and has a reservoir fit to contain twelve months allowance of it for the whole inhabitants. It is so limpid and delicious to the taste, that connoiseurs prefer drinking it pure to the pollution of its salutary qualities with a mixture of spirituous liquors.

"The town is regularly built, and capable of lodging eight thousand men in time of a siege; though the present garrison seldom exceeds two hundred Europeans and two battalions of sepoys. The Company's officers have acquired just praise by their steady adherence to the duties of their profession, which the excellent order of their sepoys clearly confirms, and which strikes every stranger with admiration and surprise. It is hardly credible, though true, that few troops in Europe cut a better appearance upon parade; and I have been told by veterans here that, when led on by European officers, they behave in the field with astonishing conduct and intrepidity. Their uniforms have a very military appearance, consisting of a red light-infantry jacket, a white waistcoat, and a blue turban placed in a soldier-like manner upon the head, edged round with tape of the same colour with the facings, and having a tassel at the lower corner. The sepoy has a long blue sash lightly girded round his loins, the end of which,

---

[1] Some allowance must be made for Munro's disappointment after the exaggerated tales he had heard on board ship. The engineers could not spare much time to rebuild or repair the barracks when the fortifications were still incomplete.

[2] A line of defence consisting of a bastion, two curtains and two half-bastions.

passing between his legs, is fastened behind.[1] He wears a pair of white drawers, tightly fitted, which only come half way down his thigh, and, being coloured at the lower end with a blue dye, appear as if scalloped all round. A pair of sandals upon his feet, white cross belts, a firelock and a bayonet, complete the sepoy's dress. These black corps have attached to them a full complement of native as well as European officers. The former rise according to their merit from private sepoys; and, before the most of them arrive at the rank of *subidars* or captains (for higher they do not go) they become quite bald and grey in the service, and their hoary beards and whiskers cut a most venerable appearance at the head of a regiment."

But Innes Munro on Madras society is too good to miss. Military engineering, for the moment, must go by the board. He is writing in April, 1780, after a month in India :—[2]

" An entertainment given by the Governor, or any other gentleman of consequence here, is really a curious spectacle. It is the custom for each guest to go thither attended by all his retinue of servants, who wait upon him at table in great pomp; the head *dubash*[3] taking post directly behind his master that he may convey his orders to the rest, who are all arranged in the rear as far back as the diningroom walls. This ridiculous fashion, together with the steam of the meat, renders the room intolerably suffocating and disagreable during dinner. It is reckoned ungenteel upon such occasions to be attended by any domestics but your own: yet a foreigner at first feels quite in pain when he is obliged to ask for anything at table, for the sign is no sooner made than twenty servants get into rapid motion, all darting at one object, and frequently running against each other in the simple act of handing a glass of beer.

" When a young lady arrives at Madras she must, in a few days afterwards, sit up to receive company, attended by some beau as master of the ceremonies; which perhaps continues for a week or until she has seen all the fair sex and gentlemen of the settlement. This is a favourable opportunity for the display of folly and extravagance, the ladies vying with each other who shall put their husbands or parents to the most expence, and who shall cut the most ridiculous figure, with high heads, flying feathers, jewels and silken robes. They are seldom seen before, and never visit until the candles are lighted up in the evening; and then four or five are quite sufficient at one time to fill up all the couches and chairs in any house, being obliged from the extravagant width of their bell-hoops to sit three or four yards asunder. Many of them have the weakness to affect such airs of pomp and ceremony as render their company extremely disgusting in any public place."

[1] The familiar *dhoti* of to-day.
[2] *A Narrative of the Military Operations on the Coromandel Coast*, by Captain Innes Munro, p. 52, Letter VI, April, 1780.   [3] Steward.

CHAPTER X.

THE MYSORE WARS, 1780–1799.

THE Madras Government, under Sir Thomas Rumbold in 1779, repeatedly sent warnings to the Governor-General, Warren Hastings, that an attack by Haidar Ali was imminent and that they were too weak to resist it. But Hastings was convinced that the Mysore ruler would remain friendly, and brought Rumbold round to this view before the latter sailed for England in April, 1780. As events proved, he was wrong. In June, Haidar Ali marched from Seringapatam into the Carnatic plain at the head of nearly 80,000 men, including a contingent of 400 European troops under French leadership. He sacked Porto Novo, south of Pondicherry, where he left 5,000 cavalry under his son Karim Sahib, and, marching then on Madras, reached Conjeveram, only 42 miles south-west of it.[1] At the same time he sent his eldest son, Tipu, at the head of a division, towards the Penner River, 100 miles north of Madras, to intercept a British force under Colonel William Baillie which was at Guntur on the Kistna River, still farther to the north. Madras was unprepared and the British forces were scattered in all directions. Colonel Baillie, with nearly 3,000 men, was far away in the northern Carnatic; to southward, Colonel Braithwaite, with 1,500 men, was held immobile at Pondicherry by Haidar Ali, who awaited an opportunity to take him in flank if he tried to march northwards; Colonel Cosby, with 2,000 men at Trichinopoly, still farther to the south, was threatened by the cavalry at Porto Novo; and, in Madras itself, the strength of the main body of the British army did not exceed 5,000 men. Haidar Ali saw the opportunity to crush these isolated forces in detail. He succeeded in one case, and failed in another only because luck was against him.

The Commander-in-Chief in Madras, at the time of the Mysore invasion, was Sir Hector Munro. He had earned a great reputation in Bengal as a leader in the field, but he failed to maintain it in the Carnatic. Although he decided rightly to concentrate his scattered troops, he accepted the advice of Muhammad Ali, Nawab of the Carnatic, and ordered Baillie to join the main British army at Conjeveram, an undefended town to the west of Madras, instead of at Madras itself. Braithwaite was told to move from Pondicherry on Madras, and Cosby, at distant Trichinopoly, was instructed to operate against Haidar Ali's communications. Braithwaite marched

[1] See the sketch map of Southern India and Burma at the end of this volume.

northwards as directed, risking an attack on his left flank until he cleverly seized and fortified Wandiwash on that flank before Haidar Ali could reach it, and the Mysore leader, foiled in this scheme, then retired to invest Arcot. Munro, with the main body, set out from Madras on August 26th to meet Baillie at Conjeveram, when the latter was already within 28 miles of him and could as easily have joined him in Madras.

Then Baillie made a very serious mistake. Having reached the small river Cortelaur, north-west of Madras, he camped before crossing it. On the following morning it was in flood and he was unable to cross, nor could he do so for several days. Haidar Ali, who had recalled Tipu to Arcot, saw Baillie's dilemma, and sent Tipu at once with 5,000 infantry, 6,000 cavalry and 18 guns to intercept him. The British commander, however, managed to cross the Cortelaur in time, and reached Perambakkam, west of Madras, on September 6th, where he encountered Tipu and repulsed him; but the delay had enabled Haidar Ali to interpose his whole army between the two British forces, Munro being still at Conjeveram. Except that he sent reinforcements of picked troops to Baillie, it is surprising to find that Munro did nothing during this critical period to interfere with the Mysore strategy, his excuse being that he was unable to move from Conjeveram because he had no transport for his stores.[1]

In a last attempt to join Munro at Conjeveram, Baillie marched four miles in that direction to Pollilur, but Nemesis then overtook him. He was beset and surrounded on September 10th by the whole of Haidar's army, including Tipu's division. His artillery was silenced after some tumbrils had blown up; he was charged repeatedly by cavalry and his sepoys fled in panic; and at last his British troops, with commendable steadiness, formed a square and prepared to fight to the end. They made a desperate but hopeless resistance. Of 86 British officers, 36 were killed or died of wounds, and, when the force surrendered, only 16 were unwounded of the 50 officers who became prisoners. Out of a total of more than 500 British officers and soldiers, only 200 were captured alive, and most of them were wounded, including Baillie himself. They, poor wretches, were marched in irons to Seringapatam to languish in the dungeons of the Mysore capital.

It may well be asked what Munro was doing while this tragedy was being enacted almost under his eyes. Apparently he dared not leave Conjeveram or its vicinity. He made an ineffective demonstration while Baillie was making his last stand, and, when all was over, threw his heavy guns and stores into a tank and marched to Chingleput where Cosby joined him from the south: then to Saidapet near Madras, a discredited and broken man.

[1] *A History of the British Army*, by the Hon. J. W. Fortescue, Vol. III, pp. 448 and 449.

There was little scope for military engineering in this brief and disastrous campaign. It was a war of movement—for the most part ill-conceived on the British side, and redeemed only by British heroism. Vibart writes[1] that he cannot ascertain the names of the engineer officers with Munro, but a Captain John Pringle commanded the " Guides "[2] with that force. It is recorded, however, that Captain John Theobald, of the Madras Engineers, was in command of the engineers with Baillie. As no trace of him was found after the fight, it is presumed that he fell at Pollilur. Vibart records also that a certain Ensign Brunton of the Madras Engineers was with Baillie and was taken prisoner and carried to Seringapatam where he died.[3] But the catastrophe at Pollilur infused new vigour into the reform of the Company's army, and, among other things, it helped, no doubt, towards a notable advance in military engineering, nothing less than the establishment of trained companies of Pioneers in the Madras Army, who became in time the Madras Sappers and Miners. For that reason, if for no other, the tale of Baillie's defeat should find a place in engineering history.

It happened that Lieutenant Joseph Moorhouse of the Madras Artillery, Commissary of Stores, was in charge of working parties of labourers in Fort George and elsewhere while this campaign against Mysore was in progress and found them not only inefficient but apt to " down tools " and fly on the first appearance of an enemy. These labourers were employed to supplement the temporary companies of Pioneers which were formed from time to time and broken up when no longer needed. Moorhouse brought forward a scheme for raising two regular companies of Pioneers to replace his " Momaty Men."[4] It was approved by the Select Committee, and the Government of Madras issued the following order on September 30th, 1780 :—

" The Honourable the President and Select Committee are pleased to direct that two companies of Pioneers be raised as soon as possible by the Commissary of Stores, each company consisting of 2 Sergeants, 3 Corporals, 5 Havildars,[5] 5 Naicks[6] and 100 Black Pioneers. The Havildars to be paid $3\frac{1}{2}$ Pagodas per month, the Naicks $2\frac{1}{2}$ Pagodas, and the private Pioneers to have 2 Pagodas per month.[7] . . . The Pioneers to be clothed in blue jackets, and to be armed, 50 of each

---

[1] *The Military History of the Madras Engineers*, by Major H. M. Vibart, Vol. I, p. 150.
[2] Raised by Sir Hector Munro in March, 1780. Total strength, 70 officers and men. See *Madras Consultations*, March 18th, 1780, Vol. LXIX.
[3] He is said to have been appointed in 1778, but his name does not appear in the List of Officers of the Corps of Royal Engineers, from 1660 to 1898, by Captain T. W. J. Connolly, R.E., edited by Captain R. F. Edwards (1898).
[4] *Madras Consultations*, September 28th, 1780. The Madras labourer used, and still uses, a *Momaty*, or *Mamuti*, an implement like a hoe with a large head and short handle.
[5] *Havildar*, an Indian serjeant.
[6] *Naick* or *Naik*, an Indian corporal.
[7] Equivalent to about sixpence a day.

company with light pistols, and 50 with pikes 6 feet long. When these Pioneers are raised, they are to be employed with the army to clear and mend roads, etc., instead of mamooty men, for whom no charge is then to be made."

This was the beginning of the regular private soldier of engineers in southern India,[1] and this was the birth of the famous corps now known as Queen Victoria's Own Madras Sappers and Miners. The honours and distinctions of that corps—The Carnatic, Sholinghur, Mysore, Seringapatam, Egypt, Assaye, Java, Nagpur, Ava and many others—form a sufficient tribute to its services and show that its soldiers have taken part not only in almost every campaign in southern India but in some far beyond its borders.

The formation of the first two companies of Madras Pioneers was a step in the right direction, but there were anomalies connected with it which led to much trouble. The Pioneers were under the orders of the Commander-in-Chief in Madras and were officered from the Infantry or Artillery. The officers of Engineers were under the orders of the Governor of Madras. Yet in time of war, when the Engineers might require assistance for some specific work such as a siege, the Pioneers came under their orders, and they had to work with men in whose training they had had no part. Naturally this was far from pleasing to the Engineers. Lieutenant Edward Lake, of the Madras Engineers, writing in 1825,[2] has much to say on the point. For instance, he remarks :—

"During the whole of the wars that have been hitherto carried on in India, the Company's Engineer Officers have never had a man employed under them who understood beforehand any one of the duties which he was required to execute. Now, if we were told that the Artillery of any Power consisted of a body of officers with an establishment of guns and stores, who, instead of having a permanent corps of skillful Gunners under their orders, were only supplied with men to fight their guns on the day of battle, and that they were under the necessity of teaching these men how to load and fire, and to perform all the other necessary manœuvres of Artillery, in the presence of the enemy, every military man would naturally laugh at such an arrangement as the height of absurdity. Yet, absurd as it may appear, such is a correct picture of what has hitherto been the actual state of the Engineer Department of the Company's Armies.

"The only men generally available for the duties of that Department have been the Pioneers, and it has been the hard fate of the Engineer Officers to be obliged to teach them every thing that was to be done, either when exposed to fire or at least when in the pre-

---

[1] In Bombay, a company of "Pioneer Lascars" had been raised in December, 1777, by Major Nilson, Chief Engineer.
[2] *Journals of the Sieges of the Madras Army*, by Lieutenant Edward Lake, Madras Engineers, p. 236 *et seq.*

sence of the enemy, and thus to waste those precious moments, when skill, energy, and activity were most wanted, in the irksome and laborious drudgery of superintending a multitude of little details. It is a fact that, in our sieges, the Officer of Engineers in person, has often had to teach a Pioneer how to make a gabion or a fascine, and to stand over him in the execution of the work. Even in the first and simplest operations of an irregular siege, such as the construction of a portion of a parallel, with a common battery or two, these difficulties have always been sufficient to exhaust the bodies, if they could not subdue the spirit, of the Engineer Officers. What prospect of success, therefore, could an Engineer have had in the execution of the sap under close musketry fire without Sappers, and the execution of mines without Miners ? "

The tragedy of Baillie's annihilation and Munro's disgrace roused Warren Hastings to instant and drastic action in military as well as civil affairs. He faced his enemies with dauntless courage. First he ordered General Goddard, on the Bombay side, to make peace if possible with the Marathas and thus to reduce the number of states arrayed against the British. Goddard tried to do so by advancing towards Poona, in an unfortunate attempt to overawe the Peshwa, and in this he failed. Then Hastings turned on the corrupt Government of Madras. He suspended Whitehill, the Governor, and sent the Commander-in-Chief in India, the veteran Sir Eyre Coote, from Bengal to assume personal command in the Carnatic, arming him with civil as well as military powers, and giving him every European soldier who could be spared from the north. Hastings decided rightly to hold off the Marathas by concessions and negotiations whilst he concentrated the whole of his available strength against Mysore, and, to help in the southern campaign, he sent Colonel Pearce in January, 1781, on a famous march from Bengal to Madras with a large column of all arms. Next he managed to detach two of the Maratha states—Berar and Gwalior—from alliance with Mysore, and then, through their help, pacified the remainder, concluding, with the whole confederacy, the treaty of Salbai in May, 1782.

On November 5th, 1780, Eyre Coote landed at Madras with some hastily collected troops, but he was unable to take the field at once as he found the army in great confusion. However, on January 13th, 1781, he marched towards Pondicherry at the head of 7,400 men and 50 guns, and by so doing drew Haidar Ali after him and caused him to relinquish the sieges of several British posts in the Carnatic. Coote hoped to obtain provisions at Pondicherry, but found none ; and so, in quest of food, he was drawn still farther south to Cuddalore, while his retreat, and supplies by sea, were cut off by a French squadron which had appeared before Madras. He was tied to Cuddalore, and was only saved from capitulation by the sudden disappearance of the blockading squadron. "Thus," writes Fortescue,[1] "by happy fortune the British Army and the British empire in India were saved."

The two newly-formed companies of Pioneers marched with Sir Eyre Coote and received their baptism of fire. They were commanded by officers of the line,[2] but worked under the direction of the Engineers. The Commanding Engineer was Captain Alexander Dugood, and with him were Captains James Johnston and William Gent, one subaltern and three ensigns, all of the Madras Engineers. Of these, the most noted is William Gent who rose to be a Major-General and Chief Engineer. Dugood, who was reported to be a "valuable and experienced officer," was unfortunately killed at the siege of Chittoor in 1781, but otherwise the engineers escaped lightly during the Second Mysore War.

After five months of inaction at Cuddalore, Coote heard that Haidar Ali had copious supplies at Chillumbrum, a further 26 miles to the south, so he set out to attack that fortress. Immediately, Haidar Ali occupied and fortified a position between him and Cuddalore, and the British, retiring to Porto Novo, found themselves surrounded on July 1st by the Mysore army of more than 80,000 men. There followed a brilliant action in which Coote, with only 8,000 men, attacked in échelon and inflicted a crushing defeat on Haidar Ali. Coote then moved towards Madras, and, after relieving Wandiwash, which Tipu was besieging, joined forces with the Bengal contingent under Pearce on August 2nd. Continuing northwards he reached Pollilur, the scene of Baillie's disaster in the previous September, and drove Haidar Ali from a strong position after a critical fight. Lack of transport and supplies prevented him from following up his victory, and made him so disgusted that he wrote resigning his command as a protest against keeping an army in the field which was tied to its bases of supply; but he was induced to withdraw the application because Sir Hector Munro was ill and about to sail for England. On September 21st, Coote marched again to relieve Vellore, and Haidar Ali took up a position at Sholinghur to oppose him. Attacking as usual, Coote then won a complete victory which appears among the battle honours of the Q.V.O. Madras Sappers and Miners. Skirmishes ensued in various parts of the Carnatic, and the British assaulted Chittoor, where Dugood was killed. November 22nd, however, saw the army retreating to Madras, half-starved and decimated, and the campaign of 1781 closed in torrential rain. Still, the results were good. Haidar Ali recognized Coote as his superior in battle, and began to evacuate the Carnatic preparatory to returning to Mysore.

In June of the same year, Lord Macartney had arrived in Madras as

[1] *A History of the British Army*, by the Hon. J. W. Fortescue, Vol. III, p. 456.
[2] One was commanded by a Lieutenant Innes.

Governor, bringing with him news of a state of war with Holland. He decided to capture Negapatam, the Dutch settlement in Tanjore, and also Trincomalee in Ceylon, and all the smaller Dutch settlements. Eyre Coote was against the Negapatam expedition as he was deeply involved already in the war with Mysore, but Macartney persisted and appointed Sir Hector Munro to undertake it. The siege of Negapatam began on October 21st and was pushed with vigour. Major Thomas Geils, of the Madras Engineers,[1] who was the Chief Engineer, had under his orders a detachment of the Madras Pioneers. The Dutch made a spirited resistance, but surrendered on November 11th, 1781. News of this event caused great rejoicing in England and was hailed by a general salute of all the guns of the new Fort William in Bengal. Munro then set about demolishing the fortifications of the Dutch stronghold. At the close of 1782 this work was far advanced, under the direction of Captain James Johnston, and it was completed by March, 1783.

Geils left Negapatam soon after the place surrendered to join a naval expedition under Admiral Hughes[2] against Trincomalee. When Hughes invited the Dutch Governor of that settlement to surrender, the summons was entrusted to Geils, who landed and delivered it but was not blindfolded. Vibart writes[3] that Geils reported on his return that Trincomalee might be taken by assault, but that it would be well to send a second summons by him in order that he might be more exact in his observations on the defences! This was done, and, as the Governor still refused to capitulate, Trincomalee was assaulted and captured on January 11th, 1782.[4] Coupled with the loss of Negapatam and Trincomalee, the fall of the minor Dutch settlements in India then completed the discomfiture of Holland.

But the British had soon to face a disaster comparable with that of Baillie at Pollilur. While Coote was defeating Haidar Ali, Tipu, with an army of 20,000 horse and foot and 400 Frenchmen, entered Tanjore and surrounded a detachment of nearly 2,000 men under Colonel Braithwaite. The British commander tried to retreat to Negapatam but failed, and, after 26 hours of desperate fighting, was compelled to surrender on February 18th, 1782. Every British officer present, except one, was either killed or wounded, and the survivors, including Braithwaite, were sent to Seringapatam to join the remnants of Baillie's detachment in captivity. Geils had been for a time the engineer with Braithwaite's force, but, luckily for him,

---

[1] He reverted later to the Artillery.

[2] The doughty opponent of the French Admiral Suffren in many a bloody sea fight during the Second Mysore War.

[3] *The Military History of the Madras Engineers and Pioneers*, by Major H. M. Vibart, Vol. I, p. 165.

[4] The company of Pioneers at Negapatam, under Lieutenant Abbott, reinforced by volunteers from the 9th and 23rd Native Battalions, embarked about January 1st, 1782, for service in Ceylon and were present at this siege.

had been detached for duty with the expedition to Ceylon, so he escaped the fate of the remainder. Even more fortunate was Lieutenant Charles Salmon, of the Madras Engineers, who was actually on his way to join Braithwaite, and quite close to him, when the detachment was surrounded. The capture of this force greatly encouraged Tipu, and when French troops arrived in March to reinforce him at Porto Novo, he marched at once to Cuddalore and wrested it from the Company.[1]

The remainder of the Second Mysore War was occupied with manœuvre and counter-manœuvre, small battles in various parts, a campaign by General Mathews on the west coast which began well and ended badly after a surrender to Tipu at Bednore, and a hard tussle with the French in front of Cuddalore. At Cuddalore we find Colonel Patrick Ross again as Chief Engineer under General Stuart.[2] He had reached India in May, 1782, 14 months after leaving England, having accompanied an expedition to attack the Dutch possessions at the Cape of Good Hope. Haidar Ali was then growing old and had been for some time in declining health, and so it happened that, on December 7th, 1782, news reached Tipu that Haidar had died and that he, Tipu, had become Nawab of Mysore. Eyre Coote did not long survive his noted enemy, for he succumbed on April 26th, 1785, and by his death Major-General Stuart was left as Commander-in-Chief to oppose Mysore and the French. Mangalore fell to Tipu after a gallant defence by Colonel Campbell, and peace was concluded on March 11th, 1784. So ended a long struggle against Mysore, which nearly cost England the possession of India. Victory in the Carnatic was followed by defeat in the south-west; and the net result was a stalemate which was bound to lead to renewed hostilities.

Although the engineering operations of the Second Mysore War were of no great importance, the campaign certainly brought about a clearer recognition of the value of engineers with an army, and more particularly of engineering units of trained men. It seems that the Corps of Madras Engineers was adequately staffed in 1782, for, in addition to Colonel Patrick Ross, it included Majors Maule and Geils, Captains Johnston, Banks, Byres, Gent and Prescott, three subalterns and ten ensigns.[3] Colonel Fullarton, however, who commanded in a campaign in the extreme south towards the close of the war, was not satisfied and reported to headquarters that "it is further extremely requisite that your establishment of pioneers should be increased, not only for expertness and despatch in the preparation of a siege, but to facilitate the rapid movement of your

---

[1] *Madras Consultations*, April 6th and 8th, 1782, Vol. LXXIX.
[2] A detachment of Pioneers, 284 strong, served at Cuddalore under Lieutenant Mitchell.
[3] *The Military History of the Madras Engineers and Pioneers*, by Major H. M. Vibart, Vol. I, p. 182.

G

armies. Hyder seldom maintained less than 5,000 pioneers. The next material object is the Department of Engineers, including not only preparations for besieging, but also the defensive condition of your forts. You have a respectable corps of engineers under an officer distinguished for his talents of arrangements—Lieutenant-Colonel Ross." This and other representations had their due effect in the course of the next 20 years. The fortress engineer became the field engineer with trained men to carry out his orders.

Madras was exhausted after the war against Mysore, and no serious military operations were undertaken until renewed hostilities against that state became inevitable at the end of 1789; but, during this lull, some political and military changes occurred which should be mentioned. Warren Hastings left India in February, 1785, to stand his trial in England, and was succeeded, as Governor-General, first by Sir John Macpherson and then, in 1796, by Lord Cornwallis, the soldier who, only five years before, had surrendered at Yorktown and so assured the independence of the United States. In Madras, on April 6th, 1786, that famous military engineer, Major-General Sir Archibald Campbell, K.B., became Governor and Commander-in-Chief. Throughout his term of office the country had a rest from the devastating wars of Macartney's time, and so he devoted himself to the development of peaceful institutions. He founded a Military Board which absorbed the duties of the Committee of Works, a Hospital Board, a Board of Revenue and a Board of Trade; he reorganized the Police, established an Exchange and a Bank, built an Astronomical Observatory and constituted an Orphan Asylum. In fact, there was hardly a department of the civil administration in which he did not labour to secure improvement and order, and Madras sustained a serious loss when, overcome by illness, he was forced to leave India in February, 1789, only to die two years later at the early age of 52. It may be said of Campbell that he was the most brilliant of the engineers who served in India during the eighteenth century.

The political events which led up to the Third Mysore War are outside the scope of this narrative, but history shows that the pretext on which the Company declared war against Tipu Sultan was his invasion of Travancore at the end of 1789, that state being nominally under British protection. Accordingly, in May, 1790, Major-General William Medows, then Governor and Commander-in-Chief at Madras, began operations against Tipu in the districts of Coimbatore and Dindigul with Major Maule as his Chief Engineer in the field. The results of this campaign, however, were so poor that Lord Cornwallis decided to come to Madras to assume command in person as soon as he had arranged for the co-operation of the Marathas and Hyderabad on the British side, and he landed at Fort St. George on December 12th, 1790, to begin his thrust at Mysore. His troops were better organized than in the previous war, his engineers were more experienced, and the establishment of Pioneers had been increased to five companies.

Cornwallis decided that, based on Madras, he would invade Mysore from the north-east and capture Bangalore which was said to be the strongest fortress in Tipu's domains: then he would strike at Seringapatam, his final objective. In these operations he counted on the help of a Bombay army under Sir Robert Abercromby advancing from Tellicherry on the west coast, and also on the assistance of Hyderabad and the Marathas, whose rulers had agreed to invade Mysore from the north. It was to be a converging movement on exterior lines, and, like all such operations, was dependent for success on exact timing and perfect organization. These could hardly be expected in a country such as India before the days of telegraphy and trained staffs, and particularly when two of the converging forces were native armies. However, it was a great attempt, and, by clever feints, Cornwallis reached Bangalore unhindered, through the Mugli Pass, in the early days of March, 1791. Tipu had been watching the southern passes, but he turned at once on the invader, and Cornwallis then had the unenviable task of laying siege to a strong fortress in the presence of a superior force when he was unprotected by a covering army. He was liable, in fact, to be stabbed in the back while engaging the enemy in front.

Colonel Patrick Ross was not present at the siege of Bangalore as his duties called him elsewhere, so Major George Maule became Chief Engineer with the force, assisted by Captain Charles Ogg, Lieutenants Norris, Lennon and Colin Mackenzie, and five ensigns among whom was young Caldwell who became afterwards General Sir James Caldwell, G.C.B. There were two detachments of Madras Pioneers with the army, one under Lennon and the other under Lieutenant Dowse of the Infantry, and these regular units were assisted by a small corps of European Pioneers raised for temporary duty from British battalions. The Engineer officers who marched with Cornwallis adopted naturally the manners and customs of their brother officers. When all was going well they moved in leisurely state, and, to appreciate what that implies, we cannot do better than listen to Innes Munro on the subject,[1] making some allowance for the fact that the luxuries of travel may have decreased somewhat during the ten years which had elapsed since he wrote:—

" The preparations for war carry nothing hostile in their appearance, ease and comfort being far more studied upon these occasions than dispatch. It would be absurd for a captain to think of taking the field without being attended by the following enormous retinue, viz, a dubash, cook and boy; and as in these times bullocks

---

[1] *A Narrative of the Military Operations on the Coromandel Coast,* by Captain Innes Munro, Letter XIII, p. 186 *et seq.*

are not to be had, he must assemble fifteen or twenty coolies to carry his baggage, who, with an horse-keeper and grass-cutter, and sometimes a dulcinea and her servants, complete his train, having occasionally the assistance of a barber, washerman, and ironer in common with the other officers of his regiment. It might be thought improper, on such occasions as that of taking the field, to allow a captain a palanquin, although I have known many of them permitted to enjoy this luxury at very important seasons, which of course must add nine bearers to his suite. His tent is furnished with a good large bed, mattress, pillows, etc., a few camp stools and chairs, a folding table, a pair of shades for his candles, and six or seven trunks with table equipage; his stock of linens (at least twenty-four suits); some dozens of wine, brandy and gin; tea, sugar and biscuit; an hamper of live poultry, and his milch goat."

Bangalore, like Madras, had a fort, with a *pettah*, or fortified town, outside it. This lay-out was a feature of almost all the cities or settlements in India, the fort providing a place of refuge for most of the inhabitants if the *pettah* was in danger of capture. The fort at Bangalore had a perimeter of about one mile; it was of solid masonry, surrounded by a wide ditch which was commanded from 26 towers placed at intervals along the ramparts. To its north lay the *pettah*, several miles in circumference and protected by an indifferent rampart, a deep belt of thorn and cactus, and a small ditch. Altogether Bangalore was not a place which invited attack. But Cornwallis had no choice in the matter. To advance on Seringapatam he must mask or capture Bangalore. His army was too weak to mask it, therefore he must capture it. Like the French before Madras in 1758, he decided to attack the *pettah* as a preliminary operation, and, with this object, sent Maule and other engineers to reconnoitre the position on March 6th. Their report being favourable, he attacked on the following morning and captured the town while the defenders retreated to the fort. An attempt by Tipu to recover the town was defeated with heavy loss to his army.

Maule and his officers then began their siege works for an attack on Bangalore Fort. These progressed steadily, interrupted only on March 17th when Tipu attempted to interfere. The situation was peculiar. As Fortescue remarks,[1] " the besiegers, as at Delhi two generations later, were themselves in a fashion besieged, for the garrison opposed to them was constantly relieved, while the whole of the enemy's field-force lay in constant menace before them." The British guns made a breach in the walls on the 18th, and two days later, it was wide enough for an assault. The Engineers were as busy as the Gunners, for they had reached the crest of the glacis by sapping from the nearest battery. In 12 days Maule had established eight

[1] *A History of the British Army*, by the Hon. J. W. Fortescue, Vol. III, p. 577.

COLONEL COLIN MACKENZIE, C.B., F.R.S.

batteries, dug several parallels, and had driven a sap to the edge of the great ditch.

Tipu was fully aware of the intended assault; but preferring to wait with two corps to take it in flank after it was launched, he moved after dark on March 21st to within one and a half miles of the Mysore Gate. The situation then appeared so serious to Cornwallis that he resolved to storm the fort at once, hoping that his men would be able to cross the ditch by a narrow causeway. At eleven o'clock, the leading troops crept forward in perfect silence, and with them Lieutenant Colin Mackenzie[1] of the Madras Sappers; they crossed the ditch with scaling ladders, mounted the breach and entered the fort, while behind them the batteries kept up a heavy fire with blank ammunition. The main body of stormers then rushed in, and after a hand-to-hand fight in which the enemy lost 1,000 killed, the fort was in Cornwallis's hands. On the British side, the Pioneers, always in the van, lost more men in proportion to their strength than any unit except the 52nd. They proved their worth in a bloody fight.

Leaving a garrison in Bangalore, Cornwallis then marched northwards, and, three weeks later, effected a junction with a corps of 10,000 cavalry from Hyderabad and some reinforcements from Madras. Meanwhile Abercromby, with his army of nine battalions from Bombay, had ascended the "ghauts"[2] from Tellicherry, and, by May 15th, lay only 40 miles west of Seringapatam, awaiting orders for the final advance. He waited in vain. Tipu was devastating the country in all directions, and Cornwallis, in dire straits through lack of transport and threatened by starvation, could barely move. So bad was the situation that women and boys were bribed to carry cannon balls, and each British officer undertook to carry a few on his charger. Finally, when the heavy guns had to be dragged by the exhausted troops and the army was almost within sight of Seringapatam, Cornwallis was forced to admit failure, and, after ordering Abercromby to retire to Malabar, destroyed the whole of his battering-train and heavy equipment which he could move no farther; then "fasting, dispirited, and chilled by bleak wind and drizzling rain, the army crept away in misery to the northward."[3] By the irony of fate Cornwallis met the Maratha army on May 28th soon after he began his retreat, but this addition to his strength was too late to help him; without heavy guns to batter down the gigantic bastions of Seringapatam he was powerless. He could do no more than continue his retirement to Bangalore.

Foiled in his thrust at the capital, Cornwallis turned to less

---

[1] Afterwards Colonel Colin Mackenzie, C.B., F.R.S., whose portrait is in the Royal Engineers Officers' Mess at Chatham, and is reproduced in this chapter. He served with distinction in the Mysore wars, in Ceylon and in Java, became Surveyor-General of India in 1816, and died near Calcutta in 1821. He was the founder of archæology in India, and a great collector of antiquities.

[2] Range of mountains.

[3] *A History of the British Army*, by the Hon. J. W. Fortescue, Vol. III, p. 585.

ambitious, but, to his engineers, most enthralling, operations. Thirty-six miles to the north of Bangalore lay the mighty stronghold of Nandidroog, three miles in circumference and towering on a mountain of granite 2,000 feet above the surrounding country. The precipices were said to be unscalable except on one side, and there the entrance to the fort was barred by formidable walls and an outwork to cover the gateway. Yet Nandidroog was captured. The Gunners, assisted probably by Colin Mackenzie[1] and the Pioneers, accomplished this amazing feat, for the credit should go to them rather than to the assaulting troops who climbed into this eagle's nest. On October 2nd, 1791, they hauled six[2] guns to the top of an adjoining hill by drag-ropes made fast to posts and trees, and opened fire on the 4th. To this attack was added another on the mountain side itself where eight guns were dragged up to within 500 yards of the walls by harnessing two elephants to each gun and using crowds of men on ropes. A breach resulted, and, on October 18th, the fortress which had defied Haidar Ali himself for three years, was wrested from his son Tipu in three weeks. The operations were a triumph of engineering and gunnery, and called forth unstinted praise from the Commander-in-Chief who tendered his best thanks to Mackenzie for his " skill and indefatigable industry," adding that " although the services of the Pioneers are less brilliant[3] than those of the troops, they are of peculiar value in such operations."

The scene shifts from Nandidroog, 20 miles north of Bangalore, to Savandroog, the " Rock of Death," some 30 miles west of it. Here Patrick Ross was sent to direct the engineering work in person. He was confronted by a fortress crowning a mountain of granite at least eight miles in circumference, which towered above a wide belt of malarial jungle. The fort on this gigantic *massif* was in two parts separated by a yawning chasm, and the whole mountain was girdled by a lower tier of ramparts. The attacking force, under Lieutenant-Colonel Stuart, advanced on December 10th, 1791, accompanied by Ross and a division of Pioneers under Dowse of the Infantry. With incredible labour they hacked a road through a dense jungle of bamboos and over rocky hills, while behind them the troops hauled the battering-train of heavy guns to its position. The obstacles were so great that some days elapsed before five 18-pounders and three 12-pounders could open fire at about 800 yards' range, and even then the guns had to be elevated to 23° and could do little damage to the massive ramparts far above them. Other guns, however, were hauled up higher, and these made a breach through which the stormers poured on December 21st while the band of the 52nd played

---

[1] Mackenzie was the senior Engineer with the force. Under him were Ensigns James Caldwell and William Farquhar of the Madras Engineers, and Ensign Joseph Stokoe of the Bengal Engineers.
[2] Two 24-pounders, two 18-pounders and two 12-pounders.
[3] Presumably he meant " conspicuous."

CORNWALLIS BESIEGES SERINGAPATAM. 167

"Britons, strike Home." Thus Savandroog fell after 12 days of strenuous battle against natural obstacles rather than the troops of Mysore. Again the Engineers and Pioneers had justified their existence, and their work drew from Lord Cornwallis an order complimenting Colonel Ross on his achievement. Soon afterwards, the capture of the even more precipitous Ootradroog deprived Tipu of the last of the more important mountain strongholds, and all was ready for another attempt on Seringapatam.

On January 22nd, 1792, Major-General Robert Abercromby,[1] with 9,000 men, set out again from the western mountains towards Mysore, and, three days later, Cornwallis's army of 22,000 men combined at Savandroog with 18,000 horsemen from Hyderabad to form the main thrust at the capital. Major John Conrad Sartorius, of the Bombay Engineers, was the Chief Engineer of the western army under Abercromby, and under Cornwallis was the redoubtable Patrick Ross, with Colin Mackenzie as his Aide-de-Camp and a staff of 5 subalterns and five Ensigns of the Madras Engineers. Sartorius had five Bombay Engineers, and there were present also five Bengal Engineers under Captain Alexander Kyd[2]—a respectable total of 24 Engineer officers in all. The Pioneers were formed into three divisions, led respectively by Lieutenant Lennon, Madras Engineers, Lieutenant Dowse, Madras Infantry, and Ensign Stokoe, Bengal Engineers. At the head of their armies, now well equipped and thirsting for vengeance, Cornwallis and Abercromby converged on Seringapatam where the Mysore army awaited them.

The island of Seringapatam, in the Cauvery River, is four miles long by one and a half miles broad at the middle, whence it falls in height to both ends. At the west, or upstream, end in 1792 was a quadrangular fort stretching eastwards for a mile, while at the east end, separated from the fort by broken ground and many buildings, was the *pettah*, or town, and the Lal Bagh where Tipu had built a new palace amid beautiful gardens. On the left, or north, bank of the river—the bank towards which Cornwallis advanced—the most formidable obstacle was a "Bound Hedge" of thorny shrubs, defended by a number of redoubts on small hills. Of the redoubts, the most important were the Eadgah (Idgah) or Mosque Redoubt within the hedge on the west flank, and an unfinished work on Carighaut (Karighatta) Hill outside the other flank. The river, though fordable in places, had a rocky and uneven bottom and a rapid current.[3]

Details of the attack have been recorded fully by many historians. It must suffice to say here that Cornwallis advanced in three columns,

---
[1] He was a younger brother of the celebrated Sir Ralph Abercromby, who fell in Egypt in 1801.
[2] Captain Alexander Kyd, B.E., became Surveyor-General with the army before Seringapatam.
[3] A plan of Seringapatam in 1792, by Captain Kyd, Surveyor-General, is included for reference.

the right under General Medows, the centre under his own command, and the left under Lieutenant-Colonel Maxwell. To each column was allotted some Engineer officers and a division of Pioneers with scaling ladders. After dark on February 6th, 1792, under the light of a rising moon, the columns moved off. Maxwell, on the left, soon captured the Carighaut Hill, and, pushing across a stream, entered the enemy's camp within the Bound Hedge. Cornwallis, with the centre column, also did his part. The head of this column struck through the middle of the camp, chased the enemy through the northern channel of the Cauvery and almost captured Tipu ; but the leading troops then lost touch with the remainder, and their blow lost its force. Unfortunately the general plan of attack was upset by the right column under Medows which, through a mistake in an order, was led to assault the Eadgah or Mosque Redoubt instead of masking it and pushing on to keep in touch with Cornwallis in the advance to the island. The delay was fatal. Medows, when free to resume his advance, wandered as far eastwards as Carighaut Hill in a vain attempt to find the centre column, and nearly one-half of the British force was thus out of the fight. In the attack on the Eadgah Redoubt fell Lieutenant Patrick Stewart of the Bengal Engineers, who was killed while gallantly pressing forward to the ditch at the head of a body of Lascars with scaling ladders.

It was not till four o'clock in the morning that Cornwallis at last found Medows near Carighaut Hill, and by that time the advantage of an attack under cover of complete darkness had passed. The British forces were revealed to Tipu, scattered about the island and across the river, and he proceeded to counter-attack them where success seemed probable. In these ventures, however, he failed, and, when the sun was up and Cornwallis had crossed to the island, there was not a Mysore soldier to be seen outside the walls of the fort. Cornwallis divided the island with Tipu : the one in the *pettah*, the other in the fort. The attempt to capture Seringapatam by a *coup de main* had failed, although a crushing defeat, with great loss, had been inflicted on the Mysore army. Nothing then remained but to begin preparations for a regular siege in which the Bombay army, which had arrived on February 16th, was ready to take its part. The Engineers and Pioneers had already prepared large numbers of gabions, fascines and piquets, and the troops were eager to fight.

The first idea was to attack the east face of the fort by approaches from the Daulat Bagh towards the north-east angle ; but Ross, after reconnoitring the north side, recommended instead that the attack should be launched across the branch of the river against the north face because its curtain was weak and damaged, the flanking defences poor, the ditch dry, and the interior commanded from across the river. It seemed possible also, by repairing a dam, to divert the water of the northern branch of the Cauvery into the southern

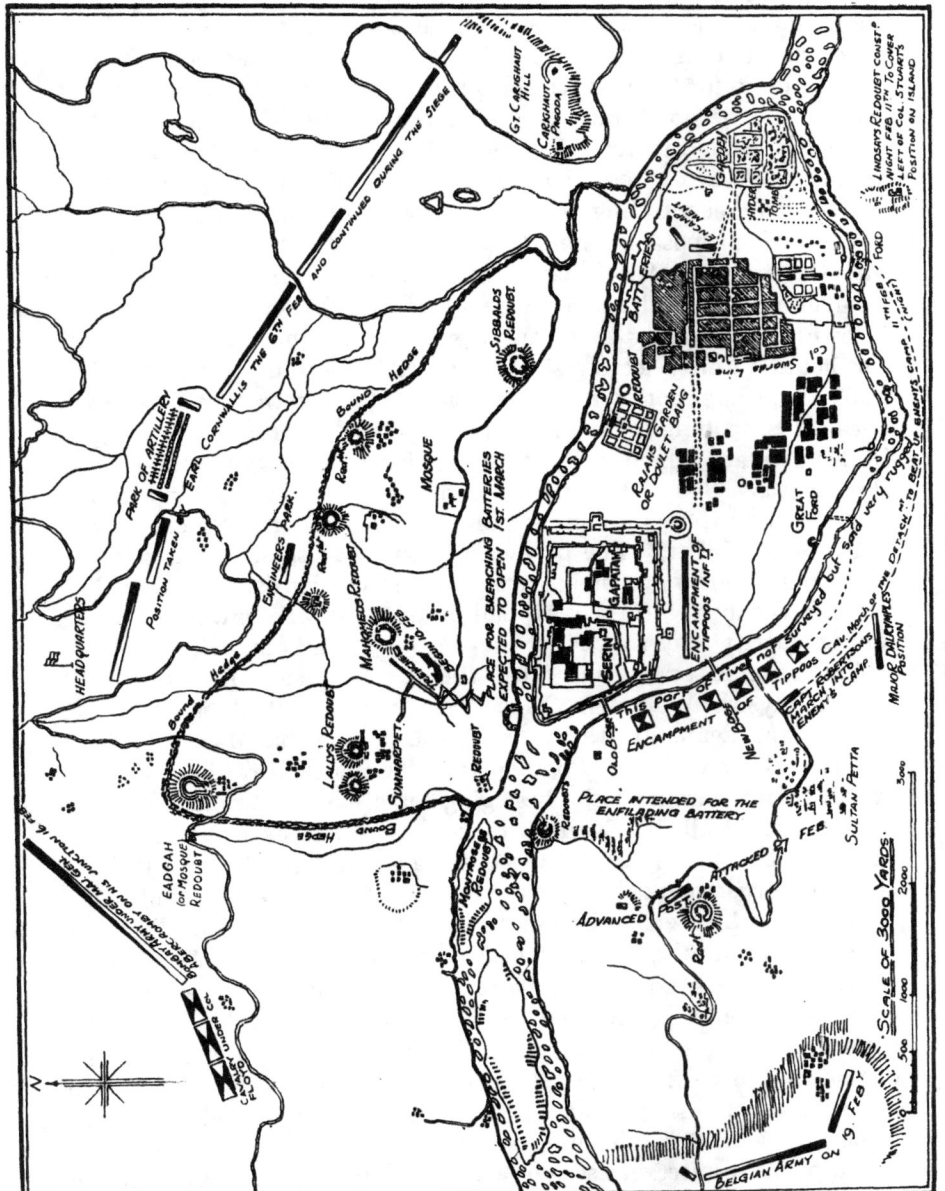

SERINGAPATAM, 1792.

From a Plan drawn by Capt. Kyd, Surveyor General with the Army.

channel and thus to secure a dry crossing. His plan having been accepted, an Engineers' Park[1] was established near the Bound Hedge, and the European and Indian Pioneers were placed, as a Corps, under the orders of the Chief Engineer for the period of the siege and rated as a distinct unit. The Engineers then proceeded to break ground for the first parallel on February 19th within breaching distance of the north face, and for a second, two days later, within 600 yards, while Lieutenant-Colonel Stuart strengthened a line which he had taken up across the middle of the island. Tipu, however, was already negotiating for peace, and Cornwallis had agreed to consider his proposals although he would not allow them to interfere with the progress of the siege. In a last effort, the defenders made a sortie on the 22nd and were repulsed with heavy loss, so, on the following day, noting that the Engineers had finished their second parallel and were selecting sites for batteries within 500 yards of the walls, Tipu abandoned hope and accepted the terms laid down by Cornwallis, sending in, at the same time, two of his sons as hostages. Under a treaty which was signed on March 19th, 1792, one-half of Mysore was ceded to the British and their allies, and an indemnity of more than three millions sterling was demanded. So ended the Third Mysore War. The power of Mysore was shaken, but not yet shattered. One more trial of arms against the British was needed to lay it in the dust. Haidar Ali had brought his kingdom to greatness and prosperity: his son, Tipu, was destined to accomplish its ruin.

A few small operations filled the gap between the Third and Fourth Mysore Wars. In June, 1793, news reached Madras that France was again at war with England, and the Madras Council decided to recapture Pondicherry. Colonel Braithwaite was appointed to command the besieging force, and recommended, as a first step, that all the Engineer officers, with two exceptions, should be ordered to assemble for the siege; also that the "very useful" Pioneer Corps should be increased from 450 to 600 men under the command of Lieutenant Dowse.[2] Two parties of European Pioneers were recruited also from the European Battalion. As Colonel Patrick Ross had gone to England after the Third Mysore War, the duties of Chief Engineer fell to Lieutenant-Colonel George Maule, assisted by almost all the Madras Engineers and by six temporary engineers drafted from the Artillery and Infantry. There is little to record about the siege of Pondicherry in 1793. It lasted only three weeks and ended in unconditional surrender on August 24th; but unhappily it resulted in a serious loss to the Madras Engineers through the death of Colonel Maule who was killed by a cannon ball on August 15th. Captain Elisha Trapaud then acted as Chief Engineer for the

---

[1] A depot for the equipment of tools, stores, etc., for the siege.
[2] On July 11th, 1793, the increase was sanctioned. The Pioneers were then recognized as a Corps and were formed into six companies with 5 British officers and 648 Indian officers and "other ranks."

remainder of the siege as Major William Gent was on the sick list. By September 2nd the Pioneers had levelled the French trenches and battery positions; and, by the middle of 1794, Dowse and his Pioneers, with 3,000 labourers, had completed the demolitions. The ditch had then been filled in, and the ramparts levelled " so that a body of horse might charge into the place." As a military base, Pondicherry ceased to exist.[1]

In July, 1795, an expedition under Colonel James Stuart was despatched against the Dutch settlements in Ceylon, since England and Holland were again at war. Two companies of Pioneers sailed with the force, and were joined later by two more. Six officers of the Madras Engineers, under Captain John Norris, accompanied the expedition, among them being Lieutenants Colin Mackenzie and Thomas Fiott de Havilland, both of whom did notable work in later years. Stuart captured Trincomalee without much difficulty, and, on January 15th, 1796, took Colombo. It was at the siege of Colombo that Mackenzie, as Chief Engineer, was disgusted to see his carefully-prepared fascines and gabions served out to the troops as firewood because the Dutch resistance did not materialize. In 1795, also, a small expedition sailed to the Malay Peninsula, with Lieutenant William Farquhar[2] as Chief Engineer, assisted by one company of Pioneers. The British took Malacca and Amboyna, and occupied the Spice Islands until peace was concluded with Holland in 1802. With an expedition under General Craig in 1797, against Manilla in the Philippine Islands, we find Captain Colin Mackenzie as Chief Engineer with 300 Pioneers, and he was present in Hyderabad in the following year when a British force compelled a contingent of 13,000 French troops in the service of the Nizam to lay down their arms and disband. These were some of the small operations which filled the interval of seven years preceding the outbreak of the final war against Tipu Sultan; but, in that interval, the Madras Engineers and Pioneers were adding steadily to their reputation by useful work in India and overseas, and to such purpose that, when the last Mysore War began in 1799, the combatant establishment of the Madras Pioneers was increased to ten companies, with five British officers, eleven British non-commissioned officers, and nearly 1,100 Indian officers and men[3]—a most useful adjunct to any army though still insufficiently officered and deficient in military training.

It should be recorded here that Lieutenant-General George Harris[4] arrived in March, 1797, as Commander-in-Chief at Madras, and, in

---

[1] It was restored, however, to the French on the conclusion of peace.
[2] He rose to be a Major-General and distinguished himself in later campaigns.
[3] Captains 2   Serjeant-Major... 1   Naicks ... 30
    Captain-Lieutenant ... 1   Serjeant ... 10   Privates ... 1000
    Lieutenant 1   Jemadars ... 11   Pakhalis ... 10
    Assistant Surgeon ... 1   Havildars ... 30
[4] He became Lord Harris of Seringapatam and Mysore in 1815.

1798, the Earl of Mornington,[1] the new Governor-General, touched there on his voyage to Calcutta. Learning that Tipu had been promised help, not only from the French Governor of Mauritius, but from Napoleon himself who was smarting under his defeat at the battle of the Nile, Lord Mornington decided to take the initiative and ordered General Harris to mobilize his army and select a base for an invasion of Mysore in co-operation with a Bombay army advancing from the west coast and another from Hyderabad State whose assistance he had secured. For the moment, the Marathas remained neutral. Harris, however, was faced by grave difficulties of transport, an empty treasury, and a scattered army. He found that he would require 20,000 bullocks, and, as these could not be collected for some time, he was obliged to postpone his advance, although he began to concentrate gradually at Vellore and Walajabad near Madras.

Early in February, 1799, Harris started with the Madras, or "Grand" Army, marching from Vellore on the 11th and joining hands with the Hyderabad army of 16,000 men at Ambur (Amboor) nine days later. He was then at the head of 31,000 fighting men, including 6,000 British cavalry and infantry, and he had also a force of 6,000 cavalry from Hyderabad. He expected the Bombay army of 6,000 men under Lieutenant-General James Stuart to join him before Seringapatam, and that expedition duly marched from Cannanore on February 21st and, by March 2nd, was near Periapatam (Peripatam), 50 miles west of the Mysore capital. The Hyderabad army, though nominally under Mir Alam, was virtually directed by Colonel Arthur Wellesley, so that its co-operation was not likely to be limited to gestures alone. Possessing the districts of Baramahal and Coimbatore, which had been shorn from Mysore by the previous war, Harris could rely on collecting supplies during his march if he could get sufficient transport to carry them. The crux of the problem was transport.

Weighed down by the paraphernalia of his army, Harris advanced slowly in a hollow formation with his transport in the middle. The space enclosed by his marching troops—some seven miles long and two miles wide—swarmed with an incredible multitude of men and beasts. There were 60,000 bullocks, mostly pack animals, for the baggage and stores, and another 20,000 for grain; a further 36,000 bullocks for the Nizam's army, and a rabble of followers, coolies, elephants and camels. The migration of this horde is well described by a Madras Engineer, Ensign George Rowley.[2] "The marches of an Indian army," he writes, "are so impeded by the cumbrous train of baggage which necessity, as well as luxury, induces it to transport,

[1] Richard Colley Wellesley, elder brother of Arthur Wellesley who became the Duke of Wellington.
[2] *Journal of the Second Siege of Seringapatam*, by Ensign G. Rowley, M.E., p. 121, appearing in the *Professional Papers of the Madras Engineers*, Vol. IV, 1856.

that it will find more difficulty in making a march of ten miles than a light European army in performing one of twenty miles. In India, every supply must be conveyed by the invading army. The Bazar or market of General Harris' army equalled, in extent and variety of articles exposed for sale, that of a populous city. The followers of the Army are so numerous that on a moderate calculation they may be considered to exceed the number of fighting men in the proportion of *five to one*. The appearance of our Army on the march is truly surprising. It may be compared with the emigration of the Israelites from Egypt : the surrounding plains and downs appear to be in motion."

Patrick Ross, now a Major-General, was too busy at Madras to march with Harris, so the appointment of Chief Engineer in the field fell to Colonel William Gent with Captain John Norris as his Aide-de-Camp. Captain Colin Mackenzie, and Ensigns Rowley and Garrard, were with the Nizam's contingent, and the Pioneers were under Captain Dowse as usual. Many Engineers joined the Grand Army during the march or while the siege was in progress : among these were Major Elisha Trapaud, Captain George Johnstone (soon to be court-martialled and cashiered), Captain-Lieutenants James Caldwell and John Blair, four Lieutenants and five Ensigns, all of the Madras Engineers. With the Bombay army were Colonel John Sartorius as Chief Engineer, and Captain-Lieutenant John Johnson, both of the Bombay Engineers. There do not seem to have been any Bengal Engineers with either army.

As in 1792, the army had a Surveyor-General, Major (afterwards Major-General) Alexander Beatson,[1] an infantry officer whose achievements were so remarkable that they deserve more than passing notice. Here was a born engineer who was never admitted to the Corps. Beatson arrived in Madras as an infantry cadet in 1776, and, by serving with the Engineers under Colonel Patrick Ross for more than two years, acquired some knowledge of engineering. Though he wished to join the Madras Engineers, there was no vacancy for him, so he became a Quartermaster of Brigade. Because of the heavy casualties among the Engineers at the siege of Pondicherry in 1778, Sir Hector Munro proposed that Beatson should be sent to Masulipatam as Superintending Engineer with the rank of Acting-Lieutenant of Engineers, so, though still an infantryman, he became the Engineer of Masulipatam and held the post till 1782. Then he was replaced by a young Captain of Engineers from England, and was so disgusted with his treatment that he reverted to infantry work and abandoned engineering. A few years later, we find him as senior Captain of the Corps of Guides which was raised under Major Pringle in 1787, and, as a Guide, he explored the whole of the Carnatic

---

[1] Author of *A View of the Origin and Conduct of the War with Tipoo Sultaun* (1800), and other works.

and got to know more than 60 passes and defiles leading into it. His trigonometrical surveys extended from the Godavari to Tuticorin, and included a great part of Mysore. This was the man who led Cornwallis's army through the Mugli Pass in February, 1791; whose reports induced Cornwallis to alter his whole plan of attack on Bangalore and so brought speedy success to the British arms; and who, at Savandroog, is said to have advocated an attack when the Engineers were against it, and to have virtually superintended and directed the siege. It was Beatson who guided the Right Column in the assault on Seringapatam in 1792, and protested against the mistaken order which led that column astray. And it was Beatson again, who, when summoned to Calcutta by Lord Mornington in August, 1798, so impressed the Governor-General with his knowledge of Mysore, that he kept him as an Aide-de-Camp and, in the following year, sent him with General Harris in the nominal appointment of Surveyor-General but with the actual purpose that he should assist and advise the Engineers in the final attack on Seringapatam. The important part which he took in the Council of War at that place will soon appear. He seems to have been the moving spirit in its deliberations, and to have been chiefly responsible for the selection of the point of attack.[1]

On March 15th, 1799, General Harris was close to Bangalore, and, on the 21st, he was at Karkanalli (Cancanhilly) having met with little resistance and no difficulties beyond those of transport. Meanwhile Tipu, with considerable strategical insight, struck at the weaker force, the Bombay army, waylaying it near Periapatam with a picked force of 12,000 men. There, on March 6th, General Stuart fought and won the critical action of Sidasir (Sedaseer). Defeated in this venture, Tipu then hastened back to check the Grand Army which he encountered on March 27th at Malavalli (Mallavelly). He attacked it with great fury but little success, and, in the end, was forced to retire. An easy way to the capital now lay open to Harris along the high road from Malavalli to Seringapatam on the northern bank of the Cauvery, a way which Tipu fully expected him to take. But Harris outwitted him. He crossed the river at Sosili and marched along the southern bank, through an area which had not been cleared of supplies, and where he could join hands easily with Stuart. It was masterly strategy, and brought him on April 5th to a strong position two miles from the western face of Seringapatam.

The first operation of the Madras army at Seringapatam was to dislodge the enemy's outposts from the Sultanpettah Tope (wood) on the right front, and from the banks of a channel, called the " Aqueduct," which ran across the front. This was accomplished on the 6th, and the Engineers and Pioneers then fortified the line

---

[1] *East India Military Calendar* (1826), Vol. II, p. 375 *et seq.*

of the aqueduct and strengthened two posts on the flanks, known as the Sultanpettah Post on the right and Shawe's Post on the left; they busied themselves also in preparing materials for the siege. On April 9th, Gent was ordered to prepare alternative plans for an attack. He could assume, if necessary, that the British army lay astride the Cauvery, and was instructed that, allowing that assumption, one scheme should include seizing part of the island as a preliminary to the assault on the fort itself, while the other should provide for an attack without a footing on the island. Four days later, Gent submitted two plans. In the first he proposed to attack the north-west angle—the sharp upstream point—by the joint operations of two forces, one on the north bank and the other on the south bank of the Cauvery; in the second, assuming that the British had already taken part of the island, he advised an attack on the south-west angle near the bridge.[1] It is instructive to note that the preparation of a general plan of attack on a fortress was still the province of the Chief Engineer alone, and not of the Commander-in-Chief and his staff, advised by the Chief Engineer.

There was much divergence of opinion about the point to be selected for attack, and, according to the *East India Military Calendar*,[2] Beatson was opposed by Gent and Sartorius, and Beatson won. It seems that General Harris, on arrival before Seringapatam, ordered Beatson to reconnoitre and prepare his own scheme for attack. This he did, and when Gent produced that scheme, and his own, at a Council of War on April 13th in the presence of Colonel Arthur Wellesley, other Staff officers, and several Engineers including Sartorius, it was found that, while the Engineers all favoured an attack on the south-west angle, Beatson proposed to attack the north-west angle and was supported in his project by all the Council except the Engineers. After long discussion, Sartorius said that, in consequence of some of Beatson's statements, he would not give his final opinion until he had reconnoitred further; he did so, and then wrote to Harris that he was still in favour of an attack on the south-west angle near the bridge. Yet Harris decided in favour of Beatson, and so we must give this infantry soldier and surveyor the credit for the preparation of the scheme which led to the capture of Seringapatam. The Engineers had cause for complaint in their treatment by the Commander-in-Chief, and it is greatly to their credit that, when Beatson's plan won so striking a success, Sartorius shook his rival by the hand and said that, having examined the south-west angle, he was convinced at last that Seringapatam could only have been taken by Beatson's attack. It was a magnanimous action and worthy of the occasion. So, if history can be trusted, Alexander Beatson was the soul of the attack on Seringapatam.

---

[1] See plan of Seringapatam.
[2] *East India Military Calendar*, Vol. II, p. 375 *et seq.*

While Harris was considering the alternative schemes, the Bombay army arrived on April 14th, escorted into camp by a strong force of cavalry under Colonel Floyd, and this accession to his strength may have influenced the British commander in his choice. In the end, Harris issued orders on the 17th that the north-west angle should be attacked without delay. He was much disquieted at the time by the discovery of a serious shortage of provisions, and saw that he must press forward or relinquish the siege. Meanwhile the Bombay army crossed to the northern bank, taking up a position with its left on the Eadgah (Idgah) Redoubt, and, on the 17th, it seized the village of Agrar where Dowse and his Pioneers dug a battery at Hart's Post to enfilade the north-west angle. On the south bank, Harris drove the enemy from a water-course called the Little Cauvery where he established a post known as Macdonald's Post, which he linked with Shawe's Post by a communication trench. The defenders, having lost their advanced lines along both the Aqueduct and the Little Cauvery, then retreated to a third line which they dug along the southern bank of the river from the bridge to a point opposite the north-west bastion, while the Engineers used the bed of the Little Cauvery as a depot for the engineering tools and materials for the assault.

Colonel Gent organized his command into four " brigades " under Captains Colin Mackenzie, George Johnstone, James Caldwell and John Blair, each of whom had two or three junior engineers to assist him. Mackenzie's brigade worked with the Bombay army on the north bank, and the other three, in turn, with the Madras army. It was while Johnstone's brigade was on duty on April 20th that the operations to eject the enemy from his final position on the south bank were begun. A battery was placed near Sultanpettah to enfilade the hostile trenches along the river-bank, and, raked as they were by the guns from Hart's Post across the river, the Mysoreans were forced to evacuate, under a strong attack, a powder-mill on their right, which Johnstone promptly connected by a parallel to Macdonald's Post. Caldwell, coming on duty next day, marked out a battery for six 18-pounders near the captured mill to enfilade the northern face of the fortress, and Mackenzie, across the river, got ready to place another battery to fire along the western face where the assault would take place. The Indian and European Pioneers, led by Dowse and Farquhar and working under the direction of Caldwell, finished the powder-mill battery on the night of April 21st–22nd, and this achievement, coupled with the preparations at Hart's Post, so roused Tipu that he attacked the Bombay army the same night with 6,000 infantry and a French contingent, losing heavily in so doing. Two days after it was finished, the battery at Hart's Post silenced all the enemy's artillery along the western face and thus paved the way for the establishment of breaching batteries against that face.

Slowly and relentlessly Harris crept forward by zigzags towards the enemy's line on the south bank, placing battery after battery as he came, till, on the 27th, his men were able to rush the river trenches and drive the defenders across the bridge to the island. The next day Blair laid out the first breaching battery, and, by the evening of May 3rd, that battery and several others—29 guns and 6 howitzers in all—had made a practicable breach in the west curtain. As Norris of the Madras Engineers and Farquhar of the European Pioneers had almost crossed the river in a plucky reconnaissance on the 29th, Harris decided to launch his assault at once; his supplies had fallen to a dangerously low level and he had to take Seringapatam without delay or retire.

He formed his assaulting troops in two parties which were together to capture the breach and then turn right and left. The right party was under Colonel Sherbrooke, the left under Lieutenant-Colonel Dunlop, and the whole under General David Baird.[1] The 3rd Brigade of Engineers—Captain Caldwell, with Lieutenant Sydenham and Ensign Rowley—was detailed for the assault, and, with some Pioneers, was divided between the two parties. At one o'clock on May 4th, under a scorching sun, the stormers rushed and scrambled through the rocky river and up the breach against a very heavy fire, and within six minutes were on the outer ramparts. The northern and southern parties then separated, and, Caldwell having been incapacitated by a wound, Rowley accompanied the northern party, and Sydenham the southern, and fought their way with them along the ramparts in either direction. The northern party encountered Tipu himself and had a desperate struggle against the flower of the enemy's infantry at a traverse which barred the way; but finally they swept the defenders before them towards a gate which led from the exterior to the interior line of fortifications. The panic-stricken Mysoreans, jammed in this gateway, were shot down in hundreds, and Tipu himself, twice wounded already, was killed there and lay unrecognized under a heap of corpses, among which, it is said, were many of his women.[2] A similar massacre began at the eastern gateway where other fugitives were caught between the burning gate and the bayonets of the furious British troops who would give no quarter. After two hours, all resistance had ceased except at the palace, and Seringapatam, running with the blood of 10,000 slain, passed into the hands of the avenging army of England.

The menace of Mysore was removed for ever; Tipu was dead, and gigantic treasure and an enormous armament fell to the victors. The state apartments, audience chambers, galleries and storerooms of the palace were filled with gold, silver, jewels and rich

---

[1] Baird, nearly 20 years before, had been captured with Baillie's force, and was but too familiar with the interior of Seringapatam.

[2] *East India Military Calendar*, Vol. III, p. 172. Footnote on Seringapatam, giving an account of the capture from the journal of an officer who took part in it.

and valuable stuffs. The muslins, cambrics and shawls alone were estimated at 500 camel-loads. Tipu's throne of solid gold, raised about four feet from the ground on the back of a golden tiger, with silver steps leading up to it, was broken up; but the treasure and jewels, valued at over one million sterling, were assigned to the army. More than 900 guns, howitzers and mortars, and about 99,000 muskets became the property of the Company, together with 500,000 cannon balls and 200 tons of powder. It was a stupendous capture and a glorious victory, which earned a marquisate for the Governor-General and brought about a treaty on June 22nd, 1799, under which the Company acquired from Mysore the districts of Kanara, Coimbatore, Nilgiri and Wynaud, while Bellary and Cuddapah went, for the time being, to the Nizam.

General Baird handed over charge of the fortress to Colonel Arthur Wellesley on the day after the assault; and while the Pioneers were burying the dead, and the troops were being brought to order and discipline after their mad orgy of bloodshed and plunder, General Harris issued a General Order in which the Engineers and Pioneers received their meed of praise. "The Commander-in-Chief," he writes, "requests that Colonel Gent, and the Corps of Engineers under his orders, will accept his thanks for their unremitting exertions in conducting the duties of that very important department. In thus publicly expressing his sense of their good conduct, the Commander-in-Chief feels himself called upon to notice in a most particular manner the exertions of Captain Dowse and his Corps of Pioneers, which during the present service have been equally marked by unremitting labour and the ability with which that labour was applied."

Colonel Gent selected Colin Mackenzie and James Caldwell for particular praise, and was himself honoured by being made the bearer of Tipu's sword and turban when these were sent by General Harris to Marquis Cornwallis as trophies of victory.[1] Becoming a Major-General two years after the siege, Gent retired to a well-earned rest in England, where he died in 1817. The Fourth Mysore War was ended. It had tested the military engineers and pioneers of India to the core, but, under Gent, they stood that fiery ordeal and emerged with honour.

[1] General Harris to Marquis Cornwallis, letter dated June 30th, 1800.

CHAPTER XI.

THE FIRST MARATHA WAR, 1774–1782.

THE desperate struggles against Mysore in the last quarter of the eighteenth century overshadowed the campaigns in other parts of India. There were many nations, however, in the west and north who were eager to deal a blow at the rising supremacy of England, and prominent among these was the great confederacy of the Marathas, in which, luckily for the British, the ruling emotions of greed, suspicion and fear prevented complete combination and perfect co-operation. Baroda was usually friendly or neutral; but Poona, Indore and Berar were distinctly hostile unless one or other had something to gain by a spurious and evanescent friendship. The character of the Marathas is clearly shown in their history. They could ravage, but could not rule: their only trade was war, and they lived by extortion. Once masters of almost the whole of India, they were crushed by the Afghans at the battle of Panipat in 1761; yet such was their spirit and enterprise that they soon returned to the north from their homes near Bombay, reoccupied Delhi, overran the fertile land between the Ganges and Jumna known as the Doab, and devastated Rohilkhand to its north. The province of Oudh was only saved from them by British intervention, and, in self-protection, its Nawab Vizier (Shuja-ud-daula) concluded an offensive-defensive alliance with the Rohillas of Rohilkhand in 1772. Again the Marathas invaded Rohilkhand, and a quarrel ensued between that state and Oudh, which caused the Nawab Vizier to appeal to Warren Hastings for assistance to punish the Rohillas. So the Governor-General sent a brigade against them in April, 1774, under Colonel Alexander Champion, who defeated them at Miranpur Katra and thus ended what is known as the First Rohilla War.

This expedition, and another which was sent against the Raja of Benares in 1781, illustrate the trivial nature of the military operations which took place in northern India in the latter part of the eighteenth century. While the military engineers of Madras were fighting in the Carnatic and Mysore, and the Bombay Engineers were sharing in their exploits or marching against the Marathas in western or central India, the Bengal Engineers were mostly deprived of any chance of winning honour and glory on the field of battle. Ensigns Nevil Cameron and Alexander Murray were engaged in the First Rohilla War; Captain Alexander Kyd and Lieutenants Patrick Stuart, Joseph Stokoe and James Blunt fought in the Third Mysore

War of 1791–92; and Lieutenant James Mouat acted as Aide-de-Camp to Sir Robert Abercromby at the battle of Bitaura in a second expedition against the Rohillas in 1794. The list is small indeed. Of these fortunate officers, Nevil Cameron is the most distinguished. He and Alexander Murray joined the Rohilla Force from the "Select Picket," a company of gentlemen cadets for whom, on arrival in India, there were no vacancies as Ensigns. After fighting in the First Maratha War, taking part in Popham's capture of Gwalior and becoming Chief Engineer at Fort William in 1793, Cameron left India in 1805, having served for 33 years without any leave, and retired three years later as a Lieutenant-General.

Yet, though they were excluded from the wars in southern India, the Bengal Engineers worked hard in their more peaceful surroundings. Encouraged by Warren Hastings, they completed the building of Fort William and extended Calcutta; they helped to establish the British garrisons at Allahabad, Cawnpore and other places on the Ganges, in proper barracks and cantonments; and—their greatest contribution to the advancement of India—they produced the best surveyors of their age. James Rennell,[1] of the Bengal Engineers is honoured as the father of the Survey of India, and others such as Sir Mark Wood and his brother Thomas, Francis Wilford, John Macdonald, Charles and James Mouat, and Thomas Robertson, were noted experts with the theodolite and plane-table. War came to few engineers in Bengal, though it came with all its glories and hardships to those other engineers of Bombay and Madras who were caught in the storms of the Maratha campaigns in western and central India.

The immediate cause of the First Maratha War was the anxiety of the ambitious Government of Bombay to obtain the island of Salsette to the north of their settlement, the port of Bassein which lay 28 miles to the north, and certain islets near Bombay—Elephanta Hog Island, Karanja and Kanara—all of which were in Maratha hands. They hoped to secure these, without fighting for them, by supporting Raghunath Rao, otherwise Raghuba, in his claim to the office of Peshwa at Poona which was in dispute after the death of Madhu Rao in 1772. However, although Raghuba undertook to cede Salsette and Bassein in return for military support, difficulties arose which made the Bombay Council resolve to seize Salsette without delay, especially as they heard that a Portuguese expedition might forestall them; and so they despatched a small force under Brigadier Robert Gordon at the end of 1774 to besiege Thana, the chief fortress of Salsette, and other detachments to occupy the fort of Vesava and the island of Karanja. After one failure, Gordon accomplished his mission, and, by New Year's Day, Salsette was in British hands.

---

[1] James Rennell was a midshipman in the Royal Navy who was commissioned in the Bengal Engineers on April 9th, 1764, and became the first Surveyor-General of India, under Lord Clive, in 1766, with the rank of Captain.

This petty expedition would not be worth mentioning but for the fact that in it, for the first time in the history of India, an Engineer officer held military command of a force in the field. So notable an advance in the status of the Corps should not pass unnoticed. The detachment which besieged and took Fort Vesava in the north of Salsette after two failures, and captured the island of Karanja on December 30th, 1774, was under the command of Lieutenant-Colonel Thomas Keating who, for ten years, had been Chief Engineer of Bombay.[1] Keating held his military rank as an officer of the Artillery, as at that time the Engineers could not hold rank as such in the army, and his seniority in the garrison entitled him to be considered for a command in the field; and so he was selected to serve with the expedition led by Gordon and abandoned his bricks and mortar for the last two years of his service.

While Keating was fighting in Salsette, the Bombay Government was shocked to learn that two powerful Maratha states, which had till then been acting with them in support of Raghuba, had seceded from his cause. These were Indore and Gwalior, whose rulers, Tukoji Rao Holkar and Mahadji Sindhia, were the best military leaders of the Maratha confederacy. However, the Government, stubborn and ambitious, continued to treat with Raghuba and concluded a treaty with him in March, 1775, by which he agreed to cede Bassein, Salsette and other territory, and to pay heavily in cash for military assistance to establish him as Peshwa. The Directors had increased the strength of the Bombay army after Colonel Archibald Campbell's report on the fortifications, and the extra expense thus incurred could only be met by revenue from new territories. Raghuba could supply the land if he became Peshwa, and on the whole his prospects seemed good; but actually the conclusion of a treaty with him was a false move, for it led to the First Maratha War.

In support of their favourite, the Bombay Government despatched Keating with some 1,500 men to Surat, where he arrived on February 27th, 1775. There he met Raghuba and learnt that his forces had already been defeated by Holkar, Sindhia and other Marathas, and that he had retreated with a remnant of his army to Cambay, 100 miles to the north; so Keating sailed again with Raghuba and reached Cambay on March 18th where he managed to join hands with the defeated troops. His army then comprised about 2,000 Company's soldiers and 35,000 irregulars belonging to Raghuba and another friendly Maratha.

Keating moved slowly northward, as Raghuba wished to capture Ahmadabad, but he was directed by Government to march on Poona, and so turned eastward towards Narad (Neriad) and thence to the banks of the Mahi. While marching slowly and in sweltering heat near Adas (Arras) on May 18th, in a deep and sandy road leading

[1] See Chapter VI.

through enclosed country, he was ambushed by a large body of the enemy and nearly cut up. The Marathas blocked the lane with elephants and their cavalry caused a panic among some of Keating's men; but Fortescue records[1] that, handling his artillery with great skill, he drove back the enemy at last with very heavy loss, and that the Marathas themselves admitted that the battle was undoubtedly a victory for the British. The critical nature of this fight is shown by the fact that the British force lost 222 men of whom 86 were Europeans, and among these, 11 officers.[2] Keating next moved to Broach, and then to Dabhoi near Baroda, where, on his own responsibility, he negotiated a treaty with the Gaikwar which was cancelled by the Supreme Government when they heard of it. The Governor-General condemned the whole venture, and sent Lieutenant-Colonel John Upton from Bengal to conclude the unfortunate Treaty of Purandhar in place of Keating's treaty, washing his hands of Raghuba though he retained Salsette for the Company.

It is interesting to note how an Engineer acquitted himself when in command of troops for the first time. Keating showed good tactical ability, but he was over-confident and tried to dabble in politics which were none of his affair. Grant Duff writes:[3] " Governor Hornby (of Bombay) seems to have had an idea that his fifteen hundred men might overcome the whole Maratha army: nor is the confidence and inexperience of Colonel Keating less apparent, for on meeting the forlorn Raghuba at Surat, he congratulates the Bombay Government on their good fortune at finding the ex-Peishwa so entirely dependent on them for his future success. Colonel Keating was not authorized to act in any political capacity beyond the tenor of his orders; but, from an injudicious and excessive zeal, often as prejudicial to the public service as its opposite defect, he was ambitious of distinguishing himself as a politician and entered into correspondence with Futih Sing,[4] shortly after he landed at Cambay, for the purpose of detaching him from the ministerial party.[5] Nothing, under the circumstances, was to be expected from negotiating, especially with a Mahratta, but humiliation and disappointment. He even entered into a treaty on April 22nd, secret, as he supposed and as Futih Sing pretended; but Colonel Keating knew so little of the people as to be insensible of the derision to which his notable diplomacy exposed him."[6]

Unfortunately Keating had incurred the bitter animosity of

[1] *A History of the British Army*, by the Hon. J. W. Fortescue, Vol. III, p. 147.
[2] *Bombay General Orders.* Colonel Keating to Government. Letter dated May 19th, 1775, in which Keating admits that the victory was " dearly purchased."
[3] *A History of the Marathas*, by J. G. Duff, Vol. II, p. 289.
[4] Fateh Singh, Gaikwar of Baroda.
[5] The hostile Maratha federation of states, organized by the minister at Poona, Nana Farnavis.
[6] In justice to Keating, however, it should be noted that the compiler of the *East India Military Calendar* remarks in Vol. II, p. 83, that Keating was highly distinguished both in his military *and political* capacity.

General Robert Gordon during or after the expedition against Salsette in 1774. We may guess the cause, for Gordon had accused him, not only of dishonourable conduct, but of introducing into Bombay as his wife a lady who had no claim to that distinction.[1] The Government refused to admit these charges, and Gordon lay low for a time. His opportunity came, however, when Keating fell into bad odour with the Government at the end of his short campaign, and Gordon then wrote a long letter on April 23rd, 1776, accusing him of misconduct, incapacity, ignorance and neglect during the operations, and asking that he should be tried by a General Court-Martial on about 17 charges including the original ones of 1774 about the lady. To this the Government agreed, except that they again rejected the accusations of 1774, and they directed that a court-martial should assemble.

The trial began in Bombay in June under Major Emanuel Henry as President, and it ended in an honourable acquittal on all the charges[2] in spite of the animosity and vindictiveness of General Gordon who attempted to brow-beat the members into a finding adverse to Keating. However, the trial having resulted as stated, Keating was ordered to return to duty, but he did so only to retire from the Service and leave India as soon as possible. The Treaty of Purandhar, which replaced the one which he had negotiated, was worthless and was never carried into effect, while many people considered that his own treaty might have had a good and lasting result. He left India a disappointed and broken man. Yet he had shown that an Engineer could lead an army in the field. If he strayed unwisely into the mazes of diplomacy, he should not have been condemned so strongly for his fault. Keating was a man of energy and action, and those qualities were badly needed in 1775.

After the victory of Adas, the Bombay Government recommended that a proper and separate cadre of Engineers should be formed[3] and that it should consist of one Major, one Captain and three Lieutenants, who would continue to hold their rank in the Artillery. But in 1777 the Government went beyond these modest suggestions:

"BOMBAY GENERAL ORDER, DECEMBER 9TH, 1777.

"The Hon. the Court of Directors approve of the separation now to take place of the Artillery and Engineer Corps, and have fixed the pay and emoluments of the latter corps conformable to the establishment at Madras, which is to receive no pay or emoluments from any other corps whatever.

"In consequence of the above order, the Hon. the President and Council have been pleased to direct that in future the Engineers shall

---

[1] *Bombay Letters Received*, Vol. V, June 6th, 1776.
[2] *Bombay Public Consultations*, October 21st, 1776.
[3] *Bombay General Orders*, August 2nd, 1775.

be an entirely distinct and separate Corps, and is to consist of 1 Major, Engineer-in-Chief, 3 Captains, 2 Lieutenants and 4 Ensigns.[1] Practitioner Engineers to be increased as occasion may require.

"The Officers of this Corps are to be:—

Major	Nilson. Chief Engineer.
Captains	Spaith / McNeill / Turner
Lieutenants	Nicholson. / Sartorius
Ensigns	Doidge / Daser / Christie."

Of these Bombay Engineers,[2] only Lawrence Nilson, Robert Nicholson and John Sartorius rose to high rank or saw much active service. Most of the original cadre left the Corps or the Service as Captains, and this is not surprising in view of the conditions of service in India. A short digression from military history will show what those conditions were.

The army in India was officered by men who were promoted by seniority alone, and there were no age limits. Selection being practically unknown, the result was a terrible block in promotion in every branch of the Service which was mitigated only by the large mortality in all ranks. The purchase of commissions, which was allowed in England in corps other than the Artillery and Engineers, was not recognized in India, though it was well known that many senior officers received large sums from their juniors to send in their papers.[3] The only financial inducement to an honest Engineer to stay in India was the highly paid post of Chief Engineer: if he got that appointment, and kept it for a few years, he could retire in affluence. The wise Chief Engineer retired before his health failed, but some remained fit and strong for many years and blocked all promotion.[4] Patrick Ross, for instance, was Chief Engineer of Madras for 32 years.

Many officers who failed to become Chief Engineers stayed for years in the country to collect sufficient money to keep themselves from penury in their old age. They could not take leave to Europe,

[1] After a few years the establishment was expanded, and the Chief-Engineership was held by a substantive Colonel.
[2] Major (afterwards Brigadier-General) Lawrence, or Laurence, Nilson; Captains David Spaith, or Spaeth, James McNeill and Charles Turner; Lieutenant (afterwards Lieutenant-General) Robert Nicholson; Lieutenant (afterwards Colonel) John Sartorius; and Ensigns Richard Doidge, Paul Dacer and Daniel Christie.
[3] A Major in the Infantry might get as much as 30,000 rupees from his junior officers to retire rather than take command when the post of Commanding Officer fell vacant.
[4] All subalterns, however, were automatically promoted to the brevet rank of Captain after 15 years' service in their rank, though the promotion carried no extra pay.

partly because of the prohibitive cost of passage for themselves and their families, which might amount to hundreds of pounds for the double journey, and also because, prior to 1796, any officer who went to Europe had to resign the Service and received no pay whatever whilst on leave.[1] To return to India he had to apply for reinstatement, and there was no guarantee that this would be granted. No married officer could afford to take leave unless he had made his fortune, and thus the regulations had the effect of encouraging illicit dealings. A change for the better, however, occurred in 1796 when the Directors issued furlough regulations under which an officer was allowed one furlough of three years' length during his service and could draw pay for two and a half years of his absence; but subalterns had to serve for ten years before they could get any leave. An officer could retire, after 25 years' service, on the full infantry pay of his rank; and half-pay was granted on retirement to men whose health had failed and who had served for certain periods according to their rank. On the whole, however, one may say that, even after 1796, there were few attractions in engineering service in India. The climate, the pay, the prospects and the isolation did not appeal to Engineers of the King's Army, very few of whom came to the East; and the adventurous five who were in the country in 1771[2] were removed from the royal establishment on the ominous date of April 1st.

The President and Council of Bombay tried to foster a military spirit in their army. Indeed, as early as 1770, they went so far as to issue a General Order that " A soldier should be as attached to, and careful of, his musket, as his mistress,"[3] an injunction which, no doubt, carried great weight under the rather lax code of morals of that day. But some of the Bombay Engineers, having little or no fighting to do, were inclined to drop their military duties and the study of war, and the position of such officers came under heated discussion when Engineers were accorded military rank in the army. They had much touring, and they did it on horseback or in palanquins, horse-drawn vehicles, or bullock carts, and as they made very slow progress, they broke their journeys for days, or even weeks, at out-stations where junior officers of the Cavalry, Artillery or Infantry held command. Let us imagine that the Chief Engineer of Bombay, a Colonel, has arrived at a station and proposes to stay there for three weeks to rest his weary bones. Should he, as a combatant officer, take command of the troops although he has not done any military duty for years and has attained his rank only by his length of service, the solidity

---

[1] *History of the Indian Medical Service*, by Lieutenant-Colonel D. G. Crawford, Vol I, Chapter XIX.
[2] Captain-Lieutenants Archibald Campbell, Patrick Ross and Henry Watson, Lieutenant James Lillyman and Ensign John Wittever.
[3] " The Bombay Engineer Officer in 1800," by " Arthur Vincent," appearing in *The R.E. Journal*, Vol. XLII, 1928.

of his fortifications, and the fine adjustment of his accounts? The President, the Councillors and the Commander-in-Chief considered the problem and scratched their heads.

The difficulty was met in 1796 by tactful warnings to touring Engineers that they should not interfere in administration and discipline at out-stations. Most of them were glad to be relieved of the extra responsibility; but a few were more ambitious, and among them Lieutenant-Colonel John Sartorius who commanded the Bombay Engineers before Seringapatam in 1792. Sartorius protested and insisted on his right of command till he wrung an order from Government that he could, if he pleased, " give out the parole and countersign "—a small concession, but with great implications, for it set the seal of official recognition on the proper status of the Engineer officer. Nevertheless, more explicit orders were needed, and these appeared in 1797 and applied to the whole of India. It was then decided that touring Engineers were to receive the full honours of their rank, but that the command and administration of the troops in any out-station were to remain with the permanent commander. " No person," writes the Commander-in-Chief, " entertains a more respectable opinion of the professional importance of the Corps of Engineers; but it is evident that an officer employed in repairing or constructing works, cannot afford the requisite attention to the duties of detail and discipline which is undoubtedly the peculiar province of the infantry officer, whose leisure and education best qualify him to conduct this part of the service." In the same letter, however, he adds that if an Engineer officer is stationed *permanently* in a garrison, he should command all the troops in that garrison. Thus, before the close of the eighteenth century, the Engineer officer in India was recognized in almost all circumstances as a combatant soldier with full power of command.

Government unfortunately showed a distrust in the probity of their Engineers which was bad for the self-respect of these officers and for the prestige of their Corps. For instance, when a work had been executed by contract, the officer in charge, whatever his rank, had to affirm on his honour that he had had no concern in providing or selling the materials, and had not derived any benefit from the work other than his Government allowances. Even the bitter experiences of former years can hardly be said to have justified the demand of such a certificate from a commissioned officer, though the demand came from a commercial body who represented the King in India and not from His Majesty's Government.

The prize of a Chief-Engineership fell only to the man who had outstanding professional ability backed by influence and a cast-iron constitution. This was a post worth holding. In the Company's army at the end of the eighteenth century there were two scales of pay, one for garrison duty and the other for service in the field, and they differed enormously.[1] Engineer officers, with the exception of the Chief Engineer, were paid no more than officers of other branches. A Lieutenant-Colonel of the Bombay Engineers, however, who was lucky enough to be promoted Chief Engineer, found his peace salary raised suddenly from Rs. 630 to Rs. 2,340 a month; and when he went on service, his pay as Chief Engineer, amounting then to Rs. 2,419, was increased by 11 rupees a day as "table money" and an allowance for the keep of two horses. It is true that, of his princely stipend, a sum of Rs. 1,200 was "an Establishment in lieu of commission on public works and all contingencies," but we may presume that he cut down his contingencies to a low figure and pocketed the equivalent of £9 a day in the field or £8 a day in garrison. If these amounts are compared with the garrison pay of a Chief Engineer in the King's Army, amounting to £2 4s. a day, no further explanation is required of the fact that, in spite of the hardships of service in India, men could be recruited by the Company as Engineers.

And what did the Engineer officer of Bombay look like in his full regimentals? In some ways he resembled his brother of the Royal army; for instance, in 1800, he wore the blue coat with gold embroidery and black velvet facings, cuffs and collar, which had been introduced by the King for his own Engineers on December 24th, 1782,[2] and a very uncomfortable coat it must have been in the sticky heat of Bombay. On his shoulders were epaulettes with eight embroidered stripes of gold on a strap with a black ground. He sported a white waistcoat and breeches as in the Royal army, and encased his feet and legs in "half boots, cut round at the top." On his head was a round black hat with a cockade on the left side, and around his damp neck a black leather stock. With a sash of crimson silk at his left side, an oval breastplate, brown leather gloves, and dozens of large brass buttons bearing the Company's crest, he was ready to captivate the hearts of the country-born beauties of Bombay and the new importations from home. They could fix his rank and value by his epaulettes. Subalterns and Captains had only one epaulette, worn on the right shoulder; Majors, an epaulette on each shoulder, while Lieutenant-Colonels carried a six-pointed spangled star, and Colonels two stars, on each epaulette. Generals and staff officers were so weighed down with gold and decoration that Solomon in all his glory was not arrayed like one of them and they seemed to be hardly mortal. So there we have the Engineer officer of every rank under John Company—his conditions of service, pay, prospects and dress—and so we will leave his personal affairs and appearance and return to the campaigns and adventures in which he took

[1] The monthly rates for a Lieutenant-Colonel were Rs. 630 and Rs. 1,009 respectively. For an Ensign they were Rs. 129 and Rs. 200.
[2] *History of the Corps of Royal Engineers*, by Major-General W. Porter, Vol. I, Chapter IX, p. 227.

part, and the evolution of the engineering troops which he commanded.

The Government records of Keating's time in Bombay are so full of references to difficulties in conducting the siege of Thana on the island of Salsette, delays by Keating before Vesava, badly-built gun-platforms and carriages, collapsing houses, defective materials and miscalculations of time and cost in fortifying the settlement, that they leave an impression of slackness on the part of the Engineers and even a suspicion of dishonesty ; but they miss the chief cause of these failures, which was that the Engineers could not get skilled craftsmen to carry out their work, and especially so when on active service. It was left to Ensign Charles Henry Witman,[1] of the Bombay Infantry, to draw attention to this matter and to show in a letter to the President and Council of Bombay, written on February 11th, 1776, how crippling was the want of efficient carpenters, sawyers, blacksmiths and other artisans. The special interest which attaches to Witman's remarks, and to his startling proposal that Government should recruit from Germany a whole company of Military Artificers, officers included, is that they are apparently the origin of the formation of the distinguished corps now known as the Royal Bombay Sappers and Miners. Witman certainly let his pen run away with him, but a few extracts from his long letter will show what he proposed :—

" ENSIGN HENRY WITMAN TO THE PRESIDENT AND COUNCIL OF BOMBAY.[2]

" From the different services I have been employed upon since my arrival in this country I have observed a very great want of proper artificers which might be attended with the worst consequences, especially in case of a distant service. To remedy this a plan has occurred to me which I now beg leave to submit to your consideration.

" It is the custom in Germany with every Prince who maintains a body of troops to have a company of artisans to every battalion of artillery. In time of peace, or whilst the army is in garrison, these artisans are employed in the arsenals, laboratories and foundries. In time of war they accompany the army and are employed in the repair of arms and carriages, in short in all the various occasions which daily arise in an army for artificers of every different occupation. Besides this, the artisans are kept in constant discipline ; and in action or in sieges, such as are not immediately wanted on works become an addition to the strength of the army by acting with the artillery. There seems to be no improvement which could be adopted in the military system of the Honourable Company at once

---

[1] Also written " Whitman " and " Wittman." He had served only one year when he put forward his scheme. Witman became a Brevet-Captain in 1784, and died in February, 1788. He earned distinction in the field in 1780.

[2] *Bombay Public Diary*, No. 69, of 1776. Letter dated February 11th, 1776, appearing in the *Bombay Gazetteer*, Vol. XXVI, Part II, Section II, pp. 425–430.

so beneficial and important as the establishment of such a company.

"Every person must allow it to be a great disadvantage burthening an army with a number of followers that are wholly useless in time of action. This must ever be the case when Indian artificers are to be employed. The little work they are capable of doing renders it necessary to have a great number of them : add to this that almost every carpenter must have his man to move, carry and turn the piece of timber he is at work upon. With Europeans, where there are six persons at present, there need be only one. After all, when you have the native artificers, their work of every kind is so miserably executed that it is almost useless. Imagine the delays this must occasion should there be a necessity for erecting several works at once. Oppose to these delays the great advantage that would accrue on service, and especially in sieges, if the engineers had workmen they could depend upon, to whom they need only give verbal direction or a drawing of what they mean to have done.

"The company might consist of 100 privates or more if necessary, all versed in some business. The non-commissioned officers should be masters or very able workmen in the different trades. I could also engage experienced officers versed in every branch of the artillery, such as making powder, casting guns, etc. The company might be kept constantly complete by recruits from Europe which I could annually send to London by means of agents established in Germany. Exclusive of their utility to the Company, these artificers would be of great convenience to the place, and, as many of them would bring out their wives and children, they might in time produce a race which would be at once useful inhabitants and considerably add to the strength of the place in case of a siege."

Charles Witman was certainly a far-sighted young man who could think not only constructively but even eugenically. There was nothing original, however, in his idea of recruiting foreigners for military service under the Company, for complete Hanoverian units had served already under the Government of Madras, and Swedes, Danes, Dutchmen, Germans, Frenchmen and Portuguese had been officers of the Company in various parts of India. But his proposal to form a regular unit of skilled foreign artisans was new and caught the fancy of the Government of Bombay ; and, although the scheme met with little success, it led to great results in the end. The President laid the letter before his Council who resolved[1] that Witman should be given a passage to Europe to submit his proposals to the Directors, noting at the same time that General Gordon advised that miners should be added to the company of artificers. Soon afterwards Witman sailed for Europe, where he managed to recruit only

[1] *Bombay Government Consultations*, February 13th, 1776. *Public Diary*, No. 69, of 1776.

25 of his Germans.[1] Still, there can be no doubt that the letter of February, 1776, impressed the Bombay Government with the necessity of forming a regular unit of engineer soldiers, for, on December 13th, 1777, after the separation of the Bombay Artillery and Engineers into distinct corps, a company of " Pioneer Lascars " was raised by Major Lawrence Nilson, Chief Engineer of Bombay, with an establishment of one Sarang,[2] four Tindals and 100 " Private Men."[3] This little unit was the origin of the present 18th Field Company, Royal Bombay Sappers and Miners, and, within a year of its formation, proved its value in the First Maratha War which was resumed after the abortive treaty of Purandhar.

During the lull in hostilities, Governor Hornby viewed the political situation with growing anxiety and told his Council in October, 1777, " that they were fast verging to a period which must compel the English nation, either to take some active and decisive part in the Maratha affairs, or relinquish for ever all hopes of bettering their own situation on the West of India."[4] A French adventurer named St. Lubin had arrived at Poona, and had offered French troops and money to the clever old minister, Nana Farnavis. This statesman, being consistently hostile to England, was intrigued by the proposal; but, before he could act on it, a rival party at Poona, who supported Raghuba, appealed to the British for help. Although Bombay was still on Raghuba's side, Warren Hastings cared nothing for him or his pretensions; the machinations of St. Lubin, however, seemed a more serious matter, and he induced his refractory Council at Calcutta to agree to overawe the Marathas by a military display. Hence General Goddard's wonderful march across India from Bengal, not in support of Raghuba, but to form an alliance with the Raja of Berar, and, by establishing that ruler as nominal head of the Maratha states, to defeat the ambitions of Nana Farnavis and the French who were backed by Sindhia and Holkar.

But the Governor and Councillors of Bombay were disgusted with this policy dictated by the Governor-General, and, without waiting for the arrival of Goddard with his six battalions and some cavalry, resolved to send their own expedition against Poona in support of their dearly-beloved Raghuba, thus defying openly the authority of the Supreme Government. To add to their folly, they selected to command their force of 4,000 men, Colonel Egerton, a " bed-ridden commander,"[5] who, as Grant Duff says,[6] " was extremely weak and totally unacquainted with India, its natives or its warfare." General Gordon having died, Egerton, as the acting Commander-in-Chief in Bombay, claimed his right to lead the expedition, and was appointed

---

[1] Court to Bombay, letter dated May 27th, 1779. *Public Department Courts' Letters*, Vol. X, of 1778–1782.
[2] A head-man. [3] *Bombay General Orders*, December 13th, 1777.
[4] *A History of the Marathas*, by J. G. Duff, Vol. II, p. 343.
[5] *Historical Sketches of the South of India*, by Colonel Mark Wilks.
[6] *A History of the Marathas*, by J. G. Duff, Vol. II, p. 362.

subject to the control of two civilian " field deputies."[1] So the little army started up the *ghats* under a council of three—a sick and useless commander, watched and hindered by two astute politicians—while Sindhia and Holkar massed 50,000 men to oppose them. The audacity of the move was only equalled by its stupidity: the expedition was doomed to failure and it met its just fate.

It toiled up the mountainside to Khandala, and then advanced towards Poona at a snail's pace of six furlongs a day under incessant attacks by the Marathas. Egerton fell ill and handed over his command to Lieutenant-Colonel Cockburn, though he retained his seat in the council of management. The column struggled on to Talagaon; but when Cockburn wished to continue to Poona, only 18 miles farther, Egerton insisted on a retirement which began on January 11th, 1779, after Cockburn had thrown his heavy guns into a lake and destroyed most of his stores. Only the gallantry of Captain James Hartley of the Bombay Infantry, and the desperate resistance made by the rearguard under his command, saved the Bombay army from annihilation during the retreat. Cockburn led his men to the village of Wargaum,[2] and repulsed several attacks by the Marathas; but the precious Council of Three had had enough, and on January 13th concluded a treaty with the victorious Mahadji Sindhia by which they agreed to resign everything acquired from the Marathas since 1772, to give up the revenues from Broach and Surat, to ensure that Goddard should advance no farther, and to pay 41,000 rupees to Sindhia's servants. The expedition was then allowed to return to Bombay, humiliated and dejected, and the Bombay Government immediately repudiated the Convention of Wargaum and dismissed not only Carnac and Egerton but also the unfortunate Cockburn.

Goddard soon heard of this fiasco, and, by a forced march of 300 miles, completed his great adventure and entered Surat on February 26th. He tried without success to gain over the Gaikwar of Baroda to the British side, and, as a counter-move, Nana Farnavis set to work to form a confederacy of Mysore, Hyderabad and the Marathas against the British. But while Goddard was engaged for months in fruitless diplomacy, the chastened Government of Bombay was not idle. Hornby mobilized a fresh force under the gallant Hartley and sent it to reinforce Goddard at Surat before the end of 1779. The patience of the British general became strained at last to breaking point. Fateh Singh, the Gaikwar, shuffled and turned, and no definite agreement could be reached either with him or with Nana

[1] Messrs. John Carnac and Daniel Draper. Grant Duff remarks (Vol. II, p. 362) that many officers of rank came to India to make their fortunes. Their pay was inadequate, and the shameless corruption which prevailed excited the jealousy of the Government. This was one cause of the appointment of Carnac and Draper to act with Egerton, leaving only " the mere detail of duty and of march as the sole occupation separately entrusted to the senior military officer of their army."

[2] Also spelt " Wargaon " and " Wadgaon."

Farnavis at Poona, so on New Year's Day, 1780, Goddard advanced to gain by force what he could not get by fair words.

Although there is no record that any Engineers accompanied the unfortunate expedition under Egerton, we know that Major David Spaith of the Bombay Engineers, and Lieutenants Charles Reynolds, George Prole and Alexander Caldwell marched with Goddard in 1780.[1] Reynolds afterwards had a brilliant career and ended his service as a Lieutenant-General and Surveyor-General of India. He prepared the first General Map of India " fighting his way through territories which now acknowledge British sway, while others were totally inaccessible to Europeans or any avowed agent."[2] His profession was surveying, but, for 12 years after his arrival in 1772, he acted as an Engineer in expeditions against the Marathas and also against Tipu Sultan. Prole belonged to the Bengal Infantry. He volunteered for service under Goddard, acting occasionally as an Engineer, until he was severely wounded at Ahmadabad. In 1814 he retired as a Major-General. The fact that, when Bombay sent expeditions against the Marathas, it was necessary to recruit most of the Engineers from outside services, indicates how serious was the deficiency in the engineering establishment at this time. The Western Presidency was indeed very far behind Madras in organization for war.

Goddard began his operations in January, 1780, by taking the Gaikwar's fort of Dabhoi, near Baroda, this being the only way to bring the shifty Fateh Singh to reason. It was a sound move, for the Gaikwar immediately concluded an offensive and defensive alliance with the British. Though the siege was a brief affair, it added something to the reputation of the Engineers, for Goddard wrote:[3] " I am happy at an opportunity of mentioning to you the satisfaction I have received from the skill and assiduity of Major Spaith, the Chief Engineer, in constructing and completing the battery with so much expedition. Lieutenant Charles Reynolds, who acted under him and showed himself exceedingly alert and active in his duty, received a wound in the thigh from a matchlock, which I hope will not prove any way dangerous." Advancing rapidly from Dabhoi upon Ahmadabad, the capital of Gujarat, Goddard next carried that place by assault on February 15th after bombarding it for five days. Lieutenant-Colonel Hartley conducted the attack, and the Engineers played a most conspicuous part in it. Spaith was mentioned particularly[4] for his work in helping, with his Pioneer Lascars, to fill up the ditch for the passage of the Bombay Grenadiers. During

[1] Reynolds was from the Bombay Army, and Prole and Caldwell from the Bengal Army. All three were temporary engineers. (See *East India Military Calendar*, Vols. I and III.)
[2] *East India Military Calendar*, Vol. III, p. 88.
[3] *Bombay General Orders*. General Goddard to the Government of Bombay. Letter dated January 20th, 1780.
[4] *Ibid.*, Letter dated February 15th, 1780.

the work he was wounded in seven places by sabre cuts, while Prole and Caldwell were wounded also. Reynolds had rejoined for duty, but was incapable of doing much. Every Engineer with the small force had been incapacitated by wounds when only two actions had been fought.

When Ahmadabad had fallen, Goddard heard that Sindhia and Holkar had crossed the Narbada River and were advancing upon Baroda at the head of 20,000 cavalry, so he turned his little force southward to meet them. The two Maratha chiefs hoped to persuade the Gaikwar of Baroda to break his treaty and combine with them, a fact which is shown by a letter which came into Goddard's hands and must have caused him some amusement :—[1]

"After compliments. I have observed what you wrote about the monkeys' force. As soon as we came to know this, Shrimant Sindhia with his two forces marched from Jamgaon the 28th Mohurum and encamped at Dhoolay. . . . The love and friendship of the Shrimant Sindhia is much upon Fattesing. Soon as he knew that the monkeys' forces were after him he despatched Bhagiratrav and other Sirdars with forces to assist him, and hope they have arrived. Now his own army, commanded by himself, is coming. You must tell Fattesing so, and desire him to continue to do as he has done before to stop the monkeys till our forces come against them. Fattesing has, by his patience and courage, not yet come under the monkeys."

But when Sindhia got news that the Company's "monkeys" under Goddard were on the march against him, his heart failed him, and, taking a leaf from Fateh Singh's book, he began to temporize. In Goddard, however, he found his match; and, before the British retired to the Narbada for the rainy season, they had secured the whole of Gujarat for the Company, though Sindhia and Holkar were still undefeated and Nana Farnavis was pursuing his intrigues at Poona. Captain William Popham had already done great things in Central India at Gohad and in storming the fort of Lahar, and, on August 3rd, assisted by Lieutenant William Cameron of the Bengal Engineers,[2] he took the almost impregnable fortress of Gwalior by escalade. But these deeds did not bring complete victory over the Maratha confederacy, so Goddard was ordered to besiege Bassein while Hartley lay to the east of it with a covering force.

Goddard sat down before Bassein on November 13th, 1780, and began his attack from the north. He had powerful siege artillery, and, by the 28th, had made batteries for 12 large guns and mortars within 900 yards of the walls and had started his approaches and

---

[1] Balaji Govind to Balkrishna Anant. Letter received on February 23rd, 1780, at Broach, appearing in *Selections from the Despatches and Other State Papers preserved in the Bombay Secretariat*, Maratha Series, Vol. I, Part II, by G. W. Forrest, p. 401.

[2] *East India Military Calendar*, Vol. I, p. 50.

H

parallels. A few days later, he writes :[1] " The enemy have not once ventured to sally from the walls or interrupt the operations otherwise than by a very hot fire of artillery, which, owing to the skill of the Engineer in constructing the works, though served remarkably well, has done us very little damage." Bassein surrendered on December 11th, and Goddard wrote on the following day : " I cannot help on this occasion doing justice to the merit of Captain Theobald, the Engineer, who had the constructing and carrying on of the works, to whose able management and skill in his profession must be in a great measure attributed the preservation of the lives of the troops, as well as the successful issue of the siege." Who was this Captain Theobald ? He does not appear in Conolly's list of the Bombay Engineers,[2] nor was there any officer of that name in the Bengal Engineers. He could not have been Captain John Theobald of the Madras Engineers, for that officer was killed with Baillie's force in the disaster at Pollilur near Madras two months before the fall of Bassein. His name does not even appear in the Indian Army List by Dodwell and Miles. One can only suppose that Theobald of Bassein was a temporary officer and engineer, or even a sailor acting as an engineer ; but, whoever and whatever he was, he shone at Bassein. The place was very formidable, accessible only from the north and surrounded on every other side by swamps when the tide was high. Theobald had the honour of helping to add this important base to the meagre possessions of the Company in Western India, and he was ably assisted by Lieutenant Charles Reynolds, who had recovered from his wound, and by Ensign (afterwards Lieutenant-General) William Blachford of the Bombay Engineers.

It is curious that the Chief Engineer of Bombay, Lieutenant-Colonel Lawrence Nilson, took no part in the operations. He had had some experience of war for he had served at the siege of Mangalore, at the siege of Broach in 1772, and under Gordon in Salsette in 1774. Yet in 1780 we find a record that " he succeeded to the command of the garrison and troops on the Bombay establishment which he held for a considerable period with the situation of Chief Engineer." Probably the urgency of the fortification work in Bombay, and some financial irregularities which had come to light in connection with it, may have prevented him from leaving the place. In the opinion of Government, Nilson was such an excellent engineer, and so efficient as a soldier, that in 1784 they made him a Brigadier-General and appointed him as Commander-in-Chief of all the forces on the western coast, with a seat as second in the Bombay Council ; and when he retired, after 37 years of service in India, he received the thanks of Government and a special annuity of £1,000 a year.

[1] *Bombay General Orders.* General Goddard to the Government of Bombay. Letter dated December 4th, 1780.
[2] *List of Officers of the Corps of Engineers from 1660 to 1898*, by Captain T. W. J. Conolly, R.E., edited by Captain R. F. Edwards, R.E.

Wisely, perhaps, Nilson made no effort to command in the field. The Government of Bombay was naturally rather suspicious of Engineers after Keating's political experiments.

While Goddard was besieging Bassein, Hartley screened him from the Maratha General, Hari Pant Phadke; and afterwards, by repulsing another leader, Ramchandra Ganesh, in the Konkan,[1] he cleared that tract of any considerable hostile force. Then, with the approval of Bombay, Goddard proposed terms of peace to the Marathas, which, however, were treated with such contempt that in January, 1781, he resumed the offensive and captured the fort of Arnala on an island north of Bombay. It seemed after this that a direct advance on Poona would be more likely to persuade the Peshwa to make peace than wasting time, men and money in besieging dozens of hill forts, so he advanced towards the mountain passes leading to the Maratha capital. This was bad strategy and worse policy. He threatened the enemy without having the power to carry his threat into execution. Hari Pant retired towards Poona, leaving the crest of the Bor Ghat guarded by Holkar with 15,000 horse and a host of irregulars. On February 9th, Goddard reached Khopuli at the foot of the ghat and found the defile held by 4,000 men with many guns.[2] He began his march up the ghat at night, and in the early hours of the morning captured two defended posts, the second of which, called the Darwaja,[3] was taken chiefly by the action of the Bombay Pioneers[4] and some Bengal Grenadiers who, having gained the heights above the road, advanced along them towards the Darwaja and assisted the troops by flanking fire. Lieutenant Daniel Christie, of the Bombay Engineers, was conspicuous in this and other operations during the advance and earned a mention in despatches. Finally the British force, under Colonel Parker, reached Khandala at the head of the ghat where it maintained a precarious footing while negotiations began once more. The Marathas were neither defeated nor alarmed, and the movement by which Goddard had hoped to gain a great advantage had failed miserably. It drew upon him, also, the displeasure of Sir Eyre Coote, the Commander-in-Chief in India, who protested in the strongest terms[5] that Goddard should have avoided hostilities against the Marathas in order to invade Malabar and so divert some of Haidar Ali's troops from the war in the Carnatic.[6]

The Marathas now took the offensive, and converged on the unfortunate Goddard. Their main body under Hari Pant and Tukoji Holkar, with Nana Farnavis in attendance, marched on Khandala, while a force of 12,000 men descended into the Konkan to cut the

---

[1] *Konkan* or *Concan*. The plain between Bombay and the ghats.
[2] General Goddard to the Government of Bombay, letter dated February 9th, 1781.
[3] *Darwaza*, a door.
[4] A body of 200 Pioneers and Lascars accompanied the force whose total strength was 6,152 men.
[5] Sir Eyre Coote to General Goddard, letter dated March 1st, 1781.
[6] The Second Mysore War.

British communications with Bombay. Goddard asked for permission to build a fort and establish a strong garrison at the head of the Bor Ghat, hoping in this way to maintain his position; but he was overruled and ordered back to the coast. He retreated down the ghat in the middle of April, harassed on every side by large bodies of Marathas, and arrived in Panvel near Bombay on the 23rd with the loss of nearly 500 men killed and wounded. The rearguard naturally bore the brunt of the fighting, and among the casualties in that part of the force was Lieutenant-Colonel Charles Reynolds, who was twice wounded in the retreat[1] after coming unscathed through the siege of Ahmadabad and the capture of Arnala. This was almost his last appearance as an Engineer. When he recovered, he reverted chiefly to infantry work, and then became Surveyor-General.

For some months longer, the First Maratha War lingered on; but Mahadji Sindhia was getting tired of it, and his weariness was the first rift which showed through the lowering clouds. Negotiations were opened which led to a treaty with him in October, 1781, and the Poona Government then decided to follow suit. The war ended in March, 1782; but the Treaty of Salbai, which was concluded in the following May, was not ratified until February, 1783. This treaty was a great political achievement. It not only secured Salsette to the British and gave Raghuba a pension, but it brought peace with the Marathas for 20 years and made England the controlling power in all except southern India; and it was a triumph for Warren Hastings, for it helped towards the ultimate fall of Mysore.

As early as 1782 the question of altering the status and nature of the Pioneer Corps began to receive serious attention in Bombay and elsewhere. A certain Major George Burghall, who is said to have belonged to the Madras Engineers,[2] had addressed the Directors in 1781 and the nature of his proposals is shown in the following reply, which reached Bombay on September 5th, 1782:—[3]

" Major George Burghall, late of our Corps of Engineers at Fort St. George, having submitted to our consideration a plan proposing sundry improvements in the mode of fortification at present adopted in India, and that an Inspector and Director of Fortifications throughout India should be appointed, also that a Corps of Miners and Pioneers should be established at each of our Presidencies, we enclose a copy thereof and direct that you take the opinion of the Commander-in-Chief at your Presidency on its utility and expediency, whose report thereon must be forwarded to England by the first ship."

[1] *East India Military Calendar*, Vol. III, p. 90.
[2] His name does not appear in the *List of Officers of the Corps of Royal Engineers*, by Captain T. W. J. Conolly, R.E.
[3] *Bombay General Orders*, October 27th, 1782.

OFFICER, MADRAS PIONEERS, 1780.

(Coat, blue with black facings; vest and trousers, white; red sash; black hat, plume and spats.)

It seems, however, that Burghall's scheme joined a number of others in the pigeon-holes of Leadenhall Street. No action was taken for many years either to change the Pioneer Corps into a Corps of Miners and Pioneers or to appoint an Inspector-General of Fortifications. Except in the opinion of the Engineers themselves, the Pioneers were meeting all requirements; and the Chief Engineers of Calcutta, Madras and Bombay were naturally jealous of any curtailment of their powers, or a system of dual control, which might result from the appointment of an Inspector-General of Fortifications. So the Pioneers remained the Pioneers; and the Chief Engineers retained their dignity—and their allowances.

As soon as the Bombay Government had signed a treaty with the Marathas, they were free to make greater exertions to help Sir Eyre Coote in the Second Mysore War. General Mathews sailed on December 12th, 1782, and landed six days later on the Malabar coast where he took the fort of Rajamandroog[1] by storm and then laid siege to the port of Honavar (Onore), some 15 miles farther south. He captured this place on January 5th, and before the end of the month had seized the fortress of Bednore. Then, on March 9th, 1783, he reduced Mangalore, although he had neither supplies, transport nor ammunition adequate for a campaign so far from his base. Haidar Ali had died, and the Bombay Government, eager to retrieve their reputation after Goddard's failure, urged Mathews on to the point of recklessness in the hope of embarrassing Tipu Sultan and thus easing the situation on the Madras side. Unfortunately Mathews was a willing tool. Not content with Bednore and Mangalore, he proceeded to reduce many hill forts, and frittered away his small army to such an extent in garrisoning them that in Bednore he had finally only 400 Europeans and 1,200 sepoys. By this time Tipu was on his way from the east with a large army. He soon arrived before Bednore where his French engineers began a regular siege, and in the end forced Mathews to capitulate after a desperate resistance. The entire garrison was then put in irons and marched away as prisoners, and it is believed that the General and many others were forced to drink poison and died as a result. After the fall of Bednore every other place except Honavar gave way in succession until Tipù arrived at Mangalore which, owing to a very spirited defence of some months under Major John Campbell of the 73rd, put a stop to his victorious career.

A few of the Bombay Engineers served in this campaign in Malabar. Captain John Sartorius sailed with General Mathews in command of a detachment of Pioneers and was present at the capture of Mangalore. Captain Daniel Christie was Field Engineer to a force which recaptured Cannanore on December 14th, 1783, when the tide had

[1] Eighty miles south of Goa.

turned in favour of the British after the defence of Mangalore.[1] Under him was Ensign (afterwards Major-General) William Atkins,[2] who had been sent as Engineer with a detachment under General Norman McLeod to the relief of Mangalore. Another Engineer in Malabar was Lieutenant William Blachford, who was at the capture of Honavar and was the only Engineer officer in the garrison when Major Torriano defended the place successfully for eight months. Lieutenant-Colonel Charles Reynolds, the temporary Engineer of Goddard's campaign, had recovered sufficiently from his wounds to be on service also in Malabar, though holding an infantry command. Only those who have travelled in that country can imagine the hardships which these men had to endure. They were poorly equipped and badly fed, and they worked in fever-stricken jungles. Their commanders were reckless, and the enemy merciless and cruel.

The conclusion of peace with Tipu in March, 1784, ended for a time the active service of these few Engineers; but, as in Madras, the years prior to the outbreak of the Third Mysore War in 1790 were not wasted, for the Bombay Engineers did much surveying in Malabar, the Konkan, Bassein, Salsette and Bombay. Although the fort at Bombay had been finished, there was work to be done in improving the town and extending the docks and harbour. Changes occurred in the establishment of the Bombay Pioneers. Early in 1789 the Corps was reduced to one company; but, when hostilities began against Tipu in the following year, it was expanded and served in Mysore in the latter stages of the war under Lieutenant (afterwards Major-General) William Brooks of the Bombay Engineers. At the end of the war the Corps was reduced again to one company, but was expanded once more in 1797, when it reached the respectable total of four companies, each of 100 men, under the command of Captain-Lieutenant Bryce Moncrieff of the Bombay Engineers. Several of the Bombay Engineers in addition to Brooks went to the south, among them being Major John Sartorius who, in March, 1790, was in command of a British contingent at Dharwar, where the Marathas were besieging the Mysoreans. Sartorius had a brilliant career before his untimely death in 1801; but he had his misfortunes also, for we read in a Bombay General Order of October 2nd, 1791, the ambiguous entry that " Major Sartorius will be pleased to proceed as soon as possible to Cannanore where a Court-Martial will be held for his trial." He was probably more pleased by the acquittal which followed, and by his appointment later as Chief Engineer of the Bombay army, under Abercromby, in the Third Mysore War.[3] In 1795 he was fortifying Cannanore with Ensign William Cowper, and, four years afterwards, was conspicuous in the Fourth Mysore War as

---

[1] *Bombay General Orders.* Bombay Record Office, Vol. LXV, 1795-1815.
[2] Atkins became Chief Engineer of Bombay in 1806, and held the post for many years. He died in Bombay in 1822.
[3] See Chapter X.

Chief Engineer of the Bombay army under Stuart.[1] His name bears an honourable place in the records of the Royal Bombay Sappers and Miners.

Space does not admit of a further description of the exploits of the Bombay Engineers in the last quarter of the eighteenth century. They earned their pay by the sweat of their brows on the steamy coasts of Malabar and Kanara, in the malarial tracts of the Konkan and Gujarat, and in the crowded areas of Bombay. And so we leave them for a time and journey to other parts to follow some of the minor expeditions which preceded the outbreak of the Second Maratha War.

After the fall of Seringapatam in 1799, the British unfortunately released from its dungeons a Maratha free-booter named Dhundia Nagh,[2] who became so troublesome that he had to be hunted down. He had collected a large force, and was a constant menace to our detachments and convoys. During the course of operations which began in June under Colonel Stevenson, a column under Colonel Dalrymple had to cross the Tungabhadra to the north of Mysore to capture the fort of Honalli. Here, some of the Madras Engineers and Pioneers distinguished themselves, and especially Ensigns John Blair and William Garrard. They found the river in flood and had no pontoons or boats of any great size, so, as speed was essential, they brought their inventive faculties into play. Seeing how unreliable were the round basket-boats or coracles used by the natives, they proceeded to build a barge of bamboo framing, covered it with raw hides, and fitted it with a mast, sail and rudder. Garrard then volunteered to steer the contraption across stream in the face of the enemy, laden not only with men but with a six-pounder gun on its carriage. He landed his cargo safely, and afterwards made several trips, so that a battery was soon erected before Honalli and the enemy bolted. It was a daring exploit, bravely carried through.

In May, 1800, Wellesley himself took the field against Dhundia with two brigades of cavalry, three of infantry and a body of Pioneers under Captain Heitland of the Madras Infantry. Capturing the forts of Bednore, Kunigal and Dummal, he surprised Dhundia at Konagal on July 30th, and on September 10th, defeated and killed him under the fort at Manoli, thus ending a brief and decisive campaign. The operations emphasized the need for pontoons when an army is fighting in a country intersected by rivers, but no action seems to have been taken in the matter till more serious difficulties arose during the Second Maratha War. The Madras Pioneers were engaged in the same year in an expedition under Colonel Agnew against the savage Poligars of the impenetrable jungles in the extreme south, and earned the praise of the commander who reported that

---
[1] See Chapter X.
[2] Spelt also " Dhoondiah Waug," and other ways.

" the labour undergone by them was extremely severe and frequently performed under fire."[1]

After this came the expedition to Egypt, under Major-General David Baird, which sailed from Bombay in February, 1801. It was sent to co-operate with a British army under Sir Ralph Abercromby, which was despatched from England to eject the French from Egypt. The Indian units belonging to it had the honour of being the first to serve outside Asia. Baird hoped to join Abercromby in time to take his share in the fighting, but he was disappointed. He was delayed by the monsoon, and had to land at Kosseir near the head of the Red Sea ; thence he marched to the Nile, and so, by land and river, to northern Egypt. When at last he arrived in Rosetta on August 31st, Alexandria had surrendered already to the British, and Abercromby was dead. Lieutenants Thomas de Havilland of the Madras Engineers, and Samuel Goodfellow of the Bombay Engineers, sailed with Baird, and also a Lieutenant and two Ensigns of the Bengal Engineers and a Captain of the Royal Engineers.[2] They had a very arduous march across the desert from Kosseir to Keneh on the Nile when the thermometer rose to 115°. It seems that it was the custom in those days to be liberal to the British troops in the way of liquid refreshment, and some of the instructions for the march make curious reading : " In the morning, half a pint of wine should be issued to each man. The men's canteens should be filled with congee,[3] and just previous to their marching (at night) another half-pint of wine should be given them to mix with their congee. You will find fresh water at Moilah and Legaitha, which you will issue to your men ; also spirits, as your wine must be issued only on marching days. You have with you one gallon of wine for each European soldier. You will endeavour to dissuade your men from drinking a great quantity of water, which has been found very hurtful and weakening."

The expedition did not return to India till July, 1802, and de Havilland not till the middle of 1804, for he was captured in January of that year by a French privateer and was allowed to rejoin at Madras only on parole. While he was absent, great changes took place in the Madras Engineers and Pioneers. Major-General Patrick Ross and Colonel William Gent left India, and Colonel Elisha Trapaud became Chief Engineer, with Lieutenant-Colonel John Norris and 21 other Engineers under him. The Madras Pioneers developed into a large and important corps, for, on January 28th, 1803, their establishment was increased from 14 to 16 companies of 100 men each, the whole forming two battalions, one under Captain W. P. Heitland and the other under Captain J. Fitzpatrick, both of the Madras Infantry. In authorizing the new establishment the Com-

---
[1] *The Military History of the Madras Engineers and Pioneers*, by Major H. M. Vibart, Vol. I, p. 352.
[2] *Ibid.*, Vol. I, p. 356. The Captain was Howard Elphinstone, who came from the Cape of Good Hope to be C.R.E.
[3] *Kanji*. Rice-water ; gruel ; starch. In this case, gruel.

mander-in-Chief wrote that "the services of the Pioneers in this country always repay their expenses in war by the additional facility which they give to the movements of an army, and in peace by the useful labour which they perform." The impressive array of engineering talent in Madras seems to have stimulated Bengal into action, for, on July 28th, 1803, a General Order was issued in Calcutta for the raising of a corps of Bengal Pioneers at Cawnpore, consisting of three companies of 75 men each. Captain Thomas Wood, of the Bengal Engineers, recruited the men and was the first commandant, but soon handed over charge to Lieutenant John Swinton of the Bengal Infantry, a man distinguished both for his amazing courage and his leadership. So, before the outbreak of the Second Maratha War, Madras had 18 companies of Pioneers, Bombay four companies, and Bengal three. The figures are instructive.

The career of John Swinton, the father of the Bengal Sappers and Miners, deserves some mention. As an Assistant Engineer under Captain Thomas Wood, he took part, early in 1803, in some operations in the "Doab," between the Ganges and the Jumna. This brief campaign became known as the "Mud War" because certain mud forts—Sasni, Bijagarh and Kachaura—were besieged and captured. At Sasni, in January, Swinton made the batteries and was wounded while his men were carrying the ladders to the breach for an assault; and again, at Bijagarh, he led a party of 12 Europeans in storming an outwork near the breach.[1] His services were so conspicuous also at the capture of Kachaura in March that he was placed in command of the Bengal Pioneers for the campaign under General Lake in the Second Maratha War. A better choice could not have been made. Swinton was no engineer, but an officer of infantry; yet the officers and men of the King George's Own Bengal Sappers and Miners of to-day will admit that no man could have done more for the Corps in its embryo stage than this officer of another arm of the Service. Swinton commanded the Bengal Pioneers at the battle of Koil in August, 1803; he helped to carry the ladders at the storm of Aligarh in September, and greatly distinguished himself in the assault: he was at Laswari in November, at Gwalior in December, and afterwards in the relief force before Delhi. He carried the ladders, and was lamed for life, in the storm of Dig, but nevertheless rejoined his corps at Bhurtpore in time for the final attack on Holkar's camp in 1805. Then he marched with Lake in pursuit of the Marathas to the Punjab, and, though severely wounded in the following year at Komona, was present again at the capture of Fort Ganouri. A few years later we find him in the thick of the Nepal War, and then at the siege of Hathras. Wherever there was fighting, there was Swinton, lame but indomitable. His men worshipped the ground on which he trod, and he was, indeed, a born leader of Indian soldiers.

[1] *East India Military Calendar*, Vol. III, p. 415 *et seq.*

CHAPTER XII.

THE SECOND MARATHA WAR, 1803–1806.

IN the campaigns of 1803 to 1806 which, grouped together, form the Second Maratha War, our Engineers had often to direct siege operations against fortresses whose defences were made of mud, or rubble and mud, instead of stone. To many of them, this was a new experience, although a few had had a foretaste of it in the " Mud War " in the Doab. Most of the mud fortresses of India were not really formidable if attacked in the right way. Their design was often primitive and their defenders easily cowed by a resolute advance. Lieutenant Edward Lake, of the Madras Engineers, had a poor opinion of them, and of the native methods of siege warfare. " The natives of India," he writes in 1825,[1] " do not seem to be aware of the importance of that maxim which is the ground-work of European Fortification, namely that every work of a Fortress should be defended or flanked by some other. Their system is that of a simple inclosure, consisting of a continued wall with round towers at intervals ; but to some of their more important places they have added one and sometimes two ditches, together with outworks, the bottom generally containing *dead ground* close to the scarp to which the besiegers may attach their miners with perfect safety. The Natives appear to be utterly ignorant of the advantage of attacking a salient angle, or of the art of conducting approaches by Sap ; and, generally speaking, they are also unacquainted with Mining. When one of their armies sits down before a place, the object appears rather to be to harass the besieged than to effect an entrance by breaching the walls. At night, to guard against a sally, the guns are withdrawn to the camp, and this ridiculous process is continued till the besieged are tired out."

He adds an account by an eye-witness of the siege of the Nizam's town of Biscondah by the Marathas in 1815. It was a leisurely affair :—

" The besieging army consisted principally of horse and about four guns which were drawn out in the open plain at about fifty yards asunder. The besiegers had a Portuguese, who levelled each gun himself and appeared to have the direction of the attack. They fired about once in a quarter of an hour, and if by chance a shot struck any part of the wall so as to raise a dust, the air resounded with

[1] *Journals of the Sieges of the Madras Army in the Years* 1817, 1818 *and* 1819, by Edward Lake, p. 10.

acclamations in praise of the Portuguese, who seemed in no small degree flattered thereby. The siege was brought to a conclusion in a curious way. A small party of Europeans were pitched near the place about three weeks after, and five or six of them stole out of camp at night to assist the besiegers, and fired the guns so fast that the town was found evacuated next morning. Two of the Europeans were wounded in this frolic."

Edward Lake's opinion, however, that generally speaking the natives of India were ignorant of mining, is not supported by the anonymous writer of *Observations on the Attack of Mud Forts* (1815). He describes how, in 1804 and 1805, the native defenders of such works drove mine galleries from their counterscarp and arranged to fire each mine by strewing loose powder on a platform at its entrance, and, when the enemy advanced, throwing live coals at the powder from across the ditch. But the cream of his remarks is his account of the steps taken by the native attackers to destroy such mines before the assault. "*Bhungees*," he says, " who are men usually employed to perform the most menial offices, are also engaged by the natives to execute the most dangerous services : among others, that here mentioned. Two or three of these are generally employed. They strip themselves naked, take each a pot filled with live coal, and having in the day reconnoitred, they go at night up to the ditch and strew the fire along the counter-scarp so as to roll down and fall upon the loose powder on the platform and fire the mine. If they succeed, and escape the explosion and the enemy, they receive a handsome reward ; if they do not escape, it is invariably given to their families. In this way the natives sometimes succeed in springing the enemy's countermines ; but we shall not presume to recommend it further than by saying that a trial can do no harm (!). It was suggested at Bhurtpore (in 1805) and, on the 19th February, three Bhungees were procured, who undertook the execution of it for a reward of a thousand rupees each if they should succeed. They asked a few rupees, which was readily granted ; and being provided with everything they required, two confidential men were sent along with them to see that they were guilty of no deception. When they had taken leave, however, they bought a quantity of spirits with the money they received, which so intoxicated them that, by the time they reached the trenches, they were totally incapable of doing anything and the plan failed." We presume that the two " confidential men " shared in the festivities of this band of martyrs.

Military engineering during the Maratha wars was still in the experimental stage, and many extraordinary suggestions were advanced by amateur enthusiasts. An instance occurs in an idea put forward by the author of *Observations on the Attack of Mud Forts*. He prefaces his remarks by explaining that the natives of Hindustan were capable gunners but mediocre engineers, so that their forts had always a few weak points ; they relied on lofty ramparts, although, in his opinion, a large and deep ditch would have been a more formidable obstacle. They never used drawbridges, and accordingly the entrance gateway was easy to assault as there was no ditch at that point. So far, he is sound in his views. But then comes his masterpiece which draws upon him the ridicule of Edward Lake.[1] He proposes that, in order to make the outer defences untenable, an " elevated battery " for three 18-pounders should be built within 80 yards of the counterscarp to destroy the defences by plunging fire. The gun platforms are to be raised some 30 feet above the ground on a gigantic mound of earth so that the parapet of this monstrosity would be quite 37 feet above the surrounding plain ; and he fondly hopes and believes that 100 men could raise this hill under the fire of the enemy in 40 hours ! It is needless to say that his theory was never put into practice.

When the nineteenth century began, England had extended her frontiers in all parts of India over conquered territories, or by subsidiary alliances with native states, until they touched the Maratha dominions on every side. The Marathas were naturally alarmed by this expansion, but for a time they avoided hostilities. This was due chiefly to the influence of Nana Farnavis, their minister at Poona, who had steered their ship of state through the troubles about Raghuba, the negotiations which led to the Treaty of Salbai, and the war against Hyderabad when all the Maratha states, in combination for the last time, defeated the Nizam at the battle of Kharda. But Nana Farnavis died on March 13th, 1800, and with him departed all cohesion and moderation in the great confederacy. Mahadji Sindhia of Gwalior, and Tukoji Rao Holkar of Indore, had been succeeded by Daulat Rao Sindhia and Jaswant Rao Holkar ; and at Poona, eclipsed by the martial power of Gwalior and Indore, was Baji Rao, " the most worthless, the wickedest and the falsest of the Peshwas."[2] After Nana's death, Sindhia and Holkar fought for the right to control the wretched Baji Rao, and for a time Sindhia had the best of the struggle ; but when Holkar had defeated him and Baji Rao at Poona in October, 1802, Baji Rao fled to Bassein and appealed to Marquis Wellesley, the Governor-General, for help. This seemed to be a good opportunity to strengthen the British power in the Maratha empire, so Wellesley agreed to restore the Peshwa to his throne at Poona, and, on December 31st, 1802, executed with him, as nominal head of the Marathas, the Treaty of Bassein. Under this agreement a subsidary force of the Company was to be stationed in the Poona state, and the Peshwa was to surrender territory producing revenue amounting to 26 lakhs of rupees yearly—a typical example of the

---

[1] *Journals of the Sieges of the Madras Army*, by Edward Lake, p. 219, and *Observations on the Attack of Mud Forts*, p. 46.
[2] *India under Wellesley*, by P. E. Roberts, p. 26.

alliances by which the Company habitually extended its sway, and which ended normally in annexation.

The Treaty of Bassein committed the Company either to control the Maratha states or to fight them. "Wellesley's subsidiary troops," says Sir Alfred Lyall,[1] "were encamped at the capitals of the four great Indian powers—at Mysore, Hyderabad, Lucknow and Poona." Sindhia, Holkar and the Raja of Berar were greatly alarmed when they heard of the treaty, and regarded it as an open surrender of independence. Even Baji Rao began to have misgivings. He sent envoys to Sindhia and Berar to excuse himself and invite them to advance on Poona, and Sindhia then crossed the Narbada and came to within 20 miles of the frontier of Hyderabad. Baji Rao was restored to his throne by Arthur Wellesley's troops on May 13th, with much pomp and ceremony, and immediately the situation became threatening, for Sindhia was found to be concerting plans with Raghuji Bhonsla, the Raja of Berar, and his army was so placed that he could either march easily on Poona or raid Hyderabad. After some fruitless protests, Wellesley therefore sent an ultimatum to Sindhia on July 14th, in which he required him to separate his army from that of Berar and retire across the Narbada. Neither Sindhia nor Berar, however, would move; and so, on August 3rd, 1803, the British declared war against these two chiefs, while Holkar, hating both the British and Sindhia, held aloof in sullen but watchful isolation.

The opening campaign of the Second Maratha War, against Daulat Rao Sindhia and the Raja of Berar, was one of the most successful ever fought by the British in India. The Government had been preparing for it for months, and no plans could have worked out with greater precision than theirs. Swift and crushing blows were dealt to the enemy in four separate theatres—the northern Deccan, Gujarat, Hindustan and Orissa—by 50,000 soldiers of the Company pitted against five times their number of Marathas, of whom 40,000 had been organized and drilled by Sindhia's French adventurer, De Boigne, and his successor, Perron.[2] The defeat of Perron's trained army in northern India was the first objective of Lieutenant-General Gerard Lake, the British Commander-in-Chief. Afterwards he proposed to capture Agra and Delhi, to take over the authority of the senile Mughal emperor, to form an alliance with the petty states of Rajputana south of the Jumna, and to annex Bundelkhand which lay to the east of those states. These several objectives in the north were to be attained by the "Grand Army," 10,500 strong, under Lake himself, whose headquarters were at Cawnpore. The objectives assigned by him to his subordinate commanders elsewhere were of

[1] *The Rise and Expansion of the British Dominion in India*, by Sir Alfred Lyall.
[2] Sindhia had given M. Perron (or Piron) some land on the banks of the Jumna, and the Frenchman had formed it almost into an independent state, garrisoned by most of Sindhia's regular infantry.

less importance. Colonel Arthur Wellesley in the Deccan was to defeat the southern army of Sindhia, which had been reinforced by an army from Berar, and to keep these forces from marching southwards on Poona or Hyderabad. Colonel Murray, with whom was Captain John Cliffe of the Bombay Engineers,[1] was to fight the Marathas in Gujarat on the western coast and protect the loyal Gaikwar of Baroda from the vengeance of Sindhia. In the east was Colonel Harcourt,[2] with Captain James Blunt of the Bengal Engineers as his Chief Engineer. His task was to deal with the Raja of Berar, and, by taking Cuttack and Balasore on the eastern coast, to complete a line of British territory from Calcutta to Madras. The western and eastern campaigns, under Murray and Harcourt, were fully successful before the end of September, 1803; but as they were of minor importance, and involved no engineering work of note, we will pass to the operations conducted by Wellesley and Lake.

Wellesley, fresh from his triumph over Dundhia Nagh, was far away on the northern border of Mysore before the war began, and lay with a powerful force at Harihar (Hurryhur); but he soon began to move northward, crossing the Tungabhadra in March, and the Kistna in April, preparatory to installing Baji Rao on the throne at Poona. Thus, on a political pretext, the Governor-General cleverly secured some concentration of his armies and brought a great commander into the field of possible warfare to face Sindhia and Berar. Wellesley waited impatiently at Poona while these chiefs were playing their game of procrastination and intrigue. He knew the mobility of his adversaries, and wished to fight them when the rivers were in flood. He had prepared most carefully for a campaign in the rainy season, and, many months before, had ordered the boats and pontoons from Bombay which would enable him to cross the flooded rivers anywhere while Sindhia searched the banks for fords. But, through the incapability or obstruction of Jonathan Duncan, Governor of Bombay, no boats or pontoons had reached him by June. A Pontoon Train had been formed in Bombay in May, 1803, and placed under the command of Lieutenant Samuel Goodfellow of the Bombay Engineers[3] with orders to join Wellesley; but though it started on its journey towards the interior, and progressed for a few miles, the carriages broke down in the torrential rain and the unit was obliged to return to Bombay. For a time it was employed in Gujarat under Colonel Murray, and then, in July, a second and successful attempt was made to send it to Wellesley. But even when it reached him, it could not always keep pace with him—perhaps through lack of bullocks—for he had no pontoons at the critical battle of Assaye and was terribly handicapped by that fact.

[1] John Cliffe distinguished himself at the capture of the town of Broach in Gujarat, when a force under Colonel Woodington took it on August 25th, 1803.
[2] The original commander of the eastern force was Lieutenant-Colonel Campbell, who, however, was invalided soon after the operations began.
[3] *Bombay General Orders*, May 20th, 1803.

If Wellesley had not been a master of strategy he would have been a notable engineer. No further proof of this is needed than that supplied in the memoranda on basket-boats, and on the manner of laying a bridge of boats across a river, which he wrote before he left the Mysore border.[1] For instance, he describes in minute detail how a basket-boat should be made. It should be 10 feet in diameter and 2 feet 3 inches high : the leather covering should overlap the gunwale and be lashed to a framework, the nature, dimensions and construction of which are all given in full. Again, in his memorandum on floating bridges, he directs his engineers how to stretch a cable across a river, to float their boats down to it, to attach them to it by rings, to lay a downstream cable if required, to cross-brace the line of boats, and to lay shore-transoms, baulks and chesses. Every contingency is foreseen, every preparation made. It was this attention to detail, in combination with great tactical ability, courage and clear judgment, which brought Wellesley at last to the pinnacle of his fame as Duke of Wellington.

With just over 11,000 men, including 1,600 Europeans, and assisted by some thousands of native horse, Wellesley advanced northwards upon Ahmadnagar on August 8th, 1803. The walled town outside the fort was strongly garrisoned by Sindhia's regular infantry and 1,000 Arabs, and its lofty bastions and massive curtains presented a formidable obstacle. A column under Colonel Harness was repulsed in the first attempt at an escalade, but another gained the crest, and in a few hours the town was captured. "These English are a strange people and their General a wonderful man," wrote a Maratha chief. " They came here in the morning, looked at the pettah-wall, walked over it, killed all the garrison, and returned to breakfast."[2] The fall of the *pettah* was followed, four days later, by the surrender of the fort which, with bastions 60 feet high and a wide dry ditch, was considered by Wellesley to be one of the strongest in India. Some Engineers and Pioneers took part in these operations, and Captain John Johnson of the Bombay Engineers and Captain W. P. Heitland of the Pioneers were mentioned in despatches. Johnson was Chief Engineer with the force, and also, for a time, Commandant of the Guides in place of Ensign George Rowley,[3] of the Madras Engineers, who had died of exposure in June while holding that appointment. Ensign John Blakiston, also of the Madras Engineers, was present at the siege ; but curiously enough, there is no record that any Bombay Engineer other than Johnson took part in it. Johnson was very junior to hold so important and responsible a post as that of Chief Engineer with the army under

---

[1] *Wellington Despatches*, by S. J. Owen, pp. 618, 619. Memoranda dated March 27th, 1803.
[2] *A History of the British Army*, by the Hon. J. W. Fortescue, Vol. V, p. 17.
[3] Ensign Rowley took part in the capture of Seringapatam in 1799, and was a good descriptive writer. (See Chapter X.)

Wellesley, and it is odd that General Robert Nicholson,[1] the Chief Engineer in Bombay, did not take the field. Perhaps he was too senior.

By capturing Ahmadnagar, Wellesley established himself in a strong position on the northern frontier of Hyderabad; also he prevented Sindhia from moving on Poona, and deprived him of a vast store of supplies and munitions. It was a great stroke, and confined Sindhia to his second plan of a raid into Hyderabad, which he proceeded to put into execution. Wellesley, however, was ready with a counter-move and marched to Aurangabad, arriving there on August 29th after crossing the swollen river Godavari in the wicker boats which he had designed a few months before. Already the value of his engineering ability and careful preparation was becoming evident. But he reached Aurangabad in great straits for lack of transport and supplies for his stupendous horde of followers. To picture Wellesley's army in camp or on the march we may glance at a few extracts from a description by Major William Thorn of the 25th Light Dragoons :—[2]

" It is obvious that in a country where no regular supplies can be depended upon, necessaries must be provided before-hand, or obtained from a train of followers whose desire of gain attaches them to the service. Hence the line of march increases the appendages to an army, particularly where an enemy, like the one to whom we were opposed, spreads devastation in every direction.

" The camp followers in such a case become exceedingly numerous, and may be fairly estimated at ten persons to every fighting man; so that where the force consists of ten thousand soldiers, there will be one hundred thousand non-combatants consisting of the following descriptions. First, an attendant to every elephant, of which valuable animals there are several hundreds, for carrying the public camp equipage, besides some thousands of camels, to every three of whom there is at least one attendant, with a proportionate number of tent Lascars who are employed in pitching and striking the tents, a service not to be dispensed with in a country where bivouacking under the canopy of heaven would soon destroy an army.

" Every horse, whether of the cavalry or not, has in addition to the rider, for the most part two attendants. Besides an immense number of draught bullocks for the use of the artillery, park and heavy ordnance carts, to every three of which there is at least one driver, large droves of Brinjarree (Bhandari) bullocks, from eighty to one hundred thousand, are employed in carrying grain. These Brinjarrees are a peculiar class of Hindoos who live by collecting

---

[1] Robert Nicholson retired in May, 1804, and was followed by Colonel Joseph Bland. Early in 1806, Bland died, and was succeeded at the end of that year by Lieutenant-Colonel William Atkins.

[2] *Memoir of the War in India conducted by Lord Lake and Sir Arthur Wellesley,* 1803–06, by William Thorn (1818), p. 84.

LIEUT.-GENERAL ROBERT NICHOLSON.

grain in districts where it is easily procured and selling it in places where the harvests have been less abundant. To these purveyors of the army, who, with their connexions, surpass calculation, must be added the palankeen and doolie bearers for the conveyance of the sick and wounded. An army is further numerically increased by the servants which every officer is under the necessity of employing to take charge of his live and dead stock, for the officers must provide their own poultry, sheep and particular goats to supply them with milk for their tea. The attendants, therefore, which these services render expedient, may be estimated at ten to a subaltern, twenty to a captain, thirty to a field officer, and so on in proportion."

After Wellesley had marched into Aurangabad he learnt that Sindhia's cavalry had entered the Nizam's territory through the Ajanta Pass; so he, with his main army, and Colonel Stevenson with a detached force, executed a series of manoeuvres to foil the enemy's designs on Hyderabad. At the end of this period of marching and counter-marching, Wellesley decided that the time had come to give battle to Sindhia, who then lay near Jafarabad, about 50 miles northeast of Aurangabad, and, on September 21st, he made a plan with Stevenson for a combined movement to attack from opposite directions three days later. The operation failed because Stevenson's guides misled him; and when, on the 23rd, Wellesley came suddenly upon Sindhia's army of 40,000 men encamped on a small peninsula formed by the rivers Kaitna and Jua, he was without Stevenson's assistance. Nevertheless, he launched his troops to the glorious action of Assaye against an enemy who outnumbered him by five to one and held a position which had every strategical advantage.

Wellesley planned to turn the left flank of the Maratha army, and directed Captain John Johnson, his Chief Engineer, to ride forward and examine the road and then to lead the infantry to the attack.[1] The only known ford across the Kaitna was under the direct fire of the enemy's artillery, and, sad to say, Wellesley could not bridge the river because his pontoon train was absent. But he noticed that, farther along the bank, two small villages were immediately opposite each other, and concluded rightly that there must be a ford between them. It was a clever deduction; and Johnson, who reconnoitred, reported that there was indeed a ford at that spot. He led the troops to it, and they pushed through the stream and up the bank, only to find, however, that Sindhia was changing position so that they could not outflank him. The details of the desperate battle which followed are well known. How our troops captured the first and second lines; how they were charged in flank and rear by cavalry and were decimated by the close fire of 100 guns; how the British cavalry

[1] *The Military History of the Madras Engineers and Pioneers*, by Major H. M. Vibart, Vol. I, p. 379.

and their Indian comrades covered themselves with glory; and how Wellesley and his splendid infantry at last carried the village of Assaye by storm—these are phases of the battle which are recorded by many historians. The British army lost more than 1,500 men, but the results were worth the price.

The Madras Pioneers, under Heitland, were in the thick of the fight, and contributed 71 casualties towards the total. Their commandant escaped uninjured although his horse was shot under him. After the battle the men were engaged in burying the dead, and an incident is recorded by Vibart which shows how comedy can be mixed with tragedy in war. In their wanderings over the field of battle the Pioneers found several enemy standards, and were much impressed by their gay colours. The flags were naturally torn and soiled, so, as they seemed of no great value, the men gave them to their wives to use as petticoats, " from which ignoble use," as Vibart says, " they were afterwards rescued."

Having won the battle of Assaye, " a triumph more splendid than any recorded in Deccan history,"[1] Wellesley had no more fighting for a time. The offensive was taken up by his subordinate, Colonel Stevenson, who rejoined him on September 24th, while the defeated Marathas retired to guard Burhanpur and their celebrated fortress of Asirgarh. Screened by the manœuvres of the main army, Stevenson crossed the Tapti, captured Burhanpur on October 15th and besieged Asirgarh till it surrendered six days later. The last of Sindhia's possessions in the Deccan having then been wrested from him, Wellesley resolved to subdue the Raja of Berar by taking his mountain fortress of Gawilgarh lying 80 miles to the east of Burhanpur. Sindhia was so much discouraged by the loss of Asirgarh that he sued for peace on November 11th, and, on the 22nd, Wellesley agreed to a truce with him as he hoped thus to be free to crush Berar more easily. It soon appeared, however, that Sindhia had no intention of observing the terms of the armistice, so Wellesley resumed the offensive and brought him and the Raja to action on November 29th, 1803, at Argaon (Argaum), 50 miles south-east of Burhanpur. There he gained a decisive victory over the combined Maratha armies, totalling 30,000 men, capturing 38 guns, many standards and quantities of ammunition, and driving the enemy from the field with the loss of 3,000 men, while his own did not amount to 400.

Ensign John Blakiston, of the Madras Engineers, watched the cavalry pursuit after Argaon, and was much interested in the way in which the British troopers attacked the flying Marathas. The bodies of the native horsemen were protected by padded clothing, and their heads covered by large turbans, and Blakiston describes[2]

---

[1] *A History of the Marathas*, by J. G. Duff, Vol. III, p. 243.
[2] Extracts from " Twelve Years' Military Adventures," by Major John Blakiston, appearing in *The Military History of the Madras Engineers and Pioneers*, by Major H. M. Vibart, Vol. I, p. 386.

GAWILGARH.

how each trooper of the 19th Dragoons, in order to cut down a fugitive, first gave point at his turban and, having knocked it off, got a fair blow at the head underneath. It was a bloody business, but war is not an affair of kid gloves. Blakiston records also a more peaceful and amusing scene which he watched from his tent at a time when the cattle in the camp were very short of forage. "I observed one of my cattle," he writes, "stretching out his head to a turban. After giving it a turn or two with his nose he seized the loose end in his mouth and began to swallow it. He swallowed and swallowed until, of about ten yards of stuff, a small bit only remained pendant. I observed his operations for about an hour. At this critical moment the owner returned, and beheld the end dangling from the mouth of the animal. With an oath he flew at the bullock, and seizing the end, pulled and pulled, hand over hand and oath upon oath, while the cloth came forth like a measuring tape. The man's rage and gestures, and the beast's astonishment at the novel kind of emetic he was undergoing, formed a scene absolutely irresistible."

After his victory at Argaon, Wellesley moved eastwards to lay siege to Gawilgarh, and was close to that place on December 6th. "The fort itself," writes Fortescue,[1] "was situated on a lofty mountain in a range of hills. . . . and, by a natural configuration of the ground, the stronghold was divided into two distinct parts, a main fort or citadel fronting to the south, and an outer or lesser fort which covered the approach to the inner on the north. Between the two forts was a deep gorge. . . . One and all of the defences were well built of stone with ramparts and towers, but without a ditch. The roads which led to the fort were three. The first reached the citadel from the south and was not only very long and steep, but so narrow as to be impracticable for cattle. The second started from the outer fort on the north-west side, circled round the western face of the main fort within range of its guns for a long distance, and finally formed the main communication with the country to the southward. But it was too narrow to be used as a regular approach, besides which the rock on each side of the gate had been scarped. There remained a third road on the north side, leading to the outer fort directly from the village of Labada,[2] and here the ground was level with the works. But on the other hand the road to Labada from Ellichpur wound for thirty miles through mountains and jungle, offering terrible obstacles to the transport of guns and stores. . . . In fact, as Wellesley said, the great difficulty in attacking Gawilgarh was to approach it at all."

The ubiquitous Captain John Johnson was sent forward to reconnoitre the south side of the fortress which was the nearest to Ellichpur, but he found that front so forbidding that he decided that no attack could succeed against it. Then he started on a circuitous

---

[1] *A History of the British Army*, by the Hon. J. W. Fortescue, Vol. V, p. 41.
[2] A village 500 yards north of the north gate, occupying approximately the position of the letter A in the plan of Gawilgarh.

expedition into the mountains, taking young Blakiston with him, and, after marching hard for two days, managed to approach Gawilgarh from the north and saw that the outer fort was connected on that side to a small table-land by a neck about 300 yards in width, closed only by a strong wall without a ditch. In spite of the enormous difficulties of an approach from the north, Johnson decided to recommend that operation, and Wellesley accepted his proposal. Accordingly, on December 7th, Wellesley advanced at the head of a force of infantry and all the cavalry, and sent Stevenson with the remainder of the army, including the Pioneers[1] and a siege train, to march through the mountains to attack Gawilgarh from the north. Johnson guided Stevenson, and Blakiston remained with Wellesley to direct the engineering operations in the southern or secondary attack.

For four days the Madras Pioneers under Heitland sweated and laboured, with the Pioneers from Bombay, to make a practicable road for the heavy guns which Stevenson's men hauled along in their wake. " The exertions of the army," says Blakiston, " in cutting a road through the mountains was such as to call forth the warmest applause of the General. The Pioneers, as usual, performed their task in a most efficient manner ; but the conduct of Captain Johnson of the Engineers was the theme of admiration from the General downwards. To great natural and acquired talents, he joined a zeal and an ardour which I never saw equalled." The work of Johnson and the Pioneers before Gawilgarh in 1803 reminds one of the exploits of Patrick Ross and his men before Savandroog in 1791. The conditions were similar, and each Engineer showed the same indomitable energy and perseverance in the face of extraordinary obstacles. The sieges of these mountain fortresses gave unique opportunities for the display of skill and resource, and, to their credit be it said, our Engineers seldom failed to rise to the occasion.

When darkness had fallen on December 12th, Stevenson was able to erect two batteries fronting the north face of the outer fort, while Wellesley, on the southern side, threw up a battery to breach the wall near the South or " Peer puttee " Gate and to divert attention from the main attack. Only the northern batteries could make any impression on the solid masonry, but they were sufficiently effective to allow Stevenson to assault the outer fort on the 15th, while Wellesley pushed forward towards the southern and north-western gates. Stevenson's troops were soon in the outer fort, and were joined there by Wellesley's men through the north-western gate. Then, to their surprise, they saw that the outer fort was separated

---

[1] A detachment of 262 Bombay Pioneers accompanied Stevenson. It is believed that they were two companies from Kanara and Malabar. If so, they took part not only in the siege of Gawilgarh but also in the siege of Asirgarh and the battle of Argaon, but they were not present at Assaye. (See *A Brief History of the Royal Bombay Sappers and Miners*, p. 3.) A large contingent of the Madras Pioneers, under Captain Heitland, was present at Gawilgarh.

PLAN OF GAVILGARH.

A Site of batteries. N. attack
B N.W gate - attacked by Chalmers
C South gate on which a subsidiary attack was made
D Wall escaladed after capture of outer fort
E Breach.

Furlongs 0 2 4 6

from the citadel by a deep gorge defended by more walls which, however, they escaladed under a heavy fire and were shortly in possession of the whole of Gawilgarh. Vast numbers of the enemy were killed, and the victorious troops searched busily for the immense treasure which the fortress was said to contain; but in this they were disappointed, for the specie and jewels had been removed secretly by the defenders before the place was assaulted.

With the fall of Gawilgarh,[1] the subsidiary campaigns of the Second Maratha War drew to a close. Colonel Harcourt had already ended his campaign in Cuttack with the capture of the fort of Barabati, and this, coupled with the loss of Gawilgarh, was too much for the Bhonsla Raja of Berar who proceeded to conclude with the Company the Treaty of Deogaon (Deogaum) on December 17th, 1803, under which he ceded Cuttack, Balasore and other territory to the victors. Sindhia then found himself deserted by his ally and hastened to save what he could by signing the Treaty of Surji Arjangaon on December 29th, surrendering all his land between the Ganges and the Jumna, his territories south of the Ajanta Hills, Broach, Ahmadnagar and many forts, in return for Asirgarh, Burhanpur, Gujarat and some other tracts which were given back to him. Wellesley marched in triumph towards Poona, and there we will leave him to follow General Lake from victory to victory in the north.

Lake's campaign was as brilliant as it was brief. Its primary objective may be summed up in one phrase—to defeat Perron's army in the field. Fortescue writes[2] of Lake that on the field of battle he was not only a grand leader, but a great commander, adored by all ranks of his army, and that although his failure at Bhurtpore stands out as a sad example of his rough and ready methods, an honourable place in the history of the army must always be reserved for this indomitable Guardsman. At last the Company had found two Generals of the first calibre, Wellesley and Lake; and while Wellesley was beginning his advance on Aurangabad, Lake marched with the Grand Army from Cawnpore on August 7th, 1803, to capture Aligarh where Perron had concentrated his troops.

The fort at Aligarh had inner and outer walls, both with circular towers at intervals, and the whole was surrounded by an immense wet ditch in which, as Lake said,[3] "a seventy-four might sail." The Grand Army had no bridging equipment; and so, as the ditch could only be crossed by a causeway leading to the outer gateway, Lake decided to assault at that point and erected two batteries on September 3rd to breach the outworks near it. At dawn on the following day, the stormers rushed at the gateway where they were met by heavy fire from three directions, but they managed to hold their

---

[1] The fortifications of Gawilgarh no longer exist. They were dismantled in 1858. (See *Berar Gazetteer*, 1870, edited by A. C. Lyall, p. 144.)
[2] *A History of the British Army*, by the Hon. J. W. Fortescue, Vol. V, pp. 135–137.
[3] *Wellesley Despatches*, Vol. III, p. 293.

position till the gate was broken down by a 12-pounder; then they dashed along a circular road to a second gate which was quickly carried. The island outwork defending the entrance being now in their hands, they had next to gain the main fortifications. Hurrying across a second causeway, they seized the third gate before the enemy could close it, and then, turning to the left, charged for a quarter of a mile to the final gateway leading into the interior of the fortress. They found this gate shut, and the 12-pounder could make little impression on it, so they were forced to halt under a devastating fire at point-blank range until some hero contrived to force an entrance through a small wicket gate and gained the ramparts with his men. There followed a scene of terrible carnage. The defenders jumped by hundreds into the ditch and were drowned: hundreds more were bayoneted by the furious stormers. It is said, indeed, that more than 2,000 of Sindhia's troops perished in these few hours.

The man who won Aligarh for the British was the brave fellow who, courting certain death, jumped first through the wicket gate, and we may well ask who he was. If the writer of the *East India Military Calendar* is to be believed, he was Lieutenant John Swinton of the Bengal Pioneers. "On September 4th, 1803," according to the *Calendar*, " he (Swinton) carried the ladders at the storm of Aligarh and was the first who entered the wicket at the last gateway." Fortescue remarks[1] that Major M'Leod of the Seventy-sixth succeeded in passing the wicket and ascending the ramparts, and he does not mention Swinton. But Engineers will prefer to claim the honour for Swinton, who probably showed the way to M'Leod and his gallant Highlanders. Lieutenant William Forrest of the Pioneers helped Swinton in the attack, and it seems that the Engineer with the force was Lieutenant Henry Carmichael-Smyth[2] of the Bengal Corps, who underwent his baptism of fire at Aligarh.

After a few days spent in strengthening the defences of Aligarh, Lake marched for Delhi, much pleased by the news that Perron and other French officers had quitted the service of Sindhia, and that an inferior man named Louis Bourquin[3] had taken command. Having covered 18 miles on September 11th, Lake found Bourquin with 19,000 soldiers and 100 guns occupying a position eight miles south-east of Delhi with the Jumna in his rear. The British General could put only 4,500 tired men into the fight, and so resorted to a clever strategem to help him towards victory. He lured the Marathas[4]

[1] *A History of the British Army*, by the Hon. J. W. Fortescue, Vol. V, p. 51.
[2] *East India Military Calendar*, Vol. II, p. 337. Henry Carmichael-Smyth was the brother of the Commanding Engineer in the Netherlands and France in 1814–18, who was present at Waterloo and rose to be Major-General Sir James Carmichael-Smyth, Bt., C.B., etc.
[3] Bourquin had been a cook and a manufacturer of fireworks before he became the Commander-in-Chief of Sindhia's northern army.
[4] It is convenient to allude to the enemy as " Marathas," but actually they were mostly recruited from the present United Provinces and Punjab, and included men of all the martial races of the north.

from their trenches by a sudden retirement of his cavalry who, when pursued by the enemy, wheeled to either flank and exposed their infantry drawn up in battle array. These opened a tremendous fire on the advancing Marathas and then dashed forward with the bayonet. The enemy broke and fled, and the cavalry pursued them to the Jumna in which large numbers of the fugitives were drowned. The Marathas lost 3,000 men and 86 guns in the battle of Delhi, and, when Lake entered the Mughal capital on the 16th, he had already received the surrender of Bourquin and his officers and had extinguished the French power in northern India. His main objective had been attained.

Sindhia was tottering to his fall. Assaye ended his ambitions in Central India on September 23rd, and Lake, marching from Delhi, reached Muttra on October 9th, where he made a treaty with the Raja of Bhurtpore which was designed to relieve the latter from Sindhia's domination. The way then lay open to Agra, the " key of Hindustan," and Lake took that fortress without much difficulty on the 18th, Carmichael-Smyth being his Engineer, and Swinton and Forrest assisting him with their Bengal Pioneers. Vast quantities of stores and many trophies of victory[1] were secured, and the troops received large sums in prize-money. Yet there still remained in the field a remnant of Sindhia's army under a Frenchman named Dudrenec, so Lake set out after this force till he brought it to bay at Laswari, about 80 miles south of Delhi. There, on November 1st, 1803, he annihilated the last battalions of the so-called " Deccan Invincibles " trained by de Boigne. The fight was desperate in the extreme, the enemy's gunners standing to their guns till they were bayoneted and the infantry and cavalry dying like heroes. Of the great confederacy which had threatened the life of the Company, only Holkar then remained as a possible foe.

Jaswant Rao Holkar of Indore had been an interested spectator of the campaigns of 1803. He was glad to watch the humiliation of his enemy Sindhia, but he drew a false conclusion from the fact that he was left severely alone by the Company. Swollen with ambition and pride, he became at last so obstructive, and the position which he took up near Ajmer was so menacing, that Lake marched to the east of Jaipur in February, 1804, to be ready to take action when required. But when the Governor-General learnt that Holkar was attempting to induce Sindhia to break his treaty and join with him against the British, he saw that war against Indore was inevitable, and on April 16th ordered Lake to take the field against this new enemy.

The plan of campaign was sound and accurate. British forces,

---

[1] Among the trophies was a gigantic piece of ordnance known as the " great gun of Agra." It was of brass, about 14 feet in length and with a calibre of 23 inches. Its weight was 43 tons, and it threw a shot weighing 1,500 lb. Unfortunately it was sunk in the Jumna when on its way to Calcutta, and, when recovered, was destroyed by order of Lord William Bentinck.

in co-operation with the armies of Sindhia and the Gaikwar, were to attack Holkar from Gujarat, Malwa and the Deccan, while Lake drove him from Hindustan. At first, all went well. Holkar retired before Lake to Kotah, and, on May 15th, a column under Colonel Don captured Rampura where Carmichael-Smyth and Forrest were mentioned for good work. But Lake then made his first mistake. Instead of pressing on southwards in pursuit of the Marathas, he withdrew northwards to Agra and Cawnpore, leaving two detachments under Colonels Don and Monson to block the passes in the mountains through which the enemy might return from Malwa to invade Hindustan. He discarded the initiative, and assumed a defensive role, though Holkar continued his retreat almost to Ujjain, drawing Monson on as far as Kotah. Then unfortunately Monson went far beyond his instructions and advanced through the Mukundwara (Mokundra) Pass to attack the Marathas with the help of a column which he knew to be coming from Gujarat. The columns failed to meet, and Monson was forced to begin a most disastrous retreat on July 8th, which ended only when, on August 31st, the remnants of his force straggled into Agra, having lost their guns, ammunition and baggage.[1] The rain fell in torrents during this march, all the rivers were in flood, and at every river-crossing the men were harried by cavalry and bombarded by artillery. There were no pontoons or boats with the force, and for this the blame must rest on Lake. It is unbelievable that Wellesley would have been guilty of such an omission; but Lake, though as gallant a soldier as ever stepped, was not a Wellesley.

Monson's retreat had grave results. Holkar advanced jubilantly into Hindustan : Sindhia began to waver, and the Raja of Bhurtpore made plans to break his treaty and join the enemy. However, Lake lost no time in taking effective action. Marching from Cawnpore on September 3rd, he concentrated near Agra to collect supplies and then advanced towards Muttra on October 1st to deal with Holkar's cavalry who were watching him while the Maratha infantry and guns went northwards to capture Delhi. Fortunately an able man, Colonel Ochterlony, was the British Resident at the Mughal capital, and he, with a small force under Lieutenant-Colonel W. Burn, made a very gallant and successful resistance against the Maratha army which, on Lake's approach, decamped towards Dig (Deig), 30 miles west of Muttra, while Holkar himself with a large force of cavalry crossed the Jumna to raid the Doab.

[1] Monson's retreat was a sad blow to British prestige, and was perpetuated by the following native doggerel :—
" *Ghore par Hauda !*
Hathi par Zin !
Dauro ! Dauro !
General Monseen ! "

(Literally : " The howdah on the horse ; the saddle on the elephant ! Run ! Run ! General Monson ! ")

Lake went after Holkar, and when he came up with him at Farrukhabad on November 17th, after a march of 58 miles in 24 hours, surprised and defeated him so completely that it was only with the greatest difficulty that the Maratha chief managed to rejoin the remainder of his army near Dig. Meanwhile General Frazer had defeated the enemy before Dig where he was killed in the fight. Monson, who then took command, wished to fall back on Agra, but Lake hurried to Dig himself and on December 13th was encamped on the western side of the fortress. With its powerful defences, encircled by marshes and lakes, it was a forbidding sight. The town was surrounded by a mud wall, with round bastions and a deep ditch, the defences running up to a rocky peak at the south-west corner called the Shah Burj, in front of which was a strongly fortified castle. Within the town lay a square citadel with circular bastions and a deep ditch guarded by massive gateways and towers, and, outside the town, a small redoubt and a dozen batteries defended the only open ground between a lake and an impassable morass. Lake began his operations by engaging the outlying batteries, and, after some days of heavy fighting, drove in the defenders and then made a breach with his own guns in the Shah Burj. On the 23rd he assaulted that peak in three columns, captured it, and took the castle, though not without desperate fighting in the narrow streets. The Marathas then lost heart, and by Christmas morning the whole of Dig was in British hands. Both divisions of Holkar's army had now been defeated, and in the south the British armies of the Deccan had seized all his possessions south of the Tapti. The war seemed to be finished, and so it would have been had not Lake made his second mistake—his insane attempt to carry Bhurtpore by a *coup de main*.

The Engineers and Pioneers covered themselves with honour at the siege of Dig. Captain Thomas Robertson of the Bengal Engineers, ably assisted by Lieutenant Carmichael-Smyth, was in charge of the siege operations, and both did so well that Lord Lake reported that " the officers of the Engineer department, Captain Robertson and Lieutenant Smyth, have peculiar merit and are entitled to my best thanks and approbation."[1] The Bengal Pioneers were led as usual by the gallant Swinton and were in the thick of the fight. They dug the batteries and trenches in the advance to the fortress, and, when the Shah Burj was stormed, carried the ladders and planted them against the walls ; but they paid a heavy price, for John Swinton was struck in the thigh by a cannon ball and lamed for life, and William Forrest, his subaltern, received more than 22 wounds and lost an arm. Their services, however, and those of their men, did not go unrecognized. " The Corps of Pioneers," writes Lord Lake,[2] " under the orders of Captain Swinton, command my warmest praise for the

---

[1] *East India Military Calendar*, Vol. II, p. 338.
[2] Lord Lake to Marquis Wellesley. Despatch dated Deeg, December 26th, 1804, quoted in the *East India Military Calendar*, Vol. III, p. 30.

cheerfulness with which they perform their laborious duties, and particularly for the alacrity displayed on the night of the 22nd instant. Too much praise cannot be bestowed on Captain Swinton, who on this and every former occasion, has been most zealous and active. I am sorry to add that this excellent officer is severely wounded, as is Lieutenant Forrest of the same corps, whose conduct was equally meritorious."

We come now to the tragedy of the Second Maratha War; an act which changed victory to defeat, lowered the prestige of England, prolonged the struggle for months, and sullied the reputation of a brave commander. Unbroken success is bad for any man, and it had its effect on Lake. He became too impetuous, and when he arrived before the fortress of Bhurtpore on January 2nd, 1805, he underestimated its strength and the bravery of its defenders, and rashly decided to teach the treacherous Raja a lesson by taking it out of hand. Now Bhurtpore was a vast stronghold, held by most determined and gallant soldiers. In circumference the town and fort measured some eight miles. This perimeter was enclosed by a mud wall of great height and enormous thickness, with round bastions mounting scores of guns and a gigantic ditch full of water. At the eastern end was the fort, with still higher walls and a larger ditch, and surrounding the whole place, a belt of jungle and swamp. Such a fortress could only be taken by deliberate and careful operations; instead it was attacked in 1805 with a carelessness which was as appalling as it was unnecessary.

Between January 9th and February 21st, in four separate attacks, failure was crowded on failure. In the first assault on the 9th, Lake concentrated his whole force opposite the south-west angle of the city and advanced in three columns. No practicable breach had been made in the mud wall, and the few men who got near to the crest were unsupported by their comrades; the ditch had not been properly reconnoitred, and most of the troops were unable to cross it. Again and again they tried to gain a footing; but every attempt failed and the casualties mounted steadily until, when the task was seen to be hopeless, they withdrew to their trenches. A new breach was made on the 16th farther to the south, but it could not be ascended as the defenders stockaded it as rapidly as the crumbling rubble of the walls slid into the ditch under the fire of Lake's artillery. The mud fortress of Bhurtpore was teaching a bitter lesson.

After this failure, Lake, for the first time, tried to provide some means of crossing the enormous wet ditch, and his Engineers made a light bridge of bamboos and inflated skins, to carry infantry in single file, and so arranged it that it could be taken forward and pushed out from the counterscarp. On January 21st, a gallant band of 11 volunteers under Serjeant John Shipp[1] rushed for the ditch, followed

[1] For a graphic and personal account of the siege of Bhurtpore the reader should study *The Memoirs of John Shipp*, Vol. I, pp. 146–214.

by the bridge-carriers, and under a terrific fire the bridge was actually launched. Alas, it proved to be much too short as the defenders had cleverly increased the width of the ditch by adding more water to it. The stormers tried desperately to prolong the bamboo structure with scaling ladders, but to no purpose for it soon upset and floated away useless. Under a hail of bullets from three directions the survivors of the storming party then retreated to their trenches while the enemy swarmed out to murder the wounded and mutilate the dead. The second attempt had ended in greater disaster than the first.

For a time the siege languished. Supplies were running short, the artillerymen and pioneers were worked to death, and the infantry disheartened. Then a convoy arrived, and also a division of the Bombay army under Major-General Richard Jones, and Lake, learning something from his previous failures, prepared for a third assault. He was now a very different man from the one who tried to rush the defences on January 9th: he sapped to the edge of the ditch, he made a new breach and placed mortar batteries to enfilade it, and he provided sandbag protection for the light artillery which he placed so as to give close support to the attack. It is said that at the time he was satisfied with the work of his Engineers and decided to storm the breach as soon as the batteries had swept away a stockade which had been built in it by the defenders.[1] On February 20th, he put his fortune to the test. Again he assaulted in three columns, but this time even his European troops had lost confidence and could not be induced to press home the attack which failed in consequence even more disastrously than the two preceding ones.

On the following day the British units, having been harangued by Lake, were eager to retrieve their reputation, and a forlorn hope was ready once again under Serjeant Shipp. The advance was sounded, and the men went forward steadily and bravely. For two long hours they tried to scale the crumbling walls, in desperation driving their bayonets into the rubble one above the other to form ladders; but they were hurled down again and again while bullets and shot tore through their crowded ranks. At last they reached the limit of human endurance, and the contest ended, as it was bound to do, in failure. Bhurtpore towered proud and defiant above the remains of more than 3,000 of Lake's best soldiers who had perished since he began the siege. Forced to admit defeat, he drew off six miles to the north-east and spent the next few weeks in harrying an army under Holkar which was near at hand. Ranjit Singh, the Raja of Bhurtpore, then thought it best to come to terms with the British, and signed a treaty on April 10th, 1805, which put an end to hostilities against him.

Failure brings criticism in its train. Everyone was criticized for Bhurtpore: Lake for his carelessness, the infantry for their conduct,

[1] *A History of the British Army*, by the Hon. J. W. Fortescue, Vol. V, p. 122.

the gunners for the impassable breaches, and the engineers for their work. An anonymous writer, in the course of an article on the siege,[1] has much to say on the matter : " The Infantry of the Army, the Artillery, the Engineers, the Staff, the General, the Government, all were glanced at—but the head of the Engineer department, being found to be a sort of ideal personage, was finally fixed upon. Who the Commanding Engineer was, I have met nobody who would exactly tell. I believe that the office passed through the hands of several individuals during the siege,[2] but none of them was of sufficient character, either in respect of influence or experience, to take upon himself the responsibility attached to so important a situation. But even if an officer of the required ability and experience had been present it is doubtful whether he would have been attended to, so confident was our fighting General in the resistless bravery of his troops. The Government, feeling itself responsible for the shamefully deficient state of his equipment, discreetly abstained from censuring either his first attack or his perseverance after that attack became hopeless. The General, grateful alike to the Government and to the devoted gallantry of his army, could not bring himself to censure either. His staff, again, he looked upon but as the shadow of himself ; and nothing, therefore, remained but to throw the entire blame upon the scientific branches of the service. The Artillery, however, had been supplied on such a ridiculously low scale that it was adjudged neither just nor prudent to let it bear any responsibility ; and therefore the whole weight of it developed (devolved ?) by an easy process upon the Engineers alone.

" Accordingly Lord Lake expresses himself as follows in July, 1805 :—[3] ' However zealous my Engineer Officers were, neither their abilities, knowledge nor experience were adequate for the occasion ; and this cause had doubtless considerable influence in preventing that success which had hitherto attended every operation of my army.' Now when it is recollected that we attacked this immense fortress with little more than eight thousand men, having, besides the usual equipment of light artillery, only six battering guns and a few small mortars and howitzers, it must be confessed that it was taxing energy and professional skill a little too highly to expect the Engineers to succeed without some assistance of a more material nature. Bhurtpore was so large a place that its wall presented a fortified line in

[1] An article entitled " Military Auto-biography," appearing in the *East India United Service Journal*, Vol. III, July–December, 1834, p. 229 *et seq*.
[2] There is no record of their names. Captain-Lieutenant William Cowper, Bombay Engineers, arrived with General Richard Jones and may have been the Chief Engineer in the last two attacks. Captain John Johnson, of the same Corps, was near Aurangabad after some successful siege operations against Chandur and Jalna. Lieutenant-Colonel George Prole, who acted occasionally as an Engineer, was with Colonel Martindell in Bundelkhand. Possibly Captain-Lieutenant Thomas Robertson and Lieutenant Henry Carmichael-Smyth, both of the Bengal Engineers, had charge of the engineering work early in the siege. It is not known who commanded the Pioneers. Swinton did not rejoin till after the siege.
[3] Lord Lake to Marquis Wellesley. State Paper, dated July 1st, 1805.

which there was no point more exposed to attack than another. It was precisely on one of these long lines that we attacked it, and, in order to protect the approaches from enfilade fire, it would have been necessary to make every angle of the advance so small that very little would have been gained. The only remedy was to advance by the double sap under a powerful direct fire of artillery, or to select another point of attack. The latter, however, was quite out of the question as the selection was made by the General himself. As to the former, as we had no regular corps of Sappers and Miners in those days, it is hardly fair to assume the apparent want of skill of our Engineers as showing them deficient in scientific and professional knowledge. Whilst Lord Lake had but six battering guns in his train, whole ranges of them were lining every avenue in Fort William. A few of these would, no doubt, have called forth that skill and energy on the part of the Engineers the absence of which His Excellency failed to discover till some months after the siege had ended."

The young Engineers at Bhurtpore cannot justly be held responsible for the disaster. They were too inexperienced and too much in awe of their despotic leader, who, in the eyes of the Government, could do no wrong. Lake himself may be censured for his precipitancy and overweening confidence, but the greatest blame must rest on Marquis Wellesley who allowed the Commander-in-Chief to embark on his mad venture with a badly-equipped and inadequate force. The enemies of the Governor-General lost no time in pressing home their advantage on this score, and, adding it to their other accusations, secured his supercession by Lord Cornwallis in July, 1805.

After Bhurtpore the war developed into a pursuit of Holkar, who marched for the Punjab where he hoped to persuade the Sikhs to join with him against the British. Lake, with a large force,[1] followed him to Delhi in November, and reached the banks of the Beas in December when the Maratha leader was at Amritsar. Then at last Holkar gave in and signed an absurdly lenient treaty which brought little advantage to England. Cornwallis had died, and Sir George Barlow, who had succeeded temporarily to the post of Governor-General, restored to Holkar the whole of his lost dominions. The Second Maratha War ended in disappointment. Indore, Gwalior and Berar had all been humbled, and then, by a misplaced clemency which was mistaken for weakness or fear, they were raised again to challenge the power of England at the first opportunity. This, however, was no affair of the army. The soldiers, in spite of their reverse at Bhurtpore, had completed their task with skill and courage, and not the least conspicuous among them were the Engineers and Pioneers of Bengal, Bombay and Madras.

[1] Including Swinton and the Bengal Pioneers.

CHAPTER XIII.

THE NEPAL AND THIRD MARATHA WARS, 1814–1819.

BRITISH prestige suffered terribly by the failure to capture Bhurtpore in 1805. The conquests of Cornwallis, Lake and Wellesley had fostered a belief in the invincibility of the British soldier, but it had been shown that even he could suffer defeat. The greater part of the Maratha armies had been dispersed after the war, and these soldiers, penniless and desperate, banded themselves together under the name of Pindaris and lived by organized plunder. There was a rebellion in Travancore in the extreme south; while in the far north-west the great Ranjit Singh led his Sikhs across the Sutlej and threatened the security of Upper India. Afghanistan was unsettled, the Burmese were advancing slowly towards Calcutta, and the Gurkhas were encroaching on the north. Discipline in the army was none too good: in Madras there was actually a mutiny of British officers.[1]

The Oriental style of correspondence affected by the Company's agents was often carried to such lengths that any eastern potentate might gather from it a false idea of the attitude of the British. To go back more than a century, the Governor of Fort St. George once addressed the King of Ava[2] as follows when asking for trade facilities in 1695:[3] " To His Imperial Majesty who blesseth the noble city of Ava with his Presence, Emperour of Emperours, and excelling the Kings of the East and West in glory and honour, the clear firmanent of Virtue, the fountain of Justice, the perfection of Wisdom, the Lord of Charity and Protector of the Distressed; the first mover in the Sphere of Greatness, President in Council, Victorious in War; who feareth none and is feared by all; Center of the Treasures of the Earth and of the Sea, Lord Proprietor of Gold and Silver, Rubys, Amber and all precious Jewells, favoured by Heaven and honoured by Men, whose brightness shines through the World as the light of the Sun, and whose great name will be preserved in perpetual memory."

It is easy to imagine the effect of this seeming humility on the then ignorant, credulous and conceited inhabitants of Burma. In 1810, when England was at war with France, a Burmese minister said that if the King of Ava had received an application in suitable terms he

[1] The " White Mutiny " of 1809.
[2] Ava, near Mandalay, was the ancient capital of Burma.
[3] Letter dated September 10th, 1695, quoted in *Our Burmese Wars*, by Colonel W. F. B. Laurie, p. 4.

would have deigned to send an army to capture France for the British;[1] and the Burmese Government once drafted a letter to Lord Minto—which, however, the King refused to sign—declaring that the King of England was certainly a vassal of the King of Burma. On the outbreak of the Burmese War in 1824, a Burmese general boasted that he would capture Calcutta and then march to England after binding golden fetters on the noble limbs of the Governor-General. In Nepal, the Gurkhas were hardly less contemptuous, though not so garrulous. In Hindustan, the Pindari bands of robbers found that they could spread devastation over the country without interference. The Sikhs were rising to the supremacy of the Punjab. On every side war threatened, and from almost every side it came.

The Government of India was immersed in a sea of correspondence, and it is a pity that its representatives did not learn something from an experience of John Blakiston, Madras Engineer and author. That young man once filled a sheet of foolscap with arguments when asking for remuneration for some money which had been stolen on the road between Bangalore and Arcot. When his native clerk had copied the letter, Blakiston enquired if he understood it. "Oh, yes," said the *babu*, " money lost : please give."[2] That clerk was certainly wasted in the Engineer's office ; he should have been editing the foreign correspondence of the Governor-General.

After the end of the Second Maratha War the Engineers and Pioneers of India went from strength to strength. Lake's failure in 1805 had shown that, without an adequate cadre of engineer soldiers, siege operations against large fortresses were most difficult. In open warfare it had been proved that an army was handicapped unless it had experts to bridge rivers and make roads. So the cadres of Engineers in all three Presidencies were increased till, in 1810, Madras alone had 30 officers under Colonel Elisha Trapaud as Chief Engineer.[3] Bengal and Bombay were not so well supplied, yet their cadres appeared to be sufficient for minor operations. The expansion of the three corps of Pioneers, however, and their change into Sappers and Miners, are such important features of this period, that some space must be devoted to these technical matters of reorganization.

In Bengal, the Pioneer Corps, which had done so well under Swinton, was increased in 1808 to eight companies of 90 men each, with two British serjeants and a few miners to each company. It became known as the " Corps of Pioneers and Sappers."[4] A company of " Miners " was also raised for field service, and was placed under

---

[1] *Our Burmese Wars*, by W. F. B. Laurie, p. 65.
[2] *Twelve Years Military Adventure*, by Major J. Blakiston, Madras Engineers, Vol. I, p. 329.
[3] *The Military History of the Madras Engineers and Pioneers*, by Major H. M. Vibart, Vol. I, p. 447.
[4] *The Services of the Bengal Native Army*, by Lieut. F. G. Cardew, p. 114.

the command of an officer of the Bengal Engineers.[1] The Bengal Pioneer was smartly dressed. He wore a green tunic, with facings of the same colour, adorned with yellow lace and black buttons.[2] On his head was a tall black hat, built up on a bamboo framework to resemble the British soldier's headgear, and on his legs, loose white trousers.[3] The private was shod with *chapplies*,[4] and the Indian officer with high boots. Black leather accoutrements completed a turn-out which must at least have attracted attention. The Pioneers of Bengal continued to be commanded by Infantry officers, as there were not enough Engineers for this duty, and their establishment remained at eight companies, and one company of Miners, till they were changed into Sappers and Miners in 1819.

Bombay was poorly supplied with Pioneers, as with everything else. In 1809, owing to reductions, there were only two companies —one permanent and the other temporary—and it was not till 1812 that this establishment was increased to four companies[5] under Captain Peter Delamotte, of the Bombay Infantry. From this year the Pioneers were officered solely from the Infantry. The corps saw very little active service till the outbreak of the Third Maratha War, but their martial spirit ran high, if one may judge by that of the Bombay Army as a whole. For instance, when a small force had besieged Nawanagar in 1812, and the Jam Sahib had surrendered his capital without serious resistance, the British commander wrote:[6] " I may be permitted to regret, in common with all the Officers and men of this Detachment, a result so full of disappointment." The Bombay Army was indeed spoiling for a fight.

A few days after the increase of the Bombay Pioneers to four companies, a momentous despatch was written by the Commander-in-Chief explaining the status and duties of the corps. It was issued on July 17th, 1812, and a few extracts from it must suffice :—[7]

" The Hon. the Governor-General in Council having been pleased to direct that a regular Corps of Pioneers should be formed on a plan detailed in the General Orders, the Corps will be raised to the same Honourable Level with the other Corps of the Hon. Company's regular army. . . . While these advantages are held out to the Pioneer Corps, the Commander-in-Chief considers it proper that they should be fully apprised of the duties expected from them. In time of peace they will be employed in making, clearing and repairing roads, in the construction and repairs of fortifications, in the demolition of dismantled forts and in giving assistance in magazines.[8] In time of war they will be employed in making, clearing

---

[1] *History and Digest of Service, K.G.O. Bengal Sappers and Miners*, p. 3.
[2] General Order by the Commander-in-Chief, December 8th, 1809.
[3] Short white drawers were worn till 1809.   [4] Sandals.
[5] Each company was commanded by a Captain with two British officers, two serjeants and two Indian officers. It had an establishment of 106 of all ranks.
[6] *Bombay General Orders*, Despatch dated February 24th, 1812.
[7] *Ibid.*, July 17th, 1812.   [8] Arsenals.

I

and repairing roads for the Troops, Artillery and Baggage of the Army, and, at sieges, in carrying on the approaches, parallels, etc.; while it will be a further part of their duty to prepare Fascines, Gabions, Pickets, etc. The Commander-in-Chief desires that it may be explained to the men that no degrading work, or work unusual for Pioneers to perform, will at any time be exacted from them."

We turn now to Madras where, in 1810, there were 16 companies of Pioneers formed into two battalions.[1] So they remained for many years. The tide of war was receding from the south and spreading northwards, and reduction was to be expected rather than expansion. The organization of a battalion of Madras Pioneers had become very complete,[2] and the unit was competent to undertake any small technical work as well as extensive unskilled work. In 1813 it was decided that each battalion should have two captains, six subalterns and an assistant-surgeon, and, in the following year, an adjutant was added to each. When the Government embarked on the Third Maratha War in 1817, the Madras Pioneers, although far from perfect, were certainly the best trained engineering soldiers in India, far outnumbering their brethren of Bengal and Bombay and with more experience in war.

A great impetus to military engineering was given by the Third Maratha War. In 1818, the Bengal Government decided to form a corps of "Sappers and Miners," and a draft of British non-commissioned officers, trained at Chatham, was sent to India and posted to it. The new corps was to consist of this draft and six companies of Indian soldiers, officered entirely from the Corps of Bengal Engineers, which was to be increased for that purpose. So, in February, 1819, the Bengal Sappers and Miners came into being.[3] At first they were commanded by an adjutant only, but in a short time a Commandant was appointed in the person of Major (afterwards Major-General Sir Thomas) Anbury, of the Bengal Engineers, who is noted not only as the first Commandant of a distinguished Corps but as the Chief Engineer at the capture of Bhurtpore in 1826. He was assisted at Allahabad, where the Bengal Sappers and Miners were formed, by Captain (afterwards Lieutenant-General) Richard Tickell. Each of the six companies contained 120 men, a nucleus being provided in each company by drafting selected men from the Pioneers; the remainder were obtained by recruitment. Apart from British officers, the Bengal Sappers and Miners in 1819 had a

---

[1] General Order by the Governor-General, dated January 28th, 1803.
[2] A battalion had seven British officers, eight Indian officers, 57 Indian non-commissioned officers, and 700 privates, and in addition a number of serjeants and a few expert bricklayers, sawyers and men of other trades. This establishment was authorized in G.O.G.G. (General Order by the Governor-General) dated October 12th, 1810.
[3] G.O.G.G., dated February 13th, 1819, and G.O.C.C., dated February 19th, 1819. (See the *History and Digest of Service, K.G.O. Bengal Sappers and Miners*, p. 5.)

strength of 816 Indian, and 39 British, soldiers of all ranks. Their uniform was made as like as possible to that of the Royal Sappers and Miners in England. It consisted of a red tunic, with blue collar and cuffs, ornamented with gold braid for Indian officers and yellow braid for the lower ranks; blue trousers with a broad red stripe; and a blue *paggari* (turban) having a yellow fringe (gold for Indian officers), with a red *kullah* (centre cap). For two years the headquarters remained at Allahabad; they were then moved to Cawnpore, Aligarh, Delhi, Meerut and Ludhiana till they came to rest finally in 1854 at Roorkee, the home and centre of military engineering in northern India.

The four companies of Bombay Pioneers did so well in the Third Maratha War that it was only natural that they should share in the expansion which followed that struggle. So we find that on December 16th, 1819, two more companies were added, and on May 6th, 1822, the Corps was increased to eight companies and became the Battalion of Bombay Pioneers.[1] As early as 1799, Major-General Nicholson, Chief Engineer and Commander-in-Chief of Bombay, had raised a small unit of 32 men from which developed the Pontoon Train of 1803 under Lieutenant Samuel Goodfellow. This was expanded in 1820 into a company of Bombay Sappers and Miners under Captain (afterwards Major-General) Thomas Dickenson, of the Bombay Engineers, with much the same establishment as in Bengal. The formation of this Sapper and Miner unit did not affect the battalion of Bombay Pioneers, which continued at full strength.[2]

The Madras Government decided to establish a Corps of Sappers and Miners at about the same time as the Government of Bengal. In March, 1818,[3] when the Maratha War was at its height, an order was issued for the formation of a corps to consist of one European and two Indian companies. The experiment failed, and the corps was disbanded in May, 1821, without ever having exceeded a strength of 50 Europeans and 32 Indians, although Bengal and Bombay still retained their Sapper and Miner Companies. The explanation may be found in the history of the Madras Pioneers. When the Maratha War ended, recruiting for the Pioneers ceased, and the two battalions fell much below their proper strength; but, early in 1821, recruiting was resumed on the application of Sir Thomas Munro,[4] who insisted that he needed Pioneers to keep open the mountain passes leading to the interior and for building work in military stations.[5] This was a

---

[1] *A Brief History of the Royal Bombay Sappers and Miners*, pp. 5 and 6.
[2] After an expansion in 1822, the battalion included ten British officers, 16 Indian officers, nine British warrant and non-commissioned officers, 80 Indian non-commissioned officers, 800 privates, and about 48 smiths, carpenters, etc., on the active service scale. (Bombay General Orders, May 6th, 1822.)
[3] G.O.C.C., dated March 24th, 1818.
[4] Governor and Commander-in-Chief of Madras.
[5] *Historical Record of the Q.V.O. Madras Sappers and Miners*, p. 30.

respite only: one battalion of the Madras Pioneers was soon to become the Madras Sappers and Miners, and the second battalion was destined to follow suit.

In November, 1821, a keen reformer, Major Thomas De Havilland, then Chief Engineer of Madras, submitted a gigantic report on his ideas of the status, duties and organization of Engineers, Pioneers, and Sappers and Miners, and, like all reformers, he drew upon himself vials of wrath. He remarked, among other things, that the Quartermaster-General was always interfering in engineering matters; that it was unfortunate that, because the Pioneers were under that officer and the Engineer officers under the Governor, the Commander-in-Chief could not appoint Engineers to command the Pioneers; and that if, as the Directors seemed to wish, a Corps of Sappers and Miners was formed, the Pioneers as such would become unnecessary and could be transferred to a corps which might be called the "Regiment of Engineers" and include one European company, another of "Men of Colour," and eight Indian companies.

The Quartermaster-General rose up in fury at the suggestion that the Pioneers should be removed from his control, and a most acrimonious and amusing correspondence followed. "The Chief Engineer," writes the Q.M.G.,[1] "may still maintain that the Pioneer officers have neither studied the profession of engineering nor have any pretensions to it, but it is almost farcical to talk of science when speaking of the construction of roads or opening of passes. It is a fact that the best road-maker now in England is a *ci-devant* purser of a ship.[2] The Chief Engineer's proposal is evidently that the Corps to which he belongs should engross every duty and service of a scientific nature. These lofty pretensions of the Corps of Engineers are nothing new; and when they assumed in the French service the proud title of the Corps of Genius,[3] they showed the extent to which they were inclined to push their exclusive claims to all scientific requirements. In general they are ignorant of the manner in which troops manœuvre: they even object to (attaining) that knowledge. Considering their own as the first of all arts, they look down with disdain on every other branch of the service. If this prejudice is kept alive amongst them by the fine name of Genius, I beg leave to inform them that the word 'Engineer' is derived, not from Genius, but from the word 'Engine.'"

But the much abused De Havilland was so persistent that his proposals were given serious consideration in London, and the Directors decreed in 1823 that, as Pioneers should certainly be

---

[1] Extracts from *The Military History of the Madras Engineers and Pioneers*, by Major H. M. Vibart, Vol. II, pp. 28-31.

[2] Mr. J. L. McAdam, who died in 1836 after introducing the Macadam process of road construction.

[3] *Corps du Génie.*

commanded by Engineer officers, one of the two Madras battalions should be transferred to the Engineers and its infantry officers should return to their battalions of the line. However, the Governor of Madras found that he could not get enough Engineer officers for a battalion of Pioneers, and so advised that both battalions should remain for a time as they were, and that meanwhile some non-commissioned officers of the Royal Engineers should be sent from Chatham to Madras. The Court agreed, but did not send the European draft until 1831, when the reorganization was considered once more. Then, in spite of further opposition, the change was carried out, and the 1st Battalion of Madras Pioneers became the Corps of Madras Sappers and Miners,[1] officered from the Madras Engineers[2] and composed of eight companies with a Captain as Commandant, assisted by an Adjutant and eight other British officers. The Corps then came under the sole control of the Chief Engineer. Thus Madras gained at last a body of engineer soldiers, well commanded, and better trained than the Pioneers.

The end of the 2nd Battalion of Madras Pioneers was in sight. Money was scarce, and India free from serious war. So, in 1833, the Directors ordered the reduction of the Sappers and Miners, or of the Pioneers, "whichever they might be called," to one battalion. Naturally, the Pioneers had to go; and in December the order went forth[3] that on February 1st, 1834, the 2nd Battalion of Madras Pioneers should be absorbed into the Sappers and Miners. With this, the Madras Pioneers disappeared from the Indian Army, leaving behind them a record second to none.

The Pioneers of Bengal and Bombay suffered a similar fate. In 1824, as in Madras, orders were issued in both Presidencies for the amalgamation of the Pioneers with the Sappers and Miners, and, as in Madras, the change was postponed. But in November, 1833,[4] the fiat went forth that the Bengal Pioneers[5] should be incorporated with the Sappers and Miners, and the corps so ably commanded by Swinton vanished in February, 1834.[6] Any remaining infantry officers rejoined their regiments, and men who were not transferred to the Sappers and Miners were drafted into the Infantry or took their pensions.

In Bombay, a second company of Sappers and Miners was formed

[1] *Madras General Orders*, May 24th, 1831.
[2] The Corps was so officered up to 1839, when, through lack of Engineers, some Infantry officers were posted to it. From that year till 1879 there were always a few Infantry officers with the Corps.
[3] G.O.C.C., dated December 27th, 1833.
[4] *Ibid.*, dated November 28th, 1833.
[5] Known also as the "Bengal Pioneers *or* Sappers."
[6] In September, 1847, however, the Bengal Sappers and Miners were remodelled into three companies of Sappers and Miners and seven companies of Pioneers, the latter to be officered from the Infantry. The Corps of Bengal Sappers and Pioneers had a short life. On March 20th, 1851, it became again the "Corps of Bengal Sappers and Miners," with a strength of twelve companies to which no more Infantry officers were posted.

on December 4th, 1826, under Engineer officers,[1] and, three years later, the Corps was moved from Bombay to Ahmadnagar and became known as the " Bombay Engineers " instead of the " Bombay Sappers and Miners."[2] The headquarters then assumed the curious title of " The Engineer Institution," and the clothing of the men was " assimilated to that of the Engineer officers." The headquarters did not stay long in Ahmadnagar, for in 1830 they were moved to Sirur and thence in 1837 to Poona, where, in the cantonment of Kirkee, they have since remained, with the exception of a five years' transfer to Karachi from 1843 to 1848. The rise of the Bombay Sappers and Miners was one cause of the reduction and final absorption of the Bombay Pioneers. On November 1st, 1830, before either Bengal or Madras had carried out the amalgamation of their Pioneers and Sappers, the Bombay Pioneers were reduced from eight to six companies and incorporated with the Sappers and Miners as an " Engineer Corps." " The Corps " ran the Order in Council,[3] " will be commanded by an officer of the Engineers and have a Regimental Staff of Engineer Officers consisting of an Adjutant and Quarter Master. Other officers of Engineers, for whom there is no specific duty, will be attached to this Corps, and all Engineer Officers will on their first arrival be employed under the Commandant." The Commander-in-Chief added that any men disliking the prospect of the " fatigue and exertion " of the drill and discipline of Sappers and Miners could take their discharge. But the Bombay Sappers and Miners (or Engineer Corps[4]) were caught in 1834 in the same scheme of retrenchment which caused the absorption of the 2nd Battalion of Madras Pioneers. By order of the Supreme Government,[5] the Bombay Corps was then reduced from eight to four companies, with a total strength of 456 Indian soldiers of all ranks, the two existing " Sapper and Miner " companies forming No. 1 Company and the six " Pioneer " companies providing Nos. 2, 3 and 4 Companies.

This brief and condensed survey of the metamorphosis of the Pioneer into the Sapper and Miner—a most important change from an engineering point of view—may be concluded by quoting some remarks of a subaltern of the Madras Engineers which show that, even in 1836, the sweeping reorganizations which had been carried out had not produced the perfect Sapper. " The Sappers and

[1] The Commandant of the Corps was Lieutenant Stephen Slight, who was succeeded in 1828 by Lieutenant Alexander Peat with Lieutenant (afterwards General) Henry Turner as Adjutant. The Sappers and Miners wore a uniform similar to that of the Pioneers (dark green), but the cap, breastplate and buttons were like those of the Bombay Engineer officers, and the pouches and belts were of black leather.

[2] *Bombay General Orders*, December 23rd, 1829.

[3] *Bombay Order in Council*, dated September 29th, 1830.

[4] In 1837 the Corps is referred to again as the " Bombay Sappers and Miners," so perhaps official approval had then been accorded to that title.

[5] G.O.G.G., published in Bombay General Orders, June 21st, 1834.

Miners," he writes,[1] " are at present but old friends with a new face. In this Presidency their duties are utterly undefined—imperfectly organized, they are nondescript in equipments, character and occupation. They are maintained to perform certain duties in time of war, for which, strange to say, they are imperfectly, or not at all, trained in time of peace. I believe economy to be one motive, but it arises also out of the greater error which would confound the duties of Sappers and Miners with those of Pioneers. The Corps of Pioneers has always maintained a character for gallantry and usefulness in the field. There, however, they have invariably been called upon to perform, not the duties of Pioneers, but of Sappers and Miners. Far more discipline and training are required to form a Sapper than any other soldier. Though the opinion may appear abrupt, I consider the corps of Pioneers to have been a useless institution. In a country where the peasant's labour is cheaper than that of the soldier, to give military organization to men who are merely to make roads and break stones is certainly a work of supererogation. There is no corps of Pioneers in the British service."

The reasons for the abolition of the Pioneer from the Indian Army are evident. With the advance of military science, an Engineer soldier, more highly trained than the Pioneer, was required for operations in the field; the East India Company was obliged to put quality before quantity because of the expense of the war in Burma; the cadres of Engineers were too small to officer both the Sapper and Miner companies and the Pioneers; and lastly, the Pioneer could no longer compete with civilian labour and thus earn his daily bread in time of peace. Yet the gallant work of the ancient Pioneers should not go unrecorded; and so, having done with reorganizations, we go back some 26 years to a period when, most of India being quiet, the Pioneers sailed overseas with expeditions against the French and Dutch to protect the commerce of the British Empire.

Apart from a rebellion during 1809 in Travancore, which the Madras Engineers and Pioneers helped to quell, the chief military operations preceding the Nepal War were expeditions against the French in Réunion (Bourbon) and Mauritius (Ile de France), and against the Dutch in Java. Since 1803, France had been at war with England, and, though the French could do little to embarrass the British in India, their privateers, sailing from Mauritius, Réunion and the island of Rodriguez, inflicted severe damage on British shipping; so Rodriguez was seized in 1809, and in June, 1810, more than three thousand soldiers sailed from Madras and effected a landing on Réunion. For a time their operations were successful; but a French squadron then defeated the British men-of-war, and

[1] Extracts from a letter entitled "Sappers and Miners," appearing in the *East India United Service Journal*, June, 1836.

the invaders were blockaded on the island. In the autumn, however, large reinforcements arrived, and the British Commander-in-Chief, Sir John Abercromby, sailed with 10,000 men on November 22nd to attack Mauritius. After severe fighting before Port Louis, he received the surrender of the French Governor on December 2nd, and with it the possession of the island. Detachments of the Madras Pioneers did useful work in Réunion and in the attack on Port Louis, and the engineering operations were directed by Major James Caldwell of the Madras Engineers. Réunion was ultimately returned to France, but Mauritius was retained by England as a Crown Colony.

The expedition against Java in 1811 was preceded by a successful venture against the minor Dutch settlements in the Moluccas or Spice Islands. This paved the way for an attack on the chief seat of the Dutch Empire in the East. The Dutch were in alliance with, and under the control of, the French, and Napoleon hoped to make Java a base for attacks on the British possessions and shipping. Its capital, Batavia, had been strongly fortified by the Dutch, who had made good roads throughout the island and had prepared an entrenched camp at Cornelis, six miles from the city. An expeditionary force, taken from the Madras and Bengal armies, and commanded by Lieutenant-General Sir Samuel Auchmuty, concentrated at Malacca, and, proceeding by Singapore and along the coast of Borneo, prepared to land in Java at a place called Chillingching, ten miles east of the capital. The expedition was well equipped with engineers. The Chief Engineer was Lieutenant-Colonel Colin Mackenzie of the Madras Engineers, and Major William Farquhar, of the same Corps, commanded the Guides. Lieutenant John Blakiston was Aide-de-Camp to General Auchmuty. Lieutenant William Garrard and several Ensigns of the Madras Engineers —mostly newly-joined from Addiscombe[1]—accompanied the army. From Bengal came Captains Henry Carmichael-Smyth and Robert Smith,[2] and the Pioneers were represented by a contingent of 300 men from Madras, under Captains T. Smithwaite and R. McCraith, with several Lieutenants.

Colin Mackenzie and young Blakiston went ahead of the army to reconnoitre for a landing place, and had some exciting adventures. They disembarked on the coast of Java on July 14th, dressed as sailors, and having completed their reconnaissance of the northern coast, guided the fleet to its anchorage off Chillingching, where the troops were duly landed on August 5th. Auchmuty then advanced

---

[1] A Military School which was opened near Croydon in 1809 for the education of cadets for the Company's Engineers and Artillery in India. From 1816, cadets were admitted for the Infantry also. The school was closed in 1861. Cadets first arrived in India from Addiscombe in time to take part as Ensigns in the fighting in Java.

[2] *The Military History of the Madras Engineers and Pioneers*, by Major H. M. Vibart, Vol. I, p. 464.

on Batavia, which he entered without difficulty on the 8th. His main objective was the entrenched camp at Cornelis, but first it was necessary to defeat a Dutch division which lay two miles from the camp. This was done on August 11th, the Pioneers taking part in the attack, and three days later Auchmuty had concentrated his whole army before Cornelis.

The defences of Cornelis appeared to be so formidable that Mackenzie began regular siege approaches, but it soon became evident that these would take too long to complete. Auchmuty was pressed for time, so he determined to put his fortune to the test by assaulting as soon as he had damaged the place sufficiently by artillery fire. The Pioneers had been very busy and had already lost two officers in the early operations. In the final assault on August 26th, Blakiston and the Madras Pioneers under Smithwaite accompanied the principal attack under Colonel Robert Gillespie against the enemy's right; and although the Dutch commander made a very gallant resistance, he was driven from his redoubts and trenches with enormous loss, and pursued in the open country by Auchmuty's small body of cavalry. The enemy rallied for one more fight three weeks later, and then surrendered Java to the British on September 17th, 1811. The capture of the island was essential to defeat the designs of the French and Dutch, but England had no desire to keep the Dutch settlements and colonies permanently; so between 1814 and 1816 Holland received back all her eastern possessions except the Cape of Good Hope, and among them the island of Java. Mackenzie remained in the island long after the troops had returned to India, and explored every part of it, earning the praise of Government for his "extraordinary application and zeal." The army lost a good soldier when he became Surveyor-General of India in 1815.

Lord Hastings, who succeeded Lord Minto as Governor-General in 1813, found a crop of troubles awaiting him on his arrival. The timid policy of non-intervention in outside affairs, which had been ordered by the Directors, had been carried out faithfully by Lord Cornwallis, with gusto by Sir George Barlow, and, as far as he was able, by Lord Minto. The first result was a serious menace from the southern slopes of the Himalayas, where a hardy race of Mongolian type, known as the Gurkhas, lived in isolation near the snows. These hillmen of Nepal were some of the best fighters east of Suez; small, but wonderfully strong, active and brave. In 1814 their territories extended over the whole of the hill region of the Himalayas from the frontier of Bhutan on the east to the River Sutlej on the west, bordering for 700 miles on British territory or that of friendly states. Unfortunately the Gurkhas were aggressive, warlike, and fond of raiding across their frontier. Sir George Barlow had always yielded to them, and Lord Minto had tried, without success, to

I*

negotiate with them; but when, in May, 1814, they attacked three British outposts, Lord Hastings knew that war must come, and arranged for an army of over 30,000 men to take the field. The declaration of war against Nepal was made on November 1st, 1814.

The Company's soldiers had never met an enemy who bore any resemblance to the Gurkha; and in the campaign which now opened they were to have their first experience of that most difficult and specialized form of warfare—hill fighting. The Gurkha army did not exceed sixteen thousand men; but it was in its own country and could fight in its own way, and, though poorly armed, it was unhampered by transport and baggage. The country was wild and precipitous in the extreme, a jumble of mountain ridges, densely wooded and intersected by deep ravines. There were no roads and few paths. Against the Gurkhas came the disciplined soldiers from the plains, twice their strength but altogether inexperienced in mountain warfare. They brought with them their artillery, baggage, tents and even elephants; and their slow and ponderous movements gave their agile enemies opportunities for surprise attack which they did not hesitate to take. The junior officers, and rank and file, of the Company's army faced these difficulties with courage and resolution, making up in gallantry what they lacked in experience, but it must be recorded with regret that most of the British generals seemed unable to adapt themselves to the strange conditions. Indeed, the advent of the Company's army into hill warfare was a most unhappy one, although in the end that army defeated the brave mountaineers who opposed it.

The plan of campaign against Nepal was devised by Lord Hastings himself,[1] and it provided for simultaneous attacks at four points along the frontier. In theory it was sound enough, and its failure in practice may be attributed justly to bad leadership in all except one of the four theatres in which fighting took place. Of all the generals whom Hastings selected, Ochterlony alone came out of the early operations with credit. These operations will be followed more easily if a reference is made to the sketch map of Northern India which appears at the end of this volume.

The war in Nepal may be divided into two phases—the first from October, 1814, to May, 1815: the second from December, 1815, to March, 1816. In the first phase, Major-General David Ochterlony, at the head of the 1st Division, was to attack the western extremity of the enemy's frontier, while Major-General Robert Gillespie, the victor of Cornelis, occupied Dehra Dun and then besieged Jaitak (Jytuk) with the 2nd Division. The task of the 3rd Division, under Major-General John Wood, was to advance from Gorakhpur through Butwal to Palpa; while a powerful 4th Division under Major-General Bennet Marley was to march from Patna through

[1] Hastings was both Governor-General and Commander-in-Chief of Bengal.

Makwanpur to capture the Gurkha capital of Katmandu. The general idea was that Ochterlony and Gillespie, converging from Ludhiana and Saharanpur respectively on the Gurkha general, Amar Singh Thappa, who lay with a powerful force in the hills bordering on the Sutlej, should pin him down and defeat him in his isolated situation while Wood cut his communications with Nepal proper and Marley advanced on Katmandu. It was thought that, as soon as Amar Singh found that his communications towards the capital were in danger, he would hasten eastwards, and if by so doing he cleared himself of Ochterlony he would run into Gillespie, who commanded the stronger of the two western columns. Actually, he stayed where he was and fought Ochterlony (who happened to be the only commander without any British infantry) and thus showed himself to be a leader of more than ordinary courage and determination.

No attempt can be made to describe in detail the strategy and tactics of the Nepal War, but some of the experiences of Engineers and Pioneers in the more important battles and movements may find a place in this history. Gillespie, marching from Saharanpur on October 19th, 1814, captured Dehra Dun three days later. With him were the 5th and 6th Companies of Bengal Pioneers under Lieutenant Elliott and Ensign Ellis, and also Captain Henry Carmichael-Smyth and Lieutenant George Blane, both of the Bengal Engineers. The local Gurkha leader made no attempt to defend Dehra Dun, but concentrated his men in the hill fort of Kalanga situated in dense jungles about five miles from the town. Gillespie assaulted Kalanga on the 31st, when two of his four columns had lost their way, and so deadly was the fire from the Gurkha stockades that the attack wavered and was finally repulsed with heavy loss. Gillespie himself was killed, and, of the Pioneers, Ellis was killed and Elliott badly wounded. Carmichael-Smyth was then sent up to superintend the operations,[1] and the attack was renewed on November 7th under Colonel Mawbey: again it was repulsed, and with still heavier loss. Mawbey then sat down to bombard the fort while the Engineers and Pioneers cut the channel which supplied it with water. The defenders, however, had no intention of standing a regular siege, so they evacuated the place after dark on the 30th and retreated into the jungle while Mawbey took possession of the dilapidated stockades whose capture had cost more than 700 casualties. On December 20th, Major-General Gabriel Martindell assumed command of the 2nd Division, and, after he had occupied Nahan, tried to seize Jaitak. In this he failed completely and was then content to carry on a passive blockade which was of no value in the general operations. There we may leave him and the unfortunate Engineers who were with him.

[1] *History of the Bengal Artillery*, by Major F. W. Stubbs, p. 8.

The repulse at Kalanga added to the difficulties of General Ochterlony in the west. Amar Singh concentrated his main force at Arki,[1] and, relinquishing any idea of retirement, occupied a number of advanced posts on a succession of high ridges. Range after range of forest-clad hills barred the advance of the British, rising to a height of six thousand feet or more, and each range fortified and strongly held. However, Ochterlony was not deterred, and advanced through the foothills on November 2nd towards the first Gurkha post at Nalagarh. Naturally cautious, and realizing the difficulties ahead of him, he brought up his heavy artillery and bombarded the place so effectively that the garrison surrendered on the 5th, together with the garrison of another post. This first success, so cheaply won, was a welcome relief after Kalanga.

It is a remarkable fact that Ochterlony employed elephants to haul his 18-pounders into position before Nalagarh. The 3rd and 4th Companies of Bengal Pioneers had already cut a track of some sort through the forest and had raised a fascine battery within a furlong of the stockades. An eyewitness describes how the guns were brought up :[2] "The eighteen-pounders were now dragged from the camp by working parties of the troops, each followed by one, or where there was room, by two elephants. This animal sometimes applying his proboscis to the circumference of the carriage wheels would at once lift and push it forward; sometimes twisting the same trunk round one of the spokes, he would raise the wheel out of a hollow or even a projecting piece of rock; and when the ground became tolerably even, a sign of the driver made him lay his forehead to the gun carriage in order to haul it along. By this means the battering train arrived in perfect order, and opened on the morning of the 4th."

While on the subject of the use of elephants in mountain warfare we may quote the imaginative John Shipp,[3] leader of forlorn hopes at Bhurtpore in 1805. At a later date in the campaign, the army had been toiling up a ravine to turn the Gurkha positions. "Having got all the men up except the rearguard," writes Shipp, "the Pioneers went to work with their pickaxes, some making a road, the others felling trees. Having cut a good deal of the most prominent part of the hill away, and lain trees on the ascent as a footing for the elephants, these animals were made to approach it, which the first did with some reluctance and fear. He looked up, shook his head, and when forced by his driver, he roared piteously. But the moment some little alteration had been made, he seemed willing to approach. He then commenced his examination and scrutiny by pressing with his trunk the trees that had been thrown across; and after this he put his fore leg on with great caution. This done, he seemed

---

[1] A few miles west of where Simla now stands.
[2] *Military Sketches of the Goorka War in India* (1822), p. 5.
[3] *Memoirs of John Shipp*, Vol. II, p. 70 et seq.

satisfied. The next step was a projecting rock, and the next against a tree, but this he did not like. Here the driver made use of the most endearing epithets, such as ' Wonderful, my life '—' Well done, my dear '—' My dove '—' My own '—' My wife '—but all these endearing appellations, of which elephants are so fond, would not induce him to try again. Force was at length resorted to, and the elephant roared terrifically but would not move. Something was then removed: he seemed satisfied as before, and in time ascended the stupendous ghaut. On his reaching the top his delight was visible; he caressed his keeper, and threw dirt about in a most playful manner. Another elephant, a much younger animal, was now to follow. When he saw his comrade up he evinced his pleasure by giving a salute like the sound of a trumpet. When this elephant was near the top, the other extended his trunk to his assistance, round which the younger entwined his, and thus reached the summit in safety. Having both accomplished their task, they embraced each other, and stood face to face for a considerable time, as if whispering congratulations. Their driver then made them salaam to the General, who ordered them five rupees each for sweetmeats. On this reward of their merit being ordered, they immediately returned thanks by another salaam."[1]

When Amar Singh learnt that Ochterlony had taken Nalagarh, he advanced from Arki and occupied a strong position at Ramgarh. This was a more formidable proposition than Nalagarh, and the Pioneers spent a whole month in constructing roads for the passage of guns towards it. The moving spirit of the British army was quite a young officer—Lieutenant Peter Lawtie, who was Ochterlony's Field Engineer and Aide-de-Camp. No praise can be too high for this Bengal Engineer. He carried out the most daring reconnaissances, acted as the eyes of the force, and was the right-hand man of the General in every operation. Fraser says[2] that, in one of his reconnaissances, Lawtie and 40 men were cut off by the Gurkhas but managed to break through them and occupied a small fort. There they held out, with some reinforcements, against repeated attacks, and it was not till their ammunition failed that they were overpowered at last. A massacre followed, from which only Lawtie and a few men contrived to escape. Twice Ochterlony issued orders for the assault on Ramgarh, and twice he countermanded them on the strength of Lawtie's reports about the ground and the defences. In the end he relinquished the plan of a direct attack, and decided

---

[1] The distinction of having the last elephant of the Army in India rests with the K.G.O. Bengal Sappers and Miners. This elephant ("Sonepat") was advertised for sale in October, 1931, at the age of sixty-five years. In 1900, four elephants were transferred from the Artillery and attached to the Sappers and Miners at Roorkee "for field telegraph purposes." Permission was obtained later to keep them for the transport of heavy stores over difficult ground. "Tuni" and "Raghnathpur" died in 1914 and "Ghazipur" in 1930, leaving "Sonepat" the sole survivor.

[2] *Journal of a Tour through the Himalaya Mountains*, by James Fraser, p. 18.

instead to strike at Amar Singh's communications with Arki and Bilaspur by moving around Ramgarh. This operation had the effect of obliging the Gurkha general to throw back his left to cover the approaches to his main position, which lay on the Malaon ridge to the north, but he still clung to Ramgarh with his right. Ochterlony, however, continued to march towards Arki, until, in the middle of January, he had turned the Malaon ridge. Then he diverted his course northwards towards Bilaspur, and Amar Singh, being cut off from Arki, retreated to the heights of Malaon which protected his communications with Bilaspur.

On February 16th, Ramgarh fell to Colonel Cooper, who then proceeded to clear the remainder of this ridge by taking the forts at Taragarh and Chamba (Chambagarh) thus shielding the left flank of the main attack on Malaon. Both these operations were planned and conducted by Lawtie " in a manner that reflected the highest credit on himself, and without any loss."[1] Amar Singh now awaited Ochterlony's assault on the Malaon position, which extended for four miles along the ridge of that name from Surajgarh by Deothal (Deonthul) to Malaon. The fortified posts in the southern area— Surajgarh, Deothal and others—were captured in a series of operations on April 14th-15th, during which Lawtie again distinguished himself, and Ensign George Hutchinson, of the Bengal Engineers, with Lieutenant Armstrong of the Pioneers, won fame for gallantry in serving a gun after the whole of its detachment had been killed. When the enemy retreated at last to Malaon, it was Lawtie who, at the head of a corps of irregulars, harried the Gurkha rearguard.

Amar Singh then stood at bay at Malaon, outmanœvred by Ochterlony and outfought by the Indian troops. He counter-attacked with desperate gallantry against Deothal on April 16th, but was thrown back with terrible loss. " A body of Goorkas advancing to the charge," writes an officer who was present,[2] " bears no resemblance to a European column. Several huge trumpets, putting forth a harsh but stirring noise, set the multitude in motion, who, except some that carry shields, grasping each a matchlock in his left hand and a broad sword[3] in his right, rush on, disregarding all regularity, very like a pack of hounds in full cry." The Gurkhas proved their valour before Deothal, whose slopes were covered with dead and dying before they relinquished the assault; but their sacrifice was in vain, and they were forced to retire again to their last defences at Malaon. In the construction of these works they had shown their usual speed and ingenuity; their organization was perfect, their industry extraordinary, and their designs well suited to the sites.

Ochterlony laid his plans most carefully for the final assault. The

---

[1] *Journal of a Tour through the Himalaya Mountains*, by James Fraser, p. 37.
[2] *Military Sketches of the Goorka War* (1822), p. 13.
[3] The curved knife of the Gurkhas known as the *kukri*.

Pioneers continued their endless road-making operations, and, by the first week in May, 1815, one battery was in position before Malaon. But the Gurkhas were fast losing confidence, and, on May 11th, after his stockades had been bombarded for three days, Amar Singh capitulated and so ended a remarkable struggle of six months' duration against the greatly superior forces of the British. A week before this surrender, young Lawtie died at Ratnagarh, worn out by illness and fatigue. Of him Fraser says: " The happy issue of the campaign was clouded by the death of one individual whose exertions had greatly contributed to it; whose energy and zeal were the soul of every enterprise in which he was engaged; whose skill and judgment at a glance perceived the measures and the moment to employ them; and whose activity rendered him of the first utility in this new and uncommon warfare. Rarely does it happen that the loss of an officer of inferior rank excites so much sorrow." So Peter Lawtie sleeps under the swaying pines of the lonely Himalayas, where he earned so much fame in so short a time.

Little need be said about the operations of the 3rd Division under Major-General John Wood, or of the 4th Division under Major-General Marley. Wood, with a force including the 8th Company of Bengal Pioneers and Lieutenant William Morrieson[1] of the Bengal Engineers, advanced in December, 1814, from Gorakhpur, and on January 3rd attacked the Gurkhas near Butwal. The attack succeeded, though with considerable loss,[2] but Wood insisted on retreating from the position he had won. From that day he appeared to suffer from an inferiority complex. Maintaining that his force was too small, he settled down to a passive defence of the frontier covering Gorakhpur. Still worse was the conduct of General Marley. Soon after he started from his base at Patna to advance on Katmandu, the Gurkhas overwhelmed some of the frontier posts ahead of him, and this so disheartened him that he hesitated to enter the hills. Then, on February 10th, an event occurred which is happily without parallel in the annals of the British Army—Marley, let us hope through insanity, deserted his command. A new commander was found in Major-General George Wood, who, however, was little better than the deserter. He declared that, as the fever season was approaching, he dared not attempt an advance in force, and, after he had marched along the edge of the forest, he camped without seeing a Ghurka. It was a pitiful exhibition of irresolution and incompetence, for he commanded the main striking force and was liberally supplied with artillery and Pioneers. The 1st, 2nd and 7th Companies of Bengal Pioneers under Captain John Swinton[3] were with this division, and we may imagine the disgust of their fire-eating leader when he was forced to remain inactive. The names of his

---

[1] Sometimes spelt " Morrison."
[2] Morrieson was mortally wounded in this fight.
[3] *East India Military Calendar*, Vol. III, p. 417.

fellow-sufferers of the Bengal Engineers are not recorded; but as Captain Richard Tickell, Lieutenant Robert Smith and Ensign (afterwards General) Edward Garstin served in the Nepal War and are not mentioned in other theatres, it is possible that at least one of these was with General George Wood. Reviewing the first phase of the war as a whole, we may say that, with the exception of Ochterlony's defeat of Amar Singh Thappa, and the capture of Almora by a small column operating in Kumaon, the campaign of 1814-15 ended in lamentable failure and loss of prestige. The Gurkhas had been subdued only in the west, and their Government at Katmandu naturally refused to ratify the treaty which was prepared after Ochterlony's victory.

The second phase of the Nepal War opened when Ochterlony took the field in February, 1816, with four brigades, in a concentrated attack on Katmandu itself. The 1st Brigade under Colonel Kelly was to enter Nepal by Hariharpur; the 2nd, under Colonel Nicolls, was to penetrate by Ramnagar; while the 3rd and 4th, under Ochterlony, struck towards Makwanpur on the road to Katmandu. Ochterlony advanced with his usual care, consolidating as he went, and found that the Chariagati Pass leading to Makwanpur was strongly held by the enemy; but his reconnoitring parties discovered an unguarded route and reached the summit of the range on February 11th. For seven days the Pioneers laboured hard to construct a road up the mountain, and by the 18th it was ready for the guns and transport. On the 27th the British took Makwanpur, where Nicolls rejoined the main body, and, as Kelly had also been successful at Hariharpur, the prospect of capturing Katmandu seemed good. The Gurkhas, however, had had enough fighting, and sent envoys to Ochterlony proposing terms of peace. Negotiations then began which led to the signature of the Treaty of Sagauli on March 3rd, 1816, by which the first and last Nepal War was brought to a close. The Government of Nepal gave up most of their lowlands bordering on British territory, withdrew from Sikkim, and surrendered the provinces of Garhwal and Kumaon and the district of Dehra Dun, and the Company thus acquired the sites of several modern hill-stations such as Simla,[1] Mussoorie, Naini Tal, Almora, and Ranikhet.

Before we pass to the medley of the Third Maratha War, the siege of Hathras in 1817 may claim our attention. This was a town not far from Aligarh in the present United Provinces, and belonged to a landowner named Dayaram, who had fortified it with the idea of creating a second Bhurtpore to defy the British power. The Governor-General was about to crush the Pindari bands who roamed through Hindustan, and, not wishing that Dayaram should interfere with the coming operations, he decided to subdue him without delay. Accordingly he sent three divisions under Major-Generals Marshall,

[1] The first house in Simla—a thatched cottage—was built in 1819.

Donkin and Brown to invest the place, and the whole force under Marshall was grouped about Hathras on February 12th. Taught by the experiences of his predecessors, Lord Hastings made no attempt to economize in troops and material: at Hathras, indeed, he was justifiably lavish in his preparations. The walled town was surrounded by a ditch 100 feet wide and 40 to 70 feet deep, the escarp being revetted with good masonry; and, about 700 yards from the town, lay a powerful fort enclosed by a broad wet ditch. The siege operations were planned by the Chief Engineer, Captain Thomas Anbury, who had with him Captains Henry Carmichael-Smyth and Robert Tickell, and Ensigns Archibald Irvine and George Hutchinson, all of the Bengal Engineers.[1] The Pioneers were led as usual by Swinton; and the company of Miners, which had been raised in Bengal in 1808, was present also. Marshall had about 100 guns, six regiments of cavalry (including two of British cavalry) and nine battalions of infantry (including two of British infantry).[2] It was an imposing array for the reduction of a fortified town.

Preparations were made to besiege the town as a preliminary to an attack on the fort, and, during some days of negotiation before the fighting began, the engineers were able to walk up the glacis and examine the huge ditch. Four batteries were then constructed and a heavy bombardment opened on February 22nd. Before dawn on the 24th, Tickell reconnoitred the breaches in the town wall and also the ditch, plumbing the latter with a 6-pounder shot and finding that it was about 70 feet deep.[3] An assault, however, proved unnecessary, for the enemy evacuated the town on the following day and concentrated in the fort to which Marshall then turned his attention.

More batteries were brought into action, four of them firing from the walls of the captured town, and the hail of shells was supplemented by showers of rockets from a Rocket Troop attached to the artillery which set fire to many houses in the fort. The Engineers pushed forward their approaches and tried to reconnoitre the defences when opportunity offered; in one such reconnaissance on the 26th, without an escort, Carmichael-Smyth and Hutchinson were nearly captured by the enemy. By that time, Anbury was running a parallel from the south-east corner of the town to pass along the southern face of the fort, and several companies of Bengal Pioneers, assisted by working parties of infantry, were hard at work, so that, by the 28th, the parallel was opposite the southern face and four more batteries were in position along it. A general bombardment was opened on March 2nd and the fort soon fell.

Dayaram, the cause of all the trouble, escaped through the lines

---

[1] Article entitled "Early Indian Campaigns," by Major H. Biddulph, R.E., appearing in *The R.E. Journal*, Vol. XVIII, July-December, 1913, p. 234.
[2] *The Services of the Bengal Native Army*, by Lieutenant F. G. Cardew, p. 127.
[3] *History of the Bengal Artillery*, by Major F. W. Stubbs, p. 52.

of investment; but his power was gone, and his fortifications were destroyed by Marshall's Engineers, who were complimented in the Field Army Orders of March 6th on their science and skill during the siege. Of the Pioneers it was said that they had given another proof, to the many already on record, of their coolness in the most trying situations and their extraordinary skill in their work.[1] The siege occupied only nine days and forms an excellent example of the true economy of overwhelming strength, for the casualties on the British side were only seven men killed and ten wounded. The speedy fall of Hathras went far to restore the prestige lost by England in many theatres of the war in Nepal.

From the close of the Second Maratha War until the arrival of Lord Hastings in 1813, Rajputana and Central India were ravaged by Marathas, Pathans and Pindaris. Sindhia, Holkar and the Bhonsla invaded Rajputana when and where they pleased; bands of Pathan marauders, under their leader, Amir Khan, made their own raids or assisted the Marathas; and the Pindaris, on the same errand, outdid the others in rapacity and brutality. The Pindaris were not a people but a collection of the refuse of many lands bound together by a common love of plunder. They raided in bodies of 2,000 or 3,000 mounted men, riding sometimes 50 miles to the destination selected by their leader, and then dispersing to loot. When the favoured district had been swept clear of cattle and property, they burnt the villages, carried off the young women, reunited, and rode home. It was a merry life till Hastings took the field.

The close of the rainy season in 1817 was the time selected for the beginning of the operations against the Pindaris, and it was evident that they would have to be on a very large scale. The rounding up of numerous columns of mobile enemies always needs great strength. In 1817 there was a strong probability also that the operations against the Pindaris would extend into a war against the Marathas, especially if the former were not overwhelmed in the first few months. As P. E. Roberts aptly puts it,[2] while one cordon of the army, facing inwards, had to encircle the robber bands, a wider ring facing outwards had to check the attempts of the Maratha states to break through to their assistance. The forebodings of the Governor-General were realized. The Pindaris were a source of revenue to several of the Maratha states, and these could not bear to see their friends, the bandits, wiped out of existence. So the hunt of the Pindaris became merged in the Third Maratha War.

For the operations which are known as the Third Maratha War, under which title are included both the Pindari and Maratha campaigns, Lord Hastings mobilized two armies. In the north, under his own command, was the "Grand Army," more than 44,000 strong,

---

[1] *East India Military Calendar*, Vol. I, pp. 395, 396.
[2] *History of British India*, by P. E. Roberts, p. 283.

SCHEME OF THE PINDARI CAMPAIGN.

including native contingents, and consisting of four divisions and two small columns. Towards the south was the "Army of the Deccan," under Lieutenant-General Sir Thomas Hislop, Commander-in-Chief in Madras, with over 70,000 men formed in seven divisions.[1] The whole constituted the largest British army which had ever taken the field in India. Excluding all irregular troops, Hastings and Hislop together commanded some 13,000 Europeans, and 74,000 Indian soldiers with 282 guns. Against them were pitted about 15,000 Pindari horse with a few guns, 22,000 Pathan cavalry and infantry with 200 guns, and later, the armies of Sindhia, Holkar, the Peshwa, the Bhonsla Raja of Berar and the Nizam—amounting to a further 130,000 cavalry and 76,000 infantry with 369 guns.[2] These figures show how this war transcended in size any previous campaign in India.

The movements of the British divisions in their chase of the Pindari bands, their pursuit of the Peshwa, and their operations against the other Maratha princes, were so exceedingly intricate that it is impossible to follow them in detail in the space of a few pages. An outline only will be attempted here, with some description of the work and exploits of Engineers in a few battles and sieges. The plan of campaign evolved by the Governor-General provided for a vast encircling movement to confine the Pindaris to their haunts in the Narbada Valley in the neighbourhood of Ujjain, which lay between Bhopal and the dominions of Sindhia and Holkar. He wished to surround them by columns operating from Bengal on the north and east, from Gujarat on the west, and from the Deccan on the south, all driving inwards towards a place called Hindia on the Narbada River south-east of Ujjain ; but the drive was to be prosecuted more by the strong southern army acting in a northerly direction than by the weaker northern army moving towards the south. The northern divisions were, in fact, to act as "stops" rather than as "beaters." To protect the south of India from stray bands which might break back, a chain of posts was established running for part of its length along the Kistna River. This was the scheme for dealing with the Pindaris ; but it had to be modified considerably through the actions of the Maratha powers.

Before the Pindari drive began, the demeanour and conduct of the Peshwa were so threatening that, in June, 1817, Lord Hastings made him sign a rigorous treaty, hoping that he could thus be kept neutral. In the east, Appa Sahib, the Bhonsla Regent of Berar, had already formed an alliance with the British which seemed likely

[1] *History of the Bengal Artillery*, by Major F. W. Stubbs, pp. 64, 65. The Divisional Commanders in the north were Generals T. Brown, R. Donkin, D. Marshall and Sir D. Ochterlony ; and, in the south, Generals Sir T. Hislop, J. Doveton, Sir J. Malcolm, and L. Smith, Colonel J. W. Adams, and Generals Sir W. Keir and Sir T. Munro.
[2] *Memoir of the Operations of the British Army in India during the Maratha War of* 1817, *and* 1819, by Lieutenant-Colonel V. Blacker, p. 19. The figures which are given here must be taken as rough approximations only.

to endure. Holkar, for the moment, made a show of friendship; but Sindhia's attitude was very doubtful. Hastings desired to keep all these Maratha princes out of the field while he exterminated the Pindaris, and so, when he marched to battle in the autumn of 1817 at the head of the Grand Army, he went straight for Gwalior where, on November 5th, he forced the vacillating Sindhia to sign a treaty which was designed to retain him on the British side. Having thus, as he imagined, disarmed the Maratha states, he turned on the Pindaris. But he was mistaken in thinking that the Peshwa was subdued, for, on the very day that Sindhia put his signature unwillingly to the treaty pressed upon him, Baji Rao sacked the British Residency at Poona and declared himself an enemy. Appa Sahib, at Nagpur, followed suit, and thus, from the very outset, the British were confronted not merely by the Pindaris but by the armies of two of the Maratha states.

Under their leaders Chitu, Karim Khan and Wazil Muhammad, the Pindaris caused the British a great deal of trouble during the war, but were never really dangerous, for they were not fighters but robbers. Karim Khan and Wazil made for Gwalior to escape from Hislop's Deccan Army, and were headed towards the north-west, where they were overtaken in December by a division of the Grand Army under Marshall and turned back by another under Donkin. They retreated some distance, ran into part of the Deccan Army, and fled towards the south-west, reduced to little more than two thousand men. Chitu fared no better, for he had meanwhile been badly mauled by Donkin. After this, the remnants of the Pindaris were left undisturbed for a time while more dangerous enemies claimed the attention of the British, but the pursuit was resumed by several columns at the end of 1817 in the direction of Jawad, in Gwalior. Throughout January, 1818, the three Pindari leaders were hunted backwards and forwards till their followers were finally dispersed by Colonel Adams near Kotah. There we may leave them.

The first serious battle was fought on November 5th, 1817, at Kirkee, outside Poona, where Colonel Burr with only 3,000 men and four guns defeated Baji Rao with 8,000 men and 14 guns in a strong position between a river and a ravine. One company of the Bombay Pioneers was present but was not heavily engaged. As a result of this reverse, Baji Rao fled to the south; and on the 17th, the British troops under General Smith, after a difficult march involving the crossing of several rivers, entered Poona, among them being two companies of the Bombay Pioneers and two of the Madras corps. The Peshwa's misfortune, however, did not discourage Appa Sahib at Nagpur. The latter rose against the British on November 25th, and on the following day sent a force of 3,000 Arab mercenaries to attack the Nagpur Residency. The small garrison took up a position on the Sitabaldi Hills, near the city, where, for 18 hours, they resisted heavy attacks by 18,000 men with 36 guns, and finally routed them. Although negotiations were then begun, they led to nothing, so General Doveton was ordered to attack Nagpur and he defeated Appa Sahib there on December 16th. This, however, did not end the struggle, for the Arabs of the Nagpur army refused to admit defeat and took refuge in the citadel, where they made a stubborn defence for five days.

The siege of Nagpur began on December 19th, 1817, and proved to be a difficult affair. From an engineering point of view its chief interest lies in the fact that a small body of Sappers and Miners was formed locally, consisting partly of 34 Europeans and 33 Indians,[1] to reinforce the inadequate establishment of Pioneers and Engineers. It is remarkable that, although a whole division was besieging Nagpur, the Engineer in charge of the operations was an officer of only eight years' service (Lieutenant Thomas Davies) and that he was assisted only by one other (Ensign Charles Nattes). Some bundles of sandbags represented the whole of the engineering stores, and the only entrenching tools were such as could be borrowed from line regiments. In spite of such handicaps, however, the British advanced on the 24th to assault one of the city gateways, headed by Davies with the European Sappers and a detachment of Pioneers, but the Arabs rushed to repel them and they had to retire after Davies and Nattes had both been severely wounded. Doveton then awaited the arrival of his battering train. Before the guns could appear, however, the Arabs surrendered. The British Government then deposed Appa Sahib, and annexed a large part of his territory. With the end of 1817, matters looked more hopeful; the Bhonsla had been taught a lesson, the Peshwa was a fugitive, and Sindhia had been coerced—but trouble was brewing from Holkar.

Edward Lake criticizes severely the state of the engineering equipment with the Deccan Army in 1817, and few will deny that, after Nagpur, he was justified in his remarks. "The Engineering Department," he writes,[2] "was utterly disproportional to the strength of the army. A few scaling ladders, intrenching tools for fifty men, with two or three platform carts containing small stores, formed the Engineer Park. None of the peculiar tools required in Mining, or in the Sap, were provided. Nor was there any equipment for Pontoons, or other stores useful for the Military Passage of Rivers. These have never been supplied in India." Blacker agrees that the army was badly equipped with engineers:[3] "In an army which has generally found a wider field for the display of bravery and discipline than occasion for scientific resources, the

[1] *Sieges of the Madras Army*, by Edward Lake, p. 42.
[2] *Ibid.*, p. 28.
[3] *Memoir of the Operations of the British Army in India during the Maratha War*, 1817, 1818, 1819, by Lieutenant-Colonel V. Blacker, pp. 236 and 331.

Engineering branch of the service is not likely to meet the encouragement which it deserves or which in fact is necessary. It may indeed be fairly asserted that this establishment is far below its proportion in India and seldom able to furnish for field service officers possessing the rare combination of talents and experience while permanent employment in Civil works is considered as paramount to the Military demands of the service. With all the Madras troops in the field during the war, there was no officer of engineers above the rank of Lieutenant." It is indeed wonderful that junior subalterns of the Corps did so well in the Third Maratha War with the few trained men and the wretched equipment at their disposal.

After the Bhonsla had been subdued at Nagpur, the Pindari leader Chitu, flying northwards before Malcolm's division of the Deccan Army, came to rest near Holkar's army in the neighbourhood of Mehidpur[1] and was cordially received by the Maratha prince. They joined forces, and Holkar announced that he would march on Poona to assist Baji Rao. Meanwhile the other Pindaris, Karim Khan and Wazil Muhammad, were invited by Sindhia, in contravention of his treaty, to join him against the British, and, although they were held off by Marshall and Donkin, the invitation showed that Sindhia was false. Holkar's attitude, however, was so openly hostile that General Hislop, with the 1st Division of his Deccan Army, and Malcolm with the 3rd Division, advanced upon him in the position which he had taken up at Mehidpur. The Maratha left rested on the River Sipra, their right was covered by a deep ravine, and they had massed 63 guns in the position. The odds were heavily against the British, who could muster only 9,000 men with 18 small guns; but nevertheless they crossed the river by a ford on December 21st, 1817, assaulted the position, and routed the defenders, who lost 3,000 men and all their artillery. Four companies of the Madras Pioneers, under Captain R. McCraith, took part in the Battle of Mehidpur,[2] and their work was described as "highly meritorious and essentially useful." The Engineers present were Lieutenants Alexander Anderson and John Purton of the Madras Corps, and, strange to say, an officer of the Royal Engineers, Lieutenant T. H. Elliott.[3] Holkar was thoroughly cowed by this defeat, and signed a treaty on January 1st, 1818, under which he surrendered a large amount of territory. Thus one more enemy was removed, and, as already related, the Pindaris were soon afterwards hunted to their end.

The scene now shifts to the chase of the Peshwa, Baji Rao, between the Godavari and the Kistna by two divisions of the Deccan Army

---

[1] A town in the Indore State.
[2] "Early Indian Campaigns," by Major H. Biddulph, R.E., appearing in *The R.E. Journal*, Vol. XVIII, p. 233.
[3] *The Military History of the Madras Engineers and Pioneers*, by Major H. M. Vibart, Vol. I, p. 507. Elliott was Aide-de-Camp to General Hislop.

under Generals Smith and Pritzler, the latter of whom had replaced Colonel Munro. The perfidious Baji Rao doubled and twisted like a hare, and eluded both his pursuers till Lord Hastings reformed their divisions into a flying column under Smith to follow the Peshwa and a siege column under Pritzler to reduce his numerous forts and occupy his territory. Smith, after a stern chase, came up with the Marathas at a place called Ashti in the present Sholapur District, and, in a purely cavalry action on February 20th, 1818, gained a complete victory over them, killed the Maratha general in command, captured the titular Raja of Satara, and put Baji Rao to flight once more. Meanwhile Pritzler advanced first against the fortress of Singhur, lying fifteen miles south of Poona. In his column were three companies of Madras Pioneers and one from Bombay; and his Engineers were Captain Justinian Nutt, Lieutenant John Macleod and Ensign Samuel Athill from Bombay, and Lieutenant Alexander Grant from Madras. Singhur looked almost inaccessible because of its precipitous sides, but it was open to bombardment from the neighbouring hills, so between February 21st and 28th Pritzler opened fire with 15 guns, howitzers and mortars, and on the 28th the garrison surrendered. This small operation was quickly followed by dozens of others of a similar nature. The hill forts of Central India were so much alike, and the methods adopted in besieging them were so uniform, that a few remarks on these defended pinnacles may not be out of place. Most of the time and energy of the military engineers in the Third Maratha War was spent in operations against them.

Edward Lake, writing of these picturesque strongholds, says :—[1]

"As the general features are the same in all, it may not be amiss to attempt a description of these extraordinary Works of Nature. The reader must imagine a series of hills rising very abruptly from 600 to 1,100 feet above the plain. He must further imagine occasional bluff rocks, perfectly perpendicular and varying in height from 80 to 100 feet, to rise from the summit of these hills. The rocks which rise from them in this manner are basaltic, being so beautifully and regularly scarped as to assume the appearance of having been formed by the chisel. The hills, which contain water on their summits, have been fortified by the Natives in periods of the most remote antiquity, and the space contained within the rocky scarp constitutes the interior of the Fort. There is seldom any work raised on them, or indeed any thing done, further than to cut flights of steps out of the solid rock and to construct a number of gateways over them. Nothing is necessary but a determined Garrison to render such positions perfectly impregnable. Fortunately for us, this latter requisite was often wanting. The fort of Unkye Tunkye set an example, the Killedar (head man) being intimidated by the determined language held out to him.

[1] *Sieges of the Madras Army*, by Edward Lake, pp. 88 to 90, and 205.

"Those vast precipices of lofty granite may equally bid defiance to the battering Gun and to the Mine; and in fact there seems no mode of reducing them, if vigorously defended, but by the tedious operation of strict blockade. It may then be asked by what means we came to reduce the whole of them with such facility? The mode of proceeding always adopted was to occupy without delay one or more positions as close to the rock as possible, and to carry up field pieces to the spot by hand. The Commanders and their Garrisons were perfectly aware that the Peishwar had been totally defeated and that the state of his affairs was hopeless. Under such impressions they only waited for the opening of the first battery to afford them a decent pretext for surrendering!"

The battles of Kirkee, Sitabaldi, Nagpur, Mehidpur and Ashti practically decided the war. It remained only to reduce the hill fortresses scattered broadcast over the country and particularly in the district of Khandesh, north-east of Bombay. This was carried out most successfully by Pritzler and other commanders during the early months of 1818. To give the names of all these forts would be superfluous. Some were very powerful, such as Wasota[1] which was surrounded by inaccessible mountains and lay on a peak in the Western Ghats towering 3,000 feet above the plains: others were small and offered no resistance. Trimbak, 26 miles from Nasik, was a mountain mass five miles in circumference, topped by sheer precipices which in some places were 400 feet high. Only the gateways were accessible, and of these there were no more than two. Yet several 8-inch mortars and howitzers were dragged into position against the place, and, after three days of siege, the garrison evacuated it. Seventeen more forts fell in the next few weeks; but it is sad to relate that an excellent young officer, Lieutenant Thomas Davies, of the Madras Engineers, who directed the operations at Trimbak, Rajdir and other sieges, was killed in May during an attack on the powerful fortress of Malegaon.[2] Lake says of him[3] that he had scarcely an equal in zeal, perseverance and activity. It is fortunate indeed that England seems able, in her hour of need, to find such young Engineers as Peter Lawtie of Nepal and Thomas Davies of Khandesh.

Early in 1819, Lord Hastings decided to reduce the great fortress of Asirgarh, which lay on the eastern border of Khandesh in one of the passes leading from the Deccan into Hindustan. The Kiladar of Asirgarh had sheltered Appa Sahib when the latter was being hunted by the British, so he had to be punished for his duplicity. Doveton's and Malcolm's divisions were accordingly sent against him, forming together the largest concentration of troops and guns

[1] Captured on April 5th, 1818.
[2] The sieges of Malegaon (Mallegaum), in Khandesh, and Chakan near Poona, were important operations in the plains. Both were successful.
[3] *Sieges of the Madras Army*, by Edward Lake, p. 118.

which had been used in siege operations during the war. Altogether the British artillery included 28 guns, 15 mortars and 19 howitzers. Asirgarh had an upper and a lower fort, with a combined circumference of two and a half miles; and not only was the upper fort surrounded by precipices 700 feet high, but the masonry ramparts which surmounted them were themselves formidable. Yet the siege, which began on March 17th, ended with the surrender of the garrison on April 9th, a result which was largely due to the excellent work of the Pioneer units from all three Presidencies.[1]

The senior Engineer at Asirgarh was Lieutenant John Coventry of the Madras Corps, and with him were only three other Lieutenants and two Ensigns. An officer who was present has something to say about this engineering establishment for the siege of such a fortress. "It was not a little remarkable," he writes,[2] "that at the siege of Asseerghur, when there were nearly 15,000 men with three Brigadier-Generals, the conduct of the siege should have been conferred upon a young Lieutenant of Engineers, whose whole experience was in the storm of Cornelis at Java. It may be asked, where were all the Colonels, Lieutenant-Colonels and other officers of the Engineers? That branch of the service is despoiled and torn away from the real exercise of their profession in the same way as the other corps of the Company." If we scan a list of all the Engineer officers who were engaged in the Third Maratha War,[3] the justice of this complaint will be evident. Thirteen Bengal Engineers, six Bombay Engineers and ten Madras Engineers fought in the various battles and sieges— a total of 29 officers. Yet among them we shall find only one Major (Anbury), and three Captains (Carmichael-Smyth, Tickell and Nutt). Where indeed were the Colonels, Lieutenant-Colonels, and the other Majors? Probably they were holding civil or military administrative appointments in the Presidency towns, and were not allowed to take the field; but such prevention was unfair, not only to them but to the youngsters who were thrust into positions of far greater responsibility than they should have been called upon to support.

The fall of Asirgarh produced an excellent effect on the political situation, and virtually ended the Third Maratha War, in which 28 battles were fought and 120 fortresses taken without a serious reverse. Order was restored at last in Central India, and England found herself ruling or controlling two-thirds of the whole peninsula. Fortescue, in reviewing this war, says that the enemy was usually contemptible and that there was no general action worthy the name except Mehidpur; also that the Engineers, Artillery and Staff were

[1] Altogether 1,000 Pioneers took part in the siege; also 125 Bengal Miners, and 35 European and 45 Indian Sappers and Miners from Madras. The Madras Pioneers, who formed the bulk of the engineering establishment, were under Captain R. McCraith.
[2] *Summary of the Mahratta and Pindaree Campaigns* (anonymous), p. 315.
[3] A list is given in "Early Indian Campaigns," by Major H. Biddulph, R.E., appearing in *The R.E. Journal*, Vol. XVIII, July-December, 1913, pp. 234, 235.

sadly deficient for so many sieges.[1] Whether, or no, the human opposition was contemptible, the obstacles provided so lavishly by Nature were certainly formidable. It was chiefly against these that the Engineers and Pioneers contended, and with remarkable success.

After the end of the Maratha War, a few minor expeditions and operations took place during the comparative lull which preceded the Burma War. In May, 1819, General Pritzler captured the stronghold of Koppaldroog[2] (Copaldroog), whose Governor had rebelled. The General was assisted by the 2nd Battalion of Madras Pioneers under Captain T. Smithwaite and by Lieutenant Alexander Grant as Senior Engineer. The assaulting columns were led as usual by the officers of the Engineers, who, with the help of volunteer artillerymen, planted the ladders which the Pioneers had carried up to the walls.[3] Bamboo poles with iron forks were used to raise the ladders, the tops of which were tied to any projections by ropes which had been secured previously to their ends. This was the customary way of preparing to escalade, and, as it had to be carried out under a point-blank fire, it explains the heavy casualties among the Engineers. One company of the Bombay Pioneers sailed to the Persian Gulf in October, 1819, with an expedition under Major-General Grant Keir, to capture Ras-al-Khaima in Arabia[4]; and, early in 1821, No. 3 Company embarked for further service in Arabia under Major-General Lionel Smith against the Bani-Bu-Ali tribe of Arabs, taking part in desperate fights on February 10th and March 2nd, before the enemy made their submission. Here, Captain (afterwards Major-General) Thomas Dickenson, of the Bombay Engineers, distinguished himself, and "Beni-Boo-Ali, 2nd March, 1821," was added to the battle honours of the Bombay Sappers and Miners. These expeditions were, however, of little importance compared to the wars which were forced upon the Company by turbulent nations such as the Gurkhas, Marathas and Burmese; and so we pass to the First Burma War, a struggle for supremacy which was bound to come and which cost the Company an immense expenditure.

[1] *A History of the British Army*, by the Hon. J. W. Fortescue, Vol. XI, p. 251.
[2] A fortress in Hyderabad State in the Deccan.
[3] *The Military History of the Madras Engineers and Pioneers*, by Major H. M. Vibart, Vol. I, p. 577.
[4] Ras-al-Khaima had been occupied also in 1809. In the expedition of 1819 the adventurous Captain (afterwards Lieutenant-General) William Monteith, Madras Engineers, became Aide-de-Camp to General Keir. Monteith had great experience of the Near East, having served with the Turks and Persians against the Russians from 1810 to 1813. In 1828 he was on the Russian side against the Turks at Kars and elsewhere, and in 1830 with the French at the capture of Algiers. (See *The Military History of the Madras Engineers and Pioneers*, by H. M. Vibart, Vol. II, pp. 120-131.)

CHAPTER XIV.

THE FIRST BURMA WAR AND THE CAPTURE OF BHURTPORE, 1824–1826.

FOR half a century the Burmese had been creeping towards India like a tide which could not be stemmed. In 1766 they had wrested Tenasserim[1] from Siam, and in 1784 they overran Arakan.[2] By 1793, they had occupied the whole of Upper and Lower Burma and were close to Chittagong, and so within measurable distance of Calcutta. During the Third Maratha War they showed every intention of invading Assam, and had the insolence to demand the cession of Chittagong, Dacca, Murshidabad and Cossimbazar. In 1822, through the prowess of Maha Bandula, their best general, the Burmese were actually in possession of both Manipur[3] and Assam and faced the British along the whole length of their eastern frontier. It was clear that they must be humbled, and the pretext for war was an attack on a British island near Chittagong in September, 1823, and other hostilities along the Assam border. Lord Amherst, the Governor-General, protested strongly but without effect; so on February 24th, 1824, he issued an ultimatum, and, on March 5th, declared war against the " White Elephant of Ava " and his subjects, little knowing what awaited his army in the approaching campaign.

Before the declaration of war, Sir Edward Paget, the Commander-in-Chief, had advised that the operations should be restricted to the maritime borders of Burma, pointing out that if the army penetrated into the country they would find, instead of armies, fortresses and cities, " nothing but jungle, pestilence and famine." He was absolutely right. The British found these in abundance in Manipur, Arakan, and on the Irrawaddy; and the war, besides costing the Government some £13,000,000 and a huge number of men,[4] was very nearly a disastrous failure. While the inhabitants of Bengal had an exaggerated respect for the Burmese soldiery, the British Government underestimated their bravery and resource and thought that the capture of Rangoon and the coastal regions of Burma might end the war. But the Burmese, after all, were neither super-men nor weaklings: they were good but ordinary fighters in their own savage style and in their natural surroundings, and, to their

---

[1] The coastal region of the present Lower Burma south of Moulmein.
[2] The coastal region bordering on the Bay of Bengal south of Chittagong.
[3] An independent state lying between Upper Burma and Assam.
[4] The cost was more than twelve times that of the Third Maratha War, and the casualties during the war amounted to $72\frac{1}{2}\%$ of the troops engaged. During the first year, while only $3\frac{1}{2}\%$ were killed in action, 45% perished from disease. (*Our Burmese Wars*, by Colonel W. F. B. Laurie, p. 14.)

credit be it said, they struggled bravely to the end. Very little was known of either the geography or the resources of their country, and it was thought that, if an advance into Upper Burma should become necessary, boats alone would suffice for transport and that these could be obtained on the spot. This was a serious miscalculation. As soon as hostilities had begun, the Burmese denuded the country of everything, and no transport whatever was available for the invaders until they had taken a large part of Burma. For a long time they were tied to their maritime bases while the Lord of the White Elephant reposed on his cushioned throne at distant Ava. The map entitled "Sketch Map of Southern India and Burma," which appears at the end of this volume, will show how far removed and how secure the King of Burma was from British guns and bayonets.

Illustrations have been given already of one trait in the character of the Burman of 1824—his belief in his invincibility—but a closer look at him may be advisable. "Born a soldier," writes Snodgrass,[1] "he is accustomed from his earliest years to consider war and foreign conquest as his trade : he seldom gives quarter or receives it, and while on foreign service is but too ready to execute the cruel orders of his chiefs. When engaged in offensive warfare the Burmese is arrogant, bold and daring : possessed of strength and activity superior to all his neighbours and capable of enduring great fatigue, his movements are rapid, and his perseverance in overcoming obstacles almost irresistible. At home the Burmese is decidedly lazy and averse to work, compelling his wife to toil hard for the support of his family while he passes his time in idleness, smoking and chewing betel. His wants are few : rice and a little pickled fish are his chief articles of food, while water is his only drink. Naturally good-humoured and contented, he seems happy and resigned, and in his own home he is kind and affectionate to his children." This was the strange mixture of activity and lethargy, kindness and cruelty, savagery and good-humour, which we met in the Burmese War.

Major-General Sir Archibald Campbell,[2] K.C.B., was appointed to command the army for the invasion of Burma. He was efficient and energetic, if somewhat bombastic in correspondence, and he had a respectable force at his disposal, drawn chiefly from the Madras Army. The Indian soldiers of Bengal, who were mostly of high caste, had a rooted aversion, on religious and other grounds, to service overseas,[3] but the more lowly men of Bombay and Madras were not so particular. Campbell's army numbered about 11,000 men with

---

[1] *Narrative of the Burmese War*, by Major Snodgrass, p. 204.
[2] He should not be confounded with the famous military engineer of the same rank and names who became Governor of Madras and died in 1791. See Chapter X.
[3] Although the Bengal sepoys had volunteered in large numbers for the Java expedition in 1811, three battalions mutinied at Barrackpore, near Calcutta, in November, 1823, when ordered on service in Arakan, which they thought might necessitate a sea-crossing. They were fired upon by artillery, and the mutiny was quelled.

42 guns. The contingents from Bengal and Madras met at the Andaman Islands on May 2nd, 1824, and three days later the combined fleets sailed for Burma and entered the Rangoon River on the 10th. It may seem curious that the month of May should have been selected for the invasion of a tropical country. The heat was sure to be terrific, and, when the rains came, malaria would decimate the force. In this case, however, the reason appears to have been that in May the rivers would be in flood and that this would simplify transport by water.

Four Madras Engineers sailed to Burma—Captain John Mackintosh, as Commanding Engineer, with Lieutenants Edward Lake,[1] George Underwood and Arthur Cotton[2] as his subalterns; and from Bengal came six Engineers—Captain (afterwards General Sir John) Cheape as Commanding Engineer, with Lieutenants Henry de Budé, James Crommelin, Joseph Tindal, William Dickson and Frederick (afterwards Major-General Sir Frederick) Abbott. The number of Engineers was perhaps adequate, but all were junior officers; indeed, John Mackintosh, the Chief Engineer with the whole army, had only sixteen years' service to his credit. These young men paid dearly for the privilege of serving in Burma. Mackintosh was invalided within three months of his arrival, and in another two months was in his grave. Captain Alexander Grant, who arrived in December from Madras to succeed him, died five months later. Underwood, Dickson and Abbott were wounded, and the remainder suffered in health.

The Pioneers who served in the First Burma War came exclusively from Madras. It was thought to be unwise to order the Bengal Pioneers " across the black water," and the Pioneers of Bombay were out of reach. So the 1st Battalion of Madras Pioneers, 552 strong, under Captain Milne, sailed with the Madras contingent. They were most eager for the fray. "No European," wrote Sir Thomas Munro,[3] " could have evinced more readiness to go on foreign service than they have done. They have been able to join only by very extraordinary exertion. A detachment of them from Hyderabad has marched at the rate of 25 miles daily for 15 days without a halt at the hottest time of the year."

The war in Burma opened at Rangoon. This town, lying about 15 miles from the sea, was a small place in 1824. It extended for 900 yards along the river-bank and was nowhere more than 700 yards wide. Upstream and downstream of it were unprotected suburbs, but the town proper was enclosed by palisades 12 feet high. The defended area had one gate in each side except on the north, where roads issued from two gates and led for two and a half miles to the

---

[1] Author of *Sieges of the Madras Army*.
[2] Afterwards General Sir Arthur Cotton, Kt., K.C.S.I., who died in 1899 after a very distinguished career as an irrigation engineer (see Volume II, Chapter II).
[3] Governor and Commander-in-Chief of Madras.

great Shwedagon Pagoda, the golden wonder of Burma. Sir Archibald Campbell had no difficulty whatever in capturing the town. Twenty minutes after his leading troops had landed on May 11th, Rangoon was in his hands; but it was a mere empty shell, for the Burmese had fled, taking with them all their cattle, provisions and valuables. Not a boat was to be had. There was nothing for the troops to eat except the salt pork and biscuits which they had brought with them, and the Burmese, stockading themselves in the jungles around, effectually blockaded the British and confined them to the town, where they rotted and died of dysentery and malaria in a never-ceasing deluge of rain.

As all hope of advancing up the Irrawaddy had to be abandoned because there was no transport and little to eat, Campbell set himself to extend his precarious holding at Rangoon. He was successful in his first brush with the enemy on May 28th when he drove them from their stockades, and this encouraged him to plan an attack on a powerful stockaded position at a place called Kemmendine, three miles up the river. He marched to the assault on June 3rd, and was repulsed. This was a most unfortunate and mismanaged affair. The Madras Pioneers who accompanied him had not been provided with either scaling ladders or axes, and the British artillery fire made little impression on the wooden defences. Doveton gives an account of this failure at Kemmendine,[1] and has much to say about the Burmese fortifications. "The stockades," he writes, "were sometimes built entirely of bamboo, at others of timber. The bamboo of Ava is remarkable for its gigantic growth, far exceeding anything met with in India. It is frequently from nine to twelve inches in diameter, and the hollow compartments, which are used by the natives for holding water, are nearly as large as a ship's bucket. The large towns, such as Rangoon, Prome and Shoe Ghein,[2] were all defended by timber stockades on a grand scale. These being permanent works, differed materially from the ephemeral productions of the jungle, which nevertheless at times bothered us and our artillery. These temporary works averaged ten to twelve feet in height, being formed of bamboo or timber, driven into the ground generally in double rows and united by transverse beams. They were loopholed for musketry, whilst larger apertures were arranged for cannon or jingals. There was a trench in the interior, the earth from which, being piled against the stockade, enabled a person standing in the trench to fire through the loopholes with little risk. Externally, the stockades were protected by an abattis formed of branches of trees carefully pointed at the ends and fixed in the ground in an outward direction. Beyond the abattis, again, rows of short bamboo spikes were planted, which being concealed by the

[1] *Reminiscences of the Burmese War in 1824-26*, by Captain F. B. Doveton, p. 52 *et seq.* and p. 38 *et seq.*
[2] Shwegyin, on the Sittang River north-east of Pegu.

STORMING A STOCKADE AT PAGODA POINT, RANGOON.

long grass, inflicted most dangerous wounds. There was often a dry ditch between the stockade and the abattis. The better description of stockade was generally defended by square bastions at intervals. These wooden walls, however barbarous, opposed difficulties by no means despicable to our disciplined troops. *Fas est hoste doceri ;* I cannot but think that our men of science (the Engineers) may have occasionally gathered a wrinkle from the uncivilized Burmans."

Campbell was not disheartened by his failure at Kemmendine on June 3rd, and made a second attempt, a week later, with three thousand men assisted by the fire of several ships. This time he took plenty of scaling ladders with him, and several heavy guns. The wily Burmese, however, made no attempt to defend the place against this powerful attack ; and when the British entered it after a heavy bombardment, the only occupant was one old woman with shattered nerves. The enemy then prepared to take the offensive in their turn, and began to mass in large numbers in the jungles around Rangoon ; so Campbell, to check this concentration, determined to capture a fortified post at a place called Pagoda Point, upstream of Kemmendine, where the Hlaing and Panhlaing join to form the Rangoon River. Underwood, of the Engineers, reconnoitred the position on July 8th, and the troops then advanced gallantly to the assault, headed by the Madras Pioneers with scaling ladders. So eager were the Pioneers that they would not even wait for a covering party.[1] Seven stockades were escaladed in half an hour, without any help from artillery fire, and 1,000 Burmese were killed at a trifling cost. Other small expeditions followed—against Siriam, east of Rangoon, and against Dalla opposite the city—and, on August 20th, a large force sailed to invade the province of Tenasserim in the south. All these minor operations were successful and served to distract the minds of the troops from the dreadful ravages which were made in their ranks by disease. Arthur Cotton was the Engineer with the Tenasserim expedition, and helped to capture Tavoy and Mergui ; but there was little scope for engineering in these small affairs, although Madras Engineers and Pioneers figured in all. In August and September, 1824, Rangoon was fairly quiet. The main Burmese army fell back to Donabyu on the Irrawaddy, fifty miles to the north-west, and the British awaited the end of the rains.

Hostilities on a small scale began again in October with varying success, and in these the Pioneers lost several of their British officers. Still, these skirmishes had one good result : the enemy began to lose confidence and refused after a time to face our European soldiers. The Burmese monarch himself recognized the difficulty of defeating the white invaders and their Indian brothers, and, recalling the

[1] *The Military History of the Madras Engineers and Pioneers,* by Major H. M. Vibart, Vol. II, p. 47.

armies he had sent into Assam and Arakan, concentrated all his forces and placed them under Maha Bandula, his favourite and most efficient general. At the end of November, 1824, Bandula, with 50,000 men, had surrounded the British in Rangoon, the Shwedagon Pagoda and Kemmendine, and was preparing to drive them into the river. The smoke from the countless bivouacs of the Burmese host could be seen rising in the north, east, and west, and in the dense forest the silence of the night was broken by the crash of falling trees as the enemy erected stockade after stockade.

At dawn on December 1st, the great attack on Rangoon was heralded by the approach of fire-rafts[1] directed against the British ships and by the steady advance of the Burmese infantry. This advance was unlike anything which the Company's soldiers had yet seen; it resembled far more an infantry advance of the present day than an operation of 1824. So remarkable, indeed, were the Burmese tactics that they must be given more than passing notice. Writing of the defence of the Shwedagon sector of the British position, Major Snodgrass says:[2] "The Great Pagoda was naturally considered the key to our position. In the course of a few hours we found ourselves completely surrounded, and as far as celerity, order and regularity are concerned, the style in which the different Burmese corps took up their stations reflected much credit on their commander. When this formation was completed, the soldiers, laying aside their spears and muskets, commenced operations with their entrenching tools with such activity that in a couple of hours their line had wholly disappeared and could be traced only by a parapet of new earth. The moving masses had sunk into the ground. To us who had watched the whole strange proceeding, it seemed the work of magic. The trenches were afterwards found to be a succession of holes capable of containing two men each and excavated so as to afford shelter both from the weather and the fire of the enemy; even a shell lighting on the trench could at most but kill two men. When one line of trench is completed, its occupiers, taking advantage of the night, push forward to where a second line is to be opened, their place being immediately taken up by fresh troops from the rear." The advance and deployment of working parties; the use of entrenching tools; traverses to localize shell bursts; front line and supports: that such methods of deliberate warfare were known and used in Burma more than 100 years ago is truly surprising.

The Burmese were soon formed in a great semi-circle extending from Dalla, opposite Rangoon, round by Kemmendine and the Shwedagon Pagoda to the Pegu channel, north-east of the town.

---

[1] Each fire-raft consisted of a train of bamboo frameworks on each of which were earthen pots filled with petroleum and cotton. Some of these floating trains of fire were more than 100 feet long. If the train fouled the bow of a ship, it wrapped its blazing length around her.

[2] *Narrative of the Burmese War*, by Major Snodgrass, p. 101 *et seq.*

They attacked with scaling ladders at Kemmendine on December 2nd, and were repulsed; and they met with the same fate when they repeated the attempt two days later. Campbell, by remaining quiet at the Pagoda, then enticed Bandula forward towards that part of the line; and on the 7th, when the exultant Burmese had sapped almost up to the defences, he sallied forth with four columns and drove them back into the jungles, killing a huge number of them and capturing 240 small guns. The Burmese offensive failed everywhere, and in the end Bandula drew off; but no farther than Kokein, only four miles from the Pagoda, where he stockaded himself with extraordinary skill and judgment.

The Engineers and Pioneers did well in the defence of Rangoon and were mentioned by Sir Archibald Campbell in flattering terms:[1] " To Captain Cheape, Commanding Engineer, and every individual of the department, the greatest credit is due; and the conduct of Captain Wheeler and the Madras Pioneers is justly the theme of praise to every officer under whose command they are placed." The grit and determination shown by the Burmese commander in retiring no farther than Kokein are remarkable in view of the severity of his repulse, but he fared no better at Kokein than at Rangoon. With 20,000 men, sheltering behind enormous stockades, he failed to resist the attack of 1,300 British infantry on December 15th, and the offensive then passed definitely to the British, while the Burmese army fell back on Donabyu. In the capture of Kokein, Cheape and Underwood of the Engineers, and Crowe and Wheeler of the Pioneers, were conspicuous in directing and assisting the assault, and their services were duly acknowledged.

We have been concerned till now with the exploits of the main body only of the British army in Burma, so it may be well to describe briefly what happened during the next few months in two secondary theatres of the war. Through ignorance of the country to be traversed, the Government of India made the fatal mistake of trying to reach Burma by land as well as sea. An expedition under Brigadier-General Thomas Shuldham, consisting of two brigades, was fitted out and ordered to march through Cachar and Manipur and so to reach Upper Burma by the northern route. Another of three brigades, under Brigadier-General J. W. Morrison, was directed to march southwards from Chittagong to the town of Arakan, whence it was to cross the mountains and descend into the Irrawaddy Valley to join Campbell in his advance towards the Burmese capital. With the Cachar force was Major John Swinton at the head of four companies of Bengal Pioneers,[2] and in February, 1825, he was trying desperately to hack a road through 40 miles of almost impenetrable jungle so that Shuldham's guns could advance. It was an

[1] G.O.C.C. in Burma, dated December 8th, 1824.
[2] *History of the Bengal Artillery*, by Major F. W. Stubbs, p. 137.

impossible task; elephants, camels and bullocks perished in large numbers even in conveying supplies to the working parties, so the attempt was abandoned and the whole expedition recalled. In Arakan, partial success attended Morrison. Leaving Chittagong at the end of January, 1825, he marched southwards along the coast, and, after traversing formidable obstacles, captured the town of Arakan on April 8th, and expelled the Burmese from the whole province. So far he had done well; but in trying to find a way to cross into Burma he was completely baffled. There was nothing for it but to sit down in Arakan, where his men died by hundreds from malaria and other diseases in the pestilential monsoon. Indeed, when the Arakan force was withdrawn in September, four out of every five British soldiers had died, and Morrison himself was so ill that he succumbed on his voyage to England. The fact that he reached even so far as Arakan was due largely to his complete equipment of engineering troops, for he had with him six companies of Bengal Pioneers, one company of Madras Pioneers, a corps of Irregular (Magh) Pioneers and a Pontoon Train.[1] When Arakan had been occupied, he brought to notice the services of his Field Engineer, Lieutenant George Thomson[2] of the Bengal Corps, and admitted that the successful advance of his division could be attributed largely to Captain Wilkie and the other officers of the Pioneers who had made a road 150 miles long and had bridged innumerable *nullahs*.[3] The impossibility of reaching Burma by any land route required no further proof, and the attempt was not renewed.

We return now to Sir Archibald Campbell, who began his advance into the interior with two columns in February, 1825, his first objective being Prome on the Irrawaddy. Under his personal command was a force, about 2,400 strong, moving by land; while Brigadier-General W. Cotton, with 1,170 men, proceeded by river to open a way past Donabyu, where Bandula was entrenched. A small column was sent also towards Bassein, westwards from Rangoon. The remainder of the army, about 4,000 men, stayed in Rangoon as a reserve. To attempt to capture Upper Burma with about 3,500 men may seem absurd, and the reserve may appear to be out of all proportion to the striking force, but the truth is that Campbell could not transport or feed a greater number than he took with him; so, at the head of his little army, he marched from Rangoon on February 13th, and, three days later, Cotton sailed up the river. All went well with the river expedition until it came in sight of Donabyu, but there it was checked by Bandula on March 7th after a hard tussle. The news soon reached Campbell who had outdistanced the flotilla

---

[1] *Frontier and Overseas Expeditions*, compiled by the Intelligence Branch, A.H.Q., Simla, Vol. V, p. 46.

[2] See the obituary notice of Colonel George Thomson, c.b., in *The R.E. Journal*, Vol. 16, 1886, pp. 78-84, in which copious extracts are given from his letters describing his experience in the First Burma War.

[3] *Documents Illustrative of the Burmese War*, by H. H. Wilson, p. 129.

in his eagerness to capture Prome, and he was obliged not only to retrace his steps but to cross the wide Irrawaddy to co-operate with Cotton in forcing a way past, and taking, Donabyu. This crossing occupied five days because he had no Pontoon Train, and, before he reached Donabyu on the 24th, his Pioneers had to cut a path for nearly ten miles through grass and reeds sometimes 20 feet high.[1]

The defences which the Burmese had prepared at Donabyu were strong enough to dismay any commander of a small and isolated army, and they must have caused some misgivings to Grant, Underwood and Abbott, the engineers with the expedition. The fortified enclosure measured about one mile by half a mile, and it was held by 15,000 soldiers with 150 guns of various sorts. On its perimeter was a stockade of teak beams about 16 feet high, and behind this, brick ramparts. A wide ditch, filled with spikes and nails, surrounded the main stockade, and outside the ditch were lines of smaller stockading. Nevertheless, Donabyu was attacked and taken. The flotilla ran the gauntlet of the Burmese guns on the 27th, when Bandula made an unsuccessful sortie with seventeen elephants, and, on April 1st, Campbell opened fire. Luck was with him, for Bandula was killed on the following day by a rocket, and the panic-stricken Burmese abandoned their stockades and vanished into the jungles. This victory opened the way to Prome which fell on April 25th.

The British Commander-in-Chief then addressed the Court at Ava, urging them to accept reasonable terms; but the answer, which was heralded by the advance of a new Burmese army of 70,000 men, was that " If you wish for peace, you may go away ; but if you ask either money or territory, no friendship can exist between us. This is the Burmese custom." So Campbell launched his little force once more to battle, and gained a notable victory over the enemy on the heights of Napadi on December 1st, driving them from a strong and well-selected position of great depth, and taking all their artillery and stores. Underwood and Abbott volunteered to lead the assaulting troops in this battle, and both were wounded.

After the action at Napadi, the enemy's resistance weakened, and they sent envoys to ascertain what terms they could secure. Retreating slowly before the victorious British, and laying waste the country as they fell back, they attempted to defend Meaday, Minhla (Melloon) and other places on the Irrawaddy till at Paghamyu (Pagan), on February 9th, Campbell with only 1,300 men defeated 10,000 Burmese known as the " Retrievers of the King's Glory " or the " King's Invulnerables." The commander of these superwarriors bore a Burmese title meaning " The Prince of Darkness " (or " Prince of the Setting Sun ") and so was called by the British soldiers " The King of Hell " ! This hapless ruler of the nether regions fled to Ava with the news of his defeat, and finding King

[1] *A History of the British Army*, by the Hon. J. W. Fortescue, Vol. XI, p. 325.

Hpagyidoa in a bad temper, was immediately beheaded. The battle at Paghamyu ended the war. Campbell was within a few miles of the Burmese capital, and the "Golden-footed"[1] monarch thought best to conclude a treaty at Yandabu on February 24th, 1826, under the terms of which he was deprived of Tenasserim, Arakan, Assam, Cachar and Manipur—in fact, all his outlying provinces—and was made to pay a large indemnity; but he was allowed to retain the province of Pegu, including Rangoon, and the whole of Upper Burma. As soon as possible after the ratification of the treaty, the British army returned to the coast and sailed for India, glad, no doubt, to see the last of the jungles and swamps of Burma.

This sketch of a remarkable campaign may be concluded by quoting the garbled version of the operations which was concocted by the Burmese; a flight of fancy which shows that, in spite of their heavy defeat, they still remained the same boastful and warlike people. In the Royal Chronicle of Ava, the war is described as follows:[2] "The white strangers of the west fastened a quarrel upon the Lord of the Golden Palace. They landed at Rangoon and took that place and Prome, and were permitted to advance as far as Yandaboo; for the King, from motives of piety and regard to life, made no preparation whatever to oppose them. The strangers had spent vast sums of money in their enterprise, so that, by the time they reached Yandaboo, their resources were exhausted and they were in great distress. They then petitioned the King, who, in his clemency and generosity, sent them large sums of money to pay their expenses back, and ordered them out of the country." The methods of recording defeat vary little from age to age. We seem to remember the German strategical movements to the rear during the Great War, which were always "in accordance with a pre-arranged plan."

Every nation in India watched the course of the Burma War, and many came to the conclusion that the Burmese would defeat the British. Immediately, disturbances occurred in various parts of the country and notably at Bhurtpore. The old Raja of that place had died; and a man named Durjan Sal, cousin to the new Raja, who was a child, disputed the succession. Durjan Sal forced his way into the citadel, took charge of affairs, and obtained the support of the Jat and Pathan garrison. This act of aggression so infuriated Sir David Ochterlony, the Resident at Delhi and late commander in the Nepal War, that he promptly denounced Durjan Sal, called upon all Jats to support the British, and issued drastic orders to the usurper which the latter ignored. Ochterlony then

---

[1] Anyone who was received by the King of Burma was said to have been "at the golden feet." If the King heard any news it was said to have "reached the golden ears." Otto of roses was in favour because it was grateful to the "golden nose."

[2] *Our Burmese Wars*, by Colonel W. F. B. Laurie, p. 60.

collected some troops and was about to march on Bhurtpore when he was stopped and censured by Lord Amherst. He resigned his post, and died soon afterwards. Thus the career of a notable leader ended in disgrace when, as later events proved, he had acted rightly. The veto of the Governor-General had deplorable results, for it confirmed the Jats in the belief that the British dared not attack Bhurtpore and fostered a spirit of rebellion in other parts of the country. The ferment in Bhurtpore increased so rapidly that Lord Amherst was soon faced with the choice of the capture of that stronghold or a possible renewal of the Maratha War with an army depleted, and an exchequer drained, by the war in Burma. Under the advice of Sir Charles Metcalfe, the new Resident at Delhi, he chose to attack Bhurtpore and appointed Lord Combermere,[1] the Commander-in-Chief in India, to lead an army of more than thirty thousand men against it in December, 1825.

The die being cast, Lord Amherst left nothing to chance. A second failure before Bhurtpore would have shattered British prestige throughout the East, so he concentrated an overwhelming force under Combermere at Agra consisting of two regiments of British and six of Indian cavalry, two battalions of British and 16 of Indian infantry, with 112 siege guns[2] and 50 mobile pieces. The army had a fine array of engineering talent. The Chief Engineer was Lieut.-Colonel Thomas Anbury, C.B., who had been the senior Engineer during the Third Maratha War; and in addition there were Captains Robert Smith, Joseph Taylor, John Colvin and Charles Davidson, with nine Lieutenants and two Ensigns, all of the Bengal Engineers. They suffered heavily during the siege. Three of the four Captains were wounded, and, of the nine Subalterns, one (Joseph Tindal) was killed and four were wounded; in fact, the cadre of sixteen Engineers suffered casualties to the extent of fifty per cent. before Bhurtpore fell. Anbury had also six companies of the newly-constituted Bengal Sappers and Miners and two companies of Bengal Pioneers who had marched from Cawnpore on October 30th to join the concentration at Agra. It was generally admitted that Lake's failure in 1806 was due to lack of Engineers as much as to over-confidence, carelessness and a deficiency of siege guns; so Lord Combermere, with that disaster before him, secured the best engineers of the north to plan his siege operations and direct his assault. The siege was exclusively a Bengal affair. There is no evidence that any Engineers or Pioneers from Bombay or Madras took part in it.

Describing Bhurtpore, Fortescue remarks[3] that the fortress had

---

[1] As Major-General Sir Stapleton Cotton, Lord Combermere had been the best cavalry commander under Wellington in the Peninsula. He became Commander-in-Chief in India in 1825.
[2] Including sixteen 24-pounders, twenty 18-pounders, twelve 8-inch howitzers, two 13-inch mortars, twelve 10-inch mortars and forty-six 8-inch mortars.
[3] *A History of the British Army*, by the Hon. J. W. Fortescue, Vol. XI, p. 358.

been extended and enlarged since Lake's attack. It was about eight miles in circumference and lay in an almost level plain bounded on the west by a ridge of low rocks. The fortifications consisted of a citadel and an outer enceinte of 35 lofty semi-circular bastions connected by curtains, the whole built of mud, which was held together by straw and in many places strengthened by rows of tree-trunks buried upright. The enceinte was surrounded by a watercourse, from 20 to 35 feet wide with perpendicular banks, which had been converted into a ditch. There were nine gates, each covered by an earthwork. The citadel, which was on high ground, commanded the body of the place. Its ditch, 50 yards broad and very deep, had a counterscarp revetted with stone. From the bottom of the scarp rose a perpendicular stone wall, 80 feet high, flanked by 40 semi-circular towers; and within this was another stone wall, 74 feet in height and flanked by 11 bastions. The whole fortress was surrounded by a belt of jungle at a distance varying from 500 to 800 yards from the walls, with but one open space about a mile wide opposite the south-western angle, and the outer perimeter of this belt was little short of 20 miles. Such defences, combined with such difficulties of approach, could not be matched anywhere in India nor perhaps in the world. The problem before Anbury was to open a way through these seemingly impregnable and well-screened fortifications.

The army marched from Agra on December 8th, and two days later a strong advanced party seized an extensive swamp, called the Moti Jhil (Motee Jheel), lying two miles north-west of Bhurtpore. This was connected to the outer ditch of the fortress by a channel, and when the party arrived, the defenders had just opened a sluice which would have filled the ditch and probably flooded the country around it, as had happened in the first siege. However, the British came in the nick of time, and drove away the piquet guarding the sluice, while Lieutenant A. Irvine[1] and his Bengal Sappers and Miners stopped the flow of water by sinking a boat across the aperture and adding brushwood and other material. The result was that throughout the siege the great ditch remained almost dry, and a most difficult obstacle thus lost half its value. The paramount importance of time in military operations is shown by this exploit, for if the advanced party had arrived only eight hours later the ditch would have been full and running over.[2]

The belt of jungle around Bhurtpore prevented Lord Combermere from making a complete investment of the place even with the powerful force at his disposal, so he concentrated his infantry in an arc about six miles long on the north-east side, and held the remainder

---

[1] According to Colonel C. W. Pasley, late R.E., Lieutenant Irvine "was the chief means of the reduction of Bhurtpore" by his activities as Brigade-Major, and by planning and executing the mining operations.

[2] *Narrative of the Siege and Capture of Bhurtpore*, by J. N. Creighton, p. 5.

PLAN OF BHURTPORE.

- Col. Delamain's attack. JUGEENAH GATE
- N.E. or PATHAN BASTION (General Reynell's attack).
- Sunken Street
- SOORAJPUR GATE
- Col. Wilson's attack
- LONG NECKED BASTION.
- KADDAM
- KANDY TEMPLE (General Nicholl's)
- Extreme left Breach.
- MUTTRA GATE
- Sluice from Motee Jheel
- PALACE
- Entrance to Citadel.
- TOWN
- BEERNALAIN GATE
- KOMBHER GATE
- Lord Lake's Batteries 1804
- N.
- Scale roughly 1¾ inches to 1 mile.

of the circumference with cavalry or fortified posts. This disposition was partly due, no doubt, to the report of his Chief Engineer, who recommended an attack on the north-east angle because the flanking defences were weaker there than elsewhere. The walls of Bhurtpore presented some problems to the Engineers and Gunners. The rounded bastions were difficult to enfilade, and the mud walls absorbed cannon balls without suffering any appreciable damage. If, by a huge expenditure of ammunition, a wall was made to crumble away, the breach was found to be obstructed by the buried palisade of trees, and bombardment of the palisade resulted only in a most effective abattis. There were no shells for the guns, and the shells from the mortars did not penetrate deeply enough to bring down large masses of the parapet. However, Anbury made every preparation. Before leaving Agra he had manufactured some thousands of fascines and gabions, and, on arrival at Bhurtpore, he continued the process in his Engineer Park, where large working parties of infantry toiled day and night alongside the Sappers and Miners. On December 22nd, 1825, he was able to report that all was ready, and the attack began by the occupation of a village and a garden, each about 600 yards from the north-east angle. These posts were then connected by a trench, and eight guns and 16 mortars opened fire from them on the 24th. A second parallel was finished on the following day, about one furlong only from a prominent feature known as the Long-necked Bastion, and more guns opened from it on the 26th. So energetically did the Sappers dig that by January 4th the north-east angle was under the fire of 78 siege guns, howitzers and mortars, and the saps were within 40 yards of the huge ditch.

By that date, several breaches had been made; but Anbury would not guarantee that they were fit for assault, so the British resorted to mining and the Jat defenders replied by counter-mining. There was so much spadework to be done that Anbury engaged gangs of labourers from neighbouring villages to help his Sappers above ground. The first mine was sprung under the north-east angle on the 5th, and did considerable damage, though not enough to open a way for the stormers, so a second mine was driven. This, however, was counter-mined by the enemy and had to be abandoned. Other mines were driven and fired during the following week, when several gallant deeds were performed by the Sappers and Miners under Irvine or on their own initiative. On January 7th, for instance, Jemadar Barga (Burzoor) Singh ran up to a mine which had failed to explode, ignited the charge and was severely injured.[1] For this he was promoted on the field. Other Sappers and Miners were honoured similarly for firing mines "under circumstances of peculiar difficulty and immense risk."[2] Mine after mine went up, and still the breaches

---

[1] *Narrative of the Siege and Capture of Bhurtpore*, by J. N. Creighton, p. 28.
[2] G.O.C.C.s, January 10th and 17th, 1826.

remained unfit for assault. Meanwhile the escalading parties practised daily, and the British soldiers were trained in the use of hand-grenades.

At length Anbury was satisfied that an assault was possible. He exploded a great mine under the Long-necked or Pathan Bastion on the 16th, and, on the following day, charged the greatest of all, a 10,000-lb. mine under the north-east angle. Its explosion was to be the signal for the storm of Bhurtpore. At 8 a.m. on January 18th the train was fired. "The massive bastion trembled from level to summit, and gradually rising from its firm foundation and increasing in bulk as it rose, seemed about to precipitate its overwhelming mass upon our heads. Still it rose on high, and still it distended in one gigantic cloud of dull hue, in graceful silent sublimity, high into the blue vault of heaven. There it stood many seconds like a tower connecting earth and sky, then slowly dissipated its particles upon the breeze of morning."[1] The wreckage showered on the stormers as, led by the Engineers, they leapt from their trenches. Scrambling up the breaches, or swarming up the ladders, the columns gained a footing on the ramparts at last, and, after desperate fighting with immense loss to the defenders, took Bhurtpore the invincible. The siege lasted only six weeks and cost the British less than 1,000 men, so the victory was cheaply won. Its value lay chiefly in its political effect; but the spoils included 200 guns and half a million sterling in prize-money, so the Sappers and Miners returned to Cawnpore in high spirits.

The general opinion of the engineering work at Bhurtpore is well expressed in a letter which appeared in the *East India United Service Journal* in 1834:—[2]

"There is no one I think who will not applaud the prudence of the Engineers and the Commander-in-Chief in waiting for the splendid breaches which crowned the exertions of the Miners. The behaviour of these men throughout the whole of the operations excited the admiration of the army: to see them exposing themselves under a hot fire with the most perfect coolness and indifference might have almost made one suppose that they bore charmed lives. It is a great credit to them that they were worthy of their Engineer officers, and indeed a more efficient body than the Bengal Sappers and Miners it would be impossible to conceive. On them, of course, and on the Artillery fell the severest labour. Their precision in practice and their cheerfulness throughout their arduous work were beyond all praise."

Anbury and his officers received full credit for their achievements. The Commander-in-Chief, in addition to a special acknowledgment to his Chief Engineer, wrote[3] that "it would be difficult to appreciate

---

[1] *The Old Field Officer*, by J. H. Stocqueler, Vol. I, p. 137.
[2] Vol. III, July-December, 1834, p. 259.
[3] G.O.C.C., January 19th, 1826. Anbury became later Major-General Sir Thomas Anbury, K.C.B.

K*

fully the science, devotion and fortitude evinced by the Officers and Men of the Engineer Corps, including the Corps of Sappers and Miners," and it is safe to say that he expressed the sentiments of the Army in India. The capture of Bhurtpore in 1826 established for ever the reputation of the Bengal Sappers and Miners.

With this victory and the end of the Burma War, India, as Fortescue says, sank into the tranquillity of the overawed.[1] There was a respite of twelve years from large military operations. Lord William Bentinck, who became Governor-General in 1828, was a man of peace and an economist, and he followed strictly the policy of non-intervention in outside affairs. Some desultory fighting took place between 1829 and 1832 in Assam against the Khasias and the Singphos, and also in Central India against other tribes, and the rebellion of a sect of fanatics called Wahabis was suppressed near Calcutta; but these skirmishes were little more than police work. During 1831 and the following year, expeditions sailed to the Malay Peninsula, and in the 1832 expedition two companies of Madras Sappers and Miners were employed under Lieutenant J. H. Bell of the Madras Engineers. This is notable as the first occasion on which the Madras Pioneers went on active service as "Sappers and Miners," and they did well under their new title. In 1834 Lord Bentinck was obliged to depose the cruel Raja of Coorg in the extreme south. A force of 6,000 men was mobilized for that purpose and included 700 Madras Sappers and Miners under Captain G. A. Underwood. This was a jungle war, and the Sappers were employed chiefly in hacking roads through the forests. The siege of Jhansi at the end of 1838 may be mentioned because the commander of the investing force was Major-General Sir Thomas Anbury, the Chief Engineer at Bhurtpore. The Rani of Jhansi had rebelled against the Government, so Anbury was sent against her fortress at the head of two regiments of cavalry, four battalions of infantry, a powerful train of artillery and several companies of Bengal Sappers and Miners. There was very little resistance. Preparations were made for a siege, but the Rani was not inclined to fight; she fled from the place and Anbury marched in.

During the period covered by this chapter the military engineers of India had great adventures and witnessed sweeping alterations in organization. They sailed east, west and south; they fought in the mountains of Nepal, the ravines of Central India, and the jungles of Burma. They reached the command of trained engineering soldiers and saw them changed from Pioneers into Sappers and Miners. There can be little doubt that these experiences were of untold value to them when, in 1838, a cloud of war arose in the far north-west, that troubled area which then became, and has since remained, the danger spot of India.

[1] *A History of the British Army*, by the Hon. J. W. Fortescue, Vol. XII, p. 5.

CHAPTER XV.

THE FIRST AFGHAN WAR, AND CAMPAIGNS IN CHINA, SIND AND GWALIOR, 1839–1843.

IF ever a war was ill-conceived, badly managed, unnecessary and disastrous it was the invasion of Afghanistan which was ordered by the Governor-General, Lord Auckland, in 1839. The plan of campaign violated all principles of strategy; the leaders, for the most part mediocre in ability, were bound hand and foot by political control; the country was far from British India, mountainous, barren and almost unknown, arctic in winter, torrid in summer, and unreachable except through narrow passes. The lines of supply were badly organized, the artillery and transport unsuitable, and the troops inexperienced in mountain warfare and encumbered by hosts of non-combatants. Henry IV. of France once said of Spain: "Invade with a large force and you are destroyed by starvation; invade with a small one and you are overwhelmed by a hostile people." Such was the problem of Afghanistan.

In 1837 the Persians besieged Herat[1] and were helped by the Russians. Dost Muhammad, the ruler of Afghanistan, turned to the British as possible allies, but was rebuffed by Lord Auckland and thereupon made friends with Russia. The Governor-General, on his own responsibility, then executed a treaty[2] with Ranjit Singh, the Sikh despot of the Punjab, and Shah Shuja, a refugee ruler of Afghanistan, by which he proposed to restore Shah Shuja to the throne at Kabul and to depose Dost Muhammad. This was in July, 1838; and although the Persians raised the siege of Herat in the following September, Lord Auckland persisted in his grandiose scheme and gave orders for the assembly of the "Army of the Indus" at Ferozepore to invade Afghanistan in company with Shah Shuja and his men.

The movements of the army were directed nominally by its military commanders but actually by the Governor-General himself through his political officers in the field; and the "politicals" not only interfered continually in the plans of the generals, but failed miserably in their undertaking to arrange for depots of supplies along the difficult route to Afghanistan. To such desperation was General William Nott driven in September, 1840, that he wrote from Afghanistan: " The conduct of the one thousand and one Politicals

---
[1] On the western border of Afghanistan.
[2] Known as the " Tri-partite " Treaty.

has ruined our cause and bared the throat of every European to the sword and knife of the revengeful Affghan and bloody Belooch."[1] With the army moved the political envoy to Afghanistan, Sir William Macnaghten, scholarly, able and courageous, but impatient of opposition, autocratic in his methods and preferring to bribe rather than fight an enemy. Among his assistants were a few able men such as Eldred Pottinger; but there were also many conceited youngsters with unbounded faith in their own sagacity. Politics determined the whole form and shape of the war, and notably the line of advance. Although the final objective was Kabul, and the direct route to it lay through the Punjab and the Khaibar (Khyber) Pass, Lord Auckland, rather than offend the Sikhs of the Punjab, sent the army down to Rohri and Sukkur on the Indus,[2] up through the Bolan Pass to Quetta, through the Khojak Pass to Kandahar, and so by Ghazni to Kabul. The warning of the Commander-in-Chief, Sir Henry Fane, went unheeded. "The chance of any reverse in Afghanistan," wrote he, "should be carefully weighed, for there is the Bolan Pass and Sind behind the army in one quarter, and the Khyber Pass and Sikhs in another. The army will be in a position to be surrounded and annihilated unless due precautions are taken in time. Supposing a reverse, what is to be the army's line of retreat?"

The Army of the Indus, which assembled at Ferozepore on the Sutlej, in November, 1838, consisted at first of 16,000 men under Major-General Sir Willoughby Cotton, but when the Persians withdrew from Herat it was somewhat reduced. There were three brigades of infantry and one of cavalry, the infantry commanders being Colonel R. H. Sale, Major-General W. Nott and Lieut.-Colonel A. Roberts.[3] Some artillery was attached to the force, and also the 2nd and 3rd Companies of the Bengal Sappers and Miners under Captain Edward Sanders of the Bengal Engineers. The Chief Engineer was Captain George Thomson of the same Corps.[4] Cotton was ordered to march down the Sutlej and Indus to join a division from Bombay under Major-General T. Willshire, consisting of a brigade of cavalry, another of infantry, some light artillery, and the 1st Company, Bombay Sappers and Miners, under Captain Alexander Peat of the Bombay Engineers. A mixed force of British and Sikhs was assembled at Peshawar to operate in the Khaibar Pass, and some attempt was made to strengthen and organize Shah Shuja's following. The whole army was placed under Lieutenant-General Sir John Keane, Commander-in-Chief in Bombay, who was expected to join his command on the Indus where he would be at the head of 39,000 men including reserves. A reference to the map entitled "Sketch

[1] *The Life of Sir William Nott*, by J. H. Stocqueler, Vol. I, p. 256.
[2] This move violated a treaty with the Amirs of Sind.
[3] Afterwards General Sir Abraham Roberts, G.C.B., and father of Field-Marshal Earl Roberts.
[4] The officer who did so well in the First Burma War as Chief Engineer with Brigadier-General J. W. Morrison in the expedition in Arakan. (See Chapter XIV.)

Map of the North-West Frontier including Afghanistan," which appears at the end of this volume, will show the enormous distance to be traversed by the Army of the Indus from Ferozepore by Rohri, Quetta and Kandahar, to Kabul.

On December 2nd, 1838, Shah Shuja's force started from Ferozepore, and Cotton followed him on the 10th in five columns. The British force, as Fortescue says,[1] had all the unwieldy bulk of a moving city. It had grain for 30 days, slaughter cattle for two and a half months, 14,000 camels for supplies, 30,000 for baggage,[2] and thousands more for ordnance stores; it was further encumbered by 50,000 followers. Still, after considerable difficulties in supply, it marched into Rohri on January 24th and prepared to cross the Indus in the wake of Shah Shuja's men who had already been ferried across to Sukkur on the right bank. Meanwhile the column from Bombay was having trouble with the Amirs of Sind, who resented its passage through their country; but, when Cotton had threatened Hyderabad from the north, the Amirs gave in and he was free to cross to Sukkur.

About a week before the army marched into Rohri, Thomson, Sanders and other Engineers, with the 2nd and 3rd Companies of Bengal Sappers and Miners, had arrived there and were soon collecting and preparing materials for a bridge. The Indus at this point ran in two channels separated by the fortified island of Bukkur, the width of the western channel being 133 yards, and of the eastern, 367 yards. Given trained men, good boats or pontoons, and plenty of material to hand, to bridge such spans would not be difficult. But Thomson had every handicap. He had no pontoons and could find only eight boats at Rohri when he arrived, though he managed to collect 120 more. All good timber had to be floated 200 miles downstream from Ferozepore, and he was obliged to supplement it by felling and splitting the date palms near Sukkur. The Sappers had to make 500 cables of grass, and to manufacture all the nails they required. Their anchors were made of timber and loaded with stone.[3] They had no experience of large floating bridges and could not talk the language of the local boatmen who assisted them. The main current was rapid, the bottom rocky and uneven. Floating trees cut the anchor cables. Floods often endangered the whole structure. Yet the narrow channel was bridged with 19 boats in four days, and the wide channel with 55 boats in 16 days, and everything was ready by February 3rd.[4] It was a fine achievement and proved of great service to the army, enabling about 38,000 troops and camp-followers, 30,000 camels, the artillery and ordnance carriages and a long train of bullock carts, to cross the Indus rapidly, easily and

---

[1] *A History of the British Army*, by the Hon. J. W. Fortescue, Vol. XII, p. 45.
[2] One brigadier had 60 camels for his personal baggage alone.
[3] Obituary notice of Colonel George Thomson, C.B., late R.E., appearing in *The R.E. Journal*, Vol. 16, 1886, p. 82.
[4] *A Narrative of the March and Operations of the Army of the Indus*, by Major W. Hough, p. 27.

safely.¹ By the 18th, every man, beast and wagon was on the right bank, and the eastern section of the bridge was then dismantled so that the boats could be used as ferries.²

The history of the First Afghan War shows that, whatever the mistakes and miscalculations in the operations, the Engineers at least proved their worth. Indeed, it is remarkable how junior officers such as Thomson, George Broadfoot, Sturt and Peat became the constant advisers of their divisional and brigade commanders. There were many clever heads on young shoulders in this unfortunate campaign : the trouble was that there were also several stupid ones on old shoulders.

The next obstacle before Cotton was a march of 170 miles northwards to Dadhar below the Bolan Pass, including 100 miles of waterless and sun-baked desert. " Oh Allah ! " ran a Muhammadan saying, " wherefore make Hell when thou hast made Dadhar ? " Seven columns, hardly one-fifth of the men being combatants, left Shikarpur on consecutive days and found no supplies collected along the route. Thomson, with Sanders and his men, led the way, and after a few marches received a message from the rear that the water was so bad that the cavalry might have to turn back. The Chief Engineer replied that the Engineers would go forward, whether the cavalry followed or not.³ So the columns trailed on, harried by Baluchi robbers, half-starved, parched by thirst and decimated by sunstroke and dysentery, till they crawled into Dadhar on March 10th to find only one day's rations collected there. After halting for six days they entered the Bolan Pass, threaded its sombre defile, and reached the mud village of Quetta on the 26th with only ten days' supply in hand, their transport reduced and disabled, and Kandahar still 150 miles away. The only course was to place the whole force on reduced rations, but Cotton feared the temper of his men. In this quandary, Thomson urged his hesitating commander to instant action, assuring him that the Sappers at least would accept half-rations without a murmur ; and so Cotton was induced to place the soldiers on half and the followers on quarter rations. By his influence and advice, Thomson certainly saved the force from disaster, so that, when General Keane arrived in Quetta on April 6th, he found a despondent but living army, and supporting it were the troops from Bombay who had just reached Dadhar.

Keane marched for Kandahar on the 7th, leaving an irate Nott to garrison Quetta. Already the Sappers were at work on the next obstacle, the Khojak Pass, and by the 13th Thomson had completed three tracks, on the left a path for camels, in the centre a track for

---

[1] *The First Afghan War*, by H. M. Durand, p. 123.
[2] The Engineers who assisted Thomson were Captain E. Sanders and Lieutenants J. Anderson, H. M. Durand, J. L. D. Sturt, N. S. Macleod, James S. Broadfoot and R. Pigou, all of the Bengal Corps.
[3] *A History of the British Army*, by the Hon. J. W. Fortescue, Vol. XII, p. 55.

guns, and on the right a very rough way for bullocks, ponies and men.¹ No more could be done in the time available. The gradients were extremely stiff, and on none of the tracks could loaded camels pass each other. Through bad staff work the whole force was expected to traverse the pass in 24 hours, and the result was chaotic when the attempt was made on April 14th. The defile became hopelessly choked with men, beasts and guns. Thousands of animals, dying of exhaustion or already dead, were still in the pass on the following day, jammed together so tightly that they formed an immovable mass. The losses in transport were paralysing, and it was not till the 21st that the last camel staggered out on to the Afghanistan tableland where hardly a drop of water could be found. When Keane entered Kandahar on April 26th, 1839, his men were starving and his animals on the point of death. The march of 1,000 miles from Ferozepore had brought the advance to a standstill.

The Bombay army arrived on May 4th, but it was not till June 27th that the march could be resumed. With 7,800 fighting men, Keane plodded on through Kalat-i-Ghilzai towards Ghazni where, according to Macnaghten, there would be no resistance. Because of that assurance, and since the political officers said that the road would be impassable for 18-pounder guns, Keane made the serious mistake of leaving almost all his heavy artillery at Kandahar. Even when he came in sight of Ghazni he was told by his Political Officer, Alexander Burnes, that the place was empty. On the contrary, it was strongly held, and Keane found himself in a desperate situation. On either side lay armies of Ghilzai tribesmen who had shadowed him from Kandahar. He had only two days' rations in hand and no more than one day's supply of artillery ammunition, while beyond Ghazni lay the main Afghan army under Dost Muhammad.

In this dilemma Keane consulted Thomson, and for the third time that Engineer saved the army. After reconnoitring the defences with Peat, Thomson said that there were only two alternatives. Either Keane could mask Ghazni and advance to fight Dost Muhammad or he must carry the fortress by a surprise assault when the Engineers had blown in the Kabul Gate.² As the parapets towered 70 feet above the plain, escalading was out of the question. The wet ditch which surrounded the place rendered mining impracticable. The walls could not be breached as the heavy guns had been left in Kandahar. In any case a siege was impossible as the army was faced with starvation. So, as Keane could not spare the troops to mask Ghazni, and he must replenish his supplies at once or perish, he took an appalling risk and launched his men to the famous assault of the Kabul Gate.

The Engineers present were most of those of the Bengal Corps

¹ *A History of the British Army*, by the Hon. J. W. Fortescue, Vol. XII, p. 65.
² This gateway was believed to be used by the defenders. All other entrances had been built up.

who bridged the Indus,[1] and, in addition, Captain A. C. Peat and Lieutenants W. F. Marriott and F. Wemyss (senior) of the Bombay Corps—ten in all.[2] But the heroes of the Kabul Gate were Thomson, Peat, Durand and Macleod. Although Lord Keane of Ghazni (as he afterwards became) wrote that the credit of blowing in the gate was due entirely to Thomson, James Broadfoot, who was an eye-witness, remarks: " Whilst to Captain Thomson is due the credit for planning the demolition and the assault, to Lieutenant H. M. Durand must be assigned that of successfully carrying out the instructions." The affair was one of simple daring. Guns were massed before the Kabul Gate during the night and a demonstration arranged against the southern face. A storming party of 240 men under Lieutenant-Colonel Dennie moved to the point of assembly at Mahmud's pillars,[3] and the main attacking column under Brigadier-General Sale joined them. It was arranged that the signal for the advance should be a call sounded by a bugler who was to accompany Peat.

The Engineers and Sappers volunteered almost to a man for the Explosion Party which was to blow down the gate. Thomson then selected Peat, Durand, Macleod, three British non-commissioned officers, Subadar Debi Singh and 15 men of the Bengal Sappers and Miners, and Jemadar Bhawani Singh and five men of the Bombay Sappers and Miners. At the first streak of dawn on July 23rd the little party moved up towards the gate. They were discovered immediately and came under a heavy fire to which their covering troops and the guns replied. Pushing across a bridge, and carrying 300 pounds of powder in 12 sandbags, they neared the gate; and, while Peat with a few men entered a lower sallyport to repel any charge of swordsmen, Durand and the others reached the gate where Debi Singh laid the first bag of powder. Man after man followed with powder bags, and then others with bags full of earth to tamp the

---

[1] Thomson, Durand, Macleod, Anderson, Sturt, J. S. Broadfoot and Pigou. Of these Durand became Major-General Sir H. M. Durand, Lieutenant-Governor of the Punjab, and Macleod rose to be a Lieutenant-General.

[2] " Early Indian Campaigns," by Major H. Biddulph, R.E., appearing in *The R.E. Journal*, Vol. XVIII, July–December, 1913, p. 301. Other Engineers were serving elsewhere, viz., Captain E. Sanders, B.E., and Lieutenant C. F. North, Bo.E., on a mission from Kandahar to Herat; Lieutenant J. D. Cunningham, B.E., as Political Assistant in the Khaibar Pass with Colonel Wade; and Lieutenant J. Laughten, B.E., as Garrison Engineer on the Indus at Bukkur. (" B.E." stands for " Bengal Engineers," and " Bo.E." for " Bombay Engineers.")

[3] Sir Keith Jackson, in his *Views in Affghaunistaun*, p. 11, states: " Near the fortress of Ghuznee are two celebrated minarets of the ancient city; they are hexagonal pillars, projecting at the angles and built of brick, about 100 feet high and 12 feet in diameter at the base, gradually diminishing to above half their height whence rises a circular column terminating in a Muezzin's gallery." A " Ghazni Tower " stands on the parade ground of the K.G.O. Bengal Sappers and Miners at Roorkee. Unfortunately the lower portion was made triangular in section instead of hexagonal. The foundation stone was laid by General Viscount Kitchener in 1907, and the tower was completed four years later. It was crowned with a small dome in 1913. To commemorate the part played by the Corps in the Great War of 1914-18, the tower was surrounded by a colonnade which was completed in 1926 and opened by Field-Marshal Sir W. R. Birdwood in 1927. The tower and the colonnade bear the names of those who fell, or became distinguished, in various campaigns.

STORMING OF THE KABUL GATE, GHAZNI.

charge. Macleod superintended this work while Durand and Serjeant Robertson uncoiled a long cloth tube full of powder, attached it to the charge, and, under a hail of missiles at close quarters, laid it to an adjacent sallyport, which by pure luck it was long enough to reach. In this shelter, Durand, after one or two failures, managed to light the train and then ran to safety.[1]

Meanwhile Peat was waiting anxiously in the lower sallyport for the sound of the explosion, and, when minute by minute went by, he thought that Durand and his party must have been killed. At last he rushed from his shelter and up towards the gate, only to be thrown violently to the ground by the explosion. There he lay stunned for a time; but when he could move and his senses returned, no thought of retreat entered his head; he stumbled on towards the wrecked gate and was only driven back at last by the sight of the fierce swordsmen beyond it.

Durand heard the explosion and listened for the bugle call which was to summon the stormers. He listened in vain, for Peat's bugler had been killed and Peat himself was helpless. Realizing that something was wrong, he tried unsuccessfully to get a bugler from the nearest infantry and then hurried back to Dennie and Sale. On his way he met James Broadfoot[2] who shouted to him, "Has it failed?" "No, no," called Durand, and with that assurance Broadfoot dashed back to call up the stormers who came on with a rush accompanied by Thomson.[3] Suddenly Thomson came across Peat and Macleod, the former badly shattered, lying under a little tomb by the roadside, and Peat gasped out his tale. The din was tremendous, and Sale, who had come up and gathered from Peat's report that the Kabul Gate was still impassable, caused his own bugler to sound the retreat. Luckily Thomson saw that Dennie and the stormers were already surging through the gate and drew Sale's attention to them. The "Advance" rang out and "Fighting Bob" Sale led the main body on with all speed.

The small delay, however, had caused a gap between the stormers and the main body which the Afghan swordsmen filled in a brave attack on the head of Sale's column in the narrow passage. Thomson, who had run on to overtake the stormers, writes:[4] "It was while the rear of the advance (the storming party) was struggling out of the gateway that the Afghans made a rush from the rampart above.

---

[1] The story of this heroic deed is taken largely from Durand's book, *The First Afghan War*, pp. 177–183, supplemented by other accounts.

[2] The youngest of three famous brothers, and a Bengal Engineer. The eldest, George, was not then in Afghanistan; but the second, William, of the 1st European Regiment, was in the assault on Ghazni, serving as a volunteer because he had been posted to Shah Shuja's force which was not engaged.

[3] "Sieges and Defence of Fortified Places," by Colonel Sir E. T. Thackeray, appearing in *The R.E. Journal*, Vol. XX, July–December, 1914, p. 246.

[4] Extracts from letters from George Thomson to his brother, Captain John Thomson, dated July 25th and 29th, 1839, quoted in an obituary notice of Colonel George Thomson, C.B., late R.E., appearing in *The R.E. Journal*, Vol. 16, 1886, p. 83.

One of the Europeans who fell across my leg, was killed. Immediately a dead Afghan fell across me. Bayonets had no chance against swords. The Afghans cut down the rest of the light company of the European Regiment and then commenced on the head of the main column, wounding Sale and several officers and men. I felt exceedingly uncomfortable while struggling to get clear of the bodies above me and the timber under me, while the sabres and bayonets made a most unpleasant clashing about my ears." The end came soon. Once within the walls the British soldiers carried all before them. Many of the Afghans leaped 30 feet to their death from the ramparts rather than face the streaming bayonets. Ghazni was won, and Thomson and his men had shown how to win it.

The British army entered Kabul on August 7th, 1839, after a weary march of 1,500 miles, and forced the villainous Shah Shuja upon a hostile Afghan nation. Little need be written of the sojourn of the army in Kabul. Intrigue, weakness and inefficiency permeated the civil administration and affected the army. Keane and Macnaghten decided that one brigade of regular British troops would suffice to garrison the capital, with detachments at Kandahar and Mastung, while Shah Shuja's troops could hold Ghazni and Girishk. The Bombay army, under Willshire, marched for India on September 18th and reached Quetta at the end of October; it then captured Kalat, where Peat and some Bombay Sappers and Miners were engaged, and so made its exit from the war. Keane himself left Kabul for India on October 16th with a force mostly of cavalry but including two companies of Sappers and Miners.[1] He had to fight his way through the Khaibar Pass and to relieve the garrison of Ali Masjid, but he arrived safely in Peshawar. Macnaghten at Kabul busied himself in futile efforts to bribe the tribesmen into complacency, and the command of the small garrison[2] devolved on Cotton. Nott at Kandahar could be supported from Quetta if Sind remained quiet; but Cotton at Kabul depended for his very existence on the dubious friendship of the Sikhs of the Punjab and the effect of Macnaghten's subsidies to the Khaibar tribes. It was his duty to occupy at once an impregnable position where he would be secure from sudden attack.

When Thomson accompanied Keane to India, Durand became the senior Engineer in Kabul. He insisted that the powerful citadel known as the Bala Hissar, which overlooked the city, should be occupied by the British force; but, as Shah Shuja objected, Macnaghten vetoed the proposal and the Shah installed his harem and his useless rabble in the place. Cotton agreed to the construction of cantonments for his own soldiers on the plain to the north of Kabul, defended only by a low parapet with corner bastions, and, to crown

---

[1] One of them was No. 1 Company, Bombay Sappers and Miners.

[2] Two battalions British Infantry, six battalions Indian Infantry, two regiments Indian Cavalry and some Artillery.

his folly, allowed his supplies to be scattered in small forts between the city and the cantonments. Even the treasury was established within easy reach of the Afghans. Macnaghten frittered away the troops in small expeditions and isolated garrisons, overruling every military protest and losing in one of these ventures Lieutenant James Broadfoot[1] of the Bengal Engineers. There was much trouble on the line of communication. Kalat was recaptured by the enemy. The only ray of hope was the voluntary surrender of Dost Muhammad. At the end of 1840, Cotton left for India, and was succeeded in April, 1841, by the brave but invalid Elphinstone. Brigadier-General Robert Sale marched for Gandamak on October 20th at the head of his brigade on relief by a brigade under Colonel Shelton. Sale had some fighting with the Ghilzais in the Jagdalak Pass but arrived safely in Gandamak on the 29th, though not with his whole force for when at Tezin he left behind him some guns and three companies of "Broadfoot's Sappers" who returned to Kabul and their annihilation.

There were in Afghanistan six companies of Broadfoot's Sappers, commanded by Captain George Broadfoot of the 34th Madras Infantry, the eldest of the brothers George, William[2] and James. Though an infantry officer, George had specialized in fortification at Addiscombe, and hence his remarkable ability as an engineer. As to his corps of Sappers, he wrote from Gandamak : " My corps, 600, is 300 Hindoostanees (brave), 200 Goorkhas (braver), 100 Afghans and Hazaras (heroes)." In 1840 he was ordered to join Shah Shuja's contingent in Afghanistan and to raise a regiment of Sappers, so he travelled up-country from Agra, collecting Hindustanis and Gurkhas and receiving finally a corps of Hazaras and Afghans recruited near Bamian[3] by his brother William. A stiffening was provided by a draft from the Bengal Sappers and Miners,[4] and, under the stern discipline of Broadfoot and his regular soldiers, the many desperate characters in the battalion became efficient and gallant Sappers. The unit did not reach Kabul till early in July, 1841, as its progress was hampered by an enormous convoy including 600 *zenana* ladies for Shah Shuja and his retinue—an enjoyable addition, perhaps, to the rigours of campaigning, but a sad encumbrance. During a brief stay in Kabul before he marched with Sale for Gandamak, Broadfoot fought strenuously for a proper supply of tools. As he refused to march without them, he got them ; and it is not an exaggeration to say that these tools in the hands of Broadfoot's men rescued Sale's brigade from disaster at Jalalabad.

[1] James Broadfoot was killed in action at Purwan, near Kabul, on November 2nd, 1840.
[2] William Broadfoot was killed in Kabul during the insurrection in November, 1841.
[3] Approximately 80 miles west of Kabul.
[4] On August 20th, 1840, the Bengal Sappers and Miners sent three British N.C.O.s, four Indian officers and 20 Indian N.C.O.s to become Jemadars and Havildars, and 20 sepoys to become Naiks.

The storm in Kabul broke on November 2nd, 1841. Its history, and that of the ghastly retreat through the Khoord Kabul and Jagdallak defiles in the depth of winter, are well known. Sturt was the only Engineer in the capital when the insurrection broke out, and he was desperately wounded on the first day; nevertheless he dragged himself from his bed a week later to implore General Elphinstone to concentrate in the Bala Hissar, but to no purpose. He died in the retreat. The British force in the cantonments numbered only 4,500 fighting men, and its provisions and money were soon captured in the outlying forts and treasury. Confusion reigned everywhere: of leadership, in the true sense, there was none. Sale was ordered to return to Kabul from Gandamak, and Nott was asked to reinforce from Kandahar; but a brigade despatched by Nott was stopped by snow, and Sale actually retreated to Jalalabad instead of fighting his way back to Kabul. Macnaghten and Burnes were murdered in cold blood. Elphinstone came to terms with his treacherous enemies who agreed to allow his soldiers, with their wives and families, through to Peshawar. But of the 16,000 people who marched from Kabul in the bitter cold of January 6th, 1842,[1] only one, Dr. Brydon, staggered into Jalalabad. With the exception of the women and children, a few prisoners and some hostages, the whole multitude perished in the snow or under the bullets and knives of the Afghans, and Elphinstone himself died later in captivity. This tragedy was the outcome of the folly of one man—Lord Auckland.

It seemed that the Afghans would now succeed in overwhelming Nott and driving the British from their country. Ghazni fell, but the little garrison of Kalat-i-Ghilzai, under Captain J. H. Craigie, put up a successful defence through the whole winter till relieved in June, 1842, from Kandahar. Among the defenders were Lieutenant R. Leech of the Bombay Engineers (Political Officer), Lieutenant T. Studdert of the same Corps, and 23 men of the Bengal Sappers and Miners.[2] Nott contrived by the aid of reinforcements to keep his hold on Kandahar, and proved the fact that he, and not Cotton or Elphinstone, should have succeeded Keane in the chief command in Afghanistan. With the possible exception of Pollock, Nott stands out head and shoulders above any other general in this war. He was a good tactician and a dour fighter.

The scene shifts to Jalalabad where Sale halted after a retreat in which George Broadfoot and his two subalterns, J. D. Cunningham and C. A. Orr,[3] distinguished themselves by their leadership and resource. In the Jagdalak Pass, according to Broadfoot, "a handful

[1] Including 300 Broadfoot's Sappers under a Captain Mathews.
[2] "Sieges and Defence of Fortified Places," by Colonel Sir E. T. Thackeray, appearing in *The R.E. Journal*, Vol. XX, July–December, 1914, p. 244.
[3] Broadfoot calls them "his two Mulls" (an abbreviation of Mulligatawny) because they came from Madras. Both were Madras Engineers. J. D. Cunningham was a brother of Major-General Sir Alexander Cunningham, a noted Bengal Engineer. (*The Career of Major George Broadfoot*, by Major W. Broadfoot, R.E., p. 39.)

of Sappers saved several hundred infantry, chiefly European, from being destroyed by the Afghans." There were three outstanding exploits by Engineers in the First Afghan War, two of which, the bridging of the Indus and the demolition of the Kabul Gate at Ghazni, have been mentioned already. The third is George Broadfoot's defence of Jalalabad. I say advisedly " George Broadfoot's defence " for he, and not Sale, was the soul of the garrison, and though he was an Engineer only by adoption, we claim him for the Corps. His energy, judgment and iron will triumphed over every difficulty, every objection. For a time he alone upheld the honour of his country, till by his example he put new life into wavering hearts. This is the tale of Jalalabad.

When Sale marched into the place on November 11th, 1841, he took possession of a ruin. He found only a quadrilateral enclosure, a mile and a quarter in circuit, buried amid houses and gardens, without a ditch, and with low and crumbling earthen walls topped by a large number of small bastions. Instantly he was attacked, but survived the ordeal, and Broadfoot then set to work to repair the defences, using the tools which he had collected with such difficulty in Kabul. On January 9th, Sale received an order from Elphinstone at Kabul, directing him to evacuate Jalalabad and retire on Peshawar. This was one of the stipulations of the victorious Afghans, but Sale rightly disregarded it. Unfortunately, he decided also to remain inactive in Jalalabad which was, as Durand puts it,[1] " a place of no military strength or importance, without magazines, in utter disrepair and so situated that to coop up a brigade within its dilapidated walls served no conceivable purpose." At Gandamak, Sale might have kept the passes open for Elphinstone: at Jalalabad he was an object lesson in futility. So thought George Broadfoot, and on the 13th, when the destruction of the Kabul force was known and he doubted if relief would arrive soon from Peshawar, he suggested to Sale that unless he was prepared to hold Jalalabad to the last man he should evacuate it instantly and fight his way through the Khaibar Pass to India.[2] " Surely," wrote Broadfoot,[3] " a superb brigade should not lie down to be destroyed as to efficiency by half-armed savages because it has been ill-supplied with money, provisions and stores. Should it not rather, while it is able, fight its way to where these things are procurable, and then, refitting, turn back and save the honour of our arms ? " But Sale declined to move, and, to avoid having to feed his transport animals, turned them loose for the Afghans to take.

Then, when news arrived that an attempt to relieve Jalalabad had failed, Sale called his famous Council of War in which every officer,

---

[1] *The Afghan War*, by H. M. Durand, p. 360.
[2] *The Career of Major George Broadfoot*, by Major W. Broadfoot, R.E., p. 61.
[3] Article entitled " The Defence of Jalalabad," by Major W. Broadfoot, R.E., appearing in *The R.E. Journal*, Vol. 21, 1891, p. 125.

except Broadfoot, voted for capitulation on an agreement with the Afghans that the brigade should be escorted safely to Peshawar. Broadfoot, with the fate of Elphinstone before him, fought his case single-handed. For days the arguments went on, while he converted the opposition one by one to his view. "Safety," said he, " is to be consulted, but not safety only ; nor ever except subordinately to the good of our country." Only Sale and the Political Officer, Macgregor, remained adamant, and even they were overruled in the end. The Council was finally dissolved on February 12th, and by that date not only had all idea of surrender been given up but the defences were much improved. When the brigade first arrived from Gandamak, the sentries on the walls were protected by piling hundreds of camel saddles, two deep and two high, where there was no parapet,[1] but Broadfoot's working parties soon built up the walls with materials secured from dismantled houses and cleared a field of fire around the place. Alas, the labours of three months were almost destroyed in a severe earthquake on February 19th. For more than a minute the earth seemed to roll like the waves of the sea, and men could only stand with difficulty. Parapets and bastions collapsed on every side. Several great breaches appeared through which the Afghans could easily have stormed the place. Luckily they made no attempt to enter, and by desperate exertions the walls were rebuilt till safety was secured once more. The siege dragged on, and in a skirmish on March 24th, Broadfoot was shot through the hip and handed over his command to Orr. But his work was done, the crisis was past ; and the garrison, restored in morale and strength, sallied out on April 7th to attack their besiegers and routed them utterly. Nine days later, the "Avenging Army," under Major-General Sir George Pollock,[2] marched in from Peshawar, and the curtain fell on the drama of Jalalabad.

With Pollock came Captain F. Abbott and Lieutenants J. W. Robertson, A. G. Goodwyn and J. R. Becher of the Bengal Engineers, and also the 5th Company, Bengal Sappers and Miners, and a semi-civil Corps of Pioneers. These, with the three companies of Broadfoot's Sappers under Orr, formed a strong body of engineering troops. The army under Pollock comprised four infantry brigades and one brigade of cavalry, and it seemed that he should be able to force a passage to Kabul easily and quickly. But it was not to be. Transport difficulties and politics intervened. On May 17th at Kandahar, Nott received an order from Lord Ellenborough, the new Governor-

---

[1] *From Cadet to Colonel*, by T. Seaton, p. 165.
[2] A distinguished Artillery officer who had served at Bhurtpore in 1805, in the Nepal War, and in the First Burma War. In 1844 the British inhabitants of Calcutta subscribed Rs. 11,000 to institute a gold medal in recognition of General Pollock's services in Afghanistan. It was called the "Pollock Medal" and was awarded twice a year at Addiscombe to the cadet passing out at the head of the list. The first medal was presented in December, 1847. Since December, 1861, the medal has been awarded twice yearly to the senior cadet passing out of the Royal Military Academy, Woolwich.

General, to retire to Quetta, and, at about the same time, Pollock was told to retreat to Peshawar. Ellenborough was determined to drag the army at once from the welter of Afghanistan. However, Pollock managed to wring a half-hearted permission from Government to " strike a severe blow at the enemy," and Nott was informed that he might " retreat by Ghazni and Kabul " if he so desired. Both seized the opportunity and advanced on Kabul, Broadfoot's Sappers being given the post of honour at the head of Pollock's army. Marching from Jalalabad on September 7th, 1842, Pollock was in Kabul in eight days, and Nott arrived there on the 17th from Ghazni.[1] Together they destroyed the great bazaar, collected all British prisoners and started for Peshawar on October 12th. The return journey was easy, and the combined forces reached the Punjab without serious fighting.

To minimize the disastrous political effect of the First Afghan War, the returning troops were accorded a grand official welcome in India, and honours were showered on the commanders; but, as Fortescue remarks,[2] the people of the East were not deceived, and particularly the Baluchis of Sind and the Sikhs of the Punjab. Viewed as a whole, the war was a mistake and a failure; and few departments of the army, other than the Engineers, emerged from it with credit. But the deeds of Thomson, George Broadfoot, Peat, Durand and Sturt will go down to posterity as models of military skill and devotion to duty.

While the Indian Government was embarrassed with the war in Afghanistan, a small campaign was in progress overseas. This was the first war against China which was initiated, not by Lord Auckland, but the Home Government. Popularly known as the " Opium War," because the importation of opium into China by British merchants in Canton and elsewhere was a bone of contention, its immediate cause was the destruction by the Chinese of British property and factories in the country. This led to the despatch of an expeditionary force from India in 1840. It was really a naval expedition backed up by a small body of soldiers. As the British force in Afghanistan seemed for the moment to be securely installed in Kabul, Lord Auckland could spare some troops to assist the naval commander-in-chief in restoring British trade in the Far East, and he arranged for the despatch of British troops and a few Indian troops from Bengal[3] and the remainder of the Indian troops from Madras. The Afghan War had been a Bengal and Bombay affair. Of the Madras Engineers only Cunningham and Orr saw much fighting in

[1] With Nott were Major E. Sanders and Lieutenant C. F. North of the Bengal Engineers, and Lieutenants R. Leech and T. Studdert of the Bombay Engineers; also a detachment of Bengal Sappers and Miners (from the 2nd and 3rd Companies) and half of " C " Company, Madras Sappers and Miners.
[2] *A History of the British Army*, by the Hon. J. W. Fortescue, Vol. XII, p. 277.
[3] *Frontier and Overseas Expeditions*, Vol. VI, p. 368. Three battalions of British Infantry, and one battalion of volunteers from ten regiments of Indian Infantry.

it; and, of the Madras Sappers, "C" Company alone represented the Corps. The China War, however, was a Madras affair and gave the Madras Sappers their chance. The operations were tedious and disjointed, interrupted continually by long periods of fruitless negotiation which were initiated by the Chinese to gain time. Promises were broken, and treaties repudiated almost before the ink had dried on the paper. The enemy was badly armed, poorly led and commonly lacking in spirit. The real adversary was the deadly climate which caused far more casualties than the stink-pots, bullets and arrows of the Chinese.

Singapore was selected as the *rendezvous* for what was called the " Eastern Expedition " under the naval commander-in-chief, Commodore Sir Gordon Bremer, the troops being commanded at first by Colonel Burrell of the 18th Regiment. The land force comprised three battalions of British Infantry, the Bengal Volunteers, two batteries of light artillery, and "A" and "B" Companies of the Madras Sappers and Miners under Captain (afterwards Major-General Sir Thomas) Pears, of the Madras Engineers, as Chief Engineer. Singapore was reached early in May, 1840, and the fleet sailed for the north at the end of that month. A few weeks later it blockaded the entrance to Canton, and then, resuming its passage northwards, landed the troops on the island of Chusan on July 5th. Here the force remained under appallingly unhealthy conditions for several months; indeed, by New Year's Day, 1841, a British regiment which had disembarked 900 strong could muster only 110 effectives.[1] The Indian units escaped more lightly, but the ravages of disease were nevertheless extremely serious. Pears beguiled his time in strengthening the British position and fortifying a height known as " Joss-House Hill." After marking out several battery positions, he found that he would have to remove a mound which was apparently part of the hill. It proved to be a vast pile of coffins ! However, it had to go, and the coffins provided a funeral pyre for their contents.[2]

A force was detached to proceed southwards early in January, 1841, and captured the fort of Chuenpi in the Canton estuary. The Chinese then opening negotiations, the British evacuated Chusan and, on January 26th, occupied Hongkong near Canton. Hostilities were resumed in February when the British attacked and captured the Bogue Forts guarding the waterway to Canton, in which operation "A" Company, Madras Sappers and Miners, took part under Lieutenant W. I. Birdwood, M.E., with Brevet-Captain F. C. Cotton, M.E., as Chief Engineer.[3] Major-General Sir Hugh Gough, K.C.B.,

[1] *A History of the British Army*, by the Hon. J. W. Fortescue, Vol. XII, p. 304.
[2] *The Military History of the Madras Engineers and Pioneers*, by Major H. M. Vibart, Vol. II, p. 137.
[3] The Madras Engineers who took part in the First China War were Captains T. T. Pears and W. I. Birdwood, Brevet-Captain F. C. Cotton, Lieutenants J. C. Shaw and J. W. Rundall, and 2nd-Lieutenants J. Ochterlony, J. G. Johnstone, and H. W. Hitchens. (*Historical Record of the Q.V.O. Madras Sappers and Miners*, p. 47.) Pears, Cotton, Birdwood and Hitchens rose to be Major-Generals.

then arrived from Madras to command the troops and finish the campaign. Towards the end of May, Gough attacked Canton, took four powerful forts overlooking the city, and, with 2,500 soldiers assisted by 1,000 sailors, defeated 45,000 Chinese. He did not storm Canton, however, as negotiations put a stop to the fighting. The enemy paid a portion of a heavy ransom, and Gough then withdrew to Hongkong. " A " and " B " Companies were in the engagements near Canton, and Rundall was severely wounded.

As usual the negotiations came to nothing, so the war was resumed at the end of August. Peking being out of reach, it was decided to advance against Nanking on the Yang-tse-kiang, dealing with other places on the way. Amoy fell on August 24th, and the expedition voyaged once more to Chusan to assault the town of Tinghai. Pears led the escalading party on October 1st when the place fell to the British with trifling loss. The next town to be captured was Chinhai at the mouth of the Ningpo. Here the Chinese had blocked the river with sunken junks and piling, and held both banks strongly, the fortified town itself being on the left bank. The ensuing operation was a combined naval and military one, as was common in this war. While Gough landed and attacked on the right bank, the sailors, with a detachment of Madras Sappers and Miners under Cotton, disembarked on a promontory forming the left bank and carried Chinhai by escalade. Pears directed the engineering work, and was the first to climb a ladder and gain the ramparts which were 26 feet in height. The enemy's losses were enormous. This victory ended the campaign of 1841, and the British force then went into winter quarters.

The Chinese attacked at Ningpo in March, 1842, but were repulsed; and Gough, largely reinforced from India, proceeded with his advance against Nanking. His first objective was Chapu, 35 miles from Hangchau. It fell on May 18th, Pears again distinguishing himself by laying a 50-pound charge and blowing a breach in the wall. This led to the occupation of Shanghai on June 19th, and in another month Gough was close to Chinkiang-Fu on the Yang-tse-kiang and within measurable distance of Nanking. The battle at Chinkiang-Fu on July 21st decided the war. The British force, now of 9,000 soldiers, was grouped in three brigades, and Pears had under his orders " A," " B " and " F " Companies of the Madras Sappers and Miners.[1] Some of the enemy's Tartar troops offered a stubborn resistance, but the defences were soon carried by assault, Johnstone of the Engineers being one of the first two men on the walls. Pears, Rundall and a party of their men demolished the city gates under heavy fire and did their work so effectively that, although the gates were five feet thick,[2] they were blown completely down. The Chinese were crushed by this defeat. The remnants of their army at Chinkiang-Fu killed

---

[1] Details of " C," " D " and " E " Companies also served in the First China War.
[2] *The Military History of the Madras Engineers and Pioneers*, by Major H. M. Vibart, Vol. II, p. 176.

their wives and children and finally themselves, and their general burnt himself to death. There followed the Treaty of Nanking on August 17th, 1842, and the war was ended. Although "F" Company and other troops remained for some years to garrison Hongkong, the bulk of the expedition returned forthwith to India.

This brief sketch of the First China War may be concluded by an illustration of Eastern serenity. "The red-bristled barbarians," wrote a Chinese General on the Yang-tse-kiang, "are wildly careering in the Celestial Waters, but the lightnings of the Empire have cleared them from the coast." "Most right," scrawled the Emperor on this despatch. "Let our servants be merciful."[1] As with the Burmese, so with the Chinese. Neither nation seemed to know when it was beaten, and both rose to fight again.

We return now to India to trace some changes which occurred in the three Corps of Sappers and Miners while the Afghan, China, Sind and Sikh wars were in progress. Before and during the First Afghan War, the headquarters of the Bengal Sappers and Miners were at Delhi. Captain George Thomson, the Commandant, having joined the Army of the Indus in November, 1838, the command devolved first on Captain E. Swetenham and then on Captain P. W. Willis. It was during the tenure of Swetenham that, on June 30th, 1841, working pay was first introduced for the men. The Bengal Sappers still consisted of six companies, each of 100 men. The original establishment in 1819 had provided for 120 men per company, and this was increased by 40 men per company in October, 1825, but subsequent reductions brought the units to more convenient proportions. Broadfoot's Sappers did so brilliantly in Afghanistan that it was decided that they should not be wholly disbanded when the war was over; and so, in January, 1843, selected men were formed into two companies, the 7th and 8th of the Bengal Sappers and Miners. Two more companies, the 9th and 10th, were added to the Corps on March 21st, 1844, so that Bengal was strong in engineering soldiers when the Army of the Sutlej took the field in the First Sikh War of 1845-46.

It has been mentioned already that the "Pioneer" disappeared from the Bengal Army in February, 1834.[2] But in September, 1847, a curious thing happened: the "Pioneer" made a brief reappearance in the Bengal Sappers and Miners. It is presumed that, after the First Sikh War, money was scarce. Reduction was certainly the order of the day in all branches of the army, and the Bengal Sappers did not escape the financial axe. The order went forth that the Corps should be remodelled into three companies of Sappers and seven companies of Pioneers,[3] amounting practically to a separation into

---

[1] *Six Months with the Chinese Expedition*, by Lord Jocelyn, p. 134.
[2] See Chapter XIII. On that date 31 Indian officers, 57 Indian N.C.O.s and 422 privates of the Pioneers joined the Sappers and Miners.
[3] Each Sapper or Pioneer company was 100 strong.

first and second line troops. The Sapper companies were to be of selected men, officered by Engineers, and the Pioneer companies of the remainder, on lower rates of working pay, officered from the Infantry and dressed in dark green uniforms. The change was duly carried out, and vacancies in the Sapper units were afterwards filled only by selected men from the Pioneer units. The Bengal Sappers and Miners then became the " Bengal Sappers and Pioneers," a designation which may have caused some surprise to military students of the Sikh wars.

When this sweeping change took place, the headquarters of the Bengal Sappers were in Meerut with Lieut.-Colonel B. Y. Reilly, of the Bengal Engineers, as Commandant. Gradually, attracted by the magnet of war in the north-west, the headquarters were moving upcountry, and soon afterwards we find them at Ludhiana with Captain Henry Siddons in command. Although the Pioneer companies were under the Commandant and formed an integral part of the Corps, they were numbered separately and had their own roster for promotion. This bifurcation of the Corps into Sappers and Pioneers must have proved a failure, for although it persisted till after the end of the Sikh wars, it was abolished on March 20th, 1851, when the Corps of " Bengal Sappers and Miners " reappeared in the Army List under Captain J. A. Weller as Commandant. The invidious distinction between Sappers and Pioneers then vanished, the number of companies was raised to 12, and Engineer officers were posted to the Corps as quickly as possible to replace the Infantry officers of the former Pioneer companies.

As regards the Bombay Engineers, it will be remembered that in 1843 six companies of these soldiers were changed into three companies of Bombay Sappers and Miners, forming with the existing Sappers a total of four companies. During the First Afghan War the Corps still consisted of four companies, one of which was sent to Aden in December, 1840.[1] In spite of the excellent services rendered by the Bombay Sappers in Afghanistan, in Sind, at Multan, and during the second war against the Sikhs in the Punjab, no increase was made in the establishment till December 15th, 1855, when the Corps was expanded to five companies.[2]

The Madras Pioneers became Sappers and Miners in 1834, as did their comrades in Bengal and Bombay, and the Madras Sappers and Miners then consisted of eight companies, four at the headquarters in Bangalore, one in Madras, and the remainder in out-stations, each company having 80 men in the ranks. A reorganization was effected in February, 1837, when the Corps was placed under the direct control of the Commander-in-Chief;[3] but a more important change

---
[1] This was the first Sapper and Miner unit to land in Aden. The place had been captured from the Arabs in January, 1839, by a small expedition from Bombay.
[2] *A Brief History of the Royal Bombay Sappers and Miners*, p. 12.
[3] G.O.C.C., dated February 3rd, 1837.

occurred in December of the same year. The eight companies were then reduced to six, and the strength of each company was increased from 80 to 120 men.[1]

The "Subadar" made his appearance as a Company Commander, the number of Indian officers rose from eight to twelve, and the number of Naiks was doubled. Much greater efficiency was thus secured in each company. It was arranged in 1838[2] that in peace time, while four companies should be lent to the Revenue Board for employment on civil works, two companies should be undergoing instruction at Bangalore in sapping, mining and field engineering generally, reliefs being carried out biennially. The proper instruction of the whole Corps in military engineering, and sufficient practice in civil engineering, were thus ensured. Each company became complete in itself and capable of independent action. A very generous equipment of tools was authorized: axes, crowbars, bill-hooks, hammers, jumpers and *mamooties*[3] were supplied in abundance. Altogether, the organization, training and equipment of a Madras Company was very complete before the First Afghan War began.

The Madras Sapper of 1840 was small,[4] but wiry and active. It was laid down that "special regard should be had to the nature of Sapper duties which require the men to be of a firm, muscular and athletic frame, capable of enduring every species of bodily labour." So efficient and intelligent did the Madras Sappers prove themselves during the First China War that the Corps was increased to nine companies during the campaign and remained at that strength for many years. The intelligence of the men is illustrated by the following tale. In 1855 the Governor of Madras made a complimentary speech to the Corps couched in the high-flown Urdu of the north, and, having finished his harangue, asked the senior Subadar if the men had understood him. "No, sir," replied the Subadar, " but I did." " Then translate my remarks into a language which the men can understand," said the Governor. When the Subadar, turning round, gave the speech in *English*. Remarkable, but true.

Although the Sappers and Miners in all three Presidencies were trained soldiers, the arms which they carried, and their training in musketry, left much to be desired. Up to January, 1844, the Bengal Sappers were armed with "fusils" and bayonets, but on January 13th of that year the fusil was replaced by the "Sapper carbine."[5] The Bombay Sappers also carried the fusil and bayonet till the end of 1844,[6] when they were rearmed with the Brunswick rifle.[7] From

[1] G.O.G., dated December 26th, 1837.   [2] G.O.C.C., dated February 15th, 1838.
[3] A digging implement like a hoe with a short handle.
[4] The standard of height was 5 feet 5 inches.
[5] G.O.C.C., dated January, 1844. The "fusil" was a light musket.
[6] The fusil was introduced in Bombay on December 4th, 1826.
[7] The Brunswick rifle remained till January 2nd, 1866, when it was replaced by the Lancaster rifle as used by the Royal Engineers. In 1875, the Lancaster rifle was discarded for the Snider carbine. The Corps was rearmed with the Martini-Henry rifle (·450) in 1888, with the Lee-Metford rifle (·303) in 1900, and with the Lee-Enfield short rifle (·303) in 1909. The Bengal and Madras Corps were similarly rearmed.

1838 the Madras Sappers were armed, some with fusils and "bayonet knives," and others with pistols; in 1846, however, "Sapper carbines" were issued to all the men.[1] It is curious to read[2] that in 1844, while a musketry course was authorized for the cavalry trooper and the infantry soldier, the infantryman being allowed to fire up to 200 yards' range and the cavalryman to only 150 yards, no practice whatever was allowed to the unfortunate Madras Sapper and Miner. The records of the Madras Corps are more complete than those of either the Bengal or Bombay Corps, but it may be said in general that the more important reorganizations in any one Corps were followed by similar changes in the others. They maintained close contact, though belonging to separate armies.

Scarcely had the last shots been fired in the Afghan and China wars than Lord Ellenborough found himself involved in troubles in Sind, that desert land which stretches northwards from Karachi to beyond Rohri and Sukkur. The Government of India was most anxious to obtain control of the Indus for commercial and strategic reasons, and it was evident that while the Amirs of Sind held the banks of the river they could interfere with traffic on its waters. The chiefs of Upper and Lower Sind, and of Mirpur or Eastern Sind, had been most unfriendly and suspicious since Lord Auckland had forced them to allow the Army of the Indus to traverse their country on its journey to Afghanistan; but so determined was Lord Ellenborough to gain the Indus that he seems to have deliberately provoked a war against the Amirs. He selected, as a kind of military dictator in Sind, a very remarkable man—Major-General Sir Charles Napier. "His appearance," writes Fortescue,[3] "was so strange that the Baluchis might well have mistaken him for a demon. Beneath a huge helmet of his own contrivance there issued a fringe of long hair at the back, and in front a large pair of round spectacles, an immense hooked nose and a mane of moustache and whisker reaching to the waist." His nature was in some ways fitted to his appearance for Napier was aggressive, dictatorial and at times merciless; but he was as brave as a lion, a good tactician, a sound administrator and popular with his men. He had no illusions about his task. "We have no right to seize Sind," he wrote,[4] "yet we shall do so; and a very advantageous, useful, humane piece of rascality it will be." So perhaps "*Peccavi*," his alleged[5] laconic announcement of the capture of Sind, may have had a double meaning. Such was the leader who arrived in Sukkur on October 5th, 1842, and announced the annexation of a part of northern Sind in December of that year.

[1] G.O.C.C., dated February 15th, 1838, and G.O.G., dated July 17th, 1846.
[2] G.O.C.C., dated November 12th, 1844.
[3] *A History of the British Army*, by the Hon. J. W. Fortescue, Vol. XII, p. 290.
[4] *The Life and Opinions of General Sir C. Napier*, by Sir W. Napier, Vol. II, p. 218.
[5] Actually, the only "authority" for the story is *Punch*, which, moreover, did not attribute the saying to Napier. The verse in *Punch* ran as follows:—
"Peccavi! I've Scinde," said Lord Ellen so proud:
Dalhousie, more modest, said, "Vovi, I've Oudh."

Major C. Waddington,[1] of the Bombay Engineers, was the Chief Engineer with the force of 8,000 men under Napier, and Lieutenant T. Studdert of the same Corps was his assistant. The Sappers and Miners were represented by "C" Company from Madras under Captain R. Henderson,[2] with Lieutenant C. A. Orr and 2nd-Lieutenant A. J. M. Boileau, all of the Madras Engineers. The only Bengal Engineer in the campaign was Lieutenant E. J. Brown, who was Secretary to the Political Resident at Hyderabad, Colonel James Outram.[3] "C" Company, it will be remembered, had been in Afghanistan, and it concentrated at Rohri only just in time for the operations of the Sind campaign.

Napier himself did not wish to force a war upon the Amirs if he could induce them to relinquish their country by other means, so he tried the effect of a ruthless display of power before any declaration of war. The Amirs had two fortresses, Imamgarh and Shahgarh, far out in the desert to the east, to which they might retire for refuge, and Napier decided to raid and destroy Imamgarh. He organized a flying column of 250 British Infantry mounted in pairs on camels, some Sind Horse, a few light guns, and half of "C" Company, Madras Sappers and Miners, and plunged on January 5th into the waterless desert which stretched for 100 miles to his goal. With him went Waddington, Henderson, Brown and Boileau. They reached the fortress a week later and found it empty, so the Engineers and Sappers set to work to mine the walls and soon completed 24 galleries and charged the chambers with powder which they discovered in the place. On the 15th Studdert lit the trains of powder and took cover, when, to his horror, he saw Waddington bending over one of the trains. "The other mines are going to burst," he shouted. "That may be," said the Chief Engineer, "but this mine must burst also," and calmly adjusting the defective match he walked away, shielding his head from the debris thrown up as the other mines exploded. The destruction of Imamgarh was completed by igniting a charge of 7,000 pounds of powder stored in one room, and the troops then set out on their return journey, well pleased with their work. But the demolitions at Imamgarh failed to impress the Amirs; so Napier moved southwards towards Hyderabad, and war became inevitable.

In February, 1843, matters came to a head. The Sindians demanded that Colonel Outram should withdraw from Hyderabad, and, because he refused to do so, attacked the Residency on the 15th with 8,000 men when Napier with less than 3,000 was some 35 miles to the north-west. Brown, of the Engineers, helped Outram to put up a gallant defence, and, when resistance was no longer possible,

---

[1] Afterwards Major-General Charles Waddington.
[2] Afterwards Major-General Robert Henderson.
[3] This list of Engineer Officers is taken from "Early Indian Campaigns," by Major H. Biddulph, R.E., appearing in *The R.E. Journal*, Vol. XVIII, July-December, 1913, p. 336.

boarded a steamer with him and joined Napier above Hyderabad. On hearing the news, Napier advanced on February 17th to attack the Sind Army which had taken up a position at Miani near the capital. He found the enemy strongly posted in and beyond the dry bed of the Fuleli River, a tributary of the Indus, and with both flanks resting on jungle which was impassable for cavalry. The Sindians numbered about 20,000 men, and Napier could not muster even 3,000 and was obliged to make a frontal attack in a confined area. Nevertheless, after parking his baggage,[1] he advanced in échelon of regiments with "C" Company, Madras Sappers and Miners, covering the flank of his artillery on the right. To his surprise he was held up by a large force of hostile infantry hidden in the bed of the Fuleli, whose course had not been properly reconnoitred, and the Sappers were crowded out of the line by a block caused through the change in direction of a high wall which bounded the right of the advance. The British Infantry came under a point-blank fire from the river-bed, and for a time there was some confusion; but the Madras Sappers made a breach in the wall so that the Gunners were able to point a gun through it and sweep the enemy in the river-bed and a wood beyond it. More guns came into action; and finally the infantry, and Henderson with his Sappers, leapt down among the enemy and ended four hours of strenuous battle with a decisive victory. On the next morning the Amirs sent emissaries to ask what terms Napier would grant. "Life and nothing more," said he, "and I require your decision before noon." On February 19th he marched into Hyderabad, and on March 12th announced the annexation of the whole of Sind.

This, however, was by no means the end of the campaign. Mirpur, or Eastern Sind, was not yet subdued, and its ruler, Sher Muhammad, proceeded to collect 20,000 men at Dabo, close to Hyderabad, to defy the 5,000 whom Napier could now bring against him. Here Napier fought him on March 24th, 1843, in an action generally known as the Battle of Hyderabad; and although Sher Muhammad was strongly entrenched in two parallel watercourses, with his right flank resting on the village of Dabo and the Fuleli River, Napier's cavalry turned his left flank and the infantry broke through and drove him in utter rout from the position. It is recorded that when the British were nearing the enemy's lines, Waddington and two others rode coolly for 300 yards along the front to reconnoitre the position. It was a deed worthy of the Corps, and it helped Napier to select a weak point for his assault. The Baluchi Infantry of Sind fought gallantly to the last; 800 dead bodies were counted afterwards in and about Dabo alone, and the country beyond was literally strewn with dead. Sher Muhammad fled, his cities of Mirpur and Umarkot fell, and the

---

[1] Napier was wise enough to insist on a minimum of baggage and transport with his army.

conquest of Sind was complete. For another year " C " Company remained in the captured territory till it embarked at Karachi for Bombay in March, 1844, after more than three years of foreign service. " No troops," wrote Napier, " have more honourably conducted themselves. You did your duty bravely in the battles of Meannee and Hyderabad."

Although no Bombay Sappers and Miners served under Napier, No. 3 Company of that Corps distinguished itself in a subsequent campaign in Sind under Major-General de la Motte at the end of 1844, and took part in the storming of the fortress of Panalla on December 1st of that year. The unit was commanded by Lieutenant (afterwards Major-General) G. B. Munbee of the Bombay Engineers. Lieutenant W. D. Graham of that Corps was also present and was the first to reach the top of the breach, and Major Alexander Peat, of Afghanistan fame, was as usual in the front rank in this affair.[1]

Before we proceed to the stormy events of the two Sikh wars in the Punjab, a brief reference is necessary to the exploits of the Engineers and Sappers and Miners who fought in what is known as the " Gwalior Campaign." Early in 1843 the death occurred of Jankoji Rao Sindhia,[2] the Maratha ruler of Gwalior, and, in the intrigue and confusion which followed, the Gwalior army of 40,000 men with 200 guns took charge of the affairs of the state. Some months later the Sikh army in the Punjab got completely out of hand after some assassinations and intrigues, and its 70,000 soldiers, longing for conquest and plunder, became a real peril to northern India. Lord Ellenborough was fully aware that a war in the Punjab was imminent, and he wished to avoid at all costs the danger of a combination of the unruly Sikh and Gwalior armies against him, so he concentrated against Gwalior what he called an " Army of Exercise," and when that gesture failed, sent the two wings of a force known as the " Army of Gwalior," under General Sir Hugh Gough,[3] to attack the Marathas from Agra in the north and Jhansi in the south.

The two wings of the Army of Gwalior advanced in December, 1843. With the Right Wing[4] under Gough himself were the 3rd, 4th, 5th and 7th Companies[5] of the Bengal Sappers and Miners, marching from Agra southwards; and with the Left Wing[6] under Major-General Sir John Grey, the 1st Company, marching from Jhansi northwards. Major E. J. Smith, of the Bengal Engineers, was Chief Engineer to the army, and had with him in the Right Wing,

---

[1] *A Brief History of the Royal Bombay Sappers and Miners*, p. 11.
[2] Son of Daulat Rao Sindhia.
[3] Sir Hugh Gough had been made Commander-in-Chief in India in recognition of his services in the First China War.
[4] Two divisions and attached troops.
[5] Major H. Biddulph, R.E., in his " Early Indian Campaigns " (*The R.E. Journal*, Vol. XVIII, July–December, 1913, p. 337), omits the 5th Company; but the *History and Digest of Service of the 1st K.G.O. Sappers and Miners* records on p. 9 that the 3rd, 4th, 5*th* and 7th Companies were present at the battle of Maharajpur.
[6] One division and attached troops.

Lieutenants W. Abercrombie, T. Renny-Tailyour, S. Pott, and C. B. Young as Company Commanders, and 2nd-Lieutenants J. D. Campbell, W. D. A. R. Short and J. E. T. Nicolls as Company Officers, all of the Bengal Corps.[1] Lord Ellenborough himself accompanied the force, and on his staff we find Major E. Sanders, B.E., as Deputy-Secretary, Military Department, and Captain H. M. Durand, B.E., as Private Secretary. It will be seen that this wing of the army was very strong in Engineers. The Left Wing, on the other hand, had only Lieutenant (afterwards Major-General) J. H. Maxwell, B.E., at the head of the 1st Company of Bengal Sappers and Miners. Durand had already been caught up into the Political Service, that heaven of all ambitious young officers.

On December 23rd, 1843, Gough and the Governor-General crossed the Chambal and advanced on Gwalior, which act was taken by the Marathas as a declaration of war. It was not long before Gough, with about 6,000 men and 30 light guns, came upon an army of 18,000 Marathas drawn up in strongly entrenched positions in front of the villages of Maharajpur and Chonda, their main position being near the latter place which lay more than one mile from Maharajpur. The opportunity was taken to attack the isolated force at Maharajpur, and a bloody fight ensued. The enemy's gunners stood to their weapons till they were bayoneted, and their infantry fought with the utmost desperation. However, the position was carried at last by a frontal assault, and afterwards the main position also at Chonda, the Marathas being routed with the loss of 56 guns and all their ammunition. In this hard-fought battle on December 29th, 1843, the British losses in infantry were very heavy, but the Engineers and Sappers escaped more lightly, though Major E. Sanders was killed. Although the four companies of Sappers were not closely engaged they earned the thanks of Sir Hugh Gough for their services prior to the action, for it was due to their efforts in bridging *nullahs* and cutting tracks through eight miles of most difficult country intersected by deep ravines that Gough was able to bring his artillery into action against the well-served Maratha guns.

On the same day that Maharajpur was fought, the Left Wing under General Grey gained a decisive victory at Panniar, 12 miles south-west of Gwalior, where it encountered a force of 12,000 Marathas. The enemy attacked Grey's cumbrous train of baggage, so he assaulted a position which they had taken up on high ground to the east and, after two hours' fighting, captured it together with 24 guns and every round of ammunition. The Maratha losses were so heavy that, combined with the effect of the defeat at Maharajpur, the battle of Panniar ended the Gwalior Campaign. The 1st

---

[1] Young, Campbell and Nicolls rose to be Lieutenant-Generals and Pott to be a Major-General.

Company, Bengal Sappers and Miners, took a very conspicuous part in this fight. When his baggage was attacked, Grey sent forward the Buffs and the Sappers alone to reconnoitre over the crest of some hills to his right. They discovered the enemy in force, and, in spite of their small numbers, promptly attacked. There, in the words of the Commander-in-Chief, " they were exposed to a most galling fire from the Mahratta guns but most gallantly carried every position before them, drove the enemy from hill to hill, and captured eleven guns and a standard."[1] The good work of the Buffs and Sappers and Miners was completed by reinforcements who followed, and the Sappers then returned in triumph to the British camp with their trophies. It was three months after this that two additional companies, the 9th and 10th, were added to the establishment of the Bengal Sappers and Miners who had proved so clearly that they could use the bayonet as skilfully as the pick and shovel. The battle of Panniar established a link of comradeship between a famous British Regiment and a gallant Indian Corps.

[1] Despatch from General Sir Hugh Gough, dated December 30th, 1843.

KHELAT-I-GHILJIE.

From Sale's *Defence of Jelalabad*.

CHAPTER XVI.

THE SIKH, SECOND BURMA AND SECOND CHINA WARS, 1845–1860.

WHILE the Gwalior Campaign was running its brief course, more serious and widespread trouble was brewing in the Punjab, where the Sikh army had got out of hand after the death of Ranjit Singh in 1839. War came soon, and it was caused, as so often, by a combination of ambition, greed and fear. The soldiers of the Khalsa, or military order, gazed with longing eyes on the riches of the Jumna *Doab* and Delhi, and noted at the same time the British advance from the Jumna to the Sutlej, the garrisons which they were building up at Ferozepore and Ludhiana on the frontier, the new base at Ambala, and the general movement of troops along new roads leading towards the Punjab. The fate of Sind was not forgotten. Ferozepore lay only 50 miles to the south of the Sikh capital at Lahore, and it leaked out that the British intended to establish a bridge of boats across the Sutlej at their frontier post. The Government indeed sent 60 boats from Bombay to the Indus in February, 1845, " to serve as a flotilla and also a bridge of boats,"[1] with confidential instructions that the purposes for which they were needed should be kept secret because of the turbulence of the Sikh army. They added also that the boats should be moved at once to Sukkur and later possibly to Ferozepore, where, as a fact, they arrived in August, 1845.[2] When the guiding hand of Ranjit Singh was removed, the Sikh army practically usurped all power in the Punjab; and the Sikh chiefs, particularly Lal Singh and Tej Singh who feared the Khalsa, looked about for a means to destroy it. No better instrument was available than the British army, so they deliberately encouraged the ambitions of their own soldiers and thus precipitated the First Sikh War. In November, 1845, the Sikhs began to move southwards from Lahore, and before the middle of December an army of about 50,000 men with 100 guns, under Lal Singh and Tej Singh, crossed the Sutlej near Ferozepore. A reference to the map entitled " Sketch Map of Northern India," which appears at the end of this volume, will show how critical was the situation created by this sudden invasion which violated every existing treaty.

[1] *The Career of Major George Broadfoot*, by Major W. Broadfoot, R.E., p. 283. Broadfoot became Political Agent in November, 1844.

[2] Lieutenant A. Taylor, B.E., the officer in charge, was ordered to sink these boats when the Sikh invasion was imminent. He did so, but they were refloated later to make a bridge for Gough after the victory at Sobraon. (*Life of General Sir Alex. Taylor*, by A. C. Taylor, Vol. I, p. 44.)

In July, 1844, Lieutenant-General Sir Henry Hardinge, a veteran of the Peninsular War, had replaced Lord Ellenborough as Governor-General. Impressed by the despatches of George Broadfoot from Lahore, he foresaw a crisis but hoped to avoid actual war. Still, as a soldier, he took steps to meet a possible invasion, reinforcing the troops at Ferozepore, Ludhiana, Ambala and elsewhere, till he had 32,000 men with 68 field guns near the Sutlej, with a further 10,000 at Meerut. Shortly before the Sikh invasion he began to concentrate his troops into the "Army of the Sutlej," and placing the whole force under General Sir Hugh Gough, the Commander-in-Chief, took the field himself as Gough's second-in-command. The army soon amounted to three Cavalry brigades, four Infantry divisions,[1] a number of batteries, and a gradually increasing body of Sappers and Miners, which included finally the whole of the Bengal Corps. Gough moved forward to defend Ferozepore, and war was announced by proclamation on December 13th.

In March, 1845, the 1st and 6th Companies of the Bengal Sappers and Miners formed part of the Ferozepore garrison, so that these units were available for engineering work when the Sikhs broke into the North-West Province; but it was not till the proclamation of war in December that the remainder of the Corps was ordered to the front, and there were no Sappers and Miners in the first battle at Mudki. The only Engineer officers who took part in this fight were Major Robert C. Napier and Lieutenant J. E. T. Nicolls, both of the Bengal Corps. From an engineering point of view, accordingly, the battle has little interest except that in it a most famous military engineer had his baptism of fire. Robert Napier, later to become Field-Marshal Lord Napier of Magdala, began his Indian career in 1828 as an Assistant Engineer on the Eastern Jumna Canal under Captain P. T. Cautley[2] of the Bengal Artillery, and had as close neighbours two other young Bengal Engineers who also rose to high office—Captain W. E. Baker[3] and Lieutenant H. M. Durand, then working on the Western Jumna Canal. From canal work Napier went to road construction at Darjeeling, and then, after a transfer to Karnal, we find him laying out a new cantonment in 1844 at Ambala. Before he could finish this work he was summoned to join the Army of the Sutlej, and so went on active service for the first time after 17 years of civil employment.[4] At Mudki his horse was killed under him; at Ferozeshah a second horse was killed under him and he was severely wounded.

General Gough, at the head of part of his army, reached Mudki,

---

[1] The Divisional Commanders were Major-Generals Sir Harry G. Smith, W. R. Gilbert, Sir J. M'Caskill and Sir J. Littler.

[2] Afterwards Colonel Sir Proby Cautley, designer and builder of the Ganges Canal.

[3] Afterwards Lieutenant-General Sir William Baker, an eminent irrigation and railway expert.

[4] Obituary notice of Field-Marshal Lord Napier of Magdala, appearing in *The R.E. Journal*, Vol. 20, 1890, pp. 61–67.

18 miles from Ferozepore, on December 18th after six days of forced marching and heard that the Sikhs were advancing to the attack. He pushed forward and discovered them in position with 40 guns close to Mudki; but, undeterred by heavy losses[1] from artillery fire, he sent his cavalry to turn the enemy's left flank while his infantry assaulted in front. A day of confused fighting in difficult country found the British victorious in the end and with 17 captured guns, but the action was costly and by no means decisive. The enemy retired during the night to their main position at Ferozeshah, eight miles to the north-west, where Lal Singh awaited Gough while another Sikh army, under Tej Singh, lay watching General Littler's division at Ferozepore.

On December 21st Gough marched to attack Lal Singh at Ferozeshah, expecting to be joined early by Littler from Ferozepore. In this, however, he was disappointed, for Littler had first to give Tej Singh the slip and did not appear till early in the afternoon. When Gough wished to attack without him, Hardinge suddenly discarded his role as second-in-command, and, assuming that of Governor-General, forbade the attempt. At length, when Littler came up, the British force of 18,000 men with 69 guns advanced against the much larger and more powerfully armed Sikh host entrenched around the village of Ferozeshah, the right of the attack being under Gough and the left under Hardinge. Littler's division on the extreme left was repulsed, but Gilbert's and M'Caskill's divisions in the centre made progress under a storm of shell from the Sikh heavy guns. Sir Harry Smith's division (the Reserve) was then thrown in and fought a way through where Littler had failed, its work being completed by a gallant charge of cavalry. It was too late, however, to gain a complete victory, and the British force was in great confusion when darkness fell. The Sikhs clung tenaciously to a part of their position, while Gough's men spent a miserable night under heavy fire, hungry, thirsty and half-frozen. Still they carried the remainder of the Sikh trenches at dawn and found that the bulk of the enemy had withdrawn. Hardly had the position been won when Tej Singh appeared with 30,000 men from Ferozepore and opened a heavy artillery bombardment. The exhausted British troops, however, showed a bold front, the cavalry charged the enemy's horse, and Tej Singh retreated. On December 22nd the British were victorious, but at what a cost! Seven hundred men were dead, and 1,700 wounded and among them 115 British officers.

There was not much scope for engineering in the battle of Ferozeshah. It was a confused and desperate struggle in which men fought hand to hand, but No. 6 Company, Bengal Sappers and Miners, was in it with Littler's division, and also Major Robert Napier and

---

[1] Major-General Robert Sale, the Commander of the Jalalabad garrison in the First Afghan War, was among the killed.

Lieutenant (afterwards Major-General) E. J. Lake[1] of the Bengal Engineers. The saddest event of the day was the death of Captain George Broadfoot, the defender of Jalalabad. He was riding with the Governor-General as a Political Aide-de-Camp when he was wounded through both thighs and thrown from his horse. He remounted and was almost immediately shot through the heart and fell dead.[2] On Christmas Day, 1845, he was laid to rest in Ferozepore, and in Madras may be found a memorial which records that he was " as brave as he was able, and second to none in all the great qualities of an accomplished officer." His loss was recorded as a public calamity in both Houses of Parliament. It removed a brilliant figure from Indian history.

After Ferozeshah, Tej Singh retreated across the Sutlej by a ford at Sobraon, 20 miles north of the battlefield, and, on January 6th, 1846, Gough received large reinforcements from Meerut including another company of Sappers. The Sikhs proceeded to bridge the Sutlej at Sobraon, so Gough moved up from Ferozepore on January 12th to watch them. They were allowed to recross the river in large numbers at Sobraon for Gough saw the trap into which they were falling, cooped up as they would be in a re-entrant bend of the Sutlej with the river behind them and only one bridge by which to recross it. They began to fortify their bridge-head position on the left bank and to reinforce it by rear and flanking defences on the high right bank while the British awaited the arrival of their heavy artillery.

In the meantime another Sikh army under Sardar Ranjodh Singh had crossed the Sutlej farther upstream and was threatening Ludhiana and the British communications with Ambala. Sir Harry Smith was sent to deal with him, and, after much manœuvring, brought him to battle on January 28th, 1846, at Aliwal, west of Ludhiana. The Sikh general took up a position with his back to the Sutlej and held it in a most determined manner with 18,000 men and 67 guns to which Sir Harry Smith could oppose only 12,000 with 32 guns. The only Engineer unit in the British force was a detachment of the 6th Company, Bengal Sappers and Miners. Several Bengal Engineer officers, however, were at Aliwal or sufficiently near the battle to receive the clasp to their " Army of the Sutlej " medal ; these were Brevet-Captain J. D. Cunningham (Political Service), Lieutenant (afterwards Lieut.-General Sir Richard) Strachey, Lieutenants R. Baird Smith and E. J. Lake, and 2nd-Lieutenants G. P. Hebbert and Alexander (afterwards General Sir Alexander) Taylor. The fight was short and decisive. The Sikh left was turned and their line rolled up and taken in reverse. For a time the crack battalions on the enemy's right—men trained by the Italian General,

---

[1] Then a Political Officer.
[2] *The Career of Major George Broadfoot*, by Major W. Broadfoot, R.E., p. 400.

Avitabile[1]—fought hard to cover the line of retreat to the river, but the 16th Lancers broke through them and finally the whole Sikh army was driven into and across the Sutlej with enormous slaughter and the loss of all their guns and supplies. This brilliant victory had a great moral effect. The Sikhs retreated everywhere across the Sutlej except at Sobraon, and Sir Harry Smith marched back to join Sir Hugh Gough in his assault on the last position held by the enemy.

The Sikh position on the left bank of the Sutlej at Sobraon was a veritable fortress. It was powerfully entrenched and its flanks were swept by massed batteries of heavy guns from a second position across the river. The two positions were held by Tej Singh with 30,000 regular troops supported by at least 70 guns. Against them Gough could bring only 16,000 men and 65 guns, and his artillery could not throw the weight of metal of the Sikh weapons. The position on the left bank was not only strongly fortified but very extensive, the southern front alone being nearly two miles in length. So forbidding was the outlook that, after a reconnaissance on February 9th, Gough's artillery officers advised him that an assault was bound to fail; but Major (afterwards Major-General Sir Frederick) Abbott, of the Bengal Engineers, and Major Henry Lawrence, the Political Agent, were for immediate attack, and Gough accepted their view. The battle opened on the 10th with a heavy bombardment between the opposing guns, and the 3rd Division (Dick) then advanced on the left; but, although it was supported by all the British heavy artillery and penetrated into the Sikh trenches, it was driven back with heavy loss by a spirited counter-attack. Feints in the centre and right by the 2nd and 1st Divisions (Gilbert and Smith) were then converted into serious attacks and pressed home, and this diversion enabled the troops of the 3rd Division to rally and renew their assault. The Sappers and Miners under Major B. Y. Reilly then made openings through the Sikh entrenchments on the extreme left through which the Third Light Dragoons passed in single file, reformed in the Sikh position, and charged wildly upon the enemy's batteries and infantry. The defenders wavered at last and began to fall back towards their bridge of boats, but found to their horror that the bridge was broken and that all the fords were impassable through a rise in the river. Panic then took them. Under a hail of grape from the British guns they were driven by thousands into the rushing waters which soon ran red with blood. Some say that 10,000 Sikhs perished in this holocaust. Gough had gained a brilliant victory and had broken the Sikh army, though at a cost of some 2,400 casualties.

The whole Corps of Bengal Sappers and Miners except the 9th and

---

[1] Ranjit Singh had employed several foreign Generals, such as Ventura, Allard, Court and Avitabile, to train his troops.

10th Companies had already concentrated on the Sutlej, and these two companies joined the army at Lahore shortly after the war had ended.[1] It appears that after the battle Gough ordered a bridge to be thrown across the Sutlej near Ferozepore, and that the 1st, 2nd, 7th and 8th Companies were making preparations there on February 9th under Abbott ; of these units, the 1st and 8th Companies remained at Ferozepore while the 2nd and 7th marched that day to Sobraon, where Abbott himself reconnoitred the Sikh position and advised the Commander-in-Chief. Accordingly the 2nd, 3rd, 4th, 5th, 6th and 7th Companies were in the assault, the 5th Company being with General Gilbert's division, and the whole Corps was under Major B. Y. Reilly. The Chief Engineer with the army was Lieut.-Colonel (local Brigadier) E. J. Smith. Lieut.-Colonel (local Brigadier) A. Irvine, who was senior to Smith, had only recently arrived and refused to supersede him. Captain Robert Napier was at Sobraon as a Brigade-Major, and six other Captains, seven Lieutenants and seven 2nd-Lieutenants of the Bengal Engineers were in the assault or engaged in bridging the Sutlej at Ferozepore. Twenty-five Engineer officers in all received the clasp for Sobraon.[2]

On February 12th, 1846, the Army of the Sutlej crossed the river by the new bridge completed that morning,[3] and eight days later entered Lahore in triumph. By a treaty concluded in March, the Sikh army was reduced and all Sikh territory on the British side of the Sutlej was given up. The Sikhs also relinquished Kashmir which was then bestowed on Gulab Singh, the Raja of Jammu, on payment of three-quarters of a million sterling. In the Jullundur *Doab* there was some trouble during April as the *kiladar* of the hill fort of Kangra refused to submit ; but when Napier, by skilful engineering and the help of elephants, had got a few siege guns within range, the *kiladar* changed his mind and surrendered.[4] The Sikh army had been heavily defeated, but the fighting spirit of the Khalsa yet remained. All the battles had been fought on British soil. Not a British soldier had been seen north of the Ravi. Every indication pointed to a renewal of the conflict, and, as later events proved, the portents were true.

Some space may now be devoted to a review of the cadres of Engineer officers in Bengal, Bombay and Madras, and the expansions which took place in those establishments between the end of the First Burma War and the outbreak of the Indian Mutiny. In 1829 Bengal had outstripped Madras in the number of her Engineers and had the largest cadre of the three Presidencies—a total of 58 officers.

---

[1] *History and Digest of Service, 1st K.G.O. Sappers and Miners*, p. 11.
[2] "Early Indian Campaigns," by Major H. Biddulph, R.E., appearing in *The R.E. Journal*, Vol. XIX, January–June, 1914, p. 46.
[3] *Life of General Sir Alex. Taylor*, by A. C. Taylor, Vol. I, p. 55.
[4] Two companies of Bengal Sappers and Miners, under Lieutenants H. Drummond and J. H. Dyas, carried out the engineering work ; and Lieutenant W. A. Crommelin assisted Napier. Captains J. D. Cunningham and J. Abbott, of the Bengal Engineers, were present as Political Officers. (Obituary notice of Lieut.-General W. A. Crommelin appearing in *The R.E. Journal*, Vol. 17, 1887, p. 10.)

Madras had only 46 Engineers, and Bombay 32. At about this time the establishment of Engineer officers for Madras was fixed at 40, and continued at this figure till 1845. On June 10th, 1844, however, a representation was made to the Court of Directors by certain Madras Engineers because promotion was so slow that they were being superseded continually in the army by officers of other branches, and the result was the addition of four Lieutenants and two 2nd-Lieutenants to the Madras cadre in January, 1845; but no further change was made till 1854. Madras had become, in some ways, a "backwater," and the eyes of the Directors were turned on the north.

By 1840, after the Afghan war had begun, the number of Engineer officers on the Bengal establishment had increased to a remarkable extent. The Army Lists of that year show that in the northern Presidency there were then 77 Engineers as compared with 58 of 11 years before, and that even in Bombay the total had risen from 32 to 42, not counting a few supernumerary 2nd-Lieutenants. The outbreak of the First Sikh War in 1845 naturally stimulated the Bengal Army, so that in the following year we find 92 Engineers on the Calcutta list when Bombay could muster only 40 and Madras 46. Eight years later, in 1854, the Bengal establishment of Engineer officers had risen to 125, the Bombay establishment to 57, and that of Madras (where a third battalion of Sappers and Miners had been added on August 1st, 1854) to 54. Thus Madras, the most favoured Presidency at the beginning of the nineteenth century, had sunk to the lowest position on the list before the outbreak of the Indian Mutiny. No clearer indication can be given of the "sweeter atmosphere" which had spread over southern India since the Mysore wars.

If we examine a list of the military engineers in any Presidency during the period under review, and the nature of their employment, we may be surprised at the enormous preponderance of officers in civil or civil engineering posts. Take, for example, the Bengal cadre for the year 1846, when Colonel John Cheape, C.B., was Chief Engineer. Of four Lieut.-Colonels under Cheape, only one appears to be in military employment (on the Military Board); of the remaining three, two are Superintending Engineers in the Department of Public Works and one in civil non-engineering employment. Of the four Majors on the list, one (B. Y. Reilly) commands the Bengal Sappers and Miners, two are in the Department of Public Works, and one in extra-regimental employment. Of 20 Captains, one is on the Military Board and one in the Sappers and Miners; three others are shown respectively as "Surveyor-General,"[1] "employed on the projected Railway"[2] and "in political service,"[3] and

---

[1] Captain A. S. Waugh.
[2] Captain A. H. E. Boileau. Private promoters sent their schemes for the first Indian railway to the Directors in May, 1845, and in 1853 the first railway line in India was opened—a length of 21 miles from Bombay to Kalyan. In 1854 the East Indian Railway opened 23 miles of track from Calcutta to Hugli.
[3] Captain H. M. Durand, the hero of the Kabul Gate at Ghazni.

the remaining 15 are in the Department of Public Works. Of 40 Lieutenants only two are doing military duty, and it falls to the cadre of 20 2nd-Lieutenants to provide 14 youngsters to command the Bengal Sappers and Miners under a sprinkling of older men and assisted by Infantry officers.

There are several explanations of this peculiar distribution. The Department of Public Works was concerned not only with what are considered nowadays as " public works " in India, such as canals, bridges, civil roads and buildings, but also with fortifications, barracks and other military structures. There was no reserve of civil engineers in India on which Government might draw in case of war, and engineers could not be sent quickly from England; consequently it was essential to keep a considerable number in India for whom no military employment could be found except in war. In the time of the Afghan and Sikh campaigns, the Madras and Bombay Sappers and Miners in particular were still officered largely by Infantrymen[1] who had been trained in field engineering in command of Sapper troops, and it was economical to continue for a time to employ them with the Sappers while the available Engineers were placed on large works for which greater technical knowledge was required. By 1846, large engineering schemes were plentiful, and particularly in the North-West Province which bordered on the Sikh domains in the Punjab. Behind the frontier of that province, marked by the River Sutlej, the country was being opened up by roads and canals; new cantonments were being laid out, and old ones enlarged; hundreds of rivers and streams were bridged in the course of a few years, and lines of survey run in all directions. It was an era of intensive effort, and the land a paradise for the engineer who could stand the extreme heat of the northern summer. There were no civil engineers to do the work, so the young Bengal Engineer entered into it with zeal, well knowing that rapid advancement could best be secured by civil engineering if, alas, the golden doors of the Political Department were closed against him.

A further glance at the list of the Engineer subalterns of Bengal for the year 1846 will reveal the facts that, of the 38 officers in civil employment, 26 were in the Department of Public Works, and that nearly one-half of these were building roads, bridges and buildings in the North-West Province. At the same time the Bengal Sappers and Miners were officered, as regards Engineers, by one Major, one Captain, one Lieutenant and 14 2nd-Lieutenants of less than two years' service in India. It is most remarkable that satisfactory engineering was carried out by the Sapper companies in war when, apart from Infantry commanders, they were officered only at the last moment by engineers drafted hurriedly from civil employment who

---

[1] For instance, " C " Company, Madras Sappers and Miners, was commanded in the First Afghan War by Captain Outlaw, 26th Madras Native Infantry.

could have had little or no knowledge of their men. The credit for the efficiency shown by all three Corps of Sappers and Miners in India should be given largely to the excellent British non-commissioned officers who were attached permanently to the units in times of peace and war.

The respite secured in the Punjab by the Treaty of Lahore, and another treaty which followed it in December, 1846, was short indeed. For a time, under the able guidance of Colonel Henry Lawrence and his famous staff—his brothers George and John, Hodson, Nicholson, Edwardes, Abbott and Lumsden—the Sikh Government and the whole province were kept in order; but when Lord Hardinge left India in January, 1848, and the Earl of Dalhousie became Governor-General, there were signs of rebellion once more, and the partial autonomy granted to the Sikhs was already proving a failure. Hardinge might have tried to annex the Punjab at the end of the First Sikh War. At that time, however, the Army of the Sutlej was so reduced in numbers, the Sikh forces were still so large, and their fortresses of Multan and Peshawar so strong, that the attempt would have been dangerous, and both Lord Gough (as he had become) and Sir Charles Napier advised against it. So Hardinge embarked on the experiment of allowing the defeated Sikhs a form of self-government, and by so doing brought war upon Dalhousie within three months of his landing in Calcutta.

The torch which set the Punjab aflame was a rebellion at Multan, a city lying near the Chenab River some 40 miles east of the Indus, and forming, with Lahore, Amritsar and Peshawar, the most powerful fortresses of the Khalsa. Diwan Mulraj, the Governor, being in disgrace, a new Governor had been appointed; and two young British officers—Vans Agnew and Anderson—were sent to Multan to see him installed. Both were foully murdered by Mulraj on April 18th, 1848, and he then proceeded to proclaim a religious war. It was the duty of the Sikh Government at Lahore to punish their rebellious Muhammadan deputy, but they contented themselves with sending four columns of disaffected Sikh troops to Multan under disloyal leaders, one of whom was a chief named Sher Singh. Lieutenant Herbert Edwardes[1] then swept suddenly across the Indus at the head of some Pathan irregulars, and with the aid of General Van Cortlandt, of the Sikh service, and a Bahawalpur army under Lieutenant E. J. Lake of the Bengal Engineers,[2] defeated Mulraj in two battles and drove him back into Multan. He proposed to lay siege to the place provided he could be given "a few heavy guns, a mortar battery, as many Sappers and Miners as could be spared, and Major Napier to plan the operations." But the terrible heat of the Punjab summer was approaching, and Lord Gough would not allow

---

[1] Political Agent in the Derajat or country bordering the Indus.
[2] Lake was acting as a Political Officer.

Napier or any troops to be sent on what seemed to be a mad venture, although Napier himself, contrary to his usual calm judgment, wished to make the attempt. The acting Resident at Lahore, however, considered that it was too late to draw back after Edwardes' raid, and on his own responsibility despatched a column[1] under Major-General William Whish to capture Multan. The force arrived at its destination on August 19th and was joined by a siege train on September 4th.

In the first phase of the siege the Chief Engineer was Major Robert Napier. Under his orders were the 1st, 2nd and 3rd Companies of Sappers,[2] and the 2nd and 3rd Companies of Pioneers, of the reconstituted Corps of " Bengal Sappers and Pioneers " then stationed at Ludhiana.[3] The Commandant of the Corps, Captain H. Siddons, led the five companies in the field. The cadre of Engineers was a large one, and all came from Bengal. In addition to Napier and Siddons, Captains W. Abercrombie and J. R. Western, Lieutenants J. H. Maxwell, P. Garforth, G. W. W. Fulton and E. J. Lake (Political) and 16 2nd-Lieutenants were at Multan in the early days of the siege.[4] No Bombay Engineers or Sappers and Miners were present during the first phase of the operations, and no Madras Engineers or Sappers and Miners took any part whatever in the Sikh wars or in the siege of Multan.

It was common knowledge that the defences of Multan were most powerful. Massive walls and bastions, a wide ditch, and the usual towering citadel, all were there ; so when Napier was appointed Chief Engineer his first problem was to get his engineering stores, and the siege guns and ammunition, some 200 miles down the Sutlej from Ferozepore. Remembering the boats collected at that place he asked young Alexander Taylor if he would undertake to float the guns, ammunition and stores downstream to a village opposite Bahawalpur where they would be within 40 miles of Multan. Taylor gladly undertook the task, and Napier embarked with him. On July 30th they left Ferozepore, reaching Bahawalpur 16 days later after a most adventurous voyage. Their huge cargo was then transported safely across the desert, and, when it had arrived, a plan of attack was considered.

Napier came forward with two schemes. Either General Whish might try to capture Multan by a *coup-de-main* by advancing to within battering distance of Khuni Burj or " Bloody Bastion " at the south-east corner, breaching it, and then launching his whole force to the assault, or he might march round to the northern side, where the citadel lay, and attack by regular approaches. Unless an immediate

---

[1] Two brigades of infantry, with cavalry, artillery and Sappers and Miners.
[2] Also a detachment of the 5th Company.
[3] As already mentioned, the Bengal Sappers and Miners became the " Bengal Sappers and Pioneers " on October 20th, 1847.
[4] " Early Indian Campaigns," by Major H. Biddulph, appearing in *The R.E. Journal*, Vol. XIX, January–June, 1914, p. 104.

victory was necessary for political reasons, Napier favoured the more cautious and deliberate plan of the northern approach, especially as it seemed that the mere capture of Multan would no longer check a general rising in the Punjab. But Lake, as commander of the Bahawalpur contingent, had other views. He was for a regular approach against the Khuni Burj, and this was the plan finally approved by Whish. A long parallel was begun by nearly 3,000 men on September 6th, and the working parties made such good progress that several batteries had been established by the 9th within one mile of the Khuni Burj and about five furlongs from some outlying entrenchments which the enemy began to throw up to the south of the city. There was much difficulty about the digging as two-thirds of Whish's men were irregulars; the heat was so great that the European troops could dig only at night, and the Pathans of Edwardes' force would not dig except for themselves! Lieutenant (afterwards General) Charles Pollard, Lieutenant (afterwards General Sir Frederick) Maunsell and Lieutenant Edward Lake did so well in this arduous work and in the subsequent attack that they drew from Edwardes the remark that "a finer body of men than the Engineer staff at Multan was never collected in any Indian army."[1] Ever to the fore was Robert Napier, brave, cool, resourceful. The reckless daring which he seemed at times to show was the confident boldness of careful preparation. This was the essence of his character.

By September 13th the Engineers were within 600 yards of the Khuni Burj, and a great breaching battery was begun on a mound; but the treachery of Sher Singh and his 4,000 Sikhs then upset all plans. They went over to the enemy, and Whish was obliged in consequence to raise the siege for a time and withdraw to a camp near Bahawalpur. Napier had recently been wounded, and it was only by the gallantry of Alexander Taylor that the engineering stores were saved from the enemy for they had been forgotten in the retreat. Taylor returned without an escort and, under cover of darkness, got them safely away. This ended the first phase of the siege of Multan. Every advantage had been lost through the duplicity of an ally.

The renewed attempt, which forms the second phase, began on December 21st, 1848. In the meantime Colonel (afterwards General Sir John) Cheape, of the Bengal Engineers, had become Chief Engineer, and Nos. 1 and 4 Companies of the Bombay Sappers and Miners, under Major (afterwards General) Walter Scott, with six subalterns of the Bombay Engineers, had just arrived as part of a large column from the Western Presidency. Mulraj was known to be intriguing with Dost Muhammad of Afghanistan to whom he promised Peshawar if the Afghans would invade the Derajat; and close to the north-east lay for a month the traitor Sher Singh with a rapidly-growing army of Sikh rebels. Sher Singh, however, marched

---
[1] *A Year on the Punjab Frontier*, by Major Herbert Edwardes, Vol. II, p. 513.

away on October 9th, and with the arrival of the Bombay troops the British army was strong enough to resume the offensive. During the lull in the operations, Napier and his men had prepared more than 15,000 gabions and 12,000 fascines for siege operations. All was ready for the attack.

The final advance was made against the north-eastern corner and the eastern face. On December 27th, the troops were entrenched within 500 yards of the citadel. Many gallant deeds were performed by the Engineers and Sappers during the approach. In those days it was usual to protect the head of a sap by rolling forward a large bundle of brushwood called a "sap-roller." One day, on sloping ground, the sap-roller rolled away, but Sapper Asan Singh immediately jumped out, and, although wounded by heavy fire, tied a rope to the roller by which it was hauled back. Several men of the Bengal Sappers and Pioneers gained the Indian Order of Merit for such deeds. A terrific explosion occurred on the 30th when Mulraj's largest magazine blew up. "At a vast height," writes Edwardes, "the heavy cloud stood still like some great tree, and its shadow fell as night over the camp below." Two breaches were made by our guns, one in the Khuni Burj and the other near the Delhi Gate in the eastern face. To Alexander Taylor was assigned the honour of leading the stormers through the Khuni Burj while the assault near the Delhi Gate was guided by Napier. The columns rushed to the attack on January 2nd, 1849, and by evening Multan City had fallen, though not without many casualties on the British side.[1] The citadel held out till January 22nd, when Mulraj was forced to surrender. By that time the attention of Government was fully occupied elsewhere. The Punjab had risen, and the battle of Chilianwala had been fought, so Whish and most of his troops marched northwards to join Lord Gough and reached him on February 20th before the battle of Gujarat.

Shortly after the first shots had been fired at Multan, the general discontent in the Punjab developed into a serious menace. In the Hazara country north of Rawalpindi, Chattar Singh[2] raised a force of rebels with which Major George Lawrence, and his assistant Major James Abbott, could not cope. Attock and its valuable bridge across the Indus fell to the enemy. The Sikh troops at Bannu, on the Afghan frontier, mutinied and marched to join Sher Singh who was on his way up the Chenab from Multan to meet Chattar Singh. The Sikhs in Peshawar rose, and Lawrence had to ride for Kohat. Already Chattar Singh had opened negotiations with Dost Muhammad resulting in the despatch of an Afghan army towards the Punjab.

[1] Lieutenants Garforth and Taylor of the Bengal Engineers, and Lieutenants J. Hill and J. A. Fuller of the Bombay Engineers were wounded. Earlier in the siege Major Napier and Lieutenants Lake, Gulliver, Pollard and Garnett had been wounded, so the Engineers did not escape lightly.
[2] Father of Sher Singh, the traitor of Multan.

By the end of October, 1848, the northern part of the province was at the mercy of the rebels. When Sher Singh marched his army into Ramnagar, 25 miles from Wazirabad, it seemed that his junction with Chattar Singh and the Afghans could not long be delayed. It was Lord Gough's task to prevent this meeting, and this is why the battles of the Second Sikh War were fought in a small area between Wazirabad and Jhelum, which was untouched by the first campaign.

While a crisis was approaching in the north, the Government had not been idle. By an order published on October 13th, the "Army of the Punjab" was assembled under Lord Gough. It numbered about 21,000 men including 5,000 under Major-General Whish at Multan, where, unfortunately for Gough, the three companies of Bengal Sappers were still engaged. The troops who concentrated at Ferozepore comprised a cavalry division under Brigadier-General C. R. Cureton, two infantry divisions under Major-Generals Sir W. R. Gilbert and Sir J. Thackwell, 11 batteries of artillery, and the 4th, 5th, 6th and 7th Companies of the Bengal Pioneers under Major (afterwards Major-General) G. B. Tremenheere of the Bengal Engineers. With these companies were Captain (afterwards Major-General) J. Glasfurd, Captains B. W. Goldie, H. M. Durand and A. Cunningham, and Lieutenants C. B. Young, R. Baird Smith, A. G. Goodwyn, H. Yule, T. S. Irwin, W. E. Morton and W. A. Crommelin. Napier, Siddons and other experienced officers, and all the 2nd-Lieutenants of the Corps of Bengal Sappers and Pioneers, were still far away at Multan. Gough had the use of a pontoon train under Crommelin at Ferozepore, but the absence of the highly-trained engineering units at Multan must have been a severe handicap when he took the field.

The campaign opened in November, 1848, with an advance against Sher Singh in his position at Ramnagar on the Chenab, where he was holding the fords of the river with 30,000 men and 28 guns pending the arrival of his fellow-conspirators, Chattar Singh and Dost Muhammad, from the north-west. Proceeding by Lahore, Gough crossed the Ravi on the 16th when Cureton and the cavalry, with a brigade of infantry, had already reached the Chenab at a spot some eight miles from Ramnagar. The main body joined the cavalry on the 21st, only to find that Sher Singh had retreated with most of his troops across the river. Gough, however, decided to attack some outposts still remaining on the left bank, and there followed the unsatisfactory cavalry action of Ramnagar which, although it cleared the left bank of Sikhs, cost the British cavalry heavy casualties, including Cureton killed, and raised the morale of the enemy. So deadly was the sword play of the Sikh horsemen in this fight that the British officers afterwards took to wrapping rolls of cloth round the back of their shakos, leaving the ends hanging down their backs. Gough and his staff adopted a leather cap with a peak in front and a large flap behind which had, says a contemporary writer, " the fantastic appearance of those hats so peculiar to the fraternity of coal-heavers ! "[1] The cap had a white linen cover as a protection against the rays of the sun.

The 4th and 6th Companies of Bengal Pioneers were spectators of the cavalry battle at Ramnagar but had no part in it. The Chenab now lay between Gough and his quarry, and the problem before the British Commander-in-Chief was how to cross it in the face of a powerful foe with numerous guns. His siege guns reached him on November 25th, and he then decided to detach a force[2] under Major-General Sir Joseph Thackwell with orders to cross the river at either of two fords about 12 miles above Ramnagar and, turning left, to march downstream against Sher Singh's flank while the main British army tried to force a direct crossing under the fire of its heavy guns. If Thackwell was unable to cross at the selected fords he was to march farther upstream to Wazirabad and attempt to gain the right bank at that place.

Thackwell set off after dark on December 1st, while Lieutenant C. S. Paton of the Bengal Engineers went ahead to reconnoitre the fords. Paton returned with the report that both fords were strongly held by the Sikhs, and that they were difficult for guns and impracticable for pontoons because of quicksands near the far bank—opinions which were confirmed later by other Engineers—so Thackwell decided to continue to Wazirabad. He sent forward Captain John Nicholson,[3] his Political Officer, with Baird Smith and Yule of the Engineers, and when he marched into Wazirabad in the afternoon he found that Nicholson and the others had already collected 17 boats and staked out two fords which enabled most of the troops to cross the Chenab during the night. The pontoon train under Crommelin was found to be superfluous and was sent back under escort towards Ramnagar. Thackwell then marched down the right bank, while Gough at Ramnagar began to bombard the Sikh position opposite to him preparatory to an attempt at crossing. The pontoon train halted six miles upstream of the main army and bridged the Chenab on December 3rd, so that one brigade from the left bank was able to reinforce Thackwell during his descent upon the left of the Sikh position. Sher Singh, however, did not remain inactive. Unknown to Gough, he withdrew most of his troops from their position and advanced to meet the isolated force under Thackwell, with the result that on December 3rd a small action was fought at a place called Sadulapur in which some of the Pioneers were involved. The attempt to overwhelm Thackwell having ended in failure, Sher Singh retired northwards to the Jhelum with Thackwell in pursuit. On

---

[1] *The Second Seikh War*, by E. J. Thackwell, p. 59.
[2] One brigade cavalry, three brigades infantry, some artillery, two companies Bengal Pioneers, Pontoon Train.
[3] The hero of the siege of Delhi.

December 8th, Gough crossed the Chenab by an excellent bridge of boats constructed at Ramnagar by Lieutenant C. B. Young[1] of the Bengal Engineers, and shortly afterwards joined hands with Thackwell.

After Sadulapur there was a break in the operations. The Governor-General was anxious about the continued resistance of Multan and the probability that Sher Singh would be reinforced on the Jhelum by Chattar Singh and perhaps by Dost Muhammad, and he practically forbade Gough to advance. The Commander-in-Chief himself was in favour of awaiting the fall of Multan and the arrival of Whish before he risked a general action on the Jhelum, especially as he was having considerable difficulties with supply. Then came news of the capture of Multan City, and, on the 10th, that Chattar Singh had taken Attock and was on his way to reinforce Sher Singh who had already 30,000 men with 62 guns at his disposal. No time was to be lost. Gough advanced to fight the Sikhs at Chilianwala near Rasul on the Jhelum, and with his army marched the four companies of Bengal Pioneers under Tremenheere.

Chilianwala, the "evening battle fought by a brave old man in a passion," was an action forced suddenly upon the British by an attack launched by the Sikhs. It was attended with such heavy losses, and caused such consternation in India and England, that the Home Government ordered the supersession of Lord Gough by Sir Charles Napier from Sind. Only by his skilful tactics at Gujarat did Gough retrieve his reputation. Chilianwala was fought on January 13th, 1849, when the Sikhs were entrenched with their backs to the Jhelum. Gough had reached the vicinity about noon, and, having sent his Engineers forward to reconnoitre, was preparing to camp with the intention of fighting on the 14th. But Sher Singh forestalled him by advancing in force and opening fire, and a furious battle began at one o'clock in the afternoon. The extreme length of the Sikh position made a frontal attack unavoidable; this attack, also, had to be made through dense scrub in which communication was very difficult. The enemy fought courageously, but in the end their right flank was rolled up and they were pressed slowly back towards the river with a loss estimated at 7,000 men. They were saved only from a repetition of Sobraon by the approach of darkness. In this desperate fight there was not much scope or time for engineering, but Tremenheere and his officers, with the 4th, 5th, 6th and 7th Companies of Bengal Pioneers were in the thick of it. Several mistakes were made by Gough's subordinates, particularly in the handling of the cavalry. Though Sher Singh was driven from the field, Gough lost 89 officers, more than 2,300 men, four guns and three regimental

[1] *The Second Seikh War*, by E. J. Thackwell, p. 112. Lieutenant Young became afterwards Major-General Charles Young. Another Young was serving at Multan—2nd-Lieutenant R. Young, B.E., who became Major-General Richard Young.

standards; thus one of the fiercest battles of Indian history brought no more than a Pyrrhic victory to the British.

After Chilianwala, Sher Singh retreated only three miles to an entrenched position near Rasul where he was soon joined by Chattar Singh and his army, fresh from the capture of Attock. Dost Muhammad had advanced to the Indus, and some Afghan cavalry had already reached the Sikhs on the Jhelum. The British had lost so heavily at Chilianwala that Gough dared not move until the division under Whish arrived from Multan. So things remained for a time until, on February 11th, the Sikhs began to march eastwards in the direction of Gujarat to attack the British communications. On the 13th, Cheape arrived from Multan as Chief Engineer to the army and marched with it on the 15th towards Ramnagar, news having been received that the enemy had taken up a position covering the sacred city of Gujarat. By the 20th Gough had diverted his march eastwards towards the Sikh position and had been reinforced by most of the troops from Multan.

The battle of Gujarat, popularly known as "the battle of the guns," was fought on February 21st, 1849. The Sikhs were drawn up in the form of a crescent facing south about a mile to the south of the city. Their right was covered by a dry sandy *nullah*; their left rested on a stream; and their centre, which was held by regular troops, was entrenched behind two fortified villages. Their strength was estimated at 60,000 men with 59 guns, to which Gough could oppose 20,000[1] with 96 guns. Thus, for the first time, the British were superior in artillery. Gough's plan was to penetrate the centre and left of the Sikh position and drive the enemy back on their right, and accordingly he advanced his right and his heavy guns, keeping back his left to deal the *coup-de-grace*. The Sikh artillery were overwhelmed by the British guns early in the battle, and our infantry were able to advance with few casualties. Handled with great skill and boldness, our guns broke down all resistance offered by the Sikh infantry and inflicted enormous losses on them. By one o'clock the position was captured, the enemy streaming in wild flight over the plain and falling by scores beneath the sabres of the cavalry. For 15 miles the pursuit continued, and, at daylight on the 22nd, Major-General Sir W. R. Gilbert was despatched with a strong force to follow the defeated host to the north. The pride of the Khalsa was humbled.

Almost all the Bengal Engineers who fought in the Second Sikh War were present at Gujarat under Brigadier Sir John Cheape—a total of 29 officers.[2] Two Lieutenants of the Bombay Corps were there also.[3] The Bengal Sappers and Pioneers under Siddons were

---
[1] Four brigades of cavalry and four divisions of infantry, with artillery and Sappers and Pioneers.

[2] "Early Indian Campaigns," by Major H. Biddulph, R.E., appearing in *The R.E. Journal*, Vol. XIX, January-June, 1914, p. 105.

[3] W. Kendall and J. W. Playfair (afterwards Major-General John Playfair).

represented by the 2nd and 3rd Companies of Sappers and the 2nd, 3rd, 4th, 5th, 6th and 7th Companies of Pioneers ; and the Bombay Sappers and Miners by the 1st Company of that Corps. Such an array of engineering talent had not been seen since Sobraon. Before the battle the Engineer officers spent their time in reconnoitring the Sikh position, and during it they were engaged with their men in clearing away obstacles to the advance of the guns, for which work they were duly mentioned in despatches. Captain A. Cunningham and Lieutenant C. S. Paton of the Bengal Corps were praised also for their success in bringing up boats from Ramnagar and placing them so that a force on the left bank was able to cross in time to join in the fray.[1]

Major-General Gilbert, with two divisions, including the 1st, 2nd and 3rd Companies of Bengal Sappers and the 1st Company of Bombay Sappers, followed by a pontoon train under Crommelin, pursued the Sikhs to Rawalpindi. The 5th and 6th Companies of Bengal Pioneers joined the column during the march.[2] Sher Singh, Chattar Singh, and the whole Sikh army laid down their arms at Rawalpindi on March 14th, 1849 ; and Gilbert, entering Peshawar a week later after Dost Muhammad had fled through the Khaibar Pass, brought the war to an end. In these final operations Robert Napier was the Chief Engineer, with Alexander Taylor as his adjutant ; and during the march they added to their exploits the construction of a fine bridge across the Indus at the Attock defile. On March 29th, 1849, Lord Dalhousie proclaimed the annexation of the Punjab. "That which Alexander attempted," wrote Gough, " the British Indian Army has accomplished."

Within three years of the grim slaughter of Chilianwala, Sikh soldiers were fighting on the British side in Burma. The term of peace which might have been expected after the conquest of the Punjab was rudely disturbed by the insolence of the Burmese, and the Government of India was entangled in another war before the country had recovered from the strain of the Sikh campaigns. British merchants in Rangoon were insulted, and the captain of a ship was placed in the stocks and fined 900 rupees by the Burmese Governor of the city. In retaliation, Lord Dalhousie demanded the removal of the Burmese official and the payment of £900, which, as some wag remarked, " was the price only of four or five golden spittoons in the palace of Ava." When even this trivial compensation was refused with scorn, the British naval envoy seized a Burmese vessel, the Burmese opened fire, the envoy replied, and in the spring of 1852 the Second Burma War began.

This war was unlike the haphazard affair of 1824–26. Every

---

[1] *A Contemporary Account of the Battle of Gujarat*, by Major-General Sir Alex. Cunningham, appearing in *The R.E. Journal*, Vol. XLI, March-December, 1927, p. 624.
[2] *History and Digest of Service*, 1st K.G.O. *Sappers and Miners*, p. 13.

contingency was foreseen. Tests of the effect of artillery fire on stockades were carried out at Dumdum near Calcutta, and the British troops were trained in escalading. Experiments were made to ascertain the powder charge required to blow down a stockade, and it was found that 200 pounds, properly laid and tamped, would ensure a demolition.[1] Warned by the experiences of the first war, Lord Dalhousie arranged that the expedition to Burma should land well before the beginning of the rainy season; its equipment was carefully scrutinized; its commissariat and transport were properly organized. Scaling ladders were provided, and a good supply of explosives. A fleet of steamers was chartered to navigate the Irrawaddy. Nothing, in fact, was left to chance. The chief command was given to Major-General H. Godwin, who had fought in the first war in Burma, and a force of nearly 6,000 men was collected from Bengal and Madras[2] consisting of two brigades of infantry, five companies of artillery, and " A " and " B " Companies of the Madras Sappers and Miners (under Brevet-Captain J. W. Rundall of the Madras Engineers) who were soon joined near Rangoon by " C " and " E " Companies. The appointment of Chief Engineer was filled by Major Hugh Fraser of the Bengal Corps who brought with him from the Northern Presidency a staff of eight Engineer subalterns, many of whom reached high rank. C. B. Young, H. Drummond, G. A. Craster and W. S. Trevor became Major-Generals, and the last-named gained the Victoria Cross; J. D. Campbell became a Lieut.-General, and A. Fraser and E. C. Sparshott Williams rose to be Generals.[3] The Engineer officers with the Madras Sappers and Miners under Rundall[4] were Lieutenant J. Carpendale, 2nd-Lieutenant (afterwards Lieut.-General) J. Mullins, 2nd-Lieutenant (afterwards Major-General) H. T. Rogers, and 2nd Lieutenants G. Dennison, J. G. Ryves, J. O. Mayne, H. Vaughan and R. F. Oakes. Brigadier Sir John Cheape, the Chief Engineer of Multan and Gujarat, joined the expedition, though not as an Engineer. Excluding Cheape, the total number of Engineer officers with the original force was 18;[5] but the Madras Sappers and Miners had ten infantry subalterns doing duty as Engineers, and consequently the actual strength of the Engineering Department reached the satisfactory total of 28 officers.

Hostilities began with the arrival of General Godwin and the

[1] *The Second Burmese War*, by W. F. B. Laurie, p. 26.
[2] No Bombay troops fought in the Second Burma War. Most of the British units came from Bengal, and most of the Indian units from Madras. No Bengal Sappers and Miners were present.
[3] The eighth subaltern, 2nd-Lieutenant L. Donaldson, was killed in action at the White House Stockade, near Rangoon, on April 12th, 1852.
[4] Captain J. W. Rundall died at Prome on November 12th, 1852. The command of the Madras Sappers then devolved on Lieutenant A. J. Carpendale.
[5] Other Engineers joined in 1853, viz., Lieutenant C. D. Newmarch and Lieutenant (afterwards Sir Henry) Yule from Bengal; also Lieutenant C. V. Wilkieson and 2nd-Lieutenants T. E. Gahagan and A. S. Moberly (afterwards Major-General Arthur Moberly) from Madras.

Bengal Brigade off the mouth of the Rangoon River on April 2nd, 1852. As the Madras Brigade had been delayed, Godwin steamed eastwards with the Bengal Brigade[1] to Moulmein and captured Martaban on the 5th. He then returned to the mouth of the Irrawaddy, met the Madras contingent, and proceeded up the river to Rangoon where, the troops having been landed on the right bank, he marched on April 12th against the defenders of the Shwedagon Pagoda. Rangoon had changed since 1824. A new and strongly-fortified town had sprung up, a mile from the river and about that distance also from the old town. It had a mud wall 16 feet high, surrounded by a ditch and some abattis, and at its northern corner stood its citadel, the great Pagoda; it copied, in fact, the layout of the fortified towns of India and was held by 20,000 Burmese with a number of guns. During his march to the Pagoda, Godwin had to deal with a work called the White House Stockade on his right flank. This he did in two columns supporting a storming party composed of British infantry and some Madras Sappers under Rundall, accompanied by Major Fraser as Chief Engineer. The party came under such heavy fire that the Sappers had to ground their ladders and return it; then, advancing with great bravery, they raised the ladders against the stockade in spite of heavy losses. Three of the Sappers were seen to lift a ladder when four others had already been shot down in the attempt. Here Donaldson was mortally, and Trevor seriously, wounded. The stockade was soon captured, and Godwin, marching on, took the Shwedagon Pagoda with a rush. Fortunately the resistance was feeble, for the defences were powerful and intricate. First there was a ditch, then ten yards of abattis with a palisade in it, then a barrier of a triple row of tree trunks placed vertically followed by another of trees laid horizontally, and finally a gigantic rampart of earth. The Burmese version of the taking of Rangoon stated that more than 1,000 Europeans were killed! This is on a par with the Burmese Governor's report to the King of Ava when the British squadron was first sighted in the Irrawaddy. "English ships have brought foreign soldiers to the mouth of the river," he wrote. "They are my prisoners; cut me some thousands of spans of rope to bind them."[2]

But the Burmese, proud and bombastic, could fight well at times in spite of very poor equipment. Their muskets were mostly condemned English flint-locks, firing a rough ball of mixed lead and iron, beaten into shape. The round shot of their cannon were supplemented by pieces of scrap-iron, necks of bottles, stones and even small brass idols. For hand-to-hand work they used the *dha*,[3] or they fastened a captured bayonet onto a spear handle. The men, however, were always in the pink of condition. They raced in boats,

---
[1] Including "A" and "B" Companies of the Madras Sappers and Miners.
[2] *Our Burmese Wars*, by W. F. B. Laurie, p. 132.
[3] A short square-ended sword with a long wooden handle.

wrestled, rode buffaloes in buffalo-fights, and played their own peculiar game of football with a wicker-work ball. Twenty-five years after the Second Burma War they were playing Rugby football. No wonder that in 1852 they were hard to beat in their native jungles; but beaten they were by trained soldiers, good leadership and proper organization and equipment.

After the fall of Rangoon on April 12th, the Burmese tried unsuccessfully to recapture Martaban. On May 17th Godwin despatched a small expedition westwards to Bassein, and, nine days later, the enemy again attempted without success to retake Martaban. On June 2nd another small expedition was sent north-eastwards to Pegu which was occupied without trouble. It was then handed over to a friendly tribe of Talaings and recaptured from them by the Burmese within a week or two of the withdrawal of the British. In July, a naval flotilla steamed up the Irrawaddy as far as Prome, to reconnoitre for a possible advance in force. These small affairs helped to keep the British force in good spirits during the rains, and detachments of Sappers and Miners took part in all of them. However, despite the loss of the Rangoon coast, the King of Ava remained defiant, so Lord Dalhousie visited Rangoon on July 27th to examine the situation on the spot and then decided to reorganize and reinforce the army in Burma. The result was that, on August 13th, Godwin's command was formed into two divisions,[1] a Bengal Division under Brigadier-General Sir John Cheape and a Madras Division under Brigadier-General S. W. Steele, and orders were issued for an advance up the Irrawaddy on Prome.

All arrangements being completed, Godwin embarked on September 27th, 1852, at the head of one brigade (including a company of Sappers) and occupied Prome with trifling loss on October 9th; he then returned to Rangoon, leaving Cheape in command at Prome. Owing to the unremitting labour of the Sappers at Rangoon, and the splendid work of Major Fraser, "the builder of Rangoon," not only was the town being improved out of recognition but the Shwedagon Pagoda was so strongly fortified that it formed a secure base for operations in any direction. So, on November 18th, Godwin led another small expedition against Pegu, captured it on the 21st, and was back at Rangoon three days later. Hardly was he settled at his base before Pegu was besieged by the enemy, and yet another expedition was necessary to relieve the small garrison of 500 men. Lieutenant J. D. Campbell of the Bengal Engineers, and 40 Madras Sappers under Lieutenant Harris of the infantry, were the only engineering troops in Pegu; but so well did they fortify the place that it held out without difficulty till the relief force arrived on December 14th. Meanwhile Cheape at Prome had repulsed a heavy attack which had been encouraged by his isolation and the weakness

[1] The strength of the reorganized force amounted to about 20,000 men.

of his force. By the end of the year the province of Pegu was annexed and the British were firmly established in a large part of Burma.

The end of the main operations came suddenly. When Godwin visited Prome on January 5th, 1853, he was informed that the enemy had vanished. It appears that a revolution had occurred at Ava, and every Burmese soldier wanted his share of the probable loot. Nothing remained to be done but to march through outlying districts, deal with large gangs of freebooters, and settle the terms of peace. Accordingly a column of 2,000 men under Brigadier-General Steele, including Lieutenant Fraser, B.E., and 70 Madras Sappers, was despatched in January from Martaban up the course of the Sittang River to Shwegyin and so to Toungoo, which surrendered on February 22nd and remained a British outpost. As the route was 240 miles in length and mostly through dense forest, the Sappers had very hard work in clearing a road for the guns.

The final stages of the campaign in Burma are of interest only through the operations of that celebrated Engineer, Brigadier-General Sir John Cheape, against the dacoit leader, Myat-Tun. A naval expedition had met with disaster on February 4th in attempting to round up Myat-Tun and his 7,000 followers in the jungles to the west of Donabyu; so Cheape went to Henzada, marched thence to Donabyu, and left that place on March 7th with 1,000 infantry, a few cavalrymen and guns, and 70 Madras Sappers and Miners under Mullins and Trevor. Striking westwards into the jungles he soon found his way barred by a very wide creek; and here, under fire from the opposite bank, the Sappers assembled and launched two rafts, rowed a covering party across, spanned the obstacle with two cables and then ferried the whole force to the far bank so that Cheape was able to resume his advance.[1] The Sappers had to work at the head of the column under the protection of only a few skirmishers, for a proper advanced guard could not be formed till a road had been cut; more than once they joined in storming a stockade when carrying only axes and *dhas* because their rifles were in carts in the rear. On March 19th, Cheape reached and assaulted Myat-Tun's jungle lair at Kyoukazin, where the Sappers had to cut a track under a heavy fire along the whole length of a huge stockade at a distance of only 40 yards from the face. Trevor was the first to enter the position by a narrow and obstructed path held strongly by the dacoits. Indeed, the Madras Sappers excelled themselves under Mullins and Trevor. " No men," wrote Sir John Cheape, " could have done better or have been more cool and steady under fire."

With the dispersion of Myat-Tun's dacoits, serious fighting came to an end. A proclamation which was issued on June 30th, 1853,

---

[1] *The History of the Madras Engineers and Pioneers*, by Major H. M. Vibart, Vol. II, p. 231.

terminated the Second Burma War, although some time was still occupied in subduing the rebel bands who roamed through the country. As the province of Pegu had been annexed, the Burmese kingdom was shut out from access to the sea except through British territory. No nation could thrive under such a condition, and the natural result was a third war against Burma which began in 1885 in the time of Lord Dufferin.

Soon after the end of the Second Burma War, India was drawn by the Home Government into two overseas expeditions which were not really her concern—the first to Persia, the second to China. The Foreign Office became alarmed at the seizure of Herat by Persia in 1855, and ordered the Governor-General to occupy the island of Kharak and the city and district of Bushire in the Persian Gulf, to induce the Persians to evacuate Herat. A division from India, under Major-General Stalker, captured Bushire on November 29th, 1856, and was joined there by a second division under Major-General Sir James Outram,[1] as Commander-in-Chief of the whole force, on February 1st, 1857. With Stalker were the 2nd and 4th Companies of the Bombay Sappers and Miners, and a select band of Bombay Engineers who were thus compensated for their exclusion from the war in Burma. Most of these officers became so eminent that their names must be recorded. Captain W. R. Dickinson was the senior Bombay Engineer until Captain C. F. North arrived in 1857; the others were Lieutenants J. W. Playfair, J. A. Ballard, W. W. Goodfellow, H. F. Hancock, H. Pym, J. Hills, A. Le Mesurier and C. T. Haig, the last two being in command of the Sapper companies. Playfair attained the rank of General, Goodfellow and Le Mesurier became Lieut.-Generals, and the remainder, except Pym, Major-Generals.

On February 8th, Outram defeated 11,000 Persians at Khush-ab outside Bushire, and then, leaving 3,000 men under Stalker at Bushire, embarked with 4,000 for the Shatt-al-Arab[2] on March 6th. With this force was " B " Company, Madras Sappers and Miners, which had just arrived from India, and also two Bombay companies. " B " Company was under Brevet-Major A. M. Boileau, M.E., assisted by two infantry officers and by 2nd-Lieutenants H. N. D. Prendergast and H. J. G. Gordon of the Madras Engineers, the former of whom became General Sir Harry Prendergast, V.C. Outram occupied Muhammareh at the junction of the Karun River with the Shatt-al-Arab on March 26th, after a plucky reconnaissance by Boileau and other Engineers; and then, with only 300 men in a few steamers, chased the Persians up the Karun to Ahwaz. Meanwhile

---

[1] The same Outram who had been Political Resident at Hyderabad in Sind before Sir Charles Napier's campaign, and who became an outstanding figure in the Indian Mutiny. He was a very keen pigsticker and shot. In 1823-24 he took 74 " first spears " out of 123.

[2] The Euphrates between its junction with the Tigris and its outlet into the Persian Gulf.

the Engineers and Sappers were hard at work in Muhammareh, constructing bridges, making roads, and demolishing the enemy's defences. On April 4th, Outram returned to Muhammareh and was met by the news that peace had been signed with Persia. The campaign was finished; the troops embarked in May for India; and many of them, notably Outram and Havelock (one of Outram's Brigadiers) were soon engaged in the life and death struggle of the Indian Mutiny. The achievements of the Engineers and Sappers in that critical time will form the subject of the next chapter, and their work in numerous frontier expeditions will be recorded later; but the Mutiny and the frontier expeditions were affairs chiefly of northern India, and it was on excursions such as those to Burma, Persia and China that most of the Madras Engineers saw active service and made their reputations.

Since the end of the first war in 1842, China had been very unsettled. The Treaty of Nanking was ignored, and affairs reached such a state in 1857 that an expedition was despatched from England to uphold British interests in the Far East, but it did not reach its destination because the troops were diverted to India to assist in quelling the Mutiny. At the end of the year, however, the British and French troops in China stormed and captured Canton, and a treaty of peace was signed at Tientsin in June, 1858. It proved to be of no more value than the Treaty of Nanking. The Chinese barred the mouth of the Peiho, the direct communication from the Gulf of Chihli (Pechili) to Peking, and repulsed a naval attempt to force a passage; so the British Government resolved to send a military expedition of two infantry divisions and a cavalry brigade to China to advance on Peking in co-operation with the French, and the Government of India was directed to assist. Lieut.-General Sir Hope Grant, who was selected to command the British force, had earned a great reputation in the Indian Mutiny; and his Divisional Commanders, Major-Generals Sir John Michel and Sir Robert Napier, were sound strategists and capable leaders.

It is natural, of course, that the interest of Engineers should centre chiefly in the work of the 2nd Division under the famous Napier, who was fresh from his triumphs at Lucknow and in Central India. With his usual care he superintended at Calcutta every detail of the supply and equipment of the Bengal portion of his division before it embarked, and to this may be attributed largely the success of his operations. No Engineer officers from Bombay embarked for China, and only one from Bengal other than Napier—Lieutenant-Colonel (afterwards Major-General) W. W. Greathed. The only Sapper and Miner units in the campaign were " A " and " K " Companies of the Madras Corps under 2nd-Captain (afterwards Major-General) J. H. M. S. Stewart, with Lieutenants H. J. G. Gordon,[1] D. H. Trail and

---

[1] Drowned in China on July 11th, 1860.

A. J. Filgate, all of the Madras Engineers,[1] the Company Commanders being Captains Dakeyne and Swanston of the Madras Infantry. All the engineering troops with the army in China were brigaded together under Lieutenant-Colonel (afterwards Major-General) G. F. Mann, R.E. To Michel's division were allotted the 10th, 23rd and half of the 8th Companies of the Royal Engineers; and to Napier's division, "A" and "K" Companies of the Madras Sappers and Miners.

After some delay in concentration, the combined British and French forces voyaged up the China coast and landed on August 1st, 1860, on the south bank of the Paitang River, to avoid having to force a passage past the Taku Forts which guarded the mouth of the Peiho ten miles to the south. "The disembarkation," writes Fortescue,[2] " took place on a bank of deep mud, and the General led the way with his trousers, boots and socks slung over his sword, which he carried over his shoulder, and nothing left on him but a large white helmet, a dirty serge jacket and a very narrow margin of grey flannel shirt below it." The whole force followed in this airy dress. It must have been an impressive sight! On August 12th, Hope Grant and the French General, Montauban, occupied Sinho, and two days later captured Tangku, which established them in rear of the Taku Forts lying on both banks of the Peiho. Hope Grant decided, on the recommendation of Napier and against the wishes of Montauban, to attack the forts on the northern bank, and did so on August 21st after a bridge of boats had been thrown across the river at Tangku. Napier's division led the assault, with Michel's in reserve. The defences of the first fort were very strong—a dry ditch followed in turn by some abattis, a wet ditch, a forest of bamboo spikes, another wet ditch, more spikes and lastly a stout wall with embrasures. An attempt to use pontoons having failed, Napier enquired whether the Royal Engineers and Sappers could arrange a crossing of the wet ditches by escalading ladders alone. They undertook to do so, and, advancing under a heavy fire, some of them jumped into the first ditch. There, by supporting some ladders above their heads, they enabled other men to cross, carrying bamboo ladders with which they escaladed the obstacles and defences,[3] Trail being one of the first to enter the fort. The French crossed by their own ladder bridges and the fort was soon taken. The second fort on the northern bank fell shortly afterwards and then all the southern forts. Napier had his field-glass shot out of his hand, his sword-hilt

---

[1] The East India Company had ceased to exist, and the Engineer officers of all three Corps were soon afterwards absorbed into the Royal Engineers. The amalgamation of the Royal Engineers and the Engineers of the Company's armies took place on April 1st, 1862.

[2] *A History of the British Army*, by the Hon. J. W. Fortescue, Vol. XIII, p. 408.

[3] "Deeds of the Royal Engineers," appearing in *The R.E. Journal*, Vol. XXV January-June, 1917, p. 212.

broken, three bullet holes through his coat and one in his boot.[1]

Tientsin fell at the end of August to Michel's division, and Napier then advanced to that place. Owing to bad weather the march was not resumed for a fortnight, but September 13th found the two divisions confronting a large Chinese army at Chang-kia-wan. A battle took place there on the 18th in which 4,000 British routed 20,000 of the enemy who fled to Tangchao within ten miles of Peking. Defeated again near Tangchao, the Chinese gave up hope, and the British Commander-in-Chief reached and occupied the Summer Palace at Peking on October 7th, receiving the surrender of the capital six days later. On October 18th the Summer Palace was destroyed by fire,[2] and the treaty of 1858 having been ratified, the troops left Peking on November 7th. Within another ten days the Madras Sappers and Miners watched the coast of China sink below the horizon. As the Governor of Madras remarked on their return, they had well sustained the ancient reputation of their Corps.

[1] Obituary notice of Field-Marshal Lord Napier of Magdala, appearing in *The R.E. Journal*, Vol. 20, 1890, p. 65.
[2] The Palace was destroyed because the Chinese had tortured British and Indian prisoners. It was filled, to the value of some four millions sterling, with treasures of ivory, carved wood, jewels, porcelain, silk and gold. Many valuables were taken by the French and a few by the British, notably a magnificent carved throne presented to the R.E. Headquarter Mess at Chatham by Captain C. G. Gordon, R.E., of the 8th Company, who became Major-General Charles Gordon, the hero of Khartoum.

STORMING OF THE KHOONEE BOORJ BREACH, MOOLTAN.

From Dunlop's *Sketches during the Siege of Mooltan*.

CHAPTER XVII.

THE INDIAN MUTINY: ROORKEE, MEERUT AND DELHI.

DURING the afternoon of May 11th, 1857, an unaddressed telegram flashed from Delhi to Army Headquarters at Ambala. "We must leave office," it read.[1] "All the bungalows are being burnt down by the Sepoys of Meerut. They came in this morning. We are off. Don't call to-day. Mr. C. Todd[2] is dead, we think. He went out this morning and has not returned yet. We heard that nine Europeans were killed. Good-bye." So ran the first warning of a cataclysm which ended the career of the East India Company, wrecked the Bengal Army, and sank Northern India for two years in a welter of destruction. Tragedy followed on tragedy. The fighting was bitter and to the death. For a time the fate of the British Empire in India trembled in the balance.

The causes of this terrible struggle were many. Among them were the annexation of the province of Oudh and the consequent loss of certain privileges by classes from which the Bengal Army was recruited; the astounding and evident weakness of the British garrison in India and its faulty distribution;[3] foolish suspicions that the Government had secret designs against the caste and religion of the sepoys; and finally the belief that the cartridges for the new Enfield rifle were purposely greased with the fat of pigs and oxen which would cause defilement alike to Muhammadans and Hindus.[4] The discipline of the Bengal Army had sunk very low, and, when the soldiers mutinied, every ruffian in the bazaars joined them for the sake of loot. It was fortunate indeed that the Hindu mutineers soon began to suspect the designs of the Muhammadans, that many rebels lost heart after the siege of Delhi, and that the inhabitants of the Punjab, Bombay and Madras remained mostly loyal to England.

The conflict may be divided into three phases.[5] First, the *Vital*

---

[1] *The Indian Mutiny in Perspective*, by Lieut.-General Sir G. MacMunn, p. 58.
[2] Telegraph Master at Delhi.
[3] In the regular Indian Army of 238,000 men, there were only 38,000 British soldiers in 1857. Of British infantry, three battalions were in Persia and three in Burma; twelve were in the Punjab, and only ten battalions in the remainder of India. There were no British troops in Delhi, Benares, Mirzapur, Allahabad, Fyzabad and Bareilly, and only weak garrisons in Meerut, Agra, Cawnpore and Lucknow. Between Benares and Calcutta there was only one British battalion at Dinapore.
[4] The rumour came to the sepoys from workmen employed in the ammunition factory, and an official denial served only to confirm the suspicions of the soldiers. It was found afterwards that, through incredible carelessness, such fat had actually been used.
[5] *The Sepoy Revolt*, by Lieut.-General McLeod Innes, p. 131.

Struggle, in which, during the months of July, August and September, 1857, our countrymen, unaided by help from England, were fighting for their very existence at Delhi, in the Residency at Lucknow and elsewhere. This phase ended with the capture of Delhi. Then the *Decisive Contest,* from October, 1857, to March, 1858, when they drove the rebels from Lucknow and Jhansi with the assistance of British reinforcements. Lastly, the *Suppression of the Revolt,* during the remainder of 1858 and in 1859, by mobile columns operating in various directions. In the five theatres of mutiny—the Punjab, Delhi, Oudh, the Southern and the Eastern—the Punjab escaped serious warfare, and not only so but it became the base of the operations against Delhi and the source of the new army which helped the British to stamp out all resistance. In Oudh the fighting lasted from beginning to end, but it was of secondary importance to that at Delhi, where the fate of India depended on the issue. The operations in the Southern and Eastern areas of mutiny occupied the later stages of the struggle. Small mutinies began near Calcutta early in 1857, and the unrest spread northwards and westwards till a vast organization had been established for a general rising of the Bengal Army towards the end of May. The mutineers at Meerut anticipated the date and broke loose on May 10th; then, marching to Delhi, they raised the whole of Oudh and Rohilkhand in open rebellion. Meanwhile in the Punjab, a band of political officers formed by Lord Dalhousie—John Lawrence, Edwardes, Montgomery and John Nicholson—were hard at work. At Peshawar, Ferozepore, Mianmir and other places the Indian regiments were rapidly disarmed. A strong movable column under Nicholson was formed to march against any insurgents, and the insurrection was nipped in the bud. Not so, however, in the North-West Provinces. At Lucknow, four regiments mutinied on May 30th, and were followed soon by others at Aligarh, Fategarh, Jhansi, Azamgarh, Bareilly, Fyzabad, Shahjahanpur, Moradabad and Sitapur. Two regiments rose at Benares on June 4th, and then four regiments at Cawnpore and one at Allahabad where there was a great arsenal. Meanwhile in Rajputana and Malwa, six regiments at Mhow, Nimach and Nasirabad joined the revolt and marched, as did the others, towards Delhi where all knew that the vital struggle would be fought.

At Meerut on the evening of Sunday, May 10th, as the British troops were parading to march to church, the 3rd Light Cavalry broke loose, galloped to the gaol, and released 1,200 prisoners, including 85 of their comrades who had been sentenced to long terms of imprisonment because they had refused to handle the new Enfield cartridge. Two Bengal Infantry regiments followed suit, and joined by the scum of the bazaar, burned their lines; they set fire to the private bungalows around, and killed eight British officers, two ladies, three children and a number of other Europeans. Darkness came, and for a short time the night resounded with the cries of victims, the roar of burning houses, the yells of the mutineers and the reports of their muskets. And what, it may be asked, were the British soldiers of the garrison—the 6th Dragoon Guards (Carabineers), the 60th Rifles and the Artillery—doing at this crisis? They turned out and made for the native lines, only to find the mutineers gone.[1] Then, under the orders of Major-General S. H. Hewitt, an officer of 50 years' service, they returned under Brigadier Archdale Wilson to their cantonments, and prepared to defend them against the mutineers who, they imagined, might be lurking in the groves around Meerut. No pursuit was attempted. During the night the mutineers streamed away to Delhi, which the 3rd Cavalry reached soon after dawn on the 11th, followed rapidly by the native infantry. There they freed the cut-throats in the gaols and proceeded to massacre every European in the city with revolting barbarity. Then it was that the telegram was sent to the Punjab. The cantonments outside Delhi were so far untouched, and the main guard at the Kashmir Gate of the city was still in British hands, though the loyalty of the native guard was doubtful. Brigadier-General Graves led his sepoys from the cantonments to the Kashmir Gate, where unfortunately they met some of the mutinous cavalry from Meerut and went over to them. Lieutenant Willoughby and eight other Europeans defended an expense magazine near the gate for three hours and then blew it up, regardless of the danger to themselves.[2] The mutineers stormed the main guard from which a party of officers,[3] ladies and children escaped across the ditch and, after terrible privations, made their way on foot to Meerut and other places. Delhi was lost, the East India Company had temporarily ceased to rule, and Bahadur Shah[4] had regained his throne. These were the events which heralded the entry of the Engineers and Sappers and Miners into the conflict.

In May, 1857, eight of the twelve companies of Bengal Sappers and Miners were at their headquarters at Roorkee under Captain Edward Fraser, Bengal Engineers, as Commandant. The 5th Company was

---

[1] *The Indian Mutiny in Perspective*, by Lieut.-General Sir G. MacMunn, p. 40.

[2] A graphic account of this supremely gallant exploit may be read in *The Tale of the Great Mutiny*, by W. H. Fitchett, pp. 40–44. Conductor Scully, who fired the train, and four others, vanished with hundreds of mutineers in the holocaust, but Willoughby and three companions escaped alive. This magazine stood within the city walls about 600 yards from the Kashmir Gate and was packed with guns, rifles and ammunition. The main magazine was situated some three miles up the river. Unfortunately it was not destroyed by the British on May 11th, and the mutineers used its contents against them.

[3] Including Lieutenant P. Salkeld, Bengal Engineers.

[4] The old Mughal Emperor whom the mutineers agreed to recognize as their new sovereign.

at Attock, the 6th at Peshawar and two others elsewhere.[1] The Corps at this time numbered some 1,300 men and was a fine body of trained engineering soldiers most of whom, if properly handled, would have been of inestimable value at Delhi and Lucknow. In spite of rather harsh treatment, more than 500 of the Sappers remained loyal, or nearly 40 per cent. of the whole number, including the companies who were not in the thick of the mutiny. The senior officer present in Roorkee when the mutiny began was Major Richard Baird Smith of the Bengal Engineers, then Superintendent of Canals, North-West Provinces. "It was on the 12th at daybreak," he writes,[2] "that I received the first intimation of the Meerut Mutiny and Massacre. About an hour before, Fraser, the Commandant, had received an express message from the General at Meerut ordering him to proceed with the Regiment[3] by forced marches to that place as the Native Regiments were in open revolt. I immediately suggested the Ganges Canal route instead of forced marches, and, as Fraser agreed, I had boats equal to the transport of 1,000 men ready within six hours. Just as the Corps, 713 strong, was starting another express came to say that two companies were to be left for the protection of Roorkee so that finally 500 men moved. I sent off the same morning an express to the Commandant (Major Reid) of the little Goorkhas at Deyrah (Dehra Dun), begging him to march on Roorkee where I would have another fleet ready for him in a day or two. He came with his almond-eyed Tartars and off they went too. Then came the news of the Delhi massacre and it became necessary for me to provide for the security of our little community here."

With the six companies of Bengal Sappers and Miners who embarked at Roorkee on May 12th on their voyage to the neighbourhood of Meerut, 65 miles to the south, were Captain E. Fraser (Commandant), Lieutenants F. R. Maunsell (Adjutant) and M. G. Geneste (Interpreter and Quartermaster) and 2nd-Lieutenants J. U. Champain, F. L. Tandy, D. Ward, E. T. Thackeray and J. M. McNeile, all of the Bengal Engineers ;[4] also Surgeon-Major Turnbull as Medical Officer, and 45 British non-commissioned officers of the Sappers and Miners. On the morning of the second day the fleet met a European driving furiously along the canal bank in a buggy. He would not stop but shouted that the mutineers were cutting throats like mad in Meerut and burning houses. Rowing hard the Sappers reached Sardhana, eight miles from Meerut, on the afternoon of the 14th, and

[1] When six companies left Roorkee for Meerut, two only remained in Roorkee. These eight companies, with those at Attock and Peshawar, make a total of ten companies. Yet there were *twelve* companies in the Corps (*vide Bengal Army List*, 1857, and the *History and Digest of Service, 1st K.G.O. Bengal Sappers and Miners*, pp. 17 and 25).
[2] Baird Smith to C. E. Norton. Letter dated May 30th, 1857, quoted in an article entitled "Baird Smith Papers," appearing in *The R.E. Journal*, Vol. XIX, January–June, 1914, p. 233.
[3] The Corps of Sappers and Miners.
[4] *Two Indian Campaigns*, by Colonel E. T. Thackeray, R.E., p. 3.

having landed their stores, marched to the cantonments on the following day. They found the place in a state of semi-siege, and themselves the object of the most profound suspicion. They entered Meerut between the Carabineers and the 60th Rifles drawn up on either side, and with the Artillery standing ready to their guns. However, they still retained their ammunition as Fraser had promised them that they should. But on the morning of the 16th, after two of the companies had marched out to work, Fraser changed his mind. Influenced, perhaps, by the arguments of the Meerut officers, and without explaining his reason to the men, he ordered the removal of the ammunition to a safer place although advised by Maunsell not to do so. The men of the four companies who were present suspected treachery and some of them stopped the carts. Fraser abused them, on which an Afghan Sapper shot him in the back, another killed a brave Havildar who tried to save him, and Maunsell escaped under a heavy fire. The mutinous Sappers then broke and fled from the cantonment pursued by a troop of the Carabineers and some Horse Artillery. Fifty of them were rounded up and exterminated, but the remainder escaped to Delhi. So, through an apparent breach of faith, the greater part of four companies of the Bengal Sappers and Miners joined the mutineers.

On the same morning, the two remaining companies were at work in other parts of the station. One, under Thackeray, was dismantling some old walls on the Delhi side of Meerut in anticipation of a possible attack from the south. " A little after 3 o'clock," writes Thackeray,[1] " my attention was attracted by the sound of bugles in the direction of the cantonment, and a native trooper of the 3rd Cavalry galloped down the road where my sappers were working. He was in uniform, fully armed, and he gesticulated and pointed in the direction of Delhi. I saw that many of the men had laid down their tools and had run to the piles of muskets. Before any order could be given they were running along the road following the trooper to Delhi. I then ordered the bugler to sound the assembly and by dint of threats and expostulations we[2] induced thirty-six men to fall in. I ordered the little detachment to march to the lines and before proceeding far we were joined by twenty-eight men who had finally made up their minds to rejoin. Lieutenant David Ward had on the same morning been sent out with a party of Sappers by Captain Fraser to execute some entrenching work on one side of the station. This party[3] remained faithful, and Ward brought them back to the lines." The remnant of Thackeray's company was met by a squadron of Carabineers and marched back to the lines with the cavalry in front and

---

[1] E. T. Thackeray to his brother F. St. J. Thackeray. Letter dated May 18th, 1857, quoted in " A Subaltern in the Indian Mutiny," by Colonel C. B. Thackeray, R.A., appearing in *The R.E. Journal*, Vol. XLIV, pp. 454–456.
[2] One Serjeant-Major and three British N.C.O.s were with Thackeray.
[3] One company.

rear. When the companies had been formed up on parade and Maunsell was about to dismiss them, he heard a shout of "Look out, sir," from Serjeant-Major Stuart. Noticing that one of the men was fingering his carbine, he instantly gave the order, "Fours left. Quick march," and before the men had realized his purpose they were in the Artillery lines under the loaded guns and rifles of the whole British garrison and were quietly disarmed. Thus Maunsell saved a remnant of his Corps at Meerut from open mutiny and disgrace.

Meanwhile, at the little station of Roorkee, Baird Smith took precautions for the safety of the British community. On May 15th he had been ordered to assume military command of the place and to send one of the two remaining companies of Sappers and Miners, with a convoy of stores, to Ambala. He decided to collect the 200 European and Eurasian men, women and children[1] in Roorkee within the walled enclosure of the Canal Foundry Workshops on the left bank of the Ganges Canal overlooking a bridge leading to the native city. Among the refugees only 90 were males fit to bear arms, and of these only 30 were trained soldiers; the others were mostly clerks or subordinates of the Thomason Civil Engineering College[2] which lies close to the cantonment. The soldiers were students of the college, and each had a carbine and 30 rounds of ammunition, these weapons and three old Sikh guns forming the whole available armament. Baird Smith garrisoned the Canal Workshops on May 14th, despatched Captain H. Drummond, B.E.,[3] Lieutenant Bingham of the College staff, and some British non-commissioned officers to the Sapper lines to keep order among the men and to live there with them, and sent to the lines for more ammunition and powder which arrived safely though not without protests from the Sappers. On the 16th came news of the Delhi massacres, so on that night the whole European community, except Drummond and Bingham and their subordinates, moved into the Workshops. To show his confidence in the Indian troops, Baird Smith next placed a strong Sapper guard in the hall of the College under Lieutenant W. F. Fulford, B.E., explaining to the men that it was necessary to secure Roorkee against marauding bands. The Sappers remained well disciplined and respectful under this tactful handling, and the Workshops were soon held by 90 armed Europeans and Eurasians with three guns in position to sweep the approaches. On the same day the Sapper company destined for Ambala marched during the morning from Roorkee to Sikandarpur on the road to Saharanpur. It was commanded by Lieutenant

[1] Including the wives of six British officers and N.C.O.s and their five children.
[2] Founded by Mr. James Thomason, Lieutenant-Governor of the North-West Provinces, in 1847, the first Principal being Lieutenant R. Maclagan, Bengal Engineers. Thirty-nine officers of the Royal Engineers have served on the staff of this college, seven of whom have held the post of Principal. The college is still the leading engineering institution of India.
[3] Working under Baird Smith on the Ganges Canal.

R. C. B. Pemberton, B.E., who had with him Lieutenant W. Jeffreys, B.E., and three British Warrant and non-commissioned officers.

At about noon a messenger arrived from Meerut in the Sapper lines at Roorkee with an exaggerated tale that the whole of the six companies at Meerut had been destroyed by grape from the British guns. Immediately there was an uproar; the women wailed and there was such excitement among the men that a mutiny seemed imminent. The messenger then rode on to Sikandarpur and told the same tale to Pemberton's Sappers who thereupon marched back towards Roorkee, taking the Europeans with them unharmed and allowing them to join their countrymen in the Workshops soon after their arrival. Meanwhile Drummond, Bingham and the British non-commissioned officers who were with them, were recalled by Baird Smith from the Sapper lines and concentrated in the Workshops. The approach of Pemberton's company was awaited with great anxiety. If the men intended no harm they would diverge to their right to cross the canal by the Ganeshpur bridge leading directly to their lines, and it was with much relief that Baird Smith learnt that the company had turned off towards that bridge. On May 19th at daybreak, having heard that many of the Sappers had left the station, Baird Smith sent a party under Captain Robert Maclagan, B.E., Principal of the Thomason College, to clear the Sapper lines. Maclagan found only 50 men remaining there who had been roughly handled because of their loyalty. The rest had decamped. Some crossed the Ganges and wandered to Moradabad, where they were made prisoners, disarmed, and turned adrift by loyal troops; others went to Delhi to join the active mutiny. Having avoided bloodshed at Roorkee by his fine handling of the situation, Baird Smith devoted himself to putting down unrest in the surrounding country and strengthening the defences of the Canal Workshops. Maclagan produced *The Roorkee Garrison Gazette*, a small paper designed to prevent undue alarm and despondency. So the little station remained quiet and, on June 27th, Baird Smith started for Delhi on his appointment as Chief Engineer of the besieging force. These events at Meerut and Roorkee explain why that force had so few trained Sappers and Miners. No Bombay or Madras Sappers and Miners took part in the siege and capture of Delhi, and only 129 Indian officers, non-commissioned officers and men of the Bengal Sappers and Miners.[1] Of the Engineer officers, all were Bengal Engineers except Lieutenant J. Walker of the Bombay Corps.

The Indian Mutiny spread so rapidly that Lord Canning,[2] the Governor-General, sent urgent messages for reinforcements from Ceylon, Bombay and Madras, arranging also that some British troops who were on their way from England to China should be landed

---

[1] *History and Digest of Service, 1st K.G.O. Sappers and Miners*, p. 25.
[2] Lord Canning succeeded Lord Dalhousie in 1856.

LIEUT.-COLONEL RICHARD BAIRD SMITH,
BENGAL ENGINEERS.

instead at Calcutta and sent up-country. General George Anson, the Commander-in-Chief in India, came down to Ambala from Simla on May 15th, and tried to mobilize a force for an immediate advance on Delhi. But there were no siege guns in Ambala nor transport for his stores, and it was not till the 25th that he was able to move southwards after ordering the troops from Meerut and a small siege train from Ludhiana to meet him at Baghpat, near Delhi. He marched to Karnal, and as he died there of cholera on May 26th, the command devolved on Major-General Sir Henry Barnard. On the following day Brigadier Archdale Wilson[1] led the troops from Meerut towards Delhi to join hands with Barnard, among them being the loyal Bengal Sappers and Miners. Reaching the left bank of the Hindan River near Ghaziuddin-Nagar[2] on the 30th, he found a body of mutineers in position on the far bank at a place where a suspension bridge spanned the shrunken stream. In the British camp, 14 Engineer officers lay during the morning in one single-fly tent. The heat was so intense that they wrapped wet towels round their heads and sheltered them under one camp table.[3] At three o'clock the fight began and the mutineers were driven off, only to return on the following day to be repulsed once more. The 2nd Gurkhas under Major Reid arrived on June 1st, and on the 5th Archdale Wilson began a flank march northwestwards to join Barnard's column at Alipur, near the battlefield of Panipat on the Jumna. The columns met on June 7th, after a siege train of eight 18-pounders, four 8-inch howitzers, four 8-inch mortars and twelve $5\frac{1}{2}$-inch mortars had come in from Ludhiana. At the head of 3,500 men, Barnard marched on the 8th to attack the enemy, who were strongly entrenched at Badli-ki-Serai, four miles north of Delhi. He routed them, took 13 guns, and pushing rapidly on, reached and cleared the famous Delhi Ridge on which he established his piquets and then camped behind its western slope.

Modern Delhi is well known, but it may be well to describe briefly the appearance of the city and its surroundings in 1857.[4] The fortifications were nearly seven miles in circuit, of which about two miles lay along the right bank of the Jumna facing eastwards and the remainder on the northern, western and southern land fronts. The northern front, nearly one mile in length, extended from the Water Bastion near the river, past the Kashmir Gate, to the Mori Bastion which lay within a few hundred yards of the southern end of the Ridge. The British attack was limited to this front because they had not sufficient men for a more extensive investment. The western front ran from the Mori Bastion by the Kabul Gate, the Burn Bastion and the Lahore Gate, to the Ajmer Gate—a distance of nearly two

---

[1] General Hewitt had relinquished his command.
[2] The present Ghaziabad, about ten miles from Delhi, where there is a large railway junction.
[3] *Two Indian Campaigns*, by Colonel E. T. Thackeray, R.E., p. 14.
[4] A plan of Delhi is included in this chapter opposite p. 346.

miles; while the southern front, which included the Turkman and Delhi Gates, stretched from the Ajmer Gate to the river-bank. About the middle of the river front stood the King's Palace (Delhi Fort), an enclosure with gigantic battlements sheltering some of the most exquisite palaces of marble and red sandstone to be found in India, but useless against artillery fire. From its north-east face projected the ancient Pathan fort of Salimgarh, whose guns flanked the river line and defended the bridge of boats which carried the road to Ghaziabad, Meerut and Roorkee. The city wall was about 16 feet high and 11 feet wide at the top, and on it was a loopholed parapet wall eight feet in height and three feet thick. It was flanked by small bastions at intervals and by a few towers[1] for single guns. The curtains were too narrow to carry any but the lightest guns, so all heavy artillery was concentrated by the enemy in the bastions, each of which could mount from nine to twelve heavy guns. At the foot of the city wall was a berm[2] from 15 to 25 feet wide; then came a vertical drop into the ditch of about eight feet; then a width of 20 to 30 feet of dry ditch, outside which rose a sloping counterscarp whose crest was 20 feet above the bottom, followed by a short glacis.[3] The only outwork was one in front of the Lahore Gate. The fortifications had been repaired and improved a few years earlier by Major Robert Napier who little dreamt that so many of his fellow Engineers would suffer and die before them. All the roads in the city, except the Chandni Chauk leading from the Lahore Gate to the King's Palace, were narrow and winding, and the only clear space within the walls was in the north-east corner near the Kashmir Gate. The highest point was crowned by the great Muhammadan mosque, the Jama Masjid,[4] whose domes and minarets still overlook the city. Such was Delhi in 1857. The British could do no more than attack one-seventh of its huge perimeter.

Running approximately northwards for a distance of four miles from a point half a mile west of the Mori Bastion was the Ridge, never more than 90 feet high, bare, rugged and formed of quartz rock. A worse locality for building defensive works could hardly be found for there was no earth on it. It lay, however, across the route to Karnal and the Punjab from which the British drew their reinforcements and supplies, and it covered their camp from direct assault. When General Barnard occupied the Ridge on June 8th he established a chain of posts along its southern half for a distance of more than a mile; the northern part was too far from Delhi to need attention. The key of his position was Hindu Rao's House, a large empty building, well constructed and close to several good roads; this was held throughout the siege by the Gurkhas under Reid and formed the

---

[1] " Martello " towers.
[2] A flat space (usually at ground level) between the wall and the ditch.
[3] Outer slope to ground level.
[4] Completed by the Emperor Shah Jahan in 1658.

extreme right of the line of defence. Other conspicuous points which were occupied were the "Observatory," an old building of Hindu architecture, the "Mosque," a massive Pathan structure, and, on the extreme left, "Flagstaff Tower," which was a good post of observation. An excellent macadamized road connected all these points. The triangular area between the city, the Jumna, and the Ridge was dotted with European bungalows standing in walled gardens, and was intersected by a number of deep ravines, overgrown with brushwood and bordered by trees, which were the natural drainage channels from the Ridge towards the river. One ravine in particular, running almost parallel to the northern wall of the city and less than half a mile from it, should be noticed, for it became the covered approach to the breaching batteries.[1] Near its left bank, and more than half-way from the Ridge to the river, lay Ludlow Castle ;[2] and close to its outfall was a summer palace of the Mughal Emperors known as the Kudsia Bagh. Between this palace and the city wall, and less than 200 yards from the latter, stood the "Custom House" with several outbuildings. Farther upstream on the river-bank was Metcalfe House[3] with stables, a cow-house, large grounds and many trees. It will be seen that this area offered great facilities for an attack on Delhi, provided that it could be occupied without heavy loss, and that, having been occupied, a good field of fire could be cleared. Everything depended on careful preliminary reconnaissance, complete secrecy, good organization and rapid work.

The weakest point of the British position on the Ridge was its exposed right flank, so close to the Mori Bastion and with the suburbs of Kishanganj and Paharipur and the village of Sabzi Mandi on its right and right-rear. Some protection might be afforded to this flank by the Delhi or Western Jumna Canal, and in rear by the canal or "cut" from the Najafgarh *Jhil*,[4] a drainage channel with a rapid stream which passed under an aqueduct of the Western Jumna Canal and so into the Jumna ; but the canal and the drainage channel were both crossed by several bridges, and while these existed the Ridge was open to close attack with artillery from the right flank and rear. By operating in strength to the west of the Ridge, the huge masses of the enemy could easily have forced Barnard to retire towards Karnal to save his line of communication. Fortunately the mutineers never realized this fact. So much for the British position on the Ridge. We turn now to the engineering resources for the so-called siege.

At first the cadre of Engineers consisted of 18 officers headed by Major John Laughton, B.E., as Chief Engineer. Laughton had been

[1] This ravine is marked "Dry Nullah" on the plan of Delhi included in this chapter.
[2] Now the Delhi Club.
[3] The fine residence of Sir Theophilus Metcalfe, Commissioner of Delhi. It was packed with art treasures which were destroyed by the rebels.
[4] Swamp.

a highly unpopular[1] Superintending Engineer in the Lahore Circle of the Department of Public Works, till through influence he was ordered on active service. He arrived at the front accompanied by a Persian wife, whose belongings were carried on some 20 camels and ten carts.[2] *Apropos* of this officer, Baird Smith writes :[3] " During the long month that had elapsed between the dismal catastrophe at Meerut and the triumphant establishment of the British Force on the Ridge, it seems incredible that no plan of operations had been provided. The provision of such a plan was, as a matter of course, the special duty of the Chief Engineer, but this Officer seems to have abdicated his functions and to have left his work to be done by irresponsible juniors or officers of other arms, or by anyone who was willing to do it. From Major Laughton, Sir Henry Barnard could obtain no definite opinions whatsoever." Fortunately Laughton was removed from his command and his errors were forgotten in the admiration excited by the capacity of Baird Smith and the exploits of Alexander Taylor and other Engineers. The original Engineer Brigade before Delhi was absurdly inadequate. Three small companies of Bengal Sappers and Miners, each of about 40 men, under Maunsell as both Commandant and Adjutant, and about 450 unarmed labourers called " Pioneers "—such were the rank and file of the Engineer Brigade.[4] The Brigade-Major was Lieutenant G. T. Chesney, B.E. Laughton was the only officer above the rank of Lieutenant. The equipment consisted of perhaps 600 *phaorahs*,[5] half that number of pickaxes, and a miscellaneous collection of tools from the local bazaars which furnished also the only engineering materials. With 21 heavy guns and mortars, 12 Coehorns,[6] 22 field-guns, very little ammunition and less than 4,000 men, General Barnard sat down in the terrific heat of June to besiege 9,000 trained soldiers and as many more irregulars, supplied with twice as many guns and unlimited ammunition, in a fortified city which he could not encircle. His communications were open to attack ; reinforcements were slow in coming and small in numbers ; his force dwindled every day from cholera, dysentery and sunstroke while his enemy increased daily in strength. As was usual, the whole direction of the siege operations was left in the hands of the Engineers who acted as

---

[1] " Laughton, our favourite in the Corps ! " sarcastically remarks Lieutenant A. M. Lang, B.E., his assistant in the Punjab. (See " The Diary and Letters of A. M. Lang," appearing in *The Journal of the Society for Army Historical Research*, Vol. IX, April, 1930, p. 84.)

[2] *Life of General Sir Alex Taylor*, by A. C. Taylor, Vol. I, p. 191 (footnote).

[3] *Richard Baird Smith*, by Colonel H. M. Vibart, R.E., p. 29. Baird Smith's original Engineer Diary of the Siege of Delhi, his personal diaries and reports, and the original rough tracing of the city, which was issued to John Nicholson for the assault, are in the R.E. Museum, Brompton Barracks, Chatham ; also the letters sent by General Wilson to Baird Smith during the siege, and Baird Smith's final despatch after the capture of Delhi.

[4] *Two Indian Campaigns*, by Colonel E. T. Thackeray, R.E., p. 23.

[5] Native digging implements.

[6] Light mortars of 5·5-inch or 4·4-inch calibre, named after their inventor, a Dutchman.

general staff officers rather than mere technical advisers. Who will not pity General Barnard in his precarious situation at the mercy of an inefficient Chief Engineer ? In June and July, 1857, the British were not besieging Delhi: they were themselves besieged on the Ridge.

Judged by modern standards, there was nothing very remarkable in the engineering work executed at Delhi. Alexander Taylor tried to construct and arm a great battery in the course of a single night. He failed to do so. The demolition of the Kashmir Gate was heroic, but a small affair. Our admiration is excited more by the unquenchable spirit which the Engineers showed in the face of great hardships than by what they achieved. They were brave to a man, and they had youth on their side. Baird Smith himself was only 39 years old when he became Chief Engineer and most of his officers were in the early twenties. The great John Nicholson was only 35 years of age when he met his death. Delhi was taken by the daring of British youth.

No sooner had the permanent posts along the Ridge been garrisoned on June 8th than the enemy poured out of the city and attacked the position along its whole length, supported by heavy artillery fire from the Mori and Kashmir Bastions.[1] In an attempt to subdue this fire, the Engineers began to build two batteries,[2] each for one 18-pounder gun and one 8-inch howitzer, close to Hindu Rao's House. Both opened fire on the 9th, on which day the famous Corps of Guides from the northern Punjab marched into camp and almost straight into action after covering nearly 600 miles in 27 days.[3] As the two little batteries could not cope with the enemy's fire they were enlarged and a battery of two mortars was added ; all three batteries opened fire on the 11th after another attack had been repulsed. Again, on the 12th, the whole position was assaulted and the mutineers nearly captured it ; the Flagstaff post was cut off for a time, and Hindu Rao's House was attacked heavily from Sabzi Mandi. This fight showed the weakness of the left centre of the position, so Barnard decided to seize and occupy the stables and cow-house of Metcalfe House as advanced posts and this was done the same evening. A new mortar battery opened fire from the Ridge on the 13th when the enemy advanced once more, pushing their light guns up to the crest of the Ridge from Kishanganj and enfilading the British batteries. Three young Engineer officers then came forward with a scheme to end the steady wastage of men under such constant attacks by a surprise assault on Delhi.

[1] The Kashmir Bastion is not marked on the plan of Delhi included in this chapter, but it is immediately above the word " Kashmir " in the name " Kashmir Gate " shown on the plan. The bastion lies close to the east of the gateway which has two openings.
[2] All the small batteries on the Ridge were named after officers of the force, and most of them after Engineers. Thus we find Salkeld's, Maunsell's, Perkins', and other batteries.
[3] Including five days of rest.

Lieutenants Greathed, Chesney and Maunsell, under the direct orders of General Barnard and unknown to the Chief Engineer,[1] had worked out in secret the details of the project and the disposition of the troops. Practically the whole force was to be employed in three columns of attack—one to enter by the Kashmir Gate, another by the Lahore Gate, and the third by escalade at some intermediate point. All three were then to fight their way along separate routes to the centre of the city and there unite. It was a desperate plan. If, by good luck, all three columns managed to force an entry and to meet in the heart of the labyrinth of Delhi, what would they do next? Surrounded by 20,000 armed men in a maze of narrow lanes, cut off from their supplies, without reinforcements, and with their sick and wounded beyond the Ridge at the mercy of any strong counter-attack, it is not difficult to imagine their fate. Nevertheless, Greathed, Chesney and Maunsell induced General Barnard to sanction the scheme and put it in hand. The troops were paraded suddenly at 1 a.m. on June 13th, and then for the first time the orders were explained to the Column Commanders. One British regiment, however, was absent from the parade on outpost duty at Metcalfe House, and there was such delay in getting it back to the camp that dawn was breaking before it had arrived and received its ammunition. A surprise assault being then impossible, the troops were dismissed. "The failure to give effect to the young Engineer officers' plan," writes Lord Roberts,[2] "may be looked upon as a merciful dispensation of Providence which saved us from what would almost certainly have been an irreparable disaster."

The enemy attacked for eight hours on June 15th, and two days later began to erect a battery in the suburb of Paharipur to take the Ridge batteries in flank and rear, but a British sortie cleared the suburb, and 40 Sappers under Perkins, Fulford and Jones demolished the battery. The episode drew attention, however, to the dangerous situation on the right flank, and a new three-gun battery was traced on a rocky plateau 300 yards from Hindu Rao's House to deal with reverse fire. The construction of this battery was most difficult, as every basketful of earth for the parapet had to be carried up from below the stony Ridge. It was not till the 22nd that the guns of the new battery could open fire, and meanwhile, on the 19th, masses of hostile infantry, cavalry and artillery issued from the Lahore and Ajmer Gates to attack the right flank and rear and were repulsed only after a long struggle. The Engineers then concentrated their attention on these sectors. After strengthening all the defences, a party of Sappers under Salkeld marched out on June 22nd and destroyed the bridge carrying the Grand Trunk Road from Karnal

---

[1] Major Laughton, B.E.
[2] *Forty-one Years in India*, by Field-Marshal Lord Roberts of Kandahar, Vol. I, p. 167.

over the Najafgarh Jhil Drain.¹ This successful demolition was followed by others on the next day when Maunsell and Jones ruined all the remaining bridges over the same channel close to Delhi. Thus, when the enemy launched a general attack on the 24th, the rear of the camp was not threatened, and 12 hours' fighting ended in their repulse with the loss of 1,000 men. Reports soon arrived that the mutineers intended to flood the dry ditch around the city by turning into it the waters of the Delhi or Western Jumna Canal. As this would increase the difficulties of an assault, Champain went out and cut the canal bank upstream of an aqueduct which carried the canal over the Najafgarh Jhil Drain, so turning the canal water into the drain.

On June 29th Major Laughton was removed from his post as Chief Engineer and left for the hills, being succeeded, as a temporary measure, by Captain Alexander Taylor, who had arrived from the Punjab on the previous day. Taylor soon infused new life not only into the Engineer Department but the whole force. All knew of his fine record in the siege of Multan. He settled down in the Engineer Mess in the camp behind the Ridge and began to make those daring reconnaissances which were his speciality. More reinforcements reached the camp, and from Roorkee, on July 3rd, came Lieutenant-Colonel Richard Baird Smith, exhausted by a final march of 54 miles which he undertook in order to arrive in time for an expected assault on Delhi. Taylor then became Baird Smith's second-in-command in a cadre of 22 Engineer officers which rose in time to 32.

The rumour which brought the new Chief Engineer post haste into Delhi arose as follows. Taylor had recommended to General Barnard that the question of trying to take the city by a surprise assault should be reopened, especially as there was no engineering equipment for a regular siege and no proper siege train. Casualties were increasing, and a rising in the Punjab was threatened. So Taylor drew up a plan of attack on much the same lines as the one prepared in June, but advocated five storming parties instead of three, each led by two Engineer officers.² The General considered the proposals and thought that they were sound. The assault was actually fixed for July 3rd³ when, at the last moment, all arrangements were cancelled on news of disaffection among the Indian cavalry. Taylor was always convinced that Delhi could have been captured on that day if Barnard had not hesitated,⁴ and Baird Smith was inclined to agree with him. But Taylor said of the General, " He does not know how contemptible is the enemy," and it is certain that some of the enemy, particularly the artillerymen, were by no means contemptible. As

---

¹ They used 325 lb. of powder in three chambers in the central pier. The bridge was a massive structure of brick masonry with two arches.
² *Two Indian Campaigns*, by Colonel E. T. Thackeray, R.E., p. 40.
³ *Forty-one Years in India*, by Field-Marshal Lord Roberts of Kandahar, Vol. I, p. 181.
⁴ *Life of General Sir Alex Taylor*, by A. C. Taylor, Vol. I, p. 242.

M*

one by one the rebel gunners were mowed down by the British fire on the walls of Delhi during the final assault, others took their places and died beside their weapons. These were mutineers, and fiendish in their cruelty, but they were no cowards.

The Engineer Mess was in a small bungalow in the old cantonment below the Ridge.[1] Around it clustered the tents of the more fortunate members while the others slept on the floor of the building or on an old billiard table without edges, which served also as a dining table. No better picture can be obtained of the Engineers at Delhi than that painted by Colonel C. B. Thackeray from the description given by Miss A. C. Taylor.[2] Packed heads and tails under a single *punkah* when off duty, the happy band of Engineer subalterns passed their few hours of leisure in reading, writing and endless discussions. Colonel Baird Smith, the Chief Engineer, seldom dined there. His next senior and right-hand man, Captain Alex Taylor,[3] otherwise " Musha," aged 31, was the oldest in the mess, the others being subalterns though some had over 12 years' service. Next came the witty and versatile Wilberforce Greathed, known commonly as the " Insulting Engineer," the native corruption for Government Consulting Engineer for Railways. Frederick Maunsell, *preux-chevalier*, Adjutant and then Commandant of the Sappers and Miners ; James Tennant, mathematician and astronomer, known as the " Objector-General " ; George Chesney, Brigade Major, the perfect Staff Officer, a man of brilliant parts ; Henry Brownlow, with his caustic humour ; Geneste, gallant, idle and capable, the actor and linguist of the Corps ; Philip Salkeld, fresh from his amazing escape from Delhi and destined, with Duncan Home, to win the Victoria Cross at the Kashmir Gate. There was Arthur Lang who, as all agreed, earned many Victoria Crosses but received none ; and there were Fulford who died, Tandy and young Ned Jones who were killed ; Gulliver, Hovenden and Warrand ; " Jules " Medley, the two Walkers, James (Bombay) and Edmund who died of cholera. Edward Talbot Thackeray, a lad of twenty, dubbed " My Lord Tall Boot," very correct in dress ; and his bosom friend " Robinson Crusoe " Thomason,[4] ragged in apparel and full of theories on the sun-resisting properties of green cloth. These were some of the gallant and capable youngsters whom Lord Canning spoke of as " accomplished all-round men, every one of them, of clear intellect and cool courage." Heat, sickness, wounds, anxiety and overwork could not quench their ardour. At times the whole cantonment resounded with music. There were many singers,

---

[1] The site seems to have been a little to the north-west of the so-called " Khaibar Pass " where the Delhi–Alipore Road crosses the Ridge.

[2] " A Subaltern in the Indian Mutiny," by Colonel C. B. Thackeray, R.A., appearing in *The R.E. Journal*, Vol. XLIV, December, 1930, pp. 644–646, condensed from *The Life of General Sir Alex Taylor*, by A. C. Taylor, Vol. I, pp. 216–226.

[3] Taylor was a remarkable athlete, known at Addiscombe and Chatham as the " Football King." He could jump a line of *twelve* mess chairs placed seat to back, and could run up a wall, over a picture hung low, and off again.

[4] Son of the Lieutenant-Governor of the North-West Provinces (1843–1853).

and far too many enthusiastic performers on the flute and cornet. The Engineers actually got up an instrumental quartette. Football was played almost daily, and racquets in the courts near Metcalfe House beyond that dangerous ground where " Pandies "[1] lurked. The less energetic fished solemnly in a *jhil*, and all bathed uproariously in the stream behind the camp on a Sunday morning.[2]

At the beginning of July it was estimated that there were in Delhi at least 15,000 trained soldiers and a still greater number of irregulars, while the British force did not exceed 5,500 men and suffered casualties amounting to at least 30 a day and sometimes to more than 100. It was advisable, therefore, to end the siege as quickly as possible, and, as already mentioned, Baird Smith at first agreed with Taylor that the desperate risk of a surprise assault should be taken. On the morning of July 5th the newly-arrived Chief Engineer conferred with General Barnard for three hours and tried hard to win his consent to an attack, but the General was doubtful and anxious and told him to return at noon for a decision. When Baird Smith came back, he was told that the General could not see him. Barnard had been stricken with cholera and in a few hours he

[1] All rebels were called " Pandies " because the first to be executed at Barrackpore, near Calcutta, was named Mangal Pande.

[2] It may be of interest to record the subsequent ranks and some of the services of the 32 Engineers who were at Delhi. Many of them served with distinction in other campaigns not here mentioned.

Generals and Colonels Commandant R.E. :—Sir A. Taylor, G.C.B., President, Indian Defence Committee ; President, Cooper's Hill College. Sir F. R. Maunsell, K.C.B., and Sir Æneas Perkins, K.C.B., both C.R.E.s in the Second Afghan War. Sir G. Chesney, K.C.B., C.S.I., C.I.E., *M.P.* for Oxford, Military Member of the Viceroy's Council ; President, Cooper's Hill College ; a brilliant political and military author. J. Walker, C.B., F.R.S. (Bombay Engineers), Surveyor-General of India.

Lieutenant-Generals :—H. W. Gulliver. C. T. Stewart. J. Tennant, C.I.E., F.R.S. H. A. Brownlow.

Major-Generals :—W. W. Greathed, C.B. After a very distinguished military career, became head of the Irrigation Department of India. W. E. Warrand. J. Medley. C. S. Thomason. R. S. B. Pemberton, C.S.I., Director of Railways ; Member of the Viceroy's Council.

Colonels :—R. Baird Smith, C.B., *A.D.C.* Shared with John Nicholson and Alex Taylor the chief credit for the capture of Delhi. Became Master of the Calcutta Mint. Died 1861. A. Lang. Sir John Bateman-Champain, K.C.M.G., Director of Indo-European Telegraphs. D. Ward. Sir E. T. Thackeray, V.C., K.C.B. (Civil), C.B. (Military). Chief Commissioner, St. John's Ambulance Brigade. Mentioned in despatches for services in Italy during the Great War, 1914–18, and died in 1927, aged 91, *the last survivor of the Delhi Engineer Brigade.* J. G. Forbes.

Lieutenant-Colonels :—J. Laughton. Chief Engineer, Delhi Field Force for a time. T. Hovenden.

Major :—P. Murray.

Lieutenants :—D. C. Home, V.C., and P. Salkeld, V.C. Both died within a month of winning the V.C., Salkeld of wounds received at the Kashmir Gate, and Home by the accidental explosion of a mine at Malagarh a few weeks later. F. L. Tandy. E. Jones. Died during the Mutiny. M. G. Geneste. W. Fulford. E. Walker. A. McNeile and H. A. L. Carnegie. Both retired soon after the Mutiny.

Assistant Engineers (attached) :—Captain Greensill, H.M. 24th Regiment, killed at Delhi. Lieutenants Gustavinski, Hills, Chalmers, Nuthall and Knowles, Bengal Staff Corps (Bengal Infantry), and a few other Infantry officers. Also Lieutenant Bingham from the College at Roorkee (commanding the Pioneers).

was dead. The chief command then passed to Major-General Reed, who was too ill to shoulder any responsibility and consequently forbade an attack, so Baird Smith devoted himself to other projects. His chief care was to make the position on the Ridge impregnable to assault, and with this object he sent out, between July 7th and 9th, parties of Sappers under Engineer officers to demolish almost all the remaining bridges over the canal and the drain which the enemy might cross with his artillery. He cleared the slopes of the Ridge of brushwood as far as possible, arranged better cover for the posts and batteries, and by the 14th had mounted a battery on the "General's Mound," south-west of the camp, to deal with attacks from the right and rear. The mutineers tried repeatedly to capture the Ridge by making full use of Kishanganj and Paharipur as positions of assembly; on July 9th, 14th, and again on the 18th, there was serious fighting to the south of the Ridge which cost the British many men. The casualties in the actions of July 9th and 14th were so heavy[1] that Baird Smith was obliged to recommend that all idea of carrying Delhi by assault should be given up for a time and that the alternative plan should be adopted of economizing in men and material till the walls could be breached by a proper siege train and the defences stormed by an adequate force. His opinion was accepted, and the British force sat down to wait.

On July 9th a very welcome addition was made to the strength of the Engineer Department. Six hundred unarmed "Pioneers," whom Baird Smith had recruited before he left Roorkee from among the workmen employed on the Ganges Canal, marched in under Lieutenant H. A. Brownlow, B.E., and from the north-west came 300 armed Punjab Sappers under Lieutenant H. W. Gulliver, B.E. The men from Roorkee brought with them a large supply of engineering tools and stores from the Canal Workshops at that place, sufficient to form the nucleus of a proper Engineer Park; they were skilled diggers, and, though unused to fighting, showed remarkable pluck under fire. The three companies of Punjab Sappers (or Pioneers) had been raised by Lieutenant D. C. Home from among the Mazbi[2] Sikh workmen employed on the Grand Trunk Road and other works in the Punjab. Home received the order one morning and the companies marched away the following evening under Gulliver. At the beginning of July, Home raised two more companies of Punjab Sappers, and, accompanied by Gustavinski (Assistant Field Engineer) marched for Delhi, but they did not reach the camp till August 20th.[3] The men had had very little military training, though some had

[1] About 500 men killed or wounded.
[2] Men of low caste who, though admitted as Sikhs, could never attain the full status of the true Sikh.
[3] *Biographical Notices of Officers of the Royal (Bengal) Engineers*, compiled by Colonel Sir E. T. Thackeray, V.C., K.C.B., 1900, pp. 122–3. Miss A. C. Taylor in her *Life of General Sir Alex Taylor*, Vol. I, p. 230, states that 800 Mazbi Sikh Sappers came from the Punjab to Delhi, but her authority is not known.

served with Nicholson's Movable Column for a time. Finally, Baird Smith managed to raise a local corps of 1,000 road coolies from the neighbouring villages, unarmed but accustomed to felling trees and digging. This "mixed bag" was turned gradually into a useful Engineer Brigade by the Engineer officers, assisted by the small but loyal remnant of the Bengal Sappers and Miners, and particularly by the splendid British non-commissioned officers of that Corps. Foremost among the latter were Serjeant-Major Stuart, a strict disciplinarian, and Conductor James Smith, dubbed the "Miscreant," who came with the stores from Roorkee and issued all requisites from the Park. Almost as much credit should be given to the British non-commissioned officers as to the officers for the work at Delhi, for it was men such as Stuart and Smith who trained the awkward hands which did it.

On July 17th the chief command passed to Brigadier-General Archdale Wilson. Major-General T. Reed, whom Baird Smith rather harshly describes[1] as a "feeble valetudinarian scarcely able to ride," had broken down. Archdale Wilson did his best; he brought order and discipline where there had been much laxity, and his reorganizations were beneficial; but he was not the man for the post; he was a bold soldier in action, but pessimistic and perhaps over-careful in council; he was lacking in nerve and had only recently recovered from smallpox, and, towards the end of the siege, was reduced to such a state of mental collapse that Baird Smith, querulous through ill-health, was driven almost frantic in his dealings with him.[2] The following entry appears in the Chief Engineer's diary, dated August 6th:[3] "Here is this dear old General a-fidgeting again about his rear. I try to comfort him three times a day with the assurance that though we must *watch* it well, there is no real cause for anxiety about it. It is his mania, however, and it costs me an awful amount of note-writing when the enemy moves in that direction as he is doing to-day." Dysentery and other diseases were rife in the camp, and no man was at his best. Every allowance accordingly should be made for the General's anxiety.

Archdale Wilson wrote on July 18th asking that a train of heavy artillery[4] should be sent from Ferozepore which, with the ordnance already on the Ridge, would give him a total of 63 guns. He had been doubtful whether he should not raise the siege and retreat across the Jumna, but Baird Smith had convinced him of the absolute necessity of holding on to Delhi "like grim Death," remaining strictly on the defensive, and ordering siege guns for a proper bombardment.

[1] *Richard Baird Smith*, by Colonel H. M. Vibart, R.E., p. 94.
[2] *Ibid.*, p. 135. Baird Smith writes: "I can truly say that the General was scarcely less an obstacle to be overcome than the walls of the place or the bayonets of the garrison."
[3] *Ibid*, p. 110.
[4] Six 24-pounders, eight 18-pounders, four 10-inch howitzers, ten 8-inch howitzers, six 5½-inch howitzers.

Hence the order for guns, followed by an announcement from Wilson that he was determined to hold his position to the last. The monsoon burst on the 27th, damping the ardour of the mutineers and slowing down all operations. Ammunition for the British guns was very scarce, and the Engineer Park was still deficient in materials for large projects. The position on the Ridge was now secure against capture though the enemy continued to attack the right at intervals, giving attention also to the ground between the Ridge and the river and seizing Ludlow Castle, from which they were ejected by a sortie. In time, however, they established a regular outpost in the Castle. They knew that British reinforcements were on their way from across the " black water " (the ocean), and among them Highlanders, men in petticoats whom they dreaded. C. B. Thackeray quotes a letter from a *babu* in Delhi to another on the Ridge which ran : " A regiment of women have arrived and play Old Harry with everybody, and have an awful savage appearance, and no chance for anyone seems left." A regiment coming from Ceylon were said to be cannibals ! Publicity may have its value in war.

To hinder the arrival of enemy reinforcements, the Engineers tried to destroy the bridge of boats across the Jumna near the King's Palace by floating down onto it rafts of casks and trees, each carrying in the centre a barrel of gunpowder with a pistol at full-cock inside it and so designed that a sudden jar would fire the pistol. They used to row the rafts into midstream and leave them to float down to the bridge. Two were released on August 3rd, but one exploded on a sandbank, and although the other reached the bridge it would not explode. The attempts were soon given up after there had been much chaff from spectators on the Ridge about the then equivalent of " Sapper stunts."[1] The Engineer Brigade, weakened by fever and dysentery, had to labour continually in drenching rain, and the casualties mounted steadily. Indeed, by the end of July, out of the 45 British non-commissioned officers who left Roorkee on May 14th, ten had died of disease, one had been killed and nine wounded, and of the remainder hardly one was really fit for duty. The officers escaped more lightly, but few were up to the work they had to do.

A notable day was that on which the celebrated Brigadier-General John Nicholson arrived from the Punjab. This was August 7th,[2] three days before the Siege Train started from Ferozepore on its long journey to Delhi. On the 12th, Baird Smith was wounded in the ankle by a steel splinter and was thus prevented from making those reconnaissances which form so important a part of the duty of a

---

[1] *Two Indian Campaigns*, by Colonel E. T. Thackeray, R.E., p. 55, and " The Diary of A. M. Lang," appearing in the *Journal of the Society for Army Historical Research*, Vol. IX, October, 1930, p. 202.

[2] The Movable Column from the Punjab, which Nicholson commanded, marched in on the 14th—a very welcome reinforcement.

Chief Engineer in the field. From the facts of his wound and ill-health a long discussion arose afterwards about the authorship of the plan of attack which gave Delhi to the British in September, 1857. It has been called the "Baird Smith–Taylor controversy." Some writers have attributed the origin of the plan to Baird Smith, others to Taylor; some have asserted that Baird Smith captured Delhi, others Taylor.[1] But should either be hailed as the "capturer of Delhi"? The Mughal capital was taken by the efforts of Wilson and every British officer and British soldier serving under him. Baird Smith and Taylor did splendidly in their different spheres—the one as Chief Engineer, the other as "Director of the Trenches" and second-in-command of the Engineers. Baird Smith was a fine administrator, a clear thinker, capable, brave and quick in decision. So far as his health would allow, he directed and guided the activities of all his officers; but his chief task was to advise his anxious General. Taylor was a man of phenomenal energy, resource and self-confidence, reckless in his daring and impatient of opposition. He acted as the eyes of Baird Smith, who, although he knew every house, ravine and thicket around Delhi, and every stone in the defences, could not re-explore the country to select lines for an advance and actual sites for siege batteries. Baird Smith is said to have prepared a plan of attack on Delhi *before he left Roorkee;* but if that plan was made the basis for the successful assault on the city, it could only have been through its elaboration by the details ascertained and worked out on the spot by Taylor. Whoever originated the final plan, the credit for its details at least must go to Taylor; but even if Taylor, as some say, was the author of the whole plan, the credit for the results obtained must go to Baird Smith who, as Chief Engineer, approved the plan and consequently bore, with Archdale Wilson, all responsibility for its success or failure.

The coming of John Nicholson led to some friction. He made a tour of the defences on the Ridge and was not too pleased with what he saw. He was a man of domineering character, and, as he did not mince his words, he was respected by many but loved by few. Tall, with massive chest and powerful limbs, a great black beard, well-cut features, a deep voice, an imperious manner and an indefinable air of unbounded strength and resolution—such was John Nicholson, almost deified by the loyal natives of the Punjab and dreaded by all rebels. In Alexander Taylor he found a man after his own heart, and, indeed, with some points of similarity; Nicholson and Taylor were the moving spirits in the siege and capture of Delhi. Within a few days of his arrival, Nicholson proceeded to take the offensive against the rebels. His Movable Column and other reinforcements

---

[1] See *Richard Baird Smith*, by Colonel H. M. Vibart, R.E., pp. 72–85. Also *Life of General Sir Alex Taylor*, Vol. I, by A. C. Taylor, pp. 253–256. Also *A Few Notes on the Siege of Delhi*, by General Sir F. R. Maunsell, pp. 15–20, and many other works.

had raised the strength of the British force to more than 8,000 men,[1] so a passive defence was no longer justifiable. He made a demonstration towards Rohtak on August 19th, and on the 25th marched with 2,000 men and 15 guns to attack a large body of the enemy who had moved out to intercept the approaching siege train. He routed them at Najafgarh in deluges of rain after an advance across flooded country, captured 13 guns and all their baggage and transport, and was back in camp on the following day.

On the evening of August 20th, General Wilson began once more to doubt whether he could take Delhi, and wrote complainingly to Baird Smith that Lord Canning was urging him to attack the place without realizing that it was garrisoned by 40,000 soldiers with 114 heavy guns, 60 field-guns and unlimited ammunition, and that he proposed to reply that he could not take Delhi unless some large force was sent to assist him. If his figures were correct he had certainly some reason for his misgivings. But Baird Smith in reply urged most strongly that Delhi should be assaulted as soon as proper breaches had been made and without awaiting the arrival of large reinforcements, so that the mutineers should not have time to throw up more defences. Wilson agreed, but in such a way that Baird Smith considered that he placed on his Chief Engineer's shoulders the undivided responsibility for the results of the operations.[2] Whether this was intentional is open to doubt. At a Council of War on August 23rd, however, Wilson publicly confirmed his decision to continue the siege and to assault Delhi as soon as there was a reasonable chance of success. It was fortunate, perhaps, that he took this line, for Nicholson, who was present at the meeting, wrote afterwards to John Lawrence[3] that had Wilson carried out his threat of withdrawing the guns he (Nicholson) was prepared to appeal to the army to remove him and elect a successor. There can be little doubt that the army would have elected Nicholson. However, an assent having been given by the General, preparations were pushed on rapidly for the supreme effort. The siege train arrived on September 4th, after covering a distance of 268 miles in 25 days. Its entry into the camp was a wonderful sight. For eight miles the Grand Trunk Road was packed with guns, howitzers and mortars drawn chiefly by elephants, while behind these trailed 700 bullock carts filled with ammunition.

Taylor redoubled his efforts in exploring the country between the Ridge and the river, and even penetrated in daylight with Greathed into the Kudsia Bagh close to the Water Bastion where he stayed for two hours to observe the enemy in the Custom House. His reconnaissances were made sometimes on horseback, but more often

---

[1] There were also some 3,000 irregulars from Kashmir and Jhind, but they were more ornamental than useful.
[2] *Richard Baird Smith*, by Colonel H. M. Vibart, R.E., p. 52.
[3] General Nicholson to Sir John Lawrence. Letter dated September 11th, 1857.

GENERAL SIR ALEXANDER TAYLOR, G.C.B.

on foot and alone ; he considered that he was not justified in exposing the lives of others to such desperate risks except on rare occasions. Once, having watched Ludlow Castle for some time from the Flagstaff Tower at the hour at which the enemy's piquet in the Castle was usually relieved, and having reason to believe that the place was empty, he made his way to the building and crept softly up a stair to the roof. Then, to his horror, he saw the enemy filing into the compound below him and realized that he was trapped. That meant not only death but torture. Bounding downstairs six steps at a time he reached a back door, rushed across the compound, and hurling himself onto and over a seven-foot wall under a scattered fire from the leading mutineers, escaped to the nearest British piquet.[1] Now these desperate ventures were made with one object alone—the preparation, down to the smallest detail, of a plan of attack. "It is curious," writes Maunsell,[2] "that the most striking feature of the siege of Delhi has never been noticed. It is surely unprecedented in warfare that, almost in the midst of a watchful enemy, the site for the final struggle was completely surveyed, and the position of every gun, of the artillery force and of all the approaches *clearly marked out on the ground*, and the action finally carried out exactly as originally planned." This was Taylor's achievement at Delhi.

The attack began on September 7th. It was clear that it must be made on some part of the enemy's front between the Water Bastion near the river and the Lahore Gate in the western face ; also that it should, if possible, be directed mainly against the northern face between the Kashmir Gate and the Water Bastion because the left flank of the attack would then be covered by the Jumna, there would be cover for the advancing troops, and they would be able to reform after the assault in the open spaces in the north-east corner of the city behind the Kashmir Gate. But an attack on this face was difficult because it was out of range of the batteries on the Ridge. These batteries could bombard the Mori Bastion and the curtains on either side of it, but the enemy were fully prepared for any attack in that quarter. It was obvious that in order to attack to the east of the Kashmir Gate, breaching batteries must be established close to that face, that they must be constructed very rapidly, and that every detail of the work must be planned in advance and with extreme secrecy. The scheme which was prepared to meet these requirements was submitted to General Wilson by Colonel Baird Smith for final approval on September 6th. It was designed to conceal as long as possible the intention to attack near the river, to get such command of the ground in front of the proposed siege batteries that the enemy could not attack the builders, and to make the first battery so powerful that it would quickly overwhelm the opposing guns. The duty of

[1] *Life of General Sir Alex Taylor*, by A. C. Taylor, Vol. I, p. 261.
[2] "A Few Notes on the Siege of Delhi," by General Sir F. R. Maunsell, appearing in *The R.E. Journal*, Vol. XIV, July–December, 1911, p. 20.

obtaining control of the field of operations—the first step—was to be performed by a powerful battery, No. 1, to the north of the Mori Bastion.[1] Its location would deceive the enemy into expecting an assault on that bastion, whereas its two wings or faces would actually engage the guns of all the northern bastions to cover the construction of the breaching batteries nearer the Jumna. Not more than three officers knew in advance the details of the plan—probably General Wilson; certainly Baird Smith and Taylor.[2] It was not till September 4th, three days before the attack began, that the details were explained to John Nicholson who was to lead the assault.

A preliminary step was to seize Ludlow Castle to cover the building of No. 1 Battery. General Wilson hesitated to sanction this move, so Nicholson offered to accompany Taylor on a night reconnaissance on September 5th to ascertain whether Ludlow Castle could be occupied without heavy fighting which might spoil the whole plan. The daring couple visited both the Castle and the Kudsia Bagh and reported that both were empty. Wilson then gave his final approval to the plan, and Ludlow Castle was occupied on the night of the 6th–7th, by which time some light batteries had been erected near the Sammy House at the southern end of the Ridge to protect the builders of No. 1 Battery. The Engineer Park under the direction of Henry Brownlow had been the scene of feverish activity for several weeks. The Sappers and Pioneers had been practised in throwing up all sorts of field works and batteries. Stacks of siege materials had been prepared including 100,000 sandbags, 10,000 gabions, 10,000 fascines, scaling ladders by the score and gun platforms by the dozen. Fifteen hundred camels, and hundreds of mules and bullock carts, had been collected for transport. Brownlow lived in his boots, and ate and slept when and where he could. Of the 26 officers then in the Engineer Brigade, seven were in hospital before the assault could be launched.

Alexander Taylor, as "Director of the Trenches," was in immediate charge of all the field engineering; under him were other Engineers who were responsible for particular batteries or for sections of the attack. As Directing Engineer of the Right Attack, the building of the important No. 1 Battery[3] fell to Frederick Maunsell who, assisted by Julius Medley, traced its lines during the afternoon of Sunday, September 7th. It had two faces, one towards the Mori Bastion to mount five 18-pounders and one 8-inch howitzer, and the other towards the Kashmir Gate for four 24-pounders;[4] the latter face ran down into the dry *nullah* which formed a natural parallel of the siege

---

[1] See the plan included in this chapter.
[2] *Life of General Sir Alex Taylor*, by A. C. Taylor, Vol. I, p. 273.
[3] Described as the "key" battery of the attack.
[4] The armaments quoted are those which appear on the masonry memorials at Delhi which mark the position of the batteries. The memorial of No. 1 Battery is in the Hospital compound of the Police Lines, 660 yards from the Mori Bastion.

works. "The moon rose on a busy scene," writes Medley.[1] "Hundreds of camels arriving, dropping their loads, and returning; and hundreds of men, as busy as bees, raising up a formidable work which was to be finished and ready to open fire in the morning. The night was very hot, but the excitement prevented anyone feeling fatigued. I went up to Hindoo Rao's house, and on returning found we had at length got rid of the camels; but now commenced arriving the long strings of artillery carts, laden with shot and shell. Then came the huge guns, drawn by twenty pairs of bullocks each. At three o'clock the place presented a scene of awful confusion. Sappers, pioneers, artillerymen and infantry, all mixed up together with an inert mass of carts, guns and bullocks. Scarcely another hour remained before daylight, and then we knew what to expect from the irate enemy. Men and officers worked like horses. Nevertheless, with all our exertion, we had only one gun ready for the Moree when day began to dawn; the other five platforms being still incomplete. We were now obliged to let the great bulk of the working party[2] go, but I, with two other Engineers, remained to finish the other platforms. The covering party was withdrawn and with the first break of day the enemy saw what we had been at and then we caught it." From dawn onwards Maunsell and his Sappers worked steadily, supported by a single howitzer which Major James Brind gallantly brought into action in the open; and although 70 men were killed in a few hours, No. 1 Battery fired its first salvo during the course of the morning, quickly reducing the guns on the Mori Bastion almost to silence. Meanwhile the light batteries on the Ridge were enfilading some guns and infantry which the mutineers had pushed out to hinder the work. The left face of No. 1 Battery dealt with the guns on the Kashmir Bastion and continued to do so very effectively till its fascine ramparts caught fire on the 10th and it was destroyed.[3] Taylor had guaranteed that No. 1 Battery would be built and armed in a single night; but although the task proved to be beyond Maunsell's power, the battery when completed was able to afford some protection to the workers on the breaching batteries nearer the river.

While Maunsell was still at work on No. 1 Battery, Taylor, Greathed, Lang and Thackeray traced the lines of the principal Breaching Battery No. 2, which was located in two sections, connected by a trench, to the south and east of Ludlow Castle. The left section was to be armed with nine 24-pounders to breach the curtain to the east of the Kashmir Bastion;[4] the right section, to mount two 18-pounders

---

[1] *A Year's Campaigning in India*, by Julius G. Medley, pp. 75-77.
[2] Large working parties had been detailed from the infantry units.
[3] The author was unable to find a memorial to mark the position of this wing of No. 1 Battery at Delhi. It should be in the compound of a private bungalow opposite the Hospital of the Police Lines. (See the "Delhi Guide Map," scale 4 inches to 1 mile, printed by the Survey of India Department.)
[4] Range 660 yards. The memorial can be seen in the grounds of the Delhi Club (formerly Ludlow Castle) on a bank above some tennis courts.

and seven 8-inch howitzers, was to breach the bastion itself or the curtain very close to it.[1] On the night of the 8th–9th, Medley and other officers, under the orders of Greathed as Directing Engineer of the Left Attack, began work on the right section. It progressed steadily; but meanwhile great difficulty was being experienced at the site of the next battery, No. 3, where the position selected in the Kudsia Bagh was found to be unsuitable. Taylor then decided to build No. 3 *inside* an empty office building of the Custom House still closer to the enemy,[2] and concentrated all the available Sappers on this critical operation. The platforms were ready before dawn on the 10th, but the demolition of the masonry in front of them, and the mounting of six 18-pounder guns under a heavy fire, cost many lives and was not finished till the morning of the 12th. The battery then opened fire with great effect. "The enemy's guns," writes Medley, "were dismounted or smashed almost immediately, the face of the bastion was beaten into a shapeless mass, and the parapet sent flying about in fragments. In a few hours the breach seemed almost practicable." Another battery, No. 4, containing four 10-inch and six 8-inch mortars, whose targets were the Kashmir and Water Bastions and the Kashmir Gate, had been completed on the 10th to the west of the Kudsia Bagh[3] and had opened fire the same night, followed by No. 2 Battery on the 11th. The mutineers were not idle during this period, for they established an advanced battery near the Kabul Gate which enfiladed Nos. 1 and 2 Batteries with fearful effect. The strain on every man in the British force was terrible. "We are worked," says Lang,[4] "to the very limit of human power. As I come into my tent after a night out, my eyes are closing themselves. I fling myself down and am too tired to sleep but restlessly. Again in excited dreams I set parties to work under hot fire, howl at them, urge them on, grape pouring in and loud guns drowning one's voice." But the 56 British guns continued to roar, night and day, their prelude to the last act of the great drama of Delhi—the assault on September 14th.

Several breaches could be seen in the walls on the evening of Sunday 13th, though it was not known whether they were practicable. Medley, Lang, Greathed and Hovenden undertook to find out. When the British artillery had ceased fire, Lang first reconnoitred a breach on the east side of the Kashmir Bastion, running in broad daylight right up to the edge of the ditch, lying down there, and escaping unhurt under a heavy fire. Then, with Medley, he returned after dark and descended actually into the ditch,

[1] Range 550 yards. The memorial is in the back compound of Curzon House (now a hotel) on a bank of a *nullah* above the cemetery.
[2] Range only 160 yards. The memorial is in the Kudsia Garden opposite the Water Bastion on a bank above some tennis courts.
[3] Range 550 yards. The memorial of No. 4 Battery is on a lawn in the Kudsia Garden near the Alipur Road.
[4] "The Diary and Letters of A. M. Lang," appearing in the *Journal of the Society for Army Historical Research*, Vol. X, April, 1931, p. 75.

examined the breach, and got back safely to the British batteries. Greathed and Hovenden, with almost equal daring, had meanwhile reconnoitred a breach near the Water Bastion. As all four Engineers reported that the breaches were practicable, General Wilson then decided to launch his assault at daybreak, and, with Baird Smith and the remainder of his staff, took his post on the roof of Ludlow Castle to watch the struggle on which, perhaps, the fate of India might depend. At 2 a.m. all the Engineers except the Chief assembled in the little mess behind the Ridge to read their instructions, pore over a big map of Delhi, write brief letters, buckle on their revolvers and fill their haversacks. They seemed to be in the highest spirits; but many wondered, no doubt, if they would see the setting of another sun. The orders were that no prisoners were to be made as there was no one to guard them. In the twilight which precedes dawn the British force assembled regiment by regiment before the northern face of Delhi while the guns thundered and the shells screamed overhead.

There were four columns of attack and a reserve, each including about 1,000 regular soldiers. The main attack on the left was under John Nicholson, with Alexander Taylor to direct the assault. It was formed in two columns; No. 1 led by Nicholson himself, with Lang, Medley and Bingham (an Assistant Engineer), was to storm the breach in the Kashmir Bastion; No. 2, under Brigadier-General Jones, with Greathed, Hovenden and Pemberton, was to advance near the river-bank against the breach in the Water Bastion. Column No. 3, under Colonel Campbell, with Home, Salkeld and Tandy, had orders to storm the Kashmir Gate when the Engineers had blown it in; and Column No. 4, under Colonel Reid, with Maunsell and Tennant, was to guard the right flank with the cavalry under Hope Grant, and, by advancing from Hindu Rao's House through the outlying suburbs, force an entrance into the city through the Kabul Gate. A contingent of 1,200 Kashmir irregulars was attached to this Column. The Reserve Column,[1] under Brigadier-General Longfield, with whom were Thackeray and Ward, was to act as occasion required. As regards Nicholson's two columns, the intention was that when they had stormed the breaches they should sweep westwards along the ramparts as far as the Kabul Gate. Then, joined by Reid's men, they were to continue to the Lahore Gate where, turning left, they would move down the Chandni Chauk to the Jama Masjid and the King's Palace, picking up on the way No. 3 Column which would have entered through the Kashmir Gate and advanced directly to the Masjid. The Reserve Column was to follow the main attack and to await orders in the open space within the walls near the Kashmir Gate. Such was the plan which, it was hoped, would give Delhi to the British.

[1] This column included 300 irregular soldiers.

Day had dawned when the guns ceased fire, and Nicholson gave the order to advance, leading Nos. 1 and 2 Columns himself from the Kudsia Bagh, while No. 3 issued from the vicinity of Ludlow Castle. Two hundred skirmishers of the 60th Rifles ran out from No. 2 Battery to cover the storming party, and instantly the walls of Delhi blazed with musketry. A detachment with ladders and powder bags then advanced to demolish the Kashmir Gate. It was led by Lieutenants D. C. Home and P. Salkeld of the Bengal Engineers, and consisted of three British non-commissioned officers and 14 Indian soldiers of the Bengal Sappers and Miners, ten men of the Punjab Sappers or Pioneers and a British bugler. When there was no more cover, the actual Explosion Party of all the Europeans and eight of the Indian Sappers rushed in two small parties towards the gate. Duncan Home describes what followed :[1] " Serjeants John Smith and Carmichael, Mahdo Havildar, all the Sappers[2] and myself arrived at the Cashmere Gate untouched a short time in advance of the remainder of the party under Lieutenant Salkeld, having found the palisade gate on the outside of the ditch and the wicket of the Cashmere Gate open, and three planks of the bridge across the ditch removed. As Serjeant Carmichael was laying his powder bag (containing 25 lb.) he was killed by a shot from the wicket. Havildar Mahdo was, I believe, also wounded about the same time. Lieutenant Salkeld, carrying the slow match to light the charge, now came up with a portion of the remainder of the party, and with a view to enable him to shield himself from the fire from the wicket[3] which was very severe (and the advanced party having deposited the powder bags) I slipped down into the ditch.[4] Lieutenant Salkeld being wounded in the leg from the wicket, handed over the match to Corporal Burgess who was mortally wounded while completing the operation. Havildar Tillok was at the same time wounded while assisting Corporal Burgess into the ditch ; Sepoy Rambeth (elsewhere Ram Heth) was also killed at the same time. As I was assisting Lieutenant Salkeld into the ditch I think he was wounded a second time. The charge having exploded blew in the right (proper right) leaf of the gate, on which I caused the regimental call of the 52nd Regiment to be sounded as the signal for the advance of the storming party. I caused the bugler (Hawthorne) to sound the call three times, after which the column

---

[1] Official Report from Lieutenant D. C. Home, B.E., to the Chief Engineer, Delhi Field Force, quoted in " A Subaltern in the Indian Mutiny," by Colonel C. B. Thackeray, R.A., appearing in *The R.E. Journal*, Vol. XLIV, December, 1931, pp. 604–605.

[2] The Sappers of the leading party, four in number.

[3] It is presumed that only one or two persons could get protection by pressing close up against the gate.

[4] No ditch now exists before the Kashmir Gate or for 100 yards to the west of it. The ditch then appears and continues along most of the northern front. It runs also between the Kashmir and Water Bastions. Motor traffic is heavy through the two archways of the Kashmir Gate. The walls have been allowed to remain as they were after the assault, and are much battered at the Kashmir Gate and to the west of it. The breaches are still clearly visible.

THE BLOWING IN OF THE KASHMIR GATE, DELHI, 14TH SEPTEMBER, 1857.

From the original drawing by Eyre Crowe, A.R.A., in the Royal Engineers Mess, Roorkee.

advanced to the storm and the gate was taken possession of by our troops."

The accounts of this heroic deed are to some extent conflicting, especially as regards the names of some of the Sappers, but this is only natural under the circumstances. The most reliable accounts should be those of men who served in the Explosion Party, such as that of Home, and another by Serjeant Smith which will be given later. A memorial placed outside the Kashmir Gate in 1876 by Lord Napier of Magdala when Commander-in-Chief,[1] gives the names of the Explosion Party as Lieutenants Duncan Home and Philip Salkeld (mortally wounded), Serjeants John Smith and A. B. Carmichael (killed), Corporal F. Burgess (killed),[2] Bugler Hawthorne, 52nd Foot, Subadar Toola Ram, Jemadar Bis Ram, Havildars Madhoo (wounded) and Tillok Singh (mortally wounded) and Sepoy Ram Heth (killed).[3] On this memorial the name of Sepoy Jahub Singh, who was mentioned by Home for gallantry, does not appear. On the other hand, Jemadar Bis Ram, though named on the tablet, is not mentioned by Home; and the name of Sepoy (some say Havildar) Ajudhia Pershad Pathak, who was apparently one of the Explosion Party, is omitted by Home and excluded also from the tablet.[4]

A graphic description of his experiences after reaching the gateway comes from the pen of Serjeant John Smith. Home and Bugler Hawthorne had already jumped into the ditch, and Serjeant Carmichael had been killed. A few extracts from Smith's narrative may be given.[5] "I placed my bags and then Carmichael's bag, arranged the fuse and reported 'All ready' to Lieutenant Salkeld who held the slow match. In stooping down to light the match Lieutenant

[1] Lord Napier placed this memorial tablet at the Kashmir Gate at his own expense.
[2] *Alias* Joshua Burgess Grierson.
[3] It will be noticed that only *five* Indian soldiers are named.
[4] (i) *Extract from the official report of Colonel Baird Smith,* dated September 17th, 1857: "The following native officers and sepoys of the Sappers and Miners are reported by Lieut. Home to have shown the most determined bravery and coolness throughout the whole operations:—Havildar Mahdoo who accompanied the advance under Lieut. Home; Subadar Toola, Jemadar Bis Ram, Havildars Tiluk Singh and Ramtaroy, and Sepoy Sahib Singh who were with the firing or reserve parties."
(ii) Extract from *Lectures on the Regimental History of the K.G.O. Bengal Sappers and Miners*, p. 22: "For their gallantry on this occasion the following received rewards:—Lieutenants Home, V.C., and Salkeld, V.C.; Serjt. Smith, V.C.; Subadar Tula Ram, I.O.M. (Indian Order of Merit), 1st Class; Jemadar Bis Ram, I.O.M., 2nd Class; Havildars Ajudhya Pathak, I.O.M., 3rd Class, and Ramtarai (Ramdulari), I.O.M., 2nd Class; Naiks Sheik Abdul, Nihal Khan, Debi Singh and Harpal Singh, and Sappers Thakurdin Tiwari and Ramsaful Upadhya, all I.O.M., 3rd Class."
(iii) The complete list as given by the Commandant, K.G.O. Bengal Sappers and Miners, in March, 1932, from the names on the tablet and from G.G.O. No. 579 of 1859, is as follows: Lieutenants D. C. Home and P. Salkeld, Serjeants J. Smith and A. B. Carmichael, Corporal F. Burgess, Bugler Hawthorne (H.M.'s 52nd Foot), Subadar Toola (Tula Ram), Jemadar Bis Ram, Jemadar Ramteroz (elsewhere Havildar Ramtaroy or Ramtarai or Ramdulari), Havildar Mahdoo (Madhoo), Havildar Tilok Singh (Tillok or Tiluk Singh), Havildar (elsewhere Naik) Harpal Singh, Havildar (some say Sepoy) Ajudhya Pershad Pathak, Naiks Devi Deen (Debi Singh), Sheik Abdulla (Sheik Abdul), and Nihal Khan; and Sepoys Ram Heth (Heth Ram), Thakurdin Tiwari, Ramsaful Upadhya and Sahib Singh (the "Jahub Singh" of Home's report). A total of 20 men including 14 Indian Sappers and Miners.
[5] *A Story of the Sepoy War in India*, by J. W. Kaye, Vol. III, pp. 674–675.

Salkeld was shot through the thigh and, in falling, held out the 'slow' and told me to fire the charge. Burgess was next him and took it. He turned round and said, ' It won't go off, sir ; it has gone out, sir,' not knowing that the officer had fallen into the ditch. I gave him a box of lucifers, and as he took them he let them fall into my hand—he being shot through the body—and fell over after Lieutenant Salkeld into the ditch. I was left alone. Keeping close to the charge I struck a light when the port-fire in the fuse went off in my hand, the light not having gone out as we had thought. I took up my gun and jumped into the ditch, but before I had reached the ground the charge went off. As soon as the dust cleared I saw Lieutenant Salkeld and Burgess covered with dust. Lieutenant Salkeld's arms were broken. Lieutenant Home got out of the ditch leaving me in charge of the wounded, and went to the front after the Rifles had gone in." Carmichael and Burgess died almost immediately. Salkeld, Home, Smith and Bugler Hawthorne were awarded the Victoria Cross.[1] But Salkeld lived for only two days. Before he died, when he was too weak to do more than whisper " It will be gratifying to send it home," he received the red ribbon. Within a few weeks Home also was gone—killed by the accidental explosion of a mine at the empty fortress of Malagarh. The Indian Sappers and Miners were rewarded with the Indian Order of Merit, promotion or grants of land ; none was forgotten. This is the story of the bravest deed ever performed in India by Engineers or Sappers and Miners.

Space does not permit of a detailed account of the operations of the various columns in the capture of Delhi. Columns Nos. 1 and 2 stormed the breaches in the Kashmir and Water Bastions under a devastating fire. The ladders were set up, hurled down, and set up again. Greathed and Hovenden were both struck down at the head of the ladder party at the Water Bastion. At the Kashmir Bastion, Lang and Medley were among the first to reach the top of the breach. The stormers of both columns poured through the breaches and then along the city wall and a lane behind it towards the Mori Bastion, while No. 3 Column, entering through the Kashmir Gate, fought its way towards the Jama Masjid. " On we rushed," says Lang with No. 1 Column, " cheering and shouting, swept by storms of shot from the side streets and by musketry from the house-tops. It was exciting to the verge of madness." Passing the Mori Bastion and the Kabul Gate, Nos. 1 and 2 Columns thrust southwards to the Burn Bastion, short of the Lahore Gate, and there were checked by a murderous fire. Nicholson found them some time later near the Kabul Gate ; he had been delayed at the Kashmir Gate in making arrangements with Taylor for a defended base near St. James'

---

[1] No doubt Carmichael and Burgess would also have received the coveted decoration if it had then been allowed as a posthumous award to relatives of the deceased, as nowadays.

THE STORM AND CAPTURE OF DELHI.   345

Church. He rallied the two columns at the Kabul Gate and led them in person along the lane towards the Burn Bastion, but was mortally wounded in the fight and the troops retreated again to the Gate.

Meanwhile, No. 4 Column under Reid had not only failed to reach the Kabul Gate from Kishanganj but had been repulsed by a strong counter-attack during which the Kashmir irregulars fled in panic. The column was only saved from disaster by the gallantry of Hope Grant's cavalry and some Horse Artillery. No. 3 Column, under Campbell, penetrated through the city to the Jama Masjid to make a junction with the other three columns at that point; but when there was no sign of them Campbell dared not remain isolated at the Masjid, so retreated in good order to St. James' Church. As report after report of disaster and confusion came in, General Wilson at the Kashmir Gate seriously considered the withdrawal of all the columns to the Ridge. He did not wish to retire, but feared that he might soon be forced to give the order. Baird Smith and General Chamberlain of his staff, however, were emphatic that if he moved his soldiers an inch from Delhi everything would be lost. Wilson held on, but his mind had become almost unhinged. He handed over charge shortly afterwards to Chamberlain and retired to his camp beyond the Ridge.

Two days after the assault which gave the British no more than a precarious hold on the northern face, Edward Thackeray earned the Victoria Cross by a deed of " cool intrepidity and characteristic daring,"[1] though he did not receive the award till 1862. With Major Renny of the Artillery and a few men he repulsed a determined attack on the Delhi expense magazine[2] which the British had re-occupied. The enemy gained the top of the high boundary wall, firing onto the defenders and setting fire to some thatched sheds which leant against the wall. The fire spread rapidly to the magazine buildings, and while Renny climbed on to a blazing roof and threw shells with lighted fuses among the mutineers, Thackeray followed him and had bags of water handed up to him with which he extinguished the fire before the powder could explode beneath them. All this time he was under musketry fire at close quarters and pelted with bricks and stones. The magazine was saved, and both Renny and Thackeray received the Victoria Cross.

The troops were very much out of hand after the assault. They found quantities of liquor in the city, and there was much drunkenness; but when all liquor had been destroyed, good order and discipline were restored. It was decided that, as the force was too weak to undertake street fighting, the Engineers should open a way for the infantry by sapping from house to house. But there were so few Engineers. Many were sick in hospital. Greathed, Maunsell,

---

[1] The deed was so described when the award was made.
[2] It lay between the Kashmir Gate and the King's Palace, about 600 yards from the Gate. (See plan.)

Salkeld, Chesney, Hovenden, Medley and Brownlow had been wounded outside the city, Pemberton at the Kabul Gate, and Tandy had been killed near the Jama Masjid. Only Baird Smith, Taylor, Home, Geneste, Thackeray, Lang and one or two Assistant Field Engineers remained, and of these Taylor was so exhausted by his unceasing labours that he handed over charge to Home and slept, off and on, for about 70 hours.[1] The whole force had lost 66 officers and 1,104 men in the assault. In modern parlance, it had fought itself to a standstill. However, on the 16th the house-to-house advance was begun. By burrowing through the houses and courtyards under the rifles of British snipers, the Engineers secured building after building at street corners which, when garrisoned, gave command of the streets and made them safe for infantry and guns. It was slow work, but the Burn Bastion was reached and captured on the 19th with the assistance of Taylor, Lang and Geneste, and the last stronghold on the perimeter, the Lahore Gate, was occupied on the 20th. There remained only the King's Palace. Home had the honour of blowing in the southern or Delhi Gate of that fortress on September 21st, to admit a spate of 60th Rifles and 4th Punjab Infantry who quickly put an end to the resistance and lives of all mutineers whom they found. The rebels were streaming away from Delhi. Hodson captured King Bahadur Shah, and afterwards avenged the murder of many Englishwomen by executing three princes who had been concerned in it. Fighting ceased, the Engineer Brigade moved into Darya Ganj[2] on the 22nd, and on the following day Baird Smith handed over charge to Taylor and set out for Roorkee.

The siege of Delhi is one of the most memorable in the annals of England. It lasted over 12 weeks during which the British fought more than 30 battles against vastly superior numbers. It cost them the life of John Nicholson and many another fine leader, the loss of nearly 1,000 men killed and nearly 3,000 wounded and missing, and a far greater number through sickness and sunstroke. Of the Engineer officers, two-thirds were killed or wounded.[3] The Sappers and Pioneers lost nearly 300 men. Geneste and Fulford were so worn out by exposure and overwork that they died soon after the siege was ended. Such was the price of victory, but the gain was worth the cost. The fall of Delhi broke the backbone of the Indian Mutiny and assured the ultimate success of our arms.

Columns were despatched as soon as possible to sweep the *Doab* between the Jumna and the Ganges and to deal with disloyal chiefs. One, under Colonel Greathed, which included the 10th and 11th Companies of Punjab Sappers with Home and Lang as Engineers,

---

[1] *Life of General Sir Alex Taylor*, by A. C. Taylor, Vol. II, p. 42.
[2] The residential area on the river-bank south of the King's Palace.
[3] Four Engineer officers were killed, and 16 wounded, out of a total of 32. Five out of nine Assistant Field Engineers (Infantry officers) became casualties. (See *R.E. Professional Papers*, Vol. XXIII, p. 89.)

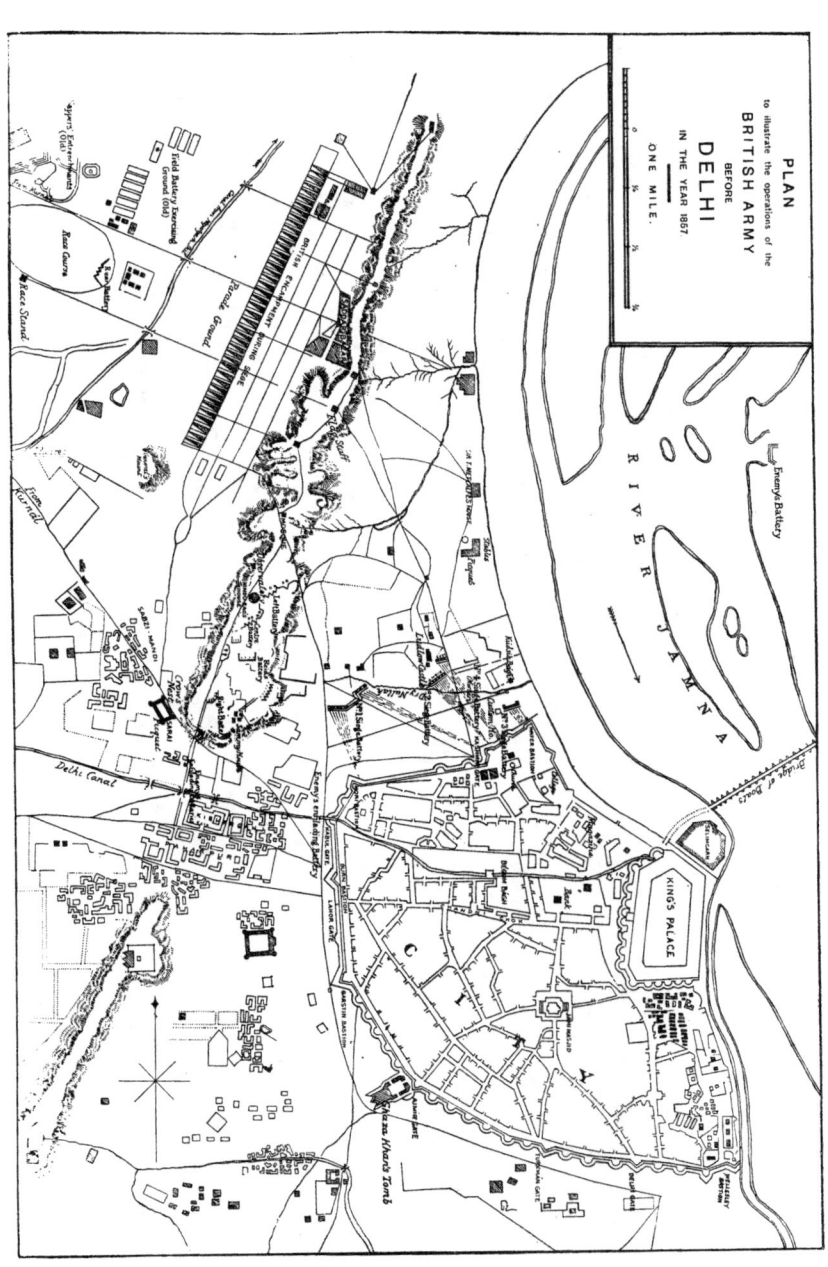

marched from Delhi on September 24th, defeated the enemy at Bulandshahr four days later, and then made for the fortress of Malagarh[1] which was found to be empty. It was there, on October 1st, that Home met his death. The Engineers were destroying the fortifications, and the last mine had failed to explode. Home ran laughing towards it. As he stooped to examine the fuse, the charge exploded and he was blown almost to pieces.[2] After escaping the desperate perils of the Kashmir Gate, he met his end before a deserted fort. The column marched sadly on and reached Agra on the 10th. There Greathed dispersed some mutineers and marched again to join the force assembling at Cawnpore. Shortly after Greathed left Delhi, another column under Brigadier Showers set out westwards and journeyed as far as the edge of the Bikaner desert. Thackeray, Humphry and two more companies of Punjab Sappers went with it. They blew up a number of forts but had no serious fighting. More trouble in the same direction, however, caused the early despatch of another column under Colonel Gerrard which had a stiff fight at Narnaul[3] on October 16th. Gerrard was killed, and Humphry of the Engineers, who was his Aide-de-Camp, was wounded in 17 places.[4] But these punitive expeditions were trivial in comparison with the serious operations then taking place in Oudh. The fall of Delhi was a doubtful boon to the British garrisons in Lucknow and other places, for it resulted in a great reinforcement of their enemies. The Delhi Mutineers streamed to the south-east to join hands with the followers of an unholy trio, Dhundhu Pant, Raja of Bithur (the infamous "Nana Sahib"), the Rani of Jhansi, the best military leader of the insurrection though a woman, and the King of Oudh, all implacable enemies of the British. The Delhi Engineer Brigade was broken up and most of the officers were ordered to Oudh to assist in the operations in the Lucknow area.

[1] Five miles north of Bulandshahr.
[2] "The Diary and Letters of A. M. Lang," appearing in the *Journal of the Society for Army Historical Research*, Vol. X, April, 1931, p. 93.
[3] About 60 miles south-west of Delhi, in the Rewari District.
[4] Humphry charged the enemy single-handed when deserted by some irregular cavalry whom he was leading. (See *Two Indian Campaigns*, by Colonel E. T. Thackeray, R.E., p. 90.)

CHAPTER XVIII.

THE INDIAN MUTINY: CAWNPORE, LUCKNOW AND CENTRAL INDIA.

THE Indian regiments at Cawnpore mutinied on June 4th, 1857, and murdered all the isolated Europeans whom they could find. Major-General Sir Hugh Wheeler, who was in command, was a gallant veteran[1] of the Afghan and Sikh Wars, but he had taken up an indefensible position in two barracks on an open plain at the eastern end of the cantonment, the nearest to Allahabad, from which direction he hoped to be reinforced. Unfortunately his magazine, which was fortified, was far away on the opposite or Delhi side of Cawnpore. He threw up a small earthen parapet around the barracks, and concentrated all the European women and children within the enclosure. When the storm burst he tried bravely to hold his own with 300 British officers and men, some civilians and a few loyal Indians against 3,000 mutineers under the Nana Sahib. The result is well known. He capitulated on June 27th under a promise from the Nana that his men and their wives and children would be given safe conduct in boats to Allahabad. All the men except four were shot down as they were embarking or soon afterwards, and the 200 British women and children were taken back to Cawnpore to be butchered in cold blood on July 15th, only one day before Brigadier-General Havelock forced his way in from Allahabad. Havelock commanded less than 2,000 men; at Bithur to the north lay the Nana's army under his general Tantia Topi, and at Kalpi to the south-west another army of mutineers was gathering from Gwalior. Yet, with remarkable daring, Havelock determined to advance to the relief of the Lucknow Residency, and summoned Colonel Neill with 200 men from Allahabad to take command at Cawnpore.

The first obstacle to an advance was the flooded Ganges. Fortunately Havelock was able to obtain the help of Captain W. A. Crommelin, B.E., the bridging expert of the Second Sikh campaign, who hurried up from Calcutta; but Crommelin did not reach Cawnpore till July 25th, when the troops had already been crossing the 1,500 yards' width of torrent and sandbank for five days. However, the operation was completed on the 28th, and Havelock moved towards Lucknow with, as Fortescue says,[2] a force of unknown strength in his front and an impassable river in his rear. He defeated the enemy in a position near Unao and again at Bashiratganj. News

---
[1] He was 75 years of age.
[2] *A History of the British Army*, by the Hon. J. W. Fortescue, Vol. XIII, p. 287.

then arrived of trouble at Dinapore which would delay his reinforcements, so he fell back on the 31st to Mangalwar where he took up a position which Crommelin proceeded to fortify. On August 4th he advanced once more, and on the 5th again defeated the enemy at Bashiratganj; but again he was forced to retreat to Mangalwar, as Neill was said to be in danger in Cawnpore. It was evident to Havelock that to keep in close touch with Neill he must bridge the Ganges; but this would require time, and meanwhile some improved means of crossing must be provided. Colonel Tytler, his Quartermaster-General, came forward with a scheme for a causeway more than a mile long over inundated land, three small floating bridges and a trestle bridge to lead up to the main channel. The work began on August 3rd under Crommelin and Lieutenant G. E. Watson, B.E., who assisted him, and was pushed on so rapidly that the main channel was reached on the 12th, when Havelock had fought a third battle at Bashiratganj. As Neill was in grave danger from the rebels at Bithur, Havelock wished to cross at once to his assistance. Crommelin did not fail him. Sixty boats, 300 boatmen, and a small steamer with a lighter attached to her were ready at the pierhead at the end of the causeway early on August 13th, and the whole force except the rearguard was ferried across to Cawnpore in five and a half hours. " I never worked harder in my life," wrote Crommelin,[1] " and whilst paddling in the water I drank freely of beer and brandy and water."

This crossing by causeway and ferry enabled Havelock to defeat the mutineers heavily at Bithur on August 16th, but it was clear that the Ganges should be bridged for a rapid advance when reinforcements arrived. Accordingly Crommelin and Watson began to prepare materials and collect boats. On September 15th they started their great work, and toiling night and day, spanned the Ganges in less than four days by a bridge 700 yards in length and containing upwards of 70 large boats. Major-General Sir James Outram and some reinforcements had arrived in Cawnpore on the 15th; and Havelock, Outram and 3,000 men crossed the bridge on September 19th and 20th to begin their advance on Lucknow.[2] Brushing aside all resistance, Havelock was within 16 miles of Lucknow on the 22nd when he fired a royal salute to put heart into the British garrison of the beleaguered Residency, and on the following day he captured and occupied a large enclosed garden called the Alam Bagh lying south of the city. On his staff was Colonel Robert Napier, B.E., who had come from Calcutta as Military Secretary with Sir James Outram.[3]

It is necessary now to trace the course of events in Lucknow itself.

[1] Obituary notice of Lieut.-General W. A. Crommelin, C.B., appearing in *The R.E. Journal*, Vol. 17, 1887, p. 11.
[2] Outram, though the senior officer, had waived his right to command in favour of Havelock who had borne the heat and burden of the day.
[3] Napier had recently arrived from furlough in England with the full intention of retiring after another three years' service.

Sir Henry Lawrence had assumed charge of the province of Oudh in March, 1857, and seeing that a serious rising was imminent, had wisely made preparations for the protection of the Europeans in Lucknow by collecting supplies and examining certain localities with a view to defence. The city was more than five miles in length and nearly three in width, and lay mostly along the right or southern bank of the River Gumti.[1] On the south and east it was bounded by a canal leading into the Gumti near a large college called La Martiniere,[2] to the south of which lay a palace named the Dilkusha. The city was very dense except at its north-eastern corner where narrow lanes and squalid buildings gave place to palatial residences, huge mausoleums and walled gardens. In the centre of the northern face, the Gumti was spanned by a so-called " stone " bridge[3] carrying a road leading to the cantonments of the troops at Mariaon and Mudkipur. Half a mile farther downstream was an iron bridge[4] with a road which bifurcated to the cantonments and to Fyzabad and extended southwards from the bridge past the British Residency, through the city, and so towards Cawnpore; it crossed the southern canal by a bridge at a garden called the Char Bagh and ran close to the Alam Bagh. Near the stone bridge on the Gumti was an old Sikh fort known as the Machhi Bhawan,[5] and to the east of the iron bridge on high ground was a group of buildings clustering around the Residency. Farther to the east, and bordering the dense mass of the city, stretched a line of great palaces—the Kaisarbagh, the Imambara and the Begum Kothi—and in a bend of the river to their north lay the Moti Mahal, Shah Najif, Kadam Rasul and a large enclosure called the Sikandar Bagh. On May 14th, when he had news of the Delhi massacres, Lawrence proceeded to put his plans into operation. He began to occupy and garrison the Machhi Bhawan with his best troops and guns, and to collect all the British families in the Residency; he marked out a line of defence to include the Residency and a number of other buildings around it and placed a part of his European troops within it. The remainder of his European troops were quartered in the southern end of the cantonment at Mariaon to keep order among the native regiments[6] and to separate them from the city. The

---

[1] A tributary of the Ganges, entering the latter below Benares. A reference to the plan of the City of Lucknow, which is included in this chapter, will enable the reader to follow the description of the locality. The plan is opposite p. 360.

[2] Designed and founded by General Claude Martin, a Frenchman, and opened in 1840. The most ornate and palatial building of the " City of Palaces."

[3] Actually of brick masonry. It was demolished in 1911 and replaced by a new bridge opened by the Viceroy (Lord Hardinge) in January, 1914.

[4] This bridge still exists. It has three spans, the centre of 90 feet width and the others of 80 feet, consisting of cast-iron arches on brick piers and abutments. The roadway is 30 feet wide. The ironwork came from England in 1798, and the bridge was built by Colonel H. Fraser, B.E., between 1842 and 1847. (See *Guide to Lucknow*, by E. H. A. Hilton.)

[5] The Machhi Bhawan no longer exists. On its site stands King George's Medical College and Hospital, opened by the Lieutenant-Governor of the United Provinces (Sir J. Hewett) in January, 1912.

[6] One regiment, the 7th Oudh Infantry, had risen on May 1st and had been disarmed.

occupation of the Machhi Bhawan was intended only as a temporary measure to cover the fortification of the Residency position. By May 17th Lawrence was holding his three positions, which commanded the passages of the Gumti, and was progressing steadily with the Residency defences. Disaffection spread rapidly, and on the 30th most of the Indian troops mutinied and marched away to join the other rebels.[1] This was the immediate result of the British disaster at Cawnpore.

It was clear that the Residency would be attacked in due course, and, at the end of June, Lawrence heard that large bodies of mutineers were approaching along the Fyzabad Road. Taking military command of a force of only 700 men with 11 guns he set out on June 30th to attack them. It was a rash move and he paid dearly for it. The British force was badly defeated at Chinhut, seven miles from the iron bridge, and was driven back into the Residency with the loss of half its strength and three guns. Although the defences were still far from complete Lawrence then decided to concentrate within them, so he withdrew the garrison of the Machhi Bhawan on July 1st when the building was blown up by Lieutenant McLeod Innes of the Bengal Engineers. The mutineers opened their bombardment of the Residency position and invested it on every side. Lawrence himself was dangerously wounded on the 2nd and died two days later. The civil charge then passed to Major Banks, and the military command to Colonel Inglis of the 32nd Foot. With a mixed force of 800 Indian soldiers and 900 Europeans including 500 British soldiers of the 32nd Foot, and with only 15 guns and seven mortars, Inglis had to defend a quadrilateral perimeter of one mile against 6,000 mutineers, who could advance under cover to within a few yards of his trenches. He was hampered by the responsibility for the defence of 600 women and children who were crowded into the lower floors of several buildings. Outside the northern face, between the defences and the river, was a clear space where the enemy could mass for an assault. On the other three fronts, houses clustered right up to the perimeter.

Only five Engineer officers were included in the garrison. These were Major J. Anderson, Captains G. W. W. Fulton and G. Hutchinson (Staff), and Lieutenant J. J. McLeod Innes, all of the Bengal Engineers, and Lieutenant J. C. Anderson of the Madras Corps.[2] There were no Sappers and Miners in the Residency, but the Engineers got some valuable help in mining operations from a few Cornish soldiers of the 32nd Foot.[3] The line of defence was divided into ten

[1] Three regiments mutinied, but some of the sepoys of each remained loyal and joined in the defence of the Residency.
[2] Brother of Lady Outram, and of the Anderson who was murdered at Multan before the Second Sikh War.
[3] They had the assistance also of Lieutenant Tulloch, 58th N.I., Lieutenant Birch, 59th N.I., and Mr. J. May, a civilian. (See *The Military History of the Madras Engineers*, by Major H. M. Vibart, Vol. II, p. 318, and *The Tourist's Guide to Lucknow*, 8th edition, by E. H. Hilton, Appendix G, giving a list of the garrison and non-combatants. Also the list of the Engineer Brigade in the *Report on the Engineering Operations at the Siege of Lucknow*, by Sir R. Napier, p. 9.)

sections including 17 posts and batteries, each post having its commandant and garrison and each being independent and self-supporting. There were no reliefs, and only one British company in the Residency building as a reserve. Fourteen large buildings lay within the perimeter, the only entrance to which was by the Baillie Guard Gate on the east side close to the Treasury, the Hospital, Dr. Fayrer's House and Saunders' House. The defenders of each post strengthened it and its vicinity as time permitted under the advice of the Engineers. Every man slept at his post with his rifle beside him. Fortunately, owing to Henry Lawrence's foresight, there was no lack of food. The water also was good and abundant. By July 9th the ceaseless labour of the whole garrison had made the defences strong enough to give hopes of a successful resistance whatever the odds.

The mutineers would not risk heavy casualties. They poured in musketry fire from surrounding houses and did considerable damage with their guns, but they preferred to keep away from British bayonets. After a few small attacks they began, on July 14th, to mine towards a projecting post on the northern front called the "Redan" in preparation for their first general attack on the 20th. The signal for this was the explosion of their mine when, under cover of a heavy musketry fire, two large bodies of mutineers tried without success to rush the Redan and Innes' Post to its west.[1] The Redan mine at Lucknow was the first attempt of the enemy at subterranean warfare,[2] and it was a complete failure; it was blown up when still 140 feet from its objective, and this although the gallery had been driven for 160 feet, the longest mine ever attempted by the mutineers.[3] Their calculations were faulty and their work was slow, but the true reason for their repeated failures was cowardice. However, it became necessary to countermine without delay, so Major Anderson, the Chief Engineer, selected eight Cornishmen[4] serving in the 32nd Foot and detailed them as instructors to the garrison of the various posts under the general supervision of Captain Fulton, the Garrison Engineer. Four new enemy galleries were soon detected by listeners, three advancing towards the south face and one towards the east face, so countermines were started. Shafts for listeners were sunk also in all the more exposed posts. If the enemy's miners were said to be near, Captain Fulton would sit, revolver in hand, at the end of a British countermine waiting for them to break through. "Some one who was looking for me," he relates, "asked one of the Europeans if I was in the mine. 'Yes, sir,' said the sergeant. 'There he has

---

[1] Innes' Post was at the extreme north-west angle.
[2] Mining by the enemy was suspected once at Delhi, but it was never proved and probably never took place.
[3] *Lucknow and Oude in the Mutiny*, by Lieut.-General McLeod Innes, R.E., p. 124.
[4] Serjeant Day and seven privates.

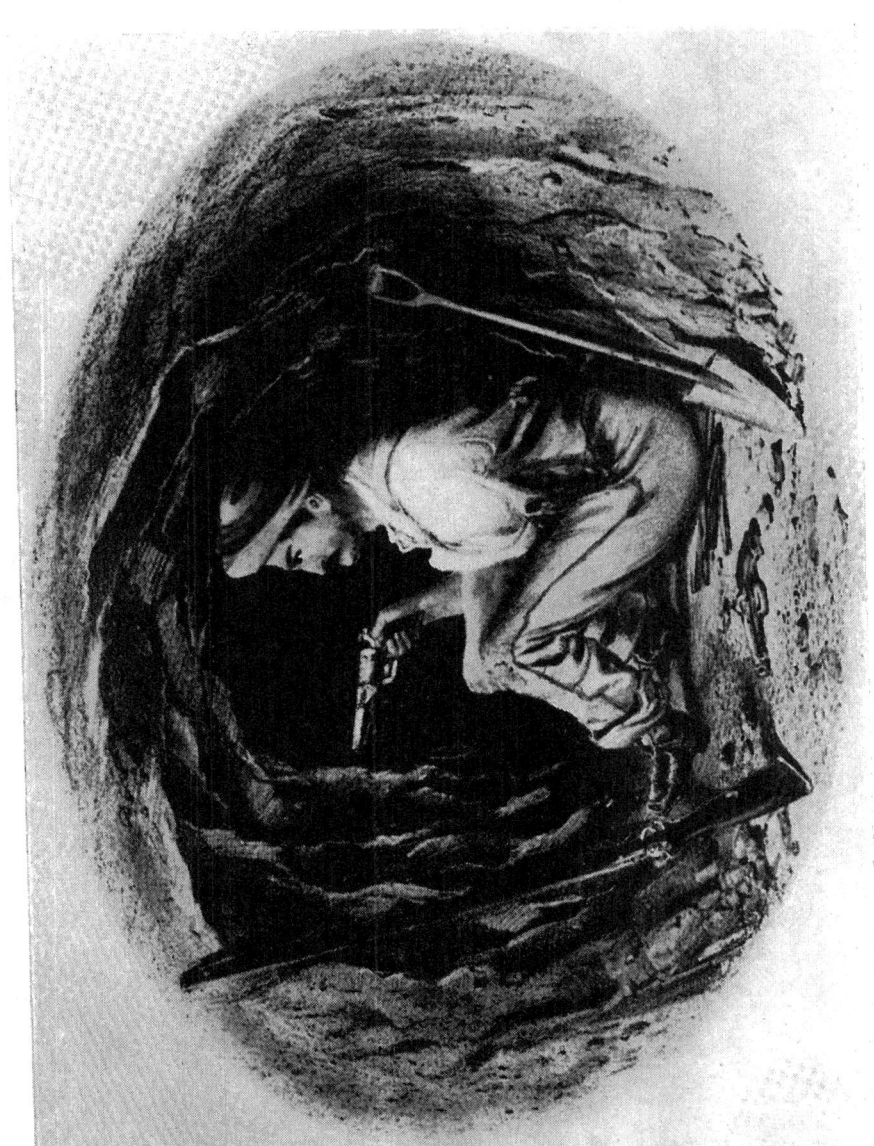

"LYING IN WAIT."
Captain G. W. W. Fulton, Bengal Engineers, at Lucknow.

been for the last two hours, like a terrier at a rat hole, and not likely to leave it either all day.' "[1]

The garrison made frequent sorties, and so hampered the enemy's operations that a general attack on August 10th was beaten off with heavy loss.[2] The mutineers then redoubled their efforts in mining, running 14 galleries before September 5th with only one success. Hutchinson had become the leader of the counterminers as the duties of Chief Engineer had devolved on Fulton owing to the death of Major Anderson on August 11th from dysentery. On September 5th the mutineers launched another general attack after exploding two mines, and once again they were repulsed. The garrison suffered a heavy loss on the 14th when Fulton was killed by a round shot. He had stopped every mine of the enemy, helped the dying Anderson, cheered the whole community by his optimism, and shot many a sniper. He is described as the life and soul of everything that was persevering, chivalrous and daring, and is said to have deserved to be called the " Defender of Lucknow." Only J. C. Anderson, Hutchinson and Innes remained to carry on the engineering work, and Anderson was in poor health.[3] But help was at hand. Cannonading was heard to the south on September 23rd and 24th; and on the 25th, in a roar of musketry, Havelock, Outram and their men entered by an embrasure and through the gate at the Baillie Guard. Havelock had forced a crossing of the canal at the Char Bagh bridge, and turning right had advanced without much difficulty by the Begum Kothi to the Sikandar Bagh. There he turned to his left and halted at the Moti Mahal within 1,100 yards of the Residency enclosure. Beyond this lay the Chattar Manzil group of palaces stretching for 800 yards along the river-bank, and to the south the great Kaisar Bagh Palace. A winding road, in which every house was a fortress, ran towards the Residency and ended in a narrow lane which led straight to the Baillie Guard Gate. Under heavy fire from all sides the British fought their way along this road, losing the gallant Colonel Neill[4] and many other good men. The rearguard was left in the Moti Mahal and was bravely rescued by a party under Napier on the following day. Thus Havelock and Outram reached their goal, but only by cutting a passage through their enemies and not by driving them away. They had merely reinforced Inglis and were too weak to extricate him and his 600 women and children. Nothing remained but to await relief in their turn by Sir Colin Campbell, the newly-appointed Commander-in-Chief.

In the second phase of the defence which now began, Outram, who had assumed command, could afford to take the offensive when

---
[1] *The Tale of the Great Mutiny*, by W. H. Fitchett, p. 184.
[2] The enemy exploded two more mines in this attack.
[3] After the final relief of Lucknow by Sir Colin Campbell in November, 1857, J. C. Anderson was so ill with scurvy that he was sent to Calcutta and granted three years' leave on medical certificate.
[4] Neill was shot by a mutineer hidden in an archway now called Neill's Arch.

opportunity offered. He sent out frequent sorties, including a very successful one under Napier on October 1st, and extended his position for about 1,000 yards eastwards, and also northwards to the river, by capturing the Chattar Manzil group of palaces. His cadre of Engineers was sufficient, though he had no Sappers and Miners. The Chief Engineer was Captain W. A. Crommelin, B.E., who, however, was incapacitated for a time by a wound received in Havelock's advance to the Residency; but Colonel Robert Napier filled the breach and acted as Chief Engineer in addition to his duties as Chief of Staff until Crommelin was able to resume his work. Under Crommelin were the three surviving Engineers of the first defence, Lieutenants J. C. Anderson, G. Hutchinson and J. J. McLeod Innes, and Lieutenants L. Russell and D. Limond who had marched in with him. All these officers, except Anderson, were Bengal Engineers.[1] They were helped by six Assistant Field Engineers, three of the original force and three who came with Havelock.[2]

The mutineers never attacked the British position seriously after it was reinforced, and most of the warfare during the second phase was underground. Sir James Outram wrote afterwards:[3] "I am aware of no parallel to our series of mines in modern war. Twenty-one shafts, aggregating 200 feet in depth, and 3,291 feet of gallery have been executed. The enemy advanced twenty mines against the palaces and outposts. Of these they exploded three which caused us loss of life and two which did no injury. Seven have been blown in, and out of seven others the enemy have been driven; results of which the Engineer Department may well be proud." It appears that the shafts averaged eight feet in depth, and the galleries were generally three feet high and two feet wide with an arched roof and usually without casing. Two galleries were run to lengths of almost 300 and 200 feet respectively without the aid of air tubes. Eight times the enemy were heard mining towards the position. Crommelin's men used to wait silently till the approaching miners broke through into their gallery. Then they fired through the opening, charged the mutineers and in every instance captured and destroyed the gallery without using any explosive.[4] The events of the final weeks of the defence make an interesting story but one which cannot

---

[1] As already stated, Anderson was a Madras Engineer. Innes rose to be a Lieut.-General, and Hutchinson, Russell and Limond became Major-Generals. Lieutenant G. E. Watson, B.E., who was with Crommelin at Cawnpore, did not take part, apparently, in Havelock's relief of the Residency at Lucknow.

[2] Lieutenants Birch and Tulloch and Mr. May of the original garrison, and Captain Oakes and Lieutenants Chalmers and Hall (all of the Native Infantry) who came with Havelock. (*History of the Corps of Royal Engineers*, by Major-General W. Porter, Vol. I, p. 486.)

[3] Sir J. Outram to Major-General Sir W. Mansfield, Chief of Staff. Extracts from a Despatch dated November 25th, 1857, published in G.O.G.G. No. 1625, dated December 22nd, 1857.

[4] Report by Captain W. A. Crommelin, B.E., quoted in the obituary notice on Lieut.-General W. A. Crommelin appearing in *The R.E. Journal*, Vol. 17, 1887, p. 12.

THE RESIDENCY, LUCKNOW, AT THE END OF THE SIEGE.

be told here. Outram established communication with Sir Colin Campbell by means of secret agents who reached the Alam Bagh where he had left a small garrison, and he suggested the lines along which Sir Colin might advance. Relief came on November 17th. Outram and Havelock with some other officers rode out to meet the Commander-in-Chief, and in that ride a musket ball found Robert Napier and laid him low for several weeks.

Sir Colin Campbell had landed at Calcutta on August 13th, and had put all his energy into sending reinforcements towards Lucknow. He followed them at the end of October and arrived in Cawnpore on November 3rd; then, leaving a small force under Major-General Windham to hold Cawnpore, he pushed on northwards and reached the Alam Bagh on November 12th. The force which was assembled there numbered about 5,000 men with 44 guns, including a heavy battery manned by sailors from H.M.S. *Shannon* under Captain Sir William Peel, R.N. It was made up of two bodies of men; one, Greathed's column from Delhi which came under the command of Colonel Hope Grant before it reached Cawnpore on October 26th; the other of various reinforcements which had arrived from the Calcutta direction. It was organized in three brigades of infantry with cavalry and artillery. An expedition had been on its way from England to China, and part of it, on reaching Singapore, was diverted to Calcutta. Among the troops so diverted was the 23rd Company of Royal Engineers under Captain A. J. Clerke, with Lieutenants W. O. Lennox, V.C.,[1] E. D. Malcolm, G. D. Pritchard and R. Harrison. This unit landed in Calcutta on August 11th, 1857, and so had the distinction of being the first company of Royal Engineers to set foot in India.[2] It was sent up to Allahabad and then to Cawnpore where it met " C " Company, Madras Sappers and Miners, under Lieutenant C. Scott, M.E., with 2nd-Lieutenant W. H. Burton, M.E., and two Infantry officers. The two companies marched together to Bani Bridge, 18 miles south of Lucknow, and, having repaired the bridge, joined the Lucknow Relief Force at Bantera towards the Alam Bagh. There they found Lieutenant A. M. Lang, B.E., and the 10th and 11th Companies of Punjab Sappers who had come with Greathed's column from Delhi. Major A. G. Goodwyn, B.E., arrived also as Chief Engineer,[3] with Lieutenant G. E. Watson, B.E., as Brigade-Major of Engineers and Lieutenant P. Stewart, B.E., as Superintendent of Electric Telegraphs. Thus Sir Colin Campbell began the second relief of Lucknow with two regular and two partly-trained companies of Engineer troops, and with a cadre of about 11

---

[1] Lieutenant W. O. Lennox, R.E., was the first Engineer officer to gain the Victoria Cross. It was awarded to him for a gallant deed performed on November 20th, 1854, during the siege of Sebastopol in the Crimea.

[2] *History of the Corps of Royal Engineers*, by Major-General W. Porter, Vol. I, p. 488.

[3] Major Goodwyn, however, fell ill on the 15th and the command then passed to Lieutenant W. O. Lennox, V.C., R.E.

Engineer officers assisted by a few Infantry officers. It was an efficient Engineer Brigade though almost all the officers were subalterns and some had no experience of India.

The Commander-in-Chief based his plan of attack on the proposals which General Outram had sent to him from the beleaguered Residency, and on maps and plans which were bravely carried through the enemy's lines by Mr. Kavanagh, a clerk, who disguised himself as a native. He set his troops in motion on November 14th, not on the direct route towards the Char Bagh Bridge as Havelock had done, but to his right towards the Dilkusha Palace which, with the Martiniere, he captured without much opposition. Lang and Burton of the Engineers were the first officers to reach the top of the Martiniere Tower where they hoisted the Union Jack. After consolidating his position on the 15th, Campbell crossed the canal on the 16th at its junction with the Gumti and advanced against the great walled enclosure of the Sikandar Bagh, the 23rd Company, Royal Engineers, and " C " Company, Madras Sappers and Miners, being with the advanced guard. A great fight and a grim slaughter followed. Lang says:[1] " We had turned Pandy's flank and he had not expected us there. Then began our work: some of our Sappers worked at knocking down a mud wall so that a big 24-pounder might play at the Sikandar Bagh; then we were at work making ramps from the street[2] up some banks, up which we pulled more heavy guns and in a little time they were smashing away at the Sikandar Bagh. The Infantry were lying under shelter ready for a rush, and some dragging away at the ropes of the heavy guns. 'Pandy' all the while keeping up no end of a fire from the walls of the Sikandar Bagh. While I was working hard I saw the 4th Punjabis yelling and shouting as they charged straight at the building.[3] Down we dropped the ropes and rushed along too: up sprung 93rd and 53rd and cheering and shouting ' Revenge for Cawnpore ' on we went, some at a breach in one of the corner towers and some (with whom I was) over a loopholed mud wall straight at the gate; axes and muskets soon smashed the gate, and then, didn't we get revenge! Right and left of the gateway ' Pandies ' lay in heaps, three or four deep. They made but little stand. It was a glorious sight to see the mass of bodies when we did get in. They shut the many thin doors and thousands of bullets were poured into the masses. The bodies have now been buried and counted—1,840 ' Pandies '." The scenes in the Sikandar Bagh, where 2,000 mutineers were trapped by

---

[1] " The Diary and Letters of A. M. Lang," appearing in the *Journal of the Society for Army Historical Research*, Vol. X, July, 1931, p. 138.

[2] A sunken road in which the column came under heavy fire and was thrown into much confusion.

[3] The south-east corner of the walled enclosure. The 93rd Highlanders, the 53rd Foot and the 4th Punjabis were all in this wild charge. A Highlander was first through the little breach and was shot dead; a 4th Punjabi Sikh was next and shared the same fate.

GENERAL SIR BINDON BLOOD, G.C.B., G.C.V.O., COLONEL-COMMANDANT ROYAL ENGINEERS, AS A COLONEL.

the furious British infantry, were terrible beyond description. This was the payment exacted for the blood of murdered Englishwomen. It was never forgotten.

During the afternoon of November 16th, the British advance continued. The Kadam Rasul was captured easily; but the Shah Najif, with bastions 40 feet in height, stopped the troops for a time. Luckily a small gap was found through which they could enter, and the defenders then fled. At last the Moti Mahal alone divided the Relief Force from Outram's men in the Chattar Manzil, but it was strongly held and well supported from the Mess House[1] to its south. On the 17th, Sir Colin Campbell proceeded to safeguard his left flank by capturing Banks House, the Barracks and the Mess House, and then, with the co-operation of Outram, the Moti Mahal itself. Cheers from house to house, battery to battery and regiment to regiment announced the junction of the relieved and relieving troops, and Outram and Havelock came out to meet Campbell. There was no question of risking another siege; immediate evacuation and a retirement to Cawnpore were obviously imperative. On November 19th the women and children[2] and the sick were moved in small parties along a lane and behind canvas screens till they were safe from fire; then to the Sikandar Bagh, and after dark to the Dilkusha. Meanwhile the attention of the mutineers in the Kaisar Bagh was engaged by heavy fire. The evacuation continued, and by the evening of the 22nd the ruined Residency was empty. Before dawn on the following day the whole force was safe in the Dilkusha. It was an admirable achievement, but the general satisfaction was marred by the death of Sir Henry Havelock who succumbed to dysentery on the 24th. Sir Colin Campbell left a division of about 4,000 men under Outram to hold a position at the Alam Bagh, and with the remainder of his army, and the women and children, set out on November 27th for Cawnpore where the situation was critical.

Outram held his own most gallantly from the end of November till the end of February. Close to his north was Lucknow with 90,000 mutineers, jubilant at Campbell's retreat. The fortified Alam Bagh —the key of his position—was in his right centre, the ruined fort of Jalalabad protected his right, and some field works his left front and left. Six times he was attacked[3] and never failed to repulse the enemy, a happy result which was due largely to the excellent defences erected by his Engineers who were headed by Lieutenant G. Hutchinson, B.E. Under Hutchinson were Lieutenant C. Scott and 2nd-Lieutenant R. G. Burton of the Madras Engineers with " C "

[1] The Kurshid Manzil, the Regimental Mess House of the 32nd Regiment whose barracks lay half a mile to the east of the Mess. (See plan.)
[2] Among them were Mrs. Brydon and her child who were present during the siege with Dr. Brydon, the sole survivor of Elphinstone's disastrous retreat from Kabul in 1842. The child, afterwards Mrs. M. A. Scott, died at Rosenberg, in Cromarty, on May 11th, 1932.
[3] On December 22nd, January 12th and 16th, and February 15th, 21st and 25th.

Company, Madras Sappers and Miners, Lieutenant C. N. Judge of the Bengal Corps, and seven Assistant Field Engineers.[1] The 23rd Company R.E. and the two companies of Punjab Pioneers (or Sappers), with their Engineer officers, had marched with Sir Colin Campbell towards Cawnpore. But when Outram began his defence of the Alam Bagh, Royal Engineers were flocking into India. The 4th Company, R.E., under Major L. Nicholson, with Lieutenants P. H. Scratchley, C. E. Wynne, G. Swetenham and W. Keith; the 11th Company, R.E., led by Captain C. E. Cumberland, with Lieutenants J. P. Maquay, D. C. Walker and J. B. Paterson, and the 21st Company, R.E., under Captain T. Fenwick, with Lieutenants J. B. Edwards, W. B. Gosset, C. E. Webber and E. R. Festing, all arrived in November, 1857, the 4th and 11th Companies disembarking at Calcutta and the 21st at Bombay.[2] Lieut.-Colonel H. D. Harness, R.E., reached Cawnpore from Malta to command the Royal Engineers under Sir Robert Napier as Chief Engineer. Other Royal Engineers who came to India were Captains A. R. V. Crease, F. E. Cox and G. Neville, and Lieutenant F. E. B. Beaumont; but of these only Cox and Beaumont took part in the final advance on Lucknow, and only the 4th and 23rd Companies, R.E., were engaged in that operation. Altogether, four companies and about two dozen officers of the Royal Engineers helped to quell the Indian Mutiny. The Royal and Company's officers soon became great friends though each got some amusement from the other; the Royals were amazed at the tattered uniforms of the Delhi veterans, and the latter smiled at the rather superior airs and side-whiskers of the newcomers and their ignorance of India.

Not long after Sir Colin Campbell had begun his march towards Cawnpore with 3,000 men and an enormous convoy, he received bad news of Windham's force which was guarding Crommelin's bridge over the Ganges.[3] Windham had rashly advanced from his entrenchment and attacked the Gwalior contingent of mutineers on November 26th, but being obliged to retire, was himself attacked by Tantia Topi and pressed back to his original position. The rebel leader then occupied Cawnpore City with his Marathas and threatened the bridge with his guns. Sir Colin Campbell realized that he would be in a desperate situation if the bridge was destroyed, so he hurried on and crossed the Ganges into Cawnpore on the 29th while the bridge

---

[1] Captain C. Oakes and Lieutenants Hon. A. Fraser and A. Tulloch of the Bengal Infantry, Ensign Ogilvie (or Ogilvy) of the Madras Infantry, Mr. Birch of the Indian Navy, and Messrs. J. May and J. Tait, Civil Engineers. (See *The History of the Madras Engineers and Pioneers*, by H. M. Vibart, Vol. II, p. 376, corrected by the list of the Engineer Brigade given by Sir Robert Napier in his *Report on the Operations at the Siege of Lucknow*.)

[2] *History of the Corps of Royal Engineers*, by Major-General W. Porter, Vol. I, p. 487.

[3] The Engineers with this force were Major N. C. MacLeod, B.E., and Captain R. H. Sankey, M.E. (See *The History of the Madras Engineers and Pioneers*, by H. M. Vibart, Vol. II, pp. 367, 368.)

was still intact. His first care was then to despatch the women, children and invalids under a strong escort to Allahabad. That done, he turned on Tantia Topi, defeated him utterly on December 6th, and followed up his victory by leading a column to Fategarh and beyond, and by sending out another under Colonel Walpole to sweep the *Doab* and ordering a third under Colonel Seaton to move from Delhi. A column under Brigadier-General Franks, which included a Nepalese contingent under Maharaja Jang Bahadur, entered Oudh from the south-east and moving on Lucknow defeated the rebels at Chanda, Hamirpur, Sultanpur and Dhaurahra. It was at Sultanpur on February 22nd, 1858, that McLeod Innes of the Bengal Engineers earned the Victoria Cross for capturing a gun single-handed. Franks' column, and the Gurkhas under Jang Bahadur, joined Sir Colin Campbell during his attack on Lucknow.

On March 2nd, 1858, the Commander-in-Chief began his advance against the rebel positions. Including Outram's division at the Alam Bagh he had an army of about 19,000 men with 120 guns, which, when strengthened later by Franks' column and the Gurkhas, was increased to 31,000 men with 164 guns. Napier had informed him in December that 20,000 men would be needed to subdue the city and that afterwards a garrison of half that strength would be required to hold it and to guard the roads to Cawnpore.[1] Early in January Napier had recovered sufficiently from his wound to rejoin Outram at the Alam Bagh as Chief of Staff. There he reconnoitred the ground on both sides of the Gumti and recommended that Lucknow should be attacked from the east. The rebels had been very busy since the British evacuation in November. Three elaborate lines of works now covered their chief citadel, the Kaisar Bagh.[2] The first was a parapet with a few batteries extending along the southern edge of Lucknow City, behind the canal, and prolonged from Banks House to the Gumti by massive earthen ramparts with bastions and batteries at close intervals. The second, with a slightly curved trace, started from the Imambara, enclosed the Mess House and the Moti Mahal, and ran northwards to the Gumti; the third, at right angles to it, was close along the front of the Kaisar Bagh.[3] All the main streets in the city were barricaded, and every important building loopholed and fortified. There were no defences on the left or northern bank of the river. The rebel garrison was believed to number at least 120,000 men.

Brigadier Robert Napier, B.E., was appointed in January, 1858, to command the Engineer Brigade before Lucknow, and soon after the attack began in March he was at the head of 1,800 officers and men. These included the 4th and 23rd Companies of Royal

---

[1] Sir Colin Campbell to Lord Canning. Memorandum dated December 22nd, 1857.
[2] See the plan included in this chapter.
[3] *Lucknow and Oudh in the Mutiny*, by Lieut.-General McLeod Innes, pp. 278–279.

Engineers under Lieut.-Colonel H. D. Harness, R.E., " C " Company, Madras Sappers and Miners, under Lieutenant C. Scott, M.E., 200 Bengal Sappers and Miners under Lieutenant F. R. Maunsell, B.E., about 750 Punjab Pioneers under Lieutenant H. W. Gulliver, B.E., and the same number of Delhi Pioneers under an Infantry officer.[1] The Royal Engineer officers numbered 13; the Bengal Engineers, headed by Alexander Taylor,[2] 23; and with Sankey, Scott and Burton of the Madras Engineers, and 19 Assistant Field Engineers or officers acting as Engineers, the cadre of Engineers, including Napier himself, reached a total of 59.[3]

The Dilkusha Palace was occupied without difficulty on March 2nd, and the Engineer Brigade moved from their depot at Jalalabad to the grounds of a house called Bibiapur, between the Dilkusha and the river. Joined by Franks' column on the 4th, Sir Colin Campbell then proceeded with his attack. The construction of two cask bridges across the Gumti was begun after dark by Major Nicholson, R.E., at a spot about one mile downstream of the Dilkusha, but only

[1] Most of the Delhi Engineer Brigade reached the camp near Lucknow on February 11th, 1858.
[2] Taylor had been transferred from Delhi at the particular request of Napier to command the Company's Engineers at Lucknow. (See *Life of General Sir Alex Taylor*, by A. C. Taylor, Vol. II, p. 124.)
[3] The figures are taken from the official *Report on the Engineering Operations at the Siege of Lucknow*, dated March 31st, 1858, by Brigadier R. C. Napier, Chief Engineer, pp. 8-11. The following list of regular Engineer officers, with their subsequent ranks in brackets, is taken from the list given by Colonel C. B. Thackeray, R.A., in his article entitled " A Subaltern in the Indian Mutiny " (*vide The R.E. Journal*, September, 1931, p. 421), supplemented by Napier's Report. Officers present at Delhi are marked (*D*); those in the defence or reliefs of the Lucknow Residency are marked (*L*).

Royal Engineers:—Lieut.-Colonel H. D. Harness (Maj.-Gen., K.C.B., Col.-Comdt.), commanding R.E. Major Lothian Nicholson (Gen., K.C.B., Col.-Comdt.), commanding 4th Coy. R.E. Captains A. J. Clerke (killed at Lucknow), commanding 23rd Coy. R.E.; F. E. Cox (Maj.-Gen.), Adjutant; Brevet-Major W. O. Lennox, ⱽ.ℭ. (*L*) (Gen., ⱽ.ℭ., K.C.B.); F. E. B. Beaumont (Col.). Lieutenants P. H. Scratchley (Maj.-Gen., K.C.M.G.); E. D. Malcolm (*L*) (Col., C.B.); G. D. Pritchard (*L*) (Lt.-Gen., K.C.B.); C. E. Wynne (died at Lucknow, 1858); R. Harrison (*L*) (Gen., G.C.B., C.M.G., Col.-Comdt.), died September 25th, 1931, the last of the Lucknow Engineers; G. Swetenham (Major); W. Keith (Col.).

Bengal Engineers:—Captain (Bt.-Major) Alexander Taylor (*D*) (Gen., G.C.B., Col.-Comdt. R.E.), commanding Indian Engineers. Lieutenants H. W. Gulliver (*D*) (Lt.-Gen.), commanding Punjab Pioneers; F. R. Maunsell (*D*) (Gen., K.C.B., Col.-Comdt.), commanding Bengal Sappers; J. A. Champain (*D*) (Col., K.C.M.G.), Adjutant; J. F. Tennant (*D*) (Lt.-Gen., C.I.E., F.R.S.); W. W. Greathed (*D*) (Maj.-Gen., C.B.); J. Medley (*D*) (Maj.-Gen.); R. S. B. Pemberton (*D*) (Maj.-Gen., C.S.I.); P. Murray (*D*) (Major); A. McNeile (*D*); J. St. J. Hovenden (*D*) (Lt.-Col.); E. P. Brownlow (killed at Lucknow); R. Young (Maj.-Gen.); G. Hutchinson (*L*) (Maj.-Gen., C.B., C.S.I.); G. E. Watson (Lt.-Col.); A. M. Lang (*D* and *L*) (Col.); J. J. McLeod Innes (*L*) (Lt.-Gen., ⱽ.ℭ., C.B., F.R.S.). 2nd-Lieutenants W. F. Fulford (*D*) (died 1858); H. A. L. Carnegie (*D*); E. T. Thackeray (*D*) (Col., ⱽ.ℭ., K.C.B.); J. G. Forbes (*D*) (Col.); C. N. Judge (Lt.-Col.); R. G. Smyth (Col.).

Madras Engineers:—Lieutenants R. H. Sankey (Lt.-Gen., K.C.B.); C. Scott (killed 1858). 2nd-Lieutenant W. H. Burton (Col.).

The establishment of Bengal Engineers in 1858 was five Colonels, five Lieut.-Colonels (including Napier), five Majors, 35 Captains, 60 Lieutenants and 25 2nd-Lieutenants, and it was almost up to strength except in 2nd-Lieutenants. It is truly remarkable, therefore, that of the 24 Bengal Engineers who served in the capture of Lucknow, 22 *were subalterns*.

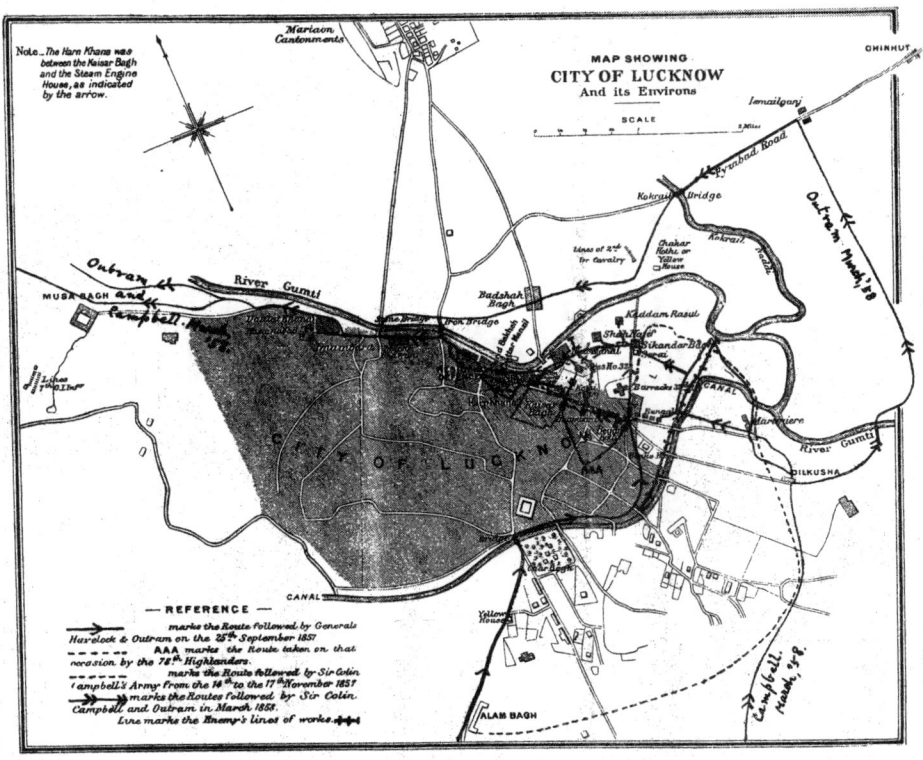

one was ready on the morning of the 5th, as there had been some miscalculation of material.[1] The second bridge was completed the same evening, and before dawn on March 6th a division under Outram was hurried across to the left bank as the bridges were found to be within range of the enemy's guns.[2] Nicholson and the 4th Company, R.E., and Hovenden with some Punjab Pioneers, marched with this force. Outram moved northwards to Ismailganj on the Fyzabad Road where he remained during the 7th and 8th; on the 9th he captured the Chakar Kothi and then the Badshah Bagh where he was in position to sweep with his heavy guns the rear and flank of the enemy's first and second lines across the Gumti. The Commander-in-Chief carried the Martiniere on the 9th,[3] and Banks House on the following day, the enemy having abandoned their first line of defence. Clerke, Harrison and the 23rd Company, R.E., then moved a cask bridge up to the end of the abandoned line.

Alexander Taylor soon threw up some batteries near Banks House which opened fire so effectively on the Begum Kothi, the first of the line of palaces extending along the Hazratganj street to the Kaisar Bagh, that it fell on the 11th.[4] After a daring reconnaissance by Medley, Lang and Carnegie, another column under General Lugard seized the Sikandar Bagh, the Kadam Rasul and the Shah Najif. Outram, across the river, took possession of the iron bridge and thus turned the enemy's second line of defence. The Gurkhas who had just arrived were preparing to fight their way through the city from the south. Led by Greathed and directed by Napier, the Engineers now sapped towards the Imambara which was assaulted and captured on March 14th. Outram asked for permission to force a crossing at the iron bridge but was given an answer which amounted to a refusal, so he was unable to help in the capture of the Kaisar Bagh which took place on the same day. Lennox and Greathed particularly distinguished themselves in this affair. It was at the iron bridge that Wynne and Serjeant Paul of the 4th Company, R.E., gained recommendations for the Victoria Cross for removing a barricade under a point-blank fire. On March 16th Outram crossed the Gumti by a floating bridge near the Sikandar Bagh and drove the enemy from the Residency and the Machhi Bhawan; and in another five days the capture of Lucknow had been completed, though most of the mutineers contrived to escape through the mishandling of the

[1] "The Diary and Letters of A. M. Lang," appearing in the *Journal of the Society for Army Historical Research*, Vol. XI, January, 1932, p. 9.
[2] They were afterwards shifted by Lennox to sites one mile farther downstream, the lower bridge on the 7th, the upper bridge on the 8th. (See Report by Lieut.-Colonel Harness to Brigadier R. Napier, dated March 19th, 1858, included in Napier's Report on the operations.)
[3] Lennox, Malcolm and Pritchard guided this attack as they had been in the Relief operations of November, 1857.
[4] Captain W. Hodson of Hodson's Horse was killed soon after the assault on the Begum Kothi, and Alexander Taylor was wounded. Captain Cox, R.E., then assumed the direction of the local engineering operations.

British cavalry by General Campbell. The rejoicings of the Engineers were marred by a sad fatality on the 17th when Clerke of the Royal Engineers, E. P. Brownlow of the Bengal Engineers, 14 men of the Royal Engineers and 30 Sikhs were killed or terribly injured by the accidental explosion of some gunpowder.

After the capture of Lucknow,[1] the army was split up into movable columns, some to operate in Oudh, others to clear Rohilkhand and ultimately to converge on Bareilly to which place Sir Colin himself advanced. The Engineer Brigade was broken up and distributed mostly among the columns. It was not till June 18th, 1858, that the loyal Bengal Sappers and Miners, with the 23rd Company, R.E., arrived once more in Roorkee, 13 months after they had started in boats down the Ganges Canal.[2] Many Engineers assisted in the general sweep of the newly-annexed province of Oudh which took place between October, 1858, and March, 1859, and ended all resistance in the north, but their exploits and adventures can find no place in this brief account of the main operations for it is necessary to turn now to the struggle in Central India.

The Bombay Army as a whole remained loyal; the Madras Army was also staunch, and Hyderabad ready to help. Thus all serious trouble was confined to the regions north of the Narbada. But had it not been for the resolute action of Lord Elphinstone, the Governor of Bombay, in despatching a movable column at once from Poona towards Mhow near Indore, the Marathas might have risen in sympathy with their countryman, the Nana Sahib. The British Resident at Holkar's capital of Indore was that renowned Bengal Engineer, Colonel H. M. Durand;[3] and although he was obliged to leave Indore on July 1st, 1857, when Holkar's troops and those at Mhow rose in mutiny, he rendered yeoman service in the brief campaign in Malwa. The column from Poona under Major-General Woodburn set out towards Aurangabad on June 8th, and was joined at that place on July 7th by " B " Company, Madras Sappers and Miners, which had landed in Bombay six days earlier on its return from Persia. The company was under Captain (Brevet-Major) A. J. M. Boileau, M.E., who had with him Captain P. A. Brown, Madras Fusiliers, Lieutenant F. R. Fox, Madras Infantry, and 2nd-Lieutenants H. N. D. Prendergast[4] and H. J. G. Gordon,[5] both of the Madras Engineers. On July 7th the column marched from Aurangabad and relieved Asirgarh on the 25th and Mhow on August 2nd. Meanwhile Brigadier-General Stuart had assumed command, with Durand as Political Officer in

---

[1] For this and subsequent operations Sir Colin Campbell was raised to the Peerage as Lord Clyde.
[2] " A Subaltern in the Indian Mutiny," by Colonel C. B. Thackeray, R.A., appearing in *The R.E. Journal*, Vol. XLIV, September, 1931, p. 432.
[3] The hero of the Kabul Gate at Ghazni in the First Afghan War. (See Chapter XV.)
[4] Afterwards General Sir Harry Prendergast, V.C., K.C.B.
[5] Drowned in China, July 11th, 1860. (See Chapter XV.)

CAMPAIGNS IN MALWA AND CENTRAL INDIA. 363

charge of the general direction of the operations. During the rains Durand collected a siege train, and by October 20th was able to send Stuart to capture the strong fortress of Dhar, 40 miles to the west of Mhow. Major Boileau, as Field Engineer, began a regular siege of the place, but the garrison evacuated it on the 31st after trying unsuccessfully to secure good terms under a flag of truce which took the form of a pair of pyjama trousers. Already the troops were feeling the strain of constant marching, and one cavalry trooper was heard to exclaim : " I say, Harry, I'm blowed if the old General hasn't been and discovered perpetual motion."[1]

Moving northwards, Durand and Stuart dispersed a rebel force at Mandasor (Mandsaur),[2] after which Durand, having suppressed and disarmed Holkar's revolted troops and ensured the loyalty of Holkar himself, returned to Indore in December, 1857, followed by Stuart and his men. The brief campaign in Malwa was ended, but a new campaign under Major-General Sir Hugh Rose[3] was about to begin. The achievements of the Central India Field Force under this gallant leader have been fully recorded in many histories. Fortescue ranks Sir Hugh Rose as, without doubt, the ablest commander in any theatre of the Indian Mutiny ;[4] and as regards his men, to use the words of Lord Derby : " In five months the Central India Field Force traversed 1,085 miles, crossed numerous large rivers, took upwards of 150 pieces of artillery, one entrenched camp, two fortified cities and two fortresses all strongly defended, fought sixteen actions, captured twenty forts ; and never sustained a check against the most warlike and determined enemy, led by the most capable commanders then to be found in any part of India." The force consisted of only two brigades,[5] the 1st under Brigadier-General Stuart of the Bombay Army, the 2nd under Brigadier-General Steuart, 14th Light Dragoons ; Sir Hugh Rose was an absolute stranger to India ; the operations were conducted in such extreme heat that men fell out by hundreds and Sir Hugh himself was prostrated five times by sunstroke. Seldom has a British general fought under worse conditions or with more consistent success.

The plan of campaign was that Sir Hugh Rose should march north-eastwards from Mhow by Jhansi to Kalpi, the chief arsenal of the insurgents on the Jumna, while a column from Madras, known as the Saugor Field Force, under Major-General Whitlock, moved from Jubbulpore (Jabalpur) northwards upon Banda. It was hoped that

---

[1] *The Campaign in Malwa and Central India*, by J. H. Sylvester, p. 11.

[2] Prendergast was dangerously wounded at Mandasor on November 21st, 1857, in saving the life of Lieutenant Dew, 11th Dragoons, in a cavalry charge. For this action, and for his later exploits at Rahatgarh and on the Betwa, he received the Victoria Cross.

[3] Afterwards Lord Strathnairn.

[4] *A History of the British Army*, by the Hon. J. W. Fortescue, Vol. XIII, p. 395.

[5] About 6,000 combatants, including cavalry, artillery and engineers.

this advance towards Oudh from the south would distract the attention of the Gwalior mutineers from the operations of Sir Colin Campbell against Lucknow besides crushing all resistance in Central India. Sir Hugh marched from Mhow with the 2nd Brigade on January 6th, 1858, and was facing the fortress of Rahatgarh, west of Saugor (Sagar), on the 24th, by which time " B " Company, Madras Sappers and Miners, had been joined by the 2nd and 5th Companies, Bombay Sappers and Miners, under 2nd-Lieutenants H. R. Meiklejohn and W. G. D. Dick of the Bombay Engineers,[1] Rahatgarh having fallen easily,[2] Sir Hugh relieved Saugor on February 3rd and, on the 11th, occupied the fortress of Garhakota to the east. The Sappers dismantled this place and Sir Hugh returned to Saugor to await the arrival of Whitlock who had been delayed. It was not till February 27th that he was able to begin his thrust with his whole force towards Jhansi. By that time the 1st Brigade had been joined by the 21st Company, R.E., under Captain T. Fenwick, with Lieutenants J. B. Edwards, W. B. Gosset, C. E. Webber and E. R. Festing, all of the Royal Engineers. While the 1st Brigade operated on its left, the 2nd Brigade drove back the enemy and was before Jhansi on March 21st.

Jhansi City had a perimeter of about four and a half miles and was surrounded by a wall from 18 to 30 feet in height with numerous bastions in which guns were mounted. At its western end was the fort, perched on a granite pinnacle with a precipitous western face. The south was the only side which offered any hope of a successful attack. The garrison was believed to number about 12,000 men with 30 to 40 guns. While the Engineers reconnoitred the place, Sir Hugh invested it with his cavalry, and Boileau, his Field Engineer, then set to work to establish breaching batteries against the southern face. The first of these opened fire on the 25th, the day before the 1st Brigade under Stuart arrived and added its guns to those of the 2nd Brigade. The rebel guns were served with remarkable skill and bravery in 13 different batteries, but gradually they were silenced and by March 30th a practicable breach existed in the city wall. All arrangements had been made for an assault when Sir Hugh learnt that Tantia Topi with 20,000 men was moving down to the relief of Jhansi. Without hesitation he advanced to meet the rebels, and, in a brilliant action on the River Betwa, on April 1st, repulsed them and took all their guns. Then, on April 3rd, he launched his assault on Jhansi. At 3 a.m., under a bright moon, the two brigades advanced to the attack. The 1st Brigade was to storm the breach and to escalade a bastion on its left, the stormers being led by Lieutenant Gosset, R.E., and the escaladers by Lieutenant Webber, R.E. The 2nd Brigade was to escalade in two columns farther to

---

[1] *A Brief History of the Royal Bombay Sappers and Miners*, p. 13.
[2] Shortly after the fall of Rahatgarh, Captain G. Neville, R.E., was killed at Barodia on January 31st, 1858.

the right, one column being led by Lieutenants Meiklejohn and Dick of the Bombay Engineers and the other by Lieutenant Bonus of the same Corps and Lieutenant Fox, an Infantry officer of the Madras Sappers.[1] The breach was carried easily by the 1st Brigade, and after a sharp fight their escaladers took the bastion; but matters did not go so well with the escaladers of the 2nd Brigade who were confronted by a wall 30 feet in height. Under a devastating fire the Bombay and Madras Sappers planted ladders in three places. Three of the ladders broke; but Dick, Meiklejohn, Bonus and Fox were soon on the ramparts at the head of the stormers. Dick was bayoneted and shot dead; Bonus, struck in the face by a stone, was hurled down; Meiklejohn was caught and cut to pieces, and Fox was shot through the neck. But this sacrifice of the Engineers enabled the British infantry to gain a footing from eight ladders. They rushed into the city and killed every armed man they saw. The Rani of Jhansi fled in the confusion. By March 6th the last of the mutineers had been destroyed and 5,000 dead lay in the streets. Before the battle of the Betwa the Sappers and Miners had had eight officers. There were now only two—2nd-Lieutenants H. J. G. Gordon, M.E., and C. A. Goodfellow, Bo.E.[2] Prendergast had been wounded in April, Bonus and Fox in the assault, Meiklejohn and Dick killed, and Brown was sick. The whole engineering work of the 2nd Brigade fell on Gordon and Goodfellow, superintended by Boileau.

After halting for three weeks, Sir Hugh Rose marched again with the 1st Brigade early on April 25th, 1858, towards Kalpi, followed by the 2nd Brigade on May 2nd. The heat was terrific. "The sun gets up," writes Thomas Lowe,[3] "and the heat and clouds of white dust well-nigh overpower the men; they begin to cry out almost hysterically for water. A shadowing of delirium begins to show itself. Men talk of home, and cool shady places, and brooks, as the hot air begins to blow over them, parching up every drop of moisture in the body; and dogs rush past with great raw wounds in their backs caused by the sun, howling for water and shade." However, the troops moved slowly on, and, passing Kunch, routed 20,000 rebels at Punch on May 7th. Three times during the battle Sir Hugh Rose collapsed from sunstroke. His men fell out by scores, many for the last time. Ahead lay Kalpi, where the Rani of Jhansi, Tantia Topi and other leading rebels had massed their armies; and on the far bank of the Jumna was a British force under Colonel Maxwell, waiting to reinforce and help the exhausted troops when they reached the wide river. By May 18th Maxwell was opposite Kalpi, and Sir Hugh

[1] *History of the Corps of Royal Engineers*, by Major-General W. Porter, Vol. I, p. 495.
[2] Afterwards Lieut.-General Charles Goodfellow, B.C. He gained the Victoria Cross for rescuing a wounded soldier under the walls of the Fort of Beyt on October 6th, 1859.
[3] *Central India during the Rebellion of* 1857 *and* 1858, by T. Lowe, Medical Officer to the Madras Sappers and Miners, p. 273.

close to Galaoli, a short distance downstream on the right bank. Then Maxwell crossed and helped to repel a powerful attack by Tantia Topi at Galaoli on the 22nd when the thermometer stood at 118°. The Sappers toiled unceasingly at roadmaking and hauling heavy guns, and when Kalpi fell on the 23rd every man in the British force had reached the end of his strength. Yet their work was not finished, for Tantia Topi, the Rani[1] and others made for Gwalior where they won Sindhia's troops over to their side, proclaimed the Nana Sahib as Peshwa of the Marathas, and forced Sindhia to fly for his life. Sir Hugh accordingly marched towards Gwalior on June 6th, and on the 18th gave the command of his 2nd Brigade to Brigadier Robert Napier, B.E., who had joined him two days before.[2] The thermometer then stood at 130°. Gwalior City was captured on June 19th, and a few days later the fort also.

Little need be said of the advance of Whitlock's division on Banda. There was no hard fighting, and the Engineers acted chiefly as orderlies to the General and as leaders of cavalry.[3] "L" Company, Madras Sappers and Miners, marched with this column, the Madras Engineers being Major S. E. O. Ludlow, Captain E. Hemery, Lieutenants F. A. Howes and J. G. Lindsay and 2nd-Lieutenant H. W. Wood. The fall of Gwalior gave Robert Napier the opportunity to show his worth as a commander in the field. He set out at once and overtook the rebels on June 22nd at Jaura Alipur, 30 miles north-west of the captured city. There he routed 4,000 of the enemy with less than 700 cavalry and artillery, and before the end of the month succeeded to the chief command when Sir Hugh Rose became Commander-in-Chief in Bombay. Then he pursued various bodies of rebels south of Gwalior, defeated Tantia Topi, and in August captured the fort of Pauri. Later he surprised and defeated Firoz Shah at Ranod (Narod) and, by February, 1859, had left only one rebel leader, Man Singh, in the field. Man Singh surrendered in due course, and Napier received the thanks of Parliament and a K.C.B.[4] Tantia Topi was chased for 3,000 miles between June, 1858, and April, 1859, but in the end he was caught and hanged. The Nana Sahib escaped, and his fate remains a mystery to this day.

Although three companies of Bombay Sappers[5] and three of Madras Sappers, with their Engineer officers, served with distinction

---

[1] The Rani of Jhansi was killed at last in a fight near Gwalior on June 17th, 1858.
[2] Since the capture of Lucknow, Napier had been engaged on a project for three fortified posts along the north side of the city and for several large roads. The completion of these works set free some 12,000 men for field operations.
[3] *The History of the Madras Engineers and Pioneers*, by H. M. Vibart, Vol. II, p. 360.
[4] A more detailed account of Napier's campaign is given in the *History of the Corps of Royal Engineers*, by Major-General W. Porter, Vol. II, pp. 477-481, in a biographical sketch of Lord Napier of Magdala.
[5] In addition to the 2nd and 5th Companies, the 3rd Company of Bombay Sappers and Miners served in the Mutiny. It was present under Lieutenant C. T. Haig, Bo.E., in the capture of Kotah in Rajputana, in October, 1857, and in three battles in 1858 and 1859.

in the Indian Mutiny, the brunt of the engineering work fell on the Bengal Engineers, their British non-commissioned officers, and their few trained Sappers and Miners in the operations at Delhi and in Oudh. More than one-half of the Bengal Engineers—64 officers—were engaged with the rebels, and of these more than one-half were killed or wounded. Thirteen were killed in action, murdered or died of exposure : 22 others were wounded.[1] " The record," wrote Lord Canning, " is very honourable to the Corps of Bengal Engineers." Three Engineers were pre-eminent in the Indian Mutiny—Napier, Baird Smith and Taylor—but the most brilliant of these was Napier.

[1] *Calcutta Official Gazette*, No. 493, dated April 12th, 1859.

IRON BRIDGE, LUCKNOW.

From engraving in *Illustrated London News*.

CHAPTER XIX.

THE SECOND AFGHAN WAR, 1878–1880.

THE mutiny of 1857 gave the deathblow to the East India Company, and although the corporation retained a formal existence until 1874, all control over Indian affairs was vested in the Crown. The Directors protested in dignified terms that the Company had laid the foundations of the Indian Empire, and that, while they admitted their share in the responsibility for the recent trouble, the burden must rest mainly on the Home Government which had for many years exercised all real power through the President of the Board of Control appointed by it. The protest was ignored. A Bill was passed through both Houses of Parliament and received the royal assent on August 2nd, 1858. In September the Directors held their last assembly and offered the Indian Empire to the Crown. " Let Her Majesty appreciate the gift," they wrote. " Let her take the vast country and the teeming millions of India under her direct control; but let her not forget the great corporation from which she has received them, nor the lessons to be learned from its success." And to their servants in India they gave a last message : " The Company has the great privilege of transferring to the service of Her Majesty such a body of civil and military officers as the world has never seen before. A government cannot be base, cannot be feeble, that has reared two such services." It was a pathetic farewell. The Company had done great things for England, but the empire which it had created had passed beyond its power of control. On November 1st, 1858, the new government was proclaimed at Allahabad by Lord Canning who then became the first Viceroy and Governor-General appointed by the Crown. A new era had dawned, an era of achievement grander than any dreamed of by Clive, Warren Hastings, Wellesley and Dalhousie, but marred, alas, by many errors of which the greatest, perhaps, was the Second Afghan War.

The Bengal Army—the largest in India—had been almost destroyed during the mutiny.[1] The moment was propitious for a complete reorganization of the Indian Army; and in the comparatively peaceful and almost humdrum atmosphere which enveloped the country for some years after the last embers of the great revolt had been extinguished, that army took on a new form. It was decided first that the British troops serving in India should form part of the Imperial British Army by their transfer to the service of

---
[1] Out of 128,000 Indian soldiers in the Bengal Army, about 120,000 had mutinied.

the Crown. The Company's European infantry became British regiments of the line, and the Bengal, Madras and Bombay European artillery were amalgamated with the Royal Artillery. By 1860, this reorganization of the British troops had been completed, and in 1861 attention was turned to the Indian troops and their British officers. A "Staff Corps" for the officers of the Cavalry and Infantry was formed in each Presidency with a general list by which promotion was regulated. The Indian Artillery was almost abolished by a stroke of the pen, and changes were made in the three Corps of Engineers which affected the establishment of the Royal Engineers as a whole.

On April 1st, 1862, the Bengal, Bombay and Madras Engineers were amalgamated with the Royal Engineers. The officers of the three Corps in India remained on their separate lists for promotion, as did the Cavalry and Infantry officers of each Staff Corps, but they were granted royal commissions and their Presidencies were indicated in brackets after their names.[1] The "Seminary" at Addiscombe was closed in June, 1861, when its last Lieutenant-Governor, Major-General Sir Frederick Abbott, late of the Bengal Engineers, retired from a most responsible post. Addiscombe had supplied the Company with military officers for 52 years, but the War Office considered that the military colleges at Woolwich and Sandhurst would suffice for the needs of the whole army, so the Engineers intended for India came in future from the Royal Military Academy at Woolwich. The incorporation of the three Indian Corps in the Royal Engineers enlarged the latter by a total of seven battalions, three for the supply of officers for Bengal and two each for Bombay and Madras; the Royal Corps thus reached an establishment of 15 battalions. Even this strength, however, was found to be insufficient to meet the voracious demands of India, and two more battalions were added on April 1st, 1874, to provide the number of officers required.[2] From the Royal Military Academy the young Engineers intended for the Indian establishment went to the School of Military Engineering, which had been formed by Major Pasley, R.E., at Chatham, in 1812.[3] There they received a specialized training which stood them in good stead when they began their work in India.

The reorganization which followed the Indian Mutiny did not affect the strength of the Sappers and Miners to any great extent. The Bombay Sappers remained with five companies; the Madras Sappers were reduced from twelve to ten companies in 1862,[4] and the

[1] A Bengal Engineer became a "Royal (Bengal) Engineer," and so also with officers of the other two Corps. In practice, however, the name of the Presidency was often omitted for the sake of brevity. Engineer officers who had belonged to the Company's armies were shown as such in the *Quarterly Lists* published with *The R.E. Journal*. This was continued until January, 1923, when there was only one survivor, Lieut-General C. Strahan.
[2] *History of the Corps of Royal Engineers*, by Major-General W. Porter, Vol. II, p. 87. [3] *Ibid.*, p. 172.
[4] G.O.C.C. No. 14, dated January 30th, 1862.

Bengal Sappers were reduced similarly in the following year.[1] In 1866, however, a scheme was prepared to improve the quality and regularity of the supply of British non-commissioned officers to these Corps by establishing three "skeleton" companies of Royal Engineers in India, one in each Presidency.[2] Each Commandant of Sappers and Miners could select men from his Skeleton Company for employment as non-commissioned officers in his Corps or in the Department of Public Works. Two Royal Engineer companies were formed at Chatham to train and supply men to the new companies in India. It was arranged also that every European engineer soldier in India should be borne on the strength of the Skeleton Company of his Presidency. On May 1st, 1868, the new companies came into being and were styled the 41st Company for Bengal, the 42nd for Madras and the 43rd for Bombay, all of the Royal Engineers.[3] Thus for the first time in the history of the Corps, units of the Royal Engineers were established permanently in India.

The number of Engineer officers in India showed a steady increase after the Mutiny. They were congregated mostly in the north where great schemes were afoot. While in 1854 Bengal had 125 Engineers, Bombay 57 and Madras 54, in 1865 the Northern Presidency had a cadre of 153, Bombay 113 and Madras 101.[4] In 11 years the number of Engineer officers in India had risen from 236 to 367. After 1865 the total establishment of Engineers did not vary appreciably for many years, but the number of Royal Engineers from home increased as the "Company's men" retired or died. Thus, in 1870, we find 57 Royal Engineers of the Imperial establishment in Bengal, in 1875, 153, and in 1885, 227. Five years later, only 15 Generals and 76 Colonels and Lieut.-Colonels of the original Company's Engineers remained in India, and when the last separate Army Lists of the Presidency armies were published in 1895 the number of Company's men had sunk to 29 and the Royal Engineers totalled 319. With the death of Lieut.-General C. Strahan in 1930, the last of the gallant band of Company's Engineers passed into the pages of history. The tale of their achievements will never be forgotten.

The Corps of Royal Engineers in India has always been maintained at a much greater strength in peace-time than would otherwise be possible by a system under which it lends its officers and other ranks for special employment in other departments of Government service when their services are not required for war. The drawback of this arrangement is that the departmental side is apt, in peace-time, to prove too attractive so that the "Military" side suffers

---

[1] The reduction was made on August 24th, 1863. (See *History and Digest of Service, 1st K.G.O. Sappers and Miners*, p. 27.)
[2] G.O.G. No. 277, dated November 20th, 1866.
[3] G.O.G.G. No. 418, dated April 22nd, 1868. Further details are given in the *Historical Record of the Q.V.O. Madras Sappers and Miners*, pp. 89–91 and 97.
[4] The 1865 figures include respectively 11, 19 and 7 Royal Engineers.

accordingly and with it the organization, preparation and equipment of the Corps for field service. This was particularly the case between the Indian Mutiny and the Second Afghan War. The Bengal Army List of 1865 affords an example. Of 15 Lieut.-Colonels in the Royal (Bengal) Engineers, *all* are employed in the Department of Public Works or the Railway or Survey Departments. There are 24 Captains[1] on the list; but F. R. Maunsell and W. W. Greathed alone are on military duty, the former as Commandant of the Bengal Sappers and Miners, the latter as Assistant Military Secretary to the Commander-in-Chief. The variety of employment among the Captains is remarkable. Although most of them are in the Department of Public Works or working on the railways or under the Surveyor-General, several have wandered far from their profession. Henry Hyde is Master of the Calcutta Mint, J. J. McLeod Innes, V.C., is a Controller of Public Works Accounts, and G. T. Chesney the Accountant-General of the Public Works Department. J. G. Medley, as Principal of the Thomason Civil Engineering College, is concerned in engineering, but only on the civil side. One 2nd-Captain alone out of 24 is soldiering, and even the 72 Lieutenants are mostly in departmental service. The truth is that there was little prospect of rapid advancement for the Engineer unless he turned to construction or surveying work or entered the Political Department. It was left to Lord Napier of Magdala to balance the scales more evenly between departmental and military service, to the lasting benefit of the three Corps of Sappers and Miners and to military engineering in India as a whole.

For many years after 1863 the strength of the Sappers and Miners did not vary greatly, but their training was improved and extended and infantry officers disappeared gradually from their cadres. In 1865 the Bengal Sappers had only one infantryman;[2] but in the Bombay and Madras Corps all were infantry officers except the Commandants—a most peculiar state of affairs. Ten years later the Bengal Corps had still one infantry officer, but Bombay had only three and Madras nine. Before 1885 all three Corps were officered entirely by Royal Engineers. This was as it should be. The infantry officers had done excellent work and had become efficient engineers, but it is a truism that engineer soldiers should be commanded by engineer officers.

The Indian Mutiny was followed by a period of 19 years of comparative inactivity for the greater part of the army; and except in the Second China War of 1860, the Abyssinian Campaign of 1867–68, the Perak Expedition of 1875–76 in the Malay Peninsula, and a number of small expeditions on the Indian frontiers, few of the Engineers or Sappers and Miners had any chance of active service.

[1] There were no Majors while the rank of 2nd-Captain existed.
[2] Lieutenant R. H. Ward, commanding the 1st and 3rd Companies at Peshawar.

Their work during the Second China War has been described already. The part which they took in the Abyssinian and Perak campaigns will be dealt with in Chapter XX, and their exploits on the frontiers of India and Burma in Chapters XXI and XXII. It may be well, however, to remark that as this narrative progresses the available information becomes more voluminous and detailed; indeed, it pours in from every side from the pens of scores of historians. The forces engaged are more highly organized, the strategy and tactics more involved. Railways, the telegraph and the heliograph[1] add to the complexity and precision of the movements. From such a tangled skein it is possible only to weave a rough fabric of the general operations on which to fasten a picture of the engineering work, for this is a history of the military engineers of India and makes no pretension to be a record of Indian wars.

The Sappers and Miners progressed steadily in efficiency, yet all was not well with them. The attention of the military authorities was focussed on the changes in the Infantry and Cavalry to the detriment of the smaller branches of the Service. It was left to Lord Napier of Magdala to put forward the claims of his own Corps. Soon after he became Commander-in-Chief of the Bombay Army in 1866, he showed to all the world what Sappers and Miners could do when he led the expedition to Abyssinia. This was an " Engineer " campaign from start to finish. And when Lord Napier was appointed Commander-in-Chief in India in 1870 he did not lose sight of his own men, but continued to watch over their interests till his final departure from the country in 1876.[2] Not long after he assumed the chief command he started an official enquiry into the organization of the three Corps of Sappers and Miners following on the reorganization of the Corps of Royal Engineers which took place after the Franco-Prussian War of 1870. The first results were small, but a beginning had been made; and after the experiences and lessons of the Second Afghan War, a great reorganization of the Sappers and Miners was effected in 1885.[3] The Afghan War, however unfortunate, brought some benefit to military engineering in India.

It may be well to mention briefly one or two events which occurred between the Indian Mutiny and the Second Afghan War. Dost Muhammad, the Amir of Afghanistan, died in 1863, and five years later his son Sher Ali, after a stormy interlude, was seated securely on the throne. Russia continued to advance slowly towards Afghanistan, and Khiva fell in 1873. Three years after this event a

---

[1] The heliograph was introduced in 1875. The original instrument, which was a modification of the " heliostat " and of the still later " heliotrope," was brought to the notice of the Indian Government by Mr. Mance in 1869. Heliographic signalling was used extensively in the Second Afghan War. Telegraphic communication was constantly interrupted by the enemy.

[2] He was seen off from Bombay on April 10th, 1876, by his personal friend Sir Frederick Roberts. (See *Forty-one Years in India*, by Field-Marshal Lord Roberts of Kandahar, Vol. II, p. 84.)

[3] This is alluded to later in this chapter.

change occurred in the policy of the Government of India. Lord Northbrook, the Viceroy, resigned and was succeeded by Lord Lytton. The unpretentious and careful sway of Gladstone as Premier and the Duke of Argyll as Secretary of State then gave way to the imperialistic and bold tactics of Disraeli and Lord Salisbury which Lord Lytton was only too ready to execute. The acquisition of Quetta in 1876 by Lord Lytton's Government made Sher Ali very suspicious, for it commanded the Bolan Pass, one of the gates of Afghanistan. On January 1st, 1877, an Imperial Assemblage was held at Delhi when Her Majesty Queen Victoria was proclaimed Empress of India in the presence of 17,000 troops among whom were the 5th, 6th, 9th and 10th Companies of Bengal Sappers and Miners. But the brilliance of this gathering was overshadowed by the storm clouds rising in the north-west, and before many months had passed it was clear that trouble with Afghanistan could not be avoided unless Sher Ali changed his attitude of partiality towards Russia.

There were at this time several schools of frontier defence. One party favoured a retirement to the line of the Indus to relieve the army from petty wars against the frontier tribes and to secure a natural barrier against invasion. Another, known as the "Forward School," wished to make the Indian frontier conterminous with that of Afghanistan by subjugating the border tribes; it even contemplated the annexation of the Amir's domains if opportunity offered. Lord Lytton, though no extremist, inclined towards the Forward School. Russia declared war on Turkey in April, 1877, and was only prevented from taking Constantinople by the resolute action of England. Foiled in the West, the Russians made peace in March, 1878, and turned their military aspirations towards Afghanistan beyond which lay India. As a first step they forced Sher Ali to receive a Russian envoy at his court, an achievement which was a triumph for them and a rebuff to Lord Lytton, whose proposal to send an envoy had already been refused. The Viceroy then despatched General Sir Neville Chamberlain, accompanied by Major Cavagnari and others, with orders to go to Kabul to represent his country. Chamberlain, however, was turned back at Ali Masjid in the Khaibar Pass, so Lord Lytton decided to resort to force. He sent an ultimatum to Sher Ali on November 2nd, demanding an apology and the immediate admission of the British envoy, adding that, unless a favourable reply was received by the 20th, war would follow. No reply came, so war was declared against Afghanistan on November 20th, 1878. The declaration had an evil effect. It upset the North-West Frontier which, between 1872 and 1877, had been peaceful and orderly under the excellent system of border defence organized by John Lawrence when Chief Commissioner of the Punjab;[1] and Sher

---

[1] *The Second Afghan War*, by H. B. Hanna, Vol. I, p. 268.

Ali, a capable ruler and not unfriendly to England, was rushed into a war for which he had no desire.

Five routes were available for the invasion of Afghanistan—the Khaibar, the Kurram, the Gomal, the Thal-Chotiali and the Bolan.[1] The Khaibar and Kurram routes lead directly to Kabul, the Thal-Chotiali and the Bolan to Kandahar, and the Gomal to Ghazni. All five traverse rugged, bare and mountainous country, but the Khaibar is the shortest and the only one which is open at all seasons; the entrance to it near Jamrud lies within a few miles of a base of supply at Peshawar, while the others are far from Rawalpindi and Multan from which they were supplied in 1878. After the Khaibar, the Bolan is the best avenue to Afghanistan; but in 1878, before the railway was extended to Sibi, it was a winter route only because it was necessary to march across the burning desert to Dadhar to reach it. The Kurram route involves the crossing of the Shutar Gardan Pass, 11,500 feet high, and is accordingly traversable only in summer. The Gomal and Thal-Chotiali lines present even greater problems of supply than the Khaibar, Kurram and Bolan approaches, so for this and other reasons they were not adopted in 1878. It was unfortunate that the invasion had to be conducted in three separate bodies —a plan which invited defeat in detail. No single road, however, could accommodate and supply the whole force required to subdue Sher Ali. The railways available for concentrating the three forces before the Khaibar, Kurram and Bolan approaches were quite inadequate. From Lahore the Great Northern State Railway ran northwards to Jhelum, where its terminus was still 173 miles from Peshawar, involving a road journey of 14 stages. Another line, the Indus Valley State Railway, extended south-westwards from Lahore as far only as Multan; in breathless haste it was pushed on to Sukkur on the Indus, but even when it was opened the trains could not travel at more than six miles an hour. Although troops could be pushed up easily to Sukkur from Karachi by the Scinde, Punjab and Delhi Railway, beyond Sukkur everything had to be transported towards Afghanistan by camels.

For the reason already given the army of invasion was formed in three columns—the Peshawar Valley Field Force of one cavalry brigade, some artillery and four infantry brigades, under Lieut.-General Sir Samuel Browne, V.C., to advance through the Khaibar Pass from Peshawar; the Kurram Valley Column of six infantry battalions with some cavalry and guns under Major-General Frederick Roberts, V.C., to proceed up the valley of that name; and the Kandahar Column[2] composed finally of two divisions under Lieut.-General D. M. Stewart to enter southern Afghanistan. One division

---

[1] The map entitled " Sketch Map of the North-West Frontier including Afghanistan," appearing at the end of this volume, shows these routes and the names of all places of importance.

[2] Also called the Quetta Field Force.

of the Kandahar Force was already at Quetta under Major-General M. A. S. Biddulph. It was to be reinforced by another under General Stewart, who would then assume the chief command in the south. Biddulph's division was provided with 40-pounder guns and 8-inch mortars in case it should have to besiege Kandahar, Kalat-i-Ghilzai or Ghazni.[1] The lesson of Keane's desperate attack on Ghazni in 1839 had not been wasted. As a reserve to the Peshawar Valley Field Force a second division under Major-General F. F. Maude, V.C., was to assemble at Rawalpindi. In lower Sind a mixed division of Bombay and Madras troops under Major-General J. M. Primrose would form a reserve for the Kandahar Force.

The Engineers and Sappers and Miners were distributed among the columns. Colonel F. R. Maunsell, R.E., was Commanding Royal Engineer of the Peshawar Force, and Major W. North, R.E., led its Sappers and Miners—the 2nd, 3rd, 6th and 8th Companies of the Bengal Corps. The 2nd and 3rd Companies were already in Peshawar, and the 6th and 8th came from Roorkee. Three companies of Madras Sappers and Miners (" B," " E " and " K "), under Major C. A. Sim, R.E., were ordered up from Bangalore to join the force and reached Jamrud between 9th and 23rd January, 1879, in time to be most useful on the line of communication through the Khaibar. The Commanding Royal Engineer with General Roberts in the Kurram Valley was Lieut.-Colonel Æneas Perkins, R.E., who had with him the 7th Company of Bengal Sappers and Miners from Rawalpindi. The division at Quetta had Lieut.-Colonel W. Hichens, R.E., as Commanding Royal Engineer, and also the 5th Company, Bengal Sappers and Miners; but when it was reinforced by the Multan Division, Lieut.-Colonel R. H. Sankey, R.E., became Commanding Royal Engineer of the whole Kandahar Force to which three more companies of Bengal Sappers, the 4th, 9th and 10th, were added. The 2nd, 3rd, 4th and 5th Companies of Bombay Sappers and Miners under Lieut.-Colonel John Hills, R.E., also joined the Kandahar Force during the early months of 1879. Thus, during the first phase of the war, 16 companies of Sappers and Miners were in the field. There were several Field Parks of a rather primitive nature, and a large number of Engineer officers who accompanied the columns as Field Engineers or Surveyors. The names of a few Royal Engineers are to be found among the Political officers, notably Lieut.-Colonels James Browne (afterwards Major-General Sir James Browne) and O. B. C. St. John, who were with the Kandahar Force. In rear of the fighting troops were the railway engineers, an energetic crew headed by Lieut.-Colonels J. G. Medley and J. G. Lindsay of the Royal Engineers. This war against Afghanistan was no petty frontier affair. The scale of the operations is shown by the fact that 171

[1] *Official History of the Anglo-Afghan War, 1878–79* (1881), Section I, p. 6.

Engineer officers earned the Afghan medal before hostilities ceased nominally in 1880.[1]

Although there was nothing spectacular in the work of the Engineers and Sappers, the very existence of every column often depended upon it. The Sappers made the roads which brought reinforcements, food and ammunition. Roadmaking and bridge-building may be prosaic and simple tasks, but when carried out in precipitous chasms, scoured by roaring torrents and under the eye of a vigilant foe, they are not so easy as they might at first appear. Great sieges offer unique opportunities to the military engineer. There he is in the front line, literally and figuratively. Generals hang upon his words: he is in his element. But in open mountain warfare he is not always in the limelight. The infantry climb, as it were, over his back to plunge into the fight; yet without that broad and patient back they would often fail to reach the foe. So it was in the Second Afghan War. Although there was no engineering exploit so striking as the blowing in of the Kabul Gate at Ghazni in 1839, the Engineers and Sappers did excellent and useful work. They bridged the Kabul River many times, constructed dozens of fortified posts, built huts, laid telegraph lines and carried out the hundred-and-one odd jobs which help an army to advance and fight. Their surveyors covered huge tracts of unknown country, triangulating and mapping as they went and always liable to attack. And far behind the fighting men, the railway engineers toiled night and day to bring their lines through desert and gorge to the advanced bases.

Sher Ali had devoted great attention to the training and equipment of his army. His soldiers were good fighters, but his officers, who were selected by favouritism, were poor in quality. The strength of the Afghan army in 1878 is uncertain. There was no Intelligence Department in India at that time. A police report estimated the numbers as 62 battalions of infantry, 16 regiments of cavalry, and 49 batteries of artillery of various sorts; altogether about 52,000 regular soldiers.[2] On the other hand the estimate given by the Russian Central Staff at St. Petersburg was 72 battalions of infantry (50,000 men), 25 regiments of cavalry (10,000 men) and a special militia consisting of 60,000 infantry and 95,000 cavalry—a total of 60,000 regulars and 155,000 irregulars.[3] Howard Hensman, in his *Afghan War*, 1879–80, states on the authority of an official report that the Afghans had 379 guns including 34 siege guns.[4] Sher Ali modelled his army on the British forces which he had seen in India during a

---

[1] A complete list of all the Engineers who received the medal is given in the *History of the Corps of Royal Engineers*, by Major-General W. Porter, Vol. II, pp. 62 and 63.
[2] Article entitled "Afghan Wars," by Colonel F. C. Molesworth, appearing in *The R.E. Journal*, December, 1929, p. 605.
[3] *The Second Afghan War*, by H. B. Hanna, Vol. I, p. 295.
[4] *The Afghan War*, 1879–80, by Howard Hensman, Special Correspondent of the *Pioneer* (Allahabad) and the *Daily News* (London), p. 326.

visit in 1869, and he did it so well that his mistakes are the more noticeable; for instance, his admiration of the Highlanders led him to put several regiments into kilts produced in his clothing factory at Kabul, but unfortunately he selected his mounted infantry for this honour! Lord Mayo once gave him four 18-pounder guns and two 8-inch howitzers. As the Amir wished to copy them he summoned one Surferaz, who had made a number of brass guns, and ordered him to set to work. The wretched man tried his best, but at the end of a few months gave up in despair; and when it was found that he had spent 12,000 rupees he was thrown into prison and all his property confiscated. But Sher Ali was not discouraged. He sent another man to be trained in Peshawar, and this hero, who was paid only 70 Kabul rupees a month, became so expert that he could turn out inferior field-guns at the rate of four or five a month at a cost of about £100 apiece. The Afghans were certainly enterprising, however poorly they were trained for war.

Sir Samuel Browne, at the head of the Peshawar Valley Field Force, opened the campaign of 1878 on the evening of November 20th by despatching the 2nd Brigade under Brigadier-General J. A. Tytler to march by a circuitous route to a position in rear of the fort of Ali Masjid, 13 miles away up the Khaibar Pass. Before dawn the 1st Brigade under Brigadier-General H. T. Macpherson marched also from Jamrud[1] to occupy some heights overlooking Ali Masjid. Sir Samuel with the 3rd and 4th Brigades started at 7 a.m. to make a direct attack on the fort, and in three hours the leading troops were on the long and stony ridge of Shagai within a mile and a half of it. Ali Masjid was a small fortified enclosure with circular towers at the four corners, standing on a detached hill towering 300 feet above the Kabul River and effectually blocking the path up the valley. It was held by nearly 4,000 Afghans, mostly regular troops, with 24 guns, and their commander, Faiz Muhammad, was brave and determined. General Browne set the Bengal Sappers to work to improve the rugged path so that he could bring forward his artillery, and when this had been done the fire of the Afghan guns was brought under control though it could not be silenced altogether. Both Macpherson and Tytler, however, were so much delayed by natural obstacles that Browne resolved to begin his attack without them. He met with a spirited resistance, and his position at one time was almost critical. The assaulting party was wavering under a murderous fire from the heights when Colonel F. R. Maunsell, R.E., who had just arrived at the foot of the hill, took command of the scattered troops, pushed up a company of Sappers to support them and called for reinforcements. Through his resolute action the attackers were extricated without serious loss and were able to retire in good order to prepare for another

---

[1] A fort of stone and mud built by the Sikhs at a distance of 11 miles from Peshawar to command the mouth of the Khaibar Pass which is about three miles from the fort.

attempt on the following morning. Before dawn two young Engineer officers and a small escort crept forward to reconnoitre the fort. They found it empty. Tytler had at last come in on the Afghan rear, and the enemy, becoming aware of this, had evacuated Ali Masjid during the night and retreated up the gorge where many of them were captured.

The fall of Ali Masjid is said to have disorganized the Afghan plan of defence.[1] It is certain that Sir Samuel Browne met with little resistance afterwards, for he was through the Khaibar Pass and had reached Dakka on November 23rd. Sher Ali's version of the affair at Ali Masjid is worth recording. "By the grace of God," he writes,[2] "a series of victories have been won by our lion-devouring warriors. At the outset there were only five regiments stationed at Ali Masjid when the British troops advanced to attack them. The said five regiments gave battle to fourteen of the infidel white regiments and for about eight hours the roaring of the cannon and musketry, together with the clashing of the swords, were incessant, till the goodness and strength of the Almighty aided the lion-catching warriors and they totally defeated the English army, when a stop was put to further fighting and each side retired to his own camp." Yet the lion-catching and lion-devouring warriors of Afghanistan thought better of facing the British Lion on the following day.

Leaving the 2nd Brigade at Dakka, Sir Samuel Browne occupied Jalalabad with the 1st and 3rd Brigades on December 20th, the 4th Brigade having been detached already to garrison Ali Masjid and to follow later. Meanwhile the 2nd Division under Lieut.-General Maude was moving up to take charge of the Khaibar line of communication. By this time Sher Ali had fled into Russian Turkestan, instructing his son Yakub Khan to treat with the British. Worn out, body and soul, Sher Ali died in exile within the next two months and the Cabinet decided to recognize the worthless Yakub as Amir. General Maude found trouble in the Khaibar with the Zakka Khel Afridis of the Bazar and Bara valleys. In December he was obliged to lead two small columns against these turbulent folk, and the company of Bengal Sappers which went with the force was occupied as usual in roadmaking and blowing up towers. These towers were by no means easy to demolish; they were of stone, round or square and often 40 feet in height, and the only access was by a rope ladder to a door near the top where there was a platform for the defenders. The expedition was successful, but another was required in January, 1879, to complete the work, and in this also the Bengal Sappers took part. Other punitive expeditions followed—two in March against the Shinwaris, and a larger one in April against the Ghilzais of the Lughman Valley when Brigadier-General Gough defeated 5,000 of

[1] *Official History of the Anglo-Afghan War, 1878-79* (1881), Section I, p. 29.
[2] Extracts from a letter from Sher Ali to the Governor of Herat, quoted in *The Second Afghan War*, by H. B. Hanna, Vol. II, p. 149.

ALI MASJID FORT IN THE KHAIBAR PASS.

the enemy at Fatehabad—and in these again the Bengal Sappers were concerned.

It was in the January expedition against the Zakka Khels that Lieutenant (afterwards General Sir Reginald) Hart, R.E., won the Victoria Cross while marching with a company of the 24th Bengal Native Infantry engaged in covering the rear of a convoy. The camels had emerged from a defile when, half a mile in rear, a few mounted messengers appeared under the escort of some troopers of the 13th Bengal Lancers. They came under the fire of Afridi marksmen, and Hart, looking back, saw one of the troopers fall and some 20 Afridis rushing down towards him. Instantly he set off on foot to his rescue, followed by another officer and six men. He completely outstripped his companions, and when, exhausted and alone, he got near the trooper he saw that the Afridis were slashing at the man with their long knives. The murderers went back a short distance as Hart approached and opened fire, but he dragged the dying trooper behind a rock and the others coming up drove off the Afridis. It was a well-earned Victoria Cross.

On the same day on which General Browne began his advance up the Khaibar, Major-General F. S. Roberts, V.C., crossed the frontier at Thal and marched up the Kurram Valley towards a formidable position held by the Afghans on the Paiwar Kotal.[1] While the 7th Company, Bengal Sappers and Miners,[2] repaired and strengthened a fort near the foot of the ascent, Roberts reconnoitred the approaches to the position which lay on a high range of pine-clad hills and precipitous cliffs. It was four miles in length and was held by 4,000 men with 24 guns.[3] The attack was planned for December 2nd. After a night march the British force surprised and turned the Afghan left on the Spin Gawai Kotal, while delivering at the same time a strong frontal attack. The enemy offered a determined resistance, but they retreated when their rear was threatened and abandoned 17 guns. During this fight Lieut.-Colonel Æneas Perkins, R.E., distinguished himself by getting two mountain guns to a position from which they were able to shell the Paiwar Kotal very effectively.[4] Roberts marched on to Ali Khel on December 6th and two days later reconnoitred the great Shutar Gardan Pass which was the chief obstacle between him and Kabul. Transport difficulties, however, deterred him from advancing farther and he had to be content to hold Ali Khel till his line of communication could be improved.

The column destined for Kandahar reached that place on January

---

[1] *Kotal.* A pass, or dip in a ridge.
[2] The Company was commanded by Lieutenant P. T. Buston, R.E., and numbered only 90 men. Its equipment was poor. For instance, it had 50 mules, but they were provided only with country straw pack saddles which required constant readjustment unless the loads balanced exactly. This caused great delay.
[3] *Official History of the Anglo-Afghan War, 1878–79,* Section I, p. 32.
[4] *History of the Corps of Royal Engineers,* by Major-General W. Porter, Vol. II, p. 46.

8th, 1879, without any serious fighting. The 2nd Division (Biddulph) from Quetta entered the Pishin Valley on November 22nd and was massed before the Khojak Pass on December 12th by which time the 1st Division under Lieut.-General Stewart was arriving at Dadhar. Stewart, who had assumed command of the whole force on December 8th, proceeded to send the 2nd Division over the Khojak Pass while he moved with the 1st Division by a route prepared by the Sappers and Miners over the Khoja Amran range to unite with Biddulph at Takht-i-Pul. The two divisions then moved on Kandahar which was abandoned by the enemy. Although the advance of the Kandahar Force was practically unopposed, it entailed very heavy work for the Sapper companies. The roads were execrable, and the difficulties of transport enormous. Major A. Le Mesurier, R.E., who was Brigade-Major with the 2nd Division, says[1] that for every fighting man it was necessary to have one follower and one camel. The mortality among the camels was at least 40 per cent. per month, and, to keep 12,000 camels at work, 1,500 fresh camels *per week* were required.[2] It was only through the unremitting toil of the Engineers, Sappers and Miners and infantry working parties under the direction of Lieut.-Colonels Sankey and Hichens of the Royal Engineers that such masses of transport were pushed through the narrow defiles and across the stony wastes of Afghanistan.

Surveying work was carried out in every area, though it progressed more rapidly in the south than in the north as the Engineers and Surveyors with the Kandahar Force were less subject to interruption than their comrades in the Khaibar and the Kurram, and their number was greater.[3] The Peshawar Valley contingent fixed many points on the mountain ranges and began an accurate survey of the route from Peshawar to Jalalabad. Captain R. G. Woodthorpe, R.E., with Roberts in the Kurram Valley, mapped a great part of the valley and accompanied the General in January, 1789, on a small expedition against the Mangals in Khost. The Kandahar Force surveyors fixed a number of peaks and did some elaborate triangulation work. As a rule they could work freely under a proper escort, and in this they were more fortunate than the Khaibar surveyors, who on several occasions had to fight for their lives. For instance, Captain E. P. Leach, R.E., found himself suddenly involved in a skirmish against the Shinwaris near Maidanak on March 17th, 1879. To cover the retirement of his party, he led a few men of the 45th

[1] *Kandahar in 1879*, by Major A. Le Mesurier, R.E., p. 85.
[2] Le Mesurier states also that to carry the rations alone for *one day* for the Kandahar Force (say, 14,000 men including followers) 1,453 *camels were needed*. (*Ibid.*, p. 87.)
[3] With the Peshawar Valley Force were Major Tanner, Bombay Staff Corps, Captain E. W. Samwells, Bengal Staff Corps, and Captain E. P. Leach and Lieutenant B. Scott of the Royal Engineers. The Kurram Valley Column had Captain R. G. Woodthorpe, R.E. The Kandahar Force had Major W. M. Campbell, Captains W. J. Heavyside, T. H. Holdich and M. W. Rogers and Lieutenant St. G. C. Gore, all of the Royal Engineers, and also two Staff Corps officers. (*Official History*, 1878–79, Section II, p. 14.)

BOUND FOR KANDAHAR!

Colonel "Jacky" Hills, R.E. First cartoon in the *Nari Gazette and Grass Widows' Chronicle*. Afghanistan, 1880.

Sikhs in a gallant charge against a large number of tribesmen, killing two or three himself and being severely wounded in the arm. By so doing he saved the whole party from annihilation, and for his bravery he was awarded the Victoria Cross.[1]

From a description given by Le Mesurier[2] it seems that the dress of the Engineers during the advance into Afghanistan was more picturesque than smart :—

"The uniform is decidedly irregular. We all have helmets, some with spikes and some without, some with leathern chin-straps, others with brass; all with hair growing promiscuously where it will, shading off from black to white. Colonel Sankey has a suit of corduroy and 'Field' boots, a Paget blade with inlaid handle; I have a suit of brown cloth and brown boots with canvas tops, a cavalry sabre and hunting spurs; Call wears a suit of brown canvas cloth, black lace boots, black gaiter-tops and a regimental sword; while Childers is in khakee. The officers with the Sappers, again, have helmets with wadded covers, khakee blouses, but their legs and feet are fitted with different patterns of trousers and boots of varying colours; and Browne, whom I met yesterday, had a suit of puttoo[3] on and a terai[4] wide-awake hat. Savage wears his patrol jacket and red stripes, with putties bound round his legs, and St. John appears in a suit of Bedford cord. The sword-belts and fittings vary with the fancy of the owner."

A parade of all the Royal Engineers would have been an interesting sight, but the variation in their kit does not seem to have affected their efficiency. They placed comfort before appearance.

On arrival at Kandahar the 1st Division under General Stewart marched on and occupied Kalat-i-Ghilzai but soon returned to Kandahar. Meanwhile the 2nd Division under General Biddulph had gone westwards to the river Helmand and Girishk. There it remained till February 23rd when it marched back to Kandahar and was broken up, a large number of the troops returning with Biddulph to India by the Thal-Chotiali route. While on the Helmand the 10th Company, Bengal Sappers and Miners, which was included with the 5th Company in Biddulph's division, executed a difficult bridging operation with the assistance of the 32nd Pioneers. A train of 12 pontoons had been sent off from Roorkee by rail, but only two of them got beyond Sukkur. These two, with their superstructure, were despatched from Sukkur to the Helmand on five wagons and carts drawn by 49 bullocks. As only two pontoons were available, Biddulph could not bridge the broad and rapid river when he wished to

---

[1] *History of the Corps of Royal Engineers*, by Major-General W. Porter, Vol. II, p. 48.
[2] *Kandahar in 1879*, by Major A. Le Mesurier, R.E., pp. 46, 47.
[3] Native homespun cloth.
[4] *Tarai*. A portion of the Naini Tal District near the foothills of the Himalayas.

cross it.¹ The best that could be done was to arrange a flying bridge, and this the 10th Company did. The fate of the Bridging Train shows how lack of transport may hinder field engineering and the movement of troops; this deficiency, indeed, eventually brought the whole of the military operations more or less to a standstill.

In the spring of 1879 the British advance had been checked everywhere, though not by the Afghans. One part of Stewart's army, pushing under Biddulph towards Herat, had been obliged to stop on the Helmand; Stewart himself had reached Kalat-i-Ghilzai only to fall back on Kandahar. Browne's forces were tied to Jalalabad, unable to move through lack of carriage. The Kurram Valley column under Roberts, compelled to withdraw from Khost and weather-bound about the Paiwar Kotal, was losing heavily through sickness. Fortunately this deadlock ended with the signature of the Treaty of Gandamak by Yakub Khan on May 26th, 1879. The Khaibar and Kurram Forces were then withdrawn except for garrisons at Landi Kotal, Ali Masjid and Jamrud, while the Kandahar Force stood fast to await the end of the hot weather. The hardships of the march from Jalalabad were very great. The temperature ranged between 110° and 118°, and cholera and sunstroke took their toll. On July 24th, 1879, Major Sir P. L. N. Cavagnari arrived at Kabul as British Resident, accompanied by a small escort, and it was thought that the war was ended. The three companies of Madras Sappers returned to Bangalore and most of the Bengal Sappers to Northern India. The Field Engineers went back to their civil appointments.

Le Mesurier gives a brief but graphic description of the Engineers in the Kandahar theatre and their work :—²

"St. John in political charge at head-quarters. Campbell and Rogers of the Survey, with Gore, Heaviside and Holdich. Savage and Dickie with the field telegraph and signalling. The road across the Khojak commenced by Ghilzai labourers under Wells and completed by Haslett and his sappers.³ Haslett, again with Jerome, in the Gwaja pass, where Sankey and his A.D.C., Childers, secured so speedily such an easy passage for the heavy guns. Nicholson, who accompanied the return force by the Thal-Chotiali line through the country where Browne had gained so much credit. The Sappers, with Browne in command, and his work at the Helmund, and again in the Arghandab at the head-works of the water-supply. Sharpe at

¹ The Helmand varies in width from 80 to 300 yards, and the current runs at 4½ miles an hour.
² *Kandahar in 1879*, by Major A. Le Mesurier, R.E., pp. 279, 280.
³ The 5th and 9th Companies of the Bengal Sappers and Miners, assisted by Pioneers, constructed a ramp for guns in the Khojak Pass, which for the first 150 yards of its length sloped at 30° and thereafter at an easier gradient for 400 yards. Lieutenant H. L. Wells, R.E., once distinguished himself by scattering a band of marauders with 36 troopers of the Indian cavalry, killing the leader, his two sons and his nephew.

Kokeran. Sankey's arrangements for sheltering the troops at Kandahar. Bisset, the field engineer, with Olivier at work in the citadel; and Call, the field-park engineer, in his endless occupation and admirable method, supervising the works of renovation and construction. Whiteford with the Bombay Sappers at work in the Bolan, and Orpen busily engaged in Katchi during the hottest season."

With Cavagnari installed in Kabul and most of the troops back in India, the Government was pleased with the results of the war, and a telegram from the envoy on September 2nd, 1879, announcing that all was well, added to the general satisfaction. But it was short-lived. Within 24 hours Cavagnari and all his escort were murdered by some discontented regiments of Afghans, and orders were issued immediately for another invasion of Afghanistan by an advance on Kabul, while the troops which had begun to leave Kandahar were directed to stand fast. The main operation was entrusted to Major-General Sir Frederick Roberts, V.C., who was to move up the Kurram Valley with one cavalry and two infantry brigades, accompanied by some artillery and engineers and supported by two more brigades in rear. At the same time a division under Major-General R. O. Bright was to assemble in the Khaibar Pass to join Roberts by that route when he reached Kabul. Lieut.-General Sir D. M. Stewart was to hold southern Afghanistan with a third division operating from Kandahar. The transport organization of the first phase of the war had been broken up and the animals dispersed, so the question of supply promised to be most difficult. To meet the situation the Government of India created a new post—that of Controller-General of Supply and Transport—and appointed an Engineer to it in the person of Lieut.-General Sir Michael Kennedy, who set to work to improvise a system based on that of the Punjab Frontier Force under which the transport of each unit was considered as part of its regimental equipment.[1] In time General Kennedy brought order out of chaos, and the movements of the troops became easier and more rapid.

Engineers, and Sappers and Miners, were allotted to each division. Roberts was given the 7th Company, Bengal Sappers and Miners, and Lieut.-Colonel Æneas Perkins, R.E., as Commanding Royal Engineer. Bright in the Khaibar had Lieut.-Colonel D. Limond, R.E., and the 2nd, 3rd, 5th and 6th Companies of Bengal Sappers and Miners under Major E. T. Thackeray, V.C., R.E.[2] Stewart with the Kandahar Field Force (afterwards called the Southern Afghanistan Field Force) had Lieut.-Colonel W. Hichens, R.E., at the head of his Engineers,

[1] *The Second Afghan War*, by H. B. Hanna, Vol. III, p. 44.
[2] Thackeray had been appointed Commandant of the Corps on September 20th, 1879, *vice* Major-General F. R. Maunsell, promoted. The 5th Company had returned to Roorkee in June, 1879, but left again for Afghanistan on December 5th.

and the 4th and 10th Companies of Bengal Sappers and Miners. On the line between Quetta and Sukkur were the 2nd, 3rd, 4th and 5th Companies of Bombay Sappers; and " A," " C " and " I " Companies of the Madras Sappers under Major R. Thompson, R.E., were soon in Afghanistan. " A " and " I " arrived from Bangalore in the middle of November, and " C " from Burma late in December. Near Landi Kotal the Madras Sappers may have seen the signpost erected in the previous campaign by some wags of their " K " Company. It lay at a road junction and its three arms were labelled respectively " To Kabul," " To Landi Kotal," and " To Madras."

General Roberts pushed rapidly up the Kurram Valley at the head of what was known as the " Kabul Field Force,"[1] his advanced guard reaching the Shutar Gardan Pass on September 11th and holding it in an entrenched position made by Lieutenant C. Nugent, R.E. Roberts then came up to Ali Khel; but it was not till October 1st that he had brought his troops by detachments over the rugged heights of the Shutar Gardan and had concentrated them at Kushi in the Logar Valley where Amir Yakub Khan presented himself in the British camp after deserting his countrymen at Kabul. The 7th Company, Bengal Sappers and Miners, assisted this advance by making a passable road up a very steep ascent three miles east of the Shutar Gardan.[2] Beyond Kushi, Roberts found his way barred by a powerful army. This was at the Sang-i-Nawishta defile north of the village of Charasiab. He attacked on October 6th, 1879, defeated the Afghans after a stubborn resistance, took all their guns, and was camped on the Sia Sang heights outside Kabul on the 9th. For a time the enemy held the Asmai heights near the city, but soon withdrew. Roberts then found himself in an uncomfortable situation, threatened by 60,000 Afghans under an enterprising leader named Muhammad Jan, with General Bright and the Khaibar Division unable to reach him through lack of transport, and with the imminent prospect of the closing of the Kurram route by the approach of winter. He contemplated the occupation of the great Bala Hissar fortress,[3] but some explosions within it made him change his mind, and early in November he moved into the Sherpur cantonments which lay a little to the north of the old British cantonments of 1841. The Sherpur enclosure had been laid out by Sher Ali and improved by Yakub Khan. It measured about 3,000 by 1,000 yards, and was commanded on the north by a range of hills known as the Bimaru Heights. The southern and western faces had a loop-holed wall 16 feet in height; but the eastern wall was unfinished, and the northern face, towards the heights, was open.

General Bright continued his efforts to get through to Kabul by

---

[1] Its strength was about 6,000 men.
[2] *Official History of the Anglo-Afghan War of 1878-80*, Section V, p. 32.
[3] Enormous quantities of Afghan war material of all sorts were in the arsenal of the Bala Hissar, and there were barracks in the fortress to hold troops.

GENERAL ROBERTS BESIEGED NEAR KABUL. 385

the Khaibar route, and on November 2nd his advanced brigade reached Jagdalak where he was met by a force from Kabul under Brigadier-General Macpherson; this route was then adopted as the line of supply to Roberts, and the Kurram route abandoned. The 7th Company of Bengal Sappers was hard at work in Kabul improving the Sherpur defences, while the 2nd, 3rd, 5th and 6th Companies under Thackeray were strung out along the road between Jagdalak and Gandamak, with " I " Company of the Madras Sappers at Jalalabad, and " A " and " C " Companies of the Corps expected soon on the line of communication between Dakka and Landi Kotal.

The inhabitants of Kabul, and the tribes around, became more and more hostile in their attitude to the British, and early in December it was rumoured that a plan had been made to surround the city and overwhelm Roberts and his 7,000 soldiers in the Sherpur cantonments. Taking the offensive, Roberts struck at the advancing hordes of Muhammad Jan but was overpowered by numbers,[1] and on December 14th was obliged to retire into Sherpur where he was soon invested closely by 100,000 of the enemy. For 48 hours continuously every available man laboured to complete the defences. It was necessary to include the Bimaru Heights in the scheme, for they were the key of the position, so the shallow ditches which connected six towers on the heights were deepened, prolonged and protected by abattis. New trenches were dug to fill any gaps in the line, and all that skill and knowledge could do to improve a defective position was done by Lieut.-Colonel Æneas Perkins and his staff of Engineers to which, at their own request, the Survey officers[2] had been attached. Sir Michael Kennedy also advised General Roberts on engineering matters. Efforts were made to provide a good field of fire around the enclosure, but a proper clearance could not be made with the few men available.

The Afghan forces made several attacks on different parts of the British position, and before dawn on December 23rd, 1879, they launched a grand assault, directed first against the village of Bimaru and a gap in the eastern wall and afterwards against the other faces. " The dense masses of the enemy, led by Ghazis," writes Hanna,[3] " were pouring across the plain, each star shell, as it flew, lighting up hundreds of fierce, eager faces. Darkness faded into dawn, and the terrible beauty of a night assault gave place to the hideous horrors of a battle by day; but still the vast mob rushed on, wave after wave, filling the air with deafening cries of *Allah-i-Allah* as they hurled themselves on the defences. But the Engineers had done their work too well. Not one succeeded in getting within the walls. On all sides the garrison was now hotly engaged, and the Afghans were

[1] Brigadier-General W. D. G. Massy was seriously defeated at Kila Kazi, near Kabul, on December 11th, and was only saved by Roberts himself.
[2] Major R. G. Woodthorpe, R.E., Captain T. H. Holdich, R.E., and others.
[3] Extracts from *The Second Afghan War*, by H. B. Hanna, Vol. III, pp. 244–247.

O

making one attempt after another to escalade the southern wall. For seven hours, without a single cannon to cover their advance and batter down the strong defences, they hurled themselves upon the abattis, and, under a murderous fire, tugged and tore at the tough telegraph wires which bound the heavy logs together. Great heaps of dead testified to the spirit by which they were inspired. That night every man in Sherpur knew that the siege was at an end."

The repulse of this assault was followed by a successful British counter-attack before which the Afghans fled in disorder. "Following in the wake of the 9th Lancers and 5th Punjab Cavalry," says Hensman,[1] "came the Sappers with every engineer officer in camp, their orders being to blow up and burn all villages and forts lately occupied by the enemy. In the villages some fanatics remained, and these were blown up in their houses by the mines laid by the engineers. A sad accident occurred. Captain Dundas, V.C., and Lieutenant Nugent, Royal Engineers, had constructed three mines, and, all being ready, went back to light the fuses. The Sappers were drawn up outside under their European non-commissioned officers and noticed that two of the mines exploded instantly. Their officers were still within the walls, and when the dust and smoke cleared away they were still missing. Search was made, and the bodies of Captain Dundas and Lieutenant Nugent were found lying under the debris. Both were dead. It is conjectured that the time-fuses, instead of burning slowly, flared up like a train of powder. We have thus lost two good officers by an accident which might have been prevented if the equipment of the Sappers had not been cut down by the parsimony of the Government. So few fuses were sent from India that the Engineers had to make others and these were of course defective."[2]

While the garrison of Sherpur was fighting for existence on December 23rd, Major E. T. Thackeray, V.C., R.E., was putting up a gallant defence against 3,000 of the enemy in a small post at the Jagdalak Kotal on the Khaibar line. He had only the 2nd and 3rd Companies of Bengal Sappers, armed with carbines, one company of the 24th Bengal Native Infantry, and 12 troopers of the 10th Bengal Cavalry. The Afghans poured in a heavy fire from all sides and Thackeray was badly wounded in the right arm; but the little garrison showed such a bold front and fired so accurately that they held out for many hours till they were finally relieved after dark. Thus the Sappers proved once again that they were as expert with their carbines as with their picks and shovels.

A few days after the battle of Kabul, Brigadier-General G. Gough, V.C., marched in from Gandamak with his brigade and so connected

---

[1] *The Afghan War*, 1878-80, by Howard Hensman, p. 255.
[2] Brigadier-General P. T. Buston, C.B., C.M.G., D.S.O., who was present as a Lieutenant, R.E., in Kabul, has written to the author as follows: "We had run out of all the safety fuze, and had had to make our own which consisted of cotton yarn soaked in gunpowder. This, of course, burnt very unevenly."

Roberts with Bright. This force included the 5th Company, Bengal Sappers and Miners, which was a welcome addition to the hard-worked 7th Company already in Kabul. There was much engineering work in hand. Every village and wall within 1,000 yards of Sherpur was levelled to the ground ; the river was bridged in three places, roads were laid out, the ramparts completed, and forts and blockhouses placed on the heights around and at other important points.[1] Sherpur, in fact, became a fortress impregnable to any Afghan attack. Meanwhile Major F. Blair, R.E., with the 2nd and 3rd Companies of Bengal Sappers, was at work on a road through the Jagdalak range, and farther down the line the Madras Sappers were doing their share. Secure in his communications with India, victorious over the enemy, and safely ensconced in Kabul, we can now leave Roberts and proceed to follow the events in the south where there had been no serious fighting.

The troops under Lieut.-General Sir D. M. Stewart had advanced from Kandahar and reoccupied Kalat-i-Ghilzai and other places. Transport was collected for a march on Kabul. The Sappers and Miners were busy on the line to Quetta, and the railway engineers were equally hard at work in the plains. In October, 1879, the Government had agreed at last to the construction of a railway line from Sukkur on the Indus to Sibi[2] at the foot of the hills, and the enterprise was put in hand. The line was easy to construct, but there were great problems of supply for the country was a barren and waterless desert. However, the ability of Lieut.-Colonel J. G. Lindsay, R.E., and his staff of military and civil engineers was such that the line to Sibi was opened for traffic on January 27th, 1880. " The execution of $133\frac{1}{2}$ miles of railway in 101 days," writes Macgregor,[3] " or an average progress of $1\frac{3}{8}$ miles per day, is a feat worthy of mention. During the fifty working days occupied in carrying the railway over ninety-three miles of inhospitable desert, the work progressed with the utmost regularity and mechanical precision." It was proposed that the line should be extended to Quetta and ultimately to Kandahar, but the end of the war made such an undertaking inadvisable.[4] In the north the railway had already reached

---

[1] In all, Lieut.-Colonel Perkins, the C.R.E., had in hand at one time 10 forts, 15 detached works, three large trestle-bridges, numerous small ones, 4,000 yards of defence, 45 miles of road, two defended posts, and quarters for 8,000 men. It will be admitted that the Engineers and Sappers earned their pay.

[2] Sanction was first accorded in September to its construction as far as Dadhar only.

[3] *Ways and Works in India*, by G. W. Macgregor, pp. 398, 399.

[4] Three years later the project of extending the railway as far as Quetta by the Harnai Pass route was revived, and Colonel James Browne, R.E., was placed in charge of the operations which were most arduous. On March 17th, 1887, the first locomotive ran through from Sibi to Quetta. Besides five companies of Bengal Sappers and huge gangs of coolies, several battalions of Pioneers were employed on this railway work in the Harnai and also in the Bolan Pass, each battalion having one wing in the Harnai and the other in the Bolan. Thus, when an awkward question was asked in Parliament about the employment of troops on railway work, the famous answer was given : " *There is not a single regiment on either the Harnai or Bolan railways.*"

Rawalpindi and extensions were contemplated to Kohat, Peshawar and Jamrud. Thus the railway engineers took their full share in the war.

On March 29th, 1880, the Ghazni Field Force, as Sir Donald Stewart's command was now called, set out from Kandahar for Kabul. It consisted of two brigades, including the 4th and 10th Companies of Bengal Sappers and Miners and seven officers of the Royal Engineers under Captain E. M. Larminie, R.E., and its place in the Kandahar area was taken by a Bombay division under Lieut.-General T. M. Primrose who had with him the 2nd, 3rd, 4th and 5th Companies of Bombay Sappers and Miners. For three weeks Sir Donald Stewart met with no opposition, but on the morning of April 19th he discovered the Afghans in great force on a range of hills at Ahmad Khel, 23 miles south of Ghazni, and made his dispositions for attack. Scarcely had his guns opened fire when masses of the enemy charged furiously down on his infantry. " The scene," says Chapman,[1] " was one which baffles description. Such an enormous body of Ghazi swordsmen had not been brought together since the battle of Meannee. Their bravery was magnificent. Nothing stopped them short of death." Nevertheless they suffered a crushing defeat, and Stewart marched on to occupy Ghazni on April 21st. Soon afterwards he joined hands with Roberts at Kabul, assumed the chief command in northern Afghanistan, and under arrangements with the newly-installed Amir, Abdur Rahman Khan, a nephew of Dost Muhammad, prepared to lead the army back to India. Some of the troops had already begun to move when the whole situation was changed by news of a disaster in the south.

Soon after Stewart had marched for Kabul there had been signs of trouble from the direction of Herat, and in June it became known that Ayub Khan, a son of Amir Sher Ali, was advancing with 20,000 men on Kandahar. The Wali of that place moved out with his own men to check him, and on July 4th General Primrose sent a brigade under Brigadier-General G. R. S. Burrows towards the River Helmand in support of the Wali. This brigade was accompanied by Lieut.-Colonel O. B. C. St. John, R.E., as Political Officer, and Major E. P. Leach, V.C., R.E., as a staff officer, and it included 41 men of the 2nd Company, Bombay Sappers and Miners, under Lieutenant T. R. Henn, with Serjeant Heapy and 1st-Corporal Ashman, all of the Royal Engineers. Its departure left Kandahar in a dangerously weak condition, for the Bombay Division was much scattered, and Lieut.-Colonel John Hills, R.E., the Commanding Royal Engineer, brought this fact to the notice of General Primrose, but without effect.[2] When the British force arrived on the Helmand, the Wali's troops deserted, and Burrows was obliged to retreat to Khusk-i-

---

[1] Article by General Chapman appearing in *Blackwoods Magazine*, February, 1902, p. 262.
[2] *The Second Afghan War*, by H. B. Hanna, Vol. III, p. 390.

Nakhud, between the Helmand and Kandahar, to replenish his supplies. The place was suitable also because it commanded all the roads by which Ayub Khan might advance from the west. On July 27th, 1880, Ayub was reported at Maiwand about 12 miles to the north-east, advancing apparently against the British line of communication, so Burrows, with Brigadier-General Nuttall in charge of his advanced guard, moved to attack him. The brigade, encumbered with baggage and sick, was soon under a heavy fire and outflanked completely by the masses of the enemy. An Indian regiment broke, others followed suit, and all was confusion. The 66th Regiment (British) fought most stubbornly and lost nearly two-thirds of its men, but it could not check the rout. Yet among the Indian soldiers were some whose courage rose as high as that of their British comrades. The Bombay Sappers and Miners under Lieutenant T. R. Henn earned undying fame on the stricken field of Maiwand. They were the last of all the troops to leave the line of battle. When the tide of retreat swept over them as they lay in support of the Horse Artillery they still remained a formed body and did not retire till they had covered the withdrawal of the guns. Henn and 14 of his men[1] then joined a party of the 66th Regiment and some Bombay Grenadiers, and these 90 soldiers made a most determined stand in a small enclosure at a place called Khig. So grim was their bearing that the Afghans dared not close with them. The defenders fired steadily, losing man after man, until only 11 were left, and these 11 charged out at last and fought to the death in the masses of the enemy. Henn was the only officer in that gallant band,[2] and he led the final charge. He did as Durnford, another Royal Engineer, had done in the previous year at Isandlwana in Zululand. He might have joined in the general retirement; but he chose instead to die, and he died in good company.[3]

In the terrible retreat of Burrows' troops during the next 33 hours through 45 miles of broken country to Kandahar, Leach shepherded and encouraged many disheartened men. No one knew the district so well as he, and he was indefatigable in collecting stragglers and indicating the route. It was not till mid-day on the 28th that the exhausted remnant staggered into the city. Out of 2,500 fighting men nearly 1,000 had been killed, and General Primrose could muster

[1] The names of these 14 Indian Sappers are among the following 15 who were killed at Maiwand: Havildar Muhammad Khan, Naik Siuram Wanjari, Bugler Shaikh Abdulla, and Privates Biru Nikam, Shaikh Pir Bakhsh, Govindrao More, Ramji Talekar, Siurattan Singh, Jangu Narsu, Rama Powar, Ambuji, Balnak Yesnak, Poshuti Piraji, Ithu Damu and Chocnak. Serjeant Heapy, R.E., and 1st-Corporal Ashman, R.E., were also killed at Maiwand. (See *A Brief History of the Royal Bombay Sappers and Miners*, p. 16.)

[2] *History of the Corps of Royal Engineers*, by Major-General W. Porter, Vol. II, p. 58.

[3] A monument to Thomas Rice Henn can be seen in St. Patrick's Cathedral in Dublin. The inscription records how he and his men covered the retreat of the whole brigade till they were killed. (See obituary notice of Lieutenant T. R. Henn, R.E., appearing in *The R.E. Journal*, Vol. 12, 1882, p. 171.) There is also a memorial window in Rochester Cathedral.

only some 4,300 soldiers to man the walls of Kandahar, 6,000 yards in length, before which Ayub Khan's army began to appear on the 29th. The cantonments had been abandoned, and the whole force concentrated in the city from which the inhabitants had been expelled. The Royal Engineers under Lieut.-Colonel Hills—Major E. P. Leach, V.C., Captain G. M. Cruickshank and Lieutenant E. A. Waller—laboured strenuously to clear a field of fire and to barricade the gates, in which work they were assisted by five non-commissioned officers and 40 men of the 2nd Company, Bombay Sappers and Miners, under Lieutenant G. Turner Jones, R.E.[1] There was little explosive available, so the houses and walls around the city had to be demolished by hand.

Ayub Khan opened fire on Kandahar on August 8th. His investing army was very powerful, for besides six regiments of cavalry and 13 of infantry, with 31 guns and 80 scaling ladders, he had many thousands of irregulars. They occupied all the nearer villages and enclosures, and fired heavily from a village called Deh Khoja. A few small sorties were undertaken from time to time, and Waller and Turner Jones were recommended for the Victoria Cross for sallying out on August 12th to rescue a wounded man.[2] At last General Primrose resolved to clear Deh Khoja and its surroundings by a powerful sortie, and at first he favoured a plan submitted by Lieut.-Colonel Hills, his Commanding Royal Engineer, for a surprise attack in force, but afterwards swung round to a scheme proposed by Brigadier-General Brooke, who was given charge of the party detailed for the enterprise. So, after a bombardment by the British guns, 800 men marched out under Brooke on August 16th. They were soon in a critical position and lost heavily. Brooke was killed, and Captain Cruickshank, R.E., mortally wounded. Hills then requested permission to take out a few men to support a retreat, but he was forbidden to do so. "It is all your doing," said General Primrose. "I am damned if it is," retorted the indignant Engineer. "You have done everything I told you was not to be done—bombardment, small force, separate attacks and wrong end of the village."[3] It was an insubordinate remark, but excusable, perhaps, under the circumstances. Terribly reduced in numbers, and followed by an ugly rush of Ghazis, the survivors of Brooke's sortie streamed in through the Kabul Gate. Primrose then sat down to await the relief which was on its way to him both from the north and south, and when the siege had lasted about one month he was relieved by Roberts from the north.

On receipt of news of the disaster at Maiwand, Stewart at Kabul

---

[1] *Official History of the Anglo-Afghan War*, 1879–1880, Section V, p. 47. This was the half-company which remained in Kandahar while the other, under Henn, marched with Burrows.

[2] Neither, however, received the award.

[3] *The Second Afghan War*, by H. B. Hanna, Vol. III, p. 451.

had appointed Roberts to the command of a "Kabul-Kandahar Force" which was to hasten to the relief of Primrose. Roberts set out on August 8th with an infantry division, a cavalry brigade and three batteries of mountain guns, and traversed the whole distance of 321 miles to Kandahar in 23 days, although he halted for one day at Kalat-i-Ghilzai and ceased to make forced marches towards the end when he came into touch with Primrose. The details of this fine performance need not be recorded here; it caught the popular fancy and will be remembered long after Stewart's more difficult journey over the same route is forgotten. But there is one curious feature in the composition of Roberts' force which is worthy of remark in this volume. Though he was allowed to pick his units, *no Sappers and Miners were included in his column.* The 7th Company of Bengal Sappers in Kabul had worked and fought under him during the siege; yet they were left behind. The only engineering establishment in the Kabul-Kandahar Force was a small Field Park hurriedly improvised by Captain W. G. Nicholson, R.E. The official history of the war contains the remark that "the absence of Sappers was met by the employment of the 23rd Pioneers, a regiment trained to all practical Engineering work, and yet furnishing 700 rifles to the fighting line."[1] It is true that Roberts had to exclude from his force everything that was not essential; for instance, he took no wheeled guns or transport; and he may have considered that the rifles of the "dual-purpose" Pioneers were worth more on this occasion than the expert work of the highly-trained Sappers; also he was obliged, for political reasons, to eliminate units which contained many Pathans.[2] But the Bengal Sappers and Miners under Captain and Brevet-Major Bindon Blood, R.E.,[3] felt the omission keenly. A number of Royal Engineer officers, however, accompanied the force. Headed by Lieut.-Colonel Æneas Perkins, the cadre included Captains W. G. Nicholson, C. F. Call, M. C. Brackenbury, F. T. Spratt and R. P. Tickell, and Lieutenants E. Glennie, T. P. Cather, Hon. M. G. Talbot, R. C. Maxwell, E. S. Childers and F. B. Longe—12 in all.[4] As it happened, there was little engineering to be done. Roberts reached

---

[1] *Official History of the Anglo-Afghan War,* 1879-80, Section V, p. 68 (footnote).

[2] *The Second Afghan War,* by H. B. Hanna, Vol. III, p. 466.

[3] Now General Sir Bindon Blood, G.C.B., G.C.V.O., the senior Colonel-Commandant of the Corps of Royal Engineers, and the writer of the foreword to this volume. He has a very distinguished record, having been engaged in the Sowaki expedition of 1877-78, South Africa (Zululand), 1879, Afghanistan, 1879-80, Egypt, 1882, Chitral, 1895, on the North-West Frontier in 1897-98, when he was in chief command, and in South Africa, 1899-1902, where he commanded a force. He officiated as Commandant of the Bengal Sappers and Miners from February, 1880, to September, 1881, in place of Lieut.-Colonel E. T. Thackeray, V.C., R.E., on leave, and was appointed Commandant in 1885. Later he held various important appointments in India. General Sir Bindon Blood retired on November 7th, 1907, and became a Colonel-Commandant on July 9th, 1914. His portrait, as a Colonel, appears in Chapter XXI.

[4] One Sub-Conductor with the Field Park, and one Serjeant as C.R.E.s clerk, accompanied the officers.

THE SECOND AFGHAN WAR, 1878–1880.

Kandahar on August 31st, 1880, just forestalling a force from Quetta under Major-General Sir R. Phayre, which arrived on September 3rd, too late for the battle of Kandahar, after a most difficult march in great heat through a whole country up in arms.

A reconnaissance had shown that Ayub Khan was holding a position north-west of Kandahar, so Roberts, then at Robat a few miles distant, marched into Kandahar on August 31st and attacked him without waiting for Phayre. The result was a brilliant victory for the British who drove the Afghans from their hills with the loss of all their guns and camp equipage and about 1,000 men killed. The battle of Kandahar brought the Second Afghan War to a conclusion. Soon after Roberts had marched from Kabul, Stewart began to withdraw the remaining troops from northern Afghanistan, and the frontier arranged by the peace of Gandamak was resumed. Followed by the Bombay troops, Roberts led part of his force from Kandahar to India, leaving Major-General Hume with a garrison in Kandahar. The retention of this city then became a much debated question, but eventually it was decided to retire from the whole of southern Afghanistan, retaining only Chaman ; so Kandahar was evacuated in 1881 after some punitive expeditions had been undertaken against recalcitrant tribes in the north and south. Amir Abdur Rahman was seated securely on the throne, and, as Sir George MacMunn writes,[1] the result of our policy of 1880 gave us 39 years of a strong and friendly Afghanistan. If the war was a mistake at the outset, the error was remedied by sound and diplomatic action at the finish. This, at least, can be said of it. Also, it brought to light many deficiencies in the army, and notably in the organization, administration and equipment of the Sappers and Miners.[2]

There is no gainsaying the fact that in Afghanistan there was not that close liaison between the Engineer Department and the Sappers and Miners on which efficiency depends so much. This was particularly evident to any Royal Engineer who came from the home establishment where the field companies worked hand-in-glove with the cadre of Engineers. On active service in India the Commanding Royal Engineer[3] had direct access to the General Officer in chief command and controlled a large staff of Field and Assistant Field Engineers. The Commandant of the Sappers and Miners, however, was denied access to the General and took his orders from the Quartermaster-General, and it often happened that few of the Royal Engineer officers serving with the companies under him in the field had been with him in peace-time. A General Order, published in

---

[1] *Afghanistan from Darius to Amanullah*, by Lieut.-General Sir George MacMunn, K.C.B., K.C.S.I., D.S.O., p. 204.

[2] At this time, none of the Bengal Sappers had any knowledge of artificer's work. They were simply trained in digging, spar-bridging and a certain amount of pontooning. Each company had five civilian artificers, two carpenters, two smiths and a mason.

[3] He was often called the " Commanding Engineer."

1879,[1] during the Afghan War, laid down that when on field service the Corps of Sappers and Miners was a "distinct body" under the command of its own officers appointed from the Royal Engineers; that Commanding Engineers had no power to interfere in the interior economy of the Sapper companies; and that the Engineer Department, though allowed to ask for Sappers for a particular work, had no control over them. Such regulations were conducive neither to harmony nor efficiency.

There were instances during the Afghan War of Field Engineers being sent to execute work on which, unknown to the Commanding Royal Engineer, the Sappers and Miners were already engaged. At Kabul, where there should have been one Mess for all the Royal Engineer officers, there were two Messes, a small one for the officers with the Sappers and Miners and a large one for those in other employment. There was no general ill-feeling or friction between the two sets of officers, but the system was certainly at fault and liable to cause trouble and duplication of work. The first improvement was one which was notified in a General Order during September, 1882,[2] about two years after the end of the war, cancelling the General Order of July, 1878, and another of January, 1880, and directing that, when on field service, the Sappers and Miners should be under the direct orders of the Commanding Royal Engineer of the force to which they were attached, though their own officers should still be responsible for the interior economy of the companies. This was an important step in the right direction, but much still remained to be done.

Three years later came the great Sapper and Miner reorganization which was the embodiment of many years of hard work. The drafting of the Army Order which introduced it was entrusted to Lieut.-Colonel Bindon Blood, R.E., who had been largely instrumental in preparing its details and in overcoming the objections which were put forward in some quarters. The Special Indian Army Circular which authorized the changes appeared in December, 1885.[3] It was a comprehensive document, and only a general idea of its more important provisions can be given here. The Bengal and Madras Corps of Sappers and Miners were each to have six Service companies, numbered 1 to 6, and two Depot companies, lettered "A" and "B." "A" Company was to include two Pontoon Sections, two Telegraph Sections, two Field Printing Sections and one Submarine Mining Section; it was to be, in fact, a company of technical experts. "B" Company was to be a Recruit Depot. The provision of special organizations in "A" Company, however, was not to interfere with the training of the Corps in general in bridging and telegraph duties. The Bombay Sappers and Miners were to have four Service companies

---
[1] Special General Order No. 88, dated July 22nd, 1879.
[2] S.G.O. No. 110, dated September 14th, 1882.
[3] I.A.C. No. 174, dated December 16th, 1885.

and one Depot company, and the post of "Superintendent of Instruction and Park and Train" was created.[1] In each of the other two Corps there was already a "Superintendent of Instruction" and a separate "Superintendent of Park and Train." The reorganization involved a renumbering of the companies in the Bengal and Madras Corps and many alterations in internal economy, but its most important feature was the principle on which it was based. This was that *the proper unit of the Engineer Service is the company and not the battalion*, and that consequently the company should be maintained in peace as well as in war as a self-contained body, ready always for independent action. In peace it should be, of course, on a reduced scale, but capable of rapid expansion on mobilization. This principle had been recognized and observed to some extent by the Madras Sappers and Miners for many years before the reorganization of 1885, but in the other two Corps there was an inclination to train and drill the companies too much as a battalion although it was known that in war they would usually act independently. In 1885 the "battalion" organization of the Sappers and Miners was abolished everywhere and a great increase in efficiency was thus secured. With a few minor alterations, and a temporary expansion of the three Corps during the Great War of 1914–18, and a recent incorporation of Pioneer units in the Sapper corps, the main provisions of the reorganization of 1885 hold to this day.[2]

The establishments of the Bengal and Madras Corps were fixed at the same strength. Each was to have 20 British officers, 43 British Warrant or non-commissioned officers, 24 Indian officers, 112 Indian non-commissioned officers,[3] 16 Buglers and 1,200 Sappers. In all three Corps the men were no longer to be called "Sepoys," but "Sappers." All the British officers were to be Royal Engineers; and the Commandants were to be officers not below the rank of Major. The Company Commanders could be Captains or Lieutenants, and the Company officers were to be Lieutenants. On field service the Company Commanders had the status of Field Engineers and the Company officers that of Assistant Field Engineers. A revised Engineer Equipment was specified, and it was laid down that each Service company was always to have with it, in barracks, in the field, or on the march, its full general service equipment. Such were the more important provisions of this reorganization.

So many defects in the military system of India were emphasized by the events of the Afghan War that the whole army was affected.

[1] *A Brief History of the Royal Bombay Sappers and Miners*, p. 18. Under the provisions, however, of an Indian Army Circular, dated November 1st, 1902, two more Service companies and one Fortress Company (at Aden) were added to the Bombay Corps.

[2] It may be well to remark that in 1903, under the provisions of I.A.O. No. 382, a general renumbering of the companies in the Madras and Bombay Corps took place. The Bengal Service companies remained as Nos. 1 to 6, the Madras companies became Nos. 9 to 14, and the Bombay companies Nos. 17 to 22.

[3] Increased to 128 in 1886.

INDIAN ARMY REFORMS.

In 1879, while the war was still in progress, Lord Lytton assembled an Army Organization Commission to make suggestions for the improvement of efficiency and the reduction of expenditure. Among other things the Commission recommended virtually that the three Presidency Armies should be abolished, a suggestion which resulted 16 years later in the merging of the three armies into one "Army of India."[1] The army was then divided into four Commands—the Punjab, including the North-Western Provinces, and the Punjab Frontier Force;[2] Bengal; Madras, including Burma; and Bombay, including Sind, Quetta and Aden. Each Command was under a Lieut.-General, and the whole under the Commander-in-Chief in India. It will be seen that the Second Afghan War had far-reaching results. It brought about not only the early reform of the Sappers and Miners but, in the course of time, the consolidation of all the forces in India.

[1] This important change came into effect on April 1st, 1895, under the provisions of G.O.G.G., Army Department, No. 981, dated October 26th, 1894.
[2] After the annexation of the Punjab a frontier brigade in the Jullundur *Doab* was moved to the Afghan border to watch the new frontier. Several new corps were added to it, recruited largely from disbanded Sikh regiments, and the Punjab Irregular Force was formed which became later the "Punjab Frontier Force." On April 1st, 1903, it and the Frontier District were distributed between the Peshawar, Kohat and Derajat Districts (G.G.O. No. 237 of 1903). Lieut.-General Sir Bindon Blood was the last commander of the Frontier Force (1901–1906). It is a curious fact that no Sappers and Miners ever formed part of it.

BALA HISSAR AND CITY OF CABOOL.

From Atkinson's *Sketches in Afghanistan*.

CHAPTER XX.

OVERSEAS EXPEDITIONS AND THE THIRD BURMA WAR.

1867-1914.

THE wars in Afghanistan and on the frontiers of India gave ample opportunities to the Bengal Sappers and Miners to gain experience and win fame. Their headquarters at Roorkee were conveniently placed for any adventure in the Himalayas. But the Madras and Bombay Corps had to look chiefly to expeditions overseas for their share of active service; and although they took part in many of the northern campaigns, they were more often on the line of communication than with the advanced guard. The difficulty of transporting Madras Sappers to the north-west frontier was certainly a deterrent, for the distance from Bangalore to Peshawar is greater than from Madrid to Warsaw, and however desirable it might be to give them experience in mountain warfare, the " overhead charges " were excessive. So, as there was no war in the south of India, the Madras and Bombay Sappers became wanderers across the seas, while their comrades of Bengal climbed and fought in the Himalayas and voyaged occasionally only, and in small numbers, to foreign shores.

The Sappers and Miners of Madras and Bombay are peculiarly well adapted to fight outside India: those of Bombay because they have the roving and adventurous spirit of some of their ancestors, the corsairs of the western coast.; the Madrassis because they are almost untrammelled by caste. In the Madras Corps, Muhammadans, Hindus, Adi Dravidians and Christians stand shoulder to shoulder in the ranks, live together, and eat the same food from the same cooking pot.[1] The Madras Sapper smokes his short pipe, and drinks his glass of beer in his canteen. He is a soldier by family, rather than racial, tradition, and his quickness and adaptability make it peculiarly easy to fit him into an expedition with British troops proceeding to distant lands. The Bengal Sapper, on the other hand, is a man of high caste and drawn from the hereditary martial races of the north. For many years he had a grave objection to voyaging overseas, though the prejudice began to wane about 1870. None can fight the Afghan, Mahsud or Waziri better than he, and this is his favourite occupation; but the realms of the fierce tribesman being

[1] Article entitled " A Short History of the Q.V.O. Madras Sappers and Miners," appearing in *The Sapper*, February, 1930, p. 179.

his common location, he does not appear so often in this chapter as the Madras or Bombay Sapper.

After the Indian Mutiny there was little warfare, except on the frontier, until the Government sent an expedition to Abyssinia in 1867. An Abyssinian named Lij Kassa, who had fought his way to the throne in 1855 and assumed the title of King Theodore, had recently imprisoned and tortured Captain Cameron, the British Consul, and other Europeans, and it was necessary to rescue them and punish the offender. Little was known of the topography and resources of the country, but it was understood that the struggle would be more against the obstacles provided by Nature than against the ill-disciplined army of King Theodore. Most careful preparation was needed for the march of some hundreds of miles from the Red Sea coast, through mountainous and barren country, to the capital at Magdala, which was reputed to be a fortress of great strength; and very wisely the British Government appointed an Engineer officer in the person of Lieut.-General Sir Robert Napier, then Commander-in-Chief in Bombay, to lead the expedition. Until that moment, as Major-General Porter asserts,[1] it had been held as an axiom at the Horse Guards that an officer of the scientific branch of the Service was for that reason incompetent to fill such a post. It was left to Sir Robert Napier to prove the fallacy of that idea. His services had been so conspicuous in India and China, and his reputation was so great, that the Government gave him a free hand to select his troops and make his arrangements. For three months he supervised every detail of the mobilization and equipment of his force, and in the end he embarked what was practically a Bombay Army to invade Abyssinia. "It is of some consequence," he wrote,[2] "in an expedition of the nature of that in contemplation . . . that the troops to be employed should know each other and their commander." All the regiments came from the Western Presidency except a few from Bengal, and there is little doubt that if Napier had thought that the small Corps of Bombay Sappers could cope with the great engineering difficulties which he foresaw, he would not have added a company of Royal Engineers from England and three companies of Sappers and Miners from Madras.

The strength of the Expeditionary Force amounted to nearly 14,000 fighting men. There were four and a half regiments of cavalry, seven batteries and one Indian company of artillery, four battalions of British infantry and ten of Indian infantry;[3] also the

[1] *History of the Corps of Royal Engineers*, by Major-General W. Porter, Vol. II, p. 9.
[2] Minute by Sir Robert Napier, dated September 5th, 1867, quoted in *The Royal (Bengal) Engineers*, by Colonel Sir E. T. Thackeray, V.C., K.C.B., p. 211.
[3] Bengal contributed only two regiments of Indian cavalry and two battalions of Indian infantry, one of which was a Pioneer battalion. No Bengal Sappers and Miners were sent. (See *The Services of the Bengal Native Army*, by F. G. Cardew, p. 316.)

10th Company, R.E., and seven companies of Sappers and Miners. It was a crushing force to bring against the Abyssinian levies. The 10th Company was commanded by Major (afterwards Lieut.-General Sir Gordon) Pritchard, R.E. ; Captain (afterwards Major-General) A. R. MacDonnell, R.E., was the senior officer with the 1st, 2nd, 3rd and 4th Companies of Bombay Sappers which were in the expedition;[1] and " G," " H " and " K " Companies of the Madras Sappers, which were also present, were led by Major (afterwards General Sir Harry) Prendergast, V.C., R.E., who was destined to command the Madras Corps for 11 years and to become the Commander-in-Chief in the field during the Third Burma War. The Commanding Royal Engineer was Lieut.-Colonel (afterwards General) H. St. C. Wilkins, R.E., at the head of a cadre of about 30 officers of his Corps including those with the companies. Napier certainly did not commit the error of underestimating the possible opposition.

On September 16th, 1867, a reconnoitring party in which were Lieut.-Colonel Wilkins and Captains W. W. Goodfellow and K. A. Jopp of the Royal Engineers, sailed from Bombay. Voyaging across the Indian Ocean and some 300 miles up the Red Sea, they selected the village of Zula in Annesley Bay as the best point on the African coast for landing the expedition.[2] Within a few weeks the leading troops began to arrive. The 3rd and 4th Companies of Bombay Sappers, with an advanced brigade from Bombay, appeared off Zula on October 21st, disembarked on the 30th, and set to work at once to build a pier on the shelving beach. For this they had to use brushwood fascines until stone could be brought from across the bay, and it was found necessary to run the pier 300 yards out from the shore to get even five feet depth of water.[3] A camp was made about one mile from the sea, 20 wells were sunk, a tramway laid to the camp, and sheds erected. Goodfellow, and the other Engineers in Zula, had never an idle moment. Meanwhile a reconnoitring party had advanced inland to examine the passes leading up to the gigantic plateau of Abyssinia. They selected the Kumayli route to Senafé as the most suitable, and when the existing track had been improved sufficiently by the Sappers, a small force advanced and occupied Senafé on December 5th. By that time a second brigade had arrived from Karachi, to be followed by " K " Company, Madras Sappers and Miners, on December 8th, and by " G " and " H " Companies on the 12th.[4] When the 10th Company, R.E., had disembarked from England, and the 1st and 2nd Companies of Bombay Sappers with other troops from India, preparations were made for an advance into the hinterland. Captain C. J. Darrah, R.E., had

---

[1] The 5th Company was divided among the other four. (See *A Short History of the Royal Bombay Sappers and Miners*, p. 15.)
[2] See the Sketch Map of North-East Africa at the end of this volume.
[3] A second pier, which was constructed later, was made with piles sent from Bombay.
[4] *Historical Record of the Q.V.O. Madras Sappers and Miners*, Vol. I, p. 94.

begun to construct a railway line from Zula to the Kumayli Pass, but the progress was very slow owing to the difficult country so the troops had to prepare to march. Sir Robert Napier landed at Zula on January 7th, 1868, and supervised in person the final arrangements for his great adventure across the plateau by Senafé and Antalo[1] to Magdala.

The engineering difficulties in reaching Senafé were enormous. Three miles after entering the Kumayli Gorge,[2] the track began to ascend steeply. The mountains grew closer and closer together till, at a place called Lower Suru, ten miles beyond Kumayli, the precipices on either side were only a few yards apart. Here the Sappers and a corps of Baluchi labourers were engaged for six weeks in making a road ten feet wide; in some places it was carried over enormous granite boulders by ramps; in others it was blasted out of the face of the precipice. Gradually the track wound up and up till it emerged at last on to the tableland at Senafé, 7,000 feet above the sea and 63 miles from Zula. Beyond Senafé the route was easier for 37 miles to Adigrat, and thence the track led across waterless uplands, destitute of supplies and impassable for wheeled traffic. As the very existence of the force when it reached the desolate tableland would depend on the efficiency of the Engineers on the coast and in the Kumayli defile, Sir Robert Napier ordered Colonel Wilkins to remain at Zula to ensure that no hitch should occur. " G " and " H " Companies of the Madras Sappers were kept also at Zula and Kumayli throughout the campaign. The various departments of engineering —railways, roads, water-supply, telegraphs, signalling and a field park—had each its small and efficient cadre of Engineer officers. There was even a Photographic Section. No commercial business could have been organized more carefully.

Napier arrived at his advanced base at Senafé on January 29th and at Adigrat on February 3rd. Captain W. W. Goodfellow, R.E., was on his staff as Commanding Royal Engineer, and Major G. D. Pritchard, R.E., was at the head of the Engineer brigade composed of the 10th Company, R.E., " K " Company, Madras Sappers, and the 2nd, 3rd and 4th Companies of Bombay Sappers. On February 26th the main body marched from Adigrat, and, through the good work of a " Pioneer " force which included the Bombay Sappers, reached the neighbourhood of Antalo at the beginning of March. The advance was resumed over bare and difficult country rising to an altitude of over 10,000 feet, till at last Napier drew near King Theodore's stronghold, and descending to the Bashilo River on April 7th, crossed it, and defeated the enemy at Arogi within ten miles of Magdala. " I thought that the people now coming were women," remarked Theodore. " I find that they are men." At daybreak the

---

[1] A place about half-way between Zula and Magdala.
[2] Seventeen miles from Zula.

King sent to sue for peace; but when he heard Napier's terms—unconditional surrender of himself, his force and his prisoners—he flew into a rage. "A warrior," replied he, "who has dandled strong men in his arms like infants, will never suffer himself to be dandled in the arms of others."[1]

Napier then advanced with 3,500 men against the stronghold of Magdala which was perched high on a mountain of granite and had only two gates. In the assault on April 13th, the Engineers led the way along a path on the side of a precipice towards one of the gates, carrying tools, ladders, and two barrels of powder. Major Pritchard, R.E., and others were wounded; but he, Lieutenant A. Le Mesurier, R.E., and a few men entered by escalade, and, joined by the 33rd Regiment, made a dash for an upper gate. There they found the body of King Theodore who had shot himself when he saw his men deserting him. The Abyssinians had lost 700 men killed and 1,200 wounded, and the British had only 20 wounded. The remnants of King Theodore's army surrendered or fled in disorder, and the war was over.

After a most difficult march back to the coast, in extremes of temperature and through defiles flooded with raging torrents, Napier embarked his troops for England and India and sailed himself for England where he received a glorious welcome and a peerage.[2] The trials and difficulties of this "Engineer" campaign are well described in his farewell to his men:—

"You have traversed, often under a tropical sun or amidst storms of rain and sleet, 400 miles of mountainous and difficult country. You have crossed many steep and precipitous ranges of mountains more than 10,000 feet in altitude where your supplies could not keep pace with you. You have stormed the almost inaccessible fortress of Magdala. You have released not only the British captives but those of other friendly nations. Magdala has been committed to the flames and remains only a scorched rock. Your gallant exploit will live in history. The Queen and the people of England will appreciate your services."

It is a far cry from Abyssinia to the Malay Peninsula where the Sappers and Miners next saw active service outside India. Mr. Birch, the Resident at Perak, a little state which faces northern Sumatra across the Malacca Straits, was murdered on November 2nd,

---

[1] *History of the Corps of Royal Engineers*, by Major-General W. Porter, Vol. II, p. 7.

[2] He sailed from Zula on June 10th, 1868. After reaching England he was thanked by Parliament and created Baron Napier of Magdala. From 1870 to 1876 he was Commander-in-Chief in India. From 1877 to 1882 he was Governor of Gibraltar. He became a Field-Marshal in 1883, in which year his statue was unveiled on the *maidan* at Calcutta. He died in London on January 14th, 1890, the most famous military engineer India has ever produced. An equestrian statue of Lord Napier can be seen opposite the Queen's Gate leading into Hyde Park in London, and his portrait forms the frontispiece of this volume.

THE DEVIL'S STAIRCASE, SURU, ABYSSINIA.

1875, and Captain W. Innes, R.E., the acting Commissioner, was shot through the heart in a skirmish a week later; so the Governor of the Straits Settlements telegraphed to India and Hongkong for troops, and a force of about 1,500 men under Brigadier-General Ross, including " C " Company, Madras Sappers and Miners, under Lieutenant A. Howlett, Madras Staff Corps, with Lieutenant H. B. Rich, R.E., was concentrated at Penang before the end of November.[1] It marched from the mouth of the Larut River[2] to Kuala Kangsa, 30 miles inland on the Perak River, preceded by the Sappers to clear the way and erect huts at its destination. The Royal Engineers with the force were Major (afterwards Major-General) J. T. Twigge, Captain C. Crawford and Lieutenants W. North, H. B. Rich, and latterly, J. Hare. Roadmaking, stockading and hutting about Kuala Kangsa were the chief duties of the Sappers. The contingent from Hongkong soon took the Perak capital at Kinta, and by December 17th the combined forces were in possession of the whole state. Then, after some desultory fighting, the little jungle war came to an end, and " C " Company embarked for India on March 22nd, 1876.[3]

In April and May, 1878, Sapper and Miner units accompanied the first military expedition ever sent from India to Europe. As a result of the advance of Russia on Constantinople, and the terms of the Treaty of San Stefano which ended the Russo-Turkish war of 1877-78, the Home Government determined to occupy Cyprus and to order the despatch of a force from India to Malta; so a " Malta Expeditionary Force " was mobilized under Major-General J. Ross, consisting of six battalions of Indian infantry and four companies of Sappers and Miners, with artillery and cavalry—about 7,000 men in all. The 3rd and 5th Companies of the Bombay Sappers under Lieutenant G. Turner Jones, R.E., and Captain F. T. Stock, Bombay Staff Corps, embarked in the sailing ship *Oriflamme* at Bombay, and " G " and " H " Companies of the Madras Corps under Lieutenants C. C. Ellis and C. B. Wilkieson, R.E., in the steamship *Canara*.[4] Colonel H. N. D. Prendergast, V.C., R.E., commanded the Engineer Brigade which included altogether 15 Royal Engineer officers. The four Sapper companies reached Malta at the end of May, and in July left for Cyprus where they landed at Larnaka. For some months they made piers, built huts and surveyed the island, until, much reduced in numbers by fever, they embarked for India on November 2nd, 1878, and arrived in Bombay on the 20th.[5] There had been no fighting and much hard work, but the men had great tales to tell

[1] " C " Company came from Rangoon.   [2] Forty miles south-east of Penang.
[3] Further details of this small expedition can be found in *The Military History of the Madras Engineers*, by H. M. Vibart, Vol. II, pp. 479-486.
[4] *Frontier and Overseas Expeditions from India*, Vol. VI, p. 24.
[5] Colonel Prendergast, V.C., R.E., left Cyprus for India on August 25th after the arrival from England of Lieut.-Colonel J. P. Maquay, R.E., who was senior to him in the Corps.

when they were back once more in their lines at Kirkee and Bangalore.

It was not long before some of the Madras Sappers and Miners[1] were voyaging westwards again. There was serious trouble in Egypt in 1881. Colonel Ahmad Bey Arabi, commonly known as "Arabi Pasha," had instigated a military revolt in Cairo, and by May, 1882, the Khedive was powerless. Great Britain and France, who were pledged to support the Khedive, sent their fleets to bombard Alexandria, but Arabi remained defiant. Great Britain became at last so much concerned about the safety of the Suez Canal, and of the small fresh-water canal which runs for some distance along its western bank, that the Home Government sent an expedition to Egypt under General Sir Garnet Wolseley and asked for a division from India. The Commander-in-Chief in India[2] prepared accordingly to mobilize a complete division under Major-General Sir H. MacPherson, V.C., K.C.B., and on July 6th, 1882, "A" and "I" Companies of the Madras Sappers, and the 2nd and 8th Companies of the Bengal Sappers, were warned for active service.[3] After "I" Company, however, had sailed for Aden with the Seaforth Highlanders in the middle of July, a telegram arrived from England curtailing the size of the force required from India and specifying that only two companies of Sappers and Miners were to be included, so the Bengal Sapper companies were denied the trip to Egypt, and "A" Company alone followed "I" Company in August. The Commanding Royal Engineer with General MacPherson's expeditionary force was Colonel James Browne, R.E., who had done so well in Afghanistan, and the cadre of Royal Engineer officers under him included Majors W. G. Nicholson,[4] J. A. Armstrong,[5] and A. F. Hamilton and nine subalterns.[6] The Madras Sapper companies arrived at Suez during August, 1882, and a section of "E" Company (telegraphists) landed on September 23rd. By the second week in September the whole of the Indian troops were concentrated on the Suez Canal at Ismailia, which had been occupied by Sir Garnet Wolseley's force on August 20th.

The Sappers and Miners arrived too late to take part in the action at Kassassin,[7] where Major-General G. Graham, V.C. (late of the Royal Engineers), when in command of the 2nd Brigade of the 1st Division, repulsed an attack by Arabi Pasha on August 28th, but they were

---
[1] Correctly the "Queen's Own" Sappers and Miners; but the original title is retained here and elsewhere for convenience.
[2] General Sir Donald Stewart.
[3] *Frontier and Overseas Expeditions from India*, Vol. VI, p. 26.
[4] Afterwards Field-Marshal Lord Nicholson of Roundhay, G.C.B., who died on September 13th, 1918.
[5] *History of the Corps of Royal Engineers*, by Major-General W. Porter, Vol. II, p. 66. Porter gives no initials, but the officer was presumably Major J. A. Armstrong.
[6] Ibid., p. 66. Major A. F. Hamilton, R.E., commanded the Madras Sappers and Miners with the expedition. The nine subalterns were Lieutenants T. P. Cather, J. Burn-Murdoch, H. S. Andrews Speed, P. B. Baldwin, W. D. Lindley, A. H. Mason, C. H. Darling, J. E. Dickie and H. E. Goodwyn.
[7] To the west of Ismailia, and between it and Zagazig near the Nile.

present at the decisive battle at Tel-el-Kebir on September 13th. After joining the force on the Suez Canal they were busily engaged in repairing the fresh-water canal, the railway from Ismailia towards Tel-el-Kebir, and the telegraph line, and in fortifying certain strong points. On September 12th they received orders to advance with Sir Garnet Wolseley's army of two divisions of infantry, a division of cavalry and the Indian contingent to attack the powerful position, four miles in length, which Arabi Pasha had prepared at Tel-el-Kebir. The movement by land and water began at 1.30 a.m. As day was breaking the infantry became engaged, and, after a sharp contest, carried the Egyptian lines. The cavalry then pursued the enemy and converted their defeat into a rout. The main body halted at Tel-el-Kebir, but MacPherson's Indian force pushed on to Zagazig. On the 14th the cavalry entered Cairo, occupied the citadel, and received the surrender of the remnants of the Egyptian army and of Arabi Pasha himself. Hostilities then came to an end.

Before and after the battle of Tel-el-Kebir the Engineers and Sappers were occupied chiefly in repairing the railway and telegraph lines, making arrangements for water supply, and removing obstacles. In the advance to Zagazig the Madras Sappers covered 26 miles in one day—a very creditable performance. Colonel Browne, R.E., wrote to General Roberts[1] that he found the men most efficient, handy and willing. "We had some very heavy pieces of work on the railway line," he added, "and the amount of work they got through, and the neat and workmanlike way in which they did it, caused the R.E. from England no little astonishment." "A" and "I" Companies remained with the British army in Cairo from September 22nd to October 8th, when they entrained for Suez. By October 30th, 1882, they were back in Bangalore after a very brief campaign in which, to their great advantage, they had been brought into intimate association with several companies of Royal Engineers. They had seen some fighting and in this were more fortunate than De Havilland of the Madras Engineers in 1801, when the Indian contingent under General Baird arrived in Egypt after the last shot had been fired.[2]

The next expedition in which Sappers and Miners took part was to the Soudan, that wild desert which lies to the west of the Red Sea and south of Egypt. Colonel Charles George Gordon, C.B., R.E.,[3] appointed Governor-General of the Soudan in 1875, had ruled the country well; but after his departure from Khartoum in 1879 there was a revolt headed by one Muhammad Ahmad who, in 1881, proclaimed himself Mahdi and set the whole of the Soudan aflame. When a small force under Major-General Hicks had been almost destroyed by the Mahdi near Khartoum, the British Government decided to

---

[1] Demi-official letter, dated November 15th, 1882. [2] See Chapter XI.
[3] "Chinese Gordon," so called because of his brilliant work in China from 1860 to 1864.

evacuate the country. But meanwhile another leader named Osman Digna had appeared with an army near Suakin, a port some 600 miles up the Red Sea, and had defeated a mixed force under Major-General Baker. As Suakin was then in danger an expedition was sent to that place under Major-General Sir G. Graham, who drove Osman Digna away and saved the situation on the coast. On the Nile, however, things were going badly. Gordon had returned to Khartoum where he was besieged by the Mahdi; and Lord Wolseley, leading an expedition up the river at the end of 1884 to rescue him, found that Khartoum had surrendered and the heroic Gordon was dead. These sad events determined the Government to recapture Khartoum and punish the Mahdi, and to carry out their intentions they proposed to make a railway from Suakin to Berber on the Nile,[1] so that troops might be concentrated near Khartoum. They appointed Lieut.-General Sir G. Graham to the command of a powerful force to protect the projected railway and to crush Osman Digna, asking at the same time for reinforcements from India. By the end of March, 1885, Graham was at Suakin, and the leading units of a brigade from India under Brigadier-General J. Hudson had joined him. One of those units was a company of Sappers and Miners.

"F" Company, Madras Sappers and Miners, under Captain C. B. Wilkieson, R.E., with Captain F. J. Romilly, R.E., and Lieutenant E. M. B. Newman, R.E., reached Suakin in the middle of March, 1885,[2] and took part in a battle at Hashin near that place on March 20th, when Graham gained an easy victory over the Arabs. The next step was to attack Osman Digna at Tamai, a few miles farther distant, but before doing so it was necessary to establish an intermediate post in the desert. So a small British force under Major-General Sir J. McNeill, with the Indian brigade including "F" Company, marched from Suakin to form a *zariba*[3] to the south-west. The construction of the *zariba* was in hand at a place called Tofrek, about six miles from Suakin, and the Sappers and the Berkshires were out cutting down the thick bush around the enclosure when, at 2.40 p.m., on March 22nd, the cavalry scouts and working parties were driven in suddenly by a furious rush of Arabs. So desperate was the charge that six companies of an Indian infantry battalion, disordered by the cavalry galloping in, broke and fled. The enemy stampeded the transport animals, and swarming into parts of the position, fought hand-to-hand with the defenders. All the British and most of the Indian soldiers stood fast, though the confusion was indescribable, and the Sappers threw themselves into the broken face

---

[1] About 200 miles downstream from Khartoum.

[2] An Indian Coolie Corps also arrived to assist in constructing the railway, with Captain T. P. Cather and Lieutenants J. A. Tanner, Godfrey Williams (now Major-General Sir Godfrey Williams, K.C.I.E., C.B.), and C. D. Learoyd, all of the Royal Engineers. In addition there was a Survey Detachment under Lieutenant F. B. Longe, R.E., who became afterwards Surveyor-General of India.

[3] *Zariba*. An enclosure surrounded usually by an abattis of thorn-bushes.

of the square. Undoubtedly they helped materially to stave off a very serious disaster, but at the cost of Romilly and Newman killed, Wilkieson seriously wounded, and 33 other casualties among the 80 Indian ranks present. The fight was over in 20 minutes. In that short period, however, 1,500 Arabs were killed and thousands wounded, while the British force suffered more than 300 casualties.[1] Wilkieson, though stabbed through the thigh, refused to go to hospital for 24 hours. "The Madras Sappers," wrote General Graham, " proved themselves first-rate troops, whether for fighting or for work."

The force returned to Suakin, and minor operations continued for a time, but no more than 20 miles of railway line had been laid when the whole project was abandoned and in May, 1885, most of the troops were recalled. " F " Company, Madras Sappers and Miners, remained with a few units in Suakin till November and then returned to Bangalore to find that half the Corps had already sailed to the north-east to fight in the Third Burma War.

The kingdom of Ava had become a purely inland territory as a result of the Second Burma War of 1852, and its Government, still proud and defiant, discouraged any friendly dealings with the British; but ten years after that war, Sir Arthur Phayre, the first Chief Commissioner of British Burma, contrived to negotiate a commercial treaty with King Mindon at Mandalay. This was followed by a second treaty in 1867 under which, for the next 12 years, the Government of India was properly represented by a Resident at the Burmese court. Yet British subjects were still badly treated, British traders were denied trade facilities, disputes were frequent, and bitterness was increased by the seemingly trivial, but actually serious, "Shoe Question." Sir Douglas Forsyth had been sent upon a mission to Mandalay in 1875, and to avoid giving offence had removed his sword and shoes before entering King Mindon's palace. He went farther, and rather than prejudice the success of his negotiations consented to squat on the floor before the King like any Burmese suppliant. Then he protested to the British Government who addressed King Mindon; but the latter insisted that the Burmese custom must be followed with the result that no British Resident would go to the palace. The incident shows the arrogance of the Burmese attitude. King Mindon died in September, 1878, and was succeeded by his fourth son, Thibaw, who was even more inimical to the British than his father had been.

Thibaw began by massacring 80 of his relations[2] and insulting British subjects in his country; and had not the British Government been saddled already with the Zulu and Afghan wars, there is no doubt that troops would have been sent at once to Burma. Matters

---

[1] *Frontier and Overseas Expeditions from India*, Vol. VI, p. 60.
[2] The story is well told in *The Lacquer Lady*, by F. Tennyson Jesse.

went from bad to worse. The British Resident was withdrawn in October, 1879, on the discovery of a plot to murder him, and Thibaw began to encourage a certain European power whose policy was to supplant the British in Burma. By the end of 1883 a large part of the country had sunk into anarchy. In September, 1884, Thibaw massacred 300 Burmese prisoners in his jails, and still the Government of India did not protest. It was not till August, 1885, that intervention became unavoidable. The Burmese Government refused insolently to allow any enquiry about an outrageous fine of 23 lakhs of rupees which they had imposed on the Bombay-Burma Trading Corporation,[1] so Lord Dufferin, the Viceroy, sent an ultimatum to King Thibaw towards the end of October, and as the reply was unsatisfactory, followed it by a declaration of war on November 10th, 1885.

Burma has been described as one vast military obstacle ; but long before 1885 its difficulties were well known and a plan of campaign had been prepared at Simla. The scheme was designed to paralyse all resistance by a rapid advance to Mandalay followed by the capture and deportation of Kind Thibaw, and the command of the expedition was entrusted in 1885 to an Engineer officer in the person of Major-General H. N. D. Prendergast, V.C., C.B., whose name has appeared frequently in this narrative.[2] This was the sixth occasion on which a British Engineer had been Commander-in-Chief of an army in the field. The first was when Lieut.-Colonel Thomas Keating of the Bombay Engineers led some 2,000 regular troops and a host of irregulars against the Marathas in 1775, and defeated them at Adas near Ahmadabad ;[3] the others were when Brigadier-General A. D'Aubant commanded in Corsica in 1794, Sir Robert Napier in Abyssinia, Sir Gerald Graham at Suakin, and Sir Charles Warren in Bechuanaland.[4]

General Prendergast's force of 9,000 fighting men was drawn from all three Presidencies and included a Naval Brigade. Coolies alone were to be used for land transport, and the steamers of the Irrawaddy Flotilla Company for the advance up the river. No cavalry were sent to Burma, but the three infantry brigades which embarked at Calcutta and Madras were well supported by artillery[5] and Sappers and

---

[1] A company trading in timber.

[2] In the Persian War of 1856-57 (see Chapter XVI), the Indian Mutiny (Chapter XVIII) and the Campaign in Abyssinia, 1867-68 (Chapter XX). Prendergast became a Lieut.-General on November 28th, 1885.

[3] See Chapter XI. General Porter in *The History of the Corps of Royal Engineers*, Vol. II, p. 85, states that General Prendergast was the *fourth* Engineer officer to command an army in the field. Apparently he was not aware of the exploits of Colonel Keating.

[4] On several occasions Engineer officers commanded large forces of all arms operating in conjunction with others, *e.g.*, Sir Robert Napier in Central India during the Mutiny, and Sir John Cheape in the Second Burma War.

[5] The artillery included twelve 25-pounders, twelve 6·3″ howitzers and 18 mountain guns. In addition the river steamers mounted 25 guns and 24 Nordenfelt or Gardner machine-guns. (See *Frontier and Overseas Expeditions from India*, Vol. V, p. 142.)

Miners. The 4th and 5th Companies of Bengal Sappers came from Roorkee; " C," " D " and " H " Companies and a Telegraph Section of " A " Company, all of the Madras Sappers, joined from Secunderabad and Bangalore; and from the western coast came the 2nd Company of Bombay Sappers.[1] Colonel (afterwards Lieut.-General) G. E. L. S. Sanford, R.E., was the Commanding Royal Engineer, with Captains W. T. Shone, S. A. E. Hickson, G. C. P. Onslow and Lieutenant J. A. Tanner as his Field Engineers. On the General's staff were Lieut.-Colonel E. W. Begbie, R.E., and Major C. B. Wilkieson, R.E., with Captain J. E. Dickie, R.E., as Superintendent of Telegraphs. Including the officers with the Sappers and Miners, about 27 Royal Engineers embarked with the original expedition to Burma, and 35 more took part in the subsequent operations.[2] As each ship arrived in Rangoon the troops were disembarked and sent in river steamers up the Irrawaddy to Thayetmyo[3] where the force concentrated for the dash to Mandalay.

General Prendergast began his advance on November 14th, 1885, crossing the frontier on the following day. His success depended on rapidity of movement by which he might take the Burmese army of 15,000 men by surprise. Like Napier in Abyssinia he had supervised every detail of the preparations, and he was rewarded with early victory. The first serious obstacles were the strong forts of Minhla and Gwegyaun, facing each other on opposite banks of the Irrawaddy, about 50 miles above Thayetmyo. Columns were landed on both banks on November 16th and carried two stockades without difficulty. On the 17th they landed again to attack Minhla on the right bank and Gwegyaun on the left, the three companies of Madras Sappers going with the right bank column.[4] The Sapper companies from Bengal and Bombay did not arrive in time to join in the attack.[5] Gwegyaun was an exceptionally powerful work designed by an Italian named Barbieri. It stood high above the river, had a huge ditch revetted with masonry, and was provided also with casemated barracks and magazines; with its 21 guns, and a garrison of 1,700 men, it bore no resemblance whatever to the stockaded enclosures of the First Burma War. However, the defenders fled on the approach of the British, and the place was occupied without loss.

Minhla was not so easily taken. It consisted of a stockaded village and a square fort with stone walls 25 feet in height, but the troops

[1] The Company Commanders, in the order named, were Lieutenant W. A. Cairns, Captains M. C. Barton, A. R. F. Dorward, H. S. Andrews Speed and J. M. T. Badgley, Lieutenant F. Glanville and Captain J. D. Fullerton, all of the Royal Engineers.
[2] *The History of the Corps of Royal Engineers*, by Major-General W. Porter, Vol. II, p. 86.
[3] See the map entitled " Sketch Map of Southern India and Burma " at the end of this volume.
[4] *Historical Record of the Q.V.O. Madras Sappers and Miners*, Vol. I, p. 129.
[5] The 5th Company, Bengal Sappers and Miners, reached Thayetmyo on the eve of the advance, and the 4th Company three days after it had started. The 2nd Company, Bombay Sappers and Miners, was then on the high seas.

forced an entry into the village, and, after some desultory fighting, carried the fort at the point of the bayonet. The defenders lost heavily, and with the fall of Minhla the resistance of the Burmese army was practically at an end. Two Italian officers, who were employed by the enemy, surrendered on the following day, and Prendergast advanced almost unopposed up the Irrawaddy. The Burmese evacuated some batteries at Pagan on November 22nd, and a force, 6,000 strong, abandoned other defences at Myingyan near the mouth of the Chindwin River on the same day.[1] On the 26th Prendergast's ships steamed past Yandabu, the extreme limit of the British advance in the war of 1824-26, and King Thibaw asked for an armistice to discuss terms of peace. The reply reminds one of that given to King Theodore by Sir Robert Napier in Abyssinia. No armistice could be granted unless the Burmese monarch surrendered himself, his army and his capital; then, if all the Europeans in Mandalay were found to be uninjured, his life would be spared. Harsh terms, no doubt, but lenient to a murderer. No answer being forthcoming, the fleet then prepared to attack Ava which was held by 8,000 of the enemy. Here, the Burmese commander surrendered after a show of resistance, and his example was followed by the commanders in other forts; but unfortunately the garrisons were allowed to escape fully armed, and thus the Burmese were able to wage a guerrilla warfare against the British for several years after King Thibaw had been dethroned. Mandalay was reached on November 28th, and on the following day Thibaw was placed with his family on board the steamer *Thooreah* and sent to Rangoon where he re-embarked for Madras and was incarcerated finally in the fortress of Ratnagiri on the Bombay coast. Thus within three weeks of the declaration of war, Thibaw was a captive and Mandalay in British hands. It was a remarkable achievement, and, but for the mistaken action at Ava, the hostilities in Burma might have ended before the summer of 1886.

Disorder and dacoity, however, spread rapidly from Mandalay with the fall of the Burmese Government. During December, 1885, armed parties of the British were scouring the country continually and operating in movable columns against the dacoits. The 5th Company, Bengal Sappers and Miners, at Pagan[2] took their share in this work. Information arrived also that the Chinese were massing on the frontier to take advantage of the general confusion by seizing Bhamo, so Prendergast with a force of 1,000 men, including the 4th Company of Bengal Sappers, proceeded up the river to that place, which he occupied without resistance on December 28th. Upper Burma was duly annexed by a proclamation on January 1st, 1886, and General Prendergast was invested with the supreme civil, as well

---

[1] The Chindwin enters the Irrawaddy a few miles below Yandabu. Myingyan lies on the left bank of the Irrawaddy close to the junction of the rivers.

[2] *History and Digest of Service, 1st K.G.O. Sappers and Miners*, p. 45.

as military, power. Military posts were soon established in various parts of the country, and several minor affairs with dacoits took place in one of which Lieutenant W. A. J. O'Meara, R.E., was very severely wounded at Pagan on January 2nd. Prendergast had achieved his primary objective and had added 140,000 square miles of territory to the British dominions; but the country was in such a turmoil that the Viceroy and the Commander-in-Chief, General Sir Frederick Roberts, took the first opportunity to visit it to co-ordinate the action required for its pacification.[1] Nevertheless, as the spring drew on, dacoities and outrages became more and more frequent, and reinforcements were sent to Burma from India.

General Prendergast vacated his command on March 31st and transferred the supreme civil authority in Upper Burma to the Chief Commissioner. Before he left, the army in Burma was separated into two commands, that in Upper Burma consisting of two brigades under Brigadier-General G. S. White,[2] V.C., with their headquarters at Mandalay and Bhamo. A hundred small engagements were fought between April 1st and July 31st, and in most of them Engineers and Sappers and Miners took their part. The construction of a railway from Toungoo to Mandalay was begun in August, 1886. There were then in Upper Burma 17,000 British and Indian troops distributed in 43 posts, and by the end of the year the number had risen to 25,000. So large was the army, and so difficult the operations, that Roberts came across again from India and spent the cold weather of 1886-87 in Mandalay to direct the movements of the troops. By that time, however, the presence of a large number of Engineers and Sappers and Miners had become unnecessary. There was no organized resistance on a large scale. Many of the companies accordingly returned to India, the 4th and 5th Companies of Bengal Sappers arriving in Roorkee on April 13th, 1887, the 1st,[3] 3rd and 4th (late "G," "C" and "D") Companies of Madras Sappers in Bangalore during May, and the 2nd Company of Bombay Sappers in Kirkee at about the same time. The 2nd Company of the Bengal Sappers had arrived in Burma during 1886, and the 2nd Company of the Madras Sappers came from Bangalore in 1887. The 2nd Company of the Bengal Corps took part in an expedition during December, 1886, to take possession of the far-famed Ruby Mines at Mogok, Kyatpin and Kathé north of Mandalay, but there was little fighting. They found the Burmese most difficult to understand. Credulous and vain as ever, no one could foretell their line of conduct. In 1886, for instance, 50 Burmans armed with *dahs*[4] set up a pseudo-king, mounted him on an elephant and advanced to capture Mandalay. In the following

---

[1] They arrived in Mandalay on February 15th, 1886.
[2] Afterwards Field-Marshal Sir George White, V.C., best known as the defender of Ladysmith in the South African War of 1899-1902.
[3] This company had been stationed in Rangoon and went up-country at the end of 1885.
[4] Burmese swords.

year the people quite close to Mandalay believed that the British were hemmed in there by a Russian army![1] It was almost too pitiful to be amusing.

It is superfluous to trace the history of the pacification of Burma which was not completed till about 1893. The military operations were extended, through force of circumstances, to the outlying territories of the Chins, Kachins, Lushais and Shans, all of which were incorporated finally in the British possessions. But before we bid farewell to the land in which three campaigns had been fought it may be of interest to describe briefly the type of defences constructed by our men during the years which followed the capture of Mandalay. When a military post was to be formed, the Engineer was told the strength of the proposed garrison and usually designed a rectangular fort with flanking bastions at two opposite angles to contain the quarters of the troops. First he erected a bamboo stockade as an obstacle, and then built outside it an earthen parapet whose sides were at the natural slope of the soil; afterwards he filled the gap between the stockade and the interior slope of the parapet with thorns or prickly pears, and added a horizontal bamboo along the stockade as a rifle rest for the defenders. Outside the parapet he dug a ditch, and planted bamboo spikes with charred and pointed ends on the berm and glacis. Sometimes, however, he might be able to get some Burmese to build him a better type of stockade, which was said to have originated in China and which could not be cut down by an enemy using a *dah*. This had vertical timber posts about ten feet high, placed at four feet intervals. On the outside, bamboo matting was fastened to a height of six feet, horizontal intervals being left for rows of split bamboo spikes which were fixed afterwards to project outwards towards the enemy. Split bamboos were interlaced above the matting, the verticals having pointed tops; and stout bamboos were lashed horizontally behind the timber uprights to strengthen the whole framework and to form attachments for the split bamboo spikes. These long and pliable spikes were bent double and passed round the horizontal bamboos so that their sharpened ends, projecting about three feet from the matting, kept an assailant from cutting at the stockade with his *dah* in much the same way as a porcupine repels a terrier. A high bamboo fence was added as an additional obstacle about eight feet outside the stockade. The Engineers and Sappers who were engaged in the Third Burma War had much of this sort of work to do, but they were occupied also in road and railway construction, surveying and building huts. Much reduced in numbers by sickness, they were not sorry when they could say good-bye to the dacoits, swamps and jungles of the Upper Irrawaddy and return to their healthy cantonments in India.

One result of the war was the raising of a Burma Company of

[1] *Frontier and Overseas Expeditions from India*, Vol. V, p. 271.

EXPEDITIONS TO SOMALILAND, THE SOUDAN AND MEKRAN. 411

Sappers and Miners. This was authorized in July, 1887,[1] and the unit was affiliated to the Madras Sappers and Miners. The Royal Engineer officers for the new unit were to be lent in rotation from the three Corps of Sappers and Miners, each officer being relieved after two years in Burma if he so desired.[2] The Indian officers were to come solely from the Madras Corps. Great difficulties were encountered at once in getting recruits, only 15 of whom had enlisted by the end of 1887 when the company at Mandalay was commanded by Captain E. W. Cotter, R.E. The first idea had been to form a unit one-half of which should be Burmans, one-quarter Kachins and Karens, and one-quarter Shans; but the Kachins and Shans would not come forward, and when the company reached its full strength for the first time in October, 1890, about four-fifths of the men were Burmans and the remainder Karens. In 1893 the Burma Company became an integral part of the Corps of Madras Sappers and Miners,[3] rendering good service for a number of years until it was finally disbanded in 1929.[4] Many officers have pleasant recollections of the jovial and intelligent Burma Sapper in his slouch hat and smart uniform in modern Mandalay.

Before the last echoes of the war in Burma had died away there was trouble once again in the Middle East. A new scene of operations opened in Somaliland where, in 1889, a section of the White Isa tribe raided a coastal town near Berbera, attacked a caravan, and murdered two French priests. To punish the offenders a small expedition of about 400 men under Captain J. R. C. Domville was sent from Aden early in January, 1890, and voyaging across the Gulf to the African shore, landed at Zeila. Thirty men of the 4th Company, Bombay Sappers and Miners, were in this force, and were followed by 40 more under Captain B. B. Russell, R.E.,[5] who commanded the company. The expedition marched south-eastwards along the coast and then turned into the interior where the men had a smart brush with the Somalis at the oasis of Husain on January 29th, 1890. The Sappers had made a *zariba*, but its thorn fence was small and thin as the troops had arrived late in camp after a long march. The enemy were quick to seize their opportunity, and before dawn a party of 25 of them burrowed under the thorns, or leapt over them using their long spears as jumping poles, and killed or wounded a number of men before they were bayoneted. There was no more fighting, and the column marched back to Zeila and embarked for Aden, but the trivial affair at Husain had its value for it proved that a *zariba* fence must at least be wide whatever its height. The lesson

---
[1] Indian Army Circular No. 117, dated July 9th, 1887.
[2] *Historical Record of the Q.V.O. Madras Sappers and Miners*, Vol. I, p. 136.
[3] Indian Army Circular No. 91, dated June 15th, 1893.
[4] The disbandment was completed by September 30th, 1929, as recorded in Indian Army Order No. 778, dated December 16th, 1929.
[5] *Frontier and Overseas Expeditions from India*, Vol. VI, pp. 96, 97, and *A Short History of the Royal Bombay Sappers and Miners*, p. 19.

was turned to good account in the later expeditions to Somaliland between 1901 and 1904.

From 1888 to 1897 the North-West Frontier of India was in such a state of turmoil with the Black Mountain, Miranzai, Mahsud, Chitral, Tochi, Malakand, Buner, Mohmand and Tirah expeditions that there was little chance of active service overseas; but the 1st Company, Madras Sappers and Miners, under Lieutenant G. A. F. Sanders, R.E., with Lieutenants J. R. Chancellor, H. A. Cameron and C. F. Anderson, R.E., was in or near Suakin on the Red Sea coast from June to December, 1896, with a brigade from India under Colonel Egerton during the expedition led by Brigadier-General Sir H. H. Kitchener (late R.E.) up the Nile from Wady Halfa to Dongola. The Sappers had no fighting but a great deal of hard work. At an out-station called Tokar the temperature rose to 119° in the officers' quarters and dust storms hardly ever ceased. Every sort of job fell to the lot of Sanders and his merry men—building barracks, digging wells, arranging for water supply, repairing boats, drainage, telegraphy, surveying, drawing, making landing stages, and even mending boots. As their C.R.E. remarked before they returned to India: " Nothing seemed to be able to get along without the Madras Sappers having a say in the matter "—which is what every true Sapper likes to hear.

About a year after the Madras Sappers had returned from the Red Sea, a detachment of the 1st Company, Bombay Sappers and Miners, under Lieutenant W. Bovet, R.E., embarked for the Mekran coast to the west of Karachi. Landing at Pasni[1] on January 27th, 1898, they joined a small force at Turbat[2] on February 2nd, after marching 40 miles on that day. On the following day they covered another 30 miles in pursuit of a rebel chief, and then proceeded by Kalat to Quetta where they arrived on April 16th, after a little expedition in which they destroyed a number of forts and created a reputation for " foot-slogging."[3]

Mekran was the scene also of a smart little fight for the Bombay Sappers at the end of 1901. A party of the 4th Company under Captain J. B. Corry, R.E., landed at Gwadur and marched with other troops to Nodiz to assist the Nazim of Mekran in besieging a band of outlaws under one Muhammad Ali. On December 20th the Sappers advanced to breach the south-west tower of the fort, and Corry, finding a hole in the wall, decided not to use explosives. The " charge " was sounded, and he and another officer, with two of the Sappers, scrambled through the aperture. They were charged furiously by Muhammad Ali and another desperado; but Corry, though wounded in the right wrist and shoulder, managed to engage the rebel leader with his left hand alone until the fellow was shot.

---

[1] Roughly 70 miles east of Gwadur.
[2] About 45 miles inland from Pasni.
[3] *A Short History of the Royal Bombay Sappers and Miners*, p. 21.

The garrison surrendered after some further resistance, and the detachment marched on to Persia where it did good work under Lieutenant W. F. Maxwell, R.E.[1]

The scene now shifts to the Far East on which the eyes of half the civilized world were focussed in 1899, when a dangerous association of brigands, who called themselves "Fists of Patriotic Union," but were commonly known as "Boxers," got beyond the control of the mandarins in China and set themselves to exterminate all foreigners. Joined by thousands of ruffians who were attracted by the prospect of loot, they advanced northwards on Peking and attacked the European legations there on June 13th, 1900. A mixed naval brigade of British, Americans, Japanese and half the nations of Europe failed to reach their besieged countrymen, and until the Boxers were driven away from Tientsin on June 23rd, that place as well as Peking was in some danger. Military assistance was summoned from all sides, and a "China Expeditionary Force" of about 10,000 men[2] under Brigadier-General Sir A. Gaselee, K.C.B., was mobilized in India and began to arrive at Taku at the mouth of the Peiho River on July 17th. The British, American, Japanese, French and Russian forces set out on their advance towards Peking on August 4th, and after successful battles at Peitsang on the 5th and Yangtsun on the 6th relieved the legations on August 14th.

Most unfortunately the Sapper and Miner units from India arrived too late to take part in the advance to Peking, but several Royal Engineers of Gaselee's division were present. Lieut.-Colonel (afterwards Major-General Sir George) Scott-Moncrieff was with the force as C.R.E., and also Captains R. E. Picton, G. H. Griffith, R. P. Lee and C. H. D. Ryder (Survey Section), and Lieutenant S. G. Loch (Telegraph Section).[3] They were much impressed by the excellent defences of the British Legation for which an American missionary was mostly responsible. There was, it is true, an architect and surveyor among the defenders; but it is said that, from force of habit, he confined himself to noting down the damages and dilapidations caused by the Boxers' artillery![4] The first Engineer unit to arrive from India was the 4th Company, Bengal Sappers and Miners, under Captain H. R. Stockley, R.E., with Lieutenants C. M. Carpenter, H. D. Pearson and M. R. Elles, R.E.; it reached Tientsin on August 5th, and Peking on the 20th. The next was the 3rd Company, Madras Sappers and Miners, under Captain J. A. S. Tulloch, R.E.,

[1] *A Short History of the Royal Bombay Sappers and Miners*, p. 23.
[2] By January 1st, 1901, the strength of the British force in China had risen to 18,229 officers and other ranks. There were then present also about 21,000 Germans, 16,000 French, 6,000 Japanese, 3,000 Russians, 2,000 Italians, 1,700 Americans and a few Austrians.
[3] Article entitled "The Work of the R.E. in the China or Boxer War of 1900–1901" (a lecture delivered by Colonel F. T. N. Spratt Bowring, late R.E.), appearing in *The R.E. Journal*, Vol. XIII, January–June, 1911, p. 172.
[4] Article entitled "Peking, June to August, 1900," by Lieut.-Colonel G. K. Scott-Moncrieff, R.E., appearing in *The R.E. Journal*, Vol. 31, 1901, p. 68.

with Lieutenants E. G. Henderson, R. E. Goldingham and J. A. Garstin, R.E., which appeared in Tientsin on the 8th. When this company was sent up later to Peking, Henderson was appointed " Garrison Engineer of the Temple of Heaven," a title of some dignity. After the Madras Sappers came the 2nd Company of the Bombay Sappers under Captain G. H. Boileau, R.E., with G. R. Pridham, J. E. Craster and W. B. Chaldecott as his subalterns. Then the Maler Kotla Sapper Company[1] arrived under Lieut.-Colonel Asuf Ali, and on September 6th a mounted detachment of 25 men of the Bengal Sappers under Lieutenant E. C. Tylden-Pattenson, R.E., to join the Cavalry Brigade. Colonel W. T. Shone, Lieut.-Colonel J. R. L. Macdonald, Majors P. G. Twining, J. E. Dickie, C. A. R. Browne, R. D. Petrie, A. R. Reynolds, T. F. B. Renny-Tailyour and a number of more junior Royal Engineers from India followed them, so that in all there were some 46 officers of the Corps in North China. Two Engineer Field Parks, located at Tientsin and Shan-Hai-Kwan, completed the Engineering establishment which was sent from India.

The Engineers and Sappers were too late to see much serious fighting, except the lucky few in the advance on Peking; but they got through a stupendous amount of useful work in building huts, laying telegraph lines, repairing railway lines and bridges, road-making and preparing camps for the troops who were to winter in China. Eighteen thousand soldiers, 14,000 followers and 10,000 animals were provided with warm shelter before the first fall of snow. So severe was the cold that sentry boxes and even drinking troughs had to be warmed. Two thousand stoves were installed, and more than seven miles of flue piping. The Bombay Engineers under Lieut.-Colonel Macdonald with Majors Browne and Twining, repaired hundreds of miles of track and scores of bridges, and assembled a dozen locomotives. The Survey parties under Major Renny-Tailyour triangulated 16,000 square miles of country and plane-tabled even more. It was a time of intensive effort. Detachments of Sappers and Miners moved frequently between Tientsin and Peking and sent parties with movable columns to operate against gangs of Boxers. When accompanying one of these columns moving from Tientsin to Tinlin, the mounted detachment under Tylden-Pattenson made a bridge of junks 48 yards long in just over one and a half hours—a remarkable feat for 25 men. After the bitter months of winter had passed the work of clearing the country of Boxers was carried out with renewed vigour, and the Engineers and Sappers continued to repair the damage done by the insurgents. It was not till September, 1901, that the three companies and the mounted detachment were back in their headquarters in India, loaded with curios and full of their adventures.

[1] Imperial Service (Indian States) Troops.

Between July, 1901, and May, 1904, some of the Bombay Sappers and Miners were on active service in the Aden Hinterland. The Turkish tribe of Humar having encroached on the territory of the Haushabi Arabs not far from Aden, a small British force was sent in July, 1901, to help the friendly Arabs to eject the invaders. This was duly carried out, and half of the 4th Company, Bombay Sappers and Miners, shared in the little fight.[1] The affair induced the Turkish authorities to propose that a proper frontier should be demarcated, and negotiations began with the Porte; but they had progressed so little by the end of 1902, and the attitude of the Turks and some Arab tribes was so threatening, that an expedition of 2,000 men, including the greater part of the 19th (late 3rd) Company of Bombay Sappers, was despatched with a Telegraph Section from Aden in January, 1903, to clear up the situation. The Turks withdrew, but the Arabs remained defiant, so the Sappers were employed during May in blowing up village towers as they were accustomed to do in punitive expeditions on the frontier of India. The 19th Company was relieved soon afterwards by the 23rd (Fortress) Company under Lieutenant Yule, R.E., from Aden, and the latter unit continued on field service till the Hinterland operations ended in the middle of 1904. These little adventures in the vast Arabian desert were dwarfed by the war in Somaliland; but it is not the lot of every Sapper to work in the limelight, and the 23rd Company, as was afterwards remarked, fully maintained the reputation of the Bombay Sappers and Miners[2] in the Hinterland campaign.

While the 23rd Company was operating north of the Gulf of Aden, other units of the Bombay Sappers were engaged in a strenuous expedition in Somaliland, that barren territory in the " Horn of Africa " which lies between the Straits of Bab-el-Mandeb and Cape Gardafui and extends southwards for 700 miles to the borders of Jubaland on the Indian Ocean. The greater part of Somaliland is a high plateau[3] covered with belts of dense thorn jungle, interspersed with open spaces. Water can usually be found by digging, but the only permanent supply is from wells excavated by the Somalis in certain rocky localities from 40 to 100 miles apart; there is, however, one tract in the interior called the Nogal Valley, some 200 miles from the northern coast, where there is a good supply from wells and where animals can graze. Unlike the grim waste called the " Sorl " or Northern Haud to its north, or the desolate Southern Haud to its south, the wide and shallow Nogal Valley is an easy country for military operations.[4] From Berbera on the northern coast a passable

[1] *A Short History of the Royal Bombay Sappers and Miners*, p. 23.
[2] The Corps was renamed the " Third Sappers and Miners " in 1903, but the older title will be retained in this narrative for convenience.
[3] A range of mountains, called the Golis, runs parallel to, and from 60 to 200 miles from, the northern coast. Behind them the plateau begins at 5,000 feet altitude and falls gradually to sea level on the Indian Ocean.
[4] *Frontier and Overseas Expeditions from India*, Vol. VI, p. 86.

caravan route ascends to the tableland by the Shaik Pass and runs by Burao and Kirrit to the important oasis of Bohotle lying to the south-west of the Nogal Valley. The only port besides Berbera from which an expedition might invade Somaliland is Obbia on the Indian Ocean 500 miles southwards from Cape Gardafui. Such was the theatre of operations between 1902 and 1904.[1]

A Mulla named Haji Muhammad began to give trouble in 1898, raiding certain districts in northern Somaliland and announcing his intention of ruling the interior and leaving the coast only to Europeans. He was driven southwards in 1901 by a small British force under Lieut.-Colonel E. J. E. Swayne, who repeated the operation with less success in the following year. As it was then deemed necessary to suppress the " Mad Mulla " completely, an expedition of about 2,000 men was landed at Obbia in January, 1903, to drive him northwards, while another of equal strength was disembarked at Berbera to seize and hold a line of communication from that port south-eastwards to Bohotle near the Nogal Valley. The Obbia Force was under Brigadier-General W. H. Manning, and included the 17th Company, Bombay Sappers and Miners, under Captain W. Bovet, R.E., with Lieutenant E. D. Tillard, R.E. The Commanding Royal Engineer was Captain W. B. Lesslie, R.E. The Berbera Force was commanded by Colonel J. C. Swann and contained a party of the 19th Company under Lieutenant A. L. Paris, R.E. General Manning marched from Obbia on February 22nd, 1903, and driving the Mad Mulla before him in spite of a disaster to a detachment at Gumburru,[2] joined hands with Swann's advanced garrison at Bohotle on June 26th. But the Mulla was still at large and a second campaign was necessary, so most of the troops moved towards Berbera[3] to concentrate for further action, while the Bombay Sappers remained in the interior to make roads and defensible posts and to arrange for water supply along the line of advance.[4]

Major-General Sir Charles Egerton landed in Berbera early in July, 1903, to take command of a force of two infantry brigades and a battalion of mounted infantry[5] for another attempt against the Mad Mulla. The remainder of the 19th Company, Bombay Sappers and Miners, under Captain W. H. Chaldecott, R.E., disembarked at Berbera from the Aden Hinterland in August, and an Engineer Field Park of the Madras Sappers under Major E. P. Johnson, R.E., arrived in the following month.[6] Several other Royal Engineer

[1] See " Sketch Map of North-East Africa " at the end of this volume.
[2] On April 17th a mixed force of 223 men under Colonel Plunkett was surrounded by 8,000 men under the Mad Mulla at Gumburru, far out in the desert south-west of Bohotle. Not a British nor Indian soldier survived.
[3] The Obbia line of communication had been rolled up and abandoned.
[4] *A Brief History of the Royal Bombay Sappers and Miners*, p. 25.
[5] Nearly 7,000 men in all, including a company of Boer mounted infantry, although the South African War had ended only a year previously.
[6] *Historical Record of the Q.V.O. Madras Sappers and Miners*, Vol. I, p. 185.

officers joined the force, and among them Major R. F. Allen as Commanding Royal Engineer. The 17th Company of Bombay Sappers was attached to the 1st Brigade and the 19th Company to the 2nd Brigade when acting independently. General Egerton marched up the Shaik Pass in November and so to Bohotle. After much manœuvring and fruitless delay in waiting for the co-operation of an Abyssinian army, the Mad Mulla was located at last with 6,000 men at a spot in the Nogal Valley called Jidballi ; so the two brigades moved forward to the attack in a large square on January 10th, 1904, the Sapper companies being in the firing line. But the Mulla took the offensive, and rushing on with great fury, tried to envelop the British force. His assault was brave and determined, yet it withered and collapsed before the accurate fire of our troops, and his army was routed utterly and with very heavy loss. It remained only to pursue the fugitive and his followers. The brigades separated, the 1st Brigade with the 17th Company sweeping down the Nogal Valley, while the 2nd Brigade with the 19th Company operated nearer to the northern coast. They did their utmost but could not catch the elusive Mulla though they chased him far to the east and back again. The campaign was brought to an end, accordingly, in the spring of 1904, and the 17th and 19th Companies of Bombay Sappers returned to Kirkee where they arrived on June 14th, much in need of proper food and rest. This was one of the hardest campaigns ever undertaken outside India.

The tale of a dozen expeditions to east and west is finished. In some the Engineers and Sappers played a most important part, as in Abyssinia : in others their duties were almost humdrum and they hardly saw a shot fired. In all, however, they lived up to the Royal Engineer's motto, "*Ubique. Quo fas et gloria ducunt.*" With the exception of two small trips by half-companies of the Bombay Sappers to the Mekran Coast in 1910 and 1911,[1] no Sappers and Miners saw any field service overseas between the end of the Somaliland campaign and the outbreak of the Great War in 1914, and, as has been recorded, only two companies served in Somaliland. But the opening years of the twentieth century are important because of the changes in the Army in India as a whole and in the Sappers and Miners. The man who initiated those changes was the greatest organizer and the most brilliant figure which the Corps of Royal Engineers has ever produced—General Viscount Kitchener of Khartoum and the Vaal and Aspall, fresh from his great achievements in the final stages of the war in South Africa. Taking up his appointment as Commander-in-Chief in India on November 28th, 1902, not

---

[1] Half the 18th Company, Bombay Sappers and Miners, under Lieutenant T. A. Swinburne, R.E., was fortifying Jask and surveying around Galag on the Mekran Coast during February and March, 1910, while an expedition against gun-runners was cruising up and down the coast. Half the 19th Company, under Captain N. W. Webber, R.E., was on service in Mekran during April, 1911. (See *A Short History of the Royal Bombay Sappers and Miners*, p. 27.)

only did he carry out many administrative reforms before he left the country seven years later, but he effected a sweeping reorganization and strategical redistribution of the British and Indian forces. He abolished the " Indian Staff Corps "[1] and evolved a scheme to divide the Army into three Corps exclusive of Aden, Burma, Chitral, Kohat and the Derajat ; and although this reorganization was never fully adopted,[2] the fact that the Army in India was mobilized so rapidly in 1914 must be attributed in a large measure to the basic principles laid down by Lord Kitchener in his great reforms.

As regards the Sappers and Miners, the relative order of precedence of the three Corps had been fixed in 1897, the senior being the Queen's Own Madras Sappers and Miners, the next the Bengal Sappers and Miners, and the junior the Bombay Sappers and Miners,[3] but there was much to be done in consolidating the three Corps into one homogeneous branch of the Service. As a first step, Kitchener set out to do this by renaming the three Corps and renumbering the companies. The Bengal Sappers and Miners became the " 1st Sappers and Miners " in October, 1903 ; the Queen's Own Sappers and Miners[4] were changed into the " 2nd Queen's Own Sappers and Miners," and the Bombay Corps emerged as the " 3rd Sappers and Miners."[5] Within another two months a general renumbering of the companies took place,[6] the service companies of the Bengal Corps alone retaining their original numbers of 1 to 6, those of the Madras Corps becoming Nos. 9 to 15 (the Burma Company), and those of the Bombay Corps Nos. 17 to 22, with the Aden Fortress Company as No. 23. Changes were made also in the lettering of the Depot companies. The names of the three Corps were altered several times in later years. In January, 1906, when H.R.H. The Prince of Wales (now H.M. King George V.) accepted the appointment of Colonel-in-Chief of the 1st Sappers and Miners, that Corps became the " 1st Prince of Wales' Own Sappers and Miners," with permission to wear the plume of three feathers on its colours and appointments ;[7] and in 1910, when the Prince ascended the throne, the title was altered to the " 1st King George's Own Sappers and Miners." After the Great War the Bengal Corps applied for and received permission to be called " King George's Own Bengal Sappers and Miners," and this is the present title of that famous body of officers and men. The 2nd Queen's Own Sappers and Miners became in due course the " 2nd Queen Victoria's Own Sappers and Miners," and are now " Queen

[1] G.G.O. No. 1 of January, 1903.
[2] In 1908, for instance, there had been so much divergence from the original plan that the Army in India consisted of a " Northern Army " and a " Southern Army," each of five divisions with a few independent brigades.
[3] G.G.O. No. 605 of June, 1897.
[4] The services of the Madras Sappers and Miners had been recognized by the grant of the title " Queen's Own " in 1876.
[5] Indian Army Order No. 181 of October, 1903.
[6] Indian Army Order No. 382 of December, 1903.
[7] Including helmets, puggris and buttons. (G.G.O. No. 1 of January, 1906.)

FIELD-MARSHAL EARL H.H. KITCHENER OF KHARTOUM AND OF THE VAAL AND ASPALL, K.P., G.C.B., O.M., G.C.S.I., G.C.M.G., G.C.I.E.
(*As a Major-General about* 1900.)

Victoria's Own Madras Sappers and Miners." The designation of the 3rd Sappers and Miners was altered to the " 3rd Royal Bombay Sappers and Miners " in 1921[1] when His Majesty bestowed this signal honour on the Corps for its services in the Great War; the title is now the " Royal Bombay Sappers and Miners."

Other changes were made before the Great War such as the abolition of the title " Service Company " which was replaced by " Field Company " in July, 1909, and the substitution in 1912 of Defence Light Sections for the small Submarine Mining Sections maintained by the three Corps at Indian ports, but such matters cannot receive their proper notice in this narrative.[2] When all the available Sappers and Miners in India were concentrated in Delhi in 1911 for the magnificent Durbar ceremonies during which Their Majesties laid the foundation stones of the new capital, no finer body of troops could be desired; and when called upon, less than three years later, to take their share in the defence of the Empire, they proved the value of their training for war.

It may be well to conclude this chapter with a few remarks about the normal military employment of those Royal Engineer officers in India who are not serving with the Sappers and Miners. In 1851 the Public Works Department, which employed so many Royal Engineers, was brought under civil control, but no separate organization was believed to be necessary for military works. After 1860 there was a boom in the construction of civil works. A large number of civil engineers were engaged by Government, and the Military Department began to lose proper control over military works. By 1871 the situation was so unsatisfactory that the control of all large military works was then transferred to a special Military Works Branch of the Public Works Department,[3] and, ten years later, this Branch (now called a Department) was placed directly under the Military Department. In 1889 the " Military Works Department " took over all the military works in India, but it was not till 1899 that it became entirely military in character and was officered wholly by Royal Engineers;[4] its title was then changed to that of the " Military Works Services," and so it remained till it became the " Military Engineer Services " in 1923.[5] The bulk of the Royal Engineer officers who proceeded to India before the Great War were employed, at least for a time, in the Military Works Department or Services, and those who go there now are distributed over the country in the Military Engineer Services after attachment to the Sappers and Miners if they are very junior. Though not in command of troops,

[1] Indian Army Order No. 821 of July, 1921.
[2] Some information about the Indian Submarine Mining Corps is given in Appendix VI, and the Defence Light Sections are alluded to in Appendices II, III and IV.
[3] In Bengal the control of *all* military works, large and small, was so transferred.
[4] The Public Works Department system of grading officers, which clashed with the system of military rank, was then abolished.
[5] *The Army in India and its Evolution*, pp. 82 and 89.

they are in constant touch with them and take part in military exercises with them, while at the same time they gather valuable experience in structural engineering work of every kind. In war they fill casualties among the Royal Engineers with the Sappers and Miners, and they work mostly on the lines of communication or at the base. They form an immense reserve of military engineering talent in India which is available immediately in an emergency such as that which arose in the fateful year 1914, and they supply those Commanding Royal Engineers and Field Engineers whose exploits on active service have been recorded so often in these pages.[1]

[1] Some details of the organization of the Military Engineer Services in India are given in Appendix I.

PRINCIPAL APPROACH TO THE GOLDEN DAGON PAGODA, RANGOON.

From Moore's *Views in Rangoon*.

CHAPTER XXI.

THE NORTH-WEST FRONTIER.

> A great and glorious thing it is
> To learn, for seven years or so,
> The Lord knows what of that and this,
> Ere reckoned fit to face the foe—
> The flying bullet down the Pass,
> That whistles clear : " All flesh is grass."
>
> A scrimmage in a Border Station—
> A canter down some dark defile—
> Two thousand pounds of education
> Drops to a ten-rupee *jezail*—
> The Crammer's boast, the Squadron's pride,
> Shot like a rabbit in a ride !
> —*Rudyard Kipling.*

BY the proclamation which extended the frontier from the Sutlej to the base of the Afghan mountains through the annexation of the Punjab in 1849, Lord Dalhousie added a great tract of valuable territory to the British Empire ; but at the same time he brought that Empire into direct contact with martial races who involved it in a succession of costly expeditions. The new boundary was ill-defined, and beyond it was a zone of country inhabited by independent tribes, mostly of Pathans in the north and of Baluchis in the south. The Pathans were fierce, treacherous and unruly : their hands against every man, and every man's hand against them. The bitter struggle for existence in an inhospitable land had produced men who were, and still are, unique, and whose reckless and cruel character is shown by some of their proverbs. " Keep a cousin poor, but use him." " When he is little, play with him. When he is grown up he is a cousin ; fight him." " Speak good words to an enemy very softly ; gradually destroy him root and branch."[1] Yet the Pathan has his good points. At times he is as brave as a lion, and he is bound by his religion to shelter and protect an enemy who comes as a suppliant, and to show hospitality to all who may demand it. He leads a wild, free and active life in his mountain fastnesses. He is a bigoted Muhammadan, proud, strong and defiant, and he values the life of a man no more than that of a jackal. All insults must be avenged in blood. At one moment he may seem a saint : at the next he is a devil. The Baluchi, on the other hand, presents a strong contrast to the Pathan in many of his characteristics. He is less turbulent, less treacherous, less bloodthirsty ; and although he

---

[1] *Record of Expeditions against the North-West Frontier Tribes,* by Lieut.-Colonel W. H. Paget, 5th Punjab Cavalry, and Lieutenant A. H. Mason, R.E., p. 7.

also is a wild son of the wildest mountains he has a better idea of faith and truth than his neighbour of the North. By far the greater number of the frontier campaigns of India have been against the Pathan, and hence this brief sketch of frontier warfare is concerned chiefly with him and his country; the Baluchi remains in the background.

The tangled mass of valleys and mountains which forms the north-west frontier of India holds a great number of tribes and clans.[1] A few of these may be mentioned. Far up in the north, beyond Kashmir and near the boundaries of Russian Turkestan and China, are the little states of Hunza and Nagar peopled by the Kanjutis and Nagaris, and between them and Kashmir proper are Gilgit and Astor. To the west of Hunza and Nagar are Yasin and Chitral, the latter being close to Afghanistan. South of these and other states, and stretching over a large area from the Black Mountain region adjoining the Indus above Attock in the east to the Afghan frontier in the west, is the country of the Yusafzai Pathans who include among their many clans the Bunerwals, Swatis, Utman Khels and Isazais. North of the Kabul River are the Mohmands, and to its south the most important and powerful of all the Pathan tribes, the Afridis who dominate the Khaibar Pass. The largest clan of the Afridi tribe is the Zakha Khel who occupy most of the Afridi Tirah,[2] which is intersected by the Bazar, Bara and Waran Valleys lying west of Peshawar. To the south of the Afridi Tirah and west of Kohat are the Miranzai and Kurram Valleys where the Orakzais, Zaimukhts and Turis have their homes, and due south of Peshawar we find the Jowakis. The country lying between the Kurram Valley and the Gomal Valley south of Bannu is the abode of the Wazirs, whose most important clans are the Darwesh Khel near the Afghan border and those daring freebooters the Mahsuds. South of the Gomal Valley, which joins the Indus below Dera Ismail Khan, live the Baluchis—the Sherani clan in the region of the Zhob Valley ascending westwards towards Quetta, and the Bozdars lower down the map near Dera Ghazi Khan. All these tribes and many others inhabit the mountains situated between the Durand Line marking the boundary of Afghanistan and the Administrative Boundary Line of British India to the west or north of the Indus.

A complete account of the work and adventures of Engineers and Sappers and Miners on the North-West Frontier of India might easily fill two volumes. Some day, perhaps, it may be written, and it will be a fascinating story; but there is no place for it here, and a mere sketch must suffice to give some idea of what these men have achieved in a few of the scores of small expeditions beyond the Indus. In

---

[1] A map entitled "Sketch Map of the North-West Frontier including Afghanistan" will be found at the end of this volume. It shows the distribution of the tribes and the more important natural features of the country.
[2] *Tirah*. Highlands.

many of these expeditions the engineering work was useful but prosaic. Roadmaking, bridging small torrents, building fortified posts and *sangars*,[1] and blowing up innumerable village towers have contributed to the success of a long series of little punitive ventures, but they do not lend themselves to detailed description. Such work is part of the daily routine of the Sapper in frontier warfare. Sometimes, however, the circumstances were so unusual, the exploits so conspicuous, or the results so remarkable that they deserve to be placed on record, and this has been attempted in the following pages.

Any history of the frontier wars of India holds a surprise for the Engineer before he has read more than the opening chapters. If ever there was a country in which one would imagine that the services of the Sapper and Miner would be indispensable during all military operations it is the bewildering maze of mountain ranges which stretches between the glaciers of Chitral and the wind-swept uplands of Quetta. Yet in most of those early expeditions into this frontier area, which crowded closely upon each other after the annexation of the Punjab, *there was rarely more than one company of Sappers and Miners*. It would almost seem that this little body of Engineer soldiers was considered sufficient for the needs of a force of any strength up to 4,000 men. In the smaller expeditions there was sometimes only a detachment of a company, and in several there were no Sappers and Miners at all. On February 2nd, 1850, the Adam Khel Afridis of the Kohat Pass cut up a party of Sappers who were making a road, and Brigadier-General Sir Colin Campbell marched from Peshawar on February 7th to punish the tribesmen. He took with him two regiments of Indian cavalry, six companies of British infantry, more than three battalions of Indian infantry and four guns —but not one Sapper and Miner. So also in other expeditions. There were no Sappers and Miners in the small force led by Major John Nicholson from Bannu and Latammar against the Umarzai Waziris in December, 1852, although it was known that the destruction of villages would be necessary. There was none in a small expedition against the Hindustani Fanatics[2] near the Black Mountain in 1853, nor in a force of nearly 3,000 men which operated during the same year against the Shiranis of the Takht-i-Suliman heights to the west of Dera Ismail Khan. Brigadier-General Sir Neville Chamberlain[3] took the field against the Orakzais north-west of Kohat in August, 1855, with a brigade of infantry, a regiment of cavalry and nine guns; yet he had no Sappers and Miners. Again, in a second expedition against the same tribe in 1868-69, there were

---

[1] Stone breastworks.
[2] The "Hindustani Fanatics" were the followers of a mulla named Ahmad Shah, who established himself on the Peshawar border in 1823 and attracted to his side a number of Pathans. He was killed in 1829, but his followers set up another leader and installed themselves near Sitana south of the Black Mountain, where they caused great trouble.
[3] Soon to become famous for his work at Delhi during the Mutiny.

no Sappers and Miners. In January, 1864, 2,000 men marched from Shabkadr against the Mohmands without a Sapper and Miner; and it should not be forgotten that Roberts refused to take any Sappers and Miners with him when he set out with a large force from Kabul towards Kandahar in 1880. In only six[1] of the 30 frontier expeditions in the North-West which were launched between 1849 and 1888 was there more than a single company of Sappers and Miners.[2]

It is evident that there must be some explanation of this extraordinary state of affairs. Possibly it may be that there were no Sappers and Miners in the Punjab Irregular Force (afterwards called the Punjab Frontier Force) which was under the direct control of the Lieutenant-Governor of the Punjab and was used by him for any small punitive expeditions which he might wish to send across the border. He could not employ Sappers and Miners without obtaining the sanction of the Commander-in-Chief, and this meant delay, especially if a Sapper company was not at hand. Again, he may have thought that Pioneers would serve his purpose, or that infantry with some engineering experience would suffice. But the most plausible explanation is that the value of properly-equipped and trained units of Sappers and Miners in frontier warfare was not recognized, and that so little attention had been paid to their organization, and particularly to their equipment, that they could not work rapidly and well and consequently their services were not in great demand. This, if true, is remarkable in view of the exploits of Broadfoot's Sappers in the First Afghan War and of the Bengal Sappers and Pioneers in the

[1] Hindustani Fanatics, 1858; Ambela, 1863; Black Mountain, 1868; Zakha Khel Afridis, 1879; Mahsuds, 1881; Zhob Valley, 1884.

[2] A list of the early expeditions, and the Sappers and Miners employed in each, is given below. The list has been compiled from *A Record of the Expeditions against the North-West Frontier Tribes*, by W. H. Paget and A. H. Mason, *Campaigns on the North-West Frontier*, by H. L. Nevill, *The Services of the Bengal Native Army*, by H. S. Cardew, *Frontier and Overseas Expeditions from India*, Vols. I and II, and the *History and Digest of Service of the 1st K.G.O. Sappers and Miners*, all of which have been used extensively in writing this chapter. Unless otherwise stated, the companies belong to the *Bengal* Sappers and Miners. The list is as follows:—(i) Swatis (Baizais), 1849, 1st Coy., Bombay Sappers. (ii) Kohat Pass Afridis (Adam Khels), 1850, *nil*. (iii) Mohmands, 1851–52, 2nd Coy. (iv) Ranizais (Swatis) and Utman Khels, 1852, 2nd Coy. (v) Waziris, 1852, *nil*. (vi) Hassanzais (Black Mountain), 1852–53, 7th Coy. (vii) Hindustani Fanatics, 1853, *nil*. (viii) Shiranis (Takht-i-Suliman), 1853, *nil*. (ix) Kohat Pass Afridis (Bori Jowakis), 1853, 2nd Coy. (x) Mohmands, 1854–55, 2nd Coy. (xi) Orakzais, 1855, *nil*. (xii) Zaimukhts and Turis (Miranzai and Kurram Valleys), 1856, detachment of 6th Coy. (xiii) Bozdars (near Dera Ghazi Khan), 1857, half-company, probably of 6th Coy. (xiv) Hindustani Fanatics (Sitana), 1858, 5th and half 6th Coys. (xv) Waziris (Kabul Khels), 1859–60, detachments of 4th and 5th Coys. (xvi) Mahsuds, 1860, 5th Coy. (xvii) Ambela Expedition (Hindustani Fanatics, Bunerwals and Swatis), 1863, 4th and 5th Coys. (xviii) Mohmands, 1863–64, *nil*. (xix) Black Mountain (Hazara Expedition), 1868, 2nd and 7th Coys. (xx) Orakzais (Bizotis), 1868–69, *nil*. (xxi) Dawaris (Tochi Valley, west of Bannu), 1872, *nil*. (xxii) Jowakis, 1877–78, 2nd, 3rd and detachment of 4th Coys. (xxiii) Zakha Khel Afridis (Bazar and Bara Valleys), 1878, half 8th Coy. (xxiv) The same, 1879, half 8th Coy. and detachments of "B" and "E" Coys., Madras Sappers. (xxv) Mohmands, 1879, "C" Coy., Madras Sappers. (xxvi) Zaimukhts, 1879, 8th Coy. (xxvii) Marris (Baluchis in the south), 1880, *nil*. (xxviii) Mahsuds, 1881, 6th and 8th Coys. (xxix) Zhob Valley Expedition, 1884, 4th and 10th Coys. (xxx) Black Mountain (Hazara) Expedition, 1888, 3rd Coy. and Telegraph Section.

THE AMBELA CAMPAIGN OF 1863.

Sikh Wars and at Multan. When the reorganization of 1885, helped so greatly by Lieut.-Colonel Bindon Blood, R.E., had produced its effect, the Sappers and Miners came into their own; and by 1890 their reputation was high and they began to take a prominent part in frontier warfare. Nevill remarks[1] that the history of the North-West Frontier wars may be divided into two sections: the period prior to 1890, and that from 1890 onwards. " It is suggested," he writes, " that the date selected marks the time when the armament of the tribesmen all along the frontier began to improve, necessitating some changes in minor tactics on both sides. Before 1890 the Pathan tribes were indifferently armed, but each campaign subsequent to 1890 marked an improvement in the armament of our enemies." As their rifles grew better and more reliable, the tribesmen began to prefer long-range fire to charging with cold steel; and with their adoption of accurate rifle fire came the need for better protection in the British camps and posts, and with that need came the demand for Sappers and Miners to give the required protection. So at last, about the year 1890, through the effects of the reorganization of 1885 and the altered conditions of frontier warfare, the Sappers and Miners began to take their full share in the work across the border, and it is from that year that it is proposed to give a sketch of some of their achievements. Most of the 30 small expeditions prior to 1890 have no technical interest to the Engineer because there was little or no engineering in them.

But the Ambela Campaign of 1863 deserves more than passing notice because it was a most severe and sanguinary contest. The " Spectre of Ambela " was not laid for many years. The object of the expedition which set out under Brigadier-General Sir Neville Chamberlain was to punish the colony of Hindustani Fanatics who had settled near Sitana on the right bank of the Indus south-west of the Black Mountain; and so confident were the authorities that the operations would resemble those of any other small punitive expedition that the affair was called " Sir Robert's picnic."[2] The Commander-in-Chief was against the project but agreed in the end to provide the troops, so Chamberlain marched towards the Ambela Pass[3] in the middle of October, 1863, at the head of over 5,000 men. Lieut.-Colonel Alexander Taylor, R.E., of Delhi fame, was the Commanding Royal Engineer, and with him were Lieutenants H. F. Blair, James Browne and T. Tupper-Carter,[4] R.E., and the 4th and 5th Companies of Bengal Sappers and Miners under Lieutenant L. H. E. Tucker of the Bengal Infantry.[5]

[1] *Campaigns on the North-West Frontier*, by Captain H. L. Nevill, D.S.O., R.A., p. 11.
[2] After Sir Robert Montgomery, Lieutenant-Governor of the Punjab.
[3] Thirty-five miles north-east of Nowshera.
[4] Carter was a Survey officer who volunteered to serve under Taylor.
[5] *Record of Expeditions against the N.W. Frontier Tribes*, by W. H. Paget and A. H. Mason, p. 136.

P*

At dawn on October 20th the advanced guard under Lieut.-Colonel A. T. Wilde began to ascend the defile; its baggage was left behind, and even without this encumbrance it did not reach the Kotal[1] till 2 p.m. Meanwhile the main body, with which were both the Sapper companies, was in great difficulties. The route lay up the bed of a stream obstructed with boulders and overgrown with jungle. The guns had to be loaded on elephants and the troops were obliged to march in single file. No transport could accompany the force, and when the weary men gained the summit late in the afternoon they had to face a night of cold and misery without cover and with scarcely any food. In spite of the efforts of Taylor and the Sappers, very little baggage arrived even on the 21st, for the obstacles were too great. It seems that the evil system of making war in luxury still survived. "Taylor himself," writes Miss A. C. Taylor,[2] " Spartan though he was, had a following of seventeen servants, six mules and three horses." Chamberlain camped just below the watershed on the western side and piqueted six of the commanding points around him, the most important being the " Eagle's Nest " to the north of the track and the " Crag " to the south.

A powerful tribe of Yusufzais called the Bunerwals, who inhabited the country to the north of the Ambela area, had agreed to remain neutral, so Taylor, with a small escort, pushed on some miles beyond the pass on the 22nd to reconnoitre for a further advance towards the haunts of the Hindustani Fanatics; but when he began to withdraw, the Bunerwals tried to cut him off and their sudden change of attitude altered the whole situation. Swati tribesmen joined them, and General Chamberlain found himself practically isolated on the Ambela Pass and threatened by a formidable army instead of being able to march at leisure against a small body of fanatical Muhammadans. When Taylor retreated from his reconnaissance, the 4th and 5th Companies of Bengal Sappers under " Buster " Browne, who were trying to improve the first two miles of road from the camp to the eastern exit from the pass, had to cease work and return to camp. There was now little possibility of an advance, and the best that could be hoped was that the force would be able to hold its own till reinforcements could be pushed up to it along a better line of communication. It was essential, accordingly, to secure such a line without delay. The Bunerwals and Swatis had assembled in thousands on the heights beyond the piquets and an immediate attack was probable. Working parties were detached to build a breastwork round the camp and to construct *sangars* surrounded by abattis for the outlying piquets, but the ground was so broken that it was difficult to prevent the tribesmen from creeping up close to the defences.

[1] Summit of the pass.
[2] *General Sir Alex Taylor*, by A. C. Taylor, Vol. II, p. 174.

After an abortive attack on October 25th, the enemy made two desperate assaults on the Eagle's Nest Piquet on the following day. Their swordsmen advanced with great determination, covered by the fire of their matchlock men, and got close up to the piquet before they were driven off. On the night of the 29th/30th they carried the Crag Piquet which was only recovered after a hand-to-hand fight. Alex Taylor and his subalterns had been occupied since the 22nd in tracing and preparing new roads along the southern spurs from Ambela to Parmali in the plains where Chamberlain wished to establish a new base, so they could not devote much time to the defences around the camp. Taylor, although a sick man, was in the saddle from dawn to sunset as at Delhi, while the Sappers and Miners blasted, dug and carpentered till they were fit to drop with fatigue. They were always exposed to attack, and on November 6th a covering party of infantry was cut off and annihilated. By November 18th, however, the new roads were practicable and a fresh position for the camp was taken up on the south side of the gorge to suit the altered lines of communication, the piquets to the north being then withdrawn.

The Crag Post changed hands three times. It was the key to the position. An eye-witness gives a graphic description of an attack by the tribesmen after darkness had fallen on November 11th. "The enemy moved silently, but the rustling of leaves and the sound of falling stones betrayed their movements. Presently the hollow in front of the Crag was full of them. They broke into yells and advanced in masses to the attack, their number being at least two thousand. I opened a rapid and well-sustained fire from our front face and it soon silenced their shouts and drove them under cover. In half an hour they rallied, and, assembling in increased numbers, rushed to the attack. They were received with the greatest steadiness and again recoiled before us. Their attacks continued until 4 a.m. each becoming weaker than the last. The post was at one time in considerable danger. The enemy clambered up, and assailing its occupants with stones from our breastworks, stunned and drove them back. But five men of the 20th Native Punjab Infantry, hurling stones on the enemy, drove them back in turn and rebuilt the parapet." On November 19th, when the Crag was lost and retaken for the third and last time, Brigadier-General Chamberlain was severely wounded and was soon obliged to relinquish his command. Major-General J. Garvock then arrived with reinforcements and took command of the force.

When a report of the situation at Ambela reached the Punjab it caused great consternation, and the Government of India ordered Chamberlain to withdraw to the plains; but here the Commander-in-Chief stepped in with a strong protest and followed it by despatching large reinforcements to the hard-pressed force on the Ambela Kotal. Fortunately also, the acting Viceroy, Lieut.-General Sir William

Denison,[1] late of the Royal Engineers, saw how disastrous a withdrawal would be and persuaded his Council to cancel their order. So the force remained on the pass and soon reached a strength of 8,000 men. Garvock took the offensive on December 15th, 1863. He stormed a peak known as Conical Hill and captured the adjacent village of Lalu, and these operations decided the issue of the struggle. The Bunerwals submitted, the Swatis vanished, and the stronghold of the Hindustani Fanatics at Malka was visited and destroyed by a few British officers under a tribal escort.

Taylor's subalterns, " Buster " Browne and " Toony " Blair, had their fill of excitement before the submission of the tribesmen. On one occasion Toony was discovered, clad in pyjamas and a helmet and armed only with a sword, fighting for his life with three tribesmen in the bottom of a nullah into which he had fallen. He had killed two, but the third was getting the better of him, which was not surprising as, when the man had been killed by a Gurkha, he was found to be encased in chain armour. Taylor put Blair under arrest for this escapade, but the offender escaped with a reprimand.[2] " I do not expect my officers to be gladiators," remarked Sir Neville Chamberlain; and thereafter Toony Blair and Buster Browne became known as " The Gladiators."

The expedition to Malka, which was to have been a military promenade of three weeks, lasted through three perilous months and cost 900 casualties.[3] Who was to blame? A distinguished officer of the Royal Engineers who inspected the Ambela position in 1898 has expressed his opinion that the lack of Sappers and Miners was the cause of many of the unfortunate incidents which occurred. Although two companies were attached to the force they were employed chiefly in the urgent and difficult task of making a passable line of communication to the plains, and neither they nor the four Engineer officers could spare much time for the defence of the camp. The trouble was that there were too few Engineers and Sappers: they could not be everywhere. If ever there was a man who could be relied upon to put every ounce of energy into his work it was the inexhaustible Taylor, and he never failed to get the most out of his men and to make the best use of his materials. It is inconceivable that he can be held responsible for the errors of Ambela. The military system which allowed the despatch of a small force, with too

---

[1] General Denison was Governor of Madras. He acted as Viceroy from December 2nd, 1863, after Lord Elgin's death, till January 12th, 1864, when Sir John Lawrence assumed charge. He is the only Engineer who has held this high post.

[2] " Buster " Browne was also in this fight. In 1884, when he had become Sir James Browne, he used to tell how his Wilkinson sword broke off at the hilt while he was fighting a Pathan, whom he then killed by a blow on the forehead, using the hilt as a boxing glove. This was why Sir James always carried an enormous weapon with a curved blade about three inches wide. He was an extremely powerful man and a great wrestler.

[3] *A History of the British Army*, by the Hon. J. W. Fortescue, Vol. XIII, p. 444.

much baggage, over an unprepared track into a land peopled by treacherous enemies, was itself at fault.

An expedition of some importance was that which Major-General J. W. McQueen, with Colonel (afterwards Major-General) B. Lovett, R.E., as his Commanding Royal Engineer, led against the turbulent Hassanzais, Akazais and other tribes in the region of the Black Mountain in Hazara during 1888. It was launched at the beginning of September and was finished by the middle of November. Thirteen Royal Engineer officers took part in it under Colonel Lovett. These were Captains S. Grant, P. T. Buston, R. A. Wahab (Survey), A. H. Mason (Intelligence), H. E. S. Abbott and H. F. Chesney, and six subalterns including J. R. L. Macdonald.[1] Yet although General McQueen had this strong cadre of Engineers, he was given only one company of Sappers and Miners—the 3rd Company from Roorkee—and a Telegraph Section, an allowance which was utterly inadequate for the task. When the Black Mountain ridge had been occupied and the Hassanzais and Akazais subdued, a column was sent northwards over the Ghoraper Pass, south of Pokal, into the Allai country, a most difficult journey owing to the steep and broken nature of the track. The last 500 feet to the summit was impracticable even for mules, and after the 3rd Company, assisted by Pioneers and coolies, had worked all day to improve it, the baggage took 12 hours to ascend the last mile on November 2nd, while 14 mules were lost by falling over the precipice. As Rudyard Kipling writes in his poem, *Sappers*—

"We blast out the rock an' we shovel the mud,
We make 'em good roads an'—they roll down the *khud*."

The work of the Engineers and Sappers was chiefly roadmaking, but they accomplished wonders in that tedious job, for they completed 222 miles of track, suitable for pack transport, in less than three months with the help of Pioneers and coolies. The Surveyors under Wahab were not idle; they mapped 177 square miles of unknown country.[2] Thus it will be seen that the Engineering Department helped materially towards the success of the expedition.

We come now to the second phase of Frontier history, which opens about the year 1890. From that time the tribesman relied more on his rifle than his sword. He developed a new technique, based on an intimate knowledge of British methods of mountain warfare. Always formidable, he became much more so. "The world," wrote Winston Churchill in 1898,[3] "is presented with that grim spectacle 'the strength of civilization without its mercy.' At a thousand yards the traveller falls wounded by the well-aimed bullet of a breech-loading rifle. His assailant, approaching, hacks him to death. Here

---

[1] Afterwards Major-General Sir J. R. L. Macdonald, K.C.I.E., C.B., who led the troops in Tibet in 1904.
[2] *Campaigns on the North-West Frontier*, by H. L. Nevill, p. 104.
[3] *The Story of the Malakand Field Force*, by Winston L. Churchill, Lieutenant, the 4th Q.O. Hussars, p. 4.

the weapons of the nineteenth century are in the hands of savages of the stone age. The tribesmen of the Afghan border afford the spectacle of a people who fight without passion and kill one another without loss of temper. Their system of ethics regards treachery and violence as virtues rather than vices. They make a sudden attack on some frontier post. They are repulsed. From their point of view the incident is closed. What puzzles them is that ' the Sirkar '[1] should regard so small an affair in a serious light." But after 1890 the affairs were often by no means small ; and a climax was reached in 1897 when the whole frontier leapt up in a blaze. The period between 1890 and 1898 is the most interesting in the history of the frontier wars, and during those eight years the Engineers and Sappers of India, reorganized and rejuvenated, took a prominent part in almost every campaign.

The 1st Company, Bombay Sappers and Miners, under Lieutenant (afterwards Major-General Sir William) Liddell, R.E., with Lieutenants E. H. De V. Atkinson, R.E.,[2] and R. E. Greer, R.E., was on service during 1890 in the Zhob Valley, that mountainous portion of Baluchistan between Quetta and the Gomal Valley in which Sir Robert Sandeman, the Chief Commissioner of Baluchistan, had established a Political Officer at Fort Sandeman on the right bank of the Zhob River. There had been trouble in previous years in the Zhob Valley, and the Sherani inhabitants had shown hostility to our people who wished to survey the Gomal route to Afghanistan. At last the Kidarzai section of the tribe became so defiant that a brigade under Major-General Sir George White, V.C., was sent against them from Fort Sandeman in October, 1890, and subdued them without difficulty. Major J. F. Garwood, R.E., accompanied the force as Field Engineer, and Captain A. H. Mason, R.E., as an Intelligence officer. Liddell and his Sappers made the usual roads and bridges. The results of the expedition were more political than military, but its success gave Lieut.-Colonel (afterwards Colonel Sir Thomas) Holdich, R.E., the eminent Survey officer with the force, great opportunities to map the Sherani country, of which he took full advantage.

Within three years of the end of the Black Mountain expedition of 1888 it became necessary to send another to that region because the tribesmen had hindered the construction of roads leading up to the ridge and were generally hostile in their attitude ; so a complete division, called the Hazara Field Force, under Major-General W. K.

---

[1] Government.
[2] Now Lieut.-General Sir Edwin Atkinson, K.C.B., K.B.E., C.M.G., C.I.E., Colonel-Commandant, R.E., an officer with a very distinguished military record in France during the Great War and in Mesopotamia and India after it. Having held the civil post of Principal of the Thomason Engineering College at Roorkee from 1902 to 1915, he went from it to France to rise to be Chief Engineer of the 4th Army in 1918. After being Chief Engineer and commanding a division in Mesopotamia in 1920 he returned as Engineer-in-Chief to India, and later became Master-General of Supply.

Elles, was concentrated at Darband and Oghi in March, 1891, for an advance up the Indus Valley against the Hassanzais and Akazais, and by the middle of June it had completed its task and brought the enemy to reason. The 4th Company of Bengal Sappers and Miners under Captain F. J. Aylmer, R.E.,[1] was the only Field Company with the force, but there were also a Pontoon Section (" A " Company) under Captain P. T. Buston, R.E., and a small Telegraph detachment of Madras Sappers under Lieutenant G. D. Close, R.E.[2] Lieut.-Colonel W. L. Greenstreet, R.E., was the Commanding Royal Engineer, with Major H. E. S. Abbott, R.E., and Captain (afterwards Major-General Sir Francis) Bond, R.E., as his Field Engineers. Other R.E. Captains with the Hazara Force were R. A. Wahab (Survey), A. H. Mason and A. E. Sandbach, and there were six subalterns besides Close, including T. Fraser[3] and H. R. Stockley. The only fault to find with an excellent Engineering Department is that it had only one company of Sappers and Miners. A great deal of road-making was done by the Sappers and Pioneers which calls for no special remark, except that its execution was much more rapid than before because proper pack saddles had at last been provided for the equipment mules so that constant stoppages to readjust loads were no longer necessary. The most interesting part of the engineering work, however, was the bridging of the Indus at Kotkai and a flying bridge constructed at Bakrai. The Bridging Train consisted of large country boats collected at Attock and towed up to Darband by crews of sturdy Attock boatmen. The rapid construction of the Kotkai Bridge reflected great credit on Captain P. T. Buston, R.E., who was in charge of the operation.[4]

The tribes of the Black Mountain were not alone in giving trouble during 1891. There was fighting in the far north in Hunza and Nagar and also in the Miranzai country lying west of Kohat. The Orakzai clans of the latter region had been hostile and defiant since the beginning of the Afghan War in 1878, and their raids across the border grew so frequent at last that a force under Brigadier-General Sir W. S. A. Lockhart was concentrated in January, 1891, in the Khanki

[1] Now Lieut.-General Sir Fenton Aylmer, V.C., K.C.B., who in 1916 commanded the force in Mesopotamia which attempted to relieve the besieged garrison of Kut-el-Amara. He served in the 3rd Burma War and many frontier campaigns, and held many responsible posts and commands in India. He appears later in this chapter.

[2] Five brothers Close obtained commissions in the Royal Engineers between 1884 and 1891. Charles (1884), Geoffrey (1885), Lewis (1888), Francis (1889) and Arthur (1891)—a remarkable record.

[3] Sandbach and Fraser rose to be Major-Generals.

[4] In a letter to the author, dated August 18th, 1932, Brigadier-General P. T. Buston, C.B., C.M.G., D.S.O., writes : " At Attock I engaged what I considered sufficient boats, and also boatmen to handle them, and I got gangs of men from villages who towed the boats up. The river at that time was low, and the only difficulty was the rapids in which we lost a certain number of boats, but we arrived (at Kotkai) with sufficient to make a bridge. We did this, and the force crossed and went up the river on the other bank. We then towed two spare boats some miles up, and made a flying bridge with them (at Bakrai) which enabled us to operate on both banks of the Indus in the enemy's country."

Valley, north of the Samana Ridge, to bring them to order. The 5th Company, Bengal Sappers and Miners, under Captain H. S. King, R.E., formed part of it. There was little fighting, and as the Orakzais soon agreed to the construction of three fortified posts on the Samana Ridge, with connecting roads and others leading southwards into the Miranzai Valley, this work was put in hand. But although victory was gained easily in this first Miranzai expedition, the Engineers and Sappers had a busy time. Major (now Lieut.-General Sir William) Shone, R.E., was the Commanding Royal Engineer, with Captain R. S. Maclagan, R.E., as a Field Engineer and Lieutenant (now Major-General) S. H. Powell and Lieutenant W. S. Nathan, R.E., as Assistant Field Engineers. Captain R. A. Wahab, R.E., was the Survey Officer, and Captain A. H. Mason, R.E., was the D.A.Q.M.G. for Intelligence. The Royal Engineer subalterns under King with the 5th Company were A. G. Hunter-Weston (now Lieut.-General Sir Aylmer Hunter-Weston, K.C.B., D.S.O.), G. A. Travers and W. M. Coldstream.

The most important part of the Sapper work was blowing up village towers, and as the conditions were typical of so many frontier expeditions they may be described. The towers were square, generally about 15 feet by 15 feet at the base, and up to 30 feet in height. They were built of solid dry stone, roughly dressed, and at every three feet in height there was a layer of very tough olive-wood poles extending completely through the structure. Above the solid base was a room with walls of sun-dried brick, loopholed all round, the loopholes being made to command the ground to within three feet of the base of the tower.[1] The only entrance was by a tiny door, two feet square, reached by a ladder. The roof had projecting eaves and a low parapet, and a dozen men could fire from it. The villages themselves were built of stones set in mud, and were each a collection of houses around a central courtyard. A blank wall, forming the backs of the houses, enclosed the village, and one or more towers commanded it. "The smells, the filth and the fleas," writes Powell,[2] "were equal to the best traditions of Pathan habitations." The method of destroying a village tower was to mine into the middle of one side till the centre of the base was reached. A well-tamped charge of 15 lb. of dynamite or 50 lb. of gunpowder was then sufficient to bring the whole structure down. Seventy towers were destroyed in this way during the two Miranzai expeditions of 1891, and so expert did the Sappers become that the destruction of a tower was once completed in ten minutes. They preferred dynamite to guncotton or powder, although in the first expedition, when 20 degrees of frost were common, the dynamite remained frozen day and night, while in the second expedition it was reduced by the heat to a sticky

---

[1] In technical language they were "machicolated."
[2] "The Miranzai Expeditions," by Lieutenant S. H. Powell, R.E., appearing in *The R.E. Journal*, Vol. 21, 1891, p. 228.

and sweating mass. In either condition it was dangerous; yet it was used without mishap, and for rapidity of work, portability and power proved to be the best explosive available.

While on the subject of demolitions a story may be told of the Isazai Expedition of October, 1892, under Major-General Sir William Lockhart.[1] Sir Fenton Aylmer, V.C., relates that at a village called Baiyo there were two high towers, and Captain W. A. Cairnes, R.E., was ordered to blow up one of them. This he did most efficiently, in the orthodox manner, with a small charge of gunpowder. There was a gentle " poof " and the tower subsided. But the General was annoyed. " That is no good," he burst out. " The tribesmen are watching for miles around." Then, turning to Captain Aylmer he ordered him to blow up the other tower properly. " I took the hint," writes Sir Fenton,[2] " and used a whole box of guncotton. A perfectly gorgeous explosion followed, and I am glad to say that none of the onlookers were killed though there were some narrow escapes. Sir William was delighted." So even fireworks may have their uses in war.

But to return to the Miranzai Expeditions. A second expedition became necessary because the Orakzais rose on April 4th, 1891, regained possession of the Samana Ridge and attacked a British camp. Twelve days later a force under Sir William Lockhart lay at the foot of the ridge, ready to advance at daybreak. Most of the Royal Engineers of the first expedition were there, with several new arrivals.[3] On the morning of the 17th two columns attacked and occupied the eastern end of the ridge, and then fought their way along it. Within another three days they had defeated the enemy heavily, and had occupied the village of Gulistan on the ridge and overrun the Chagru Valley beyond it. The operations were ended by June 4th and the force was broken up, the Sappers and some of the Engineers remaining on the ridge to complete the interrupted work of roadmaking.

We come now to the Hunza-Nagar Expedition of 1891, a campaign waged almost on the roof of the world, and justly spoken of as " a war of small parties, almost of individuals."[4] The British force was so small that success depended more upon the daring and resource shown by every soldier than in any other expedition on the North-West Frontier. The enemy were brave, and showed considerable skill in defence. They fought in a land of glaciers, forbidding precipices and raging torrents. The season was winter. In every way

---

[1] This was a small expedition against the Hassanzais, Madda Khels and Chagarzais of the Black Mountain region. The Bengal Sappers and Miners were represented in it by the 4th and 6th Companies and a Pontoon Section.
[2] Notes by Lieut.-General Sir Fenton Aylmer, V.C., K.C.B., sent to the author in June, 1932.
[3] Captain R. J. H. L. Mackenzie, and Lieutenants E. D. Haggitt, E. H. Bland, A. J. H. Swiney, C. de W. Crookshank, L. H. Close and E. C. Ogilvie.
[4] *Campaigns on the North-West Frontier*, by H. L. Nevill, p. 146.

the difficulties which confronted our troops were exceptional, but they were overcome by exceptional fortitude and heroism.

The theatre of war was the upper portion of the basin of the Hunza River which flows into the Gilgit River,[1] some two miles below Gilgit Fort. It lies close beneath the mighty peaks of the Hindu Khush, and holds the two small states of Hunza and Nagar whose rulers bore the curious title of "Thum." Sometimes the Thums were up, sometimes down; but generally up, for their truculence was matched only by their ignorance. E. F. Knight states[2] that it was the custom at the Hunza Court for a Wazir to ask, in the presence of the Thum, "Who is the greatest King of the East?"; to which the correct reply was, "Surely the Thum of Hunza, unless perhaps it be the Khan of China."[3] Nominally the Hunza and Nagar States were tributary to Kashmir, but actually their remoteness earned their virtual independence. To keep up the farce, however, they paid an annual tribute to their parent state, that of Hunza being 20 ounces of gold-dust, two horses and two hounds, and that of Nagar some gold-dust and two baskets of apricots!

There were great natural obstacles to an advance into this country. At its northernmost point, the Indus, after a course of some 800 miles in which it is fed by the mighty glaciers of the Karakoram Range, dashes through a stupendous gorge above the little valley of Haramosh and then skirts a barren plain in which lies the village of Bunji above the confluence of the Astor River. The latter skirts the huge mass of Nanga Parbat (26,620 feet) and runs in a deep gorge as far up as Astor itself. A moderate-sized stream in winter, the Astor River becomes a raging torrent in summer, and the only crossing in 1891 was by a rickety cantilever bridge of 100 feet span[4] at Ramghat, two miles from the Indus. From this bridge the old track ascended the mountain steeply for over 5,000 feet by a dangerous zigzag to the top of the Hattu Pir which lies on the route from Srinagar to Gilgit. The Gilgit River is a formidable obstacle at all times, being only passable in winter close above Gilgit Fort. The Hunza River, fed by many large glaciers, is a raging torrent in summer and unfordable even in winter as far up as Hunza. The track up it was exceptionally bad in 1891. Owing to precipitous cliffs it had to ascend by nerve-racking zigzags to great heights in certain places, the path being sometimes carried on thin poles jutting out from the face of the cliff. The Gilgit district was practically cut off from India for more than six months of the year because of the height of the Burzil[5] and other passes on the road. High up on the Hunza River was the town of

---

[1] A tributary of the Indus.
[2] *Where Three Empires Meet*, by E. F. Knight, p. 331.
[3] Meaning the Emperor of China. The prestige of China stood high in Hunza. The power of Russia was feared to some extent, but that of England was not held to be of much account.
[4] Known as the *Shaitan Nara* or "Devil's Bridge."
[5] The Burzil Pass (13,900 feet) lies between Astor and the Kashmir Valley.

Hunza, and near it, on a tributary, lay Nagar. Below them were the strong forts of Pissan, Maiun, Thol, Nilt and Chalt, the last a Kashmir Post and about half-way between Hunza and Gilgit. Such was the country which the British were called upon to traverse in 1891.

A small guard of infantry had been established already at Gilgit, where there was a British Agency, and in September the Government decided to place a garrison at Chalt, and to improve the road from Gilgit to that place. The garrison at Gilgit was strengthened, and a force under Lieut.-Colonel A. G. A. Durand then moved up to Chalt where, at the end of November, an insolent but amusing reply was received to the British ultimatum which had been sent to the Thums of Hunza and Nagar. The Thum of Hunza asked why the British had strayed into his country " like camels without nose-rings." " We will cut off your head, Colonel Durand," he wrote, " and then report you to the Indian Government. . . . The fortress of Chalt is more precious to us than the strings of our wives' pyjamas." But the threat, backed even by such an appeal, could not move Durand.

Less than 1,200 men were available for an advance from Chalt, and of these one-half were Kashmir State troops. The only regulars were 200 men of the 5th Gurkha Rifles, a small detachment of the 20th Punjab Infantry with a Gatling gun, some 80 men of No. 4 (Hazara) Mountain Battery with two 7-pounder muzzle-loading guns, a few signallers, and six men of the 4th Company, Bengal Sappers and Miners, under Captain F. J. Aylmer, R.E.[1] There was a company of Kashmir Sappers at Gilgit, but the men were of little value and were not sent forward to Chalt. Aylmer had set out from Rawalpindi on September 19th with 12 Sappers and some equipment, including explosives and a long wire rope and traveller for a flying bridge[2] at Bunji. He accompanied Durand and other officers over the difficult Burzil Pass, constructed a new bridge at Ramghat, and arrived in Bunji where he completed a flying bridge of 500 feet span in about ten days. None of the inhabitants would believe that a flying bridge could actually transport people across a river, but when a few had tried it they clamoured for another trip. At Gilgit, Aylmer found that a bridge was required at once to span the deep and rapid river, so, as skilled labour and materials were scarce, he decided to make one with a number of rough stone piers. His workmen were the soldiers of one of the Kashmir regiments, and his method of construction was as follows. From a shore pier a cantilever platform was pushed forward on which two strong men stood as far out as possible. They were kept supplied with boulders which they hurled forward into the torrent as far as they could, thus gradually forming a second pier.

[1] *Frontier and Overseas Expeditions from India*, Vol. I, p. 16.
[2] A ferry-boat or raft which is moved across a river by the combined forces of the stream and the resistance of a cable leading from the boat to a " traveller " which runs along a wire rope stretched across the river.

When this pier showed above water-level, a temporary way was made to it and it was built up readily to the proper height and the bay completed. The cantilever platform was then transferred to the new pier, and the work proceeded. By these means the river was spanned successfully in five days. Aylmer then went on with some of his Sappers to Chalt, improving the track as he passed along it, and on arrival bridged the Hunza River above Chalt. A gang of 200 wild Pathan road-coolies, who had been working on the road under Mr. Charles Spedding,[1] joined the force at Chalt as an "Engineer Corps."

On December 1st Colonel Durand moved from Chalt, and was in front of Nilt on the following day. The fort was perched on the top of a conglomerate cliff 800 feet above the Hunza River. It lay on a narrow strip of ground, covered with terraced fields, between the cliff and the mountain behind it, and in the angle formed by the junction of the Nilt Torrent from the Rakaposhi Glacier with the Hunza River. This torrent ran in a deep cleft with precipitous sides. A water-channel from the torrent passed between the fort and the mountain overlooking it; and just in front of the fort, on the side of the British approach, an overflow from the channel had formed a deep chasm impassable except near its top. The fort was accessible, therefore, only on the side facing the mountain, and it could not be seen properly until the attackers were close to it. Its walls, of large stones cemented with mud and strengthened by longitudinal timbers, were at least 14 feet high[2] and about eight feet thick. Towers at the angles, and in the faces, afforded flanking fire. The main gateway, in the corner nearest to the top of the overflow chasm, was flanked by a loopholed bastion at a few yards' distance, and was screened by a walled courtyard swept by the fire from the bastion. Outside the courtyard wall, abattis had been formed between the wall and the overflow chasm or cut. The interior of the fort was screened from the mountain above by a high parados wall. Nilt Fort was regarded locally as impregnable, and so it was until Aylmer showed the way in. The story is best told in his own words.[3]

"The plan was that, after a preliminary artillery bombardment, the fort should be rushed by the Gurkhas, the main gate being blown up with guncotton by the Sappers, and that this movement should be assisted by a detachment who were to take position on the mountain above the fort and fire down on it. Directly the explosion at the main gate was heard, the main body was to advance,[4] descend to the Nilt Torrent and storm the *sangars* above the right bank cliff, it

---

[1] A contractor engaged in making a road from Kashmir to Gilgit.
[2] Lieut.-General Sir Fenton Aylmer, V.C., K.C.B., states that the height was about 20 feet.
[3] The account which follows was given to the author by Lieut.-General Sir Fenton Aylmer, V.C., K.C.B.
[4] Across the terraced fields above the cliff and alongside the water channel.

being hoped that the defenders would be caught on the run.[1] Three of the six Sappers carried a charge of guncotton (12 lb.) with fuse, detonators, etc., and three had large axes.

"The two guns advanced with the storming party[2] to within two hundred and fifty yards of the fort and opened fire. The garrison gave us a fairly warm reception, and there was loud cheering and beating of drums. Our shells made practically no impression on the walls, so, as there was no good in waiting, the order for the assault was given. Fortunately the enemy's fire grew very wild. It was a bit uphill over the terraced fields, and I was much out of breath when I was unexpectedly pulled up by the deep overflow cut in front of the fort. Fortunately I had gone rather to the right, and by moving more in that direction I was able to let myself down into the cut where it was only twelve feet deep. Here I was at once joined by Lieutenant Boisragon[3] with ten or twelve of his Gurkhas and two of my Sappers, Abdulla Khan and Hazara Singh. After a short pause we made our way up the cut, leaving the abattis on our left, till we discovered the gate into the outer courtyard. This was attacked by Abdulla with his axe and by three Gurkhas with their *kukris*. After five minutes it had been beaten down, though one Gurkha was shot dead and another wounded.

"We then made a rush for the main gate.[4] While the Gurkhas fired at the loopholes of the flanking bastion, Hazara Singh, who providentially had a guncotton load, assisted me to lay a charge at the foot of the gate. The fuse would not light, and it had to be re-cut. The explosion was most satisfactory as the gate was entirely blown in and the men inside were killed, including the gallant commander of the fort. Just after the explosion, Lieutenant Badcock of the Gurkhas[5] arrived with two or three more of his men. We agreed that we were too weak to attempt to enter the fort, and that we must wait for more Gurkhas or the Reserve to arrive, but we waited in vain. Recognizing our precarious position, Boisragon then most gallantly volunteered to go back, with a bugler, to bring up reinforcements, and so he departed.

"The enemy began to heave big stones over the top of the wall onto our heads. It was evident that we must get under cover, and the only cover was inside the gate. Four or five of the tribesmen, with levelled guns, were posted at the end of a covered passage which led from the gate into the interior, and it was certain death for the first two or three who might try to lead our little party inside. One

---

[1] It was hoped that they would evacuate the fort, cross the Nilt Torrent beyond it, and take refuge in their outlying *sangars*.
[2] Two companies of Gurkhas under Lieutenant G. H. Boisragon, and the Sapper detachment under Captain F. J. Aylmer, R.E.
[3] Afterwards Colonel G. H. Boisragon, V.C., who died at Biarritz on July 14th, 1931.
[4] Inside the courtyard.
[5] Serving under Boisragon.

Gurkha, exposing himself, was immediately shot dead; but, by putting my revolver round the corner of the gateway and emptying it twice in the direction of the defenders, I succeeded in killing or wounding several, and, seeing the way clear, we rushed inside. We remained for a long time in the covered passage defending ourselves as best we could. Luckily the enemy were demoralized by the explosion, and did not realize how weak our party was. Having been wounded several times, I have not a very clear recollection of what happened, but Abdulla pulled me out of the gate to the cut from the water channel. Badcock with his little party continued fighting gallantly inside the gate, though he was severely wounded. Shortly after this the main body and the rest of the 5th Gurkhas arrived, and the fort was taken. The delay was due to Colonel Durand having been badly wounded, and the second-in-command not appreciating the situation. Apparently the rest of the 5th Gurkhas had gone too far to the left and had been held up by the overflow cut in front of the fort."

This is the story of one of the most gallant deeds ever performed on or beyond the Frontier. The capture of Nilt was due almost entirely to Aylmer's personal bravery and that of Boisragon, Badcock and a few of their men. Aylmer and Boisragon were awarded the Victoria Cross, and Badcock the Distinguished Service Order.[1] Sappers Abdulla Khan and Hazara Singh of the 4th Company, Bengal Sappers and Miners, and several of the Gurkhas, received the Indian Order of Merit. Both Hazara Singh and Abdulla Khan became Indian officers in due course. "Abdulla," writes Sir Fenton Aylmer, V.C., "was the most gallant fellow I ever met. Within a period of eleven years the 4th Company, Bengal Sappers, got three Victoria Crosses[2] and some eight Orders of Merit." This is surely a record for any company before the Great War.

After the fall of Nilt the enemy offered a stubborn resistance which delayed the advance for some time. For 18 days the forces remained facing each other, and the operations developed almost into siege warfare. It is seldom indeed that our soldiers are called upon to attack a position which can rest its flanks on glaciers and oppose a steep slope, covered with ice, to any advance. Yet these were the conditions under which the Hunza-Nagar Force took the fortress of Thol on December 20th, 1891, after Lieutenant T. Manners-Smith, with 50 men, had scaled a cliff 1,500 feet high and rushed the enemy's topmost *sangars* with the bayonet.[3] Maiun soon fell, Pissan was found to be empty, and on the 22nd the troops marched into Hunza and Nagar. The little war was over.

[1] Though he was recommended by Aylmer for the V.C.
[2] Captain F. J. Aylmer, R.E., for his exploits at Nilt on December 2nd, 1891, and Lieutenants T. C. Watson and J. M. C. Colvin, R.E., for their gallantry at Bilot on September 16th, 1897, as will be related.
[3] Manners-Smith (a Political officer) received the V.C. for this exploit.

A few more extracts from Sir Fenton's notes will show the nature of the engineering work which followed the defeat of the Thums. " It was two months," he writes, " before I was fit for active work, but I was constantly trying to find a solution of the problem of maintaining communications when the winter bridges were washed away. No materials could be obtained from India as all the passes were closed, but I made a thorough search at Gilgit and discovered some useful things including a few bundles of telegraph wire and a case labelled ' Old Brandy.' This was a glorious surprise. We gave a dinner party. Glasses were charged and a toast proposed, but alas ! the ' Old Brandy ' turned out to be *furniture polish*. The telegraph wire led to better results. I discovered a large amount at Bunji and had to experiment to find the best way to use the wire for constructing suspension bridge cables. At first I did not venture to have a span of more than 200 feet, but I was able to make a suspension bridge at Gilgit. I had specially selected Naik Kala Singh of the 4th Company to go with me to Gilgit. Without exception he was the ablest and most ingenious man in the Corps. Once I had chosen the site, made the calculations and started the work, I could leave him to finish any suspension bridge I had to make." Captain Aylmer, V.C., and his men constructed many other bridges. Among these may be mentioned a suspension bridge at Chalt, another half-way to Hunza from Chalt, and finally a great suspension bridge of 340 feet span across the Indus at Bunji. While this was in progress, Aylmer's health broke down, but he was able to resume work before he left Gilgit to take part in the Isazai Expedition, when he was succeeded by Lieutenant A. E. Sandbach, R.E. At this time, Captain J. E. Capper, R.E.,[1] was busily constructing permanent bridges on the Kashmir–Gilgit road. The natural obstacles encountered in and after the little Hunza-Nagar Expedition were so formidable that the Engineers had unique opportunities to show their ability, and for this reason more space has been devoted to this small campaign than to other larger ones. The exploits of individuals are often more interesting and instructive than the movements of great masses.

Two companies of Sappers and Miners were on field service in Waziristan[2] in 1894. Sir Mortimer Durand had begun to demarcate the " Durand Line " between India and Afghanistan, and before dawn on November 3rd the Mahsuds under the Mulla Powinda tried to rush the camp of the British Escort at Wana, ten miles from the border. The 2nd Company, Bengal Sappers and Miners, was there, and helped to repulse this treacherous assault. A strong force was mobilized immediately, and set out on December 18th, under Lieut.-General Sir W. S. Lockhart, to subdue the tribe. It marched

[1] Now Major-General Sir John Capper, K.C.B., K.C.V.O., Colonel-Commandant, Royal Tank Corps.
[2] The mountainous country of the Darwesh Khel and Mahsud Waziris, south-west of Bannu. The capital is Kaniguram.

in three columns, one from Wana on Kaniguram, another from Jandola on Makin, and a third from Bannu on Razmak. During the next fortnight the Mahsud valleys were overrun, and when the columns concentrated at Jandola on January 9th, 1895, all was over. The 5th Company, Bengal Sappers and Miners, shared with the 2nd Company the engineering work of this punitive expedition, consisting of roadmaking, demolitions and building defensible posts. A number of Royal Engineers took part in the operations. Lieut.-Colonel A. H. Mason was the Intelligence Officer, and Major R. A. Wahab the Survey Officer; and Captains R. S. Maclagan, E. W. Walton and A. G. Hunter-Weston and ten Lieutenants[1] were with the Sapper companies or in charge of roadmaking or other work. But the Mahsuds soon recovered from their punishment, for they joined in the general conflagration of 1897, when an expedition was sent against them in the Tochi Valley.

The scene now shifts to mountainous Chitral where, after a reverse on March 3rd, 1895, Surgeon-Major G. S. Robertson, Captains C. P. Campbell and C. V. F. Townshend[2] and a few other officers, with less than 400 men, were besieged in Chitral Fort, nearly 100 miles north of the Malakand Pass. The Government of India at once mobilized a Chitral Relief Force of 15,000 men under Major-General Sir R. C. Low, and included in it the 1st, 4th and 6th Companies of Bengal Sappers and Miners. The 6th Company, Madras Sappers and Miners, was also directed to join the force, but it arrived at Chakdarra after the military operations had finished. The Chief-of-Staff was Brigadier-General Bindon Blood, and the other Royal Engineer officers who served in the campaign were Lieut.-Colonel W. T. Shone (C.R.E.), Brevet Lieut.-Colonel H. P. Leach, Majors G. H. W. O'Sullivan, C. C. Ellis, M. C. Barton and H. E. S. Abbott, Brevet-Major F. J. Aylmer, V.C., Captains J. A. Tanner, G. Williams, B. B. Russell, G. M. Heath,[3] and W. G. R. Cordue, and 25 subalterns.[4] The bad old days were gone. Sir Robert Low had a cadre of 42 *Engineers for a force of only one strong division.* " When I found

[1] G. A. Travers, P. J. F. Macaulay (killed at Wana on November 3rd, 1894), C. L. Robertson, H. H. Austin, H. R. Stockley, L. H. Close, W. E. R. Dickson, W. S. Traill, R. S. Muter and S. H. Sheppard (now Major-General S. H. Sheppard, C.B., C.M.G., D.S.O., who became Chief-of-Staff in East Africa during the Great War). Lieutenant G. A. Travers commanded the 5th Company, and Captain A. G. Hunter-Weston the 2nd Company.

[2] Afterwards Major-General Sir Charles Townshend, K.C.B., D.S.O., the defender of Kut in the Great War.

[3] Afterwards Lieut.-General Sir Gerard Heath, K.C.M.G., C.B., D.S.O., who became Engineer-in-Chief of the British forces in France in the Great War.

[4] Lieutenants A. J. H. Swiney, G. M. Duff, J. S. Fowler (of whom more anon), A. Walpole, C. Ainslie, G. C. Kemp, E. C. Ogilvie, F. R. F. Boileau, R. F. G. Bond, H. F. Thuillier (now Major-General Sir Henry Thuillier, K.C.B., C.M.G.), A. R. Winsloe, F. N. Rees, P. G. Grant (now Major-General Sir Philip Grant, K.C.B., C.M.G.), H. W. Weekes, W. G. Hibbert, J. M. C. Colvin (later V.C.,) G. Lubbock, L. W. S. Oldham, S. D'A. Crookshank (now Major-General Sir Sydney Crookshank, K.C.M.G., C.B., C.I.E., D.S.O., M.V.O.), E. G. Farquharson, C. D. Halliday, R. H. Macdonald, H. A. L. Hepper, G. H. Boileau and H. F. E. Freeland (now Major-General Sir Henry Freeland, K.C.I.E., C.B., D.S.O., M.V.O.).

myself at the head of the staff in the Chitral Expedition," writes Sir Bindon Blood,[1] " I had under me an Engineer organization which was a marvel of efficiency. The expedition convinced everyone that Sappers and Miners are essential in every Field Force on the North-West Frontier." The reorganization of 1885 had had time to produce its full effect. Like Abyssinia, Chitral was a Sappers' war.

When Sir Robert Low received his orders, Lieut.-Colonel J. G. Kelly, with his regiment (32nd Pioneers), was making roads near Gilgit, and was directed also to attempt to relieve Chitral. In this he was so successful that he forestalled Sir Robert; but it may be well to describe briefly the advance of the main body before turning to the far north. Moving towards the Malakand Pass[2] on April 2nd, 1895, Sir Robert Low found his progress barred by the tribes of Swat and Bajaur who, it had been hoped, would remain neutral. Twelve thousand tribesmen held the pass, but it was carried on the 3rd after five hours' fighting. The Sappers and Miners worked on the track close behind the advancing infantry, and while doing so discovered an old " Buddhist " road which they converted rapidly into a passable route for mule traffic.[3] On the following day the division entered the Swat Valley and defeated the enemy at Khar. Then came the fording of the Swat River on the 7th, and the capture of Chakdarra. The history of the maintenance, for many months, of the trestle bridge which the Sappers and Miners built across the river at this spot is a record of perseverance and resource in the face of great difficulties.[4]

Soon after Sir Robert Low had carried the Malakand Pass, the improvement of the Bhuddist road was taken in hand by Major H. E. S. Abbott, R.E., with the 34th Sikh Pioneers and some coolies, and in five days it was converted into a good camel road with a gradient of 1 in 12 and a width of about eight feet. Subsequently Abbott was ordered to construct a cart road over the Pass, and, with the assistance of Lieutenants A. J. H. Swiney, S. D'A. Crookshank and G. H. Boileau, R.E., he did so by July 15th. This route was known as the " Graded Road," or " Abbott Road," and ran for a distance of nine miles from Dargai to Khar on a ruling gradient of 1 in 20 with a width of ten feet. It is the same road which, widened and improved, carries all the traffic over the Malakand Pass to-day. Practically the whole work consisted of heavy rock blasting with

[1] Letter from General Sir Bindon Blood, G.C.B., G.C.V.O., to the author, dated February 17th, 1932.
[2] Forty miles north of Nowshera.
[3] When the enemy's position had been captured, the Sappers converted several old " Buddhist " buildings into good defensible posts.
[4] It was supplemented in May, 1895, by a bridge of 12 pontoons brought up by elephants. A suspension bridge was completed by the end of June. A suspension bridge of 200 feet span was also made at Sado on the Panjkora River, and other bridges at Chutiatarn and Darora. (See *Frontier and Overseas Expeditions from India*, Vol. I, p. 547.) Major Aylmer, V.C., R.E., also constructed a suspension bridge of 290 feet span at Chitral. It was solidly built and lasted for many years.

dynamite, and its speedy completion added to the reputation which Abbott had already gained as one of the most expert road-builders on the frontier.¹

The next obstacle was the unfordable Panjkora River. Major F. J. Aylmer, V.C., R.E., with the 4th Company, Bengal Sappers and Miners, was soon trying to bridge it. There were many huge logs in the river-bed, so he took the only material at hand and made a bridge of them; but their flotation was almost nothing and the rafts were terribly unwieldy. Yet a battalion of Guides infantry succeeded in crossing the river on the night of April 12th/13th. Then a flood came down and washed the whole structure away. Nothing daunted, Aylmer set to work to make a suspension bridge of 98 feet span, of timber and telegraph wire, at a spot three miles downstream, and finished it in three days. It was a fine performance. Meanwhile Colonel Shone and his officers were accomplishing wonders in road-making.² The troops advanced, fought an action at Panjkora and another near Munda on April 17th, and with that all opposition ceased. So ends this outline of Sir Robert Low's campaign. Colonel Kelly had already relieved Chitral, and his achievement and some events in the far north call for notice because two young Royal Engineers and a few Sappers and Miners were concerned in them.

A detachment of one Indian officer and 19 " other ranks " of the Bengal Sappers and Miners under Lieutenant J. S. Fowler, R.E.,³ left Gilgit for Mastuj in February, 1895, on the road to Chitral. They joined a party of 42 men of the Kashmir Rifles under Lieutenant S. M. Edwardes at Buni beyond Mastuj, but on March 7th, at a defile beyond Reshun, found their way blocked by armed tribesmen, so they retreated under fire to Reshun and occupied and fortified a small group of houses. Here they were soon surrounded and besieged. Fowler led a successful sortie on the 10th, and on the 13th the Chitralis became suddenly friendly. Two days later, however, when Fowler and Edwardes went outside their fort to watch a native polo match,⁴ they were seized and bound, and the Chitralis, rushing the fort, killed many of the garrison and took 12 prisoners. The two British officers were dragged roughly away, and taken with the other survivors to the enemy's camp at Chitral and later to other places. They were not released till the middle of April when they joined the division under Sir Robert Low. But the little tragedy at Reshun was redeemed by the gallantry of a few men, and among these were

---

¹ For further details see the *Report on the Graded Road over the Malakand Pass*, by Major H. E. S. Abbott, R.E., dated August 8th, 1895.

² Lieutenant S. D'A. Crookshank, R.E., constructed the road up the Panjkora Valley, working with the 32nd and 34th Sikh Pioneers.

³ Now Lieut.-General Sir John Fowler, K.C.B., K.C.M.G., D.S.O., Colonel-Commandant, Royal Corps of Signals.

⁴ They had been invited to do so, and did not wish to appear suspicious by refusing to leave the fort.

Naik Kala Singh[1] and Sapper Nadir Khan, of the Bengal Sappers and Miners, who refused to surrender. When food and drink was scarce, Kala Singh had often given up his rations and water to other men; and when the fort was rushed, he killed many of the enemy and then shot himself with his last cartridge. In a defile beyond Koragh, a detachment hurrying from Mastuj to help Fowler and Edwardes was nearly overwhelmed on March 7th, and lost heavily before it regained Koragh. Another small force was besieged in Mastuj. The situation was critical until Colonel Kelly approached from Gilgit.

Kelly marched westwards from Gilgit on March 23rd with a small force which was soon joined by 40 Kashmir Sappers under Lieutenant L. W. S. Oldham, R.E.[2] His first serious obstacle was the Shandur Pass (12,230 feet) which was deep in snow. No tents were taken, and each man was limited to 15 lb. of baggage. An attempt to cross the pass on April 1st failed, but on April 3rd two companies of Pioneers with some mountain guns, and Oldham with the 40 Sappers, made a fresh start. The gun mules were soon unable to go on, so the guns, with their carriages and ammunition boxes, were unloaded from the animals and carried by the men. This was a terrible undertaking, and when camp was reached at midnight on the frozen heights, the men had to bivouac in the snow without shelter and with the poorest of camp fires. Twenty-five soldiers were incapacitated by frost-bite, and 30 by snowblindness, before the small column descended to Laspur. It was not till the 8th that the troops were fit to advance once more, and on the following day they found the enemy in position across the valley of Chokalwat. But Kelly routed the Chitralis and reached Mastuj, which had been besieged for some time; then, leaving Mastuj with reinforcements on April 13th, he attacked 1,500 of the enemy in a powerful position at a place called Nisa Gol.

" The enemy's position at Nisa Gol," writes Oldham,[3] " was extraordinarily strong. On either side of the valley rose precipitous crags to a height of many thousands of feet. The river ran close under the cliffs on the left, while on the right was a broad alluvial face cut through its centre by a nullah some 300 feet wide and with absolutely vertical sides 250 feet high. The enemy's position was in stone sangars along the further edge of this nullah, and on the mountain sides on either flank up to the snow line." Sir George Robertson takes up the tale:[4] " Noticing a long gap between the enemy's sangars and their main defences, Oldham and Beynon[5] asked leave

---

[1] Not the Naik of the same name who was with Aylmer in Gilgit.

[2] Major L. W. S. Oldham, R.E., was killed on July 26th, 1915, during the Great War.

[3] " The Defence and Relief of Chitral," by Lieutenant L. W. S. Oldham, R.E., appearing in *The R.E. Journal*, Vol. 25, 1895, p. 154.

[4] *Chitral. The Story of a Minor Siege*, by Sir G. Robertson, K.C.S.I., p. 176. (The Surgeon-Major G. S. Robertson of the siege of Chitral.)

[5] Lieutenant W. G. L. Beynon, 3rd Gurkhas (now Major-General Sir William Beynon, K.C.I.E., C.B., D.S.O.).

to hunt for a spot where the ladders and ropes, which the former had brought from Mastuj, might be utilized. The two eventually found a place, and Oldham hastened back for his Kashmir Sappers. He quickly returned and set to work. For the first forty feet the descent was comparatively easy, so that a man, by holding on with one hand to a rope made fast above, could with the other cut rough steps with a pick, but then came a vertical drop when the ladders were the only hope. The adventurous little band was all the time under a galling fire. One Sapper was soon mortally wounded, and a havildar shot through the groin. No time was to be lost. The stalwart Oldham scrambled down the rope, placed the ladder with his own hands and descended. He was followed by a dozen brave fellows, and all reached the bottom. The undaunted thirteen next attacked the opposite slope and found a goat track by which they climbed. It was a rare deed for one British officer and twelve Kashmir Sappers to cross that awful place to meet above them unknown ground and an unknown enemy; but the man who did it (an unsung hero) is a member of that famous Corps which gave Gilgit an Aylmer to blow open Nilt Gate, and a Fowler to cover himself and his comrades with glory even amidst the slaughter at Reshun." Dismayed by the sudden appearance of Oldham and his party, the enemy gave way and were soon flying in confusion. Kelly marched on and joined hands with Robertson and Townshend[1] at Chitral on April 20th. The besiegers had already dispersed.

The story of the defence of Chitral, well told by Sir George Robertson in his *Chitral—The Story of a Minor Siege*, cannot be given here. No Engineers or Sappers and Miners took part in it. During a siege lasting 46 days the enemy tried repeatedly to storm the defences and once resorted to mining which was defeated by a brilliant sortie. Captain C. F. V. Townshend, however, upheld the honour of the British flag, and but for a series of misfortunes might have repeated this performance when he commanded the ill-fated 6th Indian Division in Kut-el-Amara in 1915-16. Like so many others, a career full of promise was brought, by the irony of fate, to a disastrous end. But Kelly's march, Oldham's exploit at Nisa Gol, and Townshend's defence of Chitral, show that the word " impossible " has no place in border warfare.

The general rising of the tribes on the North-West Frontier in 1897 began by a treacherous attack on a political agent and his escort in the Tochi Valley[2] in the month of June. The trouble spread swiftly. In July the Swatis assaulted the British posts at Chakdarra and the Malakand. In August the Mohmands reached almost to Peshawar. The Afridis south of the Kabul River then took the field, and the

---

[1] Captain C. P. Campbell, of the Central India Horse, was wounded early in the defence of Chitral Fort and the command of the troops then devolved on Captain C. F. V. Townshend of the same regiment.

[2] West of Bannu.

Orakzais still farther south. Never before had the British been confronted with such a menace on their frontier. The fanatical priests of Islam proclaimed a *jihad* (holy war) and called on every true believer to join the crusade. On a gigantic scale, the situation resembled that on the British border when the Picts and Scots were trying to force the garrisons of Hadrian's wall.

The outbreak in the Tochi Valley was a very small feature in the panorama of war. The Madda Khel clan of the Darwesh Khel Wazirs assaulted a small force under Lieut.-Colonel Bunny, 1st Sikhs, at Maizar near the Afghan border on June 10th, 1897, and nearly overwhelmed it, so the Government of India despatched two brigades from Bannu and elsewhere, under Major-General Corrie Bird, to subdue them. Marching up the Tochi Valley, Bird reached Miramshah on July 9th, and his force was concentrated at Datta Khel on the 19th. He occupied Sheranni and Maizar on the following day, both places being found deserted. The 2nd Company, Bengal Sappers and Miners, which was the only Engineer unit with the force, spent the next 16 days in destroying towers and villages. There was little fighting, but much sickness, and the Madda Khels did not come to terms till November 15th, when the whole Tochi Valley had been overrun.

Service on any frontier in the early campaigns from 1854 to 1862 was recognized by the grant of the India General Service Medal with a general clasp. Special clasps were added for Ambela in 1863 and many other campaigns, and the last clasp was for " Waziristan, 1894–95." A new India Medal was inaugurated in 1895 with clasps for the defence and relief of Chitral, and, except for special clasps for " Samana " and " Tirah," all the North-West Frontier expeditions of 1897–98 were covered by one clasp to this medal. It was no longer possible to grant a clasp for almost every expedition, and similarly it is no longer possible to mention in these pages all the Royal Engineers who served in each expedition. Nearly 60,000 British and Indian troops took the field before the tribes were subdued, and the extent of the operations may be judged from the fact that 90 Royal Engineer officers received the new medal and clasp for the campaigns of 1897–98.[1] Major-General Sir Bindon Blood, K.C.B., Colonels J. W. Ottley, W. G. Nicholson, J. E. Broadbent and R. C. Hart, Lieut.-Colonels W. Peacocke, J. W. Thurburn and H. H. Hart, eight Majors, 25 Captains and no less than 49 Lieutenants of the Corps served in one or more of these campaigns. Never since the Indian Mutiny had such an array of Engineers proceeded on field service, and never since that rebellion had an Engineer in India held so important a command in the field as fell to the lot of Major-General Sir Bindon Blood when he led the expeditions into the Malakand

---

[1] *List of Officers of the Corps of Royal Engineers from 1660 to 1898*, by Captain T. W. J. Conolly, R.E., edited by Captain R. F. Edwards, R.E., pp. 40–74.

and Buner with which this story is now concerned. There was no outstanding engineering work in these operations. Their chief interest lies in the officer in command, under whom, as was natural, the Engineers and Sappers worked with particular zest in their usual roadmaking, bridging, fortification, demolition work, and surveying. Although the campaign in the Tirah was on a larger scale than those in the Malakand and Buner, there are features in Sir Bindon Blood's expeditions which differ from those of the Afridi campaign. The Swat Valley was a special centre of religious fanaticism, and this lent an added fire to the assaults of the tribesmen which only the highest discipline and training could resist. "At Malakand and Chakdarra," to quote Nevill,[1] "and in a minor degree at Nawagai, the same reckless impulse is to be seen which hurled the Mahdists against the British squares at Abu Klea, El Teb and Omdurman, for the sake of a martyr's crown." Religious madness is usually fleeting: it goes out when the bullet and sword go in. But on the Malakand and at Chakdarra it gripped the enemy for eight days. It sustained them in those elaborate night attacks which were a new feature in their tactics, and it supported them against an artillery bombardment heavier than any which they had yet encountered.

An army of Swatis threw themselves against the British defences on the Malakand Pass after dark on July 26th, 1897, and were not repulsed till dawn. On the 27th the Guides marched in from Mardan in time to join in repelling another violent night attack, which was repeated within 24 hours. The fighting was of a most desperate character, but our troops held their ground. On the night of July 30th/31st the tribesmen made their last effort, and failed. More British reinforcements arrived, followed on August 1st by Sir Bindon Blood, who then assumed the chief command. The little garrison at Chakdarra, ten miles away on the Swat River, was hard pressed and signalling for help, so a relief column was despatched on the 2nd and in a few hours had raised the siege. The garrison had repulsed every assault with great slaughter[2] and had saved the fine suspension bridge across the river. It may be said of the Malakand position that the defences did credit to the Field Engineer, Captain C. M. F. Watkins, R.E., and to Captain E. P. Johnson, R.E., and the 5th Company, Madras Sappers and Miners, who were on the Pass. The relief force which marched to Chakdarra was accompanied by half the 5th Company under Lieutenant A. R. Winsloe, R.E.,[3] who set to work at once to repair the defences.

A complete division, called the Malakand Field Force, now concentrated rapidly between Malakand and Chakdarra under Major-

---

[1] *Campaigns on the North-West Frontier*, by H. L. Nevill, p. 249.

[2] The enemy's loss before Chakdarra was estimated as 2,000 killed and many thousands wounded.

[3] Winsloe received the D.S.O. for his services during one of the night attacks by the Swatis. According to him the Madras Sappers fought with the greatest coolness and bravery, using their rifles and bayonets with marked effect.

THE MALAKAND PASS.

General Sir Bindon Blood, and was ready for action on August 7th.[1] Unfortunately the advance up the Swat Valley was delayed by bad weather, but by August 17th the division was opposite a strong position taken up by the enemy at Landakai a few miles upstream of Chakdara. Despatching three battalions and the 8th Mountain Battery to make a turning movement to the south, Sir Bindon Blood massed his remaining guns—those of the 10th Field Battery and 7th Mountain Battery—in support of his main attack. Never before had the tribesmen been under the fire of field artillery. " The principle of concentrating artillery has been admitted in Europe," wrote Winston Churchill in 1898,[2] " but Sir Bindon Blood is the first general who has applied it to mountain warfare in India. It had formerly been the custom to use the guns by twos and threes. At Landakai the Malakand Field Force had eighteen guns in action, of which twelve were in one line. The fire of this artillery drove the enemy, who were in great strength and an excellent position, from the ground. The infantry attack was accomplished with hardly any loss, and a success was obtained at the cost of a dozen lives which would have been cheap at one hundred." The Swatis soon came to terms. The 18 guns of Landakai had done their work.

The next operation was an advance westwards into Bajaur to subdue the Mamund clan of the Mohmand tribe. Leaving the 1st Brigade (Brigadier-General W. H. Meiklejohn) to guard the line of communication, Sir Bindon Blood pushed the 3rd Brigade (Brigadier-General J. H. Wodehouse) forward to Nawagai and the 2nd Brigade (Brigadier-General P. D. Jeffreys) towards the Rambat Pass, east of Nawagai. On September 14th, Sir Bindon Blood was with Wodehouse in Nawagai, and Jeffreys was in the region of the Rambat Pass from which he advanced northwards to Inayat Kila, and, working up the Mamund Valley in three small columns, attacked Shahi Tangi on the 16th and destroyed it. But in his subsequent retirement a party of Bengal Sappers and Miners, with a few men of the Buffs and four mountain guns, were caught by darkness, and Jeffreys, who was with them, decided to take shelter in the village of Bilot for the night. The Mamunds, however, forestalled him, and a bitter struggle followed for the possession of the place. This was the occasion on which two young officers of the Royal Engineers earned the Victoria Cross.

Lieutenants T. C. Watson and J. M. C. Colvin, R.E., with 43[3] " other ranks " of the 4th Company, Bengal Sappers and Miners, found themselves with a few of the Buffs in an angle outside the walls of Bilot while the enemy fired upon them from a part of the village

---

[1] The Commanding Royal Engineer was Colonel J. E. Broadbent, R.E.
[2] *The Story of the Malakand Field Force*, by Winston L. S. Churchill, p. 290.
[3] *History and Digest of Service, 1st K.G.O. Sappers and Miners*, p. 65. Some historians give the strength as 35, but the records of the Bengal Sappers show that 43 were present.

which was not in flames. To quote the official history :[1] " Lieutenant Watson at once collected a few men of the Buffs and charged several of the enemy who were firing from the north-east corner. He then pushed on and dislodged a number of men from the west side, but in so doing he was wounded in the leg. Returning to the enclosure he collected a few more men and again attacked the enemy, but was again badly wounded in the arm and hand. Thereupon Lieutenant Colvin, with some eight Sappers, worked his way into the village by a lane, and, climbing onto the roofs of some houses with a couple of men, drove the enemy away from under the walls on the outside. But they were all round him, and he was compelled to withdraw. However, he again collected a few men and climbed onto the roofs a second time though he was forced finally to retire."[2] The enemy evacuated Bilot when British reinforcements arrived at midnight. Watson, Colvin and Corporal James Smith of the Buffs, received the Victoria Cross for their gallantry,[3] and among the awards to their men was the Indian Order of Merit for Colour-Havildar Mir Khan and Naik Natha Singh of the 4th Company.

Sir Bindon Blood decided to remain at Nawagai with the 3rd Brigade under Wodehouse until he came in touch with the Mohmand Field Force under Major-General E. R. Elles. He had made every preparation against attack, and the expected assaults came on September 19th and on the following night when Wodehouse was wounded. In both actions he repulsed the enemy with severe loss.[4] " In view of the difficulty of inflicting loss on the tribesmen in their own hills," writes Sir George MacMunn,[5] " the mere fact of provoking them to attack your defensible camp must be considered a tactical triumph." On September 30th, the 4th Company, Bengal Sappers and Miners, shared in the capture by Jeffreys of the villages of Agrah and Gat, and on October 4th reinforcements arrived including the 5th Company, Madras Sappers and Miners, and the 10th Field Battery which had traversed ground where no wheeled traffic had ever been. With the destruction of a few more villages, the operations of the Malakand Field Force came to an end in the middle of October, 1897.

[1] *The Operations of the Malakand Field Force and the Buner Field Force*, 1897–98, compiled by Captain H. F. Walters, p. 56.
[2] In a letter to the author, dated July 25th, 1932, Colonel Colvin, V.C., writes : " Watson returned, hit in the thigh. He insisted on going out again, telling me to report to the General that we had only a few rounds left. While I was looking for the General, Watson reappeared, swaying about. He had been hit again, in the hand and arm, and was in great pain. I then made two abortive attempts through the village, but was brought up by high walls. Afterwards Lieut. F. A. Wynter, R.A., and I closed in our line and were eventually relieved. Wynter was always walking about and was shot through both thighs, but got all right later I am glad to say."
[3] *London Gazette*, dated May 20th, 1898.
[4] The 3rd Company, Bombay Sappers and Miners, was present in these actions in addition to the 4th Company, Bengal Sappers and Miners.
[5] *The Romance of the Indian Frontiers*, by Lieut.-General Sir George MacMunn, K.C.B., K.C.S.I., D.S.O., p. 212.

The Bunerwals alone remained defiant, and so a Buner Field Force[1] under Sir Bindon Blood was concentrated at Sanghao[2] on January 6th, 1898, with detachments at Pirsai to the east and Rustam to the south-east. It was decided that the Tanga Pass should be forced while the detachments crossed by the Pirsai Pass. The 4th Company, Bengal Sappers and Miners, and the 5th Company, Madras Sappers and Miners, were available for the engineering work, and, under the direction of Lieut.-Colonel W. Peacocke, R.E., the Commanding Royal Engineer, made the track up to the Tanga Pass fit for mule traffic in three days. The Buner Expedition went "according to plan." There was some resistance in the Tanga Pass, but little trouble afterwards. The country was soon overrun, and the Bunerwals submitted on January 17th.

Little need be said also of the Mohmand Expedition of September, 1897. The Mohmands had attacked Shabkadr Fort, 13 miles due north of Peshawar, so Major-General E. R. Elles was sent against them with two brigades and some divisional troops.[3] The 5th Company, Bengal Sappers and Miners, and later the 3rd Company of the Bombay Corps, took part in the operations, with Captain F. H. Kelly, R.E., as Field Engineer, Major G. H. W. O'Sullivan on the Staff, and Major W. J. Bythell as Survey Officer. General Elles was directed to co-operate with Sir Bindon Blood in the advance of the Malakand Field Force from Chakdarra to Nawagai, and afterwards as required. He marched up the Gandab Valley on September 14th, 1897, crossed the Karapa and Nahaki passes where the Sappers had much road-making, and met Sir Bindon Blood on the 21st to the south of Nawagai. Turning left he then proceeded to the Badmanai Pass, from which he drove the Mohmands. He destroyed Jarobi on the Afghan frontier on September 25th, and completed his circuit by returning to the Nahaki Pass. The British losses were negligible and no decisive action was fought. The Sappers burnt a number of villages,[4] and, with the submission of the tribesmen on September 29th, the Mohmand Field Force was broken up.[5]

The rising of 1897 was by no means confined to the country north of the Kabul River. In the middle of August the British authorities heard that the Afridis and Orakzais were planning simultaneous attacks, the former on the Khaibar Pass defences and the latter on the Samana Ridge and in the Kurram Valley. The Afridi onslaught in the Khaibar was launched on August 23rd against Ali Masjid and Fort Maude.[6] Both were captured and burnt to the ground. Landi

---

[1] Of two brigades, with divisional troops.
[2] Thirty miles north of Nowshera.
[3] He was joined later by the 3rd Brigade of the Malakand Field Force under Wodehouse, with the 3rd Company, Bombay Sappers and Miners.
[4] Between September 23rd and 29th, 70 towers and 20 villages were destroyed.
[5] The operations are described in detail in the official publication entitled *Operations of the Mohmand Field Force in* 1897, compiled by Captain F. A. Hoghton, 1st Bombay Infantry.
[6] A small fort situated three miles up the Khaibar Pass from its entrance at Jamrud.

Kotal held out for a time; but the Afridis took it on the 25th, and looted and abandoned it. All these forts were garrisoned only by the Khaibar Rifles.[1] The Khaibar Pass remained closed to the British until the end of December. There was trouble also in the Kurram. Some Orakzais seized the Ublan Pass, north-west of Kohat, on August 26th; while others, combining with the Afridis, threatened the British posts on the Samana Ridge and in the Kurram Valley beyond it. A small force including the 4th Company, Bombay Sappers and Miners, accordingly marched up the valley, and, arriving at Sadda[2] on September 5th, reinforced the post at that place. Other minor operations followed in the Kurram Valley, and some desperate fighting on the Samana Ridge. The enemy captured the little post of Saragarhi on September 12th and killed all the defenders. They invested Fort Gulistan, and for a time it was in grave danger; but finally they were driven from the ridge by troops advancing from Hangu, and preparations were then made to send a powerful force into the Orakzai and Afridi territory of the Tirah.

The Afridis are by far the most numerous and formidable of all the tribes on the North-West Frontier of India. In 1897, 35,000 British and Indian soldiers subdued them only after a bitter struggle. Much of the Afridi Tirah was unexplored. "It is a curious fact," says Colonel Sir Thomas Holdich, (late R.E.),[3] "that far beyond the rugged line of those frontier mountains, in the deep recesses of which dwelt those tribes that loved to call themselves 'independent,' we were, in the year 1896, better acquainted with geographical details than we were as regarded our own immediate border. Most of Afghanistan we knew by then, all of Baluchistan and much of Persia; but the comparatively narrow width of border hills which we could scrutinize with our telescopes from the windows of Peshawar houses and the stations of the Derajat was but a sketchy outline in our maps." So when Lieut.-General Sir William Lockhart set out to invade the Tirah in October, 1897, he did so at a great disadvantage. Co-ordination of movement was extremely difficult because he had few reliable maps, and one of the most important achievements of his campaign was the survey of the country which was conducted so ably by Colonel Holdich and his officers. The surveyor is the forerunner of the road-maker: the roadmaker heralds peace and prosperity.

It was decided that the advance against the Afridi and Orakzai hosts of 40,000 men should be on a single line from the south, and by October 10th, 1897, General Lockhart's Army Corps was concentrated in Kohat. With the 1st Division, under Major-General W. P. Symons, were the 3rd and 4th Companies of the Bombay Sappers and Miners and a company of Maler Kotla Imperial Service Sappers.

[1] A corps which was raised on the frontier to relieve other troops of the burden of garrison work.
[2] Half-way between Thal and Parachinar.
[3] *The Indian Borderland*, by Sir T. Holdich, p. 351.

THE TIRAH CAMPAIGN IN 1897.

The 2nd Division, under Major-General A. G. Yeatman-Biggs, included the 4th Company, Madras Sappers and Miners, and a company of Sirmur Imperial Service Sappers. The 1st and 5th Companies of the Bengal Corps were attached to the Line of Communication troops. Thus there were seven companies of Sappers and Miners in the field during the Tirah campaign, and with them, or in other employment, a large number of Royal Engineer officers. The Chief Engineer was Brevet-Colonel J. E. Broadbent, R.E., and the Commanding Royal Engineers with the two divisions were Lieut.-Colonels H. H. Hart, R.E. (1st Division) and C. B. Wilkieson, R.E. (2nd Division).

Only the barest outline of the operations can be given. Yeatman-Biggs led off on October 11th with the 2nd Division, accompanied by 43,000 transport animals. He marched by Hangu and Shinwari, and, turning northwards, carried the heights of Dargai on October 20th and dropped down into the Khanki Valley on the following day. The two divisions concentrated at Kharappa, and, advancing northwards under General Lockhart, carried the Sampagha Pass on the 28th and descended into the Mastura Valley which had never before been visited by Europeans. The transport took five days to traverse the seven miles through the pass in spite of the efforts of the Sappers and Miners and Pioneers to improve the road. Three days later the whole force, less one brigade, crossed another pass and debouched into the fertile Tirah Valley, the summer home of the Afridis, dotted with fortified villages from which the inhabitants had already fled. For eight days the surveyors under Holdich were hard at work while preparations were made for a further advance. Then came an action on November 9th fought on the Saran Sar Ridge to the north. The Waran Valley was scoured by a brigade, and three brigades advanced to Bagh and northwards to Dwatoi in the Bara Valley. The operations then extended towards the west, and at the end of November the Orakzais and Chamkannis north of Sadda had been taught their lesson. By December 6th every Afridi valley in the Tirah had been visited and laid waste.

The evacuation of the British forces began on December 7th, when Sir William Lockhart marched his two divisions eastwards by different routes converging at Barkai, 20 miles north-west of Kohat. The 1st Division had an easy passage by the Waran and Mastura Valleys; but the five days' march of the 2nd Division[1] down the Bara Valley was so difficult, and the fighting so fierce, that it has no parallel except in the disastrous retreat from Kabul in 1842. The Zakka Khel Afridis launched the most desperate attacks against the rearguard; the troops suffered severely from the cold, and the casualties were heavy. The 2nd Division reached Barkai in an exhausted condition but intact; it was joined by the 1st Division,

[1] Sir William Lockhart was with this division.

and the main operations of the Tirah Field Force came to an end. There remained only to punish the Zakka Khels of the Bazar Valley farther north and in the Khaibar Pass. This was duly accomplished by two columns, but the last of the Afridi clans did not submit until a blockade of their country had been continued till April, 1898.

The Tirah campaign was intricate and arduous. It cost the British 1,100 casualties, and the Engineers and Sappers and Miners endured great hardships in their work on the various passes. They accomplished nothing which calls for special remark, but they helped the troops and transport over formidable obstacles and destroyed dozens of villages as a just punishment for treachery.[1] With the submission of the Afridis, the last echoes of the mighty explosion on the North-West Frontier died away into silence. The British Army in India had survived an ordeal which was more severe than any since the Mutiny, a test more searching even than the Afghan War of 1878–80.

With the exception of a blockade of the Mahsud Waziris in 1901, the frontier campaigns of 1897–98 were followed by ten years of peace. No higher tribute can be paid to the policy of Lord Curzon. When that statesman became Viceroy in 1899, 10,000 troops were still quartered in Chitral, the Khaibar Pass and the Tochi Valley; but he withdrew them and replaced them by tribal levies commanded by British officers.[2] He pushed strategic railways up to Dargai, Jamrud and Thal, and limited the importation of arms and ammunition to the tribesmen. Lord Curzon showed the Pathans that Great Britain would respect their independence but would visit any outrage with condign punishment. Our relations with Afghanistan improved, and all the tribes except the Zakka Khel Afridis settled down, in what Mr. Edwin Montagu would have called a "pathetic" contentment, to enjoy the blessings of peace.[3] Only in 1908 and 1919 has that contentment been really seriously disturbed, although it was threatened in 1930.

The Zakka Khels, implacable enemies of British rule and ensconced in the isolated Bazar Valley, began to raid so persistently across the border in 1907 that the despatch of a punitive expedition against them could not be avoided. Two brigades of a division under Major-

[1] There is a tale of a Major, R.E., who nearly tamped a charge with his own body. This well-nourished officer, having placed his explosive in the centre of a tower on a solid base and lit the fuse, began to wriggle backwards through the tiny doorway. Unfortunately he stuck there, while the fuse burned merrily under his nose. His subalterns, not knowing that the fuse had been lighted, were surprised to observe his agitated legs and to listen to his muffled yells that everyone should leave him and bolt for safety. At the very last moment the human cork extracted itself, fell to the ground and rushed to cover as the tower went up.

[2] Behind the levies were small brigades of regular troops of all arms located within our frontiers. This system was economical, and it freed the regular troops to deal with any hostile action by Russia who was advancing her railway system towards the Afghan frontier on the north.

[3] Lord Curzon removed the control of the border from the Punjab and vested it in a newly-established North-West Frontier Province. This reform had a most beneficial result.

General Sir James Willcocks accordingly left Peshawar on February 13th, 1908, and concentrated near Ali Masjid in the Khaibar Pass. The 6th Company, Bengal Sappers and Miners, and the 9th Company, Madras Sappers and Miners, were the Engineer units with the force,[1] and Lieut.-Colonel W. J. D. Dundee, R.E., was the Commanding Royal Engineer. The operations which followed were models of efficiency and celerity. The preparations had been thorough, the transport was adequate, the troops well trained, and the Engineers and Sappers fully competent. For the first time a British force took the field in a frontier campaign under the commanders and Staff who had trained it in peace; and, at a total cost of £57,000, and with negligible casualties, the campaign was ended in less than three weeks.

In the hands of its keen and experienced leader, the Bazar Valley Field Force of 1908 was a perfect weapon, finely wielded; and all the entrances to the valley were seized before the enemy could concentrate to oppose an invasion. Having demonstrated towards Alachi, Sir James Willcocks marched his 1st and 2nd Brigades[2] rapidly to Chora on February 15th and pushed the 2nd Brigade up to Walai before dark. On the same day a small flying column started from Landi Kotal, and, making a surprise entry into the Bazar Valley from the north, joined the brigade at Walai on the 16th. The important village of China was destroyed during the next few days. On the 21st, the 1st and 2nd Brigades attacked and burnt Halwai, far up the Bazar Valley. The Zakka Khels, in spite of their improved armament,[3] could not stand against the British rifles and the new 10-pounder breech-loading mountain guns which used smokeless powder. On February 27th they submitted, and by March 2nd the British force had withdrawn.

The Engineers and Sappers, assisted by the Pioneers, carried out their usual tasks in this little expedition. They improved the defences of the piquet posts around Chora and made themselves generally useful. There was not much road work and no bridging. *Fougasses*[4] were prepared and used with good effect at China and elsewhere, each being charged with 30 lb. of guncotton, and nearly 30 village towers were blown up. Some of the towers were hollow, others were solid. The destruction of a hollow tower occupied about half an hour, but a solid one took three times as long. To blow up a

---

[1] The 6th Company was commanded by Captain J. R. E. Charles, R.E. (now Lieut.-General Sir Ronald Charles, K.C.B., C.M.G., D.S.O.), and the 9th Company by Captain C. M. Wagstaff, R.E. (now Major-General C. M. Wagstaff, C.B., C.M.G., C.I.E., D.S.O.).

[2] There were three brigades, the 1st Brigade under Brigadier-General C. A. Anderson, the 2nd under Major-General A. A. Barrett, and the 3rd Brigade under Major-General H. B. B. Watkis in reserve at Nowshera.

[3] They had a number of Martini rifles.

[4] *Fougasse*. A hole dug at an angle facing towards the enemy and charged with explosive overlaid with stones and earth. The explosion pelts the advancing enemy with "foreign matter" and has considerable moral, if not material, effect.

hollow rectangular tower the Engineers divided the calculated charge and placed it inside the tower at floor level in two or three corners in holes excavated to the centre of the wall. This invariably caused the collapse of the structure. The solid towers were destroyed by mining as usual into the centre of the base and exploding the whole charge at that spot.[1]

Scarcely had the Bazar Valley Field Force returned to Peshawar when reports were received that the Mohmands were rising, and troops were moved up to the administrative border beyond Shabkadr in time to repel a Mohmand attack in this quarter towards the end of April, 1908. The situation, however, was further complicated by the fact that large bodies of Afghans had reinforced the enemy; and a series of determined attacks by Mohmands and Afghans on Landi Kotal at the northern end of the Khaibar Pass during the beginning of May forced Sir James Willcocks to mass considerable forces in that neighbourhood. He drove the Afghans across their border, and then prepared to deal with the Mohmands in their own country north-west of Peshawar. For this expedition he had the 1st Brigade of the Peshawar Division under Brigadier-General C. A. Anderson, the 2nd Brigade under Major-General A. A. Barrett, and the 3rd Brigade (in reserve) under Brigadier-General J. Ramsay, and among his divisional troops were the 1st and 6th Companies of Bengal Sappers and Miners.[2] As in the expedition against the Zakka Khels, the Commanding Royal Engineer was Lieut.-Colonel W. J. D. Dundee, R.E.

Sir James Willcocks, with the 1st Brigade, crossed the Karapa Pass on May 14th, 1908, and both the 1st and 2nd Brigades were below the Nahaki Pass two days later. The 1st Brigade then crossed the Nahaki Pass, but with great difficulty for the road was execrable and the Sappers and Miners had little time to repair it. The opposition offered by the enemy was trivial until the night of May 16th/17th, when they attacked the piquets of the 1st Brigade. On the 18th, General Barrett, with the 2nd Brigade, moved westwards up the Bohai Valley; and General Anderson, with the 1st Brigade accompanied by Sir James Willcocks, advanced northwards on the 20th and occupied Lakarai on the 21st. Already the Mohmand clans were beginning to tender their submission. Anderson next turned eastwards against the Utman Khels, defeated them on the Ambahar River and marched southwards against another clan. By May 28th, Sir James Willcocks had overrun the whole Mohmand country and had subdued all the clans except one on the Afghan border. This

---

[1] *Frontier and Overseas Expeditions from India*, Vol. II, Supplement A (1908), p. 41. Report of the C.R.E. Bazar Valley Field Force. The work was not without its comic incidents. An R.E. subaltern, having measured the thickness of a hollow square tower at the doorway, bored half that distance into the wall from inside in diagonal corners and placed his charges. Unfortunately the wall happened to be thinner at the corners than at the door. The result was that, when the charges exploded, he and a brother officer only escaped a most effective " fougassing " by throwing themselves flat as the face of the wall sailed over them.

[2] Commanded by Captains J. R. E. Charles and A. H. Cunningham, R.E.

was quickly overcome, and, after an expedition lasting only 20 days, the Mohmand Field Force returned to Peshawar with a fine record of rapid marching to its credit. Its speedy success was due to excellent organization, good leadership, experienced troops, and the use of the 18-pounder quick-firing field-gun which made its first appearance in frontier warfare on this occasion. The Engineers and Sappers maintained their reputation for good work, and were employed chiefly in blowing up towers, improving roads and ensuring an adequate supply of water to the troops in a singularly dry and dusty country.[1]

Between 1908 and the outbreak of the Great War the conduct of the frontier tribes was, on the whole, exemplary. There were minor disturbances, of course, but no organized opposition on a large scale. Even when Europe had drifted to disaster and the Sultan of Turkey proclaimed a *jihad*, most of the tribes remained outwardly quiet, guided, no doubt, by the wise example set to the Afghans by Amir Habibullah Khan. There was some trouble in the Yusufzai country and in the Tochi district during the Great War, and the Mahsud Waziris had to be put down once more, but these disturbances were not very serious. With the advance of civilization, roads, and even railways, have crept forward year by year through many of the dark and sombre gorges of the North-West Frontier ; but it has remained substantially the same wild and trackless maze of crags and defiles as in the olden days, and it is still the best school of military engineering which the world has ever seen.

[1] *Frontier and Overseas Expeditions from India*, Vol. I, Supplement A (1908), Appendix III. Report of the C.R.E. Mohmand Field Force.

CHAPTER XXII.

THE NORTH-EAST FRONTIER.

A LAND of inaccessible mountains, clad in vast and dense jungle, washed for months by deluges of rain, scoured by terrific floods, infested by insect pests, and sparsely peopled by elusive and mobile savages whose features show the imprint of China—such, with the exception of the wind-swept and treeless uplands of Tibet, is the North-East Frontier of India along the line of the eastern Himalayas and down towards Burma.[1] The country and the people bear no resemblance to those of the North-West ; the tactical and strategical problems are less formidable, and war can be made only on a miniature scale. But the campaigns in the North-East have much that is novel and interesting. They have called for individual enterprise and daring greater even than those demanded on the Afghan border. The " flying bullet down the pass " and the fanatical charge of Pathan swordsmen is replaced by the cunning ambush on the narrow path, the carpet of bamboo spikes, the avalanche of stones and the shower of poisoned arrows from the hidden stockade. This is jungle warfare.

The tribes and territories along the North-East Frontier are almost as numerous and diverse as those beyond the Indus.[2] North of the Himalayas, above Nepal, lie the huge wastes of Tibet, stretching from the region of Simla in the west to the eastern gorge through which the Tsan-po or Brahmaputra enters Assam. On the southern slopes of the main range, east of Nepal and within view of Darjeeling, is the little state of Sikkim, and still farther eastwards the larger one of Bhutan. Then comes a mass of wild country in the extreme northeast corner where the Akas, Daflas, Miris, Abors, Mishmis and other tribes have their villages. South of these are the Singphos, Nagas, the tribes of the Garo, Khasi and Jaintia Hills near Shillong, and the Manipuris ; and still lower down the map, between Assam and Upper Burma, the Lushais and the Chins whose mountains extend southwards past Chittagong to the coastal province of Arakan. The impenetrable nature of the natural barrier between Assam and Burma is shown by the fact that these countries, not 200 miles apart, have yet to be linked by a railway. A succession of precipitous ranges, running north and south and washed by rains of extreme violence,

---

[1] As no frontier of India faces north, the term " North-East Frontier " is used to include the whole frontier except that in the north-west.

[2] A reference to the map entitled " Sketch Map of the North-East Frontier," which is included at the end of this volume, will show the positions of the various territories.

EARLY EXPEDITIONS.

has kept our Engineers at bay; but these inhospitable regions east of Assam have been the scene of so many small expeditions that the history of one, at least, of these must find a place in this sketch of mountain and jungle fighting and engineering.

The first expedition on the North-East Frontier in which Engineers and Sappers and Miners took any considerable share was the fourth venture into Bhutan between 1864 and 1866, soon after the desperate fighting on the Ambela Pass in the North-West.[1] A dozen small expeditions had already been launched in various directions between 1772 and 1861,[2] but no regular Sappers and Miners took part in them and only one or two Engineer officers. When Lieut.-Colonel J. C. Gawler led 1,800 men into Sikkim in 1861, his only Engineer troops were two companies of "Sibandi" Sappers,[3] irregular soldiers but sufficiently expert to bridge the Tista River (212 feet across) in 28 working hours. Most of the early expeditions were little more than police affairs, and the forces employed rarely exceeded a few hundred men. The regular Sappers and Miners were too busily engaged in fighting the Marathas or waging war in Burma, Afghanistan or the Punjab, and lastly during the Indian Mutiny, to be available for punitive work on the north-eastern boundary.

Of the expeditions after 1861, few call for much notice, and, as space is scarce, it is proposed to deal only with the Bhutan War of 1864–66, the Chin-Lushai Campaign of 1888–89, the Tibet Mission or Expedition of 1903–04, the Abor Expedition of 1911–12 and the Mishmi Mission of the same period. These five campaigns cover a wide field. They provide good examples of North-East Frontier warfare of various types, and in some of them a large number of Royal Engineers and Sappers and Miners were engaged. Among the remainder[4] the expedition against the Daflas in December, 1874, is the only one which calls for brief notice, and this not because a detachment of Bengal Sappers under Lieutenant W. J. Home, R.E., took part in it, but for a very different reason. Whooping-cough had been

---

[1] See Chapter XXI.

[2] 1st Bhutan, 1772; 1st Sikkim, 1814; Singphos, 1825; 2nd Bhutan, 1828; 3rd Bhutan, 1835–36; 1st Lushai, 1844; 2nd Lushai, 1849; 2nd Sikkim, 1850; 1st Mishmi, 1855; 1st Abor, 1858; 2nd Abor, 1859; 3rd Sikkim, 1860–61.

[3] See "Hobson-Jobson." Sibandi or Sebundy troops were irregular native soldiery (a sort of militia) for revenue or police duties. Certain local infantry regiments were officially termed Sebundy. The last official appearance of the title was in application to "The Sebundy Corps of Sappers and Miners" employed at Darjeeling in 1869. Lieutenant Robert Napier, B.E., was in charge of this Corps about 1840.

[4] Excluding the five selected expeditions, and the operations involved in pacifying Upper Burma after the Third Burma War, the list is as follows:—3rd Lushai, 1868; 4th Lushai, 1871–72 (1st and 3rd Coys., and detachment of 9th Coy., Bengal Sappers); Dafla, 1874 (detachment of 64 men of 2nd and 7th Coys., Bengal Sappers); 1st Naga, 1875; 2nd Naga, 1877–78; 3rd Naga, 1880; Aka, 1883–84 (2nd Coy., Bengal Sappers); 3rd Sikkim, 1888 (detachment 5th Coy., Bengal Sappers, under Lieutenant A. E. Sandbach, R.E.); Chin, 1888–89; 5th Lushai, 1888–89 (detachment 2nd Coy., Bengal Sappers); Tibet, 1889; Manipur, 1891; 3rd Abor, 1894; Mishmi, 1899 (detachment 5th Coy., Bengal Sappers). Between 1889 and 1893 there were many expeditions from Burma against the Kachins, Chins, Lushais and other tribes in which Madras and Burma Sapper companies took part. In 1887, the 2nd Coy., Bombay Sappers, served against the Shans.

introduced by the Daflas of the plains to the Daflas of the hills. The hill men demanded compensation, and, when this was refused, killed five " whoopers " and kidnapped 35 others. The British Government then stepped in to restore order, and 800 men voyaged up the Brahmaputra for that purpose. So the Dafla Expedition has the distinction of being the only war ever caused by the infantile affliction of whooping-cough.

We turn now to Bhutan, an exceedingly mountainous country, the northernmost zone of which, lying at a great altitude, is almost uninhabited. Below this zone the mountain slopes are less precipitous and there are wooded valleys which contain the bulk of the population. The lowest zone, nearest to the plains of India, consists of broken hills, covered with dense vegetation and separated by deep and unhealthy ravines. A violent wind blows up all the main valleys every afternoon and evening. In 1864, the Government of this strange and inhospitable land could put into the field a horde of 10,000 fighting men armed with matchlocks, bows and arrows, slings and swords, and expert in the use of catapults, booby traps and the cruelly-sharp bamboo " crows'-feet " known as *panjis* which they loved to scatter in the grass. There had already been three expeditions against the Bhutias; and a long continued series of raids, culminating in an insult to a British envoy, forced the Government of India to send another against them in December, 1864, in the form of a " Duar Field Force "[1] of one brigade and some attached troops commanded by Brigadier-General Mulcaster.

The advance was made in four columns, one from Gauhati directed against Diwangiri in the east, a second from Goalpara against Bissengiri, a third from Cooch Behar towards Buxa and Bala, and a fourth from Jalpaiguri on Daling (Dhalimkot) and Chamurtsi in the west. General Mulcaster took personal command of the two right or eastern columns, and appointed Brigadier-General Dunsford to command the two western columns. Four companies of Sappers and Miners were distributed among the columns, these being the 6th and 7th Companies of the Bengal Sappers and Miners and two companies of " Sibandi " Sappers. It is difficult to ascertain the names of the Royal Engineer officers who accompanied the columns, but a very large number served in Bhutan between 1864 and 1866, including 2nd-Captains G. N. Kelsall, F. S. Stanton, Æneas Perkins, W. S. Trevor[2] and J. L. Watts, and 19 subalterns.[3] The 2nd Company, Bengal Sappers and Miners, relieved the 7th Company in May, 1865,

---

[1] The " Bengal Duars " were the sub-montane districts south of Bhutan, north of Cooch Behar and the River Brahmaputra.
[2] Perkins rose to be a General, and Stanton and Trevor became Major-Generals.
[3] Lieutenants W. H. Collins, M. T. Sale, C. N. Judge, G. S. Hills, J. A. Armstrong, R. de Bourbel, J. H. Urquhart, F. Bailey, K. C. Pye, W. T. Whish, T. B. B. Savi, G. F. O. Boughey, T. H. Holdich, G. Strahan, C. Strahan, F. F. Cotton, W. J. Heaviside, A. J. C. Cunningham and J. Dundas who was killed by an explosion at Sherpur, near Kabul, on December 23rd, 1879. (See Chapter XIX.)

during which year the 4th, 5th and 8th Companies also went to Bhutan, so that in January, 1866, there were five regular companies in the country in addition to the " Sibandi " Sappers. The Engineer Department was certainly adequate in this war.

Marching against the Bhutias at the beginning of December, the four columns attained their objectives without much difficulty. The country was annexed, and the force was on the point of being broken up when, at the end of January, 1865, the enemy launched a series of violent attacks on the British camps at Diwangiri, Bissengiri, Buxa, Tazagong and Chamurtsi. The Bengal Sappers did well on these occasions. According to General Mulcaster, " the 7th Company covered themselves with glory on the night of the attack on our camp at Diwangiri, and were equally efficient when working with the pick and shovel or when fighting with rifle and bayonet."[1] The Sappers counter-attacked with the infantry, and unfortunately Lieutenant J. H. Urquhart, R.E., was killed in this fight. On February 4th, as the water-supply channel had been cut by the enemy, the officer in local command at Diwangiri decided to evacuate his position and retreat to the plains. This was a disastrous move. The main column lost its way in the darkness on February 5th, some of the wounded were abandoned, there was great confusion, all the baggage was lost, and the guns were thrown down a ravine.[2] In other quarters, however, the Bhutias met with little success.

Brigadier-General Henry Tombs, V.C., of Mutiny fame, soon arrived to supersede General Mulcaster, and Brigadier-General J. M. B. F. Tytler was sent to replace General Dunsford. With them came large reinforcements, including the 2nd Company, Bengal Sappers and Miners, and Tombs pushed forward his preparations for the recapture of Diwangiri. The force at his disposal was one brigade, while a second brigade under Tytler was directed against the Balla Pass, Chamurtsi and other places lying to the west of the main line of advance. Having deceived the enemy regarding his probable line of advance, Tombs launched an assault against Diwangiri on April 3rd, 1865. A storming party of three companies of Indian infantry was formed up, the advance was sounded, and, supported by the fire of a few guns, the troops rushed at the stockades. The enemy fled in large numbers, but 150 of them barricaded themselves in a wooden blockhouse to fight to the end. The only known means of entry was by climbing the blockhouse wall, which was 14 feet high, and squeezing through a gap of two feet in height between the top of the wall and the roof. Captain Trevor, R.E., Lieutenant Dundas, R.E., and an officer of the Infantry, led the way, followed by only

---

[1] There is a tradition among the Bengal Sappers and Miners that on one occasion, when a mountain gun had been abandoned under a heavy attack, a strong Sapper, named Dyal Singh, picked up the gun and carried it, unaided, a considerable distance back to the British camp.

[2] *Frontier and Overseas Expeditions from India*, Vol. IV, p. 143.

three or four men. Heavy stones were dropped on their heads, but they scrambled up the wall, crawled through the opening, and leapt down among the enemy inside the house. Others followed quickly, and after a bitter fight the Bhutias within the place were exterminated. The exploit was indeed a gallant one, and all three officers were awarded the Victoria Cross. General Tytler had already forced the Balla Pass[1] and occupied Buxa and Chamurtsi, and the enemy's losses were so heavy at Diwangiri that this engagement practically ended the war. Some show of resistance was still made, however, and it was not till the end of February, 1866, after the British had advanced farther into Bhutan, that the Bhutias laid down their arms.

Twenty-three years after the submission of Bhutan, the Lushais and their neighbours the Chins in the mountains between Chittagong and Burma were seething with the anarchy which followed the Third Burma War. Of the two, the Lushais had always been the more warlike; and the four expeditions which had already been sent against them were followed by a fifth under Colonel V. W. Tregear in March, 1889, to punish them for raids and murders and to establish British posts in their territory. Marching from Demagiri[2] with 1,100 men, Tregear conducted some punitive operations from a post in the mountains called Fort Lungleh.[3] The defences of this place were then completed by a small detachment of the 2nd Company, Bengal Sappers and Miners, and Tregear withdrew in April, when the Chins had also received a lesson from a column which had advanced against them from Burma. However, there was further trouble in the Chin and Lushai regions during the hot weather and rains, so the Government of India decided to undertake combined operations against these tribes by sending columns from Burma and Chittagong to subjugate them and also to open out the narrow strip of country which still isolated British Burma from India.

The Burma force was placed under the command of Brigadier-General W. P. Symons and consisted of two brigades, one forming a "Northern Column," to advance from Fort White[4] and containing the 5th Company, Madras Sappers and Miners, under Lieutenant C. H. Heycock, R.E., and the other, called the "Southern Column," to march from Kan[5] with the 6th and Burma Companies of the same Corps under Captain H. G. C. Swayne and Lieutenant B. A. James, R.E. The force of more than 3,000 men, including the 2nd Company, Bengal Sappers and Miners, under Captain R. D. Petrie, R.E., which was ordered to advance from Chittagong and concentrate at Fort Lungleh, was commanded by Brigadier-General V. W. Tregear.

---
[1] His success was due largely to a daring reconnaissance carried out on the night before the attack by Captain Æneas Perkins, R.E., Lieutenant R. de Bourbel, R.E., and Lieutenant Cameron, R.A., who climbed almost up to the enemy's stockades.
[2] Sixty miles north-east of Chittagong.   [3] Twenty miles east of Demagiri.
[4] Forty miles west of the Chindwin River and 70 miles north-east of Lungleh.
[5] On the Myit-Tha River, west of the Chindwin and 30 miles south-east of Haka.

From Lungleh it was to march eastwards, over a succession of precipitous hills and across many deep gorges to Haka, to join hands with the Southern Column from Burma. Major H. P. Leach, R.E., was the Commanding Royal Engineer with this column, and was assisted by Captain (afterwards Major-General Sir Herbert) Mullaly, R.E., and Lieutenant R. A. F. Kingscote, R.E. As there was much survey work to be done, Lieutenant W. J. Bythell, R.E., accompanied the Chittagong Column as Survey Officer, and Lieutenant T. F. B. Renny-Tailyour, R.E., held the same post with the Burma Force. In addition to those Royal Engineers already mentioned, Major G. Henry, Captain F. H. Oldfield and 11 subalterns[1] took part in the operations. A Telegraph Section of the Bombay Sappers and Miners was also present.

The Northern Column from Burma set out at the end of November, 1889, and by the close of the year had established several posts for the protection of the frontier from Chin raids; but the Southern Column, delayed by the extraordinary difficulties of the country, took 66 days to reach Haka from Kan instead of 12 as had been estimated. Not only the Sappers, but almost every man in the force had to be employed on roadmaking, although the route was only 64 miles in length.[2] The same difficulty confronted General Tregear who did not finish his road to Haka from the west until April 13th, 1890. But meanwhile the advance parties from east and west had met on February 26th at Tao, 52 miles by road from Haka and midway between that place and Lungleh, and after some punitive operations the campaign came to an end in May. The last of the regular troops then marched out of the Chin and Lushai countries, leaving the newly established posts to be garrisoned by detachments of the Burma Police. Every unit had suffered terribly from malaria. Of 69 British officers with the Burma Southern Force only seven escaped infection, one died, and 26 were invalided. The enemy had made elaborate defences in several places—notably at Falam, north of Haka, where they erected innumerable stockades and obstructions extending over nine miles of country—but they lacked the courage to defend them. There was, indeed, very little serious fighting against the head-hunting Chins and Lushais in 1889 and 1890, but an immense amount of laborious engineering.

The work was chiefly road construction; but there was also much bridging, and many rafts were made for river transport. Fort Tregear was built near Fort Lungleh, and several other posts on neighbouring ridges. The difficulties in linking up these posts were

[1] Lieutenants E. H. de V. Atkinson (now Lieut.-General Sir Edwin Atkinson, K.C.B., K.B.E., C.M.G., C.I.E.), H. B. H. Wright (now Major-General H. B. H. Wright, C.B., C.M.G.), L. P. Chapman, U. W. Evans, H. J. Sherwood, E. P. Johnson, G. M. Hutton, T. Fraser (now Major-General Sir Theodore Fraser, K.C.B., C.S.I., C.M.G.), C. Ainslie, H. J. M. Marshall and W. A. Harrison. (See *List of Officers of the Corps of Royal Engineers from 1660 to 1898*, by Captain T. W. J. Conolly, R.E.)

[2] *Frontier and Overseas Expeditions from India*, Vol. V, p. 333.

stupendous. The jungle was so dense that the limit of vision was less than a dozen yards, and great masses of rock were continually encountered which had to be removed by blasting. Enormous trees also had to be cut by explosives and their roots dug up. There was not a single open space between Lungleh and Haka, 55 miles apart as the crow flies and twice that distance by road; and if the jungle was not of trees matted together with thick creepers, it was of stout bamboos or elephant grass up to 20 feet high. In places a gradient of 1 in 5 was necessary, and the track had sometimes to be blasted out of solid rock. Every valley demanded a bridge. The Chittagong Column alone constructed seven bridges of 48 feet span or more, the largest being a crate and trestle bridge of 17 spans and 101 yards in length.[1] Suspension bridges of telegraph-wire rope were erected also when a clear waterway was essential. Weakened by fever, soaked by torrential rain, and bitten by leeches and mosquitoes, the Engineers and Sappers and Miners were glad to leave the dense forests of the Lushais and Chins in March and April, 1890, to return to the plains of India or the valley of the Irrawaddy.

We pass now to another "Engineer War"—the expedition into Tibet in 1904. This unique country falls into three great physical divisions. Firstly the remote, interminable and dreary plateau in the north, standing at an elevation of 15,000 feet or more above sea-level, swept incessantly by tearing winds, destitute of vegetation and dotted with hundreds of salt lakes. An early traveller in this ghastly land writes :[2] "Our journey through such infinite solitudes was one of inexpressible melancholy. Each day we traversed arid valleys, skirted blue lakes, and surmounted passes laden with snow. All nature was robed in silence except for the rushing of the wind which blew furiously as if it wished to roll aside the summits of the mountains." To the east of this arctic region lies the province of Kham, a labyrinth of wild, rugged and almost unknown mountains. To its south is the more temperate and fertile valley of the Tsan-po or Brahmaputra, separated from India by the Himalayas and containing the wonderful city of Lhasa and its peculiar inhabitants. In the valley of the Tsan-po the bulk of the Tibetans dwell happily in the most rigid isolation, suspicious of foreign instrusion, well governed by the Dalai Lama and his national assembly, but oppressed by a monastic oligarchy which has no counterpart in the world.

The Tibet Mission[3] of 1904 must always rank high among military exploits. The operations during the advance of nearly 400 miles from Siliguri to Lhasa met with natural and climatic difficulties which have never been surpassed. The country was bleak and barren

---
[1] *Official Report on the Chittagong Column, Chin–Lushai Expedition of 1889–90*, compiled by Captain O. A. Chambers, p. 39.

[2] M. F. Grenard in his *Dutreuil de Rhins. Mission Scientifique dans la Haute Asie.*

[3] It was so called because it was in the charge of a Political Officer (Colonel F. E. Younghusband) though backed by a considerable military force as an escort.

except for small tracts in the Chumbi and Gyantse-Shigatse Valleys, in the Tsan-po Valley, and around Lhasa. On two stretches, each of nearly 100 miles, no food or fuel could be obtained. The Tsan-po, which was the last obstacle before Lhasa, is rapid and dangerous. Gales and snowstorms were frequent during the winter when 50 degrees of frost were not unusual; and for 150 miles by the Gantok route, from the base at Siliguri until Phari was reached at 14,300 feet above sea-level, there was an enormous rainfall during the monsoon months. A Tibetan army of 16,000 men,[1] poorly armed but strongly posted in fortified localities and commanded by a Chinese *Amban* of Tibet,[2] was ready to oppose the British advance. Before Lhasa could be reached it was necessary to cross four ranges of mountains by passes between 14,000 and 17,000 feet in height. These were some of the difficulties encountered and overcome during the Tibet Mission.

British prospects of obtaining an entry into the country for trade purposes had been sacrificed to secure the assent of China to the annexation of Burma after the Third Burma War, and in 1888 the Tibetans invaded Sikkim and were driven out by a British force. Eleven years later, when Lord Curzon became Viceroy, the Dalai Lama began to cast off the yoke of China and to make overtures to Russia. This caused such anxiety to the Indian Government that a mission was sent up to Khamba Jong in July, 1903, under Colonel F. E. Younghusband to negotiate with China and Tibet; but the Tibetans refused to attend, and their troops began to mass in the neighbourhood. Accordingly, the Indian Government ordered, in November, that the Chumbi Valley on the main road to Tibet should be occupied, and that negotiations should be resumed by the mission at Gyantse, far towards Lhasa.

The 4th Company,[3] Madras Sappers and Miners, had been working on the Rangpo–Gantok road in Sikkim since April, 1903,[4] assisted for a time by the 23rd and 32nd Sikh Pioneers, and these units joined Younghusband's military escort, the composition of which is worthy of note. It included a battery of Mountain Artillery, a couple of machine-guns, the 3rd Company, Bengal Sappers and Miners, under Captain S. H. Sheppard, R.E., the 12th Company, Madras Sappers and Miners, under Major C. H. Heycock, R.E., a company of mounted infantry, the 23rd and 32nd Sikh Pioneers, and the 8th Gurkhas. Of its 3,000 fighting men, more than two-thirds were Engineers, Sappers or Pioneers, and it was commanded by a Royal Engineer in the person

---

[1] *Frontier and Overseas Expeditions from India*, Vol. IV, p. 74. Though the army was nominally 6,000 strong, 16,000 men took the field.
[2] Since the early years of the eighteenth century, Tibet has owned the suzerainty of China. Two Chinese officials called *Ambans*, *i.e.*, Residents or Ambassadors, were in Lhasa in 1904 and exercised considerable control over the Tibetan Government.
[3] Renumbered the "12th Company" in December, 1903.
[4] To improve the communication from Sikkim into the Chumbi Valley.

of Major (temporary Brigadier-General) J. R. L. Macdonald.[1] Seventeen other officers of the Corps served with it. These were Captain S. H. Sheppard and Lieutenants E. F. J. Hill, A. D. Walker, C. H. Haswell and G. F. B. Gough (Bengal Sappers); Major C. H. Heycock and Lieutenants J. A. Garstin, C. F. Birney, H. L. Lewis and E. K. Molesworth (Madras Sappers); Captain C. H. D. Ryder and Lieutenant H. McC. Cowie (Survey); Captain C. A. Elliott (Staff); Captain R. St. J. Gillespie and Lieutenant P. E. Hodgson (Field and Assistant Field Engineers); and Lieutenants A. F. S. Hill and L. N. Malan (in charge of two cooly corps). The preponderance of Sapper and Pioneer troops, and the size of the Engineer cadre, justify the title of " an Engineer War " for the expedition into Tibet.

Well equipped for hostilities at extreme altitudes,[2] the troops crossed the Jelep La[3] (14,390 feet), occupied Chumbi on December 15th, 1903, and seized Phari Jong[4] on the 20th, thus securing the whole Chumbi Valley. On January 7th, 1904, the Tang La (15,700 feet) was crossed and the Mission reached the wind-swept plateau of Tuna (15,300 feet), where it remained with some of the troops during the winter while Macdonald and the remainder returned to Chumbi. Three thousand Tibetans who had assembled at Guru on the shores of the frozen Bam Tso[5] a few miles to the north, blocked the road to Gyantse, and altogether these months were a period of grim strain which was shared fully by the Engineers and Sappers. Gillespie, Hodgson, A. F. S. Hill and Malan, and for a time most of the Sappers and Miners and Pioneers, were working desperately to make passable roads, and notably a new track, five feet wide, from Guntok over the Nathu La (near the Jelep La) into the Chumbi Valley. The country was a pathless jungle, and the cost of the Nathu La track having been underestimated, its progress was not helped by instructions that economy was to be the first consideration. Rain fell steadily and persistently. The track was begun at the top of the pass, working downwards on both sides to get the worst part over before the winter, but in the end it was abandoned because the expedition reached Lhasa before it was finished. Often the men laboured for hours up

---

[1] After some years of railway work on the North-West Frontier, Macdonald came to the fore as Chief Engineer on the Uganda Railway preliminary survey operations between 1891 and 1894. In 1897 he commanded the British expedition from Mombasa to forestall Marchand at Fashoda, and during the next two years quelled a mutiny of Sudanese and Waganda Muhammadans in Uganda. He was Director of Railways during the Third China War (Boxer Rebellion) in 1900. After the Tibet Expedition he commanded brigades in India, and before his retirement in 1913 was G.O.C. Mauritius. He died in 1927 as Major-General Sir Ronald Macdonald, K.C.I.E., C.B., LL.D., Colonel-Commandant R.E.

[2] Every man was issued with a long sheepskin overcoat (*poshtin*), a quilted rug (*rezai*), fur-lined gloves, two lambskin vests, quilted overalls, extra socks, felt knee-boots, comforter and goggles. During the expedition it was found necessary to fill the maxim-gun water-jackets with a mixture of water, rum and kerosene, as pure water froze hard. (The addition of kerosene oil to the rum is easily accounted for!) No lubricating oil could be used on the locks of rifles and maxims as it also froze.

[3] *La.* A pass.   [4] *Jong.* A fort.   [5] *Tso.* A lake.

THE TIBET MISSION REACHES GYANTSE.

to their knees in icy slush, and every afternoon a great slope of powdered mica flowed down the mountainside at one place, obliterating all traces of the day's work.[1] Those Engineers, Sappers and Pioneers who had not the good fortune to see the wonders of Lhasa certainly earned the Tibet medal.

Preparations for a further advance were completed by March 24th, 1904, and on that day the British force began to move forward from Chumbi and within three days was concentrated at Tuna with the exception of its Sappers and Miners who joined it later at Gyantse. The Tibetans now had 7,000 men in the field,[2] and hostilities began at Guru on March 31st when a small British force was attacked without warning by part of a horde of 2,000 Tibetans.[3] Our troops opened magazine fire, and the enemy left more than 600 dead on the field. It was a lesson which the Tibetans never forgot. The advance on Gyantse being resumed on April 4th, the enemy were encountered again in a position at the Zamdang gorge on the 10th and were routed once more with heavy loss, though they fought fanatically at close quarters with a bravery which was admirable and a hopelessness which was pitiful. The troops afterwards pushed on to Gyantse where the Jong, on its rocky pinnacle 600 feet high, being occupied on April 11th without a fight, was soon evacuated as there was no proper water supply. The Mission and its escort then took up their quarters in an adjacent hamlet called Chunglu, and after a time the bulk of the escort marched back to Chumbi. There was a skirmish on May 3rd, when four companies of infantry captured a Tibetan position at an altitude of 16,000 feet; and two days later the enemy attacked the Mission Post and were repulsed. The situation at Chunglu, however, was not too comfortable, for the Tibetans had reoccupied the empty Jong from which they could fire down on the enclosure at a range of only 1,000 yards. The Mission was practically besieged.

Although the services of most of the Sappers and Miners were so urgently needed on the line of communication that they were not available for the advanced post at Gyantse, a composite half-company reached that place on May 24th with other reinforcements. This detachment consisted of 60 men of the 3rd Company, Bengal Sappers and Miners, and 20 men of the 12th Company, Madras Sappers and Miners, under Captain S. H. Sheppard, D.S.O., R.E., with Lieutenants J. A. Garstin and A. D. Walker, R.E. The other half of the 3rd Company remained in the Chumbi Valley with Lieutenants E. F. J. Hill and C. H. Haswell, R.E., busily employed in roadmaking. The difficulties of this task are shown by the fact that the detachment had

---

[1] Letter from Colonel R. St. J. Gillespie, C.I.E., D.S.O., to the author, dated August 4th, 1932.
[2] Three thousand men at Guru, 2,000 men east of the Bam Tso, and another 2,000 men in reserve.
[3] Mr. Edmund Candler, a Press correspondent and the author subsequently of *The Long Road to Baghdad*, was severely wounded in this assault.

to blast a whole mile of the road near Chumbi out of a granite cliff.[1] Most of the 12th Company, Madras Sappers and Miners, also remained in the Chumbi Valley, working under Heycock on the road towards Phari Jong. The Royal Engineer officers who congregated at Gyantse for the operations at that place and the final advance to Lhasa were Captains Ryder, Sheppard, Elliott and Cowie, and Lieutenants Garstin, Walker and Birney.[2] Elliott was engaged chiefly in Staff work, and Ryder and Cowie were Survey officers; but all helped in the fortification of the Mission Post. The bulk of the engineering work, however, both in the stiff fighting at Gyantse and in the dash to Lhasa, fell on Sheppard and his subalterns. General Macdonald, though an Engineer, was not concerned in engineering, and he did not arrive in Gyantse till June 26th, some time after the affair at Palla Village which will now be described.

About 1,000 yards to the north of the Mission Post lay a steep hill crowned by Gyantse Jong, and beyond it, on a spur running almost north, a monastery. Houses clustered thickly around the foot of the Jong and towards the monastery. A similar distance to the north-east of the Mission Post was the fortified village of Palla, strongly held by the enemy; and 500 yards in advance of the Mission Post was a Gurkha piquet holding a house known as " Gurkha Post." As the Tibetans in Palla were preparing to mount small guns to enfilade the Mission Post it was decided to storm Palla early in the morning of May 26th and to enter it on the side farthest from the Post. Sheppard detailed four small storming or explosive parties, each of four Sappers under a British officer. He led one party himself, with another under Captain O'Connor, R.A.,[3] as a reserve. Walker commanded a third party, with a fourth under Garstin in reserve. Behind these parties came two assaulting columns, each of an officer and 60 men of the 32nd Pioneers; and on a mound called Gun Hill, beyond Palla Village, lay a reserve of the remainder of the Sappers, two companies of infantry and two mountain guns.

A night march, begun at 2.30 a.m., brought the storming parties by a circuitous route to within 300 yards of the village, unseen by the defenders.[4] They were then discovered, but Sheppard collected the parties under the village wall, and sending Walker towards the first house of the village (the one nearest to the Jong), dashed through an open gateway between that house and the second and ran almost into the arms of three Tibetans. Quick as lightning he shot two with his revolver, while the third bolted back into the first house but forgot to shut the door. Sheppard then called up Sapper Chagatta, a

---

[1] " No. 3 Company, 1st Bengal Sappers and Miners, on the Thibet Mission, 1903–1904," by Brevet-Major S. H. Sheppard, D.S.O., R.E., appearing in *The R.E. Journal*, Vol. II, July–December, 1905, p. 104.

[2] All these officers reached Lhasa except Garstin.

[3] O'Connor, though a Political Officer, had volunteered for this hazardous duty.

[4] The account which follows is based on notes given to the author by Major-General S. H. Sheppard, C.B., C.M.G., D.S.O.

soldier who afterwards distinguished himself by exceptional bravery in France during the Great War. Chagatta appeared with a box of guncotton, and though fired on heavily from all sides, Sheppard laid the charge against the wall of the second house, lit the fuse and retired, the subsequent explosion blowing a good breach in the wall. Walker was successful also in breaching the wall of the first house, and he and Sheppard, back under cover, then looked around for the assaulting columns, but they looked in vain. These columns had been attacked in flank during their advance, and having lost direction, were making their way towards the other end of the village which they entered in due course; so, as Sheppard could find no more than 20 men, he decided that it was possible only to assault the first house in which 60 Tibetans held the upper floor. Lieutenant Gurdon of the 32nd Pioneers had already led a few men into this house through the open doorway, and now he entered it again with O'Connor, and the latter placed a whole box of guncotton in the lower room and lit the fuse; and when the explosion had killed or buried half the garrison, the attackers, rushing into the miniature inferno, bayoneted the remainder or shot them as they fled.[1] It was a gallant exploit, but Garstin was mortally wounded, and Walker, O'Connor and another officer and several men, were hit. Nearly every man was knocked about by stones and bricks. Meanwhile, however, the assaulting columns had come up and soon took the remaining houses of Palla which was destined to be the starting point of the assault on the Jong itself. Thus ended a very pretty little fight.

The next task was to bridge the river near the Mission Post. This was completed in three days, a covered way was dug to Palla, and an existing way to Gurkha Post improved. There was no lack of work for the Sappers while reinforcements were awaited. General Macdonald marched in at last on June 26th with more than 3,000 men and eight guns, having stormed a large monastery south of Gyantse on his way, and preparations were then made to take the Tsechan Monastery a few miles to the north. This hive of monks and soldiers was attacked on the 28th by the 8th Gurkhas from a ridge to the south while the 40th Pathans and a small detachment of Sappers and Miners made a frontal advance across the plain, supported by the fire of the 7th Mountain Battery. The Tibetans held their walls and *sangars* until driven out at the point of the bayonet, and defended a tower in the monastery till the gates were blown in; but they had now such a wholesome dread of guncotton that they would not risk a repetition of the destruction at Palla. They fled from the monastery to a fort, and from the fort to the open, and so to the mountains for safety.

After some fruitless negotiations, Macdonald decided to assault Gyantse Jong and thus to break the enemy's resistance. This he did

[1] They accounted for 60 Tibetans apart from those killed by the explosion.

on July 6th, 1904. His plan was that three columns should emerge from behind Palla before dawn, surprise the enemy, and obtain a lodgment in the town at the foot of the Jong; but in order to do this it was necessary first to take the Chinese House, a strongly-fortified double-storeyed building with a high courtyard wall in front, the entrance to which was barred by a massive gate. With each column was an explosive party of 12 Sappers under a Royal Engineer officer, each party carrying guncotton made up in 12-lb. charges and also a couple of picks and some crowbars. Birney was in command of the left party, Sheppard of the centre, and Elliott of the right.[1] Each explosive party was followed by a company of the 32nd Pioneers and another of infantry, and Sheppard had asked for a 7-pounder mountain gun. The centre column was to capture the Chinese House, the key of the position, while the others forced an entry into walled gardens or groves on either side of it, the general idea being that the explosive parties should open a way for a rush of infantry after which the Pioneers would entrench the positions gained.

The three columns emerged from behind Palla at 3.30 a.m. and advanced easily; but the centre and right columns came under a heavy fire from their left front while still 200 yards from their objectives. Seeing that the Chinese House could not now be taken by surprise these two columns both entered the right-hand garden after Elliott had breached the wall, and there they remained for a time under a galling fire. All the Sappers were present, but most of the infantry had lost their way. However, just as dawn was breaking, the mountain gun planted three shells on the roof of the Chinese House, and the Sappers took the opportunity to blow in the entrance gate of the courtyard. This was bravely done under a point-blank fire by Sheppard assisted by Naik Usman Khan, and when the gate had fallen the Sappers and infantry charged in.[2] The enemy fled, and Sheppard then demolished the doors of the house itself while the defenders jumped from the roof. The capture of the Chinese House was the beginning of the end. The left column had attained its objective and was soon concentrating on the other columns. At 2 p.m. a company of the 8th Gurkhas, led by Lieutenant J. D. Grant[3] and supported by Royal Fusiliers, scaled the heights of the Jong under a shower of stones and bullets, and at dusk the British were masters of Gyantse. This defeat practically broke the enemy's resistance, and the way lay open to Lhasa.

The last phase of the operations began on July 14th, when Younghusband and Macdonald set out for Lhasa with 2,100 fighting men,

---

[1] *Report on the Engineer Operations of the Tibet Mission Escort,* 1903–04, p. 25.

[2] Captain S. H. Sheppard, D.S.O., R.E., was promoted for his exploits at Palla and Gyantse Jong, and Naik Usman Khan and Sapper Chagatta received the Indian Order of Merit.

[3] Grant was awarded the Victoria Cross for this exploit. He is a son of Colonel Suene Grant, late R.E.

eight guns, six maxims, 2,000 followers and 3,900 animals. A suitable garrison was left in Gyantse, and the destruction of the Jong was taken in hand. On the 16th the column reached Ralung, where Macdonald learnt that the Karo La (16,600 feet) was strongly fortified by *sangars* and by a wall extending to vertical cliffs at the snow line, but the pass was forced, nevertheless, on July 18th with slight resistance. This engagement is remarkable. It was fought at an altitude of *over* 18,000 *feet* above sea-level;[1] and when the Tibetans retreated over a glacier, some of the Gurkhas had to cut steps in the ice with their *kukris* to follow them. The advance continued, two Jongs were occupied, the expedition climbed over the Khamba La (16,400 feet) on the 24th and dropped down to Chaksam on the broad Tsan-po which is here more than 11,000 feet above the sea. A letter arrived from the Dalai Lama asking for peace; but Younghusband refused to negotiate except at Lhasa, and the Tibetan ruler then fled from his capital into the mountain wilderness of the north, leaving his national assembly and the Chinese *Amban* to make what terms they could.

The crossing of the Tsan-po at Chaksam was a fine piece of engineering. The main stream was 140 yards wide: beyond it was a sandbank and then a subsidiary channel 25 yards in width. It was necessary to cross the main stream close below the junction of two channels where the force of the current was terrific and there were many dangerous whirlpools.[2] The stores available were four Berthon boats[3] with superstructure to form two rafts, two large Tibetan ferry-boats captured at Chaksam, a few Tibetan skin boats, 200 yards of 1" steel cable and a traveller, and 640 lb. of 2" and 1½" manilla rope—a poor equipment for the transfer of 3,500 men, 3,500 animals and 350 tons of stores across a raging maelstrom. Yet Sheppard and his Sappers, assisted by the Pioneers, accomplished this feat in five and a half days. The crossing began on July 25th by rowing the Tibetan boats and Berthon boat rafts, but it was desperately slow work. The boats and rafts were carried far downstream at each trip and Major G. H. Bretherton of the Supply and Transport Corps was drowned.[4] On the following day the river had risen, and only 14 boat-loads were across after 14 hours of toil. An attempt to get a line across the main stream had failed; but on the 27th, by mooring a Berthon boat far out from each shore, connecting the two boats by a line and taking other lines out to them, a complete line was linked up at last from bank to bank. A rope soon followed, and by it a steel cable was hauled across and fixed. A ferry was then established by using a traveller to carry one end of a rope across the stream and

[1] Probably the greatest altitude at which modern war has ever been waged.
[2] The current ran at more than five miles an hour.
[3] Collapsible boats, made in sections. Each section had been carried by coolies, slowly and laboriously, all the way from India as the sections were too heavy for mules.
[4] The Berthon boats were never afterwards used in rafts.

attaching the other end to a large Tibetan boat which could thus be swung and hauled to the far bank. When empty, the boat was towed upstream and then rowed across to be reloaded, the end of the rope being sent back by the traveller as before. An ordinary flying bridge served for the crossing of the narrow channel beyond the sandbank, and thus the obstacle of the Tsan-po was overcome.

Younghusband reached the holy and mysterious city of Lhasa, the goal of so many vain endeavours, on August 3rd, 1904, and marched with his escort through the gateway below the Potala Palace, a wonderful structure whose tiers of windows and golden roofs towered far above him. Long negotiations followed until a treaty was signed on September 7th in the Throne Room of the palace, which secured British influence in Tibet. Winter was approaching. It was necessary to return at once over the passes,[1] so the Sappers and Miners set out on the 9th, with some infantry, to make arrangements for recrossing the Tsan-po at Chaksam. Additional engineering stores, however, had arrived at that place from India, and a better site for a ferry had been discovered at Partsi, 11 miles farther upstream, so all the gear was taken to Partsi and the work was begun. It progressed so rapidly that two steel-cable ferries, one of 105 yards' and the other of 140 yards' span, supplemented by a rowing ferry, were ready when the main body arrived from Lhasa on September 27th, and in another 48 hours every man and animal, and every ton of stores, had been transported to the southern bank. The return journey was uneventful. The Mission and its escort entered Gyantse in two columns on October 5th and 6th and marched on in smaller columns to India, while Captains C. H. D. Ryder and H. Wood, R.E.,[2] journeyed up the Tsan-po to examine Western Tibet as far as the sources of the Indus and Sutlej.

Every kind of work fell to the lot of the Royal Engineers and their men in this campaign among the eternal snows, but they were equal to all demands on their resources. The venture into Tibet has rightly been described as a triumph of organization and daring, and its story makes a fascinating interlude in the prosaic annals of the India that we know to-day.

The influence of the Chinese in Tibet was upset in 1911 by a mutiny of their troops in Lhasa consequent on a revolution in China, and these troops having been expelled by the Tibetans, the Dalai Lama returned to his capital after two years in exile. But China was still ambitious of regaining control in Tibet, and there were rumours that she was preparing to invade that country. This brought into prominence the need of a proper and well-defined Tibetan boundary located at a safe distance from the British administrative border north of the rich province of Assam, and hence the despatch of a

---

[1] Lhasa itself is 11,900 feet above sea-level, and the passes are far higher.
[2] Wood was sent from India for this work of exploration.

THE POTALA AT LHASA, TIBET.

military expedition into the Abor country in the far north-east to explore that territory and to punish the Abors for the murder of two Europeans and their followers in March, 1911. At the same time a friendly mission was sent into the adjacent Mishmi country to prevent the Mishmis from joining the Abors against the British and to explore their territory in order to ascertain the intentions of China.

The Abor country, lying north of Dibrugarh and Sadiya, high up the Brahmaputra, is mountainous and densely covered with forest, and roadmaking is very difficult because the ground is so shaly that it is continually slipping. The rainfall is one of the greatest in the world, and this deluge lasts from May till October. After the end of December the weather gets steadily worse, and from March onwards a thick haze adds obscurity to the shadows of the jungle. The Abors[1] about the Dihang River[2] are the most formidable of the savage tribes in the extreme north-east. They are finely developed, Mongolian in type, and fight with *dahs*,[3] spears and poisoned arrows,[4] and they are even fonder of booby traps or stone chutes[5] than their neighbours the Miris and the Bhutias farther west. They lie in wait at the corner of a jungle path, shoot their enemy, and dive headlong down a winding track prepared through the dense undergrowth. Such are their methods. It is difficult to estimate their numbers, but possibly they may have put 3,000 men into the field in 1911.

To deal with these people, a force of 2,500 men under Major-General H. Bower was sent up the Brahmaputra past Dibrugarh to Kobo, a point about six miles above the Poba tributary. It included the 1st Company, Bengal Sappers and Miners, under Captain E. C. Tylden-Pattenson, R.E., with Lieutenants W. Cave-Browne, F. S. Collin and A. F. Chater, R.E. The general idea was that the main body should move up the Dihang by Pasighat while a smaller column operated to its west in the direction of Ledum and Misshing.[6] By the middle of October, 1911, the force was concentrated at Kobo, and on the 22nd, Bower began his advance with the main body towards Pasighat which he reached four days later. The jungle was so dense that he had to move in two columns, each in file, and at every camp the men were obliged to clear some acres of undergrowth before a perimeter could be marked out. Pasighat, being the limit of navigation up the Dihang, was then converted into an advanced base and the country around reconnoitred. Advancing once more, the main body occupied Renging near the junction of the Sirpo tributary on November 9th,

[1] The name " Abor " means " remote savage."
[2] The upper portion of the Brahmaputra which is really the Tsan-po from Tibet.
[3] Short swords.
[4] The arrow-head is dipped in aconite and is loosely attached so that it will remain in the wound if the arrow is withdrawn.
[5] The stone chute is a collection of rocks supported on a scaffold of bamboos which is held in position by single canes or ropes. It is placed above a path ascending the hillside, and is liberated by cutting the canes or ropes. As the path generally runs in zigzags, it is swept in many places by the avalanche of rocks.
[6] The operations of this column were successful but require no reference in detail.

the Sappers and Miners and the 32nd Pioneers being very busy road-making. Soon afterwards heavy rain began to fall continuously, and leeches swarmed on every side. So unpleasant were the conditions that an officer who took part in the expedition has described it as a " nightmare of rain and leeches ! "

There was a small fight on November 19th during a further advance, and on the following day Bower marched to Rotung near which place he located the enemy in occupation of a large stockade on a high cliff. This position was attacked and captured on December 4th in spite of more than 100 stone chutes which the Abors had prepared ; but before the attack it was necessary to cross the Dihang, which was done with the aid of a Wheatley-bag raft[1] ferry cleverly arranged by Tylden-Pattenson and his Sappers.[2] The width of the river was nowhere less than 180 yards, and the current sometimes reached a velocity of six miles an hour. On the far bank was a sheer cliff, 30 feet high, and on the near bank, enormous boulders. Cave-Browne and five Sappers tried to row a small raft across with a light line on November 30th but found the current too strong, and an attempt to send a line to the other side by an " otter "[3] failed also. Repeated attempts to use the " otter " during the next two days met with no success till at last Cave-Browne, balanced on a small raft far out on the swirling waters, managed to catch the " otter's " tail as it ran and to join up its line with a line from the raft to the shore. A big raft of 26 bags was then rowed across, a light steel cable was pulled to the far bank and followed by a heavier one, and on the afternoon of December 3rd the attacking force was ferried over in 19 trips.[4]

The campaign was soon brought to a successful conclusion. Bower pushed up the Dihang as far as Kebang, the occupation of which on December 12th caused the Abors to submit. Extensive exploration and survey work up the river, and northwards to Damro, was then carried out by Lieutenants R. Oakes and O. H. B. Trenchard, R.E., while Lieutenant M. Everett, R.E., continued his labours on the line-of-communication roads and the Sappers and Miners made several suspension bridges. The unceasing rain, however, was washing everything away. It was time to leave the dripping forests, so a general concentration on Kobo was begun at the end of March, 1912, and before the end of May there was not a British or Indian soldier in the dreary Abor country.

[1] A raft supported by a number of waterproof canvas bags stuffed with compressed hay or dry grass.
[2] A detailed account of this bridging exploit is given in Appendix II, " Report on Engineering Operations," included in *Frontier and Overseas Expeditions from India, Official Account of the Abor Expedition*, 1911–12, pp. 199–201.
[3] An apparatus designed to drag a line across a river by the combined forces of the current on its side and the tension of a cable.
[4] The Sappers and Miners made another ferry across the Dihang at a place called Yambung on December 29th, clearing the Abors away from the opposite bank by a couple of small dynamite shells fired from " home-made " wooden mortars.

YAMBUNG FERRY, DIHANG RIVER.

Meanwhile a peaceful mission under Major C. Bliss had traversed the Mishmi country in the extreme north-east. Not only had it penetrated farther towards China than any British force has ever been, but it had actually entered that country and made contact with Chinese troops.[1] Several Royal Engineers took part in this adventure. Captain E. P. Le Breton commanded the 5th Company, Bengal Sappers and Miners, which was included in the little column of a few hundred men, and for a time he was in chief command during the absence of Major Bliss. Captain C. P. Gunter and Lieutenant H. T. Morshead[2] were the Survey officers, and Lieutenants C. H. R. Chesney, J. F. Gray and A. D. de R. Martin served with the Sapper Company, though the two last-named officers did not reach the Chinese boundary.

The distance from the base at Sadiya to the ill-defined Chinese border of the Mishmi country was nearly 200 miles, and the expedition started up the line of the Lohit Brahmaputra. During the first part of the march, through a forest of trees interlaced with creepers, the climate was that of a Turkish bath. Leeches, flies and beautiful but poisonous flowers made life a purgatory. Tigers and elephants roamed in this pestilential jungle through which the Sappers could finish no more than two miles of track in a day. They built several fortified posts, and were ready at the end of November, 1911, to advance north-eastwards with the remainder of the troops from a post named Temeimukh into the Mishmi country proper. By December 19th the column had got as far as the Del-li River,[3] a tributary of the Lohit, and two days afterwards set out towards the east, crossing deep *nullahs* by Mishmi suspension bridges of twisted bamboos,[4] hacking a way through the forest, exploring native paths which often led nowhere, and daily growing nearer to the Chinese frontier. The country changed from jungle-clad hills to bare wind-swept slopes and forbidding precipices till on January 4th, 1912, the expedition reached its goal. On some flat ground above the Lohit River there appeared a red flag with the five-toed dragon of China, and near it a wooden post bearing the inscription: " This is the Southern Limit of the Empire of the Great Pure Dynasty."

A mile or so on the Chinese side of these boundary marks, the little

---

[1] The story of the Mishmi Mission is told most graphically by Lieut.-Colonel E. P. Le Breton, R.E., in his article entitled " An Unknown Frontier," appearing in *Blackwood's Magazine*, April, 1922, pp. 427-438.

[2] Lieut.-Colonel H. T. Morshead, D.S.O., R.E., was murdered near Maymyo in Burma in 1931. He was a celebrated explorer in the Himalayas where he accompanied the Mount Everest Expeditions of 1921 and 1922, and reached a height of over 25,000 feet on the latter occasion. In 1913, with Captain F. M. Bailey, I.A., he explored South-East Tibet, and established the identity of the Tsan-po with the Brahmaputra. (See *The R.E. Journal*, Vol. XXXIII, January-June, 1921, pp. 21-40.)

[3] Twenty miles north-east of Temeimukh.

[4] One of these bridges was 350 feet long. Details of these interesting structures can be found in Appendix F, " Résumé of the Work Done by the 5th Company, 1st K.G.O. Sappers and Miners," appearing in the *Brief Narrative of the Mishmi Mission*, 1911-12 (Official), by Major C. Bliss, p. 56.

force, now of only 110 rifles of whom 80 were Sappers, camped for a month on the banks of the Yepak River, another tributary of the Lohit. Under the instructions of the Political Officer the Sappers proceeded to make a length of properly graded road—a road which never would be, or could be, used, but which went to prove that the land was within the British Empire. In due course a Chinese officer arrived with two attendants, and having been entertained with *crème-de-menthe* during an official interview, returned smiling to his headquarters at Rima. But the rivers were already rising behind the Mission, and on February 3rd, 1912, it began its return march, arriving at Sadiya on the 18th.[1]

Very few places have been named in this short account of the Mishmi Mission because hardly any place seems to have had an intelligible or permanent name. There is a story, probably grossly exaggerated, that whenever a certain officer wished to enter a name on his map he asked his interpreter (a dull-witted Assamese) to give it. The interpreter gaped. The officer prodded him. The interpreter grunted, the officer seized a pencil, and the grunt passed into history on the map. Hence such names as Nkraw, Skugh, Klok, Mpong and Glo Hawei (a particularly searching prod). One name is as good as another in the Mishmi jungles. But, fiction apart, the country was very fully explored and charted, and the political and topographical results of the expedition were of the first importance. The North-East Frontier has taught our men all that can be learnt of forest warfare and jungle engineering.

[1] The Mishmi country was visited by the 20th and 21st Companies, Bombay Sappers and Miners, under Captains A. L. Paris and J. B. Corry, R.E., during the cold weather of 1912–13, when the companies made roads and bridges and erected aerial ropeways. (See *A Brief History of the Royal Bombay Sappers and Miners*, p. 28.)

CHAPTER XXIII.

THE GREAT WAR, 1914–1918.

"Let not the world mistake us. Should any outside danger threaten us we stand shoulder to shoulder round our mighty mother, England, and her enemies will find us arrayed in solid phalanx by her side, ready to meet any danger and render any sacrifices for the sake of the great and glorious Empire of which we are proud to call ourselves citizens."—Speech by Sir Gangadhar Chitnavis in the Viceroy's Legislative Council, August, 1914.

A WAVE of patriotism spread through every community and every class in India when Great Britain declared war against Germany on August 4th, 1914. Seven hundred Indian princes offered their services: some offered all their possessions. Money rolled in. Recruits from the martial classes flocked to the colours. The intrigues of German agents were brought to an inglorious end, and in a few weeks a small though well-trained army of seven infantry divisions and five cavalry brigades, the product of Lord Kitchener's reforms, was ready for service. Though India could put only 100,000 men into the field and her army was in no sense designed to fight against the great European powers,[1] she despatched 45,000 trained British and Indian soldiers to France in the nick of time to help in checking the German thrust towards the Channel ports; and before the war had ended her troops had fought not only in France but in Mesopotamia and Persia, in East Africa, at Aden, on the Suez Canal, in North Africa, Palestine, Syria, Gallipoli and even farther afield. The Turk was their particular foe, but all came alike when everything was at stake and every bayonet was needed. And so, in 1914, the experiment was tried of sending the flower of the Indian Army to the sodden and desolate battlefields of France. There they paid a terrible price in a highly specialized and utterly barbaric type of warfare to which they were entire strangers. The Sappers and Miners and the Royal Engineer officers who voyaged to Europe shared with the infantry in the most desperate fighting in which Indian troops have ever been engaged. More than 100 of these officers left India in 1914 to reinforce the home army. Soon there was hardly a captain or a subaltern of the Corps in the Survey of India, the Railways or the Public Works departments. India drained herself dry of young Royal Engineers and followed them by a flood of junior civil engineers

---

[1] The Indian Army was deficient in artillery and machine-guns for such warfare. It had no mechanical transport, trench mortars, hand-grenades or periscopes, and its reserve organization was unsuitable and inadequate. The army was designed for the defence of India and for expeditions against uncivilized foes. For such purposes its organization was admirable.

of the Indian Army Reserve of Officers, whose services in every theatre of war were as conspicuous as they were valuable.[1] The three Corps of Sappers and Miners grew in strength from mere battalions in 1914 almost to divisions in 1918. When the war began each Corps included only six Field Companies ;[2] but the armistice found the Bengal Corps with 21 Field Companies and the Madras and Bombay Corps each with 16. In addition there were Field Troops and Squadrons, Bridging Trains, Field Parks, Railway Companies and Depot Companies galore. The Bengal Corps, which numbered 1,351 Indians in 13 units on August 4th, 1914, had increased to 8,363 Indians in 54 units by November 11th, 1918.[3] These figures will give some idea of India's engineering effort during the Great War.[4]

Official histories, war diaries and the reminiscences of a hundred writers are available for those who wish to study the military operations on the various fronts. This chapter is merely a tale of the adventures and exploits of a few Royal Engineers and Sappers and Miners from India, an incomplete tale in which much fine work and many brave deeds can find no place. It may be said that the war took India completely by surprise, yet the first transport conveying her troops to France sailed from Bombay on August 25th, 1914, and soon the whole of the 3rd (Lahore) Division, the 7th (Meerut) Division and the 9th (Secunderabad) Cavalry Brigade were on their way as an Indian Corps under the command of Lieut.-General Sir James Willcocks, K.C.B., K.C.S.I., K.C.M.G., D.S.O. With the Lahore Division, commanded by Lieut.-General H. B. B. Watkis, C.B., were the 20th and 21st Companies of the Bombay Sappers and Miners under Captains A. L. Paris and J. S. Richardson, R.E. ; and with the Meerut Division, under Lieut.-General C. A. Anderson, C.B., the 3rd and 4th Companies of the Bengal Corps, the 3rd under Captain E. F. J. Hill, R.E., and the 4th temporarily under Lieutenant E. L. Farley, R.E.[5] The Secunderabad Cavalry Brigade included a Field Troop of Bengal Sappers and Miners under Captain R. C. R. Hill, R.E.,[6] with Lieutenant F. S. Collin, R.E. Brigadier-General H. C.

[1] The I.A.R.O., which numbered only 40 in August, 1914, had supplied over 5,300 officers to all branches of the Service by the end of the war.
[2] Several of these were sent at once to Bombay or Karachi to assist in preparing transports for the expeditionary forces.
[3] The figures are taken from *A Short History of the Corps of K.G.O. Bengal Sappers and Miners during the War*, 1914-18, p. 10. Of these 8,363 Indians, 3,424 were overseas.
[4] For further details, see Appendix I. A general description of the expansion of the Indian Army is given in *The Empire at War*, by Sir Charles Lucas, Vol. V, pp. 173-201.
[5] The 4th Company was met in Egypt by its proper commander, Captain A. J. G. Bird, R.E., and his subaltern, Lieutenant C. A. Bird, R.E., and the 3rd Company by Lieutenant F. McC. Douie, R.E. All had been on leave in England.
[6] R. C. R. Hill was on his way home on leave when war was declared, and was recalled from Aden. This Field Troop was disbanded in France in September, 1915, and its personnel distributed between the 3rd and 4th Companies. Another Field Troop accompanied the 1st Indian Cavalry Division to France.

Nanton, R.E., was the Chief Engineer of the Indian Corps, and Lt.-Cols. Campbell Coffin and P. G. Twining, M.V.O., R.E., were the Commanding Royal Engineers of the Lahore and Meerut Divisions respectively. An Indian Cavalry Corps of two divisions under Lieut.-General M. F. Rimington, C.V.O., C.B., followed the other troops and arrived in France during November and December, 1914, and a number of Royal Engineer officers from the Indian establishment joined the Engineer cadre or the Sapper companies on the western front. It is said that the 20th Company, Bombay Sappers and Miners, was the first Indian unit to pass across France from Marseilles, for it reached Orleans on October 1st, closely followed by the 21st Company. The 3rd and 4th Companies of the Bengal Sappers and Miners disembarked on October 15th with the Meerut Division and were railed also to the battle area. The Indian Corps, less two brigades which had been left in Egypt, then came up gradually behind the British 2nd Corps on a general line from Givenchy round the rear of Neuve Chapelle to Fauquissart and completed its relief on October 29th.[1] But before this date the Bombay Sappers had established their reputation, as will now be told.

The Germans had gained a footing in the little village of Neuve Chapelle on October 26th and clung to it in spite of desperate counter-attacks, culminating in an assault on the 28th in which the 20th and 21st Companies under Captains Paris and Richardson, R.E., co-operated with the 47th Sikhs. "Practically only four companies definitely took part in the attack," writes Brigadier-General J. E. Edmonds.[2] "The attack of the four companies—two of the 47th Sikhs with the 20th and 21st Companies of the Sappers and Miners on either side of them—was carried out with the greatest gallantry. Their right was to have been protected by the Bhopal Regiment, but as this unit advanced it came under very heavy fire and halted and continued the action by fire from a trench that it had reached. The Sikhs and Sappers went on. Covering the seven hundred yards of open ground between them and Neuve Chapelle by rushes alternating with fire, as if on a training ground, the four companies reached the ruins of the village and drove out the Germans—reported by prisoners to be three battalions—by close hand-to-hand fighting. They even penetrated to the eastern and northern borders. Here they were met by heavy shell and machine-gun fire, and counter-attack after counter-attack was launched against them. Major S. R. Davidson, commanding the 47th Sikhs, finding that he was unsupported except by the Sappers and Miners, eventually ordered a retreat. This had to be carried out under enemy fire, and so heavy were the losses that

---

[1] The British forces under Sir John French were holding a line from Givenchy through Armentières to Ypres. The First Battle of Ypres was in progress, and the Germans were launching massed attacks against the thinly-held British line.

[2] *Military Operations, France and Belgium*, 1914, Vol. I, by Brigadier-General J. E. Edmonds, C.B., C.M.G., p. 218.

of his men he rallied only 68 out of 289 whilst of the Sappers and Miners all the officers were killed or wounded and over a third of the other ranks of each company."[1] It was a sad business; but although, as General Edmonds remarks, the use of these Engineer companies as infantry in a situation that was not desperate was a mistake which crippled the Lahore Division for a considerable period, it gave the Bombay Sappers an opportunity to show their worth in modern war and they showed it for all the world to see.

It seems that on reaching the cross-roads in the centre of Neuve Chapelle our men came under a deadly fire from snipers and machine-guns. One sniper was concealed only a few yards away, so a Punjabi Muhammadan of the Sappers, telling the others to leave the matter to him, knelt calmly in the road amidst machine-gun bullets drifting like rain, and waiting quietly until the German raised his head, shot him dead. Then he waited for another.[2] Lieutenant E. J. B. Hayes-Sadler, R.E., heading a rush against a machine-gun, was shot through the brain. Captain J. S. Richardson, R.E., was killed in an impetuous charge, and Lieutenants J. H. Rohde and R. L. Almond, R.E., fell also. Lieutenant M. A. R. G. Fitzmaurice, R.E., collapsed badly wounded, and Captain A. L. Paris, R.E., was wounded several times and then captured. At last only Lieutenants F. P. Nosworthy and R. S. Rait Kerr, R.E., with 20 of their Sappers, remained in the centre of the village. Nosworthy sent Rait Kerr with a few men to obtain help, but a bullet found Rait Kerr, who was pulled under cover and defended by one of his men, Sapper Dalip Singh, against several parties of Germans. So the message never arrived, and Nosworthy, with Subadar Ganpat Mahadeo and only 13 Sappers, built a barricade across a street and held a couple of small houses till he was relieved at 3.30 p.m. by some of the Bhopals, when, as a final exploit, he led a charge against another machine-gun. This is how the Indian Sappers and Miners fought in France. It is pleasant to record that Nosworthy, though shot through the heart in front of Ypres in 1915, is still on the active list.

The Bengal Sappers and Miners who came into the line with the Meerut Division on October 29th also had their fill of adventure. On the night of November 11th/12th, near Neuve Chapelle, half the 3rd Company, under Lieutenant F. McC. Douie, R.E., was ordered to blow up seven houses between the British and German lines. As only six were demolished before dawn, Douie took four Sappers with him to reconnoitre the seventh by daylight. They crept up to the house and were working there when a heavy fire was opened on them.

[1] Out of eight British officers, six Indian officers and some 300 Indian "other ranks," four B.O.s were killed and four wounded, one I. O. was killed and two wounded and of the I.O.R.s 45 were killed and 71 wounded. (See "The 3rd Sappers and Miners in the War," by Major A. L. Paris, R.E., appearing in *The R.E. Journal*, Vol. XXXIII, January–June, 1921, p. 15.)

[2] *The Indian Corps in France*, by Lieut.-Colonel J. W. B. Merewether, C.I.E., and The Rt. Hon. Sir Frederick Smith (afterwards Lord Birkenhead), p. 54.

At once two of the men were killed and the others wounded. Douie, while trying to lift a wounded man, was badly hit and crawled towards the British trenches. He reached them and explained what had happened. Then Jemadar Ram Rup Singh, Havildar Ram Bharose Misr and 11 Bengal Sappers jumped out of their trench under a murderous fire, raced for more than 100 yards to the house and brought back their dead and wounded comrades. At Festubert, a few nights later, the other half of the 3rd Company, under Captain E. H. Kelly, R.E., with Lieutenant E. O. Wheeler, R.E., distinguished itself in filling in German saps under heavy fire and in bayonet fighting, and in December and January the 4th Company with the two Captains Bird, R.E. (A.J.G. and C.A.) shared in heavy fighting in and near " The Orchard," north-west of Festubert, and Havildar Sucha Singh was decorated for gallantry in mining operations. Many other instances of conspicuous work by the Bengal and Bombay Sappers and Miners could be given—how the daring reconnaissances of Lieutenant R. G. G. Robson, R.E.,[1] as brave a youngster as ever stepped, ended with his death in December near " Port Arthur," and how Captain P. C. S. Hobart, R.E., Havildar Chagatta and some of the 3rd Company bombed and barricaded in a trench full of Germans in March, 1915—but space does not allow of their inclusion. The men did their duty and more than their duty. The officers were the cream of the Engineers of India.

During November and December, 1914, the Indian Corps had much heavy fighting between Givenchy and Neuve Chapelle. On November 12th the men were heartened by a visit from Field-Marshal Lord Roberts,[2] and had the honour of a visit from the King-Emperor on December 1st. The bitter cold of winter was on them, but reinforced by the Sirhind Brigade[3] from Egypt on December 7th, they fought doggedly in trenches choked with mud and water, handicapped by the strange conditions, and lacking most of the requisites for trench warfare in spite of the efforts of the Engineers to improvise this equipment. " The Indian Corps," writes General Edmonds,[4] " by virtue of its early initiation into trench warfare, had taken the lead under its Chief Engineer, Brigadier-General H. C. Nanton, R.E., in the manufacture of trench mortars, grenades, periscopes and other trench appliances[5] which the troops were driven to improvise. Little

---

[1] On November 19th, 1914, young Robson brought into action the first trench mortar used by the British forces in France. It was made by the 3rd Company, Bengal Sappers and Miners.
[2] The great Field-Marshal died three days later as the result of a chill. The day was very cold, and he would not wear an overcoat because the troops were not wearing theirs.
[3] One of the brigades of the Lahore Division.
[4] *Military Operations, France and Belgium*, 1915, Vol. III, by Brigadier-General J. E. Edmonds, C.B., C.M.G., p. 7, and footnote.
[5] Including the " Bangalore Torpedo," invented by Major R. L. McClintock, D.S.O., R.E., of the Madras Sappers and Miners. This was made of lengths of metal tubing, filled with explosive, to be pushed under or through wire entanglements and exploded in order to cut the wire. (See *The R.E. Journal*, March, 1913.) It came into constant use.

of this nature had been received from home. The official returns show that the average number of hand-grenades issued in France weekly in November was 70, and of rifle grenades 630. The Commander-in-Chief in October asked for a minimum of 4,000 and 2,000 per month, respectively, but even this very moderate total had not been reached by March, 1915. The favourite patterns of the improvised hand-grenades were the ' jam-pot,' the ' Battye bomb ' and the ' hair-brush.' The recipe for making the ' jam-pot ' was : take a tin jam-pot, fill it with shredded gun-cotton and tenpenny nails, mixed according to taste. Insert a No. 8 detonator and short length of Bickford's fuse. Clay up the lid. Light with a match, pipe, cigar or cigarette and throw for all you are worth. The Battye bomb[1] was so-called from Captain B. C. Battye, R.E., of the 21st Company, Sappers and Miners, who initiated its manufacture in an iron foundry at Bethune. The pattern was based on the design of a rifle-grenade made by Major R. L. McClintock, D.S.O., R.E., at Bangalore before the war. In the ' hair-brush ' grenade a slab of gun-cotton was made fast by wires to a flat piece of wood of hair-brush shape which afforded a convenient handle for throwing. It was ignited in the same way as the ' jam-pot ' pattern. The first of these extemporised missiles proved far from reliable. At a demonstration before more than 40 generals and their staffs, when the officer in charge threw a ' hair-brush,' only the stick went forward ; the charge dropped to the ground. Some spectators fled, others crouched to the ground, but no explosion took place. After an interval a search was made and the charge was found—under the person of a General."

On December 20th, 1914, began what may be called the Battle of Givenchy in which that village was lost and recaptured. The Germans concentrated their efforts on the much-weakened Indian Corps and forced it back with such heavy casualties that it had to be withdrawn into reserve,[2] its place being taken by the 1st Corps under General Sir Douglas Haig. Every unit was below strength, and the Bombay Sappers more than most. The reserve organization of the Indian Army could not cope with the demand for men. Only the best were good enough to send to France, and a longer period was needed to train an Indian Sapper and Miner than any other soldier in the forces of the Crown. Two of the four Sapper companies in France had been knocked almost to pieces at Neuve Chapelle ; and even as late as September, 1915, in the battle of Loos, Sappers and Miners were employed to erect wire entanglements in front of the infantry. Two parties, each of 70 men from the 3rd and 4th Companies, each erected 1,400 yards of wire obstacle at Loos in a single night although the German trenches were only 50 yards distant in

---

[1] A cast-iron cylinder about four inches long and two inches in diameter, closed at one end and serrated on the outside. The cylinder was usually filled with ammonal, and it was then closed by a wooden plug with a central hole for a detonator and fuse.

[2] The losses in the Indian Corps since it came into the line amounted to 9,579 men.

one place.¹ But should they have been allowed to perform this feat? There were barely enough Sappers and Miners in France at that time to carry out the skilled technical work which is their normal duty in war.

In March, 1915, however, all the Sappers and Miners were back in the front line for an attack on Neuve Chapelle which, it was hoped, might lead to the capture of the Aubers Ridge;² and in April the Bombay Sappers were with the Lahore Division in the second battle of Ypres, during which the 20th Company alone suffered 60 casualties in six days³ and had their first experience of poison gas. They returned to the Neuve Chapelle Sector early in May to join in those desperate assaults against the German line which ended the spring offensive and involved such losses that no further operations could be attempted for nearly four months. It was not till September, 1915, that the Indian Corps, now under Lieut.-General Sir Charles Anderson,⁴ and strengthened by the 19th (British) Division, was called upon to join in a big attack southwards from La Bassée Canal towards Loos. The troops fought bravely, but they could not hold the positions which they gained and were forced back with the loss of nearly 4,000 men. The Sappers operated phosphorous smoke bombs and other novel engines of war, blocked trenches, wired positions and were generally useful, but all to no purpose. The offensive failed, and it was decided that the battered Indian Corps would be better employed in Asia during the approaching winter. On October 31st an intimation was received that it would shortly be sent to embark at Marseilles while the Indian Cavalry Corps remained in France.⁵

On November 25th, 1915, H.R.H. The Prince of Wales read a royal message of thanks to the Indian troops on behalf of H.M. The King-Emperor, and on December 7th and 16th the transports conveying the Bengal and Bombay Sapper companies steamed out of Marseilles. By December 26th the last ship had gone. The Indian Corps had lost 1,525 officers and 32,727 other ranks in 13 months,⁶ but it had given valuable assistance to Sir John French while he awaited the arrival of the first divisions of the new army from home. More than 1,000 British officers of the Army in India had fallen. It was a heavy price. In a strange country, and under conditions

---

¹ *Lectures on the Regimental History of the K.G.O. Bengal Sappers and Miners*, p. 14.
² The 27th Division (Major-General T. D'O. Snow), mainly composed of British troops from overseas garrisons, had reinforced the Indian Corps in January.
³ *History of the 20th Field Company, Royal Bombay Sappers and Miners. Great War, 1914–1918*, by Major H. W. W. Hamilton, D.S.O., M.C., R.E., p. 26.
⁴ General Sir James Willcocks relinquished his command on September 6th, 1915.
⁵ The cavalry remained in France for nearly two years and a half after the departure of the infantry, waiting for a " break through " which never came. The greater part of the 1st Cavalry Division arrived at the front before the middle of December, 1914, and the 2nd Cavalry Division early in January, 1915. The C.R.E.s were then Lieut.-Colonels G. A. J. Leslie and H. J. M. Marshall, R.E., respectively.
⁶ The losses in Indians alone were 495 officers and 20,381 other ranks.

which were novel to them, the Sappers and Miners had given of their best, and it is recorded that when the Bombay companies left Neuve Chapelle for the last time on November 28th their pride in their work caused them to erect a notice drawing attention to Ecclesiastes ii, 18 and 19.[1] But, had they known it, their labours and sacrifices had only just begun. The battlefields of Mesopotamia and Palestine awaited them.

John Masefield once wrote a book called *O.D.T.A.A.*,[2] a title which might be used for a history of the first year of the war in Mesopotamia. Lured on, and ever on, by the lodestar of Baghdad, by the optimism engendered by easy victory, by political arguments, by the necessity of checkmating Turkish designs for an advance through Persia on India, to relieve the pressure in the Dardanelles, to seize yet one more advanced post to improve the strategical situation, the 6th Indian Division, under Major-General Charles Townshend, joined later by the 30th Brigade, advanced too far in 1915 and met its doom on April 29th, 1916, at Kut-al-Amara. The operations in Mesopotamia were designed originally to end with the occupation of Basra and the protection of the Anglo-Persian oilfields near Ahwaz by one Indian division. Actually they extended before the armistice to the subjugation of the entire country by two army corps. When Ismail Hakki surrendered with his battered troops at Sharqat on October 30th, 1918, the two field companies of Sappers and Miners who landed in November, 1914, had been replaced by 14 field companies, two field troops, four bridging trains and many other engineering units.[3] The lonely stretches of the giant Tigris then swarmed with river steamers and warships, camps and redoubts dotted its banks, railways stretched across the flat deserts, motor-cars whirled along the dusty tracks. The greater part of India at war had been transplanted to Mesopotamia.

On October 16th, 1914, 15 days before Great Britain declared war against Turkey, the 16th Infantry Brigade of the 6th (Poona) Division under Brigadier-General W. S. Delamain, C.B., D.S.O., sailed from Bombay, and with it the 22nd Company, Bombay Sappers and Miners under Captain A. M. Twiss, R.E. Waiting at Bahrein in the Persian Gulf until war had been declared, Delamain captured Fao at the entrance to the Shatt-al-Arab on November 6th and fought two small actions higher up that estuary before the remainder of the division arrived gradually under General Sir A. A. Barrett, K.C.B. The 18th Brigade soon came on the scene, accompanied by the 17th Company,

---

[1] " Yea, I hated all my labour which I had taken under the sun : because I should leave it unto the man that shall be after me. And who knoweth whether he shall be a wise man or a fool ? Yet shall he have rule over all my labour."

[2] " One damn thing after another."

[3] The 2nd, 5th, 6th, 8th, 9th, 12th, 13th, 15th, 19th, 52nd, 61st, Maler Kotla, Tehri-Garhwal, and Sirmur Field Companies, the 2nd and 5th Field Troops, the 1st, 2nd, 3rd and 7th Bridging Trains and other units, were present in October, 1918. (See *The Campaign in Mesopotamia*, 1914–1918, by Brigadier-General F. J. Moberly, C.B., C.S.I., D.S.O., Vol. IV, Appendix XLVI, pp. 384–392.)

Bombay Sappers and Miners, under Captain A. D. S. Arbuthnot, R.E., and General Barrett then advanced and took a small Turkish position at Sahil on November 17th when the two Sapper companies were used as infantry and the cadre of Engineers became sadly depleted. Lieutenant A. B. Matthews, R.E., gained the Military Cross for leading a Sapper charge and came through unscathed; but of the two Company Commanders Twiss was mortally and Arbuthnot seriously wounded, and Colonel U. W. Evans and Major H. E. Winsloe, R.E., the C.R.E.[1] and his second-in-command, were both slightly wounded. The force marched on and occupied Basra on the 22nd. The town was then a ramshackle and insanitary place with only a few good buildings on the river front. The streets were filthy. Palm trees, which, as the Arabs say, grow best with their feet in water and their heads in hell, clustered thickly near the river, and evil-smelling creeks ran in all directions. " There was a good deal of sniping by local *budmashes*," writes Colonel F. C. Molesworth,[2] " which did not stop until two or three were publicly hanged. A story is told of a football game got up by the Dorsets soon afterwards. Seeing the erection of goal-posts, a crowd of Arabs collected, but seemed to lose patience when only the apparently aimless kicking of a ball followed. At length a linguist approached and asked a Dorset, ' When is the execution coming off ? ' " Such was Basra in 1914, but the Engineers and Sappers soon changed it. Theirs was a busy life. In addition to making roads, bridging creeks, repairing buildings and installing water supplies, they converted river steamers into ironclads, mounted guns on ships and barges, laid a minefield, blew up a wreck, repaired a steam launch, electrified a house, and even designed and erected a gallows. Gradually they were followed by a stream of other engineers, military and civil, and by 1918, Basra, though still an inferno between March and October, had become a thriving modern port which coped successfully with the voracious demands of two army corps and was linked with them by a good railway.

The 17th Brigade having arrived in the country, General Barrett lost no time in striking at Qurna, 50 miles farther up the Tigris, and took it on December 9th with the 16th and 18th Brigades after Captain M. G. G. Campbell, R.E., with an Indian officer and three Sappers of the 17th Company, had swum the river with a line by which a cable was hauled across and a flying bridge established.[3] In February, 1915, the Sappers were strengthened by the arrival of a Bridging Train of Bengal Sappers and Miners, a little unit of one Indian officer (Jemadar Sadar Din) and 22 men, but bringing with it

[1] Called in those days the " D.E.C." (Divisional Engineer Commander).
[2] " Early Days in Mesopot," by Colonel F. C. Molesworth (late R.E.), appearing in *The R.E. Journal*, Vol. XLVI, June, 1931, p. 284.
[3] Campbell was awarded the M.C. for this exploit. An Indian regiment crossed at another place in two *mahailas* (country boats of very large size).

18 metal pontoons which rendered invaluable service. Captain M. G. G. Campbell, R.E., took command of this unit at Qurna, where he had already bridged the Tigris with *mahailas*, and was succeeded on April 20th by Captain E. W. C. Sandes, R.E. By that time there had been an unsatisfactory skirmish with the enemy at Ahwaz in the oilfields, the 12th Indian Division was being improvised out of the 30th Indian Brigade from Egypt (under Major-General C. J. Melliss, V.C., C.B.) and two more brigades from India and placed under Major-General G. F. Gorringe, C.B., C.M.G., D.S.O. (a Royal Engineer).[1] The 6th Indian Cavalry Brigade was expected, Major-General C. F. V. Townshend, C.B., D.S.O., had replaced General Sir Arthur Barrett in command of the 6th Division, General Sir John Nixon, K.C.B., had assumed the supreme command, and General Melliss had fought and won the battle of Shaiba[2] outside Basra, in which the 22nd Company again lost its commander (then Captain E. C. Whiteley, R.E.), who was killed in an infantry attack. A company of Sirmur Sappers with Captain C. E. Colbeck, R.E., a small Searchlight Section under Captain R. E. Stace, R.E., and the 12th Company, Madras Sappers and Miners, under Captain S. Pemberton, R.E., had arrived in Mesopotamia. Thus four field companies of Sappers and Miners were available when General Townshend started his ill-fated advance, but of these he was given only two.[3] The force in Mesopotamia had expanded to two divisions, both anxious to get beyond the swamps of the lower Tigris and Euphrates. One of them did so forthwith, and never saw those swamps again.

The story of Townshend's dash to Amara at the beginning of June, 1915, of Gorringe's capture of Nasiriya in July, of Townshend's further advance to Kut-al-Amara in September after his victory at Es-Sinn, of his still further advance on Baghdad in November, his gallant fight at Ctesiphon,[4] his long retreat, and the lingering agony of the 6th Division and 30th Brigade, besieged in Kut from the beginning of December, 1915, to the end of April, 1916, is too well known to need recapitulation here. So small was Townshend's force, so scarce his reinforcements, that in almost every battle the 17th and 22nd Companies of Bombay Sappers fought as infantry and lost accordingly. During the siege of Kut the companies were commanded by junior subalterns, Lieutenants A. B. Matthews, M.C., R.E., and K. B. S. Crawford, R.E., assisted by Engineer officers of the I.A.R.O.: all the other R.E. officers of these field units had been killed or wounded. But the companies did wonderfully well during

---

[1] Lieut.-Colonel T. C. Watson, V.C., R.E., was the first C.R.E. of this division, and Major P. H. Kealy, R.E., joined it as a Field Engineer.
[2] Fought on April 14th, 1915.
[3] The 17th and 22nd Companies, Bombay Sappers and Miners. The Bridging Train, Bengal Sappers and Miners, was also allotted to him.
[4] The commanders of both the Sapper companies, Captain E. J. Loring, R.E. (17th), and Captain M. G. G. Campbell, R.E. (22nd), were severely wounded in this battle. The 22nd Company thus lost its third commander.

the campaign and the siege, and the Bridging Train left a creditable record behind it when its last boats were blown up by Matthews, Sweet of the Gurkhas, and a few of their men after dark on December 9th at Kut to save them from capture. "This was a most gallant affair," writes General Townshend,[1] "the two officers going to the enemy's side of the river, across the bridge, while others stood by to cut the cables. With the explosion the bridge broke up. I recommended the two British officers for the Victoria Cross and the men for the Indian Order of Merit."[2] During the advance from Kut to Ctesiphon the Bridging Train, commanded by Captain E. W. C. Sandes, R.E., of 24 officers and men, assisted by half a company of Sappers, once bridged the Tigris (250 yards wide) in three and a half hours, working at night. It built 17 bridges across the river between March and December, 1915, seven of which were erected and dismantled between November 16th and 28th,[3] and this, although its pontoons would never span half the width of the river and the remainder had to be covered by Arab *danacks*, laboriously prepared and carefully handled. These were some of the engineering difficulties of the early campaign in Mesopotamia.

There were 13 officers of the Royal Engineers in the besieged garrison of Kut-al-Amara. Brigadier-General U. W. Evans, who was Chief Staff Officer and afterwards commanded a brigade, Lieut.-Colonel F. A. Wilson (C.R.E.), Majors H. E. Winsloe and J. S. Barker, Captains E. W. C. Sandes, R. E. Stace, H. W. Tomlinson and C. E. Colbeck, and Lieutenants K. D. Yearsley,[4] A. B. Matthews, M.C., K. B. S. Crawford, C. J. E. Greenwood (Wireless Section) and T. W. Abbott (R.E., Indian Army). The unlucky 13 were assisted by Lieutenant F. Mayo (Sirmur Sappers) and by Lieutenants H. H. M. Spink, W. R. Boyes and H. S. Cheshire of the I.A.R.O. (civil engineers from India). This was a small cadre for all the engineering work entailed in the defence of an important position containing a large town. Every appliance for trench warfare was lacking, so the Royal Engineers were kept very busy in designing and making periscopes, hand-grenades and mines in addition to their ordinary duties, and Stace, ever ingenious, produced an excellent bomb-gun from the cylinder of a Gnome aeroplane engine.[5] However, as all the world knows, Townshend was forced to surrender on April 29th, 1916, and the starving garrison went into a long captivity which many did not survive.[6] They had played their small part, and it may be true, as

---

[1] *My Campaign in Mesopotamia*, by Major-General Sir Charles Townshend, K.C.B., D.S.O., p. 223.

[2] Lieutenants A. B. Matthews, M.C., R.E., and R. T. Sweet, 7th Gurkha Rifles, were subsequently awarded the D.S.O. for this exploit. Sweet died as a prisoner in Turkey.

[3] *In Kut and Captivity* (1919), by Major E. W. C. Sandes, M.C., R.E., p. 142.

[4] The joint author, with Captain M. A. B. Johnston, R.G.A., of *Four-fifty Miles to Freedom*, an exciting tale of escape from Turkey.

[5] *In Kut and Captivity*, by Major E. W. C. Sandes, M.C., R.E., p. 156.

[6] *Tales of Turkey* (1924), by Major E. W. C. Sandes, D.S.O., M.C., R.E., pp. 50–55.

Sir Charles Lucas says,[1] that the dogged determination of their defence largely discounted the evil results of their eventual surrender, but more than 20,000 men were sacrificed lower down the Tigris in vain endeavours to save them.

A distinguished Royal Engineer, Lieut.-General Sir Fenton Aylmer, V.C., K.C.B.,[2] had been appointed to command the force which assembled at Ali Gharbi[3] in December, 1915, for the relief of Kut. He was confronted by appalling difficulties. His force was inadequate and it arrived piecemeal owing to lack of river transport; he was short of artillery, ammunition, medical stores, engineering equipment and even food. He had no proper staff: for a time, indeed, he had not even a Commanding Royal Engineer until Colonel E. R. B. Stokes-Roberts reached him. Lastly he had only one company of Sappers and Miners—the 13th Company of the Madras Corps under Captain E. Bradney, R.E.; and his Bridging Train, though provided with stacks of material and many inferior *danacks*, had very few pontoons. Yet, under the orders of General Nixon,[4] he launched out bravely on his desperate venture because Townshend was believed erroneously to be *in extremis*. Attacking on both banks of the Tigris from January 6th to 9th, Aylmer forced the Turks out of Shaikh-Saad, and on the 13th took Orah though with heavy loss. The enemy then retired upstream to Hanna, 15 miles below Kut, where they had prepared five lines of trenches between the river and a huge marsh, and Aylmer, attacking them on January 21st, 1916, was brought to a halt in a welter of mud and a biting gale with the loss of nearly 3,000 men. For some weeks the Relief Force was paralysed.

By the beginning of March, however, General Aylmer had been reinforced by the 3rd (Lahore) and 7th (Meerut) Divisions from France with the 20th and 21st Companies, Bombay Sappers and Miners, and the 3rd and 4th Companies of the Bengal Corps. The 12th Company, Madras Sappers and Miners, had come to the assistance of the overworked 13th Company, which, with No. 1 Bridging Train (Bengal Sappers and Miners) under Lieutenant J. M. S. Trelawny, I.A.R.O., had made a good bridge across the river at Wadi. So on March 7th, 1916, Aylmer began his second attempt to reach Kut, this time on the right bank. A long night march across the desert, ably guided by Captain K. Mason, R.E.,[5] brought nearly 20,000 British and Indian troops almost to the Dujaila Redoubt in the Turkish position at Es-Sinn, within sight of Kut. Captain A. D. S. Arbuthnot, R.E., and a few men actually entered the redoubt

---
[1] *The Empire at War*, by Sir Charles Lucas, K.C.B., K.C.M.G., Vol. V, p. 295.
[2] Formerly Captain F. J. Aylmer, R.E., who was awarded the V.C. for blowing in the gate of the fort at Nilt on the N.W. Frontier in 1891. (See Chapter XXI.)
[3] Some 50 miles downstream from Kut.
[4] General Sir John Nixon, K.C.B., was succeeded as Commander-in-Chief by Lieut.-General Sir Percy Lake, K.C.B., K.C.M.G., on January 19th, 1916.
[5] *Records of the Survey of India*, Vol. XX, *The War Record*, p. 11.

which was then empty, but they were never seen again. There was some delay, the Turks poured men into their defences to repulse the British attack, and by March 9th the attempt had failed and Aylmer withdrew. But this was not the end. A third attempt was begun on April 5th by Lieut.-General Sir George Gorringe, K.C.B., C.M.G., D.S.O., a Royal Engineer who succeeded General Aylmer in command. More reinforcements had arrived, including the 13th British Division from Egypt. This division was launched against the enemy's positions at Hanna and Falahiya on the left bank and carried them,[1] thus allowing the 7th (Meerut) Division to attack the formidable Sannaiyat position from April 7th to 9th though with little success. The main attack was then shifted to the right bank, but although the 3rd (Lahore) Division captured a Turkish position at Bait Isa on April 17th and repelled several counter-attacks with terrible slaughter, floods and rain prevented a further advance. The final attempt had failed. Kut surrendered on April 29th after a siege of 147 days.

In these operations the Sapper and Miner companies from France were engaged in trench warfare almost as fierce as that on the Western Front. The enemy's positions were designed by Germans. The Turkish regulars fought like demons and died like heroes. This was no helter-skelter affair with Arab irregulars. The Turks continually flooded low-lying areas by cutting the artificial banks which kept the swollen Tigris in its channel. Gales from the north blew the waters of the marsh as a rushing tide into the crumbling British trenches on the left bank. The mud exceeded even the mud of Flanders. No flank attacks could be made. Every advance was frontal, and every inch was gained by sapping. The saps were six feet deep and the infantry working parties could progress at no more than three feet in an hour; but the expert Sappers and Miners sometimes reached a speed of ten feet in an hour, often working ahead in the open and suffering heavy casualties in consequence. It was not their fault that Kut fell: it was not the fault of any soldier in the force.

There was now a long pause in the operations. The need for immediate action had gone. On July 11th, 1916, Lieut.-General Sir F. S. Maude, K.C.B., C.M.G., D.S.O., succeeded General Gorringe in command of the Tigris Corps and on August 28th took over the supreme command from General Lake. The brilliant series of operations by which Maude captured Baghdad are described fully in the official history of the war.[2] It must suffice to say here that by prolonged sapping,[3] followed by severe preliminary fighting from January 5th to 19th, 1917, which led to intensive trench warfare up

---

[1] Captain S. Pemberton, R.E., with the 12th and 13th Companies, Madras Sappers and Miners, then bridged the flooded Tigris at Falahiya in 24 hours.
[2] *The Campaign in Mesopotamia*, by Brigadier-General F. J. Moberly, C.B., C.S.I., D.S.O., Vol. III, pp. 1–250.
[3] Two brigades of the 3rd (Lahore) Division dug 14 miles of trench in 12 days in sapping forward towards the Khudhaira position (*ibid.*, p. 93).

to February 16th in the Khudhaira bend of the Tigris east of Kut and in the Dahra bend west of it, the Turks were cleared from the right bank. Two army corps assisted by a cavalry division, the Ist Corps under Lieut.-General Sir A. S. Cobbe, V.C., K.C.B., D.S.O., and the IIIrd Corps under Lieut.-General Sir W. R. Marshall, K.C.B., carried out the work; but the Turks still clung to their left bank positions far down the Tigris and it was necessary to cross the river to cut their communications—an operation which was duly executed and involved the most brilliant exploit in which the Sappers and Miners were concerned in Mesopotamia. At this time there were 12 companies of Engineer troops on the Tigris front : with the Ist Corps, the 1st, 3rd, 4th, 18th, 20th and 21st Companies, Sappers and Miners ; and with the IIIrd Corps the 71st, 72nd and 88th Companies, R.E., and the 12th, 13th and 15th Companies, Sappers and Miners. There were also two Field Troops and two Bridging Trains at the front, one of the latter being a " Mobile " Train[1] under Captain F. V. B. Witts, R.E. The engineering operations throughout Mesopotamia were under the able direction of Major-General J. C. Rimington, C.B., C.S.I., and it must be admitted that at this stage he was well supplied with technical troops.

Secret preparations were made by General Maude for crossing the Tigris upstream of Kut in the Shumran bend. There had been several feints at crossing below Kut, notably one on December 20th, 1916, when Captain F. V. B. Witts, R.E., commanding No. 2 (Mobile) Bridging Train, led a party of 19 Bengal Sappers across the open and down to the bank, carrying a pontoon which was launched in full view of the Turks and loaded with British infantry. The enemy then opened fire, and, as most of the party were soon killed or wounded, the project was abandoned.[2] The Shumran scheme was carefully rehearsed. The 37th Brigade[3] of the 14th Indian Division (IIIrd Corps) was to be the first formation to cross; but the leading units, and those concerned in the ferrying operations, were to be the 2nd Norfolk Regiment, 2/9th Gurkhas, 1/2nd Gurkhas, 12th and 13th Companies of the Madras Sappers and Miners, a few Burma Sappers, and strong detachments of the three R.E. Companies, the 1/4th Hampshires and the 128th Pioneers. Artillery and trench mortars would cover the crossing, and No. 2 (Mobile) Bridging Train would be assisted by the 71st Field Company, R.E., and some Welch Pioneers in making a bridge. It was decided to establish three ferries, each with 13 bi-partite pontoons, so three columns stole

[1] Each Bridging Train had 500 yards of pontoon material and a strength of 100 men in the ranks. The " Mobile " Train was supplied with land transport. Its pontoons were carried in separate halves on A.T. two-wheeled carts with specially long axles and the superstructure on G.S. wagons. (See " Pontoon Experience in Mesopotamia," by Captain and Brevet Major F. V. B. Witts, C.B.E., D.S.O., M.C., R.E., appearing in *The R.E. Journal*, Vol. XXXIV, July–December, 1921.)

[2] Witts, who was among those wounded, was awarded the Military Cross.

[3] 1/4th Devonshire Regiment, 36th Sikhs, 45th Sikhs, 1/2nd Gurkhas and No. 187 M.G. Company.

CROSSING OF THE SHUMRAN BEND, TIGRIS RIVER.

THE CROSSING OF THE TIGRIS AT SHUMRAN.   489

towards the river bank after dark on February 22nd, 1917, and launched their pontoons before dawn on the 23rd. The Tigris was nearly 300 yards wide, with a current running at five knots.

The Norfolks, crossing by a ferry immediately below the site selected for a bridge, caught the enemy by surprise. Others were not so fortunate. The 2/9th and 1/2nd Gurkhas in the second and third ferries, rowed by the Sappers of the 12th, 13th and Burma Companies and by some Hampshires, were met by a staggering fire. Many pontoons sank or drifted away, full of dead and dying, but the remainder made good. Ferrying continued steadily and by the afternoon the 37th Brigade was across. From 8.30 a.m. to 4.30 p.m., Witts and his Bengal Sappers of the Bridging Train, helped by the 71st Company, R.E., and the Welch Pioneers, laboured under artillery fire to complete their bridge. At last it reached the left bank and the troops poured across in an unceasing stream. The remainder of the 14th Division, the 13th Division and the Cavalry Division were across during the night, driving the Turks slowly back and thereby forcing the Turkish Commander-in-Chief to evacuate all his positions below Kut. The enemy, fighting bravely, retreated on Baghdad. They attempted to dispute the passage of the Diyala River beyond Ctesiphon, but the British threw a bridge across the Tigris and enfiladed them so that the IIIrd Corps (General Marshall) drove them out of their last position on March 10th. Sir Stanley Maude entered Baghdad on the following day, and his victorious troops completed the winter campaign by capturing Samarra on April 23rd. The hot weather then prevented further large operations by either side.

The fighting which took place at the end of 1917, and during 1918 up to October 30th, when the Turks were hemmed in at Sharqat below Mosul, can find no place in this story. The operations were controlled by Lieut.-General Sir W. R. Marshall, who succeeded to the chief command after the tragic death of General Maude at Baghdad on November 19th, 1917. The Turks were driven in many directions and their remnants surrendered. Engineers and Sappers and Miners were everywhere, preparing positions, consolidating gains, bridging rivers, building railways and laying out camps. They penetrated far up the Euphrates, beyond Mosul and into Persia, a vast organization catering for the needs of a huge army. A volume could be filled with an account of their achievements and adventures, but that volume still remains to be written.

Many Royal Engineers, and eight companies of Sappers and Miners served in Persia in the final stages of the war. Their work was chiefly road construction, surveying or political. The Persians were not enemies, but Russia had collapsed, the Bolsheviks were hostile to England, and in May, 1918, a Germano-Turkish advance through Persia towards Turkistan and Afghanistan was still possible. Much

R*

surveying and exploration was done in 1917 and 1918 in South and West Persia by survey parties under Major E. T. Rich and Captain W. E. Perry, R.E.[1] The " Dunsterforce "[2] was sent to the Caspian in June, 1918, to arrange for some resistance in North Persia. A military mission was despatched to North-East Persia, and an organization known as the East Persian Cordon was established between it and India with Brigadier-General W. E. R. Dickson, C.M.G., C.I.E. (late R.E.), as Inspector-General of Communications to provide a passage from Duzdab through Birjand and Meshed to Askhabad.[3] No Royal Engineers or Sappers and Miners were included in the Dunsterforce, but the 24th, 71st and 73rd Companies, Bombay Sappers and Miners, served in East Persia in 1918, where they did an immense amount of roadmaking.[4] From March, 1918, onwards, part of the British IIIrd Corps began to filter from Mesopotamia into South Persia by Qasr-i-Shirin, Karind and Kermanshah, to Hamadan ; and shortly before the armistice the 5th, 12th, 13th, 15th (Burma) and 61st Companies of Sappers and Miners, part of the 72nd Company, R.E., and the 48th and 128th Pioneers were all at work, mostly on road construction between Qasr-i-Shirin and Hamadan.[5] By that time, however, the designs of Turkey against India had been defeated. She had been overwhelmed in Palestine and checkmated in southern Arabia, to which a brief reference will now be made.

When the war began a Turkish army corps in the fertile Yemen district threatened Perim[6] and Aden, where the British had little more than two battalions, and in June, 1915, it became clear that the Turks intended to advance in force. They tried to capture Perim, and spread towards Aden. Fortunately some additional Indian troops had arrived by that time, and the Aden garrison included the 23rd (Fortress) Company, Bombay Sappers and Miners, under Captain C. F. Stoehr, R.E. It was decided that an advance should be made against the enemy in Lahej, 20 miles to the north-west, so a column of 1,000 men marched on July 3rd, 1915, towards the British outpost at Sheikh Othman, a few miles from the Aden isthmus, and beyond it into the desert ; but the men fell out in such large numbers from heat and thirst that they were compelled to retreat from Lahej on July 5th, the Bombay Sappers under Stoehr doing fine work in the rearguard. The Turks, themselves exhausted, did not press the pursuit for long, but advanced later and occupied Sheikh Othman, from which the British had retired to a position on the isthmus at

---

[1] *Records of the Survey of India*, Vol. XX, *The War Record*, 1914–1920, pp. 61–75.
[2] A small and secret mission under Major-General L. C. Dunsterville, C.B.
[3] *East Persia. A Backwater of the Great War*, by Brigadier-General W. E. R. Dickson, C.M.G., C.I.E.
[4] *A Brief History of the Royal Bombay Sappers and Miners*, p. 30.
[5] *The Campaign in Mesopotamia, 1914–1918*, by Brigadier-General F. J. Moberly, C.B., C.S.I., D.S.O., Vol. IV, pp. 251, 390.
[6] A small British island at the southern entrance to the Red Sea.

Khor Maksar. This reverse was caused more by heat than the Turks.

Help came from Egypt. The 28th (Frontier Force) Brigade, under Major-General Sir G. Younghusband, landed with two field batteries on July 18th and recaptured Sheikh Othman on the 21st. It was then replaced gradually by units from India, the first to arrive being the 5th Company, Bengal Sappers and Miners, under Captain E. P. Le Breton, R.E. From September, 1915, onwards the situation at Aden altered little. Both sides consolidated their positions, most of the Turkish army corps having been withdrawn towards Palestine. While the 5th Company was preparing a second line of defence across the polo ground and golf course at Khor Maksar, an unofficial petition arrived from Aden that the golf " brown " in the centre of the line should be spared. Accordingly it was incorporated as a traverse of exceptional size with the explanation that " traverses were being made very thick in France." Humour survived even amid sickness and hardships. There is a tale that the men of a certain unit once collected a boxful of weevils from some bad flour. But not because they loved the little insects. No. They sent them to the Supply Officer with the proper delivery vouchers and a polite request that he should weigh the weevils and substitute an equivalent amount of good flour !

The British defence of Aden was an active one, and there were many sharp fights—at Waht on September 25th, 1915, at Hatum on January 12th, 1916, a raid on Jabir on August 9th, 1916, an affair at As-sela on August 16th, 1917, and a second battle at Hatum[1] during the winter of 1917–18 ; the 5th and 23rd Companies did well in the first four, and, in the last, the 51st Company[2] (Captain R. Boal, R.E.) which had then relieved the 5th Company.[3] The Sappers and Miners were employed continually as infantry in the attack but contrived, nevertheless, to carry out some remarkable engineering work. Ably assisted by Lieutenants F. J. Salberg and A. C. Austin, I.A.R.O., Captain E. P. Le Breton, R.E., Lieutenant A. C. Lyall, R.E., and their sappers built defences at Sheikh Othman which were revetted almost entirely with mud bricks made from sand mixed with stable manure and brackish water because sandbags were not available. Le Breton also commanded a " water column " of camels, mules and vehicles to carry 10,000 gallons of liquid to thirsty troops in action ;[4] he even grew vegetables for his men to defeat the prevalent scurvy. Roadmaking never ended, and a railway was laid

---

[1] All these places are within 15 miles of Aden, and within 10 miles of Sheikh Othman.

[2] The 51st Company, Bengal Sappers and Miners, arrived in Aden from India in November, 1917. The 5th Company proceeded to Mesopotamia in December.

[3] In this battle Captain R. Boal, R.E., was seriously wounded and was afterwards awarded the D.S.O. for gallantry and fine work.

[4] It was found that, during the summer, every man required *a gallon of drinking water daily* while working or fighting in the desert.

from Aden by Captain L. M. Kent, R.E. The general position on the Aden front was a stalemate: a British advance was forbidden, and the Turks dared not tackle the Sheikh Othman defences. So this little war of raids, bombardments, sickness and thirst dragged on to the armistice with Turkey in October, 1918, and even beyond it, for the enemy's commanders in the Yemen were reluctant to carry out the terms. It was not till March, 1919, that the Aden Field Force could be demobilized. There were few opportunities and many hardships in this desert campaign outside the door of Aden.

We turn now to the shores of the Mediterranean where many Royal Engineers and Sappers and Miners from India saw heavy fighting during 1918 and a few in the previous years. India helped to defend the Suez Canal against the Turks, but she was concerned chiefly in the final operations in Palestine in which six out of the seven infantry divisions were Indian. She had little to do with the Gallipoli or Salonika campaigns. No Sapper and Miner companies served in those theatres although several Royal Engineer officers, with Indian experience, did so. For instance, Major-General Sir Godfrey Williams K.C.I.E., C.B., formerly Director-General, Military Works Services, was Chief Engineer in Gallipoli for a time and afterwards held a similar appointment in Egypt from January to June, 1916. Among others in Gallipoli was Major A. H. Cunningham, R.E., who went there in July, 1915, as C.R.E., 1st Australian Division, but was invalided in October; he did excellent work at Roorkee during the critical period of 1918, and afterwards, as Commandant of the Bengal Sappers and Miners. Lieut.-Colonel G. Walker, D.S.O.,[1] and Majors E. S. Sandys, D.S.O., and C. G. W. Hunter, D.S.O., Royal Engineers who had served with the Sappers and Miners, were at Salonika or elsewhere in Macedonia where their Indian experience stood them in good stead when they were ordered suddenly to improvise mule transport in place of wheeled transport. But the battles of Macedonia and Gallipoli do not come into this story, and the scene shifts accordingly to Egypt and particularly to the Suez Canal on which depends the life of India.

"The progress of the Entente Powers in the war," writes General Bowman-Manifold,[2] "is reflected in the campaigns of Egypt and Palestine. In 1914 and 1915, the British were on the defensive everywhere and the Turks had the initiative. During 1916, the tide began to turn. The defensive was abandoned, Sinai was retaken, and the initiative passed to the British. In 1917, the Turks were staggered by defeats entailing the loss of Mesopotamia and half of Palestine. And when the knockout blow fell in September, 1918, their collapse was complete." India took her share in these campaigns—at first a considerable share, then a small one while every man was needed for

---

[1] Now Major-General George Walker, C.B., C.B.E., D.S.O.
[2] *An Outline of the Egyptian and Palestine Campaigns, 1914 to 1918*, by Major-General Sir M. G. E. Bowman-Manifold, K.B.E., C.B., C.M.G., D.S.O., late R.E.

Mesopotamia in 1916 and 1917, and finally almost the whole burden during Allenby's sweep through Palestine and Syria in the autumn of 1918. When the war began in Europe, Egypt was still a dependency of Turkey although she had been controlled by Great Britain for more than 30 years. The Suez Canal was of immense importance to the Allies, so every effort was made to safeguard it. The 3rd (Lahore) and 7th (Meerut) Divisions landed in Egypt for a few days during their voyage to France in September, 1914, and were followed in November by the 10th and 11th Indian Divisions[1] who reinforced the small British garrison of 6,000 men. Then came the Australians and New Zealanders, but it was India who guarded the Canal at the beginning. By the end of 1914 there were more than 70,000 British, Dominion and Indian troops in the country, though only the Indians were fully trained. The first danger had passed. Egypt was firmly held, but the Suez Canal was by no means safe from attack.

The forces available at the outset to protect the 100 miles of canal between Port Said in the north and Suez in the south were so small that a passive defence, based on strong points on the Egyptian or west bank, was all that could be attempted. Until the 10th Company, Madras Sappers and Miners, under Captain T. P. Bassett, R.E., arrived on December 22nd, 1914, only one field company of Territorial Engineers was available; and when the Territorials were withdrawn on January 6th, the 10th Company was the sole engineering unit for two divisions until an Australian company joined it ten days later. For some months the only Royal Engineer officer available as a C.R.E. or Field Engineer was Captain R. E. M. Russell, R.E., who was lent by the Egyptian Army. Fortunately the Egyptian State Railways and Telegraphs Departments were managed largely by ex-officers of the Corps, and these undertook many of the duties of field companies of Engineers.[2] The 128th Pioneers, and a small engineering detachment of the Egyptian Army, gave valuable assistance, and another Territorial company came in February, 1915, but most of these troops were too late to assist in repelling the first attack on the Canal. However, the work of fortifying it was pushed on. Bridges were made at El Qantara (Kantara), Ismailia and El Kubri,[3] and eight more were thrown across the Sweet or Fresh Water Canal which runs along the western bank of the main waterway. The Engineers also built aeroplane hangars, laid water-supply systems for camps, cut the canal banks to inundate certain areas which greatly shortened the total length to be held, and prepared generally for a stubborn defence. When the 10th Company arrived in December, 1914, an advanced line was occupied in the sandy

[1] Then called I.E.F. (E) and I.E.F. (F).
[2] *Military Operations, Egypt and Palestine*, by Lieut.-General Sir George MacMunn, K.C.B., K.C.S.I., D.S.O., Vol. I, p. 33.
[3] El Qantara is 25 miles from Port Said. Ismailia is approximately half-way along the Canal to the north of the Timsah and Great Bitter Lakes through which the canal runs. El Kubri is close to Suez.

desert six miles east of the Suez Canal, and the company was put in charge of the construction of the southern section of the new defences from Gebel Murr to Ain Musa within sight of Suez. This was the first Sapper and Miner work in the Egyptian theatre of war.[1]

In January, 1915, 12,000 Turks under Djemal Pasha began a remarkable march across the Sinai Desert to attack the Suez Canal, and some of them made determined efforts on February 3rd to cross the Canal between Lake Timsah and the Great Bitter Lake; but only a few men got across in pontoons, and these having been killed or captured, Djemal withdrew. The Germans announced later that the Canal had been bridged, that five battalions had crossed it, and that the invasion of Egypt would have been accomplished if the attackers had not missed their way in a sand-storm which enabled a British cruiser to come up and sink the bridge![2] The British redoubled their efforts to strengthen their defences, and the Turks soon had no troops to spare for a renewal of their attempt. Their men were needed in Gallipoli where the British military attack opened in April, 1915. After months of bitter fighting Gallipoli was evacuated, and by the end of February, 1916, the last of our troops from the Dardanelles had reached Egypt where General Sir Archibald Murray[3] was constructing a powerful position about six miles east of the Canal.[4]

General Murray soon began to push slowly eastwards along the coast from El Qantara towards the wells at Katia and Romani, his pace being regulated by the advance of his railway and piped water supply. Having repulsed a Turkish attack at Romani on August 4th, 1916, he entered El Arish on December 21st, and with the capture of Rafa[5] in January, 1917, he cleared the Sinai Peninsula of the enemy. But here his success ended; in March and April, 1917, his attempts to capture the rapidly-growing fortress of Gaza ended in failure and he was succeeded in June by General Sir Edmund H. H. Allenby, G.C.M.G., K.C.B. The new Commander-in-Chief secured Gaza on November 6th after capturing Beersheba a week earlier; then he advanced northwards, swung eastwards, and by the end of 1917 held a strong line across Palestine from north of Jerusalem to the sea. Remarkable engineering work was done during these operations by R.E. companies and a huge Egyptian Labour Corps. Water for the army was led in large pipes[6] completely across the

---

[1] *Historical Record of the Q.V.O. Madras Sappers and Miners*, Vol. II, pp. 4, 9. For five months the 10th Company was commanded by Captain D. McA. Hogg, R.E., until Captain Bassett, R.E., resumed command on May 1st, 1916, on return from a staff appointment.

[2] *An Outline of the Egyptian and Palestine Campaigns, 1914 to 1918*, by Major-General Sir M. G. E. Bowman-Manifold, C.B., C.M.G., D.S.O., p. 13.

[3] General Sir A. J. Murray, K.C.B., K.C.M.G., C.V.O., D.S.O., commanded the Egyptian Expeditionary Force including the garrison of Egypt.

[4] The work entailed the construction of 250 miles of railways, 154 miles of pipeline and 115 miles of metalled road which were completed in six months.

[5] El Arish is 100 miles, and Rafa 128 miles, from the Suez Canal.

[6] The main pipelines were 12 inches in diameter.

Sinai Desert, a double line of railway was laid from Egypt to Palestine and hundreds of miles of roads were prepared, but only the 10th Company, Madras Sappers and Miners, represented Indian engineering in the advance towards Jerusalem. India's proper entry into the war in Palestine began in 1918 when the 3rd (Lahore) and 7th (Meerut) Divisions arrived from Mesopotamia, a large body of Indian cavalry came from France, and most of Allenby's divisions were "Indianized" so that British reinforcements could be sent to the Western Front.

A fine array of engineering talent was collected in Palestine during the summer of 1918 under Major-General H. B. H. Wright, C.B., C.M.G., as Chief Engineer. With the 7th (Meerut) Division, which had reached Egypt in January, were the 3rd and 4th Companies, Bengal Sappers and Miners, the 1st Company being allotted to the 60th (London) Division in Palestine when the latter was "Indianized." The 3rd (Lahore) Division had the 20th and 21st Companies, Bombay Sappers and Miners, and detached the 18th Company to the 10th Division. With other formations were the 10th and 16th Companies, Madras Sappers and Miners, and the 72nd Company of the Bombay Corps, making a total of nine Sapper and Miner companies in the striking force. There were also 12 Field Companies, R.E., two British and one Australian Field Squadron, and six battalions of Indian Pioneers.[1] These were the engineering troops who assisted Allenby to break the Turkish front and sweep through Palestine and Syria in September, 1918, a feat which was performed only by the perfect co-operation of all arms and most careful preparation in which the Engineers took a prominent part. As the great attack was launched from the 7th Divisional area near the coast to the north of Jaffa and the River Auja, the most interesting engineering work was performed in that sector. It is proposed, accordingly, to describe some of that work. The field companies in other sectors had similar but less important tasks.

The campaign in Palestine was emphatically an "Engineer's and Doctor's War." During April and May, 1918, the British line near the Mediterranean coast was greatly strengthened, and when this had been done the Engineers and Medical Services combined to fight the mosquito rather than the Turk. It was necessary to preserve the troops from the deadly ravages of malaria, so the Engineers were ordered to drain two marshy lakes in the 7th Divisional area. The water from the first was pumped without difficulty into the sea, but the second lake, which was a mile in length, presented a serious problem. It was in full view of the Turks and separated from the

---

[1] The 65th, 66th, 85th, 436th, 437th, 484th, 486th, 495th, 496th, 519th, 521st and 522nd Field Companies, R.E.; the 4th and 5th Field Squadrons, R.E., and an Australian Field Squadron; and the 2/32nd, 1/34th, 2/107th, 121st, 1/155th and 2/155th Pioneers. (See *Military Operations, Egypt and Palestine*, by Captain Cyril Falls, Vol. II, Part II, Appendix 3, pp. 666–673.)

sea by a ridge 200 feet in height. Luckily the Engineers found an ancient duct,[1] leading partly through the ridge, and were able to clear it of earth and connect it by a tunnel to a convenient cavern on the western side, and through these passages the water of the lake was drained into the sea in three weeks, greatly to the surprise of the Turks. Deep well pumps were installed in the few existing wells of this barren area, and perfectly pure water was obtained from shallow wells sunk quite close to the sea.[2] All the principal communications were covered with rabbit netting, 12 feet wide, stretched over a grass mat.[3] These lasted well except under the traffic of heavy lorries. The enemy came to regard the industry displayed in the 7th Divisional coastal area as quite ordinary, and were prepared to view any increase in that industry without much suspicion.

Towards the middle of June, 1918, the question of a big offensive began to receive attention. Lieut.-Colonel E. F. J. Hill, D.S.O., M.C., R.E., the C.R.E. 7th Division, was asked to report secretly if he could water five infantry divisions and three cavalry divisions in his divisional area. He replied that he could do so if he was given the necessary apparatus, and General Allenby then decided to attack on a large scale from the coastal sector.[4] Extreme secrecy was maintained. Every device which could mislead, not only the enemy but our own troops and the civilian population south of the Auja, was adopted. Every movement pointed to a British attack through the mountains near the Jordan. But meanwhile, preparations went on quietly in the 7th Divisional area near the sea. Tube wells were sunk, existing wells improved and pumping plants installed underground, until finally there were 12 large water-supply installations, capable of watering more than eight divisions, in an area only a few square miles in extent. At the same time the British front line was advanced by a series of well-planned operations to within a hundred yards of the enemy's trenches and without arousing any suspicion that a mass attack was in view. Shortly before the day of attack a number of divisions was concentrated by night near the coast and hidden in orchards. Some of the infantry and all the cavalry were located outside the area to the south of the Auja, but arrangements had been made for them to cross the river by pontoon bridges at the right moment. This had been done very cleverly by the establishment of a "school of pontooning" on the Auja which explained to inquisitive Turkish observers why there was so much material scattered on the river banks.

[1] It was four feet high and three feet wide, with heavy stone uprights and lintels, and was thought to date from the time of the Crusades or even earlier. Evidently it had been constructed for the drainage of the lake.
[2] These were square wells, nine feet deep and lined with corrugated iron. After some time the water became brackish. New wells were then dug.
[3] This use of wire netting was first made by the Royal Engineers under Lieut.-Colonel E. M. Paul, C.B., R.E., in Gallipoli.
[4] The author is indebted to Brigadier E. F. J. Hill, D.S.O., M.C., for much of the information in this narrative of the engineering operations in Palestine.

On September 19th, 1918, an irresistible assault of the 60th, 7th, 75th, 3rd and 53rd Divisions on a seven-mile front, with three cavalry divisions in rear, tore a huge rent through the Turkish defences in the short space of two hours. The task of the Engineers was to prepare two wide tracks from the British line to the rear of the enemy's positions for the advance of the artillery, cavalry and transport. Each was made by a field company and a Pioneer company, following closely on the infantry, while the remaining Engineer units were kept in reserve, and so well did the men work that two hours after the assault the leading cavalry division passed through on its long ride into Syria. The Turkish VIIth and VIIIth armies were destroyed, the victorious British armies spread north and east, and Damascus was occupied on October 1st. Our troops moved with extraordinary rapidity.[1] The 3rd and 7th Divisions, being largely on pack transport, were sent at first towards Samaria, and afterwards the 7th Division started to march up the coast in brigade groups in the wake of the advancing cavalry. Beyond Haifa the chief obstacle was a headland lying ten miles north of Acre. Here the track, known as the " Ladder of Tyre," and in places little more than a footpath, led for seven miles round the face of the Ras[2] En Nakura which rose steeply from the sea. Lieut.-Colonel Hill (C.R.E. 7th Division), with the 3rd and 4th Sapper companies, the 121st Pioneers and two infantry battalions, moved to the site and in three days made a road round the cliffs which was traversed successfully by the whole division and a battery of 60-pounder guns.

The last mile of the road was across the face of an almost vertical precipice. Here the existing track was found to cover a stone stairway—probably the original " Ladder of Tyre "—which had to be demolished to ease the gradient and widen the road. It is recorded in the official history[3] that in some places the original gradient was one in five, and that the Corps Commander,[4] when told by Hill that the whole shelf might slip into the sea during the process of blasting, demanded " time for a couple of cigarettes " in which to consider the situation. There was no other route for many miles inland, so the Sappers were ordered to make the attempt. It was completely successful. The division soon reached Beirut and marched into Tripoli shortly before the armistice with Turkey on October 31st. General Allenby had already occupied Aleppo, Liman von Sanders[5] had fled through Anatolia, and the power of Turkey was irretrievably broken. The operations which led to these results were strategically

[1] One section of a field company of Engineers was attached to each infantry brigade to arrange for its water supply. This helped to render the troops very mobile. Sometimes they covered 30 miles in a day.   [2] *Ras.* A cape.
[3] *Military Operations, Egypt and Palestine*, by Captain Cyril Falls, Vol. II, Part II, pp. 602, 603.
[4] Lieut.-General Sir E. S. Bulfin, K.C.B., C.V.O., G.O.C. XXIst Corps.
[5] The German Marshal, Liman von Sanders, commanded the Turkish and German forces in Palestine.

and tactically perfect, and the engineering work which supported those operations was a triumph of careful organization and efficiency.

One theatre of war outside India remains to be described. It is a far cry from Syria to East Africa, but that is where this narrative now leads us. In comparison with the campaigns in Europe and Asia, the operations in East Africa were small and unimportant; yet at one time Great Britain had about 80,000 soldiers between Lake Tanganyika and the Indian Ocean, of whom one-half were white, and this army was served by nearly half a million native carriers.[1] The bloodiest battle ever fought by British troops in Africa, not excluding the actions of the South African War, took place near the coast of German East Africa in July, 1917.[2] Beginning with a British failure in landing at Tanga in the north, the campaign developed into a war of attrition and extermination which is without parallel in modern times. For years the British harried and pursued the dwindling German forces, and for years the climate and the German machine-guns took a heavy toll of our men. The vastness of the country, its jungles and rivers, the dreadful mortality through sickness, and the hardships inseparable from an equatorial campaign, produced conditions which may never be seen again. In 1914 German East Africa was nearly twice the size of Germany; and Portuguese East Africa to its south, into which the operations extended in 1918, was as big as France. From the peak of Kilimanjaro, on the northern border of the pre-war German territory, to the Zambesi River forming the southern boundary of the Portuguese domains, is as far as from Paris to Leningrad. And opposed to us was a fine soldier in the person of General Von Lettow Vorbeck. Everything that mortal man could achieve with the resources at his disposal, Von Lettow accomplished. He seized every opportunity to attack, his troops were well trained and organized, his strategy and tactics masterly, his courage unquenchable. When he surrendered after the armistice, 19 out of every 20 of his men had been killed or captured. He played a lone hand to the last card in a hopeless game.

There were no roads in German East Africa. The Germans never used animal draught for wheeled traffic because of the deadly ravages of the *tse-tse* fly. Their two railways—the Northern from the port of Tanga to Moshi near Kilimanjaro, and the Central from Dar-es-Salaam by Morogoro and Tabora to Lake Tanganyika—were the principal avenues of traffic. In the rainy season the country was almost impassable, but for the greater part of the year there was little water except in the big rivers. Nine-tenths of the territory was covered with pathless bush, ranging from giant forests to elephant grass or thorny scrub, in which two forces might be no farther apart than Waterloo and King's Cross Stations and yet be unaware of each

---

[1] "Notes on Railway Work in East Africa," by Captain H. L. Woodhouse, M.C., R.E., appearing in *The R.E. Journal*, Vol. XXXVII, March–December, 1923, p. 37.
[2] The action at Narungombe, near Kilwa, on July 19th, 1917.

other's existence. The absence of roads, the loose nature of the soil, the scarcity of water in some areas and the number of rivers in others, made pioneering and engineering prominent features in this campaign. Von Lettow's *askaris*[1] required no roads : the British had to make theirs as they advanced.[2] Von Lettow retired by well-known paths to selected water supplies, destroying all bridges as he went : the British followed him into a strange country, trusting to find water and facing his machine-guns.[3] Like the campaigns on the North-East Frontier, this was a war of ambush and surprise. Like the Third Maratha War, it was a chase of an elusive foe by a number of isolated columns.

But there were enemies other than Von Lettow and his men. Malaria was more deadly than any bullets. A company of Railway Sappers which landed in June, 1917, with a strength of 150 men could muster only 35 men six months later. The *tse-tse* fly killed most horses within three months, and mules in less than five months. Elephants roamed along the newly-made roads and cut them up so that motor traffic was most difficult. Telegraph lines had to be raised to 25 feet above the ground to clear the heads of giraffes. Roaring lions stampeded the mules at night. Hippopotami attacked the boats at river crossings, and voracious crocodiles lay in wait on the banks. In the middle of a fight between two patrols a rhinoceros charged each in turn, drove them from the field, and ended the battle.[4] Never has modern war been waged under stranger conditions.

In August, 1914, the only regular forces in British East Africa and Uganda (north of the German territory) were two battalions of the King's African Rifles ; but two battalions of Indian infantry under Brigadier-General J. M. Stewart landed at Mombasa on September 1st in time to save it from capture. After a time it was decided that the Germans should be attacked north-west of Kilimanjaro and at Tanga on the coast, and an expeditionary force from India consisting of 6,000 men under Major-General A. E. Aitken appeared before Tanga on November 2nd. It had two complete brigades, with divisional troops, but included only one battalion of British infantry, one battery of mountain artillery, and not a single regular company of Sappers and Miners. The only Engineer formations were a company of Faridkot Imperial Service Sappers and Miners, a small Bridging Train[5] of Bombay Sappers and Miners under Captain E. D. Tillard, R.E., a Field Park of the Madras Corps under Major R. L.

---

[1] Native African soldiers.
[2] During the four and a half years of the war, the British made more than 3,000 miles of road passable for motor traffic.
[3] The enemy had thrice as many machine-guns as the British, and all were manned by Germans.
[4] The tale is told by a character in " At the River's Brink," an article by " Batouri " (Lieut.-Colonel R. L. McClintock, D.S.O., R.E.), which appeared in *Blackwood's Magazine*, Vol. CCIII, January, 1918, p. 10, but it is understood to be founded on fact.
[5] Known as a " Pontoon Park."

McClintock, D.S.O., R.E., a couple of Printing and Photo-Litho Sections, and the 61st Pioneers. An attempt on November 3rd to obtain the surrender of Tanga by negotiation failed. Two Indian battalions which, after an unopposed landing of the greater part of the force, advanced on the town, were driven back in panic by two and a half companies of German Colonial troops which had meantime arrived; and a like fate befell an attack of the whole force on the 4th, by which time the German troops had been strengthened by fresh arrivals.[1] The British were most fortunate to be able to re-embark without opposition on the following day and steam for Mombasa. The arrangements for this critical operation were made by Brigadier-General S. H. Sheppard, D.S.O., late R.E.,[2] who afterwards as a Brigade Commander, and finally as Chief of Staff in 1918, was a prominent figure in the campaign. After the reverse at Tanga, Brigadier-General M. J. Tighe assumed command of the British forces. Throughout 1915 there was little fighting; the British were content to protect their own territory and the valuable Uganda Railway.

But the situation changed in February, 1916, with the arrival of Lieut.-General J. C. Smuts[3] as Commander-in-Chief. Greatly reinforced, he advanced up the Uganda Railway, broke through a gap in the mountains south of Kilimanjaro, and drove the enemy along their Northern Railway and the Ruvu River towards the sea and then southwards in the direction of their Central Railway from Dar-es-Salaam. Von Lettow was often nearly surrounded by converging British columns, but always contrived to escape. He abandoned the Central Railway after destroying the bridges, and by the end of the year had been driven southwards almost to the Rufiji River. This was crossed by Sheppard's brigade on January 5th, 1917, but Von Lettow again eluded his pursuers and marched still farther south. Then came the rains, and when operations were resumed in May, 1917, under a new Commander-in-Chief, Lieut.-General J. L. Van Deventer, the British encircling tactics led to no definite result except that frequent clashes and occasional heavy fighting reduced the enemy's strength. Through the autumn and winter, Von Lettow twisted and turned, and early in 1918 he was in Portuguese territory from which he was driven northward again by Van Deventer; but his power was broken and the Government ordered the gradual withdrawal of the Indian units from East Africa. Von Lettow, with only 1,300 men, surrendered in Northern Rhodesia on November 25th, 1918.

This narrative, however, is concerned more with engineering than

---

[1] The British losses were about 40 officers and 800 men killed, wounded or missing.
[2] The author has been greatly assisted in his narrative by information supplied by Major-General S. H. Sheppard, C.B., C.M.G., D.S.O.
[3] The distinguished Boer leader in the South African War, who became afterwards Prime Minister of United South Africa and a Member of the Imperial War Cabinet.

strategy. The Faridkot Sappers, the Bridging Train, the Field Park, the 61st Pioneers, and the 25th and 26th (Railway) Companies, Bombay Sappers and Miners (who landed in Mombasa under Major C. W. Wilkinson, R.E., in November, 1914[1]) were reinforced in 1916 by two more Railway companies—the 27th and 28th—an East African Pioneer Company, and, from South Africa, a Pioneer Battalion, two Field Troops and a Water Supply Corps, the whole being under Colonel F. P. Rundle, R.E., as Chief Engineer. Early in 1918 Colonel Rundle's command was still further strengthened by the arrival of the 14th Company, Madras Sappers and Miners, under Captain W. E. Britten, R.E.,[2] and also by two Road Construction Companies, two Road Corps, and a Base Park Company.[3] By that time the operations had spread into Portuguese East Africa where the 14th Company marched 1,100 miles and made 320 miles of bush road before the end of the year. In the opening stages of the campaign there were so few engineering troops that it was often necessary to employ a whole brigade of infantry for weeks at a time in blasting, roadmaking and bridge-building. Gradually the situation improved, but to the very end the lack of regular field units of Sappers and Miners was a grievous burden.

The strategy of the opposing forces depended largely on the use of the German Northern and Central Railways, and hence the importance of the work of the Bombay Railway companies. After some road construction early in 1915, the 25th and 26th Companies built a line from Voi on the Uganda Railway to Moshi on the captured Northern Railway, and finished it in April, 1916. From May, 1916, to June, 1917, they were engaged in repairing the Northern Railway and laying two branch lines; then they set to work on the Central Railway and afterwards laid small lines from two southern ports into the interior.[4]

Before Smuts drove the Germans southwards in 1916, there were constant raids on the Uganda Railway. The enemy mined the line and blew up several trains. It was most difficult to detect these mines which were buried in the ballast, but a way was found in whitewashing the whole of the ballast so that railway patrols could see at a glance if any stones had been disturbed. The reconstruction of the Central Railway by the British began after the capture of Dar-es-Salaam in September, 1916. Although the Germans had not damaged much of the track, they had left hardly a bridge standing.

[1] *A Brief History of the Royal Bombay Sappers and Miners*, p. 35.
[2] *Historical Record, Q.V.O. Madras Sappers and Miners*, Vol. II, p. 25.
[3] *Summary of Work of Technical Units, 1916–1918*, by Colonel Frank Rundle, R.E., dated November 26th, 1918. It is recorded that between 1916 and 1918 the Engineer units, exclusive of the four Railway Companies, constructed 52 miles of trolley line, 11 flying bridges over large rivers, 118 wells, 3,421 miles of road, 133 pumping stations and many buildings.
[4] "Notes on Railway Work in East Africa," by Captain H. L. Woodhouse, M.C., R.E., appearing in *The R.E. Journal*, Vol. XXXVII, March–December, 1923 p. 38.

Sixty bridges were down within 200 miles of Dar-es-Salaam. A clever expedient, however, was adopted to make the line passable for traffic. The bridges were patched up with local material so as to carry a load of about six tons, and motor lorries with trailers were then fitted with railway trolley wheels and placed on the line to take the place of locomotives and wagons. By the end of October, 1916, the Central Railway was carrying motor traffic for a distance of 500 miles inland while new bridges were under construction. The rapid work of the four Railway Companies certainly helped Van Deventer to clear the enemy from German East Africa and thus to free a number of Indian units for service elsewhere during 1918.

It may be well, in conclusion, to review briefly the situation on the North-West Frontier of India while the bulk of the country's forces were fighting overseas. Afghanistan, under the wise rule of Amir Habibullah Khan, set an excellent example of neutrality to the turbulent tribes of the border, but nevertheless India was saddled with a number of minor campaigns in the North-West between 1915 and 1918. The frontier was held by a covering force of the best troops available. Behind it were four divisions retained in India for limited offensives and to support the defenders of the front line, but the British units of these divisions were mostly Territorials and few of the Indian units had much experience. Volunteer units assisted the regulars in garrison duties in the interior until the Indian Defence Force Act of 1917 gathered all European British subjects into an Auxiliary Force for internal security. But the entry of Turkey into the war inflamed the religious passions of the Muhammadan tribes of the border to such an extent, and they became so unsettled by the enemy's agents who penetrated even into India, that the year 1915 was one of great anxiety. The country as a whole remained staunch, but military operations became necessary across the border in Baluchistan, the Tochi Valley, Swat, Buner and the Black Mountain, and particularly against the Mohmands, and these were on a scale which involved the employment of the entire 1st (Peshawar) Division and part of the 2nd (Rawalpindi) Division.[1] They were forced upon India in self-defence.

Three *mullahs*—those of Islampur in Kunar, Babra and Chaknaur—were mainly responsible for Mohmand raids across the border in January, April, August and October, 1915, in three of which the tribe suffered severely. The fighting took place chiefly near Shabkadr, on the Michni–Abazai front north of Peshawar, and on one occasion the Mohmands lost 1,400 men. A blockade was then instituted, and the Mohmands submitted in April, 1916; but in September they began to raid again, and the blockade was resumed from a line of defensible posts and barbed wire erected by the

[1] *The Empire at War*, by Sir Charles Lucas, K.C.B., K.C.M.G., Vol. V, p. 185.

Engineers and Sappers and Miners along the Michni–Abazai front.[1] A battle took place on November 7th, 1916, when the Mohmands were dispersed by artillery fire, and it was not till July, 1917, that they made their final submission and normal relations with them were restored.[2] The 1st, 2nd and 6th Companies and a Field Troop, all of the Bengal Sappers and Miners, and the 19th Company, Bombay Sappers and Miners, served during these operations.[3] They did good work, but nothing which calls for special remark.

Although the general situation on the North-West Frontier in 1916 gave less anxiety than in the previous year, the respite was short. In 1917 the Mahsuds of Waziristan took the field and a new burden was thrust upon the army in India. It was reported on February 26th that a powerful *lashkar*[4] was moving against Sarwekai.[5] The Mahsuds attacked that post, and operations were begun under the direction of Lieut.-General Sir A. A. Barrett, K.C.B., K.C.S.I., K.C.V.O.[6] The Derajat Movable Column relieved the garrison of Sarwekai on March 9th, and then conducted punitive measures in the Khaisora and Shahur Valleys, returning to Tank on April 3rd; but within a week it had to reascend the Gomal Valley, moving by Kajuri Kach and reaching Wana on the 21st after a fight in a defile. As the Mahsuds continued to attack our convoys it became necessary to strengthen the Derajat Garrison, so a Derajat Field Force of two brigades and attached troops under Major-General W. G. L. Beynon, C.B., C.I.E., D.S.O., was concentrated at Tank. Included in it were the 7th Company, Bengal Sappers and Miners, and the 11th Company, Madras Sappers and Miners. They were not to be envied. This spot during the hot weather was truly an abomination of desolation. A catchword among the British troops was that "Hell was the hill-station of Tank," and perhaps they were right.

The Derajat Field Force was soon expanded into the "South Waziristan Field Force" by the addition of another brigade, and operations were resumed in the Khaisora Valley while a smaller "North Waziristan Field Force" under Brigadier-General the Hon. C. G. Bruce, M.V.O., prepared to co-operate in the Tochi Valley. At the end of May, 1917, hostile acts began in the Tochi while Beynon concentrated the Southern Force at Jandola for an advance up the Shahur Valley which he then traversed by Haidari Kach to Barwand

---

[1] The defensible posts were 400 yards apart, and between them was a double-apron barbed wire fence. In front of this fence was a curtain of live wire, supplied with electric current from a power house at Abazai. In May, 1917, the defensible posts were replaced by towers, and the live wire removed.
[2] *Military Report on the Mohmand Country* (General Staff, India, 1926), p. 8.
[3] The 1st Company (Captain J. F. Gray, R.E.) served on the N.W. Frontier from June, 1915, to February, 1916. The 2nd Company (Captain H. N. G. Geary, R.E.), the 6th Company (Lieutenant A. D. De R. Martin, R.E.), the 1st Field Troop (Captain E. G. Gidley-Kitchin, R.E.) and the 19th Company (Captain C. F. Stoehr, R.E.) served from October, 1916, to February or March, 1917.
[4] *Lashkar*. An army of tribesmen.
[5] North of the Gomal River, and 20 miles east of Wana.
[6] General Barrett was then G.O.C. in C., Northern Army.

in the face of considerable resistance. Next he conducted further punitive operations in the Khaisora Valley, and these brought the Mahsuds at last to reason. They submitted on August 10th, 1917. The Sapper and Miner companies were busy throughout the campaign in improving communications, bridging ravines, destroying village towers and arranging for water supply ; and two Royal Engineers on the Staff, Brigadier-General S. G. Loch, D.S.O., and Lieut.-Colonel W. E. R. Dickson, C.I.E., were highly praised for their work.

During February, March and April, 1918, part of the 52nd Company, Bengal Sappers and Miners, and the 72nd Company of the Bombay Corps were on service against the Marris between Sibi and the Indus in the neighbourhood of Quetta, but there is little of engineering interest to record about these operations. Under the energetic development of recruiting, and the consequent expansion of the Indian army, brought about by General Sir Charles Monro as Commander-in-Chief,[1] and through the increasing experience of frontier warfare gathered by the troops holding the line, the North-West Frontier seemed to be settling down contentedly ; but its placidity was apparent only, for while the exhausted nations of Europe were wrangling over the blessings of peace, the torch applied by King Amanullah of Afghanistan in 1919 started the greatest conflagration across the border which India has ever known.

---

[1] General Sir Charles Monro, G.C.S.I., G.C.M.G., K.C.B., became Commander-in-Chief in India in the autumn of 1916.

CHAPTER XXIV.

CAMPAIGNS AFTER THE GREAT WAR.

1919–1932.

THE Great War bequeathed to the civilized world a legacy of bitterness, disillusionment and strife unparalleled in history, and India did not escape the general unrest. Yet it taught many lessons, and among them that the Army in India should be provided with modern armament of European type, though modified to suit the special conditions of the North-West Frontier. Efficient equipment saves money and lives: it gives a small force increased mobility and power: it economizes in men. And so, at a time when economy was all-important, the Army in India was supplied gradually with a scale of mechanical equipment undreamed of in 1914, although it retained much of its pack transport for use in the trackless wastes of the Frontier. Efficiency and celerity of movement and action were its aims; its officers and men became highly trained, its organization carefully designed, its weapons modernized, its heavy transport mechanized. The tribesmen found themselves confronted by troops who worked with quickness and precision, guided by aerial reconnaissance, and assisted by bombing aeroplanes, machine-guns, accurate gunfire, rapid supply services, expert engineering and highly-specialized signalling. The result has been that many of the military operations against undisciplined enemies on and beyond the North-West Frontier of India since the Great War have been affairs of weeks or even days instead of months or years. But in 1919, before the Indian Army was fully reorganized and equipped, and before it was fully trained, the forces opposed to it were not wholly undisciplined. It was then that King Amanullah Khan of Afghanistan launched his mad scheme of conquest, and set his trained soldiers in motion towards the Indian Frontier in the Third Afghan War.

At this time there were serious disturbances in India and much agitation against the Rowlatt Act. Afghan agents sent news to Kabul that India was on the point of rising in open rebellion. The Army in India was in the process of demobilization. Many of its best units were still on service abroad.[1] The opportunity seemed heaven-sent. The War Party in Afghanistan seized their chance and proclaimed a *jehad*, and on April 25th, 1919, the Afghan troops

---

[1] At the outbreak of the Third Afghan War, 124 battalions and 89 squadrons were serving overseas.

began to move, while at the same time a stream of anti-British propaganda was let loose from Kabul to secure the co-operation of the Frontier tribes. Yet within ten days the Afghans were severely defeated, and on May 14th Amanullah was asking privately for an armistice which was granted on June 3rd. In less than one month of actual fighting, results were obtained which were secured in 1842 only after four years of privation and bloodshed. A Treaty of Peace was signed on August 8th, 1919, and so the war against Afghanistan came to an end; but it left the entire North-West Frontier in such a state of turmoil that it was not till December, 1920, that serious military operations ceased for a time, only to be renewed in Waziristan in 1922.

On May 3rd, 1919, the first definite acts of hostility were committed by the Afghans beyond the Khaibar Pass, and India was forced to declare war on May 6th. Three infantry divisions,[1] and several cavalry and mobile brigades, under General Sir A. A. Barrett, G.C.B., K.C.S.I., K.C.V.O., were allotted to the Peshawar line as a "North-West Frontier Force," and one division,[2] with a mounted brigade, under Lieut.-General R. Wapshare, C.B., C.S.I., to the Quetta line as a "Baluchistan Force." The Bannu and Derajat Independent Brigades, which were at first included in General Barrett's command, were separated from it in June, 1919, as a "Waziristan Force" under Major-General S. H. Climo, C.B., D.S.O. Before the outbreak of hostilities, the duty of policing the independent tribal territory beyond the Administrative Border had fallen on Militia units, Frontier Constabulary and Levies, organized in accordance with the principles laid down by Lord Curzon in 1899, one idea being that they would act as a barrier behind which the Field Army could concentrate in case of war. The Chitral Scouts, Mohmand Militia, Khyber Rifles, Kurram Militia, and North and South Waziristan Militias seemed likely to fulfil Lord Curzon's dreams, but some of them failed to stand the acid test of 1919. The general position in May of that year was that independent tribal territory was either not held at all or lightly held by these Pathan militias, the border itself being garrisoned by armed police. A striking force of two divisions and two cavalry brigades was available for a thrust into Afghanistan through the Khaibar Pass—an operation which was likely to be retarded by shortage of transport—while a defensive attitude was necessary in Chitral in the extreme north and in Waziristan in the centre. Reports estimated the Afghan army at 78 battalions of infantry and 21 regiments of cavalry, with 280 breech-loading guns and a large number of muzzle-loaders; possibly 38,000 rifles, 8,000 sabres and 4,000 artillerymen were available for actual fighting.[3] This army, however, had no staff and

[1] The 1st and 2nd Indian Divisions, with the 16th Indian Division in reserve.
[2] The 4th Indian Division.
[3] *The Third Afghan War*, 1919. *Official Account*, p. 23.

very little military organization. The infantry were brave fighters, but they were poorly led and less than half of them had small-bore rifles. The gunners were badly trained, and their weapons inefficient. The machine-gunners used archaic "Gardiners" of the Victorian era. Such an army should not have been formidable even in its own country, but the danger of the active participation of all the Frontier tribes was ever present, necessitating a wide dispersion of our forces which were composed largely of young soldiers commanded by officers who had little experience of Frontier warfare.

The days of spectacular work on a grand scale by Sappers and Miners in Eastern warfare may be said to have vanished with the appearance of the magazine rifle and the high-explosive shell. They do not now lead storming parties against enormous battlements because fortresses are rare and shells and bombs are very effective. But Frontier operations on such a scale as those of 1919 call for engineering assistance as urgently as those of the nineteenth century, and the list of the Sapper and Miner units, which served in the Third Afghan War, proves the fact. The Bengal Corps supplied six Field Companies and a Field Troop; the Madras Corps, ten Field Companies and a Field Troop; and the Bombay Corps, seven Field Companies, a Field Troop and three Railway Companies. There were also four companies of Imperial Service Sappers, two Pontoon Parks, several Field Parks and many smaller formations.[1] Never before had there been such a concentration of Engineers and Sappers and Miners on the North-West Frontier. Of the 23 regular Field Companies, General Barrett had the 7th and 56th Companies of Bengal Sappers with the 1st Division under Major-General C. A. Fowler, C.B., D.S.O., and the 11th and 64th Companies of Madras Sappers with the 2nd Division under Major-General Sir C. M. Dobell, K.C.B., C.M.G., D.S.O., while among his Corps Troops were the 53rd and 58th Companies of the Bengal Corps, the 14th Company of the Madras Corps, the 76th Company and three Railway Companies of the Bombay Corps and four battalions of Pioneers. The Waziristan Force included the 55th Company, Bengal Sappers and Miners, and the 75th Company, Bombay Sappers and Miners; and the Baluchistan Force and a force located in East Persia divided between them the 17th, 24th, 71st and 73rd Companies of the Bombay Sappers and Miners. The 57th Company of the Bengal Corps was in the Kohat Area with a division under Major-General A. H. Eustace, C.B., D.S.O. The Field Troops, the remaining companies, and the subsidiary engineering formations were distributed on the various fronts or

[1] The Bengal Sappers sent the 7th, 53rd, 55th, 56th, 57th and 58th Field Companies and No. 1 Field Troop. The Madras Sappers, the 11th, 14th, 15th, 63rd, 64th, 66th, 67th, 68th (Burma), 69th and 76th Field Companies and No. 8 Field Troop. The Bombay Sappers, the 17th, 24th, 71st, 73rd, 74th, 75th and 76th Field Companies, No. 7 Field Troop, and the 26th, 27th and 28th Railway Companies. (See *The Third Afghan War*, 1919. *Official Account*, pp. 168, 169, and records of the three Corps of Sappers and Miners.)

on the lines of communication. The organization was a huge one, and yet it was hardly large enough for the operations which took place in 1919 and 1920 between Chitral and Quetta.

On May 6th, 1919, the Afghans were massing near Bagh[1] at the western entrance to the Khaibar Pass, and were in a position to cut off the water supply of the weakly-garrisoned British fort at Landi Kotal. They occupied two prominent features, known as Tor Tsappar and Spinatsuka, five miles north of the fort, and then seized the Ash Khel ridge within a mile of it. Landi Kotal was in great danger, but it was saved by a battalion of Somersets who reached it from Peshawar on the 7th, followed by an infantry brigade under Brigadier-General G. F. Crocker, which arrived on the 8th. Crocker then cleared the Afghans off the Ash Khel ridge, and, although exposed to attack from the north, launched his troops westwards on the 9th towards a position which the enemy had occupied on the rugged slopes and ridges of Khargali, Kafir Kot and Bagh above Landi Khana. After severe fighting he regained control of the Landi Kotal water supply system, which part of the 7th Company, Bengal Sappers and Miners,[2] then repaired; but the enemy still held their main position on the Khargali ridge. General Fowler, who arrived that evening, decided to renew the attack on the 11th with the help of some reinforcements, and did so with such success that the Afghans were soon in rapid retreat towards Dakka, eight miles within the Afghan border. Our cavalry followed them while our aeroplanes bombed Dakka, and on the 13th our troops were camped south of that village. The Afghans, however, soon rallied, and advancing on the 16th, with thousands of tribesmen, against a British force to the west of Dakka, forced it to retire to the Dakka Camp. On the following day, the troops under Major-General A. Skeen, C.M.G., took the offensive and succeeded with great difficulty in driving the enemy from a strong position. The Sappers and Miners did not share in these operations as they were busily employed between Dakka and Landi Kotal. After the Royal Air Force had bombed Jalalabad and Kabul, it was proposed to advance on Jalalabad on May 26th; but the movement never took place, for on that date strong Afghan forces appeared in the Kurram Valley and reinforcements and transport had to be hurried to Kohat. This dislocated the arrangements at Dakka. King Amanullah asked officially for an armistice on May 31st, and it was granted on June 3rd. So ended the third British invasion of Afghanistan. The Afghans fought bravely enough beyond the Khaibar, but their strategy was mediocre. Their Generals were no match for ours; their artillery was poor, their machine-guns useless, and they had no

---

[1] The map inset in the "Sketch Map of the North-West Frontier and Afghanistan" at the end of this volume shows the positions of the localities mentioned.

[2] Commanded by Captain G. D. Watson, R.E.

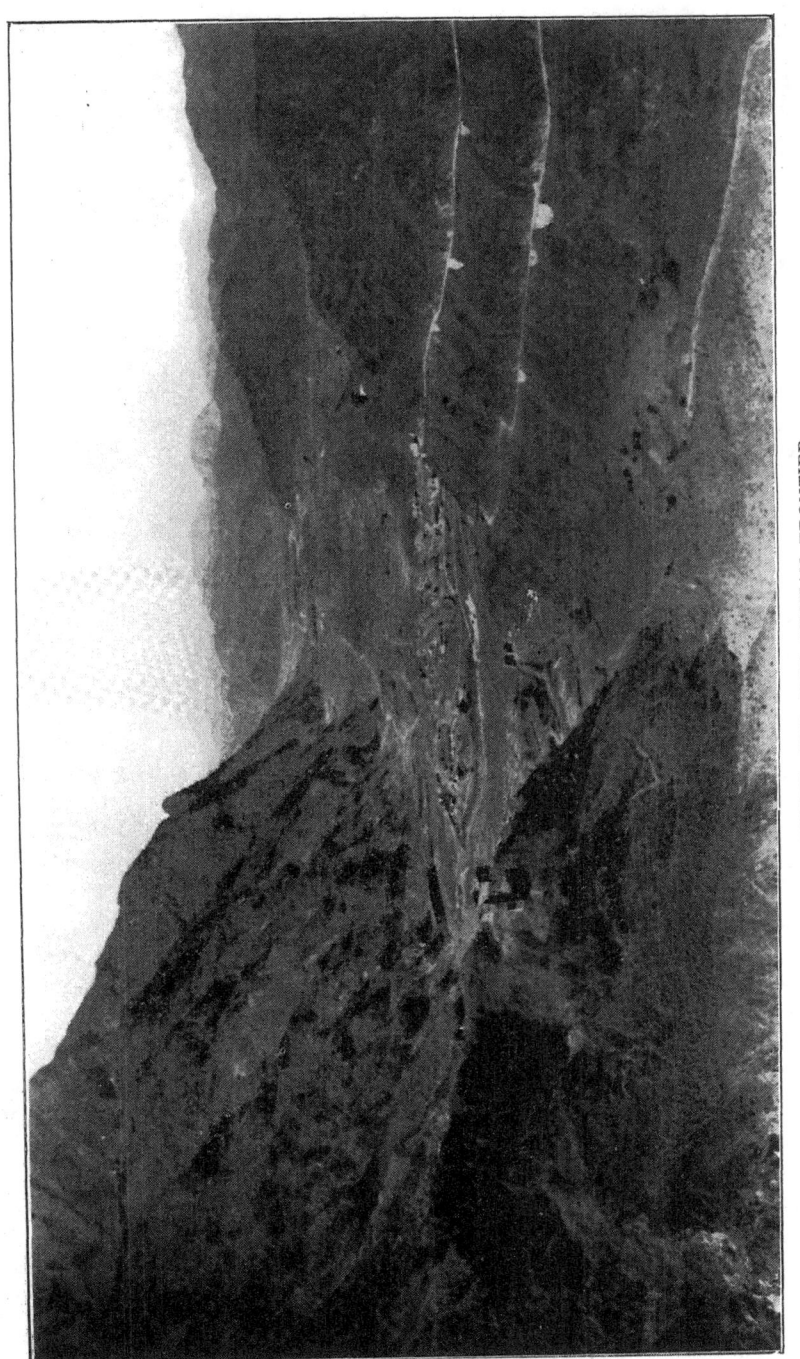

LANDI KHANA AND THE AFGHAN FRONTIER.

proper engineering troops. The British victory was cheaply won, and at express speed.

While these operations were in progress there had been trouble with the Afridis in the Khaibar Pass,[1] and it became necessary to take over the posts held by the Khyber Rifles and to disband that body. Four thousand Bajauris and Mohmands demonstrated against the Michni–Abazai line north of Peshawar and necessitated its reinforcement. Afghan troops invaded distant Chitral, where hostilities on a small scale continued till the signing of peace in August. But the most serious threat was in the Kurram Valley. Fourteen Afghan battalions with 48 guns, under General Nadir Khan,[2] began to concentrate early in May, 1919, at Matun, in the Khost salient of Afghanistan, where they could strike at either the Kurram or Tochi valleys in which our commanders were forced to stand on the defensive. It was decided that if Nadir Khan invaded the Tochi, the British posts along that river above Miramshah should be evacuated. On May 25th Nadir Khan crossed the Durand Line, west of Parachinar, and advanced against Thal while the British retired before him. He besieged and shelled the fort and camp at Thal from May 27th to 31st when the garrison was relieved by a force under Brigadier-General R. F. H. Dyer, C.B.,[3] who routed the tribal allies of the Afghans by a series of well-planned operations on June 1st, in which the 57th Company, Bengal Sappers and Miners, took part. Nadir Khan then withdrew hastily towards Khost. Punitive operations around Thal followed. During the destruction of the village of Biland Khel by the Sappers, a soldier of the 57th Company performed a deed which is a good example of the cold-blooded heroism so often demanded in frontier warfare. Bugler Narain Chand volunteered to enter a deep cave to ascertain if it was occupied by hostile tribesmen. He went in alone and unarmed and found six women whom he brought out. Then, taking one companion, he re-entered the cave and explored it thoroughly, but, fortunately for him, met no enemy.[4] Such deeds are common on the Frontier. Too often they go unobserved and unrecorded.

Nadir Khan's advance on Thal was the signal for the evacuation of the British posts in the Upper Tochi Valley, while Wana and several posts on the Gomal River were also abandoned. For the moment, a defensive attitude was unavoidable, but the effect of these retrograde movements was disastrous. Waziristan rose, the

---

[1] The trouble continued till September, 1919. In July, Major-General S. H. Sheppard, C.B., C.M.G., D.S.O., operated with a brigade in the Khaibar Pass. On September 13th, the 11th Company, Madras Sappers and Miners (Captain C. J. S. King, R.E.) was engaged with a powerful column in destroying Chora Fort, six miles west of Ali Masjid.
[2] The ex-Commander-in-Chief of the Afghan Army who is now King of Afghanistan.
[3] The officer who subdued a rebellion at Amritsar.
[4] *The Third Afghan War,* 1919, *Official Account,* p. 62.

militia organization failed, and the Government of India was forced to embark on a costly war against the Wazirs and Mahsuds in November, 1919. There was severe fighting along the Zhob River, including a serious reverse when a convoy was captured, and Fort Sandeman was besieged in July by Sheranni and Wazir tribesmen. It is impossible to describe in these pages the exploits and movements of all the British columns, but the operations of General Wapshare in Baluchistan are of engineering interest because they entailed the reduction of the Afghan stronghold of Spin Baldak, lying six miles north-west of New Chaman between Quetta and Kandahar. The political effect of this stroke was excellent, for Spin Baldak was reputed to be the second strongest fortress in Afghanistan. Wapshare concentrated two brigades and some divisional troops, including the 24th and part of the 73rd Companies of the Bombay Sappers and Miners, and attacked on May 26th, 1919, in two columns with a suitable reserve.[1] Spin Baldak was a square work, with bastioned inner and outer walls, surrounded by a ditch 25 feet deep and of similar width. It stood below the southern end of a fortified ridge close to the frontier. At the time of the First Afghan War such a fortress might have offered a stout resistance, but it fell quickly in 1919 under the accurate artillery and machine-gun fire of Wapshare's troops. The ridge was taken by a surprise attack, and Spin Baldak was then stormed by the 1/4 Gurkhas and 1/22 Punjabis, the Gurkhas entering through a breach and opening a gate to admit the Punjabis, some of whom were already scaling the walls with ladders as in the times before the Indian Mutiny. Of the 600 men who formed the garrison, 200 were killed and the remainder captured. The Bombay Sappers and Miners were not in the assault, but had a difficult task afterwards in arranging for a piped water supply to the captured work in which the existing water was undrinkable; by July 10th, however, a pipeline was completed from New Chaman to Spin Baldak. The Engineers and Sappers were also busily employed in fortifying the camp at New Chaman. The enemy made no serious attempt at retaliation for the loss of Spin Baldak, and, with the arrival of reinforcements, the British position in Baluchistan was soon secure. Six days after the signing of peace on August 8th, the battered, but cleaned and garnished, fortress was handed back to the Afghans.

Throughout the war the Engineers and Sappers and Miners, ably assisted by the Pioneers, carried out their usual duties in the field. They demolished towers, fortified positions and posts, built roads and bridges, and laid railways; they even erected aerial ropeways in the Khaibar Pass. But their most important duty in the forward areas was to supply pure water to the camps of the thirsty troops who were fighting in the heat of an Indian summer in a mountainous

[1] *The Third Afghan War*, 1919, *Official Account*, p. 99.

and barren land. The success of the operations was due largely to the efforts of the Engineer units in this utilitarian work.[1]

One of the results of the Third Afghan War was the construction of a railway line through the Khaibar Pass. Before the war, the North-Western Railway extended to Jamrud at the foot of the Pass; but the final section in the plains between Peshawar and Jamrud was a single line, roughly laid and poorly ballasted, which crossed the bed of a *nullah* where a painted post showed the engine driver whether the water, if any, was deep enough to extinguish his fires. Troops and stores had usually to be detrained at Peshawar, so the work of doubling the railway and bridging the *nullah* was put in hand as soon as the Afghan War began, and was still in progress when it ended. The transport of supplies through the Khaibar Pass, however, had proved to be so difficult during the war that in 1920 the Government of India began the construction of a single-line strategic railway 27 miles long, between Jamrud and the Afghan frontier beyond Landi Khana. A length of $20\frac{1}{2}$ miles, from Jamrud to Landi Kotal at the summit of the Pass, was opened on November 2nd, 1925,[2] and the line was soon extended to Landi Khana. It is a remarkable engineering achievement. There are two and half miles of tunnels, and seven crossings of the Khaibar *nullah*, with two very high viaducts among them. The sharpest curve is seven degrees, and the ruling gradient on the section between Jamrud and Shagai is 1 in $33\frac{1}{3}$ although the line is an adhesion one of 5' 6" gauge. This railway, reinforced by a double motor-road, has removed the difficulties of supply and transport which hampered the operations in Afghanistan in 1919. The Khaibar, and other frontier railways, afford notable examples of the work of some of the military engineers of India.[3]

[1] Brigadier-General R. F. Sorsbie, C.S.I., C.I.E. (late R.E.), was the Chief Engineer, N.W. Frontier Force; and Colonel H. A. D. Fraser, C.B. (late R.E.), C.R.E. Peshawar District and D.D.M.W. on the line of communication, was chiefly responsible for the success of its water supply arrangements. The supply of water to the troops at Landi Kotal was extremely difficult because of the shortage of plant and transport.

[2] Article entitled " The Khyber Railway," appearing in *The R.E. Journal*, Vol. XXXVIII, March–December, 1924, p. 271 (reprinted from *The Railway Gazette*, dated September 17th, 1923).

[3] Two railways leading to the Afghan frontier were built mainly by Royal Engineers. These are the Sind–Pishin Railway, built by Colonel James (" Buster ") Browne, C.B. (afterwards Colonel Sir James Browne, K.C.S.I., C.B.), and the Khaibar Railway, built by Lieut.-Colonel G. R. Hearn, D.S.O. (now Colonel Sir Gordon Hearn, C.I.E., D.S.O.). The Sind–Pishin Railway did not extend originally to the frontier, but was prolonged to it later by civilian engineers. The Mushkaf–Bolan " Cut-off " of this line was also added by civilian engineers. Major C. St. J. Lynch, D.S.O., R.E., was in charge of one of the two reconnaissance parties for the Khaibar line. This was the same officer who accompanied Colonel (then Major) Hearn on a difficult reconnaissance in 1912–13 for a railway from Tank to Fort Sandeman. The Mechanical Division of the Khaibar Railway work was ably directed by Captain E. F. Johnston, R.E. Many Royal Engineers shared in the construction and survey operations which were carried out partly by them and partly by civil engineers. Colonel Hearn was in charge of the whole project until November, 1922, when he was succeeded by Major E. P. Anderson, D.S.O., R.E., who was " Superintendent of Works " until February, 1924. The survey and construction of the Sind–Pishin and Khaibar Railways will be dealt with in Chapter IX, Volume II.

The outbreak of the Afghan War in 1919, followed by the withdrawal of the British garrisons from the Upper Tochi Valley and from Wana near the head of the Gomal route, upset the confidence and loyalty of the majority of the rank and file of the North and South Waziristan Militias. Many of the men deserted or turned against their officers, and Wazir and Mahsud raiders invaded the Derajat and Zhob. Since 1852 the British had already fought 17 campaigns in Waziristan, five of which[1] had been of a serious nature; but the Mahsuds had never offered a really protracted resistance. Nevertheless it seemed that nothing less than a permanent occupation of their country could bring them under control, and this was the policy which was adopted during the campaign which followed the Afghan War and which was sanctioned formally by the Government of India in September, 1922.

Of the four Pathan tribes which inhabit Waziristan the most troublesome have always been the Mahsuds of the central area, although the Darwesh Khel Wazirs around the Tochi Valley in the north have taken their full share in rebellion. Both tribes are brave fighters, expert marksmen, wonderfully hardy and agile, ferocious and treacherous, but these qualities are more marked in the Mahsuds than in their hereditary enemies the Wazirs. In 1919 and 1920, the Mahsuds fought with a determination and skill which were unequalled in frontier warfare, and they were defeated only by superior discipline, strategy and armament. They lacked cohesion, and had no single commander. Individually they were unsurpassed in courage and enterprise, but a collection of individuals cannot long resist a modern army. The fact that the war lasted far into 1920 was due partly to the insufficient training and knowledge of frontier warfare of the young soldiers who formed at that time the bulk of the British forces. "The chief lesson of the campaign," says the official account,[2] "is that, although a force may be equipped with the most modern weapons and appliances, it cannot command success unless its men are well trained and its officers lead them in accordance with the time-honoured and proved principles of war." There were many "regrettable incidents" in the early stages of the campaign in Waziristan, but nevertheless it ended in the submission of the enemy and the permanent occupation of their country.

The situation in Waziristan at the end of May, 1919, was critical. In the Tochi Valley, the posts at Datta Khel, Tut Narai, Spin Khaisora and Boya had been evacuated, the loyal remnants of the garrisons retiring to Miramshah and the adjacent cantonment at Dardoni. These places, and also Idak and Saidgi lower down the Tochi, were then closely invested by the Wazirs. The loyal troops at Wana had cut their way through to Fort Sandeman on the Zhob

[1] Those of 1860, 1881, 1894, 1901 and 1917.
[2] *Operations in Waziristan*, 1919-1920. *Official Account*, p. 146.

River. In the Gomal Valley, all the posts below Khajuri Kach had been abandoned, and the Mahsuds and Sherannis threatened Murtaza, Manzai, Jandola and other posts west of Tank. "It needed but the appearance of Afghan detachments provided with arms for the Wazirs and a little artillery," writes de Watteville,[1] "to set the tribesmen descending upon the plains of the Indus on an unprecedented scale." Indeed, to the Wazirs and Mahsuds, the withdrawal of the Tochi and Gomal garrisons presaged the collapse of British rule in India. Heat, cholera and the ending of the Afghan War, however, prevented any marked change in the situation during the summer months of 1919, and it was not till November 8th that a powerful force was assembled under Major-General S. H. Climo, C.B., D.S.O., to deal first with the Tochi Wazirs of Northern Waziristan.

The Waziristan Force included very few British troops, but it had six brigades of Indian infantry, four additional infantry battalions, four regiments of Indian cavalry, several batteries, a wing of the Royal Air Force, and two companies of Sappers and Miners, the 55th of the Bengal Corps and the 74th of the Bombay Corps—altogether about 29,000 men; yet such were the demands for the protection of the lines of communication that the actual Striking Force at Miramshah under Major-General A. Skeen, C.M.G., was composed of only two brigades, with divisional troops including the 55th Company, Bengal Sappers and Miners—a total of about 8,500 fighting men. It was sufficiently powerful, however, to overawe the Tochi Wazirs, who submitted when Skeen advanced to Datta Khel. On November 26th the troops were back in Dardoni, and the Striking Force (now called the Derajat Column) marched a distance of 132 miles eastwards down the Tochi, southwards to Pezu and finally westwards to the Tank–Jandola area to deal with the Mahsuds.[2] General Climo then prepared to send the Derajat Column up the Tank (or Taki) Zam defiles towards the Mahsud centres at Makin and Kaniguram. He hoped that the Mahsuds would submit to a display of force as the Wazirs had done, but the new enemy had no such intention.

Piqueting the heights carefully as he progressed, General Skeen reached Jandola with the Derajat Column on December 17th, 1919, and repulsed a fierce attack on his camp; then, advancing up the valley to Palosina, he halted there till the 29th. Throughout the campaign he was forced to collect a mass of supplies at each camp before he could undertake any further advance. Pack transport alone was possible because there were no roads, so the advance was slow. The lack of proper roads was felt at once. The 55th Company of Bengal Sappers and the 3/34th Sikh Pioneers did their best to

---

[1] *Waziristan*, 1919–1920, by H. de Watteville, p. 56.
[2] The Derajat Column reached this area on December 13th.

improve the existing track, but there was little time to do so. Every step was contested by the enemy. Desperate fighting took place while the column tried to establish permanent piquets on the ridges around Palosina. The Mahsuds attacked repeatedly. They drove our troops back time after time, only to be hurled off the captured heights in their turn. There were heavy casualties on both sides, and when Palosina was safe at last, the Mahsuds were still full of fight. Skeen advanced to Kotkai on December 29th, and halted there till January 7th when he made an abortive attempt to force a passage of the Ahnai Tangi, a narrow gorge of the Tank Zam a few miles above his new camp. Failing again on the 9th, and yet again on the 10th, he adopted the dangerous expedient of a night march, and having skilfully secured the defile by this means, passed his force through it on the 14th. In the face of further determined resistance, he arrived safely on the Sorarogha plateau on January 18th, having fought 20 actions in one month. The Mahsuds had lost heavily and their courage was beginning to wane.

The next stage of the advance up the Tank Zam was to Piaza Raghza, close below Dwa Toi and within striking distance of Makin and Kaniguram. The first obstacle was a difficult defile called the Barari Tangi, the passage of which was forced between January 23rd and 27th. The enemy's resistance became steadily less, but the operations were hindered by extreme cold. Early in February the temperature fell almost to zero, and the troops suffered severely in the piercing wind. On February 6th, the force camped at Piaza Raghza, and awaited reinforcements and supplies. As the line of communication lengthened, Waziristan absorbed more and more men; and although the Derajat Column consisted only of the 67th Infantry Brigade, with one additional battalion, two Mountain Batteries,[1] the 3/34th Sikh Pioneers, and the 55th Company, Bengal Sappers and Miners (about 10,000 combatants), the total force in the country amounted to more than 45,000 fighting men. General Skeen marched to Tauda China, close to Makin, on February 16th, and soon began a systematic devastation of the thickly populated Makin Valley. In three hours on February 20th, the Sappers and Miners and Pioneers demolished 17 towers and 160 houses; day by day they continued the work of destruction, while the howitzers bombarded the more distant villages and the aeroplanes dropped their bombs.[2] The wide valley of Makin became a smoking ruin. It was deplorable, but necessary.

On March 1st the Derajat Column retired from Makin to Dwa Toi, and on the 3rd began to ascend the Baddar Toi Valley towards the Mahsud capital of Kaniguram. The Sappers and Pioneers fortified

[1] No. 27 (Indian) Mountain Battery (2·75-inch guns), and No. 6 Mountain Battery (3·7-inch howitzers).
[2] In the campaign in Waziristan during 1919 and 1920, for the first time in Frontier warfare, aeroplanes took a prominent and decisive part in the operations.

a position at Ladha and prepared a double camel-track up the valley. Kaniguram was reached on March 6th, and there the force remained during March and April, 1920, while the Engineer units prepared a motor road between Kaniguram and Ladha and improved the fortified posts and water supply arrangements. Afterwards the entire force occupied the fortified camp at Ladha. The task of the Derajat Column was now finished, and the remainder of the campaign was concerned with punitive work and an expedition in November from Jandola by Sarwekai to Wana in which the 14th Company, Madras Sappers and Miners, took part. Wana was reoccupied without much trouble on December 22nd, 1920, and was garrisoned for several years to keep the Wana Wazirs in order. The critical operations in Waziristan during 1919 and 1920 ended in a stalemate. The Mahsuds, defeated, impoverished, sullen and exhausted, were ready nevertheless to rise again if opportunity offered. Hence the decision to occupy their country permanently, and hence the construction of the Waziristan Circular Road, the most notable and useful engineering work ever accomplished on the North-West Frontier.

The Government of India decided to establish a fortified camp at Razmak, about 7,000 feet above sea-level and within artillery range of the Makin Valley, and it was necessary, for safety, rapidity of supply, and economy of troops, to connect this camp by good roads to the existing railheads near the Administrative Boundary. Accordingly the preliminary work on a road suitable for heavy motor transport, from Isha in the Tochi Valley towards Razmak, was begun in November, 1922. It took off from an existing road along the Tochi which led to Bannu. The scheme was to connect the Isha–Razmak Road with another to be constructed from Sorarogha up the Tank Zam to Razmak, thus completing a semi-circular route between Dera Ismail Khan and Bannu through the heart of the Mahsud territory. It was realized that this road would not only facilitate the concentration of troops at any threatened point, but would help to civilize the country, encourage trade, and give employment to numbers of Mahsuds. The first C.R.E. was Major A. Campbell, C.M.G., D.S.O., R.E., but he was soon succeeded by Lieut.-Colonel C. H. Haswell, R.E. The bulk of the burden, however, fell on three R.E. officers—Major L. C. B. Deed and Lieutenants M. R. Jefferis and J. W. M. Dickson[1]—who constructed the portion from the Tochi towards Razmak, as far as the point where the road leaves the Khaisora Valley, in a period of nine months. The work was done by civil contractors and labour up to Razani. " The road was constructed in a most unorthodox way," writes Major M. Everett.[2]

[1] Lieutenant Dickson was killed by a raiding party on December 12th, 1922. Major Deed received the D.S.O., and Lieutenant Jefferis the M.C., for their work.
[2] " The Destruction of Makin in February, 1923," by Major M. Everett, D.S.O., R.E. (O.C. 21st Company, Bombay Sappers and Miners, in Waziristan), appearing in *The Journal of the United Service Institution of India*, Vol. LV, January, 1925, p. 15.

"First came the R.E. building the road, and with them the Signals building a permanent telegraph line. Many weeks and many miles behind came the Protective Troops." However, the result seems to have justified the method adopted.[1]

By the middle of January, 1923, heavy lorries were running as far as Asad Khel, nearly half-way to Razmak, and Ford vans up to Razani. The road was most carefully aligned and graded, with well-banked corners on its numerous hairpin bends. The construction of a passable track up to the Razmak Narai (Pass) in advance of the main road was a most difficult undertaking. The rugged mountains were covered with scrub jungle, and the weather was bitterly cold. Three companies of Sappers and Miners and a battalion of Pioneers, however, set to work on January 19th and completed a track with a ruling gradient of 1 in 8 on the 22nd. On the following day these units were out in the snow for 11 hours while the 7th Infantry Brigade toiled up the heights. The track became a sheet of ice, which turned later to freezing slush and mud under the pounding of camel and mule traffic; but by nightfall the whole brigade, with 1,100 mules and 1,450 camels, had surmounted the 1,200 feet ascent. The work of construction proceeded so rapidly that when the 7th Brigade reached Razmak on January 23rd, and the 5th Brigade was in Razani, the head of the main road was already past the latter place. The Engineers built a hutted camp at Razmak which developed in later years into a fine cantonment, the present garrison of which has barracks, a piped water supply, electric light, football and polo grounds, and most luxuries except feminine society. Razmak is said to be the largest enclosed camp in the world.

The construction of the motor road from Sorarogha up the Tank Zam to Razmak, to join the road to Razmak from the Tochi Valley, was completed during 1923,[2] and branch roads were put in hand from Jandola westwards to Sarwekai[3] and elsewhere. Waziristan is now intersected by large and small roads, and its inhabitants are advancing rapidly in peace and prosperity. The building of the circular road caused the greatest concentration of technical troops ever known up to that time in India. The Bengal Sappers and Miners were represented by the 3rd and 5th Companies, the Madras Sappers and Miners by the 12th and 13th Companies, and the Bombay Sappers and Miners by the 19th, 20th, 21st and 23rd Companies. Eight battalions of Pioneers worked alongside these eight Sapper companies in an undertaking on which the Government of India

[1] The duty of protection was entrusted to *Khassadars* (local armed guards) in order that Mahsud raiding parties might not be tempted by the presence of regular troops to attack them in the hope of capturing some rifles. The Sappers and Miners and other regulars were accordingly kept far down the line for a time.
[2] The work was put in hand after Razmak had been occupied.
[3] The Jandola–Sarwekai motor road was begun in May, 1923, and completed in September, 1924. Two Sapper and Miner companies and two battalions of Pioneers were employed in a difficult section, the remainder being executed by civil labour. The road was afterwards prolonged to Wana.

spent nearly one million sterling during 1923–24.[1] But it was money well spent.

It must not be imagined that the Mahsuds acquiesced in the peaceful execution of this great work. Towards the end of 1922 the Government decided to evacuate the fortified camp at Ladha near Kaniguram and to concentrate in Razmak. The rumour reached the tribesmen, who concluded at once that the British were about to leave Waziristan, and instantly they broke out into acts of hostility which necessitated the suspension of work on the motor road above Dwa Toi in the Tank Zam on December 1st. Early in January, 1923, the situation grew worse, and with the arrival of the 7th Brigade at Razmak and its subsequent junction with the 9th Brigade at Tauda China,[2] drastic punitive operations were undertaken once more against the Makin villages. The work of destroying villages, towers and orchards began on February 6th, the engineering operations being directed by Major M. Everett, D.S.O., R.E., the C.R.E. of the Makin Column. It continued for five days, assisted by aerial bombing and howitzer fire. Hundreds of houses were burnt, the usual procedure being to make holes in the roof, break open all doors and windows, fill the rooms with hay or brushwood, saturate it with kerosene oil, and apply a match. The firing operations required careful timing as otherwise the smoke interfered with the withdrawal of the troops, and on one occasion much confusion was caused through the premature ignition of a house by a native transport driver because he felt cold ! The general devastation had its effect, for on March 23rd, 1923, the Mahsuds accepted the terms imposed on them.

But trouble still brewed in Waziristan. There is a Mahsud proverb which runs, " Tell no man where you are going, the time you are starting out, or the amount of money you are taking with you." Suspicion begets hatred and fear. There was constant bickering and petty warfare between the Mahsuds and Wazirs, and the British were drawn into further operations in Waziristan in the spring of 1925 ; but after that year the pacifying effect of the circular road and the Razmak garrison became more marked, and the warring clans shook hands. For many years the North-West Frontier was quiet and apparently contented in spite of Soviet intrigues in the northern valleys of the Swat and Panjkora. Sapper and Miner units were employed in small affairs here and there, but it was not till the explosion of 1930, which will be described later, that they were massed once more in large numbers beyond the Indus.

It is necessary at this point to revert to the period of the Third

---

[1] Article entitled " Important Works Executed by the Buildings and Roads Branch of the Military Engineer Services, India," appearing in *The R.E. Journal*, Vol. XXXVIII, March–December, 1924, " Professional Notes."

[2] Ladha was evacuated by the 9th Brigade on February 1st ; and the brigade then moved by Dwa Toi and Marobi to meet the 7th Brigade at Tauda China near Makin.

Afghan War. As has been remarked already, a large number of units of the Indian Army was then serving overseas. Fortunately, most of these units were in Mesopotamia or Persia, for in 1920 Great Britain was threatened with a serious disaster in that part of the globe. Many companies of Sappers and Miners were at work in those countries during 1919, constructing roads and bridges, laying or altering railway lines, erecting blockhouses, and preparing camps and barracks. Several large projects were in hand, and early in 1920 the 2nd, 6th and 8th Companies, Bengal Sappers and Miners, built a fine bridge across the Tigris at Mosul under the direction of Lieut.-Colonel J. F. Turner, D.S.O., R.E., who was responsible for its design.[1] But the British forces, including the Sappers and Miners, were scattered over an area larger than that of the United Kingdom; and so, when General Sir J. A. Haldane, K.C.B., D.S.O., the Commander-in-Chief in Mesopotamia, was confronted with a serious insurrection of the Arabs in June, 1920, he found himself in a difficult situation.

The British army in Mesopotamia then numbered about 60,000 fighting men; but after deducting the troops required to guard many thousands of Turkish prisoners and refugees, and those employed on non-combatant duties, no more than 4,200 British and 30,000 Indian soldiers were available for field service. The army consisted of the 17th and 18th Indian Divisions[2] and some Army Troops. With the 17th Division were the 9th, 61st, 64th and 67th Companies, Madras Sappers and Miners, and with the 18th Division the 2nd, 6th and 8th Companies of the Bengal Corps. Among the Army Troops were No. 8 Field Troop, Madras Sappers and Miners, and six Railway Construction Companies; and when the reconstituted 6th Indian Division arrived in August, 1920, as a reinforcement, it brought with it the 11th, 63rd and 69th Companies of the Madras Sappers and Miners. The 19th Company, Bombay Sappers and Miners, under Captain C. F. Stoehr, R.E., was serving with the North Persia Force which had retired before the Bolshevik advance and was holding Kasvin and other places south of the Caspian;[3] and strung out along the Persian lines of communication were the 7th, 52nd and 65th Companies, Bengal Sappers and Miners. Altogether, it was a great engineering organization which had, as its Chief Engineer in Mesopotamia, Major-General E. H. de V. Atkinson, C.B., C.M.G., C.I.E., who had held a similar appointment with the 4th Army in France during 1918.

[1] This floating bridge was of novel design. Its huge pontoons, instead of being anchored, were attached to a catenary cable supported on floats from which it could lift if a change in the water-level rendered this necessary. The catenary cable had 21 three-inch wire ropes.

[2] Commanded by Major-General G. A. J. Leslie, C.B., C.M.G., and Major-General T. Fraser, C.B., C.S.I., C.M.G., respectively (both from the Royal Engineers).

[3] The work of the Sappers and Miners in North Persia is described in an article by Major C. F. Stoehr, R.E., entitled "Engineer Work with the Norperforce," appearing in *The R.E. Journal*, Vol. XXXVIII, March–December, 1924, pp. 255–266.

The Arab insurrection in Mesopotamia began with an outbreak at Tel Afar in the north-east on June 4th, 1920, followed by another at Rumaitha on the Middle Euphrates. The troops in Rumaitha were soon besieged, and the first attempt to relieve them failed; but a column under Brigadier-General F. E. Coningham, C.M.G., D.S.O., including the 61st Company, Madras Sappers and Miners, brought them away on July 20th. Many other isolated garrisons were surrounded, and there was a general demand for troops to support the civil administration. The hostile Arabs cut the Basra–Baghdad Railway and destroyed large sections of the line by hitching camels on to the rails by ropes and dragging the rails into the desert or to the nearest canal.[1] Telegraphic communication was interrupted, and following on the wholesale destruction came a disaster to a column of Manchesters on July 24th. For several weeks the situation was critical. Outlying British garrisons were withdrawn and concentrated on the essential lines of communication, or massed in important centres, such as Baghdad and Basra, which were strongly fortified. "On July 26th and 27th," writes General Haldane,[2] "accompanied by my Chief Engineer, Major-General E. H. de V. Atkinson, I fixed upon the approximate sites for a series of earthworks around Baghdad. By the middle of August, thanks in great part to the tireless energy of Lieut.-Colonel A. B. Carey, R.E., Director of Military and Civil Works, some forty brick blockhouses, which replaced the earthworks, had sprung up on a perimeter of sixteen miles, and, as material became available, was enclosed by a continuous and formidable wire obstacle." Another Royal Engineer who had a hand in the defensive arrangements of Baghdad was Brigadier-General G. A. F. Sanders, C.B., C.M.G. In a few weeks the City of the Caliphs was secure from attack.

Events moved quickly. The 67th Company, Madras Sappers and Miners, in the garrison of Hilla on the Euphrates, helped to repel Arab attacks on that place on July 27th and 31st, and the 61st Company took part with General Coningham's column in rescuing the garrison of Diwaniya and saving the Hindiya Barrage[3] from damage. General Haldane hoped to relieve the isolated garrison of Kufa near Najaf, but serious trouble north-east of Baghdad caused him to postpone the attempt. Columns set out to deal with the enemy, and among them a small one of 250 rifles under Lieut.-Colonel H. S. Gaskell, R.E., who marched on August 24th and relieved Qaraghan, a post on the railway running from Baghdad towards Persia. "On

[1] "The Arab Insurrection of 1920–21," by Captain C. M. P. Durnford, 4/6th Rajputana Rifles, appearing in the *Journal of the United Service Institution of India*, Vol. LIV, April, 1924, p. 186.
[2] *The Insurrection in Mesopotamia*, by General Sir J. Aylmer Haldane, G.C.M.G., K.C.B., D.S.O., p. 112.
[3] The great dam built across the Euphrates by that eminent engineer, Sir William Willcocks, brother of the Commander-in-Chief of the Indian Corps in France.

the 25th," writes the Commander-in-Chief,[1] " while a post to cover the bridge between the Khanikin Road and Kizil Robat was under construction, two sections of the 65th Company, Madras Sappers and Miners, were attacked by 300 tribesmen. Lieut.-Colonel Gaskell broke through the insurgents on an engine under heavy fire and made for Khanikin Road whence he brought back with him 130 rifles. With these he relieved the little garrison who, under Captain C. F. Scott-Ruffle, I.A.R.O.,[2] had held their own for two hours." Further operations took place north of Baghdad, and General Sanders re-opened communication westwards along the railway to Faluja, the entire line being provided with blockhouses by September 26th through the efforts of the 11th Company, Madras Sappers and Miners. A few days earlier, the last of a line of 173 blockhouses had been completed on the railway line between Baghdad and Kut.

The Bengal Sapper and Miner companies did good work during the insurrection, but they saw little fighting as they were mostly in the north and north-east. They were often employed as infantry when troops were scarce. Lieut.-Colonel F. G. Drew, O.B.E., R.E., records[3] that on one occasion the 2nd Company with a troop of cavalry, was sent out to " show the flag " and in due course surrounded a rebel village. But the Arabs had already fled. Enquiry elicited the information that they had mistaken the tarpaulin-covered loads of the engineer equipment mules for mountain guns and thought that a mixed column of all arms was descending on them. " After this," says Drew, " we were always careful to cover our 1st line pack equipment with tarpaulins." The mirages of the Mesopotamian plains have been responsible for many such mistakes.

The 9th, 61st and 67th Companies, Madras Sappers and Miners, had the satisfaction of being with the two brigades which relieved Kufa on October 17th after a siege lasting from July 8th ; and the 9th Company, under Major E. Bradney, R.E., distinguished itself by pushing on with the 13th Rajputs across a burning bridge to capture the town of Tuwairij during the advance.[4] Meanwhile the Chief Engineer, Major-General Atkinson, was selected by General Haldane to command a powerful column of all arms[5] destined for the relief of Samawa above Nasiriya on the Euphrates, and joined his troops at Ur on September 30th. He reached Samawa with little trouble, " the arrangements both prior to the advance and during it having

---

[1] *The Insurrection in Mesopotamia*, 1920, by General Sir J. Aylmer Haldane, G.C.M.G., K.C.B., D.S.O., p. 110.

[2] Attached to the Madras Sappers and Miners.

[3] Notes supplied to the author by Lieut.-Colonel F. G. Drew, O.B.E., R.E., who commanded the 2nd Company, Bengal Sappers and Miners, in Mesopotamia.

[4] Major Bradney was awarded the D.S.O. for this exploit.

[5] The 69th Company, Madras Sappers and Miners, and the 26th and 28th Railway Companies, Bombay Sappers and Miners, took part in operations for the relief of Samawa.

been such that they worked with admirable smoothness."[1] With the occupation of this town on October 14th, 1920, the main operations in Iraq came to an end. Rumaitha was retaken, the rebellious tribes were disarmed, and strong columns marched through the country to collect fines and ensure that the last embers of the revolt had been extinguished. Engineering continued, but fighting ceased.

We return now to India where the seditious teaching which was part of the programme of non-co-operation adopted by the Malabar[2] District Conference in 1919 culminated in 1921 in the Moplah Rebellion. This was the most serious revolt since the Indian Mutiny. It is a curious fact that, although there had been 33 large or small revolts by the Moplahs in the previous 80 years,[3] the only regular troops available at first to deal with the rebellion of 1921 were two platoons of the 2nd Battalion, Leinster Regiment, at Calicut, and a battalion of Madras Indian Infantry at Cannanore, 50 miles farther north. The country near the coast was a network of tidal creeks fringed with palms. Farther inland came ricefields and fenced enclosures, and, farther still, hills covered by extremely dense and impenetrable jungle. Mosques and villages were scattered along the numerous roads and were easily converted by the enemy into miniature fortresses. Any movement of transport or guns except by road was almost impossible, and the troops themselves could only traverse the fields or jungles with the greatest difficulty. The South Indian Railway, running through Shoranur to Tirur on the coast, and then northwards through Calicut to Cannanore, was the sole link which connected the jungles and swamps of Malabar with the rest of India. The Moplahs were fanatical Muhammadans, reckless, undisciplined swordsmen, adepts at jungle warfare and unsurpassed as scouts. This was the setting for the campaign in Southern India in 1921.

The two platoons of Leinsters at Calicut were reinforced at once by three others, and the officer in command[4] then advanced with one company to Tirurangadi[5] on August 20th, to help the civil authorities, and sent a platoon forward to the rebel centre at Malappuram.[6] He was faced by a crowd of 5,000 furious Moplahs, and was obliged to withdraw his three remaining platoons to Calicut after a sharp fight. This was the signal for a general rising. The Moplahs cut the railway line, destroyed bridges, blocked the roads, tore down the telegraph lines, and besieged the Leinster platoon in Malappuram. The police were powerless, and mob law held undisputed sway. British planters

[1] General Sir J. A. Haldane in his book *The Insurrection in Mesopotamia*, 1920, p. 228.
[2] The Malabar District, situated in the extreme south-west of India, extends along the coast from Mangalore southwards to Cochin and includes Calicut and other seaports.
[3] None of these, however, was on a scale approaching that of 1921.
[4] Captain McEnroy, D.S.O., M.C., Leinster Regiment.
[5] Fifteen miles south-east of Calicut.
[6] Twenty-three miles south-east of Calicut.

were murdered, and Hindus were massacred or forcibly converted to Islam. But meanwhile reinforcements were being sent by rail from Bangalore to the affected area—a squadron of British cavalry, a couple of field-guns, the 2nd Battalion, Dorsetshire Regiment, a company of the 64th Pioneers, some armoured cars, and two platoons (sections) of Madras Sappers and Miners (one from the 9th Company and the other from the 12th[1]), which, with some Territorial companies from Madras, were destined to form two Movable Columns in Malabar. The troops were commanded by Colonel F. W. Radcliffe, C.M.G., C.I.E., C.B.E., of the Dorsets, who conducted the operations during the first six weeks until relieved by Colonel E. T. Humphreys, C.M.G., D.S.O., of the Leinsters, when the most critical period had passed.

The first task of the military and railway engineers was to repair the railway between Shoranur and Calicut,[2] while most of the troops, detraining at Shoranur, operated northwards and reached Malappuram. The company of Leinsters at Calicut had already advanced bravely to Malappuram and had relieved the besieged platoon at that place after a desperate fight at Pukottur on August 27th, in which 400 rebels perished. The Moplahs had tried to ambush the little column, and charged repeatedly, sword in hand, against the concentrated fire of Lewis guns and rifles. This lesson, and the subsequent arrival of Colonel Radcliffe's troops, had a great moral effect. Except for an affair at Pandikkad[3] on November 14th, the Moplahs never again attempted a massed assault. Yet in spite of the arrival of further reinforcements—Gurkhas, Garhwalis and Mountain Artillery from the Himalayas, and a battalion of Kachins and Chins from Burma—the rebellion spread into the north-west of Malabar, and the re-establishment of law and order, first by small columns in definite areas and then by a general sweep south-eastwards, was a long and exhausting business. It was accomplished, however, by January 6th, 1922, and the rebellion came to an end, leaving the people impoverished and bitter, the jails full of Moplah prisoners and the hospitals overflowing with wounded. These were some of the first-fruits of the non-co-operation movement.

Only five sections of Madras Sappers and Miners worked and fought in Malabar, but their duties were difficult and responsible. When small columns were employed to traverse affected areas, each had to be self-supporting, and consequently each had to be accompanied by a small body of Sappers to clear the road for wheeled

---

[1] The remainder of the 9th Company under Captain A. V. Anderson, R.E., followed on October 12th and served in Malabar until the end of the rebellion in January, 1922. The platoon of the 12th Company returned to Bangalore on October 24th. (*Historical Record of the Q.V.O. Madras Sappers and Miners*, Vol. II, pp. 16, 17.)

[2] H.M.S. *Comus* had arrived at Calicut, and the troops and railway employees had begun to repair the line southwards. Article in *The Times of India Illustrated Weekly*, dated September 14th, 1921.

[3] Fifteen miles north of Malappuram.

transport and repair bridges. Sometimes this body was so small that it was almost invisible. On one occasion a Naik and eight Sappers had been left in charge of a dump, and the Naik was ordered by the Post Commander to detail a party of Sappers to march with a column on the following morning. When the time came it was found that only two men could be spared, but those two duly reported to the Column Commander, one with a felling axe and the other with a hand-saw! The magic of their presence was enough: the column marched proudly as a "mixed force" and completed its task.[1] But often the Sappers and Miners had very heavy labour. The Moplahs were adepts at blocking roads with bamboos and trees. One block consisted of two large piles of bamboos, each 15 feet thick, reinforced by ten teak logs, each 35 feet long and two feet square in section. The bamboo clumps could not be dragged aside owing to the thickness of the jungle; and the logs, which had been hauled into position by elephants, were most difficult to move. Nevertheless, a platoon of Sappers and Miners, and another of Pioneers, cut a way through in less than an hour.

The repair of damaged bridges occupied much time and energy. The Sappers and Miners were concerned chiefly with road bridges which were repaired at first with any material available and afterwards strengthened to take armoured cars. Camp defences were also important, and every camp had to be of enclosed type. The perimeter was sometimes formed of army transport carts and bamboos, the carts being fastened together, and the long bamboo trees, with spiky branches, tied to the carts.[2] If carts were not available, the bamboos were anchored to stout posts driven into the ground. For permanent camps, bamboo tripods about six feet high were erected and fixed at intervals of about 20 feet and then connected by wire or thin bamboos. Horizontal bamboos of a spiky nature were next tied to the legs of the tripods at three levels, both in front and rear; and finally, sharp stakes were added, pointing upwards and outwards, and lashed to two of the horizontal lines of bamboos.[3] Permanent camps usually had a central keep for one platoon, and movable lines of obstacles were arranged within the enclosed area. The campaign in Malabar provided good training in jungle warfare for a few Engineers and Sappers and Miners, and its political effect was far-reaching; but it is remarkable chiefly because it took place in that normally peaceful area, Southern India.

After the widespread fighting on the North-West Frontier during 1919 and 1920, the Arab Rebellion in Mesopotamia in 1920, and the sharp struggle in Malabar in 1921, there was little prospect of active

---

[1] "A Field Company in Malabar," by "Assaye Lines," appearing in *The R.E. Journal*, Vol. XLIII, 1929, p. 93.
[2] *Field Service Regulations*, Part II, para. 179.
[3] This horrid obstacle bears a strong resemblance to that favoured by the Burmese, and used by the British, in the Third Burma War of 1885. (See Chapter XX.) Possibly the battalion from Burma introduced it in Malabar in 1921.

service for most Royal Engineers and Sappers and Miners. It is true that there was trouble later in Waziristan, and that some of the Madras and Burma[1] Sappers and Miners were concerned in small affairs in Burma, but these operations were for the lucky few. For several years the Indian Army devoted itself to a much-needed reorganization, while politicians, to use a popular form of diction, " explored every avenue in search of a formula which might lead, in due course and through the proper channel, to responsible self-government." But the Afridis prefer direct action and took it in June, 1930, when they descended from the Tirah to raid Peshawar Cantonment. They were driven back, but returned in August and made a second abortive attempt. It was then decided that troops should occupy the Kajuri and Aka Khel Plains near Peshawar, and should occupy them permanently, thus denying to the Afridis the ground on which they grazed their cattle during the winter and the caves in which they sheltered with their families.[2] These operations were to be in three phases. First, the clearing of the Afridis from the area and the establishment of perimeter camps ; then the provision of good roads, tracks and water supply ; and finally the building of permanent camps and posts for the garrison of the area. The programme was an engineering one. In fact, the cavalry, artillery and infantry acted in these operations of 1930 and 1931 merely as a covering force for the Engineers.

The Kajuri Plain, lying a few miles south-west of Peshawar, is bounded on the north by a metalled road leading from Peshawar to Jamrud and so up the Khaibar Pass. The eastern boundary of both the Kajuri and Aka Khel Plains—the latter to the south of Peshawar—is the metalled Peshawar–Kohat road running through Matanni.[3] A third metalled road led in 1930 from Peshawar to Fort Bara on the Bara River which is a rapid torrent dividing the Kajuri and Aka Khel Plains and flowing in a deep and wide chasm with precipitous sides cut in a hard conglomerate soil. A track, ten feet wide, connected Matanni with Jamrud and formed part of the " Frontier Road." There was no surface water on the arid plains ; but in the foothills, south and west of them, were a number of springs around each of which the Afridis had dug their winter caves.

The occupation of the Kajuri Plain was easy.[4] By October 14th, 1930, the Nowshera Brigade was in position along the Frontier Road between Jamrud and Matanni, covering the operations of the 4th

[1] The 15th (Burma) Company of the Madras Sappers and Miners was separated from that Corps on January 10th, 1922, after a connection of 35 years, and became the " 4th Burma Sappers and Miners." The 62nd (Burma) Company was disbanded in September, 1921.
[2] "Operations on the Khajuri and Aka Khel Plains, 1930–31," by Major C. W. Toovey, M.C., 1st Punjab Regiment, appearing in *The Journal of the United Service Institution of India*, Vol. LXI, July, 1931, p. 287.
[3] See the sketch map of the Kajuri Plain Area on p. 527.
[4] So economical in money and lives were the Kajuri Plain operations that they became known among the British soldiers as " The Woolworth War."

Company, Bengal Sappers and Miners, and the Bombay Pioneers, who were arranging for water supply. Three days later the Jhansi Brigade advanced from Peshawar and crossed the Kajuri Plain to Miri Khel, while the Rawalpindi Brigade marched as far as Bara. On the 27th the three brigades swept the plain clear of Afridis, and preparations were made for an advance of the Rawalpindi Brigade to a more central camp at Karawal Hill. This movement, however, could not be carried out until water was brought to the site of the camp, a task which was allotted to the 3rd Company, Bengal Sappers and Miners, assisted by a company of Bombay Pioneers, and was completed by them in 15 days. They installed a powerful pump on the Bara River, two miles above Bara Fort, and laid a pipeline for more than five miles to the site of the Karawal Perimeter Camp which was occupied by the Rawalpindi Brigade on November 17th. The work might have progressed even more quickly had it not been necessary to supplement the pipeline by a road with permanent piquet posts as it advanced. Most of the infantry units were now roadmaking with great energy and increasing skill under the technical direction of the Commanding Royal Engineer. The roads intended for heavy motor transport were made 18 feet wide with a foundation of stone overlaid with earth, gravel and sand. *Nullah* crossings were ramped to a limiting gradient of 1 in 10, and covered in some cases with wire netting.[1] During the latter half of November large gangs of coolies, under Engineer officers, extended the Peshawar–Bara metalled road towards the Kandao Pass at the rate of 200 yards a day. In short, the force " dug itself in " on the Kajuri Plain rapidly, methodically, and with little interference.

While the infantry wielded their picks and shovels, most of the Engineer units were sinking wells, laying pipes or building bridges. In the second phase of the operations, between November 17th and December 9th, the 3rd, 4th and 5th Companies of the Bengal Sappers and Miners were fully occupied with the water-supply installations of the three brigade areas ; but before that phase began, the 4th Company had built a fine bridge over the Bara River close to Bara Fort. The Frontier Road between Jamrud and Matanni—a most important lateral communication—crossed the river at Bara by a ford which was often impassable during spates, so it was decided that the river should be bridged. This was a difficult problem. A bridge was required to carry a load of a ten-ton steam roller and infantry in fours, and the tubular-steel bridging material which was available (Mark I, Inglis Bridge) would not carry such a load over a span greater than 120 feet, while the necessary span was 144 feet ; but the problem was neatly solved by prolonging the bridge over its supports so that the projecting ends remained as cantilevers which were then weighted

---

[1] *Report on Engineer Work on the N.W. Frontier of India*, 1930–31, Bara Plain, Peshawar.

with concrete to reduce the stress in the centre of the main span.[1] The line of the Bara Bridge was laid out on October 29th; the launching of the girders from both banks to a central junction was completed in less than seven hours on November 13th; and on November 23rd the bridge was opened to traffic. It was a spectacular piece of engineering which reflected great credit on the Sappers and Miners, and also on the Sikh Pioneers and infantry working parties who laboured to cut the approaches in hard conglomerate soil.[2]

Another Inglis bridge, of somewhat similar size and design,[3] was erected by the 5th Company at Mazarai later in the operations; but in this case there were further complications as one bank of the Bara River was high and precipitous and the other rose to a lower level in two steps. A concrete and rubble pier was built on the lower step, and the girders launched across it to the far bank in which a very deep and long approach cutting was required. · As in the case of the Bara Bridge, the last three bays of the Mazarai Bridge were counterweighted and left permanently in cantilever—but at one end of the bridge only, instead of at both as at Bara. The pier was made 30 feet in height in order to limit the depth of the opposite approach cutting to 16 feet; but even so the Sikh Pioneers and infantry working parties who did the excavation were obliged to remove 250,000 cubic feet of very hard soil. It is creditable to all concerned that the whole undertaking was completed in 50 days.[4] The construction of the Bara and Mazarai bridges was the most important engineering work executed during the occupation of the Kajuri and Aka Khel Plains, and it has been described in some detail to show what Sappers and Miners are now called upon to do in field operations.

The third and final period, from December 9th to March 31st, began with the selection of the sites for the permanent camps and posts, and the Engineer units were soon sinking tube wells and raising defences at these places. Samghakai Post, Jhansi Post, Nowshera Post and an enlarged Fort Salop came into being, while road work continued in various directions. But in spite of a heavy programme of engineering, several small punitive expeditions were sent against Afridi villages on the outskirts of the plains. One of these, in which the Rawalpindi Brigade operated against Tauda China on February 18th, will serve as an example of the usual employment of the Engineer units. On this occasion the 3rd Company, Bengal Sappers and Miners, working with the 2nd Bombay Pioneers, demolished several towers and houses and blocked more than 100

---

[1] The last bay at each end was loaded with six tons of concrete between the roadbearers. Each end projection consisted of three bays (36 feet).
[2] The Inglis Bridge at Bara was replaced in 1932 by a reinforced concrete arch bridge, built under contract. (See " Bara Bridge Reconstruction," by Lieutenant M. C. A. Henniker, R.E., in *The R.E. Journal*, Vol. XLVI, December, 1932.)
[3] Two spans, one of 132 feet, and the other (in cantilever) of 32 feet.
[4] Full details and a complete description of this bridge are given in an article entitled " The Construction of Mazarai Bridge, Kajuri Plain Operations, 1930–31," by Captain E. F. E. Armstrong, R.E., appearing in *The R.E. Journal*, March, 1932.

THE BARA BRIDGE ACROSS THE BARA RIVER, KAJURI PLAIN.

Reproduced by permission of the Air Ministry.

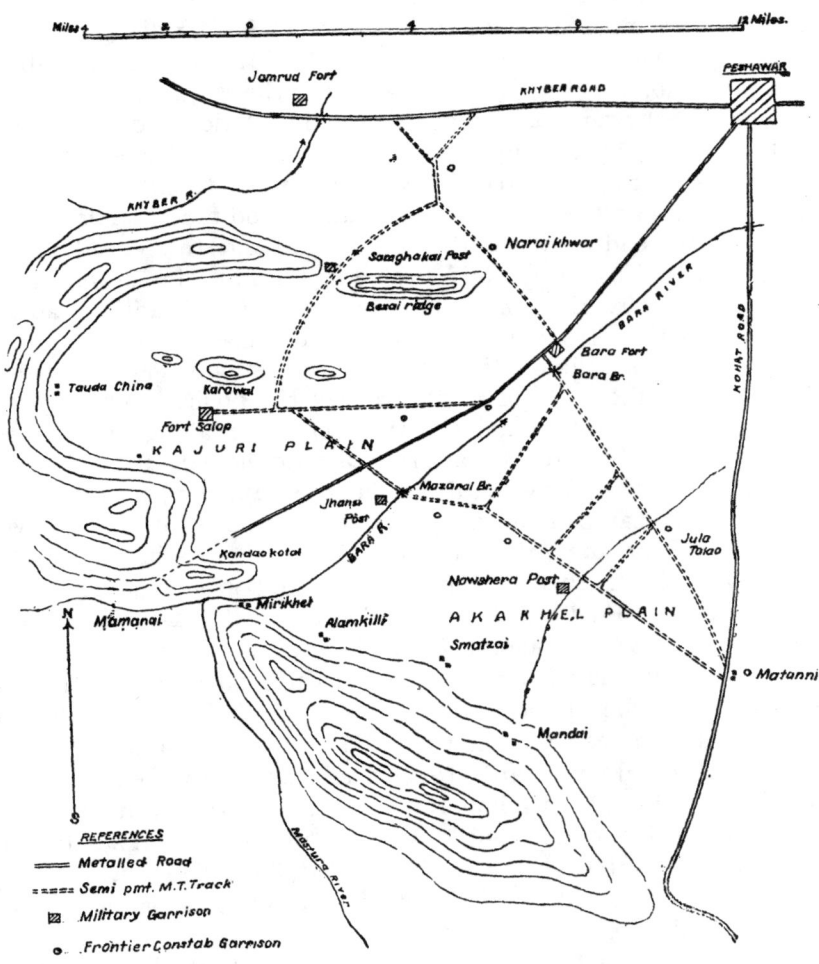

Kajuri Plain Area.

caves with thorn trees, stones and barbed wire to which they sometimes attached mines.[1] In a mined cave, any movement of the wire caused the charge to explode, and, to discourage attempts to remove the wire with a hook and a rope from a safe distance, a mine was placed occasionally at just that distance outside the cave. The results were most satisfactory—except to the Afridis. Hostilities ceased gradually, and with the approach of the hot weather all the troops except the permanent garrison left the Kajuri and Aka Khel Plains. Peshawar was safe against further Afridi raids.

Before these operations had ended, a rebellion broke out along the Irrawaddy in Burma, and one Saya San assumed the title of "King." Some troops were sent up to Tharrawaddy, 80 miles north of Rangoon, at the end of December, 1930, and others to Henzada; and outbreaks at Thayetmyo and Prome in the following spring necessitated further reinforcements and a more extended radius of action. The causes of the trouble were mainly political. By the end of 1931, after several small fights, the rebels had been subdued and the troops handed over the work of pacification to the police. Artillery was useless in the dense jungles, but wireless signalling enabled the infantry to maintain touch while rounding up the rebel gangs. There is little to record of the work of the Engineers and Sappers and Miners in this small campaign, for they were not called out until it was decided in July, 1931, that operations would be possible during the monsoon. The 14th Company, Madras Sappers and Miners,[2] and the 1st Madras Pioneers then took the field, with Major C. Preedy, O.B.E., R.E., as Commanding Royal Engineer. They reconstructed a road, 32 miles long, from Thayetmyo to Mindon, and erected many bridges, while the Public Works Department engineers built hutted camps and arranged for water supply. The Sappers and Pioneers were transferred afterwards to Henzada and improved the communications in that neighbourhood. Their work throughout was useful and well executed,[3] but it calls for little remark. It accelerated the collapse of the rebels who found that the reliance which they placed on "charmed" handkerchiefs was of little value against modern equipment and methods.

For many years the Sappers and Miners have worked alongside their brethren, the Pioneers. They have looked upon them as energetic helpers in large projects and as brave fighters when occasion has demanded that the shovel should be abandoned for the rifle. Thirteen battalions of Pioneers have formed a solid backing for the three Corps of Sappers and Miners and a link between them and the Infantry. But the conditions of modern warfare have brought about

---

[1] Caves cannot be destroyed without using large quantities of explosive, so the best method of denying their use to tribesmen is to block and mine their entrances.
[2] Under Captain E. E. G. L. Searight, M.C., R.E.
[3] A description of it appears in an article entitled "A Field Company in Burma, 1931," by "Anon," in *The R.E. Journal*, Vol. XLVII, March, 1933, pp. 89–103.

many alterations in organization, and the order has gone forth that Pioneer battalions are to vanish from the Indian Army.[1] The specialization demanded by modern war has killed the Pioneer. With the improvements in artillery, machine-guns, tanks, aeroplanes, wireless and gas, infantry tactics and duties have become so complicated that no man can be a fully competent infantry soldier and at the same time an expert in several branches of field engineering. It has been found that the organization, equipment and system of training of the Pioneers have made them Engineers more than Infantry, and so a large proportion of them are being transferred to the Sappers and Miners, and the remainder, with most of their British officers, absorbed into the Indian Infantry. The personnel of the Sappers and Miners will be greatly increased. All the field companies will have four instead of three sections, and Depot companies will be expanded and formed into a Training Battalion. These are some of the changes which are taking place in the engineering department of the Army in India. They are far-reaching indeed, but are calculated to increase efficiency and reduce expenditure. And so the Sapper and Miner welcomes the Pioneer into his ranks, remembering that he himself is descended from a Pioneer.

This story of military engineering in India comes to an end in the year 1932. Looking back, down a long vista of three centuries to the time when Cogan and Day landed on the beach at Madras and built their little fort, we see a great procession of military engineers—Gunners and their crews, hardy adventurers with a smattering of engineering, Benjamin Robins, Caroline Scott, Patrick Ross, John Call, Thomas Keating, Archibald Campbell, Henry Watson—and after them in the nineteenth century the heroes of the Indian Mutiny and the wars in Central and Northern India, Burma and Afghanistan. They stretch into the dim distance, a noble band who followed where duty and glory led and did much to create the wealth and magnificence of the India which we know to-day.

END OF VOLUME I.

[1] Some details of the scheme are given in Appendix V of this volume.

APPENDIX I.

THE MILITARY ENGINEER SERVICES.

The Military Engineer Services, whose evolution from the Public Works Department, first as the "Military Works Department" and later as the "Military Works Services," has been described briefly in Chapter XX, control all military engineering works in India and Burma except in a few small stations where these works are in charge of the Public Works Department. They control also all works of the Royal Air Force, and in addition they are in charge of all civil and military works, except railways and irrigation, in Baluchistan and the tribal areas of the North-West Frontier Province.[1]

The organization of the Military Engineer Services is complicated but well adapted for its purpose. There are three branches—the Buildings and Roads, Electrical and Mechanical, and Furniture and Stores—and the basic formation, the unit as it were, is the Subdivision. Each Buildings and Roads Subdivision is under a Subdivisional Officer (S.D.O.), who may be either a soldier or a civilian, and who is assisted by one or more civilian Overseers in charge of Sections. Where necessary, Subdivisions are formed in the Electrical and Mechanical or Furniture and Stores Branches. All Subdivisions are grouped into Divisions under Garrison Engineers,[2] who are usually assisted by one or more Assistant Garrison Engineers and a Technical Overseer. In large headquarter stations, a Garrison Engineer's staff may include officers or subordinates with special qualifications in Electrical and Mechanical or Furniture and Stores work. Divisions of the Military Engineer Services are grouped into Districts under Commanders, Royal Engineers,[3] whose functions are both executive and administrative. Each Commander, Royal Engineers, is assisted, according to the size of his District, by Assistant Commanders, Royal Engineers[4] (Works, and Electrical and Mechanical), and by a Technical Subdivisional Officer.[5] The

---

[1] The raising of the status of the North-West Frontier Province to a Governor's province, and the subsequent reorganization of the Public Works Department, led to the handing over by the Military Engineer Services to the Public Works Department of all works in the settled districts as distinct from the tribal areas. This came into effect on April 1st, 1933.

[2] The Garrison Engineer (G.E.) corresponds approximately to the Executive Engineer in the Public Works Department. He is usually a Captain or subaltern of the Royal Engineers.

[3] The C.R.E. corresponds approximately to the Superintending Engineer in the Public Works Department. He is usually a Lieut.-Colonel of the Royal Engineers.

[4] Usually Majors of the Royal Engineers.

[5] In special cases there may be also an Inspector of Royal Engineer Machinery or a Departmental Officer of the Electrical and Mechanical Branch.

organization in an Independent Brigade Area is a compromise between that of a District and a Division. The Districts, and Independent Brigade Area organizations, are grouped in the four military Commands of India—the Northern, Western, Eastern (including Burma) and Southern—those in each Command being under a Chief Engineer[1] and the whole organization under an Engineer-in-Chief.[2]

The officers of the Military Engineer Services consist of Royal Engineers, Royal Engineers (Indian Army),[3] Inspectors of Royal Engineer Machinery, Departmental Officers promoted from among the Military Subordinates of the Indian Unattached List, and civilian Assistant Engineers appointed directly or promoted from among the Civilian Subordinates. Most of the officers, however, are Royal Engineers who may be required at any moment for mobilization and meanwhile are usefully and economically employed in the Military Engineer Services. Indians (civilians) are now being recruited in increasing numbers in the lower grades of the Services except in those branches in which the requirements of mobilization necessitate the maintenance of a strong military element. Military Subordinates for the Buildings and Roads Branch were formerly recruited from British units in India and were trained at the Thomason Civil Engineering College, Roorkee; but, owing to the closing of the military class at that college in July, 1924, these subordinates are now recruited from among the Military Foremen of Works in the United Kingdom. The Military Subordinates for the Electrical and Mechanical Branch are also recruited from the United Kingdom, but those for the Furniture and Stores Branch come from British units in India.

There are substantial differences between the systems of Military Works organization in England and India. In India, Royal Engineer officers are responsible for many duties which are performed in England by separate branches such as the Lands Branch and the R.A.S.C. Barrack Department. Again, in India, there is no grade corresponding to that of Surveyor of Works, nor is there any technical audit. The whole system of accounts in the Military Engineer Services has been changed since the Great War through the assumption by the Military Accounts Department of the duty of keeping and auditing these accounts under a new Account Code, and more of the time of the Royal Engineer officer in these Services is spent in the intricacies of finance than is the case in England.

In 1914 there were three categories of Royal Engineer officers on the India establishment, (i) those in the Military Works Services, (ii) those in the Sappers and Miners, and (iii) those in civil employment such as the Departments of Public Works, the Survey of India

---

[1] A Colonel (late R.E.) with the rank of Brigadier.
[2] A Major-General (late R.E.).
[3] An establishment created during the Great War and now dying out.

and Railways. The senior Royal Engineer officer in India was called the Director-General of Military Works, and although he had an *ex-officio* position as Inspector of Sappers and Miners, his duties were actually confined almost entirely to the Military Works Services.[1] In 1921, however, his title was altered to "Director of Works" and he was placed under the Quartermaster-General. At the same time, an independent Inspector of Sappers and Miners and Pioneers was appointed. But two years later the system was changed again, and with this change came the first step towards real unity of control of all the Engineer services in India. The new organization, which was introduced on December 4th, 1923, placed all the Engineer services[2] under an Engineer-in-Chief directly responsible to the Commander-in-Chief, and included the affiliation of the four Corps of Pioneers[3] for technical training in peace and for employment in war. The Engineer-in-Chief became the technical adviser of the Commander-in-Chief on all military engineering matters through different departments of the General Staff, and he became also the Engineer Adviser to the Royal Air Force, Royal Indian Marine, Ordnance Department, and the Foreign and Political Department. He was assisted by two Deputy Engineers-in-Chief (Works, and Electrical and Mechanical), a Brigadier, R.E. (for Sappers and Miners and Pioneers), and other Staff officers.[4] The Chief Engineers of Commands became similarly the technical advisers of the General Officers Commanding-in-Chief of the Commands. The system remains substantially the same to this day, but the Works Branch is now recognized as being definitely under the control of the Quartermaster-General.

A sound knowledge of all the main departments of engineering work, as carried out in India, is demanded of each Royal Engineer officer. This he obtains by attachment to, or service with, the Sappers and Miners, and by employment in the Military Engineer Services. The difficulty, and at the same time the interest, of the work in these Services is often enhanced by the fact that in some parts of India the Engineer has to begin by making his own bricks and felling his own trees. Work is generally done by contract; but there are many cases where daily labour is used, and sometimes, as in Waziristan and on the Kajuri Plain, large numbers of Sappers and Miners and Pioneers are employed. Many and varied have been the works executed by the Military Works and Military Engineer Services. In the "'sixties" a new hill station was built at Chakrata on a site selected by Colonel Sir Frederick Roberts, V.C.[5] This

---

[1] The D.G.M.W. had the right of direct access to the Commander-in-Chief.
[2] Three Corps of Sappers and Miners and the Military Engineer Services.
[3] The Madras, Bombay, Sikh and Hazara Pioneers.
[4] The appointment of Brigadier, R.E., was abolished in 1932 for reasons of economy.
[5] Afterwards Lord Roberts of Kandahar. Lord Napier of Magdala, who was then Commander-in-Chief in India, did a great deal towards improving the accommodation for British troops and their families.

involved an approach road 77 miles long from Saharanpur, the nearest point on the railway. The road rises to a height of 7,100 feet above sea-level and has several large bridges. In the " 'nineties " a pipe-line, 22 miles long, was laid to serve the hill station of Murree, descending at one point to a depth of 1,400 feet below its mean gradient, and so forming what is believed to be the deepest antisyphon in the world. Another important work executed at this period was the preparation of defences around Attock, Rawalpindi and Quetta which, though now obsolete, were considered to be essential at that time.

Lord Kitchener's schemes for the reorganization of the Army in India from 1903 onwards entailed extensive building such as new lines for troops and vast additions to arsenals and ordnance factories. A new cantonment was built at Risalpur, close to Nowshera, many existing cantonments were greatly enlarged, and the electrification of British barracks and hospitals was begun. Up to this time almost all the buildings in the lines of Indian troops had been constructed and maintained under regimental arrangements from a " Hutting Grant " ; but Lord Kitchener established the principle that, when a set of lines had to be built or rebuilt, the work was to be carried out by the Military Works Services.[1] In later years, when the transfer of the capital of India from Calcutta to Delhi was announced[2] and the building of New Delhi was begun, 15 square miles of land were acquired for a new cantonment at Delhi and the work was started in 1913. It was retarded by the Great War, but is now complete. These are a few only of the many activities of the Military Works Services before the cataclysm of 1914.

On the outbreak of the Great War the despatch of large numbers of Royal Engineer officers and Military Subordinates on active service overseas was counter-balanced to some extent by the engagement of temporary personnel. Many officers were detached for expeditions on the North-West Frontier. Schools of instruction, extensions to arsenals, depots of various kinds, temporary lines for Indian troops,[3] and many other projects, were taken in hand. The cost of work rose, and materials (especially imported steelwork) became scarce.[4] Thus the period of the Great War was one of extreme strain, and the Armistice did not ease the situation appreciably, for it was followed soon by the Third Afghan War and the campaign in Waziristan when demobilization was arrested and large temporary building schemes had to be continued. Officers came and went, and many were inexperienced.[5] Then came the opening up of Waziristan by the great

[1] In 1919, the Hutting Grant was abolished, and *all* work, whether of construction or repair, was taken over by the Military Works Services.
[2] The transfer was sanctioned on December 12th, 1911.
[3] Temporary accommodation was constructed for nearly half a million men.
[4] The annual expenditure mounted to more than double the pre-war figure.
[5] The Rawalpindi District had 13 officers in successive charge between May, 1918, and November, 1919.

Circular Road when the staff of the Military Engineer Services worked hand-in-glove with the Sappers and Miners and Pioneers. Throughout India there were immense arrears of building and repair work caused by the Great War, coupled with a scarcity of personnel and funds and much confusion in accounts.

Gradually the tangle was straightened out, and with the return of Royal Engineer officers from field service and the reorganization of the Engineer services under an Engineer-in-Chief, large permanent works were taken in hand once more. One of the most extensive was a mechanical transport depot at Chaklala near Rawalpindi, with barracks, workshops, garages and stores covering an area of several square miles, and with the usual ancillary services of water supply, electric light and power, roads and drainage.[1] In various parts of the country the Military Engineer Services prepared aerodromes for the Royal Air Force, made provision for the needs of the Royal Corps of Signals and the Royal Tank Corps, reconstructed the lines of Indian units, and electrified and drained cantonments. India now bears little sign of the confusion created by the Great War, but the result has been achieved at considerable cost. In 1872 the annual expenditure on original military works for the entire Bengal Army amounted to no more than 28 lakhs of rupees (about £280,000), and half as much on repairs. At the present time, however, these figures are sometimes exceeded in a single district. But the Army in India to-day is housed, watered and lighted on a scale which is very different from that of 1872. This has been the achievement of the Military Engineer Services, and it has been attained because these Services have been treated since 1900 as the normal regimental employment of Royal Engineer officers in India and have been plentifully supplied with them in times of peace.

[1] Two of the workshop buildings cover an area of five acres. They were built in 1922 at a cost of £180,000.

APPENDIX II.

QUEEN VICTORIA'S OWN MADRAS SAPPERS AND MINERS.

Remarks on the history and development of the Corps of Madras Sappers and Miners have appeared from time to time in this volume, but it may be well to recapitulate some of the main features. The Corps was raised at Madras in 1780 by Lieutenant Joseph Moorhouse as two companies of Pioneers. In 1793 it was increased to six companies and formed into a battalion known as the Madras Pioneer Battalion. This formation was expanded successively to eight, ten, fourteen and finally, in 1803, to sixteen companies, organized in two battalions and styled the 1st and 2nd Battalions of Madras Pioneers. The 1st Battalion became the Corps of Madras Sappers and Miners in 1831, and the 2nd Battalion was absorbed into that Corps two years later. In 1876 the Corps became the "Queen's Own Corps of Madras Sappers and Miners," in 1903 the "2nd Queen's Own Sappers and Miners," in 1911 the "2nd Queen Victoria's Own Sappers and Miners," and in 1923 it received its present designation. It is proposed in this appendix to deal only with some of the reorganizations and changes which have taken place in the Madras Corps during the present century.

In 1900 there were six Service Companies (Nos. 1 to 6), the Burma Service Company, and "A" and "B" Depot Companies. Each Service Company was organized in two half-companies, each of which was composed of two sections which were further divided into two sub-sections. The establishment of a Service Company was two British officers, two British other ranks, three Indian officers and 168 Indian other ranks.[1] "A" Company consisted of four Telegraph Sections, two Field Printing Sections and two Field Litho Sections. A reserve of 60 men had been formed in 1899, but it was still 23 under strength in 1901. Four Service Companies, and "A" and "B" Depot Companies, were normally stationed in Bangalore; one Service Company was at Secunderabad, another on the North-West Frontier, and the Burma Company at Mandalay.

The Corps was composed of various classes of Madrassis in proportions which were fixed by the Commandant, and the units and sub-units consisted, like the Corps, of mixed classes. In 1900 the proportions of the various castes and classes were as follows:—

---

[1] Four of the Service Companies had 18 first-line equipment mules and the necessary drivers, and by 1902 the two remaining Service Companies and the Burma Company were similarly equipped.

Indian Christians and Paraiyans (or Pariahs, now called Adi-Dravidians), 50%; Tamil Hindus, 21%; Telegu Hindus, 12½%; Muhammadans, 12½%; other castes, 4%. It has always been a tradition of the Madras Corps that in Service matters, caste should not be recognized. In this respect, the Madras Sapper and Miner differs not only from his brethren of Bengal and Bombay, but from the remainder of the Indian Army.

In 1903 the Service Companies were renumbered, Nos. 1 to 6 becoming Nos. 9 to 14 respectively. The Burma Company became No. 15, and " A " and " B " Depot Companies reappeared as " C " and " D." The establishment of the reserve was raised to 274 in 1904, and to 304 in 1908. The year 1909 was chiefly remarkable for the change of the title " Service Company " to " Field Company," and for the cessation of the enlistment of Recruit or Pension boys. The establishment of Recruit boys, which had existed since 1813,[1] provided the Corps with a valuable supply of recruits whose upbringing, nutrition and training had been closely supervised. It had the further advantage that recruits joined the Corps well drilled and with an elementary knowledge of some trade. Divisional Signal Companies of Sappers and Miners were formed in 1910, and two of these became part of the Madras Corps. The result was the end of " C " Company, for the Telegraph Section of that unit was then removed from the Corps and the remaining Sections (Printing and Litho) were transferred to " D " Company. The training of recruits for the new formations began in Bangalore in 1911. The only other change prior to the Great War which calls for special remark occurred in 1912 when the Indian Submarine Mining Section at Rangoon, which had been affiliated to the Corps in 1910, was abolished and replaced by a Defence Light Section.

The Great War caused an enormous increase in the strength of the Madras Corps. While on March 31st, 1914, there were 21 British officers, 25 Indian officers, 31 British Warrant and non-commissioned officers (R.E.) and 1,509 Indian other ranks, on March 3rd, 1919, the corresponding numbers were 144, 60, 85 and 7,019.[2] On August 4th, 1914, the Corps consisted of only seven Field Companies, one Field Park, two Photo-Litho Sections, two Printing Sections, one Depot Company and a Defence Light Section; but on November 11th, 1918, it had three Field Troops, 19 Field Companies, one Bridging Train, a Chitral Section, and no less than 16 Depot Companies in addition to the Field Park and Specialist and Defence Light Sections as before.[3] Of 295 officers who served with the Corps during the war, 59 were Royal Engineers (regulars), 56 held R.E. Territorial or

---

[1] The establishment was finally abolished in 1911.
[2] In 1914, 149 recruits passed to the ranks; in 1918 the number was 3,494.
[3] The Field Troops were Nos. 2, 3 and 8. The Field Companies were Nos. 9, 10, 11, 12, 13, 14, 15, 16, 61, 62, 63, 64, 65, 66, 67, 68, 69, 70 and 94. The Bridging Train was No. 7 and from it No. 96 Field Company was raised in Mesopotamia. The units raised during the War were disbanded or abolished between 1919 and 1922.

Temporary Commissions, 14 were Indian Army officers, and 166 came from the Indian Army Reserve of Officers (I.A.R.O.). The Corps would have been in great straits for officers if it had not been supported so nobly by this reserve of civilians who were mostly engineers. As an indication of the improvisation necessary in 1914 it may be mentioned that both the Sappers and equipment of a Field Troop (No. 2), which was formed on September 10th of that year were carried in 30 *tongas*[1] obtained from the Gwalior Imperial Service troops, and it was not till 1917 that the unit was provided with horses.

During 1915, separate establishments of Indian other ranks were laid down for field service and for India; and three Depot Companies, which were finally expanded to 16, were formed at Bangalore, each of the strength of a Field Company and organized as such. Steps were taken also to augment the establishment of British Warrant and non-commissioned officers by enlisting skilled men in India for service in the Royal Engineers. No. 15 (Burma) Company was mobilized in Mandalay for service overseas in 1916, and three sections embarked at Rangoon for Mesopotamia on October 9th, leaving one section in Mandalay as a depot.[2] In 1917 a Bridging Train[3] was formed at Bangalore; it embarked for Basra in December and received its equipment after its arrival in Mesopotamia. During the period of the Great War, recruits came forward in such large numbers that the demands of each successive increase in establishment were met easily; but there were always difficulties in producing efficient training staffs and proper equipment for the new units which were raised. These units were usually raised in Bangalore,[4] and sent overseas—mostly to Mesopotamia—after a short period of training.

After the Great War, the reduction of the Corps and its reorganization on a new peace establishment were much delayed by the campaigns in Afghanistan, Waziristan, Mesopotamia[5] and Malabar, and by some punitive expeditions in Burma, to all of which the Corps had to despatch units which in some cases were due for disbandment. As a result of the findings of several committees which assembled at Army Headquarters during 1920 and 1921, some new units were authorized for all three Corps of Sappers and Miners to bring their organization into closer agreement with that of the Royal Engineers at home. Army Troops Companies were formed in the Madras Corps from existing Field Companies, reduced to about half-strength, and Divisional Headquarter Companies were added. No. 15 (Burma) Company, the Mandalay Depot and the Rangoon Defence Light

---

[1] Two-wheeled pony carriages.
[2] The three sections took part in the advance on, and capture of, Baghdad in 1917. The depot was used subsequently to raise reinforcements and extra companies.
[3] No. 7 Bridging Train, with an establishment of 118 Indian ranks and six followers.
[4] They were raised from drafts from Depot Companies. An extra Depot Company ("C") was formed in 1917 to accommodate men returning from service overseas.
[5] The Arab Insurrection (1920).

Section were removed from the Corps and became the " 4th Burma Sappers and Miners."[1]

There were other changes between 1920 and 1923—the year in which the " 2nd Q.V.O. Sappers and Miners " became the " Q.V.O. Madras Sappers and Miners."[2] The Chitral Section having been handed over to the Bengal Corps in 1920, the section posted there returned to Bangalore and was disbanded. Two Field Companies were allotted as covering troops in Waziristan, and Rawalpindi and Secunderabad were abolished as out-stations of the Corps. A Field Troop was allotted to Sialkot and posted to the 2nd Indian Cavalry Brigade. A Field Company (No. 63) was maintained in Mesopotamia, surplus to the establishment of the Corps and working under the Royal Air Force, its personnel being relieved by yearly drafts from Bangalore of about half the strength of the unit. As a result of these various reorganizations the units included in the Corps on April 1st, 1923, were two Field Troops, five Field Companies, two A.T. Companies, one Divisional H.Q. Company, two Photo-Litho and Printing Sections and three Depot Companies, together with the extra Field Company in Mesopotamia. The strength of the Corps was then 36 British officers, 56 Warrant and non-commissioned officers and 2,167 Indian ranks—an immense reduction from the total of 7,308 of all ranks in March, 1919. The distribution in peace stations was as follows :—*Bangalore*, three Field and three Depot Companies, one Field Troop, and the Army Troops and D.H.Q. Companies and Photo-Litho and Printing Sections ; *Waziristan*, two Field Companies ; *Sialkot*, one Field Troop ; *Mesopotamia*, one (extra) Field Company. Each Field Troop had two British officers, a small H.Q. Section (administrative) and two mounted half-troops each of about 40 Indian ranks, including drivers. Tool-carts had replaced pack mules as 1st Line transport, and the 2nd and 3rd Line transport was carried in A.T. carts instead of on pack mules or camels. Some motor vehicles had been provided for Army Troops and D.H.Q. Companies to carry part of the unit equipment. The organization of four Sections in a Field Company had been altered to three Sections and an H.Q. Section, with two British officers in peace-time and five in war.[3]

After 1923, although there were some changes in the terms of service and other matters, no major alterations occurred in the organization or strength of the Madras Corps until those introduced recently in connection with the abolition of Pioneers from the Indian Army. In 1925, Indian ranks were required to enrol for seven years with the colours and eight years with the reserve. A new reserve of two classes (A. and B.) was introduced. Class A. consisted of

---

[1] The 4th Burma Sappers and Miners came into existence on January 10th, 1922, under A.I.I. 20 of that year.

[2] *Gazette of India*, No. 367, of March 9th, 1923.

[3] These numbers were increased respectively to three and six in 1928.

reservists with a total service of under ten years, and Class B. of those with a total of under 15 years. In 1928, Mandalay became an out-station of the Corps, and No. 15 Company, Burma Sappers and Miners, took over one of the Corps out-stations in Waziristan. In the following year, on the disbandment of the 4th Burma Sappers and Miners, No. 63 (Burma) Company, which had returned from service in Mesopotamia, was renumbered No. 15 Field Company, and Mandalay became a permanent out-station of the Madras Corps. Henceforward, three Field Companies were stationed in Bangalore and three in out-stations. Mechanization began in 1930, during which year and 1931 the Field Troops were reorganized, the tool-carts and limbered and G.S. wagons removed, and mechanical transport substituted. One half-troop was dismounted and carried in six-wheeled vehicles. A beginning was made also in the work of mechanizing the Field Companies. In 1932 came the proposal to abolish the Pioneers, a scheme which has produced important reorganizations in the Madras Corps ; but as these changes have affected all three Corps of Sappers and Miners equally they are dealt with in Appendix V.

APPENDIX III.

KING GEORGE'S OWN BENGAL SAPPERS AND MINERS.

The Corps of Bengal Sappers and Miners had its origin in the Corps of Bengal Pioneers formed by Captain T. Wood, B.E., at Cawnpore, in 1803. Two complete companies of the Pioneers, and a large number of selected men from other companies, were taken in 1819 to form a Corps of Bengal Sappers and Miners which was raised at Allahabad by Major Thomas Anbury, B.E., and into which the remainder of the Pioneers were absorbed in 1833. The new Corps became the " Bengal Sappers and Pioneers " in 1847, reverted to the title of " Bengal Sappers and Miners " in 1851, became the " 1st Sappers and Miners " in 1903, the " 1st Prince of Wales Own Sappers and Miners " in 1906, the " 1st King George's Own Sappers and Miners " in 1910, and in 1923 took its present designation.[1] These remarks recapitulate some of the early history of the Corps which has appeared already in this volume. It is proposed to deal in this Appendix only with the reorganizations and changes in the Corps during the present century.

In 1900 the Corps of Bengal Sappers and Miners included six Service Companies (1st to 6th), a composite unit called " A " Company[2] and " B " (Depot) Company for recruits. There was also an Active Service Reserve of 250 men, which was afterwards increased. An experimental Balloon Section was formed at Rawalpindi in July and August, 1901[3] and was added to " A " Company; and in 1903 a Mounted Detachment, similar to the unit specially raised for service in China in 1900 and disbanded in 1901,[4] was included in the Company.[5] The year 1903 saw the whole Corps rearmed with Lee-Enfield magazine rifles and bandoliers in place of the Lee-Metford magazine rifles issued in 1900. In general it may be said that up

---

[1] The title " 1st Sappers and Miners " was given to the Corps in 1903 under Lord Kitchener's reform scheme of amalgamating the Presidency Armies. The change of title in 1906 took place when H.R.H. The Prince of Wales consented to become Colonel-in-Chief of the Corps. On his accession to the throne as King George V. in 1911, the title was altered by permission to the " 1st King George's Own Sappers and Miners." During the Great War, however, it was found that the numerical designation led to confusion in the field, so it was dropped and the territorial designation (Bengal) was restored.

[2] " A " Company had Printing and Photo-Litho Sections, a Telegraph Section and a Pontoon Section. It could be mobilized for field service, and was not at that time a Depot unit as it afterwards became.

[3] I.A.O. 106 of February 15th, 1901.

[4] Its strength was one B.O., one B.N.C.O. and 24 Indian ranks.

[5] With the introduction of telephones, a telephone unit was added to the Company in 1904.

to 1914 there was very little change in organization except in the composition of "A" Company, and that alterations in equipment were confined mainly to the Telegraph, Balloon, and Bridging formations.[1]

In 1907 the class composition of the Corps was fixed as follows :—[2]

No. 1 Company	½ Sikhs, ½ Punjabi-Mussalmans.
No. 2 Company	½ Sikhs, ½ Punjabi-Mussalmans.
No. 3 Company	Hindustanis.[3]
No. 4 Company	½ Sikhs, ½ Pathans.
No. 5 Company	½ Sikhs, ½ Punjabi-Mussalmans.
No. 6 Company	Hindustanis.
Balloon Section	Punjabi-Mussalmans.
Mounted Detachment	Sikhs.
"A" and "B" Companies	Mixed.

All the Service Companies were stationed in peace-time at Roorkee except one company at Peshawar and another at Rawalpindi.

The Service Companies were designated "Field Companies" in 1909, as in the Madras and Bombay Corps. Two years later, owing to the establishment of Signal Companies of Sappers and Miners, the Telegraph Section was removed from "A" Company, and Mounted Detachment, and Printing and Photo-Litho Sections, were transferred to "B" Company. The Pontoon Section of "A" Company was reduced to a cadre, and, with the abolition of the Balloon Section, "A" Company disappeared for a time from the Corps. An Indian Submarine Mining Corps had been in existence for some years, and two sections of it—at Calcutta and Karachi—were attached in 1910 to the Bengal Sappers and Miners; these were added permanently to the Bengal Corps when the Submarine Mining Corps was abolished in 1912. For some time prior to the Great War, experiments were carried out at Roorkee with hand-grenades and small mortars[4] which proved of considerable value in 1914; and the training of a few men in motor driving in 1913 foreshadowed the great mechanical transport activities of the Corps in 1929–32.

As regards the organization of the Corps before the Great War, the Headquarters (as in Bangalore) included a Commandant (a Lieut.-Colonel or Major, R.E.), a Superintendent of Park and a Superintendent of Instruction[5] (Majors or Captains, R.E.), an

---

[1] Berthon boats were purchased in 1909, and the full equipment for a Berthon boat bridge was completed in 1912. A Wireless Telegraphy Section was formed in 1912 and had the first wireless set in the Indian Army.

[2] I.A.O. 112 of 1907.

[3] The class composition of both Nos. 3 and 6 Companies was altered in 1911 to half Hindustani Hindus and half Punjabi and Hindustani Mussalmans (I.A.O. 55 of 1911).

[4] Also with the "Bangalore Torpedo," made of sections of metal tubing filled with explosive to be pushed under wire entanglements and exploded. (Designed by the Madras Sappers.)

[5] The appointment of Superintendent of Instruction was amalgamated with that of Superintendent of Park in 1915, but was revived in 1918.

Adjutant[1] (a Captain or Lieutenant, R.E.), a Medical Officer, and five Warrant and non-commissioned officers, R.E. There was no separate appointment as Quartermaster. The Bridging Train was a cadre of only 20 men, and the remainder of " B " Company consisted of recruits and instructors. Each Field Company had a peace establishment of two British officers,[2] two British non-commissioned officers (R.E.), three Indian officers and 189 Indian other ranks, including 20 Sapper drivers. There were only 18 (Ordnance) Engineer Equipment mules on the establishment although the equipment was arranged in 48 mule-loads. The Mounted Detachment consisted of a Lieutenant, R.E., one British N.C.O. (R.E.), two Indian officers and 59 Indian other ranks. Its Engineer equipment was carried on pack horses and pack mules.

The strength of the Corps increased enormously during the Great War. On August 1st, 1914, there were 21 British officers, 47 British Warrant and non-commissioned officers, 25 Indian officers and 1,396 Indian other ranks. These formed the Corps Headquarters, six Field Companies, a Mounted Detachment, three Printing Sections and three Photo-Litho Sections,[3] two Defence Light Sections and " B " (Depot) Company.[4] But when the war ended the strength of the Indian ranks, including officers, had risen from 1,421 to 8,363, and there were 54 units in the Corps—21 Field Companies, one Field Squadron, three Field Troops, three Bridging Trains, one Frontier Searchlight Section,[5] seven Printing and Photo-Litho Sections, two Engineer Field Parks, two Defence Light Sections, 13 " B " (Depot) Companies and one " A " (Depot) Company.[6] Twenty-seven new field units had been raised, including 15 Field Companies, four Field Troops, and three Bridging Trains. The supply of officers to meet this huge expansion was greatly facilitated during the opening years of the war by the Indian Army Reserve, many of whose officers were civil engineers and needed only a short course in field engineering and interior economy before being posted to units. In 1917–18, R.E. Temporary Commissioned officers became available, and in 1918 many R.E. Regular officers began to arrive from England. Altogether, 33 R.E. Regular officers, 74 R.E. Temporary Commissioned officers, and no less than 174 officers of the Indian Army

---

[1] At the end of 1917, the Adjutant was assisted by one Assistant Adjutant for Routine and two more for Training.

[2] On mobilization, however, two Lieutenants, R.E., were added by Army Headquarters from the M.W.S. or the P.W.D. or Survey Department.

[3] One of each (extra and temporary) was in China.

[4] " B " Company included a Bridging Train cadre, and had the equipment only of an Engineer Field Park.

[5] Formed on November 9th, 1917, for service in garrisons on the N.W. Frontier of India at Malakand, Fort Lockhart (on the Samana Ridge), Tank and Jandola. The unit had 20 oxy-acetylene portable searchlights. It consisted of only 20 Indian other ranks. It was disbanded in August, 1920.

[6] Formed in 1917 to equip and despatch men to, and to receive men from, service overseas.

Reserve[1] joined the Corps at Roorkee during the war. The establishment of British non-commissioned officers was maintained by the gradual transfer of 171 of these ranks from British units in India. Recruiting for the Indian ranks proceeded vigorously, the Punjabi-Mussalman being the backbone of the Corps. In 1914–15 the Oudh Hindustani Hindu did not come forward ; but from 1916 the Garhwali and Kumaoni sections[2] came in, and from 1917 the recruiting of Hindustani Hindus was general throughout Oudh. The recruiting of Trans-Frontier Pathans ceased early in 1915. Among the Sikhs, recruiting was slack until 1918 when more than 500 joined the Corps. While the total number of recruits enlisted in 1915 was only 777, it rose to 2,686 in 1918. These figures give some idea of the activities at Roorkee during the war. The Corps of Bengal Sappers and Miners in 1918 was almost as large as a division in the field ; yet it was commanded by a Lieut.-Colonel of the Royal Engineers.[3]

The years immediately following the Great War were devoted almost entirely to disbanding units specially raised for the war, and to reorganizing the remainder on the new establishments which were notified in 1921. Several new types of units were introduced as a result of experience gained in the war. An Army Troops Company, Divisional Headquarter Companies, Field Troops and a Bridging Train became part of the Corps on its peace establishment. The Field Companies were organized into three sections and a headquarters section, and the equipment was arranged so that sections could act independently. The Army Troops Company and the Divisional Headquarters Companies were organized on the lines of the British A.T. Company and Field Park Company respectively, but with smaller establishments. A Chitral Platoon was formed in 1920 and attached to the Field Company at Rawalpindi, the tour of duty in Chitral being one year ; afterwards, when the platoon became a separate Chitral Section, the tour of duty was extended to two years. Corps Headquarters at Roorkee were increased by six British officers in 1921, and there were other internal changes. By March, 1922, the reduction of strength had been pushed so energetically that the Corps had only seven Field Companies, three Field Troops, one A.T. Company, two D.H.Q. Companies, one Bridging Train, two Defence Light Sections, the Chitral Platoon and three Depot Companies,[4] and by October it had almost reached its post-war authorized establishment.

Much attention has been given at Roorkee in the last decade to the question of equipment. Before the war the Engineer equipment was manufactured largely in the Park Workshops of the Corps or

---

[1] Including a few "Non-Technical" officers.
[2] Hill men.
[3] Lieut.-Colonel A. H. Cunningham, R.E.
[4] One of these ("A" Company) had Printing and Photo-Litho Sections attached to it.

purchased locally. This system was replaced after the war by substituting articles of regular ordnance supply or specially made by the Ordnance Department. Loading tables were revised, portable water-pumping sets and canvas troughs were provided, assault bridges were designed, and from 1929 mechanization received the closest attention. In 1925, new terms of service were applied to the Sapper and Miner personnel, the men being enrolled for seven years' service with the colours and eight years with the reserve. The Calcutta Defence Light Section was reduced to cadre in the same year. In 1927, each Field Company was given a third British officer, and the Bridging Train (No. 7) was disbanded. The mechanization of one of the Field Troops and three of the Field Companies began in 1930, and the process of general mechanization continued steadily till, by the middle of 1932, the Headquarters Transport, the two Field Troops, five Field Companies, the two D.H.Q. Companies and the A.T. Company had all been mechanized. In conclusion it may be mentioned that important changes in the organization of the Corps were initiated in 1932 in connection with the abolition of Pioneers from the Indian Army. These are alluded to in Appendix V on these subjects.

APPENDIX IV.

ROYAL BOMBAY SAPPERS AND MINERS.

The first engineering unit in the Bombay Presidency was a company of Pioneer Lascars raised by Major Lawrence Nilson, the Chief Engineer, at the end of 1777. This company was reinforced gradually by other Pioneer companies so that, when the Third Maratha War began in 1817, four companies were in existence. But it was not until 1820 that Sappers and Miners made their first appearance in Bombay. On August 20th of that year a company of these men was formed by Captain Thomas Dickenson, of the Bombay Engineers, from a small Corps of Engineer Lascars and a Pontoon Train which had taken part in the Second Maratha War in 1803. Another company of Sappers and Miners was added in 1826, and at the end of 1829 the two companies were called " Engineers." These two units were incorporated with six companies[1] of the Bombay Pioneers on September 29th, 1830, to form an " Engineer Corps " which became the Corps of " Bombay Sappers and Miners " in 1840, the " 3rd Sappers and Miners " in 1903, the " 3rd Royal Bombay Sappers and Miners " in 1921, and took its present designation in 1923. This is a recapitulation of some of the early history of the Corps which has appeared already in this volume. The information given in this appendix will be confined to the reorganizations and changes which have occurred during the present century.

In 1900 the Corps of Bombay Sappers and Miners included only four Service Companies[2] (Nos. 1 to 4), " A " and " B " Depot Companies, and the equipment for one Bridging Train. Pontoon, Telegraph, Bridging, and Photo-Litho and Printing Sections were grouped in " A " Company, and " B " Company was for recruits. The establishment of the Corps consisted of a Commandant, a " Superintendent of Instruction, Park and Train," an Adjutant, a Medical Officer, six Company Commanders (British), five Company Officers (British), 22 British Warrant and non-commissioned officers, 15 Indian officers, 849 Indian other ranks, 40 Indian driver ranks and 12 recruit boys. The class composition was settled by the Commandant. The peace distribution of units provided for Headquarters, two Service Companies, and " A " and " B " Companies at Kirkee, one Service Company at Aden, and another at Quetta. In

---

[1] The Bombay Pioneers had been increased to six companies in 1819 and to eight companies in 1822.

[2] A Service Company contained 192 Sappers.

1902, two more Service Companies (Nos. 5 and 6), and also a Fortress Company, were added to the establishment.

The year 1903 saw important changes in the Corps. Not only was its title altered to " 3rd Sappers and Miners," but all the companies were renumbered and an official class composition was issued for the first time. Nos. 1, 2 and 3 Companies became Nos. 17, 18 and 19 Companies respectively, and each was to be composed of one-quarter Rajputs, one-quarter Marathas, one-quarter Mussalmans and one-quarter Mixed. Similarly, Nos. 4, 5 and 6 Companies became Nos. 20, 21 and 22 Companies with the same authorized composition but substituting Sikhs for Rajputs. The Fortress and " A " Companies were changed into No. 23 (Fortress) and " E " Companies respectively with a mixed class composition, and " B " Company emerged as " F " Company composed of all classes.[1] Of these units, one Service Company was normally at Quetta, the Fortress Company at Aden, and the remainder at Kirkee. The appointment of Superintendent of Instruction, Park and Train, was abolished in 1903 and replaced by separate appointments of Superintendent of Instruction and Superintendent of Park and Train. Beyond an expansion of " F " (Depot) Company and an increase in the Reserve,[2] nothing of much importance occurred after this until the Service Companies were renamed " Field Companies " in 1909, as in the Madras and Bengal Corps.

In 1910 a new class composition was authorized ; one-half of the men were to be Mussalmans (Punjabis), one-quarter Sikhs and one-quarter Marathas.[3] The Telegraph Section of " A " Company was absorbed into the newly-raised Signal Companies, and the Pontoon Section was reduced to cadre ; the Printing and Photo-Litho Sections, and the cadre Pontoon Section, were then transferred to " F " Company, and " E " Company vanished. In the same year an additional Field Company was transferred to Quetta from Kirkee, and the Bombay and Aden Defence Light Sections joined the Corps. They were formerly part of the Indian Submarine Mining Corps, but since 1909 their duties had been confined to defence lights, telephones and pumping installations.[4]

The Great War caused a very large expansion of the Corps. In addition to the pre-war strength of 20 British officers, 20 British

---

[1] It was laid down that the class composition of the Corps as a whole was to be one-quarter Marathas, one-quarter Mussalmans, one-quarter Mixed, one-eighth Sikhs and one-eighth Rajputs. The term " Mixed " included Brahmans in addition to Ahirs, Telegus, etc. From 1907, Mussalman recruiting was in practice confined to the Punjab.

[2] The Reserve reached a strength of 205 in 1907, 232 in 1911, and 254 in 1914.

[3] The Field Companies had not yet reached this composition in 1914. Each company then had one and a quarter Sections of Punjabi-Mussalmans, one Section of Marathas, small numbers of Mixed Hindus and Hindustani-Mussalmans, and one Section (or nearly one section) of either Sikhs or Rajputs. (These figures are approximate.)

[4] Five Defence Light Sections were formed in 1910, two of which were added to the 3rd Sappers and Miners (Bombay). The Indian Submarine Mining Corps was disbanded in June, 1912.

Warrant and non-commissioned officers, and 1,400 Indian ranks, there passed through the Corps, between August, 1914, and November, 1918, approximately 250 British officers, 90 British Warrant and non-commissioned officers, and 6,000 Indian ranks. In the same period the original six Field Companies, one Fortress Company, one Depot Company and one Pontoon Park (cadre only) developed into 16 Field Companies, one Field Squadron, two Field Troops, one Fortress Company, three Pontoon Parks, a Seistan Detachment and a Karun Section, and nine Depot Companies including " E " Company which was re-formed.[1] Reinforcements of officers came chiefly from the Indian Army Reserve and were mostly men in civil engineering work in India. The earliest reinforcements were Royal Engineer officers from the Military Works Services and the Public Works and Survey Departments, followed in 1915 and later by officers of the Indian Army Reserve, officers holding Temporary R.E. commissions and officers of the Territorial Force (R.E.). British non-commissioned officers were obtained from England and also by transfer from British units in India. The establishment of Indian ranks was maintained by increased recruiting. The losses in the 20th and 21st Companies[2] during 1914–15 were so heavy that the Maler Kotla Imperial Service Sappers and Miners were absorbed into the Corps as reinforcements for these units and so remained until early in 1916, when they were replaced by recruits from Kirkee. A further loss occurred when the 17th and 22nd Companies surrendered to the Turks at Kut-al-Amara in April, 1916. Altogether, the supply of men to replace casualties was most difficult. The great increase of strength in 1917 and 1918 necessitated the enrolment of Rajputs, Hindu Jats and other Hindus; but in general it may be said that newly-raised units were composed of two sections of Punjabi-Mussalmans and two sections of Hindus who might be either Marathas, Hindustani Hindus, or Jats. At one time during 1915 the single Depot Company (" F ") contained over 1,000 men; but it was soon expanded into four companies, and in 1917 to six companies (" F.1 " to " F.6 ") together with a new " E " Company. In 1918 the Depot had eight " F " Companies and " E " Company. In addition to training and supplying recruits, the Corps manufactured at Kirkee an enormous amount of equipment for new units and for the Indian Munitions Board.

No allusion has yet been made in this appendix to the Railway Companies of the Bombay Sappers and Miners which did such good work in East Africa and elsewhere during the Great War. Nos. 25 and 26 (Railway) Companies went to East Africa in November, 1914, after working on the North-Western Railway in India, and Nos. 27 and 28 (Railway) Companies were formed in East Africa during 1916

---

[1] Defence Light, Printing, and Photo-Litho Sections have been omitted from these lists for brevity.

[2] These were the companies which suffered so severely in France.

when the whole were combined into a Railway Battalion of Sappers and Miners. After the companies had returned to India in 1918, No. 29 Company was raised, but the battalion organization was abolished in 1921[1] and only Nos. 25 and 27 Companies retained, the latter being renumbered No. 26. The men of the Railway Companies were chiefly Punjabi-Mussalmans.

From 1919 to 1922 the Corps was in the process of reduction and reorganization. The establishment was fixed in 1920 at a Headquarters, six Field Companies, two Railway Companies, one Fortress Company, one D.H.Q. Company,[2] three Depot Companies, two Defence Light Sections (Bombay[3] and Aden) and Printing and Photo-Litho Sections. Of these the Headquarters,[4] three Field Companies, one Railway Company, the Depot Companies and the Printing and Photo-Litho Sections were stationed at Kirkee, two Field Companies were at Quetta and one at Kohat, one Railway Company was on railway work, one Defence Light Section was at Bombay, and the other and No. 23 (Fortress) Company at Aden.[5] The strength of the Corps in 1920 was 32 British officers, 49 British Warrant and non-commissioned officers, 49 Indian officers and 2,323 Indian other ranks. Nos. 17 and 22 Field Companies, which till then had each consisted of four sections (192 Indian other ranks), were reorganized in 1921 into units each with three sections and a headquarter section and a strength of two British officers, three British Warrant and non-commissioned officers, four Indian officers and 224 Indian other ranks. The equipment was also adapted to make each section self-contained. On mobilization a Field Company was to receive three additional British officers so that it would then have an Officer Commanding, a Second-in-Command and three Section Commanders.[6] The class composition at this time in all six Field Companies was one-third Marathas and one-third Punjabi Mussalmans, while the remaining one-third was of Hindustani Hindus in Nos. 17, 18 and 19 Field Companies and of Sikhs in Nos. 20, 21 and 22. The Fortress and D.H.Q. Companies were of " mixed " composition.

Both the remaining Railway Companies (Nos. 25 and 26) were disbanded in 1931, and No. 42 D.H.Q. Company was increased in strength. In the process of these alterations, the last Hindustani Hindus disappeared from the Corps. This class is no longer enlisted. At the end of 1931 the class composition was two sections of Punjabi

---

[1] Early in 1919 the Railway Battalion was officially recognized in India with headquarters and depot at Sialkot.

[2] Actually raised at Kirkee in 1921 and subsequently called No. 42 D.H.Q. Company. It was transferred to Quetta in 1924.

[3] The Bombay D.L. Section was reduced to cadre in 1923.

[4] The Headquarters were expanded in 1921, the Adjutant receiving two Assistants and the Superintendents of Instruction and Park one each.

[5] In 1927 the Aden D.L. Section and No. 23 (Fortress) Company were amalgamated as the " Aden Fortress Company," and in 1928 this unit was converted into a British Fortress Company and all the Indian ranks were withdrawn.

[6] In 1928 the peace establishment of British officers for a Field Company was increased from two to three. The war establishment then rose to six.

Mussalmans and one of Marathas in three of the Field Companies (Nos. 17, 18 and 19), and one section each of Punjabi Mussalmans, Marathas and Sikhs in the remaining Field Companies (Nos. 20, 21 and 22). The strength of the Corps was then 32 British officers, 42 British Warrant and non-commissioned officers, 40 Indian officers, 1,853 Indian other ranks, and 149 Indian driver ranks, and the Reserve had reached a total of 704 Indian other ranks. Important changes in the establishment and organization of the Corps were initiated in 1932 in connection with the scheme for the abolition of Pioneers from the Indian Army. These are alluded to in Appendix V.

APPENDIX V.

THE ABOLITION OF PIONEER CORPS AND THE REORGANIZATION OF THE SAPPERS AND MINERS IN 1932.

There have been Pioneers in the Indian Army from the middle of the eighteenth century almost to the present day, first as Engineer troops who were mostly converted into Sappers and Miners, and then as infantry with some engineering training. In the British Army they appeared before the reign of Henry VIII., and in the early part of the sixteenth century were a properly organized Corps ;[1] but they were absorbed by the Engineers in later times and did not reappear as units of that Army until a Pioneer battalion was raised during the Great War of 1914-18 for every British division of infantry. After the war it was decided that these British battalions should be amalgamated with the R.E. field companies, but the process was not applied to the Pioneer battalions of the Indian Army because their high traditions seemed to justify their continued existence. In 1923 there were four Corps of Indian Pioneers—the Madras, Bombay, Sikh and Hazara Pioneers—the first three totalling 12 battalions and the last being an independent battalion ;[2] before 1932, however, amalgamations had reduced the total to six battalions[3] and the Hazara battalion. It was soon apparent that, under modern conditions, Pioneers could hardly be both fully trained infantry and expert engineers, and that by reason of their organization and training they were better fitted to be engineers than infantry. Up to 1914 they were most useful as roadmakers in expeditions across the administrative border on the N.W. Frontier ; but as such expeditions are now rare, and the regular garrisons stationed across the border are provided with permanent roads built by civil contract, Pioneers are no longer needed for road work. It is desirable also that the Engineer troops of any division should be homogeneous. These facts, coupled with serious financial stringency, caused the Government of India to make the important decision in 1932 that Pioneers should be abolished from the Indian Army and that a part of the financial saving so effected should be applied towards an increase in the strength of the three Corps of Sappers and Miners.

[1] They were disbanded on the termination of a campaign. *History of the Corps of Royal Engineers*, by Major-General W. Porter, Vol. I, p. 22.

[2] The first Madras Pioneers were formed in 1758, the first Bombay Pioneers in 1777, the first Sikh Pioneers in 1857, and the Hazara Pioneers in 1904.

[3] The Madras, Bombay, and Sikh Corps each had two battalions.

The scheme, as approved, was that every Field Company of Sappers and Miners should be changed from a three- to a four-section basis both in peace and war, with the addition of one British officer to its establishment. There was to be a small increase in the size of a section. It was specified that the number of artificers in a Field Company should be raised from 24 to 56, and that extra transport should be allotted to the extra section. The strength of a Field Company would be raised from 234 to 320. Each Divisional Headquarter Company was to be increased by approximately the same numbers, and reorganized in Headquarters, a Field Works Section and a Workshop Section; and each Army Troops Company was to have two sections only. Minor changes were proposed in the Field Troops. The Headquarters and Depots of each Corps were to be completely reorganized into a Training Battalion of three Training and one Depot Companies, a Records unit, and Workshops. The number of Field Companies was to be reduced from 18 to 17 by the conversion of a Field Company of the Bengal Corps into an Army Troops Company, so that that Corps and the Madras Corps should each have two Army Troops Companies. The Chitral Section was to be abolished as a separate unit; Field Companies were to supply it in future. Some changes were to be made also in the locations of units.

The strengths of the three Corps of Sappers and Miners on reorganization (including recruits) were expected to be :—

Q.V.O. Madras Sappers and Miners	3,518
K.G.O. Bengal Sappers and Miners	3,365
Royal Bombay Sappers and Miners	2,925
	9,808

These large increases above the previous establishments would be provided for by extensive transfers from the Pioneers. Thus the Q.V.O. Madras Sappers and Miners were to receive approximately 715 Madrassis from the Madras Pioneers; the Bengal Corps about 160 Meos from the Bombay Pioneers, and 320 Mazhbi and Ramdassia Sikhs from the Sikh Pioneers; and the Bombay Corps about 133 Marathas and 160 Lobana Sikhs from the Bombay Pioneers, and 160 Lobana Sikhs and 320 Mazhbi and Ramdassia Sikhs from the Sikh Pioneers. Many of the Pioneers who could not be absorbed into the Sappers and Miners would be given openings in the Indian Infantry or in the machine-gun platoons of British Infantry regiments in India. The remainder would be mustered out with the usual concessions. The battalion of Hazara Pioneers would be disbanded. Most of the British officers of the Pioneer units would be absorbed into the Indian Infantry.

THE ABOLITION OF PIONEER CORPS.

It was anticipated that, with the increased numbers of British officers with the Sappers and Miners, it would be possible to provide the C.R.E. Rawalpindi District (C.R.E. 1st Indian Division) and the C.R.E. Baluchistan District (C.R.E. 2nd Indian Division) with full-time Adjutants, and that the Sapper and Miner units forming the Divisional Engineers could then be placed directly under the C.R.E.s concerned. Sapper and Miner units in other forward stations, such as Covering Troops, Field Companies, Army Troops Companies and Field Troops, would be brought gradually into closer touch with, and under the control of, the District C.R.E. Chief Engineers of Commands would carry out annual technical inspections of Sapper and Miner Headquarters, and encourage intercourse and interchange between Royal Engineer officers of the Sappers and Miners and the Military Engineer Services. Modifications are to be expected in any new scheme, but the foregoing description gives a general outline of the Sapper and Miner reorganization of 1932 including the abolition of the Pioneers.[1]

[1] Further details are given in an article entitled "Engineer Reorganization in India," by Captain H. B. Harrison, R.E., appearing in *The R.E. Journal*, Vol. XLVI, December, 1932. An important modification was made in 1933, when it was decided that there should be Sikhs of the Jat class alone in the Bengal Corps, and of the Mazhbi or Ramdassia classes alone in the Bombay Corps. This involved an extensive exchange of new personnel.

APPENDIX VI.

SUBMARINE MINING IN INDIA.

Submarine mining was first contemplated in India in 1868 in the form of " torpedo " defences (fixed mines) for Calcutta and Rangoon, but little happened until 1879 when a company of Madras Sappers and Miners, and another of the Bombay Corps, were assembled at Bombay to be instructed by a few non-commissioned officers (R.E.) who had arrived from England in charge of the first consignment of submarine mining stores. The instruction was interrupted by the outbreak of the Second Afghan War, and nothing further was done for several years. By 1885, however, a small establishment of four British officers, 38 British non-commissioned officers and 118 Indian Sappers and Miners had been authorized for the mining defences of Bombay, Calcutta, Karachi and Rangoon, and, up to 1888, schemes of defence were prepared and unsuccessful efforts were made to train the Indian ranks in their aquatic duties. The situation improved when the formation of a proper Indian Submarine Mining Company was authorized on October 15th, 1891, with an establishment of one Major, R.E., four Lieutenants, R.E., and 74 British non-commissioned officers, R.E. This unit was associated with a corps of 140 Lascars which had been formed in May, and the whole soon became an efficient body as the Indian personnel were expert watermen. Major A. M. Stuart, R.E., the O.C. Indian Submarine Mining Company,[1] began to develop electric light defence schemes in 1899, and in the following year a small section was authorized for electric defence lights, telegraphs and telephones at Aden where there was no submarine mining. An improvement was effected in 1902 by the amalgamation of the Indian Submarine Mining Company with the Corps of Submarine Mining Lascars to form an " Indian Submarine Mining Corps." In 1903, some R.E. rank and file were sent from home to make the new Corps more like a British Submarine Mining unit, and the sections at Karachi, Bombay, Calcutta and Rangoon were formed into companies; but three years later, consequent on a decision to abolish submarine mining defences on the Hugli, the Calcutta Company was reduced to a small section to operate defence lights in peace-time.[2] Then came the decision in 1907 that submarine mining should cease at all Indian ports, and the companies

---
[1] He was also Inspector of Submarine Mining Defences in India.
[2] It was to be assisted in war-time by a local company of Electrical Engineer Volunteers. Similar volunteer companies could give assistance at Karachi, Bombay and Rangoon.

were reduced to sections whose duties from 1909 were confined solely to defence lights, telephones and pumping installations. The five Submarine Mining Sections were attached in 1910 to one or other of the Sapper and Miner Corps.[1] They were replaced in 1912 by Defence Light Sections, incorporated as such in the Sappers and Miners, and in that year the Indian Submarine Mining Corps was abolished. Small Defence Light Sections have existed since that time in Karachi, Bombay, Calcutta and Rangoon,[2] though most of them were reduced to cadre between 1923 and 1925. More than 70 Royal Engineer officers served with the Submarine Miners in India before the Corps was abolished in 1912, and a large number have been in charge of the Defence Light Sections since that date.[3]

---

[1] Those at Karachi and Calcutta, to the Bengal Sappers and Miners; those at Bombay and Aden to the Bombay Sappers and Miners; and the section at Rangoon to the Madras Sappers and Miners.

[2] The section at Aden was amalgamated with No. 23 (Fortress) Company, Bombay Sappers and Miners, in 1927.

[3] Further details of the Indian Submarine Mining Service are given in the *History of Submarine Mining in the British Army*, by Lieut.-Colonel W. Baker Brown, R.E., Chapter X, pp. 189–200.

INDEX.

THE rank shown against an individual is his highest rank mentioned in the book, and not necessarily the highest rank attained by him.

Names may be found either under their own initial letters, or under general headings, such as "Engineers, Bombay," "Madras," etc.

A

Abbott, James, Punjab Govt., 1848, **299**
Abdur Rahman Khan, Amir of Afghanistan, 1880, **388**
Abercromby, Sir Robert, approaches Seringapatam, 1791, **165**; Joins Cornwallis agst. Seringapatam, 1792, **168**; Retires to Malabar, 1791, **165**; Third Mysore War, 1791, **163**
Abercromby, Sir Ralph, Egypt, 1801, **200**
Abor, 1911–12—*Country* and people, **471**; *Dihang* River crossing, **472**; *Methods* of fighting, **471**; *Plan* of operations, **471**; *Rotung* captured, **472**; *Stone* chutes, **472**; *Survey* work, **472**; *Tribe*, N.E. Frontier, **456**
Abyssinia, 1868—*Arogi*, victory at, **399**; *Baluchi* labourers, **399**; *Conclusion* of expedn., **400**; *Engineering* departments represented, **399**; *Kumayli Pass*, difficulties, **398-9**; *Losses*, **400**; *Magdala*, Antalo route to, **399**— Assault on, **400**; *Napier* apptd. to Command, **397**; *Organization* of advance, **399**; *Preparations*, **397**; *Reasons* for war, **397**; *Senafé* occupied, **398**; *Strength* of force, **397**; *Theodore*, King, **397**—Sues for peace, **400**; *War* agst. Nature, **397**; *Zula* becomes base, **398**
Adams, Col., Colm.-Comdr., Third Maratha War, **244**
Adas, Keating's victory, 1775, **181-2**
Addiscombe, history of College, f.n., **232, 369**
Aden, captured 1839, f.n., **283** (see also "Great War")
Aden Hinterland, 1901–04, operations agst. Arabs, **415**
Adyar River, French victory, 1746, **68**
Afghanistan, five routes into, **374**
Acknowledgments, author's, to helpers, **ix-x**
Afghan War, First—*Ali Masjid* relieved, 1839, **274**; *Army* of the Indus, composition, **268**; *Bala Hissar*, **274**; *Bombay* army returns to India, 1839, **274**; *Bombay* troops for Army of the Indus, 1838, **268**; *Bridge* across Indus at Rohri, 1838, **269**; *Broadfoot's Sappers*, q.v., **275**; *Burnes, A.*, murdered, 1842, **276**—Political, **271**; *Changes* in Command, 1840–41, **275**;
Conclusion, 1842, **279**; *Conditions* leading to, **267**; *Cotton's* faulty dispositions, Kabul, 1839, **274**; *Desert* march to Dadhar, **270**; *Distribution*, after occupation Kabul, 1839, **274**; *Ellenborough* orders evacuation Afghanistan, **279**; *Engineers*, junior, as advisers of Generals, **270**; *Ghazni*, defences of, **271**—Engineers at storm, **272** and f.n.—Kabul Gate, blowing in of, **272-3**—Mahmud's pillars, f.n., **272** —Recaptured by Afghans, 1842, **276**— Thomson's reconnaissance and report, **271**; *Jalalabad*, defence, 1842, **277-8** —Defences, 1841, **277**—Destroyed by earthquakes, 1842, **278**—End of defence, **278**—Occupied by Sale, 1841, **276**—Sale calls Council of War, **277-8** —Sale ordered to evacuate, 1842, **277**; *Kabul*, insurrection at, 1841, **276**— Occupied, 1839, **274**—Reoccupied, 1842, **279**—Retreat from, disastrous, 1842, **276**; *Kalat* captured by Bombay Army, 1839, **274**—Recaptured by Afghans, 1840, **275**; *Kalat-i-Ghilzai*, defence of, 1842, **276**; *Kandahar*, occupied, 1839, **271**; *Khaibar Pass* route, **268**; *Khojak Pass*, work on, **270**; *Khoord Kabul Pass*, disaster, 1842, **276**; *Nott* and Pollock, "retreat by Ghazni and Kabul," 1842, **279**; *Peshawar* Force, 1838, **268**; *Plan* of campaign, **268**; *Politicals*, **267**; *Unwieldiness* of British Force, **269**
Afghan War, Second—*Afghan* forces, numbers and training, **376-7**; *Ahmed Khel*, Stewart's victory, 1880, **388**; *Ali Masjid*, Afghan account of capture, 1878, **378**; *Captured*, 1878, **377**; *Arrangements* for second phase, **383**; *Cavagnari*, murder of, **383**; *Concluded*, **392**; *Deaths* of Dundas and Nugent, **386**; *Demolition* of towers, **378**; *End* of operations, May, 1879, **382**; *Engineers*, dress, **381**— Equipment defective, **386**—Kandahar theatre, 1879, **382**—Lack of co-ordination with S. & M., **392-3**—Works at Kabul, 1879–80, **387** and f.n.—Work of, **376**; *Events* leading up to, **372-3**; *Gandamak*, Treaty of, **382-392**; *Ghazni* Field Force, 1880, **388**; *Ghilzais*, operations agst., under Gough, **378-9**; *Helmand R.* bridged,

557

381 ; *Invading* columns, **374–5** ; *Jagdalak Post*, defence of, by Thackeray, 1879, **386** ; *Jalalabad* occupied, 1878, **378** ; *Kabul* Field Force, 1879, **384** ; *Kabul*, fighting round, 1879, **385–6**—Occupied by Roberts, 1879, **384** ; *Kalat-i-Ghilzai* occupied, **381** ; *Kandahar* Force, heavy work for Engineers, **380** ; *Kandahar*, Battle of, 1880, **392**—Evacuated, 1881, **386**—Invested by Ayub Khan, 1880, **390**—Operations for occupation, 1879, **380** ; *Khaibar* route, **374** ; *Kurram* route, **374** ; *Maiwand*, disaster at, **388–9**—Retreat from, **389** ; *Paiwar Kotal*, victory, **379** ; *Railways*, Indian, **374**—To Rawalpindi, **388**—To Sibi and Quetta, **387** and f.n. ; *Roberts' march*, Kabul–Kandahar, **391**—Absence of S. & M. on, **391**—Engineers present at, **391** ; *Second Div.* broken up, **381** ; *Sher Ali*, flight and death, **378** ; *Sherpur* cantonments, defence of, 1879, **385–6**—Description of, **384** ; *Shinwaris*, operations agst., **378** ; *Stewart's* march, Kandahar–Kabul, 1880, **388** ; *Survey* work, **380** ; *Transport* difficulties, 1879, **383** ; *War* declared, **373** ; *Yakub Khan* becomes Amir, **378** ; *Zakka Khel* Afridis, operations under Maude, **378**

Afghan War, Third—*Afghan* army, 1919, **506–7** ; *Afghans* driven back to Dacca, **508** ; *Causes* of war, **505** ; *Course* of the war, **506** ; *Engineer* troops, record concentration of, **507** ; *Engineer* work, water supply duties, **510–11** ; *Forces* engaged, **506** ; *India*, conditions in, 1919, **505** ; *Irregular* forces holding advanced posts, failure of, **506** ; *Jalalabad*, projected advance on, **508** ; *Khaibar Pass*, Afridis, trouble with, **509**—Operations agst. Afghans, **508** ; *Kurram Valley*, invasion by Nadir Khan and the results, **509** ; *Landi Kotal* threatened and relieved, **508** ; *Situation* on frontier, May, 1919, **506** ; *Spin Baldak*, capture of, **510** ; truce granted **508** ; *Waziristan*, Upper Tochi and Wana evacuated, **509**

Afridis, 1930—*Bara* bridge, **525–6** ; *Caves* blocked and mined, **526–7** ; *Kajuri* and Aka Khel Plains occupied, **524** et seq. ; *Kajuri Plain*, description, **524** ; *Mazarai* bridge, **526** ; *Permanent* posts, **526** ; *Roadmaking* and water supply, **525**

Afridis, Khaibar Pass, **422**
Agnew, Col., expedn. agst. Poligars, 1800, **199**
Agra, captured, 1803, **216** ; Visited by Hawkins, 1608, **1**
Ahmadabad, captured, 1780, **192**
Ahmad Khel, victory of Stewart, 1880, **388**
Ahmad Shah Durani sacks Delhi, 1757, **105**
Aitken, Maj.-Gen. A. E., failure at Tanga, 1914, **499, 500**

Aix-la-Chappelle, Treaty of, 1748, **68**
Akas tribe, N.E. Frontier, **456**
Alam Bagh, **349** ; held by Outram, 1857–8, **357**
Aligarh, capture of, 1803, **214**
Ali Vardi Khan, Subadar of Bengal, 1742, **45**
Aliwal, battle of, 1846, **294**
Allard, Italian, with Sikhs, f.n., **295**
Allenby, Gen. Sir Edmund, C.-in-C., E.E.F., **494**
Almora, captured, 1815, **240**
Amalgamation, Royal and Company's Engineers, f.n., **314**
Amanullah Khan, King of Afghanistan, Third Afghan War, **504–5**
Amar Singh, capitulates at Malaon, 1815, **239** ; Gurkha General, 1814, **235** ; Operations agst., **238–9**
Ambans, Chinese officials, **463**, f.n.
Ambela, 1863—*B.S. & M. Cos.* present, **425** ; *Bunerwals* join enemy, **426** ; *Chamberlain* commands, **425**—Wounded and hands over to Garvock, **427** ; *Communications*, new line constructed, **427** ; *Crag Post*, **426**—Changes hands, **427** ; *Eagle's Nest Piquet*, **426**—Attacks on, **427** ; *Hindustani Fanatics*, Sitana, 1863, **425** et seq. ; *Position* precarious, **426** ; *Proposals* to withdraw negatived by Viceroy, **428** ; *Reinforcements* arrive, **427** ; *Review* of operations, **428** ; " *Sir Robert's Picnic*," **425** ; *Swatis* join enemy, **426**
Amboyna captured, 1795, **171**
Amherst, Lord, Governor-General, **251** ; Censures Ochterlony, **261**
Anderson, murdered at Multan, 1848, **299**
Anderson, Lt.-Gen. Sir Chas., comds. Bde., Bazar Valley, 1908, **453**, f.n. ; comds. Mohmands, 1908, **454** ; comds. Div., Meerut, 1914, **476** ; comds. Indian Corps, Sept., 1915, **481**
Angria-Kanhoji, Maratha pirate, **62** ; Operations agst., **85–6**
Angria-Tulaji, pirate's stronghold destroyed, 1756, **92**
Anjidevi, expedn. lands on, 1662, **14**
Anson, Gen. G., C.-in-C., India, 1857 ; death at Karnal, **323**
Appa-Sahib, Bhonsla Regent of Berar, alliance with, **243** ; Defeated, Nagpur, 1817, **244**
Arabia, operations in, 1819, 1821, **250**
Arab mercenaries, Third Maratha War, **244**
Argaon, Battle of, 1803, **210**
Armagon, Day agent, 1639, **4**
Arms, carried by S. & M., **281**
Armstrong, Lieut., B. Pioneers, Nepal War, **238**
Army in India—*Equipment*, improvement in since 1919, **505** ; *Four Commands* established, **395** ; *Presidency* armies abolished, **395** ; *Reorganization* after Mutiny, **368–9** ; *Reorganization* by Lord Kitchener, **417–8** ; *Staff*

Corps abolished, 1903, **418**; Staff Corps formed, 1861, **369**
Army of the Indus, assembled at Ferozepore, 1838, **267**
Army Organization Committee, 1879, **395**
Arnala, captured, 1781, **195**
Ashti, battle, 1818, **247**
Asirgarh, capture of, 1803, **210**; Capture of, 1818, **249**; Lack of Senior Engineers, 1818, **249** and f.n.
Assaye, Battle of, 1803, **209–210**
Assistant Field Engineers at Alam Bagh, 358, f.n.
Astor, state, **422**
Asuf Ali, Lt.-Col., China, 1900–01, **414**
Attock, bridge captured by Sikhs, 1848, **302**
Auchmuty, Lt.-Gen. Sir S., comds. expedn. to Java, 1811, **232**
Auckland, Lord, Gov.-Gen., First Afghan War, **267** et seq.
Aungier, Gerald, introduces uniforms, 1672, **12**; President, Bombay, **12**; President, Surat, **2**
Aurangzeb, ascends throne, 1658, **31**, f.n.; Invites Charnock to return to Bengal, **31**; Peace made with, 1690, **25**
Austin, Lieut. A. C., I.A.R.O., Aden, **491**
" Avenging Army," reaches Jalalabad, 1842, **278**
Avery, J., pirate, **85**
Avitabile, Italian General with Sikhs, **295**
Ayub Khan, victor of Maiwand, 1880, **388**

B

Badcock, Lieut., 5th Gurkhas, Hunza-Nagar, **437**; awarded D.S.O., **438**
Badli-ki-Serai, mutineers defeated, 1857, **323**
Bahadur Shah, puppet emperor, 1857, **318**
Baillie, Col. W., First Mysore War, 1780, **154**; Force captured at Pollilur, **155**
Baird, Maj.-Gen. D., comds. expedn., Egypt, 1801, **200**; Prisoner, **177**; Seringapatam, 1799, **177**
Baji Rao, defeated at Kirkee, 1817, **244**; Peshwa, Poona, 1802, **204**; Sacks Residency, Poona, **244**
Baker, Maj.-Gen., defeated, Suakin, 1884, **404**
Bala Hissar, Kabul, **274**
Baluchis, characteristics, **421-2**
Bamboos of Ava, enormous size, **254**
Bangalore, defences, 1791, **164**; Siege of, 1792, **163** et seq.
Bangalore Torpedo, **479**, f.n.
Bani-Bu-Ali, battle honour, Bo.S. & M., 250
Banks, Major, succeeds Lawrence, Lucknow, 3.1
Bantam, factory in Java, founded 1603, H.Q. of E.I. Co., **3**
Barabati captured, 1803, **214**

Barlow, Sir G., Gov.-Gen., **233**
Barnard, Maj.-Gen. Sir Henry, death at Delhi, 1857, **331**; Succeeds Anson, **323**
Barnet, Commodore, off Pondicherry, 1745, **65**
Baroda, Gaikwar of, Maratha Confederacy, **143**; Treaty of, **182**
Barrett, Gen. Sir A. A., comds. Bde., Bazar Valley F.F., 1908, **453**, f.n.; Comds. Bde. Mohmands, 1908, **454**; Comds. 6th (Poona) Div., **482**; G.O.C.-in-C., Northern Army, Waziristan operations, **503**; G.O.C. N.W. Frontier Force, Third Afghan War, **506**
Barthelemy, French Comdr. of Madras, 1746, **68**
Basket boats, Wellesley's instructions for making, 1803, **207**
Bassein, captured, 1780, **194**; First Maratha War, **180**; Granted to Portugal, **13**; Treaty of, **13**; Treaty with Peshwa, **204-5**
Batavia, fortified by Dutch—occupied, 1811, **232**
Bazar Valley F.F., 1908, Willcock's three weeks' war, **453**
Beatson, Maj.-Gen. A., Madras Infy., career, **173**; Plan of attack, Seringapatam, 1799, **175**; Seringapatam, 1792, **174**; Surveyor-General, 1799, **173**
Bednore, captured, 1783, **197**; Matthews' surrender at, 1782, **161**; Recaptured by Haidar Ali, **197**
Begum Kothi Palace, Lucknow, **350**
Bellamy, Paymaster, **48**
Bellecombe, Governor of Pondicherry, 1778, **148**
Benares, Raja of, expedn. agst., 1781, **179**
Bengal—*Adams, Wm.*, Master Gunner and Engineer, 1711, **40**; *Agg, Lieut. J.*, constructed St. John's Church, **117**; *Ali Vardi Khan*, death, 1756, **57**— Subadar, 1742, **45**; *Aloffe, John*, Plans of Calcutta by—Surveyor of Works, 1728–1745, **44**; *Amphlett, T.*, Ch. Eng., 1760–62, **125**; *Azim-Ush-Shan*, grants rights in land, Calcutta, 1698, **33**; *Badara*, Dutch defeated at, 1759, **114**; *Bag Bazar Redoubt*, at Perrin's Point, **55**—Attacked by Siraj-ud-Daula, **58**; *Balasore*, **45**— Abandoned 1642, **4**—Founded 1633, **4**, **30**; *Barker, John*, on Robins' Staff, 1751, **50**; *Barker, Brig.-Gen. Sir Robert*, C.-in-C., Bengal Army, **101**, f.n.—Disgusted by coolies, **104**—On Scott's Staff, 1754, **55**—Proposals for new Ft. William, **103**—Reverts to military duties, **104**—Supersedes O'Hara as Engineer, 1757, **101**; *Bayne, R.*, examines masonry, old Ft. William, 1883, **34**; *Beard, John*, improves old Ft. William—President, retires 1704, **34**; *Black Hole*, description of, **59**; *Boddam, T.*, Councillor,

INDEX.

116; *Braddyll*, Governor, 1745, **47**; *Brohier, John*, absconds, 1760, **115**—Apptd. Engineer, 1757, **103**—Demolishes Chandernagar, **102**—Difficulties with labour, **120** *et seq.*—First proposals for Ft. William, **106**—Instructions for, **52**—On Robins' Staff, 1751, **50**—Traces out Ft. William, **108, 110**; *Calcutta*, ceded to British, 1757, **105**—Course, the, **132**—Described by Cotton, **132**—Described by Mrs. Kindersley, 1767, **131**—Development of, 1765-67, **131**—Esplanade, jungle, 1717, **42**—Extended, 1698, **33**—First fortification, **32**—Lall Dighi enlarged, **39, 41**—Origin of, **30**—Revival of, 1758, **120**—St. Anne's Church, 1709, **37**—St. John's Church, 1787, **117**—Society, 1780, **117**; *Call, John*, recommended by Robins, **51** (see "Madras"); *Campbell, Maj.-Gen. Sir Archibald*, career, f.n., **133**—Ch. Eng., 1769-1771, **133**—Destroys works at Chandernagar, 1769, **134**—Initiates Kidderpore Docks, 1770, **134**—Reforms, and reports on, works, **133** (see also "Bombay," "Madras," "Engrs., Royal," and "Engrs., Bengal"); *Carrington, N.*, on Robins' Staff, 1751, **50**; *Cave, H.*, repairs river-bank, **44**; *Chandernagar*, captured, 1757, **102**—Ft. Orleans at, **49**—French factory, 1697, **36**—Razed, **102, 113**—Secret works destroyed, 1769, **134-5**—Siraj-ud-Daula fires, **57**; *Charnock, Job*, Agent, Hugli, 1685, **30, 31**—Founds Chuttanutee, 1690, **25**—Lands at Hijili, **31**—Lands Madras, 1689, **25**—Occupies and quits Sutanuti, 1688, **31**—Reoccupies Sutanuti, **31**; *Chittagong*, raid on proposed, 1682, **30**; *Chowringhee*, new hamlet of Calcutta, 1717, **42**; *Clive, Robert, Lord*, captures Chandernagar, **102**—Death, 1774, **136**—Defeats Siraj-ud-Daula, Feb., 1757, **102**—Initiates new Ft. William, **100** *et seq.*—President and Governor, 1758, **111**—Raises first Sepoy Bns., 1757, **101**—Recaptures Calcutta, 1757, **60**—Returns 1765 as Gov., **119**—Sails for England, 1760, **114**—Victory, Plassey, June, 1757, **105**; *Colson, Joseph*, repairs at Govindpur, **44**; *Committee of Works*, formed 1751—Instructions for, **52**—Mentioned, **55, 74, 121, 123**; *Cooke*, Master Gunner and Engineer, 1711, **40**; *Corruption* of officials, 1760 onwards, **114** *et seq.*; *Cossimbazar*, captured by Siraj-ud-Daula, **57**—Factory started, 1658, **30**—Proposal for fortifying, **112-13**—Watts, chief of, **56**; *Custom House* in old Ft. William, 1766, **117**; *Dacca*, Nawab of, sanctions fortifications, Calcutta, 1696, **32**; *Da Costa*, clerk, absconds, **115**; *Diarchy*, 1704, **35**; *Dockyard*, built at Kidderpore and out-turn, **134**; *Drake*, Governor, deserts old Ft. William, 1756, **59**—Returns as Gov., 1757, **101**;

Dutch, defeated by Col. Forde, 1759, **114**; *Engineers*, earlier, not named, **35**; *Eyre, Chas.*, Agent, Sutanuti, 1693, **31**—Extends Calcutta, 1698, **33**—First President, 1700, **33**—Fortifies Calcutta, 1696, **32**; *Forde, Col.*, defeats Dutch at Badara, **114**; *Forresti*, Engineer, Patna, joins Calcutta, 1742, **46, 47**; *Forster, John*, Governor, 1747, **47**; *Fortifications*, Directors' advice, 1748, **51**—First, at Calcutta, 1693, **32**—Improved, 1696, **32**; *Fortnam*, civil architect, builds Council Chamber, 1764, **136**—Ch. Eng., 1774-76, **136**; *Fort William*, all outworks stopped by Court, 1760, **116**—As now existing, **137**—Bricklayers and carpenters imported from England, 1757-63, **122**—Brohier's first proposal, **106**—Cadres of Engineers, 1762-64, **126-128**—Ch. Engs., characters of, **133**—Civil architect imported, 1763, **122**—Completion, 1781, **136-7**—"Contracted plan" ordered by Court, **104**—Court's letter *re* cost and garrison, 1759, **112**—Description of, **108-10**—Estimate of cost, 1758, **112**—Final cost, **136**—Initiated by Clive, **100** *et seq.*—Labour troubles, **120** *et seq.*—Maidan laid out, **136**—Martin's "contracted plan," 1768, **130-31**—Martin's report on works, 1764, **128**—Military Committee controls works, **136**—Misappropriation of funds, 1760, **115, 116**—Monsoon damage, 1773, **135**—New site, selected by Clive, **107**—Private works forbidden, **120** *et seq.*—Revised estimate, **116**—River protection works 1766, **129**—Slow progress, **120** *et seq.*—Started Oct., 1757, **108, 110**—State of works, 1769, **134**—State of works, 1774, **135**—Supply of materials, **124, 125**—Work organized by A. Campbell, **133**; *French*, Engineer hired to British, 1708, **37**—Fleet, preparations agst., 1758, **111**—Found Chandernagar, 1697, **36**—Hostility, 1744, **49**; *Fulta*, refugees at, 1756, **59**; *Garden Reach*, anchorage, **44**; *Gee, Zachariah*, Master of Attendance—River works by, 1731-39, **44**; *Glass, Philip*, on Robins' Staff, **50**; *Goldbourne, Miss S.*, letters from Calcutta, **117**; *Goldsborough, Sir John*, Commissary-General, Admiral, and Chief Governor, 1693, **31**—Death, **32**—Rescues Sutanuti, **31**; *Govindpur*, new Ft. William, **60**—Origin of, **30**—Mentioned, **42, 44, 45**—Removed from site of Ft. William, **108**; *Hamilton, Robert*, proposals for defence, Calcutta, 1747, **49**; *Harnett, Capt.*, Master Gunner, 1713, **40**; *Hastings, Warren*, first Gov.-Gen., requires full report on Ft. William, 1774, **135**; *Heath*, sent to remove British, 1688, **31**; *Hedges, Robert*, President, 1716, **41**; *Hedges, William*, Agent, Hugli, 1682, **30**; *Hijili*, Charnock lands at, **31**; *Hollard,*

INDEX. 561

Ensign M. S., with Knipe, 1742, **46**; *Holwell*, obelisk in Dalhousie Square, **60**—Mentioned, **49**—President, 1760, **114**; *Hugli*, captured by Marathas, 1742, **45**—Fort built by British, 1650, **30**—Fort built by Portuguese, 16th century, **30**—Job Charnock, Agent, 1685, **31**—Recaptured, 1757, **100**; *Janoji*, invader, 1742, **45**; *Jones, Capt. J. L.*, scheme for old Ft. William, 1755, **56**; *Jones, John*, Master Mariner and Gunner, 1718, **40**; *Kalikata*, name explained, **30**; *Kidderpore Docks*, building of, **134**; *Kilpatrick, Major*, recaptures Hugli, 1757, **100**; *Kindersley, Mrs.*, description of Calcutta, 1767, **131**; *Knapton, Charles*, on Robins' Staff, **50**; *Knipe, Charles*, mily. eng., 1742, visits Calcutta, **46**; *Lennard, Robert*, Engineer, 1742, **46**; *Lillyman, Major J.*, Ch. Eng., 1772, **135**—Death, 1774, **136**; *Lowes, J.*, Asst. Eng., absconds, 1760, **115**; *Macdonald, J.*, Asst. Eng., **113**; *Mace, J.*, Ch. Eng., 1757, **104**; *Maratha, ditch*, **45**—Invasion, 1742, **45**; *Marriners*, earliest Engineers, **36**; *Martin, Capt. F.*, Ch. Eng., 1764, **128** —Resigns, 1768, **131**—Rigid economist, **130**; *Master Builder* apptd., old Ft. William, 1724, **44**; *Master Gunners* as Engineers, **40**; *Master of Attendance*, **40, 44**; *Minchin, Capt. Commandant George*, deserts garrison, old Ft. William, **58**—Incapacity of, **58**— Scheme for old Ft. William, 1755, **56**; *Mir Jafar*, Chief officer of Siraj-ud-Daula, **105**—Deposed, **115**—Made Nawab of Bengal, **105**—Plot to replace Siraj-ud-Daula supported by Clive, **105**—Restored, 1764, **119**—Treaty with, **105**; *Mir Kasim*, deposed, 1763, **119**—Succeeds as Nawab, **115**; *Morrice, Sampson*, on Robins' Staff, **50**; *Mosman, Major*, 55th Foot, Engineer adviser, 1748, **50**; *Munro, Gen. Sir Hector*, victor of Buxar, 1764, **119**; *Nawab of Bengal*, bill for entertaining, **111**; *O'Hara, Charles*, deserts old Ft. William, **58**—On Robins' Staff, **50**— Superseded by R. Barker, **101**— Transferred to Patna and dies, **101**; *Old Fort William*, Beard, J., improves, **34**—Black Hole, **59**—Building completed, 1716, **41**—Captured by Siraj-ud-Daula, 1756, **59**—Cave as Engineer, 1724, **44**—Colson as Engineer, 1728, **44**—Condition when attacked, 1756, **58**—Description of attack, 1756, **58** *et seq.*—Description of, 1700-02, **33, 34**— Ditch proposed by Winder, 1708, and reports thereon, **39**—Earlier Engineers not named, **35**—Engineers, mortality among, **56**—Final form, **42**—Fortifications improved, 1696, **32**—French Engineer hired, 1708, **37**—Holwell takes command, 1756, **59**—Houses of Europeans, **44**—Improvements, 1707-08, **38**—Jones' scheme, **56**—Lal Bagh, **42**—Lall Dighi enlarged, **39, 41**—Last days, **60, 116**—Made tenable, 1757, **102**—Minchin's scheme, 1755, **56**— Named after William III., **33**— Original masonry examined, 1883, **34, 38**—Palisading, 1716-1742, **44, 45**— Plaisted's scheme, 1747, **47**—Review of various schemes, **56**—River front improved, 1710-12, **40**—St. John's Chapel, **117**—Scott's scheme, 1754, **54** —Simson's scheme, 1756, **55**—Site, **32**—Site how now occupied, **42**— State in 1712, **40**—Surroundings, **42**— Union Jack first hoisted, 1702, **34**— Water supply, **39**; *Patna*, factory started, 1658, **30**; *Paymaster*, as Engineer, 1707, **36**; *Perrin's Point*, redoubt, **45, 55**; *Plaisted, Bartholomew*, appointments and resignations, **48**—Died, 1767, **49**—Schemes for defences, 1747, **47**—Surveyor of Works, 1745, **47**; *Plans of Calcutta*, early, **44**; *Plassey*, Battle of, **105**; *Political situation*, 1763-65, **119**; *Polier, Capt. A.*, Ch. Eng., 1762-64, **126**; *Portuguese*, in Hugli R., 1530, **30**; *Presidency*, constituted separate, 1699, **33**; *Preston, Achilles*, on Robins' Staff, **50**; *Robins, Benjamin*, death from malaria, 1751, **50**—Eng.-Gen. of all the Settlements, 1750, **50**; *Rotation Govt.*, 1704 *et seq.*, **34, 35, 37, 38**; *Russell, John*, President, grandson of Oliver Cromwell, **39**; *St. Anne's Church*, 1709, **37**; *St. John's Chapel*, old Ft. William, 1760, **117**; *St. John's Church*, 1787, **117**; *Scott, C. F.*, Lt.-Col., 29th (Fuller's) Foot, Engineer-General, **52**—Calcutta, 1753, **53**—Death at Madras, 1754, **53**— Instructions for, **53**—Schemes for Calcutta, **54**—Schemes for Maratha Ditch, **55**; *Select Committee*, orders survey, 1757, **101**; *Sepoys*, first bn. raised by Clive, 1757, **101**; *Simson, Colin*, Engineer and Surveyor, criticizes Scott's scheme, 1756, **55**— Dies in Black Hole, **58**; *Siraj-ud-Daula* (Mirza Mahomed), assassinated, **105**—Attacks and sacks Calcutta, **57-60**—Black Hole, **58**—Captures Cossimbazar, **57**—Character, **57**—Defeated at Plassey, **105**—Defeated by Clive, **102**—Nawab, 1756, **57**—Mentioned, **40, 49**; *Smith, Col.*, Member of Council, report on Ft. William, 1768, **130**; *Snow, Th.*, Gunner, 1728, **44**; *Sovereignty*, sold to British, 1765, **119**; *Steuart*, coachmaker, **132**; *Streynsham Master*, 1676, **30**; *Surveyor of Works*, John Aloffe, 1728-45, **44**; *Sutanuti* (Chuttanutee), Eyre made Agent, 1693, **31**—Mentioned, **42, 45**— Occupied and vacated, 1688, **31**— Origin of, **30**—Reoccupied by Charnock, 1690, **31**—Rescued, 1693, **31**; *Thana*, occupied by Marathas, 1742, **45**; *Tolly's Nullah*, **108**; *Twenty-four Parganas* ceded to British, **105**;

INDEX.

Vansittart, Governor, salary, **115-6**; *Verelst*, Governor, 1767, **130**; *Warren, T. G.*, Gunner, river work, 1731-39, **44**; *Watson, Admiral*, captures Chandernagar, **102**—Recaptures Calcutta, 1757, **60** (*v.* " Bombay," " Madras "); *Watson, Lt.-Col. H.*, Asst. Eng. to A. Campbell, **134**—Building of Kidderpore Docks, **134**—Ch. Eng., 1776, completes Ft. William, **136**—Seconds Francis in duel with Hastings, **136**; *Watts*, Ch. of Cossimbazar factory, **56-7**; *Wells, Lieut.*, Asst. Eng., **55**; *Weltden*, President, 1710, reports on Winder's ditch, **39**; *Winder, Jonathan*, advises ditch at Calcutta, 1708, **38-9**
Bentinck, Lord, Gov.-Gen., 1828, **266**
Berar, **143**
Betwa River, defeat of Tantia Topi, **364**
Beynon, Maj.-Gen. Sir W. G. L., 3rd Gurkhas, capture of Nisa Gol, 1895, **443**; G.O.C. Derajat (S. Waziristan) F.F., 1917, **503**
Bor Ghat, Goddard's advance on Poona, 1781, **195-6**
Bhurtpore, Raja of, joins enemy, **217**—treaty with, **216**; *Siege*, 1805—Blame for failure, **222**—Comdg. Eng. unknown, **221** and f.n.—Description of place, **219**—Efforts to cross ditch, **219**—Engineers criticized, **221**—Failures, **219-222**—Losses, **220**—Prestige lost, **223**; *Siege*, 1825—Attack, **262** *et seq.*—Capture, **265**—Description of fortress, **261**—Engineers commended, **265**—Engineers and Pioneers present, **261**—Occupied by Durjan Sal, **260**
Bhutan, 1864-66—Diwangiri, disaster, recaptured and three V.C.s won, **459**; Duar Field Force, **458**; N.E. Frontier, **456**
Biddulph, Maj.-Gen. M. A. J., Kandahar Force, 1878, **375**
Bilot, three V.C.s won, 1898, **447-8**
Bingham, Lieut., assault of Delhi, **341**; Assistant Engineer, f.n., **331**; Roorkee College Staff, 1857, **321-2**
Birch, Lieut., 58 N.I., Lucknow Residency, f.n's, **351** and **354**
Birch, Resident at Perak, murdered, 1875, **400**
Bird, Maj.-Gen. Corrie, comds. Tochi Valley, 1897, **445**
Biscondah, Maratha siege, 1815, **202**
Black Mountain, 1888, agst. Akazais and Hassanzais, **429**
Bliss, Major C., comds. Mishmi Mission, 1911-12, **473**
Boer, M.I., Somaliland, 1902-04, **416**, f.n.
Bogue forts, First China War, **280**
Boisragon, Col. G. H., V.C., 5th Gurkhas, Hunza-Nagar, 1891, **437-8**
Bolan Pass, First Afghan War, **270**; Second Afghan War, **374**
Bombay—*Aungier, Gerald, q.v.*; *Bake, Col. Herman*, Engineer and Surveyor-General, 1671, **20, 23, 27, 35**; *Barber, Robert*, Engineer, 1669, **19**; *Boone, C.*,

President, 1715, **84, 85, 86**; *Bourchier, R.*, President, 1752, **90**; *Building* entirely forbidden, **87**; *Campbell, 1st-Lieut. R. N.*, Overseer of works, 1734, **87**; *Campbell, Lt.-Col. Archibald*, reports on Dongri Hill, 1768, **96-7** (see also " Bengal," " Bombay," " Madras," " Engrs., Royal," " Engrs. Bengal "); *Castle*, in 1665, **14**—1673, **21**; *Cathedral, St. Thomas'*, 1718, **88**; *Catherine of Braganza*, dowry of, **14**; *Child, Sir John*, Governor, 1689, **22**; *Clive*, destruction of pirates, 1756, **91-2** (see " Bengal," " Madras "); *Coates*, arrives 1668, **16**; *Cockell*, Engineer, 1737, **88**; *Cooke, Humphrey*, occupies, 1665, **14, 72**—Recalled, **16**; *Cromwell* refuses to buy, **13**; *Davies, D.*, lands, 1626, **13**; *Defences*, renewed activity, 1737, **88**; *Defence wall*, 1716, **86**; *De Funck, Capt. J.*, Ch. Eng., 1753, **90**—Resigns, 1758, **91**; *Dependencies*, **16**; *Description*, 1775, **98**—Works and garrisons, 1738, **88**; *Development* by 1764, **95**; *Ditch dug*, 1740, **88**; *Docks* and harbour, **198**; *Dockyard*, **86**; *Dongri Hill*, fortifications on—Commenced 1768, **97-8**—Completed 1780, **97-8**—Disputes regarding, 1755-68, **90-97**—North end of defences, 1716, **86**; *Dutch*, approach, 1673, **21**; *Egerton, Col.*, capitulates at Wargaum, 1779, **143**—First Maratha War, **190-1**; *Engineers*, uniform, 1800, **187**; *Esplanade* cleared, 1762, **93**; *Fort St. George* on Dongri Hill, **97**; *Fortifications*,1665, **14, 16**—Early 18th century, **84**; *Garrison*, 1665-7, **16**; *Gary, H.*, Governor, 1667, **16**; *Goodwin* arrives, 1668, **16**; *Increase* of forces, 18th century, **87**; *Insanitary* State, **84**; *Keating, Capt. T.*, Principal Engineer, 1764, **94**—Reports and work on Dongri Hill, **94-96**; *Keigwin*, Comdr. of Garrison, rebels 1683, **21**; *Law, S.*, Governor, sanctions ditch, **88**; *Leased* to Garcia da Orta, 17th century, **13**; *Life* at, described, **98**; *Lighthouse*, 1769, **98**; *Lost*, except Castle, 1689, **22**; *Lucas, Sir Gervase*, Governor, 1667, **16**; *Mace, Major J.*, Ch. Eng., 1758, **91, 92**; *Manor House*, **13**; *Marathas* threaten, 18th century, **87**; *Marlborough* arrives, 1662, **14**; *Matthews, Commodore*, conduct at Bombay and agst. pirates, 1722, **85, 86**; *Mendham's Point*, south end of defences, 1716, **86**; *Mint*, site of, **13**; *Mughal War*, 1690, **22**; *Nilson, Capt. L.*, Principal Engineer, 1773, **97**; *Oxenden, Sir George*, visits, 1669, **17**; *Parsons, A.*, sailor and trader, 1775, **98**; *Pirates*, operations agst., **85**; *Policy* of Company, balance of power, **86**; *Reclamation*, 1715, **84**; *Rented* to E.I. Co. by Crown, 1668, **16**; *Shipman, Sir Abraham*, brings reinforcements, 1662, **14**; *Smith, Gen. Joseph*, career, f.n., **88**; *Smith, Capt. Samuel*,

INDEX. 563

first Ch. Eng., 1669, **17, 18**—Death, **19**; *Streynsham Master* arrives, 1668, **16**; *Surat* superseded, **22**; *Toldervy*, Engineer, 1669, **18, 19**; *Uniforms* introduced, 1672, **12**—Engineers, 1800, **187**; *Waite, N.*, begins dockyard, 1707, **86**; *Watson, Admiral*, destroys pirates, 1756, **91, 92** (see "Bengal" and "Madras"); *Werner, Capt. A.*, Sub-Engineer, 1762, **94**; *Whitehorn, Capt.*, surveys, 1669, **17**; *Women* sent out, **7**; *Young, Capt.*, arrives 1668, **16**—Depy. Gov., **17**
Bombay-Burma Trading Corporation, fined, **406**
Bombay Fusiliers, origins, **17**
Boughton, Gabriel, Agra, surgeon at, 1650, **30**
Bourquin, defeated, Delhi, 1803, **215** and f.n.
Bower, Maj.-Gen. H., Abor, 1911–12, **471**
Boxers, brigands, China, **413**
Boyes, Lieut. W. R., I.A.R.O., Kut, **485**
Bozdars, Baluchis, **422**
Braithwaite, Col., captures Pondicherry, 1793, **170**; Disaster in Tanjore, 1782, **160**; First Mysore War, **154**; Occupies Wandiwash, 1780, **155**
Bremer, Commodore Sir Gordon, naval C.-in-C., First China War, **280**
Bretherton, Major G. H., S. & T. Corps, drowned crossing Tsan-po, **469**
Bridges—Astor R., 1891, **435**; Bara R., 1930 (Bara), **525–6**—(Mazarai), **526**; Chenab R. (Ramnagar), 1848, **305**; Ganges R. (Cawnpore), 1857, **349**; Gumti R., 1858, **360**; Helmand R., 1879, **381**; Indus R. (Attock, 1849), **307**—(Kotkai, 1891), **431** and f.n.—(Rohri, 1838), **269, 270** f.n.; Sutlej R., 1846, **296**; Swat R., 1895, **441**; Tigris R. (Mosul, 1920), **518** and f.n.; Tsan-po R., 1905, **469–470**; *Suspension*—Chin-Lushai, 1890, **462**; Hunza-Nagar, **439**; Mishmi, 1911–12, **473**; Panjkora R., **442**; Swat R., f.n., **441, 446**
Bridging Train—*Absence of*, 1800, **199**; *Arakan* Colm., 1825, **258**; *Blown* up at Kut, **485**; *Crossing* of Tungabhadra R., 1799, **199**; *Gujarat*, 1803, **206**; *Mesopotamia*, **482**, f.n., **483, 485**; *Mesopotamia* mobile, **488** and f.n.; *On elephants*, Chakdarra, **441**; *Second Afghan War*, lack of transport, **381**; *Second Sikh War*, **303, 304** and f.n.; *Train* formed in Bombay, 1799 and 1803, **206, 227**; *Reaches* Wellesley, **206**; *Wellesley's* instructions re pontoons, **207**
"Brigades," Engineer, at sieges, **176**
Bright, Maj.-Gen. R. O., Khaibar Colm., 1879, **383**
British Museum, plans of Calcutta in, **44**
British N.C.O.s (S. & M.), Skeleton Cos., R.E., formed 1866, **370**; Trained at Chatham, 1819, **225**; With B.S. & M.,

1857, **319**; With B.S. & M., 1857, at Delhi, **333**; With S. & M. Corps, 1846, **299**
Broadfoot brothers, f.n., **273**
Broadfoot, Capt. George, 34th Madras Infy., his defence of Jalalabad, 1842, **276-7-8**; killed, Ferozeshah, 1845, **294**; Lahore, 1845, **292**; Memorials to, **294**; Raises Sappers, 1840, **275**; Wounded at Jalalabad, 1842, **278**
Broadfoot, William, killed, 1841, f.n., **275**
Brooke, Brig.-Gen., killed, Kandahar, **390**
Brown, Capt. P. A., M. Fusrs. and M.S. & M., Malwa Campaign, 1857, **362**
Browne, Lt.-Gen. Sir Samuel, Peshawar Valley F.F., 1878, **374**
Bruce, Brig.-Gen. Hon. C. G., N. Waziristan F.F., 1917, **503**
Brydon, Dr., sole survivor, retreat from Kabul, 1842, **276**
Buffs, with 1st Co. B.S. & M., Panniar, 1843, **290**
Bulfin, Lt.-Gen. Sir E. S., G.O.C. XXIst Corps, Palestine, **497**, f.n.
Buner F.F., Blood comds., 1898, **449**
Bunerwals, Yusafzai Pathans, **422**
Burma, contemptuous attitude of native govt., 1810, **224**
Burma Rebellion, 1931, Engineer work, **528**
Burma War, First—*Arakan*, captured, 1825—colm. withdrawn, **258**; *Burmese* account of war, **260**—Fortifications, **254**; *Cachar* Colm., failure of, **257**; *Concentration* for, 1824, **253**; *Concluded*, 1826, **260**; *Cost* in men and treasure, **251**; *Donabyu* captured, **259**; *Engineers*, youth of, **253**; *Kemmendine* captured, **255**—failure at, **254**; *Kokein* captured, 1824, **257**; *Madras* S. & M. present, **308**; *Maha Bandula*, General, 1822, **251**—Killed, Donabyu, 1825, **259**—Surrounds Rangoon, **256**; *Martaban* captured, **309**; *Napadi*, Battle of, 1825, **259**; *Outbreak* of, 1824, **251**; *Paghamyu*, Battle of, 1826, **259**; *Pagoda Point*, capture of stockades, **255**; *Prome*, advance on, 1825, **258**—Captured, **259**; *Rangoon* captured, **254**—Small expedns. round, 1824, **255**; *Tenasserim* Expedn., **255**; *Transport* arrangements, **252**; *Yandabu*, Treaty of, **260**
Burma War, Second—*Burmese* arms, **309**; *Causes* leading to, **307**; *Conclusion*, **311, 312**; *Forces* reorganized, **310**; *Martaban*, Burmese attacks, **310**; *Myat-Tun*, operations agst., **311**; *Opening* of hostilities, 1852, **309**; *Pegu*, occupied and lost, **310**; *Preparations* for, **308**; *Rangoon* captured, 1852, **309**; *Revolution* at Ava, **311**
Burma War, Third—*Ava*, advance to, **407-8**—Capture of, **408**; *Bhamo* occupied, **408**; *Burmese*, credulity and

vanity of, **409–10**; *Dacoits*, garrisons escape and become, **408**—Chase of, till 1893, **408–10**; *Events* leading up to—"shoe question," trade disputes, **405**; *Forces* engaged, **406–7**; *Gwegyaun*, capture of, **407**—Works designed by Italian, **407**; *Minhla*, capture of, **407–8**; *Military* posts, details of construction, **410**; *Mindon*, King of Burma, commercial treaty with, **405**; *Pacification* completed, 1893, **410**; *Plan* of operations, **406**; *Prendergast* in chief command, **406**; *S. & M.* return to India, **409**; *Thayetmyo*, concentration at, **407**; *Thibaw* deported, **408**—King of Burma, **405**—Massacres by, **406**; *Upper Burma* annexed, **408**—Gradual pacification, **409**—Sir George White comds. in, **409**; *Viceroy* and C.-in-C. visit Burma, 1886, **409**

Burmese, as fighters, **252**; Gradual advance towards India, **251**; Tactics, 1824, **256**

Burn, Lt.-Col. W., defends Delhi, 1804, **217**

Burnes, A., murdered, Kabul, 1842, **276**; Political, First Afghan War, **271**

Burr, Col., wins Battle of Kirkee, 1817, **244**

Burrell, Col., 18th Regt., comdg. First China War, **280**

Burrows, Brig.-Gen. G. R. S., defeated at Maiwand, 1880, **388**

Bussy, French General, captured at Wandiwash, 1760, **78**; Captures coast, **75**

Buxar, Battle of, won by Major Munro, 1764, **119**

Buxey (see "Paymaster")

C

Calcutta, *v.* "Bengal"
Calicut, Portuguese reach, **13**
Cambay, First Maratha War, **181**
Cameron, Lieut., R.A., Balla Pass, **460**, f.n.
Cameron, Capt., British Consul, Abyssinia, tortured, **397**
Campbell, Maj.-Gen. Sir Archibald, civil improvements as Governor; dies, 1791; Governor and C.-in-C., Madras, 1786; retires, 1789, **162** (see also "Bengal," "Bombay," "Madras," "Engrs., Royal," and "Engrs., Bengal")
Campbell, Maj.-Gen. Sir Archibald, Comdr., First Burma War, **252**
Campbell, Capt. C. P., defence of Chitral, **440, 444,** f.n.
Campbell, Gen. Sir Colin (Lord Clyde), Adam Khel Afridis, 1850, **423**; C.-in-C. India, **355**; Lucknow, capture, **359–362**—Relief, **355–357**; Tantia Topi defeated, **359**
Campbell, Major J., 73rd Regt., defence of Mangalore, 1783, **197**; Surrenders Mangalore, 1784, **161**

Campbell, Col., assault of Delhi, 1857, **341**
Canal Foundry Workshops, Roorkee, defence post, 1857, **321**
Canning, Lord, first Viceroy and Gov.-Gen., **368**; Gov.-Gen., 1856, **322,** f.n.
Canton, First China War, **280–1**
Carnac, J., Field Deputy, First Maratha War, **191**
Carnatic, Nawab of, attacks French in Madras, **68**
Cautley, Col. Sir Proby, Bengal Artillery, Irrigation Eng., **292** and f.n.
Cavagnari, Major Sir P. L. N., Kabul, apptd. British Resident, **382**—Envoy to, **373**—Murdered at, 1879, **383**
Cavalry, European sqn. raised, Madras, 1748, **69**; Headgear agst. Sikhs, 1848, **303**; Pursuit of Marathas, 1803, **211**
Central India F.F., 1858, **363** et seq.
Ceylon, expedn. to, 1795, **171**
Chakdarra, bridges at, **441,** f.n.; capture of, 1895, **441**; Siege and relief, 1897, **446**
Chaklala, mechanical transport depot, **535**
Chakrata, hill station and approach road, **534**
Chalmers, Lieut., N.I., Asst. Eng., Delhi, **331,** f.n.; Asst. Eng., Lucknow, **354,** f.n.
Chamberlain, Gen. Sir Neville, Ambela, 1863, **425**—Wounded and hands over Command, **427**; Kabul, envoy to, 1878, **373**; Orakzais, expedn. agst., 1855, **423**; Siege of Delhi, **345**
Champion, Col. A., defeats Rohillas, **179**
Chanda Sahib, Nawab of Carnatic, besieges Trichinopoly, 1751, **71**
Channam, plaster used at Madras, **82**
Charasiab, Roberts' victory at, 1879, **384**
Char Bagh, Lucknow, **350**
Charles II. marries Catherine of Braganza, 1661, **14**
Chattar Singh, Sikh chief, capitulates, 1849, **307**; Joins Sher Singh at Rasul, 1849, **306**; Rebels, 1848, **302**
Cheshire, Lieut. H. S., I.A.R.O., Kut, **485**
Chief Engineers, to inspect S. & M. H. Q., **553**
Chilianwala, Battle of, 1849, **305**
China War, First—*Amoy* captured, **281**; *Bogue Forts* captured, 1841, **280**; *Canton*, attacked by Gough, **281**; *Chapu* occupied, **281**; *Chinese* report of operations, **282**; *Chinhai* captured, **281**; *Chinkiang-Fu*, decisive battle, **281**; *Chuenpi* captured, 1841, **280**; *Chusan*, unhealthy, evacuated, **280**; *Gough* assumes comd., 1841, **281**; *Hong Kong* occupied, 1841, **280**; "*Opium War*," 1840, **279**; *Shanghai* occupied, **281**; *Treaty* of Nanking, 1842, **282**; *Tinghai* assaulted, **281**
China War, Second—*Canton* captured, 1857, **313**; *Concluding* engagements, 1860, **315**; *Dress*, airy, of force, **314**;

INDEX. 565

Outbreak, 1857, **313**; *Paitang R.*, landing at, **314**; *R.E. Cos.* in, **314**; *Summer Palace* destroyed, 1860, **315** and f.n.; *Taku Forts* captured, 1860, **314**; *Treaty* of Tientsin, 1858, **313**
China, 1900–01—*China* Expeditionary Force, **413**; *Defences*, British Legation, **413**; *Engineer* work, **414**; *Foreign* forces, f.n., **413**; *Pekin*, relief of Legations, **413**; *Preliminary* events, **413**; *Trouble* with Boxers, **413**
Chingleput, Naik of, grants site of Madras, **4**
Chinhut, defeat, Lucknow, 1857, **351**
Chin-Lushai, 1888–89, 1889–90, **457, 460**; Laborious engineering and malaria, **461–2**
Chins, N.E. Frontier, **456**
Chinsura, Dutch factory, **30, 57**
Chitral, 1895—*Bridge* work, **441** and f.n.; *Chakdarra* captured, **441**; *Defence* of Fort, **440, 444**; *Detachments* besieged, **442–3**; *Engineers*, strong cadre, **440**; *Fowler* and Edwardes at Reshun, **442–3**; *Kelly*, Chitral relieved by, **441, 444**—Operations by, **443–4**; *Malakand Pass* captured, **441**; *Panjkora R.* bridged by Aylmer, **442**; *Relief* force mobilized, **440**; *Road*, old Buddhist, improved by Abbott, **441**; *Sapper Cos.* present, **440**; *Sappers' War*, **441**; *Shandur Pass* crossed, **443**
Chitral, State, **422**
Chittagong, **30, 48**
Chitu, Pindari leader, 1817, **244**
Chusan, First China War, **280**
Climo, Maj.-Gen. S. H., Third Afghan War, **506**; Waziristan, 1919, **513**
Cobbe, Lt.-Gen. Sir A. S., V.C., Mesopotamia, **488**
Cockburn, Lt.-Col., First Maratha War, **191**
Cogan, Andrew, Fort St. George, founder of, **5**; Masulipatam, Agent, 1640, **4**
Colombo, captured, 1795, **171**
Combermere, Lord, C.-in-C., 1825, career, **261**, f.n.; Operations agst. Bhurtpore, 1825, **261** et seq.
Commander, Royal Engineers, to comd. S. & M. units during peace, **553**
Committee, Military, composition of, 1774, **136**
Committee of Fortifications, **107**
Committee of Secrecy, **103**
Company of Merchants of London, original E.I. Company, **1**
Conjeveram, First Mysore War, 1780, **154–5**; Mughals reach, 1687, **25**
Coningham, Brig.-Gen. F. E., relieves Rumaitha, 1920, **519**
Cooper, Col., captures Ramgarh, 1815, **238**
Coorg, Raja of, deposed 1834, **266**
Coote, Lt.-Gen. Sir Eyre, C.-in-C., India, 1780, **150**; Comds. in Carnatic, 1780, **158**; Death, 1785, **161** (see "Madras"); Defeats Haidar Ali at Pollilur, Porto Novo and Sholinghur,

1781, **159**; Movements in Carnatic, 1781, **158**
Cornelis (Java), assaulted, **233**; Entrenched camp, 1811, **232**
Cornwallis, Lord, assumes comd., Third Mysore War, 1790, **162**; Bangalore, captures, 1791, **163–5**; Gov.-Gen., 1786, **162, 233**; Reapptd. Gov.-Gen., 1805, **222**; Seringapatam, attacks, 1792, **168**—Retires from, 1791, **165**
Correspondence, Blakiston's with Govt., **224**; Oriental style of, by E.I. Co., **223**
Cosby, Col., First Mysore War, **154**
Cotton, Sir Evan, help acknowledged, **x**
Cotton, Maj.-Gen. Sir W., attacks Donabyu, 1825, **258**; Comds. Army of Indus, 1838, **268**; Kabul, 1839, **274**; Leaves Kabul, 1840, **275**
Country music, mark of grandeur, **63**
Court (Italian) with Sikhs, f.n., **295**
Craig, Gen., expedn. to Manilla, 1797, **171**
Craigie, Capt. J. H., defends Kalat-i-Ghilzai, 1842, **276**
Crocker, Brig.-Gen. G. F., Third Afghan War, **508**
Crowe, Pioneers, capture of Kokein, 1824, **257**
Cuddalore, captured by French, 1758, **75**; Captured by Tipu, 1782, **161**; Eyre Coote at, 1781, **158**; Struggle before, 1782, with French, **161**; Von Werlinhoffe to construct defences, 1698, **27** (see also "Madras")
Cureton, Brig.-Gen. C. R., Cav. Comdr., Second Sikh War; Killed, Ramnagar, 1848, **303**
Curzon, Lord, Frontier policy, **452**—tested to destruction, 1919, **506**; Speech by, 1902, **60**
Cyprus, occupation of, 1878, **401**

D

Dabhoi captured, 1780, **192**
D'Aché, Admiral, French, 1758, **75**
Daflas, tribe, N.E. Frontier, **456**; War caused by whooping cough, **458**
Dakeyne, Capt., Madras Inf., M.S. & M., Second China War, **314**
Dalhousie, Earl of, Gov.-Gen., 1848, **299**
Dalrymple, Col., captures Honalli, 1799, **199**
Danes at Tranquebar, **4**
Darwesh Khel Wazirs, **422**
Daud Khan, Rohilla chieftain, blockades Ft. St. George, **34**
Daulat Rao Sindhia succeeds to Gwalior, **204**
Davidson, Major S. R., 47th Sikhs, Neuve Chapelle, **477**
Day, Francis, Agent, Armagon, **4**; Agent, Ft. St. George, 1643, **5**; Selects Madrasapatam, **4**
Dayaram, defends Hathras, 1817, **240–2**

De Boigne, French adventurer under Sindhia, **205**; Trainer of "Deccan Invincibles," **216**
Deccan Invincibles, annihilated, 1803, **216**
Defence Light Sections, Aden Section, **555**, f.n.; B.S. & M., **542, 543, 544, 545**; Bo.S. & M., **547, 549**; Formed from Submarine Mining Sections, **419, 555**; Rangoon Section, **538-9**
Defence works, permanent, Attock, Rawalpindi, Quetta, **534**
Dehra Dun, captured, 1814, **235**; District acquired, **240**
Delamain, Brig.-Gen. W. S., captures Fao, 1914, **482**
De La Motte, Capt. P., comds. Bombay Pioneers, 1812, **225**
De La Motte, Maj.-Gen., storms Panalla, 1844, **288**
Delhi, entered by Lake, 1803, **215**; Reoccupied by Marathas, **179** (v. also " Mutiny ")
Dennie, Lt.-Col., Kabul Gate, Ghazni, 1839, **272**
Deogaon, Treaty of, 1803, **214**
D'Espréménil, French Governor of Madras, **68**
Dhar, captured, 1857, **363**
Dhundhu Pant, Raja of Bithur, 1857, **347**
Dhundia Nagh, freebooter, released 1799, **199**; Hunted down and killed, 1800, **199**
Diarchy, 1704, **35**
Dig (see " Maratha War, Second ")
Dilkusha, Palace at Lucknow, **350**
Divi, capture planned, **62**
Dobell, Maj.-Gen. Sir C. M., Third Afghan War, **507**
Domville, Capt. J. R. C., Somaliland, 1890, **411**
Don, Col., captures Rampura, 1804, **217**
Donabyu, operations agst., 1825, **259**
Dost Muhammad, death, **372**; Evacuates Peshawar, 1849, **307**; Joins Mulraj, **301**; On Indus, 1849, **306**; Ruler of Afghanistan, 1838, **267**; Surrenders to British, 1840, **275**
Doveton, Gen., besieges Nagpur, 1817, **244**; Captures Asirghur, 1818, **248**
Dowse, Lieut., M.Inf., comds. Pioneers, Bangalore, 1791, **163**; Mentioned in despatches, 1799, **178**; Pondicherry, 1793, **171**; Savandroog, 1791, **166**; Seringapatam, 1792, **168**—1799, **173**
Draper, D., Field Deputy, First Maratha War, **191**
Duar F.F. (v. " Bhutan, 1864–66 ")
Dudrenec defeated, Laswari, 1803, **216**
Dufferin, Lord, Viceroy, 1885, **406**
Dulac, French Engineer, Pondicherry, 1778, **148**
Dumas, Governor of Pondicherry, **65**
Dunlop, Lt.-Col., Seringapatam, 1799, **176**
Dunsford, Brig.-Gen., Duar F.F., **458**
Dunsterville, Maj.-Gen. L. C., " Dunsterforce," N. Persia, **490**

Dupleix, dictator of S. India, **70**; Disgraced, **75**; Governor of Pondicherry, **65**; Repudiates La Bourdonnais and seizes Madras, 1746, **68**; Repulsed from Ft. St. David, 1746, **68**; Repulses British at Pondicherry, 1746, **68**
Durand, Lt.-Col. A. G. A., Hunza-Nagar, 1891, **435**
Durand Line, **422, 439**
Durjan Sal, usurper of Bhurtpore, 1825, **260**
Dutch—*Approach* Bombay, 1673, **21**; *At* Masulipatam, etc., **4**; *At* Negapatam, 1781, **160**; *At* Trincomalee, 1781, **160**; *Attack* British on Hugli, 1759, **113, 114**; *Capture* St. Thomé, 1674, **10**; *Chinsura* (factory), **30**; *Early* Company, **1**; *Refuse* to help Siraj-ud-Daula, **57**; *Secure* Spice Is., **2**; *War* with, 1781, **160**—1795, **171**
Dyer, Brig.-Gen. R. F. H., Amritsar, **509**, f.n.; Third Afghan War, **509**
Dynamite, advantages of, **432**

E

Eadgah Redoubt, Seringapatam, 1792, **168**—1799, **176**
East India Company, ended, f.n., **314**; Farewell to, **368**; First Governor, **1**; Origin, **1**
Edwardes, Herbert, defeats Mulraj, **299**; Punjab Govt., 1848, **299**
Edwardes, Lieut. S. M., defence of Reshun, 1895, **442**
Edwards, James, Director of E.I. Co., **21**
Egerton, Maj.-Gen. Sir Charles, Somaliland, 1903, **416**
Egypt, 1801, expedn. to, instructions for march across desert, **200**
Egypt, 1882—*Arabis* revolt, **402**; *Causes* for intervention, **402**; *Concentration* at Ismailia, **402**; *Conclusion* of campaign, **403**; *Division* sent from India, **402**; *Engineer* work, **403**; *Kassassin*, **402**; *Tel-el-Kebir*, **403**
Eighty-fourth Regiment at Madras, **78**
Elambore River, Madras, **4**
Elephanta Hog Island, **180**
Elephants, bridging train, **441**; Last, of the Army in India, **237**, f.n.; Use in Nepal War, **236**
Ellenborough, Lord, Gov.-Gen., 1842, First Afghan War, **278-9**; Gwalior Campaign, **289**
Elles, Maj.-Gen. E. R., Mohmand F.F. 1897, **448**
Elles, Maj.-Gen. W. K., Hazara F.F., 1891, **431**
Elliott, Lieut., Bengal Pioneers, capture of Dehra Dun, **234**; Wounded, Kalanga, **235**
Ellis, Ensign, Bengal Pioneers, capture of Dehra Dun, **235**; Killed at Kalanga, **235**
Elphinstone, Gen., dies in captivity, 1842, **276**; Relieves Cotton at Kabul, 1841, **275**

INDEX. 567

"Emden," German cruiser, attacks Madras, 1914, **77**
Empress of India, Queen Victoria proclaimed, **373**
Engineer Field Parks, China, 1900-01, **414**; Second Afghan War, **375**
Engineer Institution, H.Q. Bombay Engineers, 1829, **230**
Engineers, Bengal—*Abbott, Maj.-Gen. Sir Fred.*, First Burma War, wounded, **253, 259**—Last Lt.-Gov. Addiscombe, **369**—Sobraon, 1846, **295**—With Pollock, 1842, **278**; *Abercrombie, Capt. W.*, Gwalior Campaign, **289**—Multan, 1848, **300**; Amalgamated with Royal Engineers, **369** and f.n.; *Anbury, Maj.-Gen. Sir T.*, Ch. Eng., Bhurtpore, 1825, **261**—Ch. Eng., Hathras, **241**—Comds. Jhansi, 1838, **266**—1st Comdt., B.S. & M., **226**; *Anderson, Major J.*, death at Lucknow, **353**—Ghazni, 1839, **272**—Lucknow Residency, **351**; *Armstrong, Major J. A.*, Bhutan, 1864, **458**, f.n.—Egypt, 1882, **402**; *Baird-Smith, Col. R.*, Aliwal, 1846, **294**—Delhi, Ch. Eng., **329**—Pre-eminence in Mutiny, **367**—Relations with Wilson, **333, 336**—Roorkee, **319, 321, 322, 346**—Second Sikh War, **303**—Services, f.n., **331**—Supt. of Canals, **319**; *Baker, Lt.-Gen. Sir W.*, canal work, **292**; *Bateman-Champain, Col. Sir John V.*, Delhi, cuts canal, 1857, **329**—Services, f.n., **331** and f.n., **360**—With B.S. & M., 1857, **319**; *Becher, Lieut. J. R.*, with Pollock, 1842, **278**; *Blunt, Capt. J.*, Ch. Eng., 1803, **206**—Third Mysore War, **179**; *Blair, Lieut. H. F.* ("Toony"), Ambela, 1863, **425, 428**—Second Afghan War, **387**; *Boileau, Capt. A. H. E.*, on projected railway, 1846, **297**; *Broadfoot, Lieut. J. S.*, Ghazni, 1839, **272**—Killed, 1840, **275**; *Brohier, J.* (see "Bengal" and "Madras"); *Brown, Lieut. E. J.*, Sind, 1842—Secy. to Outram, **286**; *Browne, Maj.-Gen. Sir James* ("Buster"), Ambela, 1863, **425**, f.n., **428**—C.R.E., I. Div., Egypt, 1882, **402**—Kandahar, 1879, **382**—Political, **375**—Rly., Sibi-Quetta, f.n., **387**—Rly., Sind-Peshin, f.n., **511**; *Brownlow, Lieut. E. P.*, killed by explosion, 1858, **362**; *Brownlow, Lt.-Gen. H. A.*, Services, f.n., **331**—Unarmed Pioneers, Delhi, **332**—Wounded, **346**; Cadres and employment, 18th century, **180**—1829-57, **296-8**; *Cameron, Lt.-Gen. N.*, career, **179-80**; *Cameron, Lieut. W.*, escalade of Gwalior, 1780, **193**; *Campbell, Maj.-Gen. Sir Archibald*, career, f.n., **133** (see "Bengal," etc.); *Campbell, Lt.-Gen. J. D.*, Gwalior Campaign, **289**—Pegu, 1852, **310**—Second Burma War, **308**; *Carmichael-Smyth, Capt. H.*, Agra, 1803, **216**—Aligarh, **215**—Dehra Dun, **235**—Dig, **218**—Hathras, **241**—Java, Expedn., **232**—Rampura, **217**; *Carnegie, Lieut. H. A. L.*, Lucknow 1858, **361**—Services, f.n., **331**; *Carter, Lieut. T. T.*, Ambela, 1863, **425**; *Cheape, Gen. Sir John*, Burma War, First, **253, 257**—Burma War, Second, **310, 311**—Sikh War, First, **297**—Sikh War, Second, **301, 306**; *Chesney, Gen. Sir G. T.*, Acct.-Gen., **371**—Delhi, 1857, **326, 328**—Services, f.n., **331**—Suggested as author, **ix**—Wounded, **346**; *Colvin, Capt. J.*, Bhurtpore, 1825, **261**; *Cotton, Lieut. F. F.*, Bhutan, 1864, f.n., **458**; *Craster, Maj.-Gen. G. A.*, Second Burma War, **308**; *Crommelin, Lieut. J. A.*, Burma, 1825, **253**; *Crommelin, Lt.-Gen. W. A.*, crossing Ganges, 1857, **348-9**—Kangra, 1846, f.n., **296**—Pontoon train, Second Sikh War, **303**—Wounded, **354**; *Cunningham, Capt. A.*, Second Sikh War, **303, 307**; *Cunningham, Lieut. A. J. C.*, Bhutan, 1864, f.n., **458**; *Cunningham, Bt. Capt. J. D.*, Aliwal, 1846, **294**—First Afghan War, f.n., **272**; *Davidson, Capt. C.*, Bhurtpore, 1825, **261**; *de Budé, Lieut. H.*, First Burma War, **253**; *Dickson, Lieut. Wm.*, First Burma War, wounded, **253**; *Donaldson, Lieut. L.*, killed, Rangoon, 1852, f.n., **308, 309**; *Drummond, Maj.-Gen. H.*, Kangra, 1846, f.n., **296**—Roorkee, 1857, **321-2**—Second Burma War, **308**; *Dundas, Capt. J.*, V.C., Bhutan, 1864, f.n., **458**—Killed, Kabul, **386**—Wins V.C., **459**; *Durand, Maj.-Gen. Sir H. M.*, Boundary Line, **422-439**—Canal work, **292**—Ghazni, 1839, **272**—Malwa, 1857, **362-3**—Pte. Secy., Gov.-Gen., Gwalior Campaign, **289**—Resident, Indore, 1857, **362**—Second Sikh War, **303**; *Dyas, Lieut. J. H.*, Kangra, 1846, f.n., **296**; *Forbes, Col. J. G.*, services, f.n., **331**; *Fraser, Gen. A.*, Second Burma War, **308**; *Fraser, Capt. Edward*, Comdt. B.S. & M., 1857, **318** et seq.—Killed by mutineers, **320**; *Fraser, Major Hugh*, "Builder of Rangoon," **310**—Ch. Eng., Second Burma War, **308-9**; *Fulford, Lieut. W. F.*, Delhi, 1857, **328**—Death from overwork, **346**—Roorkee, 1857, **321**—Services, f.n., **331**; *Fulton, Capt. G. W. W.*, "Defender of Lucknow," **353**—Killed by roundshot, **353**—Lucknow Residency, **351**—Mining, **352**—Multan, 1848, **300**; *Garforth, Lieut. P.*, Multan, 1848, **300**—Wounded, f.n., **302**; *Garstin, Gen. E.*, Nepal War, **240**; *Geneste, Lieut. M. G.*, death from overwork, 1857, **346**—Interpreter and Q.M., **319**—Services, f.n., **331**; *Glasfurd, Maj.-Gen. J.*, Second Sikh War, **303**; *Goldie, Capt. B. W.*, Second Sikh War, **303**; *Goodwyn, Major A. G.*, Relief, Lucknow, **355**—Second Sikh War, **303**—With Pollock, 1842, **278**; *Greathed, Maj.-Gen. W. W.*, Asst. M.S. to C.-in-C., **371**—Delhi, 1857, assault, **341**—

directing left attack, **339, 340**—plan for assault, June, **328**—reconnaissance of breaches, **341**—wounded, **344**—Lucknow, capture of, distinguished service, **361**—Second China War, **313**—Services, f.n., **331**; *Gulliver, Lt.-Gen. H. W.*, Delhi, Punjab Sappers, **332**—Lucknow, capture of, **360** and f.n.—Services, f.n., **331**; *Hebbert, Lieut. G. P.*, Aliwal, 1846, **294**; *Hills, Lieut. G. S.*, Bhutan, 1864, f.n., **458**; *Home, Lieut. D. C.*, V.C., assault of Delhi, **341**—Awarded V.C., **344**—Kashmir Gate, **342** *et seq.*—Killed at Malagarh, **347**—Services, f.n., **331**—With Punjab Sappers, **332**; *Hovenden, Lt.-Col. T.*, assault of Delhi, **341**—Reconnaissance of breaches, **341**—Services, f.n., **331**—Wounded, **344**; *Humphry, Lieut. E. W.*, wounded 17 places, Narnaul, 1857, **347**; *Heaviside, Capt. W. J.*, Bhutan, 1864, f.n., **458**—Kandahar, 1879, **382**—Survey, f.n., **380**; *Hutchinson, Capt. G.*, countermining, Lucknow, **351, 353**—Fortifies Alam Bagh, **357**; *Hutchinson, Ens. G.*, Hathras, 1817, **241**—Nepal War, **238**; *Hyde, Capt. Henry*, Calcutta Mint, **371**; *Innes, Lt.-Gen. McLeod*, V.C., blows up Machhi Bhawan, **351**—Controller, P.W. Accts., **371**—Wins V.C., **359**; *Irvine, Brig. A.*, Bde.Major, Bhurtpore, 1826, **262** and f.n., **264**—Hathras, 1817, **241**—Sobraon, 1846, **296**; *Irwin, Lieut. T. S.*, Second Sikh War, **303**; *Jeffreys, Lieut. W.*, Roorkee, 1857, **322**; *Jones, Lieut. E.*, Delhi, 1857, **328-9**—Services, f.n., **331**; *Judge, Lieut. C. N.*, Alam Bagh, **358**; *Kyd, Capt. A.*, Surveyor-General, Seringapatam, 1792, **168**—Third Mysore War, **179**; *Lake, Maj.-Gen. E. J.*, Aliwal, 1846, **294**—Comds. Bhawalpur Army, **299**—Ferozeshah, 1845, **294**—Multan, 1848, **300-01**; *Lang, Col. A. M.*, assault of Delhi, **341**—Batteries, **339, 340**—Kashmir Bastion breach,**344**—Reconnaissances, Delhi, **339, 340**—Reconnaissances, Lucknow, **361**—Relief of Lucknow, **355**—Services, f.n., **331**—Union Jack on Martiniere, **356**; *Laughton, Lt.-Col. J.*, Ch. Eng., Delhi, 1857, **325**—Delhi superseded, **329**—First Afghan War, f.n., **272**—Services, f.n., **331**; *Lawtie, Lieut. Peter*, A.D.C. and F.E., Nepal War, **237**—Conduct highly commended, **237-8**—Dies at Ratnagarh, 1815, **239**—" of Nepal," **248**; *Limond, Maj.-Gen. D.*, Residency, Lucknow, **354**; *Macdonald, John*, Survey of India, **180**; *Maclagan, Capt. Robert*, Principal, Thomason College, 1857, **322**; *Macleod, Lt.-Gen.*, Ghazni, 1839, **272**; *McNeile, Lieut. A.*, services, f.n., **331**; *McNeile, Lieut. J. M.*, B.S. & M., 1857, **319**; *Maunsell, Gen. Sir F. R.*, Multan, 1848, **301**; Mutiny, Delhi,

assault, **341**—Comdt. and Adjt., S. & M., **326**—construction No. 1 Battery, **338-9**—destroys bridges, **329**—plan for assault, June, **328**—wounded, **346**—Lucknow, 1858, **360** and f.n.—Meerut, Adjt., B.S. & M., **319**—attacked by mutineers, **320**—prompt action, **321**—Second Afghan War, Ali Masjid, **377**—C.R.E., Peshawar Force, **375**—Services, f.n., **331**; *Maxwell, Maj.-Gen. J. H.*, Gwalior Campaign, **289**—Multan, 1848, **300**; *Medley, Maj.-Gen. J. G.*, assault of Delhi, **341**—Batteries, Delhi, **338-340**—Kashmir Bastion breach, **344**—Principal, Thomason College, **371**—Railway Officer, 1879, **375**—Reconnaissance, Delhi,**340**—Reconnaissance, Lucknow, **361**—Services, f.n., **331**—Wounded, **346**; *Morrieson, Lieut. W.*, killed, Nepal War, **239**; *Morton, Lieut. W. E.*, Second Sikh War, **303**, *Mouat, Lieut. C.*, Survey of India, **180**; *Mouat, Lieut. J.*, Second Rohilla War; **180**—Survey of India, **180**; *Murray, Ens. A.*, First Rohilla War, **179-80**; *Murray, Major P.*, services, f.n., **331**; **Napier, F.M. Lord**, C.-in-C., Bombay, 1866, **372**—C.-in-C., India, 1870, **372**—Career up to 1845, **292**—Career after 1868, f.n., **400**—Enquiry, S. & M. organization, **372**—Memorials to, f.n., **400**—Reputation, 1867, **397**—WAR SERVICES : ABYSSINIA, 1867-8, Chief Comd., **397, 406**—Farewell address, **400**—FIRST SIKH WAR : Ferozeshah, horse shot, **293**—Kangra, **296**—Mudki, horse shot, **292**—Sobraon, **296**—MUTINY, 1857-8 : Ch. Eng. and Chief of Staff, Residency, **354**—Chief of Staff to Outram, **359**—Comds. C.I.F.F., **366**—Comds. Engineer Bde., Lucknow, 1858, **359**—Comds. 2nd Bde. C.I.F.F., **366**—Mily. Secy. to Outram, 1857, **349**—Most brilliant Engineer in, **367**—Places memorial, Kashmir Gate, **343**—Rescues rearguard, Lucknow, **353**—Thanks of Parliament, 1858, **366**—Victories in Central India, **366**—Wounded, Lucknow, 1857, **355**—SECOND CHINA WAR : capture, Taku Forts, **314-5**—Divl. Comdr., **313**—SECOND SIKH WAR : Multan, Ch. Eng., first phase, **300**—Ch. Eng., final operations, **307**—Leads assault, **302**—Wounded, **301**; *Newmarch, Lieut. C. D.*, Second Burma War, f.n., **308**; *Nicolls, Lt.-Gen. J. E. T.*, Gwalior Campaign, **289**—Mudki, **292**; *Paton, Lieut. C. S.*, reconnoitres fords of Chenab, **304**—With boats at Gujarat, 1849, **307**; *Pemberton, Maj.-Gen. R. C. B.*, assault of Delhi, **341**—Roorkee, 1857, **322**—Services, f.n., **331**—Wounded, **346**; *Perkins, Gen. Sir Æneas*, Balla Pass, reconnaissance, f.n. **460**—Bhutan, 1864, **458**—C.R.E., Kurram Force, 1879, **375**—C.R.E.,

Roberts' Colm., 1879, **383**—Delhi, 1857, **328**—Kabul, 1879, **385**—Paiwar Kotal, **379**—Roberts' march, **391**—Services, f.n., **331**; *Pigou, Lieut. R.*, Ghazni, 1839, f.n., **372**; *Pollard, Gen. Charles*, Multan, 1848, **301**; *Pott, Maj.-Gen. S.*, Gwalior Campaign, **289**; *Reilly, Lt.-Col. B. Y.*, Comdt., B.S. & M., **283, 297**—Sobraon, 1846, **295–6**; *Rennell, Capt. James*, Father of Survey of India, **180**; *Renny-Tailyour, Lieut. T.*, Gwalior Campaign, **289**; *Robertson, Lieut. J. W.*, with Pollock, 1842, **278**; *Robertson, Capt. T.*, Dig, 1804, **218**—Survey of India, **180**; *Russell, Maj.-Gen. L.*, Residency, Lucknow, **354**; *Salkeld, Lieut. P.*, 𝔙.𝔈., assault of Delhi, **341**—Awarded 𝔙.𝔈., **344**—Delhi, 1857, **328**—Dies of wounds, **344**—Escape from Delhi, **318**—Kashmir Gate, **342** *et seq.*—Services, f.n., **331**; *Sanders, Major E.*, Army of Indus, 1838, **268**—Dy. Secy., Mily. Dept., Gwalior Campaign, **289**—First Afghan War, f.n.s **272** and **279**—Killed, Maharajpore, 1843, **289**; *Short, Lieut. W. D. A. R.*, Gwalior Campaign, **289**; *Siddons, Capt. H.*, Comdt., B.S. & M., **283**—Multan, 1848, **300**; *Smith, Brig. E. J.*, Ch. Eng., Gwalior Campaign, **288**—Ch. Eng., Sobraon, **296**; *Smith, Capt. R.*, Bhurtpore, 1825, **261**—Java Expedn., 1811, **232**—Nepal War, **240**; *Sparshott Williams, Gen. E. C.*, Second Burma War, **308**; *Stanton, Maj.-Gen. F. S.*, Bhutan, 1864, **458**; *Stewart, Lt.-Gen. C. T.*, Delhi and services, f.n., **331**; *Stewart, Lieut. P.*, killed, Seringapatam, 1792, **169**; *Stewart, Lieut. P.*, Supt. of Telegraphs, Relief of Lucknow, **355**; *Stokoe, Ens. J.*, Nandidroog, 1791, **166**—Seringapatam 1792, **169**—Third Mysore War, **179**; *Strachey, Lt.-Gen. Sir R.*, Aliwal, 1846, **294**; *Strahan, Lt.-Gen. C.*, Bhutan, 1864, f.n., **458**—Last Company's Engineer on list, **370**; *Strahan, Lieut. G.*, Bhutan, 1864, f.n., **458**; *Stuart, Lieut. P.*, Third Mysore War, **179**; *Sturt, Lieut. J. L. D.*, died, retreat from Kabul, 1842, **276**—Ghazni, 1839, **272**; *Swetenham, Capt. E.*, Comdt., B.S. & M., 1838, **282**; *Tandy, Lieut. F. L.*, assault of Delhi, **341**—Killed at Delhi, **346**—Services, f.n., **331**—With B.S. & M., **319**; *Taylor, Gen. Sir Alex.*, Aliwal, 1846, **294**—Ambela, 1863, C.R.E., **425**—Delhi : assault of, **341**—daring reconnaissances, **336–7**—fatigue, **346**—laying out batteries, **339–40**—plan for assault, July, **329**—temporary Ch. Eng., **329**—Lucknow : capture of, comds. Company's Engrs., **360** and f.n.—wounded, f.n., **361**—Multan : leads assault, **302**—moves siege train, **300**—saves siege stores, **301**—wounded f.n., **302**—Pre-eminence in Mutiny, **367**—Services, f.n., **331**; *Taylor, Capt. J.*, Bhurtpore,

1825, **261**; *Tennant, Lt.-Gen. J.*, assault of Delhi, **341**—Services, f.n., **331** and f.n., **360**; *Thackeray, Col. Sir E. T.*, assault of Delhi, **341**—Battery construction, Delhi, **340**—B.S. & M., 1857, **319**—Comdt., B.S. & M., 1879, f.n., **383**—Experiences, Meerut, 1857, **320**—Services, f.n., **331**—Wins 𝔙.𝔈., Delhi, **345**—With Bright's Colm., 1879, **383**—With Shower's Colm., 1857, **347**—Wounded, Jagdalak, 1879, **386**; *Thomason, Maj.-Gen. C. S.*, services, f.n., **331**; *Thomson, Capt. G.*, Arakan Colm., 1825, **258**—Bridges Indus, 1838, **269**—Ch. Eng., Army of Indus, 1838, **268**—Comdt., B.S. & M., 1838, **282**—Ghazni, storm of, **271–4**—March to Quetta, 1839, **270**; *Tickell, Lt.-Gen. R.*, Hathras, 1817, **241**—Nepal War, **240**—Raising of B.S. & M., 1819, **226**; *Tindal, Lieut. J.*, First Burma War, **253**; *Tremenheere, Maj.-Gen. G. B.*, Chilianwala, **305**—Second Sikh War, **303**; *Trevor, Maj.-Gen. W. S.*, 𝔙.𝔈., Bhutan, 1864, **458**—Second Burma War, **308, 311**—wins 𝔙.𝔈., Diwangiri, **459**—Wounded, Rangoon, **309**; *Walker, Lieut. E.*, services, f.n., **331**; *Ward, Col. D.*, assault of Delhi, **341**—Experiences at Meerut, **320**—Services, f.n., **331**—With B.S. & M., 1857, **319**; *Warrand, Maj.-Gen. W. E.*, services, f.n., **331**; *Watson, Lt.-Col. G. E.*, Relief, Lucknow, **355**—Work on Ganges, **349**; *Watts*, 2nd-*Capt. S. L.*, Bhutan, 1864, **458**; *Waugh, Capt. A. S.*, Surveyor-General, 1846, f.n., **297**; *Weller, Capt. J. A.*, Comdt., B.S. & M., **283**; *Western, Capt. J. R.*, Multan, 1848, **300**; *Wilford, F.*, Survey of India, **180**; *Willis, Capt. P. W.*, Comdt., B.S. & M., 1842, **282**; *Wood, Sir Mark*, Survey of India, **180**; *Wood, Capt. T.*, raises Bengal Pioneers, 1803, **201**—Survey of India, **180**; *Young, Lt.-Gen. C. B.*, boat bridge, Ramnagar, **305**—Gwalior Campaign, **289**—Second Burma War, **308**—Second Sikh War, **303**; *Young, Maj.-Gen. R.*, Multan, 1848, f.n., **305**; *Yule, Col. Sir Henry*, Second Burma War, f.n., **308**—Second Sikh War, **303**—Suggested as author, **ix**

Engineers, Bombay—General—*Amalgamated* with R.E., **369** and f.n. ; *Cadre of 5*, 1775, **183** ; *Cadre of 10*, 1777, **184** ; *Cadres*, etc., 1829–57, **296–8** ; *Engineer Institution*, 1829, **230** ; *S. & M. named Bo.E.*, 1829, **230** ; *Separated from Artillery*, 1777, **183** ; *Survey work*, 1784–90, **198** ; **Officers**—*Athill, Ens. S.*, Singhur, 1818, **247**; *Atkins, Maj.-Gen. W.*, Ch. Eng., 1806, **208**—Mangalore, 1783, **198** ; *Ballard, Maj.-Gen. J. A.*, Persia, 1856, **312**; *Blachford, Lt.-Gen. W.*, Bassein, 1780, **194**—Honavar, 1783, **198** ; *Bland, Col. J.*, Ch. Eng., 1804–06, **208** ; *Bonus, Lieut.*, wounded, Jhansi, **365**;

INDEX.

Brooks, Maj.-Gen. W., Mysore War, 1790, **198**; *Christie, Capt. D.,* Bor Ghat, 1781, **195**—Cannanore, 1783, **197**—1st cadre, **184**; *Cliffe, Capt. J.,* Broach, 1803, **206**; *Cowper, Ens. Wm.,* Cannanore, 1795, **198**; *Dacer, Ens. P.,* 1st cadre, 1777, **184**; *Dick, Lieut. W. G. D.,* C.I.F.F., 1858, **364**—Killed, Jhansi, **365**; *Dickenson, Maj.-Gen. T.,* Bani-Bu-Ali, **250**—First Comdt., Bo.S. & M., 1820, **227**; *Dickinson, Maj.-Gen. W. R.,* Persia, 1856, **312**; *Doidge, Ens. R.,* 1st cadre, 1777, **184**; *Fuller, Lieut. J. A.,* wounded, Multan, f.n., **302**; *Goodfellow, Lt.-Gen. C. A.,* 𝔅.𝔒., Jhansi, 1858, **365**—Wins 𝔅.𝔒., f.n., **365**; *Goodfellow, Lieut. S.,* comds. pontoon train, 1803, **206, 227**—Egypt, 1801, **200**; *Goodfellow, Lt.-Gen. W. W.,* Abyssinia, **398**—C.R.E., **399**—Persia, 1856, **312**; *Graham, Lieut. W. D.,* Panalla, 1844, **288**; *Haig, Maj.-Gen. C. T.,* Persia, 1856, **312**; *Hancock, Maj.-Gen. H. F.,* Persia, 1856, **312**; *Hill, Lieut. J.,* wounded, Multan, f.n., **302**; *Hills, Maj.-Gen. J.,* Kandahar, 1880, **388, 390**—Kandahar Force, 1879, **375**—Persia, 1856, **312**; *Johnson, Capt. J.,* Assaye, **209**—Ch. Eng., Ahmadnagar, **207**—Comdt. of Guides, **207**—Gawilgarh, **211, 212**—Seringapatam, 1799, **173**; *Keating, Lt.-Col. T.,* character, **183**—Ch. Eng., 1764, **181**—Court-martialled, 1776, **183**—Criticized, **182**—First Engineer as C.-in-C. in field, **181, 406**—Treaty of Baroda, **182**; Victory at Adas, **182**; *Kendall, Lieut. W.,* Gujarat, 1849, **306**; *Leech, Lieut. R.,* Kalat-i-Ghilzai, **276**—Persia, 1856, **312**; *Le Mesurier, Lt.-Gen. A.,* Persia, 1856, **312**; *Macleod, Lieut. J.,* Singhur, 1818, **247**; *McNeill, Capt. J.,* 1st cadre, 1777, **184**; *Marriott, Lieut. W. F.,* Ghazni, 1839, **272**; *Meiklejohn, Lieut. H. R.,* C.I.F.F., 1858, **364**—Killed, Jhansi, **365**; *Moncrieff, Capt.-Lt. B.,* comds. Bombay Pioneers, 1797, **198**; *Munbee, Maj.-Gen. G. B.,* Panalla, 1844, **288**; *Nicholson, Lt.-Gen. R.,* Ch. Eng., **208**—1st cadre, 1777, **184**; *Nilson, Brig.-Gen. L.,* career of, **194**—C.-in-C., Bombay Forces, 1784, **194**—1st cadre, 1777, **184**; *North, Maj.-Gen. C. F.,* Ch. Eng., Persia, 1857, **312**—First Afghan War, f.n., **272**—With Nott, 1842, f.n., **279**; *Nutt, Capt. J.,* Singhur, 1818, **247**; *Peat, Maj.-Gen. A. C.,* Army of Indus, 1838, **268**—Comdt., Bo.S. & M., f.n., **230**—Ghazni, 1839, **272**—Kalat, 1839, **274**—Panalla, 1844, **288**; *Playfair, Maj.-Gen. J. W.,* Gujarat, **306**—Persia, 1856, **312**; *Pym, Capt. H.,* Persia, 1856, **312**; *Sartorius, Col. J.,* death, 1801, **198**—Dharwar, **198**—1st cadre, **184**—Later career, **198**—Mangalore, **197**—Military status of Eng., **186**—Seringapatam, 1792, **168**—Seringapatam, 1799, **173, 175**; *Scott, Gen. Walter,* Multan, 1848, **301**; *Slight, Lieut. S.,* Comdt., S. & M., 1828, f.n., **230**; *Spaith, Major D.,* Ahmadabad, **192**—Dabhoi, **191**—1st cadre, **184**—Wounded, **193**; *Studdert, Lieut. T.,* Kalat-i-Ghilzai, **276**—Sind, 1842, **286**—With Nott, 1842, f.n., **279**; *Turner, Capt. C.,* 1st cadre, 1777, **184**; *Turner, Gen. H.,* Adjt., S. & M., f.n., **230**; *Waddington, Maj.-Gen. C.,* Ch. Eng., Sind, 1842, **286**—Hyderabad, Battle of, **287**; *Walker, Gen. J.,* Delhi, 1857, **322**—Services, f.n., **331**; *Wemyss, Lieut. F.,* Ghazni, 1839, **272**; *Wilkins, Gen. H. St. C.,* C.R.E., Abyssinia, **398**; *Witman, Ens. H.,* scheme for German artificers, 1776, **188**

Engineers (General)—Amalgamation of Royal and Company's, f.n., **314**; *Bhurtpore,* 1826, casualties, **261**; *Chief,* emoluments of, 18th century, **184-7**; *Combatant* status granted, 1771, **81**; *C.s-in-C.* of armies in the field, **406**; *Conditions* of service, 18th century, **184** *et seq.*; *Considered* unfit for chief command, **397**; *Deficiencies* in Department, Third Maratha War, **245**; *Delhi,* 1857, **331**; *Difficulties* over early regular Pioneers, **228**; *Early* training, **54**; *Employment* on military works and outside S. & M., **419-20**; *Field* engineering introduced, **139**; *First,* to hold commd. in field, **181**; *How* recruited, **54**; *Increase* after Mutiny, **370**; *Increase* for field service, **138**; *Increase* in all cadres, 1810, **224**; *Lack* of skilled men, 1776, **188**; *Last* of Company's, **370**; *Lucknow* Residency, 1857, **351, 354**; *Lucknow,* Bde. for—Capture of, 1858, **359-60** and f.n.s; *Military* Engineer defined, 1763, **139**; *Military* rank granted combatant, 1771, **81**—Non-combatant, 1759, **78**—Petitions for, 1678, **23, 24**; *Military* status of, on tour, **185-6**; *Mortality* heavy among, **56**; *Probity* of, 18th century, **186**; *Q.M.G.'s* views on, 1821, **228**; *Re-organization,* 1770, **81**; *Roberts'* march, 1880, **391**; *Second Afghan War,* allotment, second phase, **383-4**—Dress, **381**—Faults of organization, **392-3**—Kandahar theatre, 1879, **382**—Numbers and work, **376**; *Second Mysore War,* effect of, on, **161**; *Seringapatam,* twenty-four present, 1792, **168**—Specially commended, 1799, **178**; *Temporary,* infy. officers at Pondicherry, 1793, **170**—In Second Burma War, **308**

Engineers, Madras—General—Amalgamation with R.E., **369** and f.n.; *Cadre,* 1782, **161**—1802, **200**—1829-57, **296-298**; *Officers*—*Anderson, Lieut. A.,* Mehidpur, 1817, **246**; *Anderson, Lieut. J. C.,* Lucknow Residency, **351, 353**; *Banks, Capt.,* 1782, **161**; *Bell, Lieut. J. H.,* Malay Expedn., 1832,

266 ; *Birdwood, Lieut. W. I.*, Bogue Forts, 1841, **280** and f.n. ; *Blair, Capt. Lt. J.*, crossing Tungabhadra R., **199**—Seringapatam, 1799, **173** ; *Blakiston, Major J.*, Ahmadnagar, **207**—Correspondence, **224**—Gawilgarh, **212**—Java Expedn., 1811, **232** ; *Boileau, Bt. Major A. J. M.*, Jhansi, 1858, **364**—Malwa Campaign, **362-3**—Sind, 1842, **286**—Persia, 1857, **312** ; *Brohier, J.* (see "Bengal" and "Madras") ; *Brunton, Ens.*, prisoner, Seringapatam, 1780, **156** ; *Burghall, Major G.*, proposals for Corps of Miners and Pioneers, 1781, **196** ; *Burton, Col. R. G.*, Alam Bagh, **357**, f.n. **360** ; *Burton, Col. W. H.*, Lucknow, capture, **360**—Relief, **355**—Union Jack on Martiniere, **356** ; *Byres, Capt.*, 1782, **161** ; *Caldwell, Gen. Sir James*, Ahmadabad, **193**—Bangalore, 1791, **163**—Nandidroog, **166**—Réunion, Ch. Eng., 1810, **232**—Seringapatam, 1799, **173, 177**—Under Goddard, 1780, **192** ; *Call, J.* (see "Madras") ; *Campbell, Capt. W.*, killed at Tanjore, **146-7** ; *Carpendale, Lieut. J.*, Second Burma War, **308** ; *Cotsford, E.*, Practitioner Eng., 1758, **76** ; *Cotton, Lieut. A.*, First Burma War, **253**—Tenasserim, **255** ; *Cotton, Bt. Capt. F. C.*, Ch. Eng., Bogue Forts, 1841, **280** and f.n.—Chinhai, **281** ; *Coventry, Lieut. J.*, Asirghur, 1818, **249** ; *Cunningham, Lieut. J. D.*, Jalalabad, 1842, **276** ; *Davies, Lieut. T.*, Ch. Eng., Nagpur, 1817, **244**—Killed, 1818, **248** ; *De Havilland, Major T. F.*, captured by French privateer, **200**—Ceylon, 1795, **171**—Egypt, 1801, **200**—Report on Engineers, etc., 1821, **228** ; *Delavaux, A.* (see "Fort St. David," and "Madras") ; *Dennison, Lieut. G.*, Second Burma War, **308** ; *Dugood, Capt. Alex.*, killed, Chittoor, **159**—Tanjore, **146** ; *Farquhar, Major W.*, Ch. Eng., Malaya, 1795, **171**—Comdt., Guides, Java, 1811, **232**—Nandidroog, **166**—Seringapatam, 1799, **177** ; *Filgate, Lieut. A. J.*, Second China War, **313** ; *Gahagan, Lieut. T. E.*, Second Burma War, f.n., **308** ; *Garrard, Lieut. Wm.*, crossing the Tungabhadra, 1799, **199**—Java Expedn., 1811, **232**—Seringapatam, 1799, **173** ; *Geils, Major T.*, cadre, 1782, **161**—Ch. Eng. Negapatam, **160**—Pondicherry, **149**—Tanjore, **146**—Trincomalee, **160** ; *Gent, Maj.-Gen. W.*, cadre, 1782, **161**—Honoured, 1799, **178**—Leaves India, **200**—Pondicherry, **148**—Seringapatam, 1799, **173, 175**—With Coote, 1781, **159** ; *Gordon, Lieut. H. J. G.*, Jhansi, 1858, **365**—Malwa, 1857, **362**—Persia, 1857, **312**—Drowned, China, **313** and f.n. ; *Grant, Capt. A.*, death, Burma, **253**—Donabyu, 1825, **259**—Koppaldroog, 1819, **250**—Singhur, 1818, **247** ;

Hemery, Capt. E., C.I.F.F., 1858, **366** ; *Henderson, Maj.-Gen. R.*, Miami, 1843, **287**—Sind, 1842, **286** ; *Hitchens*, 2nd-Lt. H. W., First China War, **280** ; *Howes, Lieut. F. A.*, C.I.F.F., 1858, **366** ; *Johnston, Capt. J.*, cadre, 1782, **161**—Negapatam, **160**—With Eyre Coote, 1781, **159** ; *Johnstone, Capt. G.*, Seringapatam, 1799, **173** ; *Johnstone, Lieut. J. G.*, First China War, **280** ; *Lake, Lieut. E.*, First Burma War, **253**—Writings quoted, **157, 202, 247** ; *Lennon, Lieut.*, Bangalore, 1791, **163**—Seringapatam, 1792, **167** ; *Lindsay, Lieut. J. G.*, C.I.F.F., 1858, **366** ; *Ludlow, Major S. E. O.*, C.I.F.F., 1858, **366** ; *Mackenzie, Col. Colin*, Bangalore, 1791, **163**—Career, f.n., **165**—Ceylon, 1795, **171**—Ch. Eng. and Explores Java, 1811, **232, 233**—Hyderabad, 1797, **171**—Manilla, 1797, **171**—Nandidroog, **166**—Seringapatam 1792, **167**—1799, **173**—Surveyor-General, 1815, **233** ; *Mackintosh, Capt. J.*, First Burma War and death, **253** ; *Maule, Capt. G.* (see "Madras") ; *Mayne, Lieut. J. O.*, Second Burma War, **308** ; *Mitchell, Lieut. A.*, Tanjore, **146** ; *Moberly, Maj.-Gen. A. S.*, Second Burma War, f.n., **308** ; *Monteith, Lt.-Gen. W.*, Ras-al-Khaima, 1819, and career, **250** and f.n. ; *Montresor, Capt. H.* (see "Madras") ; *Mullins, Lt.-Gen. J.*, Second Burma War, **308, 311** ; *Nattes, Ens. C.*, Nagpur, 1817, **244** ; *Norris, Lt.-Col. J.*, Bangalore, 1791, **163**—Cadre, 1802, **200**—Ceylon, 1795, **171**—Seringapatam, 1799, **173, 177** ; *Oakes, Lieut. R. F.*, Second Burma War, **308** ; *Ochterlony, Lieut. J.*, First China War, f.n., **280** ; *Ogg, Capt. C.*, Bangalore, 1791, **163** ; *Orr, Lieut. C. A.*, Jalalabad, 1842, **762**—Sind, 1842, **286** ; *Pears, Maj.-Gen. Sir T.*, Ch. Eng., First China War, f.n. and **280, 281** ; *Prendergast, Gen. Sir Harry*, **V.C.**, Abyssinia, **398**—C.R.E., Malta E.F., **401**—C.-in-C., Third Burma War, **406-9**—Malwa, 1857. **362**—Persia, 1856, **312**—Wins **V.C.**, **363**, f.n. ; *Prescott, Ens. J. R.*, cadre, 1782, **161** ; *Purton, Lieut. J.*, Mehidpur, 1817, **246** ; *Robins, B.* (see "Bengal," "Fort St. David," and "Madras") ; *Rogers, Maj.-Gen. H. T.*, Second Burma War, **308** ; *Ross, Maj.-Gen. Patrick*, Cape of Good Hope, 1782, **161**—Ch. Eng., Savandroog, **166, 212**—Ch. Eng., Seringapatam, 1792, **167** *et seq.*—Leaves India, 1802, **200**—Madras, 1799, **173**—Returns to India, **161**—To England, 1792, **170** (see also "Madras," and "Engrs., Royal") ; *Rowley, Ens. G.*, dies of exposure, **207**—March of an army, 1799, **172**—Seringapatam, 1799, **173, 177** ; *Rundall, Capt. J. W.*, capture, stockade, 1852, **309**—Death at Prome, f.n., **308**—First China War, f.n., **280**—Second Burma War, **308**; *Ryves, Lieut. J. G.*, Second Burma War, **308**; *Salmon, Lieut. C.*, Tanjore, **161**; *Sankey, Lt.-Gen. R. H.*, capture, Lucknow, **360** and f.n.; *Scott, Lieut. C.*, Alam Bagh, **357**—killed, 1858, f.n., **360**—Lucknow, capture, **360**—Relief, **355**; *Scott, Lt.-Col. C. F.* (see "Bengal" and "Madras"); *Shaw, Lieut. J. C.*, First China War, f.n., **280**; *Stevens, Major W.*, killed, Pondicherry, **148**; *Stewart, Maj.-Gen. J. H. M. S.*, Second China War, **313**; *Theobald, Capt. J.*, killed, Pollilur, **156, 194**; *Trail, Lieut. D. H.*, Second China War, **313**—Taku Forts, **314**; *Trapaud, Col. E.*, Ch. Eng., 1802, **200**—Pondicherry, **170**—Seringapatam, 1799, **173**; *Underwood, Capt. G. A.*, Coorg operations, 1834, **266**—Donabyu, **259**—First Burma War, **253**—Kokein, **257**—Wounded, **253, 259**; *Vaughan, Lieut. H.*, Second Burma War, **308**; *Whish, Lieut. W. T.*, Bhutan, 1864, f.n., **458**; *Wilkieson, Lieut. C. V.*, Second Burma War, f.n., **308**; *Wood, Lieut. H. W.*, C.I.F.F., 1858, **366**

Engineers, Royal—Companies—*Skeleton,* formed for India, 1866, **370**; *4th,* arrival in India, 1857, **358**—Lucknow, capture of, **359, 361**; *th,* Second China War, **314**; *10th,* Abyssinia, **398** *et seq.*—Second China War, **314**; *11th,* arrival in India, 1857, **358**; *21st,* arrival in India, 1857, **358**—C.I.F.F., 1858, **364**; *23rd,* diverted from China, **355**—first R.E. Co. to serve in India, **355**—Lucknow, Relief of, **355**—Capture of, **359, 361**—Roorkee, arrival at, **362**—Second China War, **314**; **General**—*Corps* of, in Royal Army, **54**; *Officers,* distribution, after Mutiny, **370-1**; *Officers* increased for India, **369**; *Officers* in India, 1771, **185**; **Officers**—*Abbott, Major H. E. S.*, Black Mountain, 1888, **429**—Chitral, 1895, **440**—Hazara, 1891, **431**—Malakand Pass, Buddhist and Abbott Rd., **441**; *Abbott, Lieut. T. W.*, Kut, **485**; *Addison, Maj.-Gen. G. H.*, E.-in-C., India, help acknowledged, **x**; *Ainslie, Lieut. C.*, Chin-Lushai, 1889, **461,** f.n.—Chitral, 1895, **440,** f.n.; *Allen, Major R. F.*, C.R.E., Somaliland, 1903, **417**; *Almond, Lieut. R. L.*, killed, Neuve Chapelle, **478**; *Anderson, Capt. A. V.*, Moplah rebellion, **522,** f.n.; *Anderson, Lieut. C. F.*, Suakin, 1896, **412**; *Anderson, Major E. P.*, Khaibar Rly., **511,** f.n.; *Arbuthnot, Capt. A. D. S.*, killed, Dujaila Redoubt, **487**—Wounded, Sahil, **483**; *Atkinson, Lt.-Gen. Sir Edwin*, career, **430**, f.n.—Ch. Eng., Mesopotamia, 1920, **518**—Chin-Lushai, 1889, **461,** f.n.—Relieves Samawa, 1920, **520-1**—Zhob Valley, 1890, **430**; *Austin, Lieut. H. H.*, Waziristan, 1894, f.n., **440**; *Aylmer, Lt.-Gen. Sir Fenton*

V.C., Chitral, 1895, **440**—Comds. Kut Relief Force, **486**—Hazara, 1891, **431**—Help acknowledged, **x**—Hunza-Nagar, 1891, assault of Nilt—bridge and road making—wins **V.C.**—work after, **435-9**—Isazai, 1892, **433**; *Bailey, Lieut. F.*, Bhutan, 1864, f.n., **458**; *Barker, Major J. S.*, Kut, **485**; *Barton, Major M. C.*, Chitral, 1895, **440**; *Bassett, Capt. T. P.*, Egypt, 1914, **493**; *Battye, Capt. B. C.*, "Battye bomb," France, 1914, **480**; *Beaumont, Col. F. E. B.*, Mutiny, 1857, **358**, f.n. **360**; *Begbie, Lt.-Col. E. W.*, Third Burma War, **407**; *Bird, Capt. A. J. G.*, Festubert, **479**—Meerut Div., 1914, f.n., **476**; *Bird, Capt. C. A.*, Festubert, **479**—Meerut Div., 1914, f.n., **476**; *Birney, Lieut. C. F.*, Tibet Mission, **464, 466**—Lhasa, f.n., **466**; *Bisset, Capt. W. S. S.*, Kandahar, 1879, **383**; *Bland, Lieut. E. H.*, Miranzai, 1891, f.n., **433**; *Blood, Gen. Sir Bindon*, Ch. of Staff, Chitral, 1895, **440**—Comds. Buner F.F., 1898, **445, 449**—Comds. Malakand F.F., **445, 447**—Details of service, f.n. **391**, f.n. **395**—Foreword, **vii**—Help acknowledged, **x**—Landakai, use of field artillery, **447**—Reorganization of S. & M., 1885, **393, 425**—Second Afghan War, **391**; *Boal, Capt. R.*, Aden, wounded and D.S.O., **491** and f.n.; *Boileau, Lieut. F. R. F.*, Chitral, 1895, f.n., **440**; *Boileau, Lieut. G. H.*, China, 1900-1, **414**—Chitral, 1895, f.n., **440, 441**; *Bond, Maj.-Gen. Sir Francis*, Hazara, 1891, **431**; *Bond, Lieut. R. F. G.*, Chitral, 1895, f.n., **440**; *Boughey. Lieut. G. E. O.*, Bhutan, 1864, f.n., **458**; *Bovet, Capt. W.*, Mekran, 1898, **412**—Somaliland, 1902-4, **416**; *Brackenbury, Capt. M. C.*, Roberts' march, **391**; *Bradney, Major E.*, Mesopotamia, 1920, D.S.O., **520**—Kut Relief Force, **486**; *Britten, Capt. W. E.*, E. Africa, **501**; *Broadbent, Col. J. E.*, Ch. Eng., Tirah, 1897, **451**—C.R.E., Malakand F.F., f.n., **447**—N.W. Frontier, 1897-98, **445**; *Browne, Major C. A. R.*, China, 1900-01, **414**; *Buston, Brig.-Gen. P. T.*, Black Mountain, 1888, **429**—bridges over Indus, f.n., **431**—Hazara, 1891, **431**—help acknowledged, **x**—Kabul, 1879, makeshift fuses, f.n., **386**; *Bythell, Major W. J.*, Chin-Lushai, 1889, survey, **461**—Mohmand F.F., 1898, **448**; *Cairnes, Capt. W. A.*, Isazai, 1892, **433**; *Call, Capt. C. A.*, Kandahar, 1879, **383**—Roberts' march, **391**; *Cameron, Lieut. H. A.*, Suakin, 1896, **412**; *Campbell, Maj.-Gen. Sir Archibald*, career, f.n., **133** (see "Bengal"); *Campbell, Major A.*, C.R.E., Razmak Rd., **515**; *Campbell, Capt. M. G. G.*, bridging train, **484**—M.C., Qurna, **483**—wounded, f.n., **484**; *Campbell, Major W. M.*, Kandahar, 1879, **382**—Survey, 1879, f.n.,

INDEX.   573

380 ; *Capper, Maj.-Gen. Sir John,* bridges, Hunza-Nagar, **439** ; *Carey, Lt.-Col. A. B.,* D. of W., Mesopotamia, 1920, **519** ; *Carmichael-Smyth, Maj.-Gen. Sir James,* f.n., **215** ; *Carpenter, Lieut. C. M.,* China, 1900–01, **413** ; *Cather, Lieut. T. P.,* Roberts' march, **391** ; *Cave-Browne, Lieut. W.,* Abor, 1911–12, **471**-2 ; *Chaldecott, Capt. W. H.,* China, 1900–01, **414**—Somaliland, 1903, **416** ; *Chancellor, Lieut. J. R.,* Suakin, 1896, **412** ; *Chapman, Lieut. L. P.,* Chin-Lushai, 1889, f.n., **461** ; *Charles, Lt.-Gen. Sir Ronald,* Mohmands, 1908, f.n., **454**—Zakka Khels, 1908, f.n., **453** ; *Chater, Lieut. A. F.,* Abor, 1911–12, **471** ; *Chesney, Lieut. C. H. R.,* Mishmi Mission, **473** ; *Chesney, Capt. H. F.,* Black Mountain, 1888, **429** ; *Childers, Lieut. E. S.,* Kandahar, 1879, **382**—Roberts' march, **391** ; *Clerke, Capt. A. J.,* killed, 1858, f.n., **360**, **362**—Lucknow, Relief, **355** ; *Close family,* f.n., **431** ; *Close, Lieut. G. D.,* Hazara, 1891, **431** ; *Close, Lieut. L. H.,* Miranzai, 1891, f.n., **433**—Waziristan, 1894, f.n., **440** ; *Coffin, Lt.-Col. Campbell,* C.R.E., Lahore Div., 1914, **477** ; *Colbeck, Capt. C. E.,* Kut, **485**—Sirmur Sappers, **484** ; *Coldstream, Lieut. W. M.,* Miranzai, 1891, **432** ; *Collin, Lieut. F. S.,* Abor, 1911–12, **471**—Field Troop, 1914, **476** ; *Collins, Lieut. W. H.,* Bhutan, 1864, f.n., **458** ; *Colvin, Lieut. J. M. C.,* V.C., Chitral, 1895, f.n., **440**—V.C., Bilot, 1897, **448** and f.n. ; *Cordue, Capt. W. G. R.,* Chitral, 1895, **440** ; *Corry, Capt. J. B.,* Mekran, 1901, wounded, **412**—Mishmi, 1912–13, f.n., **474** ; *Cotter, Capt. E. W.,* Burma S. & M., **411** ; *Cowie, Lieut. H. McC.,* Lhasa, f.n., **466**—Tibet, **464**, **466** ; *Cox, Maj.-Gen. F. E.,* Mutiny, 1857, **358**, f.n., **360** ; *Craster, Capt. J. E.,* China, 1900–01, **414** ; *Crawford, Capt. C.,* Perak, **401** ; *Crawford, Lieut. K. B. S.,* Kut, **484**-5 ; *Crease, Capt. A. R. V.,* Mutiny, 1857, **358** ; *Crookshank, Lieut. C. de W.,* Miranzai, 1891, f.n., **433** ; *Crookshank, Maj.-Gen. Sir Sydney,* Chitral, 1895, f.n., **440**, **441** ; *Cruickshank, Capt. G. M.,* killed, Kandahar, 1880, **390** ; *Cumberland, Capt. C. E.,* Mutiny, 1857, **358** ; *Cunningham, Major A. H.,* Comdt., B.S. & M., **492**—C.R.E., 1st Australian Div., Mohmands, 1908, **454** ; *Darrah, Capt. C. J.,* Abyssinia, **398**-9 ; *D'Aubaut, Brig.-Gen. A.,* Corsica, 1794, **403** ; *De Bourbel, Lieut. R.,* Balla Pass, f.n., **460**—Bhutan, 1864, f.n., **458** ; *Deed, Major L. C. B.,* Razmak Rd., D.S.O., **515** and f.n. ; *Denison, Lt.-Gen. Sir Wm.,* Acting Viceroy, **428** and f.n. ; *Dickie, Major J. E.,* China, 1900–01, **414**—Kandahar, 1879, **382**—Third Burma War, **407** ; *Dickson, Lieut. J. W. M.,* Razmak Rd., killed, **515** and f.n. ; *Dickson, Brig.-Gen. W. E. R.,* E. Persia Cordon, **490**—Waziristan, 1894, f.n., **440**—1917, **504** ; *Douie, Lieut. F. McC.,* Meerut Div., 1914, f.n., **476**—Neuve Chapelle, wounded, **478**-9 ; *Drew, Lt.-Col. F. G.,* help acknowledged, **x**—Mesopotamia, 1920, **520** ; *Duff, Lieut. G. M.,* Chitral, 1895, f.n., **440** ; *Dundee, Lt.-Col. W. J. D.,* C.R.E., Mohmands, 1908, **454**—C.R.E. Zakka Khels, 1908, **453** ; *Durnford, Lt.-Col. A. W.,* Isandlwana, **389** ; *Edmonds, Brig.-Gen. Sir James,* help acknowledged, **x** ; *Edwards, Lieut. J. B.,* C.I.F.F., 1858, **358**, **364** ; *Elles, Lieut. M. R.,* China, 1900–01, **413** ; *Elliott, Capt. C. A.,* Lhasa, f.n., **466**—Tibet, **464**, **466** ; *Elliott, Lieut. T. H.,* Mehidpur, 1817, **246** ; *Ellis, Major C. C.,* Chitral, 1895, **440**—Malta E.F., 1878, **401** ; *Elphinstone, Capt. H.,* Egypt, 1801, **200** ; *Evans, Brig.-Gen. U. W.,* C.S.O., Kut, **485**—Chin-Lushai, 1889, f.n., **461**—C.R.E., 6th Poona Div., wounded, **483** ; *Everett, Major M.,* Abor, 1911–12, **472**—C.R.E., Makin Colm., **517**—Waziristan, 1923, **515** ; *Farley, Lieut. E. L.,* Meerut Div., 1914, **476** ; *Farquharson, Lieut. E. G.,* Chitral, 1895, f.n., **440** ; *Fenwick, Capt. T.,* C.I.F.F., 1858, **358**, **364** ; *Festing, Lieut. E. R.,* C.I.F.F., 1858, **358**, **364** ; *Fitzmaurice, Lieut. M. A. R. G.,* Neuve Chapelle, wounded, **478** ; *Fowler, Lt.-Gen. Sir John,* Chitral, 1895, f.n., **440**—Reshun, 1895, taken prisoner, **442** ; *Fraser, Col. H. A. D.,* D.D.M.W., Third Afghan War, f.n., **511** ; *Fraser, Maj.-Gen. Sir Theodore,* Chin-Lushai, 1889, f.n., **461**—G.O.C., 18th Ind. Div., Mesopotamia, 1920, **518**—Hazara, 1891, **431** ; *Freeland, Maj.-Gen. Sir Henry,* Chitral, 1895, f.n., **440** ; *Garstin, Lieut. J. A.,* China, 1900–01, **414**—killed at Palla, **467**—Tibet Mission, **464**-7 ; *Garwood, Major J. F.,* Zhob Valley, 1890, **430** ; *Gaskell, Lt.-Col. H. S.,* Colm. Comdr., Mesopotamia, 1920, **520** ; *Geary, Capt. H. N. G.,* Mohmands, 1916–17, f.n., **503** ; *Gidley-Kitchin, Capt. E. G.,* Mohmands, 1916–17, f.n., **503** ; *Gillespie, Capt. R. St. J.,* Tibet Mission, **464** ; *Glennie, Lieut. E.,* Roberts' march, **391** ; *Goldingham, Lieut. R. F.,* China, 1900–01, **414** ; *Gordon, Maj.-Gen. C. G.,* killed at Khartoum, **403**-4—Presentation to R.E. Mess, f.n., **315** ; *Gore, Lieut. St. G. C.,* Kandahar, 1879, **382**—Survey, 1879, f.n., **380** ; *Gorringe, Lt.-Gen. Sir George,* comds. 12th Ind. Div., Mesopotamia, **484**—Succeeds Aylmer, Kut Relief Force, **487**—Vacates comd., **487** ; *Gosset, Lieut. W. B.,* C.I.F.F., 1858, **358**, **364** ; *Gough, Lieut. G. F. B.,* Tibet Mission, **464** ; *Graham, Lt.-Gen. Sir Gerald,* V.C., Ch. Comd., Suakin, **406**—Operations, Sudan, 1884–5, **404**—

574   INDEX.

Victory at Hashin, 1885, **404**—Victory at Kassassin, 1882, **402**; *Grant, Maj.-Gen. Sir Philip,* Chitral, 1895, f.n., **440**; *Grant, Capt. S.,* Black Mountain, 1888, **429**; *Gray, Lieut. J. F.,* Mishmi Mission, **473**—Mohmands, 1915-16, f.n., **503**; *Greenstreet, Lt.-Col. W. L.,* C.R.E., Hazara, 1891, **431**; *Greenwood, Lieut. C. J. E.,* Kut, **485**; *Greer, Lieut. R. E.,* Zhob Valley 1890, **430**; *Griffith, Capt. G. H.,* relief, Pekin Legation, **413**; *Gunter, Capt. C. P.,* Mishmi Mission, survey, **473**; *Haggitt, Lieut. E. D.,* Miranzai, 1891, f.n., **433**; *Halliday, Lieut. C. D.,* Chitral, 1895, f.n., **440**; *Hamilton, Major A. F.,* Egypt, 1882, **402**; *Hare, Lieut. J.,* Perak, **401**; *Harness, Maj.-Gen. H. D.,* C.R.E., Mutiny, **358**, f.n. **360**—Lucknow, capture of, **360**; *Harrison, Gen. Sir Richard,* Lucknow, capture of, f.n., **360**—Relief, **355**; *Harrison, Lieut. W. A.,* Chin-Lushai, 1889, f.n., **461**; *Hart, Col. H. H.,* C.R.E., 1st Div., Tirah, **451**—N.W. Frontier, 1897-8, **445**; *Hart, Gen. Sir Reginald,* V.C., N.W. Frontier, 1897-8, **445**—Wins V.C., 1879, **379**; *Haslett, Lieut. P.,* Kandahar, 1879, **382**; *Haswell, Lt.-Col. C. H.,* C.R.E., Razmak Rd., **515**—Tibet Mission, **464-5**; *Hayes-Sadler, Lieut. E. J. B.,* Neuve Chapelle, killed, **478**; *Hearn, Col. Sir Gordon,* Khaibar Rly., f.n., **511**; *Heath, Lt.-Gen. Sir Gerard,* Chitral, 1895, **440**—E.-in-C., France, f.n., **440**; *Henderson, Lieut. E. G.,* China, 1900-01, **414**; *Henn, Lieut. T. R.,* killed at Maiwand, memorials to, **388-9**; *Henry, Major G.,* Chin-Lushai, 1889, **461**; *Hepper, Lieut. H. A. L.,* Chitral, 1895, f.n., **440**; *Heycock, Major C. H.,* Chin-Lushai, 1889, **460**—Tibet Mission, **463, 464, 466**; *Hibbert, Lieut. W. G.,* Chitral, 1895, f.n., **440**; *Hichens, Lt.-Col. W.,* C.R.E., Quetta Div., 1879, **375**—C.R.E., Stewart's Colm., 1879, **383**; *Hickson, Capt. S. A. E.,* Third Burma War, **407**; *Hill, Lieut. A. F. S.,* Tibet Mission, **464**; *Hill, Brig. E. F. J.,* C.R.E., 7th Div., Palestine, **496-7**—Help acknowledged, **x**—Meerut Div., 1914, **476**—Tibet Mission, **464-5**; *Hill, Capt. R. C. R.,* Field Troop, 1914, **476**; *Hobart, Capt. P. C. S.,* France, March, 1915, **479**; *Hodgson, Lieut. P. E.,* Tibet Mission, **464**; *Hogg, Capt. D. McA.,* Egypt, 1916, **494**; *Holdich, Col. Sir Thomas,* Bhutan, 1864, f.n., **458**—Survey, 1879, **380**—Zhob Valley, 1890, **430**; *Home, Lieut. W. J.,* Daflas, 1874, **457**; *Hunter, Major C. G. W.,* Salonika, **492**; *Hunter-Weston, Lt.-Gen. Sir Aylmer,* Miranzai, 1891, **432**—Waziristan, 1894, **440** and f.n.; *Hutton, Lieut. G. M.,* Chin-Lushai, 1889, f.n., **461**; *Innes, Capt. W.,* killed, Perak, **401**; *James, Lieut. B. A.,* Chin-Lushai, 1889, **460**;

Jefferis, Lieut. M. R., Razmak Rd., M.C., **515** and f.n.; *Jerome, Lieut. H. J. W.,* Kandahar, 1879, **382**; *Johnson, Major E. P.,* Chin-Lushai 1889, f.n., **461**—Malakand, 1897, **446**—Somaliland, 1903, **416**; *Johnston, Capt. E. F.,* Khaibar Rly., f.n., **511**; *Jopp, Capt. K. A.,* Abyssinia, **398**; *Judge, Lieut. C. N.,* Bhutan, 1864, f.n., **458**; *Kealy, Lt.-Col. P. H.,* help acknowledged, **x**—Secretary, Instn. of R.E., **x**—12th Ind. Div., Mesopotamia, f.n., **484**; *Keith, Col. W.,* Mutiny, 1857, **358**, f.n., **360**; *Kelly, Capt. E. H.,* Festubert, **479**; *Kelly, Capt. F. H.,* Mohmand F.F., **448**; *Kelsall, 2nd-Capt. G. N.,* Bhutan, 1864, **458**; *Kemp, Lieut. G. C.,* Chitral, 1895, f.n., **440**; *Kennedy, Lt.-Gen. Sir Michael,* Controller-Gen., S. & T., 1879, **383**—Kabul, 1879, **385**; *Kent, Capt. L. M.,* Aden Rly., **492**; *King, Capt. C. J. S.,* destruction, Chora Fort, 1919, f.n., **509**; *King, Capt. H. S.,* Miranzai, 1891, **432**; *Kingscote, Lieut. R. A. F.,* Chin-Lushai, **461**; *Kitchener, Gen. Viscount,* army reorganization, **417-8**—Nile Expedn., 1896, **412**; *Larminie, Capt. E. M.,* Second Afghan War, **388**; *Leach, Capt. E. P.,* V.C., Kandahar, 1880, **390**—Maiwand, **388-9**—Wins V.C., **380-1**; *Leach, Bt. Lt.-Col. H. P.,* Chitral, 1895, **440**—C.R.E., Chin-Lushai, **461**; *Le Breton, Lt.-Col. E. P.,* Aden, 1915, **491**—Help acknowledged, **x**—Mesopotamia, 1917, f.n., **491**—Mishmi Mission, **473**; *Lee, Capt. R. P.,* relief, Pekin Legations, **413**; *Le Mesurier, Major A.,* assault of Magdala, **400**—B.M., 2nd Div., 1879, **380**; *Lennox, Gen. Sir W. O.,* V.C., Lucknow, capture of, f.n., **360, 361**—Relief, **355**—V.C., Sebastopol, f.n., **355**; *Leslie, Maj.-Gen. G. A. J.,* C.R.E., Cav. Div., France, f.n., **481**—G.O.C., 17th Ind. Div., Mesopotamia, 1920, **518**; *Leslie, Capt. W. B.,* C.R.E., Obbia Force, 1902-04, **416**; *Lewis, Lieut. H. L.,* Tibet Mission, **464**; *Liddell, Maj.-Gen. Sir Wm.,* Zhob Valley, 1890, **430**; *Limond, Lt.-Col. D.,* C.R.E., Bright's Colm., 1879, **383**; *Lindsay, Lt.-Col. J. G.,* Rly. Officer, 1879, **375**—Rly., Sukkur to Sibi, 1879-80, **387**; *Loch, Brig.-Gen. S. G.,* relief, Pekin Legation, **413**—Waziristan, 1917, **504**; *Longe, Lieut. F. B.,* Roberts' march, **391**; *Loring, Capt. E. J.,* wounded, Ctesiphon, f.n., **484**; *Lovett, Maj.-Gen. B.,* C.R.E., Black Mountain, 1888, **429**; *Lubbock, Lieut. G.,* Chitral, 1895, f.n., **440**; *Lyall, Lieut. A. C.,* Aden, **491**; *Lynch, Major C. St. J.,* Khaibar Rly., f.n., **511**; *Macaulay, Lieut. P. J. F.,* killed, Wana, 1894, f.n., **440**; *McClintock, Lt.-Col. R. L.,* "Bangalore torpedo," f.n., **479**—E. Africa, **500**; *Macdonald, Maj.-Gen. Sir J. R. L.,*

Black Mountain, 1888, **429** and f.n.—career, f.n., **464**—China, 1900–01, **414**—comds. escort, Tibet, **464**; *Macdonald, Lieut. R. H.*, Chitral, 1895, f.n., **440**; *MacDonnell, Maj.-Gen. A. R.*, Abyssinia, **398**; *Mackenzie, Capt. R. J. H. L.*, Miranzai, 1891, f.n., **433**; *Maclagan, Capt. R. S.*, Miranzai, 1891, **432**—Waziristan, 1894, **440**; *Malan, Lieut. L. N.*, Tibet Mission, **464**; *Malcolm, Col. E. D.*, Relief of Lucknow, **355**, f.n. **360**; *Mann, Maj.-Gen. G. F.*, Ch. Eng., Second China War, **314**; *Maquay, Lt.-Col. J. P.*, Cyprus, 1878, **401**—Mutiny, 1857, **358**; *Marshall, Lt.-Col. H. J. M.*, Chin-Lushai, f.n., **461**—C.R.E., 2nd Cav. Div., France, f.n., **481**; *Martin, Lieut. A. D. de R.*, Mishmi Mission, **473**—Mohmands, 1916–17, f.n., **503**; *Mason, Capt. A. H.*, Black Mountain, 1888, **429**—Hazara, 1891, **431**—Miranzai, 1891, **432**—Waziristan, 1894, **440**—Zhob Valley, 1890, **430**; *Mason, Capt. K.*, night march, Dujaila Redoubt, **486**; *Matthews, Lieut. A. B.*, Kut, **484**, **485**—M.C., Sahil, **483**; *Maxwell, Lieut. R. C.*, Roberts' march, **391**; *Maxwell, Lieut. W. F.*, Persia, 1902, **413**; *Molesworth, Lieut. E. K.*, Tibet Mission, **464**; *Morshead, Lt.-Col. H. T.*, survey, Mishmi Mission, **473** and f.n.; *Mullaly, Maj.-Gen. Sir H.*, Chin-Lushai, **461**; *Muter, Lieut. R. S.*, Waziristan, 1894, f.n., **440**; *Nanton, Brig.-Gen. H. C.*, Ch. Eng., Indian Corps, 1914, **477**; *Nathan, Lieut. W. S.*, Miranzai, 1891, **432**; *Neville, Capt. G.*, killed, 1858, f.n., **364**—Mutiny, **358**; *Newman, Lieut. E. M. B.*, killed, Tofrek, **405**—Sudan, 1885, **404**; *Nicholson, Gen. Lothian*, Lucknow, capture, **361**—Mutiny, **358**, f.n., **360**; *Nicholson, F.M. Lord (W. G.)*, Egypt, 1882, **402**—Kandahar, 1879, **382**—N.W. Frontier, 1897–98, **445**—Roberts' march, **391**; *North, Major W.*, Perak, **401**—Peshawar Force, 1878, **375**; *Nosworthy, Lieut. F. P.*, France, 1915, wounded through heart, **478**; *Nugent, Lieut. C.*, death, Kabul, 1879, **386**—Shutar Gardan Pass, **384**; *Oakes, Lieut. R.*, survey, Aborland, **472**; *Ogilvie, Lieut. E. C.*, Chitral, 1895, f.n., **440**—Miranzai, 1891, f.n., **433**; *Oldfield, Capt. F. H.*, Chin-Lushai, **461**; *Oldham, Major L. W. S.*, an unsung hero, **444**—Chitral, 1895, f.n., **440**—crossing Shandur Pass, **443**—Nisa Gol, capture of, **443–4**—Killed, 1915, f.n.' **443**; *Olivier, Lieut. H. D.*, Kandahar, 1879, **383**; *O'Meara, Lieut. A. W. J.*, severely wounded, Pagan, **409**; *Onslow, Capt. G. C. P.*, Third Burma War, **407**; *Orpen, Lieut. R. T.*, Kandahar, 1879, **383**; *O'Sullivan, Major G. H. W.*, Chitral, 1895, **440**—Mohmand F.F., 1898, **448**; *Ottley, Col. J. W.*, N.W. Frontier, 1897–98, **445**; *Paris, Capt. A. L.*, Lahore Div., 1914, **476**—Mishmi, 1912–13, f.n., **474**—Neuve Chapelle, wounded and taken prisoner, **477–8**—Somaliland, 1902–04, **416**; *Paterson, Lieut. J. B.*, Mutiny, 1857, **358**; *Paul, Lt.-Col. E. M.*, wire-netting roads, f.n., **496**; *Peacocke, Lt.-Col. W.*, C.R.E., Buner F.F., 1898, **449**—N.W. Frontier, 1897–98, **445**; *Pearson, Lieut. H. D.*, China, 1900–01, **413**; *Pemberton, Capt. S.*, bridges Tigris, **487**—Mesopotamia, **484**; *Perry, Capt. W. E.*, survey, Persia, **490**; *Petrie, Major R. D.*, China, 1900–01, **414**—Chin-Lushai, **460**; *Picton, Capt. R. E.*, relief, Pekin Legations, **413**; *Porter, Maj.-Gen. Whitworth*, **ix**; *Powell, Maj.-Gen. S. H.*, Miranzai, 1891, **432**; *Preedy, Major C.*, C.R.E., Burma rebellion, **528**; *Pridham, Capt. G. R.*, China, 1900–01; *Pritchard, Lt.-Gen. Sir G. D.*, Abyssinia, 1868, **398**—advance to Magdala, **399**—Lucknow, Relief of, **355**, f.n. **360**—wounded, Magdala, **400**; *Pye, Lieut. P. C.*, Bhutan, 1864, f.n., **458**; *Rait Kerr, Lieut. R. S.*, Neuve Chapelle, wounded, **478**; *Rees, Lieut. F. F. N.*, Chitral, 1895, f.n., **440**; *Renny-Tailyour, Major T. F. B.*, China, 1900–01, **414**—Chin-Lushai, **461**; *Reynolds, Major A. R.*, China, 1900–01, **414**; *Rich, Major E. T.*, Persia, survey, **490**; *Rich, Lieut. H. B.*, Perak, **401**; *Richardson, Capt. J. S.*, Lahore Div., 1914, **476**—Neuve Chapelle, killed, **477–8**; *Rimington, Maj.-Gen. J. C.*, E.-in-C., Mesopotamia, **488**; *Robertson, Lieut. C. L.*, Waziristan, 1894, f.n., **440**; *Robson, Lieut. R. G.*, first trench mortar, gallantry and death, France, 1914, **479**; *Rogers, Capt. M. W.*, Kandahar, 1879, **382**—Survey, 1879, f.n., **380**; *Rohde, Lieut. J. H.*, Neuve Chapelle, killed **478**; *Romilly, Capt. F. J.*, killed, Tofrek, **405**—Sudan, 1885, **404**; *Ross, Maj.-Gen. P.* (see "Bengal"); *Rundle, Col. F. P.*, Ch. Eng., E. Africa, **501**; *Russell, Capt. B. B.*, Chitral, 1895, **440**—Somaliland, 1890, **411**; *Russell, Capt. R. E. M.*, C.R.E., Egypt, 1914, **493**; *Ryder, Capt. C. H. D.*, exploration, W. Tibet, **470**—Lhasa, f.n., **466**—relief, Pekin Legation, **413**—Tibet Mission, **464**, **466**; *St. John, Lt.-Col. O. B. C.*, Kandahar, 1879, **382**—Maiwand, **388**—Political Officer, 1879, **375**; *Sale, Lieut. M. T.*, Bhutan, 1864, f.n., **458**; *Sandbach, Maj.-Gen. A. E.*, Gilgit, **439**—Hazara, 1891, **431** and f.n.; *Sanders, Brig.-Gen. G. A. F.*, Baghdad defences, 1920, **519**—Colm. Comdr., **520**—Suakin, 1896, **412**; *Sandes, Lt.-Col. E. W. C.*, bridging train, Mesopotamia, **484–5**—Foreword and Preface, **vii–xi**—Kut, **485**; *Sandys, Major E. S.*, Salonika, **492**; *Sanford, Lt.-Gen. G. E. L. S.*,

INDEX.

C.R.E., Third Burma War, **407**; *Sankey, Lt.-Col. R. H.*, C.R.E., Kandahar Force, **375**—Kandahar, 1879, **382-3**; *Savage, Lieut. G. R. R.*, Kandahar, 1879, **382**; *Savi, Lieut. T. B. B.*, Bhutan, 1864, f.n., **458**; *Scott, Lieut. B.*, survey, 1879, f.n., **380**; *Scott-Moncrieff, Maj.-Gen. Sir G.*, C.R.E., Relief, Pekin Legations, **413**; *Scratchley, Maj.-Gen. P. H.*, Mutiny, 1857, **358**, f.n. **360**; *Searight, Capt. E. E. G. L.*, Burma rebellion, f.n., **528**; *Sheppard, Maj.-Gen. S. H.*, Bde. Comdr. and Ch. of Staff, E. Africa, **500**—Crossing of Tsan-po, **469**—Gyantse Jong captured—Promoted for bravery, **468** and f.n.—Help acknowledged, **x**—Khaibar Pass, operations, 1919, **509**, f.n.—Lhasa, f.n., **466**—Palla stormed, **466-7**—Tibet Mission, **463-5**; *Sherwood, Lieut. H. J.*, Chin-Lushai, f.n., **461**; *Shone, Lt.-Gen. Sir W.*, China, 1900-01, **414**—C.R.E., Chitral, 1895, **440**—C.R.E., Miranzai, 1891, **432**—Third Burma War, **407**; *Sim, Major C. A.*, Peshawar Force, 1879, **375**; *Sorsbie, Brig.-Gen. R. F.*, Ch. Eng., N.W. Frontier Force, 1919, f.n., **511**; *Spratt, Capt. F. T.*, Roberts' march, **391**; *Stace, Capt. R. E.*, Kut, **485**—Searchlights, **484**; *Stockley, Capt. H. R.*, China, 1900-01, **413**—Hazara, 1891, **431**—Waziristan, 1894, f.n., **440**; *Stoehr, Major C. F.*, Aden, **490**—Mohmands, 1916-17, f.n., **503**—N. Persia, 1920, **518**; *Stokes-Roberts, Col. E. R. B.*, C.R.E., Kut Relief Force, **486**; *Stuart, Major A. M.*, Inspr., S.M. defences, **554** and f.n.; *Swayne, Capt. H. G. C.*, Chin-Lushai, **460**; *Swetenham, Major G.*, Mutiny, 1857, **358**, f.n. **360**; *Swinburne, Lieut. T. A.*, Mekran, 1910, f.n., **417**; *Swiney, Lieut. A. J. H.*, Chitral, 1895, f.n., **440, 441**—Miranzai, 1891, f.n., **433**; *Talbot, Lieut. Hon. M. G.*, Roberts' march, **391**; *Tanner, Capt. J. A.*, Chitral, 1895, **440**—Third Burma War, **407**; *Thuillier, Maj.-Gen. Sir H.*, Chitral, 1895, f.n., **440**; *Thurburn, Lt.-Col. J. W.*, N.W. Frontier, 1897-98, **445**; *Tickell, Capt. R. P.*, Roberts' march, **391**; *Tillard, Capt. E. D.*, E. Africa, **499**—Somaliland, 1902-04, **416**; *Tomlinson, Capt. H. W.*, Kut, **485**; *Traill, Lieut. W. S.*, Waziristan, 1894, f.n., **440**; *Travers, Lieut. G. A.*, Miranzai, 1891, **432**—Waziristan, 1894, f.n., **440**; *Trenchard, Lieut. O. H. B.*, survey, Aborland, **472**; *Tulloch, Capt. A. J. S.*, China, 1900-01, **413**; *Turner, Lt.-Col. J. F.*, floating bridge, Mosul, **518** and f.n.; *Turner Jones, Lieut. G.*, Malta E.F., 1878, **401**—Recommended 𝔙.𝔠., Kandahar, **390**; *Twigge, Maj.-Gen. J. T.*, Perak, **401**; *Twining, Lt.-Col. P. G.*, China, 1900-01, **414**—C.R.E., Meerut Div., 1914, **477**; *Twiss, Capt. A. M.*, Mesopotamia, 1914, **482**—mortally wounded, **483**; *Tylden-Pattenson, Capt. E. C.*, Abor, 1911-12, **471-2**—China, 1900-01, **414**; *Urquhart, Lieut. J. H.*, Bhutan, 1864, f.n., **458**—Killed, **459**; *Wagstaff, Maj.-Gen. C. M.*, Zakka Khels, 1908, **453**; *Wahab, Capt. R. A.*, survey, Black Mountain, 1888, **429**—Hazara, 1891, **431**—Miranzai, 1891, **432**—Waziristan, 1894, **440**; *Walker, Lieut. A. D.*, Gyantse, **465, 466**—Lhasa, f.n., **466**—Palla, **466**—Tibet Mission, **464**; *Walker, Lieut. D. C.*, Mutiny, 1857, **358**; *Walker, Maj.-Gen. G.*, Salonika, **492**; *Waller, Lieut. E. A.*, Kandahar, 1880, recommended for 𝔙.𝔠., **390**; *Walpole, Lieut. A.*, Chitral, 1895, f.n., **440**; *Walton, Capt. E. W.*, Waziristan, 1894, **440**; *Warren, Sir Charles*, Ch. Comd., Bechuanaland, **408**; *Watkins, Capt. C. F. M.*, Malakand, 1897, **446**; *Watson, Col. Sir Charles*, **ix**; *Watson, Capt. G. D.*, Third Afghan War, **508**; *Watson, Lt.-Col. T. C.*, 𝔙.𝔠., C.R.E., 12th Ind. Div., f.n., **484**—Wins 𝔙.𝔠., 1897, **448** and f.n.; *Webber, Lieut. C. E.*, C.I.F.F., 1858, **364**—Mutiny, **358**; *Webber, Capt. N. W.*, Mekran, 1911, f.n., **417**; *Weekes, Lieut. H. W.*, Chitral, 1895, f.n., **440**; *Wells, Lieut. H. L.*, Khojak Pass, 1879, f.n., **382**; *Wheeler, Lieut. E. O.*, Festubert, **479**; *Whiteley, Capt. E. C.*, killed, Shaiba, **484**; *Whiteford, Lieut. W. W. B.*, Kandahar, 1879, **383**; *Wilkieson, Lt.-Col. C. B.*, C.R.E., Tirah, 1897, **451**—Malta E.F., 1878, **401**—Sudan, 1885, **404**—Third Burma War, **407**—Wounded, **405**; *Wilkinson, Major C. W.*, E. Africa, **501**; *Williams, Maj.-Gen. Sir Godfrey*, Ch. Eng., Gallipoli and Egypt (D.G.M.W.S.), **492**—Chitral, 1895, **440**; *Wilson, Lt.-Col. F. A.*, C.R.E., Kut, **485**; *Winsloe, Lieut. A. R.*, Chitral, 1895, f.n., **440**—Malakand, 1897, D.S.O., **446** and f.n.; *Winsloe, Major H. E.*, Kut, **485**—Wounded, **483**; *Witts, Capt. F. V. B.*, Mesopotamia, wounded and M.C., **488**; *Wood, Capt. H.*, exploration, W. Tibet, **470**; *Woodthorpe, Capt. R. G.*, survey, 1879, **380**; *Wright, Maj.-Gen. H. B. H.*, Ch. Eng., Palestine, 1918, **495**—Chin-Lushai, f.n., **461**; *Wynne, Lieut. C. E.*, death, 1860—Mutiny, **358**—Recommended 𝔙.𝔠., **361**; *Yearsley, Lieut. K. D.*, Kut, **485**; **Other Ranks**—*Ashman*, 1st-Corpl., killed, Maiwand, **388-9**; *Heapy, Serj.*, killed, Maiwand, **388-9**; *Paul, Serj.*, recommended 𝔙.𝔠., **361**

Engineers, S. African, in E. Africa, **501**
England, pirate, **85**
Equipment, officers, **140, 163**
Escalading, method of, **250**
Eustace, Maj.-Gen. A. H., Third Afghan War, **507**

INDEX. 577

F

Factories, defence, general principles, **32**
—Early, on sufferance, **2**
Faiz Muhammad, Afghan General, 1878, **377**
Fane, Sir Henry, C.-in-C., 1838, **268**
Fateh Singh, Gaikwar, 1779, **191**
Ferozeshah, Battle of, 1845, **293**
Field Battery, 10th, Mohmand Valley, 1897, **448**
Field Companies, Service Cos. renamed, **419, 537, 542, 547**
Field Companies, R.E., Palestine, 1918, **495**
Field Deputies, First Maratha War, **191**
Field Squadron, R.E., Palestine, 1918, **495,** f.n.
Fire rafts, First Burma War, **256**
Fireworker, **62**
Firoz Shah, defeated, Ranod, 1858, **366**
" Fists of Patriotic Union," Boxers, China, 1900-01, **413**
Fitzpatrick, Capt. J. (M.I.), comds. Pioneer Bn., 1803, **200**
Floyd, Col., Seringapatam, 1799, **176**
Forrest, Lieut. W. (Pioneers), Agra, **217** ; Aligarh, 1803, **215** ; Loses arm at Dig, 1804, **218** ; Rampura, 1804, **217**
Forresti (Italian), plans of Calcutta in British Museum, **44**
Forsyth, Sir Douglas, Mission to Mandalay, 1875—" Shoe question," **405**
Fortifications—*British*, in India, origin of, **3** ; *Contributions* to cost of, **24** ; *Effect* on, after Adyar R., 1746, **68** ; *Inspector* and Director of, proposed, **196** ; *Lack* of foundations, 17th century, **24** ; *Permanent*, Attock, Rawalpindi, Quetta, **534**
Fort St. David—*Baker, P.*, last Gunner, **69** ; *Becomes* capital, 1746, **71** ; *Boscawen* (*Admiral*) joins Griffin, 1748, **70** ; *Brohier, J.*, apptd. Engineer, 1751, **71** (*v.* also " Bengal " and " Madras ") ; *Call, J.*, Asst. Eng., 1751, **70** (*v.* also " Madras ") ; *Clive, R.*, one of garrison, 1747, **69** ; *Defence* agst. French, 1747, **69** ; *Delavaux, A.*, arrives 1748—deserts 1749, **69-70** ; *Description* of fortifications, 1746, **69** ; *Destroyed* by French, 1758, **75** ; *Founded* at Tegnapatam, 1690, **25** ; *Griffin* (*Commodore*), relief by, 1747, **69** ; *Hugonin, F.*, Ch. Gunner, 1706, **61** ; *Jones, G.*, Engineer, 1747, **69** ; *Lawrence, Stringer*, lands 1748, **70** ; *O'Hara,* Asst. Eng., 1751, **70** ; *Relieved* by Griffin, 1747, **69** ; *Robins, B.*, Eng.-Gen., 1750, prepares plans—Dies 1751—His will, **71** ; *Von Werlinhoffe* to construct defences, 1698, **27** (see also " Madras ")
Fort St. George (see " Madras ")
Foster, Sir Wm., help acknowledged, **x**
Fougasses, **453** and f.n.
Fowler, Maj.-Gen. C. A., Third Afghan War, **507** ; Drives Afghans to Dacca, **508**

Fox, Lieut. F. R. (M.I. and M.S. & M.), killed at Jhansi, **365** ; Malwa Campaign, 1857, **362**
Franks, Brig.-Gen., Colm. Comdr., 1857, **359**
Frazer, Gen., defeats Marathas, Dig—Killed, 1804, **218**
French—*Assist* Haidar Ali, **160-1** ; *Chandernagar*, surrendered to Clive, 1757, **102** ; *Chevalier, J.*, Governor of Chandernagar, 1769, **134-5** ; *Drawn* naval battle, 1746, **67** ; *Dupleix, q.v.*; *Fleet* before Madras, 1781, **158** ; *Hyderabad*, surrender at, 1797, **171** ; *La Bourdonnais, q.v.* ; *Lally, Count, q.v.* ; *Lose* all fortified bases, **149** ; *Madras*, capture, 1746, **67**—Defence agst. Nawab of Carnatic, 1746, **68** ; *Mahé*, taken by Braithwaite, 1779, **149** ; *Mauritius*, Réunion, etc., lost 1810, **231** ; *Naval* action off Ft. St. George, 1690, **26** ; *Paradis*, Governor of Madras, routs Mughal Army, 1746, **68** ; *Perron, q.v.* ; *Pondicherry, q.v.* ; *Refuse* to help Siraj-ud-Daula, **57** ; *Renault* defends Chandernagar, 1757, **102** ; *St. Thomé* captured by, 1672, **10** ; *Sepoys* first raised by, 1740, **65** ; *Suffren, Admiral*, 1781, **160** ; *Threaten* Calcutta by sea, 1758, **111** ; *War* with England, 1744, **67**—1756, **75**—1778, **148**—1793, **170**
Frontier defence, different schools of, **373**
Frontier Militia, failure of, 1919, **506, 510** ; N. and S. Waziristan, 1919, **512**
Fullarton, Col., Report on Engineers and Pioneers, 1782, **161**
Furlough, regulations, 1796, **185**

G

Garcia da Orta, lessee of Bombay, **13, 14**
Garhwal acquired, **240**
Garo Hills, N.E. Frontier, **456**
Garvock, Maj.-Gen. J., Ambela, 1863, succeeds Chamberlain in comd., **427**
Gaselee, Brig.-Gen. Sir A., China E.F., 1900-01, **413**
Gawilgarh, capture of, 1803, **212** ; Description of, **211**
Gawler, Lt.-Col. J. C., Sikkim, 1861, **457**
German artificers, scheme for, 1776, **188**
Gerrard, Col., Colm. Comdr., killed 1857, **347**
Ghaziuddin Nagar, mutineers defeated at, 1857, **323**
Ghazni, storm of, 1839, **271** et seq. (v. also " Afghan War, First ")
Gheria, pirate stronghold, **92**
Gibraltar, soldier artificers, 1772, **139**
Gilbert, Maj.-Gen. Sir W. R., First Sikh War, **292**, f.n. ; Second Sikh War, **303**
Gilgit, State, **422**
Gillespie, Maj.-Gen. R., assault of Cornelis, 1811, **233** ; Nepal War, **234** ; Killed at Kalanga, 1814, **235**
Gingee, fall of, 1698, **26**

U

INDEX.

Goddard, Gen.—Advance on Poona, 1780, 158—1781, **195**; *Captures* Ahmadabad, **192**—Bassein, **194**—Dabhoi, **191**; *Failure* at Bhor Ghat, 1781, **195**; *March* from Bengal to Surat, **190**; *Operations* agst. Gaikwar, **191**; *Retreat* to Bombay, 1781, **196**; *Secures* Gujrat, **193**
Godwin, Maj.-Gen. H., Second Burma War, **308**
Golconda, captured by Mughals, 1687, **25**; King of, beheaded, **25**; St. Thomé captured by, 1662, **10**
Gordon, Brig. R., captures Thana, 1774, **180**
Gough, Brig.-Gen. G., Second Afghan War, **378, 386**
Gough, Hugh, Lord—*Chillianwala*, 1849, **305**; *First China War*, 1841, **280**; *First Sikh War*, **292**; *Gujarat*, Battle of, 1849, **306**; *Gwalior Campaign*, 1843, **288**; *Maharajpur*, 1843, **289**; *Second Sikh War*, **303**; *To* be superseded, 1849, **305**
Grant, Lt.-Gen. Sir Hope, assault of Delhi, **341**; Relief, Lucknow, **355**; Second China War, **313**
Grant, Lieut. J. D. (8th Gurkhas), wins ย.ᴄ., Tibet, **468** and f.n.
Greathed, Col., victory, Bulandshahr, 1857, **347**
Graves, Brig.-Gen., at Delhi, outbreak of Mutiny, **318**
Great War—**Aden**—Active operations, 1915–18, **491**; Engineer work, **491**; Garrison reinforced, **490**; Operations concluded, **492**; Perim threatened, **490**; Water Colm. and consumption, **491** and f.n.; *Bangalore* torpedo, **479**, f.n. **E. Africa**—Country and strange conditions, **498–9**; Dar-es-Salaam, capture of, **501**; Engineer troops employed, **501**; Outline of operations, **498–9**; Railway work, importance of, **501**; Smut's operations, **500**; Tanga, failure at, troops present, **499–500**; Van Deventer's operations, **500**; **Egypt**—Canal, attack on, by Turks, **494**; defence of, **493–4**; Engineer personnel, Egyptian Rlys. and Telegraphs, **493**; Garrison, 1914, reinforced from India and Australasia, **493**; Murray's advance to Palestine, **494**; **France**—Bo.S. & M., heavy losses, **478** and f.n.—Neuve Chapelle, **477**; Hand grenades, improvised varieties of, **480**; Ind. Cav. remain in France, **481**, f.n.; Indian Corps, arrival in France, **477**—Composition of, **476**—Leaves France, **481**—Neuve Chapelle, 1914, **477-8**—1915, **481**—Losses, **481**—Loos, 1915, **481**—Trench appliances devised, 1914, **479-80**—Winter, 1914–15, **479**; *Gallipoli*, R.E. officers from India, **492**; *I.A.R.O.* services, **476** and f.n.; *Indian Army*, training and equipment, **475** and f.n.; *Indian* princes offer services, **475**; *Indian* troops despatched to Europe, **475**; *Misuse* of Sapper units, **480**; **Mesopotamia**—Amara captured, **484**; Baghdad, operations for capture of, **487–8–9**; Basra, 1914 and 1918, **483**; Campaign opened, **482**; Concluding operations, **489**; Ctesiphon, Battle of, **484**; Engineer troops, 1917, **488**; Expansion of plan of campaign, **482**; Kut-al-Amara captured, **484**—bridging train at, **485**—operations for relief of, **486–7**—siege of, **484**—surrenders, **487**; Nasiriya captured, **484**; Night march to Dujaila Redoubt, **486**; Qurna captured, **483**; S. & M., 1914 and 1918, **482**; Shumran Bend—Tigris crossing, **488–9**; Trench warfare, **487**; Twelfth Ind. Div. formed, **484**; **N.W. Frontier**—Marris, operations agst., 1918, **504**; Mohmands, operations agst. and blockade, **502–3**; Organization, Indian Army, **502**; Situation, 1914–18, **502** *et seq.*; Waziristan, 1917, Derajat F.F., **503**—N. Waziristan F.F.—S. Waziristan F.F., **503–4**; **Palestine**—Allenby takes comd., **494**; Anti-malarial work, **496**; Big offensive, 1918, engineer preparation for, **496**—"Ladder of Tyre," **497**—roadmaking during, **497**; Drainage of lakes, **496**; "Engineers' and Doctors' War," **495**; Engineer troops, 1918, **495**; Engineer work, **494** *et seq.*; Indian troops arrive, 1918, **495**; Water supply on coast, **496**; Wire-netting roads, **496**; **Persia**—"Dunsterforce," **490**; East Persian Cordon, **490**; Engineer troops, S. Persia, **490**; Road construction and survey, **489–90**; *R.E.* officers from India for home army, **475**; *Salonika*, R.E. officers from India, **492**; *S. & M. Corps*, growth during War, **476**; *Theatres* where Indian Army served, **475**
Greensill, Capt. (24th Regt.), Asst. Eng., Delhi, f.n., **331**
Grey, Maj.-Gen. Sir J., Gwalior, 1843, **288**; Panniar, 1843, **289**
"Guides," Ahmadnagar, 1803, **207**; First Mysore War, 1780, **156**; Java, 1811, **232**
Guides, Corps of, march to Delhi, 1857, **327**
Gumti, R., cask bridges, 1858, **360, 361**; Tributary of Ganges, **350**
"Gunner," first British military engineer in India, **3**
Gunners, at capture of Nandidroog, 1791, **166**
Gun-room Crew, replaced by Artillery, 1748, **69**
Gurdon, Lieut. (32nd Pioneers), Palla stormed, Tibet, **467**
Gurkhas, description and territories, 1814, **233**; Delhi, **324**; Lucknow, **359**; *5th*, Hunza-Nagar, 1891, **435** *et seq.*; *8th*, Tibet Mission, 1904, **463**; (v. also "Nepal War")
Gustavinski, Lieut., Asst. Eng., Delhi, f.n., **331**

INDEX. 579

Gwalior, **143**; Captured, 1858, **366**; Escaladed by Popham, 1780, **193**
Gwalior Campaign, affairs leading up to, 1843, **288**; Chonda, **289**; Conclusion, **290**; Maharajpur, 1843, Sappers at, **289**; Panniar, 1843, Sappers at, with Buffs, **289**
Gyantse Jong (*v.* " Tibet Mission ")

H

Haidar Ali—*Advance* into Carnatic, 1780, **154**; *Army*, **145**–**6**; *Career* and character, **145**; *Death*, 1782, **161**; *Defeated* at Pollilur, Porto Novo, and Sholinghur, **159**; *Helps* French at Mahé, **149**; *Mysore War* agst. British, **143**; *Navy*, **145**
Haji Muhammad, " Mad Mulla," Somaliland, 1902–04, **416**–**7**
Haldane, Gen. Sir J. A., C.-in-C., Mesopotamia, 1920, **518**
Hall, Lieut., Asst. Eng., Lucknow, **354**, f.n.
Hand-grenades, improvised in France, **480**
Hanoverian units, **189**
Harcourt, Col., Second Maratha War, **206, 214**
Hardinge, Sir Henry, change of role at Ferozeshah, **293**; Gov.-Gen., 1844, **292**; 2nd in comd. to Gough, First Sikh War, **292**
Hariharpur, factory founded, 1633, **4**
Harness, Col., captures Ahmadnagar, 1803, **207**
Harris, Gen. Lord, C.-in-C., Madras, 1797, **171**; Fourth Mysore War, **172**; Defeats Tipu at Malavalli, 1799, **174**
Harris, Lieut. (M.I.), comds. M.S. & M., Pegu, 1852, **310**
Hartley, Capt. J. (Bo.I.), assault of Ahmadabad, 1780, **192**; Clears Konkam, **195**; Gallantry of, 1779, **191**; Reinforces Goddard, **191**
Hastings, Lord, comds. " Grand Army," Third Maratha War, **243**; Gov.-Gen., 1813, **233**–**4**
Hastings, Warren, action after Pollilur, 1780, **158**; First Maratha War, **190**; Leaves India, 1785, **162**; Policy agst. Mysore, **154**
Havelock, Sir Henry, advance towards Lucknow, **348**–**9**; Persia, 1857, **313**; Reaches Cawnpore, **348**
Hawthorne, Bugler, **V.C.** (52nd Regt.), awarded **V.C.**, Kashmir Gate, 1857, **342**–**4**
Hazara, 1891, **431** and f.n.
Headgear, as adopted agst. Sikhs, 1848, **303**
Heitland, Capt. W. P. (M.I.), comds. Madras Pioneers, at Ahmadabad, **207**; At Assaye, **210**; At Gawilgarh, **212**; In 1803, **200**; Under Wellesley, 1800, **199**
Heliograph, introduction of, **372** and f.n.

U*

Helmand R., bridged, 1879, **381**
Herat, besieged by Persians and Russians, 1837, **267**
Hewitt, Maj.-Gen. S. H., G.O.C., Meerut, 1857, **318**
Hicks, Maj.-Gen., destroyed near Khartoum, **403**
Hill Forts (*v.* " Third Maratha War ")
Hills, Lieut., Asst. Eng., Delhi, **331,** f.n.
Hindiya barrage saved, 1920, **519** and f.n.
Hindustani Fanatics, Ambela Campaign, **425** *et seq.*; Description, **423**, f.n.; Malka, stronghold destroyed, **428**
Hislop, Lt.-Gen. Sir T., comds. " Army of the Deccan," Third Maratha War, **243**; Defeats Holkar, 1817, **246**
Hodson (of Hodson's Horse), killed, f.n., **361**; Punjab Govt., 1848, **299**
Hodson, Major V. C. P., help acknowledged, **x**
Holkar (Indore), Defeat, Farrukhabad, 1804, **214**—Mehidpur, 1817, **246**; Maratha Confederacy, **143**; Operations agst., 1804, **217**
Honalli, captured, 1799, **199**
Honavar, captured, 1783, **197**; Defence of, **198**
Hong Kong, First China War, **280**
Howlett, Lieut. A. (M.S.C.), comds. Co. M.S. & M., Perak, 1875, **401**
Hpagyidoa, Burmese King, 1826, **260**
Hudson, Brig.-Gen. J., Ind. Bde., Sudan, 1885, **404**
Hughes, Admiral, captures Trincomalee, 1782, **160**; Opponent of Suffren, 1781, **160**
Hugli, British factory, abandoned, 1686—Founded, 1651, **4**; Portuguese factory, founded end 16th century, **30**
Humphreys, Col. E. T. (Leinsters), Moplah rebellion, **522**
Hunterian System of spelling, **x**
Hunza, State, **422**
Hunza-Nagar, 1891—*Bridge* and roadmaking, **435**; *Chalt* garrisoned, **435**; *Description* of country and court, **434**; *Engineer* work after expedn., **439**; *Forces* engaged, **435**; *Gilgit*, advance from, **435**; *Nilt*, Aylmer's story of capture, **436**—Description of fort and position, **436**; *Rulers*, the Thums, **434**; *Thol* captured, **438**; **V.C.s** and other awards, **438**; *War* of individuals, **433**
Hutting Grant explained, **534**
Hyderabad, Nizam of, co-operation of, 1799, **172**; Hostility of, **143**
Hyderabad, Sind, Battle of, 1843, **287**; Occupied by Napier, **287**

I

Imambara Palace, Lucknow, **350**
Imamgarh, Sind, 1842, **286**
Imperial Assemblage, 1877, **373**

Imperial Service Sappers—*Faridkot*, E. Africa, **499**; *Maler Kotla*, China, 1900–01, **414**—Mesopotamia, **482,** f.n. —Temporarily absorbed into Bo.S. & M., **548**—Tirah, 1897, **450**; *Sirmur*, Mesopotamia, **482, f.n., 484**—Tirah, 1897, **451**; *Tehri-Garhwal*, Mesopotamia, **482,** f.n.
Indian Marine, ships built at Surat, **86**
Indian Army Reserve of Officers, officering of S. & M. Corps during Great War, **538, 543-4, 548**; Services in Great War, **476** and f.n.
Indore, Maratha Confederacy, **143**
Infantry officers, as Engineers, Second Burma War, **308**; Last in S. & M. Corps, **371**
Inglis, Col. (32nd Foot), Lucknow Residency, **351**
Interloper, explained, **27**
Isazai, 1892, story concerning, **433**
Isazais, Yusafzai Pathans, **422**
Ismail Hakki, Turks under, surrender at Sharqat, **482**
Ivie, Thomas, Agent, Ft. St. George, **5** Agent, Masulipatam, **4**

J

Jagdalak, defence of post, 1879, **386**; Disaster, 1842, **276**
Jahangir, grants factory, Surat, **1**
Jam Sahib, surrenders Nawanagar, 1812, **225**
Jang Bahadur, Maharaja, joins Campbell, 1858, **359**
Janitia Hills, N.E. Frontier, **456**
Jaswant Rao Holkar, succeeds to Indore, **204**
Jaura Alipur victory, Central India, **366**
Java, expedn. agst., 1811, **232**; Restored to Dutch, 1814, **233**; Surrendered to British, 1811, **233**
Jeffreys, Brig.-Gen. P. D., Malakand F.F., 1897, captures Agrah and Gat, **448**; destroys Shaki Tangi, **447**
Jhansi, captured, 1858, **364–5**; Siege of, 1838, **266**
Jhansi, Rani of, as military leader, 1857, **347**
Jidballi, victory over Mad Mulla, **417**
Jones, Brig.-Gen., assault of Delhi, **341**
Jones, Maj.-Gen. R., siege of Bhurtpore, 1805, **220**
Joss House Hill, First China War, Coffins, **280**
Jowakis, position, **422**

K

Kadam Rasul Palace, Lucknow, **350**
Kaisar Bagh Palace, Lucknow, **350**
Kalpi captured, 1858, **366**
Kangra, capture of, 1846, **296**
Karim Khan, Pindari leader, 1817, **244**
Karim Sahib, son of Haidar Ali, **154**

Kasgassin, victory by Graham, 1882, **402**
Kashmir, sold to Raja of Jammu, 1846, **296**
Kavanagh, Mr., Residency, Lucknow, **356**
Keane, Lt.-Gen. Sir J., C.-in-C., Bombay, comds. " Army of Indus," 1838, **268**
Keir, Maj.-Gen. G., captures Ras-al-Khaima, 1819, **250**
Kelly, Lt.-Col. J. G., 32nd Pnrs., relief, Chitral, **441**
Khaibar Rifles, 1897, **450**; Disbanded, 1919, **509**
Kempe, Paymaster, **47**
Khalsa, explained, **291**
Kharda, Nizam, defeated by Marathas, **204**
Khasias, operations agst., 1830, **266**
Khasi Hills, N.E. Frontier, **456**
Khiva, fall of, **372**
Khush-Ab, victory, Persia, 1857, **312**
Kidd, Captain, pirate, **85**
Kilpatrick, Major, reaches Fulta from Madras, 1756, **59**
King-Emperor, Indian Corps, France, thanks to, **481**, visits, Dec., 1914, **479**
King's or Royal Army, first unit reaches India, **72**
Knowles, Lieut. (B.S.C.), Asst. Eng., Delhi, f.n., **331**
Konkan, explained, **195,** f.n.
Koppaldroog, captured, 1819, **250**
Kumaon acquired, **240**
Kurram Valley, 1897, Samana Ridge, heavy fighting—Saragarhi lost, **450**

L

La Bourdonnais, Mahé de, Gov. of Isles of France and Bourbon, **65**; Captures Madras, 1746, **67**; Drawn naval battle, **67**; Restores Madras on ransom, **67**
Lake, Lt.-Gen. Sir Percy, succeeds Nixon, Mesopotamia, **486,** f.n.; Vacates comd., **487**
Lake, Lord—*Agra* captured, 1803, **216**; *Aligarh* captured, 1803, **214**; *Bhurtpore*, 1805, failure at, **219–22**; *Campaign*, 1803, Second Maratha War, **214**; *Comds.* " Grand Army," 1803, **205**; *Delhi*, Battle of, 1803, **215**— Enters, **216**; *Engineers*, comments on, at Bhurtpore, 1805, **221**; *Laswari*, Battle of, 1803, **216**
Lally, Count, attacks Madras, 1758, **76**; Captured at Pondicherry, 1761, **79**; Captures Cuddalore, 1758, **75**; Defeated at Wandiwash, 1760, **78**; Destroys Ft. St. David, 1758, **75**; Sent from France to India, 1756, **75**
Lal Pultan, first Sepoy Bn., Bengal, 1757, **101**
Lal Singh, Sikh Chief, 1845, **291**
La Martiniere, College at Lucknow, **350**
Lancaster, sea captain, **1**
Lawrence, George, Punjab Govt., 1848, **299**

INDEX. 581

Lawrence, (Sir) Henry, advice at Sobraon, 1846, **295**; In Oudh, 1857, **350**; Mortally wounded, **351**; Punjab Govt., 1848, **299**
Lawrence, John (Lord), Punjab Govt., 1848, **299**
Littler, Maj.-Gen. Sir J., First Sikh War, f.n., **292**
Lockhart, Lt.-Gen. Sir Wm., Miranzai, 1891, **431**; Tirah, 1897, **450**; Waziristan, 1894, **439**
Longfield, Brig.-Gen., assault of Delhi, **341**
Low, Maj.-Gen. Sir R. C., Chitral, 1895, **440**
Lumsden, Punjab Govt., 1848, **299**
Lushais, N.E. Frontier, **456**
Lytton, Lord, Viceroy, **373**

M

McAdam, J. L., road engineer, f.n., **228**
M'Caskill, Maj.-Gen. Sir J., First Sikh War, f.n., **292**
McCraith, Capt. R., comds. Pioneers, Mehidpur, 1817, **246**; Java, 1811, **232**
McEnroy, Capt., Leinster Regt., Moplah rebellion, **521,** f.n.
Macgregor, Political Officer, Jalalabad, 1842, **278**
Machhi Bhawan, Sikh Fort, Lucknow, **350**
McLeod, Gen. N., relieves Mangalore, 1783, **198**
M'Leod, Major (76th Regt.), Aligarh, 1803, **215**
MacMunn, Lt.-Gen. Sir G., help acknowledged, **x**
Macnaghten, Sir Wm., Kabul, 1839, **274**; Murdered, Kabul, 1842, **276**; Political envoy, 1838, **268**
McNeill, Maj.-Gen. Sir J., Battle of Tofrek, 1885, **404**
Macpherson, Maj.-Gen. Sir H., Ind. Div., Egypt, 1882, **402**
Macpherson, Brig.-Gen. H. T., Ali Masjid, 1878, **377**
Macpherson, Sir John, Gov.-Gen., 1785, **162**
McQueen, Maj.-Gen. J. W., Black Mountain, 1888, **429**
Madapollam, seized by Mughals, 1689, **25**
Madhu Rao, Peshwa, died, 1772, **180**
"Mad Mulla," Somaliland, 1902–04, **416-7**
Madras and Fort St. George—*Adlercron, Lt.-Col.*, King's Army, becomes C.-in-C., 1754, **72**; *Apperley, J.*, Gunner's Mate, promoted Engineer, 1747, **70**; *Army*, growth of, 1777, **147**; *Atkinson, Robt.*, Chief Gunner, 1695–1711, **27**; *Barker, Lieut. R.*, draws Scott's scheme, **74**; *Barwick, Capt.*, 1689, **26**; *Benfield, Lieut.*, Asst. Eng. and contractor, 1764, **79-80**—Contractor, 1775, **142**; *Benyon*, Governor, 1741,

65; *Bickerstaff, L.*, Ch. Eng., 1747—Resigned, 1751, **70**; *Black Town*, 1653, **7**—Defences of, 1698, **26**—Fortified, 1700–1707, **27**; *Braithwaite*, captures Mahé, 1779, **149**; *Brohier, John*, Engineer, 1751, **51**—In charge of works, 1756, **74**—Member of Committee of Works, **74**—Submits scheme for defences, **74**—Transferred to Calcutta, 1757, **74** (v. also "Bengal"); *Bulkley, Ed.*, doctor, paymaster and engineer, 1711, **28**; *Call, J.*, baronetcy, 1791, **81**—Death, 1801, **81**—Final scheme for defences, **80**—Ft. St. David, **70**—Recommended by Robins, **51**—Remodels defences, 1762, **79**—Resigns, 1770, **81**—Scheme for Ft. St. George, 1758, **76**—Siege of Pondicherry, 1760, **78-9**—Succeeds Brohier, 1757, **75**; *Campbell, Maj.-Gen. Sir Archibald*, Gov. and C.-in-C., 1786, **162**—Inspects Ft. St. George, 1773, **141** (see "Bengal," "Bombay," "Engrs., Royal," and "Engrs., Bengal"); *Captured* by French, 1746, **67**; *Charnock, Job*, arrives from Bengal, 1689, **25**; *Charter* granted, 1727, **63**; *Clarke, Ens.*, reproved, **62**; *Clive*, besieged in Arcot, 1757, **71**—Sails for Bengal, 1756, **75**—Seizes Arcot, 1751, **71** (see "Bengal," "Bombay"); *Cogan*, founder and first Agent, **5**; *Committee of Works*, 1754, **74**; *Coote, Sir Eyre*, arrives Madras, 1759, **78**—1778, **149**—Captures Pondicherry, 1761, **78-9**—Comdg. 84th Regt., **78**—Defeats French at Wandiwash, 1760, **78** (see "Coote"); *Cost* and progress of first work, **5**; *Cotsford, E.*, Practitioner Eng., 1758, **76**; *Daud Khan*, Rohilla Chieftain, blockades, 1702, **34**; *Day, Agent*, 1643, **5, 83**; *Delavaux, Alexander*, Ch. Eng. of all the Settlements, 1748, **49** (see "Fort St. David"); *Description* of, by Mrs. Kindersley, 1765, **82**—by Munro, 1780, **152-3**; *Dixon, Hugh*, Ch. Gunner, 1658–1677, **6, 9**; *Dixon, Wm.*, Ch. Gunner, 1677, **9**—first Ingenier, 1677, **11**—Retires, **23**; *Draper, Col.*, leads sortie, 1758, **77**; *Drunkenness* reproved, **62**; *Dupleix*, q.v.; *Elambore R.* diverted, **67**; *Elwick*, Governor, **63**; "*Emden*," attack by, 1914, **77**; *Extension* of residences, 1769, **82**; *First* fort laid out, 1640, **4**; *Forces* reorganized, 1759, **78**; **Fort St. George,** *completed*, 1783, **151**—Completion plan, **151**—*Defences*, Altered by French, 1746, **69**—As in 1653, **6**—As in 1724, **28-9**—As in 1741, **65**—Plans, 1749, **70**—Progress under Ross, **147**—Remodelled by Call, **79**—Repairs agst. Marathas, **64**—Ross's project, **141**, **142**—Scott's scheme, **72-4**—Sea face reconstructed, 1779, **149**—*Final works*, 1779–82, **149**—**151**—*History* since 1783, **151**—"*Fishing Bulwarke*," fall of, **9**—*Fort Square*,

INDEX.

built, 1715, **62**—*Inner Fort*, rebuilt, 1715, **62**—*St. Mary's Church*, **12, 22**—*Water Supply* insanitary, 1740, **64**; **Foxcroft**, Agent and Governor, **9**; *Fowle, Edward*, first military engineer recruited in England, 1684, **23**—Death, **24, 27, 35**; *French* attack, 1758, **76**—Naval action, 1690, **26**; Garrison, 1673, **10**; *Goulding, J.,* Gunner, **64**; *Greenhill, H.,* Agent, 1646, **6, 8**; *Gunner*, last, **69**; *Gunroom*, as workhouse, 1724, **63**; *Gyfford, Wm.,* Governor, 1681, **22**; *Haidar Ali,* raid by, 1767, **80**; *Harris, Lord,* C.-in-C., 1797, **171**; *Harrison,* Governor, 1713, **62**; *Higginson,* Governor, 1696, **26**; *Hollard, M. S.,* Engineer, 1742, **65**; *Hugonin, F.* (Swiss), Ch. Gunner, 1706, **61**; *Hugonin, G.* (Swiss), landed, 1696, **61**; *Ivie,* Agent, 1644, **5**; *Ivory, Robert,* Engineer and Master Gunner, 1680–85, **24, 26**; *Johnson, H.,* Supervisor, 1724, **62**; *Johnson, J.,* Ch. Eng., etc., 1719, dismissed, **62**; *Kindersley, Mrs.,* description of Madras, 1765, **82**; *Knipe, C.,* death, 1743, **46, 66**—Scheme for defences, 1743, **65–6**; *Langhorn, Wm.,* Agent and Governor, 1672, **9, 22**; *Lawrence, Stringer,* reorganizes military forces, 1748, **69**—Repulses Dupleix, 1746, **68**—Returns as C.-in-C., 1752, **72**—Superseded by Aldercron, 1754, **72**; *Macartney,* Governor, 1781, **159**; *Macrae, J.,* Governor, 1725, **63**; *Mahé,* captured by Braithwaite, 1779, **149**—Political effects of capture, **149**; *Makreeth, Th.,* Provisional Surveyor, 1690, **26**; *Marathas,* effects of invasion, 1740, **64**—Rise of Confederacy, **61**; *Maule, Capt. G.,* Acting Ch. Eng., 1778, **148**—Ch. Eng., 1790, **162**—Conducts siege of Bangalore, 1791, **163–4–5**—Engineer at Tanjore, **146**—Final works, Ft. St. George, **150**—Killed, Pondicherry, 1793, **170**—Madras Engineers, 1782, **161**; *Meddowes, Th.,* Engineer, 1690, **26**; *Medows, Maj.-Gen. W.,* Governor and C.-in-C., 1790, **162**—Seringapatam, 1792, **169**; *Military* forces reorganized, 1748, **69**; *Mint,* built, 1725, **63**; *Mitchell, Lieut. Alex.,* Engineer at Tanjore, **146**; *Montresor, Capt. H.,* Ch. Eng., 1770, **141**—Death, **147**; *Morris, Jno.,* Engineer, 1646, **6**; *Morse, N.,* Governor, 1744, **66**; *Munro, Maj.-Gen. Sir Hector* (q.v.), C.-in-C. 1778, **148**—Pondicherry captured, **148**; *Murray, D.,* Engineer and Gunner, 1724, **62, 63**; *Newcome, S.,* Surveyor of Works and inventor, **63**; *Outfit* for young officer, 1780, **140**; *Paymaster* as Engineer, 1700, **28**; *Percival, W.,* Ch. Gunner, 1740, **64, 66**; *Pigot, Lord,* Governor, **142**—Revolution agst., 1776, **147**; *Pitt,* Governor, 1700, **27**—Improves defences, **28**; *Pocock, Admiral,* relieves Madras, 1759, **77**; *Presidency* established, 1684, **25**; *Putsham, Capt.,* Engineer, 1690, **26**; *Relieved,* 1759, **77**; *Restored* by French on ransom, 1746, **67**; *Restored* to England, 1748, **68**; *Revolution* agst. Governor, 1776, **147**; *Robins, B.,* Eng.-Gen., 1750, **71** (see " Fort St. David "); *Ross, Capt.-Lieut. P.,* Ch. Eng., 1770, **81**—Career of, **141**—Completes Ft. St. George, 1783, **151**—Proceeds on leave, 1778, **148**—Progress of work under, **147**—Project, Ft. St. George, **141, 142**—Returns in 1782, **150**—Siege of Tanjore, 1773, **146**; *Rumbold, Sir T.,* Governor, 1778, **148, 154**; *Scott, Lt.-Col. C. F.,* Eng.-Gen., 1752—Schemes, Ft. St. George, **72–4**—To become C.-in-C., 1754, death, **72**; *Scudimore, Giles,* Ch. Gunner's Mate, **24**; *Seized* by Dupleix, 1746, **68**; *Select Committee* formed, 1755, **78**; *Siege,* 1758, described, **76–7**; *Site* granted, **4**; *Smith, Joseph,* Engineer from Bombay, 1744, **66**—Defence schemes and death, 1745, **67**—Last Gunner, **69**; *Spencer, J.,* Ch. Gunner, 1689, blown up, **26**; *Stevens, Major W.,* Ch. Eng., killed Pondicherry, 1778, **148**; *Streynsham-Master,* Governor, **22**; *Stuart, Col.,* garrison comdr., 1776, **147**; *Surveyors of Works* in charge of civil buildings, **63**; *Sutton, Lieut.,* **9**; *Swiss* soldiers recruited, 1751, **61**; *Tanjore,* siege of, 1773, **146**; *Uniforms* introduced, 1674, **12**; *Waters, J.,* Ch. Gunner, 1743, **66**; *Watson, Admiral,* **72, 75** (v. " Bengal," " Bombay "); *Way, T.,* Alderman and death, **63**—Supervisor, 1724, **62**—Surveyor of buildings, **61**; (*Von*) *Werlinhoffe, F. M.,* **35, 61**—Dismissed, 1700, **27**—Engineer and Miner-General, 1696, **27** (see also " Cuddalore " and " Fort St. David "); *Whitehill,* Governor, suspended by Hastings, 1780, **158**; *White Town,* **7**—British take refuge in, 1698, **26**; *Wilkins, Christopher,* Engineer, 1654, **6**; *Winter, Edward,* Agent, 1662, **8**; *Women* sent out from England, **8**; *Yale, Elihu,* Governor, 1687, **25**

Madrasapatam, site of Madras, **4**
Mahadji Sindhia, leader, Maratha Confederacy, **181**
Mahsuds, Wazirs, **422**
Malacca, captured, 1795, **171**
Malaria, deaths from, **44**; Robins' death from, 1751, **50**
Malay Peninsula, expedns. to, 1795, **171**—1831–32, **266**
Malavalli, battle, 1799, **174**
Malcolm, Gen., captures Asirghur, 1818, **248**; Defeats Holkar, 1817, **246**
Malegaon, fortress captured, 1818, **248**
Malakand Field Force, 1897, operations under Sir Bindon Blood, **446–8**; Use of massed artillery, **447**

Malakand Pass, captured, 1895, **441**; Severe night attacks, 1897, **444, 446**
Malta Expeditionary Force, composition, **401**
Mamund Valley, 1897—Bilot, small force benighted—Three **V.C.s** won—Blood's operations, **447-8**
Mangalore, captured, 1783, **197**; Defended by Campbell, **197**; Recaptured by Tipu, 1784, **161**
Manilla, captured, 1797, **171**
Manipuris, N.E. Frontier, **456**
Manners-Smith, Lieut. T., **V.C.**, Hunza-Nagar, 1891—Wins **V.C.**, **438**
Manning, Brig.-Gen. W. H., Somaliland, 1902–04, **416**
Marathas—*Army* and organization, **143-4**; *Bengal* invaded, 1742, **45**; *Bombay* threatened, **87**; *Central India* ravaged, **242**; *Character* and history of, **179**; *Confederacy* agst. Madras, 1780, **143**; *Fortress Engineers*, **144**; *Treaty* of Salbai, 1782, **158**; *Under* Sivaji, 1676, **22**
Maratha War, First—*Bor Ghat*, advance on Poona, **195-6**; *Causes* of, **180**; *Conclusion* and results, **196**; *Kanara-Karanja*, **180**; *Khandala*, **191**; *Outbreak*, **190**; *Salbai*, Treaty of, **196**; *Wargaum*, Convention of, 1779, **191**; *Wargaum*, disastrous results of, **143**
Maratha War, Second—*Argaon*, Battle of, **210**; *Burhanpur* captured, **210**; *Causes* of, **1803**, **205**; *Conclusion*, 1806, **222**; *Dig*, capture of, **218**; *Gawilgarh*, capture of, **211, 212**; *Laswari*, Battle of, 1803, **216**; *Opening campaign*, **205**
Maratha War, Third—*Armies*, great size of, **243**; *Asirghur* captured, 1818, **249**; *Concluded*, **249**; *Divisional comdrs.*, f.n., **243**; *Engineering Dept.*, ill-provided, **245**; *Hathras*, capture, 1817, **240-2**; *Hill Forts* described, **247**; *Holkar* defeated, 1817, **246**; *Kirkee*, battle, 1817, **244**; *Nagpur*, siege, 1817, **244**; *Opening* plans, **242**; *Pindaris* dispersed at Kotah, 1817, **244**—Plans agst., **243**; *Review* of operations, **249**
Mariaon, cantonment, Lucknow, **350**
Marley, Maj.-Gen. B., Nepal War, **234**; Deserts his comd., **239**
Marshall, Maj.-Gen., captures Hathras, 1817, **241**
Marshall, Lt.-Gen. Sir W. R., Mesopotamia, concluding operations, **489**; IIIrd Corps, **488**
Martaban captured, 1852, **309**
Martindell, Maj.-Gen. G., Nepal War, **235**
Massy, Brig.-Gen. W. D. G., defeated at Kila Kazi, 1879, **385,** f.n.
Masulipatam, Cogan, A., Agent, 1640, **4**; Dutch at, **4**; Failure of trade, **4**; Hippon, founder, 1611, **3**; Ivie, T., Agent, 1639, **4**; Seized by Mughals, 1689, **25**

Mathews, Gen., captures many forts, 1783, **197**; Poisoned as a prisoner, 1783, **197**; Surrenders at Bednore, **161, 197**
Matross, Asst. Gunner, **9**
Maude, Maj.-Gen. F. F., Peshawar Valley F.F., 1878, **375**
Maude, Lt.-Gen. Sir F. S., Mesopotamia, captures Baghdad—Death, **487-9**
Mauritius, captured, 1810, **232**
Mawbey, Col., Nepal War, Kalanga, **235**
Maxwell, Lt.-Col., Seringapatam, 1792, **169**
May, Mr. J., Lucknow Residency, f.n.s, **351, 354**
Mayo, Lieut. F., Sirmur Sappers, Kut, **485**
Mechanization, in B.S. & M., **545**—M.S. & M., **540**
Medals, for Frontier service, **445**; N.W. Frontier, 1897-98, received by 90 R.E. officers, **445**
Mehidpur, battle, 1817, **246**
Meiklejohn, Brig.-Gen. W. H., Malakand F.F., **447**
Mekran Coast, Bo.S. & M. employed—1898, foot-slogging, **412**—1901, agst. outlaws, **412**—1910 and 1911, f.n., **417**
Melliss, Maj.-Gen. C. J., **V.C.**, Mesopotamia, wins Battle of Shaiba, **484**
Mesopotamia (see " Great War ")
Mesopotamia, 1920, Arab insurrection, **518-9**; British Army, composition of, **518**; first line mule loads mistaken for guns, **520**
Mess, R.E. H.Q., Chinese throne presented to, f.n., **315**
Metcalfe, Sir Ch., Resident, Delhi, 1825, **261**
Miani, Sind campaign, **287**
Michel, Maj.-Gen. Sir John, Second China War, **313**
Middleton, sea captain, **1**
Military Engineer, first-named British, **6**
Military Engineer Services—*Accounting* by Mily. Accts. Dept., **532**; *Chief Engineers*, **532-3**; *Commander, R.E., Asst. and duties*, **531**; *Dy. E.-in-C.* apptd., 1923, **533**; *Differences* in systems, England and India, **532**; *D.G.* of *M.W.* and *D.* of *W.*, **533**; *Engineer-in-Chief*, created, 1923, and duties, **532-3**; *Garrison* Engineers and Assts., **531**; *Growth* of annual budget, **535**; *Higher* organization, changes in, **533**; *Inspector* of S. & M. and Pioneers becomes Brigadier, R.E., **533**; *Officers*, work and qualifications, **533**; *Organization* and duties, **531-2**; *Sub-Divisional* officers, charges and recruitment, **531-2**; *Works* executed up to 1914, **534**—During Great War and to 1923, **534-5**—Since 1923, **535**
Military forces found necessary, **3**
Military policy, change from defence to attack, **138**

Military Works Department, becomes M.W. Services, 1899—Becomes Mily. Engineer Services, 1923—Undertakes all military works, 1889, **419** (v. also " P.W. Department ")

Milne, Capt., comds. Pioneers, First Burma War, **253**

Miners and Pioneers, proposals for Corps of, 1782, **198** (v. also " Pioneers ")

Mining, Bhurtpore, 1825–6, **264, 265**; Indian methods of, **203**; Lucknow Residency, **352, 354**

Minto, Lord, Gov.-Gen., **233**

Mir Alam, comds. Hyderabad army, 1799, **172**

Miranpur Katra, battle, 1774, **179**

Miranzai, 1891, **431–3**

Miris, tribe, N.E. Frontier, **456**

Mir Jumla, blockades St. Thomé, **6**; First Nawab of Carnatic, **6**

Mirpur, or Eastern Sind, **287**

Mirza Mahomed (Siraj-ud-Daula) (v. " Bengal ")

Mishmi Mission, 1911–12, enters China, **474**; Operations, **471–3**; Origin of names, survey work, **474**; Suspension bridges of bamboos, **473**

Mishmis, tribe, N.E. Frontier, **456**; Visited, 1912–13, by Bo.S. & M., f.n., **474**

Moberley, Brig.-Gen. F. J., help acknowledged, **x**

Mohmand Field Force, 1897, co-operation with Malakand F.F.—General operations—Shabkadr attacked, **448**

Mohmands, position, **422**

Mohmands, 1908, Engineer work, **455**; Outline of operations, **455**; Willcocks' second three weeks' war, **454**

Momaty Men, explained, **156**

Monson, Col., under Lake, 1804, disastrous retreat, **217**

Montauban, Gen., French Comdr., Second China War, **314**

Moorhouse, Lieut. J. (Madras Arty.), scheme for regular Pioneers, 1780, **156**

Moplah Rebellion, description of country and people, **521**; Engineer work, **522–3**

Mornington, Earl of, Gov.-Gen., 1798, **172**

Morrison, Brig.-Gen. J. W., Arakan Colm., 1825, **257**

Moti Mahal Palace, Lucknow, **350**

Mountain Battery, No. 4 (Hazara)—Hunza-Nagar, 1891, **435** et seq.

Mud fortresses, description of, **202–3**

Mudki, Battle of, 1845, **292–3**

Mud War, **202**

Mughals, Conjeveram occupied, 1687, **25**; Factories captured, 1689, **25**; Golconda besieged, 1685, **25**; St. Thomé captured, 1688, **26**; War agst., 1687, **21**

Muhammad Ali, Nawab of Carnatic, **142, 154**

Muhammad Jan, Afghan General, 1879, **385**

Mulcaster, Brig.-Gen., Duar Field Force, **458**

Mulla Powinda, attacks British, Waziristan, 1894, **439**

Mulraj, Diwan of Multan, murders British officers—Proclaims religious war, 1848, **299**

Multan—Assaulted, 1849, **302**; B.S. & M. present, **300**; Khuni Burj, attack of, **300–1**; Siege and capture of, **300–2**; Siege raised, **301**; Siege reopened, **301**; Siege train, move of, **300**

Munro, Gen. Sir Charles, C.-in-C., India, 1916–21, **504**

Munro, Sir Hector, captures Negapatam, 1781, **160**; Failure, First Mysore War, **155**; Opening dispositions, **154** (see " Madras ")

Munro, Sir Thomas, Gov. and C.-in-C., Madras, 1824, **253**

Murray, Col., Second Maratha War, 1803—In Gujerat, **206**

Murray, Gen. Sir Archibald, Egyptian E.F., **494**

Murree water supply, **534**

Museum, R.E., exhibits in, f.n., **326**

Mussoorie, site acquired, **240**

Mutiny—Army, distribution and strength, f.n., **316**; Badli-ki-Serai, victory, **323**; Bahadur Shah, Emperor, **318**; B.S. & M., mutiny of, **320**; British troops diverted from China, **322, 355**; Causes of, **316**; Cawnpore, tragedy at, **348**; Columns from Ambala and Meerut, junction, **323**; Engineers, services of, **337**; Ghaziuddin-Nagar, victory, **323**; Malwa Campaign, 1857, **362–3**; Opening telegram, **316**; Oudh, sweeping-up operations, **362**; Outbreak, general, **316**—Cawnpore, **348**—Delhi, **318**—Malwa, **317**—Meerut, **317–8**—N.W. Provinces, **317**—Punjab, **317**—Rajputana, **317**; Results of, to Govt. of India, **368**; Roorkee, events at, **319–21, 322**; Three phases of, **316, 317**

Mutiny—Central India Campaign—Dhar captured, **363**; Gwalior captured, **366**; Jhansi captured, **364–5**; Kalpi captured, **366**; Man Singh captured, **366**; Napier comds. 2nd Bde., **366**—Takes Ch. Comd., **366**—Victory at Jaura Alipur, **366**; Operations, **362–66**; Plan of campaign, **363–4**; Punch, victory, **365**; Rahatgarh captured, **364**; Saugor F.F., **363**; Tantia Topi defeated, Betwa R., **364**; Terrific heat, **365**

Mutiny—Delhi—Advance on, **323**; Artillery attack, **339, 340**; Assault, Sept. 14th, **341** et seq.—Orders for, **341**—Success of, **345, 346**; Attempts to destroy boat bridge, **334**; Baird Smith becomes Ch. Eng., **331**; Baird Smith-Taylor " controversy," **335**; Barnard, Gen., death of, **331**; Batteries named after Engineers, f.n., **327**; Battery No. 1, construction of, **338**—No. 2, construction of, **339**; British

INDEX.

Force, original, **326**; *British* N.C.O.s, B.S. & M., casualties, **334**—Good work of, **333**; *Custom House*, **325**; *Defences of city*, **323-4**; *Engineer* Bde., **326**; *Engineer* Mess, **330**; *Engineer* reinforcements, **332**; *Engineers*, exhaustion of, **346**—Plan for assault in June, **328**—Services of, **331**, f.n.—Spirit of, **327**; *Expense Magazine*, blown up by Willoughby, **318**—Saved by Renny and Thackeray, **345**; *Gurkhas* hold Hindu Rao's house, **324**; *House-to-house* advance, **346**; *Kashmir Gate*, blowing-in of, awards for, **344**—Explosion party, **342** *et seq.*—Memorial at, **343**; *King's Palace* occupied, **346**; *Kishanganj*, **325**; *Kudsia Bagh*, **325**; *Laughton* as Ch. Eng., **325**; *Ludlow Castle*, **325**—Occupied by enemy, **333**; *Metcalfe House*, **325**—Occupied, **327**; *Mori Bastion* attacked by No. 1 Battery, **339**; *Najafgarh Jhil*, **325**; *Nicholson* arrives, **334**—At assault, **341**—Mortally wounded, **344-5**—Victory, Najafgarh, **336**; *Plans* for bombardment and assault, **337**; *Reconnaissance* of breaches, **340-1**; *Reed* succeeds Barnard, **332**; *Ridge*, attacks on, **327**—Flagstaff Tower, **325**—Hindu Rao's house, **324**—Mosque, **325**—Observatory, **325**—Occupied by British, **323**—Position consolidated, **332**—Position, description of, **324-5**—Position strengthened, **328**; *Sabzi Mandi*, **325**; *Siege*, cost of, **346**; *Siege* train, arrival of, **336**—Demanded **333**; *Strengths*, opposing forces, July, **331**; *Taylor's* plan for assault, July, **329**—Reconnaissances for battery sites, **336, 337**; *Wilson* succeeds Reed, **333**

Mutiny — **Lucknow** — *Bridging* Ganges, 1857, **349**—Gumti, 1858, **361**; *City*, capture of, completed, 1858, **361**—Description of, **350**; *Defeat* at Chinhut, **351**; *Engineers*, capture of city, 1858, **360**—Garrison, **351**—Havelock's force, **349**—Relief Force, **355**; *Fatal* explosion, 1858, **362**; *Lawrence's* plans in operation, **350**; *Operations*, capture of city, 1858, **359-61**—Havelock's force, **348-9**—Relief Force, **355-7**; *Outram* at Alam Bagh, **357**; *Rebels'* defence works, 1858, **359**; *Residency*, description of position, **350**—Evacuation of, **357**—Havelock's relief, **353**—Mining, **352, 354**—Occupied, **351**—Organization of defence, **351-2**—Original garrison, **351**; *Sikander Bagh*, slaughter at, **356**

Mysore War, First—*Opening* of, 1780, **143, 154**; Pollilur, disaster, **155**

Mysore War, Second—*Operations*, **159-61**; Porto Novo, 1781, **159**; Sholinghur, 1781, **159**

Mysore War, Third—*Declaration*, 1790, **162**; *End* of, 1792, **170**; *Scheme* of operations, **163**; *Seringapatam*, attacked, 1792, **168** *et seq.*—Capture of *pettah*, **169**—*Coup de main* fails, **169**—Description of, **168**—Ross's plan of attack, **169**—Tipu capitulates, **170**

Mysore War, Fourth—*Declared*, 1798, **172**; *Description* of march, **172**; *Seringapatam*, assault of, 1799, **177**—Booty captured, **178**—Organization of Engineers, **176**—Siege, **176-8**; *Terms of treaty*, **178**

N

Nadir Khan, Afghan C.-in-C., 1919, **509**; King of Afghanistan, f.n., **509**
Nagar, State, **422**
Nagas, tribe, N.E. Frontier, **456**
Nagpur, siege of, 1817, **244**
Naini Tal, site acquired, **240**
Nalagarh captured, 1814, **236**
Names, spelling of, **x**
Nana Farnavis, death, 1800, **204**; Minister, Poona, **190**; Successful policy, **204**
Nana Sahib, Bithur, Raja of, 1857, **347**; Cawnpore, **347**; Fate unknown, **366**
Nandidroog, captured, 1791—Description of, **166**
Napadi, battle, 1825, **259**
Napier, Sir Charles, description of, 1842, **285**; Military dictator, Sind, **285**; Ordered to supersede Gough, 1849, **305**
Narwaul, fight, 1857, **347**
Narungombe, bloody battle, E. Africa, 1917, **498** and f.n.
Nawanagar, surrenders, 1812, **225**
Negapatam, Dutch factory, **4**; Captured 1781, destroyed 1783, **160**
Neill, Col., Cawnpore, 1857, **348**; Killed, Lucknow, **353**
Nepal War—*Amar Singh* surrenders, 1815, **238**; *Conclusion* of, 1816, **240**; *Declaration* of war, 1814, **234**; *End* of first phase, **240**; *Failure* of commanders, **239**; *Gurkha* attacks, **238**; *Kalanga*, fighting at, **235**; *Katmandu*, advance on, **240**; *Malaon*, Amar Singh at, **238, 239**—Capture of, **238**; *Nature* of war, 1814, **234**; *Ochterlony* captures Nalagarh, **236**; *Plan* of campaign, **234**; *Ramgarh*, capture of, 1815, **238**; *Sagauli*, Treaty of, **240**; *Second* phase, 1816, **240**
Neuve Chapelle (see " Great War, France ")
New Delhi, cantonment, **534**
Nicholson, John—*Appearance* and character, **335**; *Assault* of Delhi, **341, 344, 345**; *Expedn. v.* Umarzai Waziris, 1852, **423**; *Mortally* wounded, **345**; Punjab Govt., 1848, **299**; *Reaches* Delhi, **334**; *Relations* with Wilson, **336**; *Routs* enemy at Najafgarh, **336**
Nixon, Gen. Sir John, C.-in-C., Mesopotamia, **484**; Superseded by Lake, f.n., **486**
Northbrook, Lord, Viceroy, **373**

N.E. Frontier—*Abor Expedn.*, 1911–12, *q.v.*; *Bhutan*, 1864–66, *q.v.*; *Chin-Lushai*, 1888–89, *q.v.*; *Daflas*, 1874, *q.v.*; *Description* of terrain and countries, **456**; Lack of railway joining Burma and Assam, **456**; List of expedns. and Sappers employed, f.n., **457**; *Mishmi Mission*, 1911–12, *q.v.*; *Tibet Mission*, 1903–04, *q.v.*

N.W. Frontier—*Adam Khel* Afridis, expedn., 1850—No S. & M. employed, **423**; *Afridis*, 1930, *q.v.*; *Ambela*, 1863, *q.v.*; *Armament* of tribes before and after 1890, **425**; *Bazar Valley*, 1908, *q.v.*; *Black Mountain*, 1888, *q.v.*; *Black Mountain Expedn.*, 1853—No S. & M. employed, **423**; *Buner*, 1897–98, *q.v.*; *Chitral*, 1895, *q.v.*; *Engineers*, normal work of, **423**; *Expedns.*, 1849–88, showing S. & M. employed, f.n., **424**; *Expedns.*, 1888–97, enumerated, **412**; *Great War*, peaceable during, **455** (see also " Great War, N.W. Frontier "); *Hazara*, 1891, *q.v.*; *Hindustani Fanatics*, *q.v.*; *Hunza-Nagar*, 1891, *q.v.*; *Isazai*, 1892, *q.v.*; *Kurram Valley*, 1897–98, *q.v.*; *Mamund Valley*, 1897–98, *q.v.*, *Miranzai*, 1891, *q.v.*; *Mohmand F.F.*, 1897–98, *q.v.*; *Mohmands*, 1908, *q.v.*; *Orakzais*, expedns., 1855 and 1868–69—No S. & M. employed, **423**; *S. & M.*, absence from earlier expedns., **423, 424**—Employment after 1890, **425**; Second phase of warfare—Methods since 1890, **429**; *Shiranis* Expedn., 1853—No S. & M. employed, **423**; *Swat Valley*, 1897–98, *q.v.*; *Tirah*, 1897–98, *q.v.*; *Tochi Valley*, 1897, Madda Khels—Towers and villages destroyed, **445**; *Towers*, method of destruction, **432, 454**; *Tribes* and clans, **421, 422**; *Umarzai* Waziris, Expedn., 1852—No S. & M. employed, **423**; *Waziristan*, *q.v.*; *Zakka Khels*, 1908, *q.v.*; *Zhob Valley*, 1890, *q.v.*

N.W. Frontier, 1897-98—*Engineers* employed—Largest number since Mutiny, **445**; *General* rising, *jihad* declared, **444** *et seq.*; *Khaibar Pass* Forts, captured by Afridis—Pass closed, **449**; *Medal*, 90 R.E. officers receive, **445** (see also " N.W. Frontier ")

Nott, Gen. Sir Wm., Bde. Comdr., Army of Indus, 1838, **268**; Complains of Politicals, **267**; Holds Kandahar, 1842, **276**; " Retreat " via Kabul, **279**

Nuthall, Lieut., Asst. Eng., Delhi, f.n., **331**

Nuttall, Brig.-Gen., Maiwand, 1880, **389**

O

Oakes, Capt., Asst. Eng., Lucknow, f.n., **354**

Ochterlony, Maj.-Gen. Sir David, British Resident, Delhi, 1804, **217**; Censured and resigns, 1825, **261**; Comds. 1st. Div., Nepal War, **234**; Death, **261**

O'Connor, Capt., R.A., Palla stormed, Tibet, **466–7**

Old Fort William (see " Bengal ")

103rd Foot, origins, **17**

Ootradroog, captured, 1791, **168**

Opium War, First China War, **279**

Orakzais, expedns. agst., **423**; position of, **422**

Osman Digna, Sudan, 1884–85, **404**

" Otter " defined, f.n., **472**

Oudh, buffer State, 1765, **119**; King of, enmity, 1857, **347**

Outlaw, Capt., 26th M.N.I. and M.S. & M., f.n., **298**

Outram, Maj.-Gen. Sir James, C.-in-C., Persia Expedn., 1857, **312** and f.n.; Holds Alam Bagh, 1857–58, **357**; Joins Havelock, Sept., 1857, **349**

Oxenden, Sir George (see " Surat ")

P

Paget, Sir E., C.-in-C., 1824, advice on Burma War, **251**

Paghamyu, Battle of, 1826, **259**

Pagoda Point, capture of, 1824, **255**

Panalla stormed, 1844, **288**

Panipat, Battle of, 1761, **179**

Panniar, Battle of, 1843, **289**

Park, Engineers', defined, **170**

" Particular Persons," **62**

Pathans, characteristics of, **421**; Ravage Central India, **242**

Pathans, 40th, Tibet Mission, **467**

Pay, scales of, 1665, **11**

Paymaster as Engineer, **28, 36**

Pearce, Col., joins Coote, **159**; March from Bengal to Madras, 1781, **158**

Peel, Capt. Sir Wm., R.N., in Mutiny, **355**

Pegu, Second Burma War, **310**

Perak, Expedn. to, **400–1**

Perambakkam, fight at, First Mysore War, **155**

Perron, defeated at Aligarh, **214**; French adventurer under Sindhia, **205**

Persia, 1856–57, Ahwaz reached—Khush-Ab, victory at—Muhammerah occupied, **312-3**; Shatt-al-Arab, f.n., **312**

Persians, Herat besieged by, 1837, **267**

Phayre, Sir Arthur, Ch. Commissioner, British Burma, 1862, **405**

Phayre, Maj.-Gen. Sir R., Quetta-Kandahar Colm., 1880, **392**

Philippine Is., Expedn. to, 1797, **171**

Photographic Section, Abyssinia, 1867–8, **399**

Pindaris, methods of, **242**; Origin of, **223**; Ravage Central India, **242**; Third Maratha War, **243** *et seq.*

Pioneer Battalions, Indian Army—*Abolition*, 1932—Amalgamation with S. & M., **529–52**; *Disposal* of personnel, **553**; *Modifications*, 1933, **553**, f.n.; *Reasons* for abolition, **529, 551**;

INDEX. 587

Retention in I.A. after Great War, **551**; *Strength*, after Great War, **528, 551**; *23rd Sikh Pioneers*, Tibet Mission, 1904, **463**; *32nd Sikh Pioneers*, bridging Helmand R., 1879, **381**—Tibet Mission, 1904, **463**; *61st Pioneers*, E. Africa, **501**

Pioneers, Bengal—*Become* Corps of Pioneers and Sappers, 1808, **224**; *Become* Sappers and Miners, 1819, **226**; *Capture* of Agra, **216**—Bhurtpore, 1826, **261**—Dehra Dun, **235**—Dig, 1804, **218**—Hathras, 1817, **241**-2; *Company* of Miners formed, 1808, **224**; *Establishment*, 1809, **225**; *Incorporated* with S. & M., 1834, **229, 282**; *Increase* in 1808, **224**; *Officered* by Infantry, **225**; *Raised* at Cawnpore, 1803, **201**; *Reappearance*, 1847, **282**; *Uniform*, 1809, **225**; *With* Arakan Colm., 1825, **258**—Cachar Colm., 1825, **257**

Pioneers, Bombay—" *Battalion* of Bombay Pioneers," 1822, **227**; *Bor Ghat*, 1781, **195**; *Capture* of Ahmadabad, **192**—Gawilgarh, f.n., **212**—Mangalore, **197**; *Changes* in, 1789-97, **198**; *Duties* laid down, 1812, **225**; *Establishment*, 1809-12, **225**; *Expansions*, 1819-22, **227**; *Incorporated* with S. & M. as Corps, 1830, **230**; *Kirkee* and Poona, 1817, **244**; *Martial* spirit, 1812, **225**; *Officered* by Infantry, 1812, **225**; *Operations* agst. Hill Forts, 1818, **247**; *Persian* Gulf, 1819, **250**; *Pioneer Lascars*, formed Bombay, 1777, **190**; *Proposed* improvements, 1781, **196**

Pioneers, European, Seringapatam, 1792, **170**—1799, **176**; Temporary, Siege of Bangalore, 1791, **163**

Pioneers, General, first reference to, **31**; History of, in British Army, **551**; Introduction of, **138**; Reasons for abolition, *circa* 1834, **231**; Status considered, 1782, **196**

Pioneers, Madras—*Anomalous* administration, **157**; *Assaye*, 1803, **210**; *Baptism* of fire, 1781, **159**; *Capture* of Bangalore, 1791, **163**—Gawilgarh, **212**—Nandidroog, **166**—Negapatam, **160**—Savandroog, **166, 168**—Stockades, Pagoda Point, **255**; *Changes*, 1803, **200**; *Corps*, strength of, 1793, **170** and f.n.; *De Havilland's* report, **228**; *Early* history, f.n., **78**; *Effect* of Second Mysore War, **161**; *Establishment*, 1777, **147**—1799, **171**—1821, **227**; *Expedn.* to Ceylon, 1795, **171**; *1st Bn.*, First Burma War, **253**; *1st Bn.* becomes Madras S. & M., 1831, **229**; *First* companies raised, 1759, **77**; *Formation*, two Cos., establishment and pay, 1780, **156**; *Increase* to five Cos., 1791, **163**—ten Cos., 1799, **171** and f.n.; *Instruction* of, by Engineers, under fire, **158**; *Introduction* of, **138**; *Java* Expedn., 1811, **232**; *Letter* about, 1836, **230**;

Mauritius and Réunion, 1810, **232**; *Mehidpur*, 1817, **244**; *Mentioned* in despatches, 1799, **178**; *Officered* by Infantry, 1781, **159**; *Operations* agst. Hill Forts, 1818, **247**; *Organization*, 1810-18, **225** and f.n.; *Regular* companies formed, 1780, **156**; *Scheme* for conversion, 1823, **229**; *2nd Bn.* absorbed into S. & M., 1834, **229**; *2nd Bn.* at Koppaldroog, 1819, **250**; *Seringapatam*, 1792, **168, 170**—1799, **173**; *Under* Agnew, 1800, **199**—Wellesley, 1800, **199**; *With* Arakan Colm., 1825, **258**

Pioneers, Miscellaneous—Delhi Corps, at Delhi, 1857, **326, 332**—at Lucknow, capture, **360**; Indian, Palestine, 1918, **495**, f.n.; Magh, with Arakan Colm., 1825, **258**; Semi-civil Corps, with Pollock, 1842, **278**

Pirates, operations agst., **85**; Stronghold (Gheria) destroyed, 1756, **92**

Plantain, J., pirate, **85**

Poligars, expedn. agst., 1800, **199**

Political events, 1773-80, **142**-3

Pollilur, battles, 1780 and 1781, **155, 159**

Pollock, Maj.-Gen. Sir G., First Afghan War, **278**

Pollock Medal, f.n., **278**

Pondicherry—*Besieged* by Boscawen, 1748, **70**—British, 1746, **68**; *Captured* by British, 1760, **78-9**—1778, **148**—1793, **170**; *Eyre Coote* at, 1781, **158**; *Fortifications* destroyed, 1761, **79**—1779, **149**—1794, **171**; *Resists* Marathas, **65**

Pontoons (see " Bridging Train ")

Poona, First Maratha War, **191**

Popham, Capt. W., captures Gohad, Gwalior and Lahar, 1780, **193**

Port Louis (Mauritius), captured, 1810, **232**

Porto Novo, Battle of, 1781, **159**; Sacked by Haidar Ali, 1780, **154**

Portuguese—Bassein, granted, **13**; Bengal, pioneers in, 1530, **30**; General of the North and Viceroy of Goa, **85**; Salsette attacked by Marathas, 1737, **87**; Settled in India, 16th century, **1**

Pottinger, Eldred, Political, First Afghan War, **268**

Primrose, Lt.-Gen. M., Kandahar, 1880, **388, 390**; Kandahar Force, 1878, **375**

Pringle, Capt. J., comds. " Guides," First Mysore War, **156**

Pritzler, Gen., captures Koppaldroog, 1819, **250**; Captures Singhur, 1818, **247**

Prole, Maj.-Gen. G., under Goddard, 1780, **192**; Wounded, **193**

Public Works Department, description of, 1846, **298**; Military Works Branch, 1871, **419**; Under civil control, 1851, **419**

Pulicat, Dutch at, **4**

Punjab, annexation of, 1849, **307**; State of, between First and Second Sikh Wars, **299**

Punjab Frontier Force, f.n., **395**

INDEX.

Punjab, Irregular Force, later P.F.F.—Contained no S. & M., **424**
Purandhar, Treaty of, 1775, **182**

Q

Quartermaster-General, views on Engrs., 1821, **228**
Quetta, acquired, 1876, **373**; First Afghan War, **270**

R

Radcliffe, Col. F. W., Dorsets, Moplah Rebellion, **522**
Raghoji Bhonsla, captures Trichinopoly, 1741, **64**; Father of Janoji, **45**
Raghuba, allied with British, **143**; First Maratha War, **180** et seq.
Rahatgarh, captured, 1858, **364**
Railway Companies, Bo.S. & M., **548-9**
Railways—*Aden*, Great War, **492**; *E. Africa*, importance of, in, **501-2**; *Egypt*, Suakin to Berber, started and abandoned, 1885, **404**; *India*, extensions to Rawalpindi, Kohat, Peshawar, Jamrud, 1880, **388**—First lines opened, f.n., **297**—In 1878, **374**—Khaibar Pass, construction, 1919-24, **511** and f.n.—None joining Assam and Burma, **456**—Sind-Peshin, **511**, f.n.—Strategic extensions by Curzon, **452**—Sukkur to Sibi and Quetta, **387** and f.n.
Rajamandroog, stormed, 1782, **197**
Ramgarh, operations agst., Nepal War, **237**
Ramnagar, Cavalry action, 1848, **303**
Rampura, captured, 1804, **217**
Ramsay, Brig.-Gen. J., 3rd Bde., Mohmands, 1908, **454**
Randle, Dr. H. N., help acknowledged, **x**
Rangoon, attacked by Burmese, 1824, **256**; Captured, 1824, **253, 254**—1852, **309**
Ranikhet, site acquired, **240**
Ranjit Singh, Raja of Bhurtpore, treaty with, 1805, **220**
Ranjit Singh, Sikh despot, death, 1839, **291**; Treaty with, 1838, **267**
Ras-al-Khaima, captured, 1819, f.n., **250**
Razmak, fortified camp, Waziristan, **515**; Occupied permanently, 1923, **516**
Reed, Maj.-Gen. T., comds. at Delhi, 1857, **332**; Gives up comd., **333**
Reid, Col., assault of Delhi, **341**; Comdt., Goorkhas, Deyrah, 1857, **319**
Renny, Major, V.C., R.A., wins V.C., Delhi, 1857, **345**
Reorganizations of army (see "Army in India")
Réunion, Bourbon occupied, 1810, **231**
Reynolds, Lt.-Gen. C.—*Bassein*, 1780, **194**; *Career*, **192**; *Malabar*, 1783, **198**; *Surveyor-General of India*, **196**; *Under* Goddard, 1780, **192**; *Wounded*, Dabhoi, **192**—Twice, 1781, **198**

Riccard, Andrew, Director, E.I.C., **18**; Governor, E.I.C., **21**
Rimington, Lt.-Gen. M. F., comds. Ind. Cav. Corps, **477**
Risalpur, cantonment constructed, **534**
Roberts, Gen. Sir Abraham, Bde. Comdr., Army of Indus, 1838, **268**; Father of F.M. Earl Roberts, f.n., **268**
Roberts, F.M. Earl—*Comds.* Kabul F.F., 1879, **383** et seq.—Kurram Valley Colm., 1878, **374**; *Death*, **479**; *Invested* in Sherpur Cants., 1879, **335**; *March*, Kabul-Kandahar, 1880, **391**—Absence of S. & M., **424**; *Victory* at Paiwar Kotal, **379**; *Visits* Burma, Third Burma War, **409**—Indian Corps, France, 1914, **479**
Robertson, Surg.-Maj. G. S., defence of Chitral, **440**
Robinson, John, Director, E.I.C., **18**
Rockets used by Haidar Ali, **146**
Rodriguez seized, 1809, **231**
Roe, Sir Thomas, succeeds to Surat, 1615, **2**
Rohilla War, First, 1774, **179**—Second, 1794, **180**
Roorkee, becomes H.Q., B.S. & M., 1854, **227** (see also "Mutiny")
"Roorkee Garrison Gazette," produced, 1857, **322**
Roote, Jeremy, first named British military engineer, **6**; Sent to help Mir Jumla, **6**
Rose, Maj.-Gen. Sir Hugh, C.-in-C., Bombay, **366**; Central India F.F., 1858, **363** et seq.; Sunstroke at Punch, **365**
Rosetta, Egyptian Expedn., 1801, **200**
Ross, Maj.-Gen. J., comds. Malta E.F., 1878, **401**—Perak Expedn., 1875, **401**
Royal Air Force, works for, done by M.E.S., **535**
Rugby football, played by Burmese, **310**
Russia, envoy at Kabul, **373**; Herat besieged, 1837, **267**; War with Turkey, 1877, **373**

S

Sadras, Dutch factory, **4**
Sadulapur, action of, 1848, **304**
St. Lubin, French adventurer, 1777, **190**
St. Thomé—*Portuguese* settlement, **4**; *Blockaded* by Mir Jumla, **6**; *Captured* by Dutch, 1674, **10**—French, 1672, **10**—Golconda, 1662, **10**—Mughals, 1688, **26**; *Defences* demolished 1697, **26**
Salberg, Lieut. F. J., I.A.R.O., Aden, **491**
Sale, Maj.-Gen. R. H., Army of Indus, 1838, **268**; Defence of Jalalabad, **277-8**; Killed at Mudki, 1845, f.n., **293**; Occupies Gandamak, 1841, **275**; Retreats to Jalalabad, 1841, **276**
Salmon, Thomas, author, 1724, **28**
Salsette, First Maratha War, **180**; Secured to British, 1783, **198**
Sandeman, Sir Robert, Ch. Commissioner Baluchistan, **430**

INDEX. 589

Sappers and Miners—*Battalion* organization abolished, 1885, **394**; *British N.C.O.s*, efficiency of, **299**; *Company* becomes the Engineer unit, 1885, **394**; *Equipment* revised, 1885, **394**; *Infantry* officers cease to be employed, **371**; *Infantry* officers, employed in, 1846, **298**; *Introduction* of, **138**; *Precedence* of Corps, 1897, **418**; *Renaming* of Corps, 1903 and after, **418-9**; *Renaming* of men, 1885, **394**; *Renumbering* of companies, 1903, **418**; *Reorganization* of 1885, **372, 393, 394, 395**; *Reorganization*, 1932, on abolition of Pioneers, **552, 553**; *Under C.R.E.* on service, 1882, **393**—Q.M.G. on service, Second Afghan War, **392**

Sappers and Miners, Bengal—*Abdulla Khan*, Hunza-Nagar—Wins I.O.M., **437-8**; *Abor*, 1911-12, **471-2**; *Aden*, 1915-17, **491**; **Afghan War, First**—Army of Indus, 1838, **268**; *Kalat-i-Ghilzai*, 1842, **276**; *Pollock's Force*, 1842, **278**; **Afghan War, Second**—Bridging of Helmand R., **381**; Bright's Colm., 1879, **383**; Jagdalak, defence of, 1879, **386**; Kabul, 1879, **385**—1880, **387**—L.-of-C., 1879, **385**; Kandahar Force, 1879, **375**; Kandahar to Kabul march, **388**; Khojak Pass, 1879, f.n., **382**; Peshawar Force, 1878, **375**; Road work, 1880, **387**; Roberts' Colm., 1879, **383**; Shutar Gardan Pass, 1879, **384**; Stewart's Colm., 1879, **384**; **Afghan War, Third**—Six Field Cos. and Field Troop, **507** and f.n.; *Ajudhia Pershad Pathak*, Sepoy—Kashmir Gate, 1857, **343**; *Ambela*, 1863, **425**; *Artificers*, lack of, 1880, f.n., **392**; *Asan Singh*, Sepoy—Gallantry at Multan, **302**; *Balloon Section*, **541-2**; *Barga Singh*, Jemadar, gallantry at Bhurtpore, 1826, **264**; *Become* "Sappers and Pioneers," 1847-51, **282, 283**; *Bhurtpore*, 1826, **261-6**; *Bhutan*, 1864-66, **458-9**; *Bilot*, force benighted, **447**; *Bis Ram*, Jemadar, Kashmir Gate, 1857, **343**; *Black Mountain*, 1888, **429**; *Buner F.F.*, 1898, **449**; *Burgess, Corpl.*, killed, Kashmir Gate, 1857, **342** *et seq.*; *Burma War, Third*, **407** *et seq.*; *Carmichael, Serjt.*, killed, Kashmir Gate, 1857, **342** *et seq.*; *Chagatta*, Havildar, gallantry, France, 1915, **479** —Storming of Palla, Tibet, **467**; *Changes* in organization, f.n., **229**—1838-51, **282-3**—1885, **393-5**—1900-14, **541-3**—1914-18, **543-4**, 1932, **552, 553**; *Changes* in title, 1847-51, f.n., **229, 283**—1903 and after, **418, 541**; *China*, 1900, **413**; *Chin-Lushais*, 1889, **460**; *Chitral*, 1895, **440**; **Companies**—"Service" become "Field," **419**—1857, **318** *et seq.*—1900, **541**—1907, **542**; 1st Co. with Buffs at Paimar, 1843, **290**; 4th Co., record of, 3 V.C., and 8 I.O.M., **438** and f.n.; 7th and 8th Cos. formed from Broadfoot's Sappers, 1843, **282**; 9th and 10th Cos. formed, 1844, **282, 290**; *Comparative* strengths, 1914 and 1918, **476, 543-4**; *Debi Singh*, Subadar, explosion party, Ghazni, 1839, **272**; *Derajat F.F.*, 1917, **503**; *Equipment*, post-war, **544-5**; *Establishment*, 1819, **226**—1885, **394**; *Field Troop*, Secunderabad Cav. Bde., **476**, f.n.; *First Commandant*, **226**; *Formed*, 1819, Allahabad, **225**; *Frontier* service, special suitability for, **396**; **Great War**—Expansion during, **476, 543-4**; Festubert, "The Orchard," 1914, **479**; Meerut Div., 1914, **476**; Neuve Chapelle, **478-9** (see also "Mesopotamia" and "Palestine"); *Gwalior Campaign*, 1843, **288-9**; *Hazara*, 1891, **431**; *Hazara Singh*, Hunza-Nagar, wins I.O.M., **437, 438**; *Headquarters*, successive, **227, 283**; *How armed*, **284**; *Hunza-Nagar*, 1891, **435** *et seq.*; *Jahub Singh*, Kashmir Gate, 1857, **343**; *Kajuri Plain*, **525-8**; *Kala Singh*, Naik, Hunza-Nagar, **439**; *Kala Singh*, Naik (*dusra*), defence of Reshun, 1895, **443**; *Kurram Force*, 1879, **375**; *Kurram Valley*, 1919, **509**; *Maharajpur*, 1843, **289**; *Mahdo*, Havildar, Kashmir Gate, 1857, **342** *et seq.*; *Marris*, 1918, **504**; *Mechanization* started, **545**; **Mesopotamia**—Bridge, Mosul, 1920, **518**; Bridging Train, arrival, 1915, **483**—Relief of Kut, **486**—Shumran Bend, **488-9**; Relief of Kut, **486**; 1917, **491**, f.n.; 1920, **518, 520**; *Miranzai*, 1891, **432**; *Mir Khan, Col. Havildar*, I.O.M., Bilot, 1897, **448**; *Mishmi Mission*, **473**; *Mohmands*, 1897-98, **448**—1908, **454**—1915-17, **503**; *Mounted Detachment*, China, 1900, **414**; **Mutiny**—Delhi, 1857, **326**; Kashmir Gate, **342** *et seq.*; Lucknow, 1858, **360**; Meerut, 1857, **320**; Return to Roorkee, 1858, **362**; *Nadir Khan*, Sapper, gallantry at Reshun, 1895, **443**; *Narain Chand*, Bugler, gallantry, Third Afghan War, **509**; *Natha Singh*, Naik, I.O.M., Bilot, 1897, **448**; *Officers*, 1914-18, **543-4**; *Paiwar Kotal*, **379**; *Palestine*, 1918, **495**; *Persia L.-of-C.*, 1920, **518**; *Pioneers*, absorbed, 1834, **229**; *Pontoon* Section, Hazara, 1891, **431**; *Prince of Wales'* feathers, **418**; *Ram Bharose Misr*, Havildar, gallantry near Neuve Chapelle, **479**; *Ram Heth*, Sepoy, Kashmir Gate, 1857, **342** *et seq.*; *Ram Rup Singh*, Jemadar, gallantry near Neuve Chapelle, **479**; *Recapitulation* of history up to 1900, **541**; *Robertson, Serjt.*, explosion party, Ghazni, 1839, **273**; *Sadar Din*, Jemadar, Bridging Train, Mesopotamia, **483**; "*Sappers and Pioneers*," 1847-51, f.n., **229, 282, 283**; **Sikh War, First**—Ferozepore, **292**; Ferozeshah, **293**; Sobraon, **295**; Whole Corps engaged, **292**; **Sikh War,**

Second—Chilianwala, 1849, **305**; Corps, Sappers and Pioneers, **282, 283, 303**; Gujarat, 1849, **307**; Multan, 1848, **300, 302**; Sadulapur, 1848, **304**; *Smith, Comdr. James*, Delhi, 1857, **333**; *Smith, Serjt. John*, Kashmir Gate, 1857—Awarded V.C., **342** *et seq.*; *Stuart, Serjt.-Major*, Delhi, 1857, **333**—Meerut, 1857, **321**; *Sucha Singh*, Havildar, decorated, " The Orchard," **479**; *Tibet Mission*, **463, 465-6**; *Tillok Singh*, Havildar, Kashmir Gate, 1857, **342** *et seq.*; *Tirah*, 1897, **451**; *Tochi Valley*, 1897, **445**; *Toola Ram*, Subadar, Kashmir Gate, 1857, **343**; *Turnbull, Surg.-Major*, M.O., B.S. & M., 1857, **319**; *Uniform*, 1819, **227**; *Waziristan*, 1894, **439-40**—1919, **513**; *Working* pay introduced, 1841, **282**; *Zakka Khels*, 1908, Bazar Valley F.F., **453**

Sappers and Miners, Bombay—*Abyssinia*, **398** *et seq.*; *Aden*, first S. & M. unit lands, 1840, **283** and f.n.—Great War, **490**—Hinterland, **415**; *Afghan War, First*, Army of Indus, 1838, **268**; **Afghan War, Second**—Companies employed, **384**; Kandahar, 1880, **388**; Kandahar Force, 1879, **375**; Maiwand, 1880, last stand at, **388**—names of men, **389**, f.n.; *Afghan War, Third*, **507** and f.n.; *Bhawani Singh*, Jemadar, explosion party, Ghazni, **272**; *Bridging Train*, Pontoon Park, E. Africa, **499**; *Burma War, Third*, **407** *et seq.*; *Changes in organization*, 1820, **227**—1826, **230**—1843-55, **283**—1885, **393-5**—1900-14, **546-7**—1914-18, **548**—1919-31, **549-50**—1932, **552-3**; *Changes in title*, **230, 415** f.n., **419, 546**; *China*, 1900, **414**; *Companies, existing in* 1900, **546-7**—Original, 1834, **230**—Renumbering, 1903, **394**, f.n.—Three added, 1902, **394**, f.n.—2nd, 1826, **230**—18th, 1777, origin, **190**; *Comparative* strengths, 1914 and 1918, **476, 547-8**; *Dalip Singh*, Sapper, Neuve Chapelle, **478**; *Gaupat Mahadeo*, Subadar, Neuve Chapelle, **478**; **Great War**—E. Africa, **499, 501**; E. Persia, **490**; Expansion during, **476, 548**; Lahore Div., 1914, **476**; Neuve Chapelle, 1914, **477**—Farewell to, **482**; Palestine, **495**; Second Ypres, **481** (see also " Mesopotamia "); *Headquarters*, changes of location, **230, 282**; *How* armed, **284**; *Malerkotla* S. & M., absorbed temporarily into Corps, 1915, **548**; *Malta* E.F., 1878, **401**; *Marris*, 1918, **504**; *Mekran*, 1898 and 1901, **412**; *Mishmi*, 1912-13, **474**, f.n.; *Mohmands*, 1898, **448**—1915-17, **503**; **Mesopotamia**—17th and 22nd Cos. used as infantry, **482-4**; 20th and 21st Cos., relief of Kut, **486**; 22nd Co. loses three comdrs. in action, **483, 484** and f.n.; *Mutiny*, Central India F.F., **364**—3rd Co., **366**, f.n.; *N. Persia*, 1920, **518**; *Officers*, 1914-18, **548**; *Overseas* service, special suitability for, **396**; *Panalla*, storming of, 1844, **288**; *Persia*, 1856, **312**—1902, **413**; *Pontoon Train* formed from, 1820, **227**; *Railway* companies, **548-9**; *Recapitulation* of history up to 1900, **546**; *Sikh War, Second*, Gujarat, 1849, **307**—Multan, 1848, **301**; *Somaliland*, 1890, **411**—1902-4, **416-7**; *Spin Baldak*, 1919, water supply, **510**; *Telegraph Section*, Chin Lushai, 1889, **461**; *Tirah*, 1897, **450**; *Uniform*, 1828, f.n., **230**; *Waziristan*, 1919, **513**; *Zhob Valley*, 1890, **430**

Sappers and Miners, Burma—*Chin-Lushai*, 1889, **460**; *Mesopotamia*, Shumran Bend, **488-9**; *Organization*, affiliated to M.S. & M., 1887, **411**—Composition, **411**—Disbanded, 1929, **411, 540**—Incorporated in M.S. & M., 1893, **411**—Officers, **411**—Raised, 1887, **411**—Separated from M.S. & M., 1922, **524** f.n., **539**

Sappers and Miners, Madras—*Abyssinia*, **398** *et seq.*; *Afghan War, First*, **280**; *Afghan War, Second*, Khaibar, 1879, **385**—Second phase, **384**—Peshawar Force, **375**; *Afghan War, Third*, **507** and f.n., **509** and f.n.; *Battle* honours, **157**; *Birth* of, 1780, **157**; *Buner*, 1898, **449**; *Burma Rebellion*, **528**; *Burma War, Second*, **308**; *Burma War, Third*, **407** *et seq.*; *Caste* not recognized, **537**; *Changes* in organization, 1834, **283**—1885, **393-4-5**—1900-14, **536-7**—1914-18, **537-8**—1919-31, **538-40**—1932, **552-3**; *Changes* in title, **418-9, 536**—" Queen's Own," 1876, f.n., **418**; *China War, First*, Bogue Forts, 1841, **280**—Canton, **281**—Chinkiang-fu, **281**; *China War, Second*, **313**; *China*, 1900, **413**; *Chin-Lushai*, 1889, **460**; *Chitral*, 1895, **440**; *Companies, existing in* 1900, **536-7**—Renumbered, 1903, **394**, f.n.—Signal, formed 1910, **537**; *Comparative* strengths, 1914 and 1918, **476, 537**; *Criticism* of, 1836, **231**; *Defence Light Section*, 1912, **537**; *Derajat*, 1917, **503**; *E. Africa*, **499, 501**; *Egypt*, telegraphists, 1882, **402**—Tel-el-Kebir, 1882, **403**—1914, **493**; *European and Indian Corps*, formed 1818, disbanded 1821, **227**; *Field Park*, E. Africa, **499**; *Formed* 1831, from Pioneers, **229**; *Great War*, expansion during, **476, 537-8** (see also " Mesopotamia " and " Palestine "); *Hazara*, 1891, Telegraph Detachment, **431**; *How* armed, **284**; *Lowe, T.*, M.O., 1858, **365** and f.n.; *Malakand*, 1897, **446**; *Malay*, 1832, first services as S. & M., **266**; *Malta* E.F., 1878, **401**; *Mechanization* started, **540**; *Mesopotamia*, Kut Relief Force, **486**—Shumran Bend, **488-9**—12th Co., 1915, **484**; *Mesopotamia*, 1920, Arab insurrection, **518**—9th Co. and burning bridge, **520**—Relief of Kufa, **520**;

INDEX. 591

Mohmands, 1897, **448**; *Moplah Rebellion*, **522**; *Mutiny*, Alam Bagh, **358**—Central India, **366**—Lucknow, capture, **360**—Relief, **355**—Malwa, **362**; *Officers*, 1914–18, **538**; *Overseas* service, special suitability for, **398**; *Palestine*, advance on Jerusalem, **495**; *Perak*, 1875, **401**; *Persia*, 1857, **312**; *Recapitulation* of history, **536**; *Recruiting*, changes in 1903–14, **537**; *Sapper* of 1840, **284**; *Sholinghur*, battle honour, 1781, **159**; *Sikh War, First*, **294**; *Sind War*, 1842, **286**—Farewell order, Sir C. Napier, **288**—Miami, 1843, **287**; *Somaliland*, 1902–04, Field Park, **416**; *Sudan*, 1885, Haskin and Tofrek, **404**; *Tibet*, **463, 465, 466**; *Tirah*, 1897, **451**; *Zakka Khels*, 1908, **453**

Sappers, Miscellaneous Corps—*Broadfoot's*, First Afghan War, become 7th and 8th Cos., B.S. & M., 1843, **282**—Composition and raising, 1840, **275**—Exploits disregarded, **424**; *Local Corps*, siege of Nagpur, 1817, **244**; *Punjab*, Mutiny, 1857–58, Bulandshahr, **347**—Delhi, **332**—How raised, **332**—Kashmir Gate, **342**—Lucknow, capture of, **360-1**—Relief of, **355**; *Sibandi*, Bhutan, 1864–66, **458**—Explanation of name, f.n., **457**—Napier, R., in charge of, 1840, f.n., **457**—Sikkim, 1861, **457**

Savandroog, capture of, 1791, **166**
Scott, Mr. J. G., Librarian, help acknowledged, x
Scott-Ruffle, Capt. C. F., I.A.R.O., M.S. & M., Mesopotamia, 1920, **520**
Scully, Conductor, Delhi magazine, **318** and f.n.
Seaton, Col., Colm. Comdr., 1857, **359**
Sepoys—*Aversion* of Bengal, to overseas service, f.n., **252**; *Description* of, Madras, 1780, **152**; *First* raised by French, 1740, **65**; *Regular* Bns. formed by Clive, Bengal, 1757, **101**; *Regular* Cos. formed, Madras, 1748, **69**; *Seven* Bns. organized, 1759, **78**
Seringapatam (see "Mysore Wars")
Shah Alam, Emperor, defeated, Buxar, 1764, **119**
Shah Burj, defences of Dig, **218**
Shah Jehan, Emperor, deposed, 1658, **13**
Shah Najif Palace, Lucknow, **350**
Shah Shuja, enthroned at Kabul, 1839, **274**; Refugee, 1838, **267**
"Shannon," H.M.S., gun crews in Mutiny, **355**
Sher Ali, Amir of Afghanistan, **372**; Flight and death, **378**
Sheranis, Baluchis, **422**
Sherbrooke, Col., Seringapatam, 1799, **177**
Sher Muhammad, Amir of Eastern Sind, 1843, **287**
Sher Singh, Sikh leader, before Multan, **299**; Capitulates, 1849, **307**; Deserts, 1848, **301**

Shipp, Serjt. John, siege of Bhurtpore, 1805, **219, 220**; Use of elephants in war, **236**
Sholinghur, Battle of, 1781, **159**
Showers, Brig., Colm. Comdr., 1857, **347**
Shuja-ud-Daula, Nawab of Oudh, defeated, Buxar, 1764, **119**; Oudh restored to, **119**; Relations with Rohillas, **179**
Shuldham, Brig.-Gen. T., Cachar Colm., 1825, **257**
Shutar Gardan Pass, Kurram route, **374**; Second Afghan War, **384**
Sidasir, Battle of, 1799, **174**
Siege warfare, Indian, described, **202**; Proposed "elevated battery," **204**
Signals, Abyssinia, 1867–68, **399**
Sikandar Bagh, Lucknow, **350**
Sikhs, foreigners with, f.n., **295**; General rising of, 1848, **302**
Sikhs, 47th, Neuve Chapelle, with S. & M., **477-8**
Sikh War, First—*Aliwal*, battle, 1846, **294**—Engineers and Sappers at, **294**; *Bridge* across Sutlej, **296**; *Causes* of, **291**; *Conclusion* of, 1846, **296**; *Ferozeshah*, battle, 1845, **293**; *Mudki*, opening battle, **292-3**; *Opening* dispositions of, **292**; *Sikhs* cross Sutlej, 1845, **291**; *Sobraon*, battle, 1846, **294-5**—Engineers and Sappers at, **296**
Sikh War, Second—*Bridge*, Attock, 1849, **307**—Of boats, Ramnagar, **305**; *Chilianwala*, 1849, B.S. & P. present at, **305**—Losses, **305**; *Concentrations*, Feb., 1849, **306**; *Conclusion* of, **307**; *Gujarat*, 1849, battle, **306**—B.S. & P. present at, **307**—Engineers present at, **306**—Pursuit of Sikhs after, **307**; *Opening* of, **303**; *Ramnagar*, cavalry action, **303**; *Rawalpindi*, Sikhs lay down arms at, **307**; *Sadulapur*, action of, **304**; *Thackwell* crosses Chenab, **304**; *Troops* engaged, **303**
Simla, site acquired, **240**
Sind, Amirs of, trouble with, 1838, **269**
Sind Campaign—*Affairs* leading up to, 1842, **285**; *Concluded*, **288**; *Hyderabad*, battle, 1843, **287**—Occupied, **287**—Residency attacked, **286**; *Imamgarh*, occupied and destroyed, **286**; *Miani*, battle of, 1843, **287**; *Napier, Sir Charles*, as military dictator, 1842, **285**
Singhur, captured, 1818, **247**
Singphos, operations agst., **266**; Tribe, N.E. Frontier, **456**
Sikkim, N.E. Frontier, **456**
Sixteenth Lancers, Aliwal, 1846, **295**
Sixty-Sixth Regt., Maiwand, 1880, **389**
Sivaji, captures Gingee, 1677, **22**
Skeen, Maj.-Gen. A., Third Afghan War, **508**; Waziristan, 1919, **513**
Smith, Maj.-Gen. Sir Harry, Aliwal, wins battle of, 1846, **294**; First Sikh War, f.n., **292**
Smith, Corpl. James, V.C., Buffs, V.C. at Bilot, **448**

Smith, Maj.-Gen. Lionel, defeats Baji Rao, 1818, **247**; Defeats Bani-Bu-Ali tribes, 1821, **250**; Enters Poona, 1817, **244**
Smithwaite, Capt. T., Madras Pioneers, Java, 1811, **232**—Koppaldroog, **250**
Smuts, Lt.-Gen. J. C., C.-in-C., E. Africa, 1916, **500** and f.n.
Smythe, Thomas, first Governor of E.I.C., **1**
Snodgrass, Major, description of Burmese tactics, **256**
Snow, Maj.-Gen. T. D'O., G.O.C., 27th Div., 1915, **481**, f.n.
Soldier artificers, Gibraltar, 1772, **139**
Somaliland, 1890, causes of expedn., **411**; Zariba at Husain, **411**
Somaliland, 1902-04, operations agst. Mad Mulla, **415**; Country described, **415**; Events leading up to, **416**; Gumburru, disaster at, **416**, f.n.; Jidballi, victory at, **417**
Spice Islands, occupied, 1795, **171**; Secured by Dutch, **2**
Spink, Lieut. H. H. M., I.A.R.O., Kut, **485**
Staff Corps (see " Army in India ")
Stalker, Maj.-Gen., captures Bushire, 1856, **312**
Steele, Brig.-Gen. S. W., Madras Div., Second Burma War, **310**
Steuart, Brig.-Gen., 14th Lt. Dgns., C.I.F.F., 1858, **363** et seq.
Stevenson, Col., Asirgarh, 1803, **210**; Burhampur, 1803, **210**; Gawilgarh, **212**; With Wellesley, Second Maratha War, **209, 210**
Stewart, Gen. Sir Donald, C.-in-C., India, 1882, **402**, f.n.; Kandahar Colm., 1878, **374**; Kandahar Div., 1879, **383**; March, Kandahar to Kabul, 1880, **387-8**
Stewart, Brig.-Gen. J. M., lands at Mombasa, 1914, **499**
Stock, Capt. F. T., Bo.S.C., comds. 5th Co., Bo.S. & M., 1878, **401**
Streynsham Master, Bengal, **30**; Bombay, **16**; Madras, **22**
Stuart, Maj.-Gen., succeeds Coote as C.-in-C., 1785, **161**
Stuart, Lt.-Gen. James, captures Savandroog, 1791, **166**; Defeats Tipu at Sidasir, 1799, **174**; Expedn. to Ceylon, 1795, **171**; Seringapatam, 1792, **170**—1799, **172**
Stuart, Brig.-Gen., Malwa Campaign, 1857, **362** et seq.
Suakin, 1896, Bde. from India, **412**
Submarine mining, brief history of, **554-5**
Submarine Mining Sections become Defence Light Sections, **419**
Sudan, 1884-5, conclusion of operations, **405**; Hashin, victory of, **404**; Railway, Suakin-Berber, started and abandoned, **404**; Tofrek, square broken, **404**
Suffren, French Admiral, **160**
Surat—*Aungier*, President, **2, 17, 18**; *First Maratha War*, **181**; *Founded* 1612, by Thomas Aldworth, **1, 13**; *Hawkins* lands, 1608, **1**; *H.Q.* of E.I.C., **4**; *Oxenden, Sir George*, President, **14, 16, 17**; *Ships* built at, 1720, **86**; *Superseded* by Bombay, **22**
Surveyor-General (see " Beatson, A.")
Survey work, by Bombay Engineers, 1784-90, **198**; Second Afghan War, **380**
Suspension bridges (see " Bridges ")
Swally, seaport of Surat, **14**
Swann, Col. J. C., Berbera Force, **416**
Swanston, Capt., M.I., M.S. & M., Second China War, **314**
Swatis, Yusafzai Pathans, **422**
Swat Valley, 1897-98—*Blood* assumes comd., **446**; *Chakdara*, siege and relief, **446**; *Landakai*, use of field artillery, **447**; *Malakand F.F.* formed, **446-7**; *Malakand Pass*, night attacks, **448**; *Religious* fanaticism, **446**
Swayne, Lt.-Col. E. J. E., Somaliland, 1901-02, **416**
Swinton, Major John, Bengal Infantry—*Agra*, 1803, **216**; *Bravery*, Aligarh, 1803, **215**; *Cachar Colm.*, 1825, **257**; *Career* and gallantry of, **201**; *Comdt.*, Bengal Pioneers, 1803, **201**; *Hathras*, 1817, **241**; *Lamed* for life, Dig, 1804, **218**; *Nepal War*, **239**
Sydenham, Lieut., Seringapatam, 1799, **177**
Symons, Maj.-Gen. W. P., Chin-Lushais, 1889, **460**; Tirah, 1897, **450**

T

Tanjore, disaster, 1782, **160**; Raja of, deposed, 1773, **142**
Tank, " Hell its hill-station," **503**
Tantia Topi, captured and hanged, **366**; Defeated at Betwa R., **364**; General of Nana Sahib, **348**
Taylor, pirate, **85**
Tej Singh, Sikh chief, 1845, **291**
Telegraphs, Abyssinia, 1867-8, **399**
Thackeray, Col. C. B., help acknowledged, **x**
Thackwell, Maj.-Gen. Sir Joseph, Sadulapur, **304**; Second Sikh War, **303**
Thirty-ninth Regt., lands in India, 1754, —First King's Army unit, **72**
Thomason Civil Engineering College, Roorkee, **321** and f.n.
Thomson, Wm., Governor, E.I.C., **18**
Thorn, Major W., 25th Lt. Dgns., describes Wellesley's army, 1803, **208**
Thum, Hunza-Nagar, **434**
Tibet, N.E. Frontier, **456**
Tibet Mission—*Advance* from Chumbi, **465**; *Anti-freezing* mixture, **464**, f.n.; *Causes* of Mission, **463**; *Clothing* issued, **464**, f.n.; *Country* and climate, **462**; *Dalai Lama*, **469, 470**; *Engineers*, work of, winter, **464**; *Engineer Troops*, two-thirds escort, **463**; *Engineer* war, **462**; *Gyantse*, Engineers and S. & M. at, **465-6**;

INDEX.

Gyantse Jong, fighting round, **466-8**; *Karo-La* forced—Extreme altitude in modern war, **469,** f.n.; *Lhasa,* advance on, **469**—Entry into, **470**; *Palla* stormed, **466-8**; *Potala Palace,* **470**; *Tsan-po* crossed, **469-70**—Re-crossed, **470**; *Tsechan Monastery* captured, **467**
Tighe, Brig.-Gen. M. J., E. Africa, **500**
Tipu, son of Haidar Ali—*Becomes* Nawab, 1782, **161**; *Capitulates* at Seringapatam, 1792, **170**; *Captures* Cuddalore, 1782, **161**—Mangalore, **161**; *Character,* **145**; *Defeated* at Malaralli, 1799, **174** —At Sidasir, **174**; *On* Penner R., **154**; *Slain,* 1799, **177**; *Success* at Bednore, 1782, **161**
Tirah, 1897-98—*Country* unsurveyed, **450**; *Engineer* work, summary, **452**; *Lockhart* comds. 35,000 men, **450**; *Outline* of operations, **451**; *Second Div.,* hard fighting, **451**; *Zakka Khels* punished, **452**
Tombs, Brig.-Gen. Henry, ꓦ.ꓛ., Bhutan, 1865, **459**
Topasses, **84**
Torriano, Major, Honavar, 1783, **198**
Towers, frontier, *contretemps* with human cork, **454,** f.n.; Destruction of, method of, **432**—Method of, hollow, **454**
Townshend, Maj.-Gen. Sir Charles, defence of Chitral, **440, 444** and f.n.— Kut, **440,** f.n., **485**; 6th Div., **482, 484**
Tranquebar, Danes at, **4**
Tregear, Col. V. W., Chin-Lushais, 1889, **460**
Trelawny, Lieut. J. M. S., I.A.R.O., Bridging Train, **486**
Trench appliances (*v.* " Great War ")
Trichinopoly, captured by Marathas, **64**
Trimbak, hill fort, 1818, **248**
Trincomalee, Dutch settlement, captured, 1782, **160**—1795, **171**
Tribal Levies, Curzon's policy, **452**
Tripartite Treaty, First Afghan War, **267**
Tucker, Lieut. L. H. E., B.I., comds. S. & M., Ambela, 1863, **425**
Tukoji Rao Holkar, **181**
Tulloch, Lieut., Lucknow Residency, **351,** f.n., **354,** f.n.
Tungabhadra R., crossing of, 1799, **199**
Turban, swallowed by bullock, **211**
Turis, position of, **422**
Twentieth Punjab Infantry, Ambela, 1863, **427**; Hunza-Nagar, 1891, **435**
Tytler, Brig.-Gen. J. M. B. F., Q.M.G. to Havelock, 1857, **349**; Bhutan, 1865, **459**
Tytler, Brig.-Gen. J. A., Ali Masjid, 1878, **377**

U

Uniforms, **12, 225, 227,** f.n. **230, 381**
Upper Burma, annexed, 1886, **408**
Upton, Lt.-Col. J., Treaty of Purandhar, 1775, **182**
Utman Khels, Yusafzai Pathans, **422**

V

Van Cortlandt, Gen., defeats Mulraj, **299**
Van Deventer, Lt.-Gen. J. L., E. Africa, 1917, **500**
Vans Agnew, murdered, Multan, 1848, **299**
Vasco da Gama, reached India, 1498, **13**
de Vauban, French engineer, **108**
Ventura, Italian with Sikhs, f.n., **295**
Vesava, captured, 1774, **180**
Viceroy, Canning apptd. first, 1858, **368**; Denison acts as, 1863-64, **428,** f.n.
Vizagapatam seized by Mughals, 1689, **25**
Volunteers, electrical engineer, at ports, **554** and f.n.
Von Lettow Vorbeck, Gen., German E. Africa, **498**
Von Sanders, Liman, German Marshal, Palestine, **497** and f.n.

W

Wahabis suppressed, **266**
Wandiwash, battles of, **78, 159**
Watkis, Lt.-Gen. H. B. B., Bazar Valley, F.F., 1908, **453,** f.n.; Lahore Div., 1914, **476**
Walpole, Col., Colm. Comdr., 1857, **359**
Wapshare, Lt.-Gen. R., Baluchistan Force, 1919, **506, 510**
Ward, Lieut. R. H., Infy. officer, B.S. & M., **371,** f.n.
Wasota, hill fort, 1818, **248**
Wazil Muhammad, Pindari leader, 1817, **244**
Wazirs, Mahsuds and Darwesh Khel Wazirs, characteristics, **512**—Position, **422**; Various wars agst., **512**
Waziristan, 1894, agst. Mulla Powinda, **439, 440**
Waziristan, 1917 (see " Great War, N.W. Frontier ")
Waziristan, 1919-20—*General* situation, **512-13**; *Indian Army* untrained, **512**; *Northern* area, operations in Tochi, **513**; *Permanent* occupation decided on, **515**; *Southern* area, advance up Tank Zam, **514**—Desperate fighting, **513-15**—Kaniguram occupied, **515**— Makin Valley destroyed, **514**—Wana reoccupied, **515**
Waziristan, 1923, destruction of Makin villages, **517**
Waziristan, 1925, Mahsuds *v.* Wazirs— Tranquillizing effects of roads, **517**
Waziristan Circular Road, construction of, **515, 516, 535**
Wellesley, Col. Arthur—*At* Aurangabad, 1803, **208**; *Captures* Ahmadnagar, 1803, **207**; *Crosses* Godavari in wicker boats, **208**; *Description* of army, 1803, **208**; *Directs* Hyderabad Army, Seringapatam, 1799, **172**; *Engineering* capacity and instructions on pontooning, **207**; *Fights* and kills Dhundia, 1800, **199**; *Second Maratha War,* preparations for, **206**; *Victory* of Argaon, 1803, **210**—Assaye, 1803, **209-10**

Wellesley, Marquis, superseded after Bhurtpore, 1805, **222**
Wheeler, Maj.-Gen. Sir Hugh, Cawnpore, 1857, **348**
Wheeler, Capt., Madras Pioneers, capture of Kokein, 1824, **257**
Whish, Maj.-Gen. W., attacks Multan, 1848, **299**; Joins Gough, 1849, **306**
White, F.M. Sir George, Upper Burma, **409**; Zhob Valley, 1890, **430**
White Elephant of Ava, **251**
White Mutiny, 1809, **223**
Whitlock, Maj.-Gen., Saugor F.F., 1858, **363**
Wilde, Lt.-Col. A. T., Ambela, 1863, **426**
Wilkie, Capt., Arakan Colm., 1825, **258**
Willcocks, Gen. Sir James, comds. Indian Corps, **476**; Mohmands, 1908, **454**; Relinquishes comd., Indian Corps, **481**, f.n.; Zakka Khels, 1908, **453**
Willcocks, Sir Wm., Engineer, Hindiya Barrage, **519**, f.n.
Willoughby, Lieut., blows up magazine, Delhi, **318** and f.n.
Willshire, Maj.-Gen. T., Army of Indus, 1838, **268**
Wilson, Maj.-Gen. Archdale, character of, **333**; Delhi, decides to assault, **336**—Succeeds to comd., **333**; Meerut, march from, to Delhi, May, **323**—outbreak at, **318**
Windham, Maj.-Gen., Cawnpore, 1857, **355, 358**
Wire-netting roads, Gallipoli, first used in, **496**, f.n.; Palestine, **496**

Wodehouse, Brig.-Gen. J. H., Malakand F.F., 1897, **447**; Wounded, **448**
Wolseley, Lord, Egypt, 1882, **402**; Operations to relieve Gordon, 1884–85, **404**
Women, single, sent out to Bombay, **7, 17**—Madras, **8**
Wood, Maj.-Gen. George, failure of, Nepal War, **239**
Wood, Maj.-Gen. John, failure of, Nepal War, **239**; Third Div., **234**
Woodburn, Maj.-Gen., Colm. Comdr., 1857, **362**
Woolwich, R.M. Academy founded, **54**

Y

Yakub Khan, Amir of Afghanistan, **378**; Surrenders to Roberts, 1879, **384**
Yasin, State, **422**
Yeatman-Biggs, Maj.-Gen. A. G., Tirah, 1897, **451**
Younghusband, Col. F. E., Tibet Mission, 1904, **462** *et seq.*
Yusafzai Pathans, country of, **422**

Z

Zaimukhts, position, **422**
Zakka Khel, Afridi Tirah, **422**
Zakka Khels, 1908, Willcocks' short war, **453**
Zhob Valley, 1890, agst. Sheranis, **430**
Zulfikar Khan, Mughal Nawab, 1696, **26**

www.ingramcontent.com/pod-product-compliance
Lightning Source LLC
Chambersburg PA
CBHW060357230426
43663CB00008B/1302